Corporate Governance

Corporate Governance
Cases and Materials

SECOND EDITION

J. Robert Brown, Jr.
Lisa L. Casey

CAROLINA ACADEMIC PRESS
Durham, North Carolina

ISBN 978-1-5221-0097-3
E-Book ISBN 978-1-5221-0099-7
LCCN 2016944757

Carolina Academic Press, LLC
700 Kent Street
Durham, North Carolina 27701
Telephone (919) 489-7486
Fax (919) 493-5668
www.cap-press.com

Printed in the United States of America

To the Brown and Lee children and grandchildren,
Tessa, Beth, Ryan, Josh, Zoey, and Emerson,
all unique and astounding in their own right.
JRB

To Mom and Dad, my first and most important teachers:
you formed both my heart and my mind;
To Sean, Caitlin, Jillian and Kristen: you bring me such joy; and
To Brian: there simply are no words adequate to express my love and appreciation.
LLC

Contents

Table of Cases

Preface

A textbook on corporate governance is a particularly daunting thing to write. Like all textbooks, it must provide an overview of an area of law in a manner that is sufficiently accessible to the faculty member teaching the class and to the students who are trying to understand the area. Corporate governance, however, is a particularly challenging topic to develop in a casebook for two reasons.

First, the area involves a complicated regulatory construct, a byproduct not of reason but path dependency. Governance practices may emanate from the federal government, particularly the Securities and Exchange Commission, state government, with Delaware the predominate player, and the stock exchanges, self-regulatory organizations that are for-profit companies with regulatory responsibilities. Each regulator has a different philosophical approach and works to promote its own policy objectives. Moreover, enforcement mechanisms vary. For example, private enforcement is a significant enforcement tool under the federal securities laws but not under the rules of the stock exchanges.

At the same time, the regulatory construct has been in a state of considerable flux. Historically, matters were neatly divided between the SEC and the states. With its creation in 1934, the SEC was assigned the task of regulating corporate disclosure, particularly financial disclosure, while states continued to regulate the substantive standards of corporate governance. But in response to various corporate scandals and crises — most significantly, after the collapse of Enron and WorldCom in 2001 and 2002 — the post-Depression division of authority shifted.

In passing the Sarbanes-Oxley Act in 2002, Congress gave the SEC more extensive authority over the substance of corporate governance, particularly with respect to board structure. Congress continued this trend toward federalization by enacting the Dodd-Frank Wall Street Reform and Consumer Protection Act in 2010. Dodd-Frank, among other things, clarified the SEC's authority to allow shareholders to include their nominees for the board in the company's proxy statement and gave to the agency greater authority to define director independence.

Second, corporate governance law has become extraordinarily dynamic. For a time, the area was somewhat sleepy. Public companies were run by their executive officers with occasional intervention by boards of directors. Boards consisted mostly of company employees or other persons with financial connections to the company. Shareholders were mostly passive. To the extent investors became unhappy with management, their only real option was to exercise their rights under the Wall Street Rule; they sold their shares and exited from the company.

Much, however, has changed. Institutional investors now own about two-thirds of the outstanding shares in U.S. public companies. With the increased domination of institutional shareholders, and increased concentration of public company stock in the portfolios of the largest institutions, has come increased shareholder involvement. Shareholders have sought a greater role in corporate governance. Among other things, Congress and the SEC provided shareholders with more say in the election of directors and an advisory vote on executive compensation. At the same time, shareholders have resorted to private action for other reforms including majority vote requirements for directors and greater access to the company's proxy statement for their nominees.

Likewise, corporate boards have undergone significant structural changes. Director independence has emerged as the accepted method of reducing agency costs by management. As a result, insiders (with the exception of the CEO) have been all but eliminated from public company boards. The role of outside directors as monitors of management has been strengthened. For example, federal law requires that independent directors on the audit committee of public companies, rather than the CEO, have the authority to hire and fire the corporation's independent accountants.

The other development has been the growing involvement of public interest in the evolution of the governance process. At one time, governance was largely a matter between owners and managers. That is no longer the case. The public has taken an interest in the rulemaking efforts of the SEC. When the SEC proposed a rule seeking to require companies to disclose the ratio between the compensation paid to the median employee and the CEO, over 280,000 comment letters were received. Likewise a petition for rulemaking that sought the mandatory disclosure of political contributions garnered over a million comments. Likewise, Congress has begun to impose disclosure requirements that are aimed at the public rather than shareholders.

In Dodd-Frank, for example, Congress mandated rules that required companies to disclose their use of "conflict minerals," a requirement that had little to do with profit maximization and everything to do with publicizing corporate acquisition of minerals used to facilitate violence in parts of Africa. The mere fact that Congress has, in Sarbanes-Oxley and Dodd-Frank, chosen to intervene into the governance process suggests that reforms will increasingly be determined more by the interests of voters rather than the interests of owners and managers. This promises to add significant uncertainty to the evolutionary process.

This textbook attempts to illuminate and accommodate both the complicated regulatory framework and the dynamic nature of corporate governance law. Chapters typically cover all three areas of regulation—federal, state, and SRO. We examine corporate governance as positive law, but we also include normative and even empirical perspectives on the doctrine. We have incorporated discussions on new developments and evolving practices, often in the comments and questions following each section.

Nonetheless, this area of law, by definition, represents a complex balance that we, as authors, have attempted to depict, and that you, the faculty and students using the textbook, will discover during the pedagogical process.

Because we have written this book as a teaching tool, we have edited the cases and other materials heavily to aid in the text's readability. Citations and footnotes usually have been omitted, mostly without indication. Although this second edition does not include a separate statutory supplement, we have included, in the text, excerpts of the key statutes and regulations, and, of course, complete copies of the relevant laws and rules are readily accessible on the internet.

We would be remiss not to mention a number of people who have helped us with this textbook. Steven E. Baum did a yeoman's job in acquiring the copyright approvals, of which there were many. Sana Hamelin, JP Thibeault, Susan Beblavi, and Samual Hagreen had the unenviable task of reading chapters and eliminating the errors that can creep into a manuscript this size. They performed at the highest level. Robert Hutchison, Andrew Smith, Catherine Zung, and librarian Warren Rees contributed their excellent research skills to this project over many months, and Robert, Catherine, and Andrew also assisted with the often tedious task of editing cases and the like. Suzie Vervynckt graciously helped with formatting the text. We are grateful for all of their contributions … and their good humor!

We look forward to your comments and suggestions.

J. Robert Brown, Jr.
Lisa L. Casey
June 15, 2016

Corporate Governance

Chapter 1

An Introduction to Corporate Governance

Just thirty years ago, the term "corporate governance" seldom appeared "outside the arcane world of law school texts and academic treatises."[1] Today, however, corporate governance is a topic of substantial public interest and controversy. Corporate governance experts are quoted in recurrent press reports about public company mismanagement and executive compensation excesses. Politicians and pundits debate proposals to reform corporate governance. Institutional shareholders receive information from corporate governance advisers about how to invest their funds and vote their shares. Research firms grade public companies according to the quality of their corporate governance practices. Attorneys specialize in corporate governance practice, and law firms publish corporate governance newsletters. Not only is corporate governance an increasingly important field of professional and academic study, but corporate governance has become a subject of persistent legislative and regulatory reappraisal in the United States and internationally.

During the past decade in particular, the governance of American public companies has come under intense criticism from elected officials, shareholder advocates, and scholars. Such concerns dominated the business headlines beginning in 2002, following revelations of massive financial frauds and scandalous executive self-dealing at Enron, WorldCom, Tyco, and dozens of other major public companies. Observers reasonably asked, "Where were the directors?" And the disturbing answer, according to many critics, was that corporate board members willfully shut their eyes to management wrongdoing until it was too late. The firms failed or nearly failed. Shareholders lost billions in savings and retreated from the stock markets. Public confidence in business and corporate leaders plummeted.

In response to public outcry and tumbling share prices, the federal government took action. President George W. Bush referred to corporate governance in his 2002 State of the Union address, and Congress legislated changes in boardroom practices. The Sarbanes-Oxley Act of 2002 (Sarbanes-Oxley or SOX) mandated specific corporate governance procedures for public companies, institutionalizing reform "by converting what were previously voluntary 'should have' best practices into 'must have' minimum

---

1. Margaret M. Blair, Ownership and Control: Rethinking Corporate Governance for the Twenty-First Century 1 (1995).

standards for board structure, composition, and to some extent, responsibility."[2] Furthermore, the New York Stock Exchange and NASDAQ revised their listing requirements, modifying their rules to require that listed companies implement best boardroom practices. The erosion of investor confidence even prompted industry associations and individual companies to take voluntary action to remedy perceived deficiencies. Boards dismissed "imperial CEOs" at well-known public companies like Disney and Hewlett-Packard. Beginning in the last quarter of 2002, share prices rose steadily. Seemingly, Corporate America had recovered.

Yet, in 2008, the financial markets experienced another, even more costly, crisis. Despite both government-mandated and voluntary corporate governance reforms, corporate share prices declined more in 2008 than in any other calendar year since the Great Depression. Taxpayers bailed out the nation's too-big-to-fail financial institutions, providing some $700 billion to the mega-banks. In addition to faulting weak supervision by senior bank executives, some commentators blamed the market meltdown (or, at least, the severity of the financial crisis) on poor risk management by the boards of major financial institutions. Wall Street directors were criticized, too, for approving executive compensation practices that encouraged excessive risk-taking. Along with executives' greed, directors' dismal oversight of management was cited for the collapse of Bear Stearns, the bankruptcy of Lehman Brothers, and other corporate failures in 2008 and 2009. An op-ed in *Business Week* magazine declared, "Boards Fail—Again."[3] Another, published in the *New York Times*, asked, "Need a Job? $17,000 an Hour. No Success Required."[4]

The financial upheaval and economic recession generated renewed political support for corporate governance reform, especially at the major banks that dominate the financial sector. Activist investors and their advocates lobbied Congress and the Securities and Exchange Commission to increase their voting power by allowing shareholders to nominate directors on the corporations' ballots. Shareholders also appealed to lawmakers for a greater voice in approving executive compensation. The Dodd-Frank Wall Street Reform and Consumer Protection Act (Dodd-Frank), enacted by Congress in 2010, includes a number of provisions responsive to shareholders' demands. Whether these innovations, coupled with other voluntary corporate governance reforms, enhanced or undermined shareholder value are questions that have generated considerable discussion and disagreement.

I. What Is Corporate Governance?

Corporate governance generally refers to the host of legal and non-legal principles and practices affecting control of publicly-held business corporations. Although the

---

2. MARK J. EPSTEIN & KIRK O. HANSON, THE ACCOUNTABLE CORPORATION, Vol. 1, 6 (2005).

3. Ben W. Heineman, *Boards Fail—Again*, BUS. WEEK, Sept. 26, 2008.

4. Nicholas D. Kristof, *Need a Job? $17,000 an Hour. No Success Required*, N.Y. TIMES, Sept. 18, 2008, at A35.

term "corporate governance" apparently applies to any incorporated business association, the study of corporate governance chiefly concerns the examination of public companies; that is, corporations whose securities trade in liquid investment markets, often on regulated exchanges. Most broadly, corporate governance affects not only who controls publicly-traded corporations and for what purposes but also the allocation of risks and returns from the firm's activities among the various participants in the firm, including stockholders and managers as well as creditors, employees, customers, and even communities. However, American corporate governance doctrine primarily prescribes the control rights and related responsibilities of three principal groups: (1) the firm's shareholders, who provide capital and must approve major firm transactions, (2) the firm's board of directors, who are elected by shareholders to oversee the management of the corporation, and (3) the firm's senior executives, who are responsible for the day-to-day operations of the corporation. As the Delaware Supreme Court has stated, "The most fundamental principles of corporate governance are a function of the allocation of power within a corporation between its stockholders and its board of directors."[5] This casebook, then, focuses primarily on the relation between public company shareholders and the directors and officers charged with managing those firms.

Corporate governance guides the behavior of corporate management, encouraging the effective use of company resources and making management accountable for misuse of those resources. Applying suitable governance practices, firms hire and incentivize skilled professional managers. Robust governance structures also enable companies to better understand sources of risk, including incipient threats to the firm. Strong corporate governance helps ensure that company stewards make effective use of investment capital, reducing investment risk and contributing to growth. Proponents of strong governance argue that best practices enhance both firm performance and well-functioning securities markets.

Perhaps because "governance" evokes "government," some observers have employed the language of political science, and even transferred theories of republican institutions, in their normative accounts of the rights and duties of corporate actors. These discussants speak of "tripartite" structures, systems of "checks and balances" at work within the firm, and shareowner "suffrage" and the corporate "democracy." Theorists draw analogies between boards of directors and the legislative branch and between corporate executives and the executive branch. However, publicly-owned corporations actually employ diverse governance structures, albeit within the boundaries of applicable legal rules and securities market listing standards. Indeed, under enabling state corporation laws, the company's own constitutional documents—its charter and its bylaws—largely determine the allocation of power among the firm's board of directors, executive managers, and shareholders.

---

5. MM Companies, Inc. v. Liquid Audio, Inc., 813 A.2d 1118, 1126 (Del. 2003) (footnotes omitted).

II. Who's Who in Corporate Governance

Because a corporation can do nothing more than the individuals who act in its name or on its behalf can do, it is helpful to review briefly the identities and roles of those persons who routinely transact, affect, and are affected by the corporation.

A. Directors

Acting as a board, directors generally oversee the activities of the corporation. The precise contours of the board's powers typically are spelled out in the corporate bylaws, but most boards are responsible for selecting officers, approving major decisions, and providing shareholders with an accounting of the corporation's activities. Section 141 of Delaware's General Corporation Law requires that the firm's bylaws fix the number of directors on the board, unless that number is set forth in the certificate of incorporation.

Shareholders elect directors annually at a general meeting or, more conveniently, by proxy voting. The requirement that shareholders elect a board of directors distinguishes corporations from other forms of business organization established by state law. Nominations for the directorial ballot are made by the board or, more precisely, by a nominating committee composed of board members. Shareholders rarely nominate candidates, for reasons discussed in Chapter 8. Directors also are subject to removal by shareholders. Unless otherwise provided, a majority of the shareholders entitled to vote at any general meeting can remove a director. Delaware's General Corporation statute also permits staggering the directors' terms so that the board does not turn over completely following every election.

Importantly, directors must be natural persons, meaning that other corporations, partnerships, or entities cannot serve as board members. Delaware's Section 141(b) makes clear that directors need not be stockholders, although the certificate of incorporation or bylaws may prescribe necessary qualifications for board members. In many corporations, one or more executives will serve as directors. Directors who also are employed by the company commonly are referred to as "inside directors," and they often own equity in the corporation. By way of contrast, directors who have no management role or other position of employment with the corporation are deemed "outside directors." Because outside directors otherwise have no management function within the corporation, they often bring unique perspectives and expertise to the board. On the other hand, because outside directors are not involved in the day-to-day operations of the corporation, they usually must be apprised of relevant information before they can consider and vote on proposals made to the board. As we will see, outside directors necessarily will rely on inside directors, other corporate managers, and experts for information.

B. Officers

Sometimes referred to as the managers or executives, officers are individual employees of the corporation charged with operating the firm and making day-to-day business decisions. As discussed above, officers may serve as directors in some corporations, but many do not. The dual roles should be seen as distinct. Section 142(a) of Delaware's General Corporate Law makes clear that one individual may hold any number of offices so long as nothing in the certificate of incorporation or bylaws prohibits such service.

While Delaware's statute includes specific provisions concerning the selection of corporate directors, the same is not true for officers. Section 142(b) provides only that corporate officers shall be chosen in whatever manner the corporate bylaws prescribe. The same is true for officers' terms of service. Furthermore, the only official duty specifically described in the statute is Section 142(a)'s mandate that the proceedings of shareholders' meetings and board meetings be recorded in a book kept for that purpose. Presumably, this task could be assigned to any corporate officer. Corporate boards have broad discretion to create offices and to employ executives to fill those positions. Indeed, officers' titles and functions may and do vary substantially from company to company, depending on the firm's industry, the management needs of the business, and the market for hiring corporate executives.

In most corporations, the chief executive officer (or CEO) is the highest ranking executive. Responsible for final decisions on nearly all operational decisions, the CEO will receive reports from inferior corporate officers. CEOs are often prominent in their leadership roles, serving as the public faces of their corporations. It is not uncommon for a CEO to leave many of the regular operational decisions to other officers while functioning more actively in strategy and planning. In addition, CEOs of U.S. public companies not infrequently serve as board chairmen, although the desirability of combining the two functions has been questioned increasingly over the past decade. In corporations that have chosen to separate the roles, the chairman of the board is typically a nonexecutive (outside) director.

There is great variance in titles and functions among public companies' officers. Some corporations choose not to designate a person to serve as the firm's president. Where an executive does serve as president, that officer likely is responsible for the daily operations of the company, freeing the CEO to strategize and engage in forward-looking planning. In a corporation that does not have an officially-titled CEO, the president generally is the highest ranking officer. In some firms, the same individual may serve as both CEO and president. Corporations also may employ presidents with authority limited to single divisions or aspects of the business (i.e., marketing or sales). Some corporations decide to appoint a chief operations officer (COO) in addition to, or in lieu of, a company president. COOs generally manage the day-to-day business of the corporation. The same executive may serve as both the president and COO of the corporation.

In many large corporations, the senior officer team also will include a secretary, treasurer, and chief financial officer (CFO). The secretary records the corporate business, including by making formal records of board meetings and shareholder meetings. Increasingly, the corporate secretary serves another key role in corporate governance, engaging with investors and referring their concerns to the board and other senior executives. The treasurer, who also may act as the secretary, is responsible for corporate funds. Often both the secretary and the treasurer will report directly to the board of directors. The CFO, who also may serve as treasurer and even secretary, is responsible for corporate financial and accounting functions. In many companies, the CFO works closely with and reports directly to the corporation's CEO.

C. Shareholders

Shareholders (or stockholders) of corporations provide equity capital to firms. They do not own the corporation itself, but, as the name indicates, they own stock or shares issued by the corporation. Section 151(a) of the Delaware General Corporation Law allows a corporation to issue stock but does not require the corporation to do so. Of course, public companies — the focus of this casebook — have accepted the invitation to issue stock, often in multiple classes and with varying rights assigned to each class.

Shareholders' rights will depend on the class of stock they hold and the terms under which the corporation issued the shares. Generally, shareholders have the right to vote in the election of directors and on significant corporate matters, such as the amendment of the firm's charter, merger of the firm or sale of all or substantially all corporate assets, and dissolution of the company. Shareholders also have the right to sell their shares, and the right to receive the residual; that is, the assets remaining, if any, after the liquidating corporation has satisfied its debts. Shareholders also are said to have the right to a dividend, if one is declared. In fact, some shareholders may be entitled to a dividend while others are not, and, further, the corporation generally is not required to declare a dividend.

While all shares within a class are entitled to the same rights, there is significant potential for variance between classes. One distinction among classes of stock is that between preferred and common stock. Preferred shares often come with dividend entitlements but may be limited with regard to other rights, like voting and distributions after liquidation. Corporations also may issue multiple classes of common stock. Section 151 of Delaware's statute requires only that any right, restriction, qualification, or limitation be stated in the certificate of incorporation or in the board resolution issuing the shares. Just as in its appointment of officers, the board has great authority and flexibility in its capitalization decisions.

Unlike directors or officers, shareholders need not be natural people; institutions — such as banks, corporations, insurance companies, mutual funds, public and private pension funds, hedge funds, endowments, and foundations — also may buy, sell, or hold stock in public companies. Often institutional shareholders act as intermediaries, professionally managing investments on behalf of other persons, such as individuals who are saving for college, to buy a new home, or for retirement. Mutual funds, for example, may invest individuals' savings directly or through tax-deferred investment vehicles such as 401(k) plans. Today, institutional investors dominate the equity markets in the United States, beneficially owning roughly 75 percent of the shares of U.S. public companies. Institutions not only have enlarged their holdings of U.S. equities substantially over the past 50 years, but the ownership concentration of the largest public firms has increased substantially as well.

Over time, these capital market developments have enlarged the role of shareholders in corporate governance and, most controversially, transformed relations between shareholders and boards of directors. At least in theory, monitoring by institutional investors serves as an important check on management. Activist shareholders also have gained influence in matters of corporate governance. Activists are investors who, dissatisfied with the firm's performance, its management, or some company policy, attempt to influence corporate change without a change in corporate control. Public pension plans—that is, plans managing assets for the benefit of police officers, teachers, and other public servants—broke ground among institutional shareholders by engaging in activism in the 1980s. From that time on, the role of activist institutions in disciplining management has become a subject of debate and academic study. Most recently, attention has centered on the motivations and behavior of activist hedge funds.

D. Corporate Stakeholders

Although state corporate statutes identify the functions and broadly structure the relations of three parties—directors, officers, and shareholders—other constituents of the corporation also influence firm governance. The literature treats the company's employees, creditors, customers, suppliers, and even the community in which the firm operates as corporate stakeholders; in other words, stakeholders are groups with recognized interests in the corporation and without whose inputs and support the corporation could not operate. Internal stakeholders include individuals or entities that transact business with the corporation, while external stakeholders are affected by or can affect the corporation's actions.

Because stakeholders benefit from the company's success and may suffer harm from management errors and wrongdoing, stakeholder advocates have pursued corporate governance reforms directed at compelling directors to consider broader interests in managing the firm. Rather than operating the corporation solely with a view to maximizing shareholders' wealth, stakeholder groups propose that management consider the broader spectrum of interests affected by the corporation. The arguments for and against stakeholder participation in corporate governance are explored in Chapter 11.

E. The Advisors—Gatekeepers and Governance Experts

Accountants, attorneys, securities analysts, investment bankers, and credit rating agencies function as professional "gatekeepers" in corporate governance systems, informing and advising boards of directors, executive officers, and, on occasion, controlling shareholders. Accountants audit the firm's financial statements to ensure that the reports fairly and accurately present the company's financial condition. Corporate lawyers advise companies on transactions and provide counsel on compliance with laws requiring that firms disclose material information to shareholders. Securities analysts study firm financial data and other corporate disclosures and work to uncover new information, channeling their research to the market through reports and recommendations to investors. Investment bankers underwrite offerings of securities by the corporation and provide advice to corporations about sales of company assets, mergers, and acquisitions. Often bankers seeking advisory business will suggest potential transactions to corporate executives, and the bank also may provide deal financing. Credit rating agencies assign credit ratings for corporations that issue debt, as well as for the debt securities themselves (i.e., bonds and commercial paper). Investors, then, use credit ratings to help make investment decisions, among other things.

Certain gatekeepers, such as accountants performing audits, act as reputational intermediaries, providing verifications or certifications used by shareholders as well as creditors and other stakeholders. Other gatekeepers, including attorneys and investment bankers, deliver their professional services at critical points in corporate transactions. These gatekeepers perform an advisory role, counseling their clients on structural questions or regulatory issues and providing necessary opinions on valuation, fairness, or other requirements necessary for the transaction to close. Still other gatekeepers, for example, securities analysts and credit rating agencies, monitor corporate activities over time and publicly report their findings and related opinions. Gatekeepers may uncover corporate fraud or other wrongdoing, and some gatekeepers have a legal responsibility to investigate potential misconduct and report to the board of directors or regulatory authorities. As skilled professionals independent of the firm, gatekeepers may perform a certification function required by law (e.g., as accountants function in performing corporate audits) or by market convention (e.g., as securities analysts and credit rating agencies function in the securities markets).

The corporate scandals and financial crises of the past fifteen years have uncovered serious conflicts of interest among gatekeepers. Calls for reform have resulted in heightened regulation of gatekeepers, if not their greater accountability. Sarbanes-Oxley, for example, instituted federal regulation of public accounting firms retained to audit corporate financial statements and internal controls. Enacted in response to the massive frauds at Enron and WorldCom, among other firms, SOX included new standards for auditor independence, approval, and reporting. The Public Company Accounting Oversight Board created by SOX registers and regulates public accounting firms and sets procedures for auditing publicly traded companies. Directing its attention to credit raters, Congress next passed the Credit Rating Agency Reform Act of 2006 to improve ratings quality for investors as well as to promote accountability, transparency, and competition in the rating industry. The role of credit ratings in the near collapse of financial markets in 2008 provoked federal lawmakers to further strengthen the SEC's regulatory supervision of credit rating agencies. Among other reforms, Dodd-Frank created the Office of Credit Ratings to assist the SEC in its oversight of these gatekeepers.

Institutional shareholders also may retain experts for advice on corporate governance matters. Proxy advisory firms (sometimes called governance rating agencies) provide institutional shareholders with research and voting recommendations on matters presented to shareholders for their votes, including election of directors, approval of mergers and other significant corporate transactions, advisory approval of executive compensation (so-called "say-on-pay" votes), and shareholder-sponsored proposals. The two largest proxy advisory firms, Glass Lewis & Co. and Institutional Shareholder Services, dominate the market. In addition to assisting institutional investors with voting their shares, proxy advisors also publish corporate governance ratings and consult with public companies on corporate governance matters.

III. The Enduring Puzzle of Corporate Governance

Although corporate governance law has become a subject of focused study in recent years, the predicament driving interest in the topic is long-standing. The enduring puzzle of corporate governance is the divergence of managers' interests from the interests of passive shareholders who did not own a controlling stake in the firm. Indeed, a seminal treatise on management of the large public company, published more than 80 years ago, describes the problem well. In their landmark 1932 work, *The Modern Corporation and Private Ownership*, Adolf Berle and Gardiner Means elaborated on the puzzle:

> In discussing problems of enterprise it is possible to distinguish between three functions: that of having interests in an enterprise, that of having power over it, and that of acting with respect to it. A single individual may fulfill, in varying degrees, any one or more of these functions.... Under the corporate system, the second function, that of having power over an enterprise, has become separated from the first. The position of the owner has been reduced to that of having a set of legal and factual interests in the enterprise while the group which we have called control, are in the position of having legal and factual powers over it.... Turning then to the two new groups created out of a former single group, the owners without appreciable control and the control without appreciable ownership, we must ask what are the relations between them and how may these be expected to affect the conduct of enterprise. When the owner was also in control of his enterprise he could operate it in his own interest and the philosophy surrounding the institution of private property has assumed that he would do so....
>
> But have we any justification for assuming that those in control of a modern corporation will also choose to operate it in the interests of the owner? The

answer to this question will depend on the degree to which the self-interest of those in control may run parallel to the interests of ownership and, insofar as they differ, on the checks on the use of power which may be established by political, economic, or social conditions.

The corporate stockholder has certain well-defined interests in the operation of the company, in the distribution of income, and in the public security markets. In general, it is to his interest, first that the company should be made to earn the maximum profit compatible with a reasonable degree of risk; second, that as large a proportion of these profits should be distributed as the best interests of the business permit, and that nothing should happen to impair his right to receive his equitable share of those profits which are distributed; and finally, that his stock should remain freely marketable at a fair price....

The interests of control are not so easily discovered. Is control likely to want to run the corporation to produce the maximum profit at the minimum risk; is it likely to want to distribute those profits generously and equitably among the owners; and is it likely to want to maintain market conditions favorable to the investor? ... Are we to assume for him what has been assumed in the past with regard to the owner of enterprise, that his major aim is *personal profits?* Or must we expect him to seek some other end—prestige, power, or the gratification of professional zeal?

If we are to assume that the desire for *personal profit* is the prime force motivating control, we must conclude that the interests of control are different from and often radically opposed to those of ownership; that the owners most emphatically will not be served by a profit-seeking controlling group ...

We must conclude, therefore, that the interests of ownership and control are in large measure opposed *if* the interests of the latter grow primarily out of the desire for personal monetary gain....

In examining the break up of the old concept that was property and the old unity that was private enterprise, it is therefore evident that we are dealing not only with distinct but often with opposing groups, ownership on the one side, control on the other—a control which tends to move further and further away from ownership and ultimately to lie in the hands of the management itself, a management capable of perpetuating its own position.[6]

The risk that firm managers will take actions benefiting themselves at the expense of capital providers has long been a concern. While Berle and Means wrote about the

---

6. Adolf A. Berle & Gardiner C. Means, *The Modern Corporation and Private Property* (1932).

separation of ownership and control during the Great Depression, Adam Smith described the same problem in joint stock companies operating during revolutionary times:

> [T]he directors of companies, being managers of other people's money than their own, it cannot well be expected that they should watch over it with the same anxious vigilance with which the partner in a private copartnery frequently watch over their own. Like the stewards of a rich man, they are apt to consider attention to small matters as not for their master's honour, and very easily give themselves a dispensation from having it. Negligence and profusion, therefore, must always prevail, more or less, in the management of the affairs of such a company.[7]

Smith's oft-quoted caution makes clear the unexceptional and intractable nature of the problem.

Although elected by shareholders, corporate boards may not pursue shareholders' best interests. Directors may lack necessary education, experience, or time to fulfill their responsibilities, or directors' loyalties may lie with the firm's senior executives rather than its shareholders. Because the interests of managers and the interests of shareholders are not identical, centralizing management authority, while efficient and beneficial to the corporation, is not costless. Insofar as shareholders of large companies surrender their capital to a firm controlled by professional managers, conflicts of interest inevitably arise. When executives take actions that benefit themselves rather than the corporation, shareholders ultimately suffer the loss. More than four decades after Berle and Means published their iconic work, economists denominated conflicts between management and shareholders as "agency" problems and the resulting inefficiencies as "agency costs."[8]

Agency theory posits that corporate managers—the agents—are economically self-interested, and that, in acting to maximize their self-interest, they may harm the corporation and its shareholders—the principals. Managers may cause injury by failing to perform their responsibilities (a moral hazard problem), or by misrepresenting their skills and abilities to do the work for which they were hired (an adverse selection problem). Managers also may harm the corporation through self-dealing, by diverting corporate opportunities for themselves or competing with the company, and by extracting excessive compensation. Since shareholders own claims to the firm's residual, agency costs reduce their wealth. These problems are exacerbated because shareholders cannot determine readily whether poor corporate performance has resulted from shirking or from self-dealing by managers, nor will shareholders likely attempt to do so. Shareholders of large publicly-held corporations, owning just a fraction of the company's outstanding equity, are rationally apathetic; they lack the economic incentive to monitor management closely. Dispersed equity ownership by passive share-

---

7. Adam Smith, Wealth of Nations (1776).

8. Michael C. Jensen & William H. Meckling, *Theory of the Firm: Managerial Behavior, Agency Costs and Ownership Structure*, 3 J. Fin. Econ. 305 (1976).

holders, in combination with unchecked managerial control, enlarges public company agency costs.

In order to reduce these agency costs, some system of legal and non-legal rules and norms is needed to align the interests of management with the interests of shareholders and to incentivize management to act in the corporation's best interest. Berle and Means, who chiefly focused on the problem of management self-dealing, favored the imposition of legal constraints on management. Specifically, they called for strengthening judicially-imposed fiduciary duties on management, revising corporate law to treat corporate managers much like the law of trusts regards trustees. In addition, Berle and Means advocated for an equitable limitation on the powers of corporate management (or any other group within the corporation), requiring that management exercise its power for the ratable benefit of all shareholders.

Of course, no corporate governance system will eliminate all opportunistic behavior by management. Optimal corporate governance structures balance the risk and amount of loss from agency costs against the projected reduction in agency costs and the expenses incurred in implementing and enforcing the governance controls. Corporate scandals and massive failures, such as occurred at the beginning of this millennium, inspire government to intervene in the internal affairs of companies.

IV. The Corporate Governance Revolution

By way of introduction to the themes covered in this casebook, it is helpful to consider how the public's interest in corporate governance has grown over the past eight decades. Professor Brian Cheffins sketched the following useful history.

Brian R. Cheffins, *Did Corporate Governance "Fail" during the 2008 Stock Market Meltdown? The Case of the S&P 500*

65 Bus. Law. 1 (2009)[9]

INTRODUCTION

In 2008, corporate America experienced financial turmoil surpassing anything encountered since the Great Depression. Stock prices dropped further than they had in a single year since the 1930s. Venerable, blue chip Wall Street investment banks were sold at distress prices (e.g., Bear Stearns), ended up bankrupt (Lehman Brothers), or felt compelled to transform themselves into commercial banks (Goldman Sachs, J.P. Morgan Chase). While the commercial banking sector had to be propped up by

---

9. *Did Corporate Governance "Fail" During the 2008 Stock Market Meltdown? The Case of the S&P 500,* by Brian R. Cheffins, 2009, Business Lawyer, 65:1. © Copyright 2009 by the American Bar Association. Reprinted with permission. This information or any portion thereof may not be copied or disseminated in any form or by any means or stored in an electronic database or retrieval system without the express written consent of the American Bar Association.

governmental rescue schemes, industry leaders such as Washington Mutual and Wachovia disappeared nonetheless.

A striking aspect of the stock market meltdown of 2008 is that it occurred despite the strengthening of U.S. corporate governance over the past few decades and a reorientation toward the promotion of shareholder value. As the twentieth century drew to a close, growing institutionalization of share ownership fostered a shift to price-oriented investors, less passive in the conduct of corporate affairs than the typical individual stockholder. Boardrooms became dominated by independent directors not obviously susceptible to "capture" by corporate insiders. Executive pay became much more incentive-driven, implying that managers who delivered good results for shareholders profited handsomely. Corporate scandals that came to light at the beginning of the 2000s demonstrated weaknesses in managerial accountability, but a prompt legislative response in the form of the Sarbanes-Oxley Act of 2002 sought to fortify the existing corporate governance model.

Share prices rose smartly during the mid-2000s, implying all was well. Then came 2008, when shareholder value took a massive hit. Many are convinced the stock market meltdown proved current corporate governance arrangements are not fit for their purpose. "Boards Fail—Again," a 2008 piece in *Business Week*, claimed that "board failures represent ... a signal failure of the broad [corporate] governance movement that gained momentum at the beginning of this decade." The head of corporate governance at the California Public Employees' Retirement System ("CalPERS"), a major public pension fund, concurred in a 2009 op-ed, saying "the governance deficit ... undoubtedly exacerbated the scale and depth of the financial crisis" and "[t]he financial crisis exposed many boards as weak and incompetent." A 2009 report by the Organisation for Economic Co-operation and Development ("OECD") concluded "that the financial crisis can be to an important extent attributed to failures and weaknesses in corporate governance arrangements." Similarly, the Shareholder Bill of Rights Act of 2009, introduced to the Senate by Charles Schumer and Maria Cantwell in May 2009, contains a clause deeming Congress to have found "among the central causes of the financial and economic crises that the United States faces today has been a widespread failure of corporate governance."

THE DEVELOPMENT OF CORPORATE GOVERNANCE IN U.S. PUBLIC COMPANIES

Managerial Capitalism in the Post World War II Era

In order to assess the responsiveness of corporate governance to the stock market turmoil of 2008, it is necessary, as a preliminary matter, to identify the key corporate governance mechanisms in public companies and ascertain the role they are expected to play. On this count, history is instructive, as it reveals the corporate governance challenges that have been addressed and the logic underlying the "fixes" that have evolved....

[I]n the years immediately following World War II it seemingly mattered little whether there were mechanisms in place to ensure managers were properly accountable to shareholders. With the U.S. being the world's dominant economy and experiencing a prolonged post-war economic boom, successful corporations grew rapidly and, as an incidental byproduct, shareholders profited. Amidst this corporate prosperity, the internal governance of companies was not a high priority. The general consensus was that those who relied on corporations for employment, goods and services and investment returns could place their faith in corporate executives. Boards, supposedly guardians of shareholder rights, were expected to be collegial and supportive of management, a reasonable pre-supposition given that top executives strongly influenced the selection of directors. As for stockholders, they were "known for their indifference to everything about the companies they own except dividends and the approximate price of the stock."

With successful corporations such as IBM, General Motors, General Electric, Sears, US Steel and Alcoa becoming not merely household names but worldwide prototypes of managerial capitalism, the manager-oriented model of the corporation was pre-eminent. However, the fact executives lacked potent incentives to focus on shareholder returns became increasingly evident. CEO pay was composed primarily of salary and salary was closely correlated with company size. As a result, chief executives were typically eager to grow their companies by acquiring other firms, often operating in disparate economic sectors. Growth by acquisition, however, was frequently not good news for shareholders.

One problem was that numerous deals failed to live up to expectations and ended up destroying shareholder value. Moreover, executives struggled to maintain control over their sprawling corporate empires. Penn Central, a railway company which had diversified into pipelines, hotels, industrial parks and commercial real estate, collapsed in 1970 amidst personality clashes, mismanagement and lax board oversight. International Telephone and Telegraph, another sprawling conglomerate, was wracked in the early 1970s by allegations senior executives had authorized improper political donations to secure favorable antitrust treatment and had been involved in the controversial overthrow of a leftwing government in Chile. Subsequently, dozens of public companies, prompted by the threat of prosecution, admitted having made bribes, kickbacks or other illicit corporate payments abroad and in the United States. In the aftermath, it became clear that while senior executives typically were well aware of the payments, outside directors were too far "outside the loop" to act as a check on unethical corporate behavior.

The Corporate Governance Counter-Reaction

Widespread awareness that directors had been passive amidst the Penn Central collapse and the "questionable payments" scandal fostered a consensus that boards of public companies should proactively exercise independent oversight so as to enhance managerial accountability. In 1977, the New York Stock Exchange (NYSE), at the request of the federal Securities and Exchange Commission (SEC), amended its listing requirements to require each listed company to maintain an audit committee composed of independent directors. While regulators had not previously focused on board committees or outside directors, this initiative was not particularly radical because public companies were already restructuring their boards. Even before the NYSE amended its listing rules to provide for the establishment of audit committees, nearly 90% of the largest corporations in the U.S. had taken this step. Likewise, a 1978 report on corporate accountability based on interviews with companies in 17 countries referred to the United States as a "cauldron of experimentation," with the basic shift being toward more active and independent boards.

By the early 1980s, there was a growing consensus "the 'outside' director has won." Legal reforms sealed the victory. During the 1980s, Delaware court decisions involving derivative litigation and the invocation of takeover defenses indicated judicial acceptance of decisions taken to sidetrack derivative suits and hostile takeover bids hinged on outside directors playing a decisive role while acting in accordance with a process designed to ensure they were exercising independent judgment. In 1993, Congress endorsed the idea that executive pay should be dealt with by independent directors, stipulating that performance-based executive remuneration could only be exempted from a new $1 million deductibility cap under the Internal Revenue Code if a compensation committee made up entirely of outside directors approved the relevant arrangements.

Outside directors in turn became increasingly vigilant as monitors of management, recognizing that they had a mandate to scrutinize executives that was separate and distinct from their advisory and managerial functions. Correspondingly, by the 1990s boards increasingly evaluated managerial performance by reference to shareholder value and became more willing to fire underperforming chief executives. The board-room emphasis on shareholder returns dovetailed with other corporate governance trends. One was the rise of institutional investors (primarily pension funds and mutual funds), who became strong proponents of a shareholder-oriented model of the corporation at the same time they became the dominant group controlling the flow of money into the stock market. Traditionally, it was taken for granted among shareholders, whether individual or institutional, that the appropriate response to dissatisfaction with how a company was being run was to exercise "the Wall Street rule" and sell. During the 1980s and 1990s institutional investors began shifting away from this purely reactive approach in favor of challenging management to create value for shareholders. They did this from a position of strength, as the proportion of shares in U.S. public companies held by households and domestic institutional investors respectively shifted from 84 percent and 14 percent in 1965 to 49 percent and 44 percent, respectively, in 1985.

Institutional shareholders, in their new activist mode, initially focused on fighting anti-takeover initiatives. The 1980s was known as "the Deal Decade," exemplified by bidders relying on aggressive, innovative financial techniques to engineer daring takeover bids. Executives reacted defensively and sought to introduce management entrenchment devices such as the poison pill. Institutional investors, often sellers of large blocks of shares in takeovers, responded in turn by opposing managerial attempts to block unwelcome tender offers and by lobbying to protect their right to tender their shares to the highest bidder.

Institutional shareholders soon expanded their agenda. In the late 1980s and early 1990s they began concentrating on the board as a vehicle for improving managerial accountability and correspondingly pressed for changes designed to enhance the monitoring capabilities of directors, such as ensuring key board committees were staffed entirely with independent directors. Institutional investors also pressured companies to overhaul existing executive pay arrangements to replace the traditional bias towards "pay-for-size" in favor of pay-for-performance. The message got through, as a dramatic increase in equity-based compensation—most prominently the awarding of stock options—served to increase pay-to-performance sensitivity tenfold for CEOs between 1980 and 1998.

As the 1990s drew to a close, trends in corporate governance seemed highly positive. Boards had been strengthened, executive compensation had been restructured to align pay more closely with performance and shareholders appeared prepared to begin stepping forward to protect their interests. Economists Bengt Holmstrom and Steven Kaplan correspondingly predicted in a 2001 survey of corporate governance that "a more market-oriented corporate governance than existed up to the early 1980s is here to stay." Moreover, with corporate governance reform coinciding with strong economic growth in the U.S., ideological and market-driven momentum built up for companies elsewhere to converge towards a U.S.-style shareholder oriented corporate governance model. To quote Holmstrom and Kaplan again, "since the mid-1980s, the U.S. style of corporate governance has reinvented itself, and the rest of the world seems to be following the same path."

Then Came Enron

While Holmstrom and Kaplan strongly endorsed U.S. corporate governance in 2001, they conceded a mere four years later that "[t]o a casual observer, the United States corporate governance system must seem to be in terrible shape." A dramatic drop in share prices set the scene for disenchantment. With the demise of the late 1990s "dot-com" bull market, the Dow Jones Industrial Average ("DJIA") fell 36 percent between January 2000 and September 2002 and the S&P 500 dropped 48 percent between March 2000 and September 2002. A series of major corporate governance scandals simultaneously rocked investors, with nearly $313 billion worth of shareholder wealth being wiped out at Enron, WorldCom, Tyco, Global Crossing and Adelphia due to managerial malfeasance.

Some interpreted the corporate governance scandals as a damning indictment of the shareholder-oriented capitalism that had developed in the 1980s and 1990s and called for a profound reassessment of existing orthodoxies. Others, while prepared to acknowledge the scandals revealed various imperfections that should be addressed by regulatory intervention, argued any sort of fundamental overhaul would be unwise because the U.S. system of market-oriented capitalism had proved itself as successful in creating growth and prosperity exceeding that of all other countries. The latter view ultimately prevailed, as public officials moved quickly to introduce the federal Sarbanes-Oxley Act of 2002 (SOX) to restore confidence in the markets.

President George W. Bush said SOX encompassed "the most far-reaching reforms of American business practice since Franklin Delano Roosevelt" and the legislation was highly controversial when it was enacted. Sarbanes-Oxley did impose various new requirements on public companies and their executives and directors. Generally, however, the Act did not constitute a radical departure from past practice, building instead on existing federal regulations, state laws, accounting practices and corporate governance conventions. As a result, SOX was part [of] a larger process of strengthening corporate governance rather than a fundamental departure from past trends. As Ira Millstein, a well-known expert on corporate governance, has said: "SOX did directly what it was supposed to do: take the best practices of director independence and audit procedures and make them mandatory.... All that Sarbanes did was to take 'should' and 'could' and turned into must. And it worked."

Reforms SOX introduced concerning corporate boards and financial reporting illustrate how the legislation built upon existing corporate governance trends. With boards, audit committees were already a firmly entrenched aspect of corporate governance before Enron. From this departure point, SOX mandated changes to the NYSE and NASDAQ National Market listing rules that spelled out the formal duties of audit committees, required companies to have an audit committee composed entirely of independent directors, and obliged firms to offer an explanation if the committee lacked a member who was a "financial expert."

As for financial reporting, SOX created a new oversight panel to regulate accountants and discipline auditors, prohibited auditing firms from offering a broad range of consulting services to companies they audited, and mandated that chief executives and chief financial officers of public companies certify the accuracy and completeness of quarterly and annual financial reports. Part of the impetus for the accounting-oriented SOX reforms can be traced back to the shift from cash-based to equity-based executive compensation that began in earnest in the 1990s. As law professor Jack Coffee has pointed out, a "dark side" to option-based compensation is that more stock options tends to mean more fraud, as senior executives have powerful financial incentives to manipulate earnings in order to maximize pay-outs available from exercising the options. Earnings restatements became endemic as the 1990s drew to a close, reflecting at least in part a desire by executives to hit performance-oriented compensation targets, and complex accounting-oriented frauds designed to prop up the share price were a hallmark of the iconic Enron and WorldCom scandals. This all implied that existing checks, such as external auditors and independent boards, were an insufficient counterweight to the "dark side" of equity-based executive pay. SOX in effect aimed to redress the balance without displacing the ability of public companies to seek to motivate their executives with performance-oriented compensation.

Private Equity

According to law professor Jonathan Macey, "The most important market-inspired component of the U.S. corporate governance infrastructure is the market for corporate control." This market involves the purchasing and selling of controlling interests in companies and provides incentives to managers to maximize shareholder value because they know an unwelcome bid for control could be forthcoming if share prices are in the doldrums. It was particularly vibrant during the 1980s "Deal Decade," with the most striking type of deal being the public-to-private buyout, where financiers operating as LBO (leveraged buyout) associations would borrow heavily to buy up all of a company's publicly owned shares and take the company private.

As the 1980s drew to a close, Delaware courts and state legislatures provided strong legal backing for managers minded to fend off unwelcome tender offers. A tightening of credit markets also made it much more difficult to orchestrate public-to-private buyouts. Holmstrom and Kaplan argued in their 2001 survey of corporate governance that this sort of transaction was obsolete anyway. They reasoned that the key rationale for a public-to-private transaction, namely restructuring underperforming assets, was no longer relevant because public company executives, spurred on by incentive-based executive compensation and closer monitoring by shareholders and directors, were already seeking to maximize shareholder value. In fact, a revival of the public-to-private deal was just around the corner.

LBO associations—rechristened private equity firms—had great success through much of the 2000s securing backing for the investment funds they launched amid general enthusiasm for "alternative" investment strategies among pension funds, endowments, and wealthy private investors frustrated by uneven stock market returns to accumulate huge pools of capital available for buyouts. Private equity firms also found it was easy to borrow large sums on attractive terms, meaning they had the financial firepower required to acquire all but the very biggest public companies. Correspondingly, "[i]n 2006, the value of … 'public-to-private' buyouts surged to a record $120 billion, or about 1.5 percent of Gross Domestic Product, up from just over $70 billion in 2005."

While private equity is known for taking companies off the stock market, the surge in private equity buyouts plausibly constituted a catalyst for better corporate governance among publicly traded companies generally. Private equity bidders prefer to work in co-operation with incumbent executives rather than make "hostile" bids. Nevertheless, in buyout negotiations the bargaining position of the incumbent management team will be strengthened if the company is well-run, and underperforming executives could easily find themselves on the outside looking in on a private equity restructuring. Private equity thus potentially has a disciplinary effect on public companies something akin to old-style hostile takeover bids. As economist Irwin Stelzer said in 2007:

> We might just be entering a new phase of capitalism. Firms taken over by private equity funds will have to improve their performance; publicly owned firms competing with them will have to respond by improving their own profitability. Life at the top of corporate America will be less pleasant. Which is what dynamic capitalism is all about—change that discomfits the comfortable.

Hedge Fund Activism

The market for corporate control focuses around tender offers designed to secure a majority stake that will ensure the bidder can select the directors of the target and thereby control the corporation. An investor who targets an underperforming company alternatively might refrain from seeking to obtain voting control and instead build up "offensively" a sufficiently sizeable minority stake to capture management's attention and use that leverage to lobby for changes intended to increase shareholder value. During the 1990s, a handful of institutional shareholders — most prominently CalPERS — began analyzing the performance of executives and boards to identify underachieving companies to be targeted for shareholder action. However, pension funds and mutual funds ultimately proved reluctant to go further in challenging public companies than periodically following recommendations of a shareholder advisory service to vote against policies management supported. A key obstacle was that these investors emphasized diversification as an investment philosophy. Since improved returns in a particular company were only likely to have a marginal impact on a diversified investment portfolio and since activism was time-consuming, costly, and not always successful, the sums simply did not add up.

While neither pension funds nor mutual funds proved willing to engage in "offensive" shareholder activism, hedge fund managers began in the 2000s to step forward in earnest and target underperforming companies. The typical tactic was to build up quietly a sizeable position in the targeted company and agitate for change, with common demands being that management return cash to shareholders by way of a stock buyback or a one-off dividend payment, sell weak divisions, or even put the company itself up for sale. For activist hedge funds, the lure was the prospect of selling out at a sizeable profit after value-enhancing changes had taken place. The upside could be particularly lucrative if the hedge fund could acquire its shares at discount prices before it was forced to divulge its stake under Schedule 13D of the Securities Exchange Act of 1934, which requires the filing of an ownership report within ten days after the acquisition of 5 percent or more of a public company's shares.

Activist hedge funds are generally less likely to target big companies than small firms because a large amount of capital is required to acquire a sufficiently sizeable voting block to make offensive activism worthwhile. However, with assets under management by hedge funds growing substantially during the 2000s, and with hedge funds being able to increase their financial firepower readily through borrowing due to debt being plentiful and "cheap," hedge fund managers with a shareholder activism mandate could, and did, challenge management at very large firms. This meant that "[h]edge funds [had] become critical players in … corporate governance." The *New York Times* put the point more strongly in 2007, saying "activists have captured the center ring and are directing the main event." A *Wall Street Journal* columnist observed similarly in 2008, "Like a rebel politician declaring victory, shareholders can declare their revolution nearly complete."

Critics of hedge fund activism argued that hedge funds were hyperactive traders apt to pressure managers of a targeted company to take steps that might raise the share price in the short term but would not help the company, and might even harm it, over the long haul. Others offered a more favorable assessment, saying that hedge funds were improving corporate governance by enhancing managerial responsiveness to shareholder value. For instance, finance professors Alon Brav and Wei Jiang and law professors Frank Partnoy and Randall Thomas claimed on the basis of a detailed empirical study of hedge fund activism "that activist hedge funds occupy an important middle ground between internal monitoring by large shareholders and external monitoring by corporate raiders."

Professor Macey has put the case in favor of hedge fund activism even more strongly, saying "hedge funds ... are an extremely important addition to the market for corporate control in any nation's arsenal of corporate governance devices." He argues that the benefits do not extend merely to companies hedge funds targeted. Instead,

> the key role being played by hedge funds ... in corporate governance affects all companies in a very profound way. Even companies that want to avoid being the target of an activist fund can only do this by improving corporate governance extensively so that there are no longer any arbitrage possibilities that allow fund managers to take a position in the target company and then start agitating for reform.

To the extent this assessment is on the mark, the emergence of hedge funds as offensive shareholder activists in the 2000s would have supplemented existing corporate governance mechanisms that served to provide managers with incentives to focus on shareholder returns.

Comments and Questions

1. Professor Cheffins' account illustrates one of the recurring themes in our study of corporate governance: "Governance, like religion, does not attract followers in good times."[10] In the United States, corporate governance reforms have followed the demise of large public companies and, relatedly, post-mortem revelations of fraud, self-dealing, or other illegality by firm managers. Like the collapse of Enron some three decades later, the 1970 bankruptcy of giant conglomerate Penn Central jolted its shareholders (many of whom were railroad employees) as well as the capital markets. Government investigations into the failure of the nation's sixth largest corporation revealed not only that Penn Central management had misrepresented the firm's finances and falsified accounts to conceal losses, but also that Penn Central's directors received inadequate financial information, failed to respond to specific warnings about the company's actual financial condition, and stood by while executives paid themselves lavish salaries and traded in inside information. The SEC criticized the board for its lack of independence and for ignoring warnings about both the company's impending financial disaster and the questionable conduct of its most important officers. Similarly, a Congressional committee staff report faulted Penn Central's directors for relying on oral presentations and for failing to obtain adequate financial information necessary to effectively monitor management.

Unfortunately, Penn Central was not a lone case of corporate abuse uncovered during this period. Other corporations plagued by management fraud and self-

---

10. Roger Lowenstein, *A Boss for a Boss*, N.Y. Times (Dec. 14, 2003).

dealing—Equity Funding and Stirling Homex, to name just two—also collapsed unexpectedly. Hundreds of other corporations admitted that they paid bribes or made other illegal payments to officials in foreign countries. Federal prosecutors targeted still more companies for violating campaign finance laws at home. Following a decade of seemingly pervasive wrongdoing, a 1980 *Fortune* magazine feature story asked, "How Lawless Are Big Companies?" The article reported that some 11 percent of major American corporations had engaged in corrupt practices (not including foreign bribes and kickbacks) over the previous decade, with many firms committing multiple offenses.[11]

2. Headline-making corporate scandals in the 1970s generated widespread criticism of big business and general agreement about the need for corporate governance reform. As Professor Cheffins indicates, most proposed reforms centered on electing more outside directors to boards, persons independent of management who would monitor executives objectively and actively. Still, controversy arose over whether to regulate public company boardrooms or rely on Corporate America to restructure voluntarily. Even as companies brought more outsiders onto their boards, governance experts doubted that meaningful change would ensue absent a legal mandate. As Harvard Business School Professor Myles Mace wrote in 1979:

> It is not reasonable to expect CEOs to give up or restrict voluntarily their de facto powers of control in their respective corporations. As was the case ten years ago, CEOs still control board membership; determine what the board does and does not do; stack their boards with employees and with purveyors of professional services to the management such as investment bankers, commercial bankers, and outside legal counsel; control the agenda and management information systems; and manage the compensation packages for key executives, including perquisites. Many CEOs like it the way it is. Recommendations for any change that seems to whittle away at de facto powers of control are resisted, being dismissed as counterproductive or, as categorized in the words of one executive, unAmerican and destructive to the free enterprise system.[12]

In 1980, both houses of Congress considered bills establishing federal minimum standards for the composition of corporate boards, directors' duties, and shareholders' rights. The proposed legislation stalled, however, following the 1980 election of President Ronald Reagan and the corresponding political swing away from government regulating business. As we begin the study of corporate governance, what is your view about the need for government ordering of corporate internal affairs? Assuming the necessity of some government involvement, are corporate internal affairs best regulated by the states or by the federal government? In the next chapter, we examine the history and scope of state and federal mandates affecting corporate governance.

---

11. Ross, *How Lawless Are Big Companies?*, Fortune (Dec. 1, 1980) at 56.
12. Myles Mace, *Directors: Myth and Reality—Ten Years Later*, 32 Rutgers L. Rev. 293, 307–08 (1979).

3. Professor Cheffins notes that outside directors once were considered too far removed from corporate day-to-day operations to police against management fraud and other wrongdoing. Nonetheless, by the beginning of the 1980s, consensus developed that "the 'outside' director ha[d] won." Outside directors became entrusted with the responsibility for monitoring management in order to deter wrongdoing and thwart abuse. Even corporate executives and their advocates, such as the Business Roundtable,[13] encouraged the election of additional non-management ("outside") directors to company boards. What accounts for this change in perspective? Why might CEOs agree to nominate new directors not under their management authority?

4. Professor Cheffins' article also touches on another major theme of our study: how shifts in public company stock ownership affect corporate governance laws, rules, and norms. During the Great Depression, when Berle and Means wrote *The Modern Corporation and Private Property,* individuals (sometimes called retail investors) owned much of the outstanding stock in U.S. public companies. As Berle and Means recognized, such shareholders generally lacked both the means and the incentives to monitor corporate managers, much less control them. What did shareholders typically do if they became dissatisfied with a company's performance and/or its management?

Accepted limitations on shareholders' participation shifted as more institutional investors entered the markets, buying and selling securities offered by public companies. Over time, as institutional holdings of U.S. equities grew, shareholders' potential, if not actual, influence on corporate governance expanded as well. Because they can vote big blocks of shares, or sell their large positions and adversely affect the stock price, institutional investors enjoy the leverage to demand a more active role in firm governance than widely dispersed individual shareholders. With the skills and sophistication of professional investors, institutions may monitor more actively and seek to replace board members of poorly performing companies. By the 1970s, Congress and the SEC recognized the promise of institutional investors' participation in corporate governance, and they convened public hearings to examine shareholders' involvement.

Legislators and regulators heard competing views about shareholders' interest in becoming more active in firm governance. This finding should not have surprised lawmakers insofar as institutions are not homogeneous. Using different organizational and management structures, institutions seek to advance distinct investment objectives, using innumerable strategies, over various time frames. Institutional investors also are subject to distinct regulatory schemes (although some institutional shareholders are largely unregulated), and they face different conflicts of interest, depending on their beneficiaries and business models. Why might certain institutional shareholders seek greater voice in corporate internal affairs? What types of institutional shareholders might prefer to remain passively invested?

Lawmakers also heard that then-existing statutes and regulations, coupled with inadequate information, impeded shareholders from fully exercising their rights to

---

13. Established in 1972, the Business Roundtable is an association of CEOs of leading major U.S. companies that advocates for its members and funds research supporting its lobbying efforts.

nominate, elect, and remove board members. Responding to this feedback from investors, the SEC began to reexamine the federal proxy rules. We consider the role of the SEC in facilitating shareholders' involvement in corporate governance, beginning in the next chapter.

5. During the Deal Decade of the 1980s, the market for corporate control operated to discipline management of publicly traded companies to act in the best interests of shareholders. How does the market for corporate control motivate management? What did activist institutions do to facilitate hostile takeovers during the Deal Decade?

Among other arguments against takeovers, opponents claimed that even if shareholders profited from the transactions, they did so at the expense of other corporate stakeholders, including the firms' employees and local communities where the firms did business. We examine this contention, and how state legislatures responded to this concern, when we consider the market for corporate control in Chapter 8.

6. The article excerpt recounts a number of events leading up to the enactment of Sarbanes-Oxley in 2002, including the bursting of the technology ("dot com") stock market bubble, the bankruptcies of corporate giants Enron and WorldCom, and the revelation of widespread financial frauds and management self-dealing at still other public companies, including Tyco, Global Crossing, and Adelphia. This "perfect storm" of corporate scandals caused Congress to reconsider deregulatory policies and, especially, its serious underfunding of the SEC during the prior decade. In order to restore investor confidence, federal lawmakers passed Sarbanes-Oxley by a nearly unanimous vote.[14] According to Professor Cheffins, what benefits did the legislation provide to shareholders?

Although SOX enjoyed overwhelming bipartisan support at its enactment, some lawmakers backed calls to repeal the statute, or at least to amend it significantly, just a year later. Academics have studied whether the law's mandates ultimately helped or hurt shareholders. In Chapter 13, we review some of this research and consider whether SOX constitutes flawed regulation … "quack" corporate governance. At this point, do you suppose that better governed firms (e.g., firms with majority independent boards) provide superior investment returns for shareholders? Why or why not? If the evidence does not dependably support better returns for investors, why might shareholders nonetheless prefer corporate boards dominated by independent directors?

7. Some observers argue that Corporate America's continuing fixation with short-term performance is the most concerning governance failure of the past several decades. Management feels compelled to meet quarterly earnings estimates, understanding that missing Wall Street's forecasts by even a penny could cause the company's stock price to fall precipitously. Pressured by shareholders and the financial markets to maximize quarterly earnings, executives may take excessive risks, be tempted to

---

14. The bill passed in the House of Representatives by a vote of 423 to 3 (with eight abstentions) and in the Senate by a vote of 99 to 0 (with one abstention).

manipulate financial reports, or enter into transactions for the purpose of inflating the firm's performance. Further, management's focus on short-term stock price undermines economic growth by discouraging companies from spending capital on innovative technologies, research and development, new lines of business, and work force improvements. Companies reduce their costs and thus raise profits for shareholders in the current quarter, but firms do so at the expense of future corporate productivity, efficiency, and competitiveness.

In advance of the 2016 presidential elections, politicians have advanced various proposals to fight "quarterly capitalism" and promote sustainable economic growth. Corporate executives and their advocates seek legal reforms providing them with greater autonomy from stockholders—especially from activist hedge funds—so as to enable them to manage companies for the long-term. Executives' complaints today echo those made by their predecessors during the 1980s, when public companies that failed to meet investor expectations provoked hostile takeovers rather than activist hedge funds. Then, as now, academics debate whether corporations pursue short-term profits at the expense of long-term growth, damaging the U.S. economy, and, if so, how corporate governance affects the relevant incentives and behaviors of directors, officers, and shareholders.

Assuming that shareholders prefer that corporations maximize profits in the short-term, should the law obligate directors and officers to manage firms principally in the interest of shareholders? If incentives matter, how could corporations compensate executives to combat the "tyranny of short-termism"?

8. The growth of hedge fund activism, coupled with the greater concentration of institutional shareholders, has empowered more shareholders to exercise their voice in the new millennium. Professor Cheffins distinguishes institutional shareholder activism in the 1980s and 1990s with the newer "offensive" activist strategies employed by hedge funds beginning roughly in 2000. How does recent hedge fund activism differ from the strategies employed by LBO associations in prior decades?

Some of the most spirited debates in corporate governance over the past few years concern the benefits and costs of hedge fund activism. Strategies favored by hedge funds—such as buying back shares, paying special dividends, and selling productive assets—may provide company shareholders with immediate returns. However, detractors claim that these tactics are antithetical to long-term value. Also, insofar as hedge funds demand that target corporations slash capital expenditures in plants and equipment, abandon research and development, and terminate company efforts to develop skilled workforces, hedge funds impair long-term growth for both the firm and the economy more broadly. Hedge funds and their backers counter that even if they successfully influence corporate managers to amend their firms' business plans, their recommendations promote the efficient use of capital and strengthen target companies by optimizing their capital structures, removing underachieving managers, and selling underperforming assets. To the extent that the firms distribute excess cash reserves to shareholders, they may redeploy the capital to investments offering superior returns. Which arguments do you find more persuasive? Why?

9. Except in reaction to shareholders' challenges or corporate crises, boards of directors traditionally have not engaged directly with shareholders. Instead, management led engagement activities, often through the firm's investor relations department, corporate secretary, or chief governance officer. Recently, however, regulatory changes and evolving investor demands for unfiltered communication with directors have caused more boards to engage directly and, indeed, proactively with shareholders. In 2015, major institutional investors, including Vanguard and BlackRock, wrote letters to their portfolio companies (public companies in which they have invested) promoting enhanced engagement with directors. In the opinion of SEC Chair Mary Jo White, "[T]he board of directors is — or ought to be — a central player in shareholder engagement."[15] New organizations, such as the Shareholder-Director Exchange and the Conference Board Governance Center Task Force on Corporate/Investor Engagement, have formed to encourage dialogues, provide engagement protocols, and compile best practices for interactions between board members and investors. Why might boards of directors choose to engage directly with company shareholders? On what governance topics would shareholders prefer a dialogue with the firm's directors rather than its executives? On what governance topics might shareholders have sufficient expertise and information to communicate productively with directors? Assuming that they choose to hold their shares rather than sell them, why would investors adopt a strategy of engagement rather than simply voting their shares?

10. Publication of Berle and Means seminal work ignited a long-running academic debate about the proper role of the corporation in society. Professor Merrick Dodd claimed that business corporations exist as social institutions for the benefit of workers and communities, not solely to make profits for stockholders. Dodd further argued that corporate management should serve the community rather than simply act to maximize shareholders' wealth. Controversy regarding whether or not business firms have (or should have) social responsibilities continues today. What do you think? Should directors make shareholders' welfare their sole end? Should the law allow corporate management to pursue objectives other than maximizing shareholders' profits? Why or why not? Reconsider these questions as you study the legal duties of corporate directors in the chapters that follow. In Chapter 11, we specifically examine corporate philanthropy and corporate social responsibility as well as shareholders' proposals to influence boards to take actions benefiting the environment, human rights, and other matters of social concern.

---

15. Speech, Mary Jo White, 10th Annual Transatlantic Corporate Governance Dialogue (Dec. 3, 2013).

Chapter 2

Corporate Governance, Path Dependency, and the Sources of Regulation

Corporate governance in the United States is regulated by several different bodies, including states, self-regulatory organizations such as stock exchanges, and the federal government, particularly the Securities and Exchange Commission (SEC). Each sets the legal parameters for managers and owners. Each, however, answers to different constituencies and has different approaches to governance.

Congress created the SEC in 1934 in an attempt, ironically, not to strengthen, but to weaken enforcement of the securities laws. An "independent" federal agency, the SEC's role in the governance process was mostly limited to ensuring adequate disclosure and overseeing the proxy solicitation process. Particularly since the start of the new millennium, however, the agency has been given substantial additional responsibility and been more directly interjected into the corporate governance process.

Stock exchanges were originally private organizations that mostly provided a centralized place for trading securities. Congress, in adopting the securities laws, gave certain regulatory responsibilities to the exchanges and subjected them to oversight by the SEC. The exchanges regulate corporate governance practices primarily through the vehicle of listing standards. These are obligations assumed by companies when they agree to have their shares traded on the exchange.

At the same time, their central importance in the securities markets has declined. In recent years, both Nasdaq and NYSE have converted to for-profit companies while retaining their regulatory responsibilities. In the post-conversion period, the NYSE has seen a decline in the volume of trading for companies that it lists from 80% to around 20%. These changes suggest that the role of the exchanges in the governance process is undergoing evolution.

States are perhaps the most significant player in the corporate governance process. Under the internal affairs doctrine, the rights of directors and shareholders are determined by the state of incorporation. As a result, it is the state of incorporation that sets the fiduciary standards for directors and the voting rights for shareholders. In determining the state of incorporation, companies will pick the one with the most favorable law. In the case of large public companies, Delaware is the unquestionable favorite, with approximately 60% of the companies in the Fortune 500 incorporating in that state.

The source of regulation matters for purposes of enforcement, as will be explored more completely in this chapter. While each regulatory body has some enforcement authority, the right of private parties to bring an action varies considerably depending upon the source of the requirement. Private actions under the securities laws are typically brought as disclosure violations, something that usually requires evidence of materiality and scienter. There are no private rights of action for violations of the listing standards of the stock exchanges. As for state actions, they are typically brought as derivative suits, with high pleading standards and procedural hurdles that must be addressed.

It would be wrong to view this system of multiple regulators as a product of deliberate design. The regulatory system can more accurately be described as a matter of historical accident or path dependency. As a result, there are numerous inefficiencies. As Professor Gilson has noted: "In a path dependent environment, the influence of factors such as increasing returns and network externalities means that an observed equilibrium may not be the 'most' efficient." Ronald J. Gilson, *Path Dependence and Comparative Corporate Governance: Corporate Governance and Economic Efficiency: When Do Institutions Matter?*, 74 Wash. U. L. Q. 327, 329 (1996).

I. State Regulation

A. The Internal Affairs Doctrine

With the exception of a small number of federally chartered companies, mostly financial institutions, corporations are formed under state law. A corporation may select any state to incorporate and is not limited to the jurisdiction where it has business operations or headquarters. As a result, corporations can select a particular state for any reason, including the flexibility of the legal requirements.

The law of the state of incorporation determines the internal affairs of a corporation. The internal affairs doctrine encompasses the substantive rights of directors and shareholders. This approach avoids the possibility of inconsistent standards and requirements. *See Edgar v. Mite Corp.*, 457 US 624 (1982) ("The internal affairs doctrine is a conflict of laws principle which recognizes that only one State should have the authority to regulate a corporation's internal affairs—matters peculiar to the relationships among or between the corporation and its current officers, directors, and shareholders—because otherwise a corporation could be faced with conflicting demands."). At the same time, however, the approach provides an incentive for states to use their regulatory authority to attract corporations.

Faith Stevelman, *Regulatory Competition, Choice of Forum, and Delaware's Stake in Corporate Law*
34 Del. J. Corp. L. 57, 76–78, 80–82 (2009)[1]

As illustrated in the Dartmouth College case, early American corporations were created by the grant of a formal charter from their home state's legislature. This historic reality spawned the understanding of corporations as "creatures of state law." Furthermore, in this period, corporations were understood to possess limited powers—i.e., only those powers granted expressly in the charter. They applied for a charter from the state where they operated and were located. (Given the present state of global commerce, it is difficult to recall that as late as the mid or even late nineteenth century, most business was fundamentally local in nature.) Nor was the receipt of a charter a foregone conclusion. To increase their chances of obtaining a charter, promoters commonly cited some state interest that the company's commercial endeavors would advance. The idea of corporations "being" creatures of their incorporating state was supported, also, by the fact that states often contributed financing to these corporations, and placed representatives on their boards. Indeed, companies' separate legal personhood remained controversial; it was not self evident that their powers would be respected beyond the geographic boundaries of the state which chartered them. Against this backdrop, it is easy to see why corporations conventionally would have been conceived of as "creatures of state law." The legal and historic reality described herein, however, has long vanished. The assumptions about corporations it spawned are outmoded.

Secondly, the "corporations as creatures of state law" notion ignores the fact that Congress could federalize corporate law for companies engaged in interstate commerce (i.e., most). The fact that Congress has declined to enact a comprehensive federal corporate law reflects a concrete political reality, not an ontological or taxonomic reality that validates corporations' existence in state law.

… modern corporate legal theory undermines the rationality of conceiving corporations as belonging in any sense to the state where they charter. Under modern theory—as is reflected in Delaware's case law—corporations are conceived of as a nexus of private contracts among the factors of production. They are conceived of as private actors—legal agents of the persons who capitalize them (shareholders) and govern them (the board), rather than legal extensions of the chartering state. As modern corporate legal theory privileges this private, contractualist view of corporations, it undermines the logic of corporations being "creatures of state law." There is no umbilical cord that would tie a dispute against a corporation to the forum of the chartering state. In this private, contractualist view, Delaware's corporate law is only one example of the many legal regimes that private parties choose from in attempting to promote the wealth arising from commercial transacting. This modern, contractualist view of the corporation and corporate law is also evident in the respect courts typically afford choice of forum provisions in corporate/commercial contracts. It is also reflected

---

in the severability of choice of law and choice of forum in these contracts. Again, in this modern corporate ontology, the state has no meaningful "generative" authority which it can use to pull its corporate "creatures" back into its courtrooms. Hence choice of law and choice of forum are separate, distinct legal constructs. Choice of Delaware corporate law is simply indeterminate in regard to choice of forum.

* * *

Nevertheless, taken on its own terms, as a modern choice of law scheme, the IAD [Internal Affairs Doctrine] makes good sense. "Lex Incorporationis"—that is, the rule that the incorporating state's corporate law "sticks" to the corporation's internal affairs—provides a clear, stable rule for resolving conflicts of laws questions. Clarity in corporate choice of law is maximized by privileging the law of the state of incorporation. A different choice of law rule for corporate internal affairs—one which relied on the place of the company's principal operations or headquarters, for example—would import more subjective and changeable factors into the choice of law analysis. This would yield less certainty for courts, investors, and third parties.

As a choice of law regime, the IAD is codified in the Restatement (Second) of Conflicts of Laws. The Restatement sets forth the basic premise of the IAD—that the corporate law of the state of incorporation will govern a corporation's internal affairs irrespective of where any dispute is litigated. Second, the Restatement sets forth an expansive definition of corporate internal affairs.

The Restatement also endorses the presumption of "singularity" in the IAD—i.e., that a corporation's internal affairs should be governed exclusively by the law of the state of incorporation. In this respect, conflicts analysis in corporate law is far more streamlined or even simplistic than the conflicts of laws regime applicable to most other areas of law.

Singularity in choice of corporate law is also reflected in the Revised Model Business Corporation Act (MBCA). The MBCA provides that states complying with its choice of law dictates should refrain from "interfering" in other state's corporation laws— that is, from supplementing or amending foreign corporations' internal affairs provisions. This is set forth in section 15.05(c) of the MBCA, which provides that a state shall not "regulate the organization or internal affairs of a foreign corporation authorized to transact business in this state." Singularity in corporate choice of law allows corporate actors definitively to predict which state's laws will define their rights and obligations. Because parity is important in the treatment of shareholders, and predictability is especially important in commercial arrangements, singularity in corporate choice of law—as reflected in the IAD, the Restatement, and the MBCA— makes good sense. The singularity presumption in the IAD favors courts interpreting foreign corporation laws conservatively, in the fashion most faithful to the intent of the incorporating state. But respect for singularity in corporate choice of law (or even the goal of clarity in corporate law) does not mandate confining Delaware corporate law claims to the Delaware courts. The American civil justice system simply does not presume that the geography of adjudication will match the locus of lawmaking.

Comments and Questions

1. In the early days of the country, corporations were viewed with suspicion. As Justice Stevens has described:

> The individualized charter mode of incorporation reflected the "cloud of disfavor under which corporations labored" in the early years of this Nation. 1 W. Fletcher, Cyclopedia of the Law of Corporations § 2, p. 8 (rev. ed. 2006); *see also* Louis K. Liggett Co. v. Lee, 288 U. S. 517, 548–549 (1933) (Brandeis, J., dissenting) (discussing fears of the "evils" of business corporations); L. Friedman, A History of American Law 194 (2d ed. 1985) ("The word 'soulless' constantly recurs in debates over corporations.... Corporations, it was feared, could concentrate the worst urges of whole groups of men"). Thomas Jefferson famously fretted that corporations would subvert the Republic. General incorporation statutes, and widespread acceptance of business corporations as socially useful actors, did not emerge until the 1800's.

Citizens United v. FEC, 130 S. Ct. 876 (2010). Perhaps unsurprisingly, there were not very many corporations formed during the early period of the country's history. *Id.* (noting that only "a few hundred [were formed] during all of the 18th century.").

2. What are the advantages to the internal affairs doctrine? What are the disadvantages? Delaware is the clear winner of the competition to attract corporations. Despite having about 60% of the Fortune 500 incorporated in the state, only Du Pont actually has its headquarters in Delaware.

3. Some argue that this doctrine is critical to wealth maximization. *See* Frank H. Easterbrook & Daniel R. Fischel, *Mandatory Disclosure and the Protection of Investors*, 70 Va. L. Rev. 669, 697–98 (May 1984). Only with the internal affairs doctrine can states be counted upon to adopt wealth maximizing statutes. Do you agree with this assessment?

4. What would corporate governance look like if the internal affairs doctrine did not apply? In other countries, the rule of thumb has been that companies should incorporate in the country where they maintained their headquarters, although this is changing. What if that approach applied in this country?

5. With respect to fiduciary duties, does the internal affairs doctrine require courts in other jurisdictions to rely on the judicial interpretations of the courts or just the statutes adopted in the state of incorporation? And what happens when the courts disagree on the application of the internal affairs doctrine? *See* Gregory Scott Crespi, *Choice of Law in Veil-Piercing Litigation: Why Courts Should Discard the Internal Affairs Rule and Embrace General Choice-of-Law Principles*, 64 N.Y.U. Ann. Surv. Am. L. 85, 90 (2008) (noting that with respect to veil piercing, some courts have rejected application of the internal affairs doctrine and instead employed "a more general choice-of-law analysis" thereby allowing for the application of "local piercing law—or the law of yet another jurisdiction that is not the state of incorporation—to a piercing controversy involving an out-of-state corporation.").

6. The internal affairs doctrine dictates the law that will apply. It does not dictate where the action can actually be maintained. Thus, a derivative suit involving a company incorporated in Delaware but headquartered in San Francisco can potentially be filed in California. Delaware law will apply but the decision maker will be a judge in another state. Why might shareholders want to do this? Can companies do anything to force shareholders to actually bring the case in Delaware? Delaware courts have affirmed bylaws that require derivatives suits to be maintained in Delaware. *See Boilermakers Local 154 Retirement Fund et al. v. Chevron Corp. and ICLUB Investment Partnership v. FedEx Corp.*, 73 A.3d 934 (Del. Ch. 2013).

7. The federal government does provide for incorporation in narrow circumstances. For a discussion of these entities, see Paul E. Lund, *Federally-Chartered Corporations and Federal Jurisdiction*, 36 Fla. St. U. L. Rev. 317 (2009).

The "internal affairs" doctrine is not limited to the "state" of incorporation. The internal affairs doctrine typically applies even to companies incorporated in other countries. This can result in very different principles of corporate governance.

In re BP P.L.C. Derivative Litigation

United States District Court, Southern District of New York
507 F. Supp. 2d 302 (2007)

BAER JR, SENIOR JUDGE:

BP p.l.c., BP America, Inc., BP Products North America, Inc., BP Corp. North America, BP Exploration (Alaska) Inc. sixteen members of BP's current board of directors, nine former directors, eight current and former directors, officers and employees of BP's subsidiaries, and twenty "John Doe" defendants (collectively "Defendants" or "BP") move this Court to dismiss BP shareholders' derivative action pursuant to Fed. R. Civ. P. 12(b)(6) alleging that Plaintiffs fail to state a valid derivative claim under governing English law. Alternatively, Defendants argue, this action should be dismissed pursuant to Fed. R. Civ. P. 12(b)(2) for lack of personal jurisdiction over the movants on the ground of *forum non conveniens*. For the following reasons, Defendants' Motion to Dismiss is GRANTED in its entirety.

* * *

Defendants advance three main arguments in support of their motion to dismiss — (1) the Complaint fails to state a cognizable claim because the governing law in this instance, English law, generally prohibits a shareholder from bringing a derivative action on its behalf except in three very narrow circumstances pursuant to the Companies Act 1985; (2) none of the individual moving Defendants is subject to personal jurisdiction in New York because all are non-domiciliaries with insufficient contacts with New York to confer general jurisdiction; and (3) the Court should decline to adjudicate Plaintiffs' claims under the doctrine of *forum non conveniens* because England, not New York, has the greatest interest in this litigation. Not surprisingly, Plaintiffs challenge Defendants' three arguments and focus primarily on the proper choice of law analysis. Therefore, I will address the choice of law analysis in the first instance.

a. Internal Affairs Doctrine

This Court must apply New York's choice of law principles to determine the governing law. Klaxon Co. v. Stentor Elec. Mfg. Co., 313 U.S. 487, 496, 61 S. Ct. 1020, 85 L. Ed. 1477 (1941). New York's choice of law rules provide different choice of law doctrines depending on the nature of the claim—i.e. torts or contracts. Generally, New York law requires that claims related to corporate affairs—i.e., issues involving the rights and liabilities of a corporation—are governed by the internal affairs doctrine.

That doctrine provides that the rights of a shareholder in a foreign company (including the right to sue derivatively) are determined by the law of the place where the company is incorporated. *See* Atherton v. FDIC, 519 U.S. 213, 224, 117 S. Ct. 666, 136 L. Ed. 2d 656 (1997) ("The internal affairs [doctrine] ... seeks only to avoid conflict by requiring that there be a single point of legal reference."); Edgar v. Mite Corp., 457 U.S. 624, 645, 102 S. Ct. 2629, 73 L. Ed. 2d 269 (1982) ("The internal affairs doctrine is a conflict of laws principle which recognizes that only one State should have the authority to regulate a corporation's internal affairs—matters peculiar to the relationships among or between the corporation and its current officers, directors, and shareholders—because otherwise a corporation could be faced with conflicting demands.").

The applicability of the internal affairs doctrine in this instance turns on whether, when, and if New York State regularly applies the internal affairs doctrine in its choice of law inquiry to our facts. While there is no mechanical application of the internal affairs doctrine in New York, courts in almost every instance when faced with a choice of law inquiry in derivative actions alleging a breach of fiduciary duty have applied the internal affairs doctrine.

The internal affairs doctrine has a public policy exception, which it appears comes in two varieties. First, a public policy exception is available when the pertinent laws of the jurisdiction of incorporation are objectively "immoral" or "unjust." Second, a public policy exception applies where "application of the local law of some other state is required by reason of the overriding interest of that other state in the issue to be decided." While numerous plaintiffs have argued for a public policy exception, there are no cases in this Circuit that have acknowledged a public policy exception on our facts where defendants have minimal contacts with New York. Although Plaintiffs correctly point out that the internal affairs doctrine is not automatically applied, they fail to demonstrate that the internal affairs doctrine should not be applied to the case at bar.

* * *

Therefore, this Court agrees with Defendants that the appropriate choice of law doctrine, at least in New York, is the internal affairs doctrine, and that no public policy exception is appropriate. Since BP is incorporated in England and Wales, the law of England and Wales governs the substantive claims of this case.

i. English Law

Turning to English law as the internal affairs doctrine dictates, English law provides a narrowly tailored cause of action for a shareholder to sue on behalf of a corporation. The leading case, *Foss v. Harbottle* (1843) 2 Hare 461 (Eng.), established over 150 years ago that a shareholder may not bring a derivative action for "wrongs" to the company if those wrongs are capable of ratification by a majority of shareholders—and notably, breach of fiduciary duty is capable of ratification under English law—unless an exception applies. *Id.* There are three narrow exceptions to the *Foss v. Harbottle* rule: (1) the alleged wrong is *ultra vires*, (2) the validity of the transaction is dependent upon approval by a majority of shareholders greater than a simple majority, (3) wrongdoers profited at the expense of the company through self-dealing *and* the wrongdoers are in voting control of the company—i.e. fraud on the minority. *Id.* P17 (emphasis added).

ii. Exceptions to *Foss v. Harbottle*

The only contested exception fails since Plaintiffs have not and cannot allege control over a majority of the shares. Therefore, even if the Plaintiffs provided sufficient support for self-dealing at the expense of BP, they have not shown the necessary control to trigger the third exception.

iii. The Companies Act 2006

The United Kingdom has recently passed the Companies Act 2006, which recognizes a shareholder's derivative claim as a cognizable cause of action. The Act becomes effective in October 2007. Plaintiffs claim in their Opposition that the law's promulgation illustrates that the United Kingdom believes the common law rule enunciated in *Foss v. Harbottle* is unfair and violative of public policy. Defendants argue that the Companies Act 2006 does not apply retroactively, and therefore, is inapplicable. The U.K. Minister for Industry and the Regions, Hon. Margaret Hodge, recently issued a statement which clarified the question of retroactive application of The Companies Act 2006. Defs.' Ltr. to Hon. Harold Baer, Jr., Jun. 29, 2007. Ms. Hodge unequivocally stated that "the newer, clearer procedures should be used for all claims stated on or after 1 October 2007 [and] courts should ensure that the outcome of any claim based on acts or omissions by a director before 1 October 2007 will be what it would have been under the old, common law that applied at the time."

IV. CONCLUSION

Because I find that English law governs and prohibits derivative actions, and Plaintiffs have not plead facts sufficient to sustain this action pursuant to one of the three narrow exceptions enumerated in England's Companies Act 1985, the Complaint is dismissed pursuant to Fed. R. Civ. P. 12(b)(6) without prejudice.

Comments and Questions

1. What consequences does the internal affairs doctrine have for investors in the United States?

2. Companies with headquarters in the United States sometimes incorporate in foreign jurisdictions. Others set up subsidiaries in non-US locations. A popular area for this is the Caribbean, particularly places such as the Cayman Islands. Any idea why this is the case? What about "tax inversions?" *See* Eric L. Talley, *Corporate Inversions and the Unbundling of Regulatory Competition*, 101 Va. L. Rev. 1649 (Oct. 2015) (describing one type of tax inversion as a merger between a US and foreign company where the emerging entity is incorporated abroad and obtains tax advantages as a result of the transaction).

3. Other jurisdictions favored for overseas incorporation include Switzerland and Ireland. What accounts for the popularity of these countries? Do some jurisdictions carry greater risk than others? Accenture, the consulting arm of Arthur Andersen that emerged as an independent entity, was originally incorporated in Bermuda but moved to Ireland. In the company's proxy statement, it gave as reasons for reincorporation, among other things, "[c]ontinued criticism of companies incorporated in Bermuda" and the "global nature of Accenture's business." Proxy Statement, Accenture Ltd., June 24, 2009.

4. What other differences in governance structure might exist for companies incorporated in other countries? Much of this is discussed in Chapter 12, Comparative Corporate Governance.

Not all states are content with this approach. They have sought to adopt additional requirements designed to protect investors and shareholders by extending to them additional governance rights to foreign corporations operating in the state. California has been the most aggressive in this area.

Cal. Corp. Code § 2100. This chapter applies only to foreign corporations transacting intrastate business, except as otherwise expressly provided.

Cal. Corp. Code § 2115. Foreign corporations and foreign parent corporations subject to general corporation law; Formula for determining property, payroll, and sales factors; Applicable provisions

> (a) A foreign corporation (other than a foreign association or foreign nonprofit corporation but including a foreign parent corporation even though it does not itself transact intrastate business) is subject to the requirements of subdivision (b) commencing on the date specified in subdivision (d) and continuing until the date specified in subdivision (e) if:

> (1) The average of the property factor, the payroll factor, and the sales factor (as defined in Sections 25129, 25132, and 25134 of the Revenue and Taxation Code) with respect to it is more than 50 percent during its latest full income year and

> (2) more than one-half of its outstanding voting securities are held of record by persons having addresses in this state appearing on the books of the corporation on the record date for the latest meeting of shareholders held during its latest full income year or, if no meeting was held during that year, on the last day of the latest full income year....

(b) Except as provided in subdivision (c), the following chapters and sections of this division shall apply to a foreign corporation as defined in subdivision (a) (to the exclusion of the law of the jurisdiction in which it is incorporated):

* * *

Section 303 (removal of directors without cause);

* * *

Section 708, subdivisions (a), (b), and (c) (shareholder's right to cumulate votes at any election of directors);

* * *

Section 710 (supermajority vote requirement);

* * *

Chapter 12 (commencing with Section 1200) (reorganizations);(c) This section does not apply to any corporation (1) with outstanding securities listed on the New York Stock Exchange, the NYSE Amex, the NASDAQ Global Market, or the NASDAQ Capital Market, or (2) if all of its voting shares (other than directors' qualifying shares) are owned directly or indirectly by a corporation or corporations not subject to this section.

Comments and Questions

1. Corporations subject to the statute must, certain exceptions aside, provide for cumulative voting, the right of shareholders to remove directors without cause, and, in general, cannot adopt supermajority provisions that require a percentage above two-thirds. Why do you think California put these provisions in place?

2. What sorts of companies are subject to these requirements? Do these requirements create potential conflicts for companies incorporated in other states?

3. What companies are excluded from these requirements? Why might that be the case?

4. The provision applies to shareholders of record. Does this provide companies with a mechanism for avoiding the application of the provision?

It was one thing to adopt Section 2115 and another to ensure its application. Perhaps unsurprisingly, the judicial receptiveness to the approach has depended upon whether the relevant court is in a jurisdiction seeking to enforce the provision on companies incorporated elsewhere or in a jurisdiction where the company is incorporated. The former has upheld the approach; the latter has not.

Wilson v. Louisiana-Pacific Resources, Inc.

California Court of Appeals
138 Cal. App. 3d 216 (1982)

GRODIN, JUSTICE:

The question presented by this appeal, one of first impression and considerable significance, is whether the State of California may constitutionally impose its law requiring cumulative voting by shareholders upon a corporation which is domiciled elsewhere, but whose contacts with California, as measured by various criteria, are greater than those with any other jurisdiction.

* * *

Plaintiff Ross A. Wilson brought this action against Louisiana-Pacific Resources, Inc., a Utah corporation, seeking a declaratory judgment that the defendant met the tests of section 2115, and that he was therefore entitled to cumulative voting in accordance with section 708. The trial court found that in the years preceding the action, the average of the defendant's property, payroll, and sales in California as defined by the California corporations statute exceeded 50 percent, and that more than 50 percent of its shareholders entitled to vote resided in California, so that the statutory conditions had been met. It also found that except for being domiciled in Utah and having a transfer agent there, defendant had virtually no business connection with Utah, that its principal place of business has been in California since at least 1971, that its meetings of shareholders and directors are held in California, and that all of its employees and all of its bank accounts are in California. Finally, the court concluded, contrary to defendant's contentions, that there existed no constitutional obstacle to the application of the cumulative voting requirement to defendant, and that its "[cumulative] voting will be in effect a judicial addendum to defendant's articles of incorporation, and all of its shareholders are entitled to cumulative voting whether they are California residents or not."

* * *

I. *Full Faith and Credit*

The full faith and credit clause of the federal Constitution (art. IV, § 1) requires that "Full Faith and Credit … be given in each State to the public Acts, Records, and Judicial Proceedings of every other State.…" Although the phrase "public Acts, Records and Judicial Proceedings" has been construed to include statutes as well as judicial decisions (e.g., Bradford Elec. Co. v. Clapper (1932) 286 U.S. 145 [52 S. Ct. 571, 76 L. Ed. 1026, 82 A.L.R. 696]), the Supreme Court has recognized that "[a] rigid and literal enforcement of the full faith and credit clause, without regard to the statute of the forum, would lead to the absurd result that, wherever the conflict arises, the statute of each state must be enforced in the courts of the other, but cannot be in its own. Unless by force of that clause a greater effect is thus to be given to a state statute abroad than the clause permits it to have at home, it is unavoidable that this Court determine for itself the extent to which the statute of one state may qualify or deny rights asserted under the statute of another." (Alaska Packers Assn. v. Comm'n (1935) 294 U.S. 532, 547 [55 S. Ct. 518, 79 L. Ed. 1044, 1052].)

Under the doctrine of *Alaska Packers, supra,* determination as to application of conflicting statutes was to be made "by appraising the governmental interests of each jurisdiction, and turning the scale of decision according to their weight." (294 U.S. at p. 547 [79 L. Ed. at p. 1052].) In this balancing process it was presumed that "every state is entitled to enforce in its own courts its own statutes, lawfully enacted. One who challenges that right, because of the force given to a conflicting statute of another state by the full faith and credit clause, assumes the burden of showing, upon some rational basis, that of the conflicting interests involved those of the foreign state are superior to those of the forum." (Id., at pp. 547–548 [79 L. Ed. at p. 1052].)

Since *Alaska Packers,* the Supreme Court has abandoned the weighing-of-interests requirement in favor of a less exacting standard corresponding to the requirements of the due process clause. (Allstate Ins. Co. v. Hague (1981) 449 U.S. 302, 308, fn. 10 [101 S. Ct. 633, 66 L.Ed.2d 521, 527].) In determining whether a state's choice-of-law decision exceeds federal constitutional requirements, the current rule is that "for a State's substantive law to be selected in a constitutionally permissible manner, that State must have a significant contact or significant aggregation of contacts, creating state interests, such that choice of its law is neither arbitrary nor fundamentally unfair." (Id., at pp. 312–313 [66 L.Ed.2d at p. 531].)

We consider that test is met here; the criteria which a foreign corporation must meet in order to be subject to section 2115 assure the existence of significant aggregation of contacts. And the state interests created by those contacts are indeed substantial. California's present law requiring cumulative voting by shareholders continues in effect a policy which has existed in this state since the Constitution of 1879. 3 In Western Air Lines, Inc. v. Sobieski (1961) 191 Cal.App.2d 399 [12 Cal. Rptr. 719], the court, observing that "[it] would seem too evident to require protracted dissertation that the right of cumulative voting is a substantial right" (id., at p. 414), held that even in the absence of express statutory mandate, the Corporations Commissioner was justified in refusing to permit the elimination of cumulative voting by a "pseudo foreign" corporation, i.e., "one with its technical domicile outside of this state but one which exercises most of its corporate vitality within this state." (Id., at p. 412.) A contrary holding, the court reasoned, "would enable a foreign corporation to destroy the rights which the State of California has deemed worthy of protection by the enactment of the Corporate Securities Act." (Id., at pp. 413–414.) Section 2115 incorporates the policy reflected in *Sobieski* and applies it more generally, to all pseudo-foreign corporations meeting the statutory criteria.

Utah, on the other hand, has no interests which are offended by cumulative voting; and, whatever interest it might have in maintaining a *laissez faire* policy on that score would seem to be clearly outweighed by the interests of California, in which a majority of shareholders and the corporation's business activity is located. Thus, even on the earlier analysis of *Alaska Packers,* the full faith and credit clause provides no bar to the application of California's statute.

* * *

The "internal affairs doctrine," according to which courts traditionally looked to the law of the state of incorporation in resolving questions regarding a corporation's internal affairs (see Oldham, California Regulates Pseudo-Foreign Corporations— Trampling Upon the Tramp? (1977) 17 Santa Clara L. Rev. 85, 85–90); has no application here. That doctrine has never been followed blindly in California (see Wait v. Kern River Mining etc. Co. (1909) 157 Cal. 16, 21 [106 P. 98]; see also Western Air Lines, Inc. v. Sobieski, supra, 191 Cal.App.2d 399); it is inconsistent with the "comparative impairment" approach used by this state in resolving conflict of law problems (Offshore Rental Co. v. Continental Oil Co. (1978) 22 Cal.3d 157, 164–165 [148 Cal. Rptr. 867, 583 P.2d 721]); and it is in any event not determinative of the constitutional issue. This is not a common choice-of-law question; the Legislature has resolved the conflicts issue by mandating application of this state's law under certain conditions. The question is whether that mandate is constitutional. (See Allstate Ins. Co. v. Hague, supra, 449 U.S. at pp. 307–308 [66 L.Ed.2d at p. 527].) For the reasons we have discussed, we conclude that it is, so far as the full faith and credit clause is concerned.

II. *Commerce Clause*

Although article I, section 8, clause 3 of the federal Constitution grants Congress power "[t]o regulate commerce ... among the several States," Congress has not chosen to regulate the subject in litigation here nor has it undertaken to establish guidelines for regulation by the states. Appellant's commerce clause argument is based, therefore, upon the negative implications of dormant congressional authority.

The United States Supreme Court has established the standard for determining the validity of state statutes in such situations: "Where the statute regulates even-handedly to effectuate a legitimate local public interest, and its effects on interstate commerce are only incidental, it will be upheld unless the burden imposed on such commerce is clearly excessive in relation to the putative local benefits. If a legitimate local purpose is found, then the question becomes one of degree. And the extent of the burden that will be tolerated will of course depend on the nature of the local interest involved, and on whether it could be promoted as well with a lesser impact on interstate activities." (*Pike v. Bruce Church, Inc.* (1970) 397 U.S. 137, 142 ...)

We observe, initially, that the challenged statute "regulates even-handedly" within the meaning of the *Pike* guidelines; it applies to covered foreign corporations the same rules which are applied to corporations domiciled within the state. The statute thus imposes no special or distinct burden upon out-of-state interests. (See Tribe, American Constitutional Law (1978) pp. 326–327.)

The nature, strength, and duration of California's interest in the cumulative voting principle, and in the application of that principle to pseudo-foreign corporations have previously been considered in this opinion. There remain to be considered the effects of that application upon interstate activities.

One effect of section 2115 may well be to deter corporations from making their legal homes elsewhere for the purpose of avoiding California's protective corporate legislation, and thus to diminish the practice of "charter-mongering" among states ... but that, presumably, is not an effect which would offend the policies of the commerce clause; and appellant does not so contend. Rather, appellant contends that the application of cumulative voting requirements to pseudo-foreign corporations as provided by section 2115will have the effect of causing it and other foreign corporations already operating in California to reduce their property, payroll, and sales in this state below the 50 percent level, and will deter foreign corporations contemplating the transaction of business in this state from increasing their business activities above that level.

There is no suggestion, or evidence, that section 2115 was adopted for the purpose of deterring foreign corporations from doing business in this state; nor is there any direct evidence that it has had or will have such an effect. On the contrary, what evidence there is in the record on this point consists of testimony by appellant's president that he knew of no adverse effect on appellant's business which would be caused by cumulative voting.

Appellant argues that adverse consequences are predictable from "potentially conflicting claims of shareholders as to which state [law] governs" the method of voting by shareholders, and from the "transient nature of the applicability of the California statute." It is perhaps true that "[i]n corporation law, uncertainty about what the law is or what law is applicable to a given transaction constitutes a far more serious problem than in areas of the law which do not require comprehensive and continuous planning." (Halloran & Hammer, *Section 2115 of the New California General Corporation Law — The Application of California Corporation Law to Foreign Corporations* (1976) 23 UCLA L. Rev. 1282, 1283.) Professor Kaplan advises, however, that while the specter of "unbearable chaos and uncertainty" resulting from dual or variable sets of rules constitutes the "primary argument against the application of local law to a foreign corporation," the "precise details of such confusion are seldom stated," and the argument is "seldom challenged, though it is probably neither so cogent nor so compelling as it might at first seem." (Kaplan, *Foreign Corporations and Local Corporate Policy* (1968) 21 Vand.L.Rev. 433, 476.) Professor Kaplan observes that no such unbearable confusion has appeared from the operations of the New York statutes imposing certain duties upon foreign corporations, and opines that the "contention of the *Restatement* and of other commentators that avoidance of confusion and difficulty makes it imperative to look to the law of the state of incorporation seems belied by the experience of New York." He notes also that while extensive overlaps in state and federal regulation of many corporate matters, particularly in the area of corporate internal affairs, "has created a situation of theoretical conflict, the practical results have been accepted and viable, and the duplication of controls has resulted not so much in conflict as in cumulative standards." (*Id.*, at pp. 476–477, fn. omitted.)

The potential for conflict and resulting uncertainty from California's statute is substantially minimized by the nature of the criteria specified in section 2115. A corporation can do a majority of its business in only one state at a time; and it can have a majority of its shareholders resident in only one state at a time. If a corporation meets those requirements in this state, no other state is in a position to regulate the method of voting by shareholders on the basis of the same or similar criteria. It might also be said that no other state could claim as great an interest in doing so. In any event, it does not appear that any other state has attempted to do so. If California's statute were replicated in all states, no conflict would result. We conclude that the potential for conflict is, on this record, speculative and without substance.

What appellant refers to as the "transient nature" of the statute's applicability, i.e., its application from year to year based upon the prior year's activity, could conceivably be a problem for a corporation whose business activity within the state fluctuated widely, but the "worst-case" scenario—that such a corporation might find it necessary to adopt cumulative voting as a means of assuring compliance on a continuing basis— does not appear to be so burdensome as to result in a significant restraint upon commerce among the states. We are not told, for example, of any diminution of activity in this state by foreign corporations as a result of *Western Air Lines, Inc. v. Sobieski, supra,* 191 Cal.App.2d 399, 12 Cal.Rptr. 719.

Commentators have generally applauded the California Legislature for "providing an apparently simple and thorough determination of state interest in foreign corporations," thus resolving the uncertainties which resulted from *Western Air Lines, Inc. v. Sobieski, supra* ... and establishing a "rational means to allocate the regulation of a corporation to the state to which it is primarily related" ... through a "narrow exception to the internal affairs doctrine in situations where California's interests are clearly paramount." ... We conclude that to the extent that the cumulative voting requirement imposed by section 2115 upon pseudo-foreign corporations is shown to have any effect upon interstate commerce, the effect is incidental, and minimal in *conclusion* relation to the purpose which that requirement is designed to achieve.

Comments and Questions

1. To the extent these requirements are valid, are there any real limitations on states regulating matters that would otherwise fall within the internal affairs doctrine? Could, for example, California expand the list of substantive requirements or regulate companies with a less significant nexus to the state?

2. Is the characterization of the internal affairs doctrine accurate? In *State Farm Mutual Automobile Insurance Co. v. Superior Court,* 8 Cal. Rptr. 3d 56, 68 n. 3 (Cal. App. 2003), the court confronted allegations that the law of California should apply to the payment of dividends by a company incorporated in Illinois. In concluding that the law of the state of incorporation applied, the court observed: "In upholding the law, the court [in Wilson], in a single sentence of dictum, criticized the internal affairs doctrine. But in the 20 years since Wilson was decided, the internal affairs doctrine has *internal affairs doctrine is broadly accepted today* received broad acceptance by the courts ..." Does this suggest a shift in the court's view?

3. Another way to circumvent the internal affairs doctrine is to simply hold that the matter does not involve a company's internal affairs. In *Friese v. The Superior Courts of San Diego County,* 36 Cal. Rptr. 3d 558 (Cal. App. 4th 2005), the court dealt with a California provision which allowed derivative suits to recover from an

officer or director engaging in insider trading up to three times the amount of the gain. Defendants argued that this violated the internal affairs doctrine since the company was incorporated in Delaware (but had its headquarters in California). The court, however, determined that the provision did not implicate the internal affairs doctrine. It noted that "in general corporations are not damaged when either they or their directors engage in insider trading." Second, recovery for insider trading "does not provide the issuer with compensation for any lost opportunity the issuer itself could have lawfully realized." Finally, public interest rather than "any narrow shareholder interest" favors the provision in order to discourage insider trading. What do you make of this approach? Is it correct?

4. What do you make of the argument that Section 2115 does not violate the commerce clause? How important is it that California limited the application of the section to companies with significant operations and ownership within the state? What if the provision had not done so but had applied to any company operating in the state?

The California courts are not the only ones with a say on this issue. Those in Delaware have likewise entered the debate. Perhaps unsurprisingly, they have taken a very different view on the matter.

VantagePoint Venture Partners v. Examen, Inc.

Delaware Supreme Court

871 A.2d 1108 (2005)

HOLLAND, JUSTICE:

Examen was a Delaware corporation engaged in the business of providing web-based legal expense management solutions to a growing list of Fortune 1000 customers throughout the United States. Following consummation of the merger on April 5, 2005, LexisNexis Examen, also a Delaware corporation, became the surviving entity. VantagePoint is a Delaware Limited Partnership organized and existing under the laws of Delaware. VantagePoint, a major venture capital firm that purchased Examen Series A Preferred Stock in a negotiated transaction, owned eighty-three percent of Examen's outstanding Series A Preferred Stock (909,091 shares) and no shares of Common Stock.

On February 17, 2005, Examen and Reed Elsevier executed the Merger Agreement, which was set to expire on April 15, 2005, if the merger had not closed by that date. Under the Delaware General Corporation Law and Examen's Certificate of Incorporation, including the Certificate of Designations for the Series A Preferred Stock, adoption of the Merger Agreement required the affirmative vote of the holders of a majority of the issued and outstanding shares of the Common Stock and Series A Preferred Stock, *voting together as a single class.* Holders of Series A Preferred Stock had the number of votes equal to the number of shares of Common Stock they would have held if their Preferred Stock was converted. Thus, VantagePoint, which owned 909,091 shares of Series A Preferred Stock and no shares of Common Stock, was entitled to vote based on a converted number of 1,392,727 shares of stock.

There were 9,717,415 total outstanding shares of the Company's capital stock (8,626,826 shares of Common Stock and 1,090,589 shares of Series A Preferred Stock), representing 10,297,608 votes on an as-converted basis. An affirmative vote of at least 5,148,805 shares, constituting a majority of the outstanding voting power on an as-converted basis, was required to approve the merger. If the stockholders were to vote by class, VantagePoint would have controlled 83.4 percent of the Series A Preferred Stock, which would have permitted VantagePoint to block the merger. VantagePoint acknowledges that, if Delaware law applied, it would not have a class vote.

Chancery Court Decision

The Court of Chancery determined that the question of whether VantagePoint, as a holder of Examen's Series A Preferred Stock, was entitled to a separate class vote on the merger with a Delaware subsidiary of Reed Elsevier, was governed by the internal affairs doctrine because the issue implicated "the relationship between a corporation and its stockholders." The Court of Chancery rejected VantagePoint's argument that section 2115 of the California Corporation Code did not conflict with Delaware law and operated only in addition to rights granted under Delaware corporate law. In doing so, the Court of Chancery noted that section 2115 "expressly states that it operates 'to the exclusion of the law of the jurisdiction in which [the company] is incorporated.'"

Specifically, the Court of Chancery determined that section 2115's requirement that stockholders vote as a separate class conflicts with Delaware law, which, together with Examen's Certificate of Incorporation, mandates that the merger be authorized by a majority of all Examen stockholders voting together as a single class. The Court of Chancery concluded that it could not enforce both Delaware and California law. Consequently, the Court of Chancery decided that the issue presented was solely one of choice-of-law, and that it need not determine the constitutionality of section 2115.

Internal Affairs Doctrine

In *CTS Corp. v. Dynamics Corp. of Am.*, the United States Supreme Court stated that it is "an accepted part of the business landscape in this country for States to create corporations, to prescribe their powers, and to define the rights that are acquired by purchasing their shares." In *CTS*, it was also recognized that "[a] State has an interest in promoting stable relationships among parties involved in the corporations it charters, as well as in ensuring that investors in such corporations have an effective voice in corporate affairs." The internal affairs doctrine is a long-standing choice of law principle which recognizes that only one state should have the authority to regulate a corporation's internal affairs—the state of incorporation.

The internal affairs doctrine developed on the premise that, in order to prevent corporations from being subjected to inconsistent legal standards, the authority to regulate a corporation's internal affairs should not rest with multiple jurisdictions. It is now well established that only the law of the state of incorporation governs and determines issues relating to a corporation's internal affairs. By providing certainty and predictability, the internal affairs doctrine protects the justified expectations of the parties with interests in the corporation.

The internal affairs doctrine applies to those matters that pertain to the relationships among or between the corporation and its officers, directors, and shareholders. The Restatement (Second) of Conflict of Laws § 301 provides: "application of the local law of the state of incorporation will usually be supported by those choice-of-law factors favoring the need of the interstate and international systems, certainty, predictability and uniformity of result, protection of the justified expectations of the parties and ease in the application of the law to be applied." Accordingly, the conflicts practice of both state and federal courts has consistently been to apply the law of the state of incorporation to "the entire gamut of internal corporate affairs."

The internal affairs doctrine is not, however, only a conflicts of law principle. Pursuant to the Fourteenth Amendment Due Process Clause, directors and officers of corporations "have a significant right ... to know what law will be applied to their actions" and "stockholders ... have a right to know by what standards of accountability they may hold those managing the corporation's business and affairs." Under the Commerce Clause, a state "has no interest in regulating the internal affairs of foreign corporations." Therefore, this Court has held that an "application of the internal affairs doctrine is mandated by constitutional principles, except in the 'rarest situations,'" e.g., when "the law of the state of incorporation is inconsistent with a national policy on foreign or interstate commerce."

California Section 2115

VantagePoint contends that section 2115 of the California Corporations Code is a limited exception to the internal affairs doctrine. Section 2115 is characterized as an outreach statute because it requires certain foreign corporations to conform to a broad range of internal affairs provisions. Section 2115 defines the foreign corporations for which the California statute has an outreach effect as those foreign corporations, half of whose voting securities are held of record by persons with California addresses, that also conduct half of their business in California as measured by a formula weighing assets, sales and payroll factors.

VantagePoint argues that section 2115 "mandates application of certain enumerated provisions of California's corporation law to the internal affairs of 'foreign' corporations if certain narrow factual prerequisites [set forth in section 2115] are met." Under the California statute, if more than one half of a foreign corporation's outstanding voting securities are held of record by persons having addresses in California (as disclosed on the books of the corporation) on the record date, and the property, payroll and sales factor tests are satisfied, then on the first day of the income year, one hundred and thirty five days after the above tests are satisfied, the foreign corporation's articles of incorporation are deemed amended to the exclusion of the law of the state of incorporation. If the factual conditions precedent for triggering section 2115 are established, many aspects of a corporation's internal affairs are purportedly governed by California corporate law to the exclusion of the law of the state of incorporation.

*   *   *

Internal Affairs Require Uniformity

In *McDermott*, this Court noted that application of local internal affairs law (here California's section 2115) to a foreign corporation (here Delaware) is "apt to produce inequalities, intolerable confusion, and uncertainty, and intrude into the domain of other states that have a superior claim to regulate the same subject matter...." Professor DeMott's review of the differences and conflicts between the Delaware and California corporate statutes with regard to internal affairs, illustrates why it is imperative that only the law of the state of incorporation regulate the relationships among a corporation and its officers, directors, and shareholders. To require a factual determination to decide which of two conflicting state laws governs the internal affairs of a corporation at any point in time, completely contravenes the importance of stability within inter-corporate relationships that the United States Supreme Court recognized in *CTS*.

* * *

State Law of Incorporation Governs Internal Affairs

In *McDermott*, this Court held that the "internal affairs doctrine is a major tenet of Delaware corporation law having important federal constitutional underpinnings." Applying Delaware's well-established choice-of-law rule — the internal affairs doctrine — the Court of Chancery recognized that Delaware courts must apply the law of the state of incorporation to issues involving corporate internal affairs, and that disputes concerning a shareholder's right to vote fall squarely within the purview of the internal affairs doctrine.

Examen is a Delaware corporation. The legal issue in this case — whether a preferred shareholder of a Delaware corporation had the right, under the corporation's Certificate of Designations, to a Series A Preferred Stock class vote on a merger — clearly involves the relationship among a corporation and its shareholders. As the United States Supreme Court held in *CTS*, "no principle of corporation law and practice is more firmly established than a *State's authority* to regulate domestic corporations, including the authority to *define the voting rights of shareholders.*"

In *CTS*, the Supreme Court held that the Commerce Clause "prohibits States from regulating subjects that 'are in their nature national, or admit only of one uniform system, or plan of regulation,'" and acknowledged that the internal affairs of a corporation are subjects that require one uniform system of regulation. In *CTS*, the Supreme Court concluded that "so long as each State regulates voting rights *only in the corporations it has created*, each corporation will be subject to the law of only one State." Accordingly, we hold Delaware's well-established choice of law rules and the federal constitution mandated that Examen's internal affairs, and in particular, VantagePoint's voting rights, be adjudicated exclusively in accordance with the law of its state of incorporation, in this case, the law of Delaware. [HOLDING]

Any Forum — Internal Affairs — Same Law

VantagePoint acknowledges that the courts of Delaware, as the forum state, may apply Delaware's own substantive choice of law rules. VantagePoint argues, however, that Delaware's "choice" to apply the law of the state of incorporation to internal affairs issues—notwithstanding California's enactment of *section 2115*—will result in future forum shopping races to the courthouse. VantagePoint submits that, if the California action in these proceedings had been decided first, the California Superior Court would have enjoined the merger until it was factually determined whether *section 2115* is applicable. If the statutory prerequisites were found to be factually satisfied, VantagePoint submits that the California Superior Court would have applied the internal affairs law reflected in *section 2115*, "to the exclusion" of the law of Delaware—the state where Examen is incorporated.

In support of those assertions, VantagePoint relies primarily upon a 1982 decision by the California Court of Appeals in *Wilson v. Louisiana-Pacific Resources, Inc.* In *Wilson v. Louisiana-Pacific Resources, Inc.*, a panel of the California Court of Appeals held that section 2115 did not violate the federal constitution by applying the California Code's mandatory cumulative voting provision to a Utah corporation that had not provided for cumulative voting but instead had elected the straight voting structure set forth in the Utah corporation statute. The court in *Wilson* did not address the implications of the differences between the Utah and California corporate statutes upon the expectations of parties who chose to incorporate in Utah rather than California. As Professor DeMott points out, "[a]lthough it is possible under the Utah statute for the corporation's charter to be amended by the shareholders and the directors, that mechanical fact does not establish California's right to coerce such an amendment" whenever the factual prerequisites of section 2115 exist.

Wilson was decided before the United States Supreme Court's decision in *CTS* and before this Court's decision in *McDermott.* Ten years after *Wilson,* the California Supreme Court cited with approval this Court's analysis of the internal affairs doctrine in *McDermott,* in particular, our holding that corporate voting rights disputes are governed by the law of the state of incorporation. Two years ago, in *State Farm v. Superior Court,* a different panel of the California Court of Appeals questioned the validity of the holding in *Wilson* following the broad acceptance of the internal affairs doctrine over the two decades after *Wilson* was decided. In *State Farm,* the court cited with approval the United States Supreme Court decision in *CTS Corp. v. Dynamics* and our decision in *McDermott.* In *State Farm,* the court also quoted at length that portion of our decision in *McDermott* relating to the constitutional imperatives of the internal affairs doctrine.

Since *Wilson* was decided, the United States Supreme Court has recognized the constitutional imperatives of the internal affairs doctrine. In *Draper v. Gardner,* this Court acknowledged the *Wilson* opinion in a footnote and nevertheless permitted the dismissal of a Delaware action in favor of a California action in which a California court would be called upon to decide the internal affairs "demand" issue involving a Delaware corporation. As stated in *Draper,* we had no doubt that after the *Kamen* and *CTS* holdings by the United States Supreme Court, the California courts would "apply Delaware [demand] law [to the internal affairs of a Delaware corporation], given the vitality and constitutional underpinnings of the internal affairs doctrine." We adhere to that view in this case.

Conclusion

The judgment of the Court of Chancery is affirmed. The Clerk of this Court is directed to issue the mandate immediately.

Comments and Questions

1. What do you make of the rationale in this case? Rather than only a choice of law principle, the court suggests that the internal affairs doctrine is of constitutional magnitude. What difference does this make in the application of the doctrine? Can you reconcile the analysis of the Commerce Clause in *Wilson* and *VantagePoint*? If not, which case has the better argument?

2. *VantagePoint* and *Wilson* appear to set up a conflict between the states with companies in the middle. Is there any mechanism for addressing the disparate approaches in these two cases?

3. One commentator described the decision in *VantagePoint* as "an advisory opinion." *See* Faith Stevelman, *Regulatory Competition, Choice of Forum, and Delaware's Stake in Corporate Law*, 34 Del. J. Corp. L. 57 (2009). Another asserted that the opinion was "a signal: one intended to deter other states, such as California and New York, from seeking to regulate the affairs of Delaware entities." Timothy P. Glynn, *Delaware's VantagePoint: The Empire Strikes Back in the Post-Post-Enron Era*, 102 Nw. U. L. Rev. 91, 96 (Winter 2008). Do you agree or disagree?

4. Even without the internal affairs doctrine, Delaware has one attribute that is difficult to duplicate: a highly skilled court system. As one academic described:

> Ten judges, located for the most part along two hallways in one city, make and develop Delaware corporate law. These jurists are repeat players, in that most of the workload of the five members of the Delaware Court of Chancery arises in corporate law and a significant part of the workload for the five Delaware Supreme Court justices derives from corporate law as well. Because of this work and their own prior experiences, these judges have an expertise in corporate law that can be seen, for example, in discussions of valuation and other deal-related issues that arise. The typical federal judge who gets an occasional corporate case as part of a docket dominated by criminal and immigration matters is simply not going to have the same expertise to bring to a dispute about corporate issues. Delaware judges interact with the corporate academic and professional community in a way that is not replicated in other fields.

Robert B. Thompson, *Stockholders in Corporate Governance: Defining the Shareholder's Role, Defining A Role for State Law: Folk at 40*, 33 Del. J. Corp. L. 771, 775 (2008). Why would the quality of the court system be such an advantage for a state trying to attract corporate charters?

5. What law should apply to a wrongful termination claim brought by a former CEO of a Delaware corporation who alleged he was constructively dismissed in retaliation for complaints about possible misbehavior? Assume that under Delaware

law, the case would be dismissed. For one answer, see *Lidow v. Superior Court*, 141 Cal. Rptr. 3rd 729 (Cal. App. 2012).

6. In Delaware, the Chancery Court is not only the fact finder in the most significant corporate law disputes litigated in the United States, it is also the training ground for the Delaware Supreme Court. It is not uncommon for Justices on the Delaware Supreme Court to have first served on the Chancery Court. Why might this be the case? What information might the governor of the state glean from a jurist who first served on the Chancery Court?

7. The internal affairs doctrine has traditionally been taught as a battle between Delaware and California. That may, however, be changing. The Delaware courts have upheld bylaws that allow for the shifting of fees against owners in unsuccessful litigation (see *ATP Tour, Inc. v. Deutscher Tennis Bund*, 91 A.3d 554 (Del. 2014)) and that require shareholders to use a specified forum. *See Boilermakers Local 154 Retirement Fund v. Chevron Corp.*, 73 A.3d 934, 942 (Del. Ch. 2013). Although both have been addressed by legislation in Delaware, see DGCL 102, 109 & 115, they suggest that companies can use bylaws to regulate litigation matters. There is an argument that this authority goes beyond a company's internal affairs. *See* J. Robert Brown, Jr., *The Future Direction of Delaware Law (Including a Brief Exegesis on Fee Shifting Bylaws)*, 92 Den. U. L. Rev. Online 49 (2015). Could states adopt conflicting provisions with respect to litigation in their jurisdiction? What would be the consequences of such an approach?

B. A Race to the Bottom or to the Top?

With more than fifty jurisdictions to choose from, management can incorporate in the jurisdiction that provides the most favorable law. On that proposition, there is general agreement. The issue turns on the definition of favorable. Some view management as selecting the state where the law will permit the most self serving behavior. Those proponents characterize the evolution of state corporate law as a race to the bottom. Others see the competition for charters as something that produces the most efficient corporate law, a race to the top in other words. The appropriate characterization has been debated with considerable passion.

Renee M. Jones, *Rethinking Corporate Federalism in the Era of Corporate Reform*
29 J. Corp. L. 625 (2004)[2]

Defenders of the corporate federal system (referred to here as corporate federalists) argue that the very interstate competition that [William] Cary [former Chairman of the SEC and Professor at Columbia Law School] so excoriated, has led instead to

---

2. Copyright © 2004 The Journal of Corporation Law. Reprinted with permission.

a "race-to-the-top" in corporate law. These theorists, led by Ralph Winter [Professor at Yale Law School and judge on the US Court of Appeals, Second Circuit] agree with Cary that the federal system discourages active regulation of corporations, but they embrace this deregulatory bias as the legitimate result of the corporate law race. Race-to-the-top theorists maintain that market forces are sufficient to prevent excessive managerial self-dealing and opportunism. They take the market-based defense of the federal system a step further by arguing that not only do conventional market forces rein in management excess, but that a competitive market for corporate law works to ensure that states will adopt legal rules that appeal to managers and shareholders alike.

Thus, Winter argued, if Delaware law permitted managers to profit at the expense of shareholders, earnings of Delaware corporations would lag behind those of similar corporations chartered in other states. This would result in lower stock prices for Delaware corporations, increasing their capital costs and weakening their position in the product market, ultimately driving stock prices still lower and making such corporations attractive takeover targets. Race-to-the-top theorists thus conclude that market forces require corporate managers to seek out legal rules that are attractive to investors, which in turn encourages states to adopt legal rules that "optimize the shareholder-corporation relationship." Thus, in the view of race-to-the-top scholars, Delaware's laissez faire approach to corporate governance is superior to the interventionist model preferred by race-to-the-bottom theorists, simply because this laissez faire approach has "won" a vigorous competition among all states to attract the most corporate charters.

J. Robert Brown, Jr., *The Irrelevance of State Corporate Law in the Governance of Public Companies*

38 U. Rich. L. Rev. 317, 321–24, 326, 331 (2004)[3]

Management determines the state of incorporation and has an incentive to incorporate in a state that most meets its objectives. To the extent a state does not meet those objectives, the company can reincorporate into a jurisdiction that does. At the same time, states have an incentive to implement an approach to regulation favored by management. Companies pay a franchise tax to the state of incorporation. Delaware, one of only five states without a sales tax, obtains considerable tax revenues from companies incorporating within the state. This is true even though most of them have no significant operations within Delaware.

As long as one state puts in place a scheme of regulation favored by management, others have an incentive to do the same. Either they wish to engage in the competition for additional companies (and additional franchise taxes) or they wish to keep what

---

they have. In states that do not follow suit, at least some companies will have an incentive to leave the jurisdiction and re-incorporate in a more favorable locale.

Commentators characterize this dynamic as a competition for charters, although they vigorously disagree about the impetus for the competition. Some see the competition as a race to the top. They assert that management has an incentive to incorporate in the jurisdiction that provides the most efficient corporate law. To the extent directors elevate self-interest over efficiency, the market for corporate control will result in a change of management. Recognizing that the largest number of public companies incorporate in Delaware, the "race to the top" view requires the conclusion that the corporate law in Delaware is the most efficient.

The main problem with this approach is its excessive reliance upon the market for corporate control to ensure efficiency. The market for corporate control is not sufficiently robust to force management to select states based upon economic efficiency. Moreover, given the high costs of hostile takeovers, a great deal of inefficiency must occur before the market will become a correcting mechanism.

* * *

Others see the motivation for selecting the state of incorporation as more self-serving, characterizing the competition as a race to the bottom. Management will select a jurisdiction that favors its own self-interest. Among other things, the goal is to select the state of incorporation that permits management to extract the most benefit for itself, without regard to efficiency or the interests of shareholders.

This approach also has problems. First, changes in state corporate codes often cannot be characterized as being for or against the interests of management. Second, even if management opposes the changes, the harm must outweigh the costs (financial and reputational) before reincorporation will occur. Third, management self-interest and efficiency are not always antithetical notions.

* * *

... Only those areas important enough to management to result in reincorporation can be explained as a product of competition among states. Three areas seem likely to have paramount importance to management: (1) maximizing decision-making flexibility (particularly for self-dealing transactions); (2) minimizing liability (particularly for breach of fiduciary duties); and (3) job preservation. Moreover, even changes in these areas will not result in reincorporation unless the costs outweigh the benefits. Presumably only a small number of provisions will fall into this category.

Comments and Questions

1. The characterization of state corporate law as a race to the bottom received its modern incarnation in an article written by Professor Cary. *See* William L. Cary, *Federalism and Corporate Law: Reflections Upon Delaware*, 83 Yale L.J. 663, 701 (1974) ("The first step is to escape from the present predicament in which a pygmy among the 50 states [Delaware] prescribes, interprets, and indeed denigrates national corporate policy as an incentive to encourage incorporation within its borders, thereby

increasing its revenue."). Others preceding Cary made similar arguments. *See Louis K. Liggett v. Lee*, 288 U.S. 517, 559 (1933) (Brandeis, J., dissenting in part) (characterizing evolution of corporate law as one "not of diligence but of laxity").

2. The race to the top analysis is generally attributed to Ralph K. Winter, a professor at Yale Law School and former Chief Judge of the U.S. Court of Appeals for the Second Circuit. *See* Ralph K. Winter, Jr., *State Law, Shareholder Protection, and the Theory of the Corporation*, 6 J. Legal Stud. 251 (1977). The theory has been a staple of the law and economics movement. *See* Reza Dibadj, *Delaying Corporate Law*, 34 Hofstra L. Rev. 469, 476–77(Winter 2005) ("Digging a little deeper, however, reveals that the intellectual underpinnings of such an approach can be found in influential law and economics literature that extols the virtues of private contract; more specifically, the antiregulatory stance characteristic of the Chicago School.").

3. Some dispute that there really is a "race," contending that no state other than Delaware really seeks to attract corporations. Whether or not true, it was at least historically a "race," with an assortment of states competing for incorporations. Massachusetts was the first state to repeal restrictions on the size and duration of a corporation, encouraging larger businesses to incorporate there. For a time, New Jersey had an active role in the race. In the early part of the 20th century, Delaware took over the lead and has maintained it ever since.

4. A corporation might select the law of a particular state by incorporating there. To the extent, however, that the law becomes more favorable elsewhere, can a company change the state of incorporation? How might this occur? To the extent the approach requires shareholder approval, don't shareholders have the power to prevent the company from engaging in a race to the bottom?

5. Even if the evolution of the law can be better explained by managerial self-interest, this does not automatically conflict with efficiency. In the early days of the last century, competition among the states resulted in the removal of unnecessary restrictions on the size and duration of corporations. *See Louis K. Liggett Co. v. Lee*, 288 U.S. 517, 541 (1933) (Brandeis, J., dissenting) (noting among other things that limitations on the amount of authorized capital, although at one time "universal," were, by the 1920s, largely eliminated).

6. What are some examples of provisions that might cause management to reincorporate in Delaware? As an empirical matter, amendments to the Delaware General Corporation Law in 1986 to allow companies to waive monetary liability for breach of the duty of care by directors, a number of corporations moved to the state. Today, all 50 states have in place provisions designed to allow companies to reduce the risk of liability for directors for breach of the duty of care. What does this suggest about the importances of liability provisions in the decision of boards with respect to the location of incorporation?

7. Delaware permits liberal use of anti-takeover tactics by management of a target company, particularly poison pills. How does this fit into the characterization of state law as a race to the top? As Professor McDonnell has noted: "Since the hostile takeover

mechanism is one of the main market constraints on managers, if managers can take advantage of laws which allow them to avoid takeovers, then much of the market discipline on managers will go away." Brett H. McDonnell, *Getting Stuck Between Bottom and Top: State Competition for Corporate Charters in the Presence of Network Effects*, 31 Hofstra L. Rev. 681, 695 (Spring 2003). Do you agree?

8. It is easy enough, conceptually, to imagine a legislature willing to amend its laws to attract corporations into the state and the resulting income flow. The same is not true, however, of courts. Yet part of the Delaware advantage is a court system that can consistently clarify the law in a manner that management favors. How might that be the case? How are judges selected to the Chancery Court, the trial court that hears these cases? How are judges selected for the Delaware Supreme Court, the court that oversees the Chancery Court? Often those serving on the Supreme Court first did an apprenticeship at the Chancery Court. How might this effect the predictability of the justices on the Supreme Court?

How does the race work in practice? What is an example of a state responding in a manner that will induce corporations to move to the state? The development of waiver of liability provisions in the aftermath of the Delaware Supreme Court's decision in *Van Gorkom* is an example.

J. Robert Brown, Jr. & Sandeep Gopalan,
Opting Only In: Contractarians, Waiver of Liability Provisions, and the Race to the Bottom
42 Ind. L. Rev. 285 (2009)[4]

The contractarian strain of corporate law scholarship treats corporations as a nexus of contracts, allocating rights and obligations to the various constituencies that make up the legal fiction that is the firm. It eschews a "one size fits all" approach to regulation and instead favors the use of enabling provisions that allow companies to opt in or opt out. Unlike categorical rules imposed by the state, market actors can engage in private ordering and bargain for the most efficient arrangements. Contractarians argue that the state possesses no advantages vis-a-vis market actors in crafting rules of the game. To the extent that the state prescribes mandatory rules, they are likely to come with significant costs that could have been avoided had the parties been allowed to design their own rules.

Whatever the precise formulation of the view, contractarians, in the end, place an almost talismanic faith in private ordering and on the market as the final arbiter of efficiency. While private ordering will not ineluctably lead to greater efficiency, the market can be counted on to weed out the inefficient. In contrast, the inefficiencies arising from categorical rules are not susceptible to the same correction mechanism.

---

4. Copyright © 2009 Indiana Law Review. Reprinted with permission.

As a corollary to this approach, contractarians characterize the evolution of corporate law as a race to the top. Under state law, categorical rules have gradually been replaced with enabling provisions, sometimes by transferring authority from shareholders to the board of directors, and sometimes through shareholder and board approval mechanisms. The system, therefore, allows companies to opt in or opt out of particular legal regimes, freeing managers to negotiate and engage in the most efficient arrangements.

This Article examines an aspect of the contractarian approach to corporate law. The approach presupposes some ability of shareholders to "negotiate" with management to obtain agreements that are in the collective best interests of both groups. Presumably, the mechanism for asserting these interests in many cases is the ability to vote for or against a decision by management. This might occur, for example, where management can opt in or out of a regulatory regime through an amendment to the articles of incorporation. The need for shareholder approval would cause some companies not to seek the opt-in or opt-out authority and for others to limit the terms of the opt-in or opt-out regime in order to garner sufficient support. In other words, the regime would reflect "bargaining" between shareholders and management with the goal of achieving the most efficient relationship. If indeed some bargaining transpires between the competing interests, some degree of variance in practice would be expected.

While bargaining between competing interests is plausible in theory, in reality the management domination of the approval process and the severe problems of collective action confronted by shareholders make it all but impossible. As a result, the process of management submitting matters to shareholders cannot accurately be characterized as bargaining in any meaningful sense of the term. It is management that drafts the proposal, management that has the authority to initiate the proposal, management that decides the most propitious moment to put forth the proposal, and management that has the corporate treasury at its disposal to ensure adoption of the proposal. Moreover, once passed, shareholders typically lack the authority to initiate repeal. The consequences are stark: once management obtains adoption, the provision remains in place, irrespective of the wishes of shareholders, until management decides to initiate a change.

This Article examines whether the core claim of contractarians—that private ordering as a process of bargaining creates optimal rules—is borne out by the empirical evidence in the context of waiver of liability provisions. These provisions allow companies to eliminate monetary damages for breach of the duty of care through amendments to the articles of incorporation. With all states allowing some form of these provisions, they represent a good laboratory to examine the bargaining process between management and shareholders.

The choice of waiver of liability provisions for study is particularly appropriate because they exemplify a contractarian approach to regulation. They were a reaction to purported problems created by a mandatory approach and allowed companies to opt out of a regime that imposed liability on managers for breach of the duty of care. Moreover, as amendments to the articles, they require the assent of both managers and owners. The outcome, therefore, presumably results from negotiations between these two groups and ought to be a good example of private ordering by contract.

If a process of bargaining is at work as the contractarians claim, then the opt-in process for waiver of liability provisions ought to generate a variety of approaches. Shareholders wanting a high degree of accountability would presumably not support a waiver of damages. In other instances, shareholders might favor them in order to attract or retain qualified managers. Still other shareholders would presumably want a mix, allowing waivers only in specified circumstances.

In fact, as the analysis shows, none of the diversity predicted by a private ordering model appears in connection with waiver of liability provisions. They are permitted by every state and are used by all but one Fortune 100 company. Moreover, they are remarkably similar in effect, waiving liability to the fullest extent permitted by law. In other words, one categorical rule was merely replaced by another, with no evidence that a categorical waiver of liability was any more efficient than a categorical rule imposing liability. At the same time, the change benefited management, suggesting that the motivation was not efficiency but self-interest of one of the groups involved. Moreover, whatever one might think about the benefits of private ordering and bargaining, the evidence suggests that it is not taking place in the waiver of liability context.

Comments and Questions

1. Of the large companies studied, only one did not have a waiver of liability provision: Pepsi.

2. Does the history of Section 102(b)(7) and the pattern in other states better support a race to the top or a race to the bottom? Make the case for each.

3. When asked to approve waiver of liability provisions, shareholders typically adopt them with overwhelming support. Why do you think that is the case? Shouldn't shareholders object to a proposal designed to deprive them of compensation in the event of a breach of the duty of care?

4. Given the uniform nature of these provisions, is it accurate to characterize waiver of liability provisions as a default rule? What if shareholders wanted to eliminate the provision? Would they be able to do so?

5. The language of Section 102(b)(7) has been criticized as imprecise. For example, it excludes breaches of the duty of loyalty without defining the term. Moreover, the provision excludes both violations of good faith and the duty of loyalty. Yet Delaware courts have defined violations of good faith as a breach of the duty of loyalty. *See Stone v. Ritter*, 911 A.2d 362, 370 (Del. 2006). The waiver of liability provision in the Model Business Corporation Act extends to, among other things, "the amount of a financial benefit received by a director to which he is not entitled" and "an intentional infliction of harm on the corporation or the shareholders...." What are some possible differences in coverage between the two provisions?

6. Whether a race to the bottom or race to the top, Section 102(b)(7) had a significant impact on the market for corporate charters. Once Delaware put the provision in place, a significant number of companies reincorporated in the state. *See* Michael Bradley & Cindy A. Schipani, *The Relevance of the Duty of Care Standard in Corporate Governance*, 75 Iowa L. Rev. 1, 65 (1989) ("To date we have identified approximately 100 firms that reincorporated in Delaware between July 1, 1986 and May 1988.").

II. The SEC and Corporate Governance

A. Some History

As part of the Securities Exchange Act of 1934, Congress created the Securities and Exchange Commission, an independent agency charged with the oversight of the federal securities laws. *See* Section 4, 15 USC 78d. The birth of this agency, ironically, had a negative explanation. It was designed to weaken the existing scheme of government oversight by taking the responsibility for the securities laws away from the Federal Trade Commission.

Bevis Longstreth, *Book Review: The SEC after Fifty Years: An Assessment of Its Past and Future*

83 Colum. L. Rev. 1593, 1594–95, 1597–98 (1983)[5]

The birth of the SEC was, according to the author, "an accident." It resulted largely from a fear on the part of Senator Carter Glass and opponents of the Exchange Act that the obvious agency to administer the law—the Federal Trade Commission—was too much under the control of New Deal reformers. Foremost among this group of reformers was James Landis, appointed to the FTC in 1933. That agency's proregulatory disposition and the high caliber of its staff were believed by Exchange leaders to pose unacceptable dangers. The push for a new agency was apparently motivated in part by the (as it turned out, vain) hope that the SEC would prove less effective. Although it may well be said, as Professor Seligman suggests, that the effectiveness of the SEC over the years has been a product of the narrow scope of its jurisdiction, its birth and charter were not the product of unified design but an amalgam forged by political compromise. Ironically, New Deal reformer Landis became the second chairman of the SEC, appointed by Roosevelt in 1935.

It was through Landis's insistence on professional excellence, according to Professor Seligman, that the SEC staff developed "its esprit de corps, its enduring standards of high quality, its attractiveness to talented attorneys". Of course, the father of administrative law, Felix Frankfurter, earlier had identified the need for highly qualified expert administrators. In 1934 he wrote: "There are some things we can no longer afford ... Above all we can no longer afford to do without a highly trained, disinter-

---

5. Copyright © 1983 Columbia Law Review. Reprinted with permission.

ested governmental personnel". And as Ferdinand Pecora stressed to President Roosevelt on the day he signed the Securities Act of 1933 into law, "[i]t will be a good or bad law depending upon the men who administer it."

* * *

Throughout its history, the Commission has understood that, first, even for a so-called "independent regulatory agency," politics plays an important part in regulation and, second, that politics is the art of the possible. One must take care lest the best or better solution becomes the enemy of the good solution.

The history of securities legislation reveals a consistent pattern. For legislation to pass, a crisis, scandal or other dramatic event was required to open a "window of opportunity," through which it was possible for the Commission or other advocates of reform to move the Congress to action. Professor Seligman quotes William O. Douglas on the point: "Political and economic power only rarely diverge, and when they do, you must move rapidly" ...

Comments and Questions

1. There is a certain irony that the creation of the Securities and Exchange Commission was designed to weaken rather than strengthen securities enforcement. Overall, did the location of securities oversight (inside the FTC or in a separate entity) likely make any difference?

2. The reform of the securities markets had a high priority during the Roosevelt Administration. The first of the securities laws, the Securities Act of 1933, was adopted during Roosevelt's first 100 days in office, an indication of the priority on his agenda.

3. Joseph Kennedy was the first chairperson of the Commission. Kennedy has been described as a "a notoriously successful businessman ..." John C. Coates IV, *Private vs. Political Choice of Securities Regulation: A Political Cost/Benefit Analysis*, 41 Va. J. Int'l L. 531, 563 (2001). What might President Roosevelt have been thinking when he made this appointment?

4. The chair of the Commission was originally selected by the Commission itself. The third chairman was William O. Douglas, who later joined the Supreme Court. The authority was transferred to the President in 1950. *See* Reorganization Plan No. 10 of 1950. What strengths and weaknesses might this model provide? What happens if there are no vacancies on the Commission when a President is elected? As a practical matter, why is that not likely to occur?

5. The staff at the Commission has traditionally had a strong sense of esprit de corps, even after leaving the agency. This can be seen in part from organizations such as the Association of Securities and Exchange Commission Alumni, Inc. and the SEC Historical Society which, among other things, operates a virtual museum.

6. The author of this piece, Bevis Longstreth, is a former commissioner of the SEC. What do you make of the description that "politics plays an important part in regulation"? How might that be the case? The Commission may not have more than

a majority from a single party. *See* Section 4, 15 USC § 78d. As a result, both of the major parties are typically represented on the body. Does this increase or decrease the influence of politics on the regulatory mission of the agency?

7. What is the primary purpose of the SEC? Back in 1937, then Chairman Douglas said "[w]e have got brokers' advocates; we have got Exchange advocates; we have got investment banker advocates; and we are the investor's advocate." The SEC web site today describes the mission as "three-part" and includes the protection of investors, the maintenance of "fair, orderly, and efficient markets" and the facilitation of capital formation. Does this reflect a change in the SEC's mission? Does it influence your analysis to know that Congress in Dodd-Frank required the SEC to create an Investor Advisory Committee and appoint an Investor Advocate? See Section 951 (establishing Investor Advisory Committee) and Section 915 (establishing the Office of the Investor Advocate).

———

The Securities and Exchange Commission is considered an "independent" agency within the executive branch. Independence is often an imprecise term. Sometimes it merely refers to bureaucracies that are free standing and not part of another department. In that sense the Environmental Protection Agency is independent while the Internal Revenue Service (which is in the Department of Treasury) is not.

With respect to the SEC, however, the concept of independence has constitutional implications. Independence here means independent of the President. This arises because commissioners receive five year terms and cannot be removed by the President except for cause. Thus, a President unhappy with the regulatory policies implemented by the agency cannot automatically remove the members. At least in theory, this allows the Commission to act in a manner that is less influenced by politics. This type of independence has had a surprisingly tumultuous history that to some degree remains unsettled even today.

SEC v. Blinder, Robinson & Co.
United States Court of Appeals, Tenth Circuit
855 F.2d 677 (1988)

BRORBY, CIRCUIT JUDGE:

Blinder, Robinson and Co., Inc. and Meyer Blinder both appeal the orders of the United States District Court denying appellants' motions to vacate an injunction.

Appellant Blinder, Robinson and Co., Inc. (Blinder, Robinson) is a nationwide broker/dealer in securities. Appellant Meyer Blinder was a founder, and at all times relevant herein, was and is Blinder, Robinson's principal shareholder and president. In 1982, the United States District Court for the District of Colorado, following trial, found the Blinder, Robinson sales force practiced a program of disseminating "deliberately deceptive misinformation," orchestrated by Mr. Blinder. The court specifically found that Mr. Blinder had acted with an "intent to deceive" investors. Based upon these and other findings, the district court entered injunctions prohibiting appellants from engaging in specified practices in violation of various provisions of securities law. The injunctions can be described as ordering appellants to obey the law. Upon appeal, this court affirmed the decision of the district court in an unreported decision in September 1983. Appellants thereafter filed an action against the Securities and Exchange Commission (SEC) seeking an injunction, declaratory relief and damages. This action was predicated in part upon a continuing investigation by the SEC. Another theory of this action was that appellants were represented by incompetent or negligent counsel in the original enforcement action. This court sustained the trial court's decision which denied relief to appellants.

* * *

Appellants argue that the power of the SEC to commence a civil enforcement action in federal court is in violation of the separation of powers principle. Appellants contend that the SEC is an independent agency empowered to enforce federal law by means of civil actions for injunctions, and that the President is given sole and exclusive control over the execution of the laws under Article II of the Constitution which provides that the President shall "take care the laws be faithfully executed."

* * *

A brief overview of the SEC will be helpful in understanding the constitutional issue presented. The creation, composition, and powers of the SEC are found in the Securities Exchange Act of 1934. The commission consists of five members who are appointed by the President with the advice and consent of the Senate. The terms of the commissioners are staggered and the basic length of each term is five years. No more than three of the commissioners may be members of the same political party. The statute does not provide for a chairman. Until 1950, the Chairman was elected annually. Following Reorganization Plan No. 10 of 1950 (see, Reorganization Act of 1949, 5 U.S.C. §§ 901–913), the President designates the chairman. Pursuant to this Reorganization Plan, the chairman succeeded to most of the executive and administrative functions of the commission. The Act does not expressly give to the President the power to remove a commissioner. However, for the purposes of this case, we accept appellants' assertions in their brief, that it is commonly understood that the President may remove a commissioner only for "inefficiency, neglect of duty or malfeasance in office." While the SEC must transmit evidence of criminal misconduct to the Attorney General, there can be no doubt the SEC is authorized to institute civil actions in the federal district courts to enforce various security laws.

Several conclusions can be drawn from this brief overview. First, as the President has the power to choose the chairman of the SEC from its commissioners to serve an indefinite term, it follows that the chairman serves at the pleasure of the President. Second, as the chairman controls key personnel, internal organization, and the expenditure of funds, the chairman exerts far more control than his one vote would seem to indicate. Third, it can safely be assumed that in exercising his power of appointment, even as to commissioners who are not members of his party, the President will tend to appoint those persons who are sympathetic to his own views.

In Humphrey's Executor v. United States, 295 U.S. 602, 79 L. Ed. 1611, 55 S. Ct. 869 (1935), President Roosevelt requested Humphrey's resignation as a commissioner of the Federal Trade Commission for the reason that Humphrey and the President had differing policies concerning the administration of the commission. The statute provided that a commissioner could be removed "for inefficiency, neglect of duty, or malfeasance in office." The Supreme Court recognized the intent of Congress to create a commission that was not to be subject to anyone in the government—a body which should be independent of executive authority, *except in its selection,* and ruled that the concept of a member continuing in office at "the mere will" of the President might thwart the very ends Congress sought to realize. The Supreme Court next turned its attention to the question of whether such a limitation on the President's right to remove a commissioner is constitutional under the principles of separation of powers. The Court held that whether the power of the President to remove an officer shall prevail over the authority of Congress to condition the power by fixing a definite term and precluding removal except for cause, will depend upon the character of the office. The Court concluded "as to officers of the kind here under consideration" no removal can be made except as provided by statute. The Supreme Court noted the ruling would be equally applicable to members of the Interstate Commerce Commission. Both the FTC and the SEC are administrative bodies created by Congress to carry into effect legislative policies embodied in the statute. We conclude the same reasoning would apply to commissioners of the SEC.

More recently, in Morrison v. Olson, 487 U.S. 654, 108 S. Ct. 2597, 101 L. Ed. 2d 569 (1988), the Supreme Court decided the constitutionality of the independent counsel statutes. The law in question there provides for the appointment of an independent counsel to investigate and prosecute certain government officials for violations of federal criminal law. The law in question generally provides that upon receipt of specified information, the court shall appoint independent counsel. An independent counsel may be removed, other than by impeachment and conviction, only by the Attorney General and only for good cause, physical disability, or mental incapacity.

We note that *Morrison* is predicated in part upon *Humphrey,* which stands generally for the proposition that Congress can, without violating Article II, authorize an independent agency to bring civil law enforcement actions where the President's removal power was restricted to inefficiency, neglect of duty, or malfeasance in office. *Morrison* teaches that the real question to be answered is whether the removal restrictions impede the President's ability to perform his constitutional duty. It is a matter of fundamental law that the Constitution assigns to Congress the power to designate duties of particular officers. The President is not obligated under the Constitution to exercise absolute control over our government executives. The President is not required to execute the laws; he is required to take care they be executed faithfully. The President has the power to appoint the commissioners; he has the power to choose the chairman of the SEC who has broad powers concerning the operation and administration of the commission; the chairman serves at the President's pleasure; and, the President has the power to remove a commissioner for inefficiency, neglect of duty, or malfeasance in office. We conclude these powers give the President sufficient control over the commissioners to insure the securities laws are faithfully executed and the removal restrictions do not impede the President's ability to perform his constitutional duty.

We conclude the trial court correctly applied the proper legal standard concerning the vacation or modification of the injunction. We further conclude the civil enforcement power given to the SEC is constitutionally valid. We have carefully considered all issues raised by appellants, and those not discussed herein are found to be without merit.

For the reasons set forth herein, the judgment of the trial court is AFFIRMED.

Comments and Questions

1. What does it mean to be "independent"? What are the attributes of the SEC that earn it the characterization as independent? How might that affect the regulation of corporate governance by the SEC?

2. In the case of the independent counsel in *Morrison*, the President had no direct removal authority. That authority was vested in the Attorney General. Nonetheless, as a practical matter, the President could remove independent counsel through his/her control over the Attorney General. This occurred for example in connection with the so called Saturday Night Massacre when President Nixon dismissed two attorneys general (Elliot Richardson and William Ruckelshaus) before the third one (Robert Bork) carried out his instructions to fire Archibald Cox, the Watergate special prosecutor. *See* Senator Carl Levin (with assistance from Elise J. Bean), *The Independent Counsel Statute: A Matter of Public Confidence and Constitutional Balance*, 16 Hofstra L. Rev. 11, 12 (Fall 1987).

3. The issue of the constitutionality of the SEC's structure may be more complex than this court thought. For one thing, independence generally arises from the inability of the President to treat the commissioners as at-will employees. This right to remove "for cause" is usually set out in the statute creating the agency. Thus, commissioners serving on the Federal Trade Commission may only be removed only "for inefficiency, neglect of duty, or malfeasance in office." 15 U.S.C.S §41. The Securities Exchange Act, while providing for five year terms for commissioners, does not explicitly limit the President's right of removal. *See* 15 U.S.C. §78d. In other words, restrictions on the President's right of removal are implicit rather than explicit.

4. The issue came up in *Free Enterprise Fund v. PCAOB*, 561 US 467 (2010) (Breyer, J., dissenting). Justice Breyer had this to say about the SEC's independence:

> It is certainly not obvious that the SEC Commissioners enjoy "for cause" protection. Unlike the statutes establishing the 48 federal agencies listed in Appendix A, infra, the statute that established the Commission says nothing about removal. It is silent on the question. As far as its text is concerned, the President's authority to remove the Commissioners is no different from his authority to remove the Secretary of State or the Attorney General....

Nor is the absence of a "for cause" provision in the statute that created the Commission likely to have been inadvertent. Congress created the Commission during the 9 year period after this Court decided *Myers*, and thereby cast serious doubt on the constitutionality of all "for cause" removal provisions, but before it decided *Humphrey's Executor*, which removed any doubt in respect to the constitutionality of making commissioners of independent agencies removable only for cause. In other words, Congress created the SEC at a time when, under this Court's precedents, it would have been unconstitutional to make the Commissioners removable only for cause. And, during that 9 year period, Congress created at least three major federal agencies without making any of their officers removable for cause. *See* 48 Stat. 885, 15 U. S. C. §78d (Securities and Exchange Commission), 48 Stat. 1066, 47 U. S. C. §154 (Federal Communications Commission); 46 Stat. 797 (Federal Power Commission) (reformed post-Humphrey's Executor as the Federal Energy Regulatory Commission with "for cause" protection, 91 Stat. 582, 42 U. S. C. §7171). By way of contrast, only one month after Humphrey's Executor was decided, Congress returned to its pre-Myers practice of including such provisions in statutes creating independent commissions. *See* §3, 49 Stat. 451, 29 U. S. C. §153 (establishing National Labor Relations Board with an explicit removal limitation).

Id. at 3182–83. What do you make of this analysis? Is it correct? Does it conflict with the analysis in *Blinder, Robinson*?

5. Although Justice Breyer dissented, does his analysis reopen the issue of SEC independence? He had this to say on the subject:

> The fact that Congress did not make the SEC Commissioners removable "for cause" does not mean it intended to create a dependent, rather than an independent agency. Agency independence is a function of several different factors, of which "for cause" protection is only one. Those factors include, *inter alia*, an agency's separate (rather than presidentially dependent) budgeting authority, its separate litigating authority, its composition as a multimember bipartisan board, the use of the word "independent" in its authorizing statute, and, above all, a political environment, reflecting tradition and function, that would impose a heavy political cost upon any President who tried to remove a commissioner of the agency without cause....

561 US at 547. Is Justice Breyer correct? Does independence arise from factors other than restrictions on removal authority? In Appendix D to his dissent, he listed six criteria that "suggest independence." These include such factors as whether the agency has a multimember commission, whether the agency has independence in submitting a budget to Congress, and whether an agency has the authority to appear in court independent of the Justice Department. Do these factors ensure independence, at least if that is defined as independent of the influence of the President?

6. The independence of the SEC does translate into the right to litigate cases in federal courts without first obtaining approval of anyone in the executive branch. *See* 15 U.S.C. § 78u. There is, however, one significant limit. The SEC does not have the authority to file briefs in the U.S. Supreme Court. That authority rests exclusively with the Solicitor General within the Justice Department. Ordinarily, the Solicitor files briefs jointly written by its staff and the staff at the SEC, thereby presenting the Supreme Court with the views of the Commission. In a number of high profile cases, however, the Solicitor General has refused to file a brief on behalf of the Commission. Thus, in *Stoneridge Inv. Partners, LLC v. Scientific-Atlanta, Inc.*, 552 U.S. 148 (2008), the Commission, according to published reports, asked the Solicitor General to file an amicus brief on its behalf and the Solicitor refused. Instead, the Solicitor filed an amicus brief on the side of the case not favored by the SEC. The Supreme Court, therefore, decided an important securities case without the views of the administrative agency assigned to administer the Act under consideration. YIKES

7. The SEC sought authority to file amicus briefs in the Supreme Court without prior permission from the Solicitor General in the 1970s but never received the authority. For a discussion of what happened, see Neal Devins, *Unitariness and Independence: Solicitor General Control Over Independent Agency Litigation*, 82 Cal. L. Rev. 255 (1994). What are the pros and cons of assigning this authority to the SEC? Why might the President object?

8. Originally, the chairperson of the Commission was determined by the commissioners themselves. That changed in 1950 when the authority was assigned to the President. When administrations change, the President in theory may not have an opening to fill but will be able to designate the chair. This provides some immediate ability to influence the agency's agenda. As a practical matter, however, the tradition is for the chair appointed by the prior administration to resign. What impact does this likely have on the regulatory approach of the Commission?

———————

The role of the SEC, however, has shifted in recent years. The agency's role in the corporate governance process has become more substantive. Moreover, although still retaining its "independent" status, politics still play a role, as the next excerpt suggests.

J. Robert Brown, Jr., *The Politicization of Corporate Governance: Bureaucratic Discretion, the SEC, and Shareholder Ratification of Auditors*
2 Harv. Bus. L. Rev. 501, 501–505 (2012)

One of the most profound changes in corporate governance over the last decade has been the shift in the role of the Securities and Exchange Commission ("SEC"). Initially limited primarily to the task of ensuring adequate disclosure, the SEC mostly played a marginal role in the substance of corporate governance. It was left to the states to determine the rights and obligations of directors and shareholders. Aborted efforts by the SEC in the 1980s to engage in substantive rulemaking through the medium of listing standards were met with emphatic rejection by the courts.

The distinction between disclosure and substance, to the extent one ever really existed, has largely been dismantled. Over the last decade, Congress repeatedly transferred to the SEC direct substantive authority over the corporate governance process, first in the Sarbanes-Oxley Act of 2002 ("Sarbanes-Oxley"), then in the Dodd-Frank Wall Street Reform Act of 2010 ("Dodd-Frank"). While Sarbanes-Oxley was harshly criticized and viewed by many as an anomaly arising out of the perfect storm of the Enron scandal and rapidly approaching congressional elections, Dodd-Frank confirmed that principles of federalism in the realm of corporate governance had been permanently eroded. The Act made clear the absence of any meaningful congressional reservation on the transfer of governance authority from the states to the SEC.

The cumulative effect of these changes has been to thrust the SEC into the center of the corporate governance debate. Rather than merely addressing the informational needs of investors, the SEC has increasingly been called upon to develop substantive standards and to arbitrate the often irreconcilable positions of interest groups vying to influence the governance process.

The transfer of governance authority to the SEC will have significant consequences. For one thing, the regulatory philosophy is likely to change. Unlike the management-friendly approach employed by Delaware in determining governance standards, the SEC has as its regulatory mission the protection of shareholders and investors. The agency also has a statutory obligation to examine regulatory initiatives for their impact on efficiency, competition, and capital formation. The result will probably be, for the most part, more balanced policies.

The transfer will, however, cause increased politicization of the governance process. With changes in administration, the political makeup of the Commission typically shifts. As a result, the regulatory philosophy of the SEC more closely tracks the political philosophy of the party in power. With governance increasingly seen as a zero-sum game between investors and issuers, pressure will build with each change in administration to undo the practices of the prior SEC. The result will be increased volatility.

The volatility will be less apparent with respect to rulemaking. Rules must be adopted pursuant to notice and comment under the Administrative Procedures Act ("APA") and are difficult to undo once implemented. Moreover, efforts to change rules will be susceptible to legal challenge in an increasingly interventionist D.C. Circuit.

Staff interpretations, however, are an entirely different matter. Issued on an informal basis, often through so-called "No-Action letters," these positions are not subject to the notice and comment process mandated by the APA and in many cases are not subject to legal challenge. Moreover, the letters rarely contain meaningful analysis of the legal positions taken by the staff. They can, as a result, be changed or abandoned with little explanation.

This can be seen from shifts in the SEC staff's position under Rule 14a-8, the shareholder proposal rule. The rule allows shareholders to submit proposals to companies for inclusion in the proxy statement. Management may, under certain circumstances, exclude proposals, including those that interfere with the "ordinary business" of the company. This exclusion does not apply, however, where the proposal involves matters of important public policy.

An examination of staff interpretations under the exclusion show that they shift significantly from administration to administration, particularly with changes in the political makeup of the agency. Congress contemplated that the five-person Commission would include representatives of both major parties. When at a full complement, the Commission typically consists of three members from the party of the current administration and two members from the other major party. The replacement of a single member can cause the regulatory philosophy of the administrative agency to change.

During Republican administrations, interpretive views under Rule 14a-8 tend to minimize or eliminate consideration of social policy and more broadly allow for exclusion of shareholder proposals. During Democratic administrations, the situation is reversed. Social policy is read broadly to favor shareholders and effectively restricts management's ability to exclude proposals. Given these countervailing views, the positions of the staff often change following the advent of a new administration, sometimes leading to the reversal of previously adopted policies.

Political influence does not operate in a straight-line fashion. The ability to alter staff positions depends upon a variety of factors, including the importance of the issue, the particular views and personalities of the incumbent Commissioners, and the dynamics associated with collaborative decision making. Commissioners may need time to build coalitions favoring a particular position. Moreover, with Commissioners serving five year terms, a newly elected President often must wait several years before appointing a majority to the Commission. Finally, political influence has a logistical component, with the opportunity to intervene affected by the particular proposals submitted by shareholders and management's response.

Comments and Questions

1. Section 4(a) of the Exchange Act provides that "[n]ot more than three of such commissioners shall be members of the same political party, and in making appointments members of different political parties shall be appointed alternately as nearly as may be practicable." 15 USC 78d(a). Why do you think this requirement was inserted into the statute?

2. For much of the history of the Commission, the need for representatives of both parties likely had little impact on the decision making process of the agency. The President, after all, could likely find commissioners from both parties that reflected his or her views. At least since the 1990s, however, the practice has been for the President to appoint nominees submitted by the leadership in the Senate of the other political party. What impact might this have on the positions taken by the Commission?

3. The number of 3–2 votes in public meetings has increased significantly. Most (but not all) are votes that reflect the political divisions of the Commission. The votes on public matters are posted on the SEC's web site and can be found here: https://www.sec.gov/foia/foia-votes.shtml. Are there any patterns on the divided votes?

4. Commissioners have dissented not only on final rules but also on proposals. To the extent that a dissent at the proposal stage effectively announces opposition to any final rule, what difference might that make in the nature of the final rule? Does the staff, in drafting the language of the final rule, need to take the views of the dissenting commissioners into account? What impact might that have on the decisions of the Commission?

5. What does this article suggest will be the practical implications of decision making to the extent that the Commission remains divided on the basis of political party? Why would political differences be reflected more easily in staff interpretations?

B. Rulemaking Authority

In resolving the oversight responsibilities of the SEC, Congress provided the agency with a role in the corporate governance process. The legislative history of the Exchange Act evidenced considerable concern over the control of the voting process by directors to entrench themselves in office. As the House Report noted:

> Fair corporate suffrage is an important right that should attach to every equity security bought on a public exchange. Managements of properties owned by the investing public should not be permitted to perpetuate themselves by the misuse of corporate proxies. Insiders having little or no substantial interest in the properties they manage have often retained their control without an adequate disclosure of their interest and without an adequate explanation of the management policies they intend to pursue. Insiders have at times solicited proxies without fairly informing the stockholders of the purposes for which the proxies are to be used and have used such proxies to take from the stockholders for their own selfish advantage valuable property rights.

Congress gave the Commission the power to regulate the proxy process, primarily (though not exclusively) through disclosure. With disclosure, Congress anticipated that shareholders would be in a position to correct the most significant corporate governance abuses. This is addressed more completely in Chapter 9.

A considerable source of the Commission's involvement in the governance process occurs through rulemaking. Section 553 of the Administrative Procedures Act requires federal agencies to provide notice of proposed rules and an opportunity for comment. *See* 5 U.S.C. § 553. The proposals, therefore, provide what amounts to an open forum on corporate governance standards. The rules have, unsurprisingly, generated considerable attention and controversy. *See* Joseph A. Grundfest, *The SEC's Proposed Proxy Access Rules: Politics, Economics and the Law*, 65 Bus. Law. 361, 386 (Feb. 2010) (noting that with respect to shareholder access proposals, "more than 34,000 comments were submitted in prior rulemakings on the matter.").

In addition to any process imposed under the APA, the Commission may only adopt rules consistent with its statutory authority. Given the primary role of ensuring accurate and complete information, most of the rules affecting the governance process have involved disclosure requirements. Yet the SEC has sometimes tried to go further, using its rulemaking standards to impose substantive governance requirements.

Without direct authority to do so, the Commission sought to intervene in the corporate governance debate through the mechanism of listing standards at the stock exchanges. Under section 19(c) of the Exchange Act, the SEC had the authority to impose rules on the exchanges. *See* 15 U.S.C. §78(c). In 1988, the Commission tried to use this authority to require the exchanges to adopt a provision that regulated the voting rights of shareholders. The rule was quickly challenged.

The Business Roundtable v. Securities and Exchange Commission

United States Court of Appeals, District of Columbia Circuit
905 F.2d 406 (1990)

WILLIAMS, CIRCUIT JUDGE:

In 1984 General Motors announced a plan to issue a second class of common stock with one-half vote per share. The proposal collided with a longstanding rule of the New York Stock Exchange that required listed companies to provide one vote per share of common stock. The NYSE balked at enforcement, and after two years filed a proposal with the Securities and Exchange Commission to relax its own rule. The SEC did not approve the rule change but responded with one of its own. On July 7, 1988, it adopted Rule 19c-4, barring national securities exchanges and national securities associations, together known as self-regulatory organizations (SROs), from listing stock of a corporation that takes any corporate action "with the effect of nullifying, restricting or disparately reducing the per share voting rights of [existing common stockholders]." Voting Rights Listing Standards; Disenfranchisement Rule, 53 Fed.Reg. 26,376, 26,394 (1988) ("Final Rule"), codified at 17 CFR §240.19c-4 (1990). The rule prohibits such "disenfranchisement" even where approved by a shareholder vote conducted on one share/one vote principles. Because the rule directly controls the substantive allocation of powers among classes of shareholders, we find it in excess of the Commission's authority under §19 of the Securities Exchange Act of 1934, as amended (the "Exchange Act"), 15 U.S.C. §78s (1988). Neither the wisdom of the requirement, nor of its being imposed at the federal level, is here in question.

* * *

Two components of §19 give the Commission authority over the rules of self-regulatory organizations. First, §19(b) requires them to file with the Commission any proposed change in their rules. The Commission is to approve the change if it finds it "consistent with the requirements of [the Exchange Act] and the rules and regulations thereunder applicable" to the self-regulatory organization. §19(b)(2), 15

U.S.C. §78s(b)(2). This provision is not directly at issue here, but, as we shall see, both the procedure and the terms guiding Commission approval are important in understanding the scope of the authority the Commission has sought to exercise. That is found in §19(c), which allows the Commission on its own initiative to amend the rules of a self-regulatory organization as it

> deems necessary or appropriate [1] to insure the fair administration of the self-regulatory organization, [2] to conform its rules to requirements of [the Exchange Act] and the rules and regulations thereunder applicable to such organization, or *otherwise in furtherance of the purposes of [the Exchange Act]*.

§19(c), 15 U.S.C. §78s(c) (emphasis and enumeration added). As no one suggests that either of the first two purposes justifies Rule 19c-4, the issue before us is the scope of the third, catch-all provision.

* * *

What then are the "purposes" of the Exchange Act? The Commission supports Rule 19c-4 as advancing the purposes of a variety of sections, see Final Rule, 53 Fed.Reg. at 26,390/1, but we first take its strongest—§14's grant of power to regulate the proxy process. The Commission finds a purpose "to ensure fair shareholder suffrage." *See* Final Rule, 53 Fed.Reg. at 26,391/2. Indeed, it points to the House Report's declarations that "fair corporate suffrage is an important right," H.R.Rep. No. 1383, 73d Cong., 2d Sess. 13 (1934) ("1934 House Report"), and that "use of the exchanges should involve a corresponding duty of according to shareholders fair suffrage," id. at 14. The formulation is true in the sense that Congress's decision can be located under that broad umbrella.

But unless the legislative purpose is defined by reference to the means Congress selected, it can be framed at any level of generality—to improve the operation of capital markets, for instance. In fact, although §14(a) broadly bars use of the mails (and other means) "to solicit ... any proxy" in contravention of Commission rules and regulations, it is not seriously disputed that Congress's central concern was with disclosure. *See* J. I. Case Co. v. Borak, 377 U.S. 426, 431, 84 S. Ct. 1555, 12 L. Ed. 2d 423 (1964) ("The purpose of §14(a) is to prevent management or others from obtaining authorization for corporate action by means of deceptive or inadequate disclosure in proxy solicitation."); see also Santa Fe Industries Inc. v. Green, 430 U.S. 462, 477–78, 97 S. Ct. 1292, 51 L. Ed. 2d 480 (1977) (emphasizing Exchange Act's philosophy of full disclosure and dismissing the fairness of the terms of the transaction as "at most a tangential concern of the statute" once full and fair disclosure has occurred).

While the House Report indeed speaks of fair corporate suffrage, it also plainly identifies Congress's target—the solicitation of proxies by well informed insiders "without fairly informing the stockholders of the purposes for which the proxies are to be used." 1934 House Report at 14. The Senate Report contains no vague language about "corporate suffrage," but rather explains the purpose of the proxy protections as ensuring that stockholders have "adequate knowledge" about the "financial condition of the corporation ... [and] the major questions of policy, which are decided at stockholders' meetings." S.Rep. No. 792, 73d Cong., 2d Sess. 12 (1934) ("1934 Senate Report"). Finally, both reports agree on the power that the proxy sections gave the Commission—"power to control the conditions under which proxies may be solicited." 1934 House Report at 14. *See* also 1934 Senate Report at 12 (similar language).

That proxy regulation bears almost exclusively on disclosure stems as a matter of necessity from the nature of proxies. Proxy solicitations are, after all, only *communications* with potential absentee voters. The goal of federal proxy regulation was to improve those communications and thereby to enable proxy voters to control the corporation as effectively as they might have by attending a shareholder meeting. *Id. See* also S.Rep. No. 1455, 73d Cong., 2d Sess. 74 (1934); Sheldon E. Bernstein and Henry G. Fischer, *The Regulation of the Solicitation of Proxies: Some Reflections on Corporate Democracy*, 7 U. Chi. L. Rev. 226, 227–28 (1940).

We do not mean to be taken as saying that disclosure is necessarily the sole subject of § 14. *See* Louis Loss, Fundamentals of Securities Regulation 452-53 (1988) (asserting that § 14 is not limited to ensuring disclosure), quoted in Final Rule, 53 Fed. Reg. at 26,391 n. 163; Karmel, 36 Cath. U.L. Rev. 809, 824 (similar). But see also Dent, 54 Geo. Wash. L. Rev. 725, 733–34 (§ 14 is primarily if not exclusively directed at disclosure); Comment, 83 Nw. U.L. Rev. 1057, 1071 (similar). For example, the Commission's Rule 14a-4(b)(2) requires a proxy to provide some mechanism for a security holder to withhold authority to vote for each nominee individually. *See* 17 CFR § 240.14a-4(b)(2). It thus bars a kind of electoral tying arrangement, and may be supportable as a control over management's power to set the voting agenda, or, slightly more broadly, voting procedures. *See generally*, Dennis C. Mueller, Public Choice 38–58 (1979) (noting that difficulties inherent to majority voting, such as logrolling and cycling (in which different outcomes can be produced as coalitions reshape on successive votes), can increase the power of the agenda setter and lead to results that decrease the welfare of the voting community). But while Rule 14a-4(b)(2) may lie in a murky area between substance and procedure, Rule 19c-4 much more directly interferes with the substance of what the shareholders may enact. It prohibits certain reallocations of voting power and certain capital structures, even if approved by a shareholder vote subject to full disclosure and the most exacting procedural rules....

The Commission noted in the preamble to the Proposed Rule its conviction that collective action problems could cause even a properly conducted shareholder vote (with ample disclosure and sound procedures) to bring about results injurious to the shareholders. *See* Proposed Rule, 52 Fed. Reg. at 23,672/1 (detailing collective action problem in the shareholder voting process and expressing "concern[]" over the "effect of that vote"). We do not question these findings. But we think the Commission's reliance on them is a clue to its stretch of the congressional purposes. As the Commission itself observed, "section 14(a) contains an implicit assumption that shareholders will be able to make use of the information provided in proxy solicitations in order to vote in corporate elections." Final Rule, 53 Fed.Reg. at 26,391/3. In 1934 Congress acted on the premise that shareholder voting could work, so long as investors secured enough information and, perhaps, the benefit of other procedural protections.

It did not seek to regulate the stockholders' choices. If the Commission believes that premise misguided, it must turn to Congress.

With its step beyond control of voting procedure and into the distribution of voting power, the Commission would assume an authority that the Exchange Act's proponents disclaimed any intent to grant. Noting that opponents expressed alarm that the bill would give the Commission "power to interfere in the management of corporations," the Senate Committee on Banking and Currency said it had "no such intention" and that the bill "furnished no justification for such an interpretation." 1934 Senate Report at 10. *See* also H.R. Conf.Rep. No. 1838, 73d Cong., 2d Sess. 35 (1934) (deleting as unnecessary section 13(d) of the bill, which made explicit that the Commission could not "interfere with the management of the affairs of an issuer").

There are, of course, shadings within the notion of "management." With the present rule the Commission does not tell any corporation where to locate its next plant. But neither does state corporate law; it regulates the distribution of powers among the various players in the process of corporate governance, and the Commission's present leap beyond disclosure is just that sort of regulation. The potpourri of listing standards previously submitted to the Commission under § 19(b), see note 4 above, suggests the sweep of its current claim. These govern requirements for independent directors, independent audit committees, shareholder quorums, shareholder approval for certain major corporate transactions, and other major issues traditionally governed by state law. If Rule 19c-4 is closely enough related to the proxy regulation purpose of § 14, then all these issues appear equally subject to the Commission's discretionary control.

Surprisingly, the Commission does not concede a lack of jurisdiction over such issues. When questioned at oral argument as to what state corporation rules are not related to "fair corporate suffrage," SEC counsel conceded only that further intrusions into state corporate governance "would present more difficult situations." Tr. of Oral Argument at 29 (Nov. 21, 1989). In fact the Commission's apparent perception of its § 19 powers has been immensely broad, unbounded even by any pretense of a connection to § 14. In reviewing the previous SRO rule changes on issues of independent directors and independent audit committees, it grounded its review in a supposed mandate to "protect investors and the public interest." Midwest Stock Exchange, Inc., 52 Fed.Reg. 36,657, 36,658/2 (1987). *See* also Order Approving Amendments to the Transaction Reporting Plan With Respect to NASDAQ/NMS Securities, 52 Fed.Reg. 24,234, 24,235/2 (1987). The Commission made no attempt to limit the concept by reference to the concrete purposes of any section. Rather, it reasoned that the rule changes protected investors by "creat[ing] uniformity that helps to assure investors that all the companies traded in those markets have the fundamental safeguards they have come to expect of major companies." Midwest Stock Exchange, 52 Fed. Reg. at 36,658/1. If Rule 19c-4 were validated on such broad grounds, the Commission would be able to establish a federal corporate law by using access to national capital markets as its enforcement mechanism. This would resolve a longstanding controversy over the wisdom of such a move in the face of disclaimers from Congress and with no substantive restraints on the power. It would, moreover, overturn or at least impinge severely on the tradition of state regulation of corporate law. As the Supreme Court has said, "corporations are creatures of state law, and investors commit their funds to corporate directors on the understanding that, except where federal law *expressly* requires certain responsibilities of directors with respect to stockholders, state law will govern the internal affairs of the corporation." Sante Fe Industries, 430 U.S. at 479 (emphasis in original, quoting Cort v. Ash, 422 U.S. 66, 84, 95 S. Ct. 2080, 45 L. Ed. 2d 26 (1975)). At least one Commissioner shared this view, stating "section 19(c) does not provide the Commission carte blanche to adopt federal corporate governance standards through the back door by mandating uniform listing standards." Final Rule, 53 Fed. Reg. at 26,395/1 (Grundfest, Comm'r, concurring). *See* also Seligman, 54 Geo. Wash. L. Rev. at 715 (§ 19(c) "does not appear to authorize the SEC to amend SRO rules for the purpose of establishing a comprehensive federal corporation act (covering such matters as the number of directors or how many shall be outsiders)"). We read the Act as reflecting a clear congressional determination not to make any such broad delegation of power to the Commission.

If the Commission's one share/one vote rule is to survive, then, some kind of firebreak is needed to separate it from corporate governance as a whole. But the Commission's sole suggestion of such a firebreak is a reference to "the unique historical background of the NYSE's one share, one vote rule." Brief for Respondent at 21 n. 24. It is true that in the Senate hearings leading to enactment of the Exchange Act there were a few favorable references to that rule. *See Stock Exchange Practices: Hearings before the Senate Committee on Banking and Currency*, 73d Cong., 1st Sess., Pt. 15, 6677 (1934) (testimony of Frank Altschul, Chairman of the NYSE Committee on Stock List); *id.* at 6779–80 (questioning of Frank Altschul by Ferdinand Pecora, Senate counsel). *See* also *id* Pt. 2 at 661–62 (questioning of O. P. Van Sweringen, president of the Alleghany Corporation, by Ferdinand Pecora) (discussing a decision of the ICC denying a petition to merge several railroads on grounds that stockholders in one of the companies would be denied their vote). But these few references are culled from 9500 pages of testimony in the Senate hearings. No legislator directly discussed the NYSE's rule and no references were made to it in any of the Committee Reports. The most these references show is that legislators were aware of the rule and that it was an important part of the background. Even if we imputed the statements to a member of Congress, none comes near to saying, "The purposes of this act, although they generally will not involve the Commission in corporate governance, do include preservation of the one share/one vote principle." And even then we doubt that such a statement in the legislative history could support a special and anomalous exception to the Act's otherwise intelligible conceptual line excluding the Commission from corporate governance.

* * *

The petition for review is granted and Rule 19c-4 is vacated.

Comments and Questions

1. A subtle but important question was whether listing standards constituted "rules" as that term was used in Section 19(c). The standards are part of the listing

agreement executed by companies when they opt to have their shares traded on the exchange. As such, they have the appearance of contractual obligations. The D.C. Circuit, however, had no problem concluding that listing standards were rules, relying in part on practice. *See Business Roundtable*, 905 F.2d at 409 ("For the past fifteen years, the exchanges have routinely submitted changes in listing standards for approval and the Commission has reviewed them without any commenting party expressing doubt of its jurisdiction. Indeed, exchanges followed this practice with the proposals that led directly to the regulations challenged here."). Practice aside, is the conclusion correct? How might one argue that listing standards and "rules" are not identical?

2. The SEC had some authority under the proxy rules to regulate the shareholder voting process. Yet the court in this case seemed concerned about boundaries and limits. Had this rule been approved, could it have been used to justify the imposition of rules on the exchanges that, for example, regulated the activities of the board of directors?

3. While unable to force the adoption of corporate governance listing standards through resort to Section 19, the case did not prevent the SEC from using more informal pressure to encourage the exchanges to adopt stricter listing standards. This occurred shortly after the collapse of Enron in 2002. *See* J. Robert Brown, Jr., *Corporate Governance, the Securities and Exchange Commission, and the Limits of Disclosure*, 57 Cath. U.L. Rev. 45, 67 (2007) (noting that the SEC pressured the stock exchanges into adopting governance listing standards in the aftermath of the collapse of Enron). Is this an adequate replacement for the type of rulemaking authority rejected in *Business Roundtable*?

4. Some have contended that *Business Roundtable* was effectively overturned by the adoption of Section 301 of Sarbanes-Oxley Act of 2001 (SOX), which gave the Commission the authority to regulate audit committees through the mechanism of listing standards. Do you agree with this position? What about the fact that Congress, in adopting the Dodd-Frank Wall Street Reform Act in 2010, gave to shareholders of public companies the right to vote on compensation matters, the so called right to "say on pay," (*see* Section 951) and left to the Commission to define the matters to be voted upon and otherwise implement the requirement. Is this approach by Congress the right one? Can you make the case that the governance process would have been better off had Business Roundtable come out differently?

5. Efforts by the Commission to strengthen the governance of mutual funds also did not fare well. *See Chamber of Commerce v. SEC*, 412 F.3d 133 (D.C. Cir. 2006) (striking down rule that would require mutual fund boards to have not less than 75% independent directors and an independent chairperson). Mutual funds, however, are mostly regulated under the Investment Company Act of 1940. The 1940 Act contains a number of governance provisions not present in the earlier acts. Thus, the Act requires a minimum number of independent directors on a mutual fund board and requires funds to submit the auditor to shareholders for approval. *See* 15 USCS § 80a-10. Thus, in *Chamber of Commerce*, the court found that the SEC had the authority

to adopt the governance provisions but had failed to fulfill all of the procedural requirements for doing so. *Id.* (invalidating rule because agency relied "on materials
not in the rulemaking record without affording an opportunity for public comment").
What does this suggest about the strengths and weaknesses of using rulemaking to
establish policy? Is there another way to achieve the same results?

6. Section 3(f) of the Exchange Act requires the Commission to consider "in addition to the protection of investors, whether the action will promote efficiency, competition, and capital formation." 15 USC 78c(f). What impact might this provision
have on Commission rulemaking?

C. Enforcement Authority

The Commission can influence the corporate governance process through mechanisms other than rulemaking. One way is through enforcement proceedings. The
SEC has the authority to bring actions against those who violate the securities laws.
Some actions are brought for what amounts to a failure of the system of corporate
governance. This is particularly true where directors do not adequately supervise management, particularly where the failure results in significant disclosure violations.

In re W. R. Grace & Co.

Exchange Act Release No. 39157 (Admin. Proc. Sept. 30, 1997)

REPORT OF INVESTIGATION PURSUANT TO SECTION 21(A) OF THE
SECURITIES EXCHANGE ACT OF 1934 CONCERNING THE CONDUCT OF
CERTAIN FORMER OFFICERS AND DIRECTORS OF W. R. GRACE & CO.

* * *

The Commission is issuing this Report of Investigation to emphasize the affirmative responsibilities of corporate officers and directors to ensure that the shareholders whom they serve receive accurate and complete disclosure of information
required by the proxy solicitation and periodic reporting provisions of the federal
securities laws. Officers and directors who review, approve, or sign their company's
proxy statements or periodic reports must take steps to ensure the accuracy and
completeness of the statements contained therein, especially as they concern those
matters within their particular knowledge or expertise. To fulfill this responsibility,
officers and directors must be vigilant in exercising their authority throughout the
disclosure process.

In this case, both Grace, Jr., then the chairman of WRG's board of directors, and
J. P. Bolduc, then WRG's chief executive officer and a member of WRG's board of
directors, knew of Grace, Jr.'s substantial retirement benefits and the proposed transaction with Grace III. Eben Pyne, a non-management member of the board, also
was aware of Grace, Jr.'s benefits. Charles Erhart, another non-management member
of the board, was aware of the proposed related-party transaction. All four of these
officers and directors reviewed all or portions of the relevant documents, and all but

Pyne signed the relevant reports. Although the record does not demonstrate that Bolduc, Pyne, and Erhart acted in bad faith, the Commission concludes that they did not fulfill their obligations under the federal securities laws. Bolduc, Pyne, and Erhart each assumed, without taking the steps necessary to confirm their assumptions, that WRG's procedures would produce drafts of disclosure documents describing all matters that required disclosure.[7] Each also assumed, without taking steps necessary to confirm their assumptions, that other corporate officers, including counsel, had conducted full and informed reviews of the drafts. Bolduc, Pyne, and Erhart each had a responsibility to go beyond the established procedures to inquire into the reasons for non-disclosure of information of which they were aware.

* * *

III. GRACE, JR., BOLDUC, AND PYNE FAILED TO TAKE STEPS TO ENSURE THAT GRACE, JR.'S RETIREMENT BENEFITS WERE FULLY DISCLOSED

During the latter part of 1992, Grace, Jr.'s health was deteriorating. Pursuant to delegated authority from WRG's board of directors, WRG's Compensation, Employee Benefits and Stock Incentive Committee (the "Compensation Committee") entered into negotiations with Grace, Jr., which resulted in his retirement from WRG as its chief executive officer, effective on December 31, 1992. Pyne, then chairman of the Compensation Committee, met several times with Grace, Jr. during November and December 1992. The negotiations resulted in an agreement in principle with respect to Grace, Jr.'s proposed retirement benefits. Among the provisions of this agreement in principle was an understanding that Grace, Jr. would continue to receive in retirement various substantial perquisites which he had received while chief executive officer. On December 7, 1992, WRG's board of directors approved Grace, Jr.'s proposed retirement benefits.

Subsequently, Grace, Jr. and Pyne, on behalf of WRG, executed a letter agreement dated December 21, 1992 (the "Retirement Agreement"), which reflected the terms of this agreement in principle. The Retirement Agreement provided, among other things, that immediately following Grace, Jr.'s retirement:

All other benefits and arrangements currently provided to you [Grace, Jr.] as chief executive officer (including, but not limited to, the use of office space and corporate aircraft) will continue to be provided to you.

Pursuant to this provision of the Retirement Agreement, Grace, Jr. received the following benefits, among others, from WRG in 1993: (a) continued use of a Company-owned and maintained apartment with a market value estimated by WRG to be in excess of $3 million, with services of a cook, who was a WRG employee; (b) use of a company limousine and driver on a 24 hour basis; (c) the services of full-

---

7. [5] Indeed, this matter demonstrates that corporate disclosure mechanisms cannot compensate for the failures of individuals. WRG's procedures failed because, among other reasons, Grace, Jr. did not disclose some of his retirement benefits and the proposed transaction with his son in questionnaires which WRG distributed to officers and directors to gather information for disclosure in WRG's proxy statements and periodic reports.

time secretaries and administrative assistants; (d) the use of corporate aircraft for personal and business travel; (e) home nursing services; and (f) security services.

While there was general knowledge within management that Grace, Jr.'s Retirement Agreement provided for the continuation of benefits that he had received before retirement, specific information about Grace, Jr.'s benefits was not generally available to WRG's management. Only non-management directors were involved in the negotiation or approval of Grace, Jr.'s retirement benefits. Members of WRG's then-current management, including Bolduc and WRG's secretary and chief disclosure counsel, were asked to leave board and/or Compensation Committee meetings at which Grace, Jr.'s retirement benefits were discussed. However, Grace, Jr. and Pyne met with Bolduc in December 1992 to discuss Grace, Jr.'s retirement benefits after the negotiations over these benefits were completed. At that time, Bolduc became aware of each of the "other benefits" that WRG was providing to Grace, Jr.

The Company provided Grace, Jr. with directors' and officers' questionnaires ("D&O Questionnaires") in the course of preparing its 1992 Form 10-K and 1993 proxy statement and its 1993 Form 10-K and 1994 proxy statement. These questionnaires contained questions asking whether Grace, Jr. received certain benefits from the Company during the preceding year, including, among other things, use of Company property, including apartments; housing and other living expenses (including domestic service) provided at his principal and/or vacation residence; and other perquisites. Grace, Jr. incorrectly responded "no" to these questions.

The final version of WRG's 1993 proxy statement contained language discussing Grace, Jr.'s Retirement Agreement, including a statement that Grace, Jr. would receive "certain other benefits." WRG filed the Retirement Agreement as an exhibit to its 1992 Form 10-K, but did not further describe Grace, Jr.'s "other benefits," nor did WRG disclose the costs of providing them in any of its proxy statements or periodic reports filed with the Commission before 1995.[8]

Because WRG's senior management was excluded from the negotiation and approval of Grace, Jr.'s retirement benefits, WRG's disclosure counsel made arrangements for Pyne to review the executive compensation section of WRG's draft 1993 proxy statement, and Pyne did so. Bolduc, in his capacity as WRG's CEO, reviewed drafts of WRG's 1993 proxy statement and signed WRG's 1992 Form 10-K, which incorporated the proxy statement's section on executive compensation by reference. Grace, Jr., in his capacity as chairman, also signed the 1992 Form 10-K. Although Grace, Jr., Bolduc, and Pyne knew about the "other benefits" WRG had agreed to provide Grace, Jr. upon his retirement, they did not question the absence of information about these "other benefits" in WRG's disclosure of Grace, Jr.'s retirement benefits. Even if Bolduc

---

8. [10] After information concerning Grace, Jr.'s "other benefits" became public, WRG disclosed in its 1995 proxy statement that the benefits provided to Grace, Jr. pursuant to the "other benefits" provision cost the Company $3,601,500 in fiscal year 1993, of which approximately $2,700,000 was attributable to Grace, Jr.'s having access to corporate aircraft.

and Pyne, as each asserted, assumed that WRG's legal counsel (whose office had participated in drafting the Retirement Agreement) had considered the adequacy of the disclosure concerning Grace, Jr.'s benefits, they should not have relied upon that assumption. They should have raised the issue of disclosure of Grace, Jr.'s "other benefits," for example, by discussing the issue specifically with disclosure counsel, telling counsel exactly what they knew about the benefits, and asking specifically whether the benefits should be disclosed.[9] As a result, WRG's 1992 Form 10-K and 1993 proxy statement failed to disclose specific information about the "other benefits."

* * *

V. CONCLUSION

Serving as an officer or director of a public company is a privilege which carries with it substantial obligations. If an officer or director knows or should know that his or her company's statements concerning particular issues are inadequate or incomplete, he or she has an obligation to correct that failure. An officer or director may rely upon the company's procedures for determining what disclosure is required only if he or she has a reasonable basis for believing that those procedures have resulted in full consideration of those issues.[10]

WRG's violations resulted, in part, from its corporate culture, which reflected Grace, Jr.'s substantial influence over the Company. Given this circumstance, Bolduc, Pyne, and Erhart should have been more attentive to issues concerning disclosure of information relating to Grace, Jr. or the Grace family. Bolduc, Pyne, and Erhart did not adequately follow through on fostering accurate and complete disclosure, which should have been their touchstone as members of WRG's board of directors or as officers of WRG.

Since Grace, Jr.'s death, WRG has substantially revised the composition of its board of directors. Because of the unique circumstances presented here (including the death of Grace, Jr.), the Commission has determined not to issue cease-and-desist orders or take other action against Bolduc, Pyne, and Erhart in this matter. However, the Commission remains resolved to take enforcement action, where appropriate, against individual directors and officers who have violated or caused violations of the federal securities laws.

Dissent of Commissioner Steven M.H. Wallman

The Section 21(a) report In the Matter of W.R. Grace & Co. (the "Report") articulates a certain legal standard, and then applies that standard to these facts. I take issue with that standard specifically to the extent it suggests that officers and directors must "ensure" the accuracy and completeness of company disclosures. Moreover, I

---

9. [11] This might have established that counsel was not in fact fully informed about these benefits or that Grace, Jr. had incorrectly filed out his D&O questionnaires regarding these benefits.

10. [16] Procedures or mechanisms established to identify and address disclosure issues are effective only if individuals in positions to affect the disclosure process are vigilant in exercising their responsibilities.

do not agree that, when the appropriate legal standard is applied to the particular facts of this case as described in the Report itself, there has been a violation of law on the part of the three individuals cited.

* * *

I respectfully dissent.

Comments and Questions

1. What is a Section 21(a) Report? What flexibility does it give the Commission in articulating broad standards and legal principles? We will see other examples of these types of reports (such as the SEC's pronouncements in *In re Netflix* in Chapter 9 on the use of social media to meet the requirements of Regulation FD).

2. What is the legal basis for the Commission's decision in this case? Does it really have the authority to sanction directors under these circumstances? Given the questionable basis for the agency's authority, what was it trying to accomplish in issuing this report? Despite the broad pronouncements in the case, the Commission never really followed up on the reasoning. The case was largely overtaken by legal changes made in SOX. The law largely identified those within the company who were responsible for the corporate disclosure process.

3. What does this case suggest about the relationship between corporate governance and corporate disclosure? How far does the SEC's authority go? In *SEC v. DHB Industries, Inc.*, Litigation Release No. 21867 (Feb. 28, 2011), the SEC alleged that outside directors who also served on the audit committee missed "red flags" that resulted in disclosure violations by the company. Are these types of cases better brought under the securities laws or as state law claims for breach of fiduciary duties? Assume you represent the board of directors of a large public company. What advice would you give the board in the aftermath of this decision?

4. Assume you represent the board of directors of a large public company. What advice would you give the board in the aftermath of this decision?

5. The SEC has other remedial authority to affect the governance process in a direct way. The SEC can bar lawyers and accountants from practicing before the SEC, something that can in at least some circumstances prevent individuals from serving on the board of directors. *See In re Schneider*, Exchange Act Release No. 69922 (Admin. Proc. July 2, 2013) (SEC declined to rule that an individual who consented to a suspension from appearing or practicing before the Commission as an accountant could serve in "non-accountant positions such as positions on an audit committee or as a non-accountant CFO."). More directly, the SEC has the authority to ask a court to bar persons from serving as officers and directors of public companies. *See* Section 21(d)(2) of the Exchange Act, 15 U.S.C. §78u(d)(2). The conduct at issue, however, must demonstrate a person's "unfitness" to serve in those positions. *See SEC v. Bankosky*, 716 F.3d 45 (2d Cir. 2013). Ought this to be part of the SEC's authority? Should these decisions be left to shareholders and/or the board of directors?

6. Sometimes the governance changes are part of the relief obtained by the SEC. Thus, in *SEC v. Bank of Am. Corp.*, 2010 U.S. Dist. LEXIS 15460 (S.D. N.Y. Feb. 22, 2010), the Commission obtained a package of "prophylactic measures" that included the hiring of independent disclosure counsel to report solely to the audit committee of the board and an independent compensation consultant. What do you make of this approach? Is it likely to have any permanent effect on governance practices?

III. The Role of the Stock Exchanges and Self-Regulation

Much of the corporate governance process for public companies is dictated by stock exchanges through the use of listing standards. Stock exchanges are self-regulatory organizations. Traditionally owned by their members (brokers and dealers), stock exchanges have converted into for-profit companies. The structure raises interesting issues about the relationship between regulatory responsibilities and fiduciary obligations to shareholders.

A. A Bit More History

Roberta S. Karmel, *The Future of Corporate Governance Listing Requirements*
54 SMU L. Rev. 325, 326–29 (2001)[11]

The first NYSE listing standards were not considered a set policy by the exchange but instead were flexible terms inserted in listing agreements negotiated between each issuer and the exchange. The contractual flexibility of listing agreements meant that listing standards were not uniformly enforced and were subject to change. Also, because such standards were not retroactively applied, nonconforming issuers who had obtained listings prior to a new rule were not delisted. Thus, the NYSE employed no uniform set policy which applied to all listed companies. Nevertheless, this flexibility allowed the NYSE to change its listing agreements according to its economic needs.

As early as 1869, a Committee on Stock List, a subcommittee of the NYSE Board of Governors, was formed to evaluate applications to list with the NYSE. The Committee was primarily concerned with the qualitative character of the issuer: "the degree of national interest in the company, its standing in its particular field, the character of the market for its products, its relative stability and position in the industry, and whether or not it is engaged in an expanding activity and had prospects of maintaining its position."

---

11. Originally appearing in Vol. 54 *SMU Law Review* 1. Reprinted with permission from the *SMU Law Review* and the Southern Methodist University Dedman School of Law.

* * *

Initially, the NYSE was concerned with financial disclosure, but this emphasis precipitated several corporate governance listing standards. An annual stockholder's meeting, the first corporate governance standard, was imposed as a term within the listing agreement and was eventually linked to annual reporting requirements. By 1900, listing agreements required companies to distribute annual reports to its stockholders. By 1909, those reports had to be distributed prior to the stockholders' annual meeting. By 1914, agreements provided that a listed company notify the exchange of any change in the rights of stockholders or in the redemption of preferred stock. By 1917, agreements provided for the disclosure of a semiannual income statement and balance sheet. In 1926, the NYSE adopted a one-share, one-vote listing standard.

However, it was only after the stock market crash of 1929 that regulators began to take seriously the need for and importance of financial disclosure for listed companies. Changing public attitudes led to the establishment of a new policy on corporate publicity. The policy urged, but did not require, companies to prepare financial reports by independent accountants and to prepare detailed income statements. By 1932, independent audits became mandatory for all new listed companies. Also by 1932, companies agreed to report their earnings quarterly. Finally, with the enactment of the Exchange Act, the policies of the NYSE regarding independent audits became a matter of federal law. The value of the NYSE's listing requirements was demonstrated by the fact that "Congress closely tracked the NYSE disclosure requirements when it drafted the Exchange Act."

Prior to the enactment of the Exchange Act, listing agreements required issuers annually to disclose all significant details about their financial condition, such as changes in the character of their business, capitalization, and accounting policies, prior to the stockholders' meeting. Further, a listed company promised to have its books audited by certified public accountants and to maintain a transfer agent and registrar. Even after the promulgation of the Exchange Act, the NYSE was still concerned with the practices of its listed companies. However, the impetus for these changes may have been "the NYSE's focus during that time on bolstering trading volume." The NYSE believed that by appealing to the needs of the individual investor and improving corporate governance practices, it could attract additional investors for already listed shares.

By 1953, minimum quorum rules were established for shareholder meetings. Beginning in 1940, minimum voting rights were also required for preferred stockholders. In 1955, the NYSE required shareholder approval for any acquisition resulting in an increase of more than 20% of its shares. Then, in 1956, an independence requirement for directors was initiated, a standard of future importance and controversy. The NYSE's emphasis on corporate governance included scrutiny of the financial practices of listed companies. The NYSE's early statements regarding financial disclosure laid the groundwork for future rules; the NYSE "did not desire to list companies unless their accounting policies were sound and logical and found common acceptance among engineers and accountants." However, it was not until the 1970s that the Exchange required independent audit committee members....

Comments and Questions

1. The NYSE existed at the time of the adoption of the Exchange Act. As a result, Congress integrated the entity into the regulatory framework by authorizing the Commission to oversee the exchange. Rules of the exchange must be approved by the Commission. *See* Section 19(b), 15 U.S.C. § 78r(b). Disciplinary actions taken against members can be appealed to the Commission and from there to the U.S. Court of Appeals.

2. In the early days of oversight, the SEC and NYSE had something of a testy relationship. William O. Douglas dedicated much of his tenure as chair of the SEC to establishing tighter oversight of the NYSE. He pressured the self-regulatory organization into increasing oversight and regulation of its own members. *See* Joel Seligman, *Cautious Evolution or Perennial Irresolution: Stock Market Self-Regulation During the First Seventy Years of the Securities and Exchange Commission*, 59 Bus. Law. 1347 (August 2004).

3. Interestingly, the legislative history to the Exchange Act shows that consideration was given to imposing disclosure requirements through listing standards. *See Stock Exchange Regulation: Letter from the President of the United States to the Chairman of the Comm. On Banking and Currency with an Accompanying Report Relative to Stock Exchange Regulation* 17 (Comm. Print 1934) ("Your committee believes that each licensed stock exchange should be required to adopt listing requirements for the various classes of issues listed on the exchange which will give to the public full, complete, and pertinent information with respect to such securities, both at the time the securities are admitted to trading and periodically thereafter."). Congress, however, rejected the approach at least in part because of concerns over the enforcement of listing standards. *See* S. Rep. No. 73-1455, at 70 (1934) ("Although the New York Stock Exchange has proclaimed the searching nature of its listing requirements, evidence was adduced before the subcommittee establishing that the exchange authorities were lax in their investigation of listing applications.").

4. In the new millennium, listing standards have become a central component of the governance process. The NYSE (and Nasdaq) require that listed companies have a majority of independent directors. NYSE Rule 303A.01. Moreover, the board must have a compensation, nomination, and audit committee, each consisting entirely of independent directors. Independent and non-management directors must meet "regularly" in executive session, without management. Moreover, Congress, in regulating the compensation and audit committees of the board, did so through the mechanism of listing standards. What are the strengths and weaknesses of using listing standards to regulate board practices?

5. How much protection do shareholders really receive from listing standards? What about listing standards that can be set aside? NYSE Rule 312.03, for example, provides that shareholder approval is required prior to the issuance of shares with 20% or more

of the voting power of the company. The rule, however, also provides that the requirement may be set aside where "(1) the delay in securing stockholder approval would seriously jeopardize the financial viability of the enterprise and (2) reliance by the company on this exception is expressly approved by the Audit Committee of the Board." Rule 312.05. When JP Morgan acquired Bear Stearns in 2008, Bear Stearns apparently relied upon the exception to avoid obtaining shareholder approval. *See* Exhibit 2.2 attached to Current Report on Form 8-K filed by Bear Stearns, March 24, 2008. Should this type of decision require approval by the exchange? What difference might that make?

B. Demutualization

Stock exchanges were originally set up by broker-dealers to facilitate trading activity. As a structural matter, the NYSE was a non-profit organization owned by its members. Members elected the directors, although some also had to represent the interests of listed companies and the investing public. In the new millennium, however, the exchanges sought to change their organizational structure, transforming into for-profit corporations. In 2006, the Commission approved the merger between the NYSE and Archipelago Holdings. The transaction effectively converted the NYSE into a for-profit corporation. The change in status provided a number of advantages, not the least of which was the ability to issue shares both as compensation and as consideration in acquisitions. Not long afterwards, the NYSE acquired EuroNext, a consortium of European stock exchanges from Belgium, France, the Netherlands and Portugal, *see* Exchange Act Release No. 55293 (Feb. 14, 2007), and Amex. *See* Exchange Act Release No. 58673 (September 29, 2008) (SEC order approving acquisition).

For profit status, however, meant that the NYSE had shareholders and an obligation to act in their best interests, including the need to maximize profits. This obligation was potentially inconsistent with the organization's regulatory functions, including the enforcement of listing standards. In approving the transaction that allowed the NYSE to convert to a for-profit company, the Commission sought to ensure that the regulatory function of the NYSE was sufficiently insulated from the for profit motivations of the holding company.

To address these concerns, the NYSE took a number of steps, including the creation of a separate subsidiary, NYSE Regulation, a New York non-profit corporation, to perform most of the NYSE's regulatory functions.

Exchange Act Release No. 53382
(Feb. 27, 2006)

In connection with the Merger [between the NYSE and Archipelago, a company that owned the Pacific Stock Exchange], the NYSE proposes to reorganize so that the NYSE Group will be a for-profit, publicly traded stock corporation and the holding company for the businesses of the NYSE and Archipelago. NYSE Group will hold all of the equity interests in New York Stock Exchange LLC and Archipelago. The current

NYSE businesses and assets will be held in New York Stock Exchange LLC, NYSE Market, and NYSE Regulation.

* * *

NYSE Regulation, a New York Type A not-for-profit corporation, will be a wholly owned subsidiary of New York Stock Exchange LLC. After the Merger, NYSE Regulation will hold all of the assets and liabilities related to the regulatory functions currently conducted by the NYSE. Pursuant to the NYSE Delegation Agreement, NYSE Regulation will perform the regulatory functions of New York Stock Exchange LLC. NYSE Regulation also will perform many of the regulatory functions of the Pacific Exchange pursuant to a regulatory services agreement.

* * *

The NYSE has proposed several measures to help ensure the independence of its regulatory function from its market operations and other commercial interests. For example, all directors on the board of NYSE Regulation (other than its chief executive officer) will be required to be independent of management of NYSE Group and its subsidiaries, as well as of members and listed companies. In addition, a majority of the members of the NYSE Regulation board must be directors that are not also directors of NYSE Group. Although the NYSE will not have a regulatory oversight committee, the board of NYSE Regulation is expected to function in such capacity. Further, NYSE Regulation will have its own nominating and governance committee, rather than share the NYSE Group nominating and governance committee, and this committee also will be composed of a majority of directors that are not also directors of NYSE Group.

The chief executive officer of NYSE Regulation will function as the exchange's chief regulatory officer. This position will report solely to the NYSE Regulation board and not to any other NYSE Group entity, although he or she may attend the board meetings of such other entities as deemed appropriate to carry out his or her responsibilities.

The NYSE also proposes to establish a separate compensation committee for NYSE Regulation. This committee also will have a majority of non-NYSE Group directors. The NYSE Regulation compensation committee will be responsible for setting the compensation for NYSE Regulation employees; thus, the NYSE Group compensation committee will not have a say in this process.

The Commission further notes that the NYSE has taken steps to safeguard the use of regulatory monies. Specifically, New York Stock Exchange LLC will not be permitted to use any assets of, or any regulatory fees, fines, or penalties collected by, NYSE Regulation for commercial purposes or distribute such assets, fees, fines, or penalties to NYSE Group or any entity other than NYSE Regulation.

* * *

Several commenters believe that a for-profit structure is inconsistent with self-regulatory obligations. Nasdaq believes that it is fundamentally inconsistent with the mission of a for-profit entity for the entire regulatory apparatus to exist within the for-profit entity, given the fiduciary duty to maximize profits. IBAC also emphasizes its view that the corporate fiduciary duty of directors in a for-profit entity to maximize profits is inconsistent with SRO obligations. As long as NYSE Group controls the appointment of a majority of NYSE Regulation directors, IBAC believes that its profit motive will "reign supreme," and is concerned about compromising exchange operations in favor of short term profits....

Nasdaq believes that it is not appropriate to have all front-line member regulatory responsibilities in the overall entity that operates the trading facility. Nasdaq notes that, pursuant to its exchange registration application, it has vested most of its front-line regulatory responsibilities in NASD through contract, and that NASD will no longer be affiliated with Nasdaq. Nasdaq contrasts its structure with the NYSE's proposed structure, noting that all of the regulatory responsibilities of the New York Stock Exchange LLC and the Pacific Exchange will be vested in entities that are subject to the control of NYSE Group, a for-profit entity. IBAC requests that the Commission consider spinning off NYSE Regulation as separate not-for-profit entity completely independent of NYSE Group, while CalPERS recommends a model that has complete separation between the regulatory and non-regulatory functions, such as the enterprise model for the Public Company Accounting Oversight board. NASD believes that implementing a hybrid model of self-regulation will eliminate inherent conflicts when a regulator operates a market.

To the extent that a well-regulated market is considered by an SRO's owners to be in their commercial interests, demutualization could better align the goals of SRO owners with their statutory obligations. The NYSE believes that NYSE Group has "every incentive" to ensure robust regulatory oversight of its market, members, and listed companies because a well-regulated marketplace is essential to attracting, and retaining, listing and trading on its market. To the extent that there is a concern that profit motives may override the incentive to have a well-regulated market, as detailed above in this section the NYSE has proposed an overall structure, with several specific safeguards, designed to allow the exchange's regulatory program to function independently from its market operations and other commercial interests....

Comments and Questions

1. What do you make of this debate? Should a for profit company have regulatory responsibility of any kind? What do you make of the NYSE's solution? Do you think it is effective?

2. The NYSE opted for a "structural" separation of regulatory and "for profit" functions. NYSE Regulation was essentially walled off from the for profit holding company. Is this the only possible structure? Does the fact that some directors from NYSE Regulation can also be directors of the holding company (albeit less than a majority and only independent directors) affect your analysis? What about funding for NYSE Regulation? How is that determined?

3. Demutualization allowed the NYSE to engage in acquisitions. It also, however, made the Exchange vulnerable to being acquired. Indeed, the NYSE was acquired by and became a subsidiary of the InterContinental Exchange (ICE) in 2013. A year later,

ICE spun off Euronext through a public offering. What do you make of this? Will the role of the NYSE change now that it is a subsidiary of a much larger company?

4. Nasdaq has also become a for-profit corporation, although through a somewhat different path. Nasdaq was originally an electronic trading system developed by the NASD. The NASD eventually divested itself of all interests in Nasdaq. *See* Exchange Act Release No. 54798 (Nov. 21, 2006). Nasdaq emerged as a publicly traded for-profit company and registered with the SEC as a national stock exchange. Nasdaq used its for profit status to engage in acquisitions overseas. The Exchange sought to buy the London Stock Exchange was ultimately unsuccessful. Instead, Nasdaq acquired OMX, a holding company that controlled seven other exchanges (Sweden, Finland, Denmark, Iceland and the Baltic states).

5. Demutualization has taken place in the context of a broader change in the structure of the trading markets. When the NYSE shifted to for profit status, about 80% of the trades of equity shares of listed companies were handled over the exchange. By the second decade of the new millennium, the percentage had fallen to around 20%. Some of the trades shifted to other more recently created stock exchanges such as BATS, while others took place in less transparent centers such as dark pools. What impact might this have on the role of the NYSE in the corporate governance process?

6. What has been the practice with respect to stock exchanges outside the United States? Some of the largest have also demutualized, including Tokyo, London and the Deutsche Borse. The exchanges in China are a significant exception, as are the exchanges in the MENA region (Middle East and North Africa). *See* generally Privatization and Demutualisation of MENA Stock Exchanges, OECD, Dec. 2013.

———

Over time, the regulatory role of the NYSE declined. Most of the broker oversight function was off-loaded in the merger that created the Financial Industry Regulatory Authority (FINRA). While legal responsibility for market surveillance remained with the exchanges, the function was often assigned by contract to FINRA. *See* FINRA Press Release, May 4, 2010 (announcing FINRA's assumption of "responsibility for performing the market surveillance and enforcement functions currently conducted by NYSE Regulation"). With a reduced regulatory role, the NYSE sought a change in system for overseeing the regulatory responsibility.

Exchange Act Release No. 75991

(Sept. 28, 2015)

II. Description of the Proposal

NYSE proposes to: (i) amend the Exchange's Operating Agreement to establish a Regulatory Oversight Committee ("ROC") as a committee of the Exchange's Board of Directors ("Board") ... (ii) terminate the Delegation Agreement ("Delegation Agreement") among the Exchange, NYSE Market (DE), Inc. ("NYSE Market (DE)"), and NYSE Regulation, Inc. ("NYSE Regulation") ...

A. Establishing a ROC and Making Conforming Amendments to Exchange Rules

The Exchange proposes to add subsection (ii) to Section 2.03(h) of the Operating Agreement to establish a ROC and to delineate its composition and functions.... The ROC would be appointed annually and would have the following responsibilities:

- oversee the Exchange's regulatory and self-regulatory organization responsibilities and evaluate the adequacy and effectiveness of the Exchange's regulatory and self-regulatory organization responsibilities;

- assess the Exchange's regulatory performance; and

- advise and make recommendations to the Board or other committees of the Board about the Exchange's regulatory compliance, effectiveness and plans.

In furtherance of these functions, the Exchange proposes that the ROC shall have the authority and obligation to: (i) review the regulatory budget of the Exchange and specifically inquire into the adequacy of resources available in the budget for regulatory activities; (ii) meet regularly with the Chief Regulatory Officer ("CRO") in executive session; (iii) in consultation with the Exchange's Chief Executive Officer, establish the goals, assess the performance, and recommend the CRO's compensation; and (iv) keep the Board informed with respect to the foregoing matters.

With respect to the ROC's composition, Section 2.03(h)(ii) would provide that the ROC shall consist of at least three members, each of whom shall be a Director of the Exchange who satisfies the independence requirements of the Exchange. The Exchange states that a ROC comprised of at least three independent members has been recognized as one of several measures that can help ensure the independence of the regulatory function from the market operations and commercial interests of a national securities exchange.

In addition, Section 2.03(h)(ii) of the Operating Agreement would provide that the Board, on affirmative vote of a majority of Directors, at any time may remove a member of the ROC for cause, and also would provide that a failure of the ROC member to qualify as independent under the Company Director Independence Policy would constitute a basis to remove a member of the ROC for cause. If the term of office of a ROC member terminates, and the remaining term of office of such member at the time of termination is not more than three months, Section 2.03(h)(ii) would provide that during the period of vacancy, the ROC would not be deemed to be in violation of its compositional requirements by virtue of the vacancy. To clarify the process for filling vacancies on any committee of the Exchange, including the ROC, the Exchange also proposes to amend Section 2.03(h) of the Operating Agreement to provide that vacancies in the membership of any committee shall be filled by the Board. The Exchange believes that the proposed rule change creating an independent Board committee to oversee the adequacy and effectiveness of the performance of its self-regulatory responsibilities is consistent with previously approved rule changes for other SROs and would enable the Exchange to undertake its regulatory responsibilities under a corporate governance structure that is consistent with its industry peers. Moreover, the Exchange believes that the proposed ROC would ensure the continued independence of the regulatory process. The Exchange states that oversight of the Exchange's self-regulatory responsibilities and regulatory performance, including review of the regulatory plan, programs, budget and staffing by a ROC composed of individuals independent of Exchange management and a CRO having general supervision of the regulatory operations of the Exchange that meets regularly with the ROC is integral to the proposal.

* * *

IV. Conclusion

IT IS THEREFORE ORDERED, pursuant to Section 19(b)(2) of the Act, that the proposed rule change (SR-NYSE-2015-27) is approved.

For the Commission, by the Division of Trading and Markets, pursuant to delegated authority.

Comments and Questions

1. The Exchange has replaced a structural separation of regulatory oversight with what it describes as a functional separation. What are the advantages and disadvantages of each approach?

2. The functional separation relies on a committee of the board to oversee the responsibility for the regulatory function. Is this an adequate method of ensuring the independence of the regulatory function? For an exchange of letters discussing these reforms, see Letter from J. Robert Brown, Jr., Professor, University of Denver Sturm College of Law, to Brent J. Fields, SEC, Sept. 8, 2015, available at http://www.sec.gov/comments/sr-nyse-2015-27/nyse201527-1.pdf. For the response of the NYSE, see Letter from Martha Redding, NYSE, to Brent J. Fields, Sept. 24, 2015, available at http://www.sec.gov/comments/sr-nyse-2015-27/nyse201527-2.pdf.

3. NYSE Regulation is a non-profit; the Exchange is not. The SEC in approving the change simply noted that "there is no 'overriding regulatory reason to require exchanges to be not-for-profit membership organizations.'" Do you agree with the position of the Commission?

4. With respect to funding, NYSE provided NYSE Regulation with "adequate funding." *See* Exchange Act Release No. 53382 (Feb. 24, 2006) ("the NYSE has represented that there will be an explicit agreement among NYSE Group, New York Stock Exchange LLC, NYSE Market, and NYSE Regulation to provide adequate funding to NYSE Regulation."). How is funding determined for the regulatory function following the transfer of oversight to the Exchange? How different are they, if at all, in practice?

5. To the extent that the exchanges ultimately divested themselves of listing standards, where would the authority go? Congress has gradually given the SEC expanded authority to write listing standards. SOX provided the authority with respect to audit committees. *See* Rule 10A-3, 17 CFR 240.10A-3. In the Dodd-Frank Act, the SEC was given further authority to regulate listing standards for compensation committees.

See Section 952. In the same Act, the Commission was authorized to define the "factors" that must be considered by the exchange in determining the definition of director independence with respect to the compensation committee. Could the SEC be given all authority to write and enforce listing standards? What are the pros and cons of the approach? Why might the stock exchanges want to retain the authority over these standards?

C. Enforcement of Exchange Rules and Standards

The stock exchanges are required to enforce their listing standards, subject to review of any disciplinary action by the Securities and Exchange Commission.

Fog Cutter Capital Group Inc. v. Securities and Exchange Commission

United States Court of Appeals, District of Columbia Circuit
474 F.3d 822 (2007)

RANDOLPH, CIRCUIT JUDGE:

The National Association of Securities Dealers (NASD) delisted Fog Cutter Capital Group's public stock from Nasdaq. The Securities and Exchange Commission dismissed Fog Cutter's petition for review. *In re Fog Cutter Capital Group, Inc.*, Exchange Act Release No. 34-52993, 2005 WL 3500274, at *4 (Dec. 21, 2005). The issue in this petition for judicial review is whether the Commission's dismissal was "arbitrary, capricious, an abuse of discretion, or otherwise not in accordance with law," 5 U.S.C. § 706(2) (A).

The NASD is a registered "national securities association" under the Securities Exchange Act of 1934, 15 U.S.C. § 78o-3(b). At all times relevant to this case, the NASD operated Nasdaq, an electronic securities exchange. As a self-regulatory organization, the NASD must maintain rules to protect investors and the public interest. 15 U.S.C. § 78o-3(b)(6). One of these rules, approved by the Commission, stated that the NASD "will exercise broad discretionary authority over the initial and continued inclusion of securities in Nasdaq in order to maintain the quality and public confidence in its market." *See* NASD Marketplace Rule 4300. To that end, the NASD will delist securities if, in its "opinion," events occur that render it "inadvisable or unwarranted" to continue listing the securities "even though the securities meet all enumerated criteria for" listing. Id.

For Fog Cutter, the disqualifying events centered on the criminal investigation, indictment, and conviction of its Chief Executive Officer and Board Chairman, Andrew Wiederhorn, and the manner in which the company dealt with this development. Wiederhorn founded Fog Cutter in 1997 and, with family members, controlled approximately fifty-three percent of the company's stock. The company operated a national restaurant chain and engaged in banking, financing, and real estate investment activities.

In March 2001, federal prosecutors informed Wiederhorn and Lawrence Mendel-sohn, a former president of Fog Cutter, that they were targets of a grand jury investigation into the collapse of Capital Consultants, LLC, an investment adviser for union pension plans. Other than the fact that Wiederhorn and Mendelsohn were investigated for actions unrelated to Fog Cutter, the details of the criminal case are unnecessary to recount. Mendelsohn pleaded guilty and agreed to cooperate with the government. Wiederhorn later entered into a plea agreement and pleaded guilty to a two-count indictment charging him with giving an illegal gratuity and filing a false tax return, both felonies. The district court sentenced him to eighteen months in prison and ordered him to pay a $25,000 fine and $2 million to the Capital Consultants receiver.

On June 2, 2004, the day before Wiederhorn entered into the plea deal, he finalized a leave-of-absence agreement with Fog Cutter. The agreement acknowledged Wiederhorn's plea agreement and imminent incarceration, and provided that during his absence he would retain his titles and responsibilities. Fog Cutter agreed to pay Wiederhorn his $350,000 annual salary, bonuses, and other benefits while he was imprisoned. The company also agreed to pay him a $2 million "leave of absence payment" to retain his "good will, cooperation and continuing assistance, and in recognition of Wiederhorn's past service to the Company, to help avoid litigation and for … other reasons." Fog Cutter knew Wiederhorn would use the $2 million payment to pay the restitution his plea agreement ordered. In its filings with the Commission, Fog Cutter disclosed this information and the $4.75 million cost of its agreement with Wiederhorn.

In July 2004, NASD staff decided that it was contrary to the public interest for Fog Cutter to remain listed on Nasdaq with Wiederhorn exercising substantial influence over the company while incarcerated. *See In re Fog Cutter*, 2005 WL 3500274, at * 3. An NASD Panel determined that the Board's willingness to amend Wiederhorn's employment agreement, acquiescence to Wiederhorn's demands for financial support during his imprisonment, payment of his court-ordered restitution, and retention of him in his executive and director positions during his imprisonment were contrary to the public interest. The NASD Listing and Hearing Review Council affirmed the Panel's decision "in order to protect the quality of and public confidence in The Nasdaq Stock Market, and to protect investors and the public interest." *See id.* Fog Cutter applied to the Securities and Exchange Commission for review of the Council's decision. The Commission dismissed the application for review, focusing, as had NASD, on Wiederhorn's status as a convicted felon and the Board's actions supporting and retaining Wiederhorn on the Board and in management.

* * *

Under Section 19(f) of the Exchange Act, 15 U.S.C. §78s(f), the Commission must dismiss an application for review of an NASD delisting order if (1) the "specific grounds" "exist in fact," (2) the decision was in accordance with NASD rules, (3) the rules are and were applied in a manner consistent with the Exchange Act, and (4) the decision imposes no unnecessary or inappropriate burden on competition under the Act. Whether the Commission acted arbitrarily, capriciously, or unlawfully depends on whether its review of the NASD's decision complied with Section 19(f).

Here there was ample evidence supporting the NASD's grounds for taking action against Fog Cutter: Wiederhorn's guilty plea, the leave of absence deal and its cost to the company, the Board's determination that Wiederhorn should retain his positions with Fog Cutter, and the concern that Wiederhorn would continue to exert influence on company affairs even while he was in prison. The decision was in accordance with NASD rules giving the organization broad discretion to determine whether the public interest requires delisting securities in light of events at a company. That rule is obviously consistent with the Exchange Act, and NASD's decision did not burden competition.

Fog Cutter claims that it had to pay Wiederhorn and retain him because if it fired him in light of his guilty plea, it would have owed him $6 million. This scarcely speaks well for the company's case. The potential obligation is a result of an amendment the Board granted Wiederhorn in 2003 while he was under investigation. Wiederhorn's employment agreement stated that if terminated "for cause," he was entitled only to his base salary through the date of termination and payment of unreimbursed business expenses. If it terminated Wiederhorn without cause, Fog Cutter would have owed him three times his annual salary, three times his largest annual bonus from the last three years, unreimbursed business expenses, and accrued but unpaid base salary and bonuses—which Fog Cutter estimates would amount to $6 million—all as a lump-sum payment within ten days. Before the amendment to Wiederhorn's employment agreement in 2003, termination "for cause" included the conviction of *any* felony other than a traffic offense. In the 2003 amendment, the relevant provision allowed the Board to terminate Wiederhorn "for cause" upon conviction of a felony *involving Fog Cutter.* The Board had known about the investigation of Wiederhorn in connection with Capital Consultants for more than two years when it agreed to this amendment.

Fog Cutter thinks NASD's action was "unfair." But it was the company that bowed to Wiederhorn's demand for an amendment to his employment agreement, knowing full well that it was dramatically increasing the cost of firing him. Now it argues that terminating Wiederhorn would have been too expensive. One is reminded of the old saw about the child who murders his parents and then asks for mercy because he is an orphan. The makeup of Fog Cutter's Board was virtually unchanged between the time it amended the employment agreement and entered into the leave-of-absence agreement. *In re Fog Cutter*, 2005 WL 3500274, at *2 n.6. It was, to say the least, not arbitrary or capricious for the Commission to find that Wiederhorn exercised thorough control over the Board, and to find this troubling. We agree that the Board provided little or no check on Wiederhorn's conduct, and that the Board's actions only aggravated the concerns Wiederhorn's conviction and imprisonment raised.

That Fog Cutter did not itself violate the securities laws and that it disclosed the relevant events does not demonstrate any error in the delisting decision. The NASD's rules state that it may apply criteria more stringent than the minimum standards for listing. *See* NASD Marketplace Rule 4300. Fog Cutter's disclosure of its arrangements with Wiederhorn did not change the nature of those arrangements, which is what led the NASD to find that the company's actions were contrary to the public interest and a threat to public confidence in the Nasdaq exchange.

* * *

In delisting Fog Cutter, the NASD was concerned with the integrity and the public's perception of the Nasdaq exchange in light of both Wiederhorn's legal troubles and the Board's ongoing acquiescence to his demands. The Commission amply supported these concerns and was well within its authority to dismiss Fog Cutter's application for review of the NASD's delisting decision. We therefore deny Fog Cutter's petition for judicial review.

So ordered.

Comments and Questions

1. Nasdaq was at one time a trading system operated by the National Association of Securities Dealers, or NASD. After the NASD spun off Nasdaq, it registered with the SEC as a stock exchange. *See* Exchange Act Release No. 53128 (Jan. 13, 2006). The NASD in turn merged with the broker-dealer regulatory unit from the NYSE and was renamed the Financial Industry Regulatory Authority (FINRA). *See* Exchange Act Release No. 56145 (July 26, 2007). NASD Marketplace Rule 4300 has been renumbered Nasdaq Rule 5101.

2. Do you think this case is correct? Do the facts provide a sufficient basis for delisting Fog Cutter? What are the consequences to shareholders of the company?

3. What do you make of the role of the Commission? The SEC's review is set out in Section 19(f) of the Exchange Act. 15 USC § 78s(f). The provision limits the SEC's authority to ensuring that the SRO applied its rules in a manner consistent with its rules and with the purposes of the securities laws. Is this an adequate standard of review?

4. What remedies did the NASD [FINRA] have in this case? Are they sufficient? In *Fiero v. Financial Industry Regulatory Authority*, 600 F3d 569 (2d Cir., 2011), the Second Circuit held that FINRA, while having the authority to impose fines, see 15 U.S.C. § 78o-1, did not have the authority to collect them. As the court concluded: "the issue is one of legislative intent, and we conclude that the heavy weight of evidence suggests that Congress did not intend to empower FINRA to bring court proceedings to enforce its fines." While the case involved FINRA, the court had this to say: "It is worth noting that the power granted to SRO's by Section 15A of the Exchange Act to discipline their members applies to all SRO's, and not just to FINRA." *Id.* at 574 n.6. What does this suggest about enforcement by SROs, including stock exchanges?

5. Fog Cutter noted that two other companies with chief executives who "were convicted and imprisoned" were not delisted. The court gave little weight to the argument, describing it as "a selective prosecution argument" and noting that the company would have to show "a protected class under the Equal Protection Clause." While this may be an accurate statement of the law, ought stock exchanges, particularly in an era of demutualization, be allowed to exercise this type of discretion?

6. What about financial issues that arise as a result of the application of foreign law? In *In re Smartheat*, Exchange Act Release No. 73555 (admin proc Jan. 2, 2014), the SEC reviewed a decision of Nasdaq to delist a company over concerns about the company's liquidity. The company apparently transferred assets to subsidiaries in China and had no mechanism for obtaining a return of the funds. The company asserted that limitations on obtaining capital from Chinese subsidiaries was a byproduct of Chinese law, with "[t]he rights of a parent corporation towards its subsidiaries . . . strictly limited to the rights of a stockholder and not the rights of a manager." The SEC had this to say: "But if the constraints of Chinese law cause a listed company to operate in a way that NASDAQ deems inconsistent with the public interest, it is within NASDAQ's discretion to delist the company." Do you agree?

Despite the actions of the NASD [FINRA] in *Fog Cutter*, concerns have occasionally arisen over the adequacy of the enforcement by the exchanges of their own rules.

Exchange Act Release No. 50699
(Nov. 18, 2004)

In addition to the enhanced focus on SRO governance, recent Commission enforcement actions involving SROs have highlighted weaknesses in the effectiveness of certain SRO regulatory programs. In September 2003, for example, the Commission settled an administrative enforcement action against the CHX [Chicago Stock Exchange] for failure to enforce its trading rules. The Commission's order, among other things, included findings that the CHX's surveillance program failed adequately to detect violations by its members of the firm quote rule, trading ahead prohibitions, and the limit order display rule from 1998 through 2001. As part of the undertakings imposed by the settlement, the CHX was required, among other things, to create a regulatory oversight committee comprised almost exclusively of individuals with no material business relationship with the exchange. In addition, the CHX was required to file with the Commission various certifications by its officials confirming its ongoing compliance with its statutory obligations.

Also, recent Commission enforcement actions involving SRO members have pointed to weaknesses in the effectiveness of SROs' regulatory programs. In 2004, for example, the Commission settled enforcement actions against the seven NYSE specialist firms. The Commission found that, between 1999 and 2003, these specialist firms violated federal securities laws and NYSE rules by executing orders for their dealer accounts ahead of executable public customer orders. As part of the settlement, the firms agreed to pay a total of more than $247 million in penalties and disgorgement, and agreed to implement steps to improve their compliance procedures and systems.

Moreover, the Commission's staff recently has conducted inspections of SROs that have raised questions regarding whether, in certain circumstances, SROs have governance structures that are sufficiently independent, or whether SROs have maintained regulatory programs that are sufficiently rigorous to detect, deter, and discipline for members' violations of the federal securities laws and rules and SRO rules.

Taken together, developments involving SRO governance, as well as the concerns raised by recent enforcement actions and inspections involving SROs, have prompted the Commission to consider new regulatory measures with respect to SROs. The Commission therefore has determined to propose rules that would strengthen the governance of national securities exchanges and registered securities associations and the independence of their regulatory programs. Moreover, the Commission is proposing to enhance the level of information that would be publicly available about SROs, including with respect to their governance structures, finances, regulatory programs, and significant owners. Finally, the Commission believes that oversight of SROs would be enhanced, and inspections could be better targeted to problematic areas, if the Commission were to receive more extensive and frequent data about SRO regulatory programs in a systematic fashion. Therefore, the Commission is proposing a new SRO reporting rule that is intended to facilitate more effective Commission monitoring of SROs' regulatory programs. While the Commission is proposing other measures that would increase the transparency of SROs' operations, the information submitted under this proposed rule is intended to be used as part of the Commission's examination program and thus may not be publicly available.

Comments and Questions

1. Concerns over enforcement of exchange rules and listing standards are not new. *See* S. REP. NO. 73-1455, at 70 (1934) ("Although the New York Stock Exchange has proclaimed the searching nature of its listing requirements, evidence was adduced before the subcommittee establishing that the exchange authorities were lax in their investigation of listing applications.").

2. Does the structure of the stock exchanges raise concerns about enforcement? What impact, if any, did the conversion of the stock exchanges to for-profit companies have on the likelihood and willingness to rigorously enforce listing standards?

3. How effective is the SEC likely to be in ensuring adequate enforcement of rules and listing standards by the various exchanges? Can the SEC enforce listing standards directly? What about with respect to audit committees? *See* Rule 10A-3, 17 CFR 240.10A-3.

––––––––––

What about private enforcement? Can shareholders and other aggrieved parties sue the stock exchanges when companies violate the listing standards?

California Public Employees' Retirement System v. New York Stock Exchange, Inc.

United States Court of Appeals, Second Circuit
503 F.3d 89 (2007)

SOTOMAYOR, CIRCUIT JUDGE:

Each security listed for trading on the NYSE is assigned to a particular Firm. To execute purchases and sales of a particular security, buyers and sellers must present their bids to buy and offers to sell to the specific Specialist Firm assigned to that security. The primary method of trading on the Exchange occurs through the NYSE's Super Designated Order Turnaround System, which transmits orders to buy and sell to the Specialist Firm electronically. The orders appear on a special electronic workstation often referred to as the "display book." Each Specialist Firm has a computerized "display book" at its trading post that permits the Firm to execute orders for the market.

By acting as either the agent for investors or principal for itself in the sale and purchase of the individual securities to which they are each assigned, the Firms are required to make and display continuous two-sided quotations that accurately reflect prevailing market conditions in order to maintain a liquid and continuous two-sided public auction. When acting as agent, the Specialist Firms match the orders of buyers and sellers, whose bids and offers appear on the display book, and thus ensure the timely execution of trades at the best available price. When acting as principal, the Specialist Firms

> [a]re permitted to execute, in certain limited circumstances, trades on a "principal" or "dealer" basis, when required to do so to maintain a fair and orderly market. In such circumstances, such as if there were no matching orders to sell and orders to buy, the specialist was permitted to execute an investor's order to buy stock by selling the stock from the specialist's proprietary account, or "inventory" of stock, to the investor. Additionally, the specialist was permitted to execute an investor's order to sell stock by buying that stock and holding the stock in the investor's inventory.

In re NYSE Specialists, 405 F. Supp. 2d at 290.

The substantial powers of, and the near-total control exercised by, the Specialist Firms over any given stock on the NYSE create an opportunity to manipulate the market for self-gain. The complaint alleges that "[t]he Specialist Firm is constantly in a position to trade for its own proprietary accounts while in possession of material non-public information regarding the supply and demand for a given stock, in part through its knowledge of existing but unexecuted" orders. Consolidated Compl. P 52. Cognizant of this risk, the Exchange has promulgated internal rules that govern the conduct of Specialist Firms, including rules that require the Firms to "adhere to the principles of good business practice," NYSE Rule 401(a), and rules that prohibit any Firm from trading on its own account unless it is reasonably necessary to maintain a fair and orderly market, *see, e.g.,* NYSE Rule 104(a) ("No [Specialist Firm] shall effect on the Exchange purchases or sales of any security in which such [Firm] is registered, for any account in which [it] … is directly or indirectly interested, unless such dealings are reasonably necessary to permit such [Firm] to maintain a fair and orderly market.…"). Thus, Lead Plaintiffs allege that the rules require the Firms to act as principal only in the limited situations where doing so is necessary to maintain a fair and orderly market.

Lead Plaintiffs allege that during the Class Period, the Specialist Firms actively took advantage of their unique position to self-deal and that the NYSE neglected or abandoned its regulatory duties and oversight of the Specialist Firms by permitting and in some cases encouraging blatant self-dealing.…

* * *

We first consider whether the NYSE is entitled to absolute immunity from claims stemming from either the Exchange's active or passive complicity in the Specialist Firms' misconduct, and then turn to address whether Lead Plaintiffs have standing to bring their Rule 10b-5 claim for the Exchange's alleged misrepresentations concerning its regulatory activities and the integrity of its market.

I. Absolute Immunity

Absolute immunity affords "complete protection from suit," Harlow v. Fitzgerald, 457 U.S. 800, 807, 102 S. Ct. 2727, 73 L. Ed. 2d 396 (1982), because it gives "public officials entrusted with sensitive tasks a protected area of discretion within which to carry out their responsibilities," Barr v. Abrams, 810 F.2d 358, 361 (2d Cir. 1987), so that they will not feel "constrained in making every decision by the consequences in terms of [their] own potential liability in a suit for damages," …

Although the NYSE is not a government entity, we have recognized that in certain circumstances, it is entitled to absolute immunity for actions it takes pursuant to its quasi-governmental role in the regulation of the securities market. *See* Barbara, 99 F.3d at 58 ("Although the Exchange is a private, rather than a governmental entity, immunity doctrines protect private actors when they perform important governmental functions."). Indeed, as in other absolute immunity contexts, we focus on "the nature of the function performed, not the identity of the actor who performed it," Forrester v. White, 484 U.S. 219, 229, 108 S. Ct. 538, 98 L. Ed. 2d 555 (1988), in order to determine whether an SRO, such as the Exchange, is entitled to immunity, see D'Alessio, 258 F.3d at 104–06 (applying functional approach to determine whether the NYSE was entitled to immunity). Applying this analysis, we have found stock exchange SROs absolutely immune from suit where the alleged misconduct concerned (1) disciplinary proceedings against exchange members, Barbara, 99 F.3d at 59; (2) the enforcement of security rules and regulations and general regulatory oversight over exchange members, D'Alessio, 258 F.3d at 106; (3) the interpretation of the securities laws and regulations as applied to the exchange or its members, id.; (4) the referral of exchange members to the SEC and other government agencies for civil enforcement or criminal prosecution under the securities laws, id.; and (5) the public announcement of regulatory decisions, DL Capital Group, 409 F.3d at 98. The common thread in these cases is that absolute immunity attaches where the activity "relate[s] to the proper functioning of the regulatory system." D'Alessio, 258 F.3d at 106 (internal quotation marks omitted). Indeed, because [t]he NYSE, as a[n] SRO, stands in the shoes of the SEC in interpreting the securities laws for its members and in monitoring compliance with those laws ... [i]t follows that the NYSE should be entitled to the same immunity enjoyed by the SEC when it is performing functions delegated to it under the SEC's broad oversight authority. Id. at 105. Thus, so long as the "alleged misconduct falls within the scope of the quasi-governmental powers delegated to the NYSE," absolute immunity attaches. Id. at 106.

* * *

... The central question our SRO-immunity cases ask is not whether the SRO is acting (or not acting) "consistent with" the laws it is supposed to apply but rather whether the plaintiff's allegations concern the exercise of powers within the bounds of the government functions delegated to it. Under our precedent, the immunity protects the power to regulate, not the mandate to perform regulatory functions in a certain manner. Thus, the immunity depends only on *whether* specific acts and forbearances were incident to the exercise of regulatory power, and not on the propriety of those actions or inactions. Indeed, if "consistent with" and "capacity" meant that immunity only attaches to those who follow the law, the immunity doctrine would be effectively subverted. After all, individuals characteristically do not bring suit alleging an SRO is obeying its statutory and legal obligations; they bring suit alleging an SRO is violating the law or acting inconsistently with its legal obligations. Lead Plaintiffs here are accordingly asking us to carve out an exception that would all but swallow the doctrine whole, and this we decline to do.

In sum, the proper way to read D'Alessio's use of the terms "consistent with" and "capacity" is to focus on the specific function at issue in the allegations of misconduct to determine whether the conduct is "consistent with" the exercise of power delegated to the SRO and for which this Court has accorded absolute immunity. If such conduct was within the ambit of the SRO's delegated power, immunity presumptively attaches, even where the SRO wrongly exercises that power.

A. Application

Given this understanding of our caselaw, it is clear that the misconduct alleged by Lead Plaintiffs readily falls within the ambit of the quasi-governmental functions the SEC has delegated to the NYSE. Indeed, of the five categories of misconduct that Lead Plaintiffs allege in their complaint (interpositioning, trading ahead, freezing the book, manipulating the tick, and concealing evidence of wrongdoing), the first four involve what Lead Plaintiffs themselves characterize as the failure or abandonment of the Exchange's regulatory duties. For example, Lead Plaintiffs complain that the NYSE—either with intent, knowledge or reckless disregard—permitted the Specialist Firms (1) to engage in interpositioning in violation of the Exchange's own regulations and (2) to trade ahead and front-run stocks to their tremendous financial advantage in violation of the securities laws and regulations. Lead Plaintiffs also claim that the NYSE turned a blind eye to the manipulation of the tick price of the stock and that the practice of freezing the book was a point of contention between the SEC and the Exchange in terms of the length of time that a Specialist Firm could engage in such activity. It is clear that these claims all involve the NYSE's action or inaction with respect to trading on the Exchange, which is indisputably within the NYSE's regulatory powers. Moreover, Lead Plaintiffs' own characterizations of the above claims implicitly concede that the NYSE was acting within the realm of the oversight powers delegated to it by the SEC. *See, e.g.,* Consolidated Compl. P 5 (alleging NYSE's "deliberate failure to properly oversee, regulate or supervise its securities exchange" and that the "NYSE deliberately failed to halt, expose or discipline the illegal trading practices [of member firms] to the extent necessary to deter, stop or prevent them"). This is a tacit concession that the NYSE's decisions to act (or not to act) with respect to the Specialist Firms' conduct is "consistent with" the powers delegated to it by the SEC. Because these claims all relate to the "proper functioning of the regulatory system," D'Alessio, 258 F.3d at 106 (internal quotation marks omitted), the district court did not err when it granted immunity to the NYSE for its action or inaction with respect to these claims.

We confront a somewhat thornier question in evaluating the allegations that the NYSE knowingly permitted, or even actively encouraged, the Specialist Firms to submit doctored or altered regulatory reports to the NYSE and that it alerted the Specialist Firms to impending internal NYSE investigations so that the Firms could conceal evidence of wrongdoing. Lead Plaintiffs' allegations here focus on the NYSE's approach to weekly Form 81 Reports ("Form 81"), which every Specialist Firm was required to submit when it engaged in principal trades. The NYSE floor officials, Lead Plaintiffs claim, permitted their names and badge numbers to be used in preparing false Form 81s, essentially vouching for trades that they knew to be improper or wrong and even when the NYSE discovered a possible falsification, it would send the relevant Form 81 back to the Firm and permit the Form 81 to be resubmitted with the "correct" information. Officials at the Exchange also allegedly "tipped off" at least one of the Specialist Firms about an imminent investigation before the official announcement, permitting it, now forewarned, to alter its records to conceal its misconduct. At first glance, none of these actions appears to fall within the ambit of the powers delegated to the Exchange. The gravamen of the Lead Plaintiffs' claims, however, centers on the functions performed by NYSE in its supervisory and regulatory role: announcing investigations, signing off on regulatory reports on the stock exchange floor, and examining the Form 81s for content and legality. While these actions may not appear to form the heart of the regulatory functions delegated to the NYSE as an SRO, they are nonetheless central to effectuating the NYSE's regulatory decisionmaking....

* * *

Lead Plaintiffs contend that this case presents the "most unusual of circumstances," thus entitling them to overcome whatever grant of absolute immunity this Court might otherwise accord. While we agree that the abuse of trust fraud purportedly engaged in by the Specialist Firms and the Exchange over the years-long Class Period appears egregious, we still conclude that a fraud exception should not apply here—

even a one-time, "most unusual circumstances" exception. Indeed, courts have applied the absolute immunity doctrine without carving out a fraud exception even in cases alleging fraud in situations that directly implicate constitutionally protected personal liberty interests in the criminal context, including a case where a prosecutor allegedly committed fraud upon the courts in a criminal prosecution for capital murder, Imbler, 424 U.S. at 416 (alleged prosecutorial misconduct included knowingly permitting false testimony at trial and submitting altered evidence to the jury), or where allegedly unconstitutional restrictions were placed on a grand juror attempting to investigate official misconduct, Fields v. Soloff, 920 F.2d 1114, 1119 (2d Cir. 1990). If a fraud exception is not warranted in those situations where an individual's very liberty may be at stake, we conclude such an exception is also not appropriate here. Moreover, while Lead Plaintiffs characterize this case as representing the "most unusual of circumstances," an exception here may open a Pandora's box that would undermine the entire purpose behind the immunity doctrine. *See* DL Capital Group, 409 F.3d at 99 ("Thus, rejecting a fraud exception is a matter not simply of logic but of intense practicality since [otherwise] the [SRO's] exercise of its quasi-governmental functions would be unduly hampered by disruptive and recriminatory lawsuits.") (internal quotation marks omitted).

Lastly, we have cautioned before that courts confronted with claims of absolute immunity should consider "whether there exist alternatives to damage suits against the official as a means of redressing wrongful conduct" if absolute immunity applies. Barrett, 798 F.2d at 571 (citing Mitchell v. Forsyth, 472 U.S. 511, 521–23, 105 S. Ct. 2806, 86 L. Ed. 2d 411 (1985)). The alternatives here are manifold. The SEC, after all, retains formidable oversight power to supervise, investigate, and discipline the NYSE for any possible wrongdoing or regulatory missteps. *See*, e.g., DL Capital Group, 409 F.3d at 95 ("[I]f an SRO has violated, or is unable to comply with, *inter alia*, the provisions of the Exchange Act, its own rules, or the rules of the SEC, the SEC is authorized to suspend or even revoke an SRO's registration, as well as to impose lesser sanctions.") (citing 15 U.S.C. §78s(g)). As the facts here pellucidly illustrate, the SEC did intervene and investigate the Exchange and the Specialist Firms and extracted from them considerable settlements, which not only garnered widespread public attention but included significant monetary penalties and implemented new methods of market regulation and oversight.

For all of the reasons stated above, we conclude the NYSE is entitled to absolute immunity and affirm the district court's determination on this issue.

For the foregoing reasons, we affirm the judgment of the district court in part, vacate the judgment in part and remand for proceedings consistent with this opinion.

Comments and Questions

1. What do you think of this court's reasoning? Does the concept of self-regulation exonerate stock exchanges from private enforcement actions?

2. Does it apply to all actions by an SRO? What about misrepresentation claims based upon proxy materials submitted by the NASD to its members? In order for the

NASD and the broker-dealer oversight function of the NYSE to combine, members of the NASD had to approve certain changes to the bylaws of the SRO. An NASD member later sued and alleged that the NASD made false statements during the solicitation process. The court, however, concluded that the transfer of regulatory authority that accompanied the combination was a regulatory function entitled to immunity. Because the proxy solicitation was incident to the combination, it was also entitled to immunity. *See Std. Inv. Chartered, Inc. v. NASD*, 637 F.3d 112 (2d Cir. 2011). The court did stress, however, that the analysis was influenced by the fact that the bylaws had to receive SEC approval.

3. Judge now Justice Sotomayor noted that there were alternatives to private enforcement, including the formidable oversight power of the SEC. The SEC and the NYSE did settle charges arising out of the problems associated with the specialists. *See In re NYSE*, Exchange Act Release No. 51524 (Admin. Proc. April 12, 2005) (settled case where the SEC alleged that "[f]rom 1999 through almost all of 2002, the NYSE failed to properly detect, investigate, and discipline unlawful interpositioning and trading ahead by specialists" and, while not imposing any fines or penalties, did note that the NYSE had created a $20 million reserve fund). Is SEC oversight enough to ensure adequate enforcement of the rules of the NYSE?

4. The court also noted that the SEC had the authority to suspend or revoke an SRO's registration. How likely is this? What would happen if the SEC revoked the registration of the NYSE?

5. The court found that there is no private right of action for violations of the rules of the stock exchanges. Are listing standards rules? *See The Business Roundtable v. Securities and Exchange Commission*, 905 F.2d 406 (D.C. Cir. 1990) ("First it seems indisputable that the NYSE's proposed rule modifying its one share/one vote listing standard is a 'rule' covered by § 19(b) and, correspondingly, that Rule 19c-4 does not fall outside of § 19(c)'s ambit for any want of being a 'rule of a self-regulatory organization.' ").

6. Some early cases indicated that private parties could bring actions against companies for violations of their listing standards. *See Van Gemert v. Boeing Co.*, 520 F.2d 1373, 1381 (2d Cir. 1975) (to find there was no private right of action "would also run contrary to a position we find inviting, that to the American investing public listing on the New York Stock Exchange carries with it implicit guarantees of trustworthiness."). Subsequent decisions, however, have generally not allowed private actions.

7. Not all listing standards are the same. While generally viewed as a matter of contract between companies and exchanges, some listing standards are required by statutes. *See* Section 301 of SOX (requiring the Commission to adopt rules mandating that listed companies have audit committees with certain rights and responsibilities). In other cases, the rules of the exchange are inextricably connected with statutory requirements. *See* Rule 14b-1, 17 CFR § 240.14b-1 (requiring brokers to forward proxy materials to beneficial owners). The rules of the stock exchange regulate the right of brokers to vote shares held by beneficial owners. *See* NYSE Rule 452 and Sec-

tion 402.08 of the Manual. Is it possible that a private right of action might exist for these rules or standards?

California Public Employees' Retirement System v. New York Stock Exchange, Inc. was decided at a time when the NYSE was a non-profit corporation. As for-profit corporations, the exchanges will likely see a growth in the non-regulatory component of their business. Such functions will not be subject to immunity. Distinguishing between the two sets of activities will not, however, be easy.

Weissman v. National Association of Securities Dealers, Inc.

United States Court of Appeals, Eleventh Circuit
500 F.3d 1293 (2007) (en banc)

BARKETT, CIRCUIT JUDGE:

Between December 2000 and June 2002, Weissman purchased 82,800 shares of WorldCom stock on behalf of his minor children. In the wake of WorldCom's collapse, and after losing almost the entire investment, Weissman filed a diversity suit in federal district court against NASDAQ. In his complaint, Weissman disavowed any reliance on NASDAQ's regulatory activity as the basis for his suit, emphasizing that "[t]his action is based solely on the for-profit commercial business activity of the Defendants[, …] includ[ing] Defendants' approximately $100 million … marketing and advertising campaign during the years 2000, 2001 and 2002 to promote and sell … shares of WorldCom, Inc."

Weissman claimed that NASDAQ violated Fla. Stat. § 517.301(1) (b) by promoting WorldCom through its marketing and advertising without disclosing that its revenues were directly enhanced by increased trading in WorldCom stock; offered WorldCom shares for sale without registering as a broker, in violation of Fla. Stat. § 517.12; and committed common law fraud and/or negligent misrepresentation in its attempts to induce investors to purchase shares of WorldCom.

* * *

Under the Securities Exchange Act of 1934, Congress established a system of regulation over the securities industry, which relies on private, self-regulatory organizations to conduct the day-to-day regulation and administration of the United States' stock markets, under the close supervision of the United States Securities and Exchange Commission ("SEC"). The SEC authorized NASD to delegate its SRO functions to NASDAQ for operating and maintaining the NASDAQ stock market. *See* SEC Release No. 34-39326, Order Approving the Plan of Allocation and Delegation of Functions by NASD to Subsidiaries, 62 Fed. Reg. 62,385 (Nov. 21, 1997). Thus, NASDAQ serves as an SRO within the meaning of the Securities Exchange Act, 15 U.S.C. § 78c(a) (26), which vests it with a variety of adjudicatory, regulatory, and prosecutorial functions, including implementing and effectuating compliance with securities laws; promulgating and enforcing rules governing the conduct of its members; and listing and de-listing stock offerings. *See* 15 U.S.C. §§ 78c(a) (26), 78f(b), 78s(g); 15 U.S.C. § 78f(d); 59

Fed. Reg. 29834, 29843 (1994). At the same time, as a private corporation, NASDAQ may engage in a variety of non-governmental activities that serve its private business interests, such as its efforts to increase trading volume and company profit, as well as its daily administration and management of other business affairs. Indeed, even though the SEC has explicitly delegated regulatory functions to SROs, the SEC itself is mindful that SROs have dual status as both quasi-regulators and private businesses.

Because they perform a variety of vital governmental functions, but lack the sovereign immunity that governmental agencies enjoy, SROs are protected by absolute immunity when they perform their statutorily delegated adjudicatory, regulatory, and prosecutorial functions. *See* Barbara v. New York Stock Exch., 99 F.3d 49, 59 (2d Cir. 1996); Austin Mun. Sec., Inc. v. Nat'l Ass'n of Sec. Dealers, Inc., 757 F.2d 676, 692 (5th Cir. 1985); Sparta Surgical Corp. v. Nat'l Ass'n of Sec. Dealers, Inc., 159 F.3d 1209, 1215 (9th Cir. 1998); Zandford v. NASD, 80 F.3d 559, 1996 U.S. App. LEXIS 4574, at*2–3 (D.C. Cir. 1996). However, entities that enjoy absolute immunity when performing governmental functions cannot claim that immunity when they perform non-governmental functions. For example, municipal corporations may enjoy the same level of immunity as the government itself when "acting in their governmental capacity.... When, however, they are not acting in the exercise of their purely governmental functions, but are performing duties that pertain to the exercise of those private franchises, powers, and privileges which belong to them for their own corporate benefit, ... then a different rule of liability is applied and they are generally held responsible for injuries arising from their negligent acts or their omissions to the same extent as a private corporation under like circumstances." Owen v. City of Independence, 445 U.S. 622, 645 n.27 (quoting W. Williams, Liability of Municipal Corporations for Tort § 4, at 9 (1901)). The dual nature of SROs as private companies that carry out governmental functions is similar to that of municipal corporations.

Thus, "[t]o be sure, self-regulatory organizations do not enjoy complete immunity from suits." Sparta, 159 F.3d at 1214. Only when an SRO is "acting under the aegis of the Exchange Act's delegated authority" does it enjoy that privilege. Id. Absolute immunity is not appropriate unless the relevant conduct constitutes a delegated quasi-governmental prosecutorial, regulatory, or disciplinary function. *See* D'Alessio v. New York Stock Exch., Inc., 258 F.3d 93, 105 (2d Cir. 2001) ("a[n] SRO, such as the [New York Stock Exchange], may be entitled to immunity from suit for conduct falling within the scope of the SRO's regulatory and general oversight functions") (emphasis added); see also Austin, 757 F.2d at 692 ("NASD is entitled to absolute immunity for its role in disciplining its members and associates."); Barbara, 99 F.3d at 59 (absolute immunity granted in suit arising from disciplinary action against employee of exchange member); Sparta, 159 F.3d at 1215 (holding that decision to suspend trading was "a regulatory function cloaked in immunity").

Furthermore, because the law favors providing legal remedy to injured parties, grants of immunity must be narrowly construed; that is, courts must be "careful not to extend the scope of the protection further than its purposes require." Forrester v. White, 484 U.S. 219, 224, 108 S. Ct. 538, 98 L. Ed. 2d 555 (1988); see also Owen,

445 U.S. at 645 n.28 (1980) (citations omitted). Thus, because immunity is appropriate only when an SRO is performing regulatory, adjudicatory, or prosecutorial functions that would otherwise be performed by a government agency, it follows that absolute immunity must be coterminous with an SRO's performance of a governmental function. When an SRO is not performing a purely regulatory, adjudicatory, or prosecutorial function, but rather acting in its own interest as a private entity, absolute immunity from suit ceases to obtain. To determine whether an SRO's conduct is quasi-governmental, we look to the objective nature and function of the activity for which the SRO seeks to claim immunity. The test is not an SRO's subjective intent or motivation, *Bogan v. Scott-Harris*, 523 U.S. 44, 54, 118 S. Ct. 966, 140 L. Ed. 2d 79 (1998) (noting that the question of whether absolute immunity for a legislative act applies "turns on the nature of the act, rather than on the motive or intent" of the party performing the act), although there may be some correlation between motive and intent and the function being performed.

NASDAQ suggests that, because it serves important regulatory functions, we should adopt a rule that would find an SRO absolutely immune for all activity that is "consistent with" its powers and functions under the Exchange Act and SEC regulations. Under NASDAQ's view, even advertisements that promote the sale of a particular stock and serve no regulatory function whatsoever would be shielded by absolute immunity, because advertisements are "consistent with" NASDAQ's role as an SRO. In urging this broad test, NASDAQ argues that it is the standard followed by the Second Circuit in *D'Alessio* and that we should follow its holding. We find this argument unavailing. First, *D'Alessio* does not address the kind of conduct at issue in this case. The court in *D'Alessio* granted absolute immunity to an SRO where the complaint in that case dealt with allegations of "improper performance of its interpretive, enforcement and referral functions" in connection with the suspension of a broker—a core regulatory responsibility delegated to SROs by the SEC. *D'Alessio*, 258 F.3d at 105–106. Second, NASDAQ imperfectly represents the language of *D'Alessio* in order to arrive at the "consistent with *D'Alessio*, 258 F.3d at 105–106" test it urges. While it is true that *D'Alessio* held that an SRO "is entitled to immunity from suit when it engages in conduct consistent with the quasi-governmental powers delegated to it . . . ," it made clear that this is true only when an SRO is "acting in its capacity as a[n] SRO." *D'Alessio*, 258 F.3d at 106 (emphasis added). Thus, contrary to NASDAQ's assertions, *D'Alessio* did not apply this test "whenever" SROs engage in conduct that is simply "consistent with" their powers. (NASDAQ's Reply Brief p. 16) (emphasis added).

Indeed, every case that has found an SRO absolutely immune from suit has done so for activities involving an SRO's performance of regulatory, adjudicatory, or prosecutorial duties in the stead of the SEC. *See* Sparta Surgical Corp. v. Nat'l Ass'n of Sec. Dealers, Inc., 159 F.3d 1209, 1213–15 (9th Cir. 1998) (decision to suspend trading and delist shares of a company); D'Alessio v. New York Stock Exch., Inc., 258 F.3d 93, 104–06 (2d Cir. 2001) (disciplinary decision banning trader from the NYSE floor); Barbara v. New York Stock Exch., Inc., 99 F.3d 49, 58–59 (2d Cir. 1996) (conduct in carrying out disciplinary decision); DL Capital Group, LLC v. Nasdaq Stock

Mkt., Inc., 409 F.3d 93, 97–100 (2d Cir. 2005) (decision to suspend trading of a security, to cancel certain trades, and to announce these actions); Dexter v. Depository Trust & Clearing Corp., 406 F. Supp. 2d 260, 263–64 (S.D.N.Y. 2005), aff'd, 219 Fed. Appx. 91, 2007 WL 689542 (2d Cir. 2007) (decision setting an ex-dividend date). Therefore, we find *D'Alessio* inapplicable and hereby reject a standard that would grant SROs absolute immunity for all activity that is merely "consistent with" their delegated powers.

Thus, we now turn to Weissman's complaint to examine the nature and function of NASDAQ's actions as alleged therein. The complaint alleges the following conduct:

> NASDAQ touted, marketed, advertised and promoted WorldCom, falsely representing it as a good company and worthwhile investment and disseminating its fraudulent financial statements, without revealing that, *inter alia:*

> (i) Defendants were engaged in a partnership with WorldCom to promote the sale of its securities in order to generate trading volume and income for the Defendants;

> (ii) Defendants did not review the fraudulent WorldCom financial statements which they disseminated, thus assisting in the perpetration of the largest corporate fraud in the U.S. history;

> (iii) Defendants directly and indirectly profited from the sale of WorldCom Shares to Plaintiff; [and]

> (iv) WorldCom was not in compliance with N[ASDAQ] listing requirements....

In purchasing shares of WorldCom, Plaintiff relied on NASDAQ's advertising, which repetitively advertised WorldCom as a "successful growth company". For example, appearing in major prime time programming such as West Wing and MSNBC News with Brian Williams, NASDAQ ran TV spots for its 100 Index Trust, better known as the QQQ.... The ads feature a group of companies included in the trust, specifically including and showing WorldCom. The key message is that the world's most successful, sought after companies, can be found on the N[ASDAQ] stock market. (Complaint P 61)

Seeking to calm the markets in the wake of Enron fraud, on April 11, 2002, NASDAQ took out a two full page spread advertisement in the Wall Street Journal discussing its belief in the need for N[ASDAQ] listed companies to provide accurate financial reporting in accordance with Generally Accepted Accounted Principals ("GAAP"), "supported by a Knowledgeable Audit Committee". On one page is a picture of the N[ASDAQ] ticker with the slogan "The Responsibilities We All Share". On the opposite page under the headline "Keeping Our Markets True—It Is All About Character" is a list of the chief executives of the "good" N[ASDAQ] listed companies under the sub-heading "Our Beliefs Stand In Good Company". Listed thereunder as an endorser of these N[ASDAQ] goals is "Bernard J. Ebbers, President and Chief Executive Officer WorldCom, Inc." The message implicitly conveyed by the ad is that WorldCom and its CEO are endorsed by NASDAQ as, *inter alia*, having good character, accounting done in accordance with GAAP, and a viable audit committee in accordance with N[ASDAQ] listing requirements. Plaintiff relied on this endorsement the following day in purchasing yet additional shares of WorldCom as its price continued on a downward spiral. (Complaint P 62; see also Complaint P 96).

As noted earlier, in deciding whether NASDAQ is entitled to absolute immunity, we look to the nature and function of NASDAQ's actions as alleged in the complaint. We can find no quasi-governmental function served by the advertisements here. The allegations do not relate to NASDAQ's statutorily delegated responsibility to "prevent fraudulent and manipulative ... practices," "promote just and equitable principles of trade," "remove impediments to and perfect" the free market, or "protect investors and the public interest." 15 U.S.C. § 78o-3(b)(6). The particular advertisements alleged by the complaint were in no sense coterminous with the regulatory activity contemplated by the Exchange Act. This conduct was private business activity, and "[w]hen conducting private business, [SROs] remain subject to liability." Sparta, 159 F.3d at 1214. NASDAQ represents no one but itself when it entices investors to trade on its exchange and, specifically, when it suggests that particular companies are sound investments.

As a private corporation, NASDAQ places some advertisements that by their very nature serve the function of promoting certain stocks that appear on its exchange in order to increase trading volume and, as a result, company profits. Even if NASDAQ's status as a money-making entity does not foreclose absolute immunity for any number of its activities, its television and newspaper advertisements cannot always be said to directly further its regulatory duties under the Securities Exchange Act. These advertisements — by their tone and content — were in the service of NASDAQ's own business, not the government's, and such distinctly non-governmental conduct is not protected by absolute immunity.

Because we conclude that NASDAQ's advertising activity alleged in this case does not serve an adjudicatory, regulatory, or prosecutorial function, the district court's denial of absolute immunity to NASDAQ for the advertisements described in this case is AFFIRMED.

Comments and Questions

1. The court notes the distinction, for purposes of immunity, between the regulatory and the non-regulatory function. Does this case make the distinction clear? Can you make an argument in this case that the alleged misbehavior in fact related to a regulatory function?

2. In fact, the dissent in the case agreed with the statement of the law but disagreed with its application of the law to the facts. The opinion reasoned that the suit would "necessarily chill an SRO's ability to communicate with the marketplace" and make them afraid to "ever mention[] the name of a company, lest that act later be characterized as promotional." What do you make of this concern?

3. Does the for-profit status of the Nasdaq and the NYSE increase the risk of these types of suits? Why?

In re Facebook, Inc. IPO Securities and Derivative Litigation

United States District Court, Southern District of New York
986 F.Supp.2d 428 (2013)

Sweet, District Judge:

Facebook is a worldwide social networking company that: (i) builds tools that enable users to connect, share, discover, and communicate with each other; (ii) enables developers to build social applications of Facebook or to integrate their websites with Facebook; and (iii) offers products that enable advertisers and marketers to engage with its users. As of February 2, 2012, Facebook had 845 million monthly users and 443 million daily users.

On February 1, 2012, in preparation for its IPO, Facebook filed a Form S-1 registration statement with the SEC. Facebook subsequently amended the registration statement several times, before filing their final Form S-1/A on May 16, 2012 (the "Registration Statement"). On May 18, 2012, Facebook also filed a Form 424(b)(4) Prospectus (the "Prospectus") with respect to the IPO.

NASDAQ OMX is a global publicly-traded company whose wholly-owned subsidiaries operate securities exchanges around the world. (CAC ¶¶ 63–65.) One of those subsidiaries is the Exchange, or NASDAQ LLC, which operates the NASDAQ Stock Market in the U.S. (CAC ¶ 65.) NASDAQ OMX is not a self-regulated organization ("SRO"). At all relevant times, Defendants Greifeld and Ewing were officers of NASDAQ OMX, not the Exchange. NASDAQ OMX routinely competes for new listings and overall market share of trading in order to increase revenue and profits. (CAC ¶¶ 63–93.) Specifically, NASDAQ OMX competes against the New York Stock Exchange Euronext ("NYSE"), other exchanges and broker-dealers to secure new listings of securities and to increase its overall market share in trading activity. (*Id.* ¶¶ 66–69.)

The Exchange is an SRO and registered as a national securities exchange under Section 6 of the Exchange Act. *See* 15 U.S.C. §§ 78f & 78c(a)(26); *Findings, Opinion, and Order of the Common,* Exch. Act. Rel. No. 53, 128 (Jan. 13, 2006), 71 Fed.Reg. 3,550 (Jan. 23, 2006) ("Exchange Registration Approval Order"). Before it may permit the registration of an exchange as an SRO, the SEC must determine, among other things, that the exchange has a set of rules that are "consistent with the requirements" of the Exchange Act, 15 U.S.C. § 78s(b)(2), and thus that are designed,

> to prevent fraudulent and manipulative acts and practices, to promote just and equitable principles of trade, to foster cooperation and coordination with persons engaged in regulating, clearing, settling, processing information with respect to, and facilitating transactions in securities, to remove impediments to and perfect the mechanism of a free and open market and a national market system, and, in general, to protect investors and the public interest....

15 U.S.C. § 78f(b)(5). In addition, the SEC enforces exchanges' compliance with the Exchange Act, the SEC's rules, and the exchanges' own rules. Thus, the SEC may

bring an action to enjoin any activity by an exchange that violates the Exchange Act or any rules promulgated thereunder. 15 U.S.C. § 78u(d). The SEC also may suspend or revoke the registration of an exchange, censure it, or restrict its activities, functions, and operations,*see* 15 U.S.C. § 78s(h)(1), and can remove from office or censure an officer or director of an exchange responsible for such failure. 15 U.S.C. § 78s(h)(4).

On May 18, 2012, Facebook offered 421 million shares of its common stock to the public at $38.00 per share on the NASDAQ stock exchange, thereby valuing the total size of the IPO at more than $16 billion. The IPO was initially set to open at 11:00 a.m. Eastern Standard Time under the NASDAQ ticker symbol "FB," but was delayed. At the end of trading on the day of the initial IPO, Facebook stock closed at $31.00 per share, which was 18.42% below the IPO price.

Shortly thereafter, numerous plaintiffs filed lawsuits throughout the country raising claims about the adequacy of pre-IPO and Class Period disclosures under the federal securities laws, and federal and state claims against NASDAQ for failures relating to the Offering. All of the plaintiffs allege that they suffered some loss as a result of these events, although the causes of action they assert vary.

* * *

I. *SRO Immunity Applies in Part and is Inapplicable in Part to Plaintiffs' Allegations*

As a threshold matter, Defendants contend that all of Plaintiffs' claims arise out of actions taken (or not taken) by NASDAQ within the scope of its regulatory responsibilities and accordingly are precluded under SRO immunity, requiring dismissal of the claims and rendering any amendments to the CAC or any requests to lift the discovery stay futile. SRO immunity provides protection not only from liability, but also from the burdens of litigation, including discovery, and should be "resolved at the earliest possible stage in litigation." *Hunter v. Bryant,* 502 U.S. 224, 227, 112 S.Ct. 534, 116 L.Ed.2d 589 (1991); ...

Because Defendants are correct that an entitlement to immunity would require dismissal and preclude granting further discovery or amendments to the CAC, an initial examination as to whether Plaintiffs' claims are subject to SRO immunity is appropriate.

A. *The Applicable Standard*

"There is no question that an SRO and its officers are entitled to absolute immunity from private damages suits in connection with the discharge of their regulatory responsibilities." *Standard Inv. Chartered, Inc. v. Nat'l Ass'n of Sec. Dealers, Inc.,* 637 F.3d 112, 115 (2d Cir.2011) (quoting *DL Capital Group, LLC v. Nasdaq Stock Mkt., Inc.,* 409 F.3d 93, 96 (2d Cir.2005)); ... This immunity extends both to affirmative acts as well as to an SRO's omissions or failure to act....

The party asserting immunity bears the burden of demonstrating its entitlement. *D'Alessio,* 258 F.3d at 104. In assessing the applicability of absolute immunity to a given claim, the SRO's motive and reasonableness are not considered.... It is likewise irrelevant whether the complained of conduct complied with the securities laws. *See NYSE Specialists,*503 F.3d at 98 n. 3 ("[T]he central question ... is not whether the

SRO is acting (or not acting) consistent with the laws it is supposed to apply but rather whether the plaintiff's allegations concern the exercise of power within the bounds of the government functions delegated to it.") (internal citations omitted).

The doctrine is "of a rare and exceptional character." *Barrett v. United States,* 798 F.2d 565, 571 (2d Cir.1986) (internal quotation marks omitted). Courts examine the invocation of absolute immunity on a case by case basis, *DL Capital Group,* 409 F.3d at 97, using a functional test based upon examination of the "nature of the function performed." *Forrester v. White,* 484 U.S. 219, 229, 108 S.Ct. 538, 98 L.Ed.2d 555 (1988); *see also NYSE Specialists,* 503 F.3d at 96. Absolute immunity inheres in SROs whenever they exercise "quasi-governmental powers [ ] consistent with the structure of the securities market as constructed by Congress, … [but] when conducting private business, [an SRO] remains subject to liability." *Sparta Surgical Corp. v. Nat'l Ass'n of Sec. Dealers, Inc.,* 159 F.3d 1209, 1213–15 (9th Cir.1998). The justification for this immunity is that Congress has enabled the SROs to perform "a variety of regulatory functions that would, in other circumstances, be performed by a government," and that the government would be immune when performing these functions. *Id.* Examples of such regulatory functions entitling an SRO to immunity include (1) disciplinary proceedings against exchange members, *Barbara,*99 F.3d at 59; (2) the enforcement of security rules and regulations and general regulatory oversight over exchange members, *D'Alessio,* 258 F.3d at 106; (3) the interpretation of the securities laws and regulations as applied to the exchange or its members, *id.;* (4) the referral of exchange members to the SEC and other government agencies for civil enforcement or criminal prosecution under the securities laws, *id.;* (5) the public announcement of regulatory decisions, *DL Capital Group,* 409 F.3d at 98; and (6) an SRO's amendment of its bylaws where the amendments are inextricable from the SRO's role as a regulator, *Standard Inv. Chartered, Inc.,*637 F.3d at 116. "The common thread in these cases is that absolute immunity attaches where the activity relates to the proper functioning of the regulatory system." *NYSE Specialists,* 503 F.3d at 96 (internal quotation marks and citations omitted). "Indeed, every case that has found an SRO absolutely immune from suit has done so for activities involving an SRO's performance of regulatory, adjudicatory, or prosecutorial duties in the stead of the SEC." *Weissman v. Nat'l Ass'n of Sec. Dealers,* 500 F.3d 1293, 1296 (11th Cir.2007) (en banc) (collecting cases).

Officers and affiliates of SROs are similarly shielded by SRO immunity depending on "the nature of the function performed, not the identity of the actor who performed it." *Forrester,* 484 U.S. at 229, 108 S.Ct. 538. An SRO's officers are thus entitled to absolute immunity when they are, in effect " 'acting under the aegis' of their regulatory duties." *DL Capital,* 409 F.3d at 97 (finding NASDAQ's CEO Greenfield immune from plaintiff's claims arising from the Exchange's reporting of its decision to halt trading and cancel certain trades) (quoting *Sparta Surgical,* 159 F.3d at 1214). As such, NASDAQ, NASDAQ OMX, and its officers will be treated identically for purposes of immunity.

B. *SRO Protects in Part and is Inapplicable in Part to Plaintiffs' Negligence Claims*

The negligence allegations are separated between first, the design, testing and touting of NASDAQ's software, (the "technology negligence claims"), all executed prior to trading, and second, the decision not to halt trading or cancel the impacted trades (the "halting trade negligence claims"), determined during the IPO.

1. *The Inadequate Design, Testing and Touting of NASDAQ's Software Are Not Regulatory Actions Protected by SRO Immunity*

The technology negligence claims in the CAC arise out of the failure of NASDAQ's trading platforms during the IPO, which Plaintiffs contend was the foreseeable result of the inadequate testing of and design for a high volume of cancellations "in the face of projected demand." (CAC ¶ 251.)

Defendants mischaracterize the technology negligence claims, stating that the "negligence claims arise from the commencement of trading in Facebook" or from "NASDAQ's decisions to proceed with and not to halt trading in Facebook," (MTD Br. at 22–23.) Accordingly, Defendants cited precedent supporting immunity involves cases where exchanges determined not to cancel a trade, *see DL Capital Group, LLC v. Nasdaq Stock Market, Inc.,* 409 F.3d 93, 96 (2d Cir.2005), were accused of self-dealing regarding action or inaction with respect to trading on the exchange, *see NYSE Specialists,* 503 F.3d at 97, and de-listed stock and suspended trading, *see Sparta Surgical,* 159 F.3d at 1211, all of which Defendants correctly assert are regulatory functions protected by immunity. (Def. Mem. at 28.)

None of the CAC's allegations concerning the technology negligence claims arise from NASDAQ's commencement of trading in Facebook, or NASDAQ's statements and actions concerning its decision to proceed with and not halt trading during the IPO. (*See* CAC ¶¶ 249–269.) Rather, the technology negligence claims focus solely on the design, promotion and inadequate testing of NASDAQ's technology software prior to the Offering. NASDAQ wished to create an IPO market for companies to be newly listed and traded on its exchange. In furtherance of this venture, NASDAQ proposed, and the SEC authorized, a set of rules for conducting an opening Cross [a system designed to identify a single price for the opening of trading in a security that is the subject of an IPO] and NASDAQ then designed, implemented and tested electronic systems to perform this opening Cross function. In the months preceding the Facebook IPO, NASDAQ encouraged companies to bring new IPOs to its exchange by publicly broadcasting the capabilities and reliability of its technology in executing offerings, including on NASDAQ OMX's website (CAC ¶¶ 181–83) and during NASDAQ OMX's May 10, 2012 Investor Day Conference (CAC ¶¶ 184–89). These statements were intended to "serve [NASDAQ OMX's] private business interests, such as its efforts to increase trading volume and company profit." *Weissman,* 500 F.3d at 1296–99("NASDAQ represents no one but itself when it entices investors to trade on its exchange."). NASDAQ's software is an integral part of NASDAQ's overall business package, intended to create a market for new, revenue-producing IPO business, not in furtherance of any purported regulatory function. *See Opulent Fund,* 2007 WL 3010573, at *5 (NASDAQ's creation and promotion of the NASDAQ-100 Index was not immune "because it profits from selling the market price data" and because "NASDAQ's market facilitating actions at issue ... were nonregulatory"). There are no immunized or statutorily delegated government powers to design exchange computer software, to appropriately test computer software, or to fix computer software when it is malfunctioning before executing an Offering after touting its competence. The SEC has never engaged in the business aspects of facilitating and promoting IPOs or creating technology to increase trading, nor has Congress authorized it to do so.

Precedent has established that actions such as these, undertaken to "increase trading volume[,] are non-regulatory." *Id.* (quoting *Weissman*, 500 F.3d at 1296); *see also Sparta Surgical*, 159 F.3d at 1214 ("When conducting private business, [SROs] remain subject to liability."). Regulatory actions, including "suspending trading, banning traders, or carrying out disciplinary actions" under mandated rule, "all involve oversight of the market to protect investors." *Opulent Fund*, 2007 WL 3010573, at *6. When there is an active trading market, any decision to halt trading or cancel trades can potentially cause loss to one or another group of market participants. In contrast, actions regarding software design before an IPO or promotion of that software before trading commences does not involve such risks. NASDAQ's duty to adequately design and test software to initiate an unprecedentedly large IPO does not function to protect investors; NASDAQ represents no one but itself when it entices investors to trade on its exchange.

NASDAQ's actions functioned to create a market and increase its private trading capacities, conduct which is not protected by SRO immunity. *See, e.g., Opulent Fund*, 2007 WL 3010573, at *6; *Weissman*, 500 F.3d at 1296 ("[A]s a private corporation, NASDAQ may engage in a variety of non-governmental activities that serve its private business interests, such as its efforts to increase trading volume," which are not protected by immunity); *Sparta Surgical*, 159 F.3d at 1214–15 (mere market facilitation designed to increase trading volume is not regulatory conduct).

Securities markets have changed dramatically since the 1930s. Exchanges, like NASDAQ, have converted from non-profit mutual associations owned by their members to for-profit publicly traded corporations owned by shareholders. (*See* SIFMA letter to Mary Jo White, Chair, SEC, Re: Self-Regulatory Structure of the Securities Markets (July 31, 20130), Cappucci Aff. Ex. F ("[T]he interests, incentives and functions of the member-owned cooperative exchange of 1934 bear little resemblance to those of the for-profit publicly traded exchange of today. Since the wave of demutalizations, exchanges have rightly focused their efforts on the part of their business that earns profits to maximize the return for their shareholders, and, in some cases, minimized their actual performance of regulatory functions,").) As SEC Commissioner Gallagher stated in 2012, "the basic premises on which the self-regulatory framework ... [was] put into place almost eighty years ago—private, mutualized, self-regulating exchanges and a simple association of dealers—[are] no longer true." Daniel M. Gallagher, Comm.'s, SEC, Market 2012: "Time for a Fresh Look at Equity Market Structure and Self-Regulation," Speech at the SIFMA's 15th Annual Market Structure Conference (Oct. 4, 2012); (Cappucci Aff., Ex. E.) As exchanges have evolved into for-profit enterprises, an irreconcilable conflict has arisen, rendering independence unattainable in the context of an exchange regulating its own, for-profit business conduct.

This dual-nature of SROs, "as private companies that carry out governmental functions," renders the distinction between actions taken in a governmental capacity, which are immune, and actions taken "for corporate benefit," which cannot be, all the more critical. *Opulent Fund*, 2007 WL 3010573, at *6. Allowing Exchanges to be immune from decisions about the promotion and design of business systems implemented to increase trading volume, particularly in such expanding international markets, would allow unrestrained motives for profit to go unchecked.*See* Scott Patterson, *Dark Pools,* Cross Business New York (2012). As such, the regulatory functions of NASDAQ, including its decisions not to halt trading or announcements of those decisions, do not cloak NASDAQ's independent negligence in failing to adequately design and test its software with retroactive immunity. *Opulent Fund*, 2007 WL 3010573, at *6. ("Nasdaq's pricing conduct is much less quintessentially regulatory than deciding to suspend trading.") (internal citations omitted). If that sufficed, then every time an exchange committed a negligent or unlawful act independent of its regulatory authority, it could purport to consider whether some regulatory power existed and retroactively try to immunize itself from damages for the earlier non-immune conduct. *See* Rohit A. Nafday, *From Sense to Nonsense and Back Again: SRO Immunity, Doctrinal Bait-and-Switch, and a Call for Coherence,* 77 U. Chi. L.Rev. 847, 855 (2010) ("Nafday") (Because absolute immunity frees the recipient of its protection from civil liability unconditionally, it is fraught with potential for abuse). While the doctrine of SRO must continue to ensure regulatory independence, it cannot be applied to allow blanket protection for exchanges when they fail to exercise due care in their pursuits of profit.14 *See Weissman,* 500 F.3d at 1295 ("Grants of immunity must be narrowly construed" because they deprive injured parties of remedies); *see also Marbury v. Madison,* 5 U.S. 137, 147, 1 Cranch 137, 2 L.Ed. 60 (1803) ("It is a settled and invariable principle, that every right, when withheld, must have a remedy, and every injury its proper redress.").

Given that the technology negligence allegations involve actions taken in NASDAQ's own interest as a private entity to increase trading on its Exchange, absolute immunity from suit ceases to obtain. Accordingly, Plaintiffs' technology negligence claims are not shielded by SRO immunity.

2. *The Decision Not to Halt Trading is Protected by SRO Immunity*

In addition to the testing and design of NASDAQ's software, Plaintiffs allege that NASDAQ's decision not to halt trading during the IPO or cancel impacted trades was not a regulatory function and subjects NASDAQ to damages for negligence.

NASDAQ, during the Facebook IPO shortly after trading commenced and the technology errors began, "decided that extraordinary market activity was not occurring, and the EVP/Transactions concluded that NASDAQ therefore did not have the authority to halt trading" under Rule 4120. (SEC Order ¶ 32.) The SEC Order also determined that NASDQ did not have delegated authority to halt trading during the IPO because market trading was proceeding normally and the rule's preconditions were not satisfied. Because the decision not to halt trading was therefore not made pursuant to any official SEC rule, Plaintiffs assert that the decision was not regulatory.

In addition, Plaintiffs maintain that NASDAQ treated the system failures as business issues appropriate for discussion by officers of the holding company, and not issues reserved for independent decision-making by the regulatory arm of the Exchange, (*See* Exchange Registration Approval Order at *3 (NASDAQ OMX "will not itself carry out regulatory functions.").)

The capacity to suspend trading, irrespective of the identity of the decision-maker or the presence of an official SEC rule, is a quintessentially regulatory function. *See, e.g., DL Capital,* 409 F.3d at 96; *NYSE Specialists,* 503 F.3d at 97 (finding that the exchange had immunity given that the underlying actions involved "NYSE's action or inaction with respect to trading on the Exchange, which is indisputably within the NYSE's regulatory powers"); *Sparta Surgical,* 159 F.3d at 1211, 1215 (finding that when NASD "acts in [its] capacity to suspend trading" and de-list stocks, NASD is "performing a regulatory function cloaked in immunity" as "there are few functions more quintessentially regulatory than suspension of trading."). In *DL Capital,* the plaintiff sued NASDAQ and Greifeld for their decision to halt trading and for failing to announce timely that it was cancelling the trades at issue. 409 F.3d at 96. In affirming dismissal of the complaint on grounds of immunity, the Second Circuit confirmed that an Exchange's decision regarding "the actual suspension or cancellation of trades" is protected by SRO immunity. *Id.*at 98. This applies with equal force to NASDAQ's decision not to halt or cancel trades during the Facebook IPO. *NYSE Specialists,* 503 F.3d at 97 ("The power to exercise regulatory authority necessarily includes the power to take no affirmative action."). If an SRO's exercise "of a governmental power delegated to it deserves absolute immunity, the SRO's nonexercise of that power also entitles it to immunity." *Id.* The fact that NASDAQ determined that Rule 4120 did not apply, or that the determination was made by officers of NASDAQ OMX, *see infra* I.(A) n. 9, does not alter the nature of the underlying action. As such, Plaintiffs' negligence claims with respect to halting trading are protected by SRO immunity.

Comments and Questions

1. The court also allowed the class action under Rule 10b-5 to go forward on the basis of statements that were alleged to have "touted and detailed the purported reliability and speed of NASDAQ's technology and trading platform capabilities".

2. The case ultimately settled. *See In re Facebook, Inc. IPO Securities and Derivative Litigation,* MDL No. 12-2389 (SD NY Nov. 9, 2015). On the eve of oral argument at the Second Circuit, the action settled, with Facebook agreeing to pay $26.6 million. Counsel received one-third of the settlement fund in fees.

3. What role do you think the demutalization of NASDAQ played in the decision? Do you agree with the distinction drawn by the court between the matters that could be litigated and those that were subject to immunity?

4. In considering whether NASDAQ should have immunity for the problems associated with the Facebook IPO, does it matter that the SEC issued a cease and desist order against the company and imposed a civil penalty of $10 million. *See* Exchange

Act Release No. 69655 (admin proc May 29, 2013). Is a private enforcement mechanism necessary?

5. NASDAQ established a fund designed to reimburse members for up to $62 for losses related to the systems difficulties arising from the offering. The SEC approved the step but specifically stated that any issue of regulatory immunity was "outside of the scope" of the proposal. *See* Exchange Act Release No. 69216 (March 22, 2013).

6. Retaining a regulatory role imposes costs. Obtaining immunity, however, is one of the benefits of self regulatory status. Do the cases like *Facebook* and *Weissman* suggest that immunity may no longer have quite the same value? What impact might this have on the decision of stock exchanges to retain their self regulatory status?

D. Structural Alternatives

Can the stock exchanges be restructured to provide both the advantages of self-regulation without the drawbacks, particularly the risk of under-enforcement? Congress tried to do so when it created the Public Company Accounting Oversight Board. The Board was given the authority to oversee auditors of public companies.

On the one hand, Congress sought to reduce the risk of direct government influence in auditor oversight by setting up the PCAOB as a New York non-profit corporation rather than as a federal agency. As such, the PCAOB more closely resembled the traditional structure of stock exchanges. To reduce industry influence, however, the Board was chosen not by the entities subject to regulation but by the SEC. At the same time, the SEC could only remove Board members for cause. Cause explicitly included the failure to enforce the rules of the PCAOB.

The unique structure of the PCAOB, somewhere between the NYSE and the SEC, raised questions under the Constitution that ultimately had to be resolved by the Supreme Court.

Free Enterprise Fund v.
Public Company Accounting Oversight Board

United States Supreme Court
561 U.S. 477 (2010)

Roberts, Chief Justice:

After a series of celebrated accounting debacles, Congress enacted the Sarbanes-Oxley Act of 2002 (or Act), 116 Stat. 745. Among other measures, the Act introduced tighter regulation of the accounting industry under a new Public Company Accounting Oversight Board. The Board is composed of five members, appointed to staggered 5-year terms by the Securities and Exchange Commission. It was modeled on private self-regulatory organizations in the securities industry—such as the New York Stock Exchange—that investigate and discipline their own members subject to Commission oversight. Congress created the Board as a private "nonprofit corporation," and Board members and employees are not considered Government "officer[s] or employee[s]" for statutory purposes. 15 U.S.C. §§ 7211(a), (b). The Board can thus recruit its members and employees from the private sector by paying salaries far above the standard Government pay scale. *See* §§ 7211(f) (4), 7219.

Unlike the self-regulatory organizations, however, the Board is a Government-created, Government-appointed entity, with expansive powers to govern an entire industry. Every accounting firm—both foreign and domestic—that participates in auditing public companies under the securities laws must register with the Board, pay it an annual fee, and comply with its rules and oversight. §§ 7211(a), 7212(a), (f), 7213, 7216(a)(1). The Board is charged with enforcing the Sarbanes-Oxley Act, the securities laws, the Commission's rules, its own rules, and professional accounting standards. §§ 7215(b)(1), (c)(4). To this end, the Board may regulate every detail of an accounting firm's practice, including hiring and professional development, promotion, supervision of audit work, the acceptance of new business and the continuation of old, internal inspection procedures, professional ethics rules, and "such other requirements as the Board may prescribe." § 7213(a)(2)(B).

The Board promulgates auditing and ethics standards, performs routine inspections of all accounting firms, demands documents and testimony, and initiates formal investigations and disciplinary proceedings. §§ 7213–7215 (2006 ed. and Supp. II). The willful violation of any Board rule is treated as a willful violation of the Securities Exchange Act of 1934, 48 Stat. 881, 15 U.S.C. § 78a et seq.—a federal crime punishable by up to 20 years' imprisonment or $25 million in fines ($5 million for a natural person). §§ 78ff(a), 7202(b)(1) (2006 ed.). And the Board itself can issue severe sanctions in its disciplinary proceedings, up to and including the permanent revocation of a firm's registration, a permanent ban on a person's associating with any registered firm, and money penalties of $15 million ($750,000 for a natural person). § 7215(c)(4). Despite the provisions specifying that Board members are not Government officials for statutory purposes, the parties agree that the Board is "part of the Government" for constitutional purposes, Lebron v. National Railroad Passenger Corporation, 513 U.S. 374, 397, 115 S. Ct. 961, 130 L. Ed. 2d 902 (1995), and that its members are "'Officers of the United States'" who "exercis[e] significant authority pursuant to the laws of the United States," Buckley v. Valeo, 424 U.S. 1, 125–126, 96 S. Ct. 612, 46 L. Ed. 2d 659 (1976) (per curiam) (quoting Art. II, § 2, cl. 2); cf. Brief for Petitioners 9, n. 1; Brief for United States 29, n. 8.

The Act places the Board under the SEC's oversight, particularly with respect to the issuance of rules or the imposition of sanctions (both of which are subject to Commission approval and alteration). §§ 7217(b)–(c). But the individual members of the Board—like the officers and directors of the self-regulatory organizations—are substantially insulated from the Commission's control. The Commission cannot remove Board members at will, but only "for good cause shown," "in accordance with" certain procedures. § 7211(e)(6).

Those procedures require a Commission finding, "on the record" and "after notice and opportunity for a hearing," that the Board member

"(A) has willfully violated any provision of th[e] Act, the rules of the Board, or the securities laws;

"(B) has willfully abused the authority of that member; or

"(C) without reasonable justification or excuse, has failed to enforce compliance with any such provision or rule, or any professional standard by any registered public accounting firm or any associated person thereof." § 7217(d) (3).

Removal of a Board member requires a formal Commission order and is subject to judicial review. *See* 5 U.S.C. §§ 554(a), 556(a), 557(a), (c)(2)(B); 15 U.S.C. § 78y(a)(1). Similar procedures govern the Commission's removal of officers and directors of the private self-regulatory organizations. *See* § 78s(h)(4). The parties agree that the Commissioners cannot themselves be removed by the President except under the Humphrey's Executor standard of "inefficiency, neglect of duty, or malfeasance in office," 295 U.S., at 620, 55 S. Ct. 869, 79 L. Ed. 1611 (internal quotation marks omitted); see Brief for Petitioners 31; Brief for United States 43; Brief for Respondent Public Company Accounting Oversight Board 31 (hereinafter PCAOB Brief); Tr. of Oral Arg. 47, and we decide the case with that understanding.

* * *

As explained, we have previously upheld limited restrictions on the President's removal power. In those cases, however, only one level of protected tenure separated the President from an officer exercising executive power. It was the President — or a subordinate he could remove at will — who decided whether the officer's conduct merited removal under the good-cause standard.

The Act before us does something quite different. It not only protects Board members from removal except for good cause, but withdraws from the President any decision on whether that good cause exists. That decision is vested instead in other tenured officers — the Commissioners — none of whom is subject to the President's direct control. The result is a Board that is not accountable to the President, and a President who is not responsible for the Board.

The added layer of tenure protection makes a difference. Without a layer of insulation between the Commission and the Board, the Commission could remove a Board member at any time, and therefore would be fully responsible for what the Board does. The President could then hold the Commission to account for its supervision of the Board, to the same extent that he may hold the Commission to account for everything else it does.

A second level of tenure protection changes the nature of the President's review. Now the Commission cannot remove a Board member at will. The President therefore cannot hold the Commission fully accountable for the Board's conduct, to the same extent that he may hold the Commission accountable for everything else that it does. The Commissioners are not responsible for the Board's actions. They are only responsible for their own determination of whether the Act's rigorous good-cause standard is met. And even if the President disagrees with their determination, he is powerless to intervene—unless that determination is so unreasonable as to constitute "inefficiency, neglect of duty, or malfeasance in office." Humphrey's Executor, 295 U.S., at 620, 55 S. Ct. 869, 79 L. Ed. 1611 (internal quotation marks omitted).

This novel structure does not merely add to the Board's independence, but transforms it. Neither the President, nor anyone directly responsible to him, nor even an officer whose conduct he may review only for good cause, has full control over the Board. The President is stripped of the power our precedents have preserved, and his ability to execute the laws—by holding his subordinates accountable for their conduct—is impaired.

That arrangement is contrary to Article II's vesting of the executive power in the President. Without the ability to oversee the Board, or to attribute the Board's failings to those whom he *can* oversee, the President is no longer the judge of the Board's conduct. He is not the one who decides whether Board members are abusing their offices or neglecting their duties. He can neither ensure that the laws are faithfully executed, nor be held responsible for a Board member's breach of faith. This violates the basic principle that the President "cannot delegate ultimate responsibility or the active obligation to supervise that goes with it," because Article II "makes a single President responsible for the actions of the Executive Branch." Clinton v. Jones, 520 U.S. 681, 712–713, 117 S. Ct. 1636, 137 L. Ed. 2d 945 (1997) (Breyer, J., concurring in judgment).

Indeed, if allowed to stand, this dispersion of responsibility could be multiplied. If Congress can shelter the bureaucracy behind two layers of good-cause tenure, why not a third? At oral argument, the Government was unwilling to concede that even *five* layers between the President and the Board would be too many. Tr. of Oral Arg. 47–48. The officers of such an agency—safely encased within a Matryoshka doll of tenure protections—would be immune from Presidential oversight, even as they exercised power in the people's name.

Perhaps an individual President might find advantages in tying his own hands. But the separation of powers does not depend on the views of individual Presidents, see Freytag v. Commissioner, 501 U.S. 868, 879–880, 111 S. Ct. 2631, 115 L. Ed. 2d 764 (1991), nor on whether "the encroached-upon branch approves the encroachment," New York v. United States, 505 U.S. 144, 182, 112 S. Ct. 2408, 120 L. Ed. 2d 120 (1992). The President can always choose to restrain himself in his dealings with subordinates. He cannot, however, choose to bind his successors by diminishing their powers, nor can he escape responsibility for his choices by pretending that they are not his own.

The diffusion of power carries with it a diffusion of accountability. The people do not vote for the "Officers of the United States." Art. II, §2, cl. 2. They instead look to the President to guide the "assistants or deputies ... subject to his superintendence." The Federalist No. 72, p. 487 (J. Cooke ed. 1961) (A. Hamilton). Without a clear and effective chain of command, the public cannot "determine on whom the blame or the punishment of a pernicious measure, or series of pernicious measures ought really to fall." *Id.*, No. 70, at 476 (same). That is why the Framers sought to ensure that "those who are employed in the execution of the law will be in their proper situation, and the chain of dependence be preserved; the lowest officers, the middle grade, and the highest, will depend, as they ought, on the President, and the President on the community." 1 Annals of Cong., at 499 (J. Madison).

By granting the Board executive power without the Executive's oversight, this Act subverts the President's ability to ensure that the laws are faithfully executed—as well as the public's ability to pass judgment on his efforts. The Act's restrictions are incompatible with the Constitution's separation of powers.

Comments and Questions

1. The D.C. Circuit divided 2–1, affirming the constitutionality of the PCAOB. The Supreme Court, although reversing, was likewise divided. The decision was issued on the last day of the term and was decided by a 5–4 vote.

2. There had been some risk that the Court would strike down not only the provisions creating the PCAOB but also SOX in its entirety. Instead, the Court merely invalidated the "for cause" removal provision, essentially providing the Commission with the plenary right to remove members of the Board. What is the likely consequence of this ruling? How will it likely affect the role and independence of the PCAOB?

3. Why did Congress create this structure? Certainly, Congress intended to insulate the PCAOB from political influence. Yet at the same time, the absence of political oversight can increase the risk of capture by the agency subject to regulation. The majority acknowledged that "[o]ne can have a government that functions without being ruled by functionaries, and a government that benefits from expertise without being ruled by experts." But given the ruling in this case, will that be true with respect to the oversight of auditors for public companies?

4. The majority also noted that the "multilevel protection" created in the context of the PCAOB was a blueprint for expansion of congressional authority. Is this true?

5. What are some differences between the PCAOB and the NYSE? What are some similarities? What explains the different approach? Why didn't Congress simply put the PCAOB inside the SEC or allow it to be a self-regulatory organization modeled after the stock exchanges?

6. As the Court noted, one consequence of the structure was that the PCAOB could pay compensation to Board members "far above the standard Government pay scale." Members on the five person board are paid in excess of $500,000. *See* Speech by SEC Commissioner Paul Atkins, Statement at Open Meeting to Consider PCAOB's Proposed 2008 Budget, Dec. 18, 2007 (noting that budget for 2008 would increase salaries of board members to $532,000 and chair to $654,353). At the same time, the salary paid to the President of the United States was $400,000. Id. What is the likely justification for these salaries? Are they necessary?

7. Given the decision in this case, are we likely to see many more regulatory bodies that resemble either the PCAOB or the NYSE?

IV. Regulatory Competition: Delaware vs. the SEC

Although there is some separation in the roles of the various regulators, increasingly Delaware and the Securities and Exchange Commission seem to have the most tension. Thus, while Delaware's primacy in the realm of corporate law is uncontested at the state level, that does not mean it gets to always determine the direction of corporate governance.

To the extent Delaware can be said to have competition, therefore, the source is not the other states but federal law. According to Professor Roe, the main competition is really between Delaware and the federal government. As he has written:

> Delaware's freedom to act and its limits are not determined solely, and perhaps not even primarily, by its strength vis-a-vis other states, but by the line demarcating where the federal authorities leave it alone and where they do not. Within the area that doesn't provoke federal authorities, Delaware has autonomy.

Mark J. Roe, *Delaware's Politics*, 118 Harv. L. Rev. 2491 (2005).

Comments and Questions

1. Is it the case that there is no real competition among the states for charters? Nevada, for example, has sought to become the "Delaware of the West" by implementing law even more favorable to management. North Dakota, in turn, has attempted to compete by adopting laws even more favorable to shareholders.

2. To the extent Delaware only had to be concerned with federal intervention, the threat was rarely exercised, at least in the area of corporate governance. Thus, while Congress gave the SEC the authority to regulate tender offers in 1968, it provided for increased disclosure and prophylactic protections for tendering shareholders. The provisions, therefore, had little impact on governance. What does this tell us about any concern that Delaware might have that its approach to corporate law might result in federal intervention?

3. Is Delaware just another constituency in the groups that compete for influence in Washington, DC? The Delaware courts, for example, routinely address legal issues outside of the context of a case or controversy. *See* Myron T. Steele & J.W. Verret, *Delaware's Guidance: Ensuring Equity for the Modern Witenagemot*, 2 Va. L. & Bus. Rev. 189, 193 (2007) (noting the deliberate use of speeches and dicta in opinions to provide guidance "to signal the evolutionary direction of Court of Chancery and Delaware Supreme Court jurisprudence").

4. How might things have changed in the new millennium? In 2002, Congress adopted SOX and gave the SEC a more direct, substantive role in the governance process by allowing it to use listing standards to regulate audit committees. *See* Rule 10A-3, 17 CFR 240.10A-3. During this period, the Delaware courts issued some decisions that hinted at a more rigorous approach towards fiduciary obligations. Some

speculated that these decisions were designed to reduce the pressure for additional federal preemption. *See* John Coffee, *Post-Enron Jurisprudence*, N.Y.L.J. July 17, 2003, at 5 (noting that some recent Delaware court decisions could be explained by a desire to prevent additional federal intervention in the corporate governance process).

5. The most recent example of federal intervention occurred in connection with the Dodd-Frank Wall Street Reform Act adopted in 2010. The Act gave the Commission the authority to adopt rules regulating the compensation committee process, much the way that SOX did for the audit committee. *See* Section 952. As in SOX, the need for an independent compensation committee was limited to exchange traded companies. Going further, however, the Commission was given express authority to determine the "relevant factors" that must be considered by the exchange in defining independent directors.

6. An interesting example of the growing tension between the SEC and Delaware occurred in the litigation challenging Rule 14a-11, the shareholder access rule. For the first time, the State of Delaware filed an amicus brief in a federal case seeking to invalidate an SEC rule relating to corporate governance. The State largely took the position that the rule conflicted with the regulatory approach employed by Delaware. *See* Brief of the State of Delaware as Amicus Curiea in Support of Petitioners, *Business Roundtable v. SEC*, 10-1305, D.C. Cir., Feb. 25, 2011 ("SEC Rule 14a-11, which takes away that choice, is completely contradictory to Delaware's newly adopted statute governing proxy access."). To some degree, therefore, Delaware was trying to persuade the court that it was a better forum than the SEC for regulating certain types of governance practices. Did it succeed? *See Business Roundtable v. SEC*, 647 F.3d 1144 (D.C. Cir. 2011).

7. The debate is often viewed as almost a zero sum game. But in fact, is it possible that the mix of state authority, however it is evolving, and the mix of federal authority, however it is evolving, collectively result in the most efficient mix of governance rights? Take a look at Brian R. Cheffins, Steven A. Bank & Harwell Wells, *The Race to the Bottom Recalculated: Scoring Corporate Law Over Time*, Legal Studies Research Paper No. 2014-38, at 82 (Oct. 10, 2014) ("We demonstrate quantitatively that federally-oriented reform has bolstered considerably shareholder protection over time and indeed has more than off-set whatever diminution occurred due to state law changes. Today, shareholders, at least those in public corporations, are better protected by the amalgam of state and federal "corporation law" than were shareholders of a century or even a half-century ago."). Does this answer the question?

Chapter 3

The Public Company Board

The corporation's board of directors, as elected by the firm's shareholders, serves as the linchpin of public company governance, the ultimate decision-making body of the company. As Delaware's General Corporation Law makes clear, "the business and affairs of every corporation shall be managed by or under the direction of a board of directors."[1] Board approval is a statutory pre-requisite to corporate action on fundamental transactions, such as whether the corporation will amend its charter, buy or sell significant assets, merge with another company, or dissolve. If and when the directors recommend a transaction, shareholders will have the opportunity to veto it; however, shareholders cannot initiate transactions, nor can they amend the board's proposals. In addition, state statutes also grant to the board of directors the exclusive authority to issue stock, determine the adequacy of consideration for shares, and declare dividends. Boards of directors not only are vested with virtually irrevocable decision-making authority, but, as we will see in Chapter 4, directors' business judgments also are substantially protected from second-guessing by shareholders and the courts. In other words, corporate law confers on boards of directors substantial autonomy as well as control over company assets.

Notwithstanding their broad statutory authority, the boards of public corporations do not manage or even direct the day-to-day operations of the business. Rather, the modern public company generally is managed "under the direction of" the board of directors. Directors fulfill their responsibilities by delegating the work of running the company to the firm's officers and other senior executives employed by the corporation. The corporation's managers—including the chief executive officer but also the chief financial officer and other executives responsible for particular areas of the company's affairs—act as agents of the firm, making most of the routine operational decisions for the enterprise. The board selects these top managers, delegates duties to them, and decides their tenure and compensation. The board also provides advice to the executive team, especially on matters of strategy, long-term performance targets, vital business policy, and the like. Finally, the board assesses the company's financial and operational performance and evaluates management's leadership. In sum, public company directors function primarily in a supervisory capacity, delegating day-to-day management functions downward to the officers

---

1. Del. Gen. Corp. L. § 141(a). *See* also Model Bus. Corp. Act § 8.01(b) (2008) ("All corporate powers shall be exercised by or under the authority of, and the business and affairs of the corporation managed by or under the direction of, its board of directors....").

and other senior executives employed by the corporation, and overseeing their performance for the benefit of the firm and its shareholders. Although executives employed by the firm operate the business and make day-to-day decisions, state law also mandates that boards make fundamental decisions concerning the corporation's capital structure, mergers, acquisitions, sales of important assets, and other major transactions.

I. Why a Board?

Academics have long debated whether and why the law empowers boards of directors to control public corporations. Proponents of director primacy, like Professor Stephen Bainbridge, argue that board-centered governance promotes efficient and informed decision-making.

Stephen M. Bainbridge, *Why a Board?*
Group Decisionmaking in Corporate Governance
55 Vand. L. Rev. 1 (2002)[2]

Despite the clear advantages to the public corporation of authority-based decisionmaking and hierarchical governance, at the apex of that hierarchy is not a single autocrat, but rather a multi-member body that usually functions by consensus. To be sure, it is often said that, in the real world, boards are captured by senior management. According to this view, "managers dominate their boards by using their de facto power to select and compensate directors and by exploiting personal ties with them." Even with that caveat, however, it seems useful to think of the board as a production team.

What then does the board produce and how does it produce it? First and foremost, the board monitors and disciplines top management. Second, while boards rarely are involved in day-to-day operational decisionmaking, most boards have at least some managerial functions. Broad policymaking is commonly a board prerogative, for example. Even more commonly, however, individual board members provide advice and guidance to top managers with respect to operational and/or policy decisions. Finally, the board provides access to a network of contacts that may be useful in gathering resources and/or obtaining business. Outside directors affiliated with financial institutions, for example, apparently facilitate the firm's access to capital.

The extent to which boards actually monitor management and effectively discipline subpar performance has been the subject of considerable dispute. As noted, conventional wisdom asserts that boards are captured by senior management. The board-capture phenomenon, however, seems less valid today than it once was. Modern CEOs are constrained both from below, by other members of the top management team, and from above, by the board.

---

2. Copyright © 2002 Vanderbilt Law Review. Reprinted by permission.

During the 1980s and 1990s, several trends coalesced to encourage more active and effective board oversight. Much director compensation is now paid in stock, for example, which helps align director and shareholder interests. Courts have made clear that effective board processes and oversight are essential if board decisions are to receive the deference traditionally accorded to them under the business judgment rule, especially insofar as structural decisions are concerned (such as those relating to management buyouts). Third, director conduct is constrained by an active market for corporate control, ever-rising rates of shareholder litigation, and, some say, activist shareholders. As a result, modern boards of directors typically are smaller than their antecedents, meet more often, are more independent from management, own more stock, and have better access to information. These developments culminated in a series of high-profile board revolts against incumbent managers at such iconic American corporations as General Motors, Westinghouse, and American Express. More recently, the firing of "Chainsaw Al" Dunlap by Sunbeam's board provides yet more anecdotal evidence of board activism.

As boards become stronger and more independent of top management, moreover, the process builds momentum. For example, Westphal and Zajac have demonstrated that as board power increases relative to the CEO—measured by such factors as the percentage of insiders and whether the CEO also served as chairman—newly appointed directors become more demographically similar to the board. In any event, the institutional structure created by corporate law allows, but does not contemplate, one-man rule. If it comes to overt conflict between the board and top management, the board's authority prevails as a matter of law, if not always in practice. Indeed, it is the necessity for retaining dismissal of senior management as a potential sanction that explains why the board is at the apex of the corporate hierarchy rather than functioning as an advisory committee off to the side of the corporate organizational chart.... Acting alone, an individual director "has no power of his own to act on the corporation's behalf, but only as one of the body of directors acting as a board." Moreover, as the MBCA puts it, "directors may act only at a meeting unless otherwise expressly authorized by statute." Why this emphasis on collective rather than individual action?

The MBCA's drafters offer the following answer: "The underlying theory is that the consultation and exchange of views is an integral part of the functioning of the board." Or, as Forbes and Milliken opine, "The very existence of the board as an institution is rooted in the wise belief that the effective oversight of an organization exceeds the capabilities of any individual and that collective knowledge and deliberation are better suited to this task." These arguments run afoul of the old joke that a camel is a horse designed by a committee, but they find considerable support in the literature on individual versus group decisionmaking....

In sum, groups appear to outperform their average member consistently, even at relatively complex tasks requiring exercise of evaluative judgment. There is contested evidence as to whether groups outperform their best member, which the next section evaluates in more detail. Accordingly, it seems fair to conclude that group decision-making often is preferable to that of individuals. In addition to the specific studies recounted above, which are corroborated by those described in following sections, a number of comprehensive literature reviews confirm that conclusion. Corporate law's strong emphasis on collective decisionmaking by the board thus seems to have a compelling efficiency rationale....

Suppose the corporate hierarchy was capped by an individual autocrat rather than a board of directors. Under such circumstances, a bilateral vertical monitoring problem arises. On the one hand, the autocrat must monitor his or her subordinates. On the other hand, someone must monitor the autocrat.

As we have seen, hierarchy is an adaptive governance response to the agency cost problem. Yet that explanation raises the question of "who watches the watchers?" Because all members of the hierarchy are themselves agents of the firm with incentives to shirk, a mechanism to monitor their productivity and reduce their incentive to shirk must also be created, or one ends up with a never-ending series of monitors monitoring lower-level monitors. Alchian and Demsetz solved this dilemma by requiring that the monitor be given the residual income left after all other workers have been paid. This arrangement encourages the monitor to promote the most efficient use of the other inputs and to reduce shirking because his reward will depend upon the efficacy of his monitoring efforts. Unfortunately, their model breaks down with respect to the public corporation. Although common stockholders are the corporation's residual claimants, they also are the corporate constituency perhaps least able to monitor management behavior.

Corporate law therefore provides a series of alternative accountability mechanisms designed to constrain agency costs without the need for an unending series of monitors. Chief among them is the board of directors. Putting a group at the apex of the corporate hierarchy turns out to be a highly effective alternative solution to the problem of an otherwise unending chain of monitors.

Comments and Questions

1. Although state law vests corporate power in a deliberative body, is it intuitively obvious that groups of individuals make better decisions than individuals themselves? Does your answer depend on the qualifications, interest, and effort of the individuals making the decisions? What decisions might best be made by a qualified, well-informed individual executive rather than a group of directors?

2. Social psychologist Irving Janis famously coined the term "groupthink" to describe the tendency for members of a cohesive group to yield to their preference for consensus, resulting in defective decision-making. In the corporate boardroom, this social dynamic may impede directors from asking probing questions, considering novel or alternative ideas, evaluating proposals fully, or engaging in active debate. Commentators contend, for example, that groupthink adversely affected risk management and oversight by the directors of Lehman Brothers, Citigroup, and other financial firms devastated by the 2008 subprime mortgage crisis. How might the relatively larger size of a bank board (at the time of the meltdown, for example, Cit-

igroup had 18 directors, as compared to 11 directors on average for S&P 500 industrial company boards) make the directors more susceptible to groupthink? How might the fact that a majority of Citigroup's directors lacked significant work experience in a financial institution affect the board's vulnerability to groupthink? Can you think of ways to build a culture that encourages questioning, critical evaluation, and even dissent within the boardroom?

3. Even if small groups of informed persons generally make better decisions than a single individual or a large group of individuals, why not vest ultimate decision-making authority in the senior executive team rather than the board of directors? After all, the skilled managers with responsibility for the day-to-day operations of the business have the best, most timely information to make decisions. Also, as full time employees of the firm, senior executives presumably have the greatest interest in its success. In other words, why does the law mandate another layer of bureaucracy at the top of corporate hierarchy?

4. Although Professor Bainbridge claims that board capture "seems less valid today than it once was," many commentators disagree. They point to the growing gap between executive compensation and other employee incomes as evidence that managers continue to wield great influence over their boards, including through the director nomination process. *See, e.g.*, Lucien Bebchuk & Jesse Fried, Pay Without Performance (2004). Scholars recently reported that boards with more co-opted members (directors appointed to the board after the CEO took office) are less likely fire underperforming CEOs, more likely to approve CEO pay increases, and more likely to approve investments recommended by the CEO. Jeffrey L. Coles, Naveen D. Daniel & Lalitha Naveen, *Co-Opted Boards*, 27 Rev. Fin. Stud. 1751 (June 2014). Their research also indicates that, regardless of members' legal independence, boards with more co-opted directors tend to support CEOs. *Id.* Can you think of any benefits of co-opted boards?

5. If boards of directors are so effective, why are they not mandated for other types of entities? Limited liability companies, for example, may be managed by one or more of the owners (members), or the LLC may be managed centrally by non-member managers. Central management may consist of a board, but a single person or entity also may manage the LLC. In other words, the law does not mandate management by a board; the promoters choose the management structure. Why is corporate law more restrictive?

6. While Professor Bainbridge addresses the allocation of power between the CEO and the board of directors, state corporate law also empowers boards over shareholders. We examine the role of shareholders in corporate governance more closely in Chapter 7. Shareholders elect the board and vote on just a handful of key decisions, such as amending the corporate charter, merging the company, or dissolving the firm. Shareholders do not have the right to initiate binding resolutions concerning corporate policies, such as executive compensation, nor do they have the right to vote on most corporate decisions. Can you identify some deficiencies that would affect shareholders' ability to make fundamental decisions in the best interest of the

firm? Elsewhere, Professor Bainbridge argues that effective corporate governance requires that the law irrevocably vest decision-making authority in a small, central group rather than in a large, diffuse electorate. Stephen M. Bainbridge, *Director Primacy and Shareholder Disempowerment*, 119 Harv. L. Rev. 1735 (2006).

II. The Roles of the Board in the Public Corporation

State law specifies the authority of the corporate board of directors. Acting pursuant to that statutory authority, today's public company boards have, generally speaking, a dual mandate: (1) an oversight role, requiring the board to monitor the performance of the firm and its management; and (2) an advisory role, calling for the board to consult with management about the firm's operations and its strategy.

On day-to-day matters, then, the public company's CEO and his senior executive team make corporate decisions. However, as we briefly reviewed in Chapter 1, delegation to management leads to the agency problem in the corporation. If management opportunism is not constrained, shareholders will demand a greater premium for investing in the firm, raising the cost of capital and inhibiting economic growth. One solution to reduce agency costs is to align the interests of managers and shareholders through well-designed executive compensation arrangements.[3] We consider executive compensation at some length in Chapter 6. Another response to the agency problem is for the board of directors to monitor executives. By monitoring the firm's CEO and other senior executives, outside directors can limit the exercise of managerial discretion, thus lowering agency costs between shareholders and management.

Boards have not always functioned as watchdogs. In the mid-twentieth century, the public company board of directors often performed more like a ceremonial advisory council, a cabinet answerable only to the firm's chief executive officer. In 1971, just following the notorious collapse of the conglomerate, Harvard Business School Professor Myles Mace wrote about managerialism and weak corporate boards in his provocative and influential book *Directors: Myth and Reality*. Professor Mace, who had conducted in-depth interviews with more than 100 chief executive officers and board members, reported that corporate presidents not only had "de facto power to control the enterprise" but also that "with these powers of control it is the president who ... determines in large part what the board of directors does or does not do."[4]

Legal academics also contributed to the conversation on the role of corporate boards. Most notably, Professor Melvin Eisenberg compared the received legal model of the corporation (the board selects officers, sets policy, and generally manages the firm's business) with the public company board in practice (lacking the time, infor-

---

3. *See generally* Michael C. Jenson & William H. Meckling, *Theory of the Firm: Ownership, Behavior, Agency Costs, and Ownership Structure*, 3 J. Fin. Econ. 305 (1976).
4. Myles Mace, *Directors: Myth And Reality* 191 (1971).

mation, and incentives to manage the corporation's business or make business policy). Finding divergence between the two models, Professor Eisenberg argued for reform: boards composed of directors independent of management principally responsible for selecting and dismissing the CEO and other top managers and monitoring their performance.[5] Importantly, Professor Eisenberg recognized that in order to perform their monitoring duties effectively, directors require not just independence but sufficient information and time.

In the years following publication of Professor Mace's influential study and Professor Eisenberg's proposal for legal change, shareholders and their advocates increasingly called for outside directors to join boards and monitor senior officers and other top corporate executives. Their calls did not fall on deaf years. Revelations of illegal corporate campaign donations and corporate bribery of foreign officials lead not only to federal prosecutions but Congressional and SEC hearings on corporate governance reform. Consensus began to build around changes to board structures and reliance on independent outside directors to help deter wrongdoing by executives. In 1977, the New York Stock Exchange amended its listing requirements to require that boards of listed companies appoint audit committees composed of directors independent of management. "When the board fails to monitor effectively, disaster results—executive enrichment and corporate failure ensue. To curb managerial opportunism and protect against disastrous corporate performance, a firm must implement a corporate governance model capable of effectively monitoring the enterprise's operations."[6] The monitoring board model was born.

Although legally responsible for selecting and compensating executives and overseeing their activities, commentators still have criticized public company boards for their passivity, especially following corporate scandals and financial calamities over the past fifteen years. Massive company bankruptcies, recurrent financial frauds, executive compensation outrages, and excessive risk taking focused public attention on directors' effectiveness as monitors and their accountability to shareholders for managers' wrongdoing. Detractors have argued that directors too often "rubber stamp" managements' recommendations, making decisions without sufficient information or deliberation. As reported by the Senate subcommittee that investigated the role of the Enron board of directors in that corporation's stunning collapse:

> But much of what was wrong at Enron was not concealed from its Board of Directors. High risk accounting practices, extensive undisclosed off-the-books transactions, inappropriate conflict of interest transactions, and excessive compensation plans were known to and authorized by the Board. The Subcommittee investigation did not substantiate the claims that the Enron Board members challenged management and asked tough questions.

5. Melvin Eisenberg, *Legal Models of Management Structure in the Modern Corporation: Officers, Directors and Accountants*, 63 Calif. L. Rev. 375 (1975).

6. Charles M. Elson, et al., *Corporate Governance Reform and Reemergence from Bankruptcy: Putting the Structure Back in Restructuring*, 55 Vand. L. Rev. 1917, 1926 (2002).

Instead, the investigation found a Board that routinely relied on Enron management and Andersen representations with little or no effort to verify the information provided, that readily approved new business ventures and complex transactions, and that exercised weak oversight of company operations. The investigation also identified a number of financial ties between Board members and Enron which, collectively, raise questions about Board member independence and willingness to challenge management.

The failure of any Enron Board member to accept any degree of personal responsibility for Enron's collapse is a telling indicator of the Board's failure to recognize its fiduciary obligations to set the company's overall strategic direction, oversee management, and ensure responsible financial reporting.

SUBCOMM. ON INVESTIGATIONS, S. COMM. ON GOV'T AFFAIRS, THE ROLE OF THE BOARD OF DIRECTORS IN ENRON'S COLLAPSE, S. REP. NO. 107-70, at 7–8, 11–14 (2002).

Following the bankruptcies of Enron and WorldCom, and the discovery of dozens of other financial frauds in 2001 and 2002, commentators argued that the corporations shared a common disorder: boards of directors that failed to perform their responsibilities with vigilance. An example of such a critique follows.

Elizabeth A. Nowicki, *Director Inattention and Director Protection under Delaware General Corporation Law Section 102(b)(7): A Proposal for Legislative Reform*
33 Del. J. Corp. L. 695 (2008)[7]

The structure of the modern, publicly held corporation lends itself to problems of board inattention. Although corporations are owned by shareholders, they are managed by a board of directors elected by the shareholders. This creates a division between ownership (at the shareholder level) and control (at the director level), which raises the classic "other people's money" problem. Directors are managing a corporation representing an investment of "other people's money," yet, in theory, no one does as good a job managing a business as the business owner herself because she has the most at stake.

This "other people's money" problem is compounded by the way the modern board of directors actually fulfills its managerial obligations. While a corporation's board of directors is charged by state statute with the task of managing the business and affairs of the corporation, the board also has statutory authority to delegate management duties to officers selected by the board whom the board then "monitors." The modern board of directors is thereby a "monitoring" board, with the business of the corporation in the hands of senior corporate officers whose performance is monitored by the board. This monitoring structure removes directors from the daily operations of the corporation and limits the board in two obvious ways: (1) boards do not possess first-hand information on the day-to-day machinations of their corporate charge;

---

7. Copyright © 2008 Delaware Journal of Corporate Law. Reprinted by permission.

and (2) corporate officers, who provide the directors information regarding the corporation's operations, become informational gatekeepers with the power to limit or skew the information they relay to the board.

Because the modern board is a monitoring board and boards manage "other people's money," a director's ability and incentive to be an outstanding director are compromised. It is not surprising, then, that over the past two decades, many boards have proved themselves to be poor monitors. Many have failed to detect and squelch corporate fraud, allowing serious product failings to mar corporate reputations. In addition to a board's inability to detect corporate fraud, boards have tacitly approved a range of questionable accounting, financing, and disclosure practices. Recent corporate scandals dealing with vulgar and inexplicable executive compensation, stock option backdating, and overt looting make manifest the fact that the monitoring board may not be monitoring quite so well. Some corporate boards appear plagued by inattention, and some directors are asleep at the wheel.

Director inattention is troubling at both micro and macro levels. On an individual level, director inattention is a problem because, to the extent that corporations suffer damage due to director inattention, shareholders who hold stock in those corporations lose money when the value of their investment decreases. From a broader perspective, director inattention is a problem because it undermines investor confidence. When investors lose confidence in the management of the modern corporation, they stop investing in stocks and corporations, which tightens capital market liquidity and limits corporate expansion. Further, as an academic matter, director inattention throws into question the utility of the corporation as a business entity. One of the key benefits to the corporate form is that it allows for passive investment because management is the responsibility of directors. If the directors are inattentive, this undermines the utility of passive investment. Corporations utilize a management structure that vests "control" of the corporation into the hands of directors who are elected by shareholders. If directors are not performing their control functions, the corporation is not working as designed.

Comments and Questions

1. The independent board model of corporate governance assumes that directors will take their monitoring role seriously. However, critics long have contended that outside directors, who may accept their board nominations for reasons of status-seeking and the perquisites of board membership, lack incentives required to perform their oversight function actively. Can you think of any legislative reform that would provide incentives for directors to become more engaged, i.e., to evaluate recommendations more searchingly, seek additional information, and probe suggested strategies critically? Might the threat of legal liability cause directors to carefully analyze executives' reports and proposals? Is there a role for law in motivating directors to perform their duties more conscientiously?

2. Boards also have received criticism for being too deferential to the CEO and other members of the senior executive team. Why might this be the case? Are there

dynamics in the relationship between directors and CEOs that would encourage passivity and discourage questioning? Might the CEO's influence over director nominations to the board result in the election of individuals inclined to follow the CEO's recommendations?

3. Enron's board of directors was dominated by outside directors with outstanding credentials who appeared to be independent. However, during Congressional hearings following the Enron bankruptcy, federal lawmakers faulted directors for failing to take seriously their monitoring responsibilities. Legislators strongly criticized the firm's board for allowing Enron executives to engage in high risk accounting, for approving inappropriate conflict of interest transactions and extensive undisclosed off-the-books activities, and for awarding excessive compensation to senior executives. Congressional investigations specifically highlighted and disapproved latent relationships between supposedly independent directors and the company and/or company managers, finding that such ties compromised directors' independence and their willingness to challenge management. Even in the absence of such ties, isn't it the case that board members generally will support the CEO and senior management team? Insofar as board members will prefer collegiality to confrontation, should shareholders rely on independent directors to police the CEO and other executives?

4. Although corporate law and the firm's charter and bylaws assign ultimate management authority and major decisions to the board of directors, how can directors realistically monitor the operations of a large corporation doing business globally?

5. Even after the "corporate governance revolution," most public company boards meet less than monthly. According to a 2015 study, the boards of the largest U.S. firms meet an average of nine times annually; the boards of 52 of the top 100 companies meet less than nine times a year.[8] What does this report suggest about the ability of boards to monitor management?

6. Boards can monitor effectively only if they have timely and adequate information about what is taking place inside the company. In the era of independent directors, most of the information about the company comes to directors in preparation for and during board meetings. But who decides the agenda for the meetings of the board? Who decides what reports and documentation to send to the directors in advance of their meetings? Who decides what information directors will receive at the meeting but before making decisions?

Although the modern consensus seems to be that directors' primary responsibility is to monitor management, effective boards also are expected to perform other functions generally described as advisory in nature. Rather than simply look over the shoulders of company executives, directors additionally provide the CEO and his/

---

8. Shearman & Sterling LLP, *Corporate Governance & Executive Compensation 2015* 23 (2015).

her team with their considered advice and their expertise, contributions that presumably will improve the quality of the managers' decisions.

Report of the Task Force of the ABA Section of Business Law Corporate Governance Committee on Delineation of Governance Roles and Responsibilities
65 Bus. Law. 107 (Nov. 2009)[9]

The board of directors is vested under state law with managing or directing the business and affairs of the corporation, and therefore is recognized in law as the primary corporate decision-making body. The board in turn typically delegates significant authority for the day-to-day operations to a professional CEO and other executive officers, who in turn derive their management authority from the board of directors. To the extent that a board delegates to management, it must exercise reasonable oversight and supervision over management. Additionally, certain board functions may not be delegated. Board functions that generally are retained by the board and are central to its focus include the following:

- Selecting, monitoring, evaluating, motivating, and compensating, and, when necessary, replacing the CEO and other key members of senior management;
- Monitoring corporate performance and assessing whether the corporation is being appropriately managed by the senior management team;
- Providing strategic guidance to the senior management team and reviewing and approving financial objectives and major corporate plans and actions;
- Developing corporate policy;
- Reviewing and approving major changes in auditing and accounting principles and practices;
- Overseeing audit, internal controls, risk management and ethics, and compliance;
- In a public company, overseeing financial reporting and related disclosures;
- Declaring dividends and approving share repurchase programs;
- Making decisions on major transactions and other material events concerning the corporation for submission to the shareholders for approval; and
- Performing any other functions prescribed by law, regulation or listing rule, or the corporation's certificate of incorporation or bylaws.

In contrast to the limited powers of shareholders, the board has broad powers to initiate and adopt corporate plans, commitments, and actions. However, certain di-

---

rector powers are limited by the need for shareholder approval, and, in all cases, director powers are subject to the board's fiduciary duties to the corporation and its shareholders.

In fulfilling their mandate, directors are required to act under the high standards imposed on fiduciaries, including the duties to act with due care (focusing appropriate attention and making decisions on an informed basis), in good faith, and in the best interests of the corporation and its shareholders. Directors owe duties of care and loyalty both to the corporation and to the shareholder body as a whole. The duty of care requires that directors inform themselves of "all material information reasonably available to them" concerning a given decision prior to acting on that decision. "[T]he duty of loyalty mandates that the best interest of the corporation and its shareholders takes precedence over any interest possessed by a director … and not shared by the stockholders generally." Individual directors breach their duty of loyalty by placing the interests of anyone—whether themselves, management, a third party, or a subset of shareholders—over the corporation or the shareholders generally.

Directors are also obligated to act in a deliberative and fully informed manner, which requires access to relevant and timely information. One of the very practical challenges in corporate governance relates to the difference between managers and directors in their access to information about the corporation and the implications of this difference on the ability of part-time outside directors to hold managers accountable for the responsibilities that have been delegated to them. Increased reliance on independent directors in publicly traded companies—directors who by definition lack their own sources of information about internal corporate matters due to their lack of employment and business ties to the company—may in fact increase director dependency on management for the information that directors need to provide appropriate oversight. Nonetheless, directors must make reasonable effort to ensure that they are being kept appropriately apprised of the company's compliance with the law and its business performance.

Comments and Questions

1. Rather than advising corporate insiders about the firm's business and strategies, outside directors today must spend increasing amounts of time engaged in monitoring management and planning for management changes. Time constraints aside, some commentators contend that the collegial culture of the corporate boardroom—a culture that supports directors performing their advisory functions—impedes directors from performing their monitoring functions. Do you think that the monitoring board model inspires adversarial rather than friendly interactions between CEOs and outside directors? To the extent that directors' advisory and monitoring roles conflict, what consequences might that conflict have for the effectiveness of the board as a governing body?

2. To monitor management effectively as well as provide advice and counsel to the CEO and others on the senior executive team, directors require timely, reliable information. How do directors obtain the information that they need to function

well as advisors and monitors? What impediments might exist to outside directors acquiring essential information from management, including reports, data, and intelligence that insiders may not wish to share, i.e., bad news? How can outside directors verify the accuracy and completeness of information provided to them by company management?

———————

Some commentators have argued that post-Enron regulations aimed at strengthening the board's monitoring role have damaged boardroom collegiality and, more importantly, diverted directors' attention from providing critical advice and strategic guidance to the CEO and senior management team. Others, like Professor Brown, question the importance of the board's advisory function.

J. Robert Brown, Jr.,
The Demythification of the Board of Directors
52 Am. Bus. L.J. 131 (Spring 2015)[10]

In the debate over corporate governance, the relationship between shareholders and directors rests at the epicenter. Management has a legal obligation to act in the best interests of shareholders but sometimes does not. Shareholders have an interest in overseeing the actions of management but often cannot.

Reforms designed to address these issues frequently take the form of structural changes to the board. In the aftermath of Enron, the stock exchanges mandated the use of audit, compensation, and nomination committees, and limited membership to independent directors, thereby excluding management. Boards of listed companies were required to have a majority of independent directors. Congress in the Sarbanes-Oxley Act all but ordered the inclusion of financial expertise on the board and imposed mandatory standards for audit committees of listed companies. Dodd-Frank took a similar approach to compensation committees and tightened the definition of independent director.

These reforms have not always generated the anticipated results. This may occur in part because of an emphasis on structural reform unaccompanied by necessary changes in process. It may also occur, however, because of misconceptions about board behavior.

Two prevailing myths are used to explain board behavior at large public companies. One is the myth that directors of these companies are chosen primarily on the basis of their substantive qualifications. They are not. Companies select directors because of their predisposition toward the policies of management.

Directors have the inherent authority to intervene in corporate affairs, including the right to dismiss top officers. Moreover, in an era of independent directors and heightened shareholder organization, the potential for intervention in corporate

———————

10. Copyright © 2015. Reprinted by permission.

affairs has grown. Management, therefore, has a rational incentive to reduce this risk. Ensuring that the board consists of directors who favor the positions taken by the chief executive officer (CEO) can advance the goal. This does not render substantive qualifications irrelevant but does reduce them to a matter of secondary importance.

The other myth is that boards at large public companies perform a meaningful advisory function. Boards are commonly said to both monitor and advise management. Advising, however, increases the risk of intervention in management functions. As a result, while the role may have existed at one time, it is no longer a significant and systematic part of the board's responsibilities. Without an advisory role, the relationship between directors and management loses much of its cooperative appearance and is mostly reduced to oversight and monitoring, activities that can be more accurately characterized as adversarial.

* * *

The general assumption is that directors are selected on the basis of their substantive qualifications. This, however, is a myth. While executive experience and other types of expertise are not irrelevant, directors are selected primarily because of their willingness to support the policies of incumbent management.

The Need for Reliability

Although boards are legally responsible for managing the company, the task is in reality assigned to the officers, particularly the CEO. Boards, therefore, mostly play a monitoring role. Broadly speaking, they seek to mitigate CEO overconfidence, prevent shirking, address conflicts of interest, and otherwise ensure that managers act in the best interests of shareholders. In fulfilling these responsibilities, they will sometimes need to intervene in corporate affairs and reverse or alter the decisions of management. They may also be called upon to dismiss top officials.

The possibility of intervention is both a matter of structure and a consequence of legal obligation. CEOs serve in a manner that must be consistent with the "express desires of the board of directors." *In re Walt Disney Co. Deriv. Litig.*, 907 A.2d 693, 774 n.570 (Del. Ch. 2005). Directors in turn are obligated to act in the best interest of shareholders, something that may necessitate the dismissal of the CEO. As a practical matter, however, intervention is discretionary. Boards determine when shareholders benefit from the veto of a decision or the replacement of the CEO.

* * *

Conventional Wisdom

The second myth concerning board behavior is that directors at large public companies perform a meaningful advisory or management function. In this cooperative and interactive vision, directors are viewed as providing useful advice and historical context. They may help to hone corporate strategies, anticipate problems, and encourage CEO flexibility. Moreover, at the apex of the corporation, the board is uniquely positioned to deliver advice that management cannot easily disregard. Some have even suggested that the function has grown in importance. The vision is attractive but not a useful description of board behavior, at least with respect to the largest public companies. The need for less interventionist directors has all but eliminated a meaningful advisory role. To provide advice or participate in management, the board must be informed. Likewise, an advisory role works best with a board that contains a wide range of experiences and substantive skills, thereby allowing directors to provide management with a broader set of outcomes. The emphasis on reliability as the preeminent qualification for board service, however, conflicts with the goal of an informed and diverse board.

To the extent some suggest that an advisory or "management" function continues to exist, they often point to the board's obligation to approve certain types of transactions such as dividends and mergers. Board consideration of these transactions does provide a theoretical opportunity to advise and suggest alternatives. In reality, however, the proposals typically arrive at the board level after successful negotiation by management and a thorough vetting by outside experts. The board's role is legal sufficiency, with management seeking ratification not input.

The Case of Strategic Planning

Perhaps the closest a board comes to a formal advisory role is through participation in the strategic planning process. Strategic planning can be both advisory and cooperative, providing directors an opportunity to help determine the mission of the company. Indeed, some have argued for a strengthening of the board's role in this process.

Strategic planning is a somewhat "fuzzy" concept. Boards assign to strategic planning committees a myriad of diverse functions. This can include the obligation to determine "long-term business strategies" or, as one board put it, to ensure "that the Corporation's strategies, priorities and policies are consistent with the Corporation's overriding goals of creating and building long-term sustainable value for its stockholders." Microfinancial, Proxy Statement, at 6 (Apr. 11, 2014). The committees may alert management about alternative technologies or industry trends. Directors can suggest new products, identify acquisition candidates, or propose business opportunities.

These functions notwithstanding, strategic planning does not result in boards playing a consistent and meaningful advisory role within the company. First, not all public companies engage in the practice. Few companies have in place standing committees responsible for strategic planning with the number apparently declining in recent years, particularly among the largest public companies. Nor, when they exist, do they necessarily meet on a frequent basis. Second, the actual planning function is typically episodic and therefore occurs infrequently. Once developed, long-term goals presumably remain in place for an extended period of time.

Third, as a practical matter, strategic planning is likely influenced and guided by management. Boards are often presented with a preexisting plan. In that context, they are not devising a strategic direction but merely commenting on, or validating, management's existing vision.

Finally, the board may lack the structure needed to adequately and effectively perform a strategic planning function. Given the emphasis on reliability, boards often are devoid of the diversity of views required for a robust and meaningful discussion. Similarly, strategic planning requires informed directors. Corporate officials, however, have an incentive to withhold information in order to reduce the board's "ability to monitor management's performance." Nicola Faith Sharpe, *Informational Autonomy in the Boardroom*, 2013 U. Ill. L. Rev. 1089, 1129 (2013) (strategic plan can help improve the ability of directors to monitor management's performance).

Summary

The boards of the largest public companies do not perform an advisory role, at least in any systematic or meaningful fashion. Nor does the board "manage" the corporation. Instead, directors mostly ensure legal sufficiency and establish outer boundaries for management. They do not devise the policies or practices implemented by the company but have the authority and, sometimes, the obligation, to intervene when necessary to protect the interests of shareholders.

Comments and Questions

1. As a governing body, is the primary function of the corporate board to advise the CEO and other senior executives? Would you agree that in order to function effectively as an advisory body, the board must maintain a collegial relationship with management? Explain your responses.

2. Although it is common to attribute an advisory role to outside directors, there is little empirical evidence as to whether public company boards in fact perform this function regularly or in any meaningful way. More study is needed to determine, for example, whether, how, and how often boards engage with management in corporate strategic planning. When management consulting firm McKinsey surveyed 772 directors in 2013, only 34 percent agreed that their boards fully comprehended their companies' strategies.

As for specific mergers and acquisitions, it is unclear whether, and at what point during the deal process, corporate executives, bankers, and lawyers confer with outside directors. The board's role varies depending on the size of the transaction, its complexity, the sophistication of the directors and management, and the board's practices and culture, among other factors. Outside directors of large public companies more likely will review and approve transactions vetted by management after negotiations have concluded. These boards typically receive presentations from financial advisors and review key documents in order to understand the deal and assess its financial impact on the firm. Other boards may delegate to the audit committee responsibility for testing the economics of potential transactions and for making recommendations to the full board. Alternatively, certain individual board members may consult informally with the CEO about due diligence issues, negotiating strategies, sensitive deal points, and the like. Depending on the circumstances of the corporation and the transaction, outside directors may function as advisors, as monitors, or as both advisors and monitors.

3. Directors tend to have similar backgrounds, educations, professions, and experiences. They also likely share the same or similar affiliations and relationships,

including social ties. How might these common perspectives affect the directors' ability to function as advisors? How might directors' affinities with one another and with the CEO affect their ability to effectively counsel management? Would boards perform better as advisors if persons with diverse viewpoints were represented on the board? We will explore these questions in some depth later in this chapter and in subsequent chapters as well.

4. Professor Tamar Frankel has written that the balance of power between directors and CEOs may fluctuate depending on whether the board functions primarily as advisor to management or as management's supervisor.[11] When the board acts as advisor to the firm's CEO, the board does not have the last word concerning the subject of its advice; the board's advice may influence management, but management makes the final decisions. Conversely, when the board of directors supervises the CEO, the board acts as ultimate decision maker. Assuming this model is accurate, can you make an argument that the board's advisory function contravenes corporate law? In addition to the function performed by directors, what other factors might influence the balance of power between corporate boards and CEOs?

III. Independent Directors

In order to monitor management successfully for the benefit of the firm and its shareholders, the board of directors must include persons who are willing and able to serve as guardians of shareholders' interests. The Securities and Exchange Commission long has preferred that directors independent of management perform this oversight function; as early as 1934, William O. Douglas, a commissioner on the first SEC, argued that directors unaffiliated with management should occupy a majority of board seats.[12] With limited statutory authority, however, the Commission did not act to regulate boards until the mid-1970s. By that time, most experts in the field agreed that boards comprised of a majority of independent directors (persons not employed by or affiliated with the firm) monitor managers more effectively. Without conflicts of interest arising from their relations to the firm or its executives, independent directors presumably will exercise greater attention and objectivity. Persons not beholden to the CEO for their employment or economic well-being also will evaluate management's performance more vigorously.

In the post-Watergate era, then, independent directors became the focus of corporate governance solutions to the agency problem of executive malfeasance in public companies, and corporate governance reform efforts centered on enhancing directors' in-

---

11. Tamar Frankel, *Corporate Boards of Directors: Advisors or Supervisors*, 77 U. Cinn. L. Rev. 501 (2008) (arguing that boards more likely to fail if directors, managers, and shareholders disagree about priority of board's advisory and supervisory roles).

12. *See* William O. Douglas, *Directors Who Do Not Direct*, 47 Harv. L. Rev. 1305 (1934).

dependence from management in order to improve board oversight. The initial draft of the American Law Institute's *Principles of Corporate Governance* would have mandated that publicly held corporations include a majority of independent directors on their boards.[13] Although, the ALI had softened its position by the time it published the *Principles* in 1994 — and the independence requirement became a recommendation — the independent board movement had begun. In short order, "independent directorship ... evolved from being the subject of interesting speculation to an assumed 'best practice' for the most successful corporations in the world."[14] Public company boards transformed, as described by Professor Jeffrey Gordon in the following article.

Jeffrey N. Gordon, *The Rise of Independent Directors in the United States, 1950–2005: Of Shareholder Value and Stock Market Prices*

59 Stan. L. Rev. 1465, 1468–83 (2007)[15]

"Independent directors" — that is the answer, but what is the question?

The now-conventional understanding of boards of directors in the diffusely held firm is that they reduce the agency costs associated with the separation of ownership and control. Elected by shareholders, directors are supposed to "monitor" the managers in view of shareholder interests. Who should serve on the board of a large public firm? Circa 1950, the answer was, as a normative and positive matter, that boards should consist of the firm's senior officers, some outsiders with deep connections with the firm (such as its banker or its senior outside lawyer), and a few directors who were nominally independent but handpicked by the CEO. Circa 2006, the answer is "independent directors," whose independence is buttressed by a range of rule-based and structural mechanisms. Inside directors are a dwindling fraction; the senior outside lawyer on the board is virtually an extinct species.

The move to independent directors, which began as a "good governance" exhortation, has become in some respects a mandatory element of corporate law. For controversial transactions, the Delaware courts condition their application of the lenient "business judgment rule" to board action undertaken by independent directors. The New York Stock Exchange requires most listed companies to have boards with a majority of independent directors and audit and compensation committees comprised solely of independent directors. The NASD requires that conflict transactions be approved by committees consisting solely of independent directors. Post-Enron federal legislation requires public companies to have an audit committee comprised solely

---

13. *See* Stephen M. Bainbridge, *Independent Directors and the ALI Corporate Governance Project*, 61 Geo. Wash. L. Rev. 1034, 1037 (1993).

14. John H. Matheson & Peter D. Favorite, *Multidisciplinary Practice and the Future of the Legal Profession: Considering a Role for Independent Directors*, 32 Loy. U. Chi. L. J. 577, 609 (2001).

15. Copyright © 2007 Stanford Law Review. Reprinted by permission.

of independent directors. But why has the move to independent directors been so pronounced?

One of the apparent puzzles in the empirical corporate governance literature is the lack of correlation between the presence of independent directors and the firm's economic performance. Various studies have searched in vain for an economically significant effect on the overall performance of the firm. Some would deny there is a puzzle: theory would predict that firms will select the board structure that enhances the chance for survival and success; if competitive market pressure eliminates out-of-equilibrium patterns of corporate governance, the remaining diversity is functional. Others would note that corporate governance in the United States is already quite good, and thus marginal improvements in a particular corporate governance mechanism would expectedly have a small, perhaps negligible, effect.

The claim of this Article is that the rise of independent directors in the diffusely held public firm is not driven only by the need to address the managerial agency problem at any particular firm. "Independent directors" is the answer to a different question: how do we govern firms so as to increase social welfare (as proxied by maximization of shareholder value across the general market)? This maximization of shareholder value may produce institutions that are suboptimal for particular firms but optimal for an economy of such firms. Independent directors as developed in the U.S. context solve three different problems: First, they enhance the fidelity of managers to shareholder objectives, as opposed to managerial interests or stakeholder interests. Second, they enhance the reliability of the firm's public disclosure, which makes stock market prices a more reliable signal for capital allocation and for the monitoring of managers at other firms as well as their own. Third, and more controversially, they provide a mechanism that binds the responsiveness of firms to stock market signals but in a bounded way. The turn to independent directors serves a view that stock market signals are the most reliable measure of firm performance and the best guide to allocation of capital in the economy, but that a "visible hand," namely, the independent board, is needed to balance the tendency of markets to overshoot.

Independent directors have a comparative advantage for these different tasks. They are less dependent on the CEO and more sensitive to external assessments of their performance as directors; they are less wedded to inside accounts of the firm's prospects and less worried about the disclosure of potentially competitively sensitive information. They also have credibility in the "checking" of market signals against intrinsic measures of the firm's prospects. In other words, genuinely independent directors might create significant value in the allocation of resources, not just in their firm but more generally as other firms are forced to adapt to the best performers. Thus, one of the hallmarks of the [recent] period was the development of various mechanisms of director independence aimed at producing directors who were independent in fact.

In this time of increased shareholder activism, one important question is whether the enhanced independence of directors will create a space for a public firm to resist stock market pressure in the pursuit of currently disfavored business strategies (and whether this would be desirable) or whether the very pressures that give rise to director independence will in the end swamp this possibility.

One of the striking elements of the 1950–2005 period was the development of various mechanisms to create and enhance the independence of directors. The genesis of many of these mechanisms was the 1970s wave of corporate governance reform, which tried to establish preconditions for the monitoring board. Indeed, "independent director" entered the corporate governance lexicon only in the 1970s as the kind of director capable of fulfilling the monitoring role. Until then, the board was divided into "inside" and "outside" directors. Further developments favoring director independence occurred in the 1990s as part of the post-hostile bid settlement among institutional investors, managers, and boards. The last wave, post-2002, was spurred by the Enron, WorldCom, and other board failures, which led to new efforts to strengthen director independence in light of the board's additional role of controls monitoring as well as performance monitoring.

Analytically, these mechanisms of director independence can be broken down into four categories: (1) tightening the standards and rules of disqualifying relationships; (2) increasing negative and positive sanctions, such as legal liability for fiduciary duty breach, reputational sanctions, and stock-based compensation; (3) development of intra-board structures, such as task-specific committees and designation of a "lead director"; and (4) reducing CEO influence in director selection and retention by, for example, the creation of a nominating committee staffed solely by independent directors. Without being Panglossian, it does seem that the accumulating effects of changes in each of these mechanisms, as well as the accumulating cultural shift fostered by the successive reform efforts, should have increased the independence-in-fact of directors over the period.

A straightforward way to strengthen director independence is to select candidates who have no ongoing (or even prior) relationship with the corporation other than as a director. Over the 1950–2005 period the relationship measure of independence tightened considerably. Initially the relationship test focused narrowly on the director's employment status. Those who were not current officers were, by definition, outsiders, including non-executive directors who had what would be regarded today as a disqualifying material relationship—such as employment with a supplier or a customer, or with the firm's investment bank or law firm. This consensus was reflected by the 1962 New York Stock Exchange statement that accepted a description of an outside director as simply one who is non-management.

Standards tightened considerably in the wake of the 1970s corporate governance crisis, which for the first time produced a concerted demand for "independent" directors. The well-publicized business failures of the period led to increasing acceptance of the "monitoring model" of the board, which required independent directors. The contemporaneous revelations of widespread corporate bribery and illegal campaign contributions at home and abroad, so-called "questionable payments," spurred the SEC to insist on independent directors in the settlement of various enforcement actions.

The unresolved question was what exactly constituted "independence" — how should one deal with economic interests and personal ties that would potentially undercut independence. Federal regulatory guidance, stock exchange listing standards, state fiduciary law, and "best practice" pronouncements have all played a role in line-drawing.

The 1978 Corporate Director's Guidebook, an influential product of mainstream corporate lawyers, drew a two-level distinction: first distinguishing between "management" and "non-management" directors, and then between affiliated and non-affiliated non-management directors. A former officer or employee was to be regarded as a managerial director. A director with other economic or personal ties "which could be viewed as interfering with the exercise of independent judgment" was an affiliated non-managerial director — for example, "commercial bankers, investment bankers, attorneys, and others who supply services or goods to the corporation."

In 1978, the SEC went so far as to propose proxy disclosure that would categorize outside directors as "affiliated" or "independent, with the obvious intention of using disclosure to obtain Chairman Harold Williams' objective of boards staffed principally, if not entirely, by independent directors. In response to corporate objections, it rapidly withdrew the proposal, lamely explaining that "the ability to exercise independent judgment is not solely dependent upon the label attached to a particular director." On the NYSE front, its 1977 audit committee listing standard, which required staffing by "directors independent of management," split the difference: it permitted directors from organizations with "customary commercial, industrial, banking, or underwriting relationships with the company" to serve on an audit committee unless the board found that such relationships "would interfere with the exercise of independent judgment as a committee member." That definition remained intact until 1999, when the criterion of audit committee independence was significantly tightened in response to the prodding of the Blue Ribbon Committee on Improving Audit Committee Effectiveness. Audit committees were required to consist of at least three "independent directors," and the "customary" economic relationships of the 1977 were now off limits for committee members.

Another federal regulatory tightening of the "independence" standard came through the 1996 IRS criteria for "outside" directors who could approve performance-based remuneration that was excepted from the $1 million deductibility cap on executive compensation established by section 162(m) of the Internal Revenue Code. Those criteria disqualified a former officer of the corporation and a director who receives remuneration from the corporation "either directly or indirectly, in any capacity other than as a director." The criteria also place stringent limits on the extent to which the director could have an ownership interest in or be employed by an entity that received payments from the corporation. In turn, the IRS regulations influenced the SEC's 1996 rules specifying independent director approval of certain stock-related transactions as a condition of exemption from the short-swing profit recapture provisions of section 16(b) of the 1934 Securities Exchange Act. The definition of a "non-employee director" with such approval power followed the substance of the IRS regulation. The tests of economic distance for director independence established by these two important federal regulatory agencies were important benchmarks.

State courts grappling with the right of shareholders (as opposed to the board) to maintain derivative litigation alleging corporate wrongdoing were another important source of heightened standards of director independence midway in the period. The "questionable payments" scandal of the 1970s led to a spate of shareholder derivative suits. Corporations sought to take control of the actions to avoid their potentially disruptive effects and to eliminate alleged "strike suits." In the important decision of *Zapata Corp. v. Maldonado*, the Delaware Supreme Court held that even for a "demand-excused" derivative action, a "special committee" constituted of independent directors could nevertheless obtain dismissal of the action if it demonstrated this was in the best interests of the corporation. In its dismissal request, the special committee had the burden of demonstrating its independence. This, of course, increased the demand for directors with minimal prior connection to the corporation and its management, and helped ratchet up the independence standard. Moreover, the standards developed in derivative litigation in the 1970s and early 1980s also set criteria for the bona fides of directors who needed judicial sanction for their approval of target defensive measures in the face of a hostile bid.

Throughout the 1980s and 1990s, various panels and "blue ribbon" committees developed somewhat influential "best practice" guidelines for relationship tests. The most important exposition, the American Law Institute's ("ALI's") 1992 Principles of Corporate Governance, recommended that the board of a public corporation "should have a majority of directors who are free of any significant relationship with the corporation's senior executives." "Significant relationship" was defined in a way to disqualify many affiliated directors, both through categorical exclusions relating to the firm's principal outside law firm or investment bank, and through attention to customer/supplier relationships crossing a relatively low ($200,000) economic materiality threshold. The Principles of Corporate Governance also called for the firm's nominating committee to engage in a more individualized review of factors that could undermine the independence of particular directors. The ALI project had influence beginning in 1982 with its tentative first draft, whose "significant relationship" test was similar to the final version.

Ultimately, the Enron corporate reform wave at the end of the period worked a sea change. Seeking to avoid corporate governance legislation, the NYSE in 2002 initiated a significant revision of its board composition standards. A majority of directors were required to be independent, and stringent independence criteria applied to all such directors, not just audit committee members. Under prodding from institutional investors, issuers, and the SEC, the NYSE revised the proposals over a yearlong period, adding and subtracting stringency. The 2004 version (as further refined) contains a general standard requiring an affirmative board determination that a purportedly independent director has "no material relationship with the listed company" (including "as a partner, shareholder or officer of an organization that has a relationship with the company"). It also has a series of carefully defined exclusions and safe harbors that cover in detail the effect of prior employment, familial ties, consulting relation-ships, and charitable ties. And, of course, the SEC, exercising regulatory authority under the Sarbanes-Oxley Act, specified minimum conditions in 2003 for director independence for directors who serve on the audit committee.

Comments and Questions

1. Insiders occupied half the seats on corporate boards as late as 1950. However, as Professor Gordon indicates, executives and other firm insiders no longer dominate most public company boards. Today, populations of nominally independent directors comprise a majority and even supermajority of the boards of most public corporations. Professor Gordon estimated that the percentage of inside directors decreased from 50 percent in 1950 to about 10 percent in 2005, while the percentage of independent directors increased from approximately 20 percent to approximately 80 percent.

Indeed, despite the corporate governance failures uncovered at Enron, WorldCom, and other scandal-plagued corporations in 2002 and 2003, most lawmakers and com-mentators continued to view boards and board committees staffed with independent directors as the last, best hope to prevent and detect management, fraud, abuse, and incompetence. Following enactment of SOX, major stock exchanges adopted new governance rules for listed companies requiring that boards consist of a majority of "independent" directors, as the rules define that term. The stock exchanges also man-dated that only independent directors staff board audit committees. In addition, the NYSE required that boards establish nominating/corporate-governance and compen-sation committees staffed entirely by independent directors. While NASDAQ rules did not compel boards to establish such committees until recently, NASDAQ mandated that at least a majority of independent directors decide executive compensation and director nominee selection. Pursuant to Dodd-Frank, the SEC in 2013 approved new NYSE and NASDAQ independence standards for compensation committees and their advisors, which we examine in Chapter 6.

Importantly, as Professor Gordon indicates, the shift toward director independence predated regulatory intervention; the number of inside directors fell steadily from the mid-1970s and then dropped abruptly at the end of the century. Nor is it clear that board composition changed significantly in specific response to post-Enron reform mandates. Still, recent research suggests that the board independence trend has continued. In 2013, nearly 85 percent of directors of S&P 500 companies were considered independent, an increase of more than two percentage points since 2009.[16] Indeed, at most large public companies, the CEO occupies the only board seat held by an executive of the firm. Mid-size and small public companies report similar trends in director independence.

2. The NYSE and NASDAQ also mandate that, regardless of whether directors satisfy regulatory bright-line independence standards, listed companies affirmatively determine whether each board member is independent in fact. Does this requirement

---

16. *See* Equilar, *2014 Board Composition & Recruiting Trends Report* 13 (2014).

reflect that the independence standards are inadequate? Many of the largest U.S. public companies report that they have adopted heightened independence standards for firm directors; that is, independence standards more stringent than the listing standards. Why might a company voluntarily adopt heightened independence standards?

3. Researchers have attempted to provide both theoretical and empirical support for the propositions that (1) majority independent boards improve corporate performance, and (2) independent directors most effectively monitor management for the benefit of shareholders. Although such studies have produced mixed evidence and inconclusive results, as we will see in Chapter 13, there still is widespread agreement for the proposition that the election of independent directors is essential to good corporate governance. Without empirical proof that corporations with independent boards experience superior performance or even enhanced oversight of management, why might rational shareholders still favor such boards?

4. Now and again, corporations and their advocates have complained that director independence laws, rules, and regulations have imposed on public companies a "one-size-fits-all" solution that, in fact, may not reduce agency costs and enhance financial performance. Notably, some scholars recently have argued against the continuing imposition of these universal directives. In addition to citing studies documenting the uncertain relationship between firm financial performance and director independence, these academics proffer a host of reasons for policymakers to reconsider the regulation of board composition.[17]

Why might director independence mandates produce corporate boards lacking the necessary expertise to function effectively, whether as advisors or as monitors? Should boards include at least one member of the senior executive team (for example, the chief financial officer) in addition to the company's CEO? Why or why not?

5. Despite widespread agreement for the proposition that independent directors are indispensable to good corporate governance, there actually is no uniform definition of "independent director." Generally, "independent director" refers to a director who is not employed by the corporation and, other than serving on the board, has no economic, family, or other personal ties to the corporation and its management. Although the NYSE and NASDAQ both require that listed companies include a majority of "independent directors" on their boards, the exchanges' rules define the term using similar but not identical bright-line tests.

In contrast, Delaware law does not mandate that corporations chartered in the state include any independent directors on their boards. However, as we will see in the next several chapters, decisions made by independent directors, defined contextually in Delaware's case law, are entitled to greater deference by reviewing courts. What are the benefits and costs of disuniformity in this area? Classifying board mem-

---

17. *See, e.g.,* Roberta S. Karmel, *Is the Independent Director Model Broken?*, 37 Sea. U. L. Rev. 775 (2013); Lisa M. Fairfax, *The Uneasy Case for the Inside Director*, 96 Iowa L. Rev. 127 (2010).

bers as independent or non-independent requires careful scrutiny. Stated most simply, an independent director has no connection with the company other than his or her seat on the board. Assuming independent directors' "comparative advantages" in governing public corporations, as described by Professor Gordon, why do you think the Delaware legislature has declined to mandate their election and/or their participation on certain key board committees?

6. Commentators and even judicial opinions sometimes use the terms "independent director" and "disinterested director" interchangeably, but the two phrases actually have different meanings. A disinterested director is a person who does not have an economic or personal interest in a transaction or other matter before the board for decision. *See Rales v. Blasband*, 634 A.2d 927, 936 (Del. 1993) (a director is "interested" if he "will receive a personal financial benefit from [the] transaction that is not equally shared by the stockholders"). Disinterested directors' informed approval of conflict of interest transactions may insulate managers from legal liability for self-dealing and other breaches of loyalty to the firm, as we will see in Chapter 5. Although disinterested directors may not necessarily qualify as independent directors, independent directors' votes should qualify as disinterested, except when directors set their own compensation for service on the board.

7. As Professor Gordon documents, the "rise of independent directors" presumes that non-management board members who have no familial or financial relationships with the corporation will monitor company executives more actively for the benefit of the firm and its shareholders. Why might this assumption be misguided? What incentives/disincentives might affect directors' commitment to question or challenge senior management? Can you think of circumstances that might compromise independent directors' ability to perform their oversight functions effectively? How might CEOs influence board members to relax their supervision or otherwise insulate themselves from effective monitoring by directors who nonetheless satisfy the regulatory independence standards?

8. Professor Donald Langevoort has argued that directors' independence should signify not just the absence of financial or other relations to management but also "a willingness to bring a high degree of rigor and skeptical objectivity to the evaluation of company management and its plans and proposals."[18] In the aftermath of scandals at Enron, WorldCom, and other companies, behavioral psychologists and sociologists considered the roles of the boards of directors in the firms' demise. Although directors' conduct is not directly observable, academics theorize that the "genteel pressures of camaraderie and community between [directors] and officers, ... may have a subtly corrosive effect on their ability to monitor and exert oversight."[19] Governance experts

18. Donald C. Langevoort, *The Human Nature of Corporate Boards: Law, Norms, and the Unintended Consequences of Independence and Accountability*, 89 Geo. L.J. 797, 799 (2001).

19. John Armour & Jeffrey N. Gordon, *Systemic Harms and Shareholder Value*, 6 J. Legal Anal. 35, 66 (2014).

long have recognized the tendency of directors, like other persons who function in groups, to create harmonious work environments. Boardroom cultures, then, may promote teamwork and consensus at the expense of constructive skepticism and dissent. As Home Depot founder Kenneth Langone once explained, "Almost no one wants to be a skunk at a lawn party."

How might board committees charged with nominating new outside directors evaluate the "willingness" of potential candidates to monitor management rigorously? Is there any way for shareholders to gauge whether an outside director already sitting on the board is a "yes man" or an independent thinker who exercises "skeptical objectivity"?

9. Although cases and commentary on director independence often center on the professional, personal, and economic ties between an outside director and the firm or its executives, Delaware courts have recognized that outside directors' independence also may be compromised through control or domination by a CEO or other interested party, including by force of will. As the Delaware Supreme Court explained in *Telxon Corp. v. Meyerson*,[20] "'[i]t is the care, attention and sense of individual responsibility to the performance of one's duties … that generally touches on independence'" and "[d]irectors must not only be independent, but must act independently" in order to invoke the business judgment rule. Furthermore, a dominating director may create an atmosphere of intimidation that impairs the ability of other directors to vote independently on a transaction.[21] That said, Delaware courts "rarely" find that an outside director has been controlled.[22]

10. Regardless of their objectivity and willingness to monitor, independent directors cannot perform their oversight function effectively if they do not understand enough about the company and its industry to ask the right questions of management and its advisers. Critics of the director independence regulations include Warren Buffet, respected Chairman of Berkshire Hathaway, who famously remarked, "Over a span of 40 years, I have been on 19 public company boards and have interacted with perhaps 250 directors. Most of them were 'independent' as defined by today's rules. But their contribution to shareholder well-being was minimal at best. These people simply did not know enough about the business."

As Mr. Buffet's experience indicates, corporate governance reformers have emphasized directors' independence while largely ignoring board members' expertise. (Sarbanes-Oxley requires that at least one qualified financial expert sit on the board's

---

20. 802 A.2d 257, 264 (Del. 2002).

21. *See New Jersey Carpenters Pension Fund v. infoGROUP Inc.*, 2011 Del. Ch. LEXIS 147 (Oct. 6, 2011) (refusing to dismiss breach of duty of loyalty claim where it was reasonable to infer that interested director dominated other board members, "rendering them nonindependent" through "pattern of threats aimed at intimidating them" to approve merger).

22. Ann M. Scarlett, *Confusion and Unpredictability in Shareholder Derivative Litigation: The Delaware Courts Response to Recent Corporate Scandals*, 60 Fla. L. Rev. 589, 617 (2008).

audit committee. *See* 15 U.S.C. § 7265.) There is no requirement that directors have any knowledge of the firm's industry, much less its business. Nevertheless, research confirms that outside directors already familiar with the industry benefit their boards. Such directors impart a greater understanding of the firm's risks and opportunities within its sector of the economy, as well as understanding the key players in the industry and the regulatory environment in which the firm operates.

Academic studies also indicate that directors with experience in the company's industry more effectively monitor CEOs than board members without such experience. In a study of S&P 1500 firms, boards with a higher proportion of directors with industry experience had fewer earnings restatements, greater sensitivity to paying CEOs for performance, and were more likely replace CEOs following poor firm performance.[23] Can outside directors contribute meaningfully to the work of the board without experience in the relevant industry or a deep understanding of the business?

Is independence a reliable proxy for vigilance? Consider the following case decided by then-Vice Chancellor Leo Strine, who became Chief Justice of the Delaware Supreme Court in 2014.

Hampshire Group, Ltd. v. Kuttner

Delaware Chancery Court
2010 Del. Ch. LEXIS 144 (2010)

STRINE, VICE CHANCELLOR:

Hampshire, a Delaware corporation with its principal place of business in Anderson, South Carolina, is a leading provider of women's and men's sweaters, wovens and knits, and is a growing designer and marketer of branded apparel in the United States. Hampshire operates through three wholly-owned subsidiaries, Hampshire Designers, Inc. and Item-Eyes for women's apparel, and Hampshire Brands for men's apparel, which all offer products under several brand names as well as private label to multiple channels of distribution, including national and regional department stores and mass market retailers.

Kuttner founded Hampshire in 1977, and ran the company as its Chairman and CEO for almost three decades. He and his family owned approximately 30% of Hampshire's outstanding stock. Kuttner's lengthy term as CEO ended in September 2006 when he was asked by the board to resign due to the preliminary findings of an Audit Committee investigation. By all accounts, Kuttner was a flamboyant and energetic leader with a high public profile and a colorful way of dressing.

---

23. Ronald W. Maulis, Christian Ruzzier, Sheng Xiao & Shan Zhao, *Do Independent Expert Directors Matter?* (2012).

Many of the Hampshire directors had served on the board with Kuttner for decades. For example, Harvey Sperry had been on the board since 1977, having been a partner at Willkie Farr & Gallagher LLP during many of those years. Willkie Farr, not coincidentally, was Hampshire's outside corporate counsel for that entire time and continues in that role. Michael Jackson, a former director, served on the board from 1986 to 1996, and 2001 to May 1, 2009. Jackson was also a founding member of Ironwood Partners, LLC, a venture capital company that was retained by Hampshire as a financial consultant and with which Kuttner invested, and was involved in the deferred compensation issue Hampshire raises in this litigation. Joel Goldberg served on the Hampshire board from 1998 to March 26, 2009, at which time he resigned after admitting that he had submitted improper expense reports to the company.

The outside directors of Hampshire were aware of Kuttner's idiosyncrasies and taste for high living, and they indulged it. A good example is that Kuttner replaced his company car, a Lamborghini, with another modest vehicle, a Ferrari. As we shall see, the board was either unwilling to or unable to actually direct Kuttner even when they wanted to do so, and this case largely arose when the board's hand was forced by the Internal Review Memorandum in June 2006 from relatively new employees.

Like Sperry and Jackson, defendant Clayton was a long-time member of the Hampshire team, joining Hampshire one year after Kuttner founded the company, in 1978, as the Vice President of Finance and Controller, working out of Hampshire's South Carolina office. Five years later, in 1983, Kuttner promoted Clayton to CFO. Clayton also served as Hampshire's Treasurer and as the secretary for the Hampshire board and Audit Committee meetings. Clayton held his position as CFO until 2000 when he gave up those duties. Clayton, who is about 71 now, enjoyed only a short respite from being CFO. He was called back to that role in November 2003 when his successor departed. Clayton served as CFO from that time until April 1, 2006, and the company looked for a permanent CFO during the latter period of that stint. Like Kuttner, Clayton was terminated by the board in September 2006 due to the preliminary findings of the Audit Committee investigation. As CFO, in 2005 Clayton had earned a salary of $168,000, plus an additional $450,000 in bonuses and other compensation.

Roger Clark began his employment with Hampshire at its South Carolina office in 1998, serving as Vice President-Finance and later Principal Accounting Officer, until he was laid off in December 2006. Clark reported directly to the CFO—who was William Hodge from 2001 to 2003 until Clayton again took over the position—and was charged with overseeing Hampshire's bookkeeping functions, maintaining its ledger, and preparing its financial statements. As Principal Accounting Officer, in 2006 Clark earned $104,000, plus a bonus of approximately $30,000.

As a matter of full context, Clayton and Clark both had business relations with Kuttner during their employment with Hampshire. Specifically, in 2003, Hampshire sold Hampshire Investments, Limited ("HIL") a subsidiary that was involved in real estate investments. That subsidiary was purchased by Kuttner, Clayton, and another investor. Clark had done HIL's books when it was owned by Hampshire, and continued to fulfill that function for HIL after its sale for a modest fee. Kuttner also helped Clark, through loans, to acquire $50,000, or a 1% stake, in HIL stock....

Rancor within the long-time Hampshire crew really began when the Hampshire board received a communication it could not ignore. Between 2004 and 2006, Hampshire had hired some new high-ranking employees. Maura McNerney Langley came aboard in April 2004 as Compliance Officer after working for Hampshire's outside advisor, Deloitte & Touche LLP on the Hampshire account. Heath Golden, a former Willkie Farr lawyer, came aboard in August 2005 as Vice President of Business Development and Assistant Secretary, was promoted to General Counsel in May 2006, and eventually became CEO in April 2009. Jonathan Norwood joined Hampshire in April 2006 as Vice President and Chief Financial Officer, replacing Clayton, and later took on Clark's role of Principal Accounting Officer.

During the course of their new employment, the three became concerned about loose practices around Hampshire, even though a couple of them participated themselves in a few instances of such practices. In May 2006, these employees let fly with what they styled as an Internal Review Memorandum. The Internal Review Memorandum outlined matters that these employees suspected involved illegal activity or violations of corporate policy. The authors suspected that there was a "a long history of management utilizing Company assets for personal benefit, taking unauthorized compensation in various forms, and engaging in unauthorized related party and other transactions that unduly enriched themselves." The Internal Review Memorandum discussed issues that predominantly involved Kuttner, such as Kuttner's involvement in a stock repurchase program, problems with Kuttner's untimely and undocumented expense reports, mismanagement of deferred compensation funds by Kuttner and Clayton, and the fact that several Hampshire employees—including Clayton and Clark—worked for other companies run by Kuttner. The Memorandum recommended to the board that Kuttner, Clayton, Clark, and Kuttner's two secretaries be put on immediate leave, that they be denied access to the company, and that an internal investigation be undertaken. Absent "appropriate action by the Audit Committee," the Internal Review Memorandum authors said that they would "report [their] findings to the SEC, IRS, and other appropriate authorities."

At this point, Hampshire's board consisted of five members: Kuttner; Joel Goldberg, who served as a member of the board's Audit Committee and chair of the Compensation Committee; Harvey Sperry, a member of the Audit Committee; Irwin Winter, the chair of the Audit Committee; and Michael Jackson. The Internal Review Memorandum was explosive and could not be ignored. The Memorandum and its preliminary findings were presented to the Audit Committee on June 14, 2006. Kuttner, as well as Clark, Clayton, and Kuttner's two assistants, were placed on administrative leave the next week because of their involvement in the issues raised in the Memorandum. The board thereafter launched a full-scale investigation, and hired Navigant Consulting Inc., and the law firm of Paul, Weiss, Rifkind, Wharton & Garrison LLP as its principal outside advisors. Hampshire also hired additional outside advisors, including Ernst & Young and Dixon Hughes to investigate and remedy specific issues that were raised in the Memorandum.

The board also appointed an executive committee, consisting of all of its directors other than Kuttner, to direct the affairs of the corporation. The outside advisors were given wide latitude and a huge budget to investigate the issues in the Internal Review Memorandum, but were not authorized to consider what role the board played in the matters raised in the Memorandum. That is, it appears that the outside advisors were instructed to focus their aim on the employees put on leave and not to stir up issues that might implicate the board or other officers.

Navigant and Paul Weiss investigated all of the 23 issues raised in the Internal Review Memorandum. Their investigation "included reviews of documentation, interviews with employees of Hampshire group ... and electronic document and email searches...." Notably, the investigation did not include interviews of the employees who were put on leave—including Clark, Clayton, and Kuttner. The Audit Committee heard the preliminary findings of Navigant and Paul Weiss on September 20, 2006, and, as a result of those findings, recommended to the board that Kuttner and Clayton be terminated. Navigant and Paul Weiss found that 16 of the 23 issues were not substantiated concerns, but found that seven of the issues did raise important compliance problems. The board voted to terminate Kuttner and Clayton on September 25, 2006. A public announcement of their termination was made that same day.

The Audit Committee investigation concluded one month later on October 25, 2006, and the board was confronted with large investigation costs. Hampshire spent $2.7 million on fees for Paul Weiss, and another $2.2 million on fees for Navigant. Other outside advisors that Hampshire consulted during the investigation, including Deloitte, cost Hampshire nearly $600,000.

On December 1, 2006, Clark was notified that his employment would be terminated on December 29, 2006. At that time, Clark was admonished to use his remaining vacation time. Although Clark had been subject to investigation in the internal investigation and the results of the investigation linked him to the issues leading to the Restatement, he was not formally terminated for cause when his termination was documented. Instead, it was rationalized that his job could be performed by Langley. Two weeks after Clark was given his termination notice, Hampshire announced that it would restate its annual and quarterly financial statements for the year 2003 through the fiscal quarter ending April 1, 2006 based on the findings of the investigation. The decision to restate came in spite of the finding of Hampshire's outside advisors that there was "no evidence of misleading financial statements." That is, the internal investigation had not found evidence that Kuttner, Clayton, Clark, or others had manipulated Hampshire's earnings in any material way so as to inflate artificially the corporation's reported GAAP earnings. What problems with the books existed were largely due to a failure of the corporation to obtain proper approval for its executive compensation plan as required by § 162(m) of the Internal Revenue Code (the "§ 162(m) Plan"). After the investigation was complete, Hampshire restated its financial statements for the year 2003 through the fiscal quarter ending April 1, 2006 in the total amount of nearly $7.7 million. The record indicates that but for the failure of Hampshire to seek stockholder approval of the § 162(m) Plan after 2002, Hampshire may not have restated its financials because the other issues were not of a huge magnitude and could have been rectified in ways that did not require a restatement.

But given the need to rectify the § 162(m) Plan issue and the fact that the corporation needed to ensure that it reserved for the potential financial consequences of several of the issues investigated (for example, the potential tax implications of compensation given to Item-Eyes executives for personal expenses and deferred compensation issues), a full Restatement was made.

Hampshire accuses Clayton and Clark of breaching their fiduciary duty by their involvement in a program whereby unsold or mutilated sweaters made by Hampshire were donated to charities on behalf of various Hampshire employees who, in turn, took personal tax deductions. Hampshire could not claim a tax deduction for its surplus sweaters because they were deemed to have no value on the retail market due to their imperfections. Thus, Hampshire donated the sweaters to various charities, and requested that the charities send gift letters reflecting that the donation had been made by a Hampshire employee and attributing a value to the sweaters, which the employee could then use to take a tax deduction.

The problem is that if they had no value if contributed by Hampshire, it is difficult to see how they could have value if contributed to charities on behalf of employees. To be more concrete, one can actually see how remaindered sweaters could have real human value to people in need, as they would keep them warm. What is harder to justify is how they could have "tax value" if the sweaters had no commercial value. The sweaters were perfect for genuine charity in which the giver expects nothing in return.

But that is not what this program was about. The employees "donating" the sweaters were permitted to act as if they owned the sweaters and were personally donating them to charities. Of course, if the sweaters had value and were given to the employees by their employer, that value might, one suspects, also be considered by the IRS to be income to the employee. And Hampshire was taking the position that it could remainder the sweaters precisely because they could not be sold.

This annual sweater-fest went on for some time. The corporation annually remaindered a large number of sweaters to various charities on behalf of many company employees, officers, and directors who subsequently claimed tax deductions. For example, directors Goldberg and Jackson both took sweater deductions. Culang, who later served as CEO of Hampshire, took tax deductions for sweater donations in 2002, 2003, and 2005. Golden, the former general counsel, current CEO and Internal Review Memorandum author, took a tax deduction in 2005. Clark took just one deduction in 2003 after Kuttner gave him three "donation" receipts for $4,000. Clayton tried to take tax deductions for donations as well.

I cannot conclude that at all times Clayton knew this sweater caper was improper. I cannot conclude at any time that Clark knew. Even many trained lawyers, like Golden, and financial professionals, like Clayton and Clark, may not understand the complex rules governing charitable contributions of tangible items. Given how widespread the practice was at Hampshire, I find it hard to conclude that the program was the product of bad faith or gross negligence. The reality is that the sweaters probably had some sale value and the amounts per sweater attributed were far short of what Hampshire would profitably sell sweaters at in retail stores. Creative tax planning is, for better or worse, a quintessentially American tradition.

But the problem for Clayton is what he did after he was informed that the program should cease. In December 2004, the Audit Committee received an anonymous whistle blower call reporting the sweater donation program. The Audit Committee told Clayton, who was the CFO at the time, that the sweaters could not be treated as a gift to employees under the tax code. Winter, the chairman of the Audit Committee told Clayton that he could continue to donate sweaters to charity, and even make the donation on behalf of an employee, but that employees were not entitled to a tax deduction from the donation. Clayton confirmed that the sweaters would thereafter "be given, by the company, to charity."

But Clayton continued the sweater donation scheme through 2005 and into 2006. Clayton took tax deductions for himself in 2005 and 2006 after the Audit Committee had informed him that employees were not entitled to donations, and others, including Golden, Culang, and board members Jackson and Goldberg, did the same. The evidence convinces me that Clayton circumvented the Audit Committee's instructions because he was drafting form letters to charities that they could turn into final letters and provide Hampshire employees with documentation supporting amounts that they claim as charitable deductions.

It is true that Navigant concluded, that "[t]his issue [did] not have any financial implications for the company, only to individual employees who may have taken improper tax deductions." But Clayton nonetheless knowingly caused the corporation to engage in legally questionable activity by facilitating improper tax deductions by Hampshire's employees, board members, and officers. I find this to be a breach of the duty of loyalty.

As to Clark, by contrast, I find no evidence that he knowingly did anything improper by taking a single tax deduction in 2003, and reiterate that the current Hampshire CEO, a trained lawyer who served for three years as Hampshire's General Counsel, took a similar deduction.

Comments and Questions

1. How would you grade the Hampshire board's performance of its monitoring responsibilities before receipt of the Internal Review Memorandum? Why is it relevant that the board knew about and even "indulged" CEO Kuttner's "taste for high living" (e.g., driving a Lamborghini and then a Ferrari as his company cars)? How was the board's hand forced by its receipt of the Internal Review Memorandum? Clayton con-

tinued the sweater deduction program for more than a year after the Audit Committee instructed him to end it. What does this fact tell us about the monitoring of senior executives by the board?

2. The opinion notes that the outside law and accounting firms retained to investigate the allegations set forth in the Internal Review Memorandum "were not authorized to consider what role the board played in the matters raised in the Memorandum." The court goes so far as to suppose that "the outside advisors were instructed to focus their aim on the employees put on leave and not to stir up issues that might implicate the board or other officers." Should the Audit Committee have instructed its outside advisors to investigate the board's supervision of Kuttner and the other implicated managers?

3. From what you know of their qualifications, did Hampshire's directors have sufficient skill and expertise to monitor the firm's senior management? Why or why not? To the extent that the Hampshire board had no knowledge about certain wrongful activities (the sweater deduction scheme, for example), what does the board's ignorance suggest about its commitment to monitoring? What does the board's ignorance suggest about its processes? Regardless of their commitment to active policing, what obstacles might impede independent directors from monitoring management effectively? However impartial they might be, outside directors must have adequate, objective information to monitor executives effectively. How will outside directors likely receive the information necessary to fulfill their oversight responsibilities? Are all sources of information equally trustworthy?

4. Independent, disinterested directors perform a number of key functions under state law, as we will see. For example, they monitor corporate dealings that may be tainted by management's self-interest, including executives' compensation. Similarly, independent, disinterested directors play key decision-making roles in change of control transactions and the prosecution of derivative litigation. Directors often engage their own experts, including outside counsel, to assist them in fulfilling such responsibilities. These experts not only provide substantive advice on the decisions at hand, but they also may guide independent directors in how to discharge their fiduciary duties to the firm and its shareholders. As we will see in later chapters, state law provides that directors may rely reasonably on these advisors.

5. The tab for the outside investigation procured by the Audit Committee exceeded $4 million, an amount far exceeding Clayton's and Clark's potential liability for breaching their duties to the company. Was such an expensive outside investigation necessary? Why or why not? Could the Audit Committee simply have asked the firm's general counsel to investigate the allegations?

6. The court notes that many Hampshire directors served on the board for decades with Kuttner. We will return to directors' tenure at the end of this chapter. Furthermore, at least two board members, an attorney and a venture capitalist, had ownership interests in firms that for many years had provided important legal and financial services to Hampshire. What real incentives did these outside directors have to monitor Kuttner?

Although director independence has continued as a focal point for corporate governance reforms after Enron, courts and commentators increasingly have recognized the challenge of defining independence. We examine regulatory and judicial standards for independence and disinterestedness in the next several chapters.

Of course, independence — regardless of how it is defined — does not ensure that directors have the expertise and access necessary to provide diligent oversight of the firm's affairs. Exposure of multi-year financial reporting frauds and revelations of unabashed self-dealing by CEOs and other senior executives in the early years of the new century underscored this vulnerability. Critics of post-Enron corporate governance reforms argued further that preoccupation with director independence deprives corporate boards of the services of individuals with critical qualifications, experience, and skills. A director with no ties to management or the firm may not have the knowledge necessary to assess management misfeasance, much less the skills to ferret out fraud and self-dealing. Indeed, outside directors depend largely on management for critical information. Even if they are quite familiar with the company and its industry, outside directors almost certainly lack both the time and the firm-specific information to supervise company executives closely. Further, information asymmetries may weaken directors' decision-making authority. In addition, outside directors also may lack incentives to monitor management vigorously. "[I]ndependent directors may not be truly independent, because whatever the formal procedures, they are *de facto* selected by management, and they have insufficient personal incentive to act very independently." Directors who question executive proposals or otherwise challenge management may experience social sanctions from the CEO and other directors. We consider the increasingly higher expectations placed on independent directors — as well their ability and willingness to fulfill them — beginning in Chapter 4.

IV. Board Size, Structure, and Leadership

Directors are charged by shareholders and regulators with establishing and maintaining effective governance systems. Over the past several decades, as directors have assumed greater legal responsibility for management oversight, the size, structure, and leadership of public company boards have transformed.

On average, twelve directors serve on the boards of the largest U.S. public companies.[24] After growing in the years following enactment of Sarbanes-Oxley, large public company boards have downsized over the past few years. Heidrick & Struggles, an executive search firm, found that the number of board seats in Fortune 500 companies shrunk from 5267 in 2009 to 4637 in 2013. This trend is supported by recent

---

24. Shearman & Sterling LLP, *Corporate Governance & Executive Compensation 2015* 22 (2015) (surveying the top 100 largest U.S. public companies).

research finding that companies with fewer board members outperform their industry peers.[25] A study of corporations with at least $10 billion in market capitalization found that firms with smaller boards tended to outperform their peer companies with larger boards. Governance experts theorize that smaller boards may meet more often, engage in more robust debates, and make more timely decisions. They suggest that small board directors must assume more responsibility for the work of the board. Furthermore, boards with fewer members may monitor management more effectively than larger boards because directors cannot shirk their oversight duties as easily, nor can they simply free-ride on their colleagues policing efforts. Small boards not only supervise the performance of executives more closely, but they also are more likely to assess their own performance regularly. On the other hand, since there are fewer members to perform the board's work, small board directors necessarily carry larger work loads. Thus, while larger boards have difficulty coordinating and communicating, more members are available to divide the labor. Larger boards also facilitate diversity, networking, and information gathering.

Board leadership also has generated debate for at least four decades. Unlike their foreign counterparts in the United Kingdom, Canada, and most European countries, CEOs of American firms traditionally have chaired the corporations' boards. Directors who serve as chairmen of the board not only preside over board meetings, but they also set the agendas for each session, deciding the matters to be considered by the full board. Thus, board chairs ensure review and implementation of board resolutions and policies adopted by the board. Finally, in many companies, board chairs make committee assignments and, therefore, determine the directors responsible for various matters. Prompted by revelations that CEOs dominated corporate governance processes at corporations damaged by fraud and scandal, regulators and academics have called for companies to separate the role of CEO and board chair since the 1970s. Shareholder activists increasingly have agitated against unified leadership.

Reform advocates contend that boards cannot perform their oversight function effectively without the leadership of an independent director. Whereas unified leadership structures permit the CEO to control the flow of information to outside directors, appointment of an independent board chair reduces the cost of information gathering for outside directors, enhancing transparency and improving outside directors' ability to monitor the CEO and senior executive team. Since unity in command also may create a boardroom environment that suppresses questioning and dissent, separating leadership may boost outside directors' engagement. Issues of particular sensitivity to the CEO (developments that might portray the CEO or the senior executive team in a negative light) more likely will come before directors earlier. Outside directors may evaluate the CEO's management and decisions with greater candor and objectivity, strengthening the CEO's accountability, if not job performance. Splitting

---

25. Joann S. Lublin, *Smaller Boards Get Bigger Returns*, Wall St. J., Aug. 26, 2014.

the leadership functions also benefits the company by focusing CEOs on daily company operations and strategies. Finally, research indicates that the cost of compensating one individual as CEO and chairman is significantly higher than the cost of paying two individuals to perform those management responsibilities.

Corporate leaders and their professional associations (like the National Association of Corporate Directors) have attacked "one-size-fits-all" prescriptions for good governance, arguing that firms should adopt whatever leadership structure best suits their organization. Boards satisfied with unified command argue that there is little, if any, evidence that separating the roles of chair and CEO improves long-term corporate performance. Even if the CEO/chair does exercise weighty influence over corporate decisions, it does not follow that compelling separation improves corporate performance. According to companies with dual CEO/chairmen, unified leadership affords clear accountability and provides benefits of deep operational and industry experience. Further, because concentrating ultimate authority in a single individual is essential to effective management of many large businesses, nonexecutive board chairs actually may not (and cannot) function independently from the CEO. In short, duality enables more timely and efficient decision making.

Outside lead directors and nonexecutive chairs preside over more corporate boards today than at the beginning of the millennium. According to studies, the proportion of S&P 500 corporations with bifurcated leadership increased from 25 to 43 percent in the decade after Congress enacted Sarbanes-Oxley, and more U.S. companies have separated the roles of board chair and CEO in the most recent years. Still, many of the nation's leading corporations have resisted pressure to reform their command structures. As of 2015, CEOs continued to serve as board chairs for nearly two-thirds of the largest U.S. public companies.[26] Rather than appointing non-executives as their chairmen, these firms have augmented their boards' leadership by appointing independent directors to serve as lead directors.

Generally, lead directors (sometimes called presiding directors) do not assume the formal duties of board chair; instead, lead directors officiate at meetings of the full board only in the chairman's absence or when the need otherwise arises. Nonetheless, lead directors do preside over executive sessions or other meetings of non-management directors. The lead director also may contribute to the board's agenda (thus breaking the CEO's monopoly over agenda setting), serve as liaison between the board chairman and the outside directors, and provide leadership for the outside directors, encouraging stronger voice. Finally, lead directors may have special responsibilities in evaluating the performance and compensation of the chairman/CEO.

Nothing in federal or state law or stock exchange rules requires that corporations separate the offices of CEO and board chair. However, with activist shareholders focusing greater attention on board leadership, the SEC and the stock exchanges have

---

26. Shearman & Sterling LLP, *Corporate Governance & Executive Compensation 2015* 16 (2015).

considered the case for and against regulatory reform. As with other corporate governance initiatives, the SEC began to address investors' concerns by requiring that public companies disclose to shareholders more information about the firms' board leadership structure.

Proxy Disclosure Enhancements

Exchange Act Release No. 61175 (Dec. 16, 2009)

New Disclosure about Board Leadership Structure and the Board's Role in Risk Oversight

We proposed a new disclosure requirement to Item 407 of Regulation S-K and a corresponding amendment to Item 7 of Schedule 14A to require disclosure of the company's leadership structure and why the company believes it is the most appropriate structure for it at the time of the filing....

1. Proposed Amendments

Under the proposed amendments, companies would be required to disclose their leadership structure and the reasons why they believe that it is an appropriate structure for the company. As part of this proposed disclosure, companies would be required to disclose whether and why they have chosen to combine or separate the principal executive officer and board chair positions. In addition, in some companies the role of principal executive officer and board chairman are combined, and a lead independent director is designated to chair meetings of the independent directors. For these companies, the proposed amendments would require disclosure of whether and why the company has a lead independent director, as well as the specific role the lead independent director plays in the leadership of the company. In proposing this requirement, we noted that different leadership structures may be suitable for different companies depending on factors such as the size of a company, the nature of a company's business, or internal control considerations, among other things. Irrespective of the type of leadership structure selected by a company, the proposed requirements were intended to provide investors with insights about why the company has chosen that particular leadership structure.

2. Comments on the Proposed Amendments

Comments were mostly supportive of the proposals. Commenters believed the disclosure regarding a company's leadership structure ... would provide useful information to investors ... Some commenters opposed the disclosures. Many of these commenters believed that the proposed amendments were too vague and would likely elicit boilerplate descriptions of a company's management hierarchy ... would not provide significant insight or meaning to investors.

3. Final Rule

After consideration of the comments, we are adopting the proposals substantially as proposed with a few technical revisions in response to comments. We believe that, in making voting and investment decisions, investors should be provided with meaningful information about the corporate governance practices of companies. As we noted in the Proposing Release, one important aspect of a company's corporate governance practices is its board's leadership structure. Disclosure of a company's board leadership structure and the reasons the company believes that its board leadership structure is appropriate will increase the transparency for investors as to how the board functions.

Comments and Questions

1. The international norm for board leadership is to separate the positions of chairman and CEO. In the United States, however, the norm is reversed. Governance activists and many institutional shareholders consider separation of the two roles to be best practice. What are the pros and cons of each structure? Which arrangement is the most consistent with the monitoring board model of corporate governance?

2. Whether to separate the positions of CEO and board chair has become a hotly debated issue in corporate governance. Shareholder activists continue to pressure corporations to appoint independent board chairs, arguing that CEOs with dual titles exercise undue influence over outside directors, and boards chaired by CEOs cannot reasonably fulfill their oversight responsibilities. In the past decade, S&P 500 companies received more than 300 proxy proposals from shareholders calling for boards to strip their CEOs of the chairman role. In 2015, more than one-third of largest U.S. public companies with a dual CEO/chair received shareholder proposals calling for reform.

3. Since independent directors today hold most seats on large public company boards, the CEO—who also may serve as board chair—often is the only executive of the corporation who also serves as one of the firm's directors. Can you think of any special challenges for CEOs who chair boards operating with supermajorities of non-management directors?

4. Mandatory disclosure of the board's leadership structure became federal law when Congress passed the Dodd-Frank Act in 2010. Section 972 of the Dodd-Frank Act requires public companies to disclose whether the chairman and CEO positions are held by the same person and the reasons for the structure. Why do you think Congress enacted a statute that essentially duplicated the SEC's 2009 rulemaking? Is the federal law any more likely to satisfy shareholders concerned with CEO control over corporate boards? Regardless of whether the disclosure mandate comes from Congress or the SEC, why might disclosure change the prevailing practice of combining the two positions?

5. Surveys indicate that combining the role of CEO and chairman still is common in large public companies. In 2015, 48 percent of S&P 500 companies separated the roles of board chair and CEO between two individuals.[27] However, ten years earlier, only 29 percent of S&P 500 firms in 2005 split the positions. Whether a U.S. corporation has an independent board chair may relate to the size of the firm. Smaller

---

27. Spencer Stuart Board Services, *2015 Spencer Stuart Board Index* 20 (2015).

companies are more likely to separate the roles of chairman and CEO. Can you think of explanations for the variation in practice among differently-sized public companies? Firms that have separated the positions often made the transition during a CEO succession or other significant business change. Why do you think companies prefer to wait for some other transformative event to alter their board leadership structure?

6. Shareholder proposals to separate the roles of CEO and board chair often have failed to garner majority support. For example, JP Morgan Chase chairman and CEO Jamie Dimon retained both of his titles in 2013, the second straight year that activist shareholders failed to garner majority support for appointing an independent board chair. In fact, less than one-third of shareholders voted for the proposal (down from 40 percent the prior year) after Dimon threatened to resign if the measure passed. In recent years, other high profile companies, such as Bank of America and Disney, have recombined the roles of CEO and board chair. The firms emphasize the dearth of research proving that appointment of independent board chairs improves firm financial performance.

7. As at JP Morgan Chase, companies that combine the positions of board chair and CEO nonetheless appoint a non-management, independent board member to serve as lead director. Indeed, one recent survey reports that only eight S&P 500 corporations lacked some form of independent board leadership, either an independent board chair or an independent lead director.[28] What are some advantages and disadvantages of the lead director structure? Might the prevalence of lead directors reduce pressure on public companies to separate the roles of CEO and board chair?

8. If a listed company designates a lead director, NYSE rules require disclosure of his or her name in the listed company's annual proxy statement. Alternatively, the corporation may disclose the procedure by which a presiding director is selected for each executive session. For companies with a combined board chairman/CEO, the appointment of a lead director facilitates compliance with a NYSE rule requiring regularly scheduled executive sessions of non-management directors outside the presence of management. While stopping short of requiring its listed companies to appoint a lead independent director, can you see how the NYSE's rules have encouraged firms to do so?

The listing standards further provide that firms should hold an executive session, including only independent directors, at least once each year. The purpose of compelling these additional meetings is "to empower non-management directors to serve as a more effective check on management." How might non-management directors carry out their monitoring responsibilities differently outside the presence of the CEO or other senior executives? Further, the NYSE specifically instructs that an "independent director must preside over each executive session of the independent directors...." Corporate governance experts advise that corporate bylaws describe the process for calling both scheduled and unscheduled executive sessions. Why do governance experts

---

28. Spencer Stuart Board Services, *2015 Spencer Stuart Board Index* 23 (2015).

advise boards to hold executive sessions on a regular, scheduled — rather than an "as needed" — basis?

9. Recurring questions have arisen about the selection, functions, and authority of lead directors. Most frequently, independent directors appoint an individual from among their ranks to serve as lead director for either an indefinite term or a one-year term. Recent surveys indicate that lead directors typically have served on the board for five or more years. Other than presiding over executive sessions of fellow independent directors, lead directors have no prescribed duties, and their responsibilities vary from firm to firm. Some companies assign to lead directors the authority to call board meetings, and lead directors also may participate in setting board meeting agendas. What role ought lead directors play in corporate governance? Should the law provide greater standardization in this regard?

V. Board Committees

While it is common to speak of decisions by the board of directors (and directors only may act in consort to bind the firm), boards often administer their governance responsibilities through committees. Delaware's General Corporation Law empowers the board to appoint committees and to delegate to them a broad range of responsibilities. Del. Gen. Corp. L. § 141. Today, public company boards rely heavily on the work of committees. Indeed, among the most important innovations in board governance are (1) the implementation of standing board committees tasked with specific functions, and (2) the appointment of special board committees tasked with investigating and deciding specific legal or transactional questions.

Other than an executive committee, the board's principal standing committees include the audit committee, the compensation committee, and the nominating/governance committee. The boards of most financial institutions also utilize risk assessment committees. Much of the board's monitoring work takes place through its standing committees, and outside directors typically sit on at least one such committee. According to best practices, each standing committee is chaired by a non-management director and staffed with non-management (independent) directors. If the committee includes management directors, non-management directors may meet in executive committee sessions to provide the opportunity for candid discussions of matters (such as CEO performance) that management's presence otherwise would inhibit.

After Enron, board committees and related processes came under increasing scrutiny. Corporations engaged governance experts to educate board members on how to better fulfill their committee responsibilities. Boards adopted charters for each standing committee, defining the committee's role, responsibilities, and practices, and public companies today often make their board committee charters available publicly. Outside directors may share best committee practices from board to board, transmitting information and norms from company to company. In theory, this networking function improves the governance of public companies.

The earliest-instituted standing committee—and the board committee subject to the greatest regulation—is the audit committee. Audit committees have special responsibilities for overseeing the reliability of corporate financial statements and audits. Regulators considered proposals for mandatory audit committees as early as 1939. In 1974, the SEC instituted a rulemaking requiring public companies to disclose whether the board had established an audit committee. Four years later, the Commission published guidance regarding the audit committee's functions. The NYSE began requiring audit committees in 1977. Indeed, by 1979, virtually all NYSE-listed companies had audit committees, and for 92 percent of the firms, audit committee members were non-management directors. By the end of the 1980s, the NASDAQ and the Amex introduced audit committee requirements as well.

In 2002, greater uniformity and independence was imposed by federal legislative fiat. SOX required that public companies put in place an audit committee as a condition for listing on a stock exchange. Audit committees must be comprised entirely of independent directors. Moreover, SOX required companies to include on the audit committee one or more directors with financial expertise. SOX also mandated that the audit committee assume sole responsibility for the firm's relations with external auditors and firms' audit policies. In listed companies, it is the audit committee that has the authority to engage, compensate, oversee, and dismiss the outside auditor. In addition, the audit committee may review risk management practices, compliance with laws and regulations, and safety and environmental audit functions.

Compensation committees also have become widely used in the past two decades. The SEC did not require disclosure of the compensation committee or its membership until 1992. Previously, it was common for management directors to sit on the compensation committee, although outside directors typically constituted a committee majority. In the aftermath of Enron, however, the stock exchanges mandated that listed companies staff compensation committees with independent directors only. The Dodd-Frank Act affirmed Congress's agreement with this requirement for most public companies.

The compensation committee studies, deliberates, and makes recommendations to the full board regarding how and how much to compensate the CEO, corporate officers, and other members of the CEO's senior executive team. The committee also establishes performance guidelines for the CEO and then evaluates the CEO's performance against these standards. Finally, the compensation committee will make recommendations to the board concerning the remuneration of outside directors.

Borrowing from the statutory model adopted in SOX for audit committees, Dodd-Frank authorized compensation committees to select and retain any consultants used to advise them in determining executive pay. Congress intended board compensation committees to receive objective advice from experts independent of management.

In response to pressure from shareholders for more voice in director elections, board nominating committees (separately discussed below) have become increasingly prevalent in the past two decades. NYSE-listed companies must form a nominating committee composed entirely of independent directors. Nasdaq rules do not mandate nominating committees, but if a Nasdaq-listed firm does not establish such a committee, then independent directors constituting a majority of the board's independent directors must select or recommend candidates to the board. Each company also must have a formal written charter or board resolutions addressing the nominations process.

The nominating committee identifies, interviews, recruits, and nominates new members for the board of directors. Like the audit and compensation committees, the nominating committee will consult with outside experts (search firms) for advice. Nominating committees typically undertake additional governance responsibilities; the nominating and corporate governance committee now typically assumes a leading role in a broad array of corporate governance matters, including the development and implementation of corporate governance guidelines, establishment of director criteria and review of candidates, evaluation of the performance of the board itself and its committees, consideration of shareholder proposals and, in some cases, management succession planning. they develop corporate governance principles, recommend board committee assignments, and oversee director evaluations. The nominating/ corporate governance committee may decide outside director compensation, but in some firms, the compensation committee is responsible for that area.

The NYSE and NASDAQ require listed companies to adopt and disclose codes of business conduct and ethics for directors, officers, and employees. In addition, NYSE-listed companies must adopt and disclose corporate governance guidelines addressing director qualification standards, responsibilities, access to management and (as appropriate) independent advisors, compensation, director orientation and continuing education, annual evaluation of board performance, and succession. NASDAQ listing standards are silent regarding corporate governance guidelines.

The model for the fully independent board committee is the "special committee," a committee established under circumstances in which management's interests conflict most directly with the interests of the corporation and its shareholders. Beginning in the 1970s, this structural innovation became widely used by directors when deciding two types of issues. First, boards establish special committees to review certain change of control transactions. These transactions include management buyouts which management is part of a group that seeks to buy out the public shareholders' equity; or a parent-subsidiary merger, in which it is assumed that the target management's allegiance is likely to be towards the controlling shareholder who appointed them. Another case was a shareholder derivative suit, in which officers and directors allegedly violated a fiduciary duty to the corporation.

The nominal independence of special committees is buttressed by their retention of independent advisors, particularly independent legal counsel. Such independent advisors, whose allegiance was to the special committee rather than management, could lead the process and promote a greater sense of independence by special committee members. However, the processes employed by special committees, such as the committees' authority to retain its own expert advisors, seemed to have little impact on on-going board practice. Most often, special committees were formed and convened in "final period" situations, after which the special committee was dissolved. Moreover, the potential power exercised by a special committee advised by its own outside experts was well understood by corporate management and, in some cases, strongly resisted. Still, the lessons learned from special committees underpin contemporary best practices as well as certain contemporary regulations, such as those giving audit committees authority over the auditors' employment and giving the audit committees power to hire their own counsel and other advisors.

VI. Selection of Directors

Although shareholders elect directors (and state corporation codes set forth the voting rights of shares), neither the Delaware General Corporation Law nor the Model Business Corporate Act expressly addresses nomination rights. This omission is important insofar as the directors selected to serve certainly influence the board's performance. In practice, the board of directors exercises considerable control over board elections by nominating the slate of candidates for shareholders' review and approval at their annual meeting. Most slates nominated by incumbent boards of directors run for election unopposed. Furthermore, public company CEOs influence—if not determine outright—the individuals nominated for board seats.

Critics, then, have long questioned whether directors selected by boards of incumbent directors will act as effective monitors and evaluators of CEOs and their executive teams. Insofar as the CEO determines, or at least influences, board members' retention, it stands to reason that the involvement of CEOs in the selection process will shape directors' behavior. Directors essentially hand-picked by the CEO may feel some allegiance, even gratitude, to their backer and, relatedly, an obligation to support him. Directors' sense of fidelity, then, may weaken their oversight and discipline of the CEO. Insofar as pay, status, and other benefits of board service motivates directors to seek reappointment for additional terms, they have additional incentives to reciprocate. Finally, outside directors naturally may become more loyal to the CEO over time. On the other hand, a director whose exercise of "independent" judgment has aggravated the CEO may receive a polite request stand down for reelection. Simply put, directors may refrain from contradicting or otherwise alienating the CEO for fear that they will not be reappointed.

For more than 50 years, management has successfully resisted meaningful reforms designed to increase shareholders' influence over director selection. In particular, management has vehemently opposed proposals to give dissident shareholders "proxy access," meaning the right to include in the company's proxy materials an alternative slate of director candidates for shareholders' consideration. While granting shareholders the right to present their own candidates on the corporate proxy is substantially less expensive than waging (or defending) a proxy contest, officers and directors of public companies prevailed on the SEC twice, first in the mid-twentieth century and again in the 2000s, to bar shareholders from accessing the corporation's proxy. In the main, however, unless the corporation otherwise provides its shareholders with access, dissidents must wage a proxy contest if they wish to nominate candidates for election to the firm's board of directors. We examine proxy access and election contests in some depth in Chapter 8.

The expense and legal risks associated with proxy contests deter most shareholders from challenging director elections. The most significant impediment to dissidents is the cost — including the expense of complying with the SEC's proxy rules and especially printing, mailing, and publicity costs — of waging an election contest at a publicly-owned firm. Campaign finance rules originally promulgated in the 1950s still strongly favor managerial incumbents: shareholder dissidents must fund their campaigns from their own pockets, while management incumbents effectively have unlimited access to the corporate treasury. As a practical matter, the dissidents will receive reimbursement only if they obtain control of the board. Subsequent proposals for qualified reimbursement (for example, based on the dissident's fraction of the votes received) have failed as well. Challengers also face liability for any false or misleading statements in the proxy materials. For these reasons, among others explored in later chapters, slates nominated by incumbent boards generally run unopposed.

Then again, increasing use of board nominating committees, and the growing practice of staffing those committees with non-management directors only, may have improved the selection process. In 1979, only 19 percent of the companies sampled in a SEC study had standing board nominating committees; a subsequent SEC study showed an increase to 30 percent two years later; in 1989, a Korn/Ferry study reported that 57 percent of the responding firms had a nominating committee. As of 1992, when ALI published its Principles of Corporate Governance, best practice called for appointment of nominating committees comprised solely of non-officer directors.

For more than a decade now, the NYSE has required boards of listed public companies to use nominating committees, staffed entirely by independent directors, for director selection. The NYSE's definition of independence excludes not only officers but also most directors with affiliations to the company. Additionally, rules adopted by the SEC in 2004 require public corporations to disclose nominating committee practices, including the attributes that the nominating committee regards as essential and the process used by the committee to search for and vet candidates for the board. By learning of these procedures, shareholders may become more involved in recommending director candidates, and the CEO may exercise less influence over the process. Shareholders can propose potential candidates to the nominating committee, identifying potential bona fide candidates for the committee. In this way, the nominating committee may learn of other individuals qualified and committed to serve the best interests of the company and its shareholders.

It is not clear, however, that nominating committees of outside directors have reduced management's influence over candidate selection. Nothing in the listing standards requires boards to exclude management from participating in the selection process. Nominating committees may consult with, and accept nominees from, CEOs. CEOs likely remain active in recommending individuals for open directorships, vetting potential directors with the nominating committees, and recruiting their preferred candidates to join "their" boards. CEOs also may have involvement in the engagement of executive search firms to identify and recruit aspirants on behalf of nominating committees. On the other hand, nominating committees might work to disable CEOs from retaliating against nonconformists.

Furthermore, despite opposing proposed reforms that would have allowed shareholders access to the company's proxy, some public corporations voluntarily adopted majority voting standards for director elections, enhancing shareholders' ability to oust unresponsive or incompetent directors. Companies also have responded to activist shareholders and other critics by amending their bylaws to implement majority voting standards for uncontested elections. Finally, companies may require directors to tender their resignations if they receive more "withheld" or "against" votes than "for" votes in uncontested elections. These private ordering solutions and related developments, including key state law reforms allowing shareholder access if company by-laws so provide, are discussed in greater detail in Chapters 7 and 8.

Michael E. Murphy, *The Nominating Process for Corporate Boards of Directors: A Decision-Making Analysis*
5 Berkeley Bus. L.J. 131 (2008)[29]

Until the late 1970s, relatively few companies had any formal procedures for selecting candidates for boards of directors. While directorial elections were subject to elaborate procedures mandated by the SEC and state laws, the nomination of the slate of candidates was regarded as a personal prerogative of the CEO. On the basis of interviews in the late 1960s, Mace observed, "Most executives interviewed confirmed that the selection of new directors was controlled and decided by the president." The prevailing theory was that the CEO needed to form an effective team and the choice of directors formed part of that task. Twenty years later, Lorsch and MacIver still found many CEOs referring to the corporate board as "my directors."

The nominating committee emerged as a common feature of corporate governance in the late 1970s largely in response to the SEC investigation of shareholder participation in the corporate electoral process. Regulations issued in 1978 called for disclosure of whether a company had a nominating committee, whether its members were independent of management, and whether the committee considered shareholder recommendations for director and, if so, the procedures to be followed in making such recommendations. In proposing these regulations, the Commission stated that it believed "that the institution of nominating committees can represent a significant step in increasing shareholder participation in the corporate electoral process."

According to Conference Board [a corporate research organization providing economic and business information to its members] surveys, the percentage of companies

---

29. Copyright © 2008 by the Regents of the University of California. Reprinted from the Berkeley Business Law Journal, Vol. 5, No. 2, by permission of the Regents of the University of California.

with nominating committees stood at only eight percent in 1971, rose to fifteen percent by 1977, and roughly doubled in the next two years. By 1980, thirty-two percent of surveyed corporations reported having a nominating committee. The Conference Board study noted that management saw the nominating committee as being far preferable to the alternative of direct shareholder access to the proxy machinery. For its part, the SEC saw "the use of nominating committees as a vehicle for shareholder participation" in the nomination of directors. As we have seen, the 1980 staff report on shareholder participation in the corporate electoral process deferred consideration of direct shareholder nominations for directors pending a study of "the extent to which these [nominating] committees are considering shareholder nominations"—a study that never came to fruition.

A Corporate Director's Guidebook issued in 1976 by the ABA Committee on Corporate Laws described the nominating committee as "potentially the most significant channel for improved corporate governance." By providing a forum for shareholders to submit recommendations for directors, the nominating committee would offer "a more effective and workable method of affording access to the nominating process to individual shareholders than a direct 'right' of nominating in the corporation's proxy material." The American Law Institute (ALI) issued in 1982 Tentative Draft No. 1 of Principles of Corporate Governance, which seconded the ABA call for nominating committees composed exclusively of directors who are not officers in large public corporations. Using political terminology, an ALI consultant, Joseph Hinsey, saw the nominating committee as a screening mechanism comparable to the electoral college as originally envisioned by the founding fathers. He argued "that the independent nominating committee concept provides an effective response to the claimed erosion of so-called shareholder democracy that has been long bemoaned by corporate reformers." The committee "provides the essential link to both the effective yet practical participation of the shareholders in the corporate electoral process and the effective independent review function that is at the forefront of the board's monitoring role."

The nominating committee gained popularity in the 1980s, though it lagged behind the vision reflected in the ABA and ALI statements. By 1992, sixty-four percent of companies surveyed by the Conference Board possessed a nominating committee, but the committee met median average of only two times a year in large companies and often only once in smaller companies. The committees were increasingly composed of independent directors, though the CEO or another officer was sometimes a committee member. In any event, as one executive remarked, the CEO's membership on the committee was largely a "cosmetic" matter since he worked closely with committee members in identifying and approving candidates whether or not formally a member.

But the vision of the nominating committee as a vehicle for shareholder participation in the nominating process never became a reality. Institutional investors were rarely represented on corporate boards in the 1980s. The Conference Board's 1992 survey reported that only three percent of the firms had received suggestions concerning directorial nominees from institutional investors, and "just one company stated that it had acceded to the demand of a large shareholder that an outside director be placed on the board." After conducting some 80 interviews of corporate directors in the late 1980s, Lorsch and MacIvery concluded that "shareholders are obviously not involved [in selecting directors] until the election phase, and even at this point, their impact is negligible."

The spread of the nominating committee did not change the CEO's dominant role in the nomination process. The committee was unlikely to propose a candidate to the board over the CEO's opposition, and by most credible accounts, the CEO remained the principal source of ideas for nominees to directorships throughout the 1980s. Lorsch and MacIver reported, "In spite of these changes [involving the nominating committee], the directors' influence is still limited in comparison to the CEO's. For the most part, there is a division in responsibility between the CEO, who identifies new candidates, and the nominating committee or full board, which evaluates and formally nominates candidates."

More recently, at some point in the last 10 or 15 years, the nominating committee seems to have made a quantum shift to become a bona fide working unit of the board. In 2006, it was found in ninety-nine percent of S&P 500 companies, according to a Spencer Stuart survey. The committee met an average of 3.9 times a year and meetings typically lasted almost two hours; it nearly always operated under a written charter defining its responsibilities; and the committee members usually elected their own chairman. Today, a commentary in the Listing Company Manual of the New York Stock Exchange (NYSE) describes the nominating committee as "central to the effective functioning of the board."

The significance of nominating committee is now closely linked to the role of independent directors. Following passage of the Sarbanes-Oxley Act, both the New York Stock Exchange and the NASDAQ Exchange required listed companies to appoint independent directors, as defined by the Exchange rules, to a majority of positions on their boards. An average seventy-four percent of board members in companies with over $10 billion in revenues were independent directors in a 2004 survey. Strengthening these requirements, the Exchanges extended the policy of directorial independence to nominating committees. NYSE rules now require the nominating committee to be composed entirely of independent directors. The NASDAQ Exchange adopted a rule with much the same effect, though it contains exceptions of minor significance.

The contemporary influence of the CEO in the nominating process is difficult to assess in the absence of studies comparable to those conducted in the late 1980s, but it is clear that CEO's may have the dominant voice in the nominating process even if not included in the membership of a nominating committees composed of independent directors. The ALI Principles of Corporate Governance, adopted in 1994, note that "the chief executive officer, can be expected to be highly active in recommending to and discussing candidates with the committee and in recruiting candidates for the board," and adds that such participation of the CEO in the nominating process can be achieved "without making the CEO a member of the committee." A handbook of the National Association of Corporate Directors (NACD) suggests that these practices continue to be widespread. "Most directors," the handbook reports, "recognize the need to have the CEO closely aligned with the new director selection process. Some companies have found from personal experience that providing the CEO with veto power may be a reasonable middle ground." A sample committee charter attached to the handbook states explicitly that committee should select nominees "with direct input from the CEO."

In a minority of companies, the slowly growing movement to separate the position of CEO and Chairman of the Board may have introduced more complex patterns of interaction between the nominating committee and management, and the now common practice of appointing a "lead director" to preside over executive sessions of the independent directors may have had somewhat the same effect. Empirical evidence, however, is lacking on how these practices affect the nominating process.

For all practical purposes, institutional investors and other shareholders continue to be excluded from the nominating process. Surveys reveal that representatives of institutional investors do not figure among the populations from which directors are drawn. According to the executive director of the Council of Institutional Investors, "Our members' sense is that shareowner-suggested candidates—whether or not submitted to all-independent nominating committees—are rarely given serious consideration." To the same effect, the 2003 SEC staff report on the nominating process observed, "Although shareholders generally may recommend candidates to a company's nominating committee or group of directors fulfilling this role, shareholders have indicated that this is not effective, as companies rarely nominate candidates recommended by shareholders."

Nevertheless, the SEC adopted still more elaborate disclosure rules in 2003 with the objective of encouraging nominating committees to consider shareholder recommendations. The revised rules require, among other things: disclosure of the committee's policy regarding shareholder recommendations for directorial candidates, a description of procedures to be followed by shareholders in submitting such recommendations, whether the committee has received a recommended candidate from a shareholder or group of shareholder holding five percent of the stock of the company within 120 days of the date of the proxy statement, and whether the committee chose to nominate such candidate. A 2006 survey of Spencer Stuart, however, records no shareholder nominations three years after the effective date of the disclosure rules.

As it exists today, the original purpose of the nominating committee as an avenue for shareholder participation in the selection of directors remains unfulfilled, but the committee figures in a set of "best practices," enunciated by authoritative voices in U.S. industry. "The Corporate Handbook 2005" of the Conference Board, under the heading "Setting a New Standard for Corporate Governance," notes that "the Enron Bankruptcy, accompanied by other corporate scandals and the resulting regulatory response, has caused a sea change in the attention given corporate governance and in how directors are viewed by the public, shareholders, employees, and the courts." The functions of the nominating committee forms one of the principal chapters in the Handbook's description of best corporate governance practices. Similarly, in its "Principles of Corporate Governance," the Business Roundtable states that "the United States has the best corporate governance, financial reporting and securities market systems in the world. These systems work because of the adoption of best practices by public companies within a framework of laws and regulations." A separate statement of principles sets forth recommended practices for nominating committees.

The nominating committee practices advocated by The Conference Board and the Business Roundtable are notable in two respects: they respond to public criticism of corporations by calling on the nominating committees to follow desirable practices in selecting independent and qualified members of the board, and, in addition, they advocate a broad charter of responsibilities for these committees, which are now often designated corporate governance committees. In addition to identifying and evaluating candidates to the board, the associations recommend that nominating committees should review committee structure, recommend candidates for membership of committees, oversee efficient functioning of the board, annually evaluate performance of the board and committees, propose corporate principles, and oversee succession planning for the CEO and other senior management positions.

Comments and Questions

1. Must a system of fair corporate suffrage provide shareholders with voice in directors' nominations? What steps have been taken to increase shareholders' voice and reduce CEO influence on the selection of board members? Which reform(s) do you think are most likely to succeed? Can you think of other potential reforms?

2. Particularly during the 1990s, governance reform advocates envisaged that nominating committees would become an avenue for shareholders to participate more actively in director selection. The SEC requires companies to disclose whether they had any procedures for the shareholder submission of nominations and even required identification of any nominee submitted by a 5 percent shareholder and "whether the nominating committee chose to nominate the candidate." Item 407(c) of Regulation S-K, 17 CFR § 229.407(c). However, as the article notes, "[F]or all practical purposes, institutional investors and other shareholders continue to be excluded from the nominating process." What explains this resistance?

3. The stock exchange listing standards applicable to board nominating committees are not as exacting as those applicable to the audit and compensation committees. However, proxy advisors such as Institutional Shareholder Services (ISS) and large institutional shareholders exert important influence on the policies and practices of nominating committees. How might nominating committees structure their policies and practices to serve as dependable vehicles for shareholders seeking some say in directors' selection?

4. Notwithstanding the reforms described in Dr. Murphy's article, CEOs continue to have voice, perhaps dominating voice, in director selection. They need not sit as voting members of board nominating committees to do so. For example, Hewlett-Packard revealed in its 2011 proxy statement that five new director candidates nom-

inated by the board were identified and vetted not by its standing Nominating and Governance Committee but, rather, by a separate *ad hoc* committee of directors appointed by (and including) independent director Raymond Lane, H-P's Chairman of the Board. Lane, who previously ran Oracle Corporation as its President and Chief Operating Officer, formed the *ad hoc* committee "to assist in the identification of new director candidates and to facilitate the process of evaluating those candidates as potential directors." The company did not disclose why Lane created a separate *ad hoc* committee, tasking it with the same responsibilities delegated by the board to its chartered standing committee. Nor did the proxy statement identify the members of the *ad hoc* committee. However, in response to inquiries by ISS and the financial press, H-P revealed that Lane had appointed only one director from the Nominating and Governance Committee to serve on the *ad hoc* committee. The *ad hoc* committee also included the company's new CEO, Leo Apotheker. Defending Apotheker's direct involvement in selecting H-P's five new directors, in apparent contravention of the Nominating and Governance Committee's charter, Lane asserted in a letter to shareholders that CEO participation is ubiquitous in Corporate America. "[M]ost, if not all, other companies, large and small, public and private, involve the CEO in the identification and vetting process for new director candidates."

a. Chairman Lane's "every company does it" justification did not satisfy ISS. The proxy advisor recommended that H-P shareholders vote against reelecting members of the Nominating and Governance Committee for allowing the CEO's direct participation in the appointment of the give new directors. Do you agree with ISS's recommendation?

b. Not surprisingly, CEO Apotheker had business connections with several director candidates nominated to H-P's board. In an interview with CNBC, Lane readily acknowledged that he and Apotheker had "a lot of experience with these [new directors]." Lane also explained that the board's top priority was "to support Leo [Apotheker], to support Leo in forming his leadership, his strategy for the company, so right now to support Leo." Can the board's top priority, as described by its chairman, be squared with its responsibility to oversee management?

5. No law, rule, or regulation limits, much less prohibits, CEOs from recommending director candidates to nominating committees or the full board. Does it make sense for the nominating committee to fulfill its responsibilities without receiving advice or opinions from the CEO, at least until such time as the committee presents potential candidates to the full board for its approval? What does the continuing influence of CEOs in director selection suggest about the backgrounds, philosophies, and incentives of the outside directors serving on nominating committees?

6. Many arguments favoring CEO involvement in board selection stress the importance of board collegiality. Harvey Pitt, former chairman of the SEC and a well-respected corporate attorney, has written, "Boards should strive for collegiality and be constituted to achieve that result. Ultimately, critical board decisions are vested in the hands of a group, not a single decisionmaker. As a result, the system can only work if collegiality is fostered and actually achieved.... While pedigree and con-

stituency affinity are helpful, the most critical thing is to select people who play nicely with one another." Harvey L. Pitt, *Learning the Lessons of Hewlett-Packard*, Compliance Week (Oct. 31, 2006). Do you agree? Why or why not?

7. There is some evidence that reducing CEO influence over the director selection process results in increased value for shareholders. *See* Steven A. Ramirez, *Lessons from the Subprime Debacle: Stress Testing CEO Autonomy*, 54 St. Louis L.J. 1 (2009) ("Nevertheless, evidence supports the proposition that boards selected without CEO input enhance firm value."). Assuming this finding is accurate, why doesn't the market operate to cause companies to reduce the CEO's influence in order to maximize returns for investors?

State law authorizes shareholders to nominate their own candidates to the board, bypassing management. However, a shareholder wishing to nominate its own director candidates not only must comply with applicable state corporation law and company's charter and bylaws, but the nominating shareholder also must prepare its own proxy statement and proxy card and solicit proxies for its directors. Shareholders nominating a competing slate must bear significant expense, including solicitor fees, printing and mailing costs necessary to circulate a proxy statement as well as legal fees and costs incurred to fight off the corporation's inevitable courtroom challenges to the solicitation. To avoid this expense, shareholders alternatively might seek to include their nominees in the company's proxy pursuant to the federal shareholder proposal regulation, Rule 14a-8, promulgated under Section 14(a) of the Securities Exchange Act of 1934. In 2010, Congress enacted Section 971 of the Dodd-Frank Act to provide the SEC with express authority to adopt further "proxy access" rules that would allow qualified shareholders to place director nominees on the company's proxy ballot. Chapter 8 describes and appraises efforts to allow shareholders access to company proxy materials for the purpose of electing directors not nominated by the board.

VII. Directors' Compensation

As we have seen, expectations about directors' influence and involvement in public company governance—and, specifically, their oversight of firm management—have increased significantly in recent years. How can shareholders ensure that directors will act for their benefit, maximizing the value of the firm and, thus, shareholders' wealth? Assuming that the board controls the firm, directors must have sufficient incentives to perform their monitoring and advisory functions without having to be monitored themselves.

Until the last quarter of the 20th century, outside director compensation remained relatively low. Indeed, some directors actually served without any remuneration. Going back to the nineteenth century, corporations customarily paid a nominal fee or nothing to directors, consistent with the view that the opportunity to participate in firm governance was reward enough, especially for substantial shareholders. However, as public corporations implemented the monitoring board model, outsiders recruited to the board demanded and received greater compensation for their time and effort.

After the turn of the millenium, corporate governance reforms not only enlarged the responsibilities of board members and inflated their workloads, but new laws and regulations also generated demand for outside directors with specific (e.g., financial) expertise. These developments, coupled with mounting concerns about directors' tenure and board diversity, arguably shrunk the pool of suitable candidates, leading corporations to boost director compensation in order to attract and retain qualified board members. Total compensation to public company board members has grown significantly year-to-year over the past decade.

As director compensation has increased, corporate governance experts have focused more attention on understanding board processes for deciding self-compensation and how market forces and social norms affect these remuneration decisions. Academics and other researchers also have begun studying the impact of outside directors' compensation on their incentives and behavior. One hypothesis is that generous compensation weakens outside directors' independence. For example, directors receiving large cash fees may become, like salaried employees, beholden to management, especially if the CEO has substantial influence over board nominations. Especially as the stock markets soared in the 1990s, more companies decided to compensate outside directors with equity, ostensibly strengthening the alignment of directors' and shareholders' interests.

Despite some evidence that suggests a connection between stock-based director compensation and improved governance, equity compensation has not proven to be a panacea. Directors typically obtain their equity stakes through annual stock-based compensation rather than by an initial grant of stock options or restricted stock. Many public companies require board members to maintain minimum ownership levels in company equity. Over time, then, a director's stake likely accumulates. Still, many outside directors will not acquire a large enough interest in the corporation to produce a strong incentive effect. Furthermore, increased equity stakes actually may undercut directors' independence, aligning directors' interests more closely with management's interests. (Directors' fees are not considered in determining independence under regulatory standards.) In addition, equity-based compensation may create problematic incentives for directors. Concerned about short-term stock performance, risk adverse directors might eschew research and development projects or other capital investments with long-term payoffs. Rather than questioning the executive team about aggressive accounting practices, financial misreporting, or excessive risk-taking, compromised directors with consequential stock holdings or in-the-money options might accept management's choices. Academic studies have reached differing conclusions as to whether compensating directors with equity improves firm performance.

In any event, shareholders could not necessarily ascertain directors' compensation until 2006. While the SEC required disclosure of the amounts paid to directors, companies typically did so in narrative form and did not provide a single dollar figure on the total amount of compensation paid. In 2006, however, Item 402 of Regulation S-K was amended to require companies to reveal total compensation for directors. The changes made directors' compensation more transparent.

Proxy disclosure after 2006 showed that in many public companies, directors were paid well. Some of the most highly compensated directors sat on the boards of the largest corporations. Total compensation in some cases exceeded $1 million. Moreover, not all directors received the same pay. Increasingly, individuals who serve as lead directors and non-executive board chairs and directors who chair board committees, particularly the audit and compensation committees, receive additional amounts.

Although the actual level of pay, in general, relates to the size of the company (public companies with the highest revenues reward their directors with the highest pay), director compensation grew across firms after Congress passed Sarbanes-Oxley in 2002 and again, almost eight years later, following enactment of Dodd-Frank in 2010. The corporate governance reforms included in both statutes increased oversight demands on boards, requiring that directors devote more time to their board responsibilities. Accordingly, to attract qualified candidates and retain and motivate outside directors facing expanded workloads, companies have offered more lucrative compensation packages.

At the same time, corporations have altered director compensation structures, moving away from compensating board members through per-meeting fees and, instead, paying annual retainers to directors as base compensation. These arrangements simplify disbursements and promote directors' use of electronic communications and new technology (i.e., more frequent but shorter telephonic meetings or web conferencing) in lieu of in-person meetings. In recent years, then, directors' compensation has become increasingly similar in structure to executives' compensation.

Delaware law makes clear that directors have the authority to set their own pay. 8 DGCL § 141(h). The NYSE's governance rules also assume that the board will establish directors' compensation. Still, such decisions engender thorny conflicts. Corporate governance experts advise that disinterested directors should determine the compensation for other directors, and shareholders should ratify compensation plans. Nevertheless, directors' self-interest cannot be eliminated completely, and, recently, shareholders began challenging directors' self-compensation decisions.

Comments and Questions

1. Directors' self-compensation decisions raise obvious, inherent conflicts of interest. Nonetheless, Delaware judges historically employed a deferential standard of review to awards made by directors to directors under incentive compensation plans approved by shareholders. Applying the deferential business judgment rule, Delaware courts upheld challenged decisions unless they amounted to corporate waste; that is, the corporation received no benefit or value from the directors compensated in exchange for their services. Shareholders' approval of the plan obviated the need for the director defendants to prove, and the court to determine, the entire

fairness of the awards made to directors (i.e., whether the decision was made based on fair dealing and at a fair price).

However, as we will see in Chapter 6, a 2015 decision of the Delaware Chancery Court made clear that shareholders' advance approval of compensation plans may not suffice to insulate non-employee director compensation awards from entire fairness review. In *Calma v. Templeton*, 2015 WL 1951930 (Del. Ch. Apr. 30, 2015), shareholders brought a derivative suit for damages against the board of Citrix Systems. The complaint challenged awards of restricted stock units granted to eight non-employee directors over three years, pursuant to an equity incentive plan approved by shareholders. While the plan provided that "no beneficiary could receive more than one million shares (or RSUs) per calendar year," it did not prescribe any specific award amounts to directors, nor did the plan provide any director-specific upper limits on future awards made to them. Based on Citrix's stock price at the time plaintiffs filed suit, a director could have received grants valued at $55 million. Because the plan approved by shareholders placed no "meaningful limits" on awards made to directors, the court held that the shareholders' vote did not operate as a ratification of the awards at issue. Delaware courts, then, likely will review the entire fairness of director compensation awards unless shareholders approved the specific awards made or approved plans that included specific "meaningful limits" on either the size or the magnitude of future director compensation awards.

Would you expect this decision to lead to the filing of more shareholder derivative suits challenging directors' compensation? Why or why not? What advice would you give to a corporate board seeking to minimize its litigation risk?

2. Nevada corporate law takes a different approach. Section 78.140(5) of the Nevada statute states:

> Unless otherwise provided in the articles of incorporation or the bylaws, the board of directors, without regard to personal interest, may establish the compensation of directors for services in any capacity. If the board of directors establishes the compensation of directors pursuant to this subsection, such compensation is presumed to be fair to the corporation unless proven unfair by a preponderance of the evidence.

Faced with a breach of fiduciary duty claim by shareholders for excessive self-compensation, would director defendants prefer to litigate under Delaware law or Nevada law?

3. Directors of public companies receive compensation in the form of annual cash retainers, committee retainers, meeting fees, benefits (such as insurance and participation in matching charitable contribution programs), perquisites (such as company products and tickets to sporting events), and, increasingly, equity in the corporation. In fact, most large corporations have eliminated regular meeting fees in favor of higher annual cash/equity retainers. The mix of cash and equity paid to directors is roughly 50/50, with larger firms paying directors more than half of their compensation in equity.

4. As considered in some length in Chapter 6, executive compensation designs endeavor to provide managers with incentives to maximize the firm's share price, paying executives for improving stock performance. Similarly, in order to more closely align directors' and shareholders' economic interests, public companies now also grant shares to non-management board members. Does it make sense to pay directors for performance? How do the incentives of outside directors differ from CEOs or other inside directors? Companies typically grant full-value equity awards, rather than stock options, to outside directors. Why might shareholders have concerns about awarding stock options to outside directors?

5. Although public companies increasingly impose on directors minimum stock ownership requirements, some governance experts contend that outside directors still lack sufficient financial incentives to maximize shareholders' wealth. One proposal would require new directors to invest some portion of their own net worth in the company's equity. Another recommendation is to award each director incentive shares that would vest some number of years after the director's board service ends. What are the arguments in favor and against these ideas?

6. Over the past decade, director compensation has grown by approximately 5 percent annually. The average total compensation for directors of S&P 500 corporations was nearly $264,000 in 2014, some 6 percent higher than the average in 2013 and 24 percent greater than the average compensation in 2009. *2014 Spencer Stuart Board Index*, Spencer Stuart Board Services 7, 9 (2014). More than half of directors' compensation came in the form of equity, but over five years, the median retainer paid to non-employee directors more than doubled as well.

7. Differential director compensation has become common, too. Board leaders, such as the lead/presiding director and committee chairs, receive additional compensation in recognition of their more significant and time-consuming roles. S&P 500 companies generally pay additional compensation to directors who chair standing committees, with the chairs of the boards' audit committees and compensation committees receiving the largest retainers. When boards create special committees for particular purposes, those committees' chairs, as well as other members of the committees, often receive additional retainers as compensation for their efforts. Again, there has been a shift in the form of remuneration for board leaders and members of certain committees, from per-meeting fees to retainers.

8. Some commentators have pointed to the risk of litigation as justification for higher director compensation. Directors do incur some risk that shareholders will sue them for breach of fiduciary duty, particularly following the announcement of significant transactions or other major corporate events. However, as discussed in Chapter 10, directors at large corporations rarely face personal liability for failures of oversight, even if the firm suffered large losses or surrendered substantial penalties to government authorities. Not only is directors' risk of liability low (in general, directors who act in good faith are protected from liability), but companies indemnify their directors and provide them with insurance protection. Nevertheless, should directors compensate themselves for incurring some risk to their reputations associated

with their board service? How might directors predict litigation risk and determine reasonable compensation for such reputational exposure?

9. NYSE rules require evaluations of boards, but regulations do not mandate any specific process for such reviews, nor do the rules call for assessments of individual directors. Furthermore, U.S. public companies rarely disclose information about the framework for their board reviews (other than stating that an evaluative process exists), and corporations do not disclose the findings from recent assessments. How can shareholders gauge directors' performance? Is there a role for an independent expert in this regard? What disclosures about firms' board evaluations would investors expect to see in the corporation's annual proxy statement?

VIII. Diversity on the Board

During the past decade, investors and other stakeholders have pressured companies to enlarge the representation of women and minorities on corporate boards of directors. Boardroom diversity supports values such as fairness, justice, and equal opportunity, values much like those promoted by antidiscrimination laws. However, advocates for reform further argue that in a global economy, firms without diverse leadership suffer competitive disadvantages in the financial markets, with suppliers and customers, and in attracting desired employees. In addition, a large and growing body of behavioral psychology research, especially studies of problem solving by groups, supports diversity as a norm of good governance. This literature documents and explains how the presence of women and minorities improves group deliberations by bringing new information, opinions, and viewpoints to the discussion, thereby provoking more thoughtful analyses, generating additional solutions, and prompting greater creativity and innovation. To the extent that groups with homogeneous members reinforce biases and suffer from the perils of groupthink, diversity enhances the quality of group decisionmaking.

Given the business case bolstering the benefits of diversity, one might expect that women and minorities would have achieved greater representation on corporate boards. In fact, however, most boards include few women and even fewer people of color. White males still occupy about three-quarters of the seats in boardrooms of large U.S. companies, and women and minorities remain underrepresented, even after boards reformed membership to comply with independence mandates. Men named James, Robert, William, and John hold more seats on corporate boards than women.

Advocates for diversifying corporate boards have less evidence establishing that companies overseen by diverse boards financially outperform homogeneous boards. Some studies have reported measurable, positive correlations between board diversity and various indicators of firm performance, such as return on assets, return on equity, profit margins, dividend payments, and revenues. However, other investigators have found a negative correlation or no significant relationship, as discussed in the following article.

Renée B. Adams & Daniel Ferreira, *Women in the Boardroom and Their Impact on Governance and Performance*

94 J. Fin. Econ. 291 (2009)[30]

Women hold few corporate board seats. In the US, women held 14.8% of Fortune 500 board seats in 2007. The percentage of female directors in Australia, Canada, Japan, and Europe is estimated to be 8.7%, 10.6%, 0.4%, and 8.0%, respectively. Furthermore, the majority of firms with female directors have only one female director, a fact that is often regarded as evidence of tokenism. For example, in the top two hundred companies in Europe, 62% of companies have at least one female director, but only 28% have more than one in 2004. In Australia, 50% of ASX200 companies have at least one female director, but only 13.5% have more than one in 2006. In our data, 65% of the firms have at least one female director in 2003, but only 25% have more than one.

This situation is likely to change because boards around the world are under increasing pressure to choose female directors. Many proposals for governance reform explicitly stress the importance of gender diversity in the boardroom. In the UK, the Higgs report, commissioned by the British Department of Trade and Industry, argues that diversity could enhance board effectiveness and specifically recommends that firms draw more actively from professional groups in which women are better represented. If companies do not voluntarily reserve a minimum of 25% of their board seats for female directors, Sweden has threatened to make gender diversity a legal requirement. The most extreme promotion of gender diversity occurs in Norway, where since January 2008 all listed companies must abide by a 40% gender quota for female directors or face dissolution.[31] Although it is still too early to assess the consequences of Norway's unique experiment, Spain has followed Norway's lead by enacting a law requiring companies to increase the share of female directors to 40% by 2015.

Most of these legislative initiatives are based on the view that the presence of women on boards could affect the governance of companies in significant ways. One argument is that boards could enhance their effectiveness by tapping broader talent pools for their directors. The Higgs review, for example, points out that, although approximately 30% of managers in the UK corporate sector are female, women hold only 6% of nonexecutive director positions. Another argument is that, because they do not belong to the "old boys club," female directors could more closely correspond to the concept of the independent director emphasized in theory.

In this paper, we provide new evidence that is relevant to this debate by investigating the hypothesis that gender diversity in the boardroom affects governance in meaningful ways. In particular, we ask the following questions. First, do measures of board inputs (director attendance and committee assignments) vary with gender diversity? Second,

---

30. Copyright © 2008 Journal of Financial Economics. Reprinted with permission.

31. The law was imposed in 2006 and firms were given two years to adjust. As of February 2008, 93% of the public companies complied with the requirements, according to Statistics Norway. In April 2008, the Norwegian government announced full compliance.

does the gender composition of the board affect measures of governance, such as chief executive officer turnover and compensation? Finally, does the effect of gender diversity on governance matter sufficiently to affect corporate performance? The answers to these questions are interesting for several reasons. For example, they can help us understand the effect group composition has on board effectiveness and the likely success or failure of governance proposals advocating greater diversity. They can also shed light on whether tokenism prevents female directors from having an impact on corporate outcomes.

We find that gender diversity in boards has significant effects on board inputs. Women appear to behave differently than men with respect to our measure of attendance behavior. Specifically, women are less likely to have attendance problems than men. Furthermore, the greater the fraction of women on the board is, the better is the attendance behavior of male directors. Holding other director characteristics constant, female directors are also more likely to sit on monitoring-related committees than male directors. In particular, women are more likely to be assigned to audit, nominating, and corporate governance committees, although they are less likely to sit on compensation committees than men are.

Women also appear to have a significant impact on board governance. We find direct evidence that more diverse boards are more likely to hold CEOs accountable for poor stock price performance; CEO turnover is more sensitive to stock return performance in firms with relatively more women on boards. In our data, this effect is stronger and more robust than the previously shown effects of board independence on CEO turnover. We also find that directors in gender-diverse boards receive relatively more equity-based compensation. We do not find a statistically reliable relation between gender diversity and the level and composition of CEO pay, which is consistent with our findings that women board members are under-represented on compensation committees and thus have less involvement in setting CEO pay.

The evidence on the relation between gender diversity on boards and firm performance is more difficult to interpret. Although the correlation between gender diversity and either firm value or operating performance appears to be positive at first inspection, this correlation disappears once we apply reasonable procedures to tackle omitted variables and reverse causality problems. Our results suggest that, on average, firms perform worse the greater is the gender diversity of the board. This result is consistent with the argument that too much board monitoring can decrease shareholder value. Thus, it is possible that gender diversity only increases value when additional board monitoring would enhance firm value. To investigate this hypothesis, we examine whether gender diversity affects performance differentially in firms with different levels of shareholder rights, defined using the Investor Responsibility Research Center (IRRC) governance data. Consistent with this hypothesis, we find that gender diversity has beneficial effects in companies with weak shareholder rights, where additional board monitoring could enhance firm value, but detrimental effects in companies with strong shareholder rights.

Despite the importance of gender diversity in the policy debate, relatively little research links diversity and corporate governance. Carter, Simkins, and Simpson (2003) find a positive relation between gender and ethnic diversity of the board and corporate performance, ... Farrell and Hersch (2005) find that gender systematically impacts the selection of directors to the board. They argue that their evidence is consistent with the idea that women directors are added to the board following internal or external calls for diversity. These papers do not fully address the endogeneity problems that arise because of differences in unobservable characteristics across firms or reverse causality. Thus, their findings cannot be given causal interpretations. Our paper complements these by providing a comprehensive analysis of the consequences of gender diversity in boards. We also pay special attention to endogeneity issues that could confound the interpretation of the empirical findings.

More generally, our paper contributes to the literature on the demography of organizations, which has been studied primarily by researchers in management and organization theory and increasingly in economics and corporate finance. Empirical papers in this tradition have looked both at the effects of demography on outcomes and at the determinants of demography in organizations. In the economics and finance literatures, [researchers find that] firms appear to choose directors for their personal characteristics. [Other researchers] find that some personal characteristics of the CEO (such as tenure and age) are related to board structure.

Overall, our results suggest that gender-diverse boards are tougher monitors. Nevertheless, they reveal that mandating gender quotas in the boardroom could harm well-governed firms in which additional monitoring is counterproductive.

Comments and Questions

1. Women comprise just over half of the total workforce in the U.S., and half of all managers are women. Yet, the proportion of top leadership positions in Corporate America has changed only modestly since Professors Adams and Ferreira published their article. Fewer than one in five women serve as directors at S&P 500 companies today, compared with 16 percent five years ago. More women joined these boards during the 2015 proxy year, but they gained directorships at a reduced pace. Less than one third of new independent directors were women, an increase of approximately one percentage point over the prior year. More women also occupy the chief executives' offices in C-suites, but, again, progress toward gender parity has slowed. A 2015 study reported that only 22 women serve as CEOs at the S&P 500 companies. Catalyst, *Women CEOs of the S&P 500*, Oct. 9, 2015. The number of companies in the S&P 500 with no minority representation actually increased during the last decade, from 36 percent in 2000 to 41 percent in 2007. What might explain these statistics, including the declines?

2. Empirical researchers disagree about the effect of board diversity on firm performance. Professors Adams and Ferreira found that while boards with a higher proportion of women monitored management more closely, those firms did not enjoy better financial performance.

Other studies report that companies with diverse boards of directors outperform their peers financially. *See, e.g.,* Credit Suisse Res. Inst., *Gender Diversity and Corporate*

Performance (Aug. 2012); Catalyst, *The Bottom Line: Corporate Performance and Women's Representation on Boards* (2007). The conflicting results are not surprising; researchers review data from different time periods, countries, economies, and types of firms, and academics do not utilize the same definitions of diversity or measures of financial performance.

No studies purport to establish that board diversity *causes* superior firm performance. Might the reverse be true? Perhaps financially successful firms are better positioned to attract highly-recruited women and minority director candidates. Larger and better-performing companies may have more resources to devote to pursuing diversity. Such firms also may face more pressure from public pension plans and diversity advocates to increase the number of women and minorities in management.

3. In the absence of definitive research establishing a causal link between board diversity and firm economic performance, what are the best arguments for recruiting more women and people of color to serve as directors? Can you identify legitimate non-business rationales for increasing diversity on corporate boards? Should companies nominate more women and minorities based solely on the perceived need for greater diversity in Corporate America? Might this strategy backfire? How?

4. During the past decade, many European countries, including France, Italy, the Netherlands, and Spain, have instituted quotas designed to increase the number of women directors on corporate boards. Most recently, following months of animated debate, Germany enacted a new law requiring that women hold 30 percent of the seats on supervisory boards of listed companies by 2016. The quota applies to about 100 of Germany's largest companies. Norway, the first nation to legislate boardroom diversity in 2003, requires that boards include at least 40 percent representation of both genders. As a result, Norway has the highest representation of women on company boards. However, dozens of firms reincorporated outside the country or became private limited firms in order to circumvent the quota. Furthermore, research suggests that compliance with the mandate did not improve corporate performance in the early years after implementation. One published study reported that the Norwegian law has led to younger and less experienced boards, increases in leverage and acquisitions, and deterioration in operating performance.[32]

What do you think about laws mandating gender diversity on corporate boards? Should Congress enact a similar statute regulating U.S. public companies?

———————

What explains the continued relative scarcity of women and people of color in corporate boardrooms? Commentators have speculated on the reasons for the United

———————

32. Kenneith R. Ahern & Amy K. Dittmar, *The Changing of the Boards: The Impact on Firm Value of Mandated Female Board Representation*, 127 Q.J. Econ. 137 (2012).

States' modest record on board diversity. One explanation is the lack of a sufficient supply of women and minorities qualified to serve. This claim is considered next.

Lisa M. Fairfax, *Board Diversity Revisited: New Rationale, Same Old Story?*
89 N.C. L. Rev. 855 (2011)[33]

In the context of corporate boards, the pool problem refers to the notion that the pool of candidates that satisfy the criteria for serving on corporate boards, particularly large public corporate boards, is relatively small. Board studies reveal that corporations favor directors who have executive-level experience. Hence, in 2007, ninety-six percent of Fortune 1000 boards had one or more directors who was a retired executive, and such status reflected the most common characteristic of the directors. Indeed, most directors are active or retired CEOs or other corporate executives who have headed a division or been a functional unit leader. The number of people of color and women who fit this profile is relatively small. As a result, corporations that focus on these kinds of criteria may experience a pool problem with respect to finding diverse director candidates.

To be sure, corporations may have exaggerated the extent to which the pool problem represents a significant hurdle to board diversity. This is because there are relatively few legal requirements for board service, and none of those requirements demands that board members have specific forms of experience or backgrounds. Moreover, while it is undeniable that board service requires some understanding of financial matters and corporate affairs, there are no studies indicating that enhanced board or corporate performance is linked to ensuring that a majority or a supermajority of board members have executive-level expertise. Instead, boards or committees comprised of directors with previous managerial experience may have biases in favor of management that could undermine their ability to be independent and objective. In this regard, the focus on overpopulating the board with prior executives may have negative consequences. More importantly, the fact that corporations gravitate toward board members with particular backgrounds and experience is a function of custom rather than any legal rules. From this perspective, because the pool problem stems from custom rather than legal regimes, one may question the legitimacy of the problem.

Nevertheless, the pool problem remains a significant obstacle. Indeed, as a practical matter, boards continue to prefer particular types of experiences that too often are not typical of people of color.

Importantly, however, diversity advocates likely hoped that the business case would motivate corporations to take steps aimed at addressing the pool problem. Indeed, the pool problem is longstanding. Diversity advocates likely believed that convincing corporations of board diversity's importance to their financial bottom line would

---

33. Copyright © 2011 North Carolina Law Review.

convince them to engage in more aggressive recruiting efforts that extended beyond their traditional pool of candidates and to take steps to expand the pipeline of available diverse candidates. To be sure, some corporations and organizations have taken steps to enhance the pipeline in this area, and the results of those steps might not materialize for some time. However, it is not clear whether and to what extent corporations have actively sought to extend their search for diverse candidates. Instead, director recommendations appear to continue to come from "the usual sources," and hence, corporations have not been expansive in their search for diverse candidates.

The fact that greater embrace of the business case may not have translated into more aggressive efforts to ameliorate the pool problem suggests that the business case has not had its desired effect. Moreover, it raises concerns about whether appeals to economic impulses can prompt directors to engage in broader efforts in this area. Indeed, in many ways, overcoming the pool problem requires a leap of faith because it requires corporations to expend resources in developing a stronger pipeline without proof that this development will have immediate results. It is likely that moral or social appeals may prove more effective than those that speak solely in terms of economics because they do not require concrete data; instead, they focus on "doing the right thing." Then too, overcoming the pool problem may require directors to make personal commitments that may move them beyond their comfort zones. Characterizing diversity in market terms may have suggested that such directors need not move beyond — and may have encouraged directors to remain in — their comfort zones. By contrast, a moral or social appeal may have better luck in ensuring that directors make a personal commitment in this area. Thus, relying on market or economic terms may have served to depersonalize the board diversity issue in ways that proved unproductive.

Comments and Questions

1. Board diversity efforts continue to generate slow progress. Updating the statistics cited by Professor Fairfax, women held just over 19 percent of seats in the boardrooms of Fortune 500 companies in 2014, a small increase from 2013 and 2012, when women held about 17 percent of these directorships. In Fortune1000 companies, only 17.5 percent of board members are women. Blacks, Hispanics, and Asians also are underrepresented. Although more new directors are minorities, the total percentage of minority directors among the largest 200 S&P 500 companies has remained at 15 percent over the past decade. In fact, the percentage of those companies with at least one minority director declined from 90 percent in 2005 to 86 percent in 2015.[34] While Asian-Americans and Hispanics have made small gains, corporate boards have become less black in recent years. The Alliance for Board Diversity reports that in 2012, African-American men held 5.5 percent of board seats at Fortune 500 companies, a decline from 5.7 percent two years earlier. The percentage of African-American female

---

34. Spencer Stuart Board Services, *2015 Spencer Stuart Board Index* 17 (2015).

directors remained flat at 1.9 percent. Asian-Pacific men held 1.9 percent of directorships, and Hispanic and Latino men occupied 3.5 percent of all seats on the boards of large U.S. companies.

If "diversity breeds diversity," how can a "traditional" board become less homogeneous? Are there ways that non-diverse boards might abate unintended bias in director selection?

2. Although corporations express widespread general support for diversity, critics have questioned the true commitment at the top to achieving gender and racial equality in boardrooms and executive suites. According to a PriceWaterhouseCoopers survey of public company directors in 2015, only 35 percent of male directors agreed that it was "very important" to have women on corporate boards, and even fewer men (27 percent) agreed that racial diversity was "very important." Male and female directors disagreed, too, about the importance of diverse boardrooms. In fact, women directors were twice as likely to "very much" believe diversity leads to enhanced board effectiveness. Similarly, nearly three-quarters of female directors "very much" agreed that board diversity leads to enhanced company performance, compared to less than one-third of men. What might such findings indicate about the actual demand for women and minorities as directors at large public companies? To the extent undiversified boards seek director candidates who are good "fits" with the board's social dynamics and/or who will contribute positively to "boardroom collegiality," are they likely to recruit women and minorities?

3. Women and people of color also remain severely underrepresented in board leadership roles. White men lead the boards of nearly all Fortune 500 firms; 95 percent of board chairs and 86 percent of lead directors are white males. One-third of S&P 100 companies lack any female committee chairs, and more than half of these firms lack minority committee chairs. How might the dearth of women in board leadership positions affect diversity on corporate boards?

4. Public pension funds have agitated for greater diversity for more than a decade, adopting diversity policies to guide their investment and voting decisions and engaging informally with corporate leaders to encourage them to identify and support more diverse board candidates. Why do you think public (as opposed to private) institutional investors have led this effort? Some of these investors have used shareholder proposals to prompt changes in board recruitment policies. Since 2008, shareholders have submitted approximately 100 proposals on board diversity, more than half of which were submitted in 2013 and 2014. Typically, shareholders request that boards consider women and minorities for directorships and adopt formal policies addressing board diversity. Many firms that have received such proposals changed their board recruitment criteria to include diversity. Apple, Inc., for example, responded to threatened shareholder proposals by two institutional investors in early 2014 by agreeing to change its policies. Apple amended the charters of its board nominating and corporate governance committees, adding new language affirming that Apple was "committed to actively seeking out highly qualified women and individuals from minority groups to include in the pool from which board nominees are chosen." By the summer, Apple

announced that it had added a second woman to its then eight-member board, replacing its longest-serving member, who was retiring after 17 years of service.

5. Other organizations also have promoted gender and racial diversity on corporate boards. In 2011, for example, a group of institutional investors, senior corporate executives, government officials, leading women's organizations, and corporate governance experts joined together to form the Thirty Percent Coalition. Setting a goal of 30 percent female representation by the end of 2015, the Coalition has concentrated its efforts on "demand side" barriers to diversity by attempting to influence boards to nominate women for directorships. Each year beginning in 2012, the Coalition has sent letters to public companies with all-male boards, urging them to select women candidates. These communications have led some targeted firms to amend their director recruitment practices and nomination policies in an effort to diversify their boards. However, the Coalition obviously will not meet its stated objective.

6. Surveys of corporate directors report that men attribute continuing gender imbalance to the "[l]ack of women in executive ranks" while women perceive that the percentage of women on boards has remained fairly stagnant over the past decade because "[t]raditional networks tend to be male-oriented." What do you make of the claim that women and minorities remain underrepresented on corporate boards because they lack traditional qualifications for directorships?

7. Former CEOs comprised 47 percent of new appointments to the boards of Fortune 500 companies in 2014, as reported by the executive search firm Heidrick & Struggles. Surveys of CEOs reveal that they strongly prefer directors with experience as CEOs. Insofar as board nominating committees exclude director candidates who are not current or former CEOs, they eliminate from consideration women and minorities who might qualify but for the absence of such experience. Why are individuals with experience as CEOs and/or corporate directors considered the ideal candidates for board recruitment? How would you respond to the argument that in order to provide meaningful contributions to the board and real value to the corporation, directors should share the same background and experience as the CEO and one another?

8. Consider the following explanation for board homogeneity:

> The need for 'reliable' and 'independent' directors ... explain[s] the absence of diversity. 'Reliable' categories of directors are notoriously lacking in diversity. With respect to executive officers, few women have risen to the position of CEO of large public companies. Likewise, the pool drawn from the CEO's social and professional circle is not diverse. To the extent, therefore, that nominees are chosen from these categories, rather than the broader pool of substantively qualified candidates, diversity does, and will continue to, suffer.

J. Robert Brown, Jr., *The Demythification of the Board of Directors*, 52 Am. Bus. L.J. 131 (2015). A "reliable" director is a director who will reliably support management's policies and is unlikely to oppose the CEO, even when fully informed. According to Professor Brown, "reliable" directors include friends of management as well as current or former executive officers, especially other CEOs. How might the law prompt corporate boards to nominate less "reliable" (and more diverse) director candidates?

9. Should directors consider diversifying their boards beyond adding individuals with different socio-demographic (gender, race, ethnicity) profiles? Should diverse backgrounds, educations, experiences, and skills also count? What about diversity in an even broader context, such as viewpoint diversity? Should oil companies, for example, include environmentalists on their boards? Should companies that employ large numbers unionized workers seek one or more directors from organized labor? Would shareholders' interests be better served by such representation? How would viewpoint diversity impact boardroom culture?

10. In Norway, where a quota law requires something approaching equal gender representation, anecdotal data suggests that a small number of women hold many board positions. Women gained representation on individual boards, but the pool of women directors had not necessarily increased. What might explain this finding? Might quotas produce minimally participating "trophy" directors who fill seats mainly for the purpose of satisfying the legal requirement?

11. Although unwilling to enact compulsory quotas, several states have taken legislative action to encourage greater representation of women on corporate boards. In 2013, California passed a novel resolution calling for the state's publicly held corporations to increase gender diversity by adding women directors. The advisory measure suggested specific targets for California public companies; for example, women should hold at least three seats if the board includes nine or more directors. Following California's lead, Illinois and Massachusetts have considered similar resolutions. Do you think these initiatives will be effective? Why or why not?

While there is no legal obligation for U.S. companies to diversify their boards of directors, and the matter is left entirely to private ordering, pressure for reform intensified following the financial crisis in 2007. Two years later, the SEC promulgated a new disclosure rule, requiring that publicly-traded companies make the following disclosure in its annual proxy statements:

> Describe the nominating committee's process for identifying and evaluating nominees for director, including nominees recommended by security holders, and any differences in the manner in which the nominating committee evaluates nominees for director based on whether the nominee is recommended by a security holder and whether, and if so how, the nominating committee (or the board) considers diversity in identifying nominees for director. If the nominating committee (or the board) has a policy with regard to the consideration of diversity in identifying director nominees, describe how this policy is implemented, as well as how the nominating committee (or the board) assesses the effectiveness of its policy.

17 C.F.R. § 229.407(c)(2)(vi) (2010). In its adopting release, the Commission explained that the rule was "not intended to steer [reporting company] behavior." Instead, the

SEC enacted the rule to "provide investors with more meaningful disclosure that will help them in their voting decisions by better enabling them to determine whether and why a director candidate is an appropriate choice for a particular company."

Comments and Questions

1. As also noted by the Commission in its adopting release, numerous commentators conveyed specific interest in obtaining from reporting companies information about gender and/or racial diversity, explaining that they found the information useful in making both voting and investment decisions. Nonetheless, the SEC declined to define "diversity" in its rulemaking, explaining, "We recognize that companies may define diversity in various ways, reflecting different perspectives. For instance, some companies may conceptualize diversity expansively to include differences of viewpoint, professional experience, education, skill and other individual qualities and attributes that contribute to board heterogeneity, while others may focus on diversity concepts such as race, gender and national origin. We believe that for purposes of this disclosure requirement, companies should be allowed to define diversity in ways that they consider appropriate." Not only is diversity undefined in the rule, but the SEC also failed to require reporting companies to disclose the definition that their nominating committees (or boards) adopted. Do you agree with the SEC's approach to allow companies to give content to the rule themselves?

2. In practice, it appears that reporting companies have construed diversity quite expansively. Professor Aaron Dhir examined disclosures made by S&P 100 firms in their proxy statements filed between 2010 and 2013. He found that most companies defined diversity with regard to directors' prior business experience or other non identity-based factors (education, skills), whereas only half the companies described diversity to encompass gender, race or ethnicity. Aaron A. Dhir, Challenging Boardroom Homogeneity: Corporate Law, Governance, and Diversity (Cambridge: 2015). Why do you think many firms make no reference in their disclosures to their directors' gender, race, or ethnicity?

3. Because the Commission did not define diversity, the rule is unlikely to prompt boards to recruit more women and people of color, according to Professor Dhir. Indeed, he contends that the SEC gave reporting companies "moral cover" insofar as they can comply simply by taking into account some form of diversity. Can you think of any other unintended consequences of the SEC's disclosure rule?

4. The rule does not mandate that corporations actually adopt a diversity policy, and companies can comply without doing so. Berkshire Hathaway has disclosed, for example, that it "does not have a policy regarding the consideration of diversity in identifying nominees for director. In identifying director nominees, the ... Committee does not seek diversity, however defined." Do you think the Commission intended that its disclosure rule would encourage more corporations to adopt diversity policies? If so, how might the rule have been drafted to influence adoption of diversity policies?

5. The SEC's rule also does not compel reporting companies to disclose directors' gender, race, or ethnicity. As a result, investors who seek this information in order

to exercise their voting rights or make investment decisions must do their own investigation, which can be time-consuming, costly, and potentially inaccurate.

6. Other than promulgating this disclosure rule in 2009, the SEC has taken no further action regarding boardroom diversity, and U.S. stock exchanges make no mention of board diversity in their listed companies regulations. However, the SEC's current chair, Mary Jo White, has criticized the relatively low numbers of women in corporate leadership, expressed publicly her personal frustration at the slow progress made in diversifying boardrooms, and urged that gender and minority "underrepresentation [be] accorded the urgency that I think it deserves." What could the SEC do to accelerate board diversification at public companies?

IX. Directors' Tenure

Although less examined than board diversity, shareholder advocates and academics also have focused attention on directors' tenure in recent years. Of course, the two subjects are connected. Without turning over seats of incumbent directors, board diversification cannot progress, and corporate boardrooms remain, as governance experts say, "male, pale, and stale." In fact, studies confirm that gender diversity accelerates board renewal. Boards with at least one female director continue to add more women to their ranks, while all-male boards have lower refreshment rates. Only 57 percent of all-male boards have added a new director in the past three years. Lack of board refreshment may indicate that directors have become entrenched. Interestingly, the post-SOX elimination of classified board structures at many S&P 500 companies (in favor of annual elections) has had minimal impact on turnover of directors' seats. According to researchers, median director tenure in the S&P 1500 has increased steadily over the past eight years; in 2014, the average director served as a board member for over one year longer than in 2007.[35]

Research also verifies the aging of U.S. corporate boards. According to one study, directors age 72 years or older hold some 20 percent of board seats at S&P 1500 companies. The average age of directors at S&P 500 companies has risen from 60.5 in 2004 to 63.1 in 2014. Moreover, some 45 percent of boards have an average age of 64 or older, compared with just 16 percent a decade ago.[36] Investigators have determined that the change in average age is not merely a result of longer tenure. Rather, more companies now fill open board seats with older directors. Evidence indicates that the median age of new directors, while declining slightly in some years, generally has risen over the past decade. Indeed, retirees comprised more than half of all new non-management directors added to S&P 500 boards in 2014. Retired executives have the expertise sought by companies and the time necessary to fulfill the expanded demands of outside directors under the monitoring board model.

---

35. Equilar, *Age and Tenure in the Boardroom* (June 23, 2015), available at http://www.equilar.com/articles/19-age-and-tenure-in-the-boardroom.html.

36. *See* Spencer Stuart Board Services, *2014 Spencer Stuart Board Index* 4, 17 (2014).

Corporate America's directors have aged despite the widespread approval of director retirement policies. A 2015 survey found that most Fortune 100 firms had such policies in place, typically providing for directors' retirement at age 72. *Five-Year Outlook: Nearly 20% of Directors Poised for Board Exit*, EY Center for Board Matters 1 (2015). Not surprisingly, though, nearly half of these retirement policies expressly allow for waiver. *Id.* What's more, companies with retirement policies have raised the age for directors' exit. In S&P 500 firms, boards with a mandatory retirement age of 75 or older have increased from just 5 percent in 2004 to 30 percent ten years later. *2014 Spencer Stuart Board Index* at 18.

Boardrooms also have become increasingly gray as incumbent directors occupy their seats for longer periods of service. At present, no law, rule, or regulation prescribes term limits for directors. The average tenure of S&P 500 board members is 8.4 years. *2014 Spencer Stuart Board Index*, Spencer Stuart Board Services 5 (2014). Furthermore, fewer than 3 percent of S&P 500 companies have instituted term limits for their directors. *Id.* at 17. Of the firms that have enacted tenure policies, no corporation reportedly restricts directors' service to less than ten years. *Id.* Indeed, just four Fortune 100 companies have adopted director tenure policies as of 2015. *Five-Year Outlook* at 2. Those policies also provide for long terms, ranging from 12 to 20 years. *Id.* Target Corporation, for example, recently extended its tenure limit from 15 years to 20 years.

Like mandatory retirement policies, enforcement of term limits may cause corporate boards to lose high-performing members. Longer-tenured directors generally have substantial knowledge about the company's business, its operations and finances, and its industry. Additionally, they can provide historical perspectives that new directors simply lack. After years of board service, directors also understand the strengths and weaknesses of the executive team, facilitating more effective oversight of management. Armed with wisdom, experience, and maturity, longer-tenured directors may question senior executives more closely, challenge management's assumptions as necessary, and evaluate the CEO's performance more critically. Extended board service also may reflect a director's commitment and loyalty to the corporation and its shareholders.

On the other hand, longer tenures may compromise directors' independence. Board members with many years of service, having established close relationships with the CEO and his team, may defer to the executives more readily and otherwise fail to monitor management effectively. Some evidence also suggests that longer-tenured directors are more likely to staff board compensation and nominating committees, and their participation on compensation committees is associated with higher pay for CEOs.

Shareholders, their advisors, and academics have focused increased attention on board tenure. The Council of Institutional Investors revised its best practice policies recently to include tenure as a factor that boards should consider when determining director independence. Some governance experts have suggested term limits for public company board members, while others have recommended that directors be disqualified as independent after a certain period (e.g., ten years) of board service. Can you think of arguments for and against these proposals?

Director succession and board refreshment have become the subjects of shareholder proposals. In late 2014, shareholder activists submitted a shareholder proposal to Costco Wholesale requesting that its board adopt a bylaw requiring at least two-thirds of directors to have less than 15 years tenure on the board. Costco's board recommended that shareholders vote against the proposal, arguing that such a limit would "arbitrarily deprive Costco of qualified, experienced and effective directors." The proposal failed by a substantial margin. However, governance experts expect similar submissions at other companies. Targets will include firms where at least two-thirds of directors have served for a decade or more, especially if the board shows other signs of stagnation or entrenchment.

Chapter 4

Duties of Corporate Fiduciaries

As we have seen, state corporation statutes empower directors and their officer-delegees with authority and the full discretion to manage the company's business affairs. However, with control of corporate assets vested in its officers and directors, the company's shareholders (who own claims to the residual) become vulnerable to management misfeasance and, worse yet, opportunism. Recognizing that managers may abuse their authority, the law imposes fiduciary duties on directors and officers to regulate their otherwise self-serving behavior. As the Delaware Supreme Court explained:

> While technically not trustees, [directors and officers] stand in a fiduciary relation to the corporation and its shareholders. A public policy, existing through the years, and derived from a profound knowledge of human characteristics and motives, has established a rule that demands of a corporate officer or director, peremptorily and inexorably, the most scrupulous observance of his duty ... [in order] to protect the interests of the corporation committed to his charge.... The rule that requires an undivided and unselfish loyalty to the corporation demands that there shall be no conflict between duty and self-interest.[1]

In Delaware, where most public companies are incorporated, both directors and officers owe fiduciary duties to the company and its shareholders, and those duties, according to the Delaware Supreme Court, are the same.[2]

Unlike the vast majority of states which have codified model standards of conduct for directors and officers, Delaware's General Assembly has declined to enact statutory duties for corporate fiduciaries. Instead, judge-made law regulates the behavior standards for managers of firms incorporated in the state. This means, of course, that Delaware's fiduciary law is subject to interpretation and modification on a case-by-case basis. Some commentators view this malleability as an important advantage of Delaware doctrine, while others have denounced Delaware law as indeterminate.

Corporate directors and officers have two principal fiduciary duties: loyalty and care. The duty of loyalty functions particularly to control managers' opportunism. We examine fiduciaries' duty of loyalty in Chapter 5.

In contrast to the duty of loyalty, the duty of care requires that corporate directors and officers make lawful decisions by employing well-informed, thoughtful processes.

---

1. *Guth v. Loft, Inc.*, 5 A.2d 503, 510 (Del. 1939) (quoted in *Schoon v. Smith*, 953 A.2d 196, 206 (Del. 2008)).

2. *See Gantler v. Stephens*, 965 A.2d 695, 708–09 (Del. 2009).

As implied by its label, the duty of care refers to the obligation of corporate fiduciaries to exercise proper care in their deliberations. Generally, directors and officers must act in good faith, with the care an ordinarily prudent person would exercise under similar circumstances, and in a manner that they reasonably believe is in the best interest of the corporation.

I. The Duty of Care and the Business Judgment Rule

Corporate fiduciaries' care obligations arise in two distinct contexts. First, the duty of care applies when the board of directors exercises its decision-making function, authorizing corporate actions. Second, the duty concerns the board when it engages in its oversight function, monitoring the firm's operations and assuring that company executives fulfill their management responsibilities in compliance with applicable legal rules. In both contexts, the duty of care compels executives to be adequately informed and diligent.

At first glance, directors' and officers' duty of care appears not dissimilar from duties arising under tort law. However, corporate fiduciaries' duty of care is qualified by the business judgment rule. In the following case, Judge Ralph Winter of the Second Circuit Court of Appeals, a corporate and securities law scholar and member of the faculty of Yale Law School, explained why the law rarely holds directors and officers accountable for even their gross negligence.

Joy v. North

United States Court of Appeals, Second Circuit
692 F.2d 880 (1982)

WINTER, CIRCUIT JUDGE:

While it is often stated that corporate directors and officers will be liable for negligence in carrying out their corporate duties, all seem generally agreed that such a statement is misleading. Whereas an automobile driver who makes a mistake in judgment as to speed or distance injuring a pedestrian will likely be called upon to respond in damages, a corporate officer who makes a mistake in judgment as to economic conditions, consumer tastes or production line efficiency will rarely, if ever, be found liable for damages suffered by the corporation. Whatever the terminology, the fact is that liability is rarely imposed on corporate directors or officers simply for bad judgment and this reluctance to impose liability for unsuccessful business decisions has been doctrinally labeled the business judgment rule.

First, shareholders to a very real degree voluntarily undertake the risk of bad business judgment.... In the exercise of what is genuinely a free choice, the quality of a firm's management is often decisive and information is available from professional advisors. Since shareholders can and do select among investments partly on the basis of management, the business judgment rule merely recognizes a certain voluntariness in undertaking the risk of bad business decisions.

Second, courts recognize that after-the-fact litigation is a most imperfect device to evaluate corporate business decisions. The circumstances surrounding a corporate decision are not easily reconstructed in a courtroom years later, since business imperatives often call for quick decisions, inevitably based on less than perfect information. The entrepreneur's function is to encounter risks and to confront uncertainty, and a reasoned decision at the time made may seem a wild hunch viewed years later against a background of perfect knowledge.

Third, because potential profit often corresponds to the potential risk, it is very much in the interest of shareholders that the law not create incentives for overly cautious corporate decisions. Some opportunities offer great profits at the risk of very substantial losses, while the alternatives offer less risk of loss but also less potential profit. Shareholders can reduce the volatility of risk by diversifying their holdings. In the case of the diversified shareholder, the seemingly more risky alternatives may well be the best choice since great losses in some stocks will over time be offset by even greater gains in others.* Given mutual funds and similar forms of diversified investment, courts need not bend over backwards to give special protection to shareholders who refuse to reduce the volatility of risk by not diversifying. A rule which penalizes the choice of seemingly riskier alternatives thus may not be in the interest of shareholders generally.

Whatever its merit, however, the business judgment rule extends only as far as the reasons which justify its existence. Thus, it does not apply in cases in which the cor-

---

* Consider the choice between two investments in an example adapted from Klein, Business Organization and Finance 147–49 (1980):

Investment A

Estimated Probability of Outcome	Outcome Profit or Loss	Value
.4	+15	6.0
.4	+1	.4
.2	−13	−2.6
1.0		3.8

Investment B

Estimated Probability of Outcome	Outcome Profit or Loss	Value
.4	+6	2.4
.4	+2	.8
.2	+1	.2
1.0		3.4

Although A is clearly "worth" more than B, it is riskier because it is more volatile. Diversification lessens the volatility by allowing investors to invest 20 or 200 A's which will tend to guarantee a total result near the value. Shareholders are thus better off with the various firms selecting A over B, although after the fact they will complain in each case of the 2.6 loss. If the courts did not abide by the business judgment rule, they might well penalize the choice of A in each such case and thereby unknowingly injure shareholders generally by creating incentives for management always to choose B.

porate decision lacks a business purpose, is tainted by a conflict of interest, is so egregious as to amount to a wasteful, no-win decision, or results from an obvious and prolonged failure to exercise oversight or supervision.

Comments and Questions

1. The Delaware Supreme Court has decided that corporate directors owe "that amount of care which ordinarily careful and prudent men would use in similar circumstances."[3] However, the drafters of the Model Business Corporation Act included a subjective element in the model law's articulation of the duty of care. *See* M.B.C.A. § 8.30(a)–(b) (2008) (directors must (i) act "in good faith"; (ii) act "in a manner the director reasonably believes to be in the best interests of the corporation" [subjective]; and (iii) "discharge their duties with the care that a person in a like position would reasonably believe appropriate under similar circumstances" [objective].). Do you think that Delaware directors are disadvantaged in this regard? Why or why not?

2. If the risk of personal liability encourages drivers and other potential tortfeasors to act with reasonable (efficient) care, why not corporate directors and officers? Will corporate directors and officers act prudently if they face no real risk of personal liability for failing to do so? Is the threat of financial liability the most effective way to regulate management's behavior? What non-legal sanctions motivate corporate directors and officers to behave optimally?

3. Professor Melvin Eisenberg has argued that corporate managers' standards of conduct and standards of liability necessarily diverge because directors must make complex, inherently outcome-risky decisions.[4] In other words, if threatened with personal liability for unreasonable decisions, directors will reject risky entrepreneurial opportunities that rational shareholders, who can diversify their investment portfolios, actually prefer. Do you agree? Can you think of any flaws with this argument?

4. What are investors' expectations about whether corporate managers can be held legally responsible for their misfeasance? Do you think that shareholders of public companies understand when they invest that the firms' directors and officers will not be held legally accountable for their incompetence, regardless of how much loss they cause to the firm? Professor Rutherford Campbell thinks not. "One would have to assume that in most cases fully informed investors who are able to bargain and exercise market options would turn over their capital to managers who operate with little or no fiduciary duties or legal or financial accountability for mismanagement."[5] Is there reason to believe that rational shareholders prefer the risk of corporate managers' mismanagement, shirking, and/or incompetence to judicial error?

---

3. *Graham v. Allis-Chalmers Mfg. Co.*, 188 A.2d 125, 130 (1963) (holding that directors should be held to the actions of "ordinarily prudent and diligent men").

4. Melvin Aron Eisenberg, *The Divergence of Standards of Conduct and Standards of Review in Corporate Law*, 62 Fordham L. Rev. 437 (1994).

5. Rutheford B. Campbell, Jr., *Normative Justifications for Lax (or No) Corporate Fiduciary Duties: A Tale of Problematic Principles, Imagined Facts and Inefficient Outcomes*, 99 Ky. L. Rev. 231, 248 (2010–2011).

5. Should the law persist in classifying directors and officers as fiduciaries if they are not held accountable as fiduciaries? Relatedly, without enforcing their legal obligations, are directors' and officers' fiduciary duties illusory? Commentators have argued that fiduciary doctrine has a special narrative function. Professors Edward Rock and Michael Wachter, for example, have described Delaware's fiduciary case law as a series of cautionary tales about bad managers from which corporate directors and officers can derive reasonably determinative guidelines for their conduct.[6] Do you agree? How would corporate directors and officers learn of these cautionary tales?

6. Insofar as directors and officers will not be held liable for negligent mismanagement, when, if ever, is it in the interest of the corporation to bring suit against fiduciaries for breaching their duties of care?

II. Process Care and the Business Judgment Rule

Although the law requires corporate fiduciaries to exercise due care when discharging their duties, courts generally will not second-guess the decisions made by corporate fiduciaries acting in good faith. Even where a poor decision caused great loss to the corporation, directors and officers rarely are held to account for their misfeasance. Instead, in the main, courts apply the business judgment rule to claims that directors breached their duty of care. The business judgment rule shields directors from liability by protecting their decisions from judicial review so long as they acted in good faith, were reasonably informed under the circumstances, and rationally believed their decision was in the best interest of the corporation.

Historically, "the business judgment rule became a key feature of Delaware's jurisprudence long before the duty of care."[7] Courts justified the business judgment rule as necessary to preserve the board's authority to manage the business and affairs of the corporation. In addition, the principle recognizes the comparative expertise of directors and officers over judges in deciding business questions. More recently, however, courts and commentators have advanced other arguments in favor of the business judgment rule. For example, in his 1996 decision in *Gagliardi v. Trifoods Int'l, Inc.*, Chancellor William Allen influentially articulated various ways that the doctrine benefits the corporation and its shareholders:

> [I]n the absence of facts showing self-dealing or improper motive, a corporate officer or director is not legally responsible to the corporation for losses that may be suffered as a result of a decision that an officer made or that directors authorized in good faith. There is a theoretical exception to this general statement that holds that some decisions may be so 'egregious' that liability for

---

6. *See* Edward B. Rock & Michael L. Wachter, *Saints & Sinners: How Does Delaware Corporate Law Work?*, 44 U.C.L.A. L. Rev. 1009 (1997) (without imposing liability, Delaware judges' opinions nonetheless promote development of best fiduciary practices).

7. Lyman Johnson, *Unsettledness in Delaware Corporate Law: Business Judgment Rule, Corporate Purpose*, 38 Del. J. Corp. L. 405, 412 (2013).

losses they cause may follow even in the absence of proof of conflict of interest or improper motivation. The exception, however, has resulted in no awards of money judgments against corporate officers or directors in this jurisdiction.... Thus, to allege that a corporation has suffered a loss as a result of a lawful transaction, within the corporation's powers, authorized by a corporate fiduciary *acting in a good faith pursuit of corporate purposes*, does not state a claim for relief against that fiduciary no matter how foolish the investment may appear in retrospect.

The rule could rationally be no different. Shareholders can diversify the risks of their corporate investments. Thus, it is in their economic interest for the corporation to accept in rank order all positive net present value investment projects available to the corporation, starting with the *highest risk adjusted rate of return first.* Shareholders don't want (or shouldn't rationally want) directors to be risk averse. Shareholders' investment interests, across the full range of their diversifiable equity investments, will be maximized if corporate directors and managers honestly assess risk and reward and accept for the corporation the highest risk adjusted returns available that are above the firm's cost of capital.

But directors will tend to deviate from this rational acceptance of corporate risk *if* in authorizing the corporation to undertake a risky investment, the directors must assume some degree of personal risk relating to *ex post facto* claims of derivative liability for any resulting corporate loss.

Corporate directors of public companies typically have a very small proportionate ownership interest in their corporations and little or no incentive compensation. Thus, they enjoy (as residual owners) only a very small proportion of any "upside" gains earned by the corporation on risky investment projects. If, however, corporate directors were to be found liable for a corporate loss from a risky project on the ground that the investment was too risky (foolishly risky! stupidly risky! egregiously risky!—you supply the adverb), their liability would be joint and several for the whole loss (with I suppose a right of contribution). Given the scale of operation of modern public corporations, this stupefying disjunction between risk and reward for corporate directors threatens undesirable effects. Given this disjunction, only a very small probability of director liability based on 'negligence', 'inattention', 'waste', etc., could induce a board to avoid authorizing risky investment projects to any extent! Obviously, it is in the shareholders' economic interest to offer sufficient protection to directors from liability for negligence, etc., to allow directors to conclude that, as a practical matter, there is no risk that, if they act in good faith and meet minimal proceduralist standards of attention, they can face liability as a result of a business loss.

The law *protects shareholder investment interests* against the uneconomic consequences that the presence of such second-guessing risk would have on director action and shareholder wealth in a number of ways. It authorizes corporations to pay for director and officer liability insurance and authorizes corporate indemnification in a broad range of cases, for example. But the first protection against a threat of sub-optimal risk acceptance is the so-called business judgment rule. That 'rule' in effect provides that where a director is independent and disinterested, there can be no liability for corporate loss, unless the facts are such that no person could possibly authorize such a transaction if he or she were attempting in good faith to meet their duty.[8]

Do you agree with Chancellor Allen's arguments? What do you think motivates courts to apply the business judgment rule? Are Chancellor Allen's contentions more or less persuasive depending upon the type of decision made by the directors? For example, would directors' decisions regarding the hiring and compensation of the corporation's senior executive officers give rise to the same level and types of concerns as directors' decisions to declare dividends or to invest in a new research and development project?

In its iconic 1985 decision in the case of *Smith v. Van Gorkom*, the Delaware Supreme Court held that the business judgment rule did not protect the defendant directors from liability. There, the court reviewed a decision by the directors of Trans Union Corporation, a publicly-held Delaware company, to approve the sale of the firm to corporate raider Jay Pritzker. Defendant Jerome Van Gorkom, then Trans Union's chairman of the board and CEO, negotiated the sale of the firm to Pritzker for $55 per share in cash. Van Gorkom did not consult with outside financial experts to determine the fair value of the company, nor did he involve his own executive team in the negotiations. Following a two-hour board meeting scheduled with little advance notice, the Trans Union directors accepted Pritzker's offer at Van Gorkom's recommendation.

Smith v. Van Gorkom

Delaware Supreme Court
488 A.2d 858 (1985)

HORSEY, JUSTICE:

The Court of Chancery concluded from the evidence that the Board of Directors' approval of the Pritzker merger proposal fell within the protection of the business judgment rule. The Court found that the Board had given sufficient time and attention to the transaction, since the directors had considered the Pritzker proposal on three different occasions, on September 20, and on October 8, 1980 and finally on January 26, 1981. On that basis, the Court reasoned that the Board had acquired, over the four month period, sufficient information to reach an informed business judgment on the cash-out merger proposal. The Court ruled:

> ... that given the market value of Trans Union's stock, the business acumen of the members of the board of Trans Union, the substantial premium over

---

8. 683 A.2d 1049 (Del. Ch. 1996) (emphasis in original).

market offered by the Pritzkers and the ultimate effect on the merger price provided by the prospect of other bids for the stock in question, that the board of directors of Trans Union did not act recklessly or improvidently in determining on a course of action which they believed to be in the best interest of the stockholders of Trans Union.

The Court of Chancery made but one finding; i.e., that the Board's conduct over the entire period from September 20 through January 20, 1981 was not reckless or improvident, but informed. This ultimate conclusion was premised upon three subordinate findings, one explicit and two implied. The Court's explicit finding was that Trans Union's Board was "free to turn down the Pritzker proposal" not only on September 20 but also on October 8, 1980 and on January 26, 1981. The Court's implied, subordinate findings were: (1) that no legally binding agreement was reached by the parties until January 26; and (2) that if a higher offer were to be forthcoming, the market test would have produced it, and Trans Union would have been contractually free to accept such higher offer. However, the Court offered no factual basis or legal support for any of these findings; and the record compels contrary conclusions.

Under Delaware law, the business judgment rule is the offspring of the fundamental principle, codified in § 141(a), that the business and affairs of a Delaware corporation are managed by or under its board of directors. In carrying out their managerial roles, directors are charged with an unyielding fiduciary duty to the corporation and its shareholders. The business judgment rule exists to protect and promote the full and free exercise of the managerial power granted to Delaware directors. The rule itself "is a presumption that in making a business decision, the directors of a corporation acted on an informed basis, in good faith and in the honest belief that the action taken was in the best interests of the company." *Aronson v. Lewis*, 473 A.2d 805, 812 (Del. 1984). Thus, the party attacking a board decision as uninformed must rebut the presumption that its business judgment was an informed on.

The determination of whether a business judgment is an informed one turns on whether the directors have informed themselves "prior to making a business decision, of all material information reasonably available to them." *Id.*

Under the business judgment rule there is no protection for directors who have made "an unintelligent or unadvised judgment." *Mitchell v. Highland-Western Glass*, 167 A. 831, 833 (Del. Ch. 1933). A director's duty to inform himself in preparation for a decision derives from the fiduciary capacity in which he serves the corporation and its stockholders. Since a director is vested with the responsibility for the management of the affairs of the corporation, he must execute that duty with the recognition that he acts on behalf of others. Such obligation does not tolerate faithlessness or self-dealing. But fulfillment of the fiduciary function requires more than the mere absence of bad faith or fraud. Representation of the financial interests of others imposes on a director an affirmative duty to protect those interests and to proceed with a critical eye in assessing information of the type and under the circumstances present here.

Thus, a director's duty to exercise an informed business judgment is in the nature of a duty of care, as distinguished from a duty of loyalty. Here, there were no allegations of fraud, bad faith or self-dealing, or proof thereof. Hence it is presumed that the directors reached their business judgment in good faith, and considerations of motive are irrelevant to the issue before us.

We think the concept of gross negligence is also the proper standard for determining whether a business judgment reached by a board of directors was an informed one.

In the specific context of a proposed merger of domestic corporations, a director has a duty under §251(b), along with his fellow directors, to act in an informed and deliberate manner in determining whether to approve an agreement of merger before submitting the proposal to the stockholders. Certainly in the merger context, a director may not abdicate that duty by leaving to the shareholders alone the decision to approve or disapprove the agreement. Only an agreement of merger satisfying the requirements of §251(b) may be submitted to the shareholders under §251(c).

It is against those standards that the conduct of the directors of Trans Union must be tested, as a matter of law and as a matter of fact, regarding their exercise of an informed business judgment in voting to approve the Pritzker merger proposal.

The defendants contend that what the directors did and learned subsequent to September 20 and through January 26, 1981, was properly taken into account by the Trial Court in determining whether the Board's judgment was an informed one. We disagree with this *post hoc* approach.

The issue of whether the directors reached an informed decision to "sell" the Company on September 20, 1980 must be determined only upon the basis of the information then reasonably available to the directors and relevant to their decision to accept the Pritzker merger proposal. This is not to say that the directors were precluded from altering their original plan of action, had they done so in an informed manner. What we do say is that the question of whether the directors reached an informed business judgment in agreeing to sell the Company, pursuant to the terms of the September 20 Agreement presents, in reality, two questions: (A) whether the directors reached an informed business judgment on September 20, 1980; and (B) if they did not, whether the directors' actions taken subsequent to September 20 were adequate to cure any infirmity in their action taken on September 20. We first consider the directors' September 20 actions in terms of their reaching an informed business judgment.

On the record before us, we must conclude that the Board of Directors did not reach an informed business judgment on September 20, 1980 in voting to "sell" the Company for $55 per share pursuant to the Pritzker cash-out merger proposal. Our reasons, in summary, are as follows: The directors (1) did not adequately inform themselves as to Van Gorkom's role in forcing the "sale" of the Company and in establishing the per share purchase price; (2) were uninformed as to the intrinsic value of the Company; and (3) given these circumstances, at a minimum, were grossly negligent in approving the "sale" of the Company upon two hours' consideration, without prior notice, and without the exigency of a crisis or emergency.

As has been noted, the Board based its September 20 decision to approve the cash-out merger primarily on Van Gorkom's representations. None of the directors, other than Van Gorkom and Chelberg, had any prior knowledge that the purpose of the meeting was to propose a cash-out merger of Trans Union. No members of Senior Management were present, other than Chelberg, Romans and Peterson; and the latter two had only learned of the proposed sale an hour earlier.

Without any documents before them concerning the proposed transaction, the members of the Board were required to rely entirely upon Van Gorkom's 20-minute oral presentation of the proposal. No written summary of the terms of the merger was presented; the directors were given no documentation to support the adequacy of $55 price per share for sale of the Company; and the Board had before it nothing more than Van Gorkom's statement of his understanding of the substance of an agreement which he admittedly had never read, nor which any member of the Board had ever seen.

Under § 141(e), "directors are fully protected in relying in good faith on reports made by officers." The term "report" has been liberally construed to include reports of informal personal investigations by corporate officers. However, there is no evidence that any "report," as defined under § 141(e), concerning the Pritzker proposal, was presented to the Board on September 20. Van Gorkom's oral presentation of his understanding of the terms of the proposed Merger Agreement, which he had not seen, and Romans' brief oral statement of his preliminary study regarding the feasibility of a leveraged buy-out of Trans Union do not qualify as § 141(e) "reports" for these reasons: The former lacked substance because Van Gorkom was basically uninformed as to the essential provisions of the very document about which he was talking. Romans' statement was irrelevant to the issues before the Board since it did not purport to be a valuation study. At a minimum for a report to enjoy the status conferred by § 141(e), it must be pertinent to the subject matter upon which a board is called to act, and otherwise be entitled to good faith, not blind reliance. Considering all of the surrounding circumstances — hastily calling the meeting without prior notice of its subject matter, the proposed sale of the Company without any prior consideration of the issue or necessity therefore, the urgent time constraints imposed by Pritzker, and the total absence of any documentation whatsoever — the directors were duty bound to make reasonable inquiry of Van Gorkom and Romans, and if they had done so, the inadequacy of that upon which they now claim to have relied would have been apparent.

The defendants rely on the following factors to sustain the Trial Court's finding that the Board's decision was an informed one: (1) the magnitude of the premium or spread between the $55 Pritzker offering price and Trans Union's current market price of $38 per share; (2) the amendment of the Agreement as submitted on September 20 to permit the Board to accept any better offer during the "market test" period; (3) the collective experience and expertise of the Board's "inside" and "outside" directors; and (4) their reliance on Brennan's legal advice that the directors might be sued if they rejected the Pritzker proposal. We discuss each of these grounds *seriatim*:

(1) A substantial premium may provide one reason to recommend a merger but in the absence of other sound valuation information, the fact of a premium alone does not provide an adequate basis upon which to assess the fairness of an offering price. Here, the judgment reached as to the adequacy of the premium was based on a comparison between the historically depressed Trans Union market price and the amount of the Pritzker offer. Using market price as a basis for concluding that the premium adequately reflected the true value of the company was a clearly faulty, indeed fallacious, premise, as the defendants' own evidence demonstrates.

The record is clear that before September 20, Van Gorkom and other members of Trans Union's Board knew that the market had consistently undervalued the worth of Trans Union's stock, despite steady increases in the Company's operating income in the seven years preceding the merger. The Board related this occurrence in large part to Trans Union's inability to use its ITCs as previously noted. Van Gorkom testified that he did not believe the market price accurately reflected Trans Union's true worth; and several of the directors testified that, as a general rule, most chief executives think that the market undervalues their companies' stock. Yet, on September 20, Trans Union's Board apparently believed that the market stock price accurately reflected the value of the company for the purpose of determining the adequacy of the premium for its sale.

The parties do not dispute that a publicly-traded stock price is solely a measure of the value of a minority position and, thus, market price represents only the value of a single share. Nevertheless, on September 20, the Board assessed the adequacy of the premium over market, offered by Pritzker, solely by comparing it with Trans Union's current and historical stock price.

Indeed, as of September 20, the Board had no other information on which to base a determination of the intrinsic value of Trans Union as a going concern. As of September 20, the Board had made no evaluation of the Company designed to value the entire enterprise, nor had the Board ever previously considered selling the Company or consenting to a buy-out merger. Thus, the adequacy of a premium is indeterminate unless it is assessed in terms of other competent and sound valuation information that reflects the value of the particular business.

Despite the foregoing facts and circumstances, there was no call by the board, either on September 20 or thereafter, for any valuation study or documentation of the $55 price per share as a measure of the fair value of the Company in a cash-out context. It is undisputed that the major asset of Trans Union was its cash flow. Yet, at no time did the Board call for a valuation study taking into account that highly significant element of the Company's assets.

We do not imply that an outside valuation study is essential to support an informed business judgment; nor do we state that fairness opinions by independent investment bankers are required as a matter of law. Often insiders familiar with the business of a going concern are in a better position than are outsiders to gather relevant information; and under appropriate circumstances, such directors may be fully protected in relying in good faith upon the valuation reports of their management.

On the record before us: The Board rested on Romans' elicited response that the $55 figure was within a "fair price range" within the context of a leveraged buy-out. No director sought any further information from Romans. No director asked him why he put $55 at the bottom of his range. No director asked Romans for any details as to his study, the reason why it had been undertaken or its depth. No director asked to see the study; and no director asked Romans whether Trans Union's finance department could do a fairness study within the remaining 36-hour period available under the Pritzker offer.

Had the Board, or any member, made an inquiry of Romans, he presumably would have responded as he testified: that his calculations were rough and preliminary; and, that the study was not designed to determine the fair value of the Company, but rather to assess the feasibility of a leveraged buy-out financed by the Company's projected cash flow, making certain assumptions as to the purchaser's borrowing needs. Romans would have presumably also informed the Board of his view, and the widespread view of Senior Management, that the timing of the offer was wrong and the offer inadequate.

The record also establishes that the Board accepted without scrutiny Van Gorkom's representation as to the fairness of the $55 price per share for sale of the Company-a subject that the Board had never previously considered. The Board thereby failed to discover that Van Gorkom had suggested the $55 price to Pritzker and, most crucially, that Van Gorkom had arrived at the $55 figure based on calculations designed solely to determine the feasibility of a leveraged buy-out. No questions were raised either as to the tax implications of a cash-out merger or how the price for the one million share option granted Pritzker was calculated.

We do not say that the Board of Directors was not entitled to give some credence to Van Gorkom's representation that $55 was an adequate or fair price. Under § 141(e), the directors were entitled to rely upon their chairman's opinion of value and adequacy, provided that such opinion was reached on a sound basis. Here, the issue is whether the directors informed themselves as to all information that was reasonably available to them. Had they done so, they would have learned of the source and derivation of the $55 price and could not have reasonably relied thereupon in good faith.

None of the directors, Management or outside, were investment bankers or financial analysts. Yet, the Board did not consider recessing the meeting until a later hour that day (or requesting an extension of Pritzker's Sunday evening deadline) to give it time to elicit more information as to the sufficiency of the offer, either from inside Management (in particular Romans) or from Trans Union's own investment banker, Salomon Brothers, whose Chicago specialist in merger and acquisitions was known to the Board and familiar with Trans Union's affairs.

Thus, the record compels the conclusion that on September 20 the Board lacked valuation information adequate to reach an informed business judgment as to the fairness of $55 per share for sale of the Company.

(2) This brings us to the post-September 20 "market test" upon which the defendants ultimately rely to confirm the reasonableness of their post September 20 decision to accept the Pritzker proposal. In this connection, the directors present a two-part argument: (a) that by making a "market test" of Pritzker's $55 per share offer a condition of their September 20 decision to accept his offer, they cannot be found to have acted impulsively or in an uninformed manner on September 20; and (b) that the adequacy of the $17 premium for sale of the Company was conclusively established over the 90 to 120 days by the most reliable evidence available—the marketplace. Thus, the defendants impliedly contend that the "market test" eliminated the need for the Board to perform any other form of fairness test either on September 20, or thereafter.

Again, the facts of record do not support the defendants' argument. There is no evidence: (a) that the Merger Agreement was effectively amended to give the Board freedom to put Trans Union up for auction sale to the highest bidder; or (b) that a public auction was in fact permitted to occur.

Van Gorkom states that the Agreement as submitted incorporated the ingredients for a market test by authorizing Trans Union to receive competing offers over the next 90-day period. However, he concedes that the Agreement barred Trans Union from actively soliciting such offers and from furnishing to interested parties any information about the Company other than that already in the public domain.... Van Gorkom, conceding that he never read the Agreement, stated that he was relying upon his understanding that, under corporate law, directors always have an inherent right, as well as a fiduciary duty to accept a better offer notwithstanding an existing contractual commitment by the Board.

The defendant directors assert that they "insisted" upon including two amendments to the Agreement, thereby permitting a market test: (1) to give Trans Union the right to accept a better offer; and (2) to reserve to Trans Union the right to distribute proprietary information on the Company to alternative bidders. Yet, the defendants concede that they did not seek to amend the Agreement to permit Trans Union to solicit competing offers.

Thus, notwithstanding what several of the outside directors later claimed to have "thought" occurred at the meeting, the record compels the conclusion that Trans Union's Board had no rational basis to conclude on September 20 or in the days immediately following, that the Board's acceptance of Pritzker's offer was conditioned on (1) a "market test" of the offer; and (2) the Board's right to withdraw from the Pritzker Agreement and accept any higher offer received before the shareholder meeting.

(3) The directors' unfounded reliance on both the premium and market test as the basis for accepting the Pritzker proposal undermines the defendants' remaining contention that the Board's collective experience and sophistication was a sufficient

basis for finding that it reached its September 20 decision with informed, reasonable deliberation. *Compare Gimbel v. Signal Companies, Inc.*, 316 A.2d 599 (Del. Ch. 1974), *aff'd per curiam*, 316 A.2d 619 (Del. 1974). There, the Court of Chancery preliminary enjoined a board's sale of stock of its wholly-owned subsidiary for an allegedly grossly inadequate price. It did so based on a finding that the business judgment rule had been pierced for failure of management to give its board "the opportunity to make a reasonable and reasoned decision." 316 A.2d at 615. The Court there reached this result notwithstanding the board's sophistication and experience; the company's need of immediate cash; and the board's need to act promptly due to the impact of an energy crisis on the value of the underlying assets being sold-all of its subsidiary's oil and gas interests.

(4) Part of the defense is based on a claim that the directors relied on legal advice rendered at the September 20 meeting by James Brennan, Esquire, who was present at Van Gorkom's request. Unfortunately, Brennan did not appear and testify at trial even though his firm participated in the defense of the action.

Several defendants testified that Brennan advised them that Delaware law did not require a fairness opinion or an outside valuation of the company before the Board could act on the Pritzker proposal. If given, the advice was correct. However, that did not end the matter. Unless the directors had before them adequate information regarding the intrinsic value of the Company, upon which a proper exercise of business judgment could be made, mere advice of this type is meaningless; and, given this record of the defendants' failures, it constitutes no defense here.

A second claim is that counsel advised the Board it would be subject to lawsuits if it rejected the $55 per share offer. It is, of course, a fact of corporate life that today when faced with difficult or sensitive issues, directors often are subject to suit, irrespective of the decisions they make. However, counsel's mere acknowledgment of this circumstance cannot be rationally translated into a justification for a board permitting itself to be stampeded into a patently unadvised act. While suit might result from the rejection of a merger or tender offer, Delaware law makes clear that a board acting within the ambit of the business judgment rule faces no ultimate liability. Thus, we cannot conclude that the mere threat of litigation, acknowledged by counsel, constitutes either legal advice or any valid basis upon which to pursue an uninformed course.

We now examine the Board's post-September 20 conduct for the purpose of determining first, whether it was informed and not grossly negligent; and second, if informed, whether it was sufficient to legally rectify and cure the Board's derelictions of September 20.

The public announcement of the Pritzker merger resulted in an "en masse" revolt of Trans Union's Senior Management. The head of Trans Union's tank car operations (its most profitable division) informed Van Gorkom that unless the merger were called off, fifteen key personnel would resign.

Van Gorkom then advised Senior Management that the Agreement would be amended to give Trans Union the right to solicit competing offers through January,

1981, if they would agree to remain with Trans Union. Senior Management was temporarily mollified, and Van Gorkom then called a special meeting of Trans Union's Board for October 8.

In a brief session, the directors approved Van Gorkom's oral presentation of the substance of the proposed amendments, the terms of which were not reduced to writing until October 10. But rather than waiting to review the amendments, the Board again approved them sight unseen and adjourned, giving Van Gorkom authority to execute the papers when he received them.

The record does not affirmatively establish that Trans Union's directors ever read the October 10 amendments.

We conclude that the Board acted in a grossly negligent manner on October 8, and that Van Gorkom's representations on which the Board based its actions do not constitute "reports" under § 141(e) on which the directors could reasonably have relied.

Next, as to the "curative" effects of the Board's post-September 20 conduct, we review in more detail the reaction of Van Gorkom to the KKR proposal and the results of the Board-sponsored "market test." The KKR proposal was the first and only offer received subsequent to the Pritzker Merger Agreement. On December 2, Kravis [of KKR] and Romans hand-delivered to Van Gorkom a formal letter-offer to purchase all of Trans Union's assets and to assume all of its liabilities for an aggregate cash consideration equivalent to $60 per share. The offer was contingent upon completing equity and bank financing of $650 million, which Kravis represented as 80% complete.

Van Gorkom's reaction to the KKR proposal was completely negative; he did not view the offer as being firm because of its financing condition. It was pointed out, to no avail, that Pritzker's offer had not only been similarly conditioned, but accepted on an expedited basis. Van Gorkom refused Kravis' request that Trans Union issue a press release announcing KKR's offer, on the ground that it might "chill" any other offer.

Within a matter of hours and shortly before the scheduled Board meeting, Kravis withdrew his letter-offer. He gave as his reason a sudden decision by the Chief Officer of Trans Union's rail car leasing operation to withdraw from the KKR purchasing group. Van Gorkom had spoken to that officer about his participation in the KKR proposal immediately after his meeting with Romans and Kravis. However, Van Gorkom denied any responsibility for the officer's change of mind. At the Board meeting later that afternoon, Van Gorkom did not inform the directors of the KKR proposal because he considered it "dead."

Our review of the record compels a finding that confirmation of the appropriateness of the Pritzker offer by an unfettered or free market test was virtually meaningless in the face of the terms and time limitations of Trans Union's Merger Agreement with Pritzker as amended October 10, 1980.

Finally, we turn to the Board's meeting of January 26, 1981. The defendant directors rely upon the action there taken to refute the contention that they did not reach an informed business judgment in approving the Pritzker merger.

The Board could not remain committed to the Pritzker merger and yet recommend that its stockholders vote it down; nor could it take a neutral position and delegate to the stockholders the unadvised decision as to whether to accept or reject the merger. Under §251(b), the Board had but two options: (1) to proceed with the merger and the stockholder meeting, with the Board's recommendation of approval; *or* (2) to rescind its agreement with Pritzker, withdraw its approval of the merger, and notify its stockholders that the proposed shareholder meeting was cancelled. There is no evidence that the Board gave any consideration to these, its only legally viable alternative courses of action.

But the second course of action would have clearly involved a substantial risk— that the Board would be faced with suit by Pritzker for breach of contract based on its September 20 agreement as amended October 10. As previously noted, under the terms of the October 10 amendment, the Board's only ground for release from its agreement with Pritzker was its entry into a more favorable definitive agreement to sell the Company to a third party.... Clearly the Board was not "free" to withdraw from its agreement with Pritzker on January 26 by simply relying on its self-induced failure to have reached an informed business judgment at the time of its original agreement.

Upon the basis of the foregoing, we hold that the defendants' post-September conduct did not cure the deficiencies of their September 20 conduct; and that, accordingly, the Trial Court erred in according to the defendants the benefits of the business judgment rule.

The parties' response, including reargument, has led the majority of the Court to conclude: (1) that since all of the defendant directors, outside as well as inside, take a unified position, we are required to treat all of the directors as one as to whether they are entitled to the protection of the business judgment rule; and (2) that considerations of good faith, including the presumption that the directors acted in good faith, are irrelevant in determining the threshold issue of whether the directors as a Board exercised an informed business judgment. For the same reason, we must reject defense counsel's *ad hominem* argument for affirmance: that reversal may result in a multi-million dollar class award against the defendants for having made an allegedly uninformed business judgment in a transaction not involving any personal gain, self dealing or claim of bad faith.

Plaintiffs have not claimed, nor did the Trial Court decide, that $55 was a grossly inadequate price per share for sale of the Company. That being so, the presumption that a board's judgment as to adequacy of price represents an honest exercise of business judgment (absent proof that the sale price was grossly inadequate) is irrelevant to the threshold question of whether an informed judgment was reached.

The defendants ultimately rely on the stockholder vote of February 10 for exoneration. The defendants contend that the stockholders' "overwhelming" vote approving the Pritzker Merger Agreement had the legal effect of curing any failure of the Board to reach an informed business judgment in its approval of the merger.

The parties tacitly agree that a discovered failure of the Board to reach an informed business judgment in approving the merger constitutes a voidable, rather than void, act. Hence, the merger can be sustained, notwithstanding the infirmity of the Board's action, if its approval by majority vote of the shareholders is found to have been based on an informed electorate. The disagreement between the parties arises over: (1) the Board's burden of disclosing to the shareholders all relevant and material information; and (2) the sufficiency of the evidence as to whether the Board satisfied that burden.

The settled rule in Delaware is that "where a majority of fully informed stockholders ratify action of even interested directors, an attack on the ratified transaction normally must fail." *Gerlach v. Gillam*, 139 A.2d 591, 593 (Del. Ch. 1958). The question of whether shareholders have been fully informed such that their vote can be said to ratify director action, "turns on the fairness and completeness of the proxy materials submitted by the management to the ... shareholders." *Michelson v. Duncan*, 407 A.2d 211, 220 (Del. 1979).

This Court held that corporate directors owe to their stockholders a fiduciary duty to disclose all facts germane to the transaction at issue in an atmosphere of complete candor.... In reality, "germane" means material facts.

Applying this standard to the record before us, we find that Trans Union's stockholders were not fully informed of all facts material to their vote on the Pritzker Merger and that the Trial Court's ruling to the contrary is clearly erroneous.

The burden must fall on defendants who claim ratification based on shareholder vote to establish that the shareholder approval resulted from a fully informed electorate. On the record before us, it is clear that the Board failed to meet that burden.

To summarize: we hold that the directors of Trans Union breached their fiduciary duty to their stockholders (1) by their failure to inform themselves of all information reasonably available to them and relevant to their decision to recommend the Pritzker merger; and (2) by their failure to disclose all material information such as a reasonable stockholder would consider important in deciding whether to approve the Pritzker offer.

We hold, therefore, that the Trial Court committed reversible error in applying the business judgment rule in favor of the director defendants in this case.

On remand, the Court of Chancery shall conduct an evidentiary hearing to determine the fair value of the shares represented by the plaintiffs' class, based on the intrinsic value of Trans Union on September 20, 1980. Thereafter, an award of damages may be entered to the extent that the fair value of Trans Union exceeds $55 per share.

Reversed and remanded for proceedings consistent herewith.

McNEILLY, JUSTICE, DISSENTING:

The majority opinion reads like an advocate's closing address to a hostile jury. And I say that not lightly. Throughout the opinion great emphasis is directed only to the negative, with nothing more than lip service granted the positive aspects of this case.

It would serve no useful purpose, particularly at this late date, for me to dissent at great length. I restrain myself from doing so, but feel compelled to at least point out what I consider to be the most glaring deficiencies in the majority opinion. The majority has spoken and has effectively said that Trans Union's Directors have been the victims of a "fast shuffle" by Van Gorkom and Pritzker. That is the beginning of the majority's comedy of errors. The first and most important error made is the majority's assessment of the directors' knowledge of the affairs of Trans Union and their combined ability to act in this situation under the protection of the business judgment rule.

Trans Union's Board of Directors consisted of ten men, five of whom were "inside" directors and five of whom were "outside" directors. The "inside" directors were Van Gorkom, Chelberg, Bonser, William B. Browder, Senior Vice-President-Law, and Thomas P. O'Boyle, Senior Vice-President-Administration. At the time the merger was proposed the inside five directors had collectively been employed by the Company for 116 years and had 68 years of combined experience as directors. The "outside" directors were A.W. Wallis, William B. Johnson, Joseph B. Lanterman, Graham J. Morgan and Robert W. Reneker. With the exception of Wallis, these were all chief executive officers of Chicago based corporations that were at least as large as Trans Union. The five "outside" directors had 78 years of combined experience as chief executive officers, and 53 years of cumulative service as Trans Union directors.

Directors of this caliber are not ordinarily taken in by a "fast shuffle". I submit they were not taken into this multi-million dollar corporate transaction without being fully informed and aware of the state of the art as it pertained to the entire corporate panorama of Trans Union. True, even directors such as these, with their business acumen, interest and expertise can go astray. I do not believe that to be the case here. These men knew Trans Union like the back of their hands and were more than well qualified to make on the spot informed business judgments concerning the affairs of Trans Union including a 100% sale of the corporation. Lest we forget, the corporate world of then and now operates on what is so aptly referred to as the "fast track". These men were at the time an integral part of that world, all professional business men, not intellectual figureheads.

The majority of this Court holds that the Board's decision, reached on September 20, 1980, to approve the merger was not the product of an *informed* business judgment, that the Board's subsequent efforts to amend the Merger Agreement and take other curative action were *legally and factually* ineffectual, and that the Board did *not deal with complete candor* with the stockholders by failing to disclose all material facts, which they knew or should have known, before securing the stock holders' approval of the merger. I disagree.

At the time of the September 20, 1980 meeting the Board was acutely aware of Trans Union and its prospects. The problems created by accumulated investment tax credits and accelerated depreciation were discussed repeatedly at Board meetings, and all of the directors understood the problem thoroughly. Moreover, at the July, 1980 Board meeting the directors had reviewed Trans Union's newly prepared five-year forecast, and at the August, 1980 meeting Van Gorkom presented the results of a comprehensive study of Trans Union made by The Boston Consulting Group. This study was prepared over an 18 month period and consisted of a detailed analysis of all Trans Union subsidiaries, including competitiveness, profitability, cash throw-off, cash consumption, technical competence and future prospects for contribution to Trans Union's combined net income.

At the September 20 meeting Van Gorkom reviewed all aspects of the proposed transaction and repeated the explanation of the Pritzker transaction and repeated the explanation of the Pritzker offer he had earlier given to senior management. Having heard Van Gorkom's explanation of the Pritzker's offer, and Brennan's explanation of the merger documents the directors discussed the matter. Out of this discussion arose an insistence on the part of the directors that two modifications to the offer be made. First, they required that any potential competing bidder be given access to the same information concerning Trans Union that had been provided to the Pritzkers. Second, the merger documents were to be modified to reflect the fact that the directors could accept a better offer and would not be required to recommend the Pritzker offer if a better offer was made.

I have no quarrel with the majority's analysis of the business judgment rule. It is the application of that rule to these facts which is wrong. An overview of the entire record, rather than the limited view of bits and pieces which the majority has exploded like popcorn, convinces me that the directors made an informed business judgment which was buttressed by their test of the market.

Comments and Questions

1. The majority grounds its opinion in the determination that "Trans Union's Board was grossly negligent in that it failed to act with informed reasonable deliberation." Does this finding make sense? Did the majority conflate the standard of care with the business judgment rule? Are the policies supporting the business judgment rule offended by holding outside directors liable to shareholders for damages for conduct less culpable than intentional disloyalty?

2. After *Van Gorkom*, the Delaware legislature amended Section 141(e) of the state's general corporation law to make clear that directors were entitled to rely on reports, opinions, and statements (including financial statements) imparted by the corporation's officers or employees whom the director reasonably believes to be reliable and competent in the matters presented. Insofar as the Trans Union board relied on Van Gorkom to negotiate the sale of the company and, further, relied on Van Gorkom's judgment as to the firm's value and the adequacy of the price offered by Pritzker, why wasn't the board's reliance reasonable under the circumstances? As the owner of a substantial block of Trans Union stock, didn't Van Gorkom's interests align with the interests of shareholders generally, viz. to maximize the sales price?[9]

---

9. See Jonathan R. Macey, Smith v. Van Gorkom: *Insights About C.E.O.s, Corporate Law Rules, and the Jurisdictional Competition for Corporate Charters*, 96 NW. U. L. Rev. 607 (2002).

3. Despite their good faith and rationality, the court's majority found that Trans Union's directors breached their duty of care by failing to implement satisfactory processes to inform themselves about the true value of the company. What processes should the board have employed to make an informed business decision about the proposed merger?

4. Why do you think the Trans Union's experienced board of directors post hac delegated to Van Gorkom the authority to negotiate with Pritzker unilaterally? Did Trans Union's directors act unreasonably in doing so? Did Trans Union's directors act unreasonably by failing to object when Van Gorkom presented the board with a fully negotiated offer?

5. Why did the court's majority reject defendants' argument that they possessed the qualifications, experience, sophistication, and knowledge of the company's financial condition and prospects sufficient to make an informed decision about the adequacy of the offer? Does this make sense? Assuming Trans Union's directors already had sufficient facts and information necessary to make an informed judgment about the Pritzker offer, what would more process have accomplished?

Following *Van Gorkom*, boards often engage investment banks to provide valuations and fairness opinions for proposed mergers and acquisitions. Who benefits from hiring these outside experts? Who pays the bills for their advice and formal opinions? How might these additional costs impact the number of sale transactions? Why might shareholders receive lower returns on deals consummated?

6. Deciding shareholders' challenges to more recent mergers and acquisitions, Delaware courts have highlighted "the central role played by investment banks in the evaluation, exploration, selection and implementation of strategic alternatives" for boards considering proposed transactions. Insofar as a reviewing court must ascertain the adequacy of information considered by the board, the court "necessarily will consider the extent to which a board has relied on expert advisors."[10] Financial advisors "serve a critical function by performing a valuation of the enterprise upon which its owners rely in determining whether to support a sale. Before shareholders can have confidence in a fairness opinion or rely upon it to an appropriate extent, the conflicts and arguably perverse incentives that may influence the financial advisor in the exercise of its judgment and discretion must be fully and fairly disclosed." The Delaware courts have recognized that investment banking advisors "who guide sometimes inexperienced directors through the [mergers and acquisition] process" are "critical" to protecting shareholders' interests.[11]

7. The court rejected the plaintiffs' allegation of bad faith, but should Jerome Van Gorkom have been held liable for withholding information from his board colleagues that was material to their decision? Indeed, could plaintiffs have made a claim that Van Gorkom violated his duty of candor and, thus, breached his duty of loyalty to the firm?

---

10. *In re Atheros Communications, Inc. S'holder Litig.*, 2011 WL 864928 at *10 (Del. Ch. Mar. 4, 2011).

11. *In re Del Monte Foods Co. S'holders Litig.*, 25 A.3d 813, 831 (Del. Ch. 2011).

8. The Delaware Supreme Court remanded the case to the Court of Chancery with instructions for the lower court to determine the fair market value of plaintiffs' Trans Union shares; the defendants were ordered to pay damages to the extent the fair value exceeded $55 per share. However, before the lower court determined the shares' fair value, the case settled, with some 12,000 former Trans Union shareholders receiving an aggregate settlement of $23.5 million. Of the total settlement fund, directors' and officers' liability insurance paid $10 million, and Jay Pritzker paid the remaining $13.5 million. Given this result, was it really in the shareholders' interest to challenge the directors' good faith decision?

III. After *Smith v. Van Gorkom*

Critics strenuously denounced the Delaware Supreme Court's ruling as an incoherent departure from well-settled law, a decision that threatened the important public policies supporting deference to directors under the business judgment rule. These detractors emphasized that the merger approved by Trans Union's board had provided the firm's shareholders with almost a 60 percent premium over the market value of their shares. As concerning, the court's decision penalized qualified directors with substantial business acumen for their rational, good faith reliance on representations made by the firm's CEO.

In the weeks and months following circulation of the *Van Gorkom* decision, some directors of Delaware corporations threatened to resign. "99% of boards didn't think that anything wrong had happened. Most everybody wrote about the decision as 'the Delaware courts are going nuts.'"[12] Corporate counsel insisted that companies engage investment banks to provide nervous directors with valuations and fairness opinions. At the same time, premiums for directors' and officers' (D&O) liability insurance rose substantially. These developments created pressure on Delaware lawmakers to take legislative action. They responded in 1986 by amending the state's General Corporation Law to enable corporations to exculpate their directors.

DGCL § 102. Contents of certificate of incorporation

(b) In addition to the matters required to be set forth in the certificate of incorporation by subsection (a) of this section, the certificate of incorporation may also contain any or all of the following matters:

(7) A provision eliminating or limiting the personal liability of a director to the corporation or its stockholders for monetary damages for breach of fiduciary duty as a director, provided that such provision shall not eliminate or limit the liability of a director:

(i) For any breach of the director's duty of loyalty to the corporation or its stockholders;

---

12. *Roundtable Discussion: Corporate Governance*, 77 Chi.-Kent L. Rev. 235 (2001). *See also* Daniel R. Fischel, *The Business Judgment Rule and the* Trans Union *Case*, 40 Bus. Law 1437 (1985).

(ii) for acts or omissions not in good faith or which involve intentional misconduct or a knowing violation of law;

(iii) under § 174 of this title; or

(iv) for any transaction from which the director derived an improper personal benefit.

No such provision shall eliminate or limit the liability of a director for any act or omission occurring prior to the date when such provision becomes effective. All references in this paragraph to a director shall also be deemed to refer to such other person or persons, if any, who, pursuant to a provision of the certificate of incorporation in accordance with § 141(a) of this title, exercise or perform any of the powers or duties otherwise conferred or imposed upon the board of directors by this title.

Under Delaware's exculpatory charter statute, corporations can choose to amend their articles of incorporation to protect firm directors from liability for breaching their duty of care. Notice that Delaware corporations are not authorized to exculpate their officers, nor may corporations protect directors from liability for breaches of their duty of loyalty, improper receipt of personal benefits, knowing misconduct, authorization of illegal distributions, or decisions made in bad faith. In addition, directors remain liable to third parties.

Following the enactment of Section 102(b)(7), Delaware corporations almost invariably amended their charters to include exculpatory provisions (sometimes called "raincoat provisions"), and other states quickly followed Delaware's lead, legislating similar provisions for their own corporate statutes.[13] Like Delaware's statute, other states sanction corporate charter provisions eliminating directors' personal liability in damages for breach of the duty of care. A minority of state legislatures extended protections for fiduciaries further than Delaware. For example, some states amended their laws to allow corporations to exculpate both officers and directors, while others enacted fewer exceptions to exculpation than Delaware. A few states eliminated directors' liability directly.[14]

Today, the charters of all major U.S. corporations include broad raincoat provisions, shielding company directors from liability for violating their duty of care. Exculpatory charter provisions clearly advanced the interests of directors in Corporate America, but how does director exculpation affect the corporations' interests? Presumably, shareholders would vote against these charter amendments if their adoption, on balance, harmed the firms. Would it make sense, then, for shareholders to eliminate directors' legal incentives to behave with reasonable due care? Are there other explanations for the widespread shareholder approval of exculpation clauses? Can public companies attract quality directors without providing them with such protec-

---

13. Roberta Romano, *Corporate Governance in the Aftermath of the Insurance Crisis*, 39 Emory L.J. 1155 (1990).

14. *See* Lawrence A. Hamermesh, *Why I Do Not Teach* Van Gorkom, 34 Ga. L. Rev. 477, 490 (2000).

tion? How do we know? Consider, too, that "once management obtains adoption [of an exculpatory charter provision], the provision remains in place, irrespective of the wishes of shareholders, until management decides to initiate a change."[15]

Do raincoat provisions necessarily bar litigation of shareholders' claims alleging that directors breached their fiduciary duties? If not, how do directors enforce exculpatory charter clauses? The Delaware Supreme Court addressed these questions in the following case.

Malpiede v. Townson

Delaware Supreme Court

780 A.2d 1075 (2001)

VEASEY, CHIEF JUSTICE:

In this appeal, we affirm the holding of the Court of Chancery that allegations in the class action complaint challenging a merger do not support the stockholders' claims alleging: (1) breaches of the target board's duty of loyalty or its disclosure duties; and (2) aiding and abetting tortious interference by the acquiring corporation. We further affirm the granting of a motion to dismiss the plaintiffs' due care claim on the ground that the exculpatory provision in the charter of the target corporation authorized by § 102(b)(7), bars any claim for money damages against the director defendants based solely on the board's alleged breach of its duty of care.

Facts

Frederick's of Hollywood is a retailer of women's lingerie and apparel with its headquarters in Los Angeles, California. This case centers on the merger of Frederick's into Knightsbridge Capital Corporation under circumstances where it became a target in a bidding contest.

On June 14, 1996, the Frederick's board announced its decision to retain an investment bank, Janney Montgomery Scott, Inc. ("JMS"), to advise the board in its search for a suitable buyer for the company. In January 1997, JMS initiated talks with Knightsbridge.

On June 13, 1997, the Frederick's board approved an offer from Knightsbridge to purchase all of Frederick's outstanding Class A and Class B shares for $6.14 per share in cash in a two-step merger transaction. The terms of the merger agreement signed by the Frederick's board prohibited the board from soliciting additional bids from third parties, but the agreement permitted the board to negotiate with third party bidders when the board's fiduciary duties required it to do so. The Frederick's board then sent to stockholders a Consent Solicitation Statement recommending that they approve the transaction, which was scheduled to close on August 27, 1997.

---

15. J. Robert Brown, Jr. & Sandeep Gopalan, *Opting Only In: Contractarians, Waiver of Liability Provisions, and the Race to the Bottom*, 42 Ind. L. Rev. 285 (2009).

On August 21, 1997, Frederick's received a fully financed, unsolicited cash offer of $7.00 per share from a third party bidder, Milton Partners.

On August 27, 1997, the Frederick's board received a fully financed, unsolicited $7.75 cash offer from Veritas Capital Fund. In light of these developments, the board postponed the Knightsbridge merger in order to arrange a meeting with the two new bidders. On September 2, 1997, the board sent a memorandum to Milton and Veritas outlining the conditions for participating in the bidding process. The memorandum required that the bidders each deposit $2.5 million in an escrow account and submit, before September 4, 1997, a marked-up merger agreement with the same basic terms and the Knightsbridge merger agreement. Veritas submitted a merger agreement and the $2.5 million escrow payment in accordance with these conditions. Milton did not.

On September 3, 1997, the Frederick's board met with representatives of Veritas to discuss the terms of the Veritas offer. According to the plaintiffs, the board asserts that, at this meeting, it orally informed Veritas that it was required to produce its "final, best offer" by September 4, 1997. The plaintiffs further allege that the board did not, in fact, in form Veritas of this requirement.

The same day that the board met with Veritas, Knightsbridge and the Trusts amended their stock purchase agreement to eliminate the Trusts' termination rights and other conditions on the sale of the Trusts' shares. On September 4, 1997, Knightsbridge exercised its rights under the agreement and purchased the Trusts' shares. Knightsbridge immediately informed the board of its acquisition of the Trusts' shares and repeated its intention to vote the shares against any competing third party bids.

One day after Knightsbridge acquired the Trusts' shares, the Frederick's board participated in a conference call with Veritas to discuss further the terms of the proposed merger. During this conference call, Veritas representatives suggested that, if the board elected to accept the Veritas offer, the board could issue an option to Veritas to purchase authorized but unissued Frederick's shares as a means to circumvent the 41% block of voting shares that Knightsbridge had acquired from the Trusts.

On September 6, 1997, Knightsbridge increased its bid to match the $7.75 Veritas offer, but on the condition that the board accept a variety of terms designed to restrict its ability to pursue superior offers. On the same day, the Frederick's board approved this agreement and effectively ended the bidding process. Two days later, Knightsbridge purchased additional Frederick's Class A shares on the open market, at an average price of $8.21 per share, thereby acquiring a majority of both classes of Frederick's shares.

On September 11, 1997, Veritas increased its cash offer to $9.00 per share. Relying on (1) the "no-talk" provision in the merger agreement, (2) Knightsbridge's stated intention to vote its shares against third party bids, and (3) Veritas' request for an option to dilute Knightsbridge's interest, the board rejected the revised Veritas bid.

Before the merger closed, the plaintiffs filed in the Court of Chancery the purported class action complaint that is the predecessor of the amended complaint before us.

The Court of Chancery granted the directors' motion to dismiss the amended complaint under Chancery Rule 12(b)(6), concluding that ... the exculpatory provision in the Frederick's charter precluded money damages against the directors for any breach of the board's duty of care....

The Duty of Care Claim

Having concluded that the complaint was properly dismissed under Chancery Rule 12(b)(6) for failure to state a claim on which relief may be granted on other fiduciary duty claims, we now turn to the due care claim. The primary due care issue is whether the board was grossly negligent, and therefore breached its duty of care, in failing to implement a routine defensive strategy that could enable the board to negotiate for a higher bid or otherwise create a tactical advantage to enhance stockholder value.

In this case, that routine strategy would have been for the directors to use a poison pill to ward off Knightsbridge's advances and thus to prevent Knightsbridge from stopping the auction process. Had they done so, plaintiffs seem to allege that the directors could have preserved the appropriate options for an auction process designed to achieve the best value for the stockholders.

Construing the amended complaint most favorably to the plaintiffs, it can be read to allege that the board was grossly negligent in immediately accepting the Knightsbridge offer and agreeing to various restrictions on further negotiations without first determining whether Veritas would issue a counteroffer. Although the board had conducted a search for a buyer over one year, plaintiffs seem to contend that the board was imprudently hasty in agreeing to a restrictive merger agreement on the day it was proposed—particularly where other bidders had recently expressed interest. Although the board's haste, in itself, might not constitute a breach of the board's duty of care because the board had already conducted a lengthy sale process, the plaintiffs argue that the board's decision to accept allegedly extreme contractual restrictions impacted its ability to obtain a higher sale price. Recognizing that, at the end of the day, plaintiffs would have an uphill battle in overcoming the presumption of the business judgment rule, we must give plaintiffs the benefit of the doubt at this pleading stage to determine if they have stated a due care claim. Because of our ultimate decision, however, we need not finally decide this question in this case.

We assume, therefore, without deciding, that a claim for relief based on gross negligence during the board's auction process is stated by the inferences most favorable to plaintiffs that flow from these allegations. The issue then becomes whether the amended complaint may be dismissed upon a Rule 12(b)(6) motion by reason of the existence and the legal effect of the exculpatory provision of ... Frederick's certificate of incorporation, adopted pursuant to § 102(b)(7). That provision would exempt directors from personal liability in damages with certain exceptions (*e.g.*, breach of the duty of loyalty) that are not applicable here.

Application of *Emerald Partners*

We now address plaintiffs' argument that the trial court committed error, based on certain language in *Emerald Partners*, by barring their due care claims. Plaintiffs' arguments on this point are based on an erroneous premise, and our decision here is not inconsistent with *Emerald Partners.*

In *Emerald Partners*, we made two important points about the raising of Section 102(b)(7) charter provisions. First we said: "[T]he shield from liability provided by a certificate of incorporation provision adopted pursuant to § 102(b)(7) is in the nature of an affirmative defense." Second, we said: "[W]here the factual basis for a claim *solely* implicates a violation of the duty of care, this court has indicated that the protections of such a charter provision may properly be invoked and applied." [citations omitted]

Based on this language in *Emerald Partners*, plaintiffs make two arguments. First, they argue that the Court of Chancery in this case should not have dismissed their due care claims because these claims are intertwined with, and thus indistinguishable from, the duty of loyalty and bad faith claims. Second, plaintiffs contend that the Court of Chancery incorrectly assign to them the burden of going forward with proof.

The Court of Chancery Properly Dismissed Claims Based Solely on the Duty of Care

Plaintiffs here, while not conceding that the Section 102(b)(7) charter provision may be considered on this Rule 12(b)(6) motion, nevertheless, in effect, conceded in oral argument in the Court of Chancery and similarly in oral argument in this Court that if a complaint unambiguously and solely asserted only a due care claim, the complaint is dismissible once the corporation's Section 102(b)(7) provision is invoked. This concession is in line with our holding in *Emerald Partners* quoted above.

Plaintiffs contended vigorously, however, that the Section 102(b)(7) charter provision does not apply to bar their claims in this case because the amended complaint alleges breaches of the duty of loyalty and other claims that are not barred by the charter provision. As a result, plaintiffs maintain, this case cannot be boiled down solely to a due care case. They argue, in effect, that their complaint is sufficiently well-pleaded that—*as a matter of law*—the due care claims are so inextricably intertwined with loyalty and bad faith claims that Section 102(b)(7) is not a bar to recovery of damages against those directors.

We disagree. It is the plaintiffs who have a burden to set forth "a short and plain statement of the claim showing that the pleader is entitled to relief." The plaintiffs are entitled to all reasonable inferences flowing from their pleadings, but if those inferences do not support a valid legal claim, the complaint should be dismissed without the need for the defendants to file an answer and without proceeding with discovery. Here, we have assumed, without deciding, that the amended complaint on its face states a due care claim. Because we have determined that the complaint fails properly to invoke loyalty and bad faith claims, we are left with only a due care claim. Defendants had the obligation to raise the bar of Section 102(b)(7) as a defense, and they did. As plaintiffs conceded in oral argument before this court, if there is only an unambiguous, residual due care claim and nothing else—*as a matter of law*—then Section 102(b)(7) would bar the claim. Accordingly, the Court of Chancery did not err in dismissing the plaintiffs due care claim in this case.

The Court of Chancery Correctly Applied the
Parties' Respective Burdens of Proof

Plaintiffs also assert that the trial court in the case before us incorrectly placed on plaintiffs a pleading burden to negate the elements of the 102(b)(7) charter provision.

But we have held that the amended complaint here does not allege a loyalty violation or other violation falling within the exceptions to the Section 102(b)(7) exculpation provision. Likewise, we have held that, even if the plaintiffs had stated a claim for gross negligence, such a well-pleaded claim is unavailing because defendants have brought forth the Section 102(b)(7) charter provision that bars such claims. This is the end of the case.

And rightly so, as a matter of the public policy of this state. Section 102(b)(7) was adopted by the Delaware General Assembly in 1986 following a directors and officers insurance liability crisis and the 1985 Delaware Supreme Court decision in *Smith v. Van Gorkom.* The purpose of this statute was to permit stockholders to adopt a provision in the certificate of incorporation to free directors of personal liability in damages for due care violations, but not duty of loyalty violations, bad faith claims, and certain other conduct. Such a charter provision, when adopted, would not affect injunctive proceedings based on gross negligence. Once the statute was adopted, stockholders usually approved charter amendments containing these provisions because it freed up directors to take business risks without worrying about negligence lawsuits.

Our jurisprudence since the adoption of the statute has consistently stood for the proposition that a Section 102(b)(7) charter provision bars a claim that is found to state only a due care violation. Because we have assumed that the amended complaint here does state a due care claim, the exculpation afforded by the statute must affirmatively be raised by the defendant directors. The directors have done so in this case, and the Court of Chancery properly applied the Frederick's charter provision to dismiss the plaintiffs' due care claim.

Conclusion

We have concluded that … the amended complaint does not adequately allege a breach of the Frederick's board's duty of loyalty or its disclosure duty … [and] the exculpatory provision in the Frederick's charter operates to bar claims for money damages against the directors caused by the alleged breach of the board's duty of care…. Accordingly, we affirm the judgment of the Court of Chancery dismissing the amended complaint against the Frederick's board and Knightsbridge.

Comments and Questions

1. The Delaware Supreme Court seems to acknowledge that unless the defendant directors have failed to act in good faith or otherwise violated their duty of loyalty, Section 102(b)(7) will shield them from liability for monetary damages and no trial on the issue of entire fairness is necessary, even though a violation of the duty of care would rebut the business judgment rule. Does this decision render the duty of care

unenforceable insofar as nearly all Delaware corporations, as discussed below, have adopted exculpatory charter provisions pursuant to Section 102(b)(7)?

2. Where a corporation has adopted an exculpatory charter provision, shareholders seeking to impose liability upon corporate directors for misfeasance generally will assert that one of the statutory exceptions to exculpation applies. Often, plaintiffs will invoke the exception for acts or omissions not made in good faith; importantly, good faith is not defined in the statute, nor have the courts provided an authoritative definition of good faith. Is good faith merely the absence of bad faith? How should the law distinguish the absence of care from acts not taken in good faith? How is good faith distinct from loyalty? What are the advantages and disadvantages of allowing the courts to define good faith on a case-by-case basis?

3. Section 102(b)(7) shields directors from liability for breach of certain fiduciary duties, but the statute does not eliminate directors' duty of care. Therefore, "[d]irectors whose actions fail to pass muster under the applicable standard of review have breached their fiduciary duties, even though they are not liable for damages when exculpation applies."[16] Is this a distinction without difference? Might a corporation or its shareholders pursue equitable remedies against directors who have breached their duty of care? Under what circumstances might an aggrieved corporation sue for equitable relief? What equitable remedies might provide meaningful relief to the corporation?

4. Several months after its decision in *Malpiede*, the Delaware Supreme Court heard a third appeal in the *Emerald Partners v. Berlin* litigation ("*Emerald Partners III*"[17]). There, the controlling stockholder had been dismissed at an early stage of the litigation (as a result of bankruptcy), leaving only the disinterested directors to prove that the challenged transaction was entirely fair. The Supreme Court held that even where the disinterested directors had full protection under an exculpatory charter provision, the trial court nonetheless was "require[d] to appl[y] the entire fairness standard of judicial review ab initio at trial," and, in such a case, "a determination that director defendants are exculpated from paying monetary damages can be made only after the basis for their liability has been decided." The *Emerald Partners* opinion explained that if entire fairness is the applicable standard of review, "injury or damages becomes a proper focus only after a transaction is determined not to be entirely fair" and thus, "the exculpatory effect of a Section 102(b)(7) provision only becomes a proper focus of judicial scrutiny after the directors' potential personal liability for the payment of monetary damages has been established."

5. Practitioners and commentators recognized that *Emerald Partners III* could be read to conflict with the decision in *Malpiede*, making disinterested directors who plead exculpation worse off procedurally than disinterested directors who omitted the affirmative defense from their answer. Defendants argued that the *Emerald Partners III* decision allowed complaints without merit to survive motions to dismiss sanctioned by *Malpiede*, continuing costly litigation. For nearly fifteen years after *Emerald Partners*

---

16. *In re Rural Metro Corp. S'holders Litig.*, 88 A.3d 54 (Del. Ch. 2014), *aff'd* (Del. Nov. 30, 2015).
17. 787 A.2d 85 (Del. 2001).

III, litigating parties disputed the pleading standard applicable to minority share-holders' claims for monetary damages alleging that disinterested director fiduciaries breached their duties by negotiating, approving, or otherwise facilitating controlled shareholder deals (e.g., by serving on a special committee charged with negotiating the transaction on behalf of the firm). Defendants insisted that plaintiffs must plead specific facts raising an inference that each disinterested director defendant breached a duty not subject to exculpation. Plaintiffs disagreed, arguing that, pursuant to *Emerald Partners III*, they need only plead that (1) the controlling shareholder was on both sides of the transaction, (2) the transaction with the controlling shareholder was not entirely fair to minority shareholders, and (3) the disinterested director defendants negotiated or facilitated the deal.

The Delaware Supreme Court finally resolved the controversy, siding with dis-interested director defendants in a 2015 decision *In re Cornerstone Therapeutics*.[18] In that case, a minority shareholder objected to the company's acquisition by a con-trolling stockholder and sued not only that controlling shareholder and the directors affiliated with the controller but also the disinterested directors, persons who served on a special committee that negotiated with the controller and approved the final deal. Granting defendants' interlocutory appeal and reversing the Chancery Court, the Supreme Court held that in order to plead cognizable claims against disinterested directors who were protected by an exculpatory provision, plaintiffs must allege that each defendant violated non-exculpated duties, regardless of the underlying standard used to review the disputed transaction. Specifically, plaintiffs must plead facts supporting a rational inference that each defendant director "harbored self-interest adverse to the stockholders' interests, acted to advance the self-interest of an interested party from whom [he or she] could not be presumed to act independ-ently, or acted in bad faith." The Court distinguished *Emerald Partners III* and limited its holding to cases involving a "viable, non-exculpated loyalty claim" against a dis-interested director.

What non-exculpated claims might plaintiffs investigate against disinterested di-rectors? At the pleading stage, how might plaintiffs uncover facts giving rise to such non-exculpated claims?

Section 102(b)(7) enables Delaware corporations to protect their directors from certain specified liabilities, but the statute does not mandate that they do so. Corpo-rations can "opt in" to the exculpatory regime, either fully or partially, by amending their corporate charters, an action requiring shareholder approval. Assuming that shareholders bargain with directors, this "private ordering" approach may, in theory, lead to greater efficiency. In the following article, the authors examined how directors and shareholders of large public companies responded to enactment of the statute by the Delaware legislature.

---

18. *In re Cornerstone Therapeutics Inc., S' holder Litig.*, 115 A.3d 1173 (Del. 2015).

J. Robert Brown, Jr. & Sandeep Gopalan,
Opting Only In: Contractarians, Waiver of Liability Provisions, and the Race to the Bottom
42 Ind. L. Rev. 285 (2009)[19]

A widespread view in the academy is that corporations are best analyzed as a "nexus of contracts." As Professor Eisenberg notes, "[u]nder the nexus-of-contracts conception, the body of shareholders is not conceived to own the corporation. Rather, shareholders are conceived to have only contractual claims against the corporation." The corporation is created by a "nexus of reciprocal arrangements," and the role of the law should be to facilitate this contracting process. Managers, owners, and others bargain for the most efficient relationships, which are ones that uniquely reflect the interests of the particular parties involved.

While recognizing that managers have self-interested motivations to pursue their aims at the expense of the shareholders, contractarians rely on the "invisible hand" to constrain such behavior. Investors will punish self-interested behavior by discounting the securities issued by those companies, thus presenting an effective incentive for managers to act in ways that maximize shareholder welfare. Over a period of time companies having poor governance arrangements will be weeded out by the market, and those exhibiting optimal arrangements will thrive. Contractarians, therefore, favor enabling provisions where parties can opt-in or opt-out and eschew the one-size-fits-all approach of categorical rules. Corporate law, in this framework, should merely provide a set of default rules.

The opposition to categorical rules has influenced the view of contractarians on the evolution of corporate law. The paradigmatic example is Delaware—where companies choose to incorporate there because of its expert judiciary, sophisticated bar, and a commitment to maintaining a climate for private ordering. Contractarians view corporate law as a good that states are competing to supply and that companies choose because of the efficiency of the legal regimes offered. They characterize the predominance of companies incorporated in Delaware as a race to the top rather than to the bottom.

Section 102(b)(7)

The consternation caused by *Van Gorkom* threatened Delaware's pro-management position. Not lost on the Delaware bar and legislature, the Council of the Corporation Law Section of the Delaware State Bar Association set to work on a legislative response. That Indiana passed a statute designed to reduce liability no doubt increased the pressure on Delaware to act. Rejecting a number of other approaches, the Council ultimately settled on what was to become Section 102(b)(7). Relying on an "opt-in" approach, the provision authorized companies to insert into their articles a provision that essentially allowed for the waiver of monetary damages against the board for violations of the duty of care. In other words, companies could absolve their directors for grossly negligent behavior.

---

19. Copyright © 2009 Indiana Law Review. Reprinted with permission.

Despite the temporal proximity to *Van Gorkom*, the legislative history of the provision indicated that the impetus was the "crisis" in the D&O insurance market:

> Section 102(b)(7) and the amendments to Section 145 represent a legislative response to recent changes in the market for directors' liability insurance. Such insurance has become a relatively standard condition of employment for directors. Recent changes in that market, including the unavailability of the traditional policies (and, in many cases, the unavailability of any type of policy from the traditional insurance carriers) have threatened the quality and stability of the governance of Delaware corporations because directors have become unwilling, in many instances, to serve without the protection which such insurance provides and, in other instances, may be deterred by the unavailability of insurance from making entrepreneurial decisions. The amendments are intended to allow Delaware corporations to provide substitute protection, in various forms, to their directors and to limit director liability under certain circumstances.

Aware that the "crisis" was economic in nature (reflecting increased costs of insurance), the legislature attempted to link the reform to improved governance. Waiver of liability provisions would ensure a steady supply of qualified directors.

The rationale was suspect, solving a problem in the D&O insurance market that either did not exist or could have been more appropriately corrected by the market. First, it presupposed that the insurance "crisis" resulted from an increased risk of liability under the duty of care, an unproven assumption at the time that ultimately proved incorrect. Second, there was every reason to believe that the problem would be short-lived, with the market, in time, establishing a new equilibrium. In fact, by 1987, the "crisis" was largely over.

The purported concern over corporate governance was never established. While some anecdotal "evidence" indicated a growing number of resignations, the evidence was never marshaled to show that this resulted from problems in the D&O insurance market or that adequate replacements were unavailable. Indeed, some of the evidence suggested that directors quit not because of a threat of liability but because, in the aftermath of *Van Gorkom*, they had to work harder. Moreover, even if the pool had declined, companies had a ready mechanism for correcting the imbalance: increasing directors' fees.

The adoption of waiver of liability amounted to an overbroad response to the purported concerns about "uncertainty" in the application of the duty of care. The issues arising out of *Van Gorkom* could have been addressed in a narrower fashion, focusing, for example, on the basis for establishing an informed decision. The provision, however, went beyond the purported problems created by the decision, eliminating liability even in circumstances where no uncertainty existed.

In other words, the Delaware legislature adopted waiver of liability provisions to cure an insurance "crisis" that was short-lived, and likely structural, in order to prevent adverse consequences which were unproven for boards of directors. Rather than fix the perceived concerns with *Van Gorkom* through a narrowly tailored approach, Delaware's legislature opted for an overbroad solution that exonerated directors for breach of the duty of care in all circumstances. In short, it was a provision designed less to solve a real governance problem and more to use the surrounding din as cover to reduce director liability.

Waiver of liability did not, therefore, restore the D&O insurance market. It did, however, restore Delaware's pro-management position, something that had taken a beating in the aftermath of *Van Gorkom*. The "crisis" was little more than a cover for a substantial, pro-management change in fiduciary obligations.

Even as the insurance crisis dissipated, other states passed copycat legislation. By corporate law reform standards, the speed with which other states fell in line was nothing short of remarkable. Within a few years of the new millennium, all states had some version of waiver of liability. A modest number of states chose an "opt-out" approach, eliminating monetary damages for breach of the duty of care but allowing companies to reinstate damages through amendments to the articles. The vast majority of states, however, followed the Delaware model and relied on an "opt-in" approach.

What could be the reasons? Not the D&O insurance crisis; that was over. Not efficiency. Instead, the statutes were designed to prevent companies from moving to Delaware. Whatever Delaware's motivation, other states adopted comparable provisions not because of improved governance or efficiency, but because the statutes benefited management and avoided re-incorporation, even though some evidence suggested harm to shareholder values.

The Corporate Response

The conclusion that Delaware authorized waiver of liability provisions to restore its pro-management reputation does not necessarily preclude a finding of increased efficiency. The Delaware model relied upon an opt-in approach, which theoretically allows owners and managers to bargain for the most efficient arrangements.

In practice, however, this has not been the case. The "opt-in" approach used by the Delaware statute places exclusive authority in the hands of management to institute a waiver of liability provision and to draft the appropriate language. Structured as amendments to the articles, only the board can initiate the change. The monopoly over initiation effectively bars shareholders from opting back into the default regime. Management, therefore, can pick the most propitious moment to make a proposal, and, once in place, shareholders cannot initiate repeal. Finally, as the proponent, it is management that drafts the language in the waiver provisions.

The adoption process, predictably, contains no element of bargaining or private ordering. Instead, it is a management-dominated process. Given the benefits to management resulting from adoption, its control over the process, and the inability of shareholders to initiate repeal, it is difficult to see the opportunities for bargaining and private ordering. Instead, one could reasonably predict that over time all companies would put these provisions in place and all provisions would waive liability to the fullest extent permitted by law.

With these predictions in mind, let us turn to the empirical evidence. Many authors have already noted the popularity of waiver of liability provisions. No one, however, has studied the phenomenon systematically.

We have chosen as the initial universe for examination the Fortune 100 in the United States. Of that group, ninety-nine are incorporated under state law. Freddie Mac, a federally incorporated entity, is the only exception. Of the remainder, sixty-five are incorporated in Delaware, five in New York, four in New Jersey, Minnesota, and Pennsylvania, three in Ohio, Washington, and North Carolina, two in Illinois, and Massachusetts, and one in Virginia, Maryland, California, and Wisconsin.

Some of these states do not require charter provisions to "opt-in" to the liability waiver. In such states, the corporate code raises the level of culpability necessary for the imposition of damages, with companies allowed to "opt-out." This is true in Ohio and Wisconsin. Virginia imposes a cap but also allows elimination of liability in the articles. The rest (other than Freddie Mac) mimic the Delaware model, with some variations in language.

Among the non-federally incorporated, non-mutual companies, only one, Pepsi Co., did not have a waiver of liability provision. Pepsi was incorporated in Delaware in 1919 and re-incorporated in North Carolina in 1986. The bylaws do provide for indemnification rights "to the full extent permitted by law."

Our study of the articles of these companies shows that all waive liability to the maximum extent permitted by law. Several companies have a bare bones version of the clause containing the following language: "A director of the Corporation shall have no personal liability to the Corporation or its stockholders for monetary damages for breach of his fiduciary duty as a director to the full extent permitted by the Delaware General Corporation Law as it may be amended from time to time." The others generally repeat the language in the statute, providing that directors shall not be liable for monetary damages with some listed exceptions. Some specifically reference recklessness, while others prohibit repeal. With respect to liability for directors, none of the Fortune 100 purport to waive liability in some reduced fashion.

What explains this curious uniformity? The data shows that one categorical rule has been replaced with another. While the old rule allowed for damages in the case of a breach of the duty of care, the adoption of an "opt-in" approach to monetary damages simply resulted in everyone opting in. The results show none of the diversity that private ordering predicted.

The data shows that companies do not opt-in in the waiver of liability context. This is because of the difficulties imposed on shareholders who might want to engage in some type of negotiations. Thus, realities on the ground make change difficult despite the presence of activist shareholders. Many of these difficulties are systemic.

First, only management has the authority to propose an amendment to the articles of incorporation. Directors can pick the most propitious time to propose a matter to shareholders. The authority goes much further, however, than the power to propose. To the extent management perceives any prospect of losing a vote, it has a variety of tactics that it can deploy to affect the outcome. One example is *Mercier v. Inter-Tel (Del.), Inc.*, where a special committee of the board sought approval of a merger. When, shortly before the meeting, it became clear the proposal would fail, the committee authorized an adjournment. This occurred despite overwhelming opposition to adjournment of the meeting from shareholders.

Second, waiver of liability provisions can be implemented without the benefit of a direct shareholder vote. The provisions may be in the articles when the company goes public. In other cases, they may be inserted into the articles when the company re-incorporates, leaving shareholders with approving the entire transaction, not each individual provision in the articles. Waiver of liability provisions may also be approved in companies with controlling shareholders, making the opinions of the minority shareholders irrelevant.

Third, even when submitted for approval, shareholders confront the usual bevy of collective action problems. They lack information, often a consequence of rational apathy. To oppose management they would need to lobby other shareholders, which is both expensive and difficult due to the proxy rules.

Fourth, there are a number of reasons why shareholders are less likely to oppose waiver of liability provisions. One is the NIMBY phenomenon. Another is path dependence. Yet another is the "me-too" phenomenon, which occurs when one board has a waiver of liability provision to fall back on so every other board clamors for the same. With the provisions universally in place, shareholders would have to accept the consequences of denying the waiver to their management while all other large companies, including competitors, have the waiver in place.

Fifth, shareholders typically want to maintain positive relations with management, preferring to "vote with their feet" when dissatisfied. Thus, they will not oppose management on every proposal, even if they have reservations. In other words, opposition comes with costs attached. Given the insignificance of the duty of care under Delaware law, these costs likely outweigh the benefits that could result from opposition.

Directors might be made nervous by a provision that differs from those of other companies. In such cases, our evidence might explain the persistence of "suboptimal uniformity." The suboptimal rule waiving liability to the fullest extent allowed by the law has become uniform because learning or network externalities are significant, especially because waiver of liability provisions are drafted and proposed at the insistence of management. Given the agency cost, lawyers on the management payroll are unlikely to draft provisions that are against the interests of management, even if such provisions are in the management interests of shareholders.

The nexus-of-contracts approach is a worthy theoretical framework for the examination of issues relating to corporate governance. This is particularly true in emphasizing the importance of private ordering in the regulatory process. The usefulness, however, breaks down when the approach is used to explain the relationship between shareholders and management. There is little evidence in practice that the relationship between shareholders and managers can be accurately characterized as a process of private ordering. Instead, when the law defers to private ordering, the result is that management is allowed to impose on shareholders a categorical rule that embodies its self-interest. In the context of waiver of liability provisions, this approach has resulted in one categorical rule being replaced by another—precisely the opposite of what contractarians desire.

Thus, it would seem that the contractarian approach does not offer an adequate explanation for the situation with regard to waiver of liability provisions. Based on our evidence, the managerial model might offer better predictive power. Management would always want the reduced liability. Given learning and network effects, over time, such provisions would become universal. Management would also want protection to the fullest extent permitted. This would yield provisions consistent with the evidence that we have presented.

The evidence is consistent with a race to the bottom. The waiver of liability provisions were not designed to solve a corporate governance problem, but were intended to benefit management. Because management controls the re-incorporation process, they could move the company to Delaware to take advantage of reduced liability. Other states quickly mimicked Delaware's approach, not because it promoted good governance or efficient behavior, but because it prevented corporate flight to Delaware.

To have anything approaching an effective system of bargaining, the shareholder voting process must be meaningful. Management must know that shareholders have the ability to veto or overturn an opt-in or opt-out decision. Therefore, there must be substantial reform of the shareholder voting process.

These reforms need to do several things. First, shareholders need authority equal to that of management to initiate an opt-in or opt-out process or to change a prior decision. To do this, all opt-in or opt-out provisions either need to be in the bylaws (with shareholders receiving explicit authority to initiate, change, or repeal the bylaws) or, in the articles of incorporation with the authority to initiate an amendment to the articles.

Second, shareholders need to be given far broader authority to propose changes to the arrangements that constitute the nexus of contracts in any particular company. There are substantial areas of governance that are off-limits to shareholders. These typically arise in the context of proposals that could affect the management of the company. The argument that shareholders should not be allowed to micromanage the diurnal functioning of the company has been raised as the bogey to limit shareholder empowerment in areas that, at best, involve de minimis interference in the actual management of the company. Shareholders might condition support for a management inspired opt-in or opt-out proposal on management support for additional shareholder authority, such as an advisory vote on executive compensation.

Third, steps need to be taken to solve some of the collective action problems that impede the shareholder approval process. These issues generally relate to organization and cost. Cost issues arise most clearly in the need to solicit proxies, an expensive and time consuming process. Liberal access to the company's proxy statement for shareholder proposals would be one way to reduce costs associated with collective action.

Comments and Questions

1. Of the large companies studied, only one firm, Pepsi, did not include a waiver of liability provision in its corporate charter.

2. Section 102(b)(7) impacted the market for corporate charters significantly. Once Delaware enacted this provision, a substantial number of companies reincorporated there.[20] Understanding the circumstances leading to the enactment of Section 102(b)(7) in Delaware and the passage of similar statutes by lawmakers in other states, does this history provide evidence of a race to the top or a race to the bottom? Make the case for each.

3. Shareholders typically approve waiver of liability provisions, voting in favor of such charter amendments by wide margins. Why do you think shareholders almost invariably vote to protect corporate directors from liability? Shouldn't shareholders object proposals that serve to deprive them of compensation for damages in the event that directors breach their duties of care?

4. Given the widespread adoption of exculpatory charter provisions, is it accurate to characterize them as default rules? What if shareholders decided to eliminate the exculpatory provision in the firm's charter? Could investors so amend the articles of incorporation without action by the board of directors?

5. Commentators have criticized the language of Section 102(b)(7) as imprecise. For example, it excludes breaches of the duty of loyalty without defining the term. Moreover, the provision excludes both violations of good faith and the duty of loyalty. Yet, as we will see, Delaware courts have defined violations of good faith as a breach of the duty of loyalty. *See Stone v. Ritter*, 911 A.2d 362, 370 (Del. 2006). The parallel section in the Model Business Corporation Act excludes, among other things, "the amount of a financial benefit received by a director to which he is not entitled" and "an intentional infliction of harm on the corporation or the shareholders...." How might these differences between the law in Delaware and a MBCA state affect management's decision as to where to incorporate?

IV. Directors' Oversight and the Duty to Monitor

The business judgment rule applies to protect the decisions of directors and officers from judicial review. Fiduciaries who do not exercise their business judgment or otherwise fail to act will not receive protection from the rule. However, especially in the boardrooms of public companies today, corporate directors make relatively few discrete

---

20. *See* Michael Bradley & Cindy A. Schipani, *The Relevance of the Duty of Care Standard in Corporate Governance*, 75 Iowa L. Rev. 1, 65 (1989) ("To date we have identified approximately 100 firms that reincorporated in Delaware between July 1, 1986 and May 1988.").

decisions; rather, directors' functions chiefly involve supervision of senior executives and general oversight of firm management. What care must corporate fiduciaries exercise in fulfilling their oversight responsibilities? When should they be held accountable for failing to exercise those duties? In the next case, the Delaware Chancery Court addressed directors' liability for breach of the duty of care where the board failed to adequately supervise company employees whose misconduct caused the firm to violate the law.

In re Caremark Int'l Inc. Deriv. Litig.

Delaware Chancery Court
698 A.2d 959 (1996)

ALLEN, CHANCELLOR:

Pending is a motion pursuant to Chancery Rule 23.1 to approve as fair and reasonable a proposed settlement of a consolidated derivative action on behalf of Caremark International Inc. The suit involves claims that the members of Caremark's board of directors (the "Board") breached their fiduciary duty of care to Caremark in connection with alleged violations by Caremark employees of federal and state laws and regulations applicable to healthcare providers.

This suit was filed in 1994, purporting to seek on behalf of the company recovery of these losses from the individual defendants who constitute the board of directors of Caremark. The parties now propose that it be settled and, after notice to Caremark shareholders, a hearing on the fairness of the proposal was held on August 16, 1996.

Legally, evaluation of the central claim made entails consideration of the legal standard governing a board of directors' obligation to supervise or monitor corporate performance. For the reasons set forth below I conclude, in light of the discovery record, that there is a very low probability that it would be determined that the directors of Caremark breached any duty to appropriately monitor and supervise the enterprise.

Principles Governing Settlements of Derivative Claims

As noted at the outset of this opinion, this Court is now required to exercise an informed judgment whether the proposed settlement is fair and reasonable in the light of all relevant factors. On application of this kind, this Court attempts to protect the best interests of the corporation and its absent shareholders all of whom will be barred from future litigation on these claims if the settlement is approved. The parties proposing the settlement bear the burden of persuading the court that it is in fact fair and reasonable....

Directors' Duties To Monitor Corporate Operations

The complaint charges the director defendants with breach of their duty of attention or care in connection with the on-going operation of the corporation's business. The claim is that the directors allowed a situation to develop and continue which exposed the corporation to enormous legal liability and that in so doing they violated a duty to be active monitors of corporate performance. The complaint thus does not charge either director self-dealing or the more difficult loyalty-type problems arising from cases of suspect director motivation, such as entrenchment or sale of control contexts. The theory here advanced is possibly the most difficult theory in corporation law upon which a plaintiff might hope to win a judgment. The good policy reasons why it is so difficult to charge directors with responsibility for corporate losses for an alleged breach of care, where there is no conflict of interest or no facts suggesting suspect motivation involved, were recently described in *Gagliardi v. TriFoods Int'l Inc.*

1. *Potential liability for directoral decisions:* Director liability for a breach of the duty to exercise appropriate attention may, in theory, arise in two distinct contexts. First, such liability may be said to follow *from a board decision* that results in a loss because that decision was ill advised or "negligent". Second, liability to the corporation for a loss may be said to arise from an unconsidered failure of the board to act in circumstances in which due attention would, arguably, have prevented the loss. The first class of cases will typically be subject to review under the director-protective business judgment rule, assuming the decision made was the product of a process that was either deliberately considered in good faith or was otherwise rational. What should be understood, but may not widely be understood by courts or commentators who are not often required to face such questions, is that compliance with a director's duty of care can never appropriately be judicially determined by reference to the context of the board decision that leads to a corporate loss, apart from consideration of the good faith or rationality of the process employed. That is, whether a judge or jury considering the matter after the fact, believes a decision substantially wrong, or degrees of wrong extending through "stupid" to "egregious" or "irrational", provides no ground for director liability, so long as the court determines that the process employed was either rational or employed in a good faith effort to advance corporate interests. To employ a different rule—one that permitted an "objective" evaluation of the decision—would expose directors to substantive second guessing by ill-equipped judges or juries, which would, in the long-run, be injurious to investor interests. Thus, the business judgment rule is process oriented and informed by a deep respect for all good faith board decisions.

Indeed, one wonders on what moral basis might shareholders attack a good faith business decision of a director as "unreasonable" or "irrational." Where a director in fact exercises a good faith effort to be informed and to exercise appropriate judgment, he or she should be deemed to satisfy fully the duty of attention. If the shareholders thought themselves entitled to some other quality of judgment than such a director produces in the good faith exercise of the powers of office, then the shareholders should have elected other directors. Judge Learned Hand made the point rather better than can I. In speaking of the passive director defendant Mr. Andrews in *Barnes v. Andrews*, Judge Hand said:

> True, he was not very suited by experience for the job he had undertaken, but I cannot hold him on that account. After all it is the same corporation that chose him that now seeks to charge him ... Directors are not specialists

like lawyers or doctors … They are the general advisors of the business and if they faithfully give such ability as they have to their charge, it would not be lawful to hold them liable.…

In this formulation Learned Hand correctly identifies, in my opinion, the core element of any corporate law duty of care inquiry: whether there was good faith effort made to be informed and exercise judgment.

2. *Liability for failure to monitor:* The second class of cases in which director liability for inattention is theoretically possible entail circumstances in which a loss eventuates not from a decision but, from unconsidered inaction. Most of the decisions that a corporation, acting through its human agents, makes are, of course, not the subject of director attention. Legally, the board itself will be required only to authorize the most significant corporate acts or transactions: mergers, changes in the capital structure, fundamental changes in business, appointment and compensation of the CEO, etc. As the facts of this case graphically demonstrate, ordinary business decisions that are made by officers and employees deeper in the interior of the organization can, however, vitally affect the welfare of the corporation and its ability to achieve its various strategic and financial goals. If this case did not prove the point itself, recent business history would. Recall for example the displacement of senior management and much of the board of Salomon, Inc.; the replacement of senior management of Kidder, Peabody following the discovery of large trading losses resulting from phantom trades by a highly compensated trader; or the extensive financial loss and reputational injury suffered by Prudential Insurance as a result its junior officers misrepresentations in connection with the distribution of limited partnership interests. Financial and organizational disasters such as these raise the question, what is the board's responsibility with respect to the organization and monitoring of the enterprise to assure that the corporation functions within the law to achieve its purposes?

Modernly this question has been given special importance by an increasing tendency, especially under federal law, to employ the criminal law to assure corporate compliance with external legal requirements, including environmental, financial, employee and product safety regulations. In 1991, pursuant to the Sentencing Reform Act of 1984, the United States Sentencing Commission adopted Organizational Sentencing Guidelines which impact importantly on the prospective effect these criminal sanctions might have on business corporations. The Guidelines set forth a uniform sentencing structure for organizations to be sentenced for violation of federal criminal statutes and provide for penalties that equal or often massively exceed those previously imposed on corporations. The Guidelines offer powerful incentives for corporations today to have in place compliance programs to detect violations of law, promptly to report violations to appropriate public officials when discovered, and to take prompt, voluntary remedial efforts.

In 1963, the Delaware Supreme Court in *Graham v. Allis-Chalmers Mfg. Co.*, addressed the question of potential liability of board members for losses experienced by the corporation as a result of the corporation having violated the anti-trust laws of the United States. There was no claim in that case that the directors knew about the behavior of subordinate employees of the corporation that had resulted in the liability. Rather, as in this case, the claim asserted was that the directors ought to have known of it and if they had known they could have been under a duty to bring the corporation into compliance with the law and thus save the corporation from the loss. The Delaware Supreme Court concluded that, under the facts as they appeared, there was no basis to find that the directors had breached a duty to be informed of the ongoing operations of the firm. In notably colorful terms, the court stated that "absent cause for suspicion there is no duty upon the directors to install and operate a corporate system of espionage to ferret out wrong-doing which they have no reason to suspect exists." The Court found that there were no grounds for suspicion in that case, and, thus, concluded that the directors were blamelessly unaware of the conduct leading to the corporate liability.

How does one generalize this holding today? Can it be said today that, absent some ground giving rise to suspicion of violation of law, that corporate directors have no duty to assure that a corporate information gathering and reporting systems exists which represents a good faith attempt to provide senior management and the Board with information respecting material acts, events or conditions within the corporation, including compliance with applicable statutes and regulations? I certainly do not believe so. I doubt that such a broad generalization of the *Graham* holding would have been accepted by the Supreme Court in 1963. The case can be more narrowly interpreted as standing for the proposition that, absent grounds to suspect deception, neither corporate boards nor senior officers can be charged with wrongdoing simply for assuming the integrity of employees and the honesty of their dealings on the company's behalf.

A broader interpretation of *Graham v. Allis-Chalmers*—that it means that a corporate board has no responsibility to assure that appropriate information and reporting systems are established by the management—would not, in any event, be accepted by the Delaware Supreme Court in 1996, in my opinion. In stating the basis for this view, I start with the recognition that in recent years the Delaware Supreme Court has made it clear—especially in its jurisprudence concerning takeovers, from *Smith v. Van Gorkom* through *QVC v. Paramount Communications*—the seriousness with which the corporation law views the role of the corporate board. Secondly, I note the elementary fact that relevant and timely information is an essential predicate for satisfaction of the board's supervisory and monitoring role under Section 141 of the Delaware General Corporation Law. Thirdly, I note the potential impact of the federal organizational sentencing guidelines on any business organization. Any rational person attempting in good faith to meet an organizational governance responsibility would be bound to take into account this development and the enhanced penalties and the opportunities for reduced sanctions that it offers.

In light of these developments, it would, in my opinion, be a mistake to conclude that our Supreme Court's statement in Graham concerning "espionage" means that corporate boards may satisfy their obligation to be reasonably informed concerning the corporation, without assuring themselves that information and reporting systems exist in the organization that are reasonably designed to provide to senior management and to the board itself timely, accurate information sufficient to allow management and the board, each within its scope, to reach informed judgments concerning both the corporation's compliance with law and its business performance.

Obviously the level of detail that is appropriate for such an information system is a question of business judgment. And obviously too, no rationally designed information and reporting system will remove the possibility that the corporation will violate laws or regulations, or that senior officers or directors may nevertheless sometimes be misled or otherwise fail reasonably to detect acts material to the corporation's compliance with the law. But it is important that the board exercise a good faith judgment that the corporation's information and reporting system is in concept and design adequate to assure the board that appropriate information will come to its attention in a timely manner as a matter of ordinary operations, so that it may satisfy its responsibility.

Thus, I am of the view that a director's obligation includes a duty to attempt in good faith to assure that a corporate information and reporting system, which the board concludes is adequate, exists, and that failure to do so under some circumstances may, in theory at least, render a director liable for losses caused by non-compliance with applicable legal standards.

Analysis of Third Amended Complaint and Settlement

On balance, after reviewing an extensive record in this case, including numerous documents and three depositions, I conclude that this settlement is fair and reasonable. In light of the fact that the Caremark Board already has a functioning committee charged with overseeing corporate compliance, the changes in corporate practice that are presented as consideration for the settlement do not impress one as very significant. Nonetheless, that consideration appears fully adequate to support dismissal of the derivative claims of director fault asserted, because those claims find no substantial evidentiary support in the record and quite likely were susceptible to a motion to dismiss in all events.

In order to show that the Caremark directors breached their duty of care by failing adequately to control Caremark's employees, plaintiffs would have to show either (1) that the directors knew or (2) should have known that violations of law were occurring and, in either event, (3) that the directors took no steps in a good faith effort to prevent or remedy that situation, and (4) that such failure proximately resulted in the losses complained of....

Knowing violation for [sic] statute: Concerning the possibility that the Caremark directors knew of violations of law, none of the documents submitted for review, nor any of the deposition transcripts appear to provide evidence of it. Certainly the Board understood that the company had entered into a variety of contracts with physicians, researchers, and health care providers and it was understood that some of these contracts were with persons who had prescribed treatments that Caremark participated in providing. The Board was informed that the company's reimbursement for patient care was frequently from government funded sources and that such services were subject to the ARPL. But the Board appears to have been informed by experts that the company's practices while contestable, were lawful. There is no evidence that reliance on such reports was not reasonable. Thus, this case presents no occasion to apply a principle to the effect that knowingly causing the corporation to violate a criminal statute constitutes a breach of a director's fiduciary duty.

Failure to monitor: Since it does appear that the Board was to some extent unaware of the activities that led to liability, I turn to a consideration of the other potential avenue to director liability that the other pleadings take: director inattention or "negligence". Generally where a claim of directorial liability creating activities within the corporation, as in *Graham* or in this case, in my opinion only a sustained or systematic failure of the board to exercise oversight—such as an utter failure to attempt to assure a reasonable information and reporting system exists—will establish the lack of good faith that is a necessary condition to liability. Such a test of liability—lack of good faith as evidenced by sustained or systematic failure of a director to exercise reasonable oversight—is quite high. But, a demanding test of liability in the oversight context is probably beneficial to corporate shareholders as a class, as it is in the board decision context, since it makes board service by qualified persons more likely, while continuing to act as a stimulus to *good faith performance of duty* by such directors.

Here, the record supplies essentially no evidence that the director defendants were guilty of a sustained failure to exercise their oversight function....

The liability that eventuated in this instance was huge. But the fact that it resulted from a violation of criminal law alone does not create a breach of fiduciary duty by directors. The record at this stage does not support the conclusion that the defendants either lacked good faith in the exercise of their monitoring responsibilities or conscientiously permitted a known violation of the law by the corporation to occur....

The proposed settlement provides very modest benefits. Under the settlement agreement, plaintiffs have been given express assurances that Caremark will have a more centralized, active supervisory system in the future.... Nonetheless, given the weakness of the plaintiffs' claims the proposed settlement appears to be an adequate, reasonable, and beneficial outcome for all of the parties. Thus, the proposed settlement will be approved.

Comments and Questions

1. According to Chancellor Allen, how had trends in federal criminal law enforcement affected the need for board oversight of corporate compliance systems?

2. How did the court define bad faith with regard to the board's duty of oversight? Why did Chancellor Allen choose this standard? Are directors acting in bad faith if they do not monitor the adequacy of the corporation's compliance systems?

3. The court determined that the Caremark's board of directors had a responsibility to put into place a system designed to provide information regarding events within the corporation "to reach informed judgments concerning both the corporation's

compliance with the law and its business performance." Does this language indicate that the board's monitoring duty extends beyond oversight of the company's legal compliance to other business risks? Does Chancellor Allen's opinion offer support for a requirement that boards monitor other types of risk?

4. Federal law continues to influence directors' duties of oversight. For example, prompted by the collapse of Enron and WorldCom and Congress' enactment of Sarbanes-Oxley, the U.S. Sentencing Guidelines for Organizations were revised to emphasize the role of directors in overseeing corporate compliance programs. Effective in 2004, the amended Guidelines made clear that in order for the corporation to receive credit for having an effective compliance and ethics program, the board must be knowledgeable about its content and operation and must exercise reasonable oversight with respect to its implementation and effectiveness. In addition, companies must communicate their standards and procedures to directors by conducting effective training programs and otherwise disseminating information that is appropriate to the directors' roles and responsibilities. However, boards may delegate oversight responsibility to a subcommittee, such as the audit committee.[21]

Following the 2008 global financial crisis, the U.S. Sentencing Commission again revised the Sentencing Guidelines for Organizations. Beginning November 1, 2010, corporations with effective compliance and ethics programs may receive additional credit during sentencing, even if the offense involved high-level personnel, so long as, among other requirements, the individual responsible for the program (typically a chief compliance officer) had direct reporting obligations to the board or its designated committee.[22]

5. Chancellor Allen opined that "only a sustained or systematic failure of the board to exercise oversight—such as an utter failure to attempt to assure a reasonable information and reporting system exists—will establish the lack of good faith that is a necessary condition to liability," and that a claim for failure to monitor "is possibly the most difficult theory in corporation law upon which a plaintiff might hope to win a judgment." Subsequent decisions in Delaware often have repeated this language.[23] Given this language, do you think that *Caremark* represented a significant departure from *Graham*? Why or why not?

———————

Relying on Chancellor Allen's dicta, courts came to recognize so-called "*Caremark* claims"—causes of action alleging that the board of directors' "utter failure" or "systematic failure" to monitor legal compliance caused injury to the corporation. Directors must attempt in good faith to assure not only that the firm has a corporate information and reporting system but that the reporting system is adequate to assure the board

———————

21. *See* United States Sentencing Guidelines Manual §§ 8B2.1(b)(2)(A), 8B2.1(b)(4) and Commentary, Application Notes 2.

22. *Id.* at § 8C2.5(f)(3)(C).

23. *See, e.g., In re Massey Energy Co. Deriv. & Class Action Litig.*, 2011 Del. Ch. LEXIS 83 n.139 (Del. Ch. May 31, 2011).

that appropriate information as to compliance with applicable laws will come to its attention in a timely manner as a matter of ordinary operations. Because corporations in different industries are subject to varied federal, state, and local laws and regulations, the oversight responsibilities of corporate fiduciaries will differ depending on the firm's business; fiduciary duties will be tailored to specific facts and circumstances. In general, however, compliance with antifraud laws is essential to all corporations.

Although largely advisory, Chancellor Allen's opinion in *Caremark* generated substantial interest. For over a decade, corporate attorneys and legal scholars parsed the dicta in *Caremark*, studied subsequent decisions appraising *Caremark* claims, and debated the boundaries of oversight and the duty of good faith. Then, in 2006, the Delaware Supreme Court acknowledged the monitoring responsibilities of public company boards and attempted to clarify the doctrine.

Stone v. Ritter

Delaware Supreme Court

911 A.2d 362 (2006)

HOLLAND, JUSTICE:

This is an appeal from a final judgment of the Court of Chancery dismissing a derivative complaint against fifteen present and former directors of AmSouth Bancorporation ("AmSouth"), a Delaware corporation. The plaintiffs-appellants, William and Sandra Stone, are AmSouth shareholders and filed their derivative complaint without making a pre-suit demand on AmSouth's board of directors (the "Board"). The Court of Chancery held that the plaintiffs had failed to adequately plead that such a demand would have been futile. The Court, therefore, dismissed the derivative complaint under Court of Chancery Rule 23.1.

The Court of Chancery characterized the allegations in the derivative complaint as a "classic *Caremark* claim[...]" In *Caremark*, the Court of Chancery recognized that: "[g]enerally where a claim of directorial liability for corporate loss is predicated upon ignorance of liability creating activities within the corporation ... only a sustained or systematic failure of the board to exercise oversight—such as an utter failure to attempt to assure a reasonable information and reporting system exists-will establish the lack of good faith that is a necessary condition to liability."

In this appeal, the plaintiffs acknowledge that the directors neither "knew [n]or should have known that violations of law were occurring," *i.e.*, that there were no "red flags" before the directors. Nevertheless, the plaintiffs argue that the Court of Chancery erred by dismissing the derivative complaint which alleged that "the defendants had utterly failed to implement any sort of statutorily required monitoring, reporting or information controls that would have enabled them to learn of problems requiring their attention."

Consistent with our opinion in *In re Walt Disney Co. Deriv. Litig*, we hold that *Caremark* articulates the necessary conditions for assessing director oversight liability. We also conclude that the *Caremark* standard was properly applied to evaluate the derivative complaint in this case. Accordingly, the judgment of the Court of Chancery must be affirmed.

Facts

This derivative action is brought on AmSouth's behalf by William and Sandra Stone, who allege that they owned AmSouth common stock "at all relevant times." The nominal defendant, AmSouth, is a Delaware corporation with its principal executive offices in Birmingham, Alabama. During the relevant period, AmSouth's wholly-owned subsidiary, AmSouth Bank, operated about 600 commercial banking branches in six states throughout the southeastern United States and employed more than 11,600 people. In 2004, AmSouth and AmSouth Bank paid $40 million in fines and $10 million in civil penalties to resolve government and regulatory investigations pertaining principally to the failure by bank employees to file "Suspicious Activity Reports" ("SARs"), as required by the federal Bank Secrecy Act ("BSA") and various anti-money-laundering ("AML") regulations.... No fines or penalties were imposed on AmSouth's directors, and no other regulatory action was taken against them.

The government investigations arose originally from an unlawful "Ponzi" scheme operated by Louis D. Hamric, II and Victor G. Nance.... In August 2000 ... Nance had convinced more than forty of his clients to invest in promissory notes bearing high rates of return, by misrepresenting the nature and the risk of that investment. Relying on similar representations by Hamric and Nance, the AmSouth branch employees in Tennessee agreed to provide custodial accounts for the investors and to distribute monthly interest payments to each account upon receipt of a check from Hamric and instructions from Nance.

The Hamric-Nance scheme was discovered in March 2002, when the investors did not receive their monthly interest payments. Thereafter, Hamric and Nance became the subject of several civil actions brought by the defrauded investors in Tennessee and Mississippi (and in which AmSouth was also named as a defendant), and also the subject of a federal grand jury investigation in the Southern District of Mississippi. Hamric and Nance were indicted on federal money-laundering charges, and both pled guilty.

The authorities examined AmSouth's compliance with its reporting and other obligations under the BSA. On November 17, 2003, the USAO advised AmSouth that it was the subject of a criminal investigation.

On October 12, 2004, the Federal Reserve and the Alabama Banking Department concurrently issued a Cease and Desist Order against AmSouth, requiring it, for the first time, to improve its BSA/AML program.

FinCEN found that "AmSouth violated the suspicious activity reporting requirements of the Bank Secrecy Act," and that "[s]ince April 24, 2002, AmSouth has been in violation of the anti-money-laundering program requirements of the Bank Secrecy Act." Among FinCEN's specific determinations were its conclusions that "AmSouth's [AML compliance] program lacked adequate board and management oversight," and that "reporting to management for the purposes of monitoring and oversight of compliance activities was materially deficient."

Demand Futility and Director Independence

It is a fundamental principle of the Delaware General Corporation Law that "[t]he business and affairs of every corporation organized under this chapter shall be managed by or under the direction of a board of directors...." Thus, "by its very nature [a] derivative action impinges on the managerial freedom of directors." Therefore, the right of a stockholder to prosecute a derivative suit is limited to situations where either the stockholder has demanded the directors pursue a corporate claim and the directors have wrongfully refused to do so, or where demand is excused because the directors are incapable of making an impartial decision regarding whether to institute such litigation. Court of Chancery Rule 23.1, accordingly, requires that the complaint in a derivative action "allege with particularity the efforts, if any, made by the plaintiff to obtain the action the plaintiff desires from the directors [or] the reasons for the plaintiff's failure to obtain the action or for not making the effort."

To excuse demand under [*Rales v. Blasband,*] "a court must determine whether or not the particularized factual allegations of a derivative stockholder complaint create a reasonable doubt that, as of the time the complaint is filed, the board of directors could have properly exercised its independent and disinterested business judgment in responding to a demand." The plaintiffs attempt to satisfy the *Rales* test in this proceeding by asserting that the incumbent defendant directors "face a substantial likelihood of liability" that renders them "personally interested in the outcome of the decision on whether to pursue the claims asserted in the complaint," and are therefore not disinterested or independent.

Critical to this demand excused argument is the fact that the directors' potential personal liability depends upon whether or not their conduct can be exculpated by the section 102(b)(7) provision contained in the AmSouth certificate of incorporation. Such a provision can exculpate directors from monetary liability for a breach of the duty of care, but not for conduct that is not in good faith or a breach of the duty of loyalty. The standard for assessing a director's potential personal liability for failing to act in good faith in discharging his or her oversight responsibilities has evolved beginning with our decision in *Graham v. Allis-Chalmers Manufacturing Company*, through the Court of Chancery's *Caremark* decision, to our most recent decision in *Disney.* A brief discussion of that evolution will help illuminate the standard that we adopt in this case.

Graham *and* Caremark

Graham was a derivative action brought against the directors of Allis-Chalmers for failure to prevent violations of federal anti-trust laws by Allis-Chalmers employees.... In *Graham*, this Court held that "*absent cause for suspicion* there is no duty upon the directors to install and operate a corporate system of espionage to ferret out wrongdoing which they have no reason to suspect exists."

In *Caremark*, the Court of Chancery reassessed the applicability of our holding in *Graham* when called upon to approve a settlement of a derivative lawsuit brought against the directors of Caremark International, Inc. The plaintiffs claimed that the

Caremark directors should have known that certain officers and employees of Caremark were involved in violations of the federal Anti-Referral Payments Law. That law prohibits health care providers from paying any form of remuneration to induce the referral of Medicare or Medicaid patients. The plaintiffs claimed that the *Caremark* directors breached their fiduciary duties for having "allowed a situation to develop and continue which exposed the corporation to enormous legal liability and that in so doing they violated a duty to be active monitors of corporate performance."

In evaluating whether to approve the proposed settlement agreement in *Caremark*, the Court of Chancery narrowly construed our holding in *Graham* "as standing for the proposition that, absent grounds to suspect deception, neither corporate boards nor senior officers can be charged with wrongdoing simply for assuming the integrity of employees and the honesty of their dealings on the company's behalf."

[T]he *Caremark* Court stated, "it is important that the board exercise a good faith judgment that the corporation's information and reporting system is in concept and design adequate to assure the board that appropriate information will come to its attention in a timely manner as a matter of ordinary operations, so that it may satisfy its responsibility." The *Caremark* Court recognized, however, that "the duty to act in good faith to be informed cannot be thought to require directors to possess detailed information about all aspects of the operation of the enterprise." The Court of Chancery then formulated the following standard for assessing the liability of directors where the directors are unaware of employee misconduct that results in the corporation being held liable:

> Generally where a claim of directorial liability for corporate loss is predicated upon ignorance of liability creating activities within the corporation, as in *Graham* or in this case, ... only a sustained or systematic failure of the board to exercise oversight—such as an utter failure to attempt to assure a reasonable information and reporting system exists—will establish the lack of good faith that is a necessary condition to liability.

Caremark *Standard Approved*

As evidenced by the language quoted above, the *Caremark* standard for so-called "oversight" liability draws heavily upon the concept of director failure to act in good faith. That is consistent with the definition(s) of bad faith recently approved by this Court in its recent *Disney* decision, where we held that a failure to act in good faith requires conduct that is qualitatively different from, and more culpable than, the conduct giving rise to a violation of the fiduciary duty of care (i.e., gross negligence). In *Disney*, we identified the following examples of conduct that would establish a failure to act in good faith:

> A failure to act in good faith may be shown, for instance, where the fiduciary intentionally acts with a purpose other than that of advancing the best interests of the corporation, where the fiduciary acts with the intent to violate applicable positive law, or where the fiduciary intentionally fails to act in the face of a known duty to act, demonstrating a conscious disregard for his du-

ties. There may be other examples of bad faith yet to be proven or alleged, but these three are the most salient.

Accordingly, the Court of Chancery applied the correct standard in assessing whether demand was excused in this case where failure to exercise oversight was the basis or theory of the plaintiffs' claim for relief.

The phraseology used in *Caremark* and that we employ here — describing the lack of good faith as a "necessary condition to liability" — is deliberate. The purpose of that formulation is to communicate that a failure to act in good faith is not conduct that results, *ipso facto*, in the direct imposition of fiduciary liability. The failure to act in good faith may result in liability because the requirement to act in good faith "is a subsidiary element[,]" i.e., a condition, "of the fundamental duty of loyalty." It follows that because a showing of bad faith conduct, in the sense described in *Disney* and *Caremark*, is essential to establish director oversight liability, the fiduciary duty violated by that conduct is the duty of loyalty.

This view of a failure to act in good faith results in two additional doctrinal consequences. First, although good faith may be described colloquially as part of a "triad" of fiduciary duties that includes the duties of care and loyalty, the obligation to act in good faith does not establish an independent fiduciary duty that stands on the same footing as the duties of care and loyalty. Only the latter two duties, where violated, may directly result in liability, whereas a failure to act in good faith may do so, but indirectly. The second doctrinal consequence is that the fiduciary duty of loyalty is not limited to cases involving a financial or other cognizable fiduciary conflict of interest. It also encompasses cases where the fiduciary fails to act in good faith. As the Court of Chancery aptly put it in *Guttman* [*v. Huang*,] "[a] director cannot act loyally towards the corporation unless she acts in the good faith belief that her actions are in the corporation's best interest."

We hold that *Caremark* articulates the necessary conditions predicate for director oversight liability: (a) the directors utterly failed to implement any reporting or information system or controls; *or* (b) having implemented such a system or controls, consciously failed to monitor or oversee its operations thus disabling themselves from being informed of risks or problems requiring their attention. In either case, imposition of liability requires a showing that the directors knew that they were not discharging their fiduciary obligations. Where directors fail to act in the face of a known duty to act, thereby demonstrating a conscious disregard for their responsibilities, they breach their duty of loyalty by failing to discharge that fiduciary obligation in good faith.

Chancery Court Decision

The Plaintiffs contend that demand is excused under Rule 23.1 because AmSouth's directors breached their oversight duty and, as a result, face a "substantial likelihood of liability" as a result of their "utter failure" to act in good faith to put into place policies and procedures to ensure compliance with BSA and AML obligations.... In dismissing the derivative complaint in this action, the Court of Chancery concluded:

This case is not about a board's failure to carefully consider a material corporate decision that was presented to the board. This is a case where information was not reaching the board because of ineffective internal controls.... With the benefit of hindsight, it is beyond question that AmSouth's internal controls with respect to the Bank Secrecy Act and anti-money laundering regulations compliance were inadequate. Neither party disputes that the lack of internal controls resulted in a huge fine—$50 million, alleged to be the largest ever of its kind. The fact of those losses, however, is not alone enough for a court to conclude that a majority of the corporation's board of directors is disqualified from considering demand that AmSouth bring suit against those responsible.

Reasonable Reporting System Existed

The KPMG Report evaluated the various components of AmSouth's longstanding BSA/AML compliance program. The KPMG Report reflects that AmSouth's Board dedicated considerable resources to the BSA/AML compliance program and put into place numerous procedures and systems to attempt to ensure compliance. According to KPMG, the program's various components exhibited below a low and high degree of compliance with applicable laws and regulations.

The KPMG Report describes the numerous AmSouth employees, departments and committees established by the Board to oversee AmSouth's compliance with the BSA and to report violations to management and the Board[.]

The KPMG Report reflects that the directors not only discharged their oversight responsibility to establish an information and reporting system, but also proved that the system was designed to permit the directors to periodically monitor AmSouth's compliance with BSA and AML regulations.

The KPMG Report shows that AmSouth's Board at various times enacted written policies and procedures designed to ensure compliance with the BSA and AML regulations. For example, the Board adopted an amended bank-wide "BSA/AML Policy" on July 17, 2003—four months before AmSouth became aware that it was the target of a government investigation. That policy was produced to plaintiffs in response to their demand to inspect AmSouth's books and records pursuant to section 220 and is included in plaintiff's appendix. Among other things, the July 17, 2003, BSA/AML Policy directs all AmSouth employees to immediately report suspicious transactions or activity to the BSA/AML Compliance Department or Corporate Security.

Complaint Properly Dismissed

In this case, the adequacy of the plaintiffs' assertion that demand is excused depends on whether the complaint alleges facts sufficient to show that the defendant *directors* are potentially personally liable for the failure of non-director bank *employees* to file SARs. Delaware courts have recognized that "[m]ost of the decisions that a corporation, acting through its human agents, makes are, of course, not the subject of director attention." Consequently a claim that directors are subject to personal liability for employee failures is "possibly the most difficult theory in corporation law upon which a plaintiff might hope to win a judgment."

For the plaintiffs' derivative complaint to withstand a motion to dismiss, "only a sustained or systematic failure of the board to exercise oversight—such as an utter failure to attempt to assure a reasonable information and reporting system exists—will establish the lack of good faith that is a necessary condition to liability." As the *Caremark* decision noted:

> Such a test of liability—lack of good faith as evidenced by sustained or systematic failure of a director to exercise reasonable oversight—is quite high. But, a demanding test of liability in the oversight context is probably beneficial to corporate shareholders as a class, as it is in the board decision context, since it makes board service by qualified persons more likely, while continuing to act as a stimulus to *good faith performance of duty* by such directors.

The KPMG Report—which the plaintiffs explicitly incorporated by reference into their derivative complaint—refutes the assertion that the directors "never took the necessary steps ... to ensure that a reasonable BSA compliance and reporting system existed." KPMG's findings reflect that the Board received and approved relevant policies and procedures, delegated to certain employees and departments the responsibility for filing SARs and monitoring compliance, and exercised oversight by relying on periodic reports from them. Although there ultimately may have been failures by employees to report deficiencies to the Board, there is no basis for an oversight claim seeking to hold the directors personally liable by the employees.

Accordingly, we hold that the Court of Chancery properly applied *Caremark* and dismissed the plaintiffs' derivative complaint for failure to excuse demand by alleging particularized facts that created reason to doubt whether the directors had acted in good faith in exercising their oversight responsibilities.

Comments and Questions

1. In *Stone v. Ritter*, the Delaware Supreme Court made clear that the duty of good faith is not a separate duty of corporate fiduciaries but, rather, is an element of the duty of loyalty. Thus, although exculpated directors face liability for monetary damages only if they violate their duty of loyalty, fiduciaries may be adjudged disloyal by failing to act in good faith. Why do you think the justices focused on loyalty? Recall that Chancellor Allen's decision in *Caremark* had connected the duty of good faith to the duty of care. Insofar as most Delaware public companies have adopted exculpatory charter provisions, should corporate directors be concerned about *Stone v. Ritter*? Did the Delaware Supreme Court heighten directors' exposure to liability for money damages?

2. In *In re Walt Disney Co. Deriv. Litig.*, the Delaware Supreme Court warned of the dangers in defining good faith in such a way that it would collapse into the duty of care:

> Thus, a corporation can exculpate its directors from monetary liability for a breach of the duty of care, but not for conduct that is not in good faith. To adopt a definition of bad faith that would cause a violation of the duty

of care automatically to become an act or omission 'not in good faith' would eviscerate the protections accorded to directors by the General Assembly's adoption of Section 102(b)(7).[24]

In light of this concern, what are the practical differences between the duty of care and the duty to act in good faith?

3. In *Who's the Boss? Unmasking Oversight Liability Within the Corporate Power Puzzle*, Anne Tucker Nees argued:

> Oversight liability—directors' liability for failing to oversee the corporation in accordance with the fiduciary duty of loyalty, which requires 'good faith'—raises difficult questions because it engages in analysis close to the forbidden 'second-guessing' by courts that could discourage entrepreneurial risk taking. On the other hand, the notion that all allegations of failed oversight are beyond the purview of the shareholders and the courts is equally counterintuitive and potentially undesirable as it negates the notion of balance, opting instead to allocate total authority to directors over shareholders' investments.[25]

Should directors have any liability for failure to monitor management? Why might factfinders equate poor financial results with bad faith? Is this possibility as concerning when the court is the factfinder, as in Delaware?

4. The court makes clear that in order to impose liability on directors for breaching their oversight duty, plaintiff must make a "showing that the directors knew that they were not discharging their fiduciary obligations." Assuming that directors will not admit such knowledge, what facts could support such a showing?

5. Do you think that market forces and reputational concerns provide directors with sufficient incentives to satisfy their oversight duties? What should corporate law do, if anything, to motivate directors to be more proactive in fulfilling their monitoring responsibilities?

———————

Caremark actions presuppose that the board of directors had no knowledge of the illegal or improper activity. But what is the duty of the board to detect and prevent fraud or similar forms of wrongdoing perpetrated by employees against the corporation? How should directors respond to red flags? The parties in the next case litigated those questions.

———————

24. 906 A.2d 27, 65 (Del. 2005).
25. 35 Del. J. Corp. L. 199, 204 (2010).

Rich v. Chong

Delaware Court of Chancery
66 A.3d 963 (Del. Ch. 2013)

GLASSCOCK, VICE CHANCELLOR:

OVERVIEW

The Plaintiff here, a stockholder, made a demand to the Defendant corporation, asking the corporation to prosecute claims against its officers and directors for violating their *Caremark* duties. The individual Defendants not only failed to respond to the demand over the next two years, but allegedly took actions making a meaningful response to the demand unlikely if not impossible. Under these facts, the Plaintiff may pursue an action on behalf of the corporation derivatively, notwithstanding Court of Chancery Rule 23.1.

This Opinion concerns a motion brought by Defendant Fuqi International, Inc. and its directors to dismiss a derivative complaint alleging breaches of fiduciary duty. Fuqi, a Delaware entity whose sole asset is stock of a Chinese jewelry company, completed a public offering in the United States in 2009. In March 2010, Fuqi announced the need for restatement of its 2009 financial statements. Following this announcement, Fuqi disclosed additional problems it had, including the transfer of $120 million of cash out of the company to third parties in China. In July 2010, Plaintiff George Rich, Jr., a Fuqi stockholder, made a demand to the board of directors to remedy breaches of fiduciary duty and weaknesses in Fuqi's internal controls. Fuqi's Audit Committee commenced an investigation, which was abandoned in January 2012 upon management's failure to pay the fees of the Audit Committee's advisors. Fuqi's independent directors have since resigned.

Plaintiff Rich brought this action in June 2012, alleging breaches of fiduciary duty under *Caremark*. Now, the Defendants have moved to dismiss the Complaint under Rule 23.1, because the Fuqi board has not yet rejected the Plaintiff's demand. Having found that the Plaintiff has pled particularized facts that raise a reasonable doubt that the directors acted in good faith in response to the demand, I deny the Rule 23.1 Motion. Second, Fuqi moved to dismiss under Rule 12(b)(6) for failure to state a claim upon which relief can be granted. Notwithstanding the well-known difficulty of prevailing on a *Caremark* claim, the Plaintiff has pled facts that, assumed true, lead me to reasonably infer that the Fuqi directors knew that its internal controls were deficient, yet failed to act. Therefore, I deny the Motion to Dismiss under Rule 12(b)(6).

BACKGROUND FACTS

Parties

Plaintiff George Rich, Jr. is, and at all relevant times has been, a stockholder of Fuqi International, Inc. Nominal Defendant Fuqi is a Delaware corporation whose principle offices are located in the People's Republic of China. Fuqi is engaged in selling high quality, precious metal jewelry. Fuqi shares were traded on the NASDAQ until they were delisted in March of 2011 and now trade on the pink sheet market for approximately $1 per share.

Defendant Yu Kwai Chong is the principal founder of Fuqi and has served as Chairman of the Board since Fuqi's inception. Chong also served as Fuqi's CEO from April 2011 until June 2011. Defendant Lie Xi Zhuang has served as Fuqi's COO since April 2001 and as a director since 2008. Defendant Ching Wan Wong served as Fuqi's CFO from January 2004 until his resignation in July 2011; Wong also served as a Fuqi director from 2008 until he resigned in June 2011. Defendant Lily Lee Chen served as a Fuqi director from June 2007 until her resignation in March 2012. Defendants Eileen B. Brody and Victor A. Hollander served as Fuqi directors, and as members of the Audit Committee, from June 2007 until their resignations in January 2012. Defendant Jeff Haiyong Liu has served as a director of Fuqi from June 2007 to the present, and has also served as a member of the Audit Committee. Collectively, I refer to Defendants Chong, Zhuang, Wong, Chen, Brody, Hollander, and Liu as the "Individual Defendants."

Fuqi's Background and Organizational Structure

Fuqi's primary operations are conducted through a wholly-owned subsidiary, Fuqi International Holdings Co., Ltd., a British Virgin Islands corporation, and its wholly owned subsidiary, Shenzhen Fuqi Jewelry Co., Ltd., a company established under the laws of China.

Fuqi was born of a reverse-merger transaction involving Fuqi BVI and VT Marketing Services, Inc., a corporation formed as part of the Chapter 11 reorganization plan of visitalk.com, Inc. Prior to the Reverse Merger, Chong was the sole stockholder of Fuqi BVI. On November 20, 2006, Chong, Fuqi BVI, and VT entered into a share exchange agreement to effect the Reverse Merger. Under the agreement, Chong agreed to exchange all of his shares of Fuqi BVI for shares of VT, and VT agreed to acquire all of the issued and outstanding capital stock of Fuqi BVI. The Reverse Merger closed on November 22, 2006, and VT issued 11,175,543 shares of common stock in exchange for all of the issued and outstanding shares of Fuqi BVI. Upon the Reverse Merger's closing, VT became the 100% parent of Fuqi BVI and assumed the operations of Fuqi BVI and Fuqi China as its sole business. On December 8, 2006, VT reincorporated in Delaware, having previously been organized under the laws of Nevada, and changed its corporate name from "VT Marketing Services, Inc." to "Fuqi International, Inc."

Fuqi's Public Offering and Associated Disclosures

Fuqi's Reverse Merger facilitated Fuqi's access to the U.S. capital markets. Following the Reverse Merger, Fuqi began issuing press releases and filings with the SEC that reported strikingly strong growth. On July 31, 2009, Fuqi completed a public offering of 5.58 million of shares of common stock at a price of $21.50 per share. Gross proceeds were approximately $120 million.

Fuqi Announces Material Weakness in Accounting Methods

On March 16, 2010, Fuqi announced that its fourth quarter 10-Q and 10-K for 2009 would be delayed because Fuqi had discovered "certain errors related to the accounting of the Company's inventory and cost of sales." The press release stated that the errors identified were expected to have a material impact on Fuqi's previously issued quarterly financial statements for 2009 and that "at least one of the identified deficiencies ... constitutes a material weakness...." This press release was followed by another dated April 7, 2010, in which Fuqi disclosed that it had received a notification letter from NASDAQ that Fuqi was no longer in compliance with NASDAQ rules requiring the timely filing of SEC reports. On September 8, 2010, Fuqi announced that the SEC had initiated a formal investigation into Fuqi, related to Fuqi's failure to file timely periodic reports, among other matters.

Fuqi Stockholders File Securities and Derivative Actions Outside of Delaware

After Fuqi announced that its 2009 financial statements needed restatement, Fuqi stockholders filed several securities and derivative lawsuits on behalf of Fuqi against the Individual Defendants in federal and state courts. Ten securities class action lawsuits were filed in the United States District Court for the Southern District of New York within weeks of the March 16, 2010 press release. Three derivative suits were filed on behalf of Fuqi in April 2010, two in federal court and one in New York State court. The derivative suits allege that the directors and certain officers of Fuqi breached their fiduciary duties by failing to adequately supervise and control Fuqi, which resulted in the filing of false financial statements....

Plaintiff Rich Makes a Demand to the Fuqi Board of Directors.

On July 19, 2010, Plaintiff Rich made a demand to the Fuqi Board to commence an action against certain directors and executive officers of Fuqi (the "Demand Letter"). The Demand Letter asked the board of directors to "take action to remedy breaches of fiduciary duties by the directors and certain executive officers of the Company" as well as to "correct the deficiencies in the Company's internal controls that allowed the misconduct to occur." The Demand Letter also informed the board that if Fuqi did not respond to the letter within a reasonable period, the Plaintiff would commence a stockholder derivative action on behalf of Fuqi. Fuqi never responded to the Demand Letter in writing.

Fuqi Appoints the Special Internal Investigation Committee

On October 29, 2010, Fuqi announced the appointment of Kim K.T. Pan as a new independent member of the board of directors. In response to the demand, the directors formed a "Special Internal Investigation Committee" and appointed Pan and Chen to serve as its members (the "Special Committee"). The board authorized the Special Committee to retain experts and advisors to investigate whether the claims in the demand were meritorious. Disclosure of the Special Committee's formation was the only information Fuqi ever disclosed to the stockholders regarding the Special Committee. The Plaintiff contends that the Special Committee "never conducted any investigation or any other activity during its short-lived existence." Furthermore, by March 2012 the Special Committee effectively ceased to exist after losing both of its members, Pan and Chen, due to Chen's resignation and Pan's appointment as CEO.

Fuqi Discloses Material Weaknesses and Cash-Transfer Transactions

From the time the Plaintiff sent the Demand Letter to the present, Fuqi has released additional negative information about its accounting errors, lack of internal controls, and mismanagement of corporate resources. For instance, on March 16, 2011, Fuqi filed a Form NT 10-K with the SEC announcing that the financial statements for the quarterly periods ending March 31, 2009; June 30, 2009; and September 30, 2009 would be restated due to accounting errors. These accounting errors related to: (i) incorrect carve-out of the retail segment from the general ledger; (ii) unrecorded purchases and accounts payable, (iii) inadvertent inclusion of consigned inventory, (iv) incorrect and untimely recordkeeping of inventory movements of retail operation; and (v) incorrect diamond inventory costing, unrecorded purchases and unrecorded accounts payable.

In other words, Fuqi's financial statements were replete with basic accounting errors. The Form NT 10-K further disclosed that Fuqi had identified material weaknesses in its disclosure controls, procedures, and internal control over financial reporting. These material weaknesses include Fuqi's failure to "maintain effective controls … over its accounting and finance personnel…, the inventory and purchasing cycles, the accounting of complex and non-routine transactions, internal audit function, and treasury function."

Two weeks later, Fuqi announced that its Audit Committee was conducting an investigation relating to certain cash-transfer transactions that had been discovered by Fuqi's independent auditor during Fuqi's preparation of its restated quarterly financial statements for 2009. Fuqi made the cash-transfer transactions, between September 2009 and November 2010, to parties that are "registered legal entities in China." Chong, Fuqi's Chairman of the board, authorized the transfers pursuant to an oral agreement with Fuqi's bank. The entities receiving these cash transfers are Chinese entities, "but the Company has not been able to confirm the accuracy of their business addresses nor determine the extent and nature of their business operations, if any." As of March 2011, the company had found no evidence that the receiving entities were related to any of Fuqi's managers or directors. Fuqi has represented that "all of the outgoing cash transfers made by the Company were repaid in full by the recipient companies on a short-term basis, with no loss resulting from the transfers." However, Fuqi has not produced audited financial statements to confirm that these amounts have been repaid. The aggregate amount of the cash transfers totaled $86.3 million for 2009 and $47.5 million for 2010.

In essence, Fuqi transferred cash out of the company to third parties, outside of the U.S., who have yet to be verified as legitimate businesses. Fuqi has asserted, but not demonstrated, that the cash has been restored. The press release disclosing these events concluded with "[t]he internal investigation is ongoing." Since this press release in 2011, Fuqi has provided no additional information about the investigation to the stockholders.

The following day, because of Fuqi's ongoing failure to file timely financial statements, NASDAQ delisted Fuqi stock from the exchange. Although it once traded at close to $30 per share, Fuqi stock now trades on the pink sheets for approximately $1 per share.

Fuqi's Investigation

Although there is no evidence that the Special Committee performed any investigation, the Audit Committee did begin an investigation into Fuqi's accounting problems. Fuqi's Audit Committee, which apparently predates its disclosure problems, consisted of board members Hollander, Brody and Liu. Fuqi contends that the Audit Committee has "conducted a lengthy assessment and remediation of its internal and financial controls" resulting in "significant progress."

Fuqi's auditors requested that the Audit Committee perform an expedited investigation of the cash-transfer transactions. The Audit Committee retained a Chinese law firm to investigate the transactions and determine whether Fuqi had violated Chinese or U.S. law. In February 2011, the Audit Committee engaged special investigative counsel and a forensic accountant after Fuqi's auditors requested that the Audit Committee conclude its investigation. After the Audit Committee shared its preliminary findings with its auditors, the auditors requested that the Audit Committee expand the investigation.

Whatever progress the Audit Committee made in uncovering and correcting the causes of Fuqi's problems has allegedly stalled. According to Brody and Hollander (two of the three former members of the Audit Committee), Fuqi management failed to pay the fees of the Audit Committee's outside legal counsel, forensic specialists, and auditor. As a result, these professionals have either withdrawn from advising or suspended their services to the Audit Committee. In January 2012, Brody and Hollander resigned as Fuqi directors, and as members of the Audit Committee, in protest of the defunding.

Because the Audit Committee has failed to complete its audits of years 2009, 2010, and 2011, Fuqi has not filed any audited financial statements for over three years. As of March 28, 2012, Fuqi has represented to the SEC and to this Court that it is unable to estimate when it will file its audited financial statements.

Although Fuqi has still not completed its investigation, Fuqi has disclosed to its stockholders that the cash-transfer transactions were the result of material weaknesses in Fuqi's internal controls. For example, Fuqi has acknowledged "the Company's treasury controls did not require that internal fund transfer applications identify any specific business purpose or be accompanied by supporting documentation, such as a copy of a relevant invoice, purchase order, contract, or pre-payment statement."

Fuqi Experiences Mass Defections in Leadership

From June 2010 until March 2012, Fuqi's board of directors and executive team experienced mass defections. These defections are detailed below:

- On June 11, 2010, Xi Zhou Zhuo resigned as Marketing Director of Fuqi;

- On June 16, 2011, Wong resigned as a director but remained as Fuqi's CFO;

- On June 17, 2011, Chong resigned as Fuqi's CEO and was replaced by the previously independent director, Kim Pan;

- On July 30, 2011, Wong resigned as Fuqi's CFO, and CEO Pan also became Interim CFO, which he remained until the time of the Complaint;

- On January 3, 2012, Brody and Hollander resigned as directors;

- On January 16, 2012, Frederick Wong resigned as Vice President of Special Projects; and

- On March 31, 2012, Chen resigned as a director.

Xi Zhou Zhuo, Wong, Chong, Frederick Wong, and Chen reportedly resigned for "personal reasons." However, Brody and Hollander expressly resigned because of management's failure to pay the fees of legal, auditing, and other professional-service providers engaged by the Audit Committee, and because of management's assumption of responsibility and authority for engaging a professional accounting firm without the approval of the Audit Committee. In their words, Brody and Hollander felt compelled to resign "[b]ecause the Audit Committee's efforts to serve the shareholders of Fuqi have been completely frustrated by Management."

Fuqi responded publicly to Brody and Hollander's grievances in a Form 8-K filed on January 3, 2012. Fuqi argued that the Audit Committee's expenses had not been paid due to discrepancies with its insurer. It further contended that management had the right to select its own auditor. Brody and Hollander responded to these defenses via a letter to the Board on January 9, 2012. Without going into the details of this letter, it suffices to say that Brody and Hollander dispute the board's characterization.

The Allegations Against the Individual Defendants

As a procedural matter, the Plaintiff argues that he should not have to prove demand futility because (1) he made a demand, and (2) "the Board has not acted, is not acting, and will not act in response to the Demand." The Plaintiff draws support for this statement from the fact that the Board's Special Committee has had no meetings, released no progress reports, and now has no members. Finally, the Plaintiff alleges that the Defendants have had sufficient time to investigate this matter since over two years has passed since the Demand Letter was written.

Substantively, the Plaintiff alleges that the Individual Defendants breached their fiduciary duty of loyalty. Specifically, the Plaintiff contends that

> [E]ach of the Individual Defendants knowingly, and in a sustained and systematic manner, failed to institute and maintain adequate internal controls over Fuqi's accounting and financial reporting, failed to make a good faith effort to correct or prevent the deficiencies and accounting and financial problems caused thereby, and knowingly caused or allowed the Company to disseminate to shareholders false and misleading financial statements.

The Plaintiff alleges that the Individual Defendants were aware that Fuqi's public filings grossly misstated Fuqi's financial position. He contends that the Individual Defendants had this knowledge because they "had knowingly engaged in improper financial reporting and accounting practices, including, but not limited to, improperly reporting revenues, expenses and net income." The Plaintiff also alleges that Fuqi had "virtually no meaningful internal accounting and financial reporting controls, and ... the Individual Defendants willfully ignored the Company's obvious and pervasive lack of controls and made no good faith effort to correct or prevent the disaster that would ensue as a result." As damages, the Plaintiff seeks the costs and expenses incurred in connection with the accounting-restatement process, the SEC's investigation, and NASDAQ's delisting of Fuqi.

The Complaint in this action was filed on June 13, 2012. Fuqi moved to dismiss the Complaint on July 16, 2012.

ANALYSIS

Caremark *Claim and 12(b)(6) Analysis*

The Plaintiff alleges that Fuqi's directors are liable for failure to oversee the operations of the corporation. Fuqi argues that the Complaint fails to plead facts that show that the directors "consciously and in bad faith failed to implement any reporting or accounting system or controls." Such claims for bad-faith failure to monitor are known colloquially as "*Caremark* actions." The Defendants have moved to dismiss the action against the board generally. Because they have not articulated that claims against the Individual Defendants should be dismissed on a defendant-by-defendant basis, I refrain from undertaking that analysis.

Standard of Review Under 12(b)(6)

Under Court of Chancery Rule 12(b)(6), the Court will dismiss a complaint if the plaintiff has failed to state a claim upon which relief can be granted. The standard for reviewing a plaintiff's claims under Rule 12(b)(6) is "reasonable conceivability."

> When considering a defendant's motion to dismiss, a trial court should accept all well-pleaded factual allegations in the Complaint as true, accept even vague allegations in the Complaint as "well-pleaded" if they provide the defendant notice of the claim, draw all reasonable inferences in favor of the plaintiff, and deny the motion unless the plaintiff could not recover under any reasonably conceivable set of circumstances susceptible of proof. Dismissal is improper if, accepting all such inferences, "there is a reasonable possibility that a plaintiff could recover."

Wiggs v. Summit Midstream P'rs, LLC, 2013 WL 1286180, at *5 (Del. Ch. Mar. 28, 2013).

The Elements of a Caremark *Claim*

The essence of a *Caremark* claim is a breach of the duty of loyalty arising from a director's bad-faith failure to exercise oversight over the company. A *Caremark* claim is "possibly the most difficult theory in corporation law upon which a plaintiff might hope to win a judgment." *In re Caremark Int'l Inc. Deriv. Litig.* I am conscious of the need to prevent hindsight from dictating the result of a *Caremark* action; a bad outcome, without more, does not equate to bad faith. To survive a motion to dismiss, the plaintiff must plead facts that allow a reasonable inference that the defendants breached their fiduciary duties.

In *Stone v. Ritter*, the [Delaware] Supreme Court clarified that *Caremark* claims are breaches of the duty of loyalty, as opposed to care, preconditioned on a finding of bad faith. The Supreme Court affirmed this Court's language in *Caremark* holding that "only a sustained or systematic failure of the board to exercise oversight—such as an utter failure to attempt to assure a reasonable information and reporting system exists—will establish the lack of good faith that is a necessary condition to liability." Demonstrating lack of good faith is the reef upon which most *Caremark* claims founder. There are two possible scenarios in which a plaintiff can successfully assert a *Caremark* claim. The Supreme Court described these scenarios as being either: (a) the directors utterly failed to implement any reporting or information system or controls, *or* (b) having implemented such a system or controls, *consciously* failed to monitor or oversee its operations thus disabling themselves from being informed of risks or problems requiring their attention. Under either scenario, a finding of liability is conditioned on a plaintiff's showing that the directors knew they were not fulfilling their fiduciary duties. "Where directors fail to act in the face of a known duty to act, thereby demonstrating a conscious disregard for their responsibilities, they breach their duty of loyalty by failing to discharge that fiduciary obligation in good faith." Examples of directors' "disabling themselves from being informed" include a corporation's lacking an audit committee, or a corporation's not utilizing its audit committee.

I must analyze the facts alleged here under the lenient pleading standard of Rule 12(b)(6), drawing all reasonable inferences in favor of the Plaintiff, to see if it is reasonably conceivable that he may prevail. Because I find it so, the Motion to Dismiss for failure to state a claim must be denied.

In re American International Group, Inc. ("AIG") illustrates how Rule 12(b)(6)'s lenient pleading standard eases this Court's scrutiny of a *Caremark* claim at the motion-to-dismiss stage. In *AIG,* the underlying bases of the *Caremark* claims were several transactions, practices, and deceptive behaviors that caused AIG to restate its shareholder equity by $3.5 billion and to pay $1.6 billion to settle government investigations. Without going into the specific allegations of that case, which were quite complex, the plaintiffs alleged that the defendants had engaged in transactions designed to hide AIG's true financial situation, implemented illegal schemes to avoid taxes, sold illegal financial products to other companies, and rigged markets. The largest fraudulent transaction alleged was a $500 million phony reinsurance transaction designed to prop up AIG's financial statements.

The defendant directors, officers, and employees each moved to dismiss the complaint. In deciding whether the complaint should be dismissed, then-Vice Chancellor Strine illustrated the effect of the requirement, under 12(b)(6), that he draw all reasonable inferences in favor of the plaintiffs:

> Although the Stockholder Plaintiffs provide detailed allegations about the illegal transactions and schemes that proliferated at AIG, they are not able to tie all of the defendants directly with the specific facts to all of the schemes. In some instances … the Complaint only outlines the misconduct that occurred, or pleads the involvement of other [defendants]. But, as discussed

above, this is a motion to dismiss, and thus I must grant the Stockholder Plaintiffs the benefit of all reasonable inferences. Even the transactions that cannot be tied to specific defendants support the inference that, given the pervasiveness of the fraud, [the defendants] knew that AIG was engaging in illegal conduct.

In re Am. Int'l Group, Inc., 965 A.2d 763, 782 (Del. Ch. 2009). The Court explained that, if the case was analyzed under Rule 23.1, certain defendants would be "well positioned" to argue that the complaint needed more specifics to adequately plead knowledge on the part of the defendants. However, because the Court decided the case under Rule 12(b)(6) and because of the pervasiveness and materiality of the alleged fraud, the Court inferred that the defendants knew that AIG's internal controls were inadequate. For the purposes of a 12(b)(6) motion to dismiss, the Court inferred that "even when [the defendants] were not directly complicitous in the wrongful schemes, they were aware of the schemes and knowingly failed to stop them." I find the Court's analysis in *AIG* helpful here. My analysis follows.

Fuqi Had No Meaningful Controls in Place

One way a plaintiff may successfully plead a *Caremark* claim is to plead facts showing that a corporation had no internal controls in place. Fuqi had some sort of compliance system in place. For example, it had an Audit Committee and submitted financial statements to the SEC in 2009. However, accepting the Plaintiff's allegations as true, the mechanisms Fuqi had in place appear to have been woefully inadequate. In its press releases, Fuqi has detailed its extensive problems with internal controls. For example, Fuqi disclosed its "incorrect and untimely recordkeeping of inventory movements of retail operation." Problems with inventory are particularly troubling here, because Fuqi is a jewelry company, specializing in precious metals and gemstones which are valuable and easily stolen. Nonetheless, the Fuqi directors allowed the corporation to operate few to no controls over these vulnerable assets. Fuqi's self-disclosed accounting inadequacies include: (i) incorrect carve-out of the retail segment from the general ledger; (ii) unrecorded purchases and accounts payable, (iii) inadvertent inclusion of consigned inventory, (iv) incorrect and untimely recordkeeping of inventory movements of retail operation; and (v) incorrect diamond inventory costing, unrecorded purchases and unrecorded accounts payable.

These disclosures lead me to believe that Fuqi had no *meaningful* controls in place. The board of directors may have had regular meetings, and an Audit Committee may have existed, but there does not seem to have been any regulation of the company's operations *in China*. Nonetheless, even if I were to find that Fuqi had some system of internal controls in place, I may infer that the board's failure to monitor that system was a breach of fiduciary duty.

The Board of Directors Ignored Red Flags

As the Supreme Court held in *Stone v. Ritter,* if the directors have implemented a system of controls, a finding of liability is predicated on the directors' having "consciously failed to monitor or oversee [the system's] operations thus disabling themselves from being informed of risks or problems requiring their attention." One way that the plaintiff may plead such a conscious failure to monitor is to identify "red flags," obvious and problematic occurrences, that support an inference that the Fuqi directors knew that there were material weaknesses in Fuqi's internal controls and failed to correct such weaknesses. It is unclear how far back in time Fuqi's internal controls have been inadequate. At the very least, the Fuqi board had several "warnings" that all was not well with the internal controls as far back as March 2010.

First, Fuqi was a preexisting Chinese company that gained access to the U.S. capital markets through the Reverse Merger. Thus, Fuqi's directors were aware that there may be challenges in bringing Fuqi's internal controls into harmony with the U.S. securities reporting systems. Notwithstanding that fact, according to the Complaint, the directors did nothing to ensure that its reporting mechanisms were accurate. Second, the board knew that it had problems with its accounting and inventory processes by March 2010 at the latest, because it announced that the 2009 financial statements would need restatement at that time. In the same press release, Fuqi also acknowledged the likelihood of material weaknesses in its internal controls. Third, Fuqi received a letter from NASDAQ in April 2010 warning Fuqi that it would face delisting if Fuqi did not bring its reporting requirements up to date with the SEC.

It seems reasonable to infer that, because of these "red flags," the directors knew that there were deficiencies in Fuqi's internal controls. Furthermore, NASDAQ's letter to Fuqi put the board on notice that these deficiencies risked serious adverse consequences. The directors acknowledged as much in their March 2010 press release.

An analysis of the dates of Fuqi's disclosures demonstrates that it is reasonable, based on the facts pled, to infer that the directors knew that the internal controls were inadequate and failed to act in the face of a known duty. Fuqi announced to stockholders that it was restating its 2009 financial statements and investigating possible "material weaknesses" in its controls in March 2010. Rich sent the Demand Letter in July 2010, and the board appointed the Special Committee in October 2010. In March 2011, Fuqi announced that the cash transfer transactions had occurred between September 2009 and *November* 2010. These dates indicate that (1) Fuqi's directors knew that there were material weaknesses in Fuqi's internal controls *at the latest* in March of 2010; (2) Rich's stockholder demand in July 2010 (as well as the myriad securities litigation suits filed) put the directors on notice that the stockholders would carefully scrutinize what was going on at Fuqi; (3) Fuqi had purportedly already begun to "act" on Rich's demand by November 2010; and (4) despite their knowledge of the weaknesses in Fuqi's internal controls, the directors allowed $130 million in cash to be transferred out of the company, some as late as November 2010. The Plaintiffs have derived these facts directly from Fuqi's public disclosures. Facially, these disclosures are enough to allow me to reasonably infer scienter on the part of the Defendants.

That these cash transfers were not discovered until March of 2011, when Fuqi's auditor discovered them, reinforces the inference that the internal controls were (and possibly still are) grossly inadequate. That Chong was able to transfer $130 million out of the company's coffers, without the directors knowing about it for over a year, strains credulity. Either the directors knew about the cash transfers and were complicit, or they had zero controls in place and did not know about them. If the directors had even the barest framework of appropriate controls in place, they would have prevented the cash transfers.

When faced with knowledge that the company controls are inadequate, the directors must *act,* i.e., they must prevent further wrongdoing from occurring. A conscious failure to act, in the face of a known duty, is a breach of the duty of loyalty. At the very least, it is inferable that even if the Defendants were not complicit in these money transfers, they were aware of the pervasive, fundamental weaknesses in Fuqi's controls and knowingly failed to stop further problems from occurring. This knowing failure, as alleged by the Plaintiff, states a claim for breach of the duty of good faith under *Caremark.*

Finally, as then-Vice Chancellor Lamb explained in *David B. Shaev Profit Sharing Account v. Armstrong,* failing to establish an audit committee or failing to utilize an existing audit committee are examples of directors' "disabling themselves from being informed." Fuqi management's failure to pay the fees of the Audit Committee's advisors is a deliberate failure to utilize the Audit Committee. Therefore, I may infer that the board has disabled itself from being informed.

For the reasons above, I find that the Plaintiff has stated a claim under *Caremark* upon which relief can be granted.

Comments and Questions

1. The court found that although Fuqi had internal controls, albeit woefully inadequate controls. "Thus, in order to state a viable *Caremark* claim, and to predicate a substantial likelihood of director liability on it, a plaintiff must plead the existence of facts suggesting that the board knew that internal controls were inadequate, that the inadequacies could leave room for illegal or materially harmful behavior, and that the board chose to do nothing about the control deficiencies that it knew existed."[26] How did Vice Chancellor Glasscock infer from the facts pled that the defendant directors knew that Fuqi's internal controls were inadequate and failed to act? Did the court equate a bad outcome with bad faith?

2. What advice would you give to the board of directors of a Delaware corporation that owns significant assets and/or has significant operations overseas about how to minimize exposure to oversight liability?

---

26. *Desimone v. Barrows,* 924 A.2d 908, 940 (Del. Ch. 2007) (citing *Stone v. Ritter*) (holding that plaintiff had to plead the existence of facts suggesting that the board actually knew that the internal controls of the corporation were inadequate in detecting backdating of stock options and that the board chose to ignore the inadequacies).

3. Rather than arguing that demand was futile or otherwise excused, shareholder George Rich made a demand on the Fuqi board before eventually filing his derivative lawsuit. This choice is curious. For reasons that we will examine in Chapter 10, plaintiff shareholders rarely make demands on boards of Delaware corporations. As unusual as it is for shareholders to make a demand, it is even more unusual for the shareholder making demand to wait two years for a response from the board of directors.

4. The court notes that the outside directors' may have abdicated their duties by resigning. Vice Chancellor Glasscock emphasized that "the conscious failure to act, in the face of a known duty, is a breach of the duty of loyalty," and, further, "the business judgment rule 'has no role where directors have either abdicated their functions, or absent a conscious decision, failed to act.'" In light of these judicial admonitions, what advice would you give to a director who suspects that management has engaged in accounting fraud or other corporate malfeasance?

5. Resignation may not protect outside directors from fiduciary liability, as the directors of another Delaware public company learned in 2013. Puda Coal, like Fuqi International, became a Delaware corporation through a reverse merger with a Chinese firm and maintained its primary assets and operations in China. In 2009, the firm's chairman of the board and CEO, Ming Zhao, misappropriated Puda Coal's assets, transferring them to other companies that Zhao controlled without board authorization. The three outside directors of the firm, all Americans residing in the U.S., discovered Zhao's self-dealing from a third party more than 18 months later. Shareholders filed derivative litigation against Zhao as well as the other board members, alleging, among other claims, that the nonmanagement directors breached their duty of loyalty by failing to exercise proper oversight of the firm's assets. Although the outside directors constituted a majority of the board, they did not cause the company to join the plaintiffs' lawsuit. Instead, they resigned as from the Puda Coal board and moved to dismiss the complaint for failure to make a demand and failure to state a claim.

The court not only refused to dismiss the *Caremark* claims, but then-Chancellor Leo Strine strongly criticized defendants for resigning and leaving Puda Coal "under the sole dominion of a person [the CEO/chairman] they believe has pervasively breached his fiduciary duty of loyalty." Indeed, Strine conjectured that the outside directors may have breached their fiduciary duties by resigning: "[T]here are some circumstances in which running away does not immunize you. It in fact involves breach of duty.... If these directors are going to eventually testify that at the time they quit they believed that the chief executive officer of the company had stolen the assets out from under the company, and they did not cause the company to ... do anything, but they simply quit, I'm not sure that that's a decision that itself is not a breach of fiduciary duty."

6. Directors and officers do not act in good faith if they knowingly cause the corporation to disobey the law. Before his elevation to the Delaware Supreme Court, then-Chancellor Leo Strine made clear:

> Delaware law does not charter law breakers. Delaware law allows corporations to pursue diverse means to make a profit, subject to a critical statutory floor, which is the requirement that Delaware corporations only pursue 'lawful business' by 'lawful acts.' As a result, a fiduciary of a Delaware corporation cannot be loyal to a Delaware corporation by knowingly causing it to seek profit by violating the law.[27]

Recall, too, that Delaware's exculpation statute precludes exculpation for "a knowing violation of law." Del. Gen. Corp. L. § 102(b)(7).

V. *Caremark* Claims and Risk Management

As we have seen, Delaware law requires that boards employ reasonable information and reporting systems designed to put them on notice of potential illegal activity (fraudulent or criminal conduct) within the firm. These compliance and oversight programs allow directors to intervene, preventing wrongdoing that exposes the company to risk of criminal or civil penalties and, relatedly, massive losses. Of course, corporations are exposed to risks other than the threat that activities by the firms' executives or lower level employees will cause the company to violate civil or criminal laws or applicable regulations. Do directors have similar fiduciary duties to monitor for other types of risk?

As defaults on subprime mortgages skyrocketed, companies holding various types of mortgage-backed securities suffered massive losses. Legal analysts[28] and other observers[29] pointed to board passivity (directors "asleep at the wheel") as a contributing cause of the massive losses suffered by banks and other financial institutions, including at Citigroup, the subject of our next case. Citigroup's investments in subprime mortgages and complex debt instruments imperiled the giant bank and, eventually, threatened its survival. Citigroup posted a $27 billion loss, and its stock price fell some 77 percent, before the federal government rescued the too-big-to-fail corporation in 2008. Should Citigroup's stockholders have an opportunity to prove that the company's directors contributed to the debacle by failing to exercise proper oversight of the company's risk management function?

---

27. *In re Massey Energy Co. Deriv. & Class Action Litig.*, 2011 Del. Ch. LEXIS 83, at *73–74 (Del. Ch. May 31, 2011).

28. *See, e.g.*, Richard A. Posner, A Failure of Capitalism: The Crisis of '08 and the Descent Into Depression (2009).

29. *See, e.g.*, John Schnatter, *Where Were the Boards?*, Wall St. J., Oct. 25, 2008; Paul Myners, *Banking Reform Must Begin in Boardroom*, Fin. Times, Apr. 24, 2008.

In re Citigroup Inc. Shareholder Deriv. Litig.

Delaware Chancery Court
964 A.2d 106 (2009)

CHANDLER, CHANCELLOR:

This is a shareholder derivative action brought on behalf of Citigroup Inc. ("Citigroup" or the "Company"), seeking to recover for the Company its losses arising from exposure to the subprime lending market. Plaintiffs, shareholders of Citigroup, brought this action against current and former directors and officers of Citigroup, alleging, in essence, that the defendants breached their fiduciary duties by failing to properly monitor and manage the risks the Company faced from problems in the subprime lending market and for failing to properly disclose Citigroup's exposure to subprime assets. Plaintiffs allege that there were extensive "red flags" that should have given defendants notice of the problems that were brewing in the real estate and credit markets and that defendants ignored these warnings in the pursuit of short term profits and at the expense of the Company's long term viability.

Plaintiffs' argument is based on a theory of director liability most famously articulated by the former-Chancellor Allen in *In re Caremark*. Before *Caremark*, in *Graham v. Allis-Chalmers Manufacturing Company*, the Delaware Supreme Court, in response to a theory that the Allis-Chalmers directors were liable because they should have known about employee violations of federal anti-trust laws, held that "absent cause for suspicion there is no duty upon the directors to install and operate a corporate system of espionage to ferret out wrongdoing which they have no reason to suspect exists." Over thirty years later, in the context of approval of a settlement of a class action, former-Chancellor Allen took the opportunity to revisit the duty to monitor under Delaware law. In *Caremark*, the plaintiffs alleged that the directors were liable because they should have known that certain officers and employees were violating the federal Anti-Referral Payments Law. In analyzing these claims, the Court began, appropriately, by reviewing the duty of care and the protections of the business judgment rule.

With regard to director liability standards, the Court distinguished between (1) "*a board decision* that results in a loss because that decision was ill advised or 'negligent'" and (2) "an *unconsidered failure of the board to act* in which due attention would, arguably, have prevented the loss." In the former class of cases, director action is analyzed under the business judgment rule, which prevents judicial second guessing of the decision if the directors employed a rational process and considered all material information reasonably available—a standard measured by concepts of gross negligence.... Where directors are alleged to be liable for a failure to monitor liability creating activities, the *Caremark* Court, in a reassessment of the holding in *Graham*, stated that while directors could be liable for a failure to monitor, "only a sustained or systematic failure of the board to exercise oversight—such as an utter failure to attempt to assure a reasonable information and reporting system exists—will establish the lack of good faith that is a necessary condition to liability."

In *Stone v. Ritter*, the Delaware Supreme Court approved the *Caremark* standard for director oversight liability and made clear that liability was based on the concept of good faith, which the *Stone* Court held was embedded in the fiduciary duty of loyalty and did not constitute a freestanding fiduciary duty that could independently give rise to liability.... Thus, to establish oversight liability a plaintiff must show that the directors *knew* they were not discharging their fiduciary obligations or that the directors demonstrated a *conscious* disregard for their responsibilities such as by failing to act in the face of a known duty to act. The test is rooted in concepts of bad faith; indeed, a showing of bad faith is a *necessary condition* to director oversight liability.

Plaintiffs' Caremark Allegations

Plaintiffs' theory of how the director defendants will face personal liability is a bit of a twist on the traditional *Caremark* claim. In a typical *Caremark* case, plaintiffs argue that the defendants are liable for damages that arise from a failure to properly monitor or oversee employee misconduct or violations of law. For example, in *Caremark* the board allegedly failed to monitor employee actions in violation of the federal Anti-Referral Payments Law; in *Stone*, the directors were charged with a failure of oversight that resulted in liability for the company because of employee violations of the federal Bank Secrecy Act.

In contrast, plaintiffs' *Caremark* claims are based on defendants' alleged failure to properly monitor Citigroup's *business risk*, specifically its exposure to the subprime mortgage market. In their answering brief, plaintiffs allege that the director defendants are personally liable under *Caremark* for failing to "make a good faith attempt to follow the procedures put in place or fail[ing] to assure that adequate and proper corporate information and reporting systems existed that would enable them to be fully informed regarding Citigroup's risk to the subprime mortgage market." Plaintiffs point to so-called "red flags" that should have put defendants on notice of the problems in the subprime mortgage market and further allege that the board should have been especially conscious of these red flags because a majority of the directors (1) served on the Citigroup board during its previous Enron related conduct and (2) were members of the ARM ("Audit Risk Management") Committee and considered financial experts.

Although these claims are framed by plaintiffs as *Caremark* claims, plaintiffs' theory essentially amounts to a claim that the director defendants should be personally liable to the Company because they failed to fully recognize the risk posed by subprime securities. When one looks past the lofty allegations of duties of oversight and red flags used to dress up these claims, what is left appears to be plaintiff shareholders attempting to hold the director defendants personally liable for making (or allowing to be made) business decisions that, in hindsight, turned out poorly for the Company. Delaware Courts have faced these types of claims many times and have developed doctrines to deal with them—the fiduciary duty of care and the business judgment rule. These doctrines properly focus on the decision-making process rather than on a substantive evaluation of the merits of the decision.

Absent an allegation of interestedness or disloyalty to the corporation, the business judgment rule prevents a judge or jury from second guessing director decisions if they were the product of a rational process and the directors availed themselves of all material and reasonably available information. The standard of director liability under the business judgment rule "is predicated upon concepts of gross negligence."

Additionally, Citigroup has adopted a provision in its certificate of incorporation pursuant to § 102(b)(7) that exculpates directors from personal liability for violations of fiduciary duty, except for, among other things, breaches of the duty of loyalty or actions or omissions not in good faith or that involve intentional misconduct or a knowing violation of the law. Because the director defendants are "exculpated from liability for certain conduct, 'then a serious threat of liability may only be found to exist if the plaintiff pleads a *non-exculpated* claim against the directors based on particularized facts.'" Here, plaintiffs have not alleged that the directors were interested in the transaction and instead root their theory of director personal liability in bad faith.

A plaintiff can thus plead bad faith by alleging with particularity that a director *knowingly* violated a fiduciary duty or failed to act in violation of a *known* duty to act, demonstrating a *conscious* disregard for her duties.

The Delaware Supreme Court made clear in *Stone* that directors of Delaware corporations have certain responsibilities to implement and monitor a system of oversight; however, this obligation does not eviscerate the core protections of the business judgment rule—protections designed to allow corporate managers and directors to pursue risky transactions without the specter of being held personally liable if those decisions turn out poorly. Accordingly, the burden required for a plaintiff to rebut the presumption of the business judgment rule by showing gross negligence is a difficult one, and the burden to show bad faith is even higher.... The presumption of the business judgment rule, the protection of an exculpatory § 102(b)(7) provision, and the difficulty of proving a *Caremark* claim together function to place an extremely high burden on a plaintiff to state a claim for personal director liability for a failure to see the extent of a company's business risk.

To the extent the Court allows shareholder plaintiffs to succeed on a theory that a director is liable for a failure to monitor business risk, the Court risks undermining the well settled policy of Delaware law by inviting Courts to perform a hindsight evaluation of the reasonableness or prudence of directors' business decisions. Risk has been defined as the chance that a return on an investment will be different than expected. The essence of the business judgment of managers and directors is deciding how the company will evaluate the trade-off between risk and return. Businesses—and particularly financial institutions—make returns by taking on risk; a company or investor that is willing to take on more risk can earn a higher return. Thus, in almost any business transaction, the parties go into the deal with the knowledge that, even if they have evaluated the situation correctly, the return could be different than they expected.

It is almost impossible for a court, in hindsight, to determine whether the directors of a company properly evaluated risk and thus made the "right" business decision. Business decision-makers must operate in the real world, with imperfect information, limited resources, and an uncertain future. To impose liability on directors for making a "wrong" business decision would cripple their ability to earn returns for investors by taking business risks. Indeed, this kind of judicial second guessing is what the business judgment rule was designed to prevent, and even if a complaint is framed under a *Caremark* theory, this Court will not abandon such bedrock principles of Delaware fiduciary duty law.

The Complaint Does Not Properly Allege Demand Futility for Plaintiffs' Fiduciary Duty Claims

In this case, plaintiffs allege that the defendants are liable for failing to properly monitor the risk that Citigroup faced from subprime securities. While it may be possible for a plaintiff to meet the burden under some set of facts, plaintiffs in this case have failed to state a *Caremark* claim sufficient to excuse demand based on a theory that the directors did not fulfill their oversight obligations by failing to monitor the business risk of the company.

The allegations in the Complaint amount essentially to a claim that Citigroup suffered large losses and that there were certain warning signs that could or should have put defendants on notice of the business risks related to Citigroup's investments in subprime assets. Plaintiffs then conclude that because defendants failed to prevent the Company's losses associated with certain business risks, they must have consciously ignored these warning signs or knowingly failed to monitor the Company's risk in accordance with their fiduciary duties.

Plaintiffs do not contest that Citigroup had procedures and controls in place that were designed to monitor risk. Plaintiffs admit that Citigroup established the ARM Committee and in 2004 amended the ARM Committee charter to include the fact that one of the purposes of the ARM committee was to assist the board in fulfilling its oversight responsibility relating to policy standards and guidelines for risk assessment and risk management. The ARM Committee was also charged with, among other things, (1) discussing with management and independent auditors the annual audited financial statements, (2) reviewing with management an evaluation of Citigroup's internal control structure, and (3) discussing with management Citigroup's major credit, market, liquidity, and operational risk exposures and the steps taken by management to monitor and control such exposures, including Citigroup's risk assessment and risk management policies.

Plaintiffs nevertheless argue that the director defendants breached their duty of oversight either because the oversight mechanisms were not adequate or because the director defendants did not make a good faith effort to comply with the established oversight procedures. To support this claim, the Complaint alleges numerous facts that plaintiffs argue should have put the director defendants on notice of the impending problems in the subprime mortgage market and Citigroup's exposure thereto. Plaintiffs summarized some of these "red flags" in their answering brief as follows:

- the steady decline of the housing market and the impact the collapsing bubble would have on mortgages and subprime backed securities since as early as 2005;
- December 2005 guidance from the FASB staff— "The FASB staff is aware of loan products whose contractual features may increase the exposure of the originator, holder, investor, guarantor, or servicer to risk of non-payment or realization.";
- the drastic rise in foreclosure rates starting in 2006;
- several large subprime lenders reporting substantial losses and filing for bankruptcy starting in 2006;
- billions of dollars in losses reported by Citigroup's peers, such as Bear Stearns and Merrill Lynch.

Plaintiffs argue that demand is excused because a majority of the director defendants face a substantial likelihood of personal liability because they were charged with management of Citigroup's risk as members of the ARM Committee and as audit committee financial experts and failed to properly oversee and monitor such risk. As explained above, however, to establish director oversight liability plaintiffs would ultimately have to prove bad faith conduct by the director defendants. Plaintiffs fail to plead any particularized factual allegations that raise a reasonable doubt that the director defendants acted in good faith.

The "red flags" in the Complaint amount to little more than portions of public documents that reflected the worsening conditions in the subprime mortgage market and in the economy generally. Plaintiffs fail to plead "particularized facts suggesting that the Board was presented with 'red flags' alerting it to the potential misconduct" at the Company. That the director defendants knew of signs of a deterioration in the subprime mortgage market, or even signs suggesting that conditions could decline further, is not sufficient to show that the directors were or should have been aware of any wrongdoing at the Company or were consciously disregarding a duty somehow to prevent Citigroup from suffering losses.... Plaintiffs' allegations do not even specify how the board's oversight mechanisms were inadequate or how the director defendants knew of these inadequacies and consciously ignored them. Rather, plaintiffs seem to hope the Court will accept the conclusion that since the Company suffered large losses, and since a properly functioning risk management system would have avoided such losses, the directors must have breached their fiduciary duties in allowing such losses.

Plaintiffs cite *McCall v. Scott* to support the proposition that directors who were on the board during previous misconduct should be sensitive to similar circumstances which had previously prompted investigations. That case, however, actually shows how plaintiffs' attempt to impose a higher standard on the directors because of the Enron scandal is inadequate.... Unlike plaintiffs' allegations about Enron, the prior "experience" referenced in *McCall* was an investigation and settlement for the *same type* of questionable billing practices before the Sixth Circuit. Plaintiffs have not shown how involvement with the Enron related scandals should have in any way put the director defendants on a heightened alert to problems in the subprime mortgage market.

The Complaint and plaintiffs' answering brief repeatedly make the conclusory allegation that the defendants have breached their duty of oversight, but nowhere do plaintiffs adequately explain what the director defendants actually did or failed to do that would constitute such a violation.

It is well established that the mere fact that a company takes on business risk and suffers losses—even catastrophic losses—does not evidence misconduct, and without more, is not a basis for personal director liability. That there were signs in the market that reflected worsening conditions and suggested that conditions may deteriorate even further is not an invitation for this Court to disregard the presumptions of the business judgment rule and conclude that the directors are liable because they did not properly evaluate business risk.

The Court's recent decision in *American International Group, Inc. Consolidated Derivative Litigation* demonstrates the stark contrast between the allegations here and allegations that are sufficient to survive a motion to dismiss. In *AIG*, the Court faced a motion to dismiss a complaint that included "well-pled allegations of pervasive, diverse, and substantial financial fraud involving managers at the highest levels of AIG." ... Unlike the allegations in this case, the defendants in *AIG* allegedly failed to exercise reasonable oversight over pervasive *fraudulent* and *criminal* conduct. Indeed, the Court in *AIG* even stated that the complaint there supported the assertion that top AIG officials were leading a "criminal organization" and that "[t]he diversity, pervasiveness, and materiality of the alleged financial wrongdoing at AIG is extraordinary."

Here, plaintiffs argue that the Complaint supports the reasonable conclusion that the director defendants acted in bad faith by failing to see the warning signs of a deterioration in the subprime mortgage market and failing to cause Citigroup to change its investment policy to limit its exposure to the subprime market. Director oversight duties are designed to ensure reasonable reporting and information systems exist that would allow directors to know about and prevent wrongdoing that could cause losses for the Company. There are significant differences between failing to oversee employee fraudulent or criminal conduct and failing to recognize the extent of a Company's business risk. Directors should, indeed must under Delaware law, ensure that reasonable information and reporting systems exist that would put them on notice of fraudulent or criminal conduct within the company. Such oversight programs allow directors to intervene and prevent frauds or other wrongdoing that could expose the company to risk of loss as a result of such conduct. While it may be tempting to say that directors have the same duties to monitor and oversee business risk, imposing *Caremark*-type duties on directors to monitor business risk is fundamentally different.

To impose oversight liability on directors for failure to monitor "excessive" risk would involve courts in conducting hindsight evaluations of decisions at the heart of the business judgment of directors. Oversight duties under Delaware law are not designed to subject directors, even expert directors, to *personal liability* for failure to predict the future and to properly evaluate business risk.

Instead of alleging facts that could demonstrate bad faith on the part of the directors, by presenting the Court with the so called "red flags," plaintiffs are inviting the Court to engage in the exact kind of judicial second guessing that is proscribed by the business judgment rule. In any business decision that turns out poorly there will likely be signs that one could point to and argue are evidence that the decision was wrong. Indeed, it is tempting in a case with such staggering losses for one to think that they could have made the "right" decision if they had been in the directors' position. This temptation, however, is one of the reasons for the presumption against an objective review of business decisions by judges, a presumption that it is no less applicable when the losses to the Company are large.

Citigroup has suffered staggering losses, in part, as a result of the recent problems in the United States economy, particularly those in the subprime mortgage market. It is understandable that investors, and others, want to find someone to hold responsible for these losses, and it is often difficult to distinguish between a desire to blame *someone* and a desire to force those responsible to account for their wrongdoing. Our law, fortunately, provides guidance for precisely these situations in the form of doctrines governing the duties owed by officers and directors of Delaware corporations. This law has been refined over hundreds of years, which no doubt included many crises, and we must not let our desire to blame someone for our losses make us lose sight of the purpose of our law. Ultimately, the discretion granted directors and managers allows them to maximize shareholder value in the long term by taking risks without the debilitating fear that they will be held personally liable if the company experiences losses. This doctrine also means, however, that when the company suffers losses, shareholders may not be able to hold the directors personally liable.

Comments and Questions

1. How did Chancellor Chandler distinguish the claims plead in this case from the allegations made by the plaintiff shareholders in *Caremark*? Compare Chancellor Chandler's statements about the monitoring duties of the Citigroup board with Chancellor Allen's description of the monitoring duties owed by Caremark's directors. Do you think that Chancellor Chandler would have dismissed plaintiffs' complaint in this case if the defendants had been directors of a non-financial firm? Should Citigroup's directors have reduced responsibility for overseeing financial risks because Citigroup's business, as a financial institution, makes returns by taking on risk? Does that make sense as a matter of public policy?

2. Excessive risk taking by executives and other employees at Citigroup (as well as Bear Stearns, Lehman Brothers, AIG, and other financial institutions) focused the public's attention on corporate risk management. In the aftermath of the subprime mortgage crisis, Delaware courts examined the nexus between directors' oversight duties of directors and their risk management functions. Shareholders complained that directors failed to monitor officers and employees adequately to ensure that they

were not investing firm capital in overly risky securities or transactions. Chancellor Chandler's opinion, however, seems to deflect attention from governance inside Citigroup, attributing shareholders' losses to market declines and other economic forces beyond the control of Citigroup's board. Does his opinion suggest that Citigroup's directors had no duty to act, even if there had been red flags indicating that management had engaged in excessive risk taking? Does Chancellor Chandler's decision provide directors with incentives to inquire about the functioning of corporate risk management systems? Why or why not?

3. While acknowledging that boards must have reasonable information to monitor for fraudulent or other illegal conduct, the court characterized monitoring for business risk as "fundamentally different." Do you agree? Do *Caremark* claims for failure of oversight premised on poor risk management uniquely implicate the principles underlying the business judgment rule, even though plaintiff shareholders do not challenge a decision by the board of directors (and, therefore, the business judgment rule does not apply)? Should courts give heightened scrutiny to such claims? Why or why not?

4. Like Chancellor Chandler in *Citigroup*, courts dismissed most claims against outside directors of financial companies alleging breach of the duty of oversight. In many of these cases, plaintiffs failed to plead particularized facts demonstrating the director defendants knew or should have known about purported red flags, including internal company reports and communications that outside directors may or may not have received. Judges generally are reluctant to infer that information known by management also came to the attention of the board or even to board committees.

The shareholder plaintiffs who sued the directors of Goldman Sachs Group used a different strategy to plead a *Caremark* claim against Goldman's directors. In the case of *In re The Goldman Sachs Group, Inc. S'holder Litig.*,[30] shareholders alleged that the firm's compensation structure, approved by the board, encouraged management to take excessive risks in the subprime mortgage securities market—and eventually engage in unethical behavior and illegal conduct—in order to maximize their annual bonuses. The court dismissed plaintiffs' claims, repeating that, in the absence of red flags, judges will not second-guess directors. Citing *Citigroup*, the court also held the board's determination of the appropriate amount of risk involves business judgment and is protected by the business judgment rule. Vice Chancellor Glasscock further opined, "If an actionable duty to monitor business risk exists, it cannot encompass any substantive evaluation by a court of a board's determination of the appropriate amount of risk. Such decisions plainly involve business judgment."

5. Delaware court decisions notwithstanding, many commentators ascribed at least some blame for the 2008 meltdown on directors and officers for failing to safeguard financial institutions against excessive risk taking. Indeed, in the aftermath of the crisis, critics have blamed poor risk management oversight for the bankruptcy of Lehman Brothers and the near failure of Citigroup and other financial institutions. For example, the Financial Crisis Inquiry Commission reported to Congress that,

---

30. 2011 WL 4826104 (Del. Ch. Oct. 12, 2011).

"Lehman's failure resulted in part from significant problems in its corporate governance, including risk management, exacerbated by compensation to its executives and traders that was based predominately on short-term profits."[31] How might equity-based compensation arrangements cause executives and traders to behave recklessly?

Although courts dismissed most derivative lawsuits seeking to hold boards of financial institutions liable for lax risk oversight, the directors did not prevail in *American Int'l Group v. Greenberg*,[32] a decision that Chancellor Chandler distinguished. In *AIG*, then-Vice Chancellor Strine refused to dismiss claims against AIG's former chairman and CEO Maurice Greenberg and several inside directors (Greenberg's so-called "Inner Circle"), ruling that, "The Complaint fairly supports the assertion that AIG's Inner Circle led a—and I use this term with knowledge of its strength—criminal organization. The diversity, pervasiveness, and materiality of the alleged financial wrongdoing at AIG is extraordinary." Although the plaintiff shareholders did not plead evidence of defendants' direct knowledge of the wrongdoing, the court nonetheless implied their scienter, ruling that they "knowingly tolerat[ed] inadequate controls and knowingly fail[ed] to monitor their subordinates' compliance with legal duties." As directors and senior officers of AIG, the defendants not only held the highest positions in the firm, but they also supervised the divisions that engaged in the fraud. Moreover, the alleged wrongdoing was so widespread and so egregious that the court found it unlikely that certain illegal transactions could have taken place without their knowledge.

7. Citigroup was among a group of large financial institutions that suffered massive and, in some instances, catastrophic losses. The collapse of a "too-big-to-fail" financial institution may trigger the failure of other major financial firms, causing catastrophic losses for shareholders and, as we saw in 2008, imperiling the U.S. and worldwide economies. Not only does the business judgment rule protect directors from liability to the company and its shareholders for its good faith decisions to engage in risky business ventures, but directors have no duty whatsoever to consider how failure of their firm could cause systemic harms to other market participants and the economy. Because financial institutions pose unique systemic risks, should board oversight responsibilities extend beyond what is required for directors to satisfy their duties under *Caremark*? For one analysis of this question, see Claire A. Hill & Brett H. McDonnell, *Reconsidering Board Oversight Duties After the Financial Crisis*, 2013 U. Ill. L. Rev. 859 (proposing enlargement of directors' monitoring duties to encompass business risk, but stopping short of suggesting that directors incur legal liability for breaching those duties). Should the law require that, in evaluating business ventures, directors of systemically important corporations (like "too-big-to-fail" financial institutions) consider not only risks of to the firm and its shareholders but also risks to other firms and markets? Professor Steven Schwarcz has proposed that directors have a "public

---

31. Nat'l Comm'n on the Causes of the Financial and Economic Crisis in the United States, the Financial Crisis Inquiry Report 343 (2011).

32. 2009 WL 366613 (De. Ch. Feb. 10, 2009).

governance duty" not to engage in excessive risk taking that could systemically harm the public.[33] How could such a duty be enforced?

8. Section 165 of the Dodd-Frank Act mandates that the boards of certain publicly-traded bank holding companies (those with at least $10 billion in assets) and publicly-traded nonbank financial companies (those supervised by the Federal Reserve) establish stand-alone, board-level, risk committees. Pursuant to the statute, the risk committees must oversee enterprise-wide risk management practices and, among other things, must include at least one risk management expert with experience identifying, assessing, and managing risk exposures of large, complex firms. Are these requirements consistent with Chancellor Chandler's view of the role of Citigroup's board of directors?

9. Whether more effective board oversight could have prevented or at least mini-mized the impact of the credit meltdown on these firms, the role of directors in enterprise-wide risk management also has come under inspection by institutional shareholders, and corporate directors have heard the call to strengthen their risk over-sight. Boards of financial sector corporations as well as corporations in other industries now direct greater attention to risk management. Corporations have revised their board practices and employed new systematic mechanisms for evaluating and im-proving risk governance, with the objective of expanding the directors' oversight of enterprise-wide risks.

Surveys of public company directors reveal that a majority of boards delegate pri-mary responsibility for risk oversight to their audit committees—consistent with listing rules requiring that audit committees discuss risk assessment and risk man-agement policies—or a dedicated risk committee. Nonetheless, the full board still exercises some direct and active oversight for certain identified risks and for risks generally related to the firm's strategic direction and business plans. Corporate advisors counsel the full board to conduct annual reviews of the company's risk management system, including the risk oversight policies and procedures adopted by the board and its committees. Boards also receive periodic briefings, including from outside subject matter experts, concerning board oversight of risk culture expectations and the importance of "tone at the top." For a discussion of the board's role in enterprise risk management, see Michelle M. Harner, *Ignoring the Writing on the Wall: The Role of Risk Management in the Economic Crisis*, 5 J. Bus. & Tech. L. 45 (2010).

10. Over the past several years, directors and officers of public companies have grappled with another major business risk: exposure to cyber attacks. Not only must corporations respond to external threats from hackers, thieves, competitors, and for-mer employees, but they also must protect the company from internal threats from current employees who may intentionally misuse or inadvertently lose proprietary or commercially sensitive information. The rise of cloud computing, proliferation of mobile technology, and explosion of social media, among other developments, have exacerbated cyber security danger. Losses to corporations from cyber security breaches include business interruption and reputational damage, forensic and legal

---

33. Steven L. Schwarcz, *Misalignment: Corporate Risk-Taking and Public Duty,* 92 Notre Dame L. Rev. (2016) (forthcoming).

expenses, damage to the company's information technology and related infrastructure, mitigation and data restoration costs, and class action and other litigation filed by customers, suppliers, and employees affected by a data breach or identity theft.

In June 2014, SEC Commissioner Luis Aguilar told an audience at the NYSE that "ensuring the adequacy of a company's cybersecurity measures needs to be a part of a board of director's risk oversight responsibilities."[34] Insofar as cyber attacks have become a known-risk for public companies, well-counseled directors now monitor cyber security in connection with their oversight of the corporation's enterprise risk management structure. Commissioner Aguilar warned, "Boards that choose to ignore, or minimize, the importance of cybersecurity oversight responsibility, do so at their own peril."

Indeed, directors and officers already have faced derivative lawsuits brought by shareholders seeking to hold them liable for the harm caused to the company. The headline-making cyber attack on Target Corporation during the 2013 holiday season provides an interesting case in point. Thieves stole an estimated 70 million records containing customers' personal and financial data. Just weeks after "the worst data breach in retail history," shareholders filed at least two derivative suits against Target's directors and officers seeking monetary damages and injunctive relief in the nature of significant corporate governance reform. The complaints alleged that the defendants breached their duty of due care for failing to take reasonable steps to maintain customers' personal and financial information and failing to implement internal controls designed to detect and prevent data breaches. In addition, the plaintiff shareholders sought to hold the defendants liable for damages resulting from the company's allegedly fraudulent response to the data breach, claiming that Target's directors and officers acted in bad faith and breached their duty of loyalty by failing to provide adequate notice to customers of the data breach and by releasing incomplete and misleading information to customers. What defenses would you expect the Target defendants to plead in response to shareholders' breach of fiduciary duty claims? What claims, if any, would you expect to survive defendants' motions to dismiss?

VI. The Duty of Disclosure

Corporate directors and officers have affirmative duties of disclosure arising under federal securities statutes, duties that we will examine in detail in Chapter 9. For the most part, these complex federal laws and regulations establish the scope and substance of public companies' disclosure obligations. However, the Delaware courts also have recognized a fiduciary duty of disclosure owed by corporate directors and officers under state law. Recall that in *Smith v. Van Gorkom*, the majority found that the directors breached their duty to disclose to Trans Union shareholders "all material in-

---

34. Speech, Commissioner Luis A. Aguilar, "Boards of Directors, Corporate Governance and Cyber-Risks: Sharpening the Focus," *available at* http://www.sec.gov/News/Speech/Detail/Speech/1370542057946.

formation such as a reasonable stockholder would consider important" in deciding whether to approve the proposed merger. Delaware courts first recognized the directors' disclosure duty in connection with a request for shareholder action.[35] However, even in the absence of a request for shareholder action, directors have disclosure duties under state law, as the Delaware Supreme Court affirmed in the following case.

Malone v. Brincat
Delaware Supreme Court
722 A.2d 5 (1998)

HOLLAND, JUSTICE:

The complaint alleged that the director defendants intentionally overstated the financial condition of Mercury on repeated occasions throughout a four-year period in disclosures to Mercury's shareholders. Plaintiffs contend that the complaint states a claim upon which relief can be granted for a breach of the fiduciary duty of disclosure.

The complaint alleged that the directors "knowingly and intentionally breached their fiduciary duty of disclosure because the SEC filings made by the directors and every communication from the company to the shareholders since 1994 was materially false" and that "as a direct result of the false disclosures ... the Company has lost all or virtually all of its value (about $2 billion)."

According to plaintiffs, since 1994, the director defendants caused Mercury to disseminate information containing overstatements of Mercury's earnings, financial performance and shareholders' equity.... The complaint alleged that all of the foregoing inaccurate information was included or referenced in virtually every filing Mercury made with the SEC and every communication Mercury's directors made to the shareholders during this period of time.

The individual director defendants filed a motion to dismiss, contending that they owed no fiduciary duty of disclosure under the circumstances alleged in the complaint.

After briefing and oral argument, the Court of Chancery granted both of the motions to dismiss with prejudice. The Court of Chancery held that directors have no fiduciary duty of disclosure under Delaware law in the absence of a request for shareholder action.

We disagree, and although we hold that the Complaint as drafted should have been dismissed, our rationale is different.

This Court has held that a board of directors is under a fiduciary duty to disclose material information when seeking shareholder action: It is well-established that the duty of disclosure "represents nothing more than the well-recognized proposition that directors of Delaware corporations are under a fiduciary duty to disclose fully and fairly all material information within the board's control *when it seeks shareholder action.*"

---

35. *See Lynch v. Vickers Energy Corp.*, 383 A.2d 278 (Del. 1977).

The majority of opinions from the Court of Chancery have held that there may be a cause of action for disclosure violations only where directors seek shareholder action. The present appeal requires this Court to decide whether a director's fiduciary duty arising out of misdisclosure is implicated in the absence of a request for shareholder action. We hold that directors who knowingly disseminate false information that results in corporate injury or damage to an individual stockholder violate their fiduciary duty, and may be held accountable in a manner appropriate to the circumstances.

Fiduciary Duty Delaware Corporate Directors

An underlying premise for the imposition of fiduciary duties is a separation of legal control from beneficial ownership. Equitable principles act in those circumstances to protect the beneficiaries who are not in a position to protect themselves.

The directors of Delaware corporations stand in a fiduciary relationship not only to the stockholders but also to the corporations upon whose boards they serve. The director's fiduciary duty to both the corporation and its shareholders has been characterized by this Court as a triad: due care, good faith, and loyalty. That tripartite fiduciary duty does not operate intermittently but is the constant compass by which all director actions for the corporation and interactions with its shareholders must be guided.

Although the fiduciary duty of a Delaware director is unremitting, the exact course of conduct that must be charted to properly discharge that responsibility will change in the specific context of the action the director is taking with regard to either the corporation or its shareholders.

Director Communications Shareholder Reliance Justified

The shareholder constituents of a Delaware corporation are entitled to rely upon their elected directors to discharge their fiduciary duties at all times. Whenever directors communicate publicly or directly with shareholders about the corporation's affairs, with or without a request for shareholder action, directors have a fiduciary duty to shareholders to exercise due care, good faith and loyalty. It follows *a fortiori* that when directors communicate publicly or directly with shareholders about corporate matters the *sine qua non* of directors' fiduciary duty to shareholders is honesty.

The duty of disclosure is, and always has been, a specific application of the general fiduciary duty owed by directors. The duty of disclosure obligates directors to provide the stockholders with accurate and complete information material to a transaction or other corporate event that is being presented to them for action.

The issue in this case is not whether Mercury's directors breached their duty of disclosure. It is whether they breached their more general fiduciary duty of loyalty and good faith by knowingly disseminating to the stockholders false information about the financial condition of the company. The directors' fiduciary duties include the duty to deal with their stockholders honestly.

Shareholders are entitled to rely upon the truthfulness of all information disseminated to them by the directors they elect to manage the corporate enterprise. Delaware directors disseminate information in at least three contexts: public statements made to the market, including shareholders; statements informing shareholders about the affairs of the corporation without a request for shareholder action; and, statements to shareholders in conjunction with a request for shareholder action.

State Fiduciary Disclosure Duty Shareholder Remedy In Action Requested Context

In the absence of a request for stockholder action, the Delaware General Corporation Law does not require directors to provide shareholders with information concerning the finances or affairs of the corporation.

The duty of directors to observe proper disclosure requirements derives from the combination of the fiduciary duties of care, loyalty and good faith. The plaintiffs contend that, because directors fiduciary responsibilities are not "intermittent duties," there is no reason why the duty of disclosure should not be implicated in every public communication by a corporate board of directors. The directors of a Delaware corporation are required to disclose fully and fairly all material information within the board's control when it seeks shareholder action. When the directors disseminate information to stockholders when no stockholder action is sought, the fiduciary duties of care, loyalty and good faith apply. Dissemination of false information could violate one or more of those duties.

Fraud On Market Regulated By Federal Law

When corporate directors impart information they must comport with the obligations imposed by both the Delaware law and the federal statutes and regulations of the United States Securities and Exchange Commission.... In deference to the panoply of federal protections that are available to investors in connection with the purchase or sale of securities of Delaware corporations, this court has decided not to recognize a state common law cause of action against the directors of Delaware corporations. Here, it is to be noted, the claim appears to be made by those who did not sell and, therefore, would not implicate federal securities laws which relate to the purchase or sale of securities.

State Common Law Shareholder Remedy In Nonaction Context

Delaware law also protects shareholders who receive false communications from directors even in the absence of a request for shareholder action. When the directors are not seeking shareholder action, but are deliberately misinforming shareholders about the business of the corporation, either directly or by a public statement, there is a violation of fiduciary duty. That violation may result in a derivative claim on behalf of the corporation or a cause of action for damages.

Complaint Properly Dismissed No Shareholder Action Requested

Here, the complaint alleges (if true) an egregious violation of fiduciary duty by the directors in knowingly disseminating materially false information.

The plaintiffs, however, never expressly assert a derivative claim on behalf of the corporation or allege compliance with Court of Chancery Rule 23.1, which requires pre-suit demand or cognizable and particularized allegations that demand is excused.

If the plaintiffs intend to assert a derivative claim, they should be permitted to replead to assert such a claim and any damage or equitable remedy sought on behalf of the corporation.

Comments and Questions

1. The Delaware Supreme Court recognized plaintiffs' claim for breach of duty to disclose even in the absence of a request from the defendants for shareholders' action. From the perspective of public company shareholders, is this cause of action important? Why or why not?

2. After *Malone*, then, directors and officers may be liable for breaching their fiduciary duties if they "deliberately misinform shareholders about the business of the corporation, either directly or by a public statement." Must shareholders prove that they relied on the misinformation to their detriment? Must shareholders prove that the misinformation caused their losses?

3. The *Malone* court stated that when directors disseminate false information in the absence of a request from shareholders, they may violate one or more of the duties of care, loyalty, and good faith. Which claim would shareholders most likely assert? Why?

4. Shareholders may file a derivative action to enforce directors' duty of disclosure. *In re infoUSA, Inc. Sh'lders Litig.*, 953 A.2d 963, 990 (Del. Ch. 2007).

Chapter 5

The Duty of Loyalty

In addition to exercising proper care, directors and officers must remain loyal to the corporation that is under their governance. Indeed, loyalty is the essence of all fiduciary relations. Because of the inherent danger that corporate managers will favor themselves at the expense of the company and its shareholders, the duty of loyalty requires corporate fiduciaries to manage the business and affairs of the corporation in the best interests of the firm, placing the corporation's interests above their own personal interests or the interests of any third party.

To satisfy the duty of loyalty, then, directors and officers not only must act in good faith and with a lawful and honest corporate purpose, but managers may not engage in unfair self-dealing. Furthermore, corporate law prohibits fiduciaries from wrongly usurping the firm's business opportunities, unfairly competing with the company, or taking corporate assets or confidential company information for their own personal gain or to benefit others. More simply put, corporate fiduciaries breach their duty of loyalty if they exercise their power and authority in bad faith or for improper, non-corporate ends.

Although recognizing that human beings naturally favor themselves, courts nonetheless have condemned disloyal conduct by directors and officers using uncompromising, moralistic language. As Justice Cardozo famously described it, the "rule of undivided loyalty" imposed upon fiduciaries is "relentless and supreme," and requires "[n]ot honesty alone, but the punctilio of an honor the most sensitive." *Meinhard v. Salmon*, 164 N.E. 545 (1928). Thus, managers may not engage their self-interest without consent from the corporation following full disclosure. As explained by Vice Chancellor Leo Strine and other Delaware corporate law experts:

> Because the discretion that the DGCL affords directors is so wide, it is vitally important that directors exercise this discretion to advance the corporation's best interests, and not for improper purposes. Likewise, because the DGCL embraces a strong republican model of representation, investing corporate directors with broad managerial powers and duties during their terms in office, it is essential that directors take their responsibilities seriously by actually trying to manage the corporation in a manner advantageous to the stockholders. For these reasons, it has been traditional for the duty of loyalty to be articulated capaciously, in a manner that emphasizes not only the obligation of a loyal fiduciary to refrain from advantaging herself at the expense of the corporation, but as importantly, to act affirmatively to further the corporation's best interests. In this respect, our law has been clear that the

duty of loyalty is implicated by all director actions, because all such actions must be undertaken in good faith to advance the corporation's best interests and because directors owe an affirmative obligation to put in a good faith effort to responsibly carry out their duties.

Leo E. Strine, Jr., et al., *Loyalty's Core Demand: The Defining Role of Good Faith in Corporate Law,* 98 Geo. L. Rev 629, 633–34 (2010).

Black-letter doctrine professes to deal more harshly with the unfaithful manager than with the careless manager. For example, unlike allegations that corporate fiduciaries breached their duty of care, duty of loyalty claims purportedly are not protected from judicial review by the business judgment rule. Also, duty of loyalty claims are specifically excluded from director exculpation statutes, such as Section 102(b)(7) of the Delaware General Corporation Law.

Yet, despite continued strong condemnation of faithless corporate fiduciaries, the law has become less severe in its treatment of disloyal conduct over time. As we will see, not only have the standards of faithful conduct become less onerous, but management's duty of loyalty arguably has narrowed in scope. Furthermore, corporate law has become more tolerant of transactions between fiduciaries and the firm, allowing boards of directors to approve their colleagues' self-dealing and sheltering such agreements from demanding judicial review.

Allegations that fiduciaries breached their duty of loyalty commonly concern transactions decided by directors with conflicted interests, so-called "self-dealing" cases, or allegations that corporate fiduciaries took for themselves opportunities that they failed to present to their corporations, cases accusing directors or officers of "usurping corporate opportunities." This chapter examines managers' duty of loyalty in both contexts. Relatedly, we also consider here whether and how the duty of loyalty constrains directors and officers from competing with the corporation. To be sure, executive compensation decisions also implicate managers' duty of loyalty, as do actions by corporate boards contemplating potential change of firm control. However, we treat those subjects separately in Chapter 6 and Chapter 8, respectively.

I. Self-Dealing Transactions

Classic self-dealing transactions include not only transactions directly between the corporation and a director or officer of the firm, but also transactions between the firm and a person or entity in which the subject director or officer has an indirect interest, such as a strong personal relationship or a financial stake. Recognizing the heightened risk of opportunism when a fiduciary stands directly or indirectly on both sides of the deal, the law presumed that corporations were on the losing side of such contracts. Thus, common law courts generally voided self-dealing transactions upon objection from shareholders. By the end of the 20th century, however, shareholders' challenges to self-dealing transactions generally failed. To understand why, our examination of self-dealing transactions begins with the following much-cited article tracing the law's evolution.

Harold Marsh, Jr., *Are Directors Trustees? Conflict of Interest and Corporate Morality*
22 Bus. Law. 35 (1966–67)

In 1880 it could have been stated with confidence that in the United States the general rule was that any contract between a director and his corporation was voidable at the instance of the corporation or its shareholders, without regard to the fairness or unfairness of the transaction. This rule was stated in powerful terms by a number of highly regarded courts and judges in cases which arose generally out of the railroad frauds of the 1860's and 1870's.

Under this rule it mattered not the slightest that there was a majority of so-called disinterested directors who approved the contract. The courts stated that the corporation was entitled to the unprejudiced judgment and advice of all of its directors and therefore it did no good to say that, the interested director did not participate in the making of the contract on behalf of the corporation. "… the very words in which he asserts his right declare his wrong; he ought to have participated…." Furthermore, the courts said that it was impossible to measure the influence which one director might have over his associates, even though ostensibly abstaining from participation in the discussion or vote. "… a corporation, in order to defeat a contract entered into by directors, in which one or more of them had a private interest, is not bound to show that the influence of the director or directors having the private interest determined the action of the board. The law cannot accurately measure the influence of a trustee with his associates, nor will it enter into the inquiry…."

Perhaps the strongest reason for this inflexibility of the law was given by the Maryland Supreme Court which stated that, when a contract is made with even one of the directors, "the remaining directors are placed in the embarrassing and invidious position of having to pass upon, scrutinize and check the transactions and accounts of one of their own body, with whom they are associated on terms of equality in the general management of all the affairs of the corporation." Or, as Justice Davies of the New York Supreme Court expressed the same thought: "The moment the directors permit one or more of their number to deal with the property of the stockholders, they surrender their own independence and self control." This rule applied not only to individual contracts with directors, but also to the situation of interlocking directorates where even a minority of the boards were common to the two contracting corporations. Not only that, it was also applied to the situation where one corporation owned a majority of the stock of another and appointed its directors, even, though they might not be the same men as sat on the board of the parent corporation. It is interesting to note that the courts during this era had no difficulty in identifying so-called dummy directors, even though their inability to do so was later given as one of the reasons why this rule of law had to be abandoned.

This principle, absolutely inhibiting contracts between a corporation and its directors or any of them, appeared to be impregnable in 1880. It was stated in ringing terms by virtually every decided case, with arguments which seemed irrefutable, and it was sanctioned by age.... Thirty years later this principle was dead.

Approval by a Disinterested Majority of the Board

It could have been stated with reasonable confidence in 1910 that the general rule was that a contract between a director and his corporation was valid if it was approved by a disinterested majority of his fellow directors and was not found to be unfair or fraudulent by the court if challenged; but that a contract in which a majority of the board was interested was voidable at the instance of the corporation or its shareholders without regard to any question of fairness.

One searches in vain in the decided cases for a reasoned defense of this change in legal philosophy, or for the slightest attempt to refute the powerful arguments which had been made in support of the previous rule. Did the courts discover in the last quarter of the Nineteenth Century that greed was no longer a factor in human conduct? If so, they did not share the basis of this discovery with the public; nor did they humbly admit their error when confronted with the next wave of corporate frauds arising out of the era of the formation of the "trusts" during the 1890's and early 1900's. The only explanation which seems to have been given for this change in position was the technical one that a trustee, while forbidden to deal with himself in connection with the trust property, could deal directly with the cestui que trust if he made full disclosure and took no unfair advantage; and that the case of a director who abstained from representing the corporation but dealt in his personal capacity with a majority of disinterested directors was properly analogized to a trustee dealing with the cestui que trust....

But in no case is there any discussion or attempted refutation of the reasons previously given by the courts as 'to why it is impossible, in such a situation, for any director to be disinterested.' Some courts seem simply to admit that the practice has grown too widespread for them to cope with. In *South Side Trust Co. v. Washington Tin Plate Co.* the Supreme Court of Pennsylvania said: "The interests of corporations are sometimes so interwoven that it is desirable to have joint representatives in their respective managements, and at any rate it is a not uncommon and [therefore?] not unlawful practice."

Judicial Review of the Fairness of the Transaction

By 1960 it could be said with some assurance that the general rule was that no transaction of a corporation with any or all of its directors was automatically voidable at the suit of a shareholder, whether there was a disinterested majority of the board or not; but that the courts would review such a contract and subject it to rigid and careful scrutiny, and would invalidate the contract if it was found to be unfair to the corporation.

Effect of Shareholder Approval

One factor which we have not yet mentioned is the effect under any of the rules discussed above of shareholder ratification of the transaction, after full disclosure, even though it might otherwise have been automatically voidable because it did not meet the standards required for director action. All of the cases seem to hold that such ratification will suffice to validate the transaction with an interested director, at least in the absence of fraud or unfairness. Furthermore, the stock of the interested director or directors may be voted on the question of ratification, and *as shareholders* they may cast the deciding votes. Of course, under most of the cases even the shareholders may not effectively ratify a fraudulent transaction although according to some courts they may decide that it is inadvisable to sue and thereby block any attempt by a minority shareholder to challenge a transaction alleged to be fraudulent.

Comments and Questions

1. What are some problems with an early rule that all self-dealing contracts are presumptively voidable? What facts might cause a common law court to depart from the rule? Why not presume that conflicted directors and officers will place the firm's interest in the transaction above their own self-interest?

2. Can sophisticated managers structure transactions to conceal their own interests? How? Where a director or officer discloses her conflict fully, should the law assume that she has acted in the best interest of the firm? Why or why not?

3. While the common law did not flatly prohibit transactions between the corporation and its fiduciaries, the courts regulated such contracts more strictly in the early 20th century than they do today. According to Professor Marsh, the courts gradually shifted their review of self-dealing transactions to an analysis involving both substance (fairness of the transaction) and process (approval of the transaction by noninterested directors and/or shareholders). Should the informed approval by a majority of the disinterested directors bar judicial inquiry into the transaction's fairness? What facts would give you sufficient confidence in the process that you would feel comfortable relying on the board's approval? Is the corporation adequately protected from unfair dealings through good process? Why or why not?

4. Can directors ever really be neutral when it comes to approving a transaction between the firm and a CEO who also chairs the board of directors? What if the CEO/chair absents him/herself from the deliberation? Judge Cardozo wrote in another famous opinion, "The members of the [board] committee, hearing the contract for the first time, knew that it had been framed by the chairman of the meeting. They were assured in his presence that it was just and equitable. Faith in his loyalty disarmed suspicion." *Globe Woolen Co. v. Utica Gas and Electric Co.*, 224 N.Y. 483 (1918). Can this influence ever be entirely eliminated?

5. Professor Marsh notes that the courts required approval of self-dealing transactions by all shareholders, including those owned by the director with the conflict of interest. Does this mechanism provide better protection to the corporation than board approval? Why or why not? Does shareholder approval of the self-dealing transaction provide more or less comfort for courts reviewing contracts between public companies and corporate fiduciaries?

6. By the 1960s, according to Professor Marsh, self-dealing transactions were not voided, irrespective of the method of approval, unless unfair. Is that the right outcome? If the question turns on fairness, that is the relevance, if any, of evidence that the transaction was approved by disinterested directors or by shareholders?

———————

As judicial regulation of management self-dealing evolved during the last century, corporate doctrine became increasingly indeterminate and disuniform. Prompted by such concerns, state lawmakers opted to intervene by passing special statutory provisions designed to bring some certainty to the area. Following the lead of California and other states, Delaware's legislature enacted Section 144 of the Delaware General Corporation Law. The statute established that a covered transaction is not voidable solely based on the fiduciary's conflict of interest under certain circumstances.

DGCL § 144. Interested directors; quorum.

(a) No contract or transaction between a corporation and 1 or more of its directors or officers, or between a corporation and any other corporation, partnership, association, or other organization in which 1 or more of its directors or officers, are directors or officers, or have a financial interest, shall be void or voidable solely for this reason, or solely because the director or officer is present at or participates in the meeting of the board or committee which authorizes the contract or transaction, or solely because any such director's or officer's votes are counted for such purpose, if:

(1) The material facts as to the director's or officer's relationship or interest and as to the contract or transaction are disclosed or are known to the board of directors or the committee, and the board or committee in good faith authorizes the contract or transaction by the affirmative votes of a majority of the disinterested directors, even though the disinterested directors be less than a quorum; or

(2) The material facts as to the director's or officer's relationship or interest and as to the contract or transaction are disclosed or are known to the shareholders entitled to vote thereon, and the contract or transaction is specifically approved in good faith by vote of the shareholders; or

(3) The contract or transaction is fair as to the corporation as of the time it is authorized, approved or ratified, by the board of directors, a committee or the shareholders.

(b) Common or interested directors may be counted in determining the presence of a quorum at a meeting of the board of directors or of a committee which authorizes the contract or transaction.

Comments and Questions

1. What transactions are covered by Section 144? What transactions are outside the scope of the statute?

2. Subsection (a)(1) applies to good faith approval by the affirmative votes of a majority of the "disinterested directors." Subsection (a)(2) applies to good faith approval by a "vote of the shareholders." What is the difference between these two standards? What does this comparison tell us, if anything, about the purpose of Section 144?

3. The statute is written in the disjunctive. What is the consequence of this approach? Under the language, can a board legally enter into an unfair transaction?

What is the effect of compliance with the safe harbor statute? Assuming a transaction is not voidable under Section 144, can it be challenged nonetheless? On what grounds? Does the statute even speak to this question? Cases in Delaware initially suggested that it did not.

Fliegler v. Lawrence

Delaware Supreme Court
361 A.2d 218 (1976)

McNEILLY, JUSTICE:

In November, 1969, defendant, John C. Lawrence (then president of Agau, a publicly held corporation engaged in a dualphased gold and silver exploratory venture) in his individual capacity, acquired certain antimony properties under a lease option for $60,000. Lawrence offered to transfer the properties, which were then "a raw prospect", to Agau, but after consulting with other members of Agau's board of directors, he and they agreed that the corporation's legal and financial position would not permit acquisition and development of the properties at that time. Thus, it was decided to transfer the properties to USAC, (a closely held corporation formed just for this purpose and a majority of whose stock was owned by the individual defendants) where capital necessary for development of the properties could be raised without risk to Agau through the sale of USAC stock; it was also decided to grant Agau a long-term option to acquire USAC if the properties proved to be of commercial value.

In January, 1970, the option agreement was executed by Agau and USAC. Upon its exercise and approval by Agau shareholders, Agau was to deliver 800,000 shares of its restricted investment stock for all authorized and issued shares of USAC. The exchange was calculated on the basis of reimbursement to USAC and its shareholders for their costs in developing the properties to a point where it could be ascertained if they had commercial value. Such costs were anticipated to range from $250,000 to $500,000. At the time the plan was conceived, Agau shares traded over-the-counter, bid at $5/8 to $3/4 and asked at $1 to $1 1/4. Applying to these quotations a 50% discount for the investment restrictions, the parties agreed that 800,000 Agau shares would reflect the range of anticipated costs in developing USAC and, accordingly, that figure was adopted.

In July, 1970, the Agau board resolved to exercise the option, an action which was approved by majority vote of the shareholders in October, 1970. Subsequently, plaintiff instituted this suit on behalf of Agau to recover the 800,000 shares and for an accounting.

Plaintiff contends that because the individual defendants personally profited through the use of Agau's resources, *viz.*, personnel (primarily Lawrence) to develop the USAC properties and stock purchase warrants to secure a $300,000 indebtedness (incurred by USAC because it could not raise sufficient capital through sale of stock), they must be compelled to account to Agau for that profit. This argument pre-supposes that defendants did in fact so misuse corporate assets; however, the record reveals substantial evidence to support the Vice-Chancellor's conclusion that there was no misuse of either Agau personnel or warrants. Issuance of the warrants in fact enhanced the value of Agau's option at a time when there was reason to believe that USAC's antimony properties had a "considerable potential", and plaintiff did not prove that alleged use of Agau's personnel and equipment was detrimental to the corporation.

Nevertheless, our inquiry cannot stop here, for it is clear that the individual de-fendants stood on both sides of the transaction in implementing and fixing the terms of the option agreement. Accordingly, the burden is upon them to demonstrate its intrinsic fairness.... We agree with the Vice-Chancellor that the record reveals no bad faith on the part of the individual defendants. But that is not determinative. The issue is where the 800,000 restricted investment shares of Agau stock, objectively, was a fair price for Agau to pay for USAC as a wholly-owned subsidiary.

Preliminarily, defendants argue that they have been relieved of the burden of prov-ing fairness by reason of shareholder ratification of the Board's decision to exercise the option....

The purported ratification by the Agau shareholders would not affect the burden of proof in this case because the majority of shares voted in favor of exercising the option were cast by defendants in their capacity as Agau shareholders. Only about one-third of the "disinterested" shareholders voted, and we cannot assume that such non-voting shareholders either approved or disapproved. Under these circumstances, we cannot say that "the entire atmosphere has been freshened" and that departure from the objective fairness test is permissible.... In short, defendants have not es-tablished factually a basis for applying Gottlieb.

Nor do we believe the Legislature intended a contrary policy and rule to prevail by enacting 8 Del.C. § 144, which provides, in part:

> (a) No contract or transaction between a corporation and 1 or more of its directors or officers, or between a corporation and any other corporation, partnership, association, or other organization in which 1 or more of its di-rectors or officers, are directors or officers, or have a financial interest, shall be void or voidable solely for this reason, or solely because the director or officer is present at or participates in the meeting of the board or committee which authorizes the contract or transaction, or solely because his or their votes are counted for such purpose, if:

(1) The material facts as to his relationship or interest and as to the contract or transaction are disclosed or are known to the board of directors or the committee, and the board of committee in good faith authorizes the contract or transaction by the affirmative votes of a majority of the disinterested directors, even though the disinterested directors be less than a quorum; or

(2) The material facts as his relationship or interest and as to the contract or transaction are disclosed or are known to the shareholders entitled to vote thereon, and the contract or transaction is specifically approved in good faith by vote of the shareholders; or

(3) The contract or transaction is fair as to the corporation as of the time it is authorized, approved or ratified, by the board of directors, a committee, or the shareholders.

Defendants argue that the transaction here in question is protected by § 144(a)(2) which, they contend, does not require that ratifying shareholders be "disinterested" or "independent"; nor, they argue, is there warrant for reading such a requirement into the statute. See Folk, *The Delaware General Corporation Law—A Commentary and Analysis* 85–86 (1972). We do not read the statute as providing the broad immunity for which defendants contend. It merely removes an "interested director" cloud when its terms are met and provides against invalidation of an agreement "solely" because such a director or officer is involved. Nothing in the statute sanctions unfairness to Agau or removes the transaction from judicial scrutiny.

Agau was organized solely for the purpose of developing and exploring certain properties for potentially mineable gold and silver ore. The bulk of its cash, raised through a public offering, had been expended in "Phase I" exploration of the properties which failed to establish a commercial ore body, although it did reveal "interesting" zones of mineralization which indicated to Lawrence that "Phase II" development and exploration might eventually be desirable. However, plans for further development had been temporarily abandoned as being economically unfeasible due to Agau's lack of sufficient funds to adequately explore the properties, as well as to the falling market price of silver. It further appears that other than a few outstanding unexercised stock purchase warrants, Agau did not have any ready sources of capital. Thus, as the Vice-Chancellor found, had the option not been exercised, Agau might well have gone out of business.

By comparison, the record shows that USAC, while still considered to be in the exploratory and development stage, could reasonably be expected to produce substantial profits. At the time in question, the corporation had established a sizeable commercial ore body, had proven markets for its product, and was in the midst of constructing a major ore separation facility expected to produce a high grade ore concentrate for market.

Considering all of the above factors, we conclude that defendants have proven the intrinsic fairness of the transaction. Agau received properties which by themselves were clearly of substantial value. But more importantly, it received a promising, potentially self-financing and profit generating enterprise with proven markets and commercial capability which could well be expected to provide Agau at the very least with the cash it sorely needed to undertake further exploration and development of its own properties if not to stay in existence. For those reasons, we believe that the interest given to the USAC shareholders was a fair price to pay. Accordingly, we have no doubt but that this transaction was one which at that time would have commended itself to an independent corporation in Agau's position.

Comments and Questions

1. According to the defendants, how was the subject transaction approved? Did the process conform to the requirements of Section 144?

2. Defendants asserted that under the circumstances, the court should assume that the fairness of the transaction. Do you agree? Is this a reasonable reading of Section 144?

3. While Section 144(a)(1) requires approval by "disinterested directors," Section 144(a)(2) speaks to a "vote of the shareholders" rather than a vote of the *disinterested* shareholders. Does the different language used in the two provisions make sense? Why didn't the Delaware legislature require disinterested shareholder approval? What if the fiduciary with the conflict of interest owns a majority of the corporation's voting stock?

4. What does this decision tell us about the impact of voting by disinterested directors? If disinterested directors approve the transaction, may the reviewing court nonetheless decide whether the contract is fair to the corporation? What does Section 144 tell us? Should the reviewing court defer to the decision of the directors pursuant to the business judgment rule? On the other hand, what if the board of directors failed to approve the transaction? Perhaps the board never considered the deal, or maybe an insufficient number of directors voted to approve the transaction. May a reviewing court enforce the contract even though a majority of disinterested directors voted against it?

The Delaware Supreme Court considered Section 144 and the effect of compliance in the following 2006 decision.

Benihana of Tokyo, Inc. v. Benihana, Inc.

Delaware Supreme Court
906 A.2d 114 (2006)

BERGER, JUSTICE:

Rocky Aoki founded Benihana of Tokyo, Inc. (BOT), and its subsidiary, Benihana, which own and operate Benihana restaurants in the United States and other countries. Aoki owned 100% of BOT until 1998, when he pled guilty to insider trading charges. In order to avoid licensing problems created by his status as a convicted felon, Aoki transferred his stock to the Benihana Protective Trust. The trustees of the Trust were Aoki's three children (Kana Aoki Nootenboom, Kyle Aoki and Kevin Aoki) and Darwin Dornbush (who was then the family's attorney, a Benihana director, and, effectively, the company's general counsel).

Benihana, a Delaware corporation, has two classes of common stock. There are approximately 6 million shares of Class A common stock outstanding. Each share has 1/10 vote and the holders of Class A common are entitled to elect 25% of the directors. There are approximately 3 million shares of Common stock outstanding. Each share of Common has one vote and the holders of Common stock are entitled to elect the remaining 75% of Benihana's directors. Before the transaction at issue, BOT owned 50.9% of the Common stock and 2% of the Class A stock. The nine member board of directors is classified and the directors serve three-year terms.

In 2003, shortly after Aoki married Keiko Aoki, conflicts arose between Aoki and his children. In August, the children were upset to learn that Aoki had changed his will to give Keiko control over BOT. Joel Schwartz, Benihana's president and chief executive officer, also was concerned about this change in control. He discussed the situation with Dornbush, and they briefly considered various options, including the issuance of sufficient Class A stock to trigger a provision in the certificate of incorporation that would allow the Common and Class A to vote together for 75% of the directors.

The Aoki family's turmoil came at a time when Benihana also was facing challenges. Many of its restaurants were old and outmoded. Benihana hired WD Partners to evaluate its facilities and to plan and design appropriate renovations. The resulting Construction and Renovation Plan anticipated that the project would take at least five years and cost $56 million or more. Wachovia offered to provide Benihana a $60 million line of credit for the Construction and Renovation Plan, but the restrictions Wachovia imposed made it unlikely that Benihana would be able to borrow the full amount. Because the Wachovia line of credit did not assure that Benihana would have the capital it needed, the company retained Morgan Joseph & Co. to develop other financing options.

Abdo [John E. Abdo, a member of the board] contacted Joseph and told him that BFC Financial Corporation was interested in buying the new convertible stock. In April 2005, Joseph sent BFC a private placement memorandum. Abdo negotiated with Joseph for several weeks. They agreed to the Transaction on the following basic terms: (i) $20 million issuance in two tranches of $10 million each, with the second tranche to be issued one to three years after the first; (ii) BFC obtained one seat on the board, and one additional seat if Benihana failed to pay dividends for two consecutive quarters; (iii) BFC obtained preemptive rights on any new voting securities; (iv) 5% dividend; (v) 15% conversion premium; (vi) BFC had the right to force Benihana to redeem the preferred stock in full after ten years; and (vii) the stock would have immediate "as if converted" voting rights. Joseph testified that he was satisfied with the negotiations, as he had obtained what he wanted with respect to the most important points.

On April 22, 2004, Abdo sent a memorandum to Dornbush, Schwartz and Joseph, listing the agreed terms of the Transaction. He did not send the memorandum to any other members of the Benihana board. Schwartz did tell Becker, Sturges, Sano, and possibly Pine that BFC was the potential buyer. At its next meeting, held on May 6, 2004, the entire board was officially informed of BFC's involvement in the Transaction. Abdo made a presentation on behalf of BFC and then left the meeting. Joseph distributed an updated board book, which explained that Abdo had approached Morgan Joseph on behalf of BFC, and included the negotiated terms. The trial court found that the board was not informed that Abdo had negotiated the deal on behalf of BFC. But the board did know that Abdo was a principal of BFC. After discussion, the board reviewed and approved the Transaction, subject to the receipt of a fairness opinion.

On May 18, 2004, after he learned that Morgan Joseph was providing a fairness opinion, Schwartz publicly announced the stock issuance. Two days later, Aoki's counsel sent a letter asking the board to abandon the Transaction and pursue other, more favorable, financing alternatives. The letter expressed concern about the directors' conflicts, the dilutive effect of the stock issuance, and its "questionable legality." Schwartz gave copies of the letter to the directors at the May 20 board meeting, and Dornbush advised that he did not believe that Aoki's concerns had merit. Joseph and another Morgan Joseph representative then joined the meeting by telephone and opined that the Transaction was fair from a financial point of view. The board then approved the Transaction.

Even if the Benihana board had the power to issue the disputed stock, BOT maintains that the trial court erred in finding that it acted properly in approving the Transaction. Specifically, BOT argues that the Court of Chancery erred: (1) by applying 8 Del. C. § 144(a)(1), because the board did not know all material facts before it approved the Transaction; (2) by applying the business judgment rule, because Abdo breached his fiduciary duties; and (3) by finding that the board's primary purpose in approving the Transaction was not to dilute BOT's voting power.

Section 144 of the Delaware General Corporation Law provides a safe harbor for interested transactions, like this one, if "[t]he material facts as to the director's ... relationship or interest and as to the contract or transaction are disclosed or are known to the board of directors ... and the board ... in good faith authorizes the contract or transaction by the affirmative votes of a majority of the disinterested directors...." After approval by disinterested directors, courts review the interested transaction under the business judgment rule, which "is a presumption that in making a business decision, the directors of a corporation acted on an informed basis, in good faith and in the honest belief that the action taken was in the best interest of the company."

BOT argues that § 144(a)(1) is inapplicable because, when they approved the Transaction, the disinterested directors did not know that Abdo had negotiated the terms for BFC. Abdo's role as negotiator is material, according to BOT, because Abdo had been given the confidential term sheet prepared by Joseph and knew which of those terms Benihana was prepared to give up during negotiations. We agree that the board needed to know about Abdo's involvement in order to make an informed decision. The record clearly establishes, however, that the board possessed that material information when it approved the Transaction on May 6, 2004 and May 20, 2004.

Shortly before the May 6 meeting, Schwartz told Becker, Sturges and Sano that BFC was the proposed buyer. Then, at the meeting, Abdo made the presentation on behalf of BFC. Joseph's board book also explained that Abdo had made the initial contact that precipitated the negotiations. The board members knew that Abdo is a director, vice-chairman, and one of two people who control BFC. Thus, although no one ever said, "Abdo negotiated this deal for BFC," the directors understood that he was BFC's representative in the Transaction. As Pine testified, "whoever actually did the negotiating, [Abdo] as a principal would have to agree to it. So whether he sat in the room and negotiated it or he sat somewhere else and was brought the results of someone else's negotiation, he was the ultimate decision-maker." Accordingly, we conclude that the disinterested directors possessed all the material information on Abdo's interest in the Transaction, and their approval at the May 6 and May 20 board meetings satisfies § 144(a)(1).

BOT next argues that the Court of Chancery should have reviewed the Transaction under an entire fairness standard because Abdo breached his duty of loyalty when he used Benihana's confidential information to negotiate on behalf of BFC. This argument starts with a flawed premise. The record does not support BOT's contention that Abdo used any confidential information against Benihana. Even without Joseph's comments at the February 17 board meeting, Abdo knew the terms a buyer could expect to obtain in a deal like this. Moreover, as the trial court found, "the negotiations involved give and take on a number of points" and Benihana "ended up where [it] wanted to be" for the most important terms. Abdo did not set the terms of the deal; he did not deceive the board; and he did not dominate or control the other directors' approval of the Transaction. In short, the record does not support the claim that Abdo breached his duty of loyalty.

Based on the foregoing, the judgment of the Court of Chancery is affirmed.

Comments and Questions

1. As the Delaware Supreme Court noted, this case arose from a dispute between Benihana founder Rocky Aoki and four of his seven children, with whom the patriarch fought for control of his restaurant empire following his 2002 marriage to third wife Keiko Ono. Still embroiled in suits and countersuits with his children, Rocky Aoki died two years after the above decision came down, and costly litigation still continues between Aoki's children, his widow Ono, and the various entities Aoki established. *See* Erika Fry, "The Crazy, Bitter Battle Over Benihana," *Fortune*, Mar. 4, 2015.

2. When, as in the transactions at issue, directors owe duties of loyalty to multiple beneficiaries, how should conflicts of interest be resolved? Should Benihana have been required to consult and collaborate with someone other than Abdo?

3. What does this case say about the purpose and meaning of Section 144? What is the impact of disinterested director approval? Is the court's analysis consistent with the analysis in *Fliegler*?

4. Focusing on the language of Section 144, can you make an argument that compliance with Section 144(a)(1) does not immunize self-dealing transactions from all attacks?

5. Should the business judgment rule apply in these circumstances? Why or why not? Delaware judges have held that disinterested compliance with Section 144(a)(1) "removes" the taint of director self-interest. *See Nebenzahl v. Miller*, 1996 Del. Ch. LEXIS 113, at 10–11 (Del. Ch., Aug. 26, 1996). Do you agree?

6. Should the Delaware Supreme Court have considered the purpose of Section 144? Presumably the court deciding *Benihana* viewed its statutory interpretation as consistent with state lawmakers' intent in enacting Section 144. Yet, the opinion makes no reference to the provision's legislative history. Can you think of any reasons for this gap in the analysis? Interestingly, *Marciano v. Nakash*, the first Delaware Supreme Court decision to indicate that disinterested directors' approval was entitled to deference under the business judgment rule, also made no reference to legislative intent. 535 A.2d 400, 405 n.3 (Del. 1987). Several commentators have argued:

> Although section 144 was designed to provide a safe harbor against the specter of voidability for a limited subset of transactions in which directors of the corporation were interested and that would have been found voidable under the pre-1967 common law, it has, in the years following its adoption, been misconstrued to provide business-judgment protection to transactions complying with its terms. This result has no basis in the statute itself; the legislative history surrounding the adoption thereof, and certain cases interpreting the statute, dispel such a proposition. Section 144 is extremely limited in scope: it merely provides that a covered transaction will not be voidable solely as a result of the offending interest. That is, section 144 determines whether a covered transaction will be scrutinized under the common law of breach of fiduciary duty alone or under both the common law of breach of fiduciary duty and the common law of voidability.[1]

Why should courts consider the reason that the Delaware legislature enacted Section 144?

7. Two categories of directors are suspect for approving interested party transactions: interested directors, (those directors with a material interest in the transactions) and non-independent directors (those directors beholden to, or controlled

---

1. Blake Rohrbacher, John Mark Zeberkiewicz & Thomas A. Uebler, *Finding Safe Harbor: Clarifying the Limited Application of Section 144*, 33 Del. J. Corp. L. 719, 746–47 (2008).

by, the interested director). Section 144 speaks only to the former and not the latter. Delaware courts nonetheless have read into Section 144 the requirement that the board have a majority of disinterested and independent directors. Does approval by a majority of disinterested and independent directors on the board ensure that the transaction is fair to the company? Should other procedural requirements be met before applying the business judgment rule? For example, should the interested director and any non-independent directors be excluded from the process?

In a more recent case, the Delaware Supreme Court examined the distinct duties of directors and shareholders who approve potential self-dealing transactions.

Pfeffer v. Redstone

Delaware Supreme Court
965 A.2d 676 (2009)

STEELE, CHIEF JUSTICE:

Appellant, Beverly Pfeffer, appeals the Court of Chancery's dismissal of her claims with prejudice under Rule 12(b)(6) for failure to state a claim. Pfeffer brought a class action against the directors of Viacom and Blockbuster and against two corporations, National Amusements, Inc. (NAI) and CBS Corporation. Pfeffer asserts that the Vice Chancellor erred because she sufficiently pleaded, in connection with two transactions, that the Viacom board of directors had breached their fiduciary duties of disclosure, loyalty, and care and that NAI had breached its duty of loyalty. Because we conclude that Pfeffer failed to plead that the alleged disclosure violations were material, the Court of Chancery's judgment of dismissal is AFFIRMED.

Facts and Procedural History

This dispute arises from two transactions that resulted in Viacom divesting itself of its controlling interest in Blockbuster. As of September 2004, Sumner Redstone owned a controlling stake in NAI, which, in turn, owned a 71% voting interest in Viacom. Viacom owned approximately 82.3% of the equity value and 95.9% of the voting power in Blockbuster, a Delaware corporation. The two challenged transactions are: (1) a special $5 dividend paid to Blockbuster stockholders (the Special Dividend); and, (2) a later offer to Viacom stockholders to exchange their Viacom stock for Blockbuster stock (the Exchange Offer).

Believing Blockbuster would perform better as an independent entity, Viacom announced, on February 10, 2004, its intention to spin off 81.5% of its interest in Blockbuster. In a June 18, 2004 press release, Viacom and Blockbuster announced their preliminary divestiture plans. Before the Exchange Offer, Blockbuster would issue a Special Dividend. Thereafter, in a voluntary exchange offer, Viacom shareholders would exchange their Viacom shares for Blockbuster shares. In the press release, Viacom CEO Redstone and Blockbuster CEO John Antioco endorsed the proposed separation. Redstone stated that, after the transaction, "Viacom will devote

all its energies and resources into expanding core areas, particularly the content creation engine that we believe will drive our future growth." Antioco announced: "we
believe that by becoming a separate company we will be better able to pursue our
retailing strategy."

An independent special committee of the Blockbuster board of directors approved
the Special Dividend, which would be payable September 3, 2004 as a pro rata special
cash dividend of $5 per share. Of the Special Dividend, Viacom received over $738
million of the $905 million distributed to Blockbuster stockholders.

On September 8, 2004, Viacom issued a press release disclosing the final terms of
the voluntary Exchange Offer. A Prospectus outlining the relevant terms of the Exchange Offer soon followed. In the Exchange Offer, each tendering holder of Viacom
stock would receive 5.15 shares of Blockbuster stock in exchange for each Viacom
share tendered. Viacom disclosed that it would accept up to an aggregate of 27,961,165
shares of Class A and Class B common stock until the closing date on October 5,
2004. The Prospectus disclosed that (a) NAI would not participate in the Exchange
Offer; (b) several potential risks were associated with acquiring Blockbuster stock,
including Blockbuster's potential inability to operate with the increased debt imposed
by the Special Dividend; (c) a special committee of the Blockbuster board, comprised
of three independent directors, had recommended that the entire Blockbuster board
approve the Special Dividend and the Exchange Offer; (d) the special committee had
approved the final terms of the divestiture; and (e) neither Viacom nor Blockbuster
made a recommendation to stockholders about the Exchange Offer. Nor did the
Prospectus disclose the composition of the special committee.

Pfeffer and many other Viacom stockholders, but not including Redstone or NAI,
tendered their shares in the fully subscribed Exchange Offer.

Following the Exchange Offer, Blockbuster struggled to remain profitable. On
March 9, 2006, Blockbuster announced a restatement of its reported cash flows for
the years 2003 through 2005. After months of discussions with the SEC, Blockbuster
accounted for its new releases in its rental library as current assets, as opposed to
their earlier classification as noncurrent assets. As a result of this restatement, Blockbuster categorized those assets as operational expenses instead of capital expenses.

Pfeffer brought a class action in the Court of Chancery on behalf of all former Viacom shareholders who tendered their shares in the Exchange Offer, and on behalf
of all Blockbuster shareholders who held shares as of the August 27, 2004 record date
for the Special Dividend issued by Blockbuster. Pfeffer named 21 defendants in his
complaint, including two corporations, NAI and CBS, and several Viacom and Blockbuster directors.

Pfeffer claimed that the Viacom board of directors had violated their duty of disclosure in relation to the Exchange Offer. Specifically, Pfeffer alleged that the Viacom
directors either failed to disclose, or made material misstatements regarding, the true
state of Blockbusters' operational cash flow, the methodology used to determine the
exchange ratio, and the composition of the Viacom special committee that recom-

mended the transaction to the Viacom board. Pfeffer asserted that the Viacom board of directors knew or should have known that a Blockbuster treasury department manager had compiled a cash flow analysis seven months before the Exchange Offer, and that knowledge demonstrated that Blockbuster's operational cash flow could not support the Special Dividend or Exchange Offer. In her complaint, Pfeffer pointed to several Blockbuster announcements, including Blockbuster's cash flow restatement, as evidence that the Viacom and Blockbuster directors knew or should have known of Blockbuster's financial woes at the time they caused the Prospectus to be disseminated. Although Pfeffer attempted to establish that the directors knew or should have known of Blockbuster's financial problems, she did not allege that the announced restatement caused a market price decline for Blockbuster stock. Pfeffer also claimed that NAI and the directors had breached their duty of loyalty.

All the defendants moved to dismiss the action for failure to state a claim. On February 1, 2008, the Vice Chancellor dismissed all of Pfeffer's claims with prejudice. The Vice Chancellor held that the Viacom directors had made neither material omissions nor materially misleading statements in the Prospectus. Therefore, the complaint failed to allege a cognizable duty of loyalty violation. Because the Vice Chancellor held that NAI did not control the conduct of the Viacom directors in the transactions, NAI did not breach its duty of loyalty either.

In this appeal, Pfeffer only appeals the Court of Chancery's dismissal of the first four counts of her complaint. Those four counts allege that the Viacom directors breached their fiduciary duties of loyalty, care, and disclosure and that NAI breached its fiduciary duty of loyalty by making false misstatements or material omissions in documents distributed before the Exchange Offer. Pfeffer claims that because of Redstone's and NAI's financial interest in Viacom, the conduct complained of should have been reviewed under an entire fairness standard, thereby precluding a Rule 12(b)(6) dismissal.

Analysis

We review dismissals under Court of Chancery Rule 12(b)(6) *de novo*. This Court, like the Court of Chancery, is required to accept well pleaded allegations as true and draw reasonable inferences in favor of the plaintiff. Nevertheless, we need not accept conclusory allegations as true and accept only truly reasonable inferences. Pfeffer challenges the Vice Chancellor's determination that her allegations were conclusory and not well pleaded.

Pfeffer alleges that the Special Dividend and the Exchange Offer should be subject to entire fairness scrutiny because NAI, as the controlling stockholder of Viacom, elevated its financial interests over those of the minority holders and stood on both sides of the transactions.

The Vice Chancellor recognized that "Delaware law does not impose a duty of entire fairness on controlling stockholders making a non-coercive tender or exchange offer to acquire shares directly from the minority holders." Nor does Delaware law require entire fairness scrutiny where a corporation engaged in a voluntary, noncoercive offer. But, the Viacom directors did have a duty to structure the terms of the Exchange Offer noncoercively and to disclose all material facts relating to it.

The Vice Chancellor concluded that the Viacom directors had structured the Exchange Offer noncoercively and disclosed all material facts. We agree. Although Viacom made the Exchange Offer to its minority stockholders, the Viacom board did not recommend in the Prospectus that those stockholders exchange their shares. The Exchange Offer was purely voluntary, and the Prospectus clearly disclosed that NAI would not participate in the Exchange Offer. The Vice Chancellor properly found that the complaint did not suggest that the Viacom directors who approved the Exchange Offer structured it in a way that favored their interests over the stockholders'. Therefore, Pfeffer's complaint would state a claim for relief only if it adequately pleaded disclosure violations. That brings us to the disclosure claims.

As the Vice Chancellor correctly stated, that "[t]he duty of disclosure is not an independent duty, but derives from the duties of care and loyalty." "Corporate fiduciaries can breach their duty of disclosure under Delaware law ... by making a materially false statement, by omitting a material fact, or by making a partial disclosure that is materially misleading." "Material facts are those facts for which 'there is a substantial likelihood that a reasonable person would consider [them] important in deciding how to vote."

Pfeffer challenges the Vice Chancellor's dismissal of her complaint, which (she claims) states duty of disclosure violations in four respects. First, Pfeffer claims that she adequately pleaded that the Prospectus' disclosures about Blockbuster's operational cash flow were material. Second, Pfeffer asserts that she adequately pleaded that the Viacom board knew or should have known of Blockbuster's operational cash flow deficiencies and that the divestiture would leave Blockbuster unable to meet its operational goals. Third, Pfeffer contends that the Vice Chancellor erred by finding that the Viacom board's methodology for determining the exchange ratio was not material. Fourth, Pfeffer argues that the Vice Chancellor erred by finding the composition of the Viacom special committee who structured the divestiture to be immaterial.

The Viacom directors respond that, even if there were misstatements or omissions, they were not material. The Vice Chancellor agreed. We review those findings in the sections that follow.

Pfeffer contends that Blockbuster's accounting reclassification, which occurred approximately one and one half years after the Prospectus was distributed, demonstrates that the Prospectus was misleading and contained material misstatements. The complaint alleged that: (1) the Prospectus "misrepresented Blockbuster's cash flow—so vital to the funding of its growth plans—by more than 58%;" and that (2) the Prospectus represented that Blockbuster's ability to maintain sufficient operating cash flow was critical to funding Blockbuster's new plan. Thus, Pfeffer concludes, there being no dispute that the disclosure regarding the operational cash flow constituted misstatements, the only issue was whether those misstatements were material.

The Viacom directors respond that: "Plaintiff conceded at oral argument [in the Court of Chancery] that she has no basis by which to allege that the reclassification of Blockbuster's cash flows affected Blockbuster's earnings, total cash flow, net income, or any other accounting measure." The Viacom directors further argue that the complaint did not allege that anyone had relied on the cash flow analysis that led to the reclassification.

"To state a claim for breach of the fiduciary duty of disclosure on the basis of a false statement or representation, a plaintiff must identify (1) a material statement or representation in a communication contemplating stockholder action (2) that is false." The "issue of materiality of an alleged misstatement or omission in a prospectus is a mixed question of law and fact, but predominantly a question of fact." "Nevertheless, conclusory allegations need not be treated as true, nor should inferences be drawn unless they truly are reasonable."

The Vice Chancellor determined that "the plaintiff fail[ed] to advance well pleaded allegations of fact that a reasonable person, in deciding how to vote, would consider important the reclassification of operational and investing cash flows in this case." Although the Vice Chancellor found that some of the cash flow numbers in the Prospectus were later restated, Pfeffer did not sufficiently demonstrate why that fact was material. The Vice Chancellor recognized that the cash flow restatement merely reclassified certain cash flows, but the reclassification did not affect the total cash flows, net income, or any other reported accounting figure. Nor, (the Vice Chancellor further noted) did the complaint plead that disclosure of the restatement affected the Blockbuster stock price. Moreover, Blockbuster's certified financial statements explained its accounting methods. The Vice Chancellor concluded that the complaint failed to allege how the restatement of operating cash flows rose to the level of a material misstatement so as to constitute a disclosure violation. Therefore, Pfeffer did not allege any factual basis for her claim that the Viacom directors knew or should have known that Blockbuster's operating cash flow statements were materially misleading. We conclude that the Vice Chancellor's reasoning is correct.

Relying upon a cash flow analysis proposed by a Blockbuster treasury employee seven months before the Special Dividend and the Exchange Offer occurred, Pfeffer claims that the Viacom directors knew or should have known that Blockbuster faced operational cash flow problems before the Exchange Offer. Pfeffer contends that Redstone knew or should have known about the cash flow analysis because John Antioco, Blockbuster's Chairman and CEO, would have told him. Pfeffer asserts that her complaint adequately pleads that Viacom should have disclosed the cash flow analysis. The Viacom directors maintain, however, that they did not know of the cash flow analysis and, moreover, that the Prospectus adequately disclosed the potential cash flow problems Blockbuster might experience as a result of the Special Dividend and the Exchange Offer. They assert that Pfeffer's claim rests on no more than supposition and surmise.

For the Viacom directors to have either misstated or failed to disclose the cash flow analysis in the Prospectus, those directors must have had reasonable access to that Blockbuster information. "To state a claim for breach by omission of any duty to disclose, a plaintiff must plead facts identifying (1) material, (2) reasonably available

(3) information that (4) was omitted from the proxy materials." "[O]mitted information is *material* if a reasonable stockholder would consider it important in deciding whether to tender his shares or would find that the information has altered the 'total mix' of information available." The Viacom directors must fully and fairly disclose all material information within its control when seeking shareholder action. They are not excused from disclosing material facts simply because the Prospectus disclosed risk factors attending the tender offer. If the Viacom directors did not know or have reason to know the allegedly missing facts, however, then logically the directors could not disclose them.

The Vice Chancellor determined that Pfeffer's pleading was "based entirely on a daisy chain of surmise and illogic." Pfeffer's allegation that Redstone would know about Blockbuster's cash flows because Antioco knew this information and would have told Redstone did not persuade him. Pfeffer's allegation that Redstone would have then told the other Viacom directors similarly failed to impress the Vice Chancellor. Important in this regard is that Blockbuster's Senior Vice President of Investor Relations and Treasurer told her subordinates not to focus on the cash flow analysis. The Vice Chancellor regarded that fact as a reasonable basis to infer that even the Blockbuster Directors would not have known about the cash flow analysis. Nothing alleged in the complaint justified any contrary inference.

The Vice Chancellor did consider fact patterns where bare allegations of knowledge might suffice; for example, if a document was "of the kind routinely disclosed to boards of directors." Here, however, the cash flow analysis was not the kind of document routinely disclosed to a parent corporation's board of directors. The Vice Chancellor so concluded. Pfeffer complains that the Vice Chancellor's factual conclusions, including this one, were improper. Although there is "no reason to depart from the general pleading rules when alleging duty of disclosure violations," "it is inherent in disclosure cases that the misstated or omitted facts be identified and that the pleading not be merely conclusory." When pleading a breach of fiduciary duty based on the Viacom directors' knowledge, Pfeffer must, at a minimum, offer "well-pleaded facts from which it can be reasonably inferred that this 'something' was knowable and that the defendant was in a position to know it."

Other than conclusorily asserting that the Viacom directors would (or must) have been told this information, Pfeffer did not sufficiently plead any other facts to support that inference. The assertion that the Viacom directors knew of the cash flow analysis because Antioco would have told Redstone could not be more conclusory. Because Pfeffer failed to allege that the cash flow analysis performed by a midlevel treasury manager of a subsidiary corporation would be routinely available to the Viacom directors, the Vice Chancellor correctly dismissed this claim.

The Vice Chancellor also determined that Viacom's method for deriving the exchange ratio was not material because the Viacom directors did not specifically represent that the price offered was fair. Pfeffer claims that was error. Pfeffer stresses that Viacom's voluntary disclosure was a misleading partial disclosure, because the Viacom shareholders deserved to know how their directors calculated the exchange ratio. The Viacom directors maintain that they were not required to disclose the exact exchange ratio methodology because they neither declared that the Exchange Offer was fair nor recommended that the Viacom minority stockholders participate.

To state a claim based on partial disclosure, "a plaintiff must plead facts identifying a (1) perhaps voluntary, but (2) materially incomplete (3) statement (4) made in conjunction with solicitation of stockholder action that (5) requires supplementation or clarification through (6) corrective disclosure of perhaps otherwise material, but reasonably available information." Information material to a stockholder's decision to hold or dispose shares must be disclosed. In a non-coercive voluntary self tender, however, Delaware courts generally do not require disclosure of pricing methodology in connection with non-coercive self-tender offers. Such disclosure would be necessary where the board has a duty to offer a *fair* price ... or the board has made a partial disclosure that *implies* that the offered price is fair, thereby requiring additional disclosures to ensure a balanced presentation.

The Prospectus clearly stated that the boards of both Viacom and Blockbuster were making no recommendation regarding whether Viacom stockholders should participate in the Exchange Offer. It further disclosed that the Exchange Offer was voluntary and noncoercive. Indeed, the Prospectus disclosed that "Viacom cannot predict the prices at which shares of Viacom ... stock or Blockbuster ... stock will be trading at the expiration date of the exchange offer, and therefore, cannot predict whether stockholders who participate in this exchange will receive a premium for their shares." Although the Prospectus stated that a primary reason for the price was to induce the stockholder to tender, it did not imply that the Exchange Offer was fair or suggest that the price represented the stock's intrinsic value. For that reason, the Viacom stockholders could not reasonably rely on either the exchange ratio or the price to be fair when deciding whether to tender their shares. The Vice Chancellor correctly determined that the methodology used to determine the exchange ratio was not material. We therefore affirm the Vice Chancellor's dismissal of this claim.

Pfeffer next claims that Viacom's disclosure that a special committee existed in the Prospectus, without also disclosing the committee directors' names, breached the Viacom directors' disclosure duty.

In *Frank v. Arnelle*, the Court of Chancery held that: "the fact that a special committee, as opposed to the full Board, set the price range and other terms [is not] material." The Offer to Purchase in *Frank* did not disclose the involvement of a special committee. Here, the Viacom prospectus explicitly referenced the special committee. That caused the Vice Chancellor to frame the issue in terms of whether that disclosure was materially incomplete.

It is well settled that "[W]hen fiduciaries undertake to describe events, they must do so in a balanced and accurate fashion, which does not create a materially misleading impression." "[T]he disclosure of even a non-material fact can, in some instances, trigger an obligation to disclose additional, otherwise non-material facts in order to prevent the initial disclosure from materially misleading the stockholders."

Here, the Vice Chancellor determined, a single reference to the Viacom special committee did not require further elaboration because the Prospectus did not suggest that the committee had decided anything more significant than what the full Board could have decided. The omission was not materially misleading because "[t]here is no indication that the committee was independent of management or NAI, nor does the language in the Prospectus induce stockholders to rely on the special committee's decision to validate the transaction." The Prospectus fully disclosed that NAI was the controlling stockholder of Viacom and that Redstone was the controlling stockholder of NAI as well as Viacom's chairman and CEO.

We agree that the composition of the Viacom special committee was not material and that the Prospectus did not omit material information about the committee. We therefore hold that the Vice Chancellor correctly dismissed this claim.

Pfeffer claims that the Viacom directors designed the transaction to benefit Redstone and NAI. But, she fails to allege that the directors stood on both sides of the Exchange Offer or that they received a unique financial benefit to the exclusion of the shareholders. Pfeffer's complaint alleges conclusorily that "[e]ach of the Viacom director defendants breached their fiduciary duties of loyalty and care in approving and/or acquiescing in the Exchange Offer on terms that were unfair to Viacom's minority shareholders and unfairly benefited Viacom's controlling shareholder, NAI, and Redstone."

"[W]here there is reason to believe that the board lacked good faith in approving a disclosure, the violation implicates the duty of loyalty." Conclusory allegations that NAI unfairly benefited from the Exchange Offer, however, are insufficient to state a claim that the Viacom directors acted in bad faith, thereby breaching their duty of loyalty.

The Vice Chancellor correctly determined that 8 *Del.C.* § 144 does not apply to the Exchange Offer, because Section 144 refers to interested transactions, which this Exchange Offer was not. A transaction is interested where directors appear on both sides of a transaction or expect to derive a financial benefit from it that does not "devolve [ ] upon the corporation or all stockholders generally." This personal benefit must be so significant that it is "improbable that the director could perform her fiduciary duties ... without being influenced by her overriding personal interest."

Pfeffer complains that Redstone, through his company NAI, received an overwhelming majority of the Special Dividend. That may be true, but it does not establish a disqualifying self interest since NAI held a majority of Viacom's stock. What *is* significant is that Director Redstone and NAI received nothing unique that was otherwise unavailable to the other stockholders. Pfeffer also complains that as a result of the Exchange Offer, Redstone and NAI increased their majority control of Viacom. But, that without more, does not state a legally sufficient claim that Redstone and NAI acted in bad faith. Finally, Pfeffer alleges that Viacom directors failed to disclose facts about Blockbuster's perilous financials. As we have already held, the complaint fails to allege facts creating a reasonable inference that the Viacom directors had access to that financial information.

We conclude, for these reasons, that the Vice Chancellor properly dismissed the breach of duty of loyalty claim against the Viacom directors.

Lastly, Pfeffer claims that "NAI breached its fiduciary duties owed to the Viacom minority ... by causing the Viacom director Defendants to approve and recommend [sic] the Exchange Offer to Viacom's minority shareholders." NAI, however, did not construct or direct the Exchange Offer or the Special Dividend, and Pfeffer fails to allege any well pleaded facts showing the contrary. She merely argues that NAI failed to disclose that the Prospectus contained misleading financial statements. Had Pfeffer sufficiently pleaded that NAI engaged in crafting the transactions and then directed the Viacom directors' conduct, she may have stated a claim, but reciting alleged Prospectus disclosure omissions falls far short of implicating NAI for breach of its fiduciary duty as a controlling stockholder. For these reasons, the Vice Chancellor correctly dismissed the breach of loyalty claim against NAI.

For the foregoing reasons, we affirm the Court of Chancery's judgment.

Comments and Questions

1. How are shareholders disadvantaged by the Delaware Supreme Court's stringent pleading requirements? What guidance does the *Pfeffer* court offer to shareholders attempting to draft complaints that satisfy the threshold pleading standards?

2. Were there truly no reasonable inferences that could be drawn from the plaintiff's complaint that could have allowed it to survive dismissal? Were the court's findings of fact on materiality any less conclusory than the plaintiff's complaint? If not, who should win a tie before discovery: the court or the plaintiff?

3. The information materiality standard espoused by the *Pfeffer* court is that of the reasonable person making investment decisions. Given that the divestiture depended upon a significant cash outlay by Blockbuster, why was Blockbuster's cash flow position not deemed material?

4. How critical was the non-coercive nature of the proffered stock swap in the materiality determination? Why should this make a difference?

———————

Despite the morally charged language of its fiduciary duty decisions, the Delaware judiciary has received criticism that its jurisprudence has reduced the duty of loyalty to a toothless doctrine. The following commentary articulates some of the principal critiques of Delaware's case law.

J. Robert Brown, Jr., *Disloyalty Without Limits: "Independent" Directors and the Elimination of the Duty of Loyalty*
95 Ky. L.J. 53 (2006)[2]

Whatever one might say about the duties of corporate managers, there has been universal agreement that they must remain loyal to the company. While loyalty can

———————

2. Copyright © 2006 Kentucky Law Review. Reprinted with permission.

have a variety of meanings, the term unquestionably encompasses the notion that directors cannot use their position to profit unfairly from the company. It is this bedrock concept of fairness that theoretically places limits on self-interested transactions, particularly executive compensation.

Notwithstanding continued paeans to this proposition, Delaware courts have all but eliminated meaningful limits on self-interested transactions. Loans to officers and directors, for example, need not meet commercially reasonable standards; top officers may be paid excessive sums with no judicial oversight of the fairness of the amount; and contributions may be made to charities favored by the CEO almost without limit.

This did not all happen at once. Courts initially viewed conflict-of-interest transactions with considerable suspicion, often treating them as voidable. Over time, that approach gave way to a more workable rule requiring that the transaction be fair. Fairness amounted to a substantive limit—managers could profit from the corporation so long as they did not profit unfairly.

These limits, however, no longer apply. With little discussion, Delaware courts devised a set of procedures that rendered fairness irrelevant. So long as approved by a "neutral" decision-making body, a conflict-of-interest transaction is subject to review under the business judgment rule, a procedural standard rarely overcome and one that does not involve an examination of the terms of the transaction. This approach contains serious flaws, some practical, some analytical, and some procedural.

Analytically, the business judgment rule was not meant to apply to conflict-of-interest transactions. Instead, it arose as an over-inclusive measure designed to protect managerial risk-taking. The business judgment rule does so by rendering the consequences of a decision essentially irrelevant. As long as the process used to make the decision is adequate, liability will not attach. The rationale does not apply, however, where the harm results not from risk-taking but from a conflict of interest.

Delaware courts, however, have undone this approach. They apply the business judgment rule to cases involving a conflict of interest where a majority of the board is characterized as disinterested and independent. It makes no difference that the conflict remains present in the decision-making process. Indeed, the interested directors can sit in on the discussions, participate in the debate, and even vote on the transaction without the board losing its "neutral" status.

From a practical standpoint, Delaware courts do not adequately ensure that directors defined as independent are in fact independent. They routinely ignore evidence of a director's connections to the interested party and apply shifting and inconsistent tests. As a result, boards treated as having a majority of independent directors often in fact do not.

Procedurally, Delaware courts use pleading rules that prevent full examination of a director's relationship with the interested party. Facts rebutting the presumption of independence must be pled with particularity. Courts use this heightened standard to dismiss cases on motion without allowing for discovery. They do so even where plaintiffs have produced facts suggesting an absence of independence and where the additional information about the relationship is not publicly available.

Despite the presence of interested influence in the decision making process and the absence of truly independent directors, courts apply the business judgment rule and defer to the board's decision. The results are predictable. They effectively ensure interested approval of interested transactions.

The Presumption of Independence and Unreasonable Pleading Standards

The courts use a variety of analytically inconsistent mechanisms to dismiss challenges to a director's independence. They purport to rely on a materiality threshold but ignore it when convenient, as in the application (or non-application) to directors' fees. The courts acknowledge that personal and outside business relationships can impair independence, but apply a test that all but guarantees that these relationships never do. Mostly, though, the courts use unreasonable pleading standards to dismiss challenges before discovery has occurred.

The courts routinely require as part of the particularity standard facts that are not readily available. They often blame shareholders for the absence of the required information, insisting that it resulted from a failure to invoke inspection rights. In fact, the necessary information is rarely, if ever, available this way, something clear at least to some Delaware courts. The required use of inspection rights, therefore, does little more than delay and increase costs with little resulting advantage.

The courts also apply the higher pleading standards in an inconsistent fashion. Sometimes plaintiffs are allowed a reasonable inference from the alleged facts, but more often they are not. Other times the courts seem to change the rules mid-stream, finding that plaintiffs alleged the wrong facts. After making their own factual findings, courts sometimes dispose of the cases on a motion to dismiss.

Finally, courts simply ignore facts that indicate a disqualifying relationship. They commonly decide the issue of independence as if plaintiffs had to meet their substantive burden in the complaint, rather than merely providing a "reasonable basis." As a result, they dismiss the claims without allowing further exploration into the nature of the relationship.

Impact of the Heightened Standards

The problem is not simply that the courts impose higher standards. The standards are applied in a manner that is essentially impossible to meet, something courts have occasionally acknowledged. In the absence of discovery, plaintiffs are left with whatever information can be gleaned from public sources. While some information bearing on independence must appear in the periodic reports and proxy statements of public companies, the sources rarely provide information adequate to meet the specificity requirements. Moreover, such reports do not always disclose information about these relationships, even when legally required to do so.

The difficulty is particularly acute given the use of a subjective materiality standard. At the pleading stage, plaintiffs may need to produce facts concerning the amount of an income stream and its importance, the specific financial condition of each individual director, the compensation formula used by the firm receiving the funds, and the CEO's specific authority concerning the renewal of a lease. None of this information is typically available from public sources.

The same is true of disqualifying personal relationships. Courts have imposed a test that requires, at the pleading stage, a considerable amount of evidence about the strength of the friendship. This type of information is ordinarily difficult to discern from public sources given its personal and private nature. Yet where plaintiffs have managed to uncover public information about these relationships, the courts have nonetheless dismissed the plaintiffs' complaints for lack of specificity.

Take Beam. The plaintiffs found an interview in *Fortune* magazine of three people: Martha Stewart; Darla Moore, the allegedly non-independent director; and Charlotte Beers, another longstanding friend, who Moore replaced on the board. The three women described themselves as "best buddies" and the interview unquestionably had a relaxed and friendly tone. In addition, plaintiffs produced evidence that Moore and Stewart attended a social function that almost certainly had a restricted invitation list. Finally, Stewart owned ninety-four percent of the voting stock, giving her final say on any possible board candidate.

Plaintiffs only needed to present a "reasonable doubt" about independence. Without anything that would pass for analysis, the court concluded that "these bare social relationships clearly do not create a reasonable doubt of independence." This was a mischaracterization. Plaintiffs did more than allege "bare social relationships." The complaint specifically asserted that Stewart and Moore had a longstanding friendship and provided support for this contention. The court also failed to indicate information that would suffice and did not recognize the practical difficulties in obtaining public information about friendships.

The Search for Particularized Facts

In what has to be an odd twist, the Delaware courts ultimately recognized the difficulties imposed on plaintiffs in pleading "with specificity" facts that are not publicly available. Rather than do the obvious and either loosen the pleading requirements or permit limited discovery, they forced shareholders to invoke their inspections rights and examine the books and records of the company. Shareholders were chastised for failing to use these "tools at hand" before bringing an action to challenge director independence.

The notion that inspection rights might substitute for discovery is, in most cases, far-fetched. The likelihood that this avenue would uncover information useful in determining subjective materiality or the strength of a personal friendship is negligible. The types of records that demonstrate a lack of independence will rarely be in the possession of the corporation. Yet this is the very position taken by the courts.

The information, which the court conceded "might possibly" strengthen a claim, relates more to the issue of control over the nomination process—not to the strength of the friendship.

Using inspections rights as a substitute for discovery has other problems. Minutes of board meetings are often thin in content, and therefore will not typically reveal problems among directors or cronyism. Nor is the provision allowing inspection easy to use. Shareholders must have a proper purpose, describe the sought after records with particularity, and pay the expenses associated with any challenge, resulting in delay and additional costs with little benefit.

The emphasis on inspection rights has obscured the real problem. The failure to meet the pleading requirements does not flow from a systematic failure of shareholders to seek the necessary facts. The real problem arises from a pleading standard that imposes unrealistic burdens and is applied inconsistently. The solution is not to require an invocation of inspection rights but to permit discovery on the issue.

Case Study: The Saga of the Two Michaels

Perhaps the best single case to illustrate the problems discussed in this article is the derivative suit filed against the Disney board in connection with the employment contract awarded to Michael Ovitz. The contract was, by most measures, excessive, paying Ovitz a reported $140 million for slightly more than a year of unsuccessful service.

An employment contract for an executive who is not a member of the board would ordinarily be subject to the business judgment rule and presumed fair. To the extent that an agreement benefits someone on the board, however, the duty of loyalty applies, leaving the directors the burden of establishing fairness. To render this standard applicable, therefore, shareholders in Disney had to establish that Michael Eisner somehow benefited from the Ovitz employment contract. They asserted both that Eisner influenced the terms of the agreement out of his friendship with Ovitz and that he controlled the board.

On a motion to dismiss, without the benefit of discovery, the chancery court concluded the plaintiffs had not produced "reasonable doubt" about the independence of the Disney board. In reaching that conclusion, the court found as "independent": a director who served as an officer, a director who headed a charity that received $1 million directly from Eisner, a director who was a principal of an elementary school at one time attended by Eisner's children, a director who received $50,000 for consulting services and who worked for a law firm representing Disney, and a director whose wife received funds to start her business. This so called "independent" board was branded the worst corporate board for two years running by a magazine surveying corporate governance practices. But it was the analysis of the relationship between the two Michaels that stretched reality the furthest. Plaintiffs argued the long term "personal" and "business" relationship between the two men rendered Eisner interested in the Ovitz employment contract. Eisner, the plaintiffs argued, was motivated by friendship rather than the best interests of shareholders in negotiating with Ovitz.

The trial court treated the entire approach in a dismissive fashion, disposing of the matter in two sentences: "This argument, however, finds no support under Delaware law. The fact that Eisner has long-standing personal and business ties to

Ovitz cannot overcome the presumption of independence that all directors, including Eisner, are afforded." That was it. No analysis. No facts. No discovery.

On appeal, the Supreme Court relied on the same superficial and cursory reasoning. The decision said nothing about the close relationship between the two men and again, in two sentences, dismissed the claim.

> The Court of Chancery held that "no reasonable doubt can exist as to Eisner's disinterest in the approval of the Employment Agreement, as a matter of law," and similarly that plaintiffs "have not demonstrated a reasonable doubt that Eisner was disinterested in granting Ovitz a Non-Fault Termination." Plaintiffs challenge this conclusion, but we agree with the Court of Chancery and we affirm that holding.

Both courts rendered their decisions without allowing plaintiff to engage in discovery to explore the relationship. In other words, the courts found that the evidence did not even present "reasonable doubt" about the relationship between Ovitz and Eisner.

In the ordinary course of things, that would be the end. To guess what might have been uncovered had discovery proceeded would be a matter of speculation. But, of course, there was nothing ordinary about Disney. It continued, culminating in a lengthy trial with a voluminous record and a second appeal to the Delaware Supreme Court. The relationship between the two Michaels also became the subject of a high profile book. From these sources, considerable additional information about the relationship surfaced, including that:

> The two had been "close" friends for nearly a quarter of a century and "were very well acquainted, both socially and professionally";
>
> Ovitz was Eisner's closet friend in Hollywood;
>
> The wives of the two men were best friends;
>
> The two families vacationed as a group and spent Christmas together in Aspen in 1995;
>
> Eisner's wife called Ovitz when Eisner unexpectedly had open-heart surgery and Ovitz terminated a planned vacation to come to the hospital;
>
> Eisner invited Ovitz to be with him and his wife while awaiting the final decision on whether he would be appointed as CEO of Disney;
>
> Eisner would use effusive terms when writing to Ovitz. A letter written by Eisner in October 1996 included: "You still are the only one who came to my hospital bed—and I do remember";
>
> Ovitz would use effusive terms when writing to Eisner; and
>
> Ovitz sat on board of the New York Museum of Modern Art with Sid Bass, one of Disney's largest individual shareholders.

In other words, despite the four dismissive sentences by the Delaware courts, the two had cultivated an extraordinarily close personal relationship over a protracted period of time that encompassed their respective families. An examination of their interlocking business relationships would no doubt have added to the plaintiffs' showing of the strength of the relationship. Most of the information, however, was not in the public domain and was only uncovered by the sleuth of an author and the compulsion of a trial.

By summarily dismissing the allegations of friendship, the courts eliminated any possible claim that the contract violated the duty of loyalty. As a result, the burden remained on the plaintiffs to show a breach of the duty of care, an all but insurmountable task, as they learned. The court resolved these intensely factual issues without allowing for discovery. Had the court allowed discovery on the relationship between the two Michaels and appropriately decided the case under the duty of loyalty, the issue would have turned on the fairness of Ovitz's employment contract, with the burden on the board. This would have resulted in a proceeding that centered around the substance of the agreement rather than the minimum level of board attention permissible under the duty of care. In this long and voluminous litigation, the fairness of the agreement was never seriously examined.

Comments and Questions

1. Why would Delaware courts assume directors' independence? What policy is served by assigning to plaintiffs a strict burden of proof to overcome this presumption?

2. Would broader statutory inspection rights alleviate the plaintiffs' pleading burden? Should a plaintiff shareholder's inspection rights for pre-discovery litigation be more liberal than those accorded to shareholders for monitoring corporate conduct outside the litigation setting?

3. Professor Brown examines a number of features of the Eisner-Ovitz relationship to illustrate the refusal of the Delaware courts to seriously and consistently apply duty of loyalty principles like independence and disinterestedness. Which of the elements of that relationship most support Professor Brown's critique? Should any of these factors be beyond the scope of judicial review?

The Delaware presumption of director independence creates a high evidentiary bar for the plaintiffs, but is it truly an insurmountable defense? The following opinion, written by federal Judge Richard Posner, illustrates a more plaintiff-friendly judicial evaluation of self-dealing transactions. While reading this case, consider what policies drive the court of appeals' decision, and how those policies compare to the concerns articulated by Delaware's judiciary.

CDX Liquidating Trust v. Venrock Assoc.

United States Court of Appeals, Seventh Circuit
640 F.3d 209 (2011)

POSNER, CIRCUIT JUDGE:

This suit, brought by a trust that holds the common stock of a bankrupt company formerly known as Cadant, charges several former directors with breaches of their duty of loyalty to the corporation, and charges two venture-capital groups, which we'll abbreviate to "Venrock" and "J.P. Morgan," with aiding and abetting the disloyal directors. Trial was bifurcated. Seven weeks into the trial on liability the plaintiff rested and the defendants then moved for judgment as a matter of law. The district judge granted the motion with a brief oral statement of reasons, precipitating this appeal.

Cadant had been created in 1998 to develop what are called "cable modem termination systems," which enable high-speed Internet access to home computers. Though based in Illinois, Cadant initially was incorporated in Maryland and later was reincorporated in Delaware. The founders received common stock in the new corporation at the outset. Others purchased common stock later. Venrock and J.P. Morgan received preferred stock in exchange for an investment in the new company that they made at the beginning of 2000. Eric Copeland, a principal of Venrock, became a member of Cadant's five-member board of directors. He is the director principally accused of disloyalty to Cadant.

In April 2000 the board turned down a tentative offer by ADC Telecommunications to buy Cadant's assets for $300 million. It was later that year that the board proposed and the shareholders approved the reincorporation of Cadant in Delaware, effective January 1, 2001. The suit involves decisions by Cadant's board made both when Cadant was incorporated in Maryland and when it was reincorporated in Delaware. Illinois choice of law principles, which govern this case because it was filed in Illinois, makes the law applicable to a suit against a director for breach of fiduciary duty that of the state of incorporation. This is what is known as the "internal affairs" doctrine— "a conflict of laws principle which recognizes that only one State should have the authority to regulate a corporation's internal affairs matters peculiar to the relationships among or between the corporation and its current officers, directors, and shareholders—because otherwise a corporation could be faced with conflicting demands." The earliest challenged decision by Cadant's board—the decision not to respond to ADC's acquisition offer in April 2000—thus is easily dismissed. Maryland law applied at that time and under that law directors have no duty to "accept, recommend, or respond on behalf of the corporation to any proposal by an acquiring person."

In the fall of 2000, Cadant found itself in financial trouble. The defendants attribute this to the deflating—beginning in the spring of 2000 and continuing throughout the year and into the next year—of the dot-com bubble of the late 1990s. We'll return to the question of what caused Cadant's financial distress, but whatever the cause the company needed fresh investment. The board considered a proposal from a group of Chicago investors and a joint proposal from Venrock and J.P. Morgan, and eventually decided on an $11 million loan from Venrock and J.P. Morgan. The terms of the loan were negotiated on Cadant's behalf by Copeland. The board of directors had grown to seven members, of whom four, including Copeland, were employees of Venrock or J.P. Morgan, though one of them, defendant C.H. Randolph Lyon, resigned from J.P. Morgan before the loan was made, while remaining a director of Cadant.

The loan was a "bridge loan," which is a short-term loan intended to tide the borrower over while he seeks longer-term financing. The $11 million bridge loan to Cadant was for only 90 days, at an annual interest rate of 10 percent; it also gave the lenders warrants (never exercised) to buy common stock of Cadant. Cadant ran through the entire loan, which had been made in January 2001, within a few months. Venrock and J.P. Morgan then made a second bridge loan, in May, this one for $9 million, again negotiated on Cadant's behalf by Copeland. The loan agreement provided that in the event that Cadant was liquidated the lenders would be entitled to be paid twice the outstanding principal of the loan plus any accrued but unpaid interest on it; as a result, little if anything would be left for the shareholders. The disinterested directors of Cadant (the directors who had no affiliation with Venrock or J.P. Morgan) who voted for the loan were engineers without financial acumen, and because they didn't think to retain their own financial advisor they were at the mercy of the financial advice they received from Copeland and the other conflicted directors.

Cadant defaulted on the second bridge loan, and being in deep financial trouble agreed to sell all its assets to a firm called Arris Group in exchange for stock worth, when the sale closed in January 2002, some $55 million. That amount was just large enough to satisfy the claims of Cadant's creditors and preferred shareholders (Venrock and J.P. Morgan were both). The sale was approved by Cadant's board, but also, as required by Delaware law and the company's articles of incorporation, by a simple majority both of Cadant's common and preferred shareholders voting together as a single class and of the preferred shareholders voting separately.

The district judge gave two independent grounds for granting judgment as a matter of law for the defendants. The first was that there was insufficient evidence of proximate cause to allow a reasonable jury to render a verdict for the plaintiff, and the second was that there was likewise insufficient evidence of a breach of fiduciary duty. These grounds turn out to be intertwined. (Ordinarily the issue of duty would precede that of cause, but no matter.)

The term "proximate cause" is pervasive in American tort law, but that doesn't mean it's well understood. A common definition is that there must be proof of "some direct relation between the injury asserted and the injurious conduct alleged." But "direct" is no more illuminating than "proximate." Both are metaphors rather than definitions. What the courts are trying to do by intoning these words is to focus attention on whether the particular contribution that the defendant made to the injury for which the plaintiff has sued him resulted from conduct that we want to deter or punish by imposing liability, as in the famous case of *Palsgraf v. Long Island R.R.* The plaintiff was injured when a heavy metal scale collapsed on the railroad platform on which she was standing. The scale had buckled from damage caused by fireworks dropped by a passenger trying, with the aid of a conductor, to board a moving train at some distance from the scale. She sued the railroad; it would have been unthinkable for her to sue the scale's manufacturer, even though if heavy metal scales did not exist she would not have been injured. No one would think the scale's manufacturer should be liable, because no one would think that tort law should try to encourage manufacturers of scales to take steps to prevent the kind of accident that befell Mrs. Palsgraf. The railroad was a more plausible defendant; its conductor had tugged the passenger aboard while the train was already moving. But how could he have foreseen that his act would have triggered an explosion, as distinct from a possible injury to the boarder? If an accident is so freakish as to be unforeseeable, liability is unlikely to have a deterrent effect.

Coming closer to our case, the defendants cite our decision in *Movitz v. First National Bank of Chicago*, 148 F.3d 760 (7th Cir. 1998). The plaintiff had bought a building in Houston in reliance on what he claimed was the defendant's misrepresentation of its value. Had it not been for the misrepresentation he would not have bought it. Shortly after the purchase the Houston real estate market collapsed and his investment was wiped out. The misrepresentation had not caused that collapse but it had been a cause of the plaintiff's buying the building and thus had contributed to his loss. Yet we ruled, without using the term "proximate cause," that he could not recover from the defendant because (among other reasons) that would produce overdeterrence by making the defendant an insurer of conditions that he could not control. That would be as futile as making the manufacturer of the scale an insurer of Mrs. Palsgraf's loss.

The present case is superficially similar to *Movitz* because it is possible that what did in Cadant and hence its common shareholders (some at least of the preferred shareholders — such as Venrock and J.P. Morgan — seem to have come out all right) was not the defendants' alleged misconduct but the collapse of the dot-com bubble. And indeed the district court ruled that the plaintiff had failed to prove that the defendants' misconduct had been a "proximate cause" of Cadant's ruination, just as in *Movitz*. But we disagree with his ruling in two respects. First, the burden of proof on the issue of causation (or if one prefers, of "proximate causation") was on the defendants rather than on the plaintiff and the judge cut off the trial before the defendants presented their defenses. Second, there was enough evidence that the bursting of the dot-com bubble did not account for the entire loss to Cadant to make causation an issue requiring factfinding and therefore for the jury to resolve. The dot-com bubble was primarily in the stocks of firms that marketed their goods or services over the Internet. Cadant did not, and anyway it was in the hardware business, the fortunes of which depend on the volume of Internet traffic, which continued to increase even after the bubble burst. There may have been a crossover effect; the collapse of stock values, and the recession (mild though it was) that accompanied it, reduced the amount of venture capital available for technology companies generally, and so may have made it difficult for Cadant to obtain needed investment on reasonable terms. Our point is only that the effect of the bubble's bursting on Cadant was a jury issue, not an issue that the judge could resolve because the effect was incontestable.

The first point — that the burden of proof on the issue of causation was on the defendants — is counterintuitive. Ordinarily the burden of proving causation is on the plaintiff, since without an injury caused by the defendant there is no tort no matter how wrongful the defendant's behavior was. Delaware law, however, creates an exception for suits against directors of a corporation — an exception not to the requirement that there be proof of causation but to the requirement that the plaintiff prove causation rather than the defendant's having to prove absence of causation.

To explain: When a director is sued for breach of his duty of loyalty or care to the shareholders, his first line of defense is the business-judgment rule, which creates a presumption that a business decision, including a recommendation or vote by a corporate director, was made in good faith and with due care. But the presumption can be overcome by proof that the director breached his fiduciary duty to the corporation—his duty of loyalty and his duty to exercise due care in its performance. "If—and here we come to the nub of the causation issue in this case—the [business-judgment] rule is rebutted, the burden shifts to the defendant directors, the proponents of the challenged transaction, to prove to the trier of fact the 'entire fairness' of the transaction to the shareholder plaintiff."

Delaware law permits the shareholders to adopt (and Cadant's shareholders did adopt) a charter provision exculpating directors from liability in damages for failure to exercise due care, but does not enforce a provision exculpating them from liability for disloyalty, and that is the charge in this case. But does Delaware law govern the issue? Cadant's articles of incorporation in both Maryland and Delaware said that its directors would be exempted from liability for breaches of fiduciary duty to the fullest extent permitted by state law—and the two states' laws are, or at least may be, different. Delaware provides that articles of incorporation "shall not eliminate or limit the liability of a director ... for any breach of the director's duty of loyalty to the corporation or its stockholders," Del. General Corporation Law § 102(b)(7), while Maryland law allows a corporation to shield its directors from all liability other than for "active and deliberate dishonesty." The plaintiff presented evidence of disloyalty, as we'll see later, but we are uncertain whether it proves "active and deliberate dishonesty." The briefs virtually ignore the issue, and we cannot find a case decided by a Maryland court that construes the term. An unpublished decision by the Fourth Circuit interprets the term in the Maryland statute as including fraud, which is a possible characterization of the defendants' alleged conduct in the present case. And *Mississippi v. Richardson*, 817 F.2d 1203, 1210 (5th Cir.1987), construes the identical term appearing in a liability insurance policy to cover "willful neglect of duties," embezzlement, and fraud—and willful neglect of duties seems a pretty good description of the defendants' alleged wrongdoing. And if there was disloyalty in·this case it was deliberate, and maybe that's enough to prove "active and deliberate dishonesty."

We needn't decide, because we think the Delaware statute controls, so far as the bridge loans are concerned, and they are the focus of the suit. The negotiations leading up to the first bridge loan took place in the fall of 2000 and the loan was approved by Cadant's board on January 10, 2001—nine days after Cadant's reincorporation in Delaware took effect. Some of the plaintiff's strongest evidence of the disloyalty of the conflicted directors concerns Copeland's actions during the negotiation of the first loan, and the plaintiff argues that that loan initiated the events which led to the desperation sale of the company to Arris.

We cannot apply both states' law to the first bridge loan, and so we fall back to general choice of law principles and ask which state's law governing the duties of directors the parties would have expected to govern Cadant's internal affairs in the critical period, and which state had the greater regulatory interest in the corporation's internal affairs then. The answer to both questions is Delaware. It was on November 8, 2000, that Cadant's board formally approved the decision to reincorporate, in a resolution which stated that "the Board believes that the State of Delaware has an established body of case law that better enables the Board effectively to meet its fiduciary obligations to the stockholders of the Company." Copeland's failure to disclose disloyal acts that he committed during the negotiation was a disloyal act that caused the loan to be approved, and it was approved in January, after the company had reincorporated under Delaware law. The board would have assumed that, certainly from that day forward, the duties of the directors relating to both that loan and the second bridge loan would be governed by Delaware law.

Apart from the board's refusal to sell the company to ADC Telecommunications, moreover — an act squarely governed by Maryland law and exempted from liability by that law because it was concluded before reincorporation was resolved upon, let alone accomplished — most of the disloyal acts of which the plaintiff complains occurred while Cadant was a Delaware corporation, and most that occurred earlier occurred after the board had decided that Delaware law made a better fit with Cadant than Maryland law did. So Delaware had a greater regulatory interest than Maryland in the governance of Cadant's internal affairs in the critical period in which the events giving rise to this lawsuit occurred.

We conclude that the articles of incorporation were not effective in waiving Copeland's and the other conflicted directors' duty of loyalty, and so proof of their disloyal acts (had the jury been permitted to find that they'd indeed committed those acts) would have placed on them the burden of proving the "entire fairness" of the bridge loans. But, say our defendants, the plaintiff still had to prove proximate cause and what has "entire fairness" to do with that? In a case like this, everything. For "in the review of a transaction involving a sale of a company, the directors [once the application of the business — judgment rule is rebutted] have the burden of establishing that the price offered was the highest value reasonably available under the circumstances," — in other words, the burden of proving that the shareholders did as well as they would have done had the defendant directors been loyal and careful. That's another way of saying that the disloyal acts had no effect on the shareholders — no causal relation to their loss.

An alternative mode of rebuttal would be to prove that despite evidence of disloyalty, the directors had been loyal; and then the business-judgment rule would spring back in and insulate the directors from liability. The term "entire fairness" makes a better semantic match with this form of rebuttal than does showing that the company was sold for the highest price realistically attainable even if the directors who engineered the sale were disloyal. But what would be the need for a concept of "entire fairness" if all that was involved was that if the plaintiff's evidence of disloyalty is compelling enough to place a burden of proving loyalty on the defendant, the latter still can prevail, by proving that he was loyal after all? The alternative version of "entire fairness," which defines a distinct doctrine, is the version applicable to this case. The disloyalty of the defendant directors must be assumed because the judge aborted the trial, and so the defendants have to prove that their misconduct had no causal efficacy because Cadant made as good a deal as it would have done had the defendants been loyal. That's a simple causal question; there's no need to worry about what "proximate cause" means.

The defendants think it heresy to excuse a plaintiff from having to prove causation and to make them prove its absence. But not only is this unambiguously the Delaware rule in a case like this; shifting to the defendant the burden of proof on causation is common in other areas of law, such as employment discrimination. The shift makes sense in cases governed by the business-judgment rule, which creates such a commodious safe harbor for directors that overcoming it requires the plaintiff to make a very strong showing of misconduct. Misconduct however great can be rendered harmless by a su-pervening event such as the bursting of a commodity bubble, as in *Movitz*. But as that is exceptional, it makes sense to place the burden of proving supervening cause on the defendant; indeed that is where the burden of proving supervening cause (a cause that wipes out the defendant's responsibility for the plaintiff's injury) usually rests.

Actually there's enough proof that the alleged misconduct caused loss to Cadant's shareholders to make the issue of causation one for the jury no matter which side has the burden of proof. It was after the dot-com bubble burst, and only a few months before Cadant was sold to the Arris Group for $55 million, that a similar company, River Delta, was sold for $300 million. Cadant couldn't hold out for a comparable deal because of the terms of the bridge loans. If the plaintiff's evidence is credited, Copeland, in cahoots with an employee of J.P. Morgan named Charles Walker (a de-fendant), used information gleaned from meetings of Cadant's board to reveal to J.P. Morgan and through it to Venrock that Cadant would accept a smaller bridge loan, and for a shorter term, than Venrock and J.P. Morgan would have expected the board to insist on. Walker himself joined Cadant's board soon after the first bridge loan was made, as did another J.P. Morgan employee (Stephan Oppenheimer), who is also a defendant. There is evidence that Copeland, Walker, and Oppenheimer conspired to ensure that Cadant would accept the second bridge loan, which added to the dis-advantages to Cadant of the first loan by creating a generous liquidation preference; as mentioned earlier, in the event of a sale or liquidation of Cadant, Venrock and J.P. Morgan would be entitled to be paid twice the amount of their investment in the company, to the prejudice of the common shareholders.

The smaller the loan, the shorter the term, and the bigger the liquidation preference, the worse for those shareholders. The smaller the loan, the less it strengthens the borrower (Cadant) and thus the harder it is for the borrower to hold out for generous offers from prospective buyers. The shorter the term, the shorter the period for which the borrower can hold out for an attractive sale price. The bigger the liquidation pref-erence, the less the stockholders will realize from the sale in the event—which was looming when the bridge loans were made, and which eventually came to pass—that the firm is forced to liquidate. Uncontaminated by disloyal directors, so far as appears, River Delta, in adverse economic conditions similar to those alleged to have beset Cadant, nevertheless was sold for more than five times what Cadant was sold for a few months later. This is some evidence—and not the only evidence (but we're trying to keep this opinion as short as possible)—that Cadant's common shareholders were hurt by the defendants' misconduct, over and above the hurt inflicted by events over which the defendants had no control. Remember that the trial was bifurcated, so that all the jury had to find was that Cadant had been harmed by the directors' actions; measurement of the harm—specifically, allocating the harm between the misconduct of the defendants and the bursting of the dot-com bubble—was reserved for the trial on damages, if liability was found.

Even so, the defendants argue, retreating to their second line of defense, there was no breach of loyalty because their conflict of interest was fully disclosed. The conflict *was* fully disclosed. But that misses the point.

Section 144(a)(1) of Delaware's General Corporation Law provides, so far as relates to this case, that if "the material facts as to the director's ... relationship or interest and as to the contract or transactions are disclosed or are known to the board of directors..., and the board ... in good faith authorizes the contract or transaction by the affirmative votes of a majority of the disinterested directors," then "no contract" between the corporation (call it *A)* and another corporation *(B)* in which a director of *A* is also a director or an officer, or has some other financial interest, "shall be void or voidable solely for this reason," that is, solely because a director of *A* has an interest in *B,* with which *A* transacted. Copeland was a director of Venrock as well as of Cadant, and Venrock was a lender to Cadant, both as a preferred shareholder (which is a type of lender, not an equity owner) and as a bridge lender. The other defendant directors had a similar conflict of interest. But Copeland (and we may assume the others) fully disclosed to Cadant his (their) relationship with Venrock or J.P. Morgan, the other preferred shareholder-bridge lender, which was acting in partnership with Venrock. This meant that the transactions between it and Venrock and J.P. Morgan, disadvantageous to Cadant though they turned out to be, could not be voided solely because of the conflicts of interest. And if the conflicts thus were sterilized, the directors could not be found to have committed a breach of fiduciary duty just by virtue of the fact that they negotiated those deals.

But that is not the accusation. The accusation is that the directors were disloyal. They persuaded the district judge that disclosure of a conflict of interest excuses a breach of fiduciary duty. It does not. It just excuses the conflict. (Notice the parallel between the statutory provision and how Delaware law treats the exculpatory clause in Cadant's articles of incorporation.)

To have a conflict and to be motivated by it to breach a duty of loyalty are two different things—the first a factor increasing the likelihood of a wrong, the second the wrong itself. Thus a disloyal act is actionable even when a conflict of interest is not—one difference being that the conflict is disclosed, the disloyal act is not. A director may tell his fellow directors that he has a conflict of interest but that he will not allow it to influence his actions as director; he will not tell them he plans to screw them. If having been informed of the conflict the disinterested directors decide to continue to trust and rely on the interested ones, it is because they think that despite the conflict of interest those directors will continue to serve the corporation loyally.

Benihana of Tokyo, Inc. v. Benihana, Inc., a derivative suit much like this one, provides an illuminating contrast to this case. A director was interested but his interest was known to the board. Having settled that point, the court went on to consider whether he had breached his fiduciary duty to the corporation, and concluded that he had not. He "did not set the terms of the [challenged] deal; he did not deceive the board; and he did not dominate or control the other directors' approval of the Transaction. In short, the record does not support the claim that [he] breached his duty of loyalty." There is enough evidence that Copeland and the other defendant directors did these things to create an issue for a jury to resolve.

Only one further issue need be discussed—the potential liability of Venrock and J.P. Morgan. They of course owed no duty of loyalty or care to Cadant. But to aid and abet a breach of fiduciary duty committed by corporate directors is actionable under Delaware law, ... and the evidence of such aiding and abetting, notably by Charles Walker on behalf of both Venrock and his employer J.P. Morgan, is sufficient to create another jury issue. *Gatz* explains that "to state a claim for aiding and abetting a breach of fiduciary duty, a plaintiff must allege (1) a fiduciary relationship; (2) a breach of that relationship; (3) that the alleged aider and abettor knowingly participated in the fiduciary's breach of duty; and (4) damages proximately caused by the breach," and *Malpiede* that "a third party may be liable for aiding and abetting a breach of a corporate fiduciary's duty to the stockholders if the third party 'knowingly participates' in the breach ... Knowing participation in a board's fiduciary breach requires that the third party act with the knowledge that the conduct advocated or assisted constitutes such a breach. Under this standard, a bidder's attempts to reduce the sale price through arm's-length negotiations cannot give rise to liability for aiding and abetting, whereas a bidder may be liable to the target's stockholders if the bidder attempts to create or exploit conflicts of interest in the board," and *Gilbert* that "although an offeror may attempt to obtain the lowest possible price for stock through arm's-length negotiations with the target's board, it may not knowingly participate in the target board's breach of fiduciary duty by extracting terms which require the opposite party to prefer its interests at the expense of its shareholders." These formulas, with "lender" replacing "bidder" in *Malpiede* and "offeror" in *Gilbert*, fit this case to a T (always assuming that the plaintiff can prove his allegations). These defendants will of course avoid liability for aiding and abetting if there was no misconduct by Copeland or any of the other defendant directors for Venrock and J.P. Morgan to aid or abet, but we have just ruled that there was sufficient evidence of such misconduct to create a jury issue.

We note the questionable wisdom of granting a motion for judgment of law seven weeks into a trial that was about to end because the defendants declared that they were not going to put in a defense case. Reserving decision on the motion might have avoided a great waste of time, money, and judicial resources, as the case must now be retried from the beginning.

Reversed and remanded, with directions.

Comments and Questions

1. The court of appeals decided to evaluate the conduct of the board under Delaware law. Would the result have been any different if the court applied Maryland law instead? Would the application of Maryland law have changed the result at trial?

2. How does Judge Posner's application of Section 144 and Delaware loyalty doctrine compare to the Delaware courts' application of the same law? How is the Seventh Circuit's decision more plaintiff-friendly?

3. Judge Posner observes that "[t]o have a conflict and to be motivated by it to breach a duty of loyalty are two different things." Do you agree? Does the Delaware Supreme Court's opinion in *Benihana* support Judge Posner's decision to examine the directors' motives?

4. When should courts review a self-dealing transaction under the entire fairness standard, according to Judge Posner? Why do the defendant directors bear the burden of proof under the entire fairness standard? For discussions of the broader effect of the entire fairness review, see Randall S. Thomas & Harwell Wells, *Executive Compensation in the Courts: Board Capture, Optimal Contracting, and Officers' Fiduciary Duties*, 95 Minn. L. Rev. 846 (2011); Lisa M. Fairfax, *The Uneasy Case for the Inside Director*, 96 Iowa L. Rev. 127 (2010).

5. Judge Posner and his colleagues held that viable claims against Venrock and J.P. Morgan survived appeal because those defendants may have aided and abetted in Copeland's breach of his duty of loyalty. What facts indicate that these defendants may have knowingly participated in the alleged breach? What, if anything, could Venrock or J.P. Morgan have done to avoid potential liability for aiding and abetting? What policy justifications exist for holding corporate outsiders liable for fiduciary breaches by corporate directors? Must intent to aid in the breach be proven, or is knowledge sufficient for aiding and abetting liability?

II. Usurping Corporate Opportunities

The duty of loyalty is not limited to self-dealing transactions. It also prohibits directors and officers from usurping the company's business opportunities. Corporate law recognizes that corporate fiduciaries—especially outside directors not employed full-time by the company—may have business interests outside of the firm, interests not dissimilar to the company's current or potential operations. If fiduciaries were required to abstain from any and all personal business opportunities of interest to the company, the pool of willing, qualified, and competent directors and officers would shrink considerably. Yet, corporations still need protection from disloyal fiduciaries who would exploit the company's information, contacts, and assets to benefit themselves. The corporate opportunity doctrine attempts to balance the conflicting interests of fiduciaries and corporations through a fact-specific inquiry into the nature of the opportunity and the interests involved.

The corporate opportunity doctrine, then, represents a judicially-crafted effort to harmonize the competing demands placed on corporate fiduciaries in a modern business environment. The doctrine seeks to reduce the possibility of conflict between a director's duties to the corporation and interests unrelated to that role.

Broz v. Cellular Information Systems Inc.
Delaware Supreme Court
673 A.2d 148 (1996)

VEASEY, CHIEF JUSTICE:

In this appeal, we consider the application of the doctrine of corporate opportunity. The Court of Chancery decided that the defendant, a corporate director, breached his fiduciary duty by not formally presenting to the corporation an opportunity which had come to the director individually and independent of the director's relationship with the corporation. Here the opportunity was not one in which the corporation in its current mode had an interest or which it had the financial ability to acquire, but, under the unique circumstances here, that mode was subject to change by virtue of the impending acquisition of the corporation by another entity.

We conclude that, although a corporate director may be shielded from liability by offering to the corporation an opportunity which has come to the director independently and individually, the failure of the director to present the opportunity does not necessarily result in the improper usurpation of a corporate opportunity. We further conclude that, if the corporation is a target or potential target of an acquisition by another company which has an interest and ability to entertain the opportunity, the director of the target company does not have a fiduciary duty to present the opportunity to the target company. Accordingly, the judgment of the Court of Chancery is REVERSED.

The Contentions of the Parties and the Decision Below

Robert F. Broz ("Broz") is the President and sole stockholder of RFB Cellular, Inc. ("RFBC"), a Delaware corporation engaged in the business of providing cellular telephone service in the Midwestern United States. At the time of the conduct at issue in this appeal, Broz was also a member of the board of directors of plaintiff below-appellee, Cellular Information Systems, Inc. ("CIS"). CIS is a publicly held Delaware corporation and a competitor of RFBC.

The conduct before the Court involves the purchase by Broz of a cellular telephone service license for the benefit of RFBC. The license in question, known as the Michigan-2 Rural Service Area Cellular License ("Michigan-2"), is issued by the Federal Communications Commission and entitles its holder to provide cellular telephone service to a portion of northern Michigan. CIS brought an action against Broz and RFBC for equitable relief, contending that the purchase of this license by Broz constituted a usurpation of a corporate opportunity properly belonging to CIS, irrespective of whether or not CIS was interested in the Michigan-2 opportunity at the time it was offered to Broz.

The principal basis for the contention of CIS is that PriCellular, Inc., another cellular communications company which was contemporaneously engaged in an acquisition of CIS, was interested in the Michigan-2 opportunity. CIS contends that, in determining whether the Michigan-2 opportunity rightfully belonged to CIS, Broz was required to consider the interests of PriCellular insofar as those interests would come into alignment with those of CIS as a result of PriCellular's acquisition plans.

After trial, the Court of Chancery agreed with the contentions of CIS and entered judgment against Broz and RFBC. The court held that: (1) irrespective of the fact that the Michigan-2 opportunity came to Broz in a manner wholly independent of his status as a director of CIS, the Michigan-2 license was an opportunity that properly belonged to CIS; (2) due to an alignment of the interests of CIS and PriCellular arising out of PriCellular's efforts to acquire CIS, Broz breached his fiduciary duty by failing to consider whether the opportunity was one in which PriCellular would be interested; (3) despite the fact that CIS was aware of the opportunity and expressed no interest in pursuing it, Broz was required formally to present the transaction to the CIS board prior to seizing the opportunity for his own; and (4) absent formal presentation to the board, Broz' acquisition of Michigan-2 constituted an impermissible usurpation of a corporate opportunity. From this judgment, Broz and RFBC appeal.

Broz contends that the Court of Chancery erred in holding that he breached his fiduciary duties to CIS and its stockholders. Specifically, Broz asserts that he was under no obligation formally to present the corporate opportunity to the CIS Board of Directors. Broz further contends that PriCellular had not consummated its acquisition of CIS at the time of his decision to purchase Michigan-2, and that, accordingly, he was not obligated to consider the interests of PriCellular. We agree with Broz and hold that: (1) the determination of whether a corporate fiduciary has usurped a corporate opportunity is fact-intensive and turns on, *inter alia*, the ability of the corporation to make use of the opportunity and the company's intent to do so; (2) while presentation of a purported corporate opportunity to the board of directors and the board's refusal thereof may serve as a shield to liability, there is no *per se* rule requiring presentation to the board prior to acceptance of the opportunity; and (3) on these facts, Broz was not required to consider the interests of PriCellular in reaching his determination whether or not to purchase Michigan-2.

Facts

Broz has been the President and sole stockholder of RFBC since 1992. RFBC owns and operates an FCC license area, known as the Michigan-4 Rural Service Area Cellular License. The license entitles RFBC to provide cellular telephone service to a portion of rural Michigan. Although Broz' efforts have been devoted primarily to the business operations of RFBC, he also served as an outside director of CIS at the time of the events at issue in this case. CIS was at all times fully aware of Broz' relationship with RFBC and the obligations incumbent upon him by virtue of that relationship.

In April of 1994, Mackinac Cellular Corp. sought to divest itself of Michigan-2, the license area immediately adjacent to Michigan-4. To this end, Mackinac contacted Daniels & Associates and arranged for the brokerage firm to seek potential purchasers for Michigan-2. In compiling a list of prospects, Daniels included RFBC as a likely candidate. In May of 1994, David Rhodes, a representative of Daniels, contacted Broz and broached the subject of RFBC's possible acquisition of Michigan-2. Broz later signed a confidentiality agreement at the request of Mackinac, and received the offering materials pertaining to Michigan-2.

Michigan-2 was not, however, offered to CIS. Apparently, Daniels did not consider CIS to be a viable purchaser for Michigan-2 in light of CIS' recent financial difficulties. The record shows that, at the time Michigan-2 was offered to Broz, CIS had recently emerged from lengthy and contentious Chapter 11 proceedings. Pursuant to the Chapter 11 Plan of Reorganization, CIS entered into a loan agreement that substantially impaired the company's ability to undertake new acquisitions or to incur new debt. In fact, CIS would have been unable to purchase Michigan-2 without the approval of its creditors.

The CIS reorganization resulted from the failure of CIS' rather ambitious plans for expansion. In 1992, however, CIS' financing failed, necessitating the liquidation of the company's holdings and reduction of the company's total indebtedness. During the period from early 1992 until the time of CIS' emergence from bankruptcy in 1994, CIS divested itself of some fifteen separate cellular license systems.

On June 13, 1994, following a meeting of the CIS board, Broz spoke with CIS' Chief Executive Officer, Richard Treibick, concerning his interest in acquiring Michigan-2. Treibick communicated to Broz that CIS was not interested in Michigan-2. Treibick further stated that he had been made aware of the Michigan-2 opportunity prior to the conversation with Broz, and that any offer to acquire Michigan-2 was rejected. After the commencement of the PriCellular tender offer, in August of 1994, Broz contacted another CIS director, Peter Schiff, to discuss the possible acquisition of Michigan-2 by RFBC. Schiff, like Treibick, indicated that CIS had neither the wherewithal nor the inclination to purchase Michigan-2. In late September of 1994, Broz also contacted Stanley Bloch, a director and counsel for CIS, to request that Bloch represent RFBC in its dealings with Mackinac. Bloch agreed to represent RFBC, and, like Schiff and Treibick, expressed his belief that CIS was not at all interested in the transaction. Ultimately, all the CIS directors testified at trial that, had Broz inquired at that time, they each would have expressed the opinion that CIS was not interested in Michigan-2.

On June 28, 1994, following various overtures from PriCellular concerning an acquisition of CIS, six CIS directors entered into agreements with PriCellular to sell their shares in CIS at a price of $2.00 per share. These agreements were contingent upon, *inter alia*, the consummation of a PriCellular tender offer for all CIS shares at the same price. Pursuant to their agreements with PriCellular, the CIS directors also entered into a "standstill" agreement which prevented the directors from engaging in any transaction outside the regular course of CIS' business or incurring any new liabilities until the close of the PriCellular tender offer. On August 2, 1994, PriCellular commenced a tender offer for all outstanding shares of CIS at $2.00 per share.

PriCellular's tender offer was originally scheduled to close on September 16, 1994. At the time the tender offer was launched, however, the source of the $106,000,000 in financing required to consummate the transaction was still in doubt. PriCellular originally planned to structure the transaction around bank loans. When this financing fell through, PriCellular resorted to a junk bond offering. PriCellular's financing difficulties generated a great deal of concern among the CIS insiders whether the tender offer was, in fact, viable. Financing difficulties ultimately caused PriCellular to delay the closing date of the tender offer from September 16, 1994 until October 14, 1994 and then again until November 9, 1994.

On August 6, September 6 and September 21, 1994, Broz submitted written offers to Mackinac for the purchase of Michigan-2.

In late September of 1994, PriCellular reached agreement with Mackinac on an option to purchase Michigan-2. The exercise price of the option agreement was set at $6.7 million, with the option remaining in force until December 15, 1994. Pursuant to the agreement, the right to exercise the option was not transferrable to any party other than a subsidiary of PriCellular. Therefore, it could not have been transferred to CIS. The agreement further provided that Mackinac was free to sell Michigan-2 to any party who was willing to exceed the exercise price of the Mackinac-PriCellular option contract by at least $500,000. On November 14, 1994, Broz agreed to pay Mackinac $7.2 million for the Michigan-2 license, thereby meeting the terms of the option agreement. An asset purchase agreement was thereafter executed by Mackinac and RFBC.

Nine days later, on November 23, 1994, PriCellular completed its financing and closed its tender offer for CIS. Prior to that point, PriCellular owned no equity interest in CIS. Subsequent to the consummation of the PriCellular tender offer for CIS, members of the CIS board of directors, including Broz, were discharged and replaced with a slate of PriCellular nominees. On March 2, 1995, this action was commenced by CIS in the Court of Chancery.

At trial in the Court of Chancery, CIS contended that the purchase of Michigan-2 by Broz constituted the impermissible usurpation of a corporate opportunity properly belonging to CIS. Thus, CIS asserted that Broz breached his fiduciary duty to CIS and its stockholders. CIS admits that, at the time the opportunity was offered to Broz, the board of CIS would not have been interested in Michigan-2, but CIS asserts that Broz usurped the opportunity nevertheless. CIS claims that Broz was required to look not just to CIS, but to the articulated business plans of PriCellular, to determine whether PriCellular would be interested in acquiring Michigan-2. Since Broz failed to do this and acquired Michigan-2 without first considering the interests of PriCellular in its capacity as a potential acquiror of CIS, CIS contends that Broz must be held to account for breach of fiduciary duty.

Application of the Corporate Opportunity Doctrine

The doctrine of corporate opportunity represents but one species of the broad fiduciary duties assumed by a corporate director or officer. A corporate fiduciary agrees to place the interests of the corporation before his or her own in appropriate circumstances. In light of the diverse and often competing obligations faced by directors and officers, however, the corporate opportunity doctrine arose as a means of defining the parameters of fiduciary duty in instances of potential conflict. The classic statement of the doctrine is derived from the venerable case of *Guth v. Loft, Inc.* In *Guth*, this Court held that:

> ... if there is presented to a corporate officer or director a business opportunity which the corporation is financially able to undertake, is, from its nature, in the line of the corporation's business and is of practical advantage to it, is one in which the corporation has an interest or a reasonable expectancy, and, by embracing the opportunity, the self-interest of the officer or director will be brought into conflict with that of the corporation, the law will not permit him to seize the opportunity for himself.

The corporate opportunity doctrine, as delineated by *Guth* and its progeny, holds that a corporate officer or director may not take a business opportunity for his own if: (1) the corporation is financially able to exploit the opportunity; (2) the opportunity is within the corporation's line of business; (3) the corporation has an interest or expectancy in the opportunity; and (4) by taking the opportunity for his own, the corporate fiduciary will thereby be placed in a position inimicable to his duties to the corporation. The Court in *Guth* also derived a corollary which states that a director or officer *may* take a corporate opportunity if: (1) the opportunity is presented to the director or officer in his individual and not his corporate capacity; (2) the opportunity is not essential to the corporation; (3) the corporation holds no interest or expectancy in the opportunity; and (4) the director or officer has not wrongfully employed the resources of the corporation in pursuing or exploiting the opportunity.

Thus, the contours of this doctrine are well established. It is important to note, however, that the tests enunciated in *Guth* and subsequent cases provide guidelines to be considered by a reviewing court in balancing the equities of an individual case. No one factor is dispositive and all factors must be taken into account insofar as they are applicable. Cases involving a claim of usurpation of a corporate opportunity range over a multitude of factual settings. Hard and fast rules are not easily crafted to deal with such an array of complex situations. As this Court noted in *Johnston v. Greene*, 121 A.2d 919 (Del. 1956), the determination of "[w]hether or not a director has appropriated for himself something that in fairness should belong to the corporation is 'a factual question to be decided by reasonable inference from objective facts.'" In the instant case, we find that the facts do not support the conclusion that Broz misappropriated a corporate opportunity.

We note at the outset that Broz became aware of the Michigan-2 opportunity in his individual and not his corporate capacity. As the Court of Chancery found, "Broz did not misuse proprietary information that came to him in a corporate capacity nor did he otherwise use any power he might have over the governance of the corporation to advance his own interests." This fact is not the subject of serious dispute. In fact, it is clear from the record that Mackinac did not consider CIS a viable candidate for the acquisition of Michigan-2. Accordingly, Mackinac did not offer the property to CIS. In this factual posture, many of the fundamental concerns undergirding the law of corporate opportunity are not present (*e.g.*, misappropriation of the corporation's proprietary information). The burden imposed upon Broz to show adherence to his fiduciary duties to CIS is thus lessened to some extent.

We turn now to an analysis of the factors relied on by the trial court. First, we find that CIS was not financially capable of exploiting the Michigan-2 opportunity. Although the Court of Chancery concluded otherwise, we hold that this finding was not supported by the evidence. The record shows that CIS was in a precarious financial position at the time Mackinac presented the Michigan-2 opportunity to Broz. Having recently emerged from lengthy and contentious bankruptcy proceedings, CIS was not in a position to commit capital to the acquisition of new assets. Further, the loan agreement entered into by CIS and its creditors severely limited the discretion of CIS as to the acquisition of new assets and substantially restricted the ability of CIS to incur new debt.

The Court of Chancery based its contrary finding on the fact that PriCellular had purchased an option to acquire CIS' bank debt. Thus, the court reasoned, PriCellular was in a position to exercise that option and then waive any unfavorable restrictions that would stand in the way of a CIS acquisition of Michigan-2. The trial court, however, disregarded the fact that PriCellular's own financial situation was not particularly stable. PriCellular was unable to finance the acquisitions of CIS through conventional bank loans and was forced to use the more risky mechanism of a junk bond offering to raise the required capital. [T]he fact that PriCellular had available resources of financing is immaterial to the analysis. At the time that Broz was required to decide whether to accept the Michigan-2 opportunity, PriCellular had not yet acquired CIS, and any plans to do so were wholly speculative. Thus, contrary to the Court of Chancery's finding, Broz was not obligated to consider the contingency of a PriCellular acquisition of CIS and the related contingency of PriCellular thereafter waiving restrictions on the CIS bank debt. Broz was required to consider the facts only as they existed at the time he determined to accept the Mackinac offer and embark on his efforts to bring the transaction to fruition.

Second, while it may be said with some certainty that the Michigan-2 opportunity was within CIS' line of business, it is not equally clear that CIS had a cognizable interest or expectancy in the license. Under the third factor laid down by this Court in *Guth*, for an opportunity to be deemed to belong to the fiduciary's corporation, the corporation must have an interest or expectancy in that opportunity. As this Court stated in *[Johnston v. Greene,]* "[f]or the corporation to have an actual or expectant interest in any specific property, there must be some tie between that property and the nature of the corporate business." Despite the fact that the nature of the Michigan-2 opportunity was historically close to the core operations of CIS, changes were in process. At the time the opportunity was presented, CIS was actively engaged in the process of divesting its cellular license holdings. CIS' articulated business plan did not involve any new acquisitions. Further, as indicated by the testimony of the entire CIS board, the Michigan-2 license would not have been of interest to CIS even absent CIS' financial difficulties and CIS' then current desire to liquidate its cellular license holdings. Thus, CIS had interest or expectancy in the Michigan-2 opportunity.

Finally, the corporate opportunity doctrine is implicated only in cases where the fiduciary's seizure of an opportunity results in a conflict between the fiduciary's duties to the corporation and the self-interest of the director as actualized by the exploitation of the opportunity. In the instant case, Broz' interest in acquiring and profiting from Michigan-2 created no duties that were inimicable to his obligations to CIS. Broz, at all times relevant to the instant appeal, was the sole party in interest in RFBC, a competitor of CIS. CIS was fully aware of Broz' potentially conflicting duties. Broz, however, comported himself in a manner that was wholly in accord with his obligations to CIS. Broz took care not to usurp any opportunity which CIS was willing and able to pursue. Broz sought only to compete with an outside entity, PriCellular, for acquisition of an opportunity which both sought to possess. Broz was not obligated to refrain from competition with PriCellular. Therefore, the totality of the circumstances indicates that Broz did not usurp an opportunity that properly belonged to CIS.

Presentation to the Board

In concluding that Broz had usurped a corporate opportunity, the Court of Chancery placed great emphasis on the fact that Broz had not formally presented the matter to the CIS board. In so holding, the trial court erroneously grafted a new requirement onto the law of corporate opportunity, viz., the requirement of formal presentation under circumstances where the corporation does not have an interest, expectancy or financial ability.

The teaching of Guth and its progeny is that the director or officer must analyze the situation ex ante to determine whether the opportunity is one rightfully belonging to the corporation. If the director or officer believes, based on one of the factors articulated above, that the corporation is not entitled to the opportunity, then he may take it for himself. It is not the law of Delaware that presentation to the board is a necessary prerequisite to a finding that a corporate opportunity has not been usurped.

The numerous cases decided since Guth are in full accord with this view of the doctrine. For instance, in Field v. Allyn, the Court of Chancery held that a director or officer is free to take a business opportunity for himself once the corporation has rejected it or if it can be shown that the corporation is not in a position to take the opportunity. The Field court held this to be true even if the fiduciary became aware of the opportunity by virtue of the fiduciary's position in the corporation. Notably, this Court affirmed the Field holding on the basis of the well reasoned opinion of the court below.

Alignment of Interests Between CIS and PriCellular

Broz was under no duty to consider the interests of PriCellular when he chose to purchase Michigan-2. As stated in Guth, a director's right to "appropriate [an] ...

opportunity depends on the circumstances existing at the time it presented itself to him without regard to subsequent events." At the time Broz purchased Michigan-2, PriCellular had not yet acquired CIS. Any plans to do so would still have been wholly speculative.

Whether or not the CIS board would, at some time, have chosen to acquire Michigan-2 in order to make CIS a more attractive acquisition target for PriCellular or to enhance the synergy of any combined enterprise, is speculative. The trial court found this to be a plausible scenario and therefore found that, pursuant to the factors laid down in *Guth*, CIS had a valid interest or expectancy in the license. This speculative finding cuts against the statements made by CIS' Chief Executive and the entire CIS board of directors and ignores the fact that CIS still lacked the wherewithal to acquire Michigan-2, even if one takes into account the possibility of PriCellular's financing.

In reaching our conclusion on this point, we note that certainty and predictability are values to be promoted in our corporation law. Broz, as an active participant in the cellular telephone industry, was entitled to proceed in his own economic interest in the absence of any countervailing duty. The right of a director or officer to engage in business affairs outside of his or her fiduciary capacity would be illusory if these individuals were required to consider every potential, future occurrence in determining whether a particular business strategy would implicate fiduciary duty concerns. In order for a director to engage meaningfully in business unrelated to his or her corporate role, the director must be allowed to make decisions based on the situation as it exists at the time a given opportunity is presented. Absent such a rule, the corporate fiduciary would be constrained to refrain from exploiting any opportunity for fear of liability based on the occurrence of subsequent events.

In the instant case, Broz adhered to his obligations to CIS.

Comments and Questions

1. If the corporation lacks the financial ability to exploit the subject opportunity, may the fiduciary take the prospect for herself? Must the corporation first reject the opportunity? Does proof of financial incapacity disqualify a potential investment as a "corporate opportunity," or is financial incapacity more properly regarded as a defense to a claim of breach? Why does it matter? Specifically with regard to this case, consider the following questions:

> If Broz did indeed receive the opportunity to purchase the license in his individual capacity, why would the court's decision have been differently if CIS actually did have the ability and intent to purchase the license? The court, in heavily weighing CIS' inability to pay for the license, appears to imply that Broz would have had a greater fiduciary duty to CIS if it had been able to go ahead with the purchase. This potential result would certainly be illogical if Broz held only a simple majority interest in RFB, and thus consequently owed a duty of loyalty to its minority shareholders. Under such a scenario, what justification can be offered for weighing the fiduciary duty owed to CIS more heavily?

Terence Woolf, *The Venture Capitalist's Corporate Opportunity Problem*, 2001 Colum. Bus. L. Rev. 473 (2001).

2. In determining whether an investment constitutes a corporate opportunity, should the factfinder consider how the fiduciary learned of the prospect? Why? Won't defendants invariably claim that they discovered the opportunity in their individual capacities?

3. Courts have articulated a variety of tests for identifying corporate opportunities. A number of jurisdictions have adopted the American Law Institute's definition of corporate opportunity, which provides:

> 1. Any opportunity to engage in a business activity of which a director or senior executive becomes aware, either:
>
>> a. In connection with the performance of functions as a director or senior executive, or under circumstances that should reasonably lead the director or senior executive to believe that the person offering the opportunity expects it to be offered to the corporation; or
>>
>> b. Through the use of corporate information or property, if the resulting opportunity is one that the director or senior executive should reasonably be expected to believe would be of interest to the corporation; or
>
> 2. Any opportunity to engage in a business activity of which a senior executive becomes aware and knows is closely related to a business in which the corporation is engaged or expected to engage.

Principles of Corporate Governance § 5.05 (1992). How does the ALI standard differ from the standard established in *Broz*?

4. Should Broz have been required to formally present the opportunity to the CIS board? Why or why not?

5. The Delaware legislature now has enacted Section 122(17), which provides:

> Every corporation created under this chapter shall have power to: …
>
> (17) Renounce, in its certificate of incorporation or by action of its board of directors, any interest or expectancy of the corporation in, or in being offered an opportunity to participate in, specified business opportunities or specified classes or categories of business opportunities that are presented to the corporation or one or more of its officers, directors or stockholders.

Commentators have criticized Section 122(17) insofar as "it suggests that a Delaware corporation has the power to expand the fiduciary duties of a stockholder beyond duties that exist under Delaware law." Could the board of a corporation compel a minority investor to direct all of its software, broadband, content, or interactive media opportunities to that corporation?

When the fiduciary accused of usurping a corporate opportunity is the inventor who founded the company, other public policies may come into play, as we see in the next case.

AngioScore, Inc. v. Trireme Medical, Inc.

2015 WL 4040388 (N.D. Cal. July 1, 2015)

ROGERS, DISTRICT COURT JUDGE:

Introduction

This case staged a tension between the inveterate, established law of fiduciary duties held by corporate directors and breach of fiduciary duty claims that arise when directors of emerging companies are innovators in the technology themselves. In such an instance, plaintiff AngioScore would have innovation subverted to duty; defendants would have duty subverted to innovation. Neither party's position admits of any balance, and neither can be wholly right. As set forth in this Order, the Court finds that where transparency, loyalty, and good faith predominate, a director's fiduciary duties and his drive to innovate can co-exist, albeit with the duties to the corporation taking precedence.

AngioScore brings state law claims for breach of fiduciary duty against one of its founders and former directors, Eitan Konstantino, alleging that while he was a member of AngioScore's board, Konstantino developed a medical device directly competitive with AngioScore's flagship product. Rather than offer the opportunity to acquire the new device to AngioScore, AngioScore maintains that Konstantino instead took it for himself. Defendants disagree, arguing in part that the duty was not breached either because no opportunity existed, or because AngioScore was not entitled to Konstantino's intellectual property as a matter of law.

Following a six-day bench trial on AngioScore's claims, the parties submitted proposed findings of fact and conclusions of law. Having reviewed the evidence of record, the arguments of the parties, and relevant case law, for the reasons set forth in these findings of facts and conclusions of law, the Court hereby FINDS for AngioScore in all material respects and AWARDS a remedy accordingly.

Background

The Parties

Since its founding in 2003, AngioScore has designed, manufactured, and marketed specialty angioplasty balloon catheters that are used for the treatment of cardiovascular disease. Its signature product line, sold under the brand name AngioSculpt, consists of an nylon balloon surrounded by a nitinol structure. The AngioSculpt is sold in an array of dimensions and lengths to meet varying patient needs, although the structure of the balloon and cage remain unchanged in all material respects at each available sizing option. The purpose of the AngioSculpt is to treat cardiovascular disease, whereby plaque deposits along a blood vessel's wall, forming what are called lesions. The plaque deposits harden and block, or occlude, blood flow, with potentially severe health risks. The AngioSculpt is used to open occluded or narrowed blood vessels at lesion sites by inflating the balloon to compress the plaque deposits against a vessel wall. As the balloon inflates, the AngioSculpt's nitinol wire cage expands. The expanded cage sits atop the balloon and impresses upon plaque, "scoring it," in an effort designed to "crack" the plaque and open the blood vessel, without injuring or puncturing the vessel wall. It is to this scoring feature that AngioScore owes its name. After use, the device can then deflate, returning to its original form, for removal from the patient's body.

Defendant Eitan Konstantino invented the AngioSculpt. An engineer by training with a doctorate in laser surface treatment, optical design, and materials science, Konstantino was a cofounder, President, and Chief Scientist of AngioScore, Inc. In this role, Konstantino sought to develop and bring the AngioSculpt to market, which involved gaining approval both in Europe and through the United States Food and Drug Administration ("FDA"). To accomplish these goals, Konstantino sought funding from investors, who in turn acquired seats on AngioScore's board of directors. Among those directors were Tom Raffin, a partner with the venture capital firm Telegraph Hill Partners, and Lisa Suennen, a partner at Psilos, another such firm.

In 2005, the board decided that Konstantino would be better suited to a role directed to research and development. Tom Trotter then became AngioScore's chief executive officer. When Trotter assumed the position, he and Konstantino discussed what role was most appropriate for Konstantino moving forward. In light of that conversation, Trotter offered Konstantino the role of Executive Vice President of Research and Development and Chief Scientific Officer.

AngioScore wanted Konstantino to remain on the AngioScore team because of his central role at the company as a co-founder, and his skill as an engineer. Konstantino, however, expressed a desire to leave and work full time as President and CEO of TriReme Medical, Inc., a company he had founded for the purpose of developing bifurcation stents. Accordingly, in the fall of 2005, Trotter started to look for a replacement for Konstantino. Both he and Konstantino interviewed the candidates. At the same time, Konstantino requested that he be given permission to work on a developing technology with TriReme: endovascular bifurcation stents and delivery systems for the same. Although bifurcation stents are not competitive with specialty balloon angioplasty catheters, AngioScore's board took this request seriously, ultimately adopting a resolution that granted Konstantino permission to pursue this limited goal, and waived AngioScore's interest in the bifurcation stent technology.

In late 2006, the role of AngioScore's Vice President of Research and Development transitioned from Konstantino to Feridun Ozdil. While the details remain unclear, the relationship between Konstantino and Ozdil soon became strained and culminated in a physical altercation. Both Konstantino and Ozdil are intelligent scientists, but both are egotistical and authoritarian. The "he said"/"he said" personality conflict was never resolved definitively.

In April 2007, Konstantino's employment with AngioScore terminated, although he remained on its Board of Directors. In his capacity as a board member, he continued to attend AngioScore's board meetings and received updates about AngioScore's financial well-being and the status of its new product development up until he was asked to resign in February 2010.

318 · THE DUTY OF LOYALTY

Chocolate, the Device at Issue

In the fall of 2009, Konstantino and his brother-like friend and colleague, Tanhum Feld, conceived of what was to become "Chocolate" during a telephone "brainstorming" session. Feld was discussing frame ideas for a balloon; Konstantino offered the notion of a balloon surface defined by pillows and grooves. The concept was that a nitinol cage would surround a nylon balloon. As the balloon inflated, it would protrude through the cage. The inflated balloon would then display a pattern of pillows and grooves, exerting force against plaque lining a vessel wall.

With the concept for Chocolate established, Feld undertook to engineer the device, directing and coordinating efforts of TriReme employees with Konstantino's approval. By October 2009, Konstantino applied for a provisional patent application, naming himself and Feld as co-inventors. Within just a few months, Chocolate had progressed from an intellectual concept to physical prototypes. In January 2010, Konstantino and other TriReme employees attended animal testing at Stanford for a Chocolate prototype.

Along with supervising and directing the employees at TriReme in their efforts to develop Chocolate, Konstantino assumed the role of the businessman, conceptualizing the marketing of Chocolate and pitching it to investors under the guise of a corporate entity called "Proteus." During the second half of 2009, Konstantino met with twenty to thirty investors, offering them the opportunity to invest in Chocolate. In these pitches, Konstantino represented that the Chocolate was being developed by "Proteus," and that Chocolate's intellectual property, design, prototypes, business model, team, and partnerships were all completed. With representations of this sort, he secured a grant from the Singapore Economic Development Board and continued to solicit additional investors.

The similarities between AngioSculpt and Chocolate are obvious. Both are specialty angioplasty balloon catheters. Both are comprised of a nylon balloon surrounded by a nitinol structure. Both are used to treat peripheral and coronary artery disease by inflating to open occluded blood vessels. Neither leaves any metal behind in a blood vessel after use, unlike a stent. Both are sold to the same customers and make overlapping marketing claims. Both are sold at premium pricing with roughly identical list prices. Given the similarities between the devices, Konstantino himself identified AngioScore as a partner for the Chocolate opportunity in investor presentations in 2009 and 2010.

Konstantino knew that the devices would compete with one another and contemporaneous documents show that not only did he so intend, but this information was used as part of his investment pitch. In pricing Chocolate, Konstantino and employees at TriReme purposefully priced Chocolate exactly $25 below the list prices for AngioSculpt and targeted the same customers. Communications between Konstantino, Feld, and TriReme employees and officers from late 2009 into 2010 confirm that all those involved with the development of Chocolate—Konstantino, TriReme, and Quattro—were purposefully seeking to compete with the AngioSculpt in the specialty balloon catheter market. This included touting Chocolate for all its competitive advantages, including its potential as a drug-eluting balloon.

While he directed the development of Chocolate as both a medical device and business opportunity, Konstantino nonetheless remained on AngioScore's board of directors. Pursuant thereto, he was privy to all manner of confidential financial information, market information, and competitive information regarding the performance of the AngioSculpt device and AngioScore's highly sensitive risk assessments. He knew that AngioScore was having difficulty developing a 100mm version of its AngioSculpt as of July 2009. And, he knew that the company was interested in pursuing a drug coated specialty balloon. In addition, Konstantino knew that the financial status of AngioScore in late 2009 to early 2010 was relatively strong. AngioScore was in a prime position to raise further capital, had considerable cash reserves, and was in the process of dedicating resources to improving its presence in the specialty balloon catheter market, even though it had just emerged from the expense of an unwarranted investigation. Indeed, AngioScore's December 2009 Monthly Report, distributed for the board meeting, reflected that cash on hand totaled $15.3 million. The report described this figure as an "[o]utstanding result." That AngioScore could have exploited the Chocolate opportunity, had it been offered, is not subject to reasonable dispute.

Notably, in December 2009, Konstantino had a conversation with AngioScore's CEO, Trotter, regarding TriReme's development of a plain old balloon angioplasty ("POBA") device called "Glider." At trial, both Trotter and Konstantino confirmed that this conversation took place. Konstantino told Trotter that TriReme was too small to commercialize the Glider product, and that he was in search of a funder. He offered the Glider to AngioScore for distribution purposes. In his deposition, Konstantino explained that conversation as follows:

> I share[d] with him the specifics of the product, the technical features of this product. I share[d] with him how do we think this product may fit in the marketplace, what we view [are] the features or the advantages of this product. And I offered him to do some sort of collaboration. Specifically we discussed—or I offered two collaborations or two opportunities. I don't mean opportunities in a legal context. One was to distribute these. Told him, Tom, we are a small company. We don't have commercial capabilities. You have that. This is not a product you put in the bag. We don't have commercial capabilities. You do. This is another product you can put in the bag. You can reduce the overhead or the overhead location on sale slips. There are many perceived benefits. And I also talked with him about the what you call the fact, maybe, that AngioSculpt was not a highly deliverable product, at least this is in the perception of physicians who are using the product.

Trotter confirmed that when Konstantino revealed that TriReme had been working on the Glider, he expressed concern that TriReme was venturing into angioplasty balloons at all. Because Konstantino had presented TriReme's Glider as an ordinary

POBA, however, the Glider would not be acutely competitive with AngioSculpt. Notably absent from this conversation was any mention of Chocolate, which had been in development for months, offered to others as a corporate opportunity, and was about to undergo porcine testing.

After sitting through the February 3, 2010 AngioScore board meeting, Konstantino approached Trotter and asked to meet privately. Referencing the December 2009 conversation in which he had offered AngioScore the Glider POBA balloon, Konstantino told Trotter that TriReme was "considering developing a specialty balloon catheter for peripheral indications," and that TriReme had been actively working on "something for the future" in specialty balloon catheters. To say that Konstantino "downplayed" the facts surrounding Chocolate would be an understatement. Konstantino did not inform Trotter that the development of TriReme's specialty balloon, which by that point had been called Chocolate for several months, was well underway. He did not disclose his personal role in the development and conceptualization of the device, nor did he disclose that a prototype had been created, a patent application and been submitted, animal testing had occurred, or that he had already engaged potential investors and funding sources. Trotter was nonetheless shocked by this news. Specialty balloons were AngioScore's focus. He was of the belief that prior to that point, TriReme had been focusing on bifurcation stents and had only recently started to consider POBA devices, and even then, only the Glider POBA. Trotter informed Konstantino that he did not think further discussion was appropriate and asked him to leave.

Immediately following that meeting, Trotter relayed the conversation with Konstantino to members of AngioScore's board. The board expressed a universal belief that Konstantino should resign as soon as possible. If TriReme developed a specialty balloon, Konstantino would have direct a conflict of interest. The board was concerned that TriReme was considering potentially competing with AngioScore. At that point, no one at AngioScore knew that a competitive specialty balloon device had been developed under Konstantino's direction and control.

The next day, Trotter sent Konstantino an email entitled "Board of Directors Position," copying AngioScore's attorney, John Sellers. In it, Trotter restated his concerns about TriReme moving into the specialty balloon market, and stated that the board members with whom he had spoken saw this as a "clear conflict of interest." The "consensus opinion" was that Konstantino "need[ed] to resign from the Board immediately [and] probably should not have participated in yesterday's Board Meeting." Trotter told Konstantino that Sellers would be in touch to make arrangements for his resignation.

Konstantino's response was brief. Again, he did not disclose the existence, or development status of the Chocolate device, nor did he disclose his intimate involvement with the project. Rather, and importantly, he began his campaign of active misdirection. Thus, he responded: "TriReme has not made any decision to make such [a] change and I was giving you very early heads up to *something that may take place in the future, or may never happen*[.]" (emphasis supplied).

On February 4, 2010, John Sellers responded to Konstantino in an email. Sellers informed Konstantino that "e[ ]ven if you are just contemplating ... you have important fiduciary duties [and] ongoing confidentiality obligations." Later that day, the two men spoke on the telephone for five to ten minutes. Sellers again emphasized Konstantino's fiduciary obligations to AngioScore as a director, including that a conflict of interest would exist if TriReme developed a potentially competing technology. They also discussed the logistics of Konstantino's resignation from the Board.

The next day, February 5, 2010, Konstantino replied to Sellers, copying Trotter, Suennen, and Raffin:

> As we discussed, I'm surprised and disappointed that you and the company jumped to the conclusion that I should resign from the board based on assumptions after receiving bits and pieces of information. I am *keenly aware of my obligations* as a board member and this is precisely why I am coming to AngioScore [now]; *before any new project is started.*

AngioScore only learned that Chocolate existed a year and a half later, in the second half of 2011, when a sales representative called the Washington Hospital Center and heard that a presentation had been made on a new device called "Chocolate."

Conclusions of Law

The Corporate Opportunity Doctrine Framework

Under Delaware law, "[t]he elements of misappropriation of corporate opportunity are: (1) the opportunity is within the corporation's line of business; (2) the corporation has an interest or expectancy in the opportunity; (3) the corporation is financially able to exploit the opportunity; and (4) by taking the opportunity for his own, the corporate fiduciary is placed in a position inimical to his duties to the corporation." Once the plaintiff has shown the breach of the director's duty of loyalty, the burden switches to the fiduciary to show that he or she did not seize a corporate opportunity "because either the corporation was presented the opportunity and rejected it, or because the corporation was not in a position to take the opportunity." Delaware courts further recognize that "a director or officer may take a corporate opportunity if: (1) the opportunity is presented to the director or officer in his individual and not his corporate capacity; (2) the opportunity is not essential to the corporation; (3) the corporation holds no interest or expectancy in the opportunity; and (4) the director or officer has not wrongfully employed the resources of the corporation in pursuing or exploiting the opportunity." *Broz,* 673 A.2d at 155

The rule set forth in the Delaware cases accords with economic and public policy, and civic accountability. Put simply, men are not angels. We require structures to govern conduct. *See* FEDERALIST NO. 51. The corporate structure necessarily requires a separation of ownership and control, which produces a conflict: the shareholders are the principle bearers of risk, but the board of directors are vested with the power to make managerial decisions. Centralizing decisionmaking authority in a board of directors presents efficiencies insofar as shareholders can diversify their interests, which, in turn, has contributed to substantial economic growth and development. However, the concentration of decisionmaking power in individuals who do not necessarily bear the risk creates a misalignment of interests. The general purpose of corporate governance principles, specifically, the duties of care and loyalty, is to control for the moral hazards that arise when directors either shirk their responsibilities or self-serve. Without strong corporate governance principles, the trust that underpins a shareholder's decision to invest will dissolve, with broader economic consequences to follow.

Whether a corporate opportunity has been usurped is "a factual question to be decided by reasonable inferences from objective facts." *Guth*, 5 A.2d at 513.

The Corporate Opportunity Doctrine Applies to a Director Who Is Also an Inventor

Throughout this case, defendants have argued that the corporate opportunity doctrine cannot apply where, as here, a director invents a technology, even where such technology is directly competitive with that of the corporation he serves. Defendants maintain that because Chocolate was intellectual property belonging to Konstantino and the product of his own innovation, this necessarily obviates any fiduciary obligation to offer Chocolate to AngioScore. The Court disagrees.

The fact of inventorship does not absolve a director of his fiduciary obligations with respect to inventions he may develop that compete with the corporation he serves. To hold otherwise would work an absurdity. Directors of corporations would be free to invent and develop competing technologies for their own benefit, concealing the same from the companies they serve, even where elements of those inventions would likely benefit the companies. This scenario stands in stark opposition to the foundational principles of corporate governance, which demand that directors exalt the interests of the companies they serve above their own. *Guth*, 5 A.2d at 510 ("the rule ... demands of a corporate officer or director, peremptorily and inexorably, the most scrupulous observance of his duty, not only affirmatively to protect the interests of the corporation committed to his charge, but also to refrain from doing anything that would work injury to the corporation, or to deprive it of profit or advantage which his skill and ability might properly bring to it, or to enable it to make in the reasonable and lawful exercise of its powers."). Most seriously, the extension of defendants' preferred rule would have directors entertain divided loyalty. The position is untenable. *See id.* ("[t]he rule ... demands that there shall be no conflict between duty and self-interest"). The rule makes logical sense. A director can leave the corporation thereby dissolving the duties he owes. A corporation cannot and therefore relies on untarnished fidelity....

At the same time, AngioScore's position is equally untenable. AngioScore posits that by virtue of Konstantino's position as a director, AngioScore had a right to the Chocolate outright, and that therefore Konstantino was obligated to *give* the opportunity to AngioScore. The logical extension of this position demonstrates its implausibility. Were this the case, Konstantino's invention assignment agreement would have been superfluous in the first instance, and so, too, would all invention assignment agreements between directors and the corporations they serve. The Court cannot overlook the effect such a rule would work in the context of intellectual property and emerging technologies. Critically, holding that directors who are also innovators must relinquish to the corporations they serve technologies falling within that corporation's line of business, in which the corporation has an interest or expectancy, or which aligns with its business purpose and objectives, would serve to undermine innovation. Indeed, holding as AngioScore requests would subvert fundamental principles of intellectual property respecting inventors' rights, which are designed to encourage, not discourage, ingenuity and innovation. The fact that this case concerns a medical device, which is currently being used in medical procedures in this country, only serves to underscore the public interest in innovation.

With these positions, the parties posit a tension: do fiduciary duties extend so far as to compromise, potentially fatally, innovation; or, by contrast, does a director's ingenuity and innovation provide an escape route from his fiduciary duties? Neither extreme prevails. A court must apply the principles of the law in such a way that balances the wise public policy behind the *Guth* rule, with the public policy counseling in favor of innovation. For this reason, the Court finds that although AngioScore was owed fiduciary duties by Konstantino, those duties did not entitle AngioScore to outright ownership of the Chocolate opportunity at any point in time. Rather, what Konstantino's fiduciary duty demanded was that he offer AngioScore the *opportunity to acquire* the rights to the Chocolate. The Court need not venture as to specifics of such a transaction, but having chosen to remain on AngioScore's board, the offering must occur to satisfy both the law of fiduciary duties and the public interest in innovation. Offering an opportunity to AngioScore meets Delaware's demand that directors not undertake any activity that would work harm to the corporation they serve and prioritize the interests of those corporations above their own. It also accords with directors' duty not to "do anything" that would "deprive" the corporations they serve "of profit or advantage which [their] skill and ability might properly bring to it." *Guth*, 5 A.2d at 510. And, it remains faithful to the general principle that a director can establish conclusively no breach of his fiduciary duty where, in keeping the interests of the corporation he serves first in mind, the corporation is presented the opportunity and rejects it. By ensuring that transparency and good faith predominate, the application of the rule in this manner assures that any conflict will be resolvable.

Application of the Corporate Opportunity Doctrine

Longstanding law requires that certain "opportunities" be offered to the corporation. The definition of an "opportunity" is "a favorable juncture of circumstances" or "a good chance for advancement or progress." Merriam-Webster, *New Collegiate Dictionary* (9th ed. 1988). The evidence adduced in this case establishes conclusively that as of the date Konstantino resigned from AngioScore's board of directors, Chocolate was a concrete business opportunity. By that point, Chocolate had developed from a mere idea into a concrete opportunity. It had been in development for approximately five months. The initial "brainstorming" discussions in the second half of 2009 had resulted in the creation of many engineering design models, followed by physical models and prototypes. By January of 2010, the Chocolate design was so complete that prototypes were suitable for testing, and in fact, was the subject of a porcine study at Stanford, which TriReme employees and Konstantino attended.

Not only was Chocolate sufficiently developed to enable testing, development of Chocolate had advanced to the point that Konstantino felt it appropriate to market it as an opportunity for investors.

If the Chocolate opportunity was sufficiently concrete for twenty to thirty investors, it was sufficiently developed to be offered to AngioScore. The Court so finds.

* * *

An opportunity is within a corporation's line of business if it is "an activity as to which [the corporation] has fundamental knowledge, practical experience and ability to pursue, which, logically and naturally, is adaptable to its business having regard for its financial position, and is one that is consonant with its reasonable needs and aspirations for expansion." This factor is to be broadly construed.

The Court finds that Chocolate falls within AngioScore's line of business. Since its founding in 2003, AngioScore has designed, manufactured, and marketed angioplasty balloon catheters surrounded by a nitinol structure that are used for the treatment of cardiovascular disease and sold under the brand name AngioSculpt. The evidence demonstrates conclusively that AngioSculpt and Chocolate are similar in both purpose and function.

Under Delaware law, the "line of business" element is to be broadly construed. The Court finds it met here. The similarities in terms of purpose and function establish that AngioScore had "fundamental knowledge and practical experience" to pursue Chocolate. That AngioScore has historically focused on products that "scored" plaque is of no moment, for the devices are materially similar and their differences amount to variations on a common theme. Further, given the overlapping features and design, AngioScore's manufacturing and distribution process could have easily been modified to accommodate Chocolate. All of Chocolate's component parts were essentially the same as those of the AngioSculpt.

Based on the above findings, the conclusion is inescapable that Chocolate is "logically and naturally ... adapt[ed] to [AngioScore's] business."

* * *

"[F]or a corporation to have an expectant interest in any specific property, there must be some tie between the property and the nature of the corporate business." By requiring a tie to the 'nature of the corporate business,' this factor "implicates many of the issues" discussed above concerning AngioScore's line of business. Even if there is a "tie" between the line of a corporation's business and the potential opportunity, however, the Court may decline to find an interest or expectancy where facts establish that a corporation is shifting away from its historical line of business, where it disavows such interest, and where it lacks the capacity to capitalize on the interest. In *Broz*, for example, the Delaware Supreme Court found that there was no interest or expectancy where a corporation was divesting in the area of venture from which the potential opportunity arose, and where its business plan did not contemplate any new acquisitions.

Broz, 673 A.2d at 156. The inquiry requires a court to use its judgment to discern whether, given the factual context of each particular case, the corporation had an interest, "*actual or in expectancy,*" or whether the acquisition of property for a director's own use "may hinder or defeat the plans and purposes of the corporation in the carrying on or development of the legitimate business for which it was created."

As detailed in the preceding discussion, the Court finds that "some tie" exists between Chocolate and the nature of AngioScore's business. The devices are both angioplasty balloon catheters that serve similar purposes and are constructed from the same materials. Well beyond the loose connection that the "some tie" standard evokes, however, the Court finds that in 2009 and early 2010, AngioScore had an actual and expectancy interest in Chocolate by virtue of its then-existing needs and business purposes, as well as Chocolate's unique features and potential benefits to AngioScore. The Court so finds for three main reasons: (1) Chocolate's design configuration could have proven helpful, and at a minimum, would have been seriously considered in solving AngioScore's then-existing problem with creating AngioSculpt devices at 100mm lengths; (2) Chocolate's potential as a drug-eluting specialty balloon technology was in keeping with AngioScore's business goal to bring such a device to market; and (3) AngioScore had an interest in keeping a direct competitor out of the relatively small specialty balloon market. Collectively, these conclusions compel a finding that AngioScore had an interest and expectancy in Chocolate as of, at the latest, the date Konstantino resigned from its board.

Accordingly, the Court finds that AngioScore had an interest and expectancy in the Chocolate opportunity.

AngioScore Had the Financial Capacity to Exploit the Chocolate Opportunity

The Court finds that AngioScore had the financial ability to exploit Chocolate. In so finding, the Court is mindful that under Delaware law, this prong implicates broader policy concerns more favorable to the corporation. Such concerns stem from the inherent conflict between, on the one hand, a director who has control and responsibility for the financial security of the corporation he serves, and on the other hand, the director's potential personal interest in ensuring that the company not have secured financial footing so as to permit usurpation of what otherwise might be a corporate opportunity. Thus, once the plaintiff has made such a *prima facie* showing of financial ability, a fiduciary "faces a significant burden in establishing that a corporation was financially unable to take advantage of a corporate opportunity." Defendants have not established AngioScore's inability to capitalize on the Chocolate opportunity. To the contrary, AngioScore has established that it could have capitalized on Chocolate had Konstantino offered the opportunity.

Evidence regarding what it would have cost to develop Chocolate varies, but in all events, reflects an initial amount that fell *below* the amount of cash AngioScore had on hand at the end of 2009 and beginning of 2010. According to an email from November 17, 2009, Konstantino estimated capital requirement of approximately $3 million. By May 2010, Konstantino had secured sufficient capital to pursue the Chocolate "all the way to first commercial sale"; the total raised to that point was $4.5 to 5 million. Finally, with respect to the amount of money required to acquire an assignment of the intellectual property rights to Chocolate, the record places that value in the amount of $370,000 cash and a royalty of 5%. In the event such right was acquired, however, there is nothing to suggest that AngioScore would have been obligated to develop Chocolate.

Based on the above figures, even assuming that Chocolate would have cost $5 million to develop, the Court finds that AngioScore was able to exploit this opportunity through several avenues. First, AngioScore had approximately $17 million cash on hand in October 2009, and in excess of $15 million cash on hand at the end of 2009. Second, as a going concern with existing relationships, AngioScore could have obtained funds from external investors, such as Oxford Finance, or other venture capital funds. In December 2009, for example, Oxford Capital expressed a willingness to lend between $10 and $20 million to AngioScore. Third, AngioScore could have redirected research and development money it was currently using to fix the design problems for its 100mm AngioSculpt product. This financial position existed notwithstanding the downsizing and resources expended in response to a Department of Justice investigation.

The practicalities of new technology companies further support the Court's conclusion. Konstantino himself admitted that startup companies in Silicon Valley, such as AngioScore and TriReme, are frequently short on cash and face the prospect of running out of money. He further stated that the fact that such a company is not "profitable" doesn't mean that the company is "not successful." For example, TriReme was not able to sell its Antares product, a stent, in the United States, and Antares made only negligible sales abroad. Despite TriReme's limited financial position, TriReme was able to develop Chocolate.

Based on the foregoing, the Court finds that AngioScore was able to exploit the Chocolate opportunity. Despite having been privy to AngioScore's confidential financial documents as a member of AngioScore's board of directors, Konstantino never broached the subject of Chocolate with AngioScore.

By Taking the Chocolate for Himself, Konstantino Placed Himself in a Position Inimical to his Fiduciary Duties to AngioScore.

The result of the above findings compels the conclusion that by taking the Chocolate opportunity for himself and companies he preferred, to the exclusion of AngioScore, Konstantino placed himself in a "position inimicable to his duties to the corporation." *Broz*, 673 A.2d at 155. In essence, he became a competitor to AngioScore. It is axiomatic that as such, absent some knowing waiver by AngioScore, Konstantino could never fulfill his duty of loyalty to AngioScore. Any financial gain Konstantino enjoyed stemmed from Chocolate's success in the limited specialty balloon market, in which AngioScore is a key player. Indeed, while sitting on AngioScore's board, Konstantino participated in a strategy where, by design, Chocolate would compete with AngioScore. Chocolate's price was explicitly tied to AngioSculpt pricing, *i.e. exactly* $25 less than AngioScore's products. That Chocolate was priced just below the AngioSculpt was intended to "drive rapid adoption" and "get faster uptick" in the specialty balloon catheter market. Moreover, Konstantino himself extolled the advantages of Chocolate compared to scoring balloons, including AngioScore's devices, as he sought to secure funding for Chocolate.

This factor is therefore met, as is each element of AngioScore's breach of fiduciary duty claim.

Remedy

Legal Framework

The law abhors one who betrays his or her fiduciary duty. Thus, "[i]f an officer or director of a corporation, in violation of his duty as such, acquires gain or advantage for himself, the law charges the interest so acquired with a trust for the benefit of the corporation, at its election, while it denies to the betrayer all benefit and profit." *Guth*, 5 A.2d at 510. The bounds of this rule are considerable, for it rests upon the "broader foundation of a wise public policy that, for the purpose of *removing all temptation*, *extinguishes all possibility* of profit flowing from a breach of the confidence imposed by the fiduciary relation. Given the relation between the parties, a certain result follows; and a constructive trust is the remedial device through which precedence of self is compelled to give way to the stern demands of loyalty." Where a plaintiff has proved that its interests have been subverted by a disloyal fiduciary, "the corporation may elect to claim all of the benefits of the transaction for itself, and the law will impress a trust in favor of the corporation upon the property, interests and profits so acquired."

While it is true that damages flowing from a breach of fiduciary duty are to be liberally calculated, the Delaware Supreme Court has held that where certain claimed damages were not proximately caused by the breach, those damages were not recoverable. Thus, causation remains a consideration for damages even in the context of fiduciary duty breaches.

Defense of Causation

Defendants have argued throughout this case that AngioScore has failed to prove that defendants' behavior caused harm to AngioScore either because (i) the devices do not compete, or (ii) Feld had an independent right to develop Chocolate. The Court is unpersuaded.

First, Chocolate and AngioSculpt compete. More than sufficient evidence exists in the record to support a finding that Chocolate's presence in the market has harmed AngioScore.

Defendants' second argument is that due to Feld's independent right to assign his interest in Chocolate, defendants enjoyed an independent right to develop Chocolate. Thus, they reason that AngioScore cannot demonstrate that their actions caused AngioScore's harm, and that AngioScore cannot establish that had the opportunity been offered by Konstantino, it would have been able to acquire an exclusive right to Chocolate. The Court rejects this conclusion as contrary to the facts of record and reasonable inferences therefrom.

Remedy Awarded

Konstantino may retain no benefit he received as a result of his breach.

Under *Guth,* the remedies available in a breach of duty case are designed to "den[y] to the betrayer all benefit and profit." *Guth,* 5 A.2d at 510. AngioScore has proved that its interests have been subverted by a disloyal fiduciary, and may now "elect to claim all of the benefits of the transaction for itself."

Accordingly, Konstantino may retain no benefit of his breach. The result, while potentially viewed as harsh, is designed to deter such conduct from occurring in the first place. It differs from contractual remedies and does more than return AngioScore to the position that it would have been in had the breach never occurred. It serves to deter future transgressions.

The Court awards AngioScore its past and future lost profits as the most appropriate equitable remedy.

In light of the fact that the underlying claim is equitable in nature, the Court has broad discretion to address inequity. Beyond the disgorgement of benefits Konstantino personally received as a result of his breach, the Court finds it appropriate, given the totality of the circumstances, to fashion a remedy in order that defendants may be deterred from future breaches and to compensate AngioScore, as "the beneficiary must not be harmed by such conduct."

As set forth above, AngioScore has proved that Chocolate's market presence has cost it market share and resulted in lower profits; the causation element is satisfied. But it must be noted that the harms resulting from defendants' wrongdoing are difficult to quantify, especially given the industry and the infancy of Chocolate. The Court, "fortunately, has broad discretion to tailor remedies to suit the situation as it exists."

The Court finds that AngioScore's calculated lost profits, reflective of both its harm to this point and into the future, is sufficiently well-established to remedy AngioScore's harm, and represents an appropriate degree of opprobrium for defendants' wrongful behavior. Thus, the Court awards AngioScore (i) its current lost profits of $2.97 million, representing the profits it would have generated had business not been diverted to defendants, and (ii) its future lost profits where, as here, the Court declines to issue an injunction and permits Chocolate to stay on the market. That value is $17.064 million, representing AngioScore's lost profits on future sales from 2014 through the second quarter of 2019.

Conclusion

In summary, the Court finds that Konstantino not only breached his fiduciary duties, he actively hid his transgressions to avoid detection. As a result, he exploited the Chocolate opportunity for his own gain rather than providing the opportunity to AngioScore, as he was duty bound to do. While such a duty would not have existed had he resigned before Chocolate became an opportunity, Konstantino's breach resulted in measurable harm to AngioScore.

A director's duty to the corporation he serves cannot be ignored under the mantra of innovation. Should a director walk that path, the innovation must be offered, the conduct transparent, and the fidelity to one's duty paramount. While conflicts between the desire to innovate and the obligations of board membership may arise, a director always has the option to resign. Here, Konstantino did neither, and thus, a remedy must be awarded to address the breach.

Accordingly, the Court **ORDERS** the following measures of damages:

1. Konstantino shall disgorge the benefits he obtained by way of his breach; and

2. Defendants are liable for AngioScore's past and future lost profits, totaling $2.97 million and $17.064 million, respectively, for a total of $20.034 million....

Comments and Questions

1. Why did the court decide that, at least in this case, fiduciary duties trump innovation rights? How does the court know that general policies encouraging innovation must yield to Kostantino's duties as a member of the board of directors?

2. AngioScore's board of directors specifically disclaimed an interest in bifurcation stents when Kostantino requested, and the board approved, permission for him to start a new company, TriReme. Why wasn't that disclaimer, made pursuant to Del. Gen. Corp. L. § 122(17), effective to protect Kostantino from liability in this case?

3. Insofar as the court held that Chocolate was a corporate opportunity, why did the court reject AngioScore's claim that it owned the rights to the technology?

Review and approval by independent directors serves as a substitute for external regulation, particularly with respect to certain transactions. Pay close attention while reading the following case to the court's treatment of the various fiduciary claims and the pleading requirements and defenses applicable to each challenge to the same transaction.

Orman v. Cullman

Delaware Chancery Court
794 A.2d 5 (2002)

CHANDLER, CHANCELLOR:

This purported class action involves alleged breaches of fiduciary duty in connection with the cash-out merger of the public shareholders ("Unaffiliated Shareholders" or "Public Shareholders") of General Cigar Holdings, Inc. ("General Cigar" or the "Company"). According to the complaint, plaintiff Joseph Orman, is and was the owner of General Cigar Class A common stock at all times relevant to this litigation. Orman brings this suit on behalf of himself and the Public Shareholders of General Cigar Class A common stock against General Cigar and its eleven-member board of directors.

On January 19, 2000 the Board unanimously approved a merger agreement pursuant to which a subsidiary of an unaffiliated third party, Swedish Match AB, would purchase the shares owned by the Unaffiliated Shareholders of General Cigar. On April 10, 2000 the Company filed with the Securities and Exchange Commission an amended proxy statement relating to this proposed merger.

The complaint first alleges breaches of fiduciary duty with respect to the Board's approval of (and the fairness of) the proposed merger. Orman contends that Board approval of the merger was ineffective and improper because a majority of the defendant directors was not independent and/or disinterested. He further alleges that the defendant directors violated their fiduciary duty of loyalty by entering into a transaction that was unfair to the Public Shareholders of General Cigar and usurped for themselves corporate opportunities rightfully belonging to all General Cigar shareholders.

Orman also asserts that the Board breached its duty of disclosure. Specifically, he alleges that the Proxy Statement soliciting shareholder approval of the proposed merger omitted material facts necessary for the Public Shareholders to make a fully informed decision with regard to their vote for or against the merger.

The defendants moved pursuant to Court of Chancery Rule 12(b)(6) to dismiss the complaint on the grounds that: 1) Orman failed to plead facts sufficient to overcome the presumption of the business judgment rule with respect to the Board's approval of the merger transaction; 2) the merger was ratified by a fully informed majority vote of the Public Shareholders of General Cigar; and 3) Orman failed to plead cognizable disclosure claims. Moreover, even if Orman had successfully pled cognizable disclosure claims (defendants argue), any possible liability arising from those claims is barred by an exculpatory provision in the Company's certificate of incorporation, adopted pursuant to § 102(b)(7) of the Delaware General Corporation Law, because only a duty of care violation is implicated by those disclosure claims.

I conclude that the defendants' motion to dismiss must be granted in part and denied in part. The motion to dismiss the duty of loyalty claims must be denied, as Orman has pled facts from which is it reasonable to question the independence and disinterest of a majority of the General Cigar Board. The motion to dismiss Orman's disclosure claims is granted as to all but one claim which, at this stage of the litigation, I cannot say is immaterial as a matter of law. Because I conclude that one of Orman's disclosure claims must survive as a matter of law, I am unable to find that any possible breaches of fiduciary duty in connection with the challenged transaction were ratified by a fully informed vote of a majority of the Company's disinterested shareholders. Finally, as I conclude that the complaint does not unambiguously state only a duty of care claim, it would be premature for me to consider the effect of the Company's exculpatory charter provision.

FACTUAL HISTORY

General Cigar, a Delaware Corporation with its principal executive offices located in New York, New York, is a leading manufacturer and marketer of premium cigars. The Company has exclusive trademark rights to many well-known brands of cigars, including seven of the top ten brands that were previously manufactured in Cuba.

The Company went public in an initial public offering ("IPO") of 6.9 million shares of Class A stock at $18.00 per share on February 28, 1997. As of March 30, 2000, the Company had approximately 13.6 million shares of Class A and 13.4 million shares of Class B common stock outstanding. Class A stock was publicly traded and Class B stock was not publicly traded. Class A stock had one vote per share and Class B had ten votes per share. Even though Class B shares had ten times the voting power of Class A shares, the Company's Certificate of Incorporation required equal consideration in exchange for Class A and Class B shares in the event of a sale or merger. At the time of the proposed merger, the Cullman Group owned approximately 162 shares of Class A and 9.9 million shares of Class B. Although this aggregated to approximately 37% of the Company's total outstanding stock, the Cullman Group had voting control over the Company because the 9.9 million Class B shares it owned represented approximately 74% of that class, which enjoyed a 10:1 voting advantage over Class A shares. The Cullman Group's equity interest, therefore, gave it approximately 67% of the voting power in the corporation.

In the early fall of 1999, Swedish Match approached certain members of the Cullman Group (the "Cullmans") about purchasing the interest in General Cigar owned by its Public Shareholders. This was seen to be a logical business combination because General Cigar had a strong presence in the United States premium cigar market and Swedish Match had strength in the international cigar and smokeless tobacco markets through its established network of international contacts and resources. At a November 4, 1999 General Cigar board meeting, the Cullmans informed the Board of Swedish Match's interest. The Board then authorized the Cullmans to pursue discussions with Swedish Match assisted by defendant director Solomon's financial advising firm, Peter J. Solomon & Company ("PJSC").

Negotiations between the Cullmans and Swedish Match continued during November and December 1999. By the end of December 1999 the structure for a proposed transaction had been determined. That structure included: 1) a sale by the Cullman Group of approximately one-third of its equity interest in the Company to Swedish Match at $15.00 per share; 2) immediately following the Cullman Group's private sale, a merger in which all shares in the Company held by the Unaffiliated Shareholders would be purchased for $15.00 per share; 3) Cullman Sr. and Cullman Jr. maintaining their respective positions as Chairman and President/Chief Executive Officer of the surviving company and having the power to appoint a majority of the board; 4) three years after the merger, the Cullman Group having the power to put its remaining equity interest to the Company and the Company having the power to call such interest; and 5) an agreement by the Cullman Group that should the proposed transaction with Swedish Match not close, it would vote against any other business combination for a period of one year following the termination of the proposed transaction.

Once the negotiations reached agreement on the above points, the Board created a special committee (the "Special Committee"), consisting of outside defendant directors Lufkin, Israel, and Vincent, to determine the advisability of entering into the proposed transaction. The Special Committee retained independent legal and financial advisors—Wachtell, Lipton, Rosen & Katz and Deutsche Bank Securities, Inc., respectively—to assist them in this endeavor. In early January 2000 the Special Committee received copies of the proposed agreements previously reached between the Cullmans and Swedish Match. After a review of these proposals by the Special Committee and its legal and financial advisors, the Special Committee directly negotiated with Swedish Match over the terms of the agreement. The substantive changes in the terms of the transaction resulting from negotiations by the Special Committee appear to be that the amount of consideration to be received by the Unaffiliated Shareholders for each of their Class A shares increased from $15.00 to $15.25 and the length of time the Cullman Group would not vote in favor of another business combination if the challenged merger failed to close increased from twelve to eighteen months. On January 19, 2000 the Special Committee unanimously recommended approval of the transaction as modified as a result of their negotiations. That same day, the General Cigar Board unanimously approved the transaction.

The relevant terms of the final transaction recommended to the Company's shareholders, and subject to approval of the Unaffiliated Shareholders, included an initial private sale by the Cullman Group of 3.5 million shares of its Class B stock, representing about one-third of its General Cigar equity interest, to Swedish Match for $15.00 per share. The Cullman Group was to retain its remaining equity interest, which would then consist of approximately 162 Class A shares and 6.4 million Class B shares. Following the merger, that remaining interest would aggregate to approximately 36% of the total outstanding equity interest in the Company. Immediately following this private sale, a merger would take place in which all publicly owned Class A and Class B shares (those not owned by the Cullman Group) would be purchased for $15.25 per share.

In addition to the Cullman Group's continuing equity position and voting control in the surviving company, several provisions of the proposed transaction assured ongoing participation of the Cullman Group in the day-to-day operations of that company. Cullman Sr. would retain his position as Chairman of the Board of the surviving company and Cullman Jr. would continue to serve as President and CEO of the surviving company. The Cullman Group would have the power to appoint a majority of the board of the surviving company after the merger.

Additionally, beginning three years from the date of the merger, the Cullman Group would have the option to put some or all of its remaining equity interest to the surviving company and the surviving company would have a reciprocal right to call some or all of the company's stock retained by the Cullman Group. The Cullman Group also agreed to vote against any proposed merger transaction for eighteen months should the transaction with Swedish Match not be consummated.

Finally, the transaction was structured in such a way that the Cullman Group could not dictate its approval. Despite the fact that the Cullman Group possessed voting control over the Company both before and after the proposed transaction, approval of the merger required that a majority of the Unaffiliated Shareholders of Class A stock, voting separately as a class, vote in favor of the transaction.

ANALYSIS

Fiduciary Duty Claims

Orman alleges that the Board's approval of the Company's merger with Swedish Match was ineffective and improper because a majority of the Board was not disinterested and independent and that the directors breached their duty of loyalty by approving a transaction that was unfair to the public shareholders. Orman asserts that he has pled facts sufficient to rebut the presumption of the business judgment rule and that this Court should employ an "entire fairness" analysis. He contends that a determination that entire fairness is the appropriate standard would preclude dismissal at this stage of the litigation regardless of upon whom the Court ultimately were to place the burden of proving, or disproving, the transaction's entire fairness. The defendants contend that these claims must be dismissed because Orman has not pled facts sufficient to overcome the business judgment rule presumption and in such a case the actions of a board should be respected.

"A cardinal precept of the General Corporation Law of the State of Delaware is that directors, rather than shareholders, manage the business and affairs of the corporation." The business judgment rule is a recognition of that statutory precept. The rule "is a presumption that in making a business decision the directors of a corporation acted on an informed basis, in good faith and in the honest belief that the action taken was in the best interests of the company." Therefore, the judgment of a properly functioning board will not be second-guessed and "[a]bsent an abuse of discretion, that judgment will be respected by the courts." Because a board is presumed to have acted properly, "[t]he burden is on the party challenging the decision to establish facts rebutting the presumption."

As a general matter, the business judgment rule presumption that a board acted loyally can be rebutted by alleging facts which, if accepted as true, establish that the *board* was either interested in the outcome of the transaction or lacked the independence to consider objectively whether the transaction was in the best interest of its company and all of its shareholders. To establish that a *board* was interested or lacked independence, a plaintiff must allege facts as to the interest and lack of independence of the *individual members* of that board. To rebut successfully business judgment presumptions in this manner, thereby leading to the application of the entire fairness standard, a plaintiff must normally plead facts demonstrating "that a *majority* of the director defendants have a financial interest in the transaction or were dominated or controlled by a materially interested director." I recognize situations can exist when the material interest of a number of directors *less* than a majority may rebut the business judgment presumption and lead to an entire fairness review. That is when an "'interested director *fail[ed] to disclose his interest* in the transaction to the board *and* a reasonable board member would have regarded the existence of the material interest as a significant fact in the evaluation of the proposed transaction.'" Nevertheless, in this case the interest that may be attributed to the Cullman Group or other Board members *was* disclosed to the Board and, therefore, Orman still must establish that a majority of the Board was interested and/or lacked independence.

If a plaintiff alleging a duty of loyalty breach is unable to plead facts demonstrating that a majority of a board that approved the transaction in dispute was interested and/or lacked independence, the entire fairness standard of review is not applied and the Court respects the business judgment of the board. Whether a particular director is disinterested or independent is a recurring theme in Delaware's corporate jurisprudence. We reach conclusions as to the sufficiency of allegations regarding interest and independence only after considering all the facts alleged on a case-by-case basis.

The *Aronson* Court set forth the meaning of "interest" and "independence" in this context. It defined interest as "mean [ing] that directors can neither appear on both sides of a transaction nor expect to derive any personal financial benefit from it in the sense of self-dealing, as opposed to a benefit which devolves upon the corporation or all stockholders generally." This definition was further refined in *Rales v. Blasband* when our Supreme Court recognized that "[d]irectoral interest also exists where a corporate decision will have a materially detrimental impact on a director, but not on the corporation and the stockholders." It should be noted, however, that in the absence of self-dealing, it is not enough to establish the interest of a director by alleging that he received *any* benefit not equally shared by the stockholders. Such benefit must be alleged to be *material* to that director. Materiality means that the alleged benefit was significant enough "*in the context of the director's economic circumstances,* as to have made it improbable that the director could perform her fiduciary duties to the ... shareholders without being influenced by her overriding personal interest."

On the separate question of independence, the *Aronson* Court stated that "[i]ndependence means that a director's decision is based on the corporate merits of the subject before the board rather than extraneous considerations or influences." Such extraneous considerations or influences may exist when the challenged director is controlled by another. To raise a question concerning the independence of a particular board member, a plaintiff asserting the "control of one or more directors must allege particularized facts manifesting 'a direction of corporate conduct in such a way as to comport with the wishes or interests of the corporation (or persons) doing the controlling.' The shorthand shibboleth of 'dominated and controlled directors' is insufficient." This lack of independence can be shown when a plaintiff pleads facts that establish "that the directors are 'beholden' to [the controlling person] or so under their influence that their discretion would be sterilized."

In determining the sufficiency of factual allegations made by a plaintiff as to either a director's interest or lack of independence, the Delaware Supreme Court has rejected an objective "reasonable director" test and instead requires the application of a subjective "actual person" standard to determine whether a *particular* director's interest is material and debilitating or that he lacks independence because he is controlled by another.

General Cigar had an eleven-member board. In order to rebut the presumptions of the business judgment rule, Orman must allege facts that would support a finding of interest or lack of independence for a majority, or at least six, of the Board members. Orman asserts, and defendants appear to concede, that the four members of the Cullman Group were interested because they received benefits from the transaction that were not shared with the rest of the shareholders. Orman, therefore, would have to plead facts making it reasonable to question the interest or independence of two of the remaining seven Board members to avoid dismissal based on the business judgment rule presumption. With varying levels of confidence, Orman's complaint alleges that each of the seven remaining Board members—Israel, Vincent, Lufkin, Barnet, Sherren, Bernbach, and Solomon—were interested and/or lacked independence.

Directors Israel and Vincent

Perhaps the weakest allegations of interest and/or lack of independence are aimed at directors Israel and Vincent, who were both members of the Special Committee that investigated the advisability of the merger and negotiated with Swedish Match. The complaint states that these two defendants "had longstanding business relations with members of the Cullman Group which impeded and impaired their ability to function independently and outside the influence of the Cullman Group." The only fact pled in support of this assertion is the mere recitation that Israel and Vincent had served as directors of General Cigar since 1989 and 1992, respectively. In his brief opposing defendants' motion to dismiss, Orman apparently concedes that Israel and Vincent are independent by omitting these two directors from his contention that, in addition to the Cullman Group, "[p]laintiff has sufficiently pled that Sherren, Bernbach, Solomon and Lufkin also suffer disabling conflicts of interest and lack of independence in connection with the transaction."

At this stage of the litigation, however, the Court must address itself to the allegations contained in the complaint. To make clear my opinion as to the independence of directors Israel and Vincent, therefore, I conclude that the allegations in the complaint with regard to the lack of independence of these two directors fail as a matter of law. The naked assertion of a previous business relationship is not enough to overcome the presumption of a director's independence.

Director Lufkin

Orman asserts that director Lufkin, who was the third member of the Special Committee, lacked independence and was also interested in the merger transaction. With regard to Lufkin's purported lack of independence, Orman makes the same allegations as were directed at Israel and Vincent, namely, Lufkin "had longstanding business relations with members of the Cullman Group which impeded and impaired [his] ability to function independently and outside the influence of the Cullman Group. Defendant Lufkin had been a Board member of General Cigar or its predecessor since 1976." For the reasons stated above, such bare allegation fails as a matter of law to assert a lack of independence on the part of director Lufkin.

Director Barnet

The *only* fact alleged in support of Orman's allegation of director Barnet's interest is that he "has an interest in the transaction since he will become a director of the surviving company." No case has been cited to me, and I have found none, in which a director was found to have a financial interest *solely* because he will be a director in the surviving corporation. To the contrary, our case law has held that such an interest is not a disqualifying interest. Even if I were to infer that Orman was alleging that the fees Barnet was to receive as a director with the surviving company created a disabling interest, without more, that assertion would also fail. Because Orman alleges no facts in addition to the assertion of continued board membership on the part of Barnett, his assertion of interest fails as a matter of law.

Director Bernbach

Orman alleges that director Bernbach was both interested in the merger and lacked the independence to make an impartial decision regarding that transaction because he has "a written agreement with the Company to provide consulting services [and that] [i]n 1998 ... Bernbach was paid $75,000 for such services ... and additional funds since that date." Orman further asserts that the Proxy Statement did not reveal the existence of the consulting contract, which was executed in 1997, or "that that the surviving company inherits the Company's contractual obligations to Defendant Bernbach." Contrary to defendants' assertion that Orman has failed to plead any continuing obligation on the part of General Cigar to Bernbach, his complaint clearly states such a continuing obligation.

Orman asserts that Bernbach has a written consulting contract with General Cigar, and that he had received, and continued to receive, payments under this contract. He further alleges that the surviving company will be obligated to uphold the contracts of the existing company. Such well-pleaded facts, accepted as true on a motion to dismiss, plainly allege a continuing obligation. Unfortunately for Orman, however, this clearly stated allegation is fatal to his assertion that Bernbach was interested in the transaction. As this Court has stated previously, "a director is considered interested when he will receive a personal financial benefit *from a transaction* that is not equally shared by the stockholders." Accepting Orman's allegations as true reveals that Bernbach does not meet this definition of "interest." Bernbach had a contract with General Cigar. If the merger were consummated, he would have a contract that the surviving company would be obligated to honor. If the merger were not consummated he would still have his contract with the existing General Cigar that it would be obligated to honor. Therefore, director Bernbach would have received no benefit *from the transaction* being challenged that was not shared by the other General Cigar shareholders. As a result of the merger, shareholder Bernbach would be cashed out and receive the same consideration for his General Cigar stock as the rest of the Unaffiliated Shareholders. Since he was to receive the same benefit as the Company's other shareholders, his interest in getting as high a price as possible for the Company's stock from the merger transaction was aligned with the Unaffiliated Shareholders. Orman's complaint, therefore, fails to plead adequately that director Bernbach was interested in the merger.

This conclusion obviates the need to examine, for the purpose of determining whether a disabling interest existed, the defendants' further assertion that even if some interest were sufficiently alleged, Orman failed to plead the materiality of that contract to Bernbach.

Orman also argues that Bernbach's consulting agreement suggests a lack of independence. At this stage of the litigation, the facts supporting this allegation are sufficient to raise a reasonable inference that director Bernbach was controlled by the Cullman Group because he was beholden to the controlling shareholders for future renewals of his consulting contract. In addition to the facts specifically set forth in the complaint, the Proxy Statement reveals that, at the time of the challenged transaction, Bernbach's principal occupation was "Chairman and Chief Executive officer of the Bernbach Group, Inc." Accepting as true all the well-pled allegations and the inferences reasonably drawn therefrom in this case, I believe it is reasonable to question the objectivity of a director who has a consulting contract with his company and will continue to have a consulting contract with the surviving company. This is particularly true when, regardless of whether the merger is approved or not, the challenged director is beholden to the identical group of controlling shareholders favoring the challenged transaction. The Cullman Group would continue to be in a position to determine whether particular contracts are to be renewed as well as the extent to which the company will make use of the consulting services already under contract. Even though there is no bright-line dollar amount at which consulting fees received by a director become material, at the motion to dismiss stage and on the facts before me, I think it is reasonable to infer that $75,000 would be material to director Bernbach and that he is beholden to the Cullman Group for continued receipt of such fees. Although not determinative, the inference of materiality is strengthened when the allegedly disabling fee is paid for the precise services that comprise the principal occupation of the challenged director.

Director Solomon

Orman alleges that "Defendant Solomon has an interest in the transaction since his company, PJSC, stands to reap fees of $3.3 million if the transaction is effectuated." The reasonable inference that can be drawn from this contention is that if the merger is consummated PJSC will receive $3.3 million. If the merger is not consummated PJSC will not receive $3.3 million. PJSC, therefore, has an interest in the transaction. Because director Solomon's principal occupation is that of "Chairman of Peter J. Solomon Company Limited and Peter J. Solomon Securities Company Limited," it is reasonable to assume that director Solomon would personally benefit from the $3.3 million *his* company would receive if the challenged transaction closed. I think it would be naïve to say, as a matter of law, that $3.3 million is immaterial. In my opinion, therefore, it is reasonable to infer that director Solomon suffered a disabling interest when considering how to cast his vote in connection with the challenged merger when the Board's decision on that matter could determine whether or not his firm would receive $3.3 million.

Directors Bernbach and Solomon, at this stage, cannot be considered independent and disinterested. Orman has thus pled facts that make it reasonable to question the independence and/or disinterest of a majority of the General Cigar Board—the four Cullman Group directors, plus Bernbach and Solomon, or six out of the eleven directors. Accordingly, I cannot say, as a matter of law, that the General Cigar Board's actions are protected by the business judgment rule presumption. Defendants' motion to dismiss the fiduciary duty claims—based as it is on a conclusion that the challenged transaction was approved by a disinterested and independent board—must be denied.

Reaching this decision with regard to the loyalty of the Board that approved the merger, however, does not rebut the business judgment presumption at this stage of the litigation. It merely means that the business judgment presumption may not be used as the basis to dismiss Orman's fiduciary duty claims for failure to state a cognizable claim.

Comments and Questions

1. What is the substantive result of Chancellor Chandler's denial of the plaintiff's claim for breach of the duty of loyalty? Has the evidentiary burden shifted as a result of this decision?

2. Chancellor Chandler articulates a two-prong standard for automatic application of the entire fairness standard: "an entity [must] stand on both sides of the transaction and that such entity is a controlling shareholder." Which prong prevented the application of entire fairness review in this case? How might Chancellor Chandler's decision have been different if entire fairness was deemed to be the appropriate standard of review and the burden was shifted to the defendants?

3. Chancellor Chandler observes that Delaware courts apply a subjective test when considering the independence of directors rather than an objective reasonable director test. What are the advantages of such an approach? Would defendants generally fare better under a more objective standard? Does Chancellor Chandler's application of the test to Bernbach make sense? Should hypothetical renewals of consulting contracts be enough to undermine the disinterestedness of a director, or would it have made more sense for Chancellor Chandler to ground his discussion in the current contractual relationship between Bernbach and General Cigar? Compare Chancellor Chandler's discussion of the potential renewals of Bernbach's contract to the benefits Solomon would receive from consummation of the merger. Does Chancellor Chandler's brief consideration of the materiality of the potential financial interests of Bernbach and Solomon conform to the *Rales'* standard for materiality established earlier in the case? Which director is least likely to be disinterested in the merger? Should the board reasonably have foreseen that the independence of these directors would be questioned seriously?

4. Two years after this decision, Chancellor Chandler dealt the final blow to Orman's case, granting the defendants' final motion for summary judgment. *See Orman v. Cullman*, 2004 Del. Ch. LEXIS 150 (Oct. 20, 2004). By that time, Orman's claims had been stripped down until his only remaining ground for a fiduciary breach was his allegation that the 18-month lockout provision against the Cullman Group coerced the unaffiliated shareholders into approving the merger. What impact, if any, could

this provision actually have had on the Class A shareholders when they cast their votes on the proposed merger? Can you imagine a different set of circumstances where such a deal protection mechanism could be coercive to the entire shareholder constituency? What other mechanisms also could have such an effect? The leading cases in Delaware on deal protection mechanisms are *Unocal Corp. v. Mesa Petroleum Co.*, 493 A.2d 946 (Del. 1985) and *Omnicare, Inc. v. NCS Healthcare, Inc.*, 818 A.2d 914 (Del. 2003). For a discussion of these cases and the impact and limits of deal protection mechanisms, *see* Christina M. Sautter, *Rethinking Contractual Limits on Fiduciary Duties*, 38 Fl. St. U. L. Rev. 55 (2010).

III. Competing with the Corporation

The claim that a fiduciary usurped the corporation's opportunity is closely related to another potential breach of the duty of loyalty: the allegation that the defendant competed with the corporation unfairly. Like the corporate opportunity doctrine, courts closely scrutinize claims of unfair competition through detailed factual examination in order to differentiate permissible economic activity from fiduciary breaches. In unfair competition cases, however, the alleged breach is not the acquisition of a single commercial transaction or client but, rather, entry into the market as a direct corporate rival. As the following case demonstrates, the corporation often suffers losses caused by the fiduciary's taking of information, valuable employees, and/or customers from the corporation. The corporation's breach of loyalty claim is strengthened if the company can prove that the fiduciary misappropriated these corporate assets before she resigned from the firm.

Riggs Inv. Mgmt. Corp. v. Columbia Partners, L.L.C.

United States District Court, District of Columbia
966 F. Supp. 1250 (1997)

LAMBERTH, DISTRICT JUDGE:

Plaintiff Riggs Investment Management Corporation ("RIMCO") manages investment funds for individuals, pension funds, and other corporate and institutional investors. RIMCO is a wholly-owned subsidiary of Plaintiff Riggs Bank, N.A. ("Riggs").

In June 1989, defendant Robert von Pentz left a competitor, American Securities Bank Capital Management ("ASB"), to become RIMCO's Managing Director of Equity Strategy and Management. When von Pentz became CEO of RIMCO in January 1990, he hired Philip Tasho, a former ASB colleague, as von Pentz's replacement as the head of equities at RIMCO. Von Pentz served as Chief Executive Officer, Chief Investment Officer and Chairman of the Board of RIMCO from late 1989 until his resignation on September 28, 1995.

Von Pentz renewed his employment contract with RIMCO [in July, 1994]. The contract, which extended through December 31, 1995, entitled von Pentz to an annual salary of $175,000, as well as additional incentive compensation based on RIMCO's profits and performance. In July 1995, Tim Coughlin and Henry Dudley—successor to George Grosz, head of Financial Services at Riggs Bank—met with von Pentz to discuss a possible extension of his employment contract, which was set to expire December 31, 1995. Von Pentz was not eager to enter into a new contract, but was willing to listen to Riggs' proposal. He wanted an equity interest in RIMCO as an inducement to enter into any new contract, but when Dudley and Coughlin finally presented von Pentz with a draft employment agreement in late September, it contained no provision for an equity interest in RIMCO, and the changes in terms from the existing contract were not particularly favorable to von Pentz. Von Pentz found the terms in the draft contract to be unacceptable, and told them he would not sign it given the other opportunities he had available to him.

On September 28, 1995, more than three months before his contract was to expire, von Pentz resigned without advance notice. He immediately went to work for defendant Columbia Partners, an investment company in which he holds a ten percent interest. Within two days, von Pentz hired eight RIMCO employees to join him at Columbia Partners, including everyone involved in marketing, client service, and equity investment.

On Monday, October 2, 1995, Columbia Partners officially opened for business at fully appointed offices on Pennsylvania Avenue, and Columbia Partners was actively soliciting investment clients, including RIMCO clients. As a result of defendant von Pentz's actions in starting up his new business and hiring away RIMCO employees, plaintiffs have alleged breaches of fiduciary duty by von Pentz. As a result of the alleged actions of Columbia Partners, plaintiffs charge Lanham Act and unfair competition violations.

Formation of Columbia Partners

The evidence establishes that from at least February of 1995, von Pentz participated in developing projections for Columbia Partners, and from at least April of 1995, shared information about RIMCO's employees and customers for inclusion in those projections. Galway needed the projections to ensure the feasibility of the project and to recruit investors.

In order to create a budget for the new firm so that he would know how much start-up capital was needed, Fant asked Collins and von Pentz to provide estimates of certain expenses such as employee salaries and the revenues from potential clients for the new firm. Beginning in April, 1995, von Pentz sent spreadsheets to Collins and later, Pant, which contained his estimates of potential revenues and expenses for the new firm. These spreadsheets contained the names of several RIMCO clients and information concerning the size of the client's account, the fees that client paid, and von Pentz's estimate of the probability that the client would transfer its account to the new firm. Von Pentz's spreadsheets also listed the names and salaries of the RIMCO employees whom he hoped to recruit for the new venture.

Defendants admit that some of the information provided by von Pentz to Collins and Fant was confidential to RIMCO, but contend it was not the type of confidential information which was particularly useful to a competitor, or which would cause competitive harm to RIMCO if disclosed. For example, the names of RIMCO's institutional clients are printed in its promotional materials, and von Pentz testified that many clients willingly disclose the amount of assets they have with different money managers. However, von Pentz also disclosed information about the assets that RIMCO clients had under management and the fees that each client generated. Von Pentz admitted that he had never previously shared such information about clients with any competitors, and that he did not have clients' consent to share information about their accounts. Von Pentz further acknowledged that the fees charged by investment managers are "a factor in the competitive balance between firms," though he believed it to be one of the least important elements in picking a money manager.

The projections von Pentz and Collins provided to Galway listed RIMCO employees and RIMCO clients that von Pentz intended to recruit for the new company, identified which RIMCO marketing employees had relationships with which targeted RIMCO clients, and estimated the probability that each client could be switched to the new venture. Von Pentz also shared information about salaries and bonuses that would be needed to recruit RIMCO employees.

Throughout the summer of 1995, von Pentz and Collins provided input and approval concerning "pretty much every detail" of establishing Columbia Partners. Von Pentz's input was sought on everything from finding office space and furniture, purchasing computer software, and designating the office layout, to placing phone outlets, and even selecting coffee for the office. Von Pentz also worked on setting salary and commission structures.

RIMCO Employees

Von Pentz acknowledged that in the summer of 1994, when he and Collins were seeking investors, he disclosed to RIMCO employees that he planned to start his own business, and that he hoped to take them with him. In July 1995, von Pentz told Curt Winsor of his "dream" to run his own company. That conversation prompted Winsor to discuss the subject with Tom O'Neill. At approximately the same time, von Pentz had similar conversations with Louise Toler and Colleen Kelly.

Throughout September 1995, von Pentz informed RIMCO employees of his imminent departure from RIMCO. On September 6, 1995, von Pentz told Lane that he would soon be leaving to start his own company, and asked Lane to join him. This conversation occurred as the two were flying to meet with Texas Scottish Rite Hospital, a client von Pentz had identified as one that Lane might bring over to Columbia Partners. On September 19, 1995, von Pentz took Lane for a tour of Columbia Partners' future offices and informed Lane that he would be resigning on September 28. Lane acknowledged that even though he was a RIMCO officer, he did not disclose to Riggs' management von Pentz's imminent departure out of personal loyalty to von Pentz.

On September 14, 1995, von Pentz discussed his imminent departure with O'Neill on a flight back from Kentucky, where they had attended a meeting with Modern

Welding and had entertained a trustee of the UIU Pension Trust ("UIU"). Von Pentz had identified Modern Welding and UIU as RIMCO clients that would likely follow O'Neill and von Pentz, respectively, to the new firm. Von Pentz told O'Neill that he would be leaving RIMCO in the next several weeks; that he would be joining resources with another well-known entity; and that he would be running the equity side of the new venture.

On September 26, 1995, von Pentz and Winsor discussed Columbia Partners over lunch. Von Pentz told Winsor that he would be leaving at the end of the week and discussed Winsor's joining the new firm with responsibilities in marketing. Winsor's understanding was that he had a job offer, and that he had accepted it, though not explicitly.

On September 27, 1995, von Pentz gave Louise Toler a tour of Columbia Partners' future offices, told her he was joining forces with Collins, and showed her a letter specifying the terms of her offer of employment at Columbia Partners.

Each of these RIMCO employees resigned on September 28, 1995. Even though Winsor and O'Neill typically met with 10 to 20 prospective clients a month, as of their resignations from RIMCO on September 28, 1995 Winsor had only one scheduled RIMCO appointment and O'Neill had none. Von Pentz resigned, business cards for O'Neill, Winsor, and Lane had already been printed and were available at Columbia Partners. Four other employees targeted by von Pentz resigned within days of von Pentz's resignation. Several offered to stay on at RIMCO while RIMCO made arrangements for their replacement, but RIMCO generally declined.

RIMCO Clients

In September 1995, von Pentz and Lane or O'Neill met with representatives of RIMCO clients targeted for Columbia Partners: Texas Scottish Rite, Modern Welding and UIU. Von Pentz had identified each client as a prospect to be brought to Columbia Partners by either himself, Lane, or O'Neill. Lane first denied that it was unusual for him to travel so frequently and to travel with both O'Neill and von Pentz, as they had on the trip to see Modern Welding and the UIU trustee, but was impeached on this very point. Von Pentz admitted that he had never previously visited the UIU trustee at his home in Kentucky.

Von Pentz told two RIMCO clients that he would be resigning before he told Riggs management: UIU, one of RIMCO's largest accounts, and National Electrical Contractors Association (NECA). However, with respect to NECA, this notification preceded Riggs' notification by merely a few hours, and in the case of UIU this prior "notice" came during the course of a cocktail conversation with Howard Kluttz, a long-time friend of von Pentz and an informal advisor to UIU. Furthermore, Richard Hoffman, a UIU executive most importantly connected to the transfer of funds from RIMCO to Columbia Partners, testified that he first learned that von Pentz was leaving RIMCO after he had resigned. The news was a surprise to Mr. Hoffman. UIU and NECA both transferred their accounts to Columbia Partners in the first few days of the company's existence.

Negotiations with Riggs' Management

At no time before September 28 did von Pentz tell Riggs' management of his intention to resign before the expiration of his contract. Nor did von Pentz ensure that RIMCO would continue to operate after his resignation. But dark clouds were clearly on the horizon. In fact, Dudley testified that he sought new contract negotiations with von Pentz in the summer of 1995 because he feared von Pentz would leave.

Von Pentz testified that he told Dudley a week before his departure that he saw no reason to sign a new contract given that RIMCO provided him with nothing new or beneficial. He did say, however, that he would look over the contract again. Von Pentz did not officially tell Dudley of his intention to resign until the evening of September 27, 1997. At the time, Dudley was visiting a RIMCO client north of Pittsburgh, Pennsylvania. Though plaintiffs desire to show just how devastating von Pentz's resignation was to the organization, it is worth noting that Dudley did not fly back to Washington to perform even some modicum of damage control even though von Pentz called him the night before he quit to give warning. Von Pentz even offered to fly Dudley down to Washington on a private plane, but Dudley instead remained in Pennsylvania to play golf. The next day, von Pentz tendered his resignation to Tim Coughlin and Fred Bollerer. He declined a request to serve out his contract.

The day after Columbia Partners opened for business, UIU, one of RIMCO's largest clients, transferred its account to von Pentz's new operation. Richard Hoffman, counsel to UIU, was concerned that a "disaster" could occur in the time it would take RIMCO to hire von Pentz's successor. But, Hoffman also stated, "[w]e liked the performance that Mr. von Pentz had given us. And he knew our portfolio. He knew — he knew us. And weighing all these factors, we decided to move the money." Hoffman recommended that UIU move its funds immediately.

The issue now is what legal consequences attach to these actions.

Breach of Fiduciary Duty

As the Chairman of the Board and CEO of RIMCO from mid-1994 through September 1995, von Pentz owed a fiduciary duty to both RIMCO and its sole shareholder, Riggs. This duty included an obligation of "undivided and unselfish loyalty" to his employer. *Maryland Metals, Inc. v. Metzner*, 382 A.2d, 564, 568 (1978). Furthermore, as an agent, von Pentz had a duty to act solely for the benefit of his employer in all matters within the scope of his employment and to avoid conflicts of interest between his duty to his employer and his own self interest. *Id.*

But just as von Pentz owed a duty of loyalty to RIMCO, it is also clear that an agent may make arrangements or plan to go into competition with his principal before terminating his agency, "provided no unfair acts are committed or injury done his principal." *Mercer Management Consulting v. Wilde*, 920 F. Supp. 219, 232 (D.D.C. 1996), citing *Science Accessories Corp. v. Summagraphics Corp.*, 425 A.2d 957, 962 (Del. 1980). Thus, the privilege to compete is limited. The question in this case is whether von Pentz, stepped over the line between privilege and disloyalty. The court finds he did.

Von Pentz argues that his discussions throughout 1994 and into 1995 are properly privileged and preparatory. The fact that von Pentz was under contract with RIMCO at the time, or that he had some basic meetings with Collins, or even that he sent "feelers" out to possible investors does not breach the fiduciary duty of loyalty. However, it is clear that von Pentz shared confidential information about wages paid to RIMCO employees and fees paid by its clients. Von Pentz admits that this information was confidential to RIMCO but attempts to whitewash the situation by suggesting that, at least with respect to client fees, clients often disclose this information themselves, so no there was no harm done. The court believes otherwise. The disclosure of this type of information to Collins—who at that point was simply a RIMCO competitor—clearly breaches von Pentz's duty of loyalty to RIMCO. If the plan to establish Columbia Partners had fallen through, there was nothing to stop Collins from using that information against RIMCO. True, information about who RIMCO managed money for and what fees it charged may have been obtained from third party sources, but not without considerable effort. For von Pentz to just hand it over goes beyond his privilege to prepare for future competition—not to mention that von Pentz had pledged RIMCO that he would keep confidential exactly the type of information he in the end shared.

The evidence also shows just how involved von Pentz was in even the most minute details of this "turnkey" operation—right down to whose office would go where and what kind of stationery would be used.

It is also clear that von Pentz pre-solicited employees, though these pre-solicitations were generally close to the time of his departure. Perhaps von Pentz was simply very excited about his upcoming job and wanted to share his happiness with his co-workers by offering them jobs as well. Whatever the reason, the evidence is clear that von Pentz was careless (or crafty) about letting co-workers know about his imminent departure, giving several the clear indication he was offering them jobs at Columbia Partners even though von Pentz was still Chairman of the Board at RIMCO. Most strikingly, the two marketing employees at RIMCO, Winsor and O'Neill, had nothing on their calendars for the month of October or thereafter, even though they testified it was normal to have up to 20 appointments. Their lack of credible explanation for this deficiency was offensive to the court and is stark evidence of what the only credible explanation for their lack of planning could have been-that they knew, well in advance, that they were heading to Columbia Partners in October of 1995.

It is also worth noting that Ruff Fant of Galway Partners, Columbia Partners' bankroller, warned Collins in a letter of January 17, 1995 that neither he nor anyone else associated with the new business were to breach any duties to their employers. Fant informed Collins that this would slow down Columbia Partners' opening, but said that it was central to the business operation to avoid any illegality. It placed special emphasis on pre- and post-resignation conduct, and included two court cases outlining breaches of duties by corporate officers. Though this may have been what is commonly called a "CYA" letter, it nevertheless put Collins on notice of how he was to behave. Collins forwarded these materials to von Pentz with a note stating that the letter made for "stomach churning" reading. That von Pentz would then violate exactly the types of behavior cautioned against by his own backer indicates that von Pentz did not just make some mistakes, but instead knowingly breached his duties to RIMCO resulting in exactly the type of litigation of which Fant warned him.

Thus, there is no doubt that von Pentz breached his duty of loyalty to RIMCO. But for damages purposes, the question is when the breach occurred. Plaintiffs, obviously, seek to push this date back as far as possible. The court finds by a preponderance of the evidence, however, that von Pentz began to breach his duty of loyalty in April of 1995 when he shared salary information with Collins. As von Pentz knew the salaries of the RIMCO employees he wanted to bring over, he had to ensure that Columbia Partners could sweeten the deal to entice defections. But von Pentz had no right to disclose this clearly confidential information to Collins, even for budgeting purposes. True, this presents a difficulty to upper level executives who seek to build turnkey operations, but such is the price of being a highly paid corporate confidant.

It is true that while von Pentz was in breach of duty, RIMCO was performing exceptionally well in the marketplace. Von Pentz is obviously a talented money manager. But this does not excuse his disclosure of confidential RIMCO information to Collins. In preparing to compete an employee may not commit fraudulent, unfair, or wrongful acts, such as the misuse of confidential information, or solicitation leading to a mass resignation of the firm's employees. *Science Accessories*, 425 A.2d at 965. Von Pentz did misuse such protected information, and he also pre-solicited employees while still an employee of RIMCO himself. The fact that RIMCO's entire current equity team followed von Pentz to Columbia Partners is proof positive that von Pentz's scheme worked.

Plaintiffs seek to recover von Pentz's compensation for the time during which he was in breach. As no compensation is owed an employee who has breached his duty of loyalty to his employer, plaintiff is entitled to its return. *Radio TV Reports, Inc. v. Ingersoll*, 742 F. Supp. 19, 23 (D.D.C. 1990). Given the court's finding that this occurred in April of 1995, he must forfeit any compensation he earned from that point until his resignation on September 28, 1995—a six month period. As Von Pentz earned an annual salary of $175,000 during this time, he must tender one-half of this to the plaintiffs, plus any bonus money earned during that period. He must also tender any other compensation earned during the breach.

Plaintiffs seek as well to recover a portion of the equity fees earned by Columbia Partners from clients who transferred their accounts from RIMCO, arguing that disgorgement of profits earned as a result of a breach of fiduciary duty is an appropriate remedy. *United States v. York*, 890 F. Supp. 1117, 1139 (D.D.C. 1995). RIMCO argues that the fees Columbia Partners earned during the first three months of its existence are a "conservative measure" of the damages von Pentz caused. Alternatively, it seeks the fees UIU, one of RIMCO's largest clients, paid, totaling over $100,000. It is clear from the evidence that while von Pentz may have pre-solicited employees, he cannot be said to have pre-solicited clients who transferred their assets under management from RIMCO to Columbia Partners. There is no real evidence of pre-solicitation of any RIMCO client, except for the fact that von Pentz made an unusual trip to a trustee's home in Kentucky shortly before he resigned, but this appears to have been more about pre-soliciting a RIMCO employee, O'Neill, on the way down than anything else. There is no palpable evidence that von Pentz did any actual pre-solicitation of any client at the time, however.

With respect to UIU, it is certain that von Pentz's breach of duty towards RIMCO had nothing to do with its transfer of funds. Columbia Partners cannot be penalized simply because UIU likes Richard von Pentz and wants him to continue to manage its money. Hoffman, instrumental in moving the funds, testified he was surprised to learn that von Pentz was leaving, and even though he was nervous that bad things could happen at RIMCO in the time it would take to hire a new Chairman, UIU above all wanted von Pentz in the picture. Columbia Partners cannot be forced to disgorge fees so earned.

Thus, on plaintiffs' breach of fiduciary duty count, von Pentz is ordered to pay six months wages to plaintiffs (April 1 through September 28, 1995) in the amount of $87,500.

Though this court has seen only a glimpse of the investment management profession, if anything is clear, it is that at its essence is the race for the buck, and those who can't grab it fast enough fall behind. That is not to say, however, that this is an evil business. Investment drives our economy, employs Americans, feeds families. But as the average person has no idea how to invest, there are experts who show us which businesses we can do the most for, and which will do the most for us. We thus reward those experts, investment managers, who successfully direct our hard-earned funds to companies and corporations which are productive to our society. By appropriately compensating these individuals, we encourage them to be more careful with our money, and lure those with great talent in this area to use that talent in the investment arena, as opposed to other, perhaps less lucrative occupations.

In this case, the court is presented with a man who may not have been paid according to his worth. The problem, however, is that some of the steps he took to increase his compensation—in conjunction with forming a new company in which he would have an equitable share in the profits—were forbidden by law. And that new company, in an effort to compete in a very intense marketplace, would also violate the law. Perhaps some of these behaviors were economically efficient, but our common law and our Congress have determined that efficiency is not always of paramount importance. Loyalty and fair-play are also prized values. Riggs and RIMCO do not necessarily hold a moral high ground in this litigation. They are just as competitive as Columbia Partners. But this is not a morality contest, it is about who violated the law. On that score, von Pentz and Columbia Partners overstepped their legal bounds, and for that the court will appropriately sanction them, providing proper relief for plaintiffs in the process.

For the reasons stated above, Robert von Pentz must forfeit the salary he earned from RIMCO between April 1, 1995 and September 28, 1995 in the amount of $87,500 for his breaches of his duty of loyalty to his employer.

Comments and Questions

1. The classic Delaware case on unfair competition is *Guth v. Loft, Inc.*, 5 A.2d 503 (Del. 1939). There, the Delaware Supreme Court announced that "a corporate officer or director is entirely free to engage in an independent, competitive business, so long as he violates no legal or moral duty with respect to the fiduciary relation that exists between the corporation and himself." *Id.* at 514. The court in *Guth* also referenced a famous passage in *Meinhard v. Salmon*, insisting that "the fiduciary relation demands more than the morals of the market place." *Id.* at 515. Given the emphasis on the moral dimension of a reviewing court's judgment, one might expect director competition to be a second source of litigation. In over 70 years, however, *Guth* only has been cited in about 50 cases. Why might potential litigants choose not to pursue relief under this claim? What other litigation options do potential plaintiffs have when directors misappropriate information and improperly compete with the corporation?

2. Why didn't von Pentz's decision to form a competing firm constitute liable conduct? What conduct actually gave rise to von Pentz's liability in this case? What steps could von Pentz have taken to mitigate his potential liability? Was the court's remedy sufficient to reverse the harm caused by von Pentz's actions? If not, what could the court have done instead?

3. The court emphasizes the turnkey nature of von Pentz's plans for his new company. Does this case indicate that a director who is planning to compete with his current employer can never take any of his current associates with her? Does this case suggest proper methods by which a director could recruit and hire employees of the corporation for the new firm without violating the director's duties of loyalty to the corporation?

Chapter 6

Executive Compensation

Compensation paid to top officers, particularly the Chief Executive Officer, has been a much debated topic. Compensation dipped in 2008, following the onset of the financial crisis. The drop was short lived, however. The compensation paid to the 200 highest paid CEOs increased by 9% from 2013 to 2014, compared with economic growth of 2.4%.

Although there is plenty of disagreement, CEO compensation is often used as the premier example of problems with the system of corporate governance. Compensation for top officers is typically determined by the board of directors. The form and amount must, therefore, be consistent with the board's fiduciary obligations.

These payments have traditionally been tested under the duty of loyalty, at least where the compensated officer also served on the board of directors. In these circumstances, the board has the burden of establishing that the amount paid is "fair" to the corporation. Fairness means that the amount paid is commensurate with the benefit received. In short, fairness depends upon an examination of the terms of the compensation and an analysis of the services provided.

But as we will explore in this Chapter, the role of fairness has changed. Mostly, the need to ensure substantive fairness in the area of executive compensation has been replaced by process. It is enough to show that a majority of the board consists of independent directors. In those circumstances, the obligation to establish the fairness of the terms or amount is essentially eliminated and the duty of loyalty is replaced by the duty of care. We will explore how the law developed in this fashion.

We will also discuss what is a growing federalization of the executive compensation process. The Securities and Exchange Commission has long required at least some disclosure of executive compensation in the proxy statement. Congress, however, has increased the level of disclosure, requiring such things as the ratio between CEO compensation and the median employee, and has given shareholders of public companies the right to an advisory on executive compensation (say on pay).

I. Is The Problem of Executive Compensation a New One?

A. Some History

Much of the explosion in executive compensation comes in large part from the widespread use of bonuses and other forms of incentive compensation. This appears, however, to be a relatively new approach.

Harwell Wells, *"No Man Can Be Worth $1,000,000 a Year":* *The Fight over Executive Compensation in 1930s America*
44 U. Rich. L. Rev. 689, 697–702 (2010)[1]

Before World War I, it appears that little thought was given to whether senior executives needed to be compensated differently from other employees. There is only one useful study of executive compensation during the pre-World War I era: a survey of four hundred manufacturing firms by economists F.W. Taussig and W.S. Barker. In the largest firms, those with capital over $1.5 million, they found an average senior executive's salary was only $9,958, equivalent to $217,234 in today's dollars, a sum the author deemed modest. While some executives had enough ownership in their firms to make up for a comparatively low salary (i.e., they were owner-managers), quite a few did not. Half of the largest corporations reported executives owned less than one-fifth of their stock, with more than one-tenth of the largest corporations reporting that executives owned no stock at all.

Nor did most of the firms offer executives additional incentives. No more than five percent regularly gave executives extra compensation based on firm performance. The authors found this surprising in light of the widespread use of such bonus systems in Europe, where executives typically received "not fixed salaries, but sums which vary with the earnings of the business which they manage." Taussig and Barker attributed this lack of special incentives in part to Americans' reluctance to mix what they perceived as two very different things: wages and profits. Wages paid to executives were seen as no different from wages paid to other employees and were clearly distinguished from profits, which were the rightful property of shareholders: "The business profits of corporations are received by the stockholders and these only. Their dividends ... are alone the rewards of enterprise, risk, judgment."

Even this early in the era of the salaried executive, however, a few perceptive business leaders recognized the problems posed by senior managers who directed firms but had no further stake in their economic success. In response, some influential shareholders of firms that separated ownership and management implemented bonus plans that paid senior employees bonuses linked to firm profits. These plans were explicitly intended to replicate the incentive once provided by ownership and mitigate the principal/agency problems raised by the separation of ownership and control.

---

1. Copyright © 2010 University of Richmond Law Review. Reprinted with permission.

Bethlehem Steel had one of the first bonus plans, adopted at the instigation of president Charles Schwab, a protégé of Andrew Carnegie who saw how "the awarding of partnerships and financial shares in the company [had] secured the commitment of those who were chosen" for top management positions at Carnegie Steel. Bethlehem's bonus program began in 1902 and paid executives a percentage of the steelmaker's net profits. It grew until, during the late 1920s, some top executives took home in bonuses almost as much as shareholders received in dividends. United States Steel adopted a similar — though less generous — plan the same year. At the nation's largest tobacco company, American Tobacco, a bonus plan intended to replicate the incentives of ownership was implemented at the turn of the century by James B. Duke, who believed that executives needed to "feel and realize that they are part owners of the business and that their personal success and prosperity are measured by the success and prosperity they achieve for the company." After the tobacco giant's breakup in 1911, successor firms including a new American Tobacco adopted similar plans as discussed below.

Executive bonus plans flourished in the 1920s. While few companies reported using bonus plans in the prewar era, a survey of one hundred large industrial companies found that in 1928, 64% paid executives both salaries and annual bonuses linked to firm performance. At firms paying bonuses, they constituted 42% of total executive compensation in 1929 (admittedly, a high water-mark for bonus payments) although there were great variations among particular plans. Among the surveyed firms, bonus payments ranged from 0–1% of an executive's compensation to 96 or 97%, and firms also differed on which members of senior management could participate. Firms also calculated bonuses differently, although most used some formula that placed a percentage of earnings into a bonus pool to be distributed annually among top management, with the bonus most often being paid in cash but sometimes in firm stock. Stock options were less frequently offered. Linking executive pay to performance was clearly seen as the wave of the future. In 1925, Forbes magazine editorialized that "companies that refuse to share profits with managers will have to be satisfied with second-rate executives, for the number of enterprises adopting profit-sharing is increasing as never before."

There are several reasons why executive bonus plans became so popular. From a present-day perspective, the obvious reason is that bonus plans promised to align the incentives of executives with those of shareholders, so that executives would be properly incentivized to increase shareholder value. Therefore, the plans became more popular as non-owner management spread. Proponents of managerial bonus plans identified shareholders as the plans' major beneficiaries, with some proponents specifically identifying the creation of a "mutuality of interest" between managers and stockholders as a goal.

Reasons particular to the 1920s, however, also encouraged their spread. First, in a time that still valorized independent proprietors, bonus plans were a means of persuading talented executives to work for large corporations rather than "start their own firm or purchase a large share of an existing company." Second, many of the corporations for which these executives labored had only recently been assembled out of smaller firms, and a bonus system linked to firm-wide profits was to persuade executives to place the interests of the entire firm ahead of the interests of their particular divisions. Finally, executive bonus plans fit well with the rhetoric, and even practice, of the 1920s' "new economy." During that decade, corporations trumpeted profit-sharing and stock-ownership plans for workers as a cure for the split between labor and capital. Profit-sharing plans for workers were sold as a way to make ordinary laborers "capitalists" and participants in the enterprise—though many such plans paid little to laborers, who in any event hated the uncertainty the plans engendered and preferred steady wages. While the public face of bonus plans in the 1920s were those for workers, more widespread were those for executives.

With the new executive compensation schemes came higher executive compensation. How much were executives making? While comparisons are difficult in the era before standardized reporting, a study of one hundred large industrial firms found the median compensation earned by a president in 1929 was $69,728, equivalent in 2009 dollars to $880,648. The study also revealed sharp variations. Presidents' compensation ranged from $10,000 a year to $1,635,753. Though thirty presidents received compensation above $100,000, the million-dollar pay package was an outlier. The next highest-paid president received $605,613, and only four of the hundred received compensation above $300,000.

Comments and Questions

1. Professor Wells concludes that before WWI, executive compensation, even based upon today's dollars was "modest." What happened that changed these modest amounts?

2. What role did the separation of ownership and management have on compensation practices?

3. In the early days of the prior century, compensation apparently did not have a significant performance-based component. What does that mean? What is performance-based compensation and how might that cause compensation to escalate?

4. Professor Wells traces the growth in executive compensation to the separation of ownership and management identified by Berle and Means. What does this tell us about dynamics underlying the issue of executive compensation?

5. The article also identifies the early trend towards bonus plans. What sorts of benefits and harms might arise out of a compensation system where executive officers are paid in large part through bonuses?

6. At the time of the adoption of the federal securities laws in the 1930s, executive compensation and bonuses were considered a significant problem that required legislative intervention. *See* 78 Cong. Rec. 7861 (1934) (statement of Rep. Rayburn) (noting the use of proxies to obtain approval of "vast bonuses out of all proportion to what legitimate management would justify."). As we will come to later in the chapter, Congress sought to solve the problem through disclosure. With this infor-

mation, shareholders could exercise control over the amounts paid. Did this approach work?

7. According to one paper, CEO compensation prior to the 1970s reflected "low levels of pay, little dispersion across top managers, and moderate pay-performance sensitivities." Carola Frydman & Dirk Jenter, *CEO Compensation*, Working Paper No. 77, Rock Center for Corporate Governance, Stanford University, at 1 (Mar. 19, 2010). What might explain this change? In fact, the authors further note that no theory "offers a fully convincing explanation for the apparent regime change that occurred in the 1970s." *Id.* Do you have any thoughts on what the explanation might be?

B. Compensation and the Market: A Debate

Some argue that compensation is a matter for the market. CEOs are paid what they are worth after negotiations with the board of directors. Moreover, if shareholders do not like the amount paid to top executives, they can sell their shares and go elsewhere. That debate recently came to the fore in a slightly different context.

Jones v. Harris Associates, L.P.

United States Court of Appeals, Seventh Circuit
527 F.3d 627 (2008), *rev'd*, 559 U.S. 335 (2010)

EASTERBROOK, CHIEF JUDGE:

Harris Associates advises the Oakmark complex of mutual funds. These open-end funds (an open-end fund is one that buys back its shares at current asset value) have grown in recent years because their net returns have exceeded the market average, and the investment adviser's compensation has grown apace. Plaintiffs, who own shares in several of the Oakmark funds, contend that the fees are too high and thus violate § 36(b) of the Investment Company Act of 1940, 15 U.S.C. § 80a-35(b), a provision added in 1970 [which imposes a fiduciary obligation on advisors in setting fees]....

* * *

The district court followed *Gartenberg v. Merrill Lynch Asset Management, Inc.*, 694 F.2d 923 (2d Cir. 1982), and concluded that Harris Associates must prevail because its fees are ordinary. *Gartenberg* articulated two variations on a theme:

> [T]he test is essentially whether the fee schedule represents a charge within the range of what would have been negotiated at arm's-length in the light of all of the surrounding circumstances.

694 F.2d at 928. And

> [t]o be guilty of a violation of § 36(b) ... the adviser-manager must charge a fee that is so disproportionately large that it bears no reasonable relationship to the services rendered and could not have been the product of arm's-length bargaining.

Ibid. Oakmark Fund paid Harris Associates 1% (per year) of the first $2 billion of the fund's assets, 0.9% of the next $1 billion, 0.8% of the next $2 billion, and 0.75% of anything over $5 billion....

* * *

Having had another chance to study this question, we now disapprove the Gartenberg approach. A fiduciary duty differs from rate regulation. A fiduciary must make full disclosure and play no tricks but is not subject to a cap on compensation. The trustees (and in the end investors, who vote with their feet and dollars), rather than a judge or jury, determine how much advisory services are worth.

* * *

... Business corporations ... though not trusts are managed by persons who owe fiduciary duties of loyalty to investors. This does not prevent them from demanding substantial compensation and bargaining hard to get it. Publicly traded corporations use the same basic procedures as mutual funds: a committee of independent directors sets the top managers' compensation. No court has held that this procedure implies judicial review for "reasonableness" of the resulting salary, bonus, and stock options. These are constrained by competition in several markets—firms that pay too much to managers have trouble raising money, because net profits available for distribution to investors are lower, and these firms also suffer in product markets because they must charge more and consumers turn elsewhere. Competitive processes are imperfect but remain superior to a "just price" system administered by the judiciary. However weak competition may be at weeding out errors, the judicial process is worse—for judges can't be turned out of office or have their salaries cut if they display poor business judgment.

* * *

Today thousands of mutual funds compete. The pages of the *Wall Street Journal* teem with listings. People can search for and trade funds over the Internet, with negligible transactions costs. "At the end of World War II, there were 73 mutual funds registered with the Securities and Exchange Commission holding $1.2 billion in assets. By the end of 2002, over 8,000 mutual funds held more than $6 trillion in assets." Paul G. Mahoney, *Manager-Investor Conflicts in Mutual Funds*, 18 J. Econ. Perspectives 162, 162 (Spring 2004). Some mutual funds, such as those that track market indexes, do not have investment advisers and thus avoid all advisory fees. (Total expenses of the Vanguard 500 Index Fund, for example, are under 0.10% of assets; the same figure for the Oakmark Fund in 2007 was 1.01%.) Mutual funds rarely fire their investment advisers, but investors can and do "fire" advisers cheaply and easily by moving their money elsewhere. Investors do this not when the advisers' fees are "too high" in the abstract, but when they are excessive in relation to the results—and what is "excessive" depends on the results available from other investment vehicles, rather than any absolute level of compensation.

New entry is common, and funds can attract money only by offering a combination of service and management that investors value, at a price they are willing to pay. Mutual funds come much closer to the model of atomistic competition than do most other markets. Judges would not dream of regulating the price of automobiles, which are produced by roughly a dozen large firms; why then should 8,000 mutual funds seem "too few" to put competitive pressure on advisory fees? A recent, careful study concludes that thousands of mutual funds are plenty, that investors can and do protect their interests by shopping, and that regulating advisory fees through litigation is unlikely to do more good than harm. *See* John C. Coates & R. Glenn Hubbard, Competition in the Mutual Fund Industry: Evidence and Implications for Policy, 33 Iowa J. Corp. L. 151 (2007).

It won't do to reply that most investors are unsophisticated and don't compare prices. The sophisticated investors who do shop create a competitive pressure that protects the rest. *See* Alan Schwartz & Louis Wilde, Imperfect Information in Markets for Contract Terms, 69 Va. L. Rev. 1387 (1983). As it happens, the most substantial and sophisticated investors choose to pay substantially more for investment advice than advisers subject to § 36(b) receive. A fund that allows only "accredited investors" (i.e., the wealthy) to own non-redeemable shares is exempt from the Investment Company Act. *See* 15 U.S.C. § 80a-6(a) (5) (A) (iii). Investment pools that take advantage of this exemption, commonly called hedge funds, regularly pay their advisers more than 1% of the pool's asset value, plus a substantial portion of any gains from successful strategies. *See* Rene M. Stulz, *Hedge Funds: Past, Present, and Future*, 21 J. Econ. Perspectives 175 (Spring 2007). *See* also Joseph Golec & Laura Starks, *Performance fee contract change and mutual fund risk*, 73 J. Fin. Econ. 93 (2004). When persons who have the most to invest, and who act through professional advisers, place their assets in pools whose managers receive more than Harris Associates, it is hard to conclude that Harris's fees must be excessive.

* * *

Federal securities laws, of which the Investment Company Act is one component, work largely by requiring disclosure and then allowing price to be set by competition in which investors make their own choices. Plaintiffs do not contend that Harris Associates pulled the wool over the eyes of the disinterested trustees or otherwise hindered their ability to negotiate a favorable price for advisory services. The fees are not hidden from investors — and the Oakmark funds' net return has attracted new investment rather than driving investors away. As § 36(b) does not make the federal judiciary a rate regulator, after the fashion of the Federal Energy Regulatory Commission, the judgment of the district court is affirmed.

Comments and Questions

1. In effect, Judge Easterbrook is favoring some aspect of the Wall Street Rule, where shareholders and investors vote with their feet. If they are unhappy with executive compensation, they should sell their shares and go elsewhere. Is this an effective solution to any concern over compensation?

2. For Judge Easterbrook, the *sin qua non* of regulation is disclosure. With full disclosure, the market can take over and discipline those who charge excessive fees or receive excessive amounts of compensation. Is disclosure enough?

3. The opinion likens the issue with mutual funds to executive compensation at public companies. Judge Easterbrook notes that managers "bargain[] hard" to get their compensation. Is that an accurate description of the compensation dynamic in place at most public companies?

4. The opinion notes that corporations that overpay in compensation will have reduced profits and, as a result, have a more difficult time raising capital. Is the connection between compensation and capital raising as clear as Judge Easterbrook makes it sound?

5. As we will explore later, he correctly notes that where public companies use the proper process, there is no additional review for the reasonableness of the amount paid. More accurately, there is no review of the fairness of the amount paid. Is this an appropriate standard?

6. In any event, he believes that it is not the role of the courts to assess the reasonableness of compensation. Do you agree?

———————

The entire Seventh Circuit declined to rehear the case. Judge Posner dissented and took issue with the market analysis articulated by Judge Easterbrook.

Jones v. Harris Associates, L.P.

United States Court of Appeals, Seventh Circuit
537 F.3d 728 (2008) (dissent from hearing en banc)

POSNER, CIRCUIT JUDGE, with whom Circuit Judges ROVNER, WOOD, WILLIAMS, and TINDER join, dissenting from denial of rehearing en banc.

The panel bases its rejection of *Gartenberg* mainly on an economic analysis that is ripe for reexamination on the basis of growing indications that executive compensation in large publicly traded firms often is excessive because of the feeble incentives of boards of directors to police compensation.... Directors are often CEOs of other companies and naturally think that CEOs should be well paid. And often they are picked by the CEO. Compensation consulting firms, which provide cover for generous compensation packages voted by boards of directors, have a conflict of interest because they are paid not only for their compensation advice but for other services to the firm—services for which they are hired by the officers whose compensation they advised on....

Competition in product and capital markets can't be counted on to solve the problem because the same structure of incentives operates on all large corporations and similar entities, including mutual funds. Mutual funds are a component of the financial services industry, where abuses have been rampant, as is more evident now than it was when Coates and Hubbard wrote their article. A business school professor at Northwestern University recently observed that "business connections can mitigate agency conflicts by facilitating efficient information transfers, but can also be channels for inefficient favoritism." She found "evidence that connections among agents in [the mutual fund industry] foster favoritism, to the detriment of investors. Fund directors and advisory firms that manage the funds hire each other preferentially based on past interactions. When directors and the management are more connected, advisors capture more rents and are monitored by the board less intensely. These findings support recent calls for more disclosure regarding the negotiation of advisory contracts by fund boards." Camelia M. Kuhnen, "Social Networks, Corporate Governance and Contracting in the Mutual Fund Industry" (Mar. 1, 2007), http://ssrn.com/abstract=849705 (visited July 28, 2008). The SEC's Office of Economic Analysis (the principal adviser to the SEC on the economic aspects of regulatory issues) believes that mutual fund "boards with a greater proportion of independent directors are more likely to negotiate and approve lower fees, merge poorly performing funds more quickly or provide greater investor protection from late-trading and market timing," although "broad cross-sectional analysis reveals little consistent evidence that board composition is related to lower fees and higher returns for fund shareholders." "OEA Memorandum: Literature Review on Independent Mutual Fund Chairs and Directors," Dec. 29, 2006....

* * *

The panel opinion points out that courts do not review corporate salaries for excessiveness. That misses the point, which is that unreasonable compensation can be evidence of a breach of fiduciary duty.

Comments and Questions

1. How does Judge Posner differ in his analysis of the issue from Judge Easterbrook? Why does he not view the market as necessarily adequate to resolve compensation issues?

2. What are some of the structural issues raised by Judge Posner? What do you make of them? Do they require reform?

3. Some assert that executive compensation is and should be entirely market driven. Such an approach assumes an effective market with respect to executive compensation. Professor Macey at Yale in his book *Corporate Governance, Promises Kept, Promises Broken*, describes boards of directors as having been "captured" by the CEO. Assuming this is the case, what impact would that likely have on any market for executive compensation?

4. Does the analysis change when a CEO is joining the company for the first time? Thus, John Thain, the CEO of Merrill Lynch, was one of the highest paid CEOs in 2007, receiving total compensation of over $80 million. Yet he had been the CEO of the NYSE. In other words, the large compensation package was what he negotiated in return for leaving one company to join another. Do compensation packages in these circumstances raise the same concerns? Would it affect your analysis to know that Thain departed from Merrill Lynch in early 2009, shortly after the investment bank was acquired by Bank of America?

The Supreme Court ultimately weighed in and reversed the decision by Judge Easterbrook.

Jones v. Harris Associates, L.P.

United States Supreme Court
130 S. Ct. 1418 (2010)

ALITO, JUSTICE:

... [I]f the disinterested directors considered the relevant factors, their decision to approve a particular fee agreement is entitled to considerable weight, even if a court might weigh the factors differently. Cf. id., at 485, 99 S. Ct. 1831, 60 L. Ed. 2d 404. This is not to deny that a fee may be excessive even if it was negotiated by a board in possession of all relevant information, but such a determination must be based on evidence that the fee "is so disproportionately large that it bears no reasonable relationship to the services rendered and could not have been the product of arm's-length bargaining." Gartenberg, supra, at 928.

In contrast, where the board's process was deficient or the adviser withheld important information, the court must take a more rigorous look at the outcome. When an investment adviser fails to disclose material information to the board, greater scrutiny is justified because the withheld information might have hampered the board's ability to function as "an independent check upon the management." Burks, supra, at 484, 99 S. Ct. 1831, 60 L. Ed. 2d 404 (internal quotation marks omitted). "Section 36(b) is sharply focused on the question of whether the fees themselves were excessive." Migdal v. Rowe Price-Fleming Int'l, Inc., 248 F.3d 321, 328 (CA4 2001); see also 15 U.S.C. § 80a-35(b) (imposing a "fiduciary duty with respect to the *receipt of compensation* for services, or of payments of a material nature" (emphasis added)). But an adviser's compliance or noncompliance with its disclosure obligations is a factor that must be considered in calibrating the degree of deference that is due a board's decision to approve an adviser's fees.

It is also important to note that the standard for fiduciary breach under § 36(b) does not call for judicial second-guessing of informed board decisions. *See* Daily Income Fund, supra, at 538, 104 S. Ct. 831, 78 L. Ed. 2d 645; see also Burks, 441 U.S., at 483, 99 S. Ct. 1831, 60 L. Ed. 2d 404 ("Congress consciously chose to address the conflict-of-interest problem through the Act's independent-directors section, rather than through more drastic remedies"). "[P]otential conflicts [of interests] may justify some restraints upon the unfettered discretion of even disinterested mutual fund directors, particularly in their transactions with the investment adviser," but they do not suggest that a court may supplant the judgment of disinterested directors apprised of all relevant information, without additional evidence that the fee exceeds the arm's-length range. Id., at 481, 99 S. Ct. 1831, 60 L. Ed. 2d 404. In reviewing compensation under § 36(b), the Act does not require courts to engage in a precise calculation of fees representative of arm's-length bargaining. *See* 527 F.3d at 633 ("Judicial price-setting does not accompany fiduciary duties"). As recounted above, Congress rejected a "reasonableness" requirement that was criticized as charging the courts with rate-setting responsibilities. *See Daily Income Fund, supra, at 538–540, 104 S. Ct. 831, 78 L. Ed. 2d 645.* Congress' approach recognizes that courts are not well suited to make such precise calculations. Cf. GMC v. Tracy, 519 U.S. 278, 308, 117 S. Ct. 811, 136 L. Ed. 2d 761 (1997) ("[T]he Court is institutionally unsuited to gather the facts upon which economic predictions can be made, and professionally untrained to make them"); Verizon Communs., Inc. v. FCC, 535 U.S. 467, 539, 122 S. Ct. 1646, 152 L. Ed. 2d 701 (2002); see also Concord v. Boston Edison Co., 915 F.2d 17, 25 (CA1 1990) (opinion for the court by Breyer, C. J.) ("[H]ow is a judge or jury to determine a 'fair price'?"). Gartenberg's "so disproportionately large" standard, 694 F.2d at 928, reflects this congressional choice to "rely largely upon [independent director] 'watchdogs' to protect shareholders interests." Burks, supra, at 485, 99 S. Ct. 1831, 60 L. Ed. 2d 404.

By focusing almost entirely on the element of disclosure, the Seventh Circuit panel erred. *See* 527 F.3d at 632 (An investment adviser "must make full disclosure and play no tricks but is not subject to a cap on compensation"). The *Gartenberg* standard, which the panel rejected, may lack sharp analytical clarity, but we believe that it accurately reflects the compromise that is embodied in § 36(b), and it has provided a workable standard for nearly three decades. The debate between the Seventh Circuit panel and the dissent from the denial of rehearing regarding today's mutual fund market is a matter for Congress, not the courts.

Comments and Questions

1. At least from the perspective of Justice Alito's opinion, who won the debate, Judge Posner or Judge Easterbrook?

2. According to Justice Alito, what is the mechanism that is supposed to ensure reasonable compensation? He places considerable weight on process, including informed disinterested directors. Yet that presumably requires courts to ensure that, for example, disinterested directors are truly disinterested. Is this in fact the case?

3. Deference to process (disinterested and informed directors) is the system generally used by courts in reviewing executive compensation. Does it work? Is Justice Alito suggesting reliance on a system that is in fact broken?

4. The Court in *Harris* accepts that even if properly approved, fees can be so disproportionate to the services provided that they violate fiduciary duties. Is this enough of a "safety valve" in the event that the process does not ensure reasonable compensation? How, in the executive compensation area, might one determine whether compensation was disproportionate? Delaware courts allow for the review of compensation even where the process is proper under a waste standard. The test for waste, however, is compensation that is "so one sided that no business person of ordinary, sound judgment could conclude that the corporation has received adequate consideration." Are these standards the same? Would the Delaware standard act as a sufficient safety valve?

5. Justice Alito notes that the standard for breach of fiduciary duty should not involve "judicial second-guessing" of board decisions. This is a common mantra. Courts ought not to be acting as surrogate directors and making day to day business decisions. Does this mean that there should be no room for courts in reviewing compensation?

C. More on the Structural Issues

CEO compensation is typically determined by the board of directors. The directors in turn are elected by shareholders. As a result, shareholders can oust a board that pays what is perceived to be excessive compensation. Yet this straightforward system is not quite as straightforward as it seems.

Richard A. Posner, *Essay: Are American CEOs Overpaid, and, if so, What if Anything Should Be Done About It?*
58 Duke L.J. 1013, 1020–21, 1023–25 (2009)[2]

American CEOs are paid on average about twice as much as their counterparts in other countries. This is not because Americans at all levels earn more than their foreign counterparts; the margin is much smaller below the CEO level, and sometimes is negative. The proximate cause of American CEOs' higher incomes is that ... salaries are a much smaller fraction of their compensation than of foreign CEOs' incomes— less than half—with the rest consisting partly of bonuses but mainly of stock options. The difference in the structure of compensation may be due in part to the fact that foreign firms, inhibited by culture and sometimes by law in their ability to economize on labor costs, have less power to influence the profitability and hence market cap-italization of their firms.

* * *

The more effective shareholder monitoring is, the less need there is for incentive-based compensation: the stick is substituted for the carrot. This is a clue that agency costs may indeed lead to overcompensation in corporations in which ownership is widely dispersed, for otherwise why should greater stockholder concentration result in lower CEO compensation?

Yet it might seem that such dispersion should not matter because the CEO's com-pensation is determined by the board of directors, who are elected by the shareholders. But the board of directors does not solve the problem of agency costs that arises from the dispersed ownership of a publicly held corporation. The more dispersed that ownership, the weaker the incentive of shareholders to base their vote for the slate of proposed directors on a careful study of the candidates, especially because only rarely are there competing slates. Shareholder election of directors resembles the system of voting in the Soviet Union and other totalitarian nations.

Monitors who are not monitored are imperfect agents of their principal, and so in the absence of effective monitoring of directors by the shareholders, boards have weak incentives to limit CEO compensation. The problem is exacerbated by the fact that a board of directors is likely to be dominated by highly paid business executives, including CEOs of other companies. They have a conflict of interest, since they have a financial

---

2. Copyright © 2009 Duke Law Journal. Reprinted with permission of the Duke Law Journal and the author.

stake in high corporate salaries, their own salaries being determined in part by the salaries paid to persons in comparable positions in other companies. They also have a natural psychological tendency to believe that the high salaries of corporate executives accurately reflect executives' intrinsic worth. People are strongly inclined to exaggerate their own merit; many people feel underpaid; virtually none feels overpaid.

In addition, directors devote only a fraction of their time to the company. And if they are inside directors (that is, full-time employees of the firm), they have a palpable conflict of interest, while if they are outside (independent) directors, they have less access to information about the company than insiders and a smaller stake in the corporation's success. That explains why there is no persuasive evidence that corporate performance is positively correlated with the percentage of independent directors on the corporation's board. Many outside directors have no business experience.

CEOs, moreover, influence the selection of outside as well as inside directors; and there is evidence of mutual back scratching—the directors authorizing generous compensation for the CEO and the CEO supporting generous fees for the directors. CEOs hire and pay the auditors who certify the correctness of the corporation's financial statements, dangle consulting contracts in front of auditors who also offer consulting services, and can influence securities analysts' reports by steering underwriting fees to investment banks whose analysts give their companies glowing reports.

Still another reason to doubt that boards of directors ride herd on CEO compensation is that they can shield themselves from criticism, should the firm perform poorly, by pointing out that they paid top dollar for the CEO. Presumably therefore he was the best candidate for the post, and so in picking him they made the best choice they could have made and should not be blamed for his failures. The generosity of the compensation package they gave him thus becomes evidence that he was indeed the best choice ex ante. Conversely, if to economize they paid a second-best candidate less than they would have had to pay the best, then should he prove a bust they invite a charge of having been penny wise and pound foolish.

The consulting firms that boards of directors hire to advise them on selection and compensation of a CEO play to the self-protective instincts of directors by invariably recommending that the board hire as CEO someone who will demand compensation in the 75th or higher percentile of the CEOs of the firms that the consultant has identified as comparable to the board's firm. The result is an upward ratchet in CEO compensation; the old 75th percentile becomes the new 50th percentile, making the new 75th percentile higher than the old one. The compensation consultants have a conflict of interest because, like many accounting firms, they sell other consulting services to the firm.

* * *

And almost always the CEO is a member of the board of directors. The reason is that the board of directors of a corporation, unlike the board of trustees of a university, has responsibilities that go far beyond the selection and monitoring of the CEO. (That, along with fund raising and the management of endowment funds, is the principal function of a university's board.) The corporate board participates in shaping corporate strategy. This makes it complicit in the CEO's decisions and reluctant by firing him or cutting his pay to acknowledge a mistake for which it may be jointly responsible.

Comments and Questions

1. Judge Posner notes differences in the structure of executive compensation between CEOs in the United States and elsewhere. What might be the impact of this difference in structure, particularly the more common use of stock options as a significant portion of compensation in the United States?

2. What does it mean to have shareholders "monitor" compensation? How might this occur? What are some limits on shareholder monitoring?

3. Is the problem one of executive compensation or of CEO compensation? The amount of compensation paid to CEOs relative to other officers has increased. *See* Carola Frydman & Dirk Jenter, *CEO Compensation*, Working Paper No. 77, Rock Center for Corporate Governance, Stanford University, at 3 (Mar. 19, 2010) ("The median ratio of CEO compensation to that of the other highest-paid executives was stable at about 1.4 prior to 1980 but has since then risen to almost 2.6 in the 2000–05 period."). Moreover, as Judge Posner notes, the difference in compensation paid to officers below the CEO is less pronounced. What do you make of these observations?

4. Responsibility for setting compensation foremost falls to the board of directors. Directors are elected by shareholders. Isn't the power to replace the board enough to ensure effective monitoring? Why not?

5. How is the executive compensation dynamic different in companies where there is no separation of ownership and management? What about companies with a controlling shareholder, the common model in foreign companies? Do these companies have the same issues?

6. Compensation seemed to escalate in the 1990s. As one commentator described:

> Between 1992 and 2000 alone, the compensation of chief executive officers (CEOs) at S&P 500 companies more than quadrupled, from $3.5 million to $14.7 million. In 1991, the average large company CEO earned 140 times the wage of the average company employee; by 2003 it was 500 times. In 2005 alone, the average CEO's pay rose 27%, compared to a rise of 38% in 2004, while ordinary workers' wages remained stagnant. Quite often, these increases in compensation continue even when the corporation is struggling. The question persists whether executive compensation rewards CEO performance or gains unrelated to the efforts of the executive.

Jennifer S. Martin, *The House of Mouse and Beyond: Assessing the SEC's Efforts to Regulation Executive Compensation*, 32 Del. J. Corp. L. 481, 483–84 (2007). What accounts for this change? What does this tell us about the evolution of executive compensation?

7. At least one of the causes, ironically, may have been congressional efforts to limit compensation. In the 1990s, Congress adopted Section 162(m) of the Internal

Revenue Code. The provision prohibited corporations from deducting any amount of compensation for the CEO and four highest paid officers in excess of $1 million. The limit, however, did not apply to certain performance-based compensation. What impact would this provision likely have on compensation practices?

8. Equity compensation might come in the form of stock or options. Sometimes the compensation is based upon stock appreciation rights, a device that allows recipients to profit on increases in share prices without actually owning the underlying shares. These types of compensation only provide a return if share prices increase. Yet this does not take into account practices such as backdating or repricing. What impact does the ability to reprice have on managerial incentives? *See* Lucian Arye Bebchuk, Jesse M. Fried & David I. Walker, *Managerial Power and Rent Extraction in the Design of Executive Compensation*, 69 U. Chi. L. Rev. 751, 814 (Summer 2002) (describing practice of repricing as providing officers with "ex post indexing on the downside").

9. Options can also be timed in a manner that provides a windfall. Spring-loaded options are a term used to describe options issued just before a positive development that will increase share prices. As a result, the options quickly become "in the money." Backdated options are the practice of issuing options on one date but determining the exercise price on a prior date when share prices were lower. This effectively allows for the issuance of stock options that are in the money. It is not illegal to backdate stock options. Companies, however, failed to disclose the backdated nature of the options, creating the impression that the options were actually issued at market price. What legal issues might arise in connection with these practices? For some answers, take a look at *In re Tyson Foods, Inc. Consol. Shareholder Litig.*, 2007 Del. Ch. LEXIS 120 (Del. Ch. August 15, 2007).

10. The financial crisis that began in the fourth quarter of 2008 was perceived to have been caused at least in part by a compensation scheme that encouraged short term profits. This was particularly true for compensation based on one year results and paid in cash. One of the responses to these practices was to encourage the use of stock rather than cash bonuses and to encourage vesting schedules for the shares. How might these compensation practices affect management's behavior?

II. Fiduciary Duties and the Standard of Review

Executive compensation is usually determined by the board of directors. As such, the decisions are subject to the board's fiduciary obligations. Boards have both a duty of care and a duty of loyalty. The standard of review can, in this area, be outcome determinative. The duty of care is primarily a process standard. Courts largely defer to decisions taken by independent and informed directors. In effect, the terms (and amount) of compensation are largely irrelevant to the analysis.

The duty of loyalty, in contrast, leaves with the board the affirmative obligation to show that the amount of compensation is fair to the corporation. In these circumstances, the substantive terms and amount are very relevant. Boards will have to justify why an executive officer deserved the particular compensation and how it benefited the corporation.

A. Entire Fairness

The duty of loyalty applies to compensation decisions that affect members of the board. The standard most often applies to directors and officers such as the CEO who also serve on the board. The duty of loyaly imposes on the board the burden of establishing entire fairness. Entire fairness in turn includes two components—fair dealing and fair price. How does this analytical framework apply in the context of executive compensation?

Julian v. Eastern States Construction Service, Inc.

Delaware Chancery Court
2008 Del. Ch. LEXIS 86 (July 8, 2008)

PARSONS, VICE CHANCELLOR.

These are the facts as I find them after trial.

Plaintiff is Gene Julian who currently owns stock in ESCS, Benchmark, and ESD.C., but no longer works for any of the companies.

Defendant ESCS is a Delaware corporation formed on September 14, 1983. Nominal Defendant Benchmark is a Delaware corporation formed on November 28, 1988. Defendant Steven Bomberger is the President of Benchmark and serves as a director of Benchmark, along with Defendants Francis and Richard Julian. Nominal Defendant ESD.C. is a Delaware corporation formed on June 2, 1958. Eastern States Group Management Company, Inc. is a Delaware corporation formed on December 13, 2004 (together with ESCS, Benchmark, and ESD.C., the "Julian Businesses").

A. The Early Years

In the early 1970's, Gene, Francis, and Richard worked for Eastern States Construction Company and First State Enterprises. Eastern States Construction Company was owned by the Julian Brothers' father and their uncle, James Julian, along with several minority shareholders. First State Enterprises was owned by the brothers' father and a company owned by their Uncle James, in equal shares. In 1976 the brothers' father died and the Julian Brothers took on increasing responsibilities in the companies. By the mid-1980s the brothers wanted to buy Eastern States Construction Company, which by that time they ran. Among other things, they objected to the continuing need to pay dividends to Uncle James, who had no active role in the company. The brothers successfully bought out all of the minority interests in the company, except for Uncle James. The brothers attempted to purchase Uncle James' shares, but could not come to terms with him. Consequently, they liquidated Eastern States Construction Company and formed ESCS.

* * *

F. Benchmark Bonuses

At a meeting of the Benchmark board of directors on December 20, 2005, the board approved a $1,000,000 bonus to Eastern States Group Management Company (the "Management Group Bonus") and a $300,000 bonus to Bomberger (the "Bomberger Bonus," collectively the "Benchmark Bonuses") for calendar year 2005. Defendants allege the board discussed two business reasons for the bonuses—to reward management for a good year and to reduce retained earnings so that fewer assets would be at risk in the event of a lawsuit. The meeting took less than half an hour and no legal or financial advisors attended.

Before the December 20, 2005 meeting, Francis discussed the possibility of awarding bonuses with Richard for approximately fifteen minutes. Both Francis and Richard recognized that payment of any bonuses would decrease the net book value of Benchmark, and thereby benefit Benchmark in the event of a buyback of Gene's shares. Yet, the Benchmark directors did not consult anyone else before deciding to pay the bonuses. Several days after the board meeting, Benchmark issued a check to Eastern States Management Group for $1,000,000, which then distributed the bonus in equal shares to Francis and Richard. Benchmark paid the Bomberger Bonus in 2006.

The Benchmark Bonuses constituted 22.28% of Benchmark's adjusted income in 2005. For historical context, from 1996 to 1998, Benchmark paid no bonuses. Between 1999 and 2004, Benchmark's bonuses ranged from 3.30% to 3.36% of its adjusted income. Further, the Bomberger Bonus was the first bonus Bomberger received during his career at Benchmark beyond the compensation provided for in his Employment Agreement. A portion of Bomberger's contractual compensation in 2005 and earlier years was based on a percentage of Benchmark's gross profit or income before taxes.

Additionally, the portion of the Benchmark Bonuses paid to Francis, Richard, and Bomberger directly correlates to their respective stock ownership in Benchmark. Specifically, Francis and Richard each own 250 shares of Benchmark stock and Bomberger owns 150 shares. Their respective bonuses each translate into a payment to them of $2,000 per share.

* * *

Gene asserts that the Benchmark Bonuses represent self-interested transactions, and therefore Defendants must establish that the bonuses were entirely fair. According to Gene, the Benchmark Bonuses resulted from unfair dealing and reflect an unfair price. Regarding fair dealing, Gene questions the timing of the bonuses, noting Defendants approved them shortly after Gene resigned from ESCS and ESD.C., and most of the bonuses were paid shortly before the end of 2005, thereby intentionally causing a reduction in Benchmark's net asset value (the metric to be used for the purchase price of Gene's stock). Gene criticizes the process used as involving three interested directors of Benchmark who approved self-compensation, without any independent protections. According to Gene, Francis dominated the process and Richard and Bomberger went along, spending no more than half an hour considering the bonuses and failing to seek any review by an independent consultant or other disinterested person before approving them. Finally, Gene contends the amount of the Benchmark Bonuses, $1.3 million, was unfair and not commensurate with past practices of the Julian Businesses. In terms of relief, Gene seeks damages for the alleged breach of fiduciary duty, including disgorgement by Francis, Richard, and Bomberger of the bonuses they received and reimbursement for his attorneys' fees.

Francis and Richard respond by defending the entire fairness of the Benchmark Bonuses. They stress that the Julian Businesses are family run companies with three to four member boards of directors and very few shareholders. The length and nature of the December 20, 2005 Benchmark board meeting at issue matched the procedures attendant to other Benchmark director actions. Thus, Defendants contend the Benchmark Bonuses resulted from fair dealing. Additionally, according to Francis and Richard, the amount or "price" of the bonuses, given the circumstances, was historically comparable and fair.

Bomberger also defends the Benchmark Bonuses as entirely fair. In particular, Bomberger denies having breached his fiduciary duty when he voted in favor of those bonuses. Bomberger argues that as one of three directors his vote was not necessary to authorize the $1 million paid to Eastern States Management Group. According to Bomberger, he had not discussed the prospect of paying any bonuses before the December 20 meeting. Additionally, Bomberger contends that after the meeting he confirmed that the Julian Businesses had paid similar bonuses in the past. Moreover, Bomberger relies on an expert, Trey Stevens, who testified Bomberger's bonus was fair and comported with the "Independent Investor Test."

Self-interested directorial compensation decisions made without independent protections, like other interested transactions, are subject to entire fairness review. Directors of a Delaware corporation who stand on both sides of a transaction have "the burden of establishing its entire fairness, sufficient to pass the test of careful scrutiny by the courts." They "are required to demonstrate their utmost good faith and the most scrupulous inherent fairness of the bargain." The two components of entire fairness are fair dealing and fair price. Fair dealing "embraces questions of when the transaction was timed, how it was initiated, structured, negotiated, disclosed to the directors, and how the approvals of the directors and the stockholders were obtained." Fair price "assures the transaction was substantively fair by examining 'the economic and financial considerations.'"

The two aspects of entire fairness are not independent. Rather, "the fair dealing prong informs the court as to the fairness of the price obtained through the process. The court does not focus on the components individually, but determines the entire fairness based on all aspects of the entire transaction."

The circumstances of the Benchmark Bonuses give rise to suspicion about their fairness. Eleven days after Gene submitted his letter of retirement and resignation from ESD.C. and ESCS, the Benchmark board approved the Benchmark Bonuses. Francis initiated the process just days after Gene's notice of retirement. He approached Richard before the December 20, 2005 board meeting and proposed making the bonuses. The brothers discussed the concept for fifteen minutes, and consulted no one else. Francis and Richard concede that they knew any bonus would decrease the net book value of Benchmark, consequently decreasing the value of the shares they contemporaneously were trying to force Gene to sell back.

The size of the bonuses, given their historical context, also raises questions. Before the December 20, 2005 meeting, the Benchmark board had not approved bonuses near the magnitude of $1.3 million. While the record is imperfect, it suggests Benchmark paid no bonuses from 1996 through 1998. From 1999 through 2004, Benchmark's bonuses as a percentage of adjusted income hovered between 3.30% and 3.36%. In contrast, the challenged 2005 bonuses constituted 22.28% of adjusted income. Additionally, 2005 marked the first time Bomberger received a bonus beyond the performance-based compensation set forth in his Employment Agreement.

I do not find credible Defendants' argument that the board approved the Benchmark Bonuses as a reward for a good year in 2005 or to reduce retained earnings in the event of a lawsuit. Regarding the reward for a good year, Benchmark had a better year in 2004 than 2005, and the bonuses in 2004 were still only 3.36% of adjusted income. Moreover, when asked about the discrepancy between the bonuses in 2004 and 2005, Richard responded:

He [Gene] didn't leave, either [in 2004]. We were in shock when he left, to tell you the truth.... We were in shock. You know, here's somebody you sweat with and be successful with for 30 years—30-plus years—gives you not as much notice as most of your good truck drivers give us when they decide to retire. In other words, more than anything else, the bonuses represented a knee-jerk reaction to Gene's precipitous retirement, which Francis and Richard considered a betrayal.

To summarize, the Benchmark Bonuses were the product of an unfair process. The record indicates no coherent, credible reason for the bonuses other than in reaction to Gene's retirement. Additionally, there was no notice, meaningful deliberation, or independent advice or research before the board's action. In fact, as to the Management Group Bonus, Bomberger had no clear idea what he was approving. In addition, the price was also unfair. There was no historical precedent for the size of the bonus. For example, Gene, who worked for the Eastern States Group through nearly all of 2005, received nothing. Finally, I do not find Stevens' expert testimony persuasive. His "Independent Investor Test" is so subjective and unsupported by work of other experts in the relevant field, that I find it unreliable and unhelpful in the circumstances of this case. I also note Bomberger could not cite any Delaware law that has adopted or supported Stevens' theory. Therefore, I conclude Francis, Richard, and Bomberger failed to demonstrate the Benchmark Bonuses were entirely fair and breached their fiduciary duty of loyalty to Benchmark when they approved them.

* * *

As to the claims regarding the Benchmark Bonuses, the Court has concluded that Francis, Richard, and Bomberger have breached their fiduciary duties in approving and accepting those bonuses. To remedy that breach, the Court will require Francis,

Richard, and Bomberger (1) to disgorge the total of $1.3 million in Benchmark Bonuses they received and return that money to Benchmark with interest at the legal rate, compounded quarterly, and (2) to reimburse Gene for his reasonable attorneys' fees and costs incurred in the prosecution of the Benchmark Bonuses claim.

Comments and Questions

1. In general, the board must show that the conflict of interest transaction retained "the earmarks of an arm's length bargain." *Byelick v. Vivadelli*, 79 F. Supp. 2d 610, 629 (E.D. Va. 1999) (quoting *Moneta v. Willard Building Supply Co.*, 515 S.E.2d 277, 287 (Va. 1999)). As one commentator noted, fairness represented what "would have been approved by a disinterested board negotiating at arm's length with a stranger." Joel Seligman, *The New Corporate Law*, 59 Brook. L. Rev. 1, 7 (1993).

2. What is fair dealing? What goes into the consideration of fair dealing? As one court described: Fair dealing "embraced questions of when the transaction was timed, how it was initiated, structured, negotiated, disclosed to the directors, and how the approvals of the directors and the stockholders were obtained." *Weinberger v. UOP*, 457 A.2d 701, 710 (Del. 1983).

3. How did the board try to establish the fairness of the bonuses in this case? Can directors establish fairness by comparing the amounts to other employees within the company? For some thoughts on that issue, see *Zutrau v. Jansing*, C.A. No. 7457-VCP (Del. Ch. July 31, 2014).

4. Had the bonuses been consistent with those paid in the past, the court suggests that they would have been treated as fair. Can you draw a general rule from this implication? Would it always be the case that such bonuses would be treated as fair?

5. How else might the board have demonstrated the fairness of the bonuses? Do you think that industry practice matters? If these bonuses were typical in amount for their industry (large financial institutions, for example, tend to pay significant bonuses), would that have been sufficient to show fairness? How important is the particular "peer group" used in making the comparison. The issue came up in *Zutrau v. Jansing*, C.A. No. 7457-VCP (Del. Ch. July 31, 2014).

6. We will examine process and fair dealing in more detail in the next case. What role did it play here? What could the board have done to ensure fair dealing? Had there been "fair dealing," would the outcome have been different?

7. The duty of loyalty does not apply unless an interested director receives a benefit not shared by the other shareholders. Thus, a dividend paid to all shareholders will not result in the application of the business judgment rule even where a director gets the largest portion of the payment. *See Pfeffer v. Redstone*, 965 A.2d 676 (Del. 2009). Could the bonuses have been structured to fall within that exception to the duty of loyalty?

———

What about the amount of compensation paid to directors? Does this compensation also have to meet standards of fairness?

CALMA v. Templeton

Delaware Chancery Court
114 A.3d 563 (2015)

BOUCHARD, VICE CHANCELLOR:

I. INTRODUCTION

Over the past six decades, Delaware courts have issued numerous decisions concerning ratification of compensation paid to non-employee directors. This Opinion surveys that jurisprudence to determine whether stockholder approval of a compensation plan subjects the self-interested payment of compensation to non-employee directors under such a plan to judicial review under a waste standard instead of an entire fairness standard.

In this derivative action, a stockholder challenges awards of restricted stock units (RSUs) that were granted to eight non-employee directors of Citrix Systems, Inc. ("Citrix" or the "Company") in 2011, 2012, and 2013 (the "RSU Awards"). The majority of the directors' compensation consisted of these RSU Awards, which the board's compensation committee granted under the Company's 2005 Equity Incentive Plan (the "Plan"). That Plan, along with subsequent amendments thereto, was approved by a majority of Citrix's disinterested stockholders in informed and uncoerced votes.

Citrix's directors, officers, employees, consultants, and advisors were all beneficiaries under the Plan. The only limit on compensation the Plan imposed is that no beneficiary could receive more than one million shares (or RSUs) per calendar year. There were no sub-limits based on the beneficiary's position at Citrix. Based on Citrix's stock price when this action was filed, one million RSUs were worth over $55 million.

The plaintiff contends that the RSU Awards were, when combined with the cash payments that Citrix's non-employee directors received, "excessive" in comparison with the compensation received by directors at certain of Citrix's "peers." The plaintiff seeks to recover against the defendants, the members of Citrix's board, under three theories of liability: (i) breach of fiduciary duty (Count I); (ii) waste of corporate assets (Count II); and (iii) unjust enrichment (Count III).

The plaintiff does not contend that Citrix stockholders failed to approve the Plan; that Citrix stockholders were not fully informed when they approved the Plan; or that the RSU Awards violated the Plan. Rather, he asserts that the defendants must establish the entire fairness of the RSU Awards as conflicted compensation decisions because the Plan does not have any "meaningful limits" on the annual stock-based compensation that Citrix directors can receive from the Company.

The defendants moved to dismiss the complaint in its entirety under Court of Chancery Rule 12(b)(6) for failure to state a claim upon which relief may be granted, and under Court of Chancery Rule 23.1 for failure to make a pre-suit demand upon Citrix's board or to plead facts excusing such a demand. The defendants' primary argument is a ratification defense, but they concede that Citrix stockholders were not asked to ratify the specific RSU Awards at issue here. Instead, the defendants contend that Citrix stockholders ratified the Plan so that any award of RSUs to the directors under the generic one million RSU limit in the Plan must be reviewed under a waste standard. They further contend that it is not reasonably conceivable that the RSU Awards constituted waste.

In this opinion, I conclude that the plaintiff has established that demand is futile because a majority of the Citrix board in office when the complaint was filed were interested by virtue of receiving the RSU Awards. Thus, the defendants' Rule 23.1 motion is denied.

I further conclude that the defendants have not established that Citrix stockholders ratified the RSU Awards because, in obtaining omnibus approval of a Plan covering multiple and varied classes of beneficiaries, the Company did not seek or obtain stockholder approval of any action *bearing specifically on the magnitude of compensation to be paid to its non-employee directors*. Accordingly, because the RSU Awards were self-dealing decisions, the operative standard of review is entire fairness, and it is reasonably conceivable that the total compensation received by the non-employee directors was not entirely fair to the Company.

* * *

B. Citrix's 2005 Equity Incentive Plan

On May 25, 2005, a majority of Citrix's stockholders approved the Plan. The Plan was adopted in part "to advance the interests of Citrix Systems, Inc.... by encouraging ownership of Stock by employees, directors, officers, consultants or advisors of the Company" and by "attracting and retaining the best available individuals for service as directors of the Company."

The Plan initially encompassed 10.1 million total shares, of which 500,000 shares could be awarded as RSUs. Those terms have since been amended several times. The Plan currently encompasses 48.6 million total shares, of which 16 million shares can be awarded as RSUs. As of the filing of the Complaint, there were over 16 million shares available under the Plan, with 11 million shares available to be granted as RSUs.

* * *

Under *Rales,* Plaintiff's derivative claims must be dismissed under Court of Chancery Rule 23.1 unless, based on the particularized facts alleged, Plaintiff creates "a reasonable doubt that, as of the time the complaint is filed, the board of directors could have properly exercised its independent and disinterested business judgment in responding to a demand." In this analysis, all particularized allegations in the Complaint are accepted as true, and all reasonable inferences logically flowing from those particularized allegations are drawn in Plaintiff's favor. Most relevant here, a director is not disinterested if he or she "appear[s] on both sides of a transaction [or] expect[s] to derive any personal financial benefit from it in the sense of self-dealing."

Defendants argue that a director is not deemed interested simply because he or she received compensation from the corporation unless Plaintiff is able to show that the compensation received was material to that individual, which they contend Plaintiff has not done. In opposition, Plaintiff contends that where, as here, there are derivative claims challenging the compensation received by directors, those directors are interested for demand futility purposes because they "have a personal financial interest in their compensation for their service as directors," regardless of whether the compensation they received was material to them personally. Accordingly, Plaintiff submits that demand is excused here because he challenges the RSU Awards received by a majority of the Board in office when the Complaint was filed. I agree with Plaintiff.

Under Delaware law, directors are generally not considered interested ... "simply because [they] receive compensation from the company." But, a derivative challenge to director compensation is different because the law is skeptical that an individual can fairly and impartially consider whether to have the corporation initiate litigation challenging his or her own compensation, regardless of whether or not that compensation is material on a personal level.

Drawing on Chancellor Allen's analysis in *Steiner v. Meyerson,* I concluded in *Cambridge Retirement System v. Bosnjak* that, in a derivative challenge to director compensation, there is a reasonable doubt that the directors who received the compensation at issue—regardless of whether that compensation was material to them on a personal level—can be sufficiently disinterested to consider impartially a demand to pursue litigation challenging the amount or form of their own compensation. In my view, this conclusion has even more force where, as here, the directors received equity compensation from the corporation because those individuals "have a strong financial incentive to maintain the status quo by not authorizing any corrective action that would devalue their current holdings or cause them to disgorge improperly obtained profits."

Here, eight of the nine Citrix directors in office when Plaintiff filed the Complaint received the RSU Awards from the Company. Plaintiff alleged with sufficient particularity that those eight directors are "interested" by identifying the amount and form of the RSU Awards they received from the Company during 2011–2013. As in *Steiner* and *Bosnjak,* Plaintiff need not establish that the RSU Awards were material to the Company's non-employee directors. Since a majority of the Board is interested, Plaintiff has raised a reasonable doubt as to the ability of the Board to impartially consider whether or not to pursue a claim challenging the RSU Awards....

* * *

Delaware courts examine the merits of a claim for breach of fiduciary duty through one of (primarily) three doctrinal standards of review: business judgment, enhanced scrutiny, and entire fairness. Where a stockholder cannot rebut the presumptive business judgment standard, the stockholder must show that the board's decision cannot be attributed to any rational business purpose—which, in effect, is the standard for waste under Delaware law. But, where a stockholder rebuts the business judgment standard—for example, by establishing that at least half of the directors who approved a business decision are not independent or disinterested—the Court reviews the directors' decision under the entire fairness standard, in which case the directors must establish "to the *court's* satisfaction that the transaction was the product of both fair dealing *and* fair price."

The Compensation Committee approved the RSU Awards to the Company's non-employee directors in 2011, 2012, and 2013. These were conflicted decisions because all three members of the Compensation Committee received some of the RSU Awards. As the Delaware Supreme Court observed in *Telxon Corp. v. Meyerson,* director self-compensation decisions are conflicted transactions that "lie outside the business judgment rule's presumptive protection, so that, where properly challenged, the receipt of self-determined benefits is subject to an affirmative showing that the compensation arrangements are fair to the corporation." This is not a case where disinterested directors approved the compensation of other directors; the Compensation Committee approved their own compensation and that of the other non-employee directors. Thus, in my view, Plaintiff has rebutted the presumptive business judgment standard of review.

2. Stockholder Ratification Concerning Director Compensation

To avoid the entire fairness standard, Defendants raise the affirmative defense of common law stockholder ratification and contend that the RSU Awards must be reviewed under a waste standard. Specifically, Defendants submit that the RSU Awards "were the result of the Board administering the shareholder-approved 2005 [Plan] and were made pursuant to, and in full compliance with, that [P]lan." Plaintiff counters that, even though the RSU Awards were granted under the stockholder-approved Plan, Defendants still bear the burden to establish the entire fairness of the RSU Awards because the Plan "has no meaningful limits" on the total equity compensation that the Company's non-employee directors could hypothetically receive....

The question before me is whether advance stockholder approval of a compensation plan with multiple classes of beneficiaries and a single generic limit on the amount of compensation that may be awarded in a given year is sufficient to establish a ratification defense for the RSU Awards that were granted to Citrix's non-employee directors.... Given Defendants' contention that sixty years of precedent supports their position, I review those decisions before applying the key principles from them to the allegations here.

* * *

In my view, this case law discussed above supports two principles of common law stockholder ratification relevant to director compensation.

One principle is that the affirmative defense of ratification is available only where a majority of informed, uncoerced, and disinterested stockholders vote in favor of a *specific decision* of the board of directors. Indeed, this is the standard about the scope of ratification pronounced by the Delaware Supreme Court in *Gantler v. Stephens.* There, the defendants argued that stockholders had ratified the directors' purportedly interested decision to recommend that stockholders approve a stock reclassification proposal. Although *Gantler* ultimately rejected the ratification defense because the complaint adequately alleged that the stockholder vote was not fully informed, the Supreme Court held, as a matter of law, that "the only director action or conduct that can be ratified is *that which the shareholders are specifically asked to approve.*" As support for this ratify the board's approval of any deal protection provisions in the merger agreement because, in that case, the stockholders did not "*specifically vote in favor*" of those proposition, *Gantler* cites to *In re Santa Fe Pacific Corp. Shareholder Litigation,* where the Supreme Court earlier had concluded that a stockholder vote in favor of a merger did not defensive measures.

* * *

The second principle is well-established and non-controversial: valid stockholder ratification leads to waste being the doctrinal standard of review for a breach of fiduciary duty claim. Approval by a mere majority of stockholders does not ratify waste because "a waste of corporate assets is incapable of ratification without unanimous stockholder consent."

Important policy considerations support these two principles of common law stockholder ratification in the context of director compensation. Specifying the precise amount and form of director compensation in an equity compensation plan when it is submitted for stockholder approval "ensure[s] integrity" in the underlying principal-agent relationship between stockholders and directors "by making the directors suffer the ugly and enjoy the good that comes with a consistent, non-discretionary approach" to their compensation. Likewise, obtaining stockholder approval of director compensation on an annual or regular basis facilitates the disclosure of inherently conflicted decisions and empowers stockholders with a meaningful role in the compensation of their fiduciaries.

3. Citrix's Stockholders Did Not Ratify the RSU Awards

Turning to the present case, Citrix stockholders initially approved the Plan in 2005. Because Plaintiff does not allege otherwise, I treat the Citrix stockholder approval of the Plan in 2005 (and of the amendments thereto) as a vote of approval by a majority of informed, uncoerced, and disinterested stockholders.

The Plan specified the total shares available (Section 4), the beneficiaries under the Plan (Section 6.1(a)), and the total number of shares that any beneficiary could receive in a calendar year (Section 6.1(b)). But the Plan did not specify the amount or form of compensation to be issued to the Company's non-employee directors. Rather, the only limit on director compensation appears in Section 6.1(b): directors, like every other eligible recipient under the Plan, may receive up to 1 million shares (or equivalent RSU awards) per calendar year. To repeat, based on Citrix's stock price at the time, one million RSUs were worth over $55 million when this action was filed.

In my view, Defendants have not carried their burden to establish a ratification affirmative defense at this procedural stage because Citrix stockholders were never asked to approve—and thus did not approve—any *action bearing specifically on the magnitude of compensation for the Company's non-employee directors.* Unlike in *Steiner* or *Vogelstein,* the Plan here does not set forth the specific compensation to be granted to non-employee directors. And, unlike in *3COM,* the Plan here does not set forth any director-specific "ceilings" on the compensation that could be granted to the Company's directors.

I see no meaningful difference between the allegations here and those in *Slager,* which I do not read (for the reasons discussed above) as a departure from Delaware precedent as Defendants have argued. Here, as in *Slager,* the Plan does not specify any amounts (or director-specific ceilings) of equity compensation that Citrix directors would or could receive independent of the generic annual limit applicable to all the varied classes of beneficiaries under the Plan. Under *Sample* and *Slager,* the upfront stockholder approval of the Plan was not a "blank check" or "*carte blanche*" ratification of any compensation that the Compensation Committee might award to the Company's non-employee directors. Thus, in my opinion, upfront stockholder approval by Citrix stockholders of the Plan's generic limits on compensation for all beneficiaries under the Plan does not establish a ratification defense for the RSU Awards because, when the Board sought stockholder approval of the broad parameters of the Plan and the generic limits specified therein, Citrix stockholders were not asked to approve any *action specific to director compensation.* They were simply asked to approve, in very broad terms, the Plan itself. For this reason, as in *Sample* and *Slager,* I cannot conclude that the Company's stockholders ratified the RSU Awards such that those awards would be limited to challenge under a waste standard.

At the Company's annual meetings in 2012 and 2013, Citrix stockholders voted in favor of amendments to the Plan to increase the total number of shares available under the Plan and to "ratif[y], confirm[ ] and approve[ ]" the Plan in all respects. But, in those proxy statements, Citrix stockholders were not specifically asked to ratify the RSU Awards granted the prior year. Nonetheless, Defendants argue that because the relevant proxy statements *589 disclosed the specific compensation that was granted to non-employee members of the Board during the prior years (*i.e.,* the RSU Awards issued in 2011 and 2012), the vote to "ratify, confirm, and approve" the Plan was the functional equivalent of a vote in favor of the RSU Awards. I disagree. Unlike in *Bosnjak,* the Company's proxy statements in 2012 and 2013 did not seek stockholder approval of the specific compensation that had been (or that would be) awarded to the non-employee members of the Board. Instead, the Citrix stockholder approval of the Plan in 2012 and 2013 ratified only the adoption and terms of the Plan.

For these reasons, I conclude that Defendants have not carried their burden to show that the Company's stockholders ratified the RSU Awards.114 Accordingly, the operative standard of review remains entire fairness with the burden on Defendants.

4. It is Reasonably Conceivable that the RSU Awards were Not Entirely Fair

Where, as here, the entire fairness standard of review applies, Defendants must establish that the decision "was the product of both fair dealing *and* fair price." The fact that the entire fairness standard applies "normally will preclude dismissal of a complaint on a Rule 12(b)(6) motion to dismiss." But, "[e]ven in a self-interested transaction in order to state a claim a shareholder must allege some facts that tend to show that the transaction was not fair."

The parties frame the issue of whether the RSU Awards were entirely fair as a matter of whether Citrix's non-employee director compensation practices were in line with those of the Company's "peer" group. Defendants argue that Citrix's peer group for director compensation purposes is the fourteen companies identified by the Company as its peers in its filings with the Securities and Exchange Commission. Plaintiff, on the other hand, submits that the appropriate peer group should be limited to only five of the Company's fourteen self-selected peers based on comparable market capitalization, revenue, and net income metrics.

In my view, Plaintiff has raised meaningful questions as to whether certain companies with considerably higher market capitalizations, revenue, and net income—such as Amazon.com, Google, and Microsoft—should be included in the peer group used to determine the fair value of compensation for Citrix's non-employee directors. These factual questions about the fairness of the RSU Awards in comparison to the director compensation practices at public companies that are comparable to Citrix, however, cannot be resolved at the procedural stage of the present Rule 12(b)(6) motion. Thus, Count I states a claim for breach of fiduciary duty.

Comments and Questions

1. Director compensation must be disclosed in proxy statements distributed by public companies. Amounts can be significant. The proxy statement filed in 2011 for Apple, for example, showed total compensation of over $1 million for two directors. That year, the board met four times. What impact might disclosure have on the amount of compensation?

2. Conceptually, why are director compensation decisions more likely to be subject to the entire fairness standard than decisions affecting the CEO? How might directors structure the approval process in order to obtain the benefit of the business judgment rule?

3. In this case, directors argued that shareholders had ratified the decision, entitling them to the protection of the business judgment rule. Why did the defense fail? In the future, how would directors need to structure the approval process to obtain the benefits of shareholder ratification?

4. How might directors establish that the amount of compensation was "fair." Are the standards the same for showing fairness of CEO compensation?

5. Assuming the application of the business judgment rule to director compensation decisions, what is the legal standard for challenging the payments? How easily will it be, for example, to argue that directors were overpaid given their "minimal participation and lack of qualifications"? *Friedman v. Dolan*, CA No. 9425 (Del. Ch. Jan. 23, 2015) (Delaware law).

B. The Duty of Care

Not all compensation decisions are subject to the duty of loyalty. Sometimes the relevant officer is not on the board of directors. This was the case, for example, with respect to Michael Ovitz at Disney. In those circumstances, the courts typically apply the duty of care.

Brehm v. Eisner

Delaware Supreme Court
906 A.2d 27 (2006)

JACOBS, JUSTICE:

In August 1995, Michael Ovitz ("Ovitz") and The Walt Disney Company ("Disney" or the "Company") entered into an employment agreement under which Ovitz would serve as President of Disney for five years. In December 1996, only fourteen months after he commenced employment, Ovitz was terminated without cause, resulting in a severance payout to Ovitz valued at approximately $130 million.

* * *

In 1994 Disney lost in a tragic helicopter crash its President and Chief Operating Officer, Frank Wells, who together with Michael Eisner, Disney's Chairman and Chief Executive Officer, had enjoyed remarkable success at the Company's helm. Eisner temporarily assumed Disney's presidency, but only three months later, heart disease required Eisner to undergo quadruple bypass surgery. Those two events persuaded Eisner and Disney's board of directors that the time had come to identify a successor to Eisner.

Eisner's prime candidate for the position was Michael Ovitz, who was the leading partner and one of the founders of Creative Artists Agency ("CAA"), the premier talent agency whose business model had reshaped the entire industry. By 1995, CAA had 550 employees and a roster of about 1400 of Hollywood's top actors, directors, writers, and musicians. That roster generated about $150 million in annual revenues and an annual income of over $20 million for Ovitz, who was regarded as one of the most powerful figures in Hollywood.

Eisner and Ovitz had enjoyed a social and professional relationship that spanned nearly 25 years. Although in the past the two men had casually discussed possibly working together, in 1995, when Ovitz began negotiations to leave CAA and join Music Corporation of America ("MCA"), Eisner became seriously interested in recruiting Ovitz to join Disney. Eisner shared that desire with Disney's board members on an individual basis.

* * *

Russell [a Disney director and chairman of the compensation committee] assumed the lead in negotiating the financial terms of the Ovitz employment contract. In the course of negotiations, Russell learned from Ovitz's attorney, Bob Goldman, that Ovitz owned 55% of CAA and earned approximately $20 to $25 million a year from that company. From the beginning Ovitz made it clear that he would not give up his 55% interest in CAA without "downside protection." Considerable negotiation then ensued over downside protection issues. During the summer of 1995, the parties agreed to a draft version of Ovitz's employment agreement (the "OEA") modeled after Eisner's and the late Mr. Wells' employment contracts....

The proposed OEA sought to protect both parties in the event that Ovitz's employment ended prematurely, and provided that absent defined causes, neither party could terminate the agreement without penalty. If Ovitz, for example, walked away, for any reason other than those permitted under the OEA, he would forfeit any benefits remaining under the OEA and could be enjoined from working for a competitor. Likewise, if Disney fired Ovitz for any reason other than gross negligence or malfeasance, Ovitz would be entitled to a non-fault payment (Non-Fault Termination or "NFT"), which consisted of his remaining salary, $7.5 million a year for unaccrued bonuses, the immediate vesting of his first tranche of options and a $10 million cash out payment for the second tranche of options.

* * *

On September 26, 1995, the Disney compensation committee (which consisted of Messrs. Russell, Watson, Poitier and Lozano) met for one hour to consider, among other agenda items, the proposed terms of the OEA. A term sheet was distributed at the meeting, although a draft of the OEA was not. The topics discussed were historical comparables, such as Eisner's and Wells' option grants, and also the factors that Russell, Watson and Crystal [an executive compensation consultant] had considered in setting the size of the option grants and the termination provisions of the contract. Watson testified that he provided the compensation committee with the spreadsheet analysis that he had performed in August, and discussed his findings with the committee. Crystal did not attend the meeting, although he was available by telephone to respond to questions if needed, but no one from the committee called. After Russell's and Watson's presentations, Litvack [Disney's general counsel] also responded to substantive questions. At trial Poitier and Lozano testified that they believed they had received sufficient information from Russell's and Watson's presentations to exercise their judgment in the best interests of the Company. The committee voted unanimously to approve the OEA terms, subject to "reasonable further negotiations within the framework of the terms and conditions" described in the OEA.

Immediately after the compensation committee meeting, the Disney board met in executive session. The board was told about the reporting structure to which Ovitz had agreed, but the initial negative reaction of Litvack and Bollenbach [Disney's CFO] to the hiring was not recounted. Eisner led the discussion relating to Ovitz, and Watson then explained his analysis, and both Watson and Russell responded to questions from the board. After further deliberation, the board voted unanimously to elect Ovitz as President.

At its September 26, 1995 meeting, the compensation committee determined that it would delay the formal grant of Ovitz's stock options until further issues between Ovitz and the Company were resolved. That was done, and the committee met again, on October 16, 1995, to discuss stock option-related issues. The committee approved amendments to the Walt Disney Company 1990 Stock Incentive Plan (the "1990 Plan"), and also approved a new plan, known as the Walt Disney 1995 Stock Incentive Plan (the "1995 Plan"). Both plans were subject to further approval by the full board of directors and the shareholders. Both the amendment to the 1990 Plan and the

Stock Option Agreement provided that in the event of a non-fault termination ("NFT"), Ovitz's options would be exercisable until the later of September 30, 2002 or twenty-four months after termination, but in no event later than October 16, 2005. After approving those Plans, the committee unanimously approved the terms of the OEA and the award of Ovitz's options under the 1990 Plan.

B. Ovitz's Performance As President of Disney

Ovitz's tenure as President of the Walt Disney Company officially began on October 1, 1995, the date that the OEA was executed. When Ovitz took office, the initial reaction was optimistic, and Ovitz did make some positive contributions while serving as President of the Company. By the fall of 1996, however, it had become clear that Ovitz was "a poor fit with his fellow executives." By then the Disney directors were discussing that the disconnect between Ovitz and the Company was likely irreparable and that Ovitz would have to be terminated.

* * *

In our view, a helpful approach is to compare what actually happened here to what would have occurred had the committee followed a "best practices" (or "best case") scenario, from a process standpoint. In a "best case" scenario, all committee members would have received, before or at the committee's first meeting on September 26, 1995, a spreadsheet or similar document prepared by (or with the assistance of) a compensation expert (in this case, Graef Crystal). Making different, alternative assumptions, the spreadsheet would disclose the amounts that Ovitz could receive under the OEA in each circumstance that might foreseeably arise. One variable in that matrix of possibilities would be the cost to Disney of a non-fault termination for each of the five years of the initial term of the OEA. The contents of the spreadsheet would be explained to the committee members, either by the expert who prepared it or by a fellow committee member similarly knowledgeable about the subject. That spreadsheet, which ultimately would become an exhibit to the minutes of the compensation committee meeting, would form the basis of the committee's deliberations and decision.

Had that scenario been followed, there would be no dispute (and no basis for litigation) over what information was furnished to the committee members or when it was furnished. Regrettably, the committee's informational and decisionmaking process used here was not so tidy. That is one reason why the Chancellor found that although the committee's process did not fall below the level required for a proper exercise of due care, it did fall short of what best practices would have counseled.

The Disney compensation committee met twice: on September 26 and October 16, 1995. The minutes of the September 26 meeting reflect that the committee approved the terms of the OEA (at that time embodied in the form of a letter agreement), except for the option grants, which were not approved until October 16 — after the Disney stock incentive plan had been amended to provide for those options. At the September 26 meeting, the compensation committee considered a "term sheet" which, in summarizing the material terms of the OEA, relevantly disclosed that in the event of a non-fault termination, Ovitz would receive: (i) the present value of his salary ($1 million per year) for the balance of the contract term, (ii) the present value of his annual bonus payments (computed at $7.5 million) for the balance of the contract term, (iii) a $10 million termination fee, and (iv) the acceleration of his options for 3 million shares, which would become immediately exercisable at market price.

Thus, the compensation committee knew that in the event of an NFT, Ovitz's severance payment alone could be in the range of $40 million cash, plus the value of the accelerated options. Because the actual payout to Ovitz was approximately $130 million, of which roughly $38.5 million was cash, the value of the options at the time of the NFT payout would have been about $91.5 million. Thus, the issue may be framed as whether the compensation committee members knew, at the time they approved the OEA, that the value of the option component of the severance package could reach the $92 million order of magnitude if they terminated Ovitz without cause after one year. The evidentiary record shows that the committee members were so informed.

On this question the documentation is far less than what best practices would have dictated. There is no exhibit to the minutes that discloses, in a single document, the estimated value of the accelerated options in the event of an NFT termination after one year. The information imparted to the committee members on that subject is, however, supported by other evidence, most notably the trial testimony of various witnesses about spreadsheets that were prepared for the compensation committee meetings.

The compensation committee members derived their information about the potential magnitude of an NFT payout from two sources. The first was the value of the "benchmark" options previously granted to Eisner and Wells and the valuations by Watson of the proposed Ovitz options. Ovitz's options were set at 75% of parity with the options previously granted to Eisner and to Frank Wells. Because the compensation committee had established those earlier benchmark option grants to Eisner and Wells and were aware of their value, a simple mathematical calculation would have informed them of the potential value range of Ovitz's options. Also, in August and September 1995, Watson and Russell met with Graef Crystal to determine (among other things) the value of the potential Ovitz options, assuming different scenarios. Crystal valued the options under the Black-Scholes method, while Watson used a different valuation metric. Watson recorded his calculations and the resulting values on a set of spreadsheets that reflected what option profits Ovitz might receive, based upon a range of different assumptions about stock market price increases. Those spreadsheets were shared with, and explained to, the committee members at the September meeting.

The committee's second source of information was the amount of "downside protection" that Ovitz was demanding. Ovitz required financial protection from the risk of leaving a very lucrative and secure position at CAA, of which he was a controlling partner, to join a publicly held corporation to which Ovitz was a stranger, and that had a very different culture and an environment which prevented him from completely controlling his destiny. The committee members knew that by leaving CAA and coming to Disney, Ovitz would be sacrificing "booked" CAA commissions of $150 to $200 million—an amount that Ovitz demanded as protection against the risk that his employment relationship with Disney might not work out. Ovitz wanted at least $50 million of that compensation to take the form of an "up-front" signing bonus. Had the $50 million bonus been paid, the size of the option grant would have been lower. Because it was contrary to Disney policy, the compensation committee rejected the up-front signing bonus demand, and elected instead to compensate Ovitz at the "back end," by awarding him options that would be phased in over the five-year term of the OEA.

It is on this record that the Chancellor found that the compensation committee was informed of the material facts relating to an NFT payout. If measured in terms of the documentation that would have been generated if "best practices" had been followed, that record leaves much to be desired. The Chancellor acknowledged that, and so do we. But, the Chancellor also found that despite its imperfections, the evidentiary record was sufficient to support the conclusion that the compensation committee had adequately informed itself of the potential magnitude of the entire severance package, including the options, that Ovitz would receive in the event of an early NFT.

The OEA was specifically structured to compensate Ovitz for walking away from $150 million to $200 million of anticipated commissions from CAA over the five-year OEA contract term. This meant that if Ovitz was terminated without cause, the earlier in the contract term the termination occurred the larger the severance amount would be to replace the lost commissions. Indeed, because Ovitz was terminated after only one year, the total amount of his severance payment (about $130 million) closely approximated the lower end of the range of Ovitz's forfeited commissions ($150 million), less the compensation Ovitz received during his first and only year as Disney's President. Accordingly, the Court of Chancery had a sufficient evidentiary basis in the record from which to find that, at the time they approved the OEA, the compensation committee members were adequately informed of the potential magnitude of an early NFT severance payout.

Comments and Questions

1. Should this case have been analyzed under the duty of loyalty? Plaintiff certainly argued that it should be. Plaintiff asserted that Eisner, the CEO, was interested in the transaction because he would benefit from the high amount of compensation paid to Ovitz. The court, however, dismissed the argument.

> Plaintiffs' theory is that Eisner was advancing Ovitz' interests primarily because a lavish contract for Ovtiz would redound to Eisner's benefit since Eisner would thereby gain in his quest to have his own compensation increased lavishly. This theory appears to be in the nature of the old maxim that a "high tide floats all boats." But, in the end, this theory is not supported by well-pleaded facts, only conclusory allegations.

Brehm v. Eisner, 746 A.2d 244 (Del. 2000). What do you make of this argument?

2. Plaintiff, however, also alleged that Eisner was interested in the transaction because of his close friendship with Ovitz. The Chancery Court dispatched the contention this way:

> Plaintiffs suggest that Eisner's long-time personal relationship with Ovitz caused him to be interested in obtaining the Board's approval of the Employment Agreement. This argument, however, finds no support under Delaware law. The fact that Eisner has long-standing personal and business ties to Ovitz cannot overcome the presumption of independence that all directors, including Eisner, are afforded.

In re Walt Disney Co. Derivative Litig., 731 A.2d 342 (Del. Ch. 1998), *See In re The Walt Disney Co. Derivative Litig.*, 731 A.2d 342, 356 (Del. Ch. 1998), *aff'd in part, rev'd in part sub nom. Brehm v. Eisner*, 746 A.2d 244, 253 (Del. 2000). In other words, the Chancery Court suggested that friendship and outside business relationships were not enough as a matter of law to render a director interested. What do you think of this analysis? On appeal, the Delaware Supreme Court seemed to affirm this position. *See Brehm v. Eisner*, 746 A.2d 244, 258 (Del. 2000) ("The Court of Chancery held that 'no reasonable doubt can exist as to Eisner's disinterest in the approval of the Employment Agreement, as a matter of law,' ... Plaintiffs challenge this conclusion, but we agree with the Court of Chancery and we affirm that holding."). To the extent suggesting that friendship could never render a director "interested" or deprive a director of his/her independence, can the position be reconciled with the analysis in *Beam v. Stewart*, 845 A.2d 1040 (Del. 2004)?

3. Had Eisner been treated as an "interested" director, would the board have been independent? Members included an administrator at the elementary school where the Disney CEO sent his children and the President of a university where the CEO contributed over a million dollars. *See In re The Walt Disney Co. Derivative Litig.*, 731 A.2d at 356. Certainly, some in the market had their doubts. *See* John A. Byrne, *The Best and Worst Boards*, Bus. Wk., Dec. 8, 1997, at 90 ("Disney's directors have won the dubious distinction of being named the worst board in America in Business Week's second annual analysis of the state of corporate governance."). The Chancery Court, however, concluded that the board was independent.

4. Had the case been examined under a fairness analysis, what difference would it have made? Was the "fairness" of the compensation package ever examined?

5. What does this case tell us about the difficulty in challenging a compensation decision under the duty of care? How "informed" must the directors be to pass muster under this duty?

6. The court suggests that the compensation committee was informed in part because it knew that Ovitz would want compensation for the commissions that he was leaving behind at CAA, an amount put at between $150 and $200 million. Assuming this is the case, is there any evidence that, at the time of the compensation decision, the committee knew that Ovitz would receive something approaching this amount if he departed one year later?

7. What is the tension between the legal obligations to be informed and "best practices"? Do boards have any incentive to engage in "best practices"?

8. The court also considered whether it was appropriate for only the compensation committee, rather than the entire board, to approve the package awarded to Ovitz. The court responded this way:

> The Delaware General Corporation Law (DGCL) expressly empowers a board of directors to appoint committees and to delegate to them a broad range of responsibilities, which may include setting executive compensation. Nothing in the DGCL mandates that the entire board must make those decisions. At Disney, the responsibility to consider and approve executive compensation was allocated to the compensation committee, as distinguished from the full board. The Chancellor's ruling—that executive compensation was to be fixed by the compensation committee—is legally correct.

In effect, this allows the board to off-load the compensation decision to a committee. What difference does this make? Should the decision be something that requires approval of the entire board?

The courts apparently view such a board as providing sufficient protection to shareholders to warrant application of the business judgment rule. The approach, however, depends upon the vitality of the definition of independent director.

The issue of director independence typically comes up in the context of demand excusal, a topic discussed in Chapter 10. Nonetheless, courts use the same analysis in determining whether the board is independent for purposes of the duty of loyalty. The courts in Delaware assume that directors are independent and impose on plaintiffs an obligation to plead facts that cast a reasonable doubt about independence. Independence can be lost where the director is "beholden" or under the control of the interested director and, as a result, cannot consider the transaction "objectively." Control in turn typically arises where the interested director can terminate a material benefit. Materiality is determined on a subjective basis.

The case below, another one of the decisions arising out of the litigation by shareholders over the contract between Michael Ovitz and Disney illustrates the analysis used by the courts in determining independence.

In re the Walt Disney Co. Derivative Litigation

Delaware Chancery Court
731 A.2d 342 (1998), *rev'd on other grounds*, 746 A.2d 244 (Del. 2000)

CHANDLER, CHANCELLOR

2. Eisner's Alleged Domination of the Board

I turn now to the Disney directors whom Plaintiffs allege were under Eisner's control, to consider whether they could have exercised their business judgment independently of Eisner.

* * *

e. Wilson

Plaintiffs allege that director Gary L. Wilson lacked independence from Eisner as well. Wilson served under Eisner as Disney's executive vice president and chief financial officer from July 1985 through December 1989, receiving substantial compensation from Disney over which, Plaintiffs' allege, Eisner had considerable influence. Plaintiffs also assert that Wilson is beholden to Eisner because Eisner, by virtue of his authority as chairman, rewarded Wilson handsomely when the latter retired from Disney. Finally, Plaintiffs allege that Wilson's independence is further compromised because in 1995 Disney paid $121,122 to a design firm owned by Wilson's wife.

Plaintiffs' claims do not raise a reasonable doubt that Wilson is interested in the [Ovitz] Employment Agreement. Whatever rights Wilson had when he left Disney have already been paid to him. Nothing indicates that Wilson expects to receive additional financial benefits from Disney for acceding to Eisner's wishes in connection to the Employment Agreement. Nor have Plaintiffs alleged particularized facts that would lead one to infer that Wilson is beholden to Eisner. The $121,122 payment to Wilson's wife's design firm for services performed is immaterial to Wilson, a man who received a bonus and stock options that, by Plaintiffs' own estimations, have resulted in over $70 million in income realized so far.

f. O'Donovan

Plaintiffs also allege that Father Leo J. O'Donovan, involved only in the decision to honor the Employment Agreement, is incapable of rendering independent business judgment. O'Donovan is the president of Georgetown University, the *alma mater* of one of Eisner's sons and the recipient of over $1 million of donations from Eisner since 1989. Accordingly, Plaintiffs allege that O'Donovan would not act contrary to Eisner's wishes.

The closest parallel to O'Donovan's situation faced by this Court occurred in *Lewis v. Fuqua*. Any reliance by Plaintiffs on that case, however, would be misplaced. In *Lewis*, the allegedly disinterested director, Sanford, was the President of Duke University. Duke was the recipient of a $10 million pledge from the dominant board member, Fuqua. Nevertheless, several differences exist that serve to distinguish that matter from the present one. First and foremost, Sanford had "numerous political and financial dealings" with Fuqua, while Plaintiffs here have not alleged any such relationship between Eisner and O'Donovan. Secondly, Fuqua and Sanford served as directors together both on the Board whose actions were being challenged and on the Duke University Board of Trustees. Such an interlocking directorship, a situation that would likely lead to a reasonable doubt of O'Donovan's independence, does not exist here, as Eisner has no formal relationship with Georgetown University. These two differences are sufficient to demonstrate that *Lewis* does not apply here.

The question, then, is whether Eisner exerted such an influence on O'Donovan that O'Donovan could not exercise independent judgment as a director. Plaintiffs do not allege any personal benefit received by O'Donovan—in fact, they admit that

O'Donovan is forbidden, as a Jesuit priest, from collecting any director's fee. Plaintiffs cite the case of *Kahn v. Tremont Corp.* "Eisner's philanthropic largess to Georgetown is no less disqualifying than the financial arrangements enjoyed by the special committee members in *Kahn.*" In that case, however, two of the three special committee members received a direct, personal financial benefit from their affiliation with the interested party, and the third sought membership on the boards of other entities controlled by the interested party. The distinction between *Kahn* and this matter then is clear, and I do not believe that Plaintiffs have presented a reasonable doubt as to the independence of O'Donovan.

g. Bowers

Director Reveta F. Bowers is the principal of the elementary school that Eisner's children once attended. Plaintiffs suggest that because Bowers' salary as a teacher is low compared to her director's fees and stock options, "only the most rigidly formalistic or myopic analysis" would view Bowers as not beholden to Eisner.

Plaintiffs fail to recognize that the Delaware Supreme Court has held that "such allegations [of payment of director's fees], without more, do not establish any financial interest." To follow Plaintiffs' urging to discard "formalistic notions of interest and independence in favor of a realistic approach" expressly would be to overrule the Delaware Supreme Court.

Furthermore, to do so would be to discourage the membership on corporate boards of people of less-than extraordinary means. Such "regular folks" would face allegations of being dominated by other board members, merely because of the relatively substantial compensation provided by the board membership compared to their outside salaries. I am especially unwilling to facilitate such a result. Without more, Plaintiffs have failed to allege facts that lead to a reasonable doubt as to the independence of Bowers.

h. Mitchell

Plaintiffs question the independence of Senator George J. Mitchell. Mitchell acts as special counsel to a law firm that has been engaged by Disney on various matters and that was paid $122,764 for its services in 1996. Disney has also retained Mitchell on an individual basis to provide consulting services to the Company. Plaintiffs allege that during 1996, Disney paid Mitchell $50,000 for performing these services. Accordingly, Plaintiffs allege that Mitchell is incapable of making business decisions independently of Eisner.

First, Plaintiffs have not indicated that Mitchell, as "special counsel" (and not "partner") shared in the legal fees paid to his firm. Second, Plaintiffs have not alleged that the $50,000 in consulting fees was even material to Mitchell, a nationally known legal and political figure. Plaintiffs have not alleged any particularized facts that raise a reasonable doubt that Mitchell voted in favor of the Employment Agreement in order to obtain a specific financial benefit. Without such allegations, Plaintiffs' conclusory assertion that Mitchell was under Eisner's influence or otherwise interested in any aspect of the Employment Agreement is insufficient as a matter of law to raise a reasonable doubt as to Mitchell's independence.

Comments and Questions

1. Directors must be independent and disinterested. What is the difference between the two terms?

2. Despite the court's conclusion that the board had a majority of independent directors, others apparently did not agree. Business Week in January 2000 labeled the Disney board the "worst in America" in a ranking based upon governance practices and noted that "[i]nstitutional shareholders want Eisner to put more independent directors on a board that, despite some improvement, remains packed with Eisner chums." What does this suggest about the approach to independence used by the Delaware courts?

3. In general, the Delaware courts disqualify as independent those directors who receive a material income stream from the company. Did the court apply this analysis to the principal of the elementary school attended by Eisner's children? What does this suggest about the rule with respect to directors fees in Delaware?

4. Certain family relationships can also result in the loss of independence. A spouse, for example, serving on the board would likely not be treated as independent. What about other non-familial relationships such as close friends? This issue is addressed in *Beam v. Martha Stewart Living Omnimedia, Inc.*, 845 A.2d 1040 (Del. 2004), a case set out in Chapter 10.

5. Senator Mitchell worked for a law firm that received fees from Disney. In finding that payments did not result in a loss of independence, the court noted that plaintiffs had not indicated that Mitchell, as "special counsel" (and not "partner") "shared in the legal fees paid to his firm." Presumably, the court was suggesting that plaintiffs should know something about the internal allocation of fees within a large law firm and the particular application of these rules to Senator Mitchell. How likely is it that plaintiffs would, absent discovery, have this type of information?

6. What about the analysis of Father O'Donovan, the president of Georgetown University? Eisner made over $1 million in donations to the University. The court seemed to view the payment (and the prospect for future payments) as immaterial because plaintiffs did not allege that Father O'Donovan received any personal benefit from the contribution. Is it the case that the head of a non-profit is only influence by the prospect of contributions if he or she will personally benefit from the contribution? Does this case stand for the proposition that contributions, irrespective of their amount, will never result in a loss of independence unless the director benefits directly from the contributions? Do you agree with this analysis? To the extent that a president of a non-profit did benefit from the contributions, how would plaintiffs be aware of that information before any discovery has occurred?

7. What kinds of business relationships will disqualify a director as independent? In *In re Goldman Sachs*, 2011 Del. Ch. LEXIS 151 (Sept. 7, 2011), one of the directors of Goldman also served as CEO and chairman of a company that had a business relationship with the investment bank. Plaintiffs alleged that Goldman had "arranged or provided billions of euros in financing to his company" and that "[d]uring 2007

and 2008 alone, the Company had made loans to [the company] in the aggregate amount of 464 million euros." The court concluded that the evidence did not raise a reasonable doubt about the director's independence. According to the court:

> Goldman is an investment bank. The fact "[t]hat it provided financing to large ... companies should come as no shock to anyone. Yet this is all that the plaintiffs allege." The Plaintiffs fail to plead facts that show anything other than a series of market transactions occurred between [the company] and Goldman. For instance, the Plaintiffs have not alleged that [the company] is receiving a discounted interest rate on the loans from Goldman, that [the company] was unable to receive financing from any other lender, or that loans from Goldman compose a substantial part of [the company's] funding.

What do you make of this analysis? Is it correct?

8. The issue of director independence can come up in the context of a motion to dismiss for failure to make demand or for failure to state a claim. The former requires the plaintiff to meet the higher pleading standards in Rule 23.1 while the latter need only meet the traditional notice pleading standards. *See In re INFOUSA, Inc. Shareholders Litig.*, 953 A.2d 963 (Del. Ch. 2007). Can these differences be outcome determinative? Does this raise any additional implications concerning the approach taken by the courts with respect to director independence?

J. Robert Brown, Jr.,
Returning Fairness to Executive Compensation
84 N.D. L. Rev. 1141, 1149–52 (2008)[3]

... Compensation and other conflict of interest transactions rarely receive the scrutiny of entire fairness. The mild obligation for boards to justify unusually large compensation awards is not typically part of the analysis. Instead, the Delaware courts extend to compensation decisions the absolute protection of the business judgment rule [even when a conflict of interest exists]. The standard makes the substantive terms essentially irrelevant. The number of options, the amount of salary, and the size of the bonuses are not generally part of the analysis. Instead, the matter turns on the number of "independent" directors on the board.

The Delaware courts came to this position through legerdemain. The business judgment rule represents an over-inclusive protection designed to protect risk taking by directors. Boards know that even if they take risks that prove in hindsight to be mistaken and harmful, they will escape liability. The presumption is not, however, designed to protect decisions motivated by a conflict of interest.

The Delaware courts avoided this traditional approach [in the context of executive compensation] largely by ignoring the existence of the conflict of interest in the decision-making process. Without any real analysis, they extended the presumption of the business judgment rule to boards containing a majority of independent direc-

---

3. Copyright © 2008 North Dakota Law Review. Reprinted with permission.

tors. It was as if the presence of this majority caused the taint of the conflict to dissipate. The courts, however, did not accompany the extension with any obligation to eliminate or quarantine the interested influence. Indeed, the business judgment rule applied even if the interested directors participated in the decision and voted on the final outcome.

There are many problems with this approach. First, it makes a mockery of the underlying rationale for the business judgment rule. By leaving the conflict in the decision-making process, the Delaware courts have extended the over-inclusive presumption beyond the traditional goal of protecting risk taking to encompass decisions motivated by a conflict of interest. The mere presence of a majority of "independent" directors in no way establishes that the decision was unaffected by the interested influence.

Second, whatever benefits flow from the presence of independent directors, the Delaware courts have done little to ensure that directors are in fact independent. They routinely ignore facts that suggest a lack of independence, employing excessive pleading standards and inconsistent tests. The courts categorically decline to consider relationships arising from structural bias and largely ignore friendship as a basis for finding a disqualifying relationship. Boards characterized as independent, therefore, may in fact have a majority of directors subject to the control and influence of the CEO.

Third, the business judgment rule requires that directors be informed. A growing body of evidence suggests that, in the context of executive compensation, the decisions are uninformed. To support compensation decisions, boards (or compensation committees) typically rely on reports from consultants. Compensation consultants often are not neutral, independent advisors, but advocates for the CEO. In those circumstances, their role may be less about fairness and more about providing a post hoc justification for predetermined amounts of compensation. In addition, they may have other business relationships with the company that impairs neutrality.

Comments and Questions

1. Is this approach correct? Should boards with a majority of independent directors be given the benefit of the business judgment rule in making compensation determinations? Give the pros and cons of each position.

2. The article states that under the duty of care, the substantive terms of the executive compensation, including the amount, rarely matter. Is this true? What implication does this have for the analysis of compensation determinations?

3. The business judgment rule is an over-inclusive protection that shields directors from liability for decisions that go awry in the absence of a conflict of interest. In other words, the presumption protects directors from their own negligence in order to avoid discouraging risk taking. Is it appropriate to apply this presumption where only a majority of the directors are independent and where the directors with the interested influence are in a position to influence the board's decision making?

4. Would the analysis change if the "conflict of interest" was isolated and excluded from the decisionmaking process? Will this effectively eliminate the influence of the interested director? How might this be accomplished?

5. The critical component of the shift in the legal standard is the independence of the board of directors. Independence requires that "a director's decision is based on the corporate merits of the subject before the board rather than extraneous considerations or influences." *Aronson v. Lewis*, 473 A.2d 805, 816 (Del. 1984). Directors lose their independence under this test if they have a material financial relationship that can be terminated by the interested director. Materiality is determined on a subjective basis. Moreover, at the pleading stage, shareholders must present evidence showing reasonable doubt as to the director's independence. These standards are not always easy to meet, particularly at the pleading stage. What does this suggest about board independence?

6. By applying the duty of care, the courts provide an incentive to put independent directors on the board. Is this enough of a benefit for shareholders to justify the shift in the standard of review for compensation matters?

7. Are there other ways of encouraging the use of independent directors without necessarily applying the duty of care? What about shifting the burden of proof to shareholders? *See Reis v. Hazelett Strip-Casting Corp.*, 2011 Del. Ch. LEXIS 11 (Del. Ch. Jan. 21, 2011) ("If the controlling stockholder permits the board to form a duly empowered and properly functioning special committee, or if the transaction is conditioned on a correctly formulated majority-of-the-minority vote, then the burden could shift to the plaintiff to prove that the transaction was unfair."). Would this be a better approach? Why or why not?

C. The Safety Valve of Waste

The "safety valve" under the duty of care is waste. Even if compensation is approved by an independent and disinterested board, the decision can still constitute waste. Waste essentially recognizes that even with proper process, there is an outer limit to how much the board can award in compensation.

It is not, as the next cases illustrate, an easy standard to meet.

Brehm v. Eisner

Delaware Supreme Court
906 A.2d 27 (2006)

Jacobs, Justice

V. *THE WASTE CLAIM*

The appellants' final claim is that even if the approval of the OEA [Ovitz employment agreement] was protected by the business judgment rule presumptions, the payment of the severance amount to Ovitz constituted waste. This claim is rooted in the doctrine that a plaintiff who fails to rebut the business judgment rule presumptions is not entitled to any remedy unless the transaction constitutes waste. The Court of Chancery rejected the appellants' waste claim, and the appellants claim that in so doing the Court committed error.

To recover on a claim of corporate waste, the plaintiffs must shoulder the burden of proving that the exchange was "so one sided that no business person of ordinary, sound judgment could conclude that the corporation has received adequate consideration." A claim of waste will arise only in the rare, "unconscionable case where directors irrationally squander or give away corporate assets." This onerous standard for waste is a corollary of the proposition that where business judgment presumptions are applicable, the board's decision will be upheld unless it cannot be "attributed to any rational business purpose."

The claim that the payment of the NFT [non-fault termination] amount to Ovitz, without more, constituted waste is meritless on its face, because at the time the NFT amounts were paid, Disney was contractually obligated to pay them. The payment of a contractually obligated amount cannot constitute waste, unless the contractual obligation is itself wasteful. Accordingly, the proper focus of a waste analysis must be whether the amounts required to be paid in the event of an NFT were wasteful *ex ante*.

Appellants claim that the NFT provisions of the OEA were wasteful because they incentivized Ovitz to perform poorly in order to obtain payment of the NFT provisions. The Chancellor found that the record did not support that contention:

> Terminating Ovitz and paying the NFT did not constitute waste because he could not be terminated for cause and because many of the defendants gave credible testimony that the Company would be better off without Ovitz, meaning that would be impossible for me to conclude that the termination and receipt of NFT benefits result in "an exchange that is so one sided that no business person of ordinary, sound judgment could conclude that the corporation has received adequate consideration," or a situation where the defendants have "irrationally squandered or given away corporate assets." In other words, defendants did not commit waste.

That ruling is erroneous, the appellants argue, because the NFT provisions of the OEA were wasteful in their very design. Specifically, the OEA gave Ovitz every incentive to leave the Company before serving out the full term of his contract. The appellants urge that although the OEA may have induced Ovitz to join Disney as President, no contractual safeguards were in place to retain him in that position. In essence, appellants claim that the NFT provisions of the OEA created an irrational incentive for Ovitz to get himself fired.

That claim does not come close to satisfying the high hurdle required to establish waste. The approval of the NFT provisions in the OEA had a rational business purpose: to induce Ovitz to leave CAA, at what would otherwise be a considerable cost to him, in order to join Disney. The Chancellor found that the evidence does not support any notion that the OEA irrationally incentivized Ovitz to get himself fired. Ovitz had no control over whether or not he would be fired, either with or without cause.

To suggest that at the time he entered into the OEA Ovitz would engineer an early departure at the cost of his extraordinary reputation in the entertainment industry and his historical friendship with Eisner, is not only fanciful but also without proof in the record. Indeed, the Chancellor found that it was "patently unreasonable to assume that Ovitz intended to perform just poorly enough to be fired quickly, but not so poorly that he could be terminated for cause."

We agree. Because the appellants have failed to show that the approval of the NFT terms of the OEA was not a rational business decision, their waste claim must fail.

Comments and Questions

1. Courts have described waste as an "outer limit." *See In re Citigroup Inc. Shareholder Derivative Litig.*, 964 A.2d 106 (Del. Ch. 2009) (noting that waste is an "'outer limit' to the board's discretion to set executive compensation"). What does that mean and why, conceptually, is this a necessary companion to the process oriented business judgment rule?

2. What do you make of the standard for waste set out in this decision? What type of burden does it impose on shareholders? Does the standard effectively impose an outer limit on executive compensation?

3. Can shareholders show waste by arguing that compensation is excessive given that the officers are "not going anywhere"? In other words, there was no need to pay significant amounts since the amounts were unnecessary to retain the officers? For some insight, see *Friedman v. Dolan*, CA No. 9425 (Del. Ch. Jan. 23, 2015) (Delaware law).

4. One commentator asserted that the doctrine "essentially lies fallow...." Andrea M. Matwyshyn, *Imagining the Intangible*, 34 Del. J. Corp. L. 965, 1004 (2009). Is this inevitable? What does this tell us about the interpretation of the test by the Delaware courts?

5. What would be the likely treatment of a claim for waste under a waiver of liability provision? While the provision specifically excludes good faith and the duty of loyalty, it does not speak specifically to waste.

Waste claims are very difficult to win. In only a few instances have the courts allowed them to go forward. The following case is an example of one that did.

In re InfoUSA

Delaware Chancery Court
953 A.2d 963 (2007)

CHANDLER, CHANCELLOR:

At the heart of the complaint lies the accusation that Vinod Gupta and, to a much lesser extent, the other individual defendants have long used infoUSA to enrich themselves at the expense of shareholders. Indeed, the bulk of the complaint presents a vast, gaudy panoply of gilded excess, expressed either through frequent and allegedly unquestioned related-party transactions or through payments made directly for the benefit of Vinod Gupta and his family.

1. Related-party payments for "business" expenses: planes, yachts, automobiles, and more

The list of related-party transactions relating to transportation alone makes for lengthy reading. Between 2001 and 2005, infoUSA paid approximately $8.2 million to Annapurna Corporation, an entity 100% owned by V. Gupta. These expenditures covered the use of private jets, the use of the *American Princess* yacht, and the use of a personal residence in California, as well as unidentified travel expenses. Vinod Gupta himself incurred much of the travel expenses, and Dolphin alleges that none of the documents provided in response to its § 220 request identified a business purpose for a substantial number of these payments. The log books of the American Princess yacht reveal little regarding the justification for these "business" expenses. Nor did defendants produce minutes or consents reflecting board approval of these substantial transactions as part of their response to Dolphin's § 220 request. Plaintiffs allege that many of these travel expenditures were either personal in nature or provided as gifts by Vinod Gupta to personal or political friends.

* * *

5. Count V: Waste

The amended consolidated complaint maintains that defendants committed two separate forms of waste: the millions of dollars of related-party transactions for the benefit of Vinod Gupta and the consultancy agreements with [former President] Clinton. The test for waste is a demanding standard. The Court must "apply a reasonable person standard and deny a claim of waste wherever a reasonable person might deem the consideration received adequate. When this difficult standard is applied in the liberal context of a motion to dismiss, in order for the complaint to survive the motion, the Court must find that in any of the possible sets of circumstances inferable from the facts alleged under the complaint, no reasonable person could deem the received consideration adequate." Plaintiffs have already failed to meet this exacting burden with regard to the contracts with Clinton.

Plaintiffs succeed, however, in alleging a successful claim for waste. The amended consolidated complaint presents a series of related-party transactions and improper benefits allowed to flow to Vinod Gupta from a board that was dominated and controlled by him. Consider, for instance, the skybox at the University of Nebraska-Lincoln Football Stadium, acquired by infoUSA from Annapurna in 2003. The remaining lease on the skybox lasted twenty-one years, for which the company paid $617,000. The company's 2006 proxy statement states that Vinod Gupta originally paid $2 million for the skybox, and the amended consolidated complaint asserts that he received a $1.3 million charitable tax deduction on the purchase. The complaint alleges that the purchase price was based upon a $29,400 per year cost of twenty-eight tickets, and yet the value of these tickets was not discounted to a present value. Further, the purchase price did not reflect any amounts paid to Annapurna for use of the skybox in prior years. These allegations, if proven, suggest that a dominated board purchased permanent rights to a skybox that it was already leasing from its CEO, while conveniently forgetting to discount the value of tickets that mature at the same time that a baby born at the time of the transaction would be legally able to buy beer from a stadium vendor. A reasonable person might well consider this a sweetheart deal for Vinod Gupta, but would be hard pressed to find that the consideration was adequate.

Like the rest of the related-party transactions, the story of the skybox supports the inference that the board of directors allowed Vinod Gupta to extract value from the company by selling his own assets to the corporation at inequitable prices. Although defendants will have the opportunity to rebut this evidence at trial, for the moment plaintiffs plead sufficient facts to maintain an action for waste.

Comments and Questions

1. What does this case suggest about the instances when a court will find waste?

2. The court seems to infer waste from the unreasonableness of the transaction. Yet Delaware courts have suggested that this approach will not be available for compensation. *See In re 3Com Shareholder Litig.*, 1999 Del. Ch. Lexis 215 (Oct. 25, 1999) ("bare allegations" that stock options were "excessive or even lavish" will not be sufficient to plead waste). Can you reconcile these views?

3. The case involved some important personalities. One of the claims of waste centered on a consulting contract with Bill Clinton. According to the opinion, the former President received payments of $3.3 million over six years and 100,000 stock options. The court dismissed the claim, concluding that "nothing in the amended consolidated complaint, beyond plaintiffs' conclusory allegations, supports a reasonable inference that it was unreasonable, let alone gratuitous and without consideration." Do you think the personality involved played any role in the court's analysis?

4. The Securities and Exchange Commission brought its own case against InfoUSA. *See In re InfoUSA, Inc.*, Exchange Act Release No. 61708 (admin proc March 15, 2010) (finding violations of Rule 14a-9 for failing to properly disclose related party transactions).

III. Compensation and the SEC

In adopting the Exchange Act, Congress provided a role for the SEC in the compensation process. The SEC was assigned the task of ensuring adequate disclosure of compensation. Congress anticipated that the resulting burst of sunlight would reduce the perceived abuse in the area. Unsurprisingly, therefore, some of the earliest regulatory initiatives by the fledgling agency involved executive compensation. *See* Exchange Act Release No. 1823 (Aug. 13, 1938) (requiring disclosure of "remuneration" for any nominee to the board who also constituted one of three highest paid officers of company).

Nonetheless, it took until 1992 before the Commission adopted a comprehensive and thorough set of rules regulating the disclosure of executive compensation. *See* Exchange Act Release No. 31327 (Oct. 16, 1992). These rules were designed to allow "market forces, rather than legislators or bureaucrats, [to] shape corporate compensation policies." Reform of Executive Compensation Disclosure Rules, Fact Sheet, 1992 SEC Lexis 2466 (Oct. 15, 1992).

Among the innovations was the use of a "summary compensation table," something described as the "linchpin of the Commission's revised executive compensation disclosure scheme." The table included all forms of compensation including salary, bonuses, stock awards, option awards, non-equity incentive compensation, deferred compensation, and "other compensation." Item 402(c), 17 C.F.R. 229.402(c). In short, the table reflected every type of compensation paid to the top officers and allowed compensation to be reduced down to a single dollar amount.

Yet the 1992 reforms were more of a start than a finish. For one thing, they did not appear to exert a downward pressure on compensation. Compensation escalated in the 1990s, causing some to argue that, by making compensation so transparent, it put upward pressure on amounts. Boards and CEOs could more easily compare the amounts paid and, if below comparable companies, argue for increases.

Substantial reforms occurred in 2006. *See* Exchange Act Release No. 54302A (August 29, 2006) (describing the amendments as "a thorough rethinking of the rules."). To some degree, the changes were designed to fill gaps left in place from the earlier requirements. Reforms substantially tightened the disclosure of perquisites paid to the top executives. The new requirements mandated disclosure of the compensation paid to the CFO, in addition to the CEO. Director compensation for the first time had to appear in tabular form that included total compensation. *See* Item 402(d), 17 C.F.R. 229.402(d).

The 2006 reforms, however, went much further than the disclosure of the amounts paid. As the Commission noted:

> The new Compensation Discussion and Analysis calls for a discussion and analysis of the material factors underlying compensation policies and decisions reflected in the data presented in the tables. This overview addresses in one place these factors with respect to both the separate elements of executive compensation and executive compensation as a whole.

Exchange Act Release No. 54302A (August 29, 2006). In other words, disclosure shifted from amount to process, presumably with the intent to influence the manner in which compensation was calculated. This would create a multitude of challenges for the Commission and corporate boards.

A. Compensation and Disclosure

Executive compensation is disclosed in the annual report on Form 10-K and in the proxy statement. As a practical matter, however, it appears in the proxy statement and is incorporated by reference into the annual report. The instructions for the disclosure of executive compensation appear in Item 402 of Regulation S-K. 17 C.F.R. 229.402. As the introductory note provides, Item 402 "requires clear, concise and understandable disclosure of all plan and non-plan compensation awarded to, earned by, or paid to the named executive officers."

The term "earned by" is deliberate. Total compensation does not reflect an amount actually paid to the relevant officer. It involves the value of certain benefits, such as perquisites or stock options, as of a specified date. Particularly with respect to compensation paid in the form of equity (stock or options), the value may have changed significantly by the time disclosure occurs.

One of the areas that has proved difficult to regulate has been the disclosure of perquisites. The summary compensation table mandated by Item 402(c) must include all "other compensation" paid to the CEO and CFO. This includes the value of any "[p]erquisites and other personal benefits, or property, unless the aggregate amount of such compensation is less than $10,000." 17 C.F.R. 229.402(c) (2). Common perquisites include personal use of the corporate aircraft, country club dues, installation of a security system in the officer's home, use of a driver, and tax gross ups.

A perk can have a business and personal purpose. Deciding which of these benefits must be treated as compensation has not always been easy. The SEC amended Item 402 and provided substantial additional guidance on this issue in the 2006 reforms.

Executive Compensation and Related Person Disclosure
Exchange Act Release No. 54302A (Aug. 29, 2006)

Among the factors to be considered in determining whether an item is a perquisite or other personal benefit are the following:

- An item is not a perquisite or personal benefit if it is integrally and directly related to the performance of the executive's duties.

- Otherwise, an item is a perquisite or personal benefit if it confers a direct or indirect benefit that has a personal aspect, without regard to whether it may be provided for some business reason or for the convenience of the company, unless it is generally available on a non-discriminatory basis to all employees.

We believe the way to approach this is by initially evaluating the first prong of the analysis. If an item is integrally and directly related to the performance of the executive's duties, that is the end of the analysis—the item is not a perquisite or personal benefit and no compensation disclosure is required. Moreover, if an item is integrally and directly related to the performance of an executive's duties under this analysis, there is no requirement to disclose any incremental cost over a less expensive alternative. For example, with respect to business travel, it is not necessary to disclose the cost differential between renting a mid-sized car over a compact car.

Because of the integral and direct connection to job performance, the elements of the second part of the analysis (e.g., whether there is also a personal benefit or whether the item is generally available to other employees) are irrelevant. An example of such an item could be a "Blackberry" or a laptop computer if the company believes it is an integral part of the executive's duties to be accessible by e-mail to the executive's colleagues and clients when out of the office. Just as these devices represent advances over earlier technology (such as voicemail), we expect that as new technology facilitates the extent to which work is conducted outside the office, additional devices may be developed that will fall into this category.

The concept of a benefit that is "integrally and directly related" to job performance is a narrow one. The analysis draws a critical distinction between an item that a company provides because the executive needs it to do the job, making it integrally and directly related to the performance of duties, and an item provided for some other reason, even where that other reason can involve both company benefit and personal benefit. Some commenters objected that "integrally and directly related" is too narrow a standard, suggesting that other business reasons for providing an item should not be disregarded in determining whether an item is a perquisite. We do not adopt this suggested approach. As we stated in the Proposing Release, the fact that the company has determined that an expense is an "ordinary" or "necessary" business expense for tax or other purposes or that an expense is for the benefit or convenience of the company is not responsive to the inquiry as to whether the expense provides a perquisite or other personal benefit for disclosure purposes. Whether the company should pay for an expense or it is deductible for tax purposes relates principally to questions of state law regarding use of corporate assets and of tax law; our disclosure requirements are triggered by different and broader concepts.

As we noted in the Proposing Release, business purpose or convenience does not affect the characterization of an item as a perquisite or personal benefit where it is not integrally and directly related to the performance by the executive of his or her job. Therefore, for example, a company's decision to provide an item of personal benefit for security purposes does not affect its characterization as a perquisite or personal benefit. A company policy that for security purposes an executive (or an executive and his or her family) must use company aircraft or other company means of travel for personal travel, or must use company or company-provided property for vacations, does not affect the conclusion that the item provided is a perquisite or personal benefit.

If an item is not integrally and directly related to the performance of the executive's duties, the second step of the analysis comes into play. Does the item confer a direct or indirect benefit that has a personal aspect (without regard to whether it may be provided for some business reason or for the convenience of the company)? If so, is it generally available on a non-discriminatory basis to all employees? For example, a company's provision of helicopter service for an executive to commute to work from home is not integrally and directly related to job performance (although it would benefit the company by getting the executive to work faster), clearly bestows a benefit that has a personal aspect, and is not generally available to all employees on a non-discriminatory basis. As we have noted, business purpose or convenience does not affect the characterization of an item as a perquisite or personal benefit where it is not integrally and directly related to the performance by the executive of his or her job.

A company may reasonably conclude that an item is generally available to all employees on a non-discriminatory basis if it is available to those employees to whom it lawfully may be provided. For this purpose, a company may recognize jurisdictionally based legal restrictions (such as for foreign employees) or the employees' "accredited investor" status. In contrast, merely providing a benefit consistent with its availability to employees in the same job category or at the same pay scale does not establish that it is generally available on a non-discriminatory basis to all employees.

Applying the concepts that we outline above, examples of items requiring disclosure as perquisites or personal benefits under Item 402 include, but are not limited to: club memberships not used exclusively for business entertainment purposes, personal financial or tax advice, personal travel using vehicles owned or leased by the company, personal travel otherwise financed by the company, personal use of other property owned or leased by the company, housing and other living expenses (including but not limited to relocation assistance and payments for the executive or director to stay at his or her personal residence), security provided at a personal residence or during personal travel, commuting expenses (whether or not for the company's convenience or benefit), and discounts on the company's products or services not generally available to employees on a non-discriminatory basis.

Comments and Questions

1. What is the purpose of this guidance and why is it tucked away in the release adopting changes to Item 402?

2. What impact does disclosure have on executive compensation? Apparently since the changes made to Item 402 in 2006, corporate expenditures for country club dues have declined. It is not clear that the same has happened for personal use of the corporate aircraft. What might explain these results?

3. Can the disclosure of perks impact share prices? Although the amount may be modest relative to a company's earnings, the answer is that it can. *See* Carola Frydman & Dirk Jenter, *CEO Compensation*, Working Paper No. 77, Rock Center for Corporate Governance, Stanford University, at 6 (March 19, 2010). Why? "[T]he available evidence indicates that at least some perk consumption is a reflection of managerial excess and reduces shareholder value." *Id.* Is this always true?

4. What are some examples of benefits that are "integrally and directly related" to job performance? Can these benefits also have a personal, non-business use? How are they different from a security system at the CEO's private residence or the board requiring the CEO to use the corporate aircraft for safety reasons?

5. Item 402 is lengthy (more than 15,000 words) and complex. Moreover, as this reading demonstrates, the regulation itself does not provide all of the answers to disclosure related issues. Many can only be found through resort to the adopting release.

Can you think of any reason why compensation disclosure in particular requires such regulatory detail?

6. The Commission has also sought to require companies to disclose the process used in arriving at executive compensation. As the Commission noted:

> We are adopting instructions to make clear that the Compensation Discussion and Analysis should focus on the material principles underlying the company's executive compensation policies and decisions, and the most important factors relevant to analysis of those policies and decisions, without using boilerplate language or repeating the more detailed information set forth in the tables and related narrative disclosures that follow....

Executive Compensation and Related Person Disclosure, Exchange Act Release No. 54302A (Aug. 29, 2006). What does this type of disclosure accomplish? How successful is this approach likely to be?

10. What impact does the absence of a private right of action have on the nature of this type of disclosure? In the 1980s, the Commission invested considerable bureaucratic and enforcement resources in attempting to improve the quality of disclosure made in Item 303 of Regulation S-K, Management's Discussion and Analysis. The efforts presumably resulted in some qualitative improvement in disclosure. Nonetheless, the Commission ultimately ceased targeting the area and moved on to other issues. What is likely to have happened to the qualitative improvements as a result of this change in enforcement priorities?

The requirements mandated by Item 402 are considered a minimum. Companies also must disclose any other information necessary to make the proxy materials accurate and complete.

In the Matter of Musclepharm Corporation

Administrative Proceeding File No. 3-16788 (Sept. 8, 2015)

ORDER INSTITUTING CEASE-AND-DESIST PROCEEDINGS PURSUANT TO SECTION 8A OF THE SECURITIES ACT OF 1933 AND SECTION 21C OF THE SECURITIES EXCHANGE ACT OF 1934, MAKING FINDINGS, AND IMPOSING A CEASE-AND-DESIST ORDER

II.

In anticipation of the institution of these proceedings, Respondent has submitted an Offer of Settlement (the "Offer") which the Commission has determined to accept. Solely for the purpose of these proceedings and any other proceedings brought by or on behalf of the Commission, or to which the Commission is a party, and without admitting or denying the findings herein, except as to the Commission's jurisdiction over it and the subject matter of these proceedings, which are admitted, Respondent consents to the entry of this Order Instituting Cease-and-Desist Proceedings Pursuant to Section 8A of the Securities Act of 1933 and Section 21C of the Securities Exchange

Act of 1934, Making Findings, and Imposing a Cease-and-Desist Order ("Order"), as set forth below.

III.

On the basis of this Order and Respondent's Offer, the Commission finds1 that:

Summary

MSLP is a Denver-based sports nutrition company that develops, manufactures, and markets sports nutrition products. When MSLP became a public company in 2010, it was unprepared for the Commission's reporting requirements and lacked sufficient infrastructure to support its rapid growth. MSLP's revenues greatly increased each year (MSLP's reported revenue was $3M in 2010, $17M in 2011, $67M in 2012 and $111M in 2013). MSLP's senior management lacked public company or accounting experience. While the company focused on revenue growth, it failed to establish sufficient internal controls and keep proper books and records. As a result, between 2010 and 2013, MSLP engaged in a series of accounting and disclosure failures that resulted in the company filing materially false and misleading filings with the Commission from 2010 through July 2014. Specifically, as described further below, MSLP failed to disclose perquisite compensation to its executive officers, failed to disclose related party transactions, failed to disclose bankruptcies of its executive officers, and committed other financial statement, accounting, and disclosure failures. Additionally, MSLP engaged in the unregistered offer and sale of its securities.

Respondent

1. MSLP is a Nevada corporation, based in Denver, Colorado, that manufactures and markets sports nutrition products. From 2010 to present, MSLP's common stock was registered with the Commission pursuant to Section 12(g) of the Exchange Act and was quoted on the OTC Bulletin Board.

MSLP's Failure to Disclose Perquisites from 2010 through July 2014

2. From 2010 through July 2014, MSLP significantly understated its disclosed perquisites by approximately $482,000 or 76% in Forms 10-K, Forms S-1, and proxy statements filed with the Commission. MSLP understated its disclosed perquisites in (1) 2010 by approximately $37,000 or 100%; (2) in 2011 by approximately $160,000 or 100%; (3) in 2012 by approximately $214,000 or 93%; and (4) in 2013 by approximately $71,000 or 35%.

3. MSLP paid its chief executive officer ("CEO") approximately $244,000 of undisclosed perquisites during this time period. The perquisites included perquisites related to meals, autos, apparel, personal professional tax and legal services, and two golf club memberships. During this time, MSLP also paid for perquisites of other executives that were not disclosed, including items such as the medical costs of the birth of a child, eye surgery, and personal golf club memberships.

4. From 2010 until mid-2012, MSLP executives knew or should have known that executive compensation was required to be disclosed in Commission filings and failed to educate themselves regarding the required reporting of executive compensation in

Commission filings or what were considered perquisites with respect to executive officers. As a consequence, MSLP did not disclose any perquisites in its filings with the Commission prior to October 2012.

5. From mid-2012 through 2013, MSLP executives failed to properly identify or fully investigate undisclosed perquisites. As a consequence, MSLP continued to fail to identify or disclose many perquisites in its filings with the Commission through July 2014.

6. In September 2012, the MSLP board of directors determined perquisites related to autos, golf club memberships, and private plane usage would be disclosed in Commission filings. MSLP, however, filed several Commission filings through July 2014, which failed to include complete disclosure of the perquisites identified at the board meeting and otherwise known by senior management.

7. By summer 2013, MSLP began an internal review to determine the amount of undisclosed perquisites paid by MSLP to its executives since 2010. MSLP identified over $100,000 of undisclosed perquisites, including jet use, autos, and golf club memberships. MSLP, however, filed a Form S-1 in August 2013 with incorrect perquisite disclosures that were identical to amounts previously disclosed before the internal review began.

8. MSLP continued its internal investigation of undisclosed perquisites from fall 2013 through spring 2014. On March 31, 2014, MSLP filed its 2013 Form 10-K. In the summary compensation table, MSLP set forth previously undisclosed perquisites for 2011 and 2012 totaling approximately $189,000 (previously undisclosed perquisites of $74,000 for 2011 and $115,000 for 2012). The table also disclosed approximately $134,000 of perquisites in 2013. These disclosures, however, still significantly understated perquisites paid to MSLP executives.

9. MSLP reexamined its perquisite investigation results from spring 2014 through fall 2014. On October 31, 2014, MSLP filed amended Forms 10-K for the years ended 2012 and 2013. The 2013 Form 10-K/A disclosed an additional $252,000 of undisclosed perquisites that were not included in the 2013 Form 10-K or its July 2014 proxy statement. The 2012 Form 10-K/A disclosed an additional $37,000 of perquisites for 2010. In total, MSLP failed to report perquisites totaling approximately $482,000 from 2010–2013.

* * *

Books, Records, and Lack of Internal Controls

24. Because MSLP improperly recorded and/or reported its **perquisites**, related parties, revenue, losses on settlement of accounts payable, sponsorship commitments, manufacturing concentration, leases, and international sales, its books, records and accounts did not, in reasonable detail, accurately and fairly reflect its transactions and dispositions of assets.

25. In addition, MSLP failed to implement internal accounting controls relating to its **perquisites**, related parties, revenue, losses on settlement of accounts payable, sponsorship commitments, manufacturing concentration, leases, and international

sales, which were sufficient to provide reasonable assurances that transactions were recorded as necessary to permit the preparation of financial statements in conformity with GAAP and to maintain the accountability of assets.

Violations

26. As a result of the conduct described above, MSLP violated Sections 17(a)(2) and 17(a)(3) of the Securities Act, which make it unlawful for any person in the offer or sale of any securities by the use of interstate commerce to obtain money or property by means of any untrue statement of a material fact or any omission to state a material fact necessary in order to make the statements made, in light of the circumstances under which they were made, not misleading; and to engage in any transaction, practice, or course of business which operates or would operate as a fraud or deceit upon the purchaser.

* * *

28. As a result of the conduct described above, MSLP violated Section 14(a) of the Exchange Act and Rule 14a-9 thereunder, which prohibits solicitations by means of a proxy statement, form of proxy, notice of meeting or other communication, written or oral, containing a statement which, at the time and in the light of the circumstances under which it was made, was false or misleading with respect to any material fact, or which omitted to state any material fact necessary in order to make the statements therein not false or misleading or necessary to correct any statement in any earlier communication with respect to the solicitation of a proxy for the same meeting or subject matter which has become false or misleading.

29. As a result of the conduct described above, MSLP violated Section 13(a) of the Exchange Act and Rules 13a-1, 13a-13, and 12b-20 thereunder, which require every issuer of a security registered pursuant to Section 12 of the Exchange Act file with the Commission information, documents, and annual and quarterly reports as the Commission may require, and mandate that periodic reports contain such further material information as may be necessary to make the required statements not misleading.

30. As a result of the conduct described above, MSLP violated Section 13(b)(2)(A) of the Exchange Act, which requires reporting companies to make and keep books, records and accounts, which in reasonable detail, accurately and fairly reflect their transactions and dispositions of assets.

31. As a result of the conduct described above, MSLP violated Section 13(b)(2)(B) of the Exchange Act, which require all reporting companies to devise and maintain a system of internal accounting controls sufficient to provide reasonable assurances that transactions are recorded as necessary to permit preparation of financial statements in accordance with GAAP and to maintain the accountability of assets.

32. Lastly, as a result of the conduct described above, MSLP violated Rule 302 of Regulation S-T of the Exchange Act, which requires that (1) a signatory to an electronic filing manually sign the signature page either before or at the time of the electronic filing; (2) the filer retain the original executed document for five years; and (3) that the filer provide the Commission staff with a copy of the document upon request.

IV. *Undertakings*

Respondent has undertaken to:

Retain an independent consultant (the "Independent Consultant") for a period of one year, not unacceptable to the staff of the Commission, to conduct a comprehensive review of MSLP's policies, procedures, controls, and training relating to payment of expenses, related party transactions, and required financial statement disclosures in accordance with GAAP; and to recommend, if and where appropriate, policies, procedures, controls, and training reasonably designed to ensure:

(a) MSLP's compliance with Item 402 of Regulation S-K requiring, among other things, the disclosure of perquisites as executive compensation;

(b) MSLP has processes and internal controls in place to reasonably ensure payments for private club memberships, private airplane use, meals and entertainment, financial services, and other expenses that have a personal element are properly evaluated for perquisite disclosure;

(c) MSLP's related party disclosures are complete, not misleading, and in accordance with Item 404 of Regulation S-K and FASB ASC Topic 850, Related Party Disclosures; and

(d) MSLP's financial statements, including related notes, for external purposes are prepared in accordance with GAAP.

Require the Independent Consultant to enter into an agreement that provides that for the period of engagement and for a period of two years from completion of the engagement, the Independent Consultant shall not enter into any employment, consultant, attorney-client, auditing or other professional relationship with MSLP, or any of its present or former affiliates, directors, officers, employees, or agents acting in their capacity. The agreement will also provide that the Independent Consultant will require that any firm with which he/she is affiliated or of which he/she is a member, and any person engaged to assist the Independent Consultant in performance of his/her duties under this Order shall not, without prior written consent of the Denver Regional Office of the Commission, enter into any employment, consultant, attorney-client, auditing or other professional relationship with MSLP or any of its present or former affiliates, directors, officers, employees, or agents acting in their capacity as such for the period of the engagement and for a period of two years after the engagement.

Certify, in writing, compliance with the undertaking(s) set forth above. The certification shall identify the undertaking(s), provide written evidence of compliance in the form of a narrative, and be supported by exhibits sufficient to demonstrate compliance. The Commission staff may make reasonable requests for further evidence of compliance, and Respondent agrees to provide such evidence....

V.

In view of the foregoing, the Commission deems it appropriate to impose the sanctions agreed to in Respondent MSLP's Offer.

Accordingly, it is hereby ORDERED that:

A. Pursuant to Section 8A of the Securities Act and Section 21C of the Exchange Act, Respondent MSLP cease and desist from committing or causing any violations and any future violations of Sections 5(a), 5(c), 17(a)(2) and 17(a)(3) of the Securities Act, Sections 13(a), 13(b)(2)(A), 13(b)(2)(B), and 14(a) of the Exchange Act and Rules 12b-20, 13a-1, 13a-13, and 14a9 thereunder, and Rule 302 of Regulation S-T of the Exchange Act.

B. Respondent shall comply with the undertakings enumerated in Section IV above.

C. Respondent shall pay civil penalties of $700,000 to the Commission....

Comments and Questions

1. How did these disclosure violations come about? What are some possible explanations for why the perquisites were not disclosed?

2. The failure to disclose information required by Regulation S-K in a periodic report can violate Section 13(a) of the Exchange Act. Such a violation, however, does not require a showing of intentional or negligent behavior. In this case, however, the Commission brought actions for violation of Rule 14a-9, the antifraud provision in the Exchange Act. What extra elements must be shown with respect to the noncompliance with Regulation S-K to make out a claim under this provision? Are those elements present in this case?

3. What do you make of the undertakings set out in this case? Will they be effective? Who selects the independent consultant? Is one year of service sufficient to ensure proper treatment of these expenses in the future?

4. Section 162(m) of the Internal Revenue Code limits the deductibility of executive compensation to $1 million. The provision does not apply, however, to compensation that is "performance-based." This provision was an early attempt by Congress to limit executive compensation. Did it work? What impact did it likely have on compensation? Note that any additional tax liability was imposed on the company, not on the officer receiving the compensation.

Have these expanded disclosure requirements worked?

Jennifer S. Martin, *The House of Mouse and Beyond: Assessing the SEC's Efforts to Regulate Executive Compensation*
32 Del. J. Corp. L. 481, 523–26 (2007)[4]

The benefit to the investing public of having full access, in a more transparent way, to executive compensation policies, practices and data cannot be understated. Brandeis' oft-quoted statement, "[s]unlight is said to be the best of disinfectants; electric light the most efficient policeman," is appropriate here. Transparency, if achieved, certainly will have an effect on the ability of executives to receive executive compen-

---

4. Copyright © 2007 Delaware Journal of Corporate Law. Reprinted with permission.

sation packages that are less linked to performance. Disclosure also ensures that investors have access to compensation information prior to making an investment. It is widely believed that access to understandable financial data, even by the market professionals alone, results in the data being reflected in the pricing of the stock. Examining compensation policies in stock prices and giving shareholders access to this information prior to investment is meaningful. However, it is not the same as providing shareholders with a means to hold decision makers accountable or to change compensation policies or processes to protect investments once made. Should we employ a regulatory approach for executive compensation that is predominately dependent on investor choice at the purchase stage? What about information overload, overconfidence in one's ability to decipher information, optimism and other barriers to disclosure-based regulation?

The SEC has often turned its focus to disclosure-based regulations, rather than merit review or substantive regulation. "[T]here is the recurrent theme throughout [the federal securities laws] of disclosure, again disclosure, and still more disclosure." The SEC believes that the market assumes investors make informed decisions with full disclosure. The advantage of disclosure as a regulatory approach is that it serves as a less invasive government intrusion into companies and allows investors to make personal choices about investments. The disclosure focus is certainly evident in the Sarbanes-Oxley Act of 2002 (Sarbanes-Oxley), which is intended "[t]o protect investors by improving the accuracy and reliability of corporate disclosures made pursuant to the securities laws." Traditional SEC disclosure-focused programs can produce results in some areas, such as making sure a prospectus in an initial public offering that contains misstatements creates liability for the issuer.

... In light of the continuing issues surrounding corporate governance, over-reliance on disclosure as a regulatory approach may be out-of-step with the current regulatory needs. First, investors do not always make rational decisions when making an initial investment. Second, investors need options other than selling to respond to disclosure of information about excessive compensation to executives. Third, the complexity of modern corporate enterprises makes clear that accurate disclosure that is understandable to shareholders is a daunting task for corporate officers. Not all investor behavior is simple buy and sell decisions in response to readily understandable disclosed information. Investors are vulnerable to corporate misdealing from the lack of information about executive compensation. Investors are also vulnerable from limits on their ability to respond to the information they have.

Using the same disclosure approach for executive compensation matters is not likely to yield the same meaningful results. The SEC-mandated disclosure to shareholders of executive compensation data lacks value if the shareholders cannot process and effectively use the information. For instance, information overload is a problem with disclosure-based regulatory systems generally, but it will particularly be a hurdle to investors in understanding executive compensation disclosure. The Revised Regulations contemplate no less than eight complex graphs and extensive narrative discussion. Additionally, the SEC is attempting to avoid "boilerplate" disclosure of compensation information with the Revised Regulations. Because lawyers draft many of the documents filed with the SEC, boilerplate language will be almost impossible to eliminate with the Revised Regulations. Further, most of the disclosure contemplated by the Revised Regulations will be received after executive compensation decisions are made. Therefore, existing shareholders have no meaningful options to change compensation policies after the fact, short of selling their shares. As discussed above, selling shares is a weak check on corporate decision makers.

Comments and Questions

1. What is the problem with trying to solve the issue of executive compensation through disclosure? Professor Martin noted that disclosure "is not the equivalent of merit review or substantive regulation of corporate conduct." As a result, she concludes that it may not have significant effect on compensation decisions, except perhaps to cause the amounts to increase. Is it an appropriate role for the SEC to be concerned about the substantive impact of disclosure on compensation decisions?

2. The level of disclosure that must take place with respect to executive compensation is extraordinary. *See* Item 402 of Regulation S-K, 17 C.F.R. 229.402. Are there particular reasons why such detailed disclosure is necessary in the area of executive compensation? Is there a point where the amount of disclosure can be characterized as counter-productive?

3. How might disclosure in this area result in an increase, rather than decrease in executive compensation? As one academic asserts: "Inflated executive egos demand inflated executive pay, especially when benchmarked to the compensation of rival executives." Kenneth R. Davis, *Taking Stock—Salary and Options Too: The Looting of Corporate America*, 69 Md. L. Rev. 419, 447 (2010). Do you agree?

4. Section 953(b) of the Dodd-Frank Act requires companies to disclose "the median" total annual compensation of all employees except the CEO, the annual total compensation of the CEO, and a ratio of these amounts. What purpose might this disclosure have? To the extent that a company wants to reduce the ratio, what steps might it take?

B. Disclosure and Substantive Changes in Behavior

The SEC does not have the power to regulate the substantive terms of executive compensation. In other words, the type and amount are mostly beyond the agency's regulatory authority. This does not, however, mean that the Commission has left substance alone. Disclosure alone can sometimes affect what happens inside the board room. Specifically, Item 402(b) of Regulation S-K, 17 C.F.R. 229.402(b), provides:

> **(b)** *Compensation discussion and analysis.* (1) Discuss the compensation awarded to, earned by, or paid to the named executive officers. The discussion shall explain all material elements of the registrant's compensation of the named executive officers. The discussion shall describe the following:
>
> > The objectives of the registrant's compensation programs; **(ii)** What the compensation program is designed to reward;**(iii)** Each element of com-

pensation; (**iv**) Why the registrant chooses to pay each element; (**v**) How the registrant determines the amount (and, where applicable, the formula) for each element to pay; (**vi**) How each compensation element and the registrant's decisions regarding that element fit into the registrant's overall compensation objectives and affect decisions regarding other elements ...

Executive Compensation and Related Person Disclosure
Exchange Act Release No. 54302A (Aug. 29, 2006)

The purpose of the Compensation Discussion and Analysis disclosure is to provide material information about the compensation objectives and policies for named executive officers without resorting to boilerplate disclosure. The Compensation Discussion and Analysis is intended to put into perspective for investors the numbers and narrative that follow it.

As described in the Proposing Release and as adopted, the Compensation Discussion and Analysis requirement is principles-based, in that it identifies the disclosure concept and provides several illustrative examples. Some commenters suggested that a principles-based approach would be better served without examples, on the theory that "laundry lists" would lead to boilerplate. Other commenters expressed the opposite view—that more specific description of required disclosure topics would more effectively elicit meaningful disclosure.

... Overall we designed the proposals to state the requirements sufficiently broadly to continue operating effectively as future forms of compensation develop, without suggesting that items that do not fit squarely within a "box" specified by the rules need not be disclosed. We believe that the adopted principles-based Compensation Discussion and Analysis, utilizing a disclosure concept along with illustrative examples, strikes an appropriate balance that will effectively elicit meaningful disclosure, even as new compensation vehicles develop over time.

We wish to emphasize, however, that the application of a particular example must be tailored to the company and that the examples are non-exclusive. We believe using illustrative examples helps to identify the types of disclosure that may be applicable. A company must assess the materiality to investors of the information that is identified by the example in light of the particular situation of the company. We also note that in some cases an example may not be material to a particular company, and therefore no disclosure would be required. Because the scope of the Compensation Discussion and Analysis is intended to be comprehensive, a company must address the compensation policies that it applies, even if not included among the examples. The Compensation Discussion and Analysis should reflect the individual circumstances of a company and should avoid boilerplate disclosure.

Comments and Questions

1. What do you think of this approach by the Commission? What impact might the disclosure of the process used in determining compensation have on the amount

paid? What implications does this type of disclosure have for purposes of a board's fiduciary obligations?

2. The Commission describes the approach as "principles-based" rather than "rule-based." What does this mean? Is it likely to work? What problems arise with a system that requires disclosure of the "individual circumstances" of each company?

3. Item 402 requires disclosure of policies that affect not only amounts but types of compensation. For example, disclosure must be made of the policies for allocating cash and non-cash compensation. What sorts of policies would be disclosed as a result of this type of requirement? Why does the type of compensation matter?

4. The discussion must also describe policies that address the recovery of certain compensation awards. SOX provides for some instances of mandatory recovery of compensation. In addition, companies receiving funds from the government during the financial crisis in 2008 had to provide for "clawbacks" of compensation in certain circumstances. Moreover, the practice ultimately extended beyond companies receiving bailout funds.

5. The most significant concern with disclosure requirements attempting to uncover the method and factors used to set compensation was the fear that it would result in boilerplate disclosure. Recall that investors have no private right of action for violations of the periodic reporting requirements and, while shareholders can sue for violations of the proxy rules, they must meet the requirements for a private right of action, including the need for the omissions or misstatements to be material. As a result, enforcement of these requirements largely fell to the Commission.

6. The staff at the Division of Corporation Finance aggressively reviewed filings containing compensation disclosure and sought to improve the quality of the disclosure provided by companies. The efforts uncovered considerable flaws in the disclosure process. As the staff observed, for example:

> We found that a number of companies discussed their compensation philosophies and decision mechanics in great detail. We asked a substantial number of companies to refocus their Compensation Discussion and Analysis presentations on the substance of their compensation decisions and to disclose how they analyzed information and why their analyses resulted in the compensation they paid. For example, where a company provided a lengthy discussion about its compensation philosophies, we suggested that it improve its Compensation Discussion and Analysis by explaining how and why those philosophies resulted in the numbers they presented in the required tables. Similarly, where a company provided a lengthy discussion about its decision-making process, we suggested that, rather than explaining the process, it explain how its analysis of relevant information resulted in the decisions it made.

Staff Observations in the Review of Executive Compensation Disclosure, Division of Corporation Finance, Oct. 9, 2007. What does this suggest about the problems confronted by the staff in ensuring that these requirements elicit meaningful disclosure?

What sorts of resources must the staff devote to this issue and what is likely to happen when the resources are used for other matters?

7. The most common problem noted by the staff concerned the use of performance targets. Companies commonly opined that compensation was dependent upon performance but, as the staff noted, "[w]e often found it difficult to understand how companies used these performance targets or considered qualitative individual performance to set compensation policies and make compensation decisions." In other words, the staff had difficulty determining the relationship between the targets and the amount of compensation actually paid. What are some possible explanations for this difficulty?

8. Does the requirement work? According to one commentator, to comply with the Compensation Discussion and Analysis, "companies need compensation consultants and lawyers with specialized expertise to help compile a report that few investors read and even fewer understand." Kenneth R. Davis, *Taking Stock—Salary and Options Too: The Looting of Corporate America*, 69 Md. L. Rev. 419, 424 (2010).

9. The Dodd-Frank Act also expanded the SEC's authority to regulate compensation. Section 956 gave to certain federal regulators, including the SEC, the authority to adopt rules prohibiting "any types of incentive-based payment arrangement" that encouraged "inappropriate risks" by certain financial institutions. In the SEC's case, the authority extended to certain brokers and investment advisors. Does this suggest that Congress will eventually allow the SEC to directly regulate the amount and type of compensation paid by public or listed companies?

Pay Ratio Disclosure

Exchange Act Release No. 75610 (August 5, 2015)

Section 953(b)(1) of the Dodd-Frank Wall Street Reform and Consumer Protection Act (the "Dodd-Frank Act") directs us to amend Item 402 of Regulation S-K ("Item 402") to require each registrant, other than an emerging growth company, as that term is defined in Section 3(a) of the Exchange Act, to disclose in any filing of the registrant described in Item 10(a) of Regulation S-K (or any successor thereto): (A) The median of the annual total compensation of all employees of the registrant, except the chief executive officer ("CEO") (or any equivalent position) of the registrant; (B) the annual total compensation of the CEO (or any equivalent position) of the registrant; and (C) the ratio of the median of the total compensation of all employees of the registrant to the annual total compensation of the CEO of the registrant. Section 953(b)(2) specifies that, for purposes of Section 953(b), "total compensation" of an employee of a registrant shall be determined in accordance with Item 402(c)(2)(x) of Regulation S-K as in effect on the day before the date of enactment of the Dodd-Frank Act. As discussed in detail below, we are adopting amendments to Item 402 to implement Section 953(b). We refer to this disclosure of the median of the annual total compensation of all employees of the registrant, the annual total compensation of the principal executive officer ("PEO") of the registrant, and the ratio of the two amounts as "pay ratio" disclosure.

Congress did not expressly state the specific objectives or intended benefits of Section 953(b), and the legislative history of the Dodd-Frank Act also does not expressly state the Congressional purpose underlying Section 953(b). As discussed below, based on our analysis of the statute and comments received, we believe Section 953(b) was intended to provide shareholders with a company-specific metric that can assist in their evaluation of a registrant's executive compensation practices. Accordingly, we have sought to tailor the final rule to meet that purpose while avoiding unnecessary costs.

In informing our understanding of the Congressional purpose of Section 953(b), we have considered the surrounding provisions of the Dodd Frank Act as well as the comments that we received during this rulemaking. Subtitle E of Title IX of the Dodd-Frank Act, headed—"Accountability and Executive Compensation" is, as explained in the Conference Report for the legislation, "designed to address shareholder rights and executive compensation practices." Its provisions, including Section 953(b), address various aspects of executive compensation with a focus on encouraging shareholder engagement in executive compensation matters by, among other things, increasing the transparency of compensation. In Section 951, for example, Congress required companies to provide for periodic shareholder votes on executive compensation. In implementing Congress's directive, we noted that a key function of the disclosures required incident to the new voting requirement was to "provide shareholders and investors with timely information" that was potentially useful to them "as they consider voting and investment decisions." Section 952 requires, in turn, that both compensation committee members of registrants and their advisors be independent. We noted that the rules implementing Section 952 could serve an informational purpose that benefits "investors to the extent they enable compensation committees to make better informed decisions regarding the amount or form of executive compensation." Further, as we noted in the release proposing implementation of Section 953(a), that section is intended to provide shareholders with metrics that will help them assess executive compensation relative to the registrant's performance.15 The Section 953(a) information is intended, among other things, to assist shareholders when exercising their say-on-pay voting rights under Section 951.

We believe that Section 953(b) should be interpreted consonant with Subtitle E's general purpose of further facilitating shareholder engagement with executive compensation. Thus, we believe that Congress intended Section 953(b) to supplement the executive compensation information available to shareholders. Particularly, Section 953(b) provides new data points that shareholders may find relevant and useful when exercising their voting rights under Section 951. Several commenters stated affirmatively that they would find the new data points, including pay ratio disclosure, relevant and useful when making voting decisions. Some commenters in the pre-proposing period suggested specifically that shareholders of public companies could use the pay ratio information, together with pay-versus-performance disclosure, to help inform their say-on-pay votes, which could also be a tool for shareholders to hold companies accountable for their CEO compensation. A significant consideration for us in fashioning a final rule implementing Section 953(b), then, is the extent to which elements of the final rule further Congress's apparent goal of giving shareholders additional executive compensation information to enhance the shareholder engagement envisioned by Section 951.

Consistent with this understanding of the Congressional purpose of Section 953(b), we believe the final pay ratio rule should be designed to allow shareholders to better understand and assess a particular registrant's compensation practices and pay ratio disclosures rather than to facilitate a comparison of this information from one registrant to another. As we noted in the Proposing Release, we do not believe that precise conformity or comparability of the pay ratio across companies is necessarily achievable given the variety of factors that could cause the ratio to differ. Consequently, we believe the primary benefit of the pay ratio disclosure is to provide shareholders with a company-specific metric that they can use to evaluate the PEO's compensation within the context of their company.

On the other hand, some commenters asserted that the pay ratio disclosure would not provide meaningful or material information to shareholders in making voting or investment decisions. In support of this contention, some of these commenters cited studies demonstrating that shareholders are not interested in this information, some commenters cited shareholder votes indicating a high level of support for executive pay and little support for shareholder proposals advocating for pay ratio disclosure, and some commenters contended that pay ratio disclosure would confuse shareholders because they would rely on it without fully considering a company's detailed narrative disclosures. Notwithstanding the disagreement among commenters on the value of the pay ratio disclosure, in adopting the final rule we have sought to implement Congress's apparent determination that the pay ratio disclosure would be useful to shareholders.

* * *

Overall, we think the final rule will provide investors with information Congress intended them to have to assess the compensation and accountability of a company's PEO while seeking to limit the costs and practical difficulties of providing the disclosure.

Finally, we recognize the possibility that, based on the specific facts and circumstances of a registrant's work force and corporate operations, the pay ratio disclosure may warrant additional disclosures from a registrant to ensure that, in the registrant's view, the pay ratio disclosure is a meaningful data point for investors when making their say-on-pay votes. While Congress appears to have believed that the pay ratio disclosure would be a useful data point, we recognize that its relative usefulness — taken alone without accompanying disclosures to provide potentially important context — may vary considerably. Rather than prescribe a one-size-fits-all catalogue of additional disclosures that registrants should provide to put the pay ratio disclosure in context, we believe it is the better course to provide registrants the flexibility to provide additional disclosures that they believe will assist investors' understanding of the meaning of pay ratio disclosure when making say-on-pay votes. In this way, we believe we can best fulfill Congress's directive in Section 953(b) while avoiding unnecessary costs and complexities that might result from mandating additional disclosures.

Comments and Questions

1. The proposed rule generated an enormous number of comments. The adopting released pointed out that the Commission had received 287,400 comment letters, the "vast majority" supporting the rule. What provoked such an outpouring for a seemingly technical rule?

2. The issue of pay ratios as a method of assessing CEO compensation has been a longstanding one. Pay ratios have been computed on the basis of such varied metrics as minimum wage and statistics on average compensation provided by the Department of Labor. None of these statistics, however, results in a ratio that is company specific. Section 953(b) altered that by requiring companies to compute and disclose a ratio based upon the compensation paid to the median employee at that company. What impact will the company specific nature of this calculation have on the value of the disclosure? Will it, as some critics contend, obscure and mislead rather than clarify or inform? If true, can the concern be alleviated by explanatory disclosure?

3. Is this information material to investors? At the same time Dodd-Frank required disclosure of pay ratios, the legislation also mandated "say on pay", an advisory vote on executive compensation by shareholders. Are the two provisions related? If there were no say on pay, would the information still be material?

4. The Commission noted that the ratio was not designed to facilitate comparisons among different companies but to "provide shareholders with a company-specific metric that they can use to evaluate" compensation. How might that be the case? Is this type of metric useful in evaluating compensation?

5. The discussion of the pay ratio has been in the context of shareholders. How might this information be used in the boardroom? Is it possible that compensation decisions by directors may be affected by the impact on the ratio?

6. One of the difficult issues that came up in the comment process was the inclusion of foreign employees. Some issuers indicated that their human resources software system could not easily capture the information, adding time and cost to the process while others were concerned with foreign privacy laws. Of course, the inclusion of foreign workers, particularly those from developing countries, could lower the median and effectively worsen the ratio. The statute required that the ratio include the median of "all employees," limiting the discretion of the Commission to completely exclude foreign employees. The final rule, however, addressed the concerns by allowing for the exclusion of employees where foreign law prevented compliance and where the total number of employees amounted 5% or less of the total number of employees (the de minimis exception). Does this fix the concerns expressed by issuers?

C. Substantive Regulation of Compensation

In recent years, however, the SEC's authority has been expanded and is no longer entirely limited to disclosure. The first modern attempt to substantively regulate compensation at the federal level probably involved Section 162(m) of the IRC. The provision disallowed the deduction of amounts paid to the CEO and other top officers in excess of $1 million. The exceptions, however, swallowed the rule. For one thing, the provision did not apply to compensation determined based upon "performance goals." One consequence of the provision was to encourage greater use of stock and options as part of the compensation package.

The Sarbanes-Oxley Act dealt with the problem of loans to executive officers. Companies made loans with terms that were far better than what was commercially available. This might include interest rates lower than what a bank would have charged or a willingness to make the loan without insisting on collateral. In some cases, the loans were forgiven, eliminating any repayment obligation. Congress addressed these problems in an unsubtle fashion. Section 13(k) of the Exchange Act simply prohibited personal loans to directors and executive officers. *See* 15 USC 78m(k).

The other issue addressed in SOX was the problem of performance-based compensation paid based upon financial statements later found to be incorrect, often because of fraud. Congress responded by adopting Section 304 of SOX. The provision made clawbacks (the return of performance-based compensation) mandatory where a restatement occurred as a result of misconduct. While not specifically expanding the Commission's authority, the provision provided a potential mechanism for affecting compensation practices.

Nonetheless, the provision sat unused for the first eight years after the adoption of SOX.

SEC v. Jenkins

United States District Court, District of Arizona
2010 U.S. Dist. LEXIS 57023 (June 9, 2010)

SNOW, J

BACKGROUND

During the time relevant to this action, CSK Auto Corporation ("CSK") was a publicly-traded retail company of automotive parts and accessories, operating under three brand names: Checker Auto Parts, Schucks Auto Supply, and Kragen Auto Parts. From January 1997 through August 2007, Jenkins was CSK's CEO and the chairman of its board of directors, receiving a base salary, bonuses, and stock option grants.

While Jenkins worked for CSK, the company engaged in a vendor allowance program called "Let's Work Together." The Complaint alleges that, by intentionally failing to properly account for receivables under this program, CSK reported greater pretax income than the company actually earned during fiscal years 2002, 2003, and 2004. Although the SEC does not allege that Jenkins personally was aware of the fraudulent concealment perpetrated by various CSK officers, Jenkins did certify the company's inaccurate financial statements for those years.

Eventually, to correct these overstatements, CSK filed two accounting restatements as required by federal securities laws, which Jenkins also certified. In 2004, CSK released its first restatement. That restatement, however, failed to write-off all known uncollectible vendor allowance receivables and incorrectly indicated that the errors were mistakes rather than fraudulent misstatements by CSK. In 2007, CSK filed a second restatement, which restated the financial statements for fiscal years 2002–2004. The Complaint does not allege that Jenkins played any role in perpetuating the scheme. In fact, the SEC has filed both civil complaints and criminal indictments against other CSK officers, alleging that those officers concealed the scheme from Jenkins.

From May 2003 through May 2005, Jenkins received over $2 million in compensation in the form of bonuses and other incentive-based and equity-based compensation. During the same period, Jenkins realized over $2 million from the sale of CSK securities. Jenkins has not reimbursed CSK for any portion of these bonuses, incentive-based compensation, equity-based compensation, or stock sale profits.

The SEC now seeks an order compelling Jenkins to reimburse CSK for this income pursuant to Section 304 of the Sarbanes-Oxley Act of 2002 ("Sarbanes-Oxley" or the "Act"), 15 U.S.C. § 7243 (2006). Section 304 of the Act requires that, if an issuer, such as CSK, must prepare an accounting restatement because of its material non-compliance with financial-reporting securities laws, and if that noncompliance was caused by CSK's misconduct, then the CEO or CFO must provide certain reimbursement to the issuer. 15 U.S.C. § 7243(a). Under the Act, such reimbursement includes any bonuses, incentive based, and equity-based compensation received during the twelve-month period following the first improper public issuance or filing. *Id.* Because the Complaint does not allege that Jenkins was personally responsible for either the Let's Work Together scheme or the incorrect SEC filings, except to the extent that Jenkins certified the SEC filings, Jenkins's liability depends on whether Section 304 requires a CEO to reimburse an issuer even where the CEO committed no personal wrongdoing. The Court is unaware of any cases discussing this issue, but the Court concludes that the Complaint properly states a claim under the statute.

* * *

DISCUSSION

Section 304 of Sarbanes-Oxley provides:

> (a) Additional compensation prior to noncompliance with Commission financial reporting requirements.

> If an issuer is required to prepare an accounting restatement due to the material noncompliance of the issuer, as a result of misconduct, with any financial reporting requirement under the securities laws, the chief executive officer and chief financial officer of the issuer shall reimburse the issuer for—

(1) any bonus or other incentive-based or equity-based compensation received by that person from the issuer during the 12-month period following the first public issuance or filing with the Commission (whichever first occurs) of the financial document embodying such financial reporting requirement; and

(2) any profits realized from the sale of securities of the issuer during that 12-month period.

(b) Commission exemption authority. The Commission may exempt any person from the application of subsection (a) of this section, as it deems necessary and appropriate.

15 U.S.C. § 7243.

I. Section 304 Does Not Require Personal Misconduct.

The overarching issue is whether the Complaint alleges facts sufficient to raise a plausible claim under Section 304. Because a motion to dismiss turns not on what facts ultimately may be proven, but rather on what the complaint plausibly alleges, the Court need not reach issues that depend on factual disputes. Accordingly, based on traditional rules of statutory interpretation, the Court concludes that the Complaint has alleged facts sufficient to state a claim under Section 304. "The purpose of statutory construction is to discern the intent of Congress in enacting a particular statute." *United States v. Daas*, 198 F.3d 1167, 1174 (9th Cir. 1999). "The starting point for the interpretation of a statute is always its language," and "[a]ny inquiry must cease if the statutory language is unambiguous and the statutory scheme is coherent and consistent." *Alvarado v. Cajun Operating Co.*, 588 F.3d 1261, 1268 (9th Cir. 2009) (citation omitted). Applying these steps of statutory interpretation, the Court holds that the text and structure of Section 304 require only the misconduct of the issuer, but do not necessarily require the specific misconduct of the issuer's CEO or CFO. Moreover, Section 304's legislative history supports this textual reading. Because Congress's intent is evident from these main methods of statutory interpretation, the Court need not resort to the additional canons raised by Defendant.

A. The Text of the Statute Requires Misconduct Only by the Issuer.

When discerning Congress's intent from a statute's text, "courts must presume that a legislature says in a statute what it means and means in a statute what it says there[.]" *Alvarado*, 588 F.3d at 1268 (citation omitted). When possible, a statute's plain meaning is determined according to its terms' "ordinary, contemporary, common meaning[,]" *Cooper v. F.A.A.*, 596 F.3d 538, 544 (9th Cir. 2010), and by "look[ing] to the entire statutory scheme[,]" *Daas*, 198 F.3d at 1174.

The relevant statutory phrase specifies that the reimbursement obligation is triggered if an issuer has to prepare an accounting restatement "due to the material noncompliance of the issuer, as a result of misconduct, with any financial reporting requirement under the securities laws." 15 U.S.C. § 7243(a). The ordinary, contemporary and common meaning of that language is that the misconduct of the issuer is the misconduct that triggers the reimbursement obligation of the CEO and the

CFO. In this case, the issuer is a corporation. In general, a corporation acts through its officers, agents or employees and is liable for the actions of such persons acting within the scope of their agency. *In re Am. Int'l Group, Inc.*, 965 A.2d 763, 802, 823 (Del. Ch. 2009). Thus, the plain language of the statute indicates that the misconduct of corporate officers, agents or employees acting within the scope of their agency or employment is sufficient misconduct to meet this element of the statute. *See* 15 U.S.C. § 7243(a). Before reimbursement can be required, however, the issuer's misconduct must also be sufficiently serious to result in material noncompliance with a financial reporting requirement under the securities laws, and must require the issuer to file an accounting restatement. *See id.*

In addition to the plain text of the relevant statutory language, Congress entitled this subsection of Sarbanes-Oxley as "Additional Compensation Prior to Noncompliance with Commission Financial Reporting Requirements." 15 U.S.C. § 7243(a). "Although statutory titles are not part of the legislation, they may be instructive in putting the statute in context." *Singh v. Gonzales*, 499 F.3d 969, 977 (9th Cir. 2007). As the title of the subsection makes plain, it was Congress's purpose to recapture the additional compensation paid to a CEO during any period in which the corporate issuer was not in compliance with financial reporting requirements. A CEO need not be personally aware of financial misconduct to have received additional compensation during the period of that misconduct, and to have unfairly benefitted therefrom. When a CEO either sells stock or receives a bonus in the period of financial noncompliance, the CEO may unfairly benefit from a misperception of the financial position of the issuer that results from those misstated financials, even if the CEO was unaware of the misconduct leading to misstated financials. It is not irrational for Congress to require that such additional compensation amounts be repaid to the issuer.

* * *

Further, in ascertaining the purposes to be served by a statute, it is appropriate to look at the larger statutory scheme of which the particular statute is a part. *See Daas*, 198 F.3d at 1174 ("To determine the plain meaning of a particular statutory provision, and thus congressional intent, the court looks to the entire statutory scheme."); *see also SEC v. Nat'l Sec., Inc.*, 393 U.W. 453, 466 (1969) (noting that the "interdependence of the various sections of the securities laws is certainly a relevant factor in any interpretation of the language Congress has chosen"). Pursuant to the immediately preceding sections of the Sarbanes-Oxley Act, particularly Section 302, an issuer's CEO and CFO are required to certify each annual or quarterly report of the issuer. 15 U.S.C. § 7241. In so doing, the CEO and the CFO also certify that they are responsible for the existence, design, and operation of effective internal controls that provide assurances as to the accuracy of the issuer's financial statements. *Id.* Section 304 provides an incentive for CEOs and CFOs to be rigorous in their creation and certification of internal controls by requiring that they reimburse additional compensation received during periods of corporate non-compliance regardless of whether or not they were aware of the misconduct giving rise to the misstated financials.

B. Legislative History Affirms the Court's Textual Reading.

Because the Court has determined that the text of the statute warrants only one interpretation, the Court "need not resort to legislative history" or other canons of statutory interpretation. *Alvarado*, 588 F.3d at 1268. In any event, legislative history actually "confirms" and "supports" the Court's holding that Section 304 requires no personal misconduct by the CEO or CFO. *See Rutti v. Lojack Corp., Inc.*, 596 F.3d 1046, 1052 (9th Cir. 2010) (holding that the "legislative history confirms the plain language" of the statute); *Guidiville Band of Pomo Indians v. NGV Gaming, Ltd.*, 531 F.3d 767, 779 n. 14 (9th Cir. 2008) (noting that "legislative history ... remains a frequently-relied-upon additional tool of statutory interpretation" and that even plain-language interpretations of statutes may also be "supported by legislative history") (internal quotations omitted). Contrary to Defendant's assertion, it is inapposite that the legislative history does not include a statement that Congress intended to create a "vicarious strict liability statute." (Dkt. # 27 at 15.)

The House and Senate passed different versions of Sarbanes-Oxley, but only the House's version, which did not become law, included language regarding the CEO or CFO's scienter in the context of disgorgement. Section 12 of H.R. 3763 (the "House Bill") directed the SEC to "conduct an analysis of whether, and under what conditions, any officer or director of an issuer should be required to disgorge profits gained, or losses avoided, in the sale of the securities of such issuer during the six month period immediately preceding the filing of a restated financial statement on the part of such issuer." H.R. Rep. No. 107-414, at 12 (2002). If the SEC determined that disgorgement regulations were appropriate, then the House Bill required the SEC to "identify the scienter requirement that should be used in order to determine to impose the requirement to disgorge." *Id.* The House Committee on Financial Services extrapolated that the SEC should require reimbursement "only in cases where the Commission can prove extreme misconduct on the part of [the] officer or director." *Id.* at 44.

On the other hand, the Senate version of the bill, S. 2673 (the "Senate Bill"), included no similar discussion of scienter. *See* S. 2673, 107th Cong. § 304 (2002). In contrast to the House Bill, the Senate Bill was passed after additional news of corporate misconduct arose, such as Adelphia's massive restatement to account for previously undisclosed loans, Tyco's former CEO's indictment for tax evasion, Worldcom's accounting scheme, and Imclone's CEO's insider trading charges. *See* John Patrick Kelsh, *Section 304 of the Sarbanes-Oxley Act of 2002: The Case for a Personal Culpability Requirement*, 59 Bus. Law. 1005, 1018 (2004). As it relates to Section 304 of the Act, the language in the Senate Bill ultimately became the version signed into law, without mentioning scienter or requiring misconduct on behalf of the officers in order to trigger reimbursement. *Compare* S. 2673 *with* 15 U.S.C. § 7243.

Additionally, the Senate had the opportunity to consider an amendment that would have limited Section 304 to the officers and directors "with knowledge, at the time of the misconduct, of the material noncompliance of the issuer." *See Arnold & Porter Legislative History: Sarbanes-Oxley Act of 2002*, P.L. 107-204, 116 Stat. 745, History

40-C, 2002 WL 32054475 (July 10, 2002). This amendment arguably would have created a personal misconduct element, but it was tabled.

Jenkins further contends that the Senate report on Section 304 implies a personal wrongdoing element because it states that CEOs and CFOs must "disgorge" certain compensation, a term that Defendants contend means relief designed to deprive a *wrongdoer* of ill-gotten gains. *See* Sen. Rep. No. 107-205, at 23 (2002); *SEC v. First Pac. Bancorp.*, 142 F.3d 1186, 1191 (9th Cir. 1998); *SEC v. Blatt*, 583 F.2d 1325, 1335 (2d Cir. 1978). Regardless of the fact that the Senate report uses the term "disgorged," Section 304's *text* utilizes the term "reimburse" rather than "disgorge." Thus, while "disgorge" may have a specialized meaning in the context of a court's preexisting common law authority to order *equitable* disgorgement, *see, e.g., First Pac. Bancorp.*, 142 F.3d at 1191, *Blatt*, 583 F.2d at 1335, it has no application to the text of the statute here.

Comments and Questions

1. What is the purpose of this provision? Why was it necessary? Is it likely to have much effect on the accuracy of financial statements?

2. Should Congress be deciding these issues? Should the matter be left to state law and the discretion of the board to determine?

3. Do you agree with this decision? Irrespective of the legal analysis, should clawbacks be required for those who did not commit wrongdoing? Should repayment be keyed to restatements? What are the strengths and weaknesses of such an approach?

4. This was the first suit brought by the Commission that relied on Section 304. Why has it not been used more often? That may, however, be changing. *See SEC v. McCarthy*, Litigation Release No. 21873 (March 4, 2011) (referencing Section 304 and disclosing that CEO agreed to reimburse company for cash bonus paid in 2006).

5. What about private parties? The trend is to find that there is no private right of action under Section 304 to enforce the provision. *See Cohen v. Viray*, 622 F.3d 188 (2d Cir. 2010); *see also In re Digimarc Corp. Derivative Litig.*, 549 F.3d 1223, 1233 (9th Cir. 2008). Could the provision have any relevance in a derivative suit?

6. Could private parties include in a settlement to securities and derivative actions a specific waiver of Section 304 that would preclude the Commission from bringing actions under the provision? In *Cohen v. Viray*, the parties sought approval of a settlement that would both waive Section 304 and indemnify the relevant officers for any payments required as a result of the provision. The SEC intervened (along with the Justice Department) and objected to the settlement. The court vacated the settlement, concluding that "companies themselves do not have the authority effectively to exempt persons from 304 liability."

7. Congress apparently liked the idea of clawbacks. The provision was strengthened and broadened in the Dodd-Frank Act. Section 954 requires the Commission to adopt rules that would provide for the repayment of incentive-based compensation upon

any restatement resulting upon a showing of "material noncompliance" with financial reporting requirements. In addition, the provision applies to current and former executive officers and applied to performance-based compensation paid within the three year period preceding the restatement. The SEC has proposed rules to implement this provision. See Exchange Act Release No. 75342 (July 1, 2015) (proposing Rule 10D-1). The proposal would mandate recovery, giving the board little discretion to forgo clawbacks. The Release noted that "allowing discretion whether to recover excess incentive-based compensation could undermine the purpose of Section 10D by permitting an issuer's board of directors to determine that an executive officer may retain incentive-based compensation to which he or she is not entitled." Discretion would exist only where recovery would impose "undue costs" or violate the laws of another country. What impact is this rule likely to have? Do you agree with the proposed lack of discretion afforded boards in seeking clawbacks?

D. Fixing the Process

Dodd-Frank also sought to regulate the process used by listed companies in determining executive compensation. The Act added Section 10C to the Exchange Act. *See* 15 USC 78j-3. The provision provides that the Commission must, by rule, require direct stock exchanges to adopt listing standards regulating compensation committees. The committee was to consist of independent directors and have the authority to retain advisers, whether compensation consultants or counsel. The committee also was to received "appropriate funding" that it would determine. The Commission did so with the adoption of Rule 10C-1.

In regulating compensation committees, Congress was particularly concerned with the use of compensation consultants. Concerns had arisen that these consultants were sometimes advocates for the CEO rather than for the company. The provision, therefore, not only gave committees the authority to retain consultants but gave the Commission the authority to define the factors that had to be considered in selecting a consultant.

Listing Standards for Compensation Committees
File No. S7-13-11
Exchange Act Release No. 67220 (June 20, 2012)

4. Compensation Adviser Independence Factors

Section 10C(b) of the Exchange Act provides that the compensation committee of a listed issuer may select a compensation adviser only after taking into consideration the five independence factors specified in Section 10C(b) as well as any other factors identified by the Commission. In accordance with Section 10C(b), these factors would apply to the selection of compensation consultants, legal counsel and other advisers to the committee. The statute does not require a compensation adviser to be independent, only that the compensation committee of a listed issuer consider the enumerated independence factors before selecting a compensation adviser. Section

10C(b)(2) specifies that the independence factors identified by the Commission must be competitively neutral and include, at minimum:

The provision of other services to the issuer by the person that employs the compensation consultant, legal counsel or other adviser;

The amount of fees received from the issuer by the person that employs the compensation consultant, legal counsel or other adviser, as a percentage of the total revenue of the person that employs the compensation consultant, legal counsel or other adviser;

The policies and procedures of the person that employs the compensation consultant, legal counsel or other adviser that are designed to prevent conflicts of interest;

Any business or personal relationship of the compensation consultant, legal counsel or other adviser with a member of the compensation committee; and

Any stock of the issuer owned by the compensation consultant, legal counsel or other adviser.

We proposed to direct the exchanges to adopt listing standards requiring the compensation committee of a listed issuer to consider the five factors enumerated in Section 10C(b) of the Exchange Act prior to selecting a compensation adviser. We are adopting the rule substantially as proposed, but with some changes in response to comments.

* * *

Many commentators urged us to add more independence factors to the list of factors that could affect the independence of a compensation adviser. Several commentators argued that we should include a comparison of the amount of fees received for providing executive compensation consulting services to the amount of fees received for providing non-executive compensation consulting services. Other commentators expressed support for requiring compensation committees to consider any business or personal relationship between an executive officer of the issuer and an adviser or the person employing the compensation adviser. Some commentators, however, opposed adding new factors to the list of factors identified in the proposed rule, although one of these commentators acknowledged that it would advise any compensation committee evaluating the independence of a potential adviser to consider the business and personal relationships between the issuer's executive officers and the adviser or adviser's firm.

* * *

c. Final Rule

After considering the comments, we are adopting the requirements substantially as proposed, but with some revisions. As discussed above, this aspect of the final rule will also apply to those members of a listed issuer's board of directors who oversee executive compensation matters on behalf of the board of directors in the absence of a board committee. We have also decided to include one additional independence factor that compensation committees must consider before selecting a compensation adviser. Under the final rule, the exchanges will be directed to adopt listing standards that require a compensation committee to take into account the five factors enumerated in Section 10C(b)(2), as well as any business or personal relationships between the executive officers of the issuer and the compensation adviser or the person employing the adviser. This would include, for example, situations where the chief executive officer of an issuer and the compensation adviser have a familial relationship or where the chief executive officer and the compensation adviser (or the adviser's employer) are business partners. We agree with commentators who stated that business and personal relationships between an executive officer and a compensation adviser or a person employing the compensation adviser may potentially pose a significant conflict of interest that should be considered by the compensation committee before selecting a compensation adviser.

Comments and Questions

1. What do you make of these reforms? Will they improve the decision making process for executive compensation?

2. The Rule does not require the selection of an independent compensation consultant, only that the board consider the prescribed factors. How then are these factors likely to effect the selection of compensation consultants?

3. Assuming the committee considers the required factors, may it still obtain input from the CEO with respect to the functions of the compensation consultant? The practice is apparently permitted under state law. *See Friedman v. Dolan*, CA No. 9425 (Del. Ch. Jan. 23, 2015) (Delaware law) (in response to allegations that compensation committee allowed CEO to "assist the Compensation Committee and its compensation consultant in determining the Company's core peer group and the peer group comparisons" court concluded that a "board is not forbidden from seeking management's input in compensation decisions"). What would you recommend and why?

4. Compensation committees get to determine their own compensation. Rule 10C-1 provided that companies must provide "appropriate funding, as determined by the compensation committee" but specified that the funding had to be sufficient "for payment of reasonable compensation to a compensation consultant, independent legal counsel or any other adviser retained by the compensation committee." Compare this with the provision applicable to the funding of audit committees in Rule 10A-3. There appropriate funding (as determined by the committee) must include compensation to the auditor, advisers, and "[o]rdinary administrative expenses ... that are necessary or appropriate in carrying out its duties." 17 CFR 240.10A-3. What impact, if any, might these differing standards have on their decision making?

5. The committee also must consist of independent directors. Section 10C gave the Commission the authority to determine the "factors" that must be considered in determining director independence for the committee. These factors engendered sig-

nificant debate among commentators. Some argued that the factors should include business and personal relationships between directors on the compensation committee and executive officers. When the NYSE adopted its listing standard, the Commission made this comment in the release:

> Although personal and business relationships, related party transactions, and other matters suggested by commenters are not specified either as bright-line disqualifications or explicit factors that must be considered in evaluating a director's independence, the Commission believes that compliance with NYSE's rules and the provision noted above would demand consideration of such factors with respect to compensation committee members, as well as to all Independent Directors on the board.

Exchange Act Release No. 68639 (Jan. 11, 2013). What impact might this standard have on the determination of independence? Is it limited only to directors on the compensation committee?

E. Compensation Practices and Remedies

The Commission has used disclosure to encourage the use of independent compensation consultants. In other instances, the SEC has employed more compulsory means to achieve the same result.

SEC v. Bank of America

United States District Court, Southern District of New York
2010 U.S. Dist. LEXIS 15460 (Feb. 22, 2010)

RAKOFF, JUSTICE:

The question before the Court is whether to grant the motion of plaintiff Securities and Exchange Commission ("S.E.C."), filed on February 4, 2010, seeking approval of a Proposed Consent Judgment that would resolve the two above-captioned cases. Given the somewhat tortured background of these cases and the difficulties the motion presents, the Court is tempted to quote the great American philosopher Yogi Berra: "I wish I had an answer to that because I'm getting tired of answering that question." However, after full consideration, the Court reluctantly grants the motion, on the terms specified below.

The Court begins where any court should: with the facts. In disapproving as neither fair, reasonable, adequate nor in the public interest the prior proposed settlement of the first of these two cases, 09 Civ. 6829 (the "Undisclosed Bonuses" case), the Court bewailed the absence of established facts supporting the proposal and expressed the hope that "the truth may still emerge." S.E.C. v. Bank of America Corp., 653 F. Supp. 2d 507, 512 (S.D.N.Y. 2009). Since then, the parties have conducted extensive discovery, assisted by the helpful decision of defendant Bank of America Corp. (the "Bank") to waive attorney-client privilege, resulting in the S.E.C.'s presentation to this Court of a 35-page Statement of Facts and a 13-page Supplemental Statement of Facts, the accuracy of which is not contested here by the Bank. In addition, in response to questions from the Court in an Order dated February 11, 2010, the parties have provided, and the Court has reviewed, hundreds of pages of deposition testimony and other evidentiary materials bearing on the case.

As a result of that review, it is clear to the Court that:

(1) the Proxy Statement that the Bank sent to its shareholders on November 3, 2008 soliciting their approval of the merger with Merrill Lynch & Co., Inc. ("Merrill") failed adequately to disclose the Bank's agreement to let Merrill pay its executives and certain other employees $5.8 billion in bonuses at a time when Merrill was suffering huge losses; and

(2) the Bank failed adequately to disclose to its shareholders either prior to the shareholder approval of the merger on December 5, 2008 or prior to the merger's effective date of January 1, 2009 the Bank's ever-increasing knowledge that Merrill was suffering historically great losses during the fourth quarter of 2008 (ultimately amounting to a net loss of $15.3 billion, the largest quarterly loss in the firm's history) and that Merrill had nonetheless accelerated the payment to certain executives and other employees of more than $3.6 billion in bonuses.

Despite the Bank's somewhat coy refusal to concede the materiality of these nondisclosures, it seems obvious that a prudent Bank shareholder, if informed of the aforementioned facts, would have thought twice about approving the merger or might have sought its renegotiation. What is far from obvious, however, is why these nondisclosures occurred. The S.E.C. and the Bank have consistently taken the position that it was, at worst, the product of negligence on the part of the Bank, its relevant executives, and its lawyers (inside and outside), who made the decisions (such as they were) to non-disclose on a piecemeal basis in which inadequate data coupled with rather narrow parsing of the disclosure issues combined to obscure the combined impact of the information being withheld. In particular, it appears that the relevant decision-makers took the position that neither the bonuses nor the mounting fourth quarter losses had to be disclosed because the bonuses were consistent with prior years' bonuses and the losses were uncertain and, in any case, roughly consistent with prior quarters. *See, e.g.,* Statement of Facts at 15, 29; Supplemental Statement of Facts at 5–8. Despite ever-growing indications that the latter assumption was erroneous, *see, e.g.,* Supplemental Statement of Facts at 8, the relevant decision-makers stuck to their previous determinations so far as disclosure of the losses was concerned and appear never to have considered at all the impact that the accelerated payment of over $3.6 billion in bonuses might have on a company that was verging on financial ruin.

* * *

The Court accordingly turns to the question of whether, … the settlement is fair, reasonable, adequate, and in the public interest. The proposed settlement has essentially two components: a package of prophylactic measures designed to prevent such nondisclosures in the future; and a penalty provision that is supposed also to serve the purpose of partially compensating victims.

The package of prophylactic measures includes, among other items, the following:

– the Bank's engagement, in consultation with the SEC, of an independent auditor to assess over the next three years whether the Bank's accounting controls and procedures are adequate to assure proper public disclosures;

– the Bank's engagement, in consultation with the SEC, of an independent disclosure counsel to report solely to the Bank's audit committee on the adequacy of the Bank's public disclosures over the next three years;

– the Bank's engagement of an outside compensation consultant to advise a fully independent compensation committee of the Bank's board as to the terms of executive compensation over the next three years; and

– the Bank's submission of executive compensation recommendations to the shareholders, for a nonbinding vote of approval or disapproval, over the next three years.

No one can quarrel that these remedial steps are helpful, so far as they go, and may help to render less likely the kind of piecemeal and mincing approach to public disclosure that led to the Bank's problems in the instant cases. Given that the apparent working assumption of the Bank's decision-makers and lawyers involved in the underlying events at issue here was not to disclose information if a rationale could be found for not doing so, the proposed remedial steps should help foster a healthier attitude of "when in doubt, disclose."

In order to further strengthen these prophylactic measures, the Court suggested at the hearing on February 8, 2010 that the independent auditor and the disclosure counsel not just be chosen in consultation with the S.E.C., but rather be fully acceptable to the S.E.C., with the Court having the final say if the two sides could not agree on the selections. The parties, by letters dated February 16, 2010, have subsequently agreed to these suggestions, which will therefore need to be incorporated in a revised Proposed Consent Judgment to be presented to the Court, as detailed below.

The Court also suggested that the compensation consultant, which the present proposal provides will be chosen solely by the Bank's compensation committee (not even in consultation with the S.E.C.), be chosen jointly by the compensation committee, the S.E.C., and the Court. The reason for this suggestion was the Court's perception that too many compensation consultants have a skewed focus when it comes to executive compensation, concentrating on what they perceive is necessary to attract and keep "talent" (however defined), and more generally favoring ever larger compensation packages, while rarely taking account of limits that a reasonable shareholder might place on such expenditures. In its letter of February 16, 2010, however, the Bank rejects this proposal outright, noting in its letter that the "SEC has consistently stated that it does not seek to enforce any particular philosophy or impose any substantive judgments on the form or amount of compensation." But the Bank's strong defense of the sacred cow of executive compensation is besides the point: the Court only suggested that giving the S.E.C. and/or the Court some role in the selection of the compensation consultant might provide a modicum of objectivity in that selection. Nonetheless, the Court does agree that the manner of selection of the compensation consultant is sufficiently peripheral to the main concerns of these cases as not to constitute a "dealbreaker," particularly in light of the requirement of a nonbinding shareholder vote on compensation for the next three years.

The part of the proposed settlement that presents the greatest difficulty is, however, the penalty package, which essentially consists of a $150 million fine. Though that amount is considerably greater than the $33 million that the Court rejected in the prior proposed settlement of the Undisclosed Bonuses case, it is still very modest in light of the fact that it now covers both cases—that is, all the nondisclosures that were material to the proposed merger with Merrill, a merger that may yet turn out well but that could have been a Bank-destroying disaster if the U.S. taxpayer had not saved the day. From this perspective, the amount of the fine appears paltry.

An even more fundamental problem, however, is that a fine assessed against the Bank, taken by itself, penalizes the shareholders for what was, in effect if not in intent, a fraud by management on the shareholders. This was among the major reasons the Court rejected the earlier proposed settlement. *See* S.E.C. v. Bank of America Corp., 653 F. Supp.2d at 509. Where management deceives its own shareholders, a fine most directly serves its deterrent purposes if it is assessed against the persons responsible for the deception. If such persons acted out of negligence, rather than bad faith, that should be a mitigating factor, but not a reason to have the shareholder victims pay the fine instead.

Although the pending complaint of the New York Attorney General against the top two Bank officials allegedly responsible for the deceptions may, if proven in court, partially serve this deterrent purpose, it is not part of the settlement pending before this Court and may have its own evidentiary weaknesses. The parties to the instant cases, however, attempt to mitigate the Court's concerns by proposing that, pursuant to the "Fair Fund" provisions of the Sarbanes-Oxley Act, the $150 million be distributed solely to Bank shareholders who were harmed by the Bank's nondisclosures (Bank "legacy" shareholders) and not to former Merrill shareholders who now own Bank stock (Merrill "legacy" shareholders), nor to Bank officers or directors who had access to the undisclosed information. Although this proposal was not specifically incorporated into the Proposed Consent Judgment presented to the Court, the parties subsequently agreed to the Court's proposal that it be incorporated, and thus any revised Proposed Consent Judgment to be presented to the Court must include such terms.

What the proposal does, in effect, is to transfer $150 million from all shareholders to those current Bank shareholders who were victimized by the non-disclosures. Since the S.E.C. in its letter dated February 16, 2010 estimates that this latter group is roughly around 50 percent of all current Bank shareholders, the effect is to transfer $75 million from Merrill "legacy" shareholders to Bank "legacy" shareholders.

Put another way, it serves to renegotiate the price that Bank shareholders would have paid to Merrill shareholders for purchasing Merrill shares if the disclosures had been made.

But the effect is very modest, amounting perhaps to no more than a few pennies per share. Moreover, while the "legacy" Merrill shareholders may have received something of a windfall as a result of the nondisclosures, they were not responsible for those nondisclosures. Rather, the responsibility was that of the Bank's executives, who, although barred from receiving any part of the $150 million fine, are not contributing to its payment in any material respect.

In short, the proposed settlement, while considerably improved over the vacuous proposal made last August in connection with the Undisclosed Bonuses case, is far from ideal. Its greatest virtue is that it is premised on a much better developed statement of the underlying facts and inferences drawn therefrom, which, while disputed by the Attorney General in another forum, have been carefully scrutinized by the Court here and found not to be irrational. Its greatest defect it that it advocates very modest punitive, compensatory, and remedial measures that are neither directed at the specific individuals responsible for the nondisclosures nor appear likely to have more than a very modest impact on corporate practices or victim compensation. While better than nothing, this is half-baked justice at best.

So should the Court approve the proposed settlement as being fair, reasonable, adequate, and in the public interest? If the Court were deciding that question solely on the merits—de novo, as the lawyers say—the Court would reject the settlement as inadequate and misguided. But as both parties never hesitate to remind the Court, the law requires the Court to give substantial deference to the S.E.C. as the regulatory body having primary responsibility for policing the securities markets, especially with respect to matters of transparency. While such deference can never be absolute—since the Judgment ultimately entered is the Court's and is enforced by the Court's contempt power—the Court would fail in its duty if it did not give considerable weight to the S.E.C.'s position.

Even more weighty, however, in this Court's view, are considerations of judicial restraint. This Court, it may be obvious, does not abdicate its role of seeking to plumb the depths of any proposal presented for its approval. But the considerable power given federal judges to assure compliance with the law should never be confused with any power to impose their own preferences. We can balk when a bank tries to escape the implications of hiding material information from its shareholders, and we can protest when the regulatory agency in charge of deterring such misconduct seems content with modest and misdirected sanctions; but, in the words of a great former Justice of the Supreme Court, Harlan Fiske Stone, "the only check upon our own exercise of power is our own sense of self-restraint." United States v. Butler, 297 U.S. 1, 79, 56 S. Ct. 312, 80 L. Ed. 477, 1936-1 C.B. 421 (1936). In the exercise of that self-restraint, this Court, while shaking its head, grants the S.E.C.'s motion and approves the proposed Consent Judgment provided that, by no later than this Thursday, February 25, 2010, the parties present the Court with a proposed Consent Judgment that includes the revised provisions to which they have consented, as set forth above.

Comments and Questions

1. This case arose when the parties approached Judge Rakoff with a settlement of a case involving only allegations of non-disclosure of the bonuses (and not the large losses incurred by Merrill Lynch) and a much smaller penalty imposed on the Bank of America. Judge Rakoff, in an unusual move, rejected the settlement. This case involves the second settlement reached in the case.

2. The case brought by the SEC involved allegations that Bank of America failed to adequately disclose bonuses that would be paid to Merrill Lynch employees. As part of the settlement, Bank of America agreed to engage an outside or independent compensation consultant. Yet when the court suggested that the consultant be chosen collectively by the court, the SEC, and the compensation committee of the board, the Bank objected. Given that the consultant had to be independent, why did the Bank object to the sharing of appointment authority? Do you think the Bank was more worried about the court or the SEC?

3. The court, in the end, opted not to require this shared authority, concluding that the manner of selection was not a "dealbreaker." What do you think of the court's approach? Should it have required, for example, the SEC's consent to the appointment of the compensation consultant?

4. This is not the only instance where the use of independent compensation consultants has been considered by the Commission. *See In re infoUSA Inc.*, Exchange Act Release No. 61708 (admin proc March 15, 2010) (taking into account remedial efforts by company including "hiring an independent compensation consultant to advise on compensation matters"). Why does the Commission care about this issue? Should the Commission be this involved in the corporate governance of boards of public companies?

5. The court indicated that the failure to disclose the $5.8 billion in bonuses was material to shareholders and may have caused them to vote down the merger. Despite the substantial amounts, is this necessarily the case?

6. In the Dodd-Frank Act, Congress provided that compensation committees for listed companies were to have the authority to select their own consultant. The Commission was given the power to identify the "factors" that the committee must consider when making the determination. *See* Section 10C, 15 USC § 78j-3. The factors mostly include those that would identify potential conflicts of interest. What is the likely concern that Congress is addressing in adopting this requirement?

7. By making clear that the responsibility for appointing and compensating the compensation consultant rests with the compensation committee, does this reduce the influence of the CEO in the selection process?

8. The requirement in the Dodd-Frank Act also adds a disclosure element. Companies must disclose any potential conflict with respect to the compensation com-

mittee that was raised and "how the conflict [was] addressed." What is the point of this requirement? What impact will it have on the committee's decision making process?

IV. "Say on Pay" and Strengthening the Role of Shareholders in the Compensation Process

Shareholders have increasingly agitated for the right to have an advisory vote on executive compensation, a practice dubbed "say on pay." Other countries such as Britain have long extended the authority to shareholders.

Some companies voluntarily allowed shareholders to vote on compensation, with Aflac becoming the first. Others were required to do so. The Commission amended the proxy rules to require an annual "say on pay" vote for companies receiving government funds during the financial crisis in 2008–2009. *See* Rule 14a-20, 17 C.F.R. § 240.14a-20.

The most significant development, however, occurred in 2010 with the adoption of the Dodd-Frank Wall Street Reform Act. Congress made "say on pay" mandatory for all public companies. *See* Section 951 (adding Section 14A of the Exchange Act, 15 U.S.C. § 78n-1). The SEC received the regulatory authority to implement the requirement. The provision reflected another expansion of the SEC's role in the corporate governance process. Moreover, Congress did not require that the SEC use the stock exchanges as an intermediary to implement the requirement. Instead, the SEC's role was direct and applied to all public companies, not just those traded on an exchange.

Shareholder Approval of Executive Compensation and Golden Parachute Compensation

Exchange Act Release No. 63768 (Jan. 25, 2011)

The [Dodd-Frank Wall Street Reform] Act amends the Exchange Act by adding new Section 14A. New Section 14A(a)(1) requires that "[n]ot less frequently than once every 3 years, a proxy or consent or authorization for an annual or other meeting of the shareholders for which the proxy solicitation rules of the Commission require compensation disclosure shall include a separate resolution subject to shareholder vote to approve the compensation of executives," as disclosed pursuant to Item 402 of Regulation S-K, or any successor to Item 402 (a "say-on-pay vote"). The shareholder vote to approve executive compensation required by Section 14A(a)(1) "shall not be binding on the issuer or the board of directors of an issuer."

Section 951 of the Act also adds new Section 14A(a)(2) to the Exchange Act, requiring that, "[n]ot less frequently than once every 6 years, a proxy or consent or authorization for an annual or other meeting of the shareholders for which the proxy solicitation rules of the Commission require compensation disclosure shall include a separate resolution subject to shareholder vote to determine whether [the say-on-pay vote] will occur every 1, 2, or 3 years." As discussed below, this shareholder vote "shall not be binding on the issuer or the board of directors of an issuer."

In addition, Section 951 of the Act amends the Exchange Act by adding new Section 14A(b)(1), which requires that, in any proxy or consent solicitation material for a meeting of shareholders "at which shareholders are asked to approve an acquisition, merger, consolidation, or proposed sale or other disposition of all or substantially all the assets of an issuer, the person making such solicitation shall disclose in the proxy or consent solicitation material, in a clear and simple form in accordance with regulations to be promulgated by the Commission, any agreements or understandings that such person has with any named executive officers of such issuer (or of the acquiring issuer, if such issuer is not the acquiring issuer) concerning any type of compensation (whether present, deferred, or contingent) that is based on or otherwise relates to the acquisition, merger, consolidation, sale or other disposition of all or substantially all of the assets of the issuer[...]." These compensation arrangements are often referred to as "golden parachute" compensation. Such disclosure must include the aggregate total of all such compensation that may be paid or become payable to or on behalf of such named executive officer, and the conditions upon which it may be paid or become payable. Under Section 14A(b)(2), "unless such agreements or understandings have been subject to [the periodic shareholder vote described in Section 14A(a)(1)]," a separate shareholder vote to approve such agreements or understandings and compensation as disclosed is also required. As with the say-on-pay vote and the shareholder vote on the frequency of such votes, this shareholder vote "shall not be binding on the issuer or the board of directors of an issuer."

In addition to their non-binding status, none of the shareholder votes required pursuant to Section 14A is to be construed "as overruling a decision by such issuer or board of directors." These shareholder votes also do not "create or imply any change to the fiduciary duties of such issuer or board of directors" nor do they "create or imply any additional fiduciary duties for such issuer or board of directors." Further, these votes will not be construed "to restrict or limit the ability of shareholders to make proposals for inclusion in proxy materials related to executive compensation." Section 14A also provides that "the Commission may, by rule or order, exempt an issuer or class of issuers" from the shareholder advisory votes required by Section 14A. In determining whether to make an exemption, the Commission is directed to take into account, among other considerations, whether the requirements of Section 14A(a) and (b) disproportionately burden small issuers.

Section 14A(b)(2) generally requires a separate shareholder advisory vote on golden parachute compensation arrangements required to be disclosed under Section 14A(b)(1) in connection with mergers and similar transactions.

Comments and Questions

1. How might an advisory vote affect executive compensation? Although an advisory vote, how much latitude, as a practical matter, does the board have to ignore shareholders when they vote down a compensation package?

2. Is this an appropriate subject for shareholders? Some have criticized the requirement, asserting that "shareholders are apt to make honest but poor decisions with respect to compensation matters." Andrew C.W. Lund, *Say on Pay's Bundling Problems*, 99 Ky. L.J. 119, 129 (2010–2011) (describing the criticisms). Professor Lund also notes that "say on pay" may "tend to homogenize compensation practices across public firms." *Id.* at 131. Why might that be the case? What would be the consequences of such an outcome?

3. The Commission codified the "say on pay" requirements in Rule 14a-21. 17 CFR 240.14a-21. The Rule was approved by a 3–2 vote of the Commission. Among other things, the dissenting commissioners objected to the failure to include an exemption from the requirement for newly public companies. What would be the advantage of such an exemption? Should it have been included in the rule?

4. In adopting the rule, the Commission provided a two year exemption from "say on pay" votes (but not advisory votes on golden parachutes) for companies with a market capitalization of less than $75 million. The Commission decided to provide smaller reporting companies with "additional time" to implement the requirement. The Commission hinted, however, that the exemption might be extended. As the Release noted: "We also believe that delayed implementation for these companies will allow us to evaluate the implementation of the adopted rules by larger companies and provide us with the additional opportunity to consider whether adjustments to the rule would be appropriate for smaller reporting companies before the rule becomes applicable to them." What do you make of this exemption? How might smaller companies take advantage of the extra time?

5. Section 14A also requires the approval of golden parachutes at the same time shareholders are asked to approve a merger. What are the benefits of this requirement?

6. Which officers are currently subject to Item 402 and therefore likely to fall within the "say on pay" requirement? *See* Item 402(a) (3), 17 C.F.R. 229.402(a) (3). Could the SEC expand the requirements of Item 402 to include all executive officers and require shareholder approval of those packages? Does this authority involve a significant change in the Commission's role in the corporate governance process?

7. Section 14A provides that the provision will not "restrict or limit the ability of shareholders to make proposals for inclusion in proxy materials related to executive compensation." This is a reference to Rule 14a-8 of the proxy rules. The provision allows shareholders to submit proposals for inclusion in the company's proxy statement. What other types of compensation proposals might shareholders submit? In 2010, shareholders of Chesapeake Energy adopted a provision that called for an advisory vote on compensation paid to directors.

———————

"Say on pay" involves an advisory vote on executive compensation. Section 14A explicitly provides that the advisory vote will not "create or imply any change to the fiduciary duties of such issuer or board of directors." Does that mean the advisory vote has no impact on these obligations?

NECA-IBEW Pension Fund v. Cox

United States District Court, Southern District of Ohio

2011 U.S. Dist. LEXIS 106161 (Sept. 20, 2011)

BLACK, JUDGE:

This civil lawsuit presents the question, among others, whether a shareholder of a public company may sue its directors for breach of the duty of loyalty when the directors grant $4 million dollars in bonuses, on top of $4.5 million dollars in salary and other compensation, to the chief executive officer in the same year the company incurs a $61.3 million dollar decline in net income, a drop in earnings per share from $0.37 to $0.09, a reduction in share price from $3.45 to $2.80, and a negative 18.8% annual shareholder return.

Normally, a board of directors is protected by the "business judgment rule" when making decisions about executive compensation, and courts "will not inquire into the wisdom of actions taken by a director in the absence of fraud, bad faith, or abuse of discretion." Radol v. Thomas, 772 F.2d 244, 257 (6th Cir. 1987). However, the business judgment rule is a presumption that may be rebutted by a plaintiff with factual evidence that board members acted disloyally, i.e., not in the best interests of the company or its shareholders. See, e.g., Koos v. Cent. Ohio Cellular, Inc., 94 Ohio App. 3d 579, 641 N.E.2d 265, 272 (Ohio Ct. App. 1994).

Under the recently enacted federal law, The Dodd-Frank Wall Street Reform Act, publicly traded companies must include a separate shareholder resolution to approve executive compensation in their proxies at least once every three years. See 15 U.S. Code § 78n-1(a) (2010). Pursuant to that requirement, the Cincinnati Bell Board included a shareholder resolution in its March 21, 2011 proxy seeking shareholder approval of the 2010 executive compensation. The Board recommended that the shareholders vote in support of the resolution. On May 3, 2011, 66% of voting shareholders voted against the 2010 executive compensation.[5] Citing, *inter alia*, the over-

---

5. [1] Some "commentators are now identifying excessive executive compensation as the No. 1 problem in corporate governance ... While private sector wages rose only 2% in 2010..., the median compensation for chief executive officers at Standard & Poor's 500 index companies was up by 18% from 2009 to an average of $12 million.... In 1965, the typical chief executive made 24 times the salary of the average worker. [Today], the typical chief executive makes 275 times the salary of the average worker.... The top 1% of earners now take in about a quarter of our nation's income and own 40% of its wealth...." Morrissey, Daniel J. "Courts Should Curb Executive Pay" The National Law Journal (Aug. 15, 2011). (See Ex. 2 to plaintiff's memo contra; Doc. 24). Against this backdrop, Congress passed the Dodd-Frank Wall Street Reform Act and included within it the "say-on-pay" provision which requires public companies to allow their shareholders an advisory vote on the compensation of their top officials. Although Dodd-Frank states that those expressions are not binding and do not alter the fiduciary duties of directors, some commentators opine that "[a] negative say-on-pay vote gives the court evidence that there's been a breach of duty. It doesn't mean there's been a breach of duty, but it can support a finding of breach." Myles, Danielle "Experts Disagree on Validity of Say-on-Pay Lawsuits" International Financial Law Review (Aug. 2011). (See Ex. 1 to plaintiff's memo contra; Doc. 24). Critics of Dodd-Frank's "say-on-pay" provisions worry that extensive, frivolous litigation will ensue, but a report issued by Shulte Roth & Zabel on the 2011 annual meeting season

whelming rejection by shareholders of 2010 executive compensation, plaintiff filed this lawsuit alleging that the Cincinnati Bell Board breached its fiduciary duty of loyalty when it decided to approve large pay raises and bonuses to its top three officers in a year when, according to plaintiff, the company performed dismally. The directors and officers, in turn, have filed their motion to dismiss the lawsuit.

* * *

B. The Business Judgment Rule Does Not Require Dismissal Because Plaintiff Adequately Pleads a Claim for Breach of Fiduciary Duty.

Directors owe two separate fiduciary duties to the corporation: the duty of loyalty and the duty of care. *Radol*, 772 F.2d at 256. The duty of loyalty requires that directors perform their duties "in good faith, in a manner the director reasonably believes to be in or not opposed to the best interests of the corporation." Ohio Rev. Code Ann. § 1701.59(B) (2011). Plaintiff alleges that Cincinnati Bell's directors breached their duty of loyalty when they approved the 2010 executive compensation.

Ohio courts follow "the business judgment rule" and "will not inquire into the wisdom of actions taken by a director in the absence of fraud, bad faith, or abuse of discretion." *Radol*, 772 F.2d at 257. Under Ohio law, directors will face liability only if it is shown by clear and convincing evidence that their actions were undertaken with "a deliberate intent to cause injury to the corporation" or "reckless disregard for the best interests of the corporation." Ohio Rev. Code Ann. § 1701.59(D) (2011).

Informed decisions on compensation rendered by disinterested directors are presumed to be the product of a valid business judgment. Prod. Res. Group LLC v. NCT Group, Inc., 863 A.2d 772, 779 (Del. Ch. 2004). Plaintiff bears the burden to establish facts rebutting the business judgment rule's presumption of good faith of directors. *Radol*, 772 F.2d at 257; *Koos*, 641 N.E.2d at 273.

However, "the business judgment rule imposes a burden of proof, not a burden of pleading." In re Nat'l Century Fin. Enters., Indiv. Litig., 504 F.Supp.2d 287, 312 (S.D. Ohio 2007); Marsalis v. Wilson, 149 Ohio App. 3d 637, 2002 Ohio 5534, 778 N.E.2d 612, 616 (Ohio Ct. App. 2002). When plaintiffs allege a breach of fiduciary duty, "the business judgment rule would impose on plaintiffs a burden at trial to present evidence to rebut the presumption the rule imposes. However, plaintiffs are not likewise obligated to plead operative facts in their complaint that would rebut the presumption." *Marsalis*, 778 N.E.2d at 616. While the Court applies federal law on matters of procedure, the federal rule is much the same, holding that while a plaintiff must plead an exception to the business judgment rule, he is "not required to plead the exception with particularity." *In re Tower Air, Inc.*, 416 F.3d 229, 236 (3d Cir. 2005).

Here, plaintiff has made adequate pleadings that "the Cincinnati Bell Board is not entitled to business judgment protection for its 2010 executive pay hikes." (Doc. 1 at

---

shows that only 1.6% of public companies which have held their annual meetings as of the end of June 2011 received negative shareholder recommendations. (See Ex. 1 to plaintiff's memo contra; Doc. 24). Cincinnati Bell is one of those companies.

¶ 4). The complaint provides factual allegations and not simply conclusory allegations.[6] These factual allegations raise a plausible claim that the multi-million dollar bonuses approved by the directors in a time of the company's declining financial performance violated Cincinnati Bell's pay-for-performance compensation policy[7] and were not in the best interests of Cincinnati Bell's shareholders[8] and therefore constituted an abuse of discretion and/or bad faith.

Defendants may offer the affirmative defense of the business judgment rule at trial, where plaintiff may well not be able to prove by clear and convincing evidence that the directors acted with "a deliberate intent to cause injury to the corporation" or "reckless disregard for the best interests of the corporation." But that all is for trial, or summary judgment—it is not fodder for dismissal. Plaintiff states a claim; no dismissal is warranted.

* * *

Conclusion

Accordingly, defendants' motion to dismiss (Doc. 3) is DENIED.

IT IS SO ORDERED.

Comments and Questions

1. Although denying the motion to dismiss, the court subsequently declined to grant a preliminary injunction. *See NECA-IBEW Pension Fund v. Cox*, 2011 U.S. Dist. LEXIS 109064 (S.D. Ohio, Sept. 26, 2011) (declining to issue an injunction and noting

---

6. [2] The Directors awarded CEO Cassidy an annual performance bonus of $1,335,840, a special bonus of $600,160, and a retention bonus of $2,100,000, bringing his total compensation to over $8.5 million, representing a 71.7% increase in his prior total yearly compensation. (Doc. 1 at ¶¶ 11–13; 30–31; Doc. 3 at 11–12). CFO Wojtaszek received an annual incentive award of $282,762, a special bonus of $531,300, and a long-term incentive award of $552,174, bringing his total compensation to over $2 million and constituting an 80.3% increase over his prior compensation. (Id.) Vice President and General Counsel Wilson was awarded an annual incentive award of $282,762 and a long-term incentive award of $538,486, bringing his total compensation to over $1.5 million and constituting a 54.3% increase over his prior yearly compensation. (Id.) All of the compensation awards were approved by the full Board. (Doc. 3 at 11–12). The awarding of these bonuses occurred in a year when the company incurred a $61.3 million dollar decline in net income, a drop in earnings per share from $0.37 to $0.09, a reduction in share price from $3.45 to $2.80, and a negative 18.8% annual shareholder return. (Doc. 1 at ¶ 28). The company's 2010 net income applicable to common shareholders and total shareholders' equity also materially declined. (Id.)

7. [3] Plaintiff alleges that the compensation violated Cincinnati Bell's written compensation policy, which states that "a significant portion of the total compensation for each of our executives is directly related to the Company's earnings and revenues and other performance factors" and that at-risk compensation should be "tied to the achievement of specific short-term and long-term performance objectives, principally the Company's earnings, cash flow, and the performance of the Company's common shares, thereby linking executive compensation with the returns realized by shareholders." (Doc. 1 at ¶ 27) (emphasis supplied).

8. [4] Plaintiff asserts that the negative shareholder advisory vote on executive compensation, in which 66% of voting shareholders voted against the 2010 executive compensation, provides "direct and probative evidence that the 2010 executive compensation was not in the best interests of the Cincinnati Bell shareholders." (Doc. 1 at ¶ 36).

that plaintiff has not shown a "strong likelihood of success on the merits" that the compensation decision was not "protected by the business judgment rule"). Moreover, few other decisions have agreed with the reasoning. *See In re Citigroup Shareholder Derivative Litig.*, No. 12 Civ. 3114c(JPO) (S.D.N.Y. Aug. 19, 2013) ("But the vast weight of authority—both now and at the time this suit was being litigated—suggests that plaintiffs should not be excused from making a demand on the board where the shareholders reject proposed executive compensation through a say-on-pay vote."). What does this suggest about the role of a negative "say on pay" vote in the context of a board's fiduciary obligations?

2. What role did the say on pay vote have in this case? In adopting the say on pay rule, Congress specifically stated that the advisory vote would not "change" the existing fiduciary obligations or "create or imply any additional fiduciary duties." Section 14A, 15 U.S.C. §78n-1. Is this case consistent with that approach?

3. Say on pay had been implemented voluntarily by some companies. Companies that received federal money during the financial crisis in 2009 were required to institute say on pay. Only with the adoption of the Dodd Frank Act, however were all public companies required to give shareholders an advisory vote on compensation. In the first year of implementation, shareholders at 37 of the 2,340 companies voted against the compensation package. Does this tell us anything about the role of the advisory vote in the governance process?

4. To the extent a board wants to prevent a negative vote, what steps might it take or strategies might it implement?

V. The Future Direction of Executive Compensation

While some assert that the system for determining executive compensation is not broken, the constant intervention by Congress at a minimum suggests that the status quo is at risk for further revision. If we step back and ask who should determine executive compensation, the board of directors seems an obvious answer. Compensation is a case by case determination that depends upon the value of a particular CEO to a particular company.

The board is in the best place to make these determinations. Moreover, with the CEO typically on the board, it would be reasonable to require that the board show the fairness of the compensation. The need to establish fairness (and the risk of liability for failing to do so) would require that the board establish a relationship between the amount paid and the benefits provided by the CEO. At a minimum, such a burden would likely provide reduced incentives to approve compensation packages that exceeded by significant amounts the compensation paid to comparable officers in other companies.

But of course, that is not the standard. The board obtains the benefit of the business judgment rule if it meets certain process requirements when approving compensation. *Disney* demonstrates that the informational requirements are at best modest. Similarly, the law on independent directors is not sufficiently robust to ensure that those approving compensation are in fact independent.

Large compensation packages, therefore, may reflect actual value to the company or may be a consequence of a faulty process. As a result, Congress has stepped in and imposed obligations designed to tighten the process used in approving compensation. In doing so, however, Congress has opted for categorical rules that are imposed on a large number of companies, listed companies in the case of compensation committees, and all public companies in the case of say one pay. Reforms at this level raise concern over whether they will work and whether the costs outweigh the benefits.

To the extent that the approach under state law is inadequate to ensure proper compensation decisions, pressure for additional federal intervention will continue. After all, Congress responds not to the wishes of managers and shareholders but voters.

Given this dynamic, is there a fix? Or are we to expect that every decade or so, Congress will further intervene and impose additional categorical requirements on public companies?

Chapter 7

The Role of Shareholders in the Governance Process

The role of shareholders in the governance process is not always an easy one to accurately characterize. At one level, they own the enterprise. Yet they have no authority to control the day-to-day activities of the company. Moreover, while they elect those on the board, the practical reality of the plurality system of voting and the costs of a proxy contest effectively limit the ability of shareholders to replace directors. Their role is further complicated by the diversity among shareholders. Investors, whether pension plans, mutual funds, hedge funds, or individuals, vary in their approach to investing and in their profit horizons.

Nonetheless, shareholders have agitated for a greater role in the governance process. They have sought to influence board practices, particularly those affecting their economic interests. Shareholders have proposed and sometimes adopted resolutions seeking to encourage the elimination of staggered boards or the cancellation of poison pills. They have also applied pressure to reform the electoral system for directors by encouraging companies to replace plurality with a majority vote system. Likewise, pressure has resulted in companies increasingly providing access to their proxy statements for shareholder nominees to the board.

As the role of shareholders becomes more important, other issues have surfaced. The logistics of voting in public companies have been, until recently, mostly overlooked. The system for allowing beneficial owners to exercise the franchise is extraordinarily complex and open to the problem of "hanging chads." Likewise, the traditional right of brokers to cast uninstructed shares held by street name owners has increasingly come under scrutiny.

The role of shareholders will, therefore, continue to evolve. It will not be a straight line process. Finding the right level of influence without untoward interference in the management of the business will amount to an ever-shifting task that likely will engender disagreement and controversy among participants in the corporate governance debate for the foreseeable future.

I. Separation of Ownership and Control

Any discussion of the role of shareholders must begin with the structural phenomena identified by Adolf Berle and Gardiner Means—the separation of ownership and control. See THE MODERN CORPORATION AND PRIVATE PROPERTY (1932). When management owned the business, there was in theory little concern that officers and directors would act in a manner inimical to the interests of shareholders.

As corporations grew larger, however, ownership and management diverged. Managers had every incentive to engage in rent-seeking behavior and maximize their return at the expense of shareholders. The task fell to shareholders to monitor management and reduce self-serving behavior. The efforts to do so, however, confronted significant agency costs. Most noticeable were problems associated with collective action. Organizing disparate groups of shareholders had to overcome an assortment of logistical problems, including rational apathy and free riding.

A. The Rise of Institutional Investors

Berle and Means identified the separation of ownership and management. At the time of their seminal work, however, the ownership configuration of most public companies was dominated by individuals. In the years since publication, that configuration has changed.

Iman Anabtawi & Lynn Stout,
Fiduciary Duties for Activist Shareholders
60 Stan. L. Rev. 1255, 1274–76 (2008)[1]

When Berle and Means wrote about shareholder powerlessness in 1932, most shareholders were individuals. This situation has changed dramatically with the rise of the "institutional investor." Institutional investors—typically pension funds and mutual funds—aggregate the savings of millions of individuals into enormous investment portfolios that buy stock in public companies. As a result, institutional investors can take far larger positions in particular companies than most individual investors ever could.

Institutions have captured a larger and larger share of the total market for public equities over time, from 8% of outstanding shares in 1950 to nearly two-thirds today. This trend has been widely recognized as undermining the realism of the assumption that shareholders in public companies are dispersed and powerless. As Professor Bernard Black put it in his influential 1990 article Shareholder Passivity Reexamined, "Collective action problems, while important, seem manageable for the large institutions who are today the dominant shareholders." "The model of public companies as owned by thousands of anonymous shareholders simply isn't true. There are a limited number of large shareholders, and they know each other."

Institutional investors are in a much more favorable position to play an activist role in corporate governance than dispersed individual investors are. Although many pension and mutual funds rely on relatively passive stock-picking strategies, especially

1. Copyright © 2008 Stanford Law Review. Reprinted with permission.

when they hold highly diversified portfolios, a number of prominent institutional investors—including both mutual funds like Fidelity and Vanguard and pension funds like CalPERS—have emerged as activist investors willing to mount public relations campaigns, initiate litigation, and launch proxy battles to pressure corporate officers and directors into following their preferred business strategy.

Comments and Questions

1. Berle and Means are credited with having identified the separation of management and ownership in public companies. What does that mean? What are some of the problems that arise as a result of the separation? The need for some mechanism designed to ensure that directors act in the best interests of shareholders is generally referred to as "agency costs."

2. Influenced by this analysis, Congress in the securities laws sought to empower shareholders through the use of disclosure. The legislative history to the proxy provisions articulated the goal of "fair corporate suffrage." Is this an effective solution to the problems raised by Berle and Means?

3. According to one commentator, scholars in the post-Berle and Means era "have searched for the corporate equivalent of the Holy Grail: a mechanism to bridge the separation by holding non-owner managers accountable for their performance." Elizabeth Cosenza, *The Holy Grail of Corporate Governance Reform: Independence or Democracy?*, 2007 BYU L. Rev. 1, 53. What are some examples of these "Holy Grails" and have they worked?

4. The increased institutionalization of the market has been particularly apparent with respect to larger public companies. *See* Carolyn Kay Brancato & Stephan Rabimov, Conference BD., *The 2008 Institutional Investment Report: Trends in Institutional Investor Assets and Equity Ownership of U.S. Corporations* 27 (2008) (noting that institutional investors owned almost 77% of shares of largest 1000 companies). Does that solve the problems posed by the separation of management and ownership?

5. In many ways, the widespread ownership of public companies in the United States is unique. *See generally* John C. Coffee, Jr., *The Future as History: The Prospects for Global Convergence in Corporate Governance and Its Implications*, 93 Nw. U. L. Rev. 641 (1999) (noting that "contemporary empirical evidence finds that, even at the level of the largest firms, dispersed share ownership is ... largely limited to the United States and Great Britain....."). The more common model is for public companies to have a controlling shareholder, often a family. What difference does this make with respect to shareholder monitoring?

6. Professor Roe notes that the problem with monitoring management is not the separation of ownership and management but "atomization." As he writes:

> Most public companies are held by thousands of shareholders, each with only a small stake. As a result, an active shareholder cannot capture all of the gains from monitoring managers. The costs of monitoring are borne by the shareholder who becomes involved, studies the enterprise, or sits on the

board of directors and thereby takes the risk of enhanced liability. But since monitoring gains would be divided among all shareholders, most fragmented shareholders rationally forego involvement.

Mark J. Roe, *A Political Theory of American Corporate Finance*, 91 Colum. L. Rev. 10, 12 (1991). Do you agree with this? To the extent true, what would have to happen in the securities markets to reduce this dynamic?

7. Perhaps an example of the problems highlighted by Professor Roe can be seen with respect to the ownership configuration of ExxonMobil. According to the Annual Report on Form 10-K filed in Feb. 2014, the Company had 4,194,690,266 shares outstanding as of Jan. 31, 2015. The same report disclosed that as of the same date, ExxonMobil had 432,983 registered holders of common stock (which presumably does not include beneficial owners). The Company had one 5% shareholder (the mutual fund family, Vanguard, with 6.0%), with the next three owning 4.26%, 2.63% and 1.52%. What sorts of problems does this configuration create for purposes of shareholder actions?

B. The Types of Institutional Investors

As equity markets have become more institutional, the types of institutions have also evolved. Insurance companies and banks (through their trust departments), both with "close ties to management," *see* Robert C. Illig, *What Hedge Funds Can Teach Corporate America: A Roadmap for Achieving Institutional Investor Oversight*, 57 Am. U. L. Rev. 225, 249 (2007), have given way to mutual funds, pension plans, and hedge funds as the largest institutional investors.

Not all institutional investors have the same goals or approaches to corporate governance. As one report described:

> In addition to differences in general holding periods and investment strategies, institutional investors may differ in a number of other key ways, such as the level of government regulation to which they are subject, their level of interest in the corporate governance of their portfolio companies, the degree to which political or social policy factors may influence their decision-making or voting decisions, and their level of corporate activism (both litigation and non-litigation based).

Report of the New York Stock Exchange Commission on Corporate Governance, at 13 (Sept. 23, 2010). These variations can result in significantly different approaches to governance.

K. A. D. Camara, *Classifying Institutional Investors*
30 J. Corp. L. 219, 235, 239–41 (2005)[2]

Public pension funds are pools of capital collected by the state and invested on behalf of state employees. The public pension fund structure provides more insulation

---

2. Copyright © 2005 The Journal of Corporation Law. Reprinted with permission.

from political forces that favor things other than shareholder wealth maximization than does direct state ownership. Different fund structures provide different levels of insulation. A directly elected controlling board is more sensitive to political forces than a controller appointed for a long, unrenewable term and subject to removal only for cause carefully shown. The tradeoff is between insulation from political forces and accountability (including accountability for maximizing shareholder wealth) to the electorate or other fund beneficiaries.

sensitivity to political forces

Although public pension funds pursue non-shareholder-wealth-maximizing agendas less often than states investing directly likely would, they are among the leaders in corporate-governance activism. This activism includes but is not limited to issues widely thought to be principally of concern to shareholders: effective staggered boards, poison pills, and other devices in the literature on the market for corporate control. Public pension funds have often taken the lead on social-responsibility issues such as environmental protection, workers' rights, and human rights in foreign regimes. While the public pension fund structure may dampen political pressures, it does not eliminate them entirely.

* * *

Private pension funds are those associated with private organizations, principally unions and corporations. Union pension funds pool capital from union members for investment while corporate pension funds pool capital from employees. Pooled capital is invested either directly or through a mutual fund or other engaged investment adviser. Voting rights are exercised by the investment adviser, fund officials, or management of the sponsoring organization. The Employee Retirement Income Security Act (ERISA) requires that votes be cast and that voting power be used to benefit plan beneficiaries, rather than the sponsoring organization. For example, it violates ERISA for a corporate pension fund knowingly to vote for an act designed to preserve managerial perquisites at the expense of shareholder value. But because almost all votes can be plausibly defended, the effect of ERISA is mainly in shaping managerial norms, mandating a veneer of investigation, and deterring the worst excesses by threat of liability. In this it is not unlike the duty of care in corporate-law proper.

ERISA) duty of care

Union pension funds, which have been among the largest supporters of the recent proposals to increase shareholder power, are concerned not only with maximizing shareholder value, but also with the employment contracts and working conditions available to member employees. Union pension funds might view favorably, for example, a corporate act, say, a larger employee benefits package, that decreases shareholder wealth but increases the wealth of employees (an expropriation of capital for the benefit of labor). Under a legal regime in which union pension funds, in concert with other institutions, can command such acts, contracting difficulties might prevent their being blocked even if the act decreases the total wealth available for distribution. Even if these contracting difficulties can be overcome, to grant such a power is to effect a distribution to employees, not to create a new control mechanism for shareholder wealth maximization. We might think of it as a mandatory, across-the-board increase in wages.

Corporate pension funds are concerned not only with maximizing shareholder value, but also with all those things with which corporate management is concerned. For example, corporate pension funds can be expected to prefer managerial insulation from the market for corporate control, large managerial compensation packages, costly acquisitions over which managers will then enjoy control, and so forth. Sympathy, understanding, and reciprocal voting encourage this concern when the shares a corporate pension fund votes are those of an unrelated corporation. Senior management feels enough of a connection and has enough hope of reciprocation to look out for other members of the group.

Comments and Questions

1. How might the governance policies of the different types of pension plans vary? Are these constrained in any meaningful way by the legal obligation to manage the assets for the benefit of the beneficiaries?

2. Perhaps the most active public pension place has been the California Public Employees' Retirement System (CalPERS). For a history of the role played by CalPERS in the corporate governance movement, see Sanford M. Jacoby, *Convergence by Design: The Case of CalPERS in Japan*, 55 Am. J. Comp. L. 239 (2007).

3. Boards of public pension plans are sometimes appointed in whole or in part by politicians. What impact might this have on the involvement of public pension plans in the corporate governance process?

4. Typically set up as trusts, pension plans are generally subject to ERISA and under the oversight of the Department of Labor. Under Section 404(a) (1) (A) of ERISA, plan fiduciaries are required to act in the best interests of beneficiaries. The regulations of the DoL allow the trustee to delegate voting authority to an investment manager. *See* 29 C.F.R. 2509.08-2(1).

5. The DoL has issued regulations providing that "the fiduciary act of managing plan assets that are shares of corporate stock includes the voting of proxies appurtenant to those shares of stock." 29 C.F.R. § 2509.08-2. The rules, however, provide that "the responsible fiduciary shall consider only those factors that relate to the economic value of the plan's investment and shall not subordinate the interests of the participants and beneficiaries in their retirement income to unrelated objectives." Some have asserted that these obligations ought to prevent shareholder activism. What do you think?

6. Some have questioned whether pension plans always act in the best interests of beneficiaries. *See* Leo E. Strine, Jr., *Toward a True Corporate Republic: A Traditionalist Response to Bebchuk's Solution for Improving Corporate America*, 119 Harv. L. Rev. 1759, 1765 (2006) ("Those institutions most inclined to be activist investors are associated with state governments and labor unions, and often appear to be driven by concerns other than a desire to increase the economic performance of the companies in which they invest."). Do you agree?

Pension plans are often managed by investment advisers. The advisers may, in addition to the selection of investments, also have the discretion to vote shares in the portfolio. This has the potential to result in conflicts of interest.

In re INTECH Investment Management LLC

Investment Advisors Act Release No. 2872 (admin. proc. May 7, 2009)

Summary

1. This case involves a registered investment adviser, INTECH, which, from at least 2003 through 2006 (the "relevant time period"), exercised voting authority over client securities without having written policies and procedures that were reasonably designed to ensure it voted its clients' securities in the best interests of its clients because those policies and procedures did not include how the adviser would address material potential conflicts of interests that may arise between its interests and those of its clients. INTECH also did not sufficiently describe its proxy voting policies and procedures to clients. In determining how to vote securities (or proxies) for those clients who had delegated such voting authority to INTECH, it selected a third-party proxy voting service's guidelines that followed AFL-CIO proxy voting recommendations. Those guidelines, offered by Institutional Shareholder Services ("ISS"), were referred to as the ISS Proxy Voter Services ("ISS-PVS"). INTECH chose to follow ISS-PVS at a time when it was participating in the annual AFL-CIO Key Votes Survey that ranked investment advisers based on their adherence to the AFL-CIO recommendations on certain votes. INTECH believed that following the ISS-PVS Guidelines would improve its ranking in the AFL-CIO Key Votes Survey and that the improved score would likely be helpful in maintaining existing and attracting new union-affiliated clients.

2. In connection with the then-newly effective Investment Advisers Act Rule 206(4)-6 (the "Proxy Voting Rule"), INTECH adopted and implemented written proxy voting policies and procedures and provided them to its clients. Contrary to the Proxy Voting Rule, INTECH's written policies and procedures did not address material potential conflicts that may have arisen between INTECH's interests and those of its clients who were not pro-AFL-CIO. Moreover, INTECH did not sufficiently describe to clients its proxy voting policies and procedures. Using ISS-PVS created a material potential conflict of interest for INTECH because INTECH chose an AFL-CIO-based voting platform for all clients without addressing and describing its potential effect on INTECH's ability to retain and obtain business from existing and prospective union-affiliated clients.

Respondents

3. INTECH, a Delaware limited liability company located in West Palm Beach, Florida, has been registered with the Commission as an investment adviser since February 28, 2002. As of September 30, 2008, INTECH had approximately 400 clients with over $55 billion in assets under management. Since 2002, INTECH has exercised voting authority with respect to those clients' proxies for which it had been delegated such authority.

* * *

5. During the relevant time period, INTECH managed institutional portfolios for pension plans, foundations, unions (including those referred to as "Taft-Hartley" clients), public funds, and public corporations (hereinafter collectively referred to as "clients"). Most of the assets invested by the public funds and corporations were related to employee pension plans. As part of its investment advisory services, INTECH exercised voting authority with respect to many of its clients' securities. In deciding how to vote client securities, INTECH chose to rely upon the recommendations of a third-party proxy voting service called Institutional Shareholder Services. ISS offered various sets or platforms of recommendations.

6. During 2002, INTECH chose one of ISS' platforms known as the ISS-General Guidelines ("ISS-General"). These guidelines typically recommended voting in accordance with corporations' management's recommendations.

7. In response to this choice, INTECH received inquiries and complaints from some of its union-affiliated clients about proxy votes that INTECH had cast on behalf of its clients as the result of following ISS-General.

INTECH Moved From a Management-Based Platform to the AFL-CIO-Based Voting Platform for All Clients

8. During the relevant time period, INTECH participated in the annual AFL-CIO Key Votes Survey ("AFL-CIO Survey"). The AFL-CIO collects the information regarding proxy voting from investment advisers and the AFL-CIO Survey summarizes and ranks investment advisers based on their proxy voting records on issues the AFL-CIO identifies as "Key Votes." The AFL-CIO Survey places investment advisers into one of three tiers based upon the percentage of votes the adviser cast that were consistent with the AFL-CIO voting recommendations on Key Votes. The AFL-CIO ranks advisers that vote all or the majority of its clients' proxies, including clients that are not pro-AFL-CIO, in accordance with AFL-CIO recommendations, higher than advisers who vote only their union-affiliated clients in accordance with the AFL-CIO recommendations. INTECH recognized this incentive in the AFL-CIO Survey.

9. On January 1, 2003, INTECH switched from ISS-General Guidelines to ISS-PVS Guidelines] for all of its clients. INTECH believed that this change could improve its score on the AFL-CIO Survey. INTECH also believed that some union-affiliated clients felt that it was important for INTECH to score well on the AFL-CIO Survey. Moreover, INTECH believed that prospective union-affiliated clients might use the AFL-CIO Survey as a factor in selecting an investment adviser. Further, INTECH made this switch to please its union-affiliated clients, which had communicated displeasure with some of INTECH's 2002 votes made while INTECH followed the ISS-General Guidelines. INTECH also believed ISS-PVS applied a reasonable standard for enhancing shareholder value as it related to corporate governance matters.

10. INTECH improved its AFL-CIO Survey score by changing to the ISS-PVS recommendations. In 2002, when INTECH followed ISS-General, INTECH scored

68.9% and was ranked in the middle tier. In 2003, when INTECH followed ISS-PVS, INTECH scored 100% and was ranked in the top tier.

11. After switching from the ISS-General Guidelines to the AFL-CIO-based ISS-PVS Guidelines, INTECH received inquiries from some clients as to why there seemed to be a higher number of votes against management on shareholder proposals.

The Proxy Voting Rule Requires Advisers to Adopt Proxy Voting Policies and Procedures

12. The Proxy Voting Rule became effective on March 10, 2003 and its compliance date was August 6, 2003. The Proxy Voting Rule requires advisers to adopt and implement policies and procedures that are reasonably designed to ensure that advisers vote clients' proxies in the clients' best interests. Such procedures must include how the adviser addresses material conflicts that may arise between the adviser's interests and those of its clients, disclose to clients how they can obtain information about how the adviser voted the proxies, and describe to clients the adviser's proxy voting policies and procedures.

13. In the Adopting Release for the Proxy Voting Rule, the Commission recognized that under the Advisers Act, "an adviser is a fiduciary that owes each of its clients duties of care and loyalty with respect to all services undertaken on the client's behalf, including proxy voting." This duty of care requires an adviser who has voting authority to monitor corporate events and vote the proxies. To satisfy its duty of loyalty, an adviser must cast the proxy votes in a manner consistent with the best interests of its client and must not subrogate a client's interest to its own. The Commission explained that the Proxy Voting Rules "were designed to prevent material conflicts of interest from affecting the manner in which advisers vote" clients' proxies.

14. The Commission noted that advisers may use a "predetermined voting policy," such as a third-party proxy voting service's platform, to vote proxies provided that the predetermined policy is "designed to further the interests of clients rather than the adviser."

INTECH Did Not Satisfy the Proxy Voting Rule Requirements

15. In an effort to comply with the new rule, INTECH drafted written proxy voting policies and procedures. Hurley, as Chief Operating Officer, reviewed and edited counsel's drafts of those policies and procedures. On July 22, 2003, INTECH sent those policies and procedures to clients along with a cover letter from Hurley. Those policies and procedures remained in effect as written until 2006. Under INTECH's proxy voting policy, Hurley, as the Chief Operating Officer, had responsibility to evaluate whether certain proxy votes created conflicts between INTECH and its clients' interests.

16. At the same time that Hurley participated in drafting the proxy voting policies and procedures, he knew that INTECH was voting all of its clients' securities in accordance with the ISS-PVS Guidelines. Hurley recognized the potential benefits to INTECH of choosing ISS-PVS, including an improved AFL-CIO Survey score. Hurley also recognized the choice created a potential conflict of interest because he acknowl-

edged that different types of clients may have made a different choice than INTECH made. Although he received some input from counsel during the drafting process, he did not discuss the potential conflict of interest with counsel during the drafting process. The policy, as finalized, did not address this potential conflict.

17. INTECH's final written policies and procedures did not address the potential conflict caused by INTECH choosing the ISS-PVS Guidelines for all of its clients while having an interest in retaining and obtaining union-affiliated clients. Moreover, INTECH told its clients in the cover letter signed by Hurley and stated in its proxy voting policy that, because it relied on a third-party proxy voting service, it did not "expect [] that any conflicts w[ould] arise in the proxy voting process."

18. In addition, INTECH did not sufficiently describe its proxy voting policies and procedures to its clients. INTECH disclosed that it intended to rely on ISS-PVS to vote clients' securities. INTECH, however, did not disclose that ISS-PVS followed AFL-CIO proxy voting recommendations. In fact, INTECH, through Hurley, described its policies and procedures without including references to the fact that the ISS-PVS guidelines it had chosen followed AFL-CIO recommendations. Although INTECH did not sufficiently describe its proxy voting policies and procedures to its clients, it did, on a quarterly basis, send to all of its clients a report showing all proxy votes cast on behalf of clients. The report, however, did not reference the guidelines that were followed that resulted in those votes.

19. In mid-2005, INTECH considered offering clients the additional option of the ISS-General Guidelines. In December 2005, after the Commission staff began inquiring about INTECH's proxy voting, INTECH offered clients a choice between the ISS-PVS and ISS-General Guidelines to begin in 2006. At that time, INTECH sent a summary of the ISS-PVS Guidelines to clients that explained that the voting recommendations were based upon the AFL-CIO proxy voting recommendations. If clients did not notify INTECH of a choice, the default choice on behalf of clients was to the ISS-PVS recommendations. Approximately 27% of INTECH's clients chose to switch voting recommendations from ISS-PVS to the ISS-General Guidelines.

20. In May 2006, INTECH, in its Form ADV, described its proxy voting policies and procedures. It described that it offered clients a choice between ISS-PVS and ISS-General. It stated that ISS-PVS recommendations are based upon the AFL-CIO proxy voting guidelines and that INTECH's policy may result in INTECH obtaining and retaining Taft-Hartley or other union-affiliated clients. If clients did not notify INTECH of a choice, the default choice on behalf of clients was to the ISS-PVS recommendations.

23. Section 206(4) of the Advisers Act makes it unlawful for investment advisers "to engage in any act, practice, or course of business which is fraudulent, deceptive or manipulative."

24. Rule 206(4)-6 under the Advisers Act provides that "it is a fraudulent, deceptive, or manipulative act, practice or course of business within the meaning of Section 206(4) of the Act for [a registered investment adviser] to exercise voting authority with respect to client securities unless [it]: (a) adopt[s] and implement[s] written

policies and procedures that are reasonably designed to ensure that [it] vote[s] client securities in the best interests of clients, which procedures must include how [it] address[es] material conflicts of interest that may arise between [its] interests and those of [its] clients … and (c) describe[s] to [its] clients [its] proxy voting policies and procedures, and, upon request, furnish[es] a copy of the policies and procedures to the requesting client."

25. If registered investment advisers do not satisfy the foregoing conditions, they engage in acts, practices or courses of business that are unlawful.

26. As a result of the conduct described above, INTECH willfully violated Section 206(4) of the Advisers Act and Rules 206(4)-6(a) and 206(4)-6(c) thereunder.

27. As a result of the conduct described above, Hurley willfully aided and abetted and caused INTECH's violations of Section 206(4) of the Advisers Act and Rules 206(4)-6(a) and 206(4)-6(c) thereunder.

IV.

In view of the foregoing, the Commission deems it appropriate and in the public interest to impose the sanctions agreed to in Respondents' Offers.

Accordingly, pursuant to Sections 203(e), 203(f) and 203(k) of the Advisers Act, it is hereby ORDERED that:

A. Respondents INTECH and Hurley shall cease and desist from committing or causing any violations and any future violations of Section 206(4) of the Advisers Act and Rules 206(4)-6(a) and 206(4)-6(c) promulgated thereunder.

B. Respondents INTECH and Hurley are censured.

C. INTECH shall, within 30 days of the entry of this Order, pay a civil money penalty in the amount of $300,000 to the United States Treasury …

D. Hurley shall, within 30 days of the entry of this Order, pay a civil money penalty in the amount of $50,000 to the United States Treasury.…

Comments and Questions

1. Pension plans may handle governance issues directly. Many, however, contract out the task to their investment advisors. *See* Stephen J. Choi & Jill E. Fisch, *On Beyond CalPERS: Survey Evidence on the Developing Role of Public Pension Funds in Corporate Governance*, 61 Vand. L. Rev. 315, 324 (2008) ("a substantial number of funds delegate corporate governance responsibility, including voting authority, to their external portfolio managers."). Why do you think they do this? Investment advisers, in turn, often rely extensively on proxy advisory firms. Why is that the case?

2. This particular case involved an apparent effort to adjust voting behavior in order to attract additional business from union-sponsored pension plans. What strategy might an advisor implement if seeking to attract business from private, corporate sponsored pension plans?

3. As in this case, the investment advisor relied for voting recommendations on a proxy advisory firm, a topic addressed later in this chapter. Sometimes, advisers will

outsource the voting process to a proxy advisory firm. The proxy advisory firm in turn votes shares in accordance with the specified policies or guidelines adopted by the adviser. What obligations does this outsourcing impose on the adviser? Is there, for example, a continuing obligation to monitor the voting process to make sure it is done correctly? For more on this topic, see Division of Investment Management Division of Corporation Finance Securities and Exchange Commission, Staff Legal Bulletin No. 20 (June 30, 2014).

Mutual funds are another large category of institutional investors. They are created as a corporation or trust and invest capital in accordance with their stated investment objectives. Many portfolios are actively managed, with investment advisors recommending the shares to purchase or sell. Some, such as index funds, may invest in accordance with a formula. Such funds may have less discretion to dispose of shares when they disagree with the approach taken by management.

Jennifer S. Taub, *Able but Not Willing: The Failure of Mutual Fund Advisers to Advocate for Shareholders' Rights*
34 J. Corp. L. 843, 847–50, 865 (2009)[3]

Mutual funds hold tremendous wealth, are ubiquitous savings vehicles for individual investors, and have consolidated power. In terms of wealth, as of the year-ended 2006, assets in mutual funds worldwide stood at $21.8 trillion. Of that, approximately 48%, or $10.4 trillion, was held in U.S. mutual funds. In terms of ubiquity, the United States has approximately 90 million mutual fund shareholders. Nearly half of all U.S. households (51.8 million households) own stocks through mutual funds. That is, approximately 77.7 million Americans invest in equities through stock mutual funds. There are more than 4000 individual equity mutual funds in the United States with more than $4 trillion in assets. With holdings of approximately 25% of outstanding U.S. stock, the bloc voting power of mutual funds can sway election outcomes on matters from board directorships and executive compensation to shareholder governance and social issues. Notwithstanding the number of mutual funds in total, their power is very concentrated. In 2005, the top 5 mutual fund families had about 37% of all fund assets, the top 10 had about 48%, and the top 25, had 71%.

* * *

A mutual fund is a legal construct — a business trust or corporation — that pools customer money to invest in a portfolio of securities. Most funds are invested in stocks, bonds, or money market instruments. Some own a mixture. A mutual fund that holds corporate stocks is considered to be the shareholder of that corporation.

---

3. Copyright © 2009 The Journal of Corporation Law. Reprinted with permission.

The person (or institution) who invests money in the mutual fund is considered to be the shareholder of the mutual fund.

* * *

Typically, a mutual fund has no employees. It has a board of trustees or a board of directors. Because the mutual fund is usually a shell, this board takes action on its behalf. The mutual fund board "hires" an investment adviser to manage the investments within the fund. Among other things, this Adviser is a fiduciary and owes the fund a duty of "utmost good faith, and full and fair disclosure." To be sure, notwithstanding the title, the Adviser provides not just advice to the fund, but also discretionary management services. In addition, by law, the board hires a transfer agent to keep track of customer information, a principal underwriter to advertise and sell shares of the mutual fund to customers, a custodian to safe-keep fund assets, auditors, and other service providers.

In reality, though, the Adviser runs the show. The Adviser is often a wholly owned subsidiary of a financial services firm. Some such adviser firms are known as "fund families" or "fund complexes" given the numerous mutual funds that each adviser firm launches and sustains. The Adviser may be a private or a public corporation. The Adviser firm that launches the fund initially selects a slate of directors to be elected by the fund shareholders and the "independent" board members who are unaffiliated with the Adviser firm continue to nominate directors on a periodic basis. The directors who are also employees of the firm are considered "interested." The directors meet on a regular basis, on average 4–5 times per year and monthly at large fund families, to ratify various agreements and fulfill legal requirements. Regardless of these procedural safeguards, the Securities and Exchange Commission (SEC) "noted that a fund adviser is frequently in a position to dominate the board because of the adviser's monopoly over information about the fund and its frequent ability to control the board's agenda."...

* * *

[T]he SEC enacted a rule concerning mutual fund proxy voting. The Disclosure of Proxy Voting Policies and Proxy Voting Records by Registered Management Investment Companies (the Fund Proxy Voting Rule) became effective April 14, 2003 with a compliance date of August 31, 2004. This rule has three main requirements. First, mutual funds must file an annual report with the SEC "not later than August 31 of each year, containing the registrant's proxy voting record for the most recent twelve-month period ended June 30." Second, mutual funds must make available free-of-charge to investors a description of their proxy voting policies and procedures. Third, mutual funds must inform investors how they may obtain free of charge the policies and procedures and the annual proxy voting records of the funds.

Comments and Questions

1. Mutual funds own a sizeable portion of the equity of public companies. According to one source, they are estimated to hold 29% of US equities at the end of

2013. *See* Chapter 1: Overview of U.S. Registered Investment Companies, 2014 ICI Fact Book. This compares with public pension funds, for example, that hold about "10 percent or more of the total U.S. equity market." Rhonda L. Brauer, et al., *Report of the Task Force of the ABA Section of Business Law Corporate Governance Committee on Delineation of Governance Roles and Responsibilities*, 65 Bus. Law. 107, 135 (2009).

2. The broad category of mutual funds can mask significant differences. According to one source, "[o]ver 30% of US stock assets under management are now held in index mutual funds or exchange-traded funds that are based on indexes." Robert C. Pozen, Institutional Investors and Corporate Short-Termism, MIT Sloan School of Management, Aug. 25, 2015. What difference might this make in voting behavior?

3. Mutual funds can be described as less active than some other institutional investors such as public pension plans and hedge funds. Given that mutual funds typically have no employees and the adviser "runs the show," does this explain the less active stance? Is this an example of rational reticence? See Ronald J. Gilson & Jeffrey N. Gordon, *The Agency Costs of Agency Capitalism: Activist Investors and The Revaluation of Governance Rights*, 113 Colum. L. Rev. 863, 895 (2013).

4. A number of studies have been undertaken with respect to mutual fund voting patterns. One study of 26 mutual fund families on proposals relating to executive compensation found that "[t]he average level of support for management proposals on compensation issues was 82% in 2007 and 84% in 2008. . . ." *Mutual Fund Proxy Voting on Executive Compensation: 2007–2008*, The American Federation of State, County and Municipal Employees, The Corporate Library and The Shareowner Education Network. What does this information suggest about mutual fund voting patterns?

5. On the other hand, another commentator noted that "[m]utual funds with large holdings are also more likely to vote against management when their votes are more likely to alter the outcome." George W. Dent, Jr., *The Essential Unity of Shareholders and the Myth of Investor Short-Termism*, 35 Del. J. Corp. L. 97, 139–40 (2010). Assuming the statement to be true, is this the desired outcome?

———————

Hedge funds have become active participants in the securities markets. These are pooled investment vehicles that offer a variety of strategies, including investment in shares of public companies. Unlike mutual funds, hedge funds are not subject to the substantive provisions of the Investment Company Act of 1940. The role of these funds is more fully developed in Chapter 8.

In the governance area, they have become increasingly active in pressuring incumbent management to alter their business strategies in an effort to boost share prices. Hedge funds typically employ a compensation structure that encourages short term profit maximization. *See* Marcel Kahan & Edward B. Rock, *Hedge Funds in Corporate Governance and Corporate Control*, 155 U. Pa. L. Rev. 1021 (2007) ("The standard hedge fund charges a base fee equal to 1–2% of the assets under management and a significant incentive fee, typically 20% of the profits earned. This fee structure gives hedge fund managers a very significant stake in the financial success of the fund's investments.").

Comments and Questions

1. As the SEC has noted, "[a] performance fee could motivate a hedge fund manager to take greater risks in the hope of generating a larger return." Hedge Funds, Investor.gov. What impact might this have on investment strategies of hedge funds? How do they differ from mutual funds? The average hedge fund has a duration of somewhere around five years. What role might the form of compensation have in this relatively short life span?

2. Hedge funds and their advisers were for most of their history largely unregulated. The SEC tried to subject advisers to registration and reporting obligations but the nascent effort was struck down by the D.C. Circuit. *See Goldstein v. SEC*, 451 F.3d 873 (D.C. Cir. 2006). Congress gave the Commission the authority to require the advisers to maintain records and file certain specified reports. *See* Sections 403 & 404, Public Law 111–203 (July 21, 2010). The registration requirements did not, however, apply to advisers with less than $150 million under management or to advisers for venture capital funds.

3. Not all hedge funds are shareholder activists. *See* Dionysia Katelouzou, *Myths and Realities of Hedge Fund Activism: Some Empirical Evidence*, 7 Va. L. & Bus. Rev. 459 (2013) ("Activist hedge funds have emerged as a distinct subset within the wider hedge fund community, of which they comprise only a relatively small portion. In terms of numbers, they are about 100 of the more than 9,000 hedge funds in the United States, while in terms of size, activist hedge funds have approximately $50 billion of assets under management and constitute just 2.7% of total global hedge fund assets."). What does this say about the role of hedge funds in the corporate governance system?

4. To the extent hedge funds can be characterized as having a short term horizon, is this necessarily harmful? Said another way, is the long term perspective always the right one? *See* Lucian A. Bebchuk, *Essay: The Myth that Insulating Boards Serves Long-Term Value*, 113 Colum. L. Rev. 1637, 1642 (2013) (contending that "insulation advocates" have "failed to provide an adequate basis" for claims that the long term effects of board insulation are positive).

5. As institutional investors, are hedge funds really that different from the types of investors that have always existed? Corporate raiders in the 1980s targeted large public companies, particularly conglomerates and were variously labeled as shareholder benefactors and a corporate scourge. *See Unocal Corp. v. Mesa Petroleum Co.*, 493 A.2d 946, 956 (Del. 1985) (noting that board opposition to a tender offer motivated in part by the fact that "the threat was posed by a corporate raider with a national reputation as a 'greenmailer'").

6. In late 2014, CALPERS, the large public pension plan from California, announced that it was divesting itself of the $4 billion in investments in hedge funds. Other funds followed by reducing or eliminating their exposure to hedge funds, including the New York City Employees' Retirement System. What are some possible motivations for this decision?

What role ought institutional investors play in the corporate governance process?

George W. Dent, Jr., *The Essential Unity of Shareholders and the Myth of Investor Short-Termism*
35 Del. J. Corp. L. 97, 143–49 (2010)[5]

For decades there have been efforts to curb CEOs by infusing boards of directors — the ostensible governing bodies — with independence. Despite some claims to the contrary, these efforts have failed. CEOs always influence, and often dominate, the selection of outside directors. Naturally they prefer candidates who look kindly on high executive compensation and perquisites and on managerial self-dealing. Many outside directors themselves have conflicts of interest. CEOs also control the information received by outside directors. The CEO can curry their favor in various ways and can threaten to remove uncooperative members. The CEO (who is almost always a director) and her allies on the board can seize the board's initiative, and "groupthink" discourages anyone inclined to oppose them. Further efforts to ensure board independence are probably doomed to failure because of the boards' "unique susceptibility to capture by the managers they are supposed to monitor."

The repeated failures of outside board majorities to curb CEO autocracy have led to repeated tightening of the definition of director independence in the hope that this will finally achieve the desired result. This strategy is doomed to defeat. The law can exclude directors who have certain affiliations that could negate independence, but that does not guarantee that the board will act diligently to maximize share value. CEOs have twisted the outsider board, which is intended to restrain them, into a tool for increasing their power. One tactic is the growth of interlocking directorates, where CEOs sit on each other's boards. Similarly, the use of independent compensation committees and consultants, which was intended to institute real pay for performance, has been twisted into another ploy for further inflating already bloated CEO compensation. Tightening the criteria for director independence may actually be damaging to corporate governance by excluding "informed and interested outside directors with significant equity stakes" at a time when "firms are becoming more complex (geographically and technologically) and bigger, making them more difficult to monitor."

* * *

Despite the persistence of CEO domination and its damage to investors, some commentators feel that shareholders have become too powerful and their rights should be curtailed. Delaware's Vice Chancellor Leo Strine, for example, wants to deny voting

---

5. Copyright © 2010 The Delaware Journal of Corporate Law. Reprinted with permission.

rights altogether to stockholders who have held their shares for less than a year or who seek control.

Tinkering with the rules for shareholder voting will accomplish little. Matters would be different if boards were actually chosen by shareholders. Directors then would know that they would be rewarded if they effectively represent the shareholders, and dismissed if they did not. If shareholders chose boards, the rewards to able directors would include a reputation that could lead to further and more lucrative directorships.

The disempowerment of shareholders is now a threat to America's ability to attract investment capital. Investors care about shareholder rights and try to improve them in other countries. Investor protection is associated with higher economic growth. Many foreign countries now have stronger shareholder rights than America does. This fact may explain why American executives receive higher compensation than their foreign counterparts. Rupert Murdoch even shifted the incorporation of News Corp. from Australia to Delaware in order to escape the stronger shareholder rights provided by the former. The Committee on Capital Markets Regulation (the "Paulson Committee") concluded that "[o]verall, shareholders of U.S. companies have fewer rights … than do their foreign competitors" and that this situation was impairing investment in the United States. It recommended strengthening shareholder rights in several respects.

Human beings are imperfect. No system that depends on them can be perfect; some people will always contrive to game every system. Accordingly, nomination of directors of public companies by a committee of the ten to twenty largest shareholders will not prove flawless, but that is no reason to reject it. The question is whether it is likely to work better than any alternative. It definitely should be superior to the dysfunctional status quo, and I am not aware of any different proposal for a new system that would be preferable.

Comments and Questions

1. Do you agree that the current model of corporate governance is one dominated by the CEO and requires correction?

2. Do institutional shareholders sometimes have too much influence in the corporate governance process? In some cases, a small number of institutions hold a sizeable percentage of a public company's shares. As one report described:

> Concentration of share ownership in the largest twenty-five companies is significant. Just ten institutional investors account for between approximately 56 percent (WalMart) and 18 percent (ExxonMobil and Procter & Gamble) of the equity ownership in the top twenty-five companies; and just twenty institutional investors account for between approximately 61 percent (WalMart) and 24 percent (ExxonMobil and Procter & Gamble).

Rhoda L. Brauer, et al., *Report of the Task Force of the ABA Section of Business Law Corporate Governance Committee on Delineation of Governance Roles and Responsi-*

bilities, 65 Bus. Law. 107, 135 (2009). Might it be the case that in these companies, shareholders can exert excessive influence on management?

3. As the debate on the role of institutional investors in the governance process got underway, some saw the increased involvement as potentially harmful. *See* John C. Coffee, Jr., *Liquidity Versus Control: The Institutional Investor as Corporate Monitor*, 91 Colum. L. Rev. 1277, 1282 (1991) (noting that "defenders of corporate management seem equally convinced that, unless their power is checked, institutional investors will soon dominate corporate managements.... Typically, these proposals have portrayed institutional investors not as highly constrained and overly regulated entities, but as financial adolescents, recklessly preoccupied with short-term profit maximization."). Over the last two decades, has this occurred?

4. According to one commentator, CEO power has been reduced by "the continued increase in shareholdings by institutional investors and the rise of mutual funds as the most significant type of institutional investor; the emergence of hedge funds as significant shareholder activists; the change by mutual funds and public pension funds to a more confrontational mode of activism; and the increased prominence and power of proxy advisory firms." Marcel Kahan & Edward Rock, *Embattled CEOs*, 88 Tex. L. Rev. 987, 995 (2010). Do you agree? Assuming this is true, is this something that should cause concern? What can be done about this?

C. The Role of Proxy Advisory Firms

Shareholders with diverse holdings must make a significant number of complicated voting decisions in a short period of time. It is not unusual, therefore, for pension plans, investment advisers, and other investors to obtain assistance from proxy advisory firms. The assistance includes voting recommendations on particular proposals. Their role in the proxy process has, however, generated controversy.

Concept Release on the U.S. Proxy System
Exchange Act Release No. 62495 (July 14, 2010)

Over the last twenty-five years, institutional investors, including investment advisers, pension plans, employee benefit plans, bank trust departments and funds, have substantially increased their use of proxy advisory firms, reflecting the tremendous growth in institutional investment as well as the fact that, in many cases, institutional investors have fiduciary obligations to vote the shares they hold on behalf of their beneficiaries. Institutional investors typically own securities positions in a large number of issuers.

Every year, at shareholders' meetings, these investors face decisions on how to vote their shares on a significant number of matters, ranging from the election of directors and the approval of stock option plans to shareholder proposals submitted under Exchange Act Rule 14a-8, which often raise significant policy questions and corporate governance issues. At special meetings of shareholders, investors also face voting decisions when a merger or acquisition or a sale of all or substantially all of the assets of the company is presented to them for approval.

In order to assist them in exercising their voting rights on matters presented to shareholders, institutional investors may retain proxy advisory firms to perform a variety of functions, including the following:

- Analyzing and making voting recommendations on the matters presented for shareholder vote and included in the issuers' proxy statements;

- Executing votes on the institutional investors' proxies or VIFs in accordance with the investors' instructions, which may include voting the shares in accordance with a customized proxy voting policy resulting from consultation between the institutional investor and the proxy advisory firm, the proxy advisory firm's proxy voting policies, or the institution's own voting policy;

- Assisting with the administrative tasks associated with voting and keeping track of the large number of voting decisions;

- Providing research and identifying potential risk factors related to corporate governance; and

- Helping mitigate conflict of interest concerns raised when the institutional investor is casting votes in a matter in which its interest may differ from the interest of its clients.

Firms that are in the business of supplying these services to clients for compensation—in particular, analysis of and recommendations for voting on matters presented for a shareholder vote—are widely known as proxy advisory firms. Institutional clients compensate proxy advisory firms on a fee basis for providing such services, and proxy advisory firms typically represent that their analysis and recommendations are prepared with a view toward maximizing long-term share value or the investment goals of the institutional client.

Issuers may also be consumers of the services provided by some proxy advisory firms. Some proxy advisory firms provide consulting services to issuers on corporate governance or executive compensation matters, such as assistance in developing proposals to be submitted for shareholder approval. Some proxy advisory firms also qualitatively rate or score issuers' corporate governance structures, policies, and practices, and provide consulting services to corporate clients seeking to improve their corporate governance ratings. As a result, some proxy advisory firms provide vote recommendations to institutional investors on matters for which they also provided consulting services to the issuer. Some proxy advisory firms disclose these dual client relationships; others also have opted to attempt to address the conflict through the creation of "fire walls" between the investor and corporate lines of business.

* * *

The use of proxy advisory firms by institutional investors raises a number of potential issues....

a. Conflicts of Interest

Perhaps the most frequently raised concern about the proxy advisory industry relates to conflicts of interest. The Government Accountability Office has issued two reports since 2004 examining conflicts of interest in proxy voting by institutional investors. The GAO Report issued in 2007 addressed, among other things, conflicts of interest that may exist for proxy advisory firms, institutional investors' use of the firms' services and the firms' potential influence on proxy vote outcomes, as well as the steps that the Commission has taken to oversee these firms. The GAO Report noted that the most commonly cited conflict of interest for proxy advisory firms is when they provide both proxy voting recommendations to investment advisers and other institutional investors and consulting services to corporations seeking assistance with proposals to be presented to shareholders or with improving their corporate governance ratings.

In particular, this conflict of interest arises if a proxy advisory firm provides voting recommendations on matters put to a shareholder vote while also offering consulting services to the issuer or a proponent of a shareholder proposal on the very same matter. The issuer in this situation may purchase consulting services from the proxy advisory firm in an effort to garner the firm's support for the issuer when the voting recommendations are made. Similarly, a proponent may engage the proxy advisory firm for advice on voting recommendations in an effort to garner the firm's support for its shareholder proposals. The GAO Report also noted that the firm might recommend a vote in favor of a client's shareholder proposal in order to keep the client's business.

A conflict also arises when a proxy advisory firm provides corporate governance ratings on issuers to institutional clients, while also offering consulting services to corporate clients so that those issuers can improve their corporate governance ranking. The GAO Report also described the potential for conflicts of interest when owners or executives of the proxy advisory firm have significant ownership interests in, or serve on the board of directors of, issuers with matters being put to a shareholder vote on which the proxy advisory firm is offering vote recommendations. In such cases, institutional investors told the GAO that some proxy advisory firms would not offer vote recommendations to avoid the appearance of a conflict of interest.

It is our understanding that at least one proxy advisory firm provides a generic disclosure of such conflicts of interest by stating that the proxy advisory firm "may" have a consulting relationship with the issuer, without affirmatively stating whether the proxy advisory firm has or had a relationship with a specific issuer or the nature of any such relationship. Some have argued that this type of general disclosure is insufficient, even if the proxyadvisory firm has confidentiality walls between its corporate consulting and proxy research departments.

b. Lack of Accuracy and Transparency in Formulating Voting Recommendations

Some commentators have expressed the concern that voting recommendations by proxy advisory firms may be made based on materially inaccurate or incomplete data, or that the analysis provided to an institutional client may be materially inaccurate or incomplete. To the extent that a voting recommendation is based on flawed data or analysis, issuers have expressed a desire for a process to correct the mistake. We understand, however, that proxy advisory firms may be unwilling, as a matter of policy, to accept any attempted communication from the issuer or to reconsider recommendations in light of such communications. Even if a proxy advisory firm entertains comment from the issuer and amends its recommendation, votes may have already been cast based on the prior recommendation. Accordingly, some issuers have expressed a desire to be involved in reviewing a draft of the proxy advisory firm's report, if only for the limited purpose of ensuring that the voting recommendations are based on accurate issuer data. Some proxy advisory firms have claimed that they are willing to discuss matters with issuers, but that some issuers are unwilling to enter into such discussions.

There also is a concern that proxy advisory firms may base their recommendation on one-size-fits-all governance approach. As a result, a policy that would benefit some issuers, but that is less suitable for other issuers, might not receive a positive recommendation, making it less likely to be approved by shareholders.

Comments and Questions

1. Proxy advisory firms are vendors that provide services to issuers and institutional investors. In this role, they are largely unregulated. Voting recommendations are, however, treated as a solicitation under the proxy rules. *See Division of Investment Management Division of Corporation Finance Securities and Exchange Commission*, Staff Legal Bulletin No. 20 (June 30, 2014) ("As a general matter, the Commission has stated that the furnishing of proxy voting advice constitutes a 'solicitation' subject to the information and filing requirements of the federal proxy rules."). Nonetheless, the firms generally remain exempt from the proxy rules (save only Rule 14a-9). *See* Rule 14a-2(b), 17 CFR § 240.14a-2(b).

2. Two firms dominate the proxy advisory firm industry, Institutional Shareholder Services (ISS) and Glass Lewis. Moreover, significant barriers to entry apparently exist, suggesting that the structure will not change anytime soon. How much of the concern over proxy advisory firms is a result of this structure?

3. Part of the need for proxy advisory firms is structural. Annual meetings for public companies are bunched together, mostly occurring during the first half of the year. The table below is a breakdown of monthly frequency provided by ISS for meetings by public companies for 2013. Statistics provided by ISS for meetings held by the S&P 500 and the Russell 3000 show the following distribution:

Month	% age
January	3%
February	3%
March	3%
April	14%
May	38%
June	16%
July	4%
August	4%
September	4%
October	3%
November	4%
December	5%
Grand Total	100%

Most of the meetings, therefore, take place in a three month period. How might this impact demand for services provided by proxy advisory firms.

4. With the advent of say on pay resolutions (something that was imposed on public companies in Dodd-Frank), the number of proposals that must be considered by investors has increased. Institutional investors, therefore, find themselves having to cast more votes in a short period of time on complicated compensation matters. What impact might this have on the services offered by proxy advisory firms?

5. Calls have arisen for greater oversight by the SEC. *See* Commissioner Daniel M. Gallagher, *Remarks at Society of Corporate Secretaries & Governance Professionals*, 67th National Conference, Seattle, Washington, July 11, 2013 ("the Commission should fundamentally review the role and regulation of proxy advisory firms and explore possible reforms, including, but not limited to, requiring them to follow a universal code of conduct, ensuring that their recommendations are designed to increase shareholder value, increasing the transparency of their methods, ensuring that conflicts of interest are dealt with appropriately, and increasing their overall accountability."). What do you make of this suggestion?

6. Perhaps the most controversial aspect of these firms concerns the impact of their recommendations on the voting process. Negative recommendations will increase the percentage of negative votes. *See Yucaipa Am. Alliance Fund II, L.P. v. Riggio*, 1 A.3d 310, 357 (Del. Ch. 2010), *aff'd*, 15 A.3d 218 (Del. 2011) ("[A]ll of the experts in the case make a point that might make the object of their commentary blush. All say that one of the key factors in the outcome of a proxy contest will be the recommendation of the firms that provide institutional investors with recommendations about how to vote, the so-called 'proxy advisory firms.'"). A portion of this increase may result from investors automatically following the recommendations of these firms. A portion, however, may also result from the "noise" that accompanies a negative recommendation.

II. Majority vs. Plurality Voting

Until the new millennium, directors were almost universally elected through a system of plurality voting. Plurality voting meant that shares were not voted for or against directors. Instead, the candidates with the most votes were elected. In the public company arena, candidates for the board were typically nominated by management and ran unopposed. In unopposed elections, a plurality system ensured that those nominated automatically won, irrespective of the number of shares voted "against" them.

Pressure to alter the system began with a "just vote no" campaign instigated by Professor Joseph Grundfest at Stanford Law School. *See* Joseph A. Grundfest, *Just Vote No: A Minimalist Strategy for Dealing with Barbarians Inside the Gates*, 45 Stan. L. Rev. 857, 862 (1993). By voting no (actually withhold) against an unopposed director, shareholders could send a message about their level of dissatisfaction about the candidate. The approach was put into actual practice when, in 2004, 45% of shareholders at The Walt Disney Corporation voted against the election of Michael Eisner, the CEO, to the board.

Unwilling to rest with symbolic messages, shareholders began to push for a system of majority voting where votes against a director mattered. Shareholders submitted proposals under Rule 14a-8 calling on directors to implement such a system and many received majority support. Quickly a large number of companies put policies in place that required directors to receive a majority of the votes cast.

The provisions, however, ran into a number of legal issues. State law continued to rely on plurality voting to elect directors. As a result, directors not receiving a majority of the votes cast were nonetheless elected under state law. The practice, therefore, arose of requiring directors who did not receive a majority of the votes to resign and leaving it to the board to decide whether to accept the resignation.

In the space of a few short years, majority vote provisions became common, at least among larger public companies. Some saw this as a victory for shareholder advocacy, others as a reaffirmation of private ordering. Yet in some cases, the value to shareholders was, in the end, not always clear.

City of Westland Police & Fire Retirement System v. Axcelis Technologies, Inc.

Delaware Chancery Court

2009 Del. Ch. LEXIS 173 (Sept. 28, 2009), *aff'd*, 1 A.3d 281 (2010)

Noble, Vice Chancellor:

* * *

Defendant Axcelis Technologies, Inc. ("Axcelis" or the "Company") is a Delaware corporation specializing in the manufacture of ion implantation and semiconductor equipment.

SHI is a Japanese company that also makes and sells semiconductor equipment. In 1983, Axcelis and SHI became equal partners in a joint venture called SEN. SEN, like Axcelis and SHI, manufactures ion implantation and semiconductor equipment. SEN was an important asset to both Axcelis and SHI.

* * *

B. *SHI's Proposals*

On February 4, 2008, SHI (along with TPG Capital LLP) made an unsolicited bid to acquire Axcelis for $5.20 per share. Shares of Axcelis closed at a price of $4.18 per share that day. Three days later, Axcelis informed SHI that it would respond to its acquisition proposal after completing discussions with certain advisers. The Board rejected SHI's proposal on February 25, 2008. The Board found that the $5.20 per share price failed to compensate shareholders adequately for the synergistic value of the SEN joint venture and ignored the substantial business opportunity to take market share back from Axcelis competitors.

On March 10, 2008, SHI again proposed to acquire Axcelis, this time at a price of $6 per share. Shares of Axcelis closed at a price of $5.45 per share that day. On March 17, 2008, the Board again rejected SHI's overtures. The Board concluded that, while "a 'one company' approach combining Axcelis and SEN could yield significant operational and commercial synergies, ... [its] view of current market conditions and of the company's prospects when market conditions do improve" led to a belief that a transaction with SHI would not be in the shareholders' best interest. The Board also noted its feeling that, in order to engage in serious, productive discussions with SHI, some exchange of confidential information would be necessary, and SHI had yet to agree to keep such information and discussions confidential.

C. *The May 2008 Axcelis Shareholders' Meeting, Director Election, and the Rejection of Director Resignations*

On May 1, 2008, Axcelis held its annual shareholders' meeting. The terms of three directors were expiring, and each ran unopposed for reelection to the Board. Those directors were Hardis, Fletcher, and Thompson (the "Three Directors"). Axcelis follows the plurality voting provisions of Delaware law, and thus a director may be elected without receiving a majority of the votes cast in a given election. Each of the Three Directors received less than a majority of the votes cast in his reelection bid. The Court assumes the Plaintiff's position to be true: that the failure of the Three Directors to receive a majority of the votes cast in their reelection bids was the result of a concerted effort by at least some Axcelis shareholders to "send a message to the board, expressing their discontent with the [C]ompany's unresponsiveness to SHI" by withholding support for each of the Three Directors facing reelection at the 2008 annual meeting.

The failure to receive at least a majority of the votes cast triggered one of Axcelis's corporate governance policies. Pursuant to this policy (the "Policy"), directors failing to receive a majority of the stockholder vote must submit their resignations to the Board's Nominating and Corporate Governance Committee, which must then consider and recommend to the Board whether such resignations should be accepted or rejected. The Board must then accept or reject any resignations submitted by its directors under the Policy. Following the May 1, 2008, vote, the Three Directors offered to resign their positions. Through a May 23, 2008, press release, the Board announced its decision not to accept those resignations.

The press release stated that:

> In making their determination, the Board considered a number of factors relevant to the best interests of Axcelis. The Board noted that the three directors are experienced and knowledgeable about the Company, and that if their resignations were accepted, the Board would be left with only four remaining directors. One or more of the three directors serves on each of the key committees of the Company and Mr. Hardis serves as lead director. The Board believed that losing this experience and knowledge would harm the Company. The Board also noted that retention of these directors is particularly

important if Axcelis is able to move forward on discussions with SHI following finalization of an appropriate non-disclosure agreement.

The Board also expressed its intention to be responsive to the shareholder concerns that gave rise to the withhold votes. The Board is seeking to engage in confidential discussions with SHI and, prior to next year's Annual Meeting, the Board will consider recommending in favor of a declassification proposal at that meeting.

* * *

E. *The Section 220 Demand*

Plaintiff delivered a Demand, dated December 9, 2008, to Axcelis by overnight mail. The Demand seeks the inspection of the following categories of books and records:

* * *

6. All minutes of agendas for meetings (including all draft minutes and exhibits to such minutes and agendas) of the Board at which the Board discussed, considered or was presented with information concerning or related to the Board's decision not to accept the resignations of Directors Stephen R. Hardis, R. John Fletcher, and H. Brian Thompson.

7. All documents reviewed considered, or produced by the Board in connection with the Board's decision not to accept the resignations of Directors Stephen R. Hardis, R. John Fletcher, and H. Brian Thompson.

* * *

G. *The Alleged Wrongdoing*

Plaintiff alleges that there is a credible basis from which this Court can infer that the Board breached its fiduciary duties to shareholders by: ... (3) retaining three candidates for the Board after a majority of the shareholders refused to support them, allegedly for their failure to negotiate with SHI; ...

* * *

B. *Has the Plaintiff Demonstrated a Proper Purpose?*

The Plaintiff here seeks an inspection of Axcelis's books and records for the purpose of investigating whether members of the Board have breached their fiduciary duties in connection with: (1) the Board's decision to retain the Three Directors whose resignations had been tendered to the Board in accordance with prevailing Board policy following an annual meeting; ...

1. The Board's Decision to Retain the Three Directors

According to the Plaintiff, the Board members retained the Three Directors for the purpose of entrenching those directors and themselves in office. The Plaintiff argues that, because of this "interference" with the shareholder franchise for the purpose of entrenchment, the Board must bear the heavy burden of justifying its actions under the compelling justification standard found in *Blasius Indus., Inc. v. Atlas Corp.* Alternatively, the Plaintiff argues that the Board must justify its actions under the reasonable and proportionate standard of *Unocal Corp. v. Mesa Petroleum Co.* because the decision to retain the Three Directors was a defensive measure designed to defeat or impede a change of control.

The Court does not need to address the proper substantive standard of review surrounding a board's behavior under these Pfizer-type policies because the Plaintiff fails to demonstrate any credible basis from which the Court might infer the foundational assumptions upon which the Plaintiff's theory rests: that the Board's decision to retain the Three Directors was either motivated by entrenchment or was defensive in nature.

There is no support in the record of any entrenchment motive. Only the Plaintiff's bare accusations suggest such a motive, and mere accusations are insufficient. The Plaintiff has not shown why the Court should suspect that the independent, outside director members of the Board were motivated to perpetuate the Three Directors in office. The Three Directors were properly reelected to the Board under Delaware corporate law's plurality voting provisions. With this fact the Plaintiffs do not, and cannot, disagree. However, because a certain number of shareholders withheld their votes, a Board-enacted governance policy was triggered requiring each of the Three Directors to submit their resignation to a Board designated committee, which would then recommend whether the Board should, it its sole discretion, accept the resignations. The Plaintiff argues that a sufficient number of shareholders withheld their votes in reliance on, and out of a desire to trigger, the Policy. If so, they were successful; these shareholders achieved their desired goal and the Policy was triggered.

The problem for the Plaintiff is that the Policy vested discretion whether to accept the resignations of the Three Directors in the Board. By refusing to accept these resignations, the Board effectuated the results of a valid shareholder election. There is no evidence that the Board identified, and then sought to thwart, the will of the shareholder franchise by refusing to accept the resignations of the Three Directors.

The Plaintiff argues that the Board's purported justifications for the retention of the Three Directors under the Policy is not logically consistent with the record, and that this inconsistency creates a credible basis from which the Court might infer wrongdoing in the form of a breach of the Board's duty of loyalty. The Plaintiff identifies this alleged inconsistency as follows: SHI claims in its public statements to have attempted to negotiate with the Axcelis Board for nearly two years, but was repeatedly rebuffed. However, the Board justifies retention of the Three Directors as essential to moving forward with any negotiations with SHI. This alleged inconsistency is not a sufficiently credible basis from which the Court might infer wrongdoing.

Moving forward with negotiations with SHI was not the sole justification for the retention of the Three Directors. The Board also credited their experience and knowledge regarding the management of Axcelis, as well as the fact that they served on a number of key Axcelis committees. The record demonstrates that, throughout the prior negotiations with SHI, the Board insisted on some form of confidentiality agreement before moving forward—a request SHI avoided. Soon after the Board's decision to retain the Three Directors was made, Axcelis and SHI entered into a confidentiality agreement and negotiations proceeded, albeit unsuccessfully. In short, the purported justifications for the retention of the Three Directors are not materially inconsistent with the record and do not demonstrate a credible basis from which to infer wrongdoing.

Nevertheless, the Plaintiff argues that the Board's exercise of discretion under the Policy warrants heightened scrutiny and a suspicion of wrongdoing. The Plaintiff's logic is not sufficiently credible to support such suspicion. The Plaintiff's position would require this Court to accept the theory that mere shareholder reliance upon a board-enacted governance policy could effectively rewrite the voting provisions contained in a corporation's by-laws. The Axcelis By-laws provide for director election by plurality vote, and the interposition of the Board's discretionary review required by the Policy cannot change that fact simply because the shareholders who chose to withhold their votes wish it to be so. Perhaps certain shareholders withheld their votes for the purpose of symbolically demonstrating their lack of confidence in the Board. If the purpose was the removal of the Three Directors, then those shareholders would have been better served by supporting an alternative slate of directors in the May 2008 election. A poor strategic choice cannot be the basis of a Section 220 action.

It further appears that the Plaintiff's position would require this Court to subject Axcelis to the burden of a Section 220 request merely for having adopted the Policy, and exercising its discretion under it in fidelity with Axcelis's By-laws. Unless enacting the Policy and then acting in accordance with it constitutes credible evidence of wrongdoing, the Plaintiff has failed to demonstrate the requisite credible basis to suspect wrongdoing under Delaware's Section 220 jurisprudence. If mere acting in accordance with the terms of a Pfizer-style policy is to be found credible evidence of wrongdoing, then its death knell has been rung. Reasonable people might disagree as to the utility and propriety of the Policy. However, this Court is not prepared to eliminate functionally its use at this juncture. Merely pointing out the Board's exercise of discretion under the Policy—an exercise which ultimately effectuated the shareholder franchise—is not credible evidence of wrongdoing on this record. The Three Directors took office, duly elected by a plurality of Axcelis shareholders. The ultimate result under the Policy was the result of the shareholder franchise, not an interference with it. Absent the Policy, the result of the May 2008 election would have been no different.

The Plaintiff's attempt to paint the retention of the Three Directors as a defensive measure requiring the application of Unocal is equally unavailing. There was no present threat to corporate control at the time of the May 2008 election. There is no evidence that the Board disloyally desired to fend off SHI's advances. Indeed, the record demonstrates the opposite. Soon after the reelection of the Three Directors, the Board engaged SHI in further acquisition discussions and executed a confidentiality agreement, the absence of which had previously hindered negotiations. There is no credible basis from which the Court might infer that the Board's negotiations were conducted in bad faith. Failed negotiations, without more, do not form a credible basis supporting an inference of wrongdoing. In short, the Plaintiff has not demonstrated a logically credible basis from which wrongdoing might be inferred from the Board's retention of the Three Directors under the Policy.

Comments and Questions

1. Delaware had a majority vote system in place until 1987. The state changed the requirement because of concern over failed elections in the event of a contest. *See* S. 93, 134th Gen. Assembly, 66 Del. Laws ch. 136, § 11 (1987), *Discussion Paper on Voting by Shareholders for the Election of Directors*, Committee on Corporate Laws of the Section of Business Law of the American Bar Association, June 22, 2005, at 5 ("The Delaware rule has been that a vote of a majority of those present is required to take stockholder action. However, it was thought that at least in the case of the election of directors, the statute should only require a plurality vote.").

2. What do you make of the board's explanation for retaining the directors? Are they sufficiently specific? Are they consistent with the board's fiduciary obligations?

3. To the extent "experience and knowledge" of the directors is a sufficient explanation for rejecting the letters of resignation, what does this suggest about the ability of shareholders to challenge a board's decision in this area?

4. What possible reasons might Axcelis have for refusing to disclose the requested documents? What would be the consequence had the information and process used by the Axcelis board been made available?

5. The decision was affirmed on appeal, although the Supreme Court used a different line of reasoning. (This case is set out and discussed in Chapter 9.) In that decision, the Court did note that shareholders had the right to access documents in order to determine whether "directors, as fiduciaries, made a disinterested, informed business judgment that the best interests of the corporation require the continued service of these directors, or whether the Board had some different, ulterior motivation." 1 A.3d at 291. What does this suggest about the standard of review that will be applied by the Delaware courts to cases challenging the board's decision to reject letters of resignation?

6. What is the practical effect of this decision with respect to the ability of shareholders to challenge a board's decision to refuse to accept resignation letters from directors who did not receive majority support?

Whatever the approach, does it really provide shareholders with a meaningful opportunity to influence board membership?

William K. Sjostrom, Jr. & Young Sang Kim,
Majority Voting for the Election of Directors
40 Conn. L. Rev. 459, 486–89 (2007)[6]

C. Smoke and Mirrors?

We examined the majority voting systems of all 371 companies included in the Majority Vote Study as well as those of several companies that adopted some form

---

of majority voting after completion of the study. In the end, we failed to find a single company that had actually adopted a form of majority voting that gives shareholders veto power over incumbent directors. Almost all adopted forms include resignation policies requiring a "losing" director to resign, but all of these resignation policies leave discretion to the board of directors as to whether or not to accept the resignation. And presumably a board's decision not to accept a resignation would be treated like any other business decision and afforded business judgment rule protection. As long as the board made the decision "on an informed basis, in good faith and in the honest belief that the action taken was in the best interests of the company," the decision would likely withstand legal challenge. Certainly, in making the decision, a board would be expected to take into account that a majority of shares were against a particular candidate and would be concerned about bad publicity. However, as former Delaware Chancellor Allen stated in Paramount Communications Inc. v. Time Inc.: "The corporation law does not operate on the theory that directors, in exercising their powers to manage the firm, are obligated to follow the wishes of a majority of shares. In fact, directors, not shareholders, are charged with the duty to manage the firm." Thus, a board decision to retain a "losing" director would be on solid legal footing.

Hence, in our view, majority voting as put in action is little more than smoke and mirrors.... under the traditional plurality standard, absent the very rare occurrence of a proxy fight, the board will be comprised of individuals selected by the existing board regardless of how shareholders vote. But the same is also true under both plurality plus and majority plus because of the discretion built into the resignation requirement, the exercise of which is protected by the business judgment rule, and the board's power to fill a vacancy if it does decide to accept a resignation. At the end of the day, under the traditional plurality standard and the new majority standards, all directors are ultimately selected by the existing board regardless of how shareholders vote. Majority voting, as implemented in practice, simply does not give shareholders veto power over directors.

This bottom line likely explains why so many companies have adopted some form of majority voting over a relatively short period of time. With no shareholder veto power, there is no risk of failed elections and therefore the objections raised by critics of majority voting (potential to destabilize the board, shrink the candidate pool, etc.) are not really implicated. Thus, the decision to implement a plurality plus or majority plus system requires minimal thought by a board of directors. By implementing it, the board gives up little, if any, control over the election of directors but can then put out a press release touting the implementation as the latest example of its "long-standing commitment to responding to the concerns of shareholders," and/or pacify activist shareholders. As a bonus, the media may even pick up the story, as it has on a number of occasions, and trumpet the company's commitment to corporate governance.

Some assert that there is substance to the shift from plurality voting to majority voting as implemented. For example, Ira Millstein, a senior partner with the law firm Weil, Gotshal & Manges has stated:

The thing I like about [majority voting] is it puts the responsibility back on the board.... Once that director is not elected by a majority, the board then has to do something. And any board that didn't do anything in the face of that, would be idiotic. It would change the dynamics of the process completely.

Presumably the "something" he is referring to is the board's obligation under a resignation policy to consider the resignation of any director who failed to secure the requisite vote. But is this really so different from the traditional plurality system? Under that system, if a director candidate receives a majority of withheld votes would not any board that didn't do anything in the face of such a result be "idiotic"? It is true that under the traditional system a candidate who receives a majority "withheld" votes is still elected and is not required to tender his resignation. It is also true that the board does not have the legal power to oust him against his will. But it seems highly unlikely that a director who does not have the confidence of the shareholders, and is therefore asked to resign by the rest of the board, would refuse to resign. In any event, the board could simply decline to re-nominate him the next time his seat is up for election. Hence, we are skeptical that majority voting as implemented has much impact on the dynamics of the process, let alone changes the process completely.

Comments and Questions

1. There is a significant discrepancy in the companies adopting majority vote provisions. Although almost universal among large cap companies, smaller businesses are less inclined to adopt the provisions. Majority vote provisions of one kind or another have become common place among larger companies. By 2014, 86% of the companies in the S&P 500 had a majority vote policy in place. The percentage falls to 56% of the S&P 400 (mid-cap) and 28% of the S&P 600 (small-cap). What are some factors that may explain this configuration?

2. What do you make of the conclusion that majority vote provisions are a "myth"? Even if this characterization is accurate, do they have any residual value? What kind of signal does it send when an incumbent director does not receive majority support? What is the profile of a director most likely to be targeted by shareholders in a withhold campaign?

3. Majority vote provisions have often been used to support the "private ordering" approach to corporate law. They are used to show that corporate governance reforms can be quickly implemented without the need for regulatory intervention. *See Letter Submitted by the Delaware State Bar Association to the Securities and Exchange Commission*, July 24, 2009, at 11 (pointing out that "a significant majority of S&P 500 companies, in the space of just three years, have adopted a majority voting rule for the election of directors, in lieu of the state law default rule of plurality voting."). What do you make of this argument?

4. The failure of directors to receive a majority of the votes cast remains relatively uncommon. *See* Annual Shareholder Meetings and the Conundrum of "Unelected" Directors, Committee on Capital Markets Regulation, Feb. 2015 ("The study com-

piled and analyzed selected governance data and related information from companies of the Russell 3000 Index, finding that among the 97,958 director elections held at Russell 3000 companies during the five years 2010, 2011, 2012, 2013, and 2014, in 270 cases (0.28%) directors failed to achieve a majority of votes cast in director elections conducted under any voting format."). Moreover, almost 85% of the directors who did not receive majority support remained on the board two years later (compared with 90.3% of directors who did receive majority support). Those not receiving a majority but remaining on the board have sometimes been termed "zombie directors." What do you think explains these statistics? Should the SEC require additional disclosure with respect to zombie directors? What form might such disclosure requirements take?

5. As a result of majority vote provisions, "vote no" campaigns against directors have become a common fixture in the proxy process. What is the value of such a campaign? Why might particular directors be targeted? Does a sizeable negative vote but one that falls short of a majority put pressure on directors to step down? In 2013, three directors on the risk committee at JP Morgan Chase received between 53% and 59% of the votes cast. *See* Form 8-K, JP Morgan Chase & Co., filed May 23, 2013. A few months later, two of the directors stepped down from the board. *See* Form 8-K, JP Morgan Chase & Co., filed July 19, 2013 (disclosing that two directors on the board had retired).

6. Not all majority vote provisions require a letter of resignation that must be submitted to the board. Section 10.22 of the MBCA permits a bylaw that treats a director not receiving a majority as elected but provides that the term must terminate on the earlier of 90 days after the voting results are determined or the date a replacement is designated by the board. Why do you think the MBCA chose this approach? Would it not have been simpler to just provide that directors not receiving majority support were not elected? Even if a director steps down after 90 days, can the board appoint the defeated director to the vacancy? For an answer, read the commentary to Section 10.22.

III. Shareholder Proposals

Shareholders may want to influence the direction of the company without necessarily changing management. They do so through the adoption of proposals designed to influence the policies of the board. While proposals may be introduced at shareholder meetings, they have no chance of adoption unless preceded by a proxy solicitation. Recognizing this, the Securities and Exchange Commission adopted what is now Rule 14a-8 in 1942. *See* Exchange Act Release No. 2376 (1942). The Rule allows shareholders to submit proposals for inclusion in the company's proxy statement.

The Rule extends to any shareholder owning the lesser of 1% or $2000 of the voting shares of the company for at least one year. The modest ownership requirement essentially means that the rule is available to most shareholders. The rule was, in its early days, used primarily by individuals who were often characterized as corporate gadflies. *See* Frank D. Emerson & Franklin C. Latcham, *The SEC Proxy Proposal Rule: The Corporate Gadfly*, 19 U. Chi. L. Rev. 807, 808 (1951). By the 1990s, however, many of the proposals were submitted by institutional investors, particularly union and public pension funds.

The Rule contains a number of logistical requirements. Shareholders cannot submit more than a single proposal. The proposal and any accompanying statement cannot exceed 500 words (although it can refer to a web site for additional information). The proposal must be submitted at least 120 days in advance of the distribution of the proxy statement (calculated based upon the distribution date of the prior year's proxy statement).

Most importantly, the Rule contains thirteen grounds for excluding a proposal. They include matters improper under state law, not significantly related to a company's business, or that have already been implemented. Perhaps the most difficult to apply and the most commonly litigated is the exclusion for proposals that involve the "ordinary business" of the company. *See* Rule 14a-8(i)(7), 17 CFR 240.14a-8(i)(7).

A. The Ordinary Business Exclusion and the Public Interest Exception

The Commission added the "ordinary business" exclusion in 1954. Exchange Act Release No. 4979 (Jan. 6, 1954). With state law assigning day-to-day oversight of the business to the board, the provision allowed management to exclude proposals that intruded into its jurisdiction. The dearth of law, however, meant that the Commission staff largely had to determine the proper division of authority between owners and managers.

The exclusion allowed for the omission of ordinary business matters even if they raised issues of significant social importance. This application allowed "issuers to exclude proposals that involve matters of considerable importance to the issuer and its security holders." Exchange Act Release No. 12598 (July 7, 1976). By the 1970s, however, shareholders increasingly sought to use Rule 14a-8 to promote debate on matters of public importance. Whether manufacturing napalm or segregating buses, shareholders increasingly wanted to use the proxy process as a means of discussing these policies.

The Commission initially resisted efforts to allow these types of proposals, viewing the proxy process as an inappropriate forum for promoting public debate. See Exchange Act Release No. 4775 (Dec. 11, 1952) ("The amended rules also permit the omission of stockholder proposals submitted primarily for the purpose of promoting general economic, political, racial, religious, social or similar causes."). Pressure from investors, along with judicial intervention, eventually caused the policy to shift. In 1976, the Commission expressly acknowledged that the "ordinary business" exclusion would be modified by consideration of the social importance of the proposal.

Adoption of Amendments Relating to
Proposals by Security Holders

Exchange Act Release No. 12999 (Nov. 22, 1976)

... [A] proposal will be excludable if it "deals with a matter relating to the conduct of the ordinary business operations of the issuer." The Commission recognizes that this standard for omission has created some difficulties in the past, and that, on occasion, it has been relied upon to omit proposals of considerable importance to security holders. Nevertheless, the Commission believes that the provision is a workable one, as evidenced by the fact that it has been in operation for over 22 years and has not, until the past year or so, generated a significant amount of controversy.

The Commission is of the view that the provision adopted today can be effective in the future if it is interpreted somewhat more flexibly than in the past. Specifically, the term "ordinary business operations" has been deemed on occasion to include certain matters which have significant policy, economic or other implications inherent in them. For instance, a proposal that a utility company not construct a proposed nuclear power plant has in the past been considered excludable.... In retrospect, however, it seems apparent that the economic and safety considerations attendant to nuclear power plants are of such magnitude that a determination whether to construct one is not an "ordinary" business matter. Accordingly, proposals of that nature, as well as others that have major implications, will in the future be considered beyond the realm of an issuer's ordinary business operations, and future interpretative letters of the Commission's staff will reflect that view.

Although [the ordinary business exclusion] will be subject to a more restrictive interpretation in the future than its predecessor, ... this should not be construed to mean that the provision will not be available for the omission of proposals that deal with truly "ordinary" business matters. Thus, where proposals involve business matters that are mundane in nature and do not involve any substantial policy or other considerations, the subparagraph may be relied upon to omit them.

Comments and Questions

1. Shareholder proposals have become common. In 2015, shareholders submitted over 900 proposals. No action requests were filed with respect to over 300 proposals. While proposals concerning staggered boards and majority vote provisions remained common, the most popular resolutions in 2014 involved political and lobbying expenditures (126), independent chair (68) and climate change (56). In 2015, the most popular were political and lobbying (110), shareholder access (109), and independent chair (76). What do these statistics suggest about the shareholder proposal process?

2. What do you make of the exception for matters of social and public importance? Should proxy proposals be used as forums to debate important social issues? How does this exception affect the role of the SEC staff in the shareholder proposal process?

3. With the dollar amounts currently at $2000, almost any shareholder is eligible to submit a proposal. Should the ownership threshold be changed? In the UK, the own-

ership threshold is more difficult to meet but companies have fewer grounds for the exclusion of a proposal. Would you recommend something similar in this country?

4. The Commission at one time avoided some of the more difficult interpretive issues by allowing the proposals to go forward when they merely called for a report by the company. The Commission, however, eventually abandoned the position, concluding that it raised "form over substance" and rendered the exclusion "largely a nullity." Exchange Act Release No. 20091 (Aug. 16, 1983). Do you agree with this position?

5. Delaware's state constitution contains a provision that allows the Securities and Exchange Commission to refer matters to the state Supreme Court for advisory opinions. *See* Section 11(8) of Article IV of the Delaware Constitution. The Commission has made one such referral. *See CA, Inc. v. AFSCME*, 953 A.2d 227 (Del. 2008). Would the authority be sufficient to clarify the meaning of the "ordinary business" exclusion? Said another way, does the exclusion depend entirely upon state law?

6. Proposals are usually precatory. In other words, they merely request the board to act. Why do you think this is the case? Can precatory proposals influence the behavior of management? In at least one case, it apparently did. *See* Marleen O'Connor-Felman, *American Corporate Governance and Children: Investing in Our Future Human Capital During Turbulent Times*, 77 S. Cal. L. Rev. 1258, 1341 (2004) (noting that after a proposal calling for nondiscriminatory policies relating to sexual orientation "passed with fifty-eight percent of the shareholder vote, the company agreed to amend its written equal opportunity policy to state that the company does not discriminate based on sexual orientation.").

The 1976 Release indicated that proposals dealing with ordinary business matters could not be excluded if addressing matters of significant social importance. The position, however, was not easy to implement. It meant that every proposal involving a company's ordinary business was susceptible to an argument that it should not be excluded based upon the public importance of the subject matter.

As a result, the staff of the Commission was inundated with no action requests. The staff had to first determine whether a proposal fell within the ordinary business of the company and, if it did, the relative importance of the matter to the public. The staff needed to do so in the absence of any inherent expertise or meaningful standards.

The Commission sought to address these concerns in connection with a proposal submitted by the New York City Employees' Retirement System to Cracker Barrel Old Country Store, Inc. The proposal involved employment policies designed to prevent discrimination based upon sexual orientation. As the proposal provided:

> RESOLVED, Shareholders request the Board of Directors to implement nondiscriminatory policies relating to sexual orientation and to add explicit prohibitions against such discrimination to their corporate employment policy statement.

The Company sought the staff's permission to exclude the proposal from its proxy statement. The staff responded with the following letter.

Cracker Barrel Old Country Store, Inc.

SEC No Action Letter (Oct. 13, 1992)

The proposal requests that the Board of Directors implement hiring policies relating to sexual orientation and incorporate such policies into the corporate employment policy statement.

The company contends that the proposal is excludable pursuant to Rule 14a-8(c)(7) [the "ordinary business" exclusion]. As a general rule, the staff views proposals directed at a company's employment policies and practices with respect to its non-executive workforce to be uniquely matters relating to the conduct of the company's ordinary business operations. Examples of the categories of proposals that have been deemed to be excludable on this basis are; employee health benefits, general compensation issues not focused on senior executives, management of the workplace, employee supervision, labor-management relations, employee hiring and firing, conditions of employment and employee training and motivation.

Notwithstanding the general view that employment matters concerning the workforce of the company are excludable as matters involving the conduct of day-to-day business, exceptions have been made in some cases where a proponent based an employment-related proposal on "social policy" concerns. In recent years, however, the line between includable and excludable employment-related proposals based on social policy considerations has become increasingly difficult to draw. The distinctions recognized by the staff are characterized by many as tenuous, without substance and effectively nullifying the application of the ordinary business exclusion to employment related proposals.

The Division has reconsidered the application of Rule 14a-8(c)(7) to employment-related proposals in light of these concerns and the staff's experience with these proposals in recent years. As a result, the Division has determined that the fact that a shareholder proposal concerning a company's employment policies and practices for the general workforce is tied to a social issue will no longer be viewed as removing the proposal from the realm of ordinary business operations of the registrant. Rather, determinations with respect to any such proposals are properly governed by the employment-based nature of the proposal.

This is to be distinguished from proposals relating to the compensation of senior executives and directors. The Commission continues to regard issues affecting CEO and other senior executive and director compensation as unique decisions affecting the nature of the relationships among shareholders, those who run the corporation on their behalf and the directors who are responsible for overseeing management performance. Consequently, unlike proposals relating to the rank and file workforce, proposals concerning senior executive and director compensation are viewed by the Commission as inherently outside the scope of normal or routine practices in the running of the company's operations.

Accordingly, it is the Division's view that the instant proposal may be excluded from the Company's proxy material in reliance upon Rule 14a-8(c)(7).

Comments and Questions

1. In an unusual step, the staff issued a second letter noting that the position in the Cracker Barrel letter had been approved by the Commission. Cracker Barrel Old Country Store, Inc. (Jan. 15, 1993) (denying NYCER's appeal to the Commission but noting that the "Commission has affirmed the Division's position that the proposal was excludable from the Company's proxy material in reliance upon rule 14a-8(c)(7).""). While aware of significant staff positions, the Commission ordinarily does not directly intervene. Why might the Commission have intervened in this case?

2. What do you make of the approach set out in the *Cracker Barrel* letter? How does it clarify the application of the "ordinary business" exclusion?

3. Is there any reason to apply the approach applies only to employment related issues? In the aftermath of the Cracker Barrel letter, companies sought to exclude other types of proposals, arguing that the public policy exception should not apply. Does the Cracker Barrel letter provide support for this approach?

4. Cracker Barrel also illustrates a commonly known dynamic of the shareholder proposal process. Rule 14a-8 is filled with vague or subjective terms that are interpreted by the staff with little guidance from the Commission. Moreover, the staff can, consistent with the Administrative Procedures Act, change an interpretation without notice and comment. *See Perez v. Mortgage Bankers Association*, 135 S. Ct. 1199 (2015). What difference might this make in the staff's interpretive approach under the Rule?

The position in *Cracker Barrel* was strongly criticized. At least one court suggested that the Commission had violated administrative process in reaching the determination. *See Amalgamated Clothing and Textile Workers Union v. Wal-Mart Stores, Inc.*, 821 F. Supp. 877 (S.D.N.Y. 1993). As pressure mounted, the Commission decided to reconsider the position.

Amendments to Rules on Shareholder Proposals
Exchange Act Release No. 40018 (May 21, 1998)

In applying the "ordinary business" exclusion to proposals that raise social policy issues, the Division seeks to use the most well-reasoned and consistent standards possible, given the inherent complexity of the task. From time to time, in light of experience dealing with proposals in specific subject areas, and reflecting changing societal views, the Division adjusts its view with respect to "social policy" proposals involving ordinary business. Over the years, the Division has reversed its position on the excludability of a number of types of proposals, including plant closings, the manufacture of tobacco products, executive compensation, and golden parachutes.

We believe that reversal of the Division's Cracker Barrel no-action letter, which the Commission had subsequently affirmed, is warranted. Since 1992, the relative importance of certain social issues relating to employment matters has reemerged as a consistent topic of widespread public debate. In addition, as a result of the extensive policy discussion that the Cracker Barrel position engendered, and through the rule-making notice and comment process, we have gained a better understanding of the depth of interest among shareholders in having an opportunity to express their views to company management on employment-related proposals that raise sufficiently significant social policy issues.

Reversal of the Cracker Barrel no-action position will result in a return to a case-by-case analytical approach. In making distinctions in this area, the Division and the Commission will continue to apply the applicable standard for determining when a proposal relates to "ordinary business." The standard, originally articulated in the Commission's 1976 release, provided an exception for certain proposals that raise significant social policy issues.

While we acknowledge that there is no bright-line test to determine when employment-related shareholder proposals raising social issues fall within the scope of the "ordinary business" exclusion, the staff will make reasoned distinctions in deciding whether to furnish "no-action" relief. Although a few of the distinctions made in those cases may be somewhat tenuous, we believe that on the whole the benefit to shareholders and companies in providing guidance and informal resolutions will outweigh the problematic aspects of the few decisions in the middle ground.

Nearly all commenters from the shareholder community who addressed the matter supported the reversal of this position. Most commenters from the corporate community did not favor the proposal to reverse *Cracker Barrel*, though many indicated that the change would be acceptable as part of a broader set of reforms.

Going forward, companies and shareholders should bear in mind that the *Cracker Barrel* position relates only to employment-related proposals raising certain social policy issues. Reversal of the position does not affect the Division's analysis of any other category of proposals under the exclusion, such as proposals on general business operations.

Comments and Questions

1. What is the effect of this action by the Commission? What problems might it cause shareholders submitting and companies receiving shareholder proposals?

2. What do you make of the Commission's explanation for the change in policy? Is it convincing? What are some alternative explanations? Is the shift in the political composition of the Commission a possible explanation? *See* J. Robert Brown, Jr., *Essay: The Politicization of Corporate Governance: Bureaucratic Discretion, the SEC, and Shareholder Ratification of Auditors*, 2 Harv. Bus. L. Rev. 61, 74–75 (2012) (noting that once President Clinton succeeded in appointing a majority of the Commission, "the Commission set about reversing *Cracker Barrel*.").

3. *Cracker Barrel* is not the only example of attempts by the staff to impose bright line tests concerning the application of the ordinary business exception, only to later be overturned. *Compare* Staff Legal Bulletin No. 14C (CF), June 28, 2005 (implanting bright line test noting that proposals relating to environment or public health could

be excluded if requiring "an internal assessment of the risks or liabilities that the company faces as a result of its operations that may adversely affect the environment or the public's health"), *with* Staff Legal Bulletin No. 14E (CF), Oct. 27, 2009 (noting that "most corporate decisions involve some evaluation of risk," staff abandoned bright line test in favor of applying "the same standards" used for "other types of proposals under Rule 14a-8(i)(7).").

4. Application of the social policy element has continued to evolve. In 2002 and 2003, the staff issued no action letters concluding that proposals concerning the use of antibiotics in animal feeds could be excluded as "ordinary business." In 2009, however, the staff reversed the position, noting that antimicrobial resistance through the use of antibiotics in livestock had generated "widespread public debate." Tyson Foods, Inc. (Dec. 15, 2009). The staff noted the ban by the European Union of the use of most antibiotics as feed additives and legislation introduced in Congress "to prohibit the non-therapeutic use of antibiotics in animals absent certain safety findings relating to antimicrobial resistance." *Id.* What do you make of the additional evidence of public debate? Was it necessary? Was it enough?

5. Shareholder proposals tend to fall into four groups: executive compensation, governance standards for the board, takeover defenses, and social/political matters. Executive compensation proposals range from limits on the amount of severance for executive officers and holding periods for stock awards. Common governance proposals include those that call for the separation of chairman/CEO and for the election of directors by majority vote. Takeover proposals involve such matters as the repeal of staggered boards, the redemption of poison pills, and the right of shareholders to call special meetings.

6. With respect to socially responsible proposals, common topics include climate change and reports on political expenditures. In general, these proposals receive less support than those addressing governance issues. Thus, in 2015, more than 35 shareholder access proposals received majority support as did seven calling for majority vote for directors. Although shareholders submitted 110 proposals addressing political and lobbying activities, they averaged only 28.8% of the votes cast and none received majority support (although three did in 2014). What explains this difference?

7. Those unhappy with the staff's determination can seek reconsideration or even appeal to the Commission. The staff acts as gatekeeper for appeals. See Rule 202.1(d) of the SEC Rules of Practice ("The staff, upon request or on its own motion, will generally present questions to the Commission which involve matters of substantial importance and where the issues are novel or highly complex, although the granting of a request for an informal statement by the Commission is entirely within its discretion."). As a practical matter, the Commission almost never hears an appeal and almost never reverses the staff's position. *See* Courtney Bartkus, *Appealing No-Action Responses under Rule 14a-8: Informal Procedures of the SEC and the Availability of Meaningful Review*, 93 Denv. L. Rev. Online 199 (2016) (noting that from 2005 through 2015, the Commission had only directly intervened once as a result of an appeal of a staff ruling under Rule 14a-8). Why might this be the case? For an unusual exception to this approach, see Statement from Chair White Directing Staff to Review

Commission Rule for Excluding Conflicting Proxy Proposals, Jan. 16, 2015 (directing the staff to review Rule 14a-8(i)(9) and report to the Commission; as a result of the instructions, the Division of Corporation Finance announced that it would "express no views" on the provision during the current proxy season).

The revisions in 1998 effectively reinstated the traditional analysis. Proposals could be excluded if they involved a company's ordinary business unless they also implicated an important issue of public policy. As a result, the concerns that led to the original position in *Cracker Barrel* remained in place. Almost any proposal involving a company's business was presumptively excludable. At the same time, however, shareholders typically targeted aspects of the business that implicated issues of public policy, creating at least an argument that the proposal should not be excluded. The difficulties in the approach surfaced in the following case.

Trinity Wall Street v. Wal-Mart Stores, Inc.
United States Court of Appeals, Third Circuit
792 F.3d 323 (2015)

Ambro, Circuit Judge:

I. INTRODUCTION

"[T]he secret of successful retailing is to give your customers what they want." Sam Walton, SAM WALTON: MADE IN AMERICA 173 (1993). This case involves one shareholder's attempt to affect how Wal-Mart goes about doing that.

Appellant Wal-Mart Stores, Inc., the world's largest retailer, and one of its shareholders, Appellee Trinity Wall Street—an Episcopal parish headquartered in New York City that owns Wal-Mart stock—are locked in a heated dispute. It stems from Wal-Mart's rejection of Trinity's request to include its shareholder proposal in Wal-Mart's proxy materials for shareholder consideration.

Trinity's proposal, while linked to Wal-Mart's sale of high-capacity firearms (guns that can accept more than ten rounds of ammunition) at about one-third of its 3,000 stores, is nonetheless broad. It asks Wal-Mart's Board of Directors to develop and implement standards for management to use in deciding whether to sell a product that (1) "especially endangers public safety"; (2) "has the substantial potential to impair the reputation of Wal-Mart"; and/or (3) "would reasonably be considered by many offensive to the family and community values integral to the Company's promotion of its brand." Standing in Trinity's way, among other things, is a rule of the Securities and Exchange Commission ("SEC" or "Commission"), known as the "ordinary business" exclusion. 17 C.F.R. §240.14a-8(i)(7) ("Rule 14a-8(i)(7)"). As its name suggests, the rule lets a company omit a shareholder proposal from its proxy materials if the proposal relates to its ordinary business operations.

Wal-Mart obtained what is known as a "no-action letter" from the staff of the SEC's Division of Corporation Finance (the "Corp. Fin. staff" or "staff"), thus signaling that there would be no recommendation of an enforcement action against the company if it omitted the proposal from its proxy materials. *See Wal-Mart Stores, Inc.,* SEC No-Action Letter, 2014 WL 409085, at *1 (Mar. 20, 2014).Trinity thereafter filed suit in federal court, seeking to enjoin Wal-Mart's exclusion of the proposal. *See Trinity Wall Street v.Wal-Mart Stores, Inc.,* 75 F.Supp.3d 617, No. 14-405-LPS, 2014 WL 6790928 (D.Del. Nov. 26, 2014). The core of the dispute is whether the proposal was excludable under the ordinary business exclusion. Although the District Court initially denied Trinity's request, it handed the church a victory on the merits some seven months later by holding that, because the proposal concerned the company's Board (rather than its management) and focused principally on governance (rather than how Wal-Mart decides what to sell), it was outside Wal-Mart's ordinary business operations. Wal-Mart appeals, seeking a ruling that it could exclude Trinity's proposal from its 2015 proxy materials and did not err in excluding the proposal from its 2014 proxy materials.

Stripped to its essence, Trinity's proposal—although styled as promoting improved governance—goes to the heart of Wal-Mart's business: what it sells on its shelves. For the reasons that follow, we hold that it is excludable under Rule 14a-8(i)(7) and reverse the ruling of the District Court.

* * *

IV. ANALYSIS

The principal issue we address is whether Trinity's proposal was excludable because it related to Wal-Mart's ordinary business operations. In doing so, we evaluate the District Court's primary and alternative holdings. To repeat, it held that Trinity's proposal doesn't meddle in the nuts-and-bolts of Wal-Mart's business because it was a directive to the Board (rather than management) to set standards to guide certain merchandising decisions. And in the alternative the proposal is not excludable because it implicates a significant social policy—the sale of high-capacity firearms by the world's largest retailer—that transcends Wal-Mart's ordinary business. In this case (and we agree with the Commission that our determination counsels a case-by-case inquiry) we conclude that the proposal is excludable under the ordinary business proviso and that the significant social policy intended by the proposal is here no exception to that exclusion.

A. Trinity's Proposal Relates to Wal-Mart's Ordinary Business Operations.

We employ a two-part analysis to determine whether Trinity's proposal "deals with a matter relating to the company's ordinary business operations [.]" 17 C.F.R. §240.14a-8(i)(7). Under the first step, we discern the "subject matter" of the proposal. *See* 1983 Adopting Release, 1983 WL 33272, at *7. Under the second, we ask whether that subject matter relates to Wal-Mart's ordinary business operations. *Id.* If the answer to the second question is yes, Wal-Mart must still convince us that Trinity's proposal does not raise a significant policy issue that transcends the nuts and bolts of the retailer's business.

1. What is the subject matter of Trinity's proposal?

Beginning with the first step, we are mindful of the Commission's consistent nod to substance over form and its distaste for clever drafting. As it reaffirmed in the 1982 and 1983 Releases, it matters little how a shareholder styles its proposal; the emphasis should always be on its substance. To illustrate its point, the SEC invoked the staff's disparate treatment of two proposals where the Commission thought the outcome should have been the same:

> [T]he staff, in a letter to Castle & Cooke ... *agreed* with the company that a proposal requesting that it alter its food production methods in underdeveloped countries could be excluded under [the ordinary business exclusion] since [it] specified the steps management should take to implement the action requested.... [Years later], however, the proponent instead asked the company *to appoint a committee to review* foreign agricultural operations with emphasis on the balance between labor and capital intensive production. The staff *refused* to apply the rule to this provision because the appointment of a special committee to study the company's foreign agricultural operations is a matter of policy.

1982 Proposing Release, 1982 WL 600869, at *17 n. 49 (emphases added). In the SEC's view, a directive to Castle & Cooke to alter its food production methods in underdeveloped countries was the functional equivalent of a request for committee review of those methods. *See id.* Because the staff concurred that the former was excludable, it should have reached the same result as to the latter. Thus, even though Trinity's proposal asks for the development of a specific merchandising policy—and not a review, report or examination—we still ask whether the *subject matter* of the action it calls for is a matter of ordinary business.

Applying that principle, we part ways with the District Court. We perceive it put undue weight on the distinction between a directive to management and a request for Board action. In the District Court's view, if the proposal had directed management to arrange its product assortment in a certain way, it would have been excludable. But because it merely asked the "*Board* [to] oversee the development and effectuation of a Wal-Mart policy," it was not. *Trinity,* 75 F.Supp.3d at 630, 2014 WL 6790928, at *9 (emphasis and bold in original); *see also id.* ("Any direct impact of adoption of Trinity's proposal would be felt at the Board level; it would then be for the Board to determine what, if any, policy should be formulated and implemented."). The concern with this line of reasoning is that the SEC in its 1976 Adopting Release rejected the proposed bright line whereby shareholder proposals involving "matters that would be handled by management personnel without referral to the board ... generally would be excludable," but those involving "matters that would require action by the board would not be." 1976 Proposing Release, 1976 WL 160410, at *8. Thus, though the District Court's rationale and holding are not implausible, we do not adopt them.

Distancing itself from the District Court's formal approach, Trinity argues that the subject matter of its proposal is the improvement of "corporate governance over strategic matters of community responsibility, reputation for good corporate citizenship, and brand reputation, none of which can be considered ordinary business," Trinity Br. 39, and the focus is on the "shortcomings in Wal-Mart's corporate governance and oversight over policy matters," *id.* at 33. We cannot agree. As the National Association of Manufacturers points out, Trinity's contention, like the District Court's analysis, relies "on how [the proposal] is framed and to whom, rather than [its] substance." Brief of *amicus curiae* Nat'l Assoc. of Mfrs. 15. Contrary to what Trinity would have us believe, the immediate consequence of the adoption of a proposal—here the improvement of corporate governance through the formulation and implementation of a merchandising policy—is not its subject matter. If it were, then, analogizing to the review context, the subject matter of a review would be the review itself rather than the information sought by it. *See* 1982 Proposing Release, 1982 WL 600869, at *17. For example, under Trinity's position, the subject matter of a proposal that calls for a report on how a restaurant chain's menu promotes sound dietary habits would be corporate governance as opposed to important matters involving the promotion of public health. Yet that is the analysis the SEC disavowed in adopting the suggestions made in the 1982 Proposing Release. The subject matter of the proposal is instead its *ultimate* consequence—here a potential change in the way Wal-Mart decides which products to sell. Indeed, as even the District Court acknowledged, if the company were to adopt Trinity's proposal, then, whatever the nature of the forthcoming policy, it "could (and almost certainly would) shape what products are sold by Wal-Mart[.]" *Trinity*, 75 F.Supp.3d at 630, 2014 WL 6790928, at *9.

This view of the subject matter of Trinity's proposal finds support in a well-established line of SEC no-action letters. The most instructive is the no-action letter issued to Sempra Energy in January 2012. The proposal there urged the Board "to conduct an independent oversight review each year of the Company's management of political, legal, and financial risks posed by [its] operations in any country that may pose an elevated risk of corrupt practices." *Sempra Energy*, SEC No-Action Letter, 2011 WL 6425347, at *2 (Jan. 12, 2012). As Trinity does here, the proposing shareholder framed the subject matter of its proposal as targeting the company's governance of a certain type of risk: "the political, legal, and financial risks" inherent in the company's operations in countries "posing an elevated risk of corrupt practices," *id.*, which could ultimately trigger a Foreign Corrupt Practices Act prosecution. *Cf.* Trinity Br. 40 (maintaining that its proposal addresses the governance of the "risks to society and Wal-Mart should a product, after it is sold, cause harm to [its] customers or its brand and reputation") (quotation marks omitted). But, as here, the staff granted no-action relief because, "although the proposal requests the board to conduct an independent oversight review of Sempra's management of particular risks, the underlying subject matter of these risks appears to involve ordinary business matters." *Sempra Energy*, 2011 WL 6425347, at *1; *see also The Home Depot, Inc.*, SEC No-Action Letter, 2008 WL 257307, at *1, *2 (Jan. 25, 2008) (granting no-action relief where the proposal asked Home Depot's Board to publish a report outlining the company's product safety policies and describing what management is doing to address recent product safety concerns because it related to "Home Depot's ordinary business operations (i.e., the sale of particular products)"); *Family Dollar Stores, Inc.*, SEC No-Action Letter, 2007 WL 3317923, at *1 (Nov. 6, 2007) (same where proposal asked for a report "evaluating Company policies and procedures for systematically minimizing customers' exposure to toxic substances and hazardous components in its marketed products" because it relates to Family Dollar's "ordinary business operations (i.e., sale of particular products)"); *Walgreen Co.*, SEC No-Action Letter, 2006 WL 5381376, at *1 (Oct. 13, 2006) (same for proposal asking for a report "characterizing the extent to which the company's private label cosmetics and personal care products lines contain carcinogens, mutagens, reproductive toxicants, and chemicals that affect the endocrine system and describing options for using safer alternatives," because the subject matter of the proposal related to Walgreen's "ordinary business operations (i.e., the sale of particular products)").

The staff's consistent focus on the underlying subject matter of a proposal is instructive. So too is Trinity's failure to cite any authority for its view of the subject matter of its proposal. *See* Trinity Br. *344 37–42. For us, the subject matter of Trinity's proposal is how Wal-Mart approaches merchandising decisions involving products that (1) especially endanger public-safety and well-being, (2) have the potential to impair the reputation of the Company, and/or (3) would reasonably be considered by many offensive to the family and community values integral to the company's promotion of the brand. A contrary holding—that the proposal's subject matter is "improved corporate governance"—would allow drafters to evade Rule 14a-8(i)(7)'s reach by styling their proposals as requesting board oversight or review. *See* Reply Br. 10. We decline to go in that direction.

2. Does Wal-Mart's approach to whether it sells particular products relate to its ordinary business operations?

Reaching the second step of the analysis, we ask whether the subject matter of Trinity's proposal relates to day-to-day matters of Wal-Mart's business. Wal-Mart says the answer is yes because, even though the proposal doesn't demand any specific changes to the make-up of its product offerings—a point on which Trinity hangs its hat, *see* Trinity Br. 38 ("[The proposal] is not a 'stop selling' proposal. Nor does it require intricate reports on Wal-Mart's products.")—it "seeks to have a [B]oard committee address policies that could (and almost certainly would) shape what products are sold by Wal-Mart." Reply Br. 9 (internal quotation marks omitted). That is, Trinity's proposal is just a sidestep from "a shareholder referendum on how [Wal-Mart] selects its inventory." Brief of *amicus curiae* the Nat'l Assoc. of Mfrs. at 11. And thus its subject matter strikes at the core of Wal-Mart's business.

We agree. A retailer's approach to its product offerings is the bread and butter of its business. As *amicus* the National Association of Manufacturers notes, "Product selection is a complicated task influenced by economic trends, data analytics, demographics, customer preferences, supply chain flexibility, shipping costs and lead-times, and a host of other factors best left to companies' management and boards of directors." *Id.* at 12; *see also* Brief of *amicus curiae* Retail Litig. Ctr., Inc. 11 ("The understanding of consumer behavior and careful tailoring of product mix is central to the success or failure of a given retailer."). Though a retailer's merchandising approach is not beyond shareholder comprehension, the particulars of that approach involve operational judgments that are ordinary-course matters.

Moreover, that the proposal doesn't direct management to stop selling a particular product or prescribe a matrix to follow is, we think, a straw man. *See* Trinity Br. 38; *Trinity,* 75 F.Supp.3d at 631, 2014 WL 6790928, at *10 ("Trinity has carefully drafted its Proposal.... not [to] dictate which products should be sold or how the policies regarding sales of certain types of products should be formulated or implemented."). A proposal need only *relate* to a company's ordinary business to be excludable. *Cf.* 17 C.F.R. § 240.14a-8(i)(7) (exclusion is proper where a proposal deals with a matter "*relating* to the company's ordinary business operations") (emphasis added). It need not dictate any particular outcome. To make the point even clearer, suppose that Trinity's proposal had merely asked Wal-Mart's Board to *reconsider* whether to continue selling a given product. Though the request doesn't dictate a particular outcome, we have no doubt it would be excludable under the SEC's 1983 Adopting Release, as the action sought relates to Wal-Mart's ordinary business operations. This is so even though it doesn't suggest any changes. The same is true here. In short, so long as the subject matter of the proposal *relates* — that is, bears on — a company's ordinary business operations, the proposal is excludable unless some other exception to the exclusion applies.

* * *

B. Trinity's Proposal Does Not Focus on a Significant Policy Issue that Transcends Wal-Mart's Day-to-Day Business Operations.

As discussed above, there is a significant social policy exception to the default rule of excludability for proposals that relate to a company's ordinary business operations. For the SEC staff this means that when "a proposal's underlying subject matter transcends the day-to-day business matters of the company and raises policy issues so significant that it would be appropriate for a shareholder vote, the proposal generally will not be excludable under Rule 14a-8(i)(7)." SEC Staff Legal Bulletin No. 14E, 2009 WL 4363205, at *2 (Oct. 27, 2009).

The difficulty in this case is divining the line between proposals that focus on sufficiently significant social policy issues that transcend a company's ordinary business (not excludable) from those that don't (excludable). Even the Commission admits that the social-policy exception "raise[s] difficult interpretive questions." 1997 Proposing Release, 1997 WL 578696, at *13. No doubt that is because the calculus is complex. Yet we cannot sidestep what some may deem an unreckonable area. Thus we wade in.

We think the inquiry is again best split into two steps. The first is whether the proposal focuses on a significant policy (be it social or, as noted below, corporate). If it doesn't, the proposal fails to fit within the social-policy exception to Rule 14a-8(i)(7)'s exclusion. If it does, we reach the second step and ask whether the significant policy issue transcends the company's ordinary business operations.

1. Does Trinity's proposal raise a significant social policy issue?

We first turn to whether Trinity's proposal focuses on a "sufficiently significant" policy issue like "significant [employment] discrimination." 1998 Adopting Release, 1998 WL 254809, at *4. The District Court said yes because the proposal at its core dealt with "the social and community effects of sales of high capacity firearms at the world's largest retailer." *Trinity,* 75 F.Supp.3d at 630, 2014 WL 6790928, at *9. However, even Trinity concedes its proposal "is not directed solely to Wal-Mart's sale of guns." Trinity Mot. for Summ. J. 17 (ECF No. 38, filed Jun. 18, 2014). Rather it asks Wal-Mart's Board to oversee merchandising decisions for *all* "products especially dangerous to reputation, brand value, or the community that a family retailer such as Wal-Mart should carefully consider whether or not to sell." Trinity Br. 44. *See also* Brief of *amici curiae* Corporate and Securities Law Professors 14–15 (arguing that the "ethical and social policy implications" of "[s]elling products that endanger public safety, Wal-Mart's reputation, and [its] core values," are "easily on par with employment discrimination, which the SEC's 1998 Release deemed a sufficiently significant policy issue to warrant inclusion of shareholder proposals relating to it").

Wal-Mart, on the other hand, contends that neither the Commission nor its staff has ever countenanced "such a broad and nebulous concept of significant policy issue." Reply Br. 21. We disagree. True enough, the Commission has adopted what can only be described as a "we-know-it-when-we-see-it" approach, *see* Palmiter at 910 (describing the Commission's "shifting approach to social/political proposals" as the "most dramatic and prominent example of SEC inconstancy" under Rule 14a-8). Yet it is hard to counter that Trinity's proposal doesn't touch the bases of what are significant concerns in our society and corporations in that society. Thus we deem that its proposal raises a matter of sufficiently significant policy.

* * *

2. Even if Trinity's proposal raises a significant policy issue, does that issue transcend Wal-Mart's ordinary business operations?

To repeat, where "a proposal's underlying subject matter transcends the day-to-day business matters of the company *and* raises policy issues so significant that it would be appropriate for a shareholder vote, the proposal generally will not be excludable under Rule 14a-8(i)(7)." SEC Staff Legal Bulletin No. 14E, 2009 WL 4363205, at *2 (Oct. 27, 2009) (emphasis added). What this means is that, to shield its proposal from the ordinary business exclusion, a shareholder must do more than focus its proposal on a significant policy issue; the subject matter of its proposal must "transcend" the company's ordinary business. *See* 1998 Adopting Release, 1998 WL 254809, at *4. The Commission used the latter term, we believe, to refer to a policy issue that is divorced from how a company approaches the nitty-gritty of its core business. *See* SEC Staff Legal Bulletin No. 14E, 2009 WL 4363205, at *3 (maintaining that CEO succession-planning "raises a significant policy issue regarding the governance of the corporation that transcends the day-to-day business matter of managing the workforce"). Thus, and contrary to the position of our concurring colleague, we think the transcendence requirement plays a pivotal role in the social-policy exception calculus. Without it shareholders would be free to submit "proposals dealing with ordinary business matters yet cabined in social policy concern." *Apache Corp. v. New York City Emps.' Ret. Sys.,* 621 F.Supp.2d 444, 451 n. 7 (S.D.Tex.2008) (rejecting the argument that "whether a proposal implicates significant social policy is the dispositive inquiry").

For major retailers of myriad products, a policy issue is rarely transcendent if it treads on the meat of management's responsibility: crafting a product mix that satisfies consumer demand. This explains why the Commission's staff, almost as a matter of course, allows retailers to exclude proposals that "concern[ ] the sale of particular products and services." *Rite Aid Corp.*, SEC No-Action Letter, 2015 WL 364996, at *1 (Mar. 24, 2015). On the other hand, if a significant policy issue disengages from the core of a retailer's business (deciding whether to sell certain goods that customers want), it is more likely to transcend its daily business dealings.

To illustrate the distinction, a proposal that asks a supermarket chain to evaluate its sale of sugary sodas because of the effect on childhood obesity should be excludable because, although the proposal raises a significant social policy issue, the request is too entwined with the fundamentals of the daily activities of a supermarket running its business: deciding which food products will occupy its shelves. So too would a proposal that, out of concern for animal welfare, aims to limit which food items a grocer sells. *Cf., e.g., Amazon.com, Inc.*, SEC No-Action Letter, 2015 WL 470145, at *1 (Mar. 27, 2015) (allowing Amazon to exclude proposal that asked it to "disclose to shareholders any reputational and financial risks that it may face as a result of negative public opinion pertaining to the treatment of animals used to produce products it sells" because the "proposal relates to the products and services offered for sale by the company"); *Papa John's Int'l, Inc.*, SEC No-Action Letter, 2014 WL 7406254, at *1 (Feb. 13, 2015) (same for proposal that encouraged the pizza franchise to "expand its menu offerings to include vegan cheeses and vegan meats in order to advance animal welfare, reduce its ecological footprint, expand its healthier options and meet growing demand for plant-based foods").

By contrast, a proposal raising the impropriety of a supermarket's discriminatory hiring or compensation practices generally is not excludable because, even though human resources management is a core business function, it is disengaged from the essence of a supermarket's business. *See Wal-Mart Stores, Inc.*, SEC No-Action Letter, 2004 WL 326494, at *1 (Feb. 17, 2004) (denying no-action relief where proposal asked for a report documenting "the distribution of [ ] equity compensation by the recipient's race and gender and discuss[ing] recent trends in equity compensation granted to women and employees of color"). The same goes for proposals asking for information on the environmental effect of constructing stores near environmentally sensitive sites. *See, e.g.,* Jenny Staletovich, *Developer Defends Walmart in Rare Forest,* The Miami Herald (Sept. 12, 2014), *available at* http://www.miamiherald.com/news/local/environment/article2092364.html.

With those principles in mind, we turn to Trinity's proposal. Trinity says it focuses on "*both* corporate policy and social policy" — specifically, the "transcendent policy issue of under what policies and standards and with what Board oversight Wal-Mart handles [ ] merchandising decisions" for products that are "especially dangerous to [the company's] reputation, brand value, or the community." Trinity Br. 44 (emphasis in original). "In an age of mass shootings, increased violence, and concerns about product safety," Trinity argues, "the [p]roposal goes to the heart of Wal-Mart's impact on and approach to social welfare as well as the risks such impact and approach may have to Wal-Mart's reputation and brand image and its community." *Id.* at 43.

But is how a retailer weighs safety in deciding which products to sell too enmeshed with its day-to-day business? We think it is in this instance. As we noted before, the essence of a retailer's business is deciding what products to put on its shelves—decisions made daily that involve a careful balancing of financial, marketing, reputational, competitive and other factors. The emphasis management places on safety to the consumer or the community is fundamental to its role in managing the company in the best interests of its shareholders and cannot, "as a practical matter, be subject to direct shareholder oversight." 1998 Adopting Release, 1998 WL 254809, at *4. Although shareholders perform a valuable service by creating awareness of social issues, they are not well-positioned to opine on basic business choices made by management.

It is thus not surprising that the Corp. Fin. staff consistently allows retailers to omit proposals that address their product menu. For example, it has indicated that a proposal trying to stop a retailer from selling or promoting products that connote negative stereotypes is excludable. *See, e.g., Federated Dep't Stores, Inc.,* SEC No-Action Letter, 2002 WL 975596, at *13 (Mar. 27, 2002) (allowing the retailer to omit a proposal asking for a report on its "efforts to identify and disassociate from any offensive imagery to the American Indian community in products, adverting [*sic*], endorsements, sponsorships and promotions"). It has done the same for proposals aiming to restrict a retailer's promotion of products that pose a threat to public health, *see e.g., Wal-Mart Stores, Inc.,*SEC No-Action Letter, 2002 WL 833445, at *1 (Apr. 1, 2002) (agreeing with Wal-Mart that it could exclude a proposal asking it to explain "its rationale for not adopting in developing nations the same policies restricting the promotion and marketing of tobacco products as in the United States"); *Walgreen Co.,* SEC No-Action Letter, 2006 WL 5381376, at *1–2 (Oct. 13, 2006) (same for proposal asking for a report regarding "the extent to which the company's private label cosmetics and personal care product lines contain carcinogens, mutagens, reproductive toxicants, and chemicals that affect the endocrine system"), as well as those proposals targeting a retailer's approach to product safety. *See, e.g., Wal-Mart Stores, Inc.,* SEC No-Action Letter, 2008 WL 670182, at *1 (Mar. 11, 2008) (Wal-Mart may exclude a proposal requesting a "report on the company's policies on nanomaterial product safety"); *The Home Depot, Inc.,* SEC No-Action Letter, 2008 WL 257300, at *2 (allowing company to exclude a proposal encouraging it "to end its sale of glue traps because they are cruel and inhumane to the target animals and pose a danger to companion animals and wildlife"); *The Home Depot, Inc.,* SEC No-Action Letter, 2008 WL 257307, at *7 (same for proposal asking for an "evaluation of company policies and practices relating to product safety").

For further support of the view that a policy issue does not transcend a company's ordinary business operations where it targets day-to-day decision-making, we look to the difference in treatment of stop-selling proposals sent to retailers and those sent to pure-play manufacturers. A policy matter relating to a product is far more likely to transcend a company's ordinary business operations when the product is that of a manufacturer with a narrow line. Here the staff often will decline a no-action request. *See, e.g., Phillip Morris Companies, Inc.,* SEC No-Action Letter, 1990 WL 286063, at *1 (Feb. 22, 1990) (denying no-action relief as to proposal that requests the Board to amend the company's charter to provide that it "shall not conduct any business in tobacco or tobacco products"); *Sturm, Ruger & Co., Inc.,* SEC No-Action Letter, 2001 WL 258493, at *1 (Mar. 5, 2001) (same where proposal asks the Board to provide a report on company policies and procedures focused on reducing gun violence in the United States).

But the outcome changes where those same policy proposals are directed at retailers who sell thousands of products. *See Wal-Mart Stores, Inc.,* SEC No-Action Letter, 2001 WL 253625, at *6 (Mar. 9, 2001) (allowing Wal-Mart to exclude a proposal aimed at stopping its sale of handguns and accompanying ammunition[ ] in any way (e.g. by special order)" because it relates to "Wal-Mart's ordinary business operations (i.e., the sale of a particular product)"); *see also Rite Aid Corp.,* SEC No-Action Letter, 2009 WL 829472, at *1 (Mar. 26, 2009) (same for proposal asking for a report on the company's response "to rising regulatory, competitive and public pressures to halt sales of tobacco products"); *Walgreen Co.,* SEC No-Action Letter, 1997 WL 599903, at *1 (Sept. 29, 1997) (same for proposal requesting that Walgreen stop the sale of tobacco in its stores, as it "is directed at matters relating to the conduct of the Company's ordinary business operations (i.e., the sale of a particular product)").

The reason for the difference, in our view, is that a manufacturer with a very narrow product focus—like a tobacco or gun manufacturer—exists principally to sell the product it manufactures. Its daily business deliberations do not involve whether to continue to sell the product to which it owes its reason for being. As such, a stop-selling proposal generally isn't excludable because it relates to the seller's very existence. Quite the contrary for retailers. They typically deal with thousands of products amid many options for each, precisely the sort of business decisions a retailer makes many times daily. Thus, and in contrast to the manufacturing context, a stop-selling proposal implicates a retailer's ordinary business operations and is in turn excludable. Although Trinity's proposal is not strictly a stop-selling proposal, it still targets the same basic business decision: how to weigh safety risks in the merchandising calculus.

Trinity's claim that its proposal raises a "significant" and "transcendent" *corporate* policy is likewise insufficient to fit that proposal within the social-policy exception to exclusion. *See* Trinity Br. 47. The relevant question to us is whether Wal-Mart's consideration of the risk that certain products pose to its "economic success" and "reputation for good corporate citizenship" is enmeshed with the way it runs its business and the retailer-consumer interaction. We think the answer is yes. Decisions relating to what products Wal-Mart sells in its rural locations versus its urban sites will vary considerably, and these are quintessentially calls made by management. Wal-Mart serves different Americas with different values. Its customers in rural America want different products than its customers in cities, and that management decides how to deal with these differing desires is not an issue typical for its Board of Directors. Indeed, catering to "small-town America" is how Wal-Mart built its business. *See* Sam Walton, SAM WALTON: MADE IN AMERICA 50 (1993) ("It turned out that the first big lesson we learned was that there was much, much more business out there in small-town America than anybody, including me, had ever dreamed of."). And whether to put emphasis on brand integrity and brand protection, or none at all, is naturally a decision shareholders as well as directors entrust management to make in the exercise of their experience and business judgment.

We also agree with Wal-Mart's contention (and seemingly the position of the Corp. Fin. staff) that a company can omit a shareholder proposal concerning its reputation or brand when what the proposal seeks is woven with the way the company conducts its business. *Cf. FedEx Corp.*, SEC No-Action Letter, 2014 WL 2358714, at *1 (July 11, 2014) (allowing FedEx to omit a proposal that asked for a report addressing how the company "can better respond to reputational damage from its association with the Washington D.C. NFL franchise team name controversy" because it "relates to the manner in which FedEx advertises its products and services"); *see also Equity Lifestyle Props., Inc.*, SEC No-Action Letter, 2012 WL 6723114, at *1 (Feb. 6, 2013) (same for proposal asking the Board to prepare a report on, among other things, "the reputational risks associated with the setting of unfair, inequitable and excessive rent increases that cause undue hardship to older homeowners on fixed incomes," as "the setting of prices for products and services is fundamental to management's ability to run a company on a day-to-day basis"); *Bank of America Corp.*, SEC No-Action Letter, 2010 WL 4922465, at *1 (Feb. 24, 2010) (same for proposal asking Bank of America's Board to publish a report describing the bank's policy regarding the "funding of companies engaged predominantly in mountain top removal coal mining and an assessment of the policy's efficacy in reducing [greenhouse gas] emissions and in protecting [its] reputation," as it "addresses matters beyond the environmental impact of [its] project finance decisions, such as [its] decisions to extend credit or provide other financial services to particular types of customers"); *Dean Foods Co.*, SEC No-Action Letter, 2007 WL 754960, at *1 (Mar. 9, 2007) (same for proposal requesting that an independent committee of the Board "review the company's policies and procedures for its organic dairy products and report to shareholders on the adequacy of the policies and procedures to protect the company's brands and reputation and address consumer and media criticism," because this concerns the company's "ordinary business operations (i.e., customer relations and decisions relating to supplier relationships)").

We thus hold that, even if Trinity's proposal raises sufficiently significant social and corporate policy issues, those policies do not transcend the ordinary business operations of Wal-Mart. For a policy issue here to transcend Wal-Mart's business operations, it must target something more than the choosing of one among tens of thousands of products it sells. Trinity's proposal fails that test and is properly excludable under Rule 14a-8(i)(7).

V. CONCLUSION

Although a core business of courts is to interpret statutes and rules, our job is made difficult where agencies, after notice and comment, have hard-to-define exclusions to their rules and exceptions to those exclusions. For those who labor with the ordinary business exclusion and a social-policy exception that requires not only significance but "transcendence," we empathize. Despite the substantial uptick in proposals attempting to raise social policy issues that bat down the business operations bar, the SEC's last word on the subject came in the 1990s, and we have no hint that any change from it or Congress is forthcoming. As one former SEC commissioner has opined, "it is neither fair nor reasonable to expect securities experts [like the Commission and its staff] to deduce the prevailing wind on public policy issues that have yet to be addressed by Congress in any decisive fashion." *Commissioner Criticizes Subjectivity, Inconsistency in SEC Review of Proposals*, BNA Corp. Couns. Wkly., 2–3 (Mar. 31, 1993) (quoting remarks of Comm. Richard Y. Roberts). That remains true today.

We have no doubt that the Commission is equipped to collect "relevant data and views regarding the best direction for its regulatory policy." Nagy at 993. We thus suggest that it consider revising its regulation of proxy contests and issue fresh interpretive guidance. In the meantime, we hold here that Trinity's proposal is excludable from Wal-Mart's proxy materials under Rule 14a-8(i)(7).

Schwartz, Circuit Judge, with whom Judge Vanaskieto Part III, concurring in the judgment.

I agree with the Majority that Wal-Mart may omit Trinity's proposal from the company's proxy materials. I write separately, however, for two reasons. First, while I agree with my colleagues that the proposal is excludable based on the ordinary business exclusion, I believe that the test that it has fashioned for determining when an exception to this exclusion applies may remove many company actions over which shareholders should have a say from shareholder oversight. Second, I write to explain that both the ordinary business and the vagueness exclusions support exclusion of the entire proposal.

Comments and Questions

1. Assuming the matter in this case involves the "ordinary business" of Wal-Mart, is it really an example of "clever drafting"? State law does not prohibit advisory proposals, even if involving day to day business. Should the exclusion prohibit what is permitted under state law?

2. In applying the exclusion at issue in this case, a company must first establish that the proposal would address the company's "ordinary business." In this case, while the substance of the proposal overlaps with the company's ordinary business, it did not actually propose any changes. Instead, the proposal essentially asked the board to study and consider the matter. Does a proposal requesting board consideration of an issue fall within a company's "ordinary business"? Make the case each way.

3. The court agreed that the proposal involved matters of "sufficiently significant policy." Nonetheless, the proposal also had to "transcend" the ordinary business of the company. The court interpreted this term to mean that the policy issue must be "divorced from how a company approaches the nitty-gritty of its core business." What are the implications of this approach? Does the analysis address some of the same concerns that arose in the context of the back and forth in *Cracker Barrel*?

4. The staff of the Commission ultimately issued guidance with respect to this case. The staff found that the test adopted by the majority opinion "differs from the Commission's statements on the ordinary business exclusion and Division practice." Staff Legal Bulletin No. 14H(CF) (Oct. 22, 2015). Moreover, "we are concerned that the new analytical approach introduced by the Third Circuit goes beyond the Commission's prior statements and may lead to the unwarranted exclusion of shareholder proposals." As a result, "[t]he Division intends to continue to apply Rule 14a-8(i)(7) as articulated by the Commission and consistent with the Division's prior application of the exclusion, as endorsed by the concurring judge, when considering no-action requests that raise Rule 14a-8(i)(7) as a basis for exclusion." What impact will this have on the use of the exclusion?

IV. The Mechanics of Voting

The voting process, particularly for public companies, is remarkably complex. The process involves three separate regulators: states, the NYSE, and the Securities and Exchange Commission. In addition, the regulatory system varies depending upon whether the shares are titled in the investor's name or in a street name account. If held in a street name account, it matters if the intermediary is a bank or a broker.

A. The Problem of Beneficial Ownership

The system of voting starts with state law. State law places voting rights in the hands of record owners, those owners appearing on the company's stock ledger. With some exceptions, state law generally restricts other substantive rights — such as voting and appraisal rights — to record owners. *But see* 8 Del. C. § 220 (extending inspection rights to beneficial owners).

The problem with reliance on record ownership is that, in public companies, most owners no longer hold title as record owners. Investors increasingly rely on street name accounts, retaining the economic attributes of the shares but leaving title in the name of their broker or bank. Brokers and banks in turn typically place the shares in a depository for safekeeping. It is the depository that appears as the owner on the list of shareholders. Moreover, this form of ownership has become very common, with more than half of the shares in the largest public companies held through depositories. This structure adds enormous complexity to the voting process.

Crown EMAK Partners, LLC v. Kurz

Delaware Supreme Court
992 A.2d 377 (2010)

HOLLAND, JUSTICE:

Prior to December 18, 2009, the Board [of EMAK Worldwide, Inc.] had six directors and one vacancy. On December 18, one director resigned, creating a second vacancy. The plaintiffs-appellees contend that on December 20 and 21, Take Back EMAK LLC ("TBE") delivered sufficient consents (the "TBE Consents") to remove two additional directors without cause, and fill three of the resulting vacancies with Philip Kleweno, Michael Konig, and Lloyd Sems. Incumbent director Donald A. Kurz ("Kurz") is a member of TBE. If valid, the TBE Consents would establish a new Board majority.

* * *

DTC's And Broadridge's Roles in TBE Consent Solicitation

TBE conducted a broad-based solicitation in which it sought to obtain consents from a large number of individual EMAK stockholders. Since EMAK's shares were publicly traded for fourteen years, a significant number of EMAK stockholders owned their shares in "street name." This practice is summarized in a leading treatise:

> The vast majority of publicly traded shares in the United States are registered on the companies' books not in the name of beneficial owners—*i.e.*, those investors who paid for, and have the right to vote and dispose of, the shares— but rather in the name of "Cede & Co.," the name used by The Depository Trust Company ("DTC").

> Shares registered in this manner are commonly referred to as being held in "street name." ... DTC holds the shares on behalf of banks and brokers, which in turn hold on behalf of their clients (who are the underlying beneficial owners or other intermediaries).

The roles of DTC and the Investor Communications Solutions Division of Broadridge Financial Services, Inc. ("Broadridge") are important in this case. Broadridge's role has been summarized as follows:

> For many years, banks and brokers maintained their own proxy departments to handle the back-office administrative processes of distributing proxy materials and tabulating voting instructions from their clients. Today, however, the overwhelming majority have eliminated their proxy departments and subcontracted these processes out to [Broadridge]. For many years, these proxy processing services were provided by Automatic Data Processing, Inc. ("ADP"), but on March 31, 2007, ADP spun off its Brokerage Services Group into a new independent company, Broadridge, which now provides these services to most banks and brokers.

> To make these arrangements work, Broadridge's bank and broker clients formally transfer to Broadridge the proxy authority they receive from DTC (via the [DTC] Omnibus Proxy) via written powers of attorney. On behalf of the brokers and banks, Broadridge delivers directly to each beneficial owner a proxy statement and, importantly, a voting instruction form (referred to as a "VIF") rather than a proxy card. Beneficial owners do not receive proxy cards because they are not vested with the right to vote shares or to grant proxy authority—those rights belong only to the legal owners (or their designees). Beneficial owners merely have the right to instruct how their shares

are to be voted by Broadridge (attorney-in-fact of the DTC participants), which they accomplish by returning a VIF.

DTC is generally regarded as the entity having the power under Delaware law to vote the shares that it holds on deposit for the banks and brokers who are members of DTC. Through the DTC omnibus proxy, DTC transfers its voting authority to those member banks and brokers. The banks and brokers then transfer the voting authority to Broadridge, which votes the shares held at DTC by each bank and broker in proportion to the aggregate voting instructions received from the ultimate beneficial owners.

For the TBE Consent Solicitation, Broadridge collected, recorded, and totaled the voting instructions it received from the beneficial owners of EMAK shares held in street name. There is no dispute that the banks and brokers properly authorized Broadridge to vote the EMAK shares held on their behalf by DTC.

What no one ever obtained, and what DTC never provided, was the DTC omnibus proxy. The evidence conflicts as to who had the responsibility to get the DTC omnibus proxy. The Court of Chancery found that neither party clearly had the obligation to secure the DTC omnibus proxy, although both could have done more, neither acted improperly or inequitably with respect to this aspect of the case.

* * *

Court of Chancery Redefines Stock Ledger

The statutory mandate in section 219(c) provides that only stockholders of record who appear on the stock ledger can vote. Therefore, the Court of Chancery continued its analysis by considering whether the Cede breakdown should be part of the stock ledger for purposes of Section 219(c). It concluded:

> There is a straightforward basis for doing so, namely our law's long recognition that the Cede breakdown is part of the stock ledger for purposes of Section 220(b). If the Cede breakdown is part of the stock ledger, then the banks and brokers who appear on the Cede breakdown have the power to vote as record holders at a meeting of stockholders or for purposes of taking action by written consent.

The history of the depository system is set forth on DTC's website. The holding of securities through DTC has significance under Delaware law because it is Cede, not the DTC-participant banks and brokers, that appears on the stock ledger of a Delaware corporation. The Court of Chancery noted that Cede is typically the largest record holder on the stock ledger of most publicly traded Delaware corporations. Under Delaware law, only stockholders who appear on the stock ledger have authority to vote at a meeting or express consent.

The DTC omnibus proxy currently serves as the mechanism by which the federally mandated depository system of indirect ownership through DTC comports with Delaware's system of direct ownership evidenced through the stock ledger. The DTC omnibus proxy operates to ensure the transfer of DTC's voting authority to the participant members. As one treatise explains: "Because DTC has no beneficial interest in its shares..., it has devised a mechanism to pass on its voting rights. This mechanism, called the 'omnibus proxy,' provides for the transfer of DTC's voting right to its clients—the bank and broker participants."

The record reflects that DTC issues the omnibus proxy as a matter of course during the interactions between issuers and DTC that are compelled by the federal securities laws. When preparing for a meeting of stockholders or a consent solicitation, issuers are required by federal law to go through DTC to identify the participant banks and brokers for purposes of distributing voting cards and solicitation materials. An issuer typically starts the process by requesting a Cede breakdown so that it can send out the broker search cards. When the entire process is complete, the issuer provides each bank and broker with sufficient copies of the proxy statement, card, and other materials for distribution to the beneficial owners.

The Court of Chancery acknowledged that under section 219(c) it is the "stock ledger" that determines who are the record holders. It concluded, however, that the Cede breakdown should be considered "part of the stock ledger for purposes of Section 219(c), just as the Cede breakdown has long been part of the stock ledger for purposes of Section 220(b)." The Court of Chancery recognized that its new interpretation "represents a change in how Delaware practitioners understand the stock ledger for purposes of voting...." In fact, based upon prior Delaware precedents, the Court of Chancery acknowledged that its own initial view was that the absence of a DTC omnibus proxy would be dispositive.

The Court of Chancery noted that the DTC system usually works well. The record reflects that the DTC omnibus proxy is routinely obtained and simply becomes another item on a preparation checklist. In this case, the absence of a DTC omnibus proxy did not result from a breakdown in the DTC system. The failure in this case was attributable to human oversight on someone's party [sic] by not making a proper and timely request. The Court of Chancery concluded that insisting on the DTC omnibus proxy would disenfranchise the beneficial owners. To avoid that result it decided that Delaware law would benefit "from treating the Cede breakdown as part of the stock ledger for purposes of Section 219(c)."

The parties have extensively briefed and argued both sides of the issue of whether the Cede breakdown is (or is not) part of the "stock ledger" for section 219 purposes. Given our ruling invalidating the votes attributable to the Boutros shares, it is unnecessary for this Court to decide that issue, because a decision either way would not alter the result we have reached nor would a gratuitous statutory interpretation resolving this difficult issue be prudent. The human failures that occurred in this case are easily avoidable in the future and may be a one-time anomaly that may not again occur.

Moreover, and in any event, a legislative cure is preferable. The DGCL is a comprehensive and carefully crafted statutory scheme that is periodically reviewed by the General Assembly. Indeed, the General Assembly made coordinated amendments to section 219 and section 220 in 2003. Any adjustment to the intricate scheme of which section 219 is but a part should be accomplished by the General Assembly through a coordinated amendment process. Therefore, the Court of Chancery's interpretation of stock ledger in section 219 is *obiter dictum* and without precedential effect.

Comments and Questions

1. The case sets out the system for voting by street name owners. How does it work? How many layers exist in the system? Does the company actually know the identity of its street name owners?

2. What is the role of the omnibus proxy? Since Cede has the voting rights under state law, why does it give them away to the brokers and banks? To the extent that Cede lacks any economic interest in the shares, cannot the same be said of brokers and banks that deposit the shares in Cede?

3. Brokers and banks must forward proxy materials to street name owners. The forwarding system is not free. Companies must reimburse intermediaries for the expenses associated with the process. *See* NYSE Rule 451 (requiring members to forward materials so long as they receive "satisfactory assurance" of payment of expenses). This can, therefore, add substantial cost to the proxy distribution process.

4. Brokers and banks must send to street name owners either a proxy card or voting instructions. What difference does it make? Why would intermediaries such as brokers favor one approach over the other? What would be the consequence of distributing to street name owners a proxy card rather than voting instructions?

5. What role does Broadridge play in the process? Most brokers and banks outsource the proxy distribution process to Broadridge. *See* Concept Release on the U.S. Proxy System, Exchange Act Release No. 62495 n. 57 (July 14, 2010) (noting that with respect to the distribution of proxy materials and the collection of voting instructions, Broadridge "currently handles over 98% of the U.S. market for such proxy vote processing services."). Why do you think this is the case? What additional complexity does the reliance on Broadridge add to the voting process?

6. Who ought to have the authority to designate the intermediary, the broker or the issuer? What difference would it make?

7. Issuers communicate with street name account holders without knowing their identity. Under the Shareholder Communication Rules, companies can obtain a list of street name owners who do not object to the disclosure of their identity (non-objecting beneficial owners or NOBOs). There are innumerable problems with these rules, not the least of which is that large numbers of street name owners routinely object to disclosure. Most designate themselves as NOBOs. *See Roundtable Discussion on Proxy Voting, Securities and Exchange Commission*, Thursday, May 24, 2007 (Statement by Cathy Kinney, President and COO of NYSE Euronext). Calls for reform have arisen. How might the system be reformed? What are some possible objections?

8. The system also has implications under state law. In some cases, state law rights inure to the benefit of record owners. For example, appraisal rights apply to a record owner who "continuously holds such shares through the effective date of the merger".

DGCL 262(a). What happens if the shareholder has the shares in a street name account and, before the effective date, the shares are transferred to a different depository? Does the street name owner lose his or her appraisal rights? The answer, at least according to one court, can be found in In re Appraisal of Dell Inc., CA no. 9322-VCL (Del. Ch. July 30, 2015).

———————

Street name owners receive proxy materials and voting instructions from the broker where they have an account. Voting instructions in turn have to be returned to the broker, tabulated, and sent to the company. This has, according to some, resulted in a "nightmare of verification." *See* Marcel Kahan & Edward Rock, *The Hanging Chads of Corporate Voting*, 96 Geo. L.J. 1227, 1255 (2008).

Concept Release on the U.S. Proxy System
Exchange Act Release No. 62495 (July 14, 2010)

... [B]eneficial owners cast their votes through a securities intermediary, which, in turn, uses a proxy service provider to collect and send the votes to the vote tabulator. Beneficial owners, particularly institutional investors, often want or need to confirm that their votes have been timely received by the vote tabulator and accurately recorded. Similarly, securities intermediaries want to be able to confirm to their customers that their votes have been timely received and accurately recorded. Issuers also want to be able to confirm that the votes that they receive from securities intermediaries on behalf of beneficial owners properly reflect the votes of those beneficial owners. We understand that, on occasion, errors have been made when a third party fails to timely submit votes on behalf of its clients.

The inability to confirm voting information is caused in part because no one individual participant in the voting process—neither issuers, transfer agents, vote tabulators, securities intermediaries, nor third party proxy service providers—possesses all of the information necessary to confirm whether a particular beneficial owner's vote has been timely received and accurately recorded. A number of market participants contend that some proxy service providers, transfer agents, or vote tabulators are unwilling or unable to share voting information with each other or with investors and securities intermediaries. There are currently no legal or regulatory requirements that compel these entities to share information with each other in order to allow for vote confirmations.

The inability to confirm that votes have been timely received and accurately recorded creates uncertainty regarding the accuracy and integrity of votes cast at shareholder meetings. At a time when votes on matters presented to shareholders are increasingly meaningful and consequential to all shareholders, this lack of transparency could potentially impair confidence in the proxy system. Because of the inability to ascertain the integrity of the votes cast by beneficial owners, concerns have been raised by investors that it may be difficult to assess the accuracy of the current proxy system as a whole.

Comments and Questions

1. What are the consequences of this nightmare? *See* Marcel Kahan & Edward Rock, *The Hanging Chads of Corporate Voting*, 96 Geo. L.J. 1227, 1253 (2008) ("The verification nightmare suggests that there may well be discrepancies—sometimes significant ones—between the ballots cast and the voting instructions given by the beneficial holders.").

2. How might a non-vote affect the approval process under state law? What are some examples of approval requirements in which a non-vote is the same as a no-vote? Does this apply to the election of directors?

3. Are these rules enforceable? To the extent that proxy materials arrive late (or not at all), is there any effective recourse? How, for example, would the company or an insurgent know?

4. What issues might arise in the context of the distribution of voting instructions? In *Larkin v. Baltimore Bancorp*, 769 F. Supp. 919 (D. Md. 1991), the court dealt with voting instructions that varied from the actual language on the proxy card. Because of the ambiguity of the language in the voting instructions, the court ordered a new election.

5. There have been some well publicized examples of mistaken tallies in connection with shareholder elections. In 2008, the CEO and founder of Yahoo, Jerry Yang, was targeted in a withhold campaign. Initial reports revealed that 15% of the shares had been withheld. Eventually, it was reported that in fact 34% of the shares had been withheld. The difference was explained as a "tabulation error." While the mistake did not affect the outcome of the election, it did show substantially greater opposition to the CEO. Yang stepped down as CEO later in the year.

B. The Problem of Overvoting

Other complexities and problems exist with respect to the system of voting street name shares. A critical concern involves the problem of overvoting. This occurs when a broker or bank submits a proxy card to the inspector of election for more shares than it is authorized to vote. One consequence may be the disqualification of the entire proxy, effectively disenfranchising all of the street name owners who properly instructed their shares.

Seidman and Associates, L.L.C v. G.A. Financial, Inc.

Delaware Chancery Court
837 A.2d 21 (2003)

LAMB, VICE CHANCELLOR:

The plaintiffs in this case mounted a proxy contest to unseat the chairman of the board of directors of a publicly held Delaware corporation at its 2003 annual meeting. The outcome of the election was close, but the independent inspector of elections preliminarily reported that the insurgents' candidate lost by over 190,000 votes. In reaching that conclusion, the inspector disqualified two proxy cards submitted by a bank representing a total of 232,376 shares after concluding that those proxy cards represented an overvote of the bank's position. Although 203,800 of those shares were voted in favor of the insurgent, 29,400 were voted in favor of the incumbent. Thus, the exclusion of those cards did not affect the outcome of the election.

In this lawsuit, the insurgents argue that the inspector of elections improperly defined the "overvote" at issue by excluding all of the shares covered by two other "omnibus" proxies given by the same bank in favor of two other banks holding shares as fiduciaries for several company-sponsored employee compensation plans. According to the insurgents, the inspector of elections should have defined the "overvote" to include all of the proxies given by the first bank because (they say) the inspector was never able to obtain adequate reliable information to form a judgment as to the validity of any of the proxies. Thus, the insurgents argue for the exclusion of all 859,430 shares voted either by the first bank or pursuant to the authority transferred in its omnibus proxies. If all of those votes are disregarded, the insurgent nominee will have gained a plurality of the votes cast and will have been elected.

The issues presented are whether the inspector of elections properly discharged its duties in defining the "overvote" in a way that disqualified some but not all of the proxy cards given by the first bank. If the answer to that question is "no," the court must then determine whether it may now take note of the facts adduced in discovery in this matter to validate the proxy cards reflecting the votes of the employee participants in those company-sponsored plans since the record shows that those proxy cards voted exactly the right number of shares.

* * *

Before the Annual Meeting, GAF [a Delaware corporation] appointed Corporate Election Services, Inc. ("CES") to serve as the inspector of elections for the Annual Meeting. In correspondence with GAF, CES described, *inter alia*, the procedures it would follow in the case of an "overvote," as follows:

> If overvoting occurs, we will attempt to resolve the overvotes. If we are unable to contact the appropriate bank or broker, we will duly note the overvote and our treatment. In all ambiguous or unresolved cases, we will look to both sides for a mutually agreed upon resolution. Lacking this resolution, we will exclude the overvote from the tabulation, but note it in the certification.

In addition, GAF retained Georgesen Shareholder Communications, Inc. and the Committee retained D. F. King & Co., Inc. to serve as their respective proxy solicitors.

B. The Overvote

On or about April 23, 2003, CES issued its Preliminary Tabulation of the votes cast at the Annual Meeting, reporting the vote with respect to the contested board seat, as follows:

Kish   2,117,179 votes
Seidman   1,926,903 votes

In conjunction with the issuance of the Preliminary Tabulation, CES issued an Overvote Report disclosing a voting discrepancy attributable to The Bank of New York ("BONY") position. According to that report, CES preliminarily determined that two proxies given by BONY to Automated Data Processing ("ADP") (which acts as agent for many banks and brokers in connection with proxy solicitations), attempting to vote 233,376 shares, overvoted the BONY position by 824 shares. Because CES had been unable to resolve the overvote issue in its communications with ADP and BONY, it invalidated those two proxies.

When it issued its Overvote Report, CES knew the following information about the source of the overvote.

- Cede & Co., the nominee name of the Depository Trust Company ("DTC"), was the record holder of 4,422,673 shares of GAF common stock as of the Record Date.

- In connection with the Annual Meeting, Cede issued an "omnibus" proxy in favor of BONY for 859,647 shares of GAF common stock, reflecting BONY's entire Record Date position at DTC. This proxy is dated as of the Record Date. This "omnibus" proxy was executed for the purpose of granting to BONY voting power over that number of shares.

- BONY in turn executed (and CES received) two further "omnibus proxies" in favor of two other banks, First Bankers Trust Company and First Bank of Clayton (Missouri). These proxies were for 625,771 shares and 1,500 shares, respectively, and were also dated as of the Record Date, although the Stipulated Record describes them as having been issued "prior to the closing of the polls."

- BONY also "voted" 233,200 shares through two proxies submitted through ADP, splitting the "vote" 203,800 for Seidman and 29,400 for Kish.

- CES held two other proxies that bore on the issue. First was a proxy given by First Bankers Trust voting only 625,554 of the shares covered by the omnibus proxy given by BONY in its favor. The second was a proxy given by First Bank of Clayton (Missouri) voting all of the 1,500 shares covered by the omnibus proxy given by BONY in its favor.

Before issuing its Overvote Report, CES took certain measures to resolve the overvote. On April 23, 2003, CES contacted the proxy clerk at ADP and explained that there was an overvote. That clerk stated that he would contact BONY and get back to CES. On April 28, 2003, the proxy clerk at ADP reported that BONY was unable to ascertain the reason or reasons for the overvote and suggested that CES contact BONY directly. CES contacted a representative of BONY the same day. According to the Stipulated Record, the BONY representative "acknowledged the issuance of" the two omnibus proxies in favor of the two banks and reported that "she had checked her system, the votes looked fine, she could not see any obvious overvote and would have to further research the issue." CES informed her that "a review and challenge session was scheduled for May 2, 2003 and she was asked to contact CES if she discovered anything with respect to the overvote." This BONY representative did not further contact CES.

Before the May 2, 2003 review and challenge session, CES remained in contact with ADP and BONY but was unable to resolve the overvote. CES reported these facts to the parties. CES did not contact First Bankers Trust (or, presumably, the First Bank of Clayton) to ascertain or verify the number of shares in its position. At the May 2, 2003 challenge session, based on the information it then knew, CES determined to include the 625,554 votes cast by First Bankers Trust through ADP and the 1,500 votes cast by First Bank of Clayton through ADP and determined that First Bankers Trust had voted 217 fewer shares than it was authorized to vote pursuant to BONY's 625,771 share Omnibus Proxy. CES also determined to disqualify the 233,376 shares voted by BONY on the two proxy cards it gave to ADP, based on its view that the "overvote" was properly limited to those two cards. D.F. King, in its capacity as Seidman and Associates representative made a timely objection to this conclusion, arguing that "the entire BONY position should be disqualified, that it was improper to pick and choose [among] the BONY votes cast, and improper to 'carve-out' part of the vote, allowing some votes to stand and disqualify others."

* * *

In Delaware, "[a] stockholder's ability to participate in corporate governance through the election of directors is a fundamental part of our corporate law." Under our law, "there is a 'general policy against disenfranchisement.'" At the same time, Delaware law recognizes the need for certainty and finality in corporate elections, in order to avoid prolonged periods of turmoil. "The necessity for an expeditious conclusion of corporate elections that is consistent with the stockholders' franchise has resulted in the development of practical and certain rules."

The Delaware General Corporation Law directly addresses itself to the situation of an apparent overvote by a bank, broker or similar person. Section 231(d) clearly permitted the inspector of elections look beyond the proxies and the corporate records in an effort to reconcile that overvote:

> In determining the validity and counting of proxies and ballots, the inspectors shall be limited to an examination of the proxies, any envelopes submitted with those proxies, any information provided in accordance with § 211(e) or § 212(c) (2) of this title, or any information provided pursuant to § 211(a) (2) (B) (i) or (iii) of this title, ballots and the regular books and records of the corporation, *except that the inspectors may consider other reliable information for the limited purpose of reconciling proxies and ballots submitted by or on behalf of banks, brokers, their nominees or similar persons which represent more votes than the holder of a proxy is authorized by the record owner to cast or more votes than the stockholder holds of record.*

Section 231, adopted in 1990, codified the general rule of common law limiting the information that an inspector is permitted to review but carved out an exception for bank and broker overvotes. The Official Synopsis explains the changes to the common law as follows:

> Subsection (d) specifies the information the inspectors may consider in determining the validity and counting proxies and ballots. This subsection is intended to be a codification of pre-existing common law with two exceptions. *One change from the pre-existing common law is that inspectors are permitted to examine "reliable information" other than the proxies, ballots and books and records of the corporation, but only for the limited purpose of reconciling bank and broker "over votes" viz., proxies and ballots which represent more votes than the holder of the proxy is authorized by the record owner to cast or move votes than the stockholder holds of record....*

* * *

The first question presented on the record in this case is whether CES had a reasonable basis in fact upon which to conclude that the First Bankers Trust and First Bank of Clayton proxies were not part of the overvote. The court is satisfied that the information reported by BONY to CES provided a reasonable basis for CES's decision to limit the "overvote" issue to the 233,376 shares BONY attempted to vote. Because CES was not able to obtain reliable information to resolve that overvote, it properly excluded the two proxy cards reflecting those votes.

CES specifically inquired of BONY about both of the omnibus proxies given by BONY in favor of the other two banks. In both cases, according to the Stipulated Record, BONY specifically "acknowledged the issuance of" those omnibus proxies and reported that, after a check of BONY's system, "the votes looked fine." In the case of omnibus proxies, this is the sort of information that CES could ordinarily be expected to regard as reliable. Unlike a proxy card that purports to "vote" shares, an omnibus proxy merely creates a paper record of a transfer of voting power to another bank or broker down the chain of ownership or title. The single piece of relevant information was the number of shares held by that other bank or broker as of the Record Date. That information should have been readily obtainable by the BONY proxy clerk from a review of BONY's internal records. Thus, it was reasonable of CES to rely upon information from BONY verifying the accuracy of the omnibus proxies.

Further, there were no other circumstances present that should have caused CES to inquire further or demand documentary proof. In particular, the fact that First Bankers Trust appeared to have undervoted its position did not give cause for concern. In the case of proxy contests, banks and brokers are precluded from voting the shares they hold on behalf of others without explicit instructions. Thus, the fact that a position is undervoted would not be expected to raise a red flag in the mind of an inspector of elections. Undervotes are common and to be expected. They are ordinarily accepted without any need for inquiry. It is only overvotes that give rise to counting problems. Moreover, CES was able to observe that the 217 share discrepancy between the number of shares reported on the omnibus proxy given in favor of First Bankers Trust and the number of shares voted was *607 shares less than the total overvote ob-*

served. Thus, even if CES had had reason to question the reliability of the information received from BONY, it would not have had reason to conclude that there was anything wrong with either the 625,554 share proxy card or the 1,500 share proxy card given to ADP by First Bankers Trust and First Bank of Clayton, respectively. This is entirely consistent with the general policy of Delaware law favoring enfranchisement.

Comments and Questions

1. What does this case suggest about the discretion of the vote tabulators when it comes to problems such as overvoting? Who typically appoints the tabulators?

2. How does overvoting even occur? Often the problem is clerical, a mistake in the broker's record keeping system. The problem commonly arises in connection with the practice of share borrowing. Brokers will sometimes "lend" shares (the transaction is actually a sale) in a customer's account in return for a payment. It is sometimes the case that brokers give to both the lenders and borrowers voting rights over the same shares, effectively double counting the shares. In these circumstances, who actually ought to have the voting rights? For beneficial owners who discover that they do not have voting rights, Professors Kahan and Rock have called this the "securities lending surprise."

3. Can the system of share lending be manipulated? Could, for example, someone "borrow" shares on the record date and then return them the next day, yet still be in a position to influence the outcome of the vote of shareholders?

4. What do you make of the lending of shares? Ought the practice to be prohibited or regulated? Should lending shareholders be notified of any loan? How might lending/borrowing of shares influence the outcome of a proxy contest?

5. Is disqualification of the relevant proxy the only way to handle the overvoting problem? As the Securities and Exchange Commission described:

> some vote tabulators accept votes from a DTC participant on a "first-in" basis up to the aggregate amount indicated in DTC's records—that is, once the votes cast by the participant exceed the number of positions indicated on the securities position listing, the vote tabulator will refuse to accept any votes subsequently remitted. Conversely, other vote tabulators, we understand, refuse to accept any votes from a securities intermediary if the aggregate number of votes submitted exceeds the vote tabulator's records for that intermediary.

Exchange Act Release No. 62495 (July 14, 2010). In short, one problem is the lack of uniformity in resolving the problem. Which of these approaches is the most appropriate default rule?

6. The NYSE has called on brokers to "focus on the prevention of overvoting," *see* NYSE Information Memo 04-58, "Supervision of Proxy Activities and Over-voting" (Nov. 5, 2004), and sanctioned members for failing to adequately safeguard against over-voting. *See In re Deutsche Bank Securities Inc.*, Board of Directors, NYSE, Feb. 2, 2006 (noting the imposition of a fine of $1 million against member firm and noting that overvoting ranged from 31 shares to 4,488,662 shares). In effect, the allegation

is that the brokers failed to maintain adequate policies and procedures to ensure that overvoting did not occur. Would the problem be solved if brokers had better record keeping systems so that ownership of the shares was always clear?

C. The Problem of Uninstructed Shares

In providing street name owners with an opportunity to vote their shares, it is not uncommon for them to fail to return their instructions to the broker. Treated as record owners under state law (assuming DTC executes an omnibus proxy), the brokers have the right to vote the uninstructed shares. By voting the shares, brokers ensure that the shares are present at the meeting, facilitating, for example, the company's ability to obtain a quorum.

The rules of the NYSE, however, impose limits on these voting rights. Brokers cannot vote shares on matters considered controversial. This includes, among other matters, those subject to a contest and "the authorization for a merger, consolidation of any matter which may affect substantially the rights and privileges of such stock." NYSE Rule 452.

Rule 452 has proved to be a controversial provision. Until recently, it allowed brokers to vote these shares in uncontested elections for the board. In a system of plurality voting, this hardly mattered. In an era of majority voting, however, broker votes could be outcome determinative. Pressure therefore rose for changes to Rule 452 to prohibit brokers from voting uninstructed shares in all board elections, contested and uncontested.

Exchange Act Release No. 60215
(July 1, 2009)

The NYSE's discretionary voting rule dates back to 1937. Historically, the majority of shareholders held their shares directly as record holders. In 1976, for example, shareholders held approximately 71% of securities of record (in their own name), while only approximately 29% of securities were held by securities intermediaries in street name. The number of beneficial owners holding securities in street name, however, has increased significantly since 1976, with the result that securities intermediaries, on behalf of beneficial owners, now hold a substantial majority of exchange traded securities....

Under Rule 451, when a public company furnishes proxy materials to its record shareholders, securities intermediaries that hold securities in street name must deliver the proxy materials to the beneficial shareholders within a certain time frame and request voting instructions from the beneficial shareholders. If beneficial shareholders return voting instructions, the securities intermediaries vote their shares accordingly. However, if beneficial shareholders do not return voting instructions, securities intermediaries may, in certain situations, vote their shares at the intermediaries' discretion. Specifically, if voting instructions have not been received by the tenth day preceding the meeting date, under current NYSE Rule 452, brokers may vote on behalf of the beneficial shareholders on certain matters where there is no contest and the item does not include authorization for a merger, consolidation, or any matter which may substantially affect the rights or privileges of the stock. The rule also contains eighteen specific items on which the broker generally may not vote without instructions from the beneficial owner. Items where the broker can vote without instructions are referred to as "routine" matters. Among other matters, the "uncontested" election of directors is considered a "routine" matter under current NYSE Rule 452, and thus can be voted by the broker in its discretion if the beneficial owner has not returned voting instructions within the required time period.

With the large proportion of shares now held in street name, the impact of the broker vote on the election of directors has become increasingly significant. In the view of some commenters, brokers tend to vote in accordance with management's recommendation. According to the NYSE, in recent years its interpretation of a "contested election" has been questioned by a variety of persons, as an increasing number of proxy campaigns have targeted a formal contest. These campaigns generally do not involve a competing slate of directors or a formal counter-solicitation opposed by management, and hence, are not considered "contests" by the NYSE under NYSE Rule 452. Examples of these campaigns include "just vote no" or "withhold" campaigns, where one or more investors express dissatisfaction with the performance of the company or its management, and urge shareholders to withhold their votes for one or more of management's nominees for director. NYSE views director elections subject to these campaigns as eligible for broker discretionary voting under current Rule 452. Concerns have been expressed that, in certain "just vote no" or "withhold" campaigns, the broker vote for management has made the difference and allowed directors subject to these campaigns to be elected, which would not have happened but for NYSE's discretionary voting rule.

* * *

[T]he Commission believes that it is reasonable and consistent with the Act for NYSE to determine that the election of directors should no longer be an item eligible for broker discretionary voting, particularly given the large proportion of shares that today are held in street name, the importance of corporate governance and accountability expressed through the election process, and the concern that the broker vote could potentially distort election results....

* * *

The Commission acknowledges commenters' concerns regarding the potential for the proposed rule change to impact the ability of some companies to achieve quorum. For example, the Proxy Working Group recognized that smaller issuers may have certain increased costs in obtaining quorum due to the high percentage of shares held by retail investors. However, as noted by several commenters, issuers with a large institutional shareholder base or with another routine matter on their proxies, such as ratification of independent auditors, should not face material additional difficulties in achieving a quorum. The Commission notes that a majority of companies other than registered investment companies include the ratification of independent auditors as a matter for shareholders to approve, even though such approval is not required by law, so that these companies should not, as a practical matter, encounter the quorum issue as articulated by the commenters. Quorum concerns for other companies, including small companies, may be addressed to the extent that these companies include an item on their ballot that may be considered a routine matter. The Commission also notes a report showing that, if NYSE's proposal were implemented, most companies would nevertheless achieve quorum, albeit at a date closer to their annual meetings than previously. More fundamentally, however, although issuers may incur increased proxy solicitation costs under the NYSE's proposal, the Commission agrees with the NYSE and the Proxy Working Group that these costs are justified by, among other things, assuring voting on matters as critical as the election of directors can no longer be determined by brokers without instructions from the beneficial owner, thereby enhancing corporate governance and accountability.

* * *

With regard to the concern that proxy advisory firm recommendations could have increased influence on director elections, the Commission notes that issues relating to the use of proxy advisory services by institutions and others, and whether that use should be further regulated, is a matter that will be considered by the Commission as it examines broader proxy issues. It is not, however, germane to, and does not need to be resolved to approve, the NYSE's proposal. While the Commission acknowledges the possibility that, with the elimination of the broker vote, the vote of institutions or others that use proxy advisory services may, at least in the short term, represent a larger percentage of the votes returned in director elections, the Commission believes the goals of the NYSE's proposal, as described above, are consistent with Section 6(b) (5) of the Act in that the proposal should protect investors and the public interest by barring brokers from voting on behalf of investors in uncontested elections of directors when they have no economic interest in the corporation or the outcome. The Commission further notes that institutional investors, whether relying on proxy advisory firms or not, must vote the institutions' own shares and, in so doing, must discharge their fiduciary duties to act in the best interest of their investors and avoid conflicts of interest; institutions are not relieved of their fiduciary responsibilities simply by following the recommendations of a proxy advisor.

* * *

Several commenters believed that companies employing a majority vote standard for director elections may have particular difficulty in obtaining majority support for director nominees were NYSE's proposal to be approved. Specifically, commenters noted that the elimination of broker discretionary voting, coupled with majority voting, would make it more difficult for these companies to obtain adequate votes to overcome a "vote no" campaign by activist shareholders, and thus would disproportionately empower minority shareholder groups. Two commenters suggested that the difficulty of obtaining a majority vote without broker discretionary voting might discourage issuers from adopting a majority vote standard.

According to an analysis submitted by one commenter, however, in calendar year 2007, NYSE-listed companies had majority vote standard for the election of directors. Analyzing the elections of those majority vote companies, the analysis found that only eight out of 2,718 directors received at least 50 percent withhold votes based on actual votes from returned proxy cards by shareholders, while six directors received at least 50 percent withhold votes using broker voting. Thus, according to the commenter, only two more directors out of 2,718 failed to receive a majority without broker votes.

Comments and Questions

1. One source estimated that approximately 19% of shares of publicly traded companies were discretionary votes under Rule 452. With this percentage in mind, what impact would this have on efforts to defeat directors under majority vote provisions? *See also* Exchange Act Release No. 60825 n. 18 (Oct. 14, 2009) (noting that percentage of "retail" shares held by beneficial owners that voted was 27.69% for those using Internet distribution of proxy materials and 31.8% for those sending hard copies of proxy materials).

2. Is a prohibition on voting the only way to handle the problem of uninstructed shares? What about requiring that the shares be voted for and against management in proportion to instructed shares? Is this a better solution than the one proposed by the NYSE and approved by the SEC?

3. What impact does this rule change have on majority voting provisions? Will they discourage companies, as some commentators suggested, from adopting them?

4. In fact, the role of uninstructed shares can be outcome determinative. In 2004, Michael Eisner, the CEO and Chairman of Disney, was subjected to a withhold campaign. Approximately 45% of the votes cast in the election for the director were withheld. Had the votes of discretionary shares cast by brokers been excluded, the percentage of withheld votes would have been a majority. *See Report and Recommendations of the Proxy Working Group to the New York Stock Exchange*, at 9 (June 5, 2006), *available at* http://www.nyse.com/pdfs/PWG_REPORT.pdf (noting that "[h]ad broker votes not counted in this election then Mr. Eisner would have received only 45% of the votes in favor of re-election, and a majority of the votes cast, 54%, would have been withheld from him.").

5. The Dodd-Frank Act provides the Commission with the authority to adopt rules in this area. *See* Section 957. Specifically, Section 6(b) of the Exchange Act was amended to require exchanges to prohibit members from voting uninstructed shares in connection with board elections, executive compensation matters, or "any other significant matter" determined by the Commission. What role does this give to the Commission in the shareholder voting process?

6. One objection to the prohibition on voting uninstructed shares in board elections is that companies will have a more difficult time obtaining a quorum. As the SEC release notes, one way to address the concern is to include an item on the meeting

agenda where this type of voting is permitted. The most obvious example is shareholder approval of the company's independent accounting firm. The right to approve the auditor is not mandated by state law. Nonetheless, approximately 90% of the companies in the S&P 500 and the Russell 3000 submit the matter to shareholders. The matter is rarely controversial and allows the uninstructed shares to be vote and, therefore, counted for quorum purposes.

7. What happens when a beneficial owner returns a partially executed voting instruction? The practice for at least some issuers is to treat the unmarked portions of the VIF as a vote consistent with the recommendations of management. What do you make of this practice? For a discussion of this issue, see Christie Nicks, *Voting Partially Instructed Shares by Brokers*, 91 Denv. U. L. Rev. Online 155 (2014).

8. VIFs are typically returned to Broadridge. Broadridge, therefore, is aware of interim results before they are reflected on a proxy card and provided to the issuer. Interim voting information can be strategically significant. Where a shareholder solicits proxies in a manner inconsistent with the interests of management (against directors in a "just say no" campaign, for example), who (if anyone) should be allowed to obtain this information? Why would either side seek the information?

D. The Problem of Empty Voting

Another problem has been the practice of "empty voting." Broadly speaking, this arises where the person voting the shares has no economic interest in the underlying securities. This can occur in a number of circumstances.

For example, the original owner may have sold the shares after the record date. Nonetheless, he or she retains the right to vote the shares. The issue can also arise in connection with borrowed shares (that can be voted at the meeting but will be "returned" to the lender) and the use of derivatives to essentially eliminate the economic risks associated with ownership. As the Commission described: "The term 'empty voting' has been defined to refer to the circumstance in which a shareholder's voting rights substantially exceed the shareholder's economic interest in the company." Concept Release on the U.S. Proxy System, Exchange Act Release No. 62495 (July 14, 2010). With voting rights detached from the underlying economic interests, owners may not have the same interests as other shareholders. *See* Henry T. C. Hu & Bernard Black, *Equity and Debt Decoupling and Empty Voting II: Importance and Extensions*, *156 U. Pa. L. Rev. 625* (2008).

Comments and Questions

1. What other circumstances give rise to empty voting? Almost any transaction that entirely eliminates the risk of ownership will likely qualify. In addition to traditional hedging techniques, insiders sometimes use collars for their shares (the simultaneous purchase of a put and sale of an option that limits trading risk to a predetermined range). Do these qualify as empty voting? Are there unique concerns associated with officers or directors engaging in empty voting?

2. This article looks at more complex forms of empty voting such as the use of derivatives to eliminate risk. Can you think of more common instances where this routinely occurs? What about any shareholder who purchases after the record date? The owner on the record date retains the voting rights under state law but has divested itself of the economic risk. How about brokers who vote uninstructed shares? Do the brokers share in any of the economic risk?

3. In some cases, the empty voter may even prefer that share prices fall rather than rise. *See* Concept Release on the U.S. Proxy System, Exchange Act Release No. 62495 (July 14, 2010) ("[A]n empty voter with a negative economic interest in the company may prefer that the company's share price fall rather than increase."). What problems does this cause with respect to shareholder behavior?

4. Is there any positive benefit to empty voting? What if informed shareholders acquired the voting (but not the economic) rights to shares of uninformed investors? What does this suggest about the problem of empty voting?

5. Under state law, courts allow for vote buying in certain circumstances. Is vote buying a form of "empty" voting? *See Crown Emak Partners LLC v. Kurz*, 992 A.2d 377 (Del. 2010). What about simply selling shares after the record date?

V. Shareholder Rights and Fiduciary Duties of the Board

The shareholder franchise can also be limited through otherwise legal actions by management. This may entail anything from the delay of a shareholder meeting to a change in the record date. Courts have struggled with these sorts of practices, particularly the standard of review.

A. Tampering with the Franchise

Blasius Industries, Inc. v. Atlas Corp.
Delaware Chancery Court
564 A.2d 651 (1988)

ALLEN, CHANCELLOR:

On December 30, 1987, Blasius [which owned 9.1% of Atlas] caused Cede & Co. (the registered owner of its Atlas stock) to deliver to Atlas a signed written consent (1) adopting a precatory resolution recommending that the board develop and implement a restructuring proposal, (2) amending the Atlas bylaws to, among other things, expand the size of the board from seven to fifteen members — the maximum number under Atlas' charter, and (3) electing eight named persons to fill the new directorships. Blasius also filed suit that day in this court seeking a declaration that certain bylaws adopted by the board on September 1, 1987 acted as an unlawful restraint on the shareholders' right, created by Section 228 of our corporation statute, to act through consent without undergoing a meeting.

The reaction was immediate. Mr. Weaver [the CEO of Atlas] conferred with Mr. Masinter, the Company's outside counsel and a director, who viewed the consent as an attempt to take control of the Company. They decided to call an emergency meeting of the board, even though a regularly scheduled meeting was to occur only one week hence, on January 6, 1988. The point of the emergency meeting was to act on their conclusion (or to seek to have the board act on their conclusion) "that we should add at least one and probably two directors to the board ..." ... A quorum of directors, however, could not be arranged for a telephone meeting that day. A telephone meeting was held the next day. At that meeting, the board voted to amend the bylaws to increase the size of the board from seven to nine and appointed John M. Devaney and Harry J. Winters, Jr. to fill those newly created positions. Atlas' Certificate of Incorporation creates staggered terms for directors; the terms to which Messrs. Devaney and Winters were appointed would expire in 1988 and 1990, respectively.

The Motivation of the Incumbent Board In Expanding the Board and Appointing New Members.

In increasing the size of Atlas' board by two and filling the newly created positions, the members of the board realized that they were thereby precluding the holders of a majority of the Company's shares from placing a majority of new directors on the board through Blasius' consent solicitation, should they want to do so. Indeed the evidence establishes that that was the principal motivation in so acting.

The conclusion that, in creating two new board positions on December 31 and electing Messrs. Devaney and Winters to fill those positions the board was principally motivated to prevent or delay the shareholders from possibly placing a majority of new members on the board, is critical to my analysis of the central issue posed by the first filed of the two pending cases. If the board in fact was not so motivated, but rather had taken action completely independently of the consent solicitation, which merely had an incidental impact upon the possible effectuation of any action authorized by the shareholders, it is very unlikely that such action would be subject to judicial nullification.... The board, as a general matter, is under no fiduciary obligation to suspend its active management of the firm while the consent solicitation process goes forward.

* * *

On balance, I cannot conclude that the board was acting out of a self-interested motive in any important respect on December 31. I conclude rather that the board saw the "threat" of the Blasius recapitalization proposal as posing vital policy differences between itself and Blasius. It acted, I conclude, in a good faith effort to protect its incumbency, not selfishly, but in order to thwart implementation of the recapitalization that it feared, reasonably, would cause great injury to the Company.

The real question the case presents, to my mind, is whether, in these circumstances, the board, even if it *is* acting with subjective good faith (which will typically, if not always, be a contestable or debatable judicial conclusion), may validly act for the principal purpose of preventing the shareholders from electing a majority of new directors. The question thus posed is not one of intentional wrong (or even negligence), but one of authority *as between the fiduciary and the beneficiary* (not simply legal authority, *i.e.*, as between the fiduciary and the world at large).

* * *

The shareholder franchise is the ideological underpinning upon which the legitimacy of directorial power rests. Generally, shareholders have only two protections against perceived inadequate business performance. They may sell their stock (which, if done in sufficient numbers, may so affect security prices as to create an incentive for altered managerial performance), or they may vote to replace incumbent board members.

It has, for a long time, been conventional to dismiss the stockholder vote as a vestige or ritual of little practical importance. It may be that we are now witnessing the emergence of new institutional voices and arrangements that will make the stockholder vote a less predictable affair than it has been. Be that as it may, however, whether the vote is seen functionally as an unimportant formalism, or as an important tool of discipline, it is clear that it is critical to the theory that legitimates the exercise of power by some (directors and officers) over vast aggregations of property that they do not own. Thus, when viewed from a broad, institutional perspective, it can be seen that matters involving the integrity of the shareholder voting process involve consideration not present in any other context in which directors exercise delegated power.

B. *Questions of this type raise issues of the allocation of authority as between the board and the shareholders.*

The distinctive nature of the shareholder franchise context also appears when the matter is viewed from a less generalized, doctrinal point of view. From this point of view, as well, it appears that the ordinary considerations to which the business judgment rule originally responded are simply not present in the shareholder voting context. That is, a decision by the board to act for the primary purpose of preventing the effectiveness of a shareholder vote inevitably involves the question who, as between the principal and the agent, has authority with respect to a matter of internal corporate governance. That, of course, is true in a very specific way in this case which deals with the question who should constitute the board of directors of the corporation, but it will be true in every instance in which an incumbent board seeks to thwart a shareholder majority. A board's decision to act to prevent the shareholders from creating a majority of new board positions and filling them does not involve the exercise of *the corporation's power* over its property, or with respect to *its* rights or obligations; rather, it involves allocation, between shareholders as a class and the board, of effective power with respect to governance of the corporation. This need not be the case with respect to other forms of corporate action that may have an entrenchment effect — such as the stock buybacks present in *Unocal, Cheff* or *Kors v. Carey*. Action designed principally to interfere with the effectiveness of a vote inevitably involves a conflict between the board and a shareholder majority. Judicial review of such action involves a determination of the legal and equitable obligations of an agent towards his principal.

This is not, in my opinion, a question that a court may leave to the agent finally to decide so long as he does so honestly and competently; that is, it may not be left to the agent's business judgment.

2. *What rule does apply: per se invalidity of corporate acts intended primarily to thwart effective exercise of the franchise or is there an intermediate standard?*

Plaintiff argues for a rule of *per se* invalidity once a plaintiff has established that a board has acted for the primary purpose of thwarting the exercise of a shareholder vote....

* * *

In two recent cases dealing with shareholder votes, this court struck down board acts done for the primary purpose of impeding the exercise of stockholder voting power. In doing so, a *per se* rule was not applied. Rather, it was said that, in such a case, the board bears the heavy burden of demonstrating a compelling justification for such action.

* * *

In my view, our inability to foresee now all of the future settings in which a board might, in good faith, paternalistically seek to thwart a shareholder vote, counsels against the adoption of a *per se* rule invalidating, in equity, every board action taken for the sole or primary purpose of thwarting a shareholder vote, even though I recognize the transcending significance of the franchise to the claims to legitimacy of our scheme of corporate governance. It may be that some set of facts would justify such extreme action. This, however, is not such a case.

3. *Defendants have demonstrated no sufficient justification for the action of December 31 which was intended to prevent an unaffiliated majority of shareholders from effectively exercising their right to elect eight new directors.*

The board was not faced with a coercive action taken by a powerful shareholder against the interests of a distinct shareholder constituency (such as a public minority). It was presented with a consent solicitation by a 9% shareholder. Moreover, here it had time (and understood that it had time) to inform the shareholders of its views on the merits of the proposal subject to stockholder vote. The only justification that can, in such a situation, be offered for the action taken is that the board knows better than do the shareholders what is in the corporation's best interest. While that premise is no doubt true for any number of matters, it is irrelevant (except insofar as the shareholders wish to be guided by the board's recommendation) when the question is who should comprise the board of directors. The theory of our corporation law confers power upon directors as the agents of the shareholders; it does not create Platonic masters. It may be that the Blasius restructuring proposal was or is unrealistic and would lead to injury to the corporation and its shareholders if pursued. Having heard the evidence, I am inclined to think it was not a sound proposal. The board certainly viewed it that way, and that view, held in good faith, entitled the board to take certain steps to evade the risk it perceived. It could, for example, expend corporate funds to inform shareholders and seek to bring them to a similar point of view....

But there is a vast difference between expending corporate funds to inform the electorate and exercising power for the primary purpose of foreclosing effective shareholder action. A majority of the shareholders, who were not dominated in any respect, could view the matter differently than did the board. If they do, or did, they are entitled to employ the mechanisms provided by the corporation law and the Atlas certificate of incorporation to advance that view. They are also entitled, in my opinion, to restrain their agents, the board, from acting for the principal purpose of thwarting that action.

I therefore conclude that, even finding the action taken was taken in good faith, it constituted an unintended violation of the duty of loyalty that the board owed to the shareholders. I note parenthetically that the concept of an unintended breach of the duty of loyalty is unusual but not novel.... That action will, therefore, be set aside by order of this court.

Comments and Questions

1. Could the board have taken the same actions at issue in this case in other circumstances without raising the concerns at issue in this case? Give some examples.

2. This case turns on motive. In expanding the size of the board and electing two additional directors, the board intended to prevent shareholders from electing a majority of directors. What interpretive issues can arise in connection with this standard?

3. "Commentators have attempted to rationalize the *Blasius* line of cases by arguing that when the board action interferes with imminent stockholder action it will be invalidated, but if the threat is not imminent and the action is not preclusive, it will survive." William J. Carney & George B. Shepherd, *The Mystery of the Success of Delaware Law: The Mystery of Delaware Law's Continuing Success*, 2009 U. Ill. L. Rev. 1, 43. Do you agree with this interpretation of *Blasius*? What can you see are some of the difficulties in implementing this test?

4. The court refused to adopt a *per se* rule prohibiting these practices and instead imposed on the board an obligation to show a "compelling justification" for any restriction on the franchise. Courts have called the standard "quite onerous." Is this the right outcome? What does it mean to show a compelling justification?

5. What are some other mechanisms within the board's authority that can be used to limit the franchise? What about changing the size of the board of directors? *See MM Cos. v. Liquid Audio, Inc.*, 813 A.2d 1118, 1132 (Del. 2003).

6. What about manipulating the record date? Delaware now allows (but does not require) companies to set one record date for the notice of the meeting and another for voting. Del. Code Ann. tit. 8, §213(a). How might a last minute change in the record date for voting influence the outcome of a shareholder vote?

7. Some have essentially asserted that *Blasius* does not go far enough. *See* Julian Velasco, *Taking Shareholder Rights Seriously*, 41 U.C. Davis L. Rev. 605, 658 (2007) ("In fact, it might make sense to extend *Blasius* beyond the intent to interfere standard

to also cover any action with a significant effect of interference with shareholder democracy."). Do you agree?

The *Blasius* standard creates an intermediate standard of review, somewhere between the duty of care and the duty of loyalty. The courts call it enhanced scrutiny. *See Reis v. Hazelett Strip-Casting Corp.*, 2011 Del. Ch. LEXIS 11 (Jan. 21, 2011). *Blasius* is one intermediate standard; *Unocal* is another. Moreover, the two standards can arise in the same context. Thus, for example, behavior implicating the *Blasiuis* standard could also constitute a defensive measure subject to *Unocal.* Some have argued that the approach should be simplified and the two standards combined.

Mercier v. Inter-Tel (Delaware), Inc.

Delaware Chancery Court
929 A.2d 786 (2007)

STRINE, VICE CHANCELLOR:

The plaintiff, Vernon Mercier, in this class action seeks to preliminarily enjoin the consummation of a stockholder approved merger in which Inter-Tel, Inc. will sell itself to Mitel Networks Corporation in an all cash, all shares merger for $25.60 a share (the "Mitel Merger"). Mercier owns 100 shares of Inter-Tel, which he has held since 1999.

* * *

After Inter-Tel set the [shareholder] meeting date [to approve the Merger with Mitel for June 29], Mihaylo [Inter-Tel's largest shareholder] entered the game again.... On June 4, Mihaylo sent a public letter to the Inter-Tel stockholders. In that letter, Mihaylo complained that the Special Committee had been secretly considering acquisition proposals and had not asked him to bid or conducted a full auction. He expressed his opposition to the Mitel Merger and proposed an alternative transaction whereby Inter-Tel would engage in a leveraged recapitalization. The Mihaylo "Recap" Proposal" involved the company using a 50–50% combination of cash on hand and new debt to acquire up to 60% of its shares for $28 a piece....

* * *

As June 29 approached, the Special Committee knew with virtual certainty that the Merger would be defeated if the special meeting was held as scheduled. By June 25, Innisfree [a proxy solicitor retained by Inter-Tel] was already reporting that every large holder who had voted had opposed the Merger. On June 26, ISS's [Institutional Shareholder Services] West Coast rival Glass Lewis also recommended a no vote on the Merger.

The next day Innisfree reported that over 73% of the shares had been voted, and that 49.6% of Inter-Tel's outstanding shares were already voted against the Merger. The vote was running even heavier against authorizing an adjournment in the event there were not enough votes to approve the Merger.

By this stage, the Special Committee was fatalistic. Stout [Inter Tel's CEO] viewed the Merger as "DOA," but he and others on the Special Committee team continued to try to make the vote closer, in part because, as its Chairman Cappello noted, a close vote would "help later when [Mihaylo] goes to dump the board." It was at this stage that Innisfree received indications from ISS that it might reconsider its position if there was a postponement. Innisfree also advised Stout and Cappello [Intel's Chairman of the Board] that "a short move in the record date would get the arbs fairly heavy in the stock."

* * *

At a lengthy meeting, the Special Committee deliberated on whether to postpone the meeting. The meeting was clearly and thoroughly "advised," shall we say, and the meeting minutes do not reflect the obvious reality driving the need for the meeting: the Merger was going down to defeat the next day. Instead, the minutes concentrate on the various factors outlined above that supposedly justified a postponement. The Special Committee ultimately decided to sleep on it. They reconvened early the next morning and decided to reschedule the meeting. One member of the Special Committee dissented. He favored the Merger but was uncomfortable rescheduling the vote.

The Special Committee believed that the special meeting should be rescheduled so that the stockholders would have the benefit of the company's second quarter results and more time to deliberate on the other factors outlined before rejecting the Merger. The Special Committee thought it was in the stockholders' best interests for them to think about it more. Although the minutes do not put it this way, the Special Committee believed the stockholders were about to make a huge mistake.

In voting to reschedule, the Special Committee was aware that if the vote were held that day, the Merger would be soundly defeated. In fact, as of that time, it was clear that an absolute majority of the outstanding shares, almost 15.5 million shares, were going to vote against the Merger, and that only around 5 million shares favored the Merger.

The Special Committee delayed the vote precisely so that it could have more time to convince the stockholders to support the Merger. In fact, Stout, the company's CEO, has admitted that he would not have favored postponing the meeting if the stockholders were poised to approve the Merger.

* * *

On July 2, Inter-Tel announced the date of the rescheduled meeting and the new record date. Because the record date was more than a week after the announcement, additional time was given to arbitrageurs as well as all other investors to buy Inter-Tel stock that could be voted at the meeting. After concerns were raised about whether the new meeting date of July 23 complied with the minimum notice requirements of §251(c) of the DGCL, the meeting was moved to August 2.

* * *

On August 2, the special meeting on the Merger was actually held. Over 87% of the outstanding shares were voted. Over 62% of Inter-Tel's 27.3 million outstanding shares were voted in favor of the Merger, with about 25% against. Of the shares voted, nearly 72% voted for the Merger. Of the shares not controlled by Mihaylo, more than 90% of the shares voted were in favor of the Merger. In fact, the stockholders this time even approved the second resolution authorizing an adjournment if necessary to gather more votes in favor of the Merger.

* * *

It would hardly be indiscreet for me to acknowledge yet again the widely known reality that our law has struggled to define with certainty the standard of review this court should use to evaluate director action affecting the conduct of corporate elections. The results in the cases make sense, as the decisions do a good job of sorting between situations when directors have unfairly manipulated the electoral process to entrench themselves against insurgents and those when directors have properly used their authority over the election process for good faith reasons that do not compromise the integrity of the election process. The problem that remains though is that there is no certain prism through which judges are to view cases like this. The great strength of *Blasius*—its reminder of the importance of the director election process and the barrier the decision draws to the acceptance of the bizarre doctrine of "substantive coercion" as to the question of who should constitute the board—came along with some overbroad language that rendered the standard of review articulated in the case too crude a tool for regular employment. As has been noted elsewhere, the trigger for the test's application—director action that has the primary purpose of disenfranchisement—is so pejorative that it is more a label for a result than a useful guide to determining what standard of review should be used by a judge to reach an appropriate result. As a result, decisions in the wake of *Blasius* tended to involve threshold exertions in reasoning as to why director action influencing the ability of stockholders to act did not amount to disenfranchisement, thus obviating the need to apply *Blasius* at all.

Blasius also employed in the corporate context language that has totemic meaning for those steeped in our legal tradition.... For that reason, our Supreme Court has candidly announced that *Blasius* is so strict a test that it is "applied rarely."

As the case law developed, it became increasingly obvious that the traditional skepticism and strong scrutiny that Delaware had always employed toward director actions that might unfairly taint the election process—a tradition that *Blasius* acknowledged and that importantly is reflected in *Schnell v. Chris-Craft Industries, Inc.*—needed to be preserved, but applied in a more workable way than *Blasius* articulated. Because cases involving electorally-directed action often arose in the M & A context, it was natural that judges would give thought to the *Unocal* standard, because they had to apply that standard anyway.

Happily, looking in that direction made logical sense, too. *Unocal*, when applied faithfully, requires directors to bear the burden to show their actions were reasonable. Implicitly, but importantly as I will soon articulate, that requires directors to convince the court that their actions are motivated by a good faith concern for the stockholders' best interests, and not by a desire to entrench or enrich themselves. In other words, to satisfy the *Unocal* burden, directors must at minimum convince the court that they have not acted for an inequitable purpose. Thus *Unocal* subsumes the question of loyalty that pervades all fiduciary duty cases, which is whether the directors have acted for proper reasons. This aspect of the test thus addresses issues of good faith such as were at stake in *Schnell.*

But *Unocal* does even more. The origins of *Unocal* as a standard of review addressing takeover defenses has probably led to too much emphasis on the word "threat" in the test. The core of *Unocal's* utility really rests in the burden it asserts on directors to: (1) identify the proper corporate objectives served by their actions; and (2) justify their actions as reasonable in relationship to those objectives....

... I believe that the standard of review that ought to be employed in this case is a reasonableness standard consistent with the *Unocal* standard....

To be specific, I believe that in this case, the burden should be on the Inter-Tel board as an initial matter to identify a legitimate corporate objective served by its decision to reschedule the June 29 special meeting on the Mitel Merger and to set a new record date. As part of meeting that burden, the directors should bear the burden of persuasion to show that their motivations were proper and not selfish. That showing, however, is not sufficient to ultimately prevail. To ultimately succeed, the directors must show that their actions were reasonable in relation to their legitimate objective, and did not preclude the stockholders from exercising their right to vote or coerce them into voting a particular way. If for some reason, the fit between means and end is not reasonable, the directors would also come up short.

* * *

As the starting point in my analysis [of the reasonableness standard from *Unocal*], I address the question of whether the Inter-Tel Special Committee has convinced me that they in fact acted for reasons that were properly motivated. On that score, the record supports the conclusion that the Inter-Tel Special Committee was motivated by a good faith concern that the Mitel Merger was in the best interests of the Inter-Tel stockholders and that if the meeting was held as scheduled on June 29, the advantages the Merger promised to the stockholders would be irretrievably lost. In so finding, I do not blanch from acknowledging that the Special Committee took action precisely because they believed—in fact, knew to a virtual certainty—that if the Merger vote went forward on June 29, the Merger would have been soundly defeated.

The plaintiff has not raised any argument at all questioning the independence of the Special Committee majority. Even as to Inter-Tel's CEO Stout, the plaintiff has been unable to suggest any substantial reason why Stout would favor a cash-out merger with Mitel over another higher-priced alternative or continuing as Mitel's CEO on a stand-alone basis if that would deliver more value. The plaintiff points to nothing about his severance package that was unusual and the plaintiff has not made any argument that Stout could have been fired with cause if Mihaylo was successful in taking over control of the board. In the event of a without cause dismissal, Stout would have stood to receive a substantial severance package.

In concluding on this record that the Special Committee acted in good faith, I note the absence of any evidence that the Special Committee failed patiently to explore the possibility of a more-valuable alternative takeover bid from interested parties. By contrast, it appears that the Special Committee diligently responded to all interested parties and tried to facilitate attractive bids. Certainly, Vector Capital received such treatment, and that was also true of even Mihaylo. And, of course, it bears repeating that the success of the Mitel Merger would speed, not slow, the departure of the Special Committee from their director offices.

* * *

In concluding that the Special Committee acted for the proper purpose of trying to do what they thought was best for the stockholders—to put the vote off so that they could rally more support for the Merger—I do not conclude they acted perfectly. As the plaintiff notes, the Special Committee's proxy solicitor indicated that a movement in the record date would not only allow actual holders of Inter-Tel stock who could not vote to do, it would do something more. A new prospective record date would, in Innisfree's view, allow arbitrageurs to buy additional shares at below the Merger price that could be voted. Because those shares could be bought at a price lower than the Merger price, arbitrageurs could make a profit by buying, voting for the Merger, and cashing in on the difference. The fact that the Special Committee dilated on this possibility in deciding to reschedule the special meeting and set a new record date was not disclosed publicly.

* * *

But the change in the record date did not unfairly tilt the odds against Mihaylo or any other Inter-Tel stockholder opposing the Merger. They remained free to convince their fellow stockholders that they would be better off economically if Inter-Tel rejected the Mitel bid and remained independent. If they made a convincing case that they were correct about where the most dollars could be had, they stood to prevail. In being inclined in this direction, I note that the plaintiff has failed to show that the agency problems resulting from the "separation of ownership from ownership"— i.e., from the fact that institutional investors have agency problems of their own because their interests are not identical to their investors'—are so substantial that stockholders will accept a merger at $25.60 per share when they stand to make more profit on a risk- and inflation-adjusted basis by rejecting it.

As important, the Special Committee has persuaded me, on this preliminary injunction record, that the change in the record date was not what determined the outcome of the ultimate Merger vote. What determined the outcome was that ISS and Inter-Tel stockholders who held on both record dates came to view the Mitel Merger as the value-maximizing option. That change in behavior also negates the plaintiff's view that the circumstances that the Special Committee considered to have been consequential on June 29 in delaying the meeting were trifles. Taken together, the fuller information the stockholders had regarding Inter-Tel's operating performance and prospects, the state of the debt markets, and the credibility and value of Mihaylo's

Recap Proposal was obviously influential. On August 2, the Inter-Tel stockholders had a much clearer understanding that their choice was down to taking the $25.60 per share Mitel bid or remaining stockholders in an independent Inter-Tel. No higher valued offer was coming from Mitel, Mihaylo, or another source.

* * *

Before concluding my determination of the main merits claim, I must deal with the question of whether a "compelling justification" supports the action of the Inter-Tel Special Committee. For the reasons I have stated, I believe that this test should be replaced by something more tempered, such as a "legitimate objective" test, so long as there is a recognition that the odd doctrine of "substantive coercion" has no proper place in jurisprudence regarding director elections. But I recognize that *Liquid Audio* and other cases seem to give continuing life to the compelling justification usage.

In this case, that standard can be addressed in two ways. The more traditional, but less convincing way, is to reason backwards out of that standard from the effect of the Special Committee's action. In prior decisions, this court has decided that because board action influencing the election process did not have the effect of precluding or coercing stockholder choice, that action was not taken for the primary purpose of disenfranchising stockholders. Because non-preclusive, non-coercive action did not have the primary purpose of disenfranchisement, the *Blasius* standard did not apply and thus no compelling justification for the board's action had to be shown. That is, the lack of disenfranchising effect provided that the trigger for the test was not pulled.

That type of reasoning backwards from effect works here, of course. The primary purpose of the Inter-Tel board was not to disenfranchise its stockholders. Rather, it was to give the stockholders more time to deliberate before exercising their right to vote. Because the Special Committee did not preclude stockholders from making a free and uncoerced choice about the Merger, its decision to reschedule the meeting does not invoke *Blasius* at all.

Approaching the issue more directly, I conclude that the Special Committee has demonstrated a compelling justification for its action, even if that standard applies. In the corporate context, compelling circumstances are presented when independent directors believe that: (1) stockholders are about to reject a third-party merger proposal that the independent directors believe is in their best interests; (2) information useful to the stockholders' decision-making process has not been considered adequately or not yet been publicly disclosed; and (3) if the stockholders vote no, the acquiror will walk away without making a higher bid and that the opportunity to receive the bid will be irretrievably lost. Stockholders invest to make moolah, cash, ching, green, scratch, cabbage, benjamins — to obtain that which Americans have more words for than Eskimos have for snow — money. When directors act for the purpose of preserving what the directors believe in good faith to be a value-maximizing offer, they act for a compelling reason in the corporate context. Of course, that does not mean that they have unlimited freedom to advance that purpose. But that is a question about the fit between the means they employ, not the end they are seeking to achieve.

Here, the means the Special Committee chose—a short delay in the meeting schedule and a new record date—were, as I have found, reasonable in relation to their objective. For all these reasons, I conclude that the plaintiff does not have a reasonable probability of success on its claim that the Special Committee breached its fiduciary duties by rescheduling the special meeting and setting a new record date.

Comments and Questions

1. What changes does the court in *Mercier* want to make to the *Blasius* doctrine? What would be the consequences of the change in the doctrine, were it to be implemented?

2. Postponement of the meeting provided the board with additional time to convince shareholders to favor the merger. The board, however, did more than postpone the meeting. It also changed the record date. What impact did this have on the outcome of the shareholder vote? Was this necessary?

3. The Vice Chancellor in this case describes the *Blasius* standard as "too crude a tool for regular employment." What do you think he means by that?

4. The opinion also noted that *Blasius* applied to interference with the franchise that occurred not just in the context of the election of directors but also in the context of other transactions involving shareholder approval, such as mergers. The court reasoned that "the reasoning of *Blasius* is far less powerful when the matter up for consideration has little or no bearing on whether the directors will continue in office." In effect, he reasoned that ordinary fiduciary obligations are sufficient. Do you agree with this?

5. In arguing that the appropriate test should be the reasonableness standard in *Unocal*, the opinion acknowledged that some had reason to believe that the Unocal standard was "being denuded into simply another name for business judgment rule review." The opinion asserted, however, that "[m]ore recent decisional law, one hopes, has been truer to the test as written." Is it appropriate to adopt a standard where there is a chance it may not be sufficient to protect shareholder because of the "hope" that it will be given more content by the courts in the future?

6. One way to address the different standards of review in *Unocal* and *Blasius* would be to impose in the takeover context not the reasonableness standard in *Unocal* but the compelling justification standard in *Blasiuis*. Why do you think the courts have not gone in this direction?

7. Does it matter whether a meeting is cancelled or, as was the case in *Mercier*, postponed? In *Perlegos v. Atmel Corp.*, 2007 Del. Ch. LEXIS 25 (Feb. 8, 2007), the court had this to say:

> The Defendants liken this [cancellation of the meeting] to "mere delay." That stockholders were not *prevented* from voting on replacing the Director Defendants but, instead, their opportunity to do so was *postponed* for seven months may, however, be a distinction without a difference. The Defendants have correctly referenced instances in which this Court has refused to apply *Blasius* where a board only postponed or delayed a stockholders meeting,

but those cases are distinguishable. Here, the Director Defendants did not simply postpone the special meeting. They cancelled it.

Does this distinction really matter?

8. The *Blasius* standard has never been applied to a poison pill? Why might that be the case? Poison pills, after all, typically prevent shareholders from forming voting blocks that exceed the triggering thresholds. For a discussion of the issue, see *Third Point LLC v. Ruprecht*, C.A. No. 9469 (Del. Ch. May 2, 2014).

B. Vote Buying

Vote buying represents another tactic that can be used to influence the outcome of a shareholder vote. This typically involves some type of payment or benefit in return for a commitment to vote the shares in the designated manner. As a result, it separates from the underlying economic attributes of the shares. Vote buying does not involve the transfer of the underlying shares. We examined this phenomenon somewhat when considering the issue of empty voting.

Vote buying was at one time prohibited, at least by management. That, however, is no longer the case.

Schreiber v. Carney

Delaware Chancery Court
447 A.2d 17 (1982)

HARTNETT, VICE CHANCELLOR:

[Texas International Airlines made a loan to Jet Capital, the owner of 35% of the shares of Texas International, in order to gain approval of a merger between Texas International and Texas Air. Jet Capital intended to vote against the merger because of negative tax implications the resulted from the ownership of warrants in Texas International. To eliminate the negative tax implications, Texas International agreed to lend Jet Capital $3.335 million in order to fund the early exercise of the warrants. Plaintiffs sued, alleging that the loan amounted to vote buying.]

… Vote-buying, despite its negative connotation, is simply a voting agreement supported by consideration personal to the stockholder, whereby the stockholder divorces his discretionary voting power and votes as directed by the offeror. The record clearly indicates that Texas International purchased or "removed" the obstacle of Jet Capital's opposition. Indeed, this is tacitly conceded by the defendants. However, defendants contend that the analysis of the transaction should not end here because the legality of vote-buying depends on whether its object or purpose is to defraud or in some manner disenfranchise the other stockholders. Defendants contend that because the loan did not defraud or disenfranchise any group of shareholders, but rather enfranchised the other shareholders by giving them a determinative vote in the proposed merger, it is not illegal *per se*. Defendants, in effect, contend that vote-buying is not void *per se* because the end justified the means. Whether this is valid depends upon the status of the law.

* * *

… [I]t is clear that Delaware has discarded the presumptions against voting agreements. Thus, under our present law, an agreement involving the transfer of stock voting rights without the transfer of ownership is not necessarily illegal and each arrangement must be examined in light of its object or purpose. To hold otherwise would be to exalt form over substance. As indicated in *Oceanic* more than the mere form of an agreement relating to voting must be considered and voting agreements in whatever form, therefore, should not be considered to be illegal *per se* unless the object or purpose is to defraud or in some way disenfranchise the other stockholders. This is not to say, however, that vote-buying accomplished for some laudable purpose is automatically free from challenge. Because vote-buying is so easily susceptible of abuse it must be viewed as a voidable transaction subject to a test for intrinsic fairness.

Comments and Questions

1. What are some concerns with vote-buying (sometimes also called "vote rental")? The court rejected a "*per se*" rule with respect to vote buying. Why?

2. Did the purchaser of the votes affect the analysis? What unique concerns can arise with vote-buying by the board of directors?

3. What is the test employed by the court for testing the legality of vote-buying arrangements? How does this test compare with the one articulated in *Blasius*, where the court likewise seemed concerned with the disenfranchising nature of the board's action?

4. Vote-buying allows for the separation of voting and economic rights. Is this appropriate?

5. Some commentators have indicated that the court in *Schreiber* approved vote buying where it was used to "better align the financial interests of the shareholder with that of the corporation." Robert B. Thompson & Paul H. Edelman, *Corporate Voting*, 62 Vand. L. Rev. 129, 165 (2009). Is that the correct way to view this case?

Hewlett v. Hewlett-Packard Co.

Delaware Chancery Court
2002 Del. Ch. LEXIS 44 (Apr. 8, 2002)

CHANDLER, CHANCELLOR:

The Hewlett Parties' allegation with regard to proxies cast in favor of the proposed merger by Deutsche Bank is essentially, although not captioned as such in the complaint, a vote-buying claim. Deutsche Bank holds at least 25 million shares of HP. The plaintiffs allege that Deutsche Bank's last-minute switch from voting 17 million of its shares against the merger to voting those shares for the merger was the result of a combination of inducement and coercion, orchestrated by HP's management, which caused Deutsche Bank to vote in favor of the proposed merger for reasons other than those based upon the merits of the transaction. The Hewlett Parties' allegations in support of this claim focus on actions taken during the four days before and the morning of the special meeting.

On or before March 15, 2002, the proxy committee of Deutsche Asset Management, Inc. conducted an independent review from which it determined to vote its shares against the proposed merger. Consistent with that decision, Deutsche Bank submitted its proxies and voted against the proposed merger. On March 15, 2002, HP closed a new multi-billion dollar credit facility to which Deutsche Bank had been added as a co-arranger. As of March 18, 2002, the day before the shareholders meeting, Deutsche Bank was concerned that HP's reaction to the proxy committee's disapproval of, and vote against, the proposed merger would be to end the ongoing, and desired future, business dealings between HP and Deutsche Bank. Allegedly at the demand of HP management, a telephone conference was held between Deutsche Bank and HP management on the morning of the March 19 vote. After that conference call, Deutsche Bank switched as many as 17 million votes to favor the proposed merger. The plaintiffs contend that this switch was elicited as a result of the inducement provided by the current HP credit facility, to which Deutsche Bank had just been added, combined with the coercion of the telephone conference from which Deutsche Bank understood that its future business dealings with HP would be jeopardized if it did not switch its votes to favor the proposed merger. The Hewlett Parties suggest that evidence of the import of this switch to HP's management is shown from HP's CEO and board chair-woman, Carleton S. Fiorina ("Fiorina"), first delaying the scheduled opening of the March 19 special stockholder meeting to wait for word from Deutsche Bank, and then announcing the closing of the polls promptly after apparently receiving word on the podium that Deutsche Bank had switched its vote. This vote-buying arrangement allegedly had the purpose and effect of defrauding and disenfranchising HP stockholders.

* * *

This Court has, on several earlier occasions, addressed so-called "vote-buying" allegations. In some instances the claims were successful and in others they were not. There does not, however, appear to be an obvious predisposition on the part of the Court one way or another toward vote-buying claims.

The appropriate standard for evaluating vote-buying claims is articulated in *Schreiber v. Carney*. Schreiber indicates that vote-buying is illegal *per se* if "the object or purpose is to defraud or in some way disenfranchise the other stockholders." *Schreiber* also notes, absent these deleterious purposes, that "because vote-buying is so easily susceptible of abuse it must be viewed as a voidable transaction subject to a test for intrinsic fairness." At first blush this proposition seems difficult to reconcile with the General Assembly's explicit validation of shareholder voting agreements in § 218(c). Significantly, however, it was the management of the defendant corporation that was buying votes in favor of a corporate reorganization in *Schreiber*. Shareholders are free to do whatever they want with their votes, including selling them to the highest bidder. Management, on the other hand, may not use corporate assets to buy votes in a hotly contested proxy contest about an extraordinary transaction that would significantly transform the corporation, unless it can be demonstrated, as it was in *Schreiber*, that management's vote-buying activity does not have a deleterious effect on the corporate franchise.

* * *

Initially, I believe the facts as alleged in the complaint support a reasonable inference that the switch of Deutsche Bank's vote of 17 million shares to favor the merger was the result of the enticement or coercion of Deutsche Bank by HP management. The Hewlett Parties allege that just four days before the stockholders meeting Deutsche Bank was named as a co-arranger of a multi-billion dollar credit facility. That same day (March 15), Deutsche Bank had submitted all of its proxies and voted 25 million shares against the merger. On Monday, March 18, it is alleged that Deutsche Bank expressed fear over losing future business as a result of HP's negative reaction to Deutsche Bank's vote against the HP management-sponsored merger. Finally, the complaint alleges that, on March 19, the date of the special stockholder meeting, HP delayed the meeting while HP management was involved in a purportedly coercive telephone conference and then closed the polls immediately after Deutsche Bank switched 17 million of its votes as a result of the understanding arrived at during that call. As stated above, however, a vote-buying agreement is not illegal *per se*, even when company management is buying votes. The more difficult question is whether or not the facts alleged support a reasonable inference that the agreement had a materially adverse effect on the franchise of the other HP shareholders.

The Hewlett Parties' primary argument as to why the alleged vote-buying agreement between HP and Deutsche Bank is illegal is that HP management used corporate funds (in essence, funds in which all of HP shareholders have a common interest as owners of HP) to purchase votes in favor of a transaction favored by management that management was required to put to a shareholder vote. Furthermore, HP management failed to use any devices, such as a ratifying vote of independent shareholders, which would protect the integrity of the vote on the proposed merger.

The allegations of the Hewlett Parties, if true, are particularly troubling. The extraordinary transaction at issue in this case is one of the limited types of transactions a corporate board cannot unilaterally cause its corporation to consummate. Because the transaction would have a fundamental impact on the ownership interests of a company's shareholders, the board must present the proposal to the shareholders for approval. If the allegations of the Hewlett Parties are true, the implication is that HP management was concerned that the proposed merger, which *they* supported, would not be supported by a majority of HP's shareholders. Despite the fact that it was for the shareholders to make the ultimate determination of whether to approve the proposed merger, HP management purportedly used the shareholders' own money (in the form of corporate funds) to buy votes in opposition to HP shareholders who did not favor the merger. These actions, if they in fact were taken impermissibly, tipped the balance in favor of HP management's view of how the vote should turn out and made it proportionally more difficult for shareholders opposing the merger to defeat the transaction. In my opinion, that is an improper use of corporate assets by a board to interfere with the shareholder franchise. Whether the shareholders disagreed with, did not believe, or even did not understand the information presented to them by HP management about the proposed merger, it was the right of the shareholders to cast their votes on the proposed merger without impermissible interference from HP management.

Schreiber is instructive in demonstrating how a vote-buying agreement in which a board expends corporate assets to purchase votes in support of a board-favored transaction may be validly consummated. There, a vote-buying agreement was being contemplated in which corporate assets were to be loaned to a 35% shareholder on favorable terms as consideration for that shareholder's agreement to vote in favor of a management-endorsed merger. The company formed a special committee to consider the merger and also the advisability of entering into the vote-buying agreement. The special committee hired independent counsel and then determined that both the merger and the shareholder agreement would be in the best interests of the company and its shareholders. After arm's-length bargaining with the 35% shareholder, the parties arrived at agreeable terms for the loan and the special committee recommended the shareholder agreement to the full board. The board of directors unanimously approved the agreement as proposed and submitted the vote-buying proposal to the shareholders for a separate vote — in effect a vote on vote-buying in that particular setting. As a condition for passage of the vote-buying proposal, a majority of outstanding shares, as well as a majority of the shares neither participating in the agreement nor owned by directors and officers of the company, had to be voted in favor of the proposal. After distribution of a proxy statement that fully disclosed the terms of the agreement, the vote-buying proposal was easily approved by the shareholders.

The *Schreiber* Court noted all of these protective measures and ultimately held that "the subsequent ratification of the [shareholder agreement] by a majority of the independent stockholders, after a full disclosure of all germane facts with complete candor precludes any further judicial inquiry." I agree with the well-reasoned opinion by then-Vice Chancellor Hartnett in *Schreiber*. Absent measures protective of the shareholder franchise like those taken in *Schreiber*, this Court should closely scrutinize transactions in which a board uses corporate assets to procure a voting agreement. This is not to say that all of the protective measures taken in *Schreiber* must be present before the Court will validate vote-buying by management using company assets. Each case must be evaluated on its own merits to determine whether or not the legitimacy of the shareholder franchise has been undercut in an unacceptable way. It is certainly possible for management to enter into vote-buying arrangements with salutary purposes. Accepting the allegations of the complaint as true in this case, however, I conclude that the plaintiffs have stated a cognizable vote-buying claim.

Because the Hewlett Parties successfully have alleged that HP bought votes from Deutsche Bank with corporate assets and because no steps were taken to ensure that the shareholder franchise was protected, HP's motion to dismiss the plaintiffs' vote-buying claim is denied. At trial, the plaintiffs will have the significant burden of presenting sufficient evidence for me to find that Deutsche Bank was coerced by HP management during their March 19, 2002 telephone conference into voting 17 million shares in favor of the proposed merger and that the switch of those votes was not made by Deutsche Bank for independent business reasons.

Hewlett v. Hewlett-Packard Co.

Delaware Chancery Court
2002 Del. Ch. LEXIS 35 (Apr. 30, 2002)

* * *

The vote-buying claim turns entirely on circumstantial evidence. The Hewlett Parties point to circumstances surrounding the arranging of the March 19 telephone conference and to one statement by Fiorina [the CEO and Chairwoman of HP] at the end of HP's presentation during that call to support their claim of illegal vote-buying. Having considered all of the testimony and exhibits offered at trial, I conclude that plaintiffs have failed to meet their burden of proving the existence of such a vote-buying arrangement.

The plaintiffs first rely upon a voicemail message left by Fiorina for Wayman [HP's CFO] on March 17 after HP management became aware that Deutsche Bank might have voted against the merger. In that message, Fiorina told Wayman:

> Talking to Alan Miller [HP's proxy solicitor] again today. He remains very nervous about Deutsche ... And so the suggestion is that you call the guy at Deutsche again first thing Monday morning. And if you don't get the right answer from him, then you and I need to demand a conference call, an audience, etc. to make sure that we get them in the right place.

> ... So if you take Deutsche ... get on the phone and see what we can get, but we may have to do something extraordinary for those two to bring 'em over the line here.

The plaintiffs contend that Fiorina's comment that HP "demand a conference call" and her reference to "doing something extraordinary" support their allegation that HP management was willing to, and did, improperly pressure Deutsche Bank to switch its vote.

The plaintiffs next question the motive behind the scheduling of the March 19, 2002, conference call. The parties acknowledge that Deutsche Bank had existing commercial relationships with HP. Deutsche Bank was also providing services to HP in connection with the merger. It is undisputed that Deutsche Bank desired to continue and expand its business relationships with HP. Because of this desire, the plaintiffs contend, Deutsche Bank was susceptible to the threat that business opportunities would be withheld if Deutsche Bank voted against the merger.

Based on these statements and inferences, the plaintiffs allege that HP management coerced Deutsche Bank by using the threat of lost future business opportunities to compel the CIB [Corporate and Investment Bank] group, through Griswold and Thornton the Deutsche Bank commercial bankers advising HP], in turn to force PCAM [Private Clients and Asset Management, a division of Deutsche Bank], of which the PWG [the Deutsche Bank Proxy Working Group, a five-member committee] was a part, to reconsider its vote against the merger. In the face of this threat, the plaintiffs insist, the PWG ignored its fiduciary duty to the beneficial owners of HP shares controlled by PCAM and voted in favor of the merger so that Deutsche Bank's CIB group might avoid the loss of some unspecified future business. Based on the evidence before me, however, I cannot agree that these circumstances are sufficient to demonstrate a vote-buying scheme.

First, I do not believe that Fiorina's voicemail evidences an intent to employ improper means to persuade Deutsche Bank to vote in favor of the merger. Fiorina testified credibly at trial that by "doing something extraordinary," she meant that HP management needed to take the steps necessary to gain an audience at Deutsche Bank for HP's presentation in favor of the merger. These steps included flying to New York for a personal presentation to Deutsche Bank, making independent HP board members available to speak to Deutsche Bank, or having someone from Compaq speak to Deutsche Bank. Under the circumstances, with the hotly contested shareholder vote less than 48 hours away, such actions would be somewhat extraordinary. In light of the proximity of the shareholder vote and the perceived narrow margin separating votes for or against the merger, I believe the contents of Fiorina's message are not sufficient to support an inference that HP management intended to coerce Deutsche Bank. Rather, Fiorina's message reflects reasonable actions taken by an executive faced with unexpected adverse information.

Second, although members of Deutsche Bank's CIB group were contacted by HP management and attempted to arrange a meeting with the PWG, the evidence does not show that the intervention of the commercial bankers resulted from a threat by HP to withdraw future business from Deutsche Bank. Other than introducing the participants in the March 19 conference call, the CIB individuals (Griswold and Thornton) neither contributed to the substantive discussions of the proposed merger nor offered any input during the PWG's consideration of how to vote the HP shares controlled by Deutsche Bank. Moreover, it appears that Griswold and Thornton helped arrange the hastily convened conference call because they were distressed that they had misled their client, HP, about the process DBAM [Deutsche Bank Asset Management] would follow in voting shares on the merger. Both Griswold and Thornton testified, without exception, that they had erroneously advised HP that shares held by DBAM as index, or passive, shares would be voted according to the ISS recommendation. Feeling "stupid," "shocked," and "embarrassed" about having misstated the facts regarding the voting process, both Griswold and Thornton believed that it was only appropriate to create an opportunity, albeit at the last minute and with no assurance as to its outcome, for the proxy contestants (and particularly their client) to present their positions on the merits of the merger to the PWG. This was the good news that Griswold and Thornton could offer HP in conjunction with the bad news that the vote was against the merger. From these circumstances, the plaintiffs contend that the only reasonable inference is that Griswold and Thornton, responding to HP's threat to withhold future business, coerced and pressured the PWG to switch its vote.

The circumstances surrounding the March 19 conference call give rise to reasonably conflicting inferences, not all of which are benevolent. It is troubling, for example, that the March 19 telephone conference was initiated at the urging of individuals from the CIB group of Deutsche Bank and that those individuals also attended the telephone conference. This fact raises clear questions about the integrity of the internal ethical wall that purportedly separates Deutsche Bank's asset management division from its commercial division. Nevertheless, no evidence credibly demonstrates that Griswold and Thornton arranged the conference call in response to a threat from HP management to withhold future business.

Ultimately, the recording of the March 19 conference call, as well as the testimonies of Fiorina, Wayman, and the individuals at Deutsche Bank participating in the call, fail to support the plaintiffs' vote-buying contention. This testimony, which I find credible, disproves the assertion that HP management improperly coerced or influenced the PWG in the ultimate deliberations about the vote. The recording reveals that the presentation made by Fiorina and Wayman on behalf of HP, the questions posed by Deutsche Bank, and the responses by Fiorina and Wayman all concerned the merits of the proposed merger and not the effect of Deutsche Bank's vote on its future business relationship with HP.

Following HP management's presentation on the merits, the PWG debated about the merger without reference to how its decision would affect business between HP and Deutsche Bank. The PWG focused instead on the harm the companies and their shareholders would suffer if the merger was not approved, as well as other substantive issues relating to the merits of the merger, such as the revenue synergy from printer pull-through. After this substantive discussion, the PWG voted 4–1, by secret ballot, in favor of the merger.

The committee then spoke to Klaus Kaldermorgen, Deutsche Bank's European Proxy Committee representative, about how he would vote the shares he controlled. Again, the discussion concerned the substantive merits of the merger and no mention was made of any threat to Deutsche Bank from a business relationship standpoint. All of this evidence indicates that the ultimate decision of the PWG to vote the shares of HP it controlled in favor of the merger was made with regard to what the PWG believed to be in the best interests of the beneficial owners of those shares. On its face, none of the evidence suggests an effort was made to coerce or manipulate the PWG's vote.

The final circumstance offered by the plaintiffs to prove that the PWG's vote was the result of improper influence from HP management is Fiorina's closing remarks during the conference call. Fiorina ended her presentation by stating:

> Gentlemen, we appreciate your time. I need to go try and get ready for a shareowner meeting. We very, very much appreciate your willingness to listen to us this morning. This is obviously of great importance to us as a company. *It is of great importance to our ongoing relationship.* We very much would like to have your support here. We think this is a crucially important decision for this company.

This is the only statement from HP management that plaintiffs point to as evidence that Deutsche Bank was coerced during the March 19, 2002, telephone conference.

That statement does not, in my opinion, demonstrate that Fiorina was attempting to coerce Deutsche Bank. Fiorina testified that the statement was the typical way she ended similar calls after making HP's standard presentation to investors. For thirty minutes prior to that closing statement, Fiorina and Wayman presented management's case for the merger and responded to concerns specifically raised by members of the PWG. The plaintiffs can point to nothing in those exchanges that indicates a threat from management that future business would be withheld by HP from Deutsche Bank and there is no indication that the PWG believed its discretion had been limited because of such a threat. Instead, the record establishes that all of the questions posed by the proxy committee—some of which were prompted by concerns raised just minutes before by Walter Hewlett's presentation in opposition to the merger—went to the merits of the transaction. Accordingly, I must find in favor of HP on the vote-buying claim.

Comments and Questions

1. What do these two cases suggest about the difficulty encountered by shareholders in establishing vote buying? What sorts of evidence would shareholders need to present to establish improper vote buying?

2. What about the perspective from the Deutsche Bank side? The Bank votes shares held by clients in favor of the merger. The SEC brought an action the Bank's asset management group (which made voting decisions). *See In re Deutsche Asset Management, Inc.*, Investment Advisors Act Release No. 2160 (admin proc August 19, 2003) ("A reasonable advisory client would want to know that its fiduciary, which was called upon to vote client proxies on a merger, had been contacted by officials of its affiliated investment bank in connection with an engagement directly related to the subject of the proxy vote."). Can the cases brought by the different regulators be reconciled?

3. How has the law developed since *Schreiber* refused to impose a *per se* rule prohibiting vote buying? Are shareholders better or worse off?

4. In assessing vote buying, Delaware courts distinguish between agreements that involve corporate assets and agreements that involve the assets of third parties. A third party cannot buy votes only if doing so would be "disenfranchising" by "creat[ing] a misalignment between the voting interest and the economic interest of [the] shares." Crown EMAK Partners, LLC v. Kurz, 992 A.2d 377, 388 (Del. 2010). What if a shareholder wants to buy votes and uses his/her own funds but promises the seller a seat on the board? *See Flaa v. Montano*, Civil Action No. 9146-VCG (Del. Ch. May 2, 2014).

Chapter 8

The Market for Corporate Control: Hostile Tender Offers and Proxy Contests

The market for control has long been viewed as a central component of the corporate governance process. To the extent dissatisfied with management, shareholders can exit the company, pushing down share prices and making the company affordable to a third party acquirer. The acquirer may purchase a majority of the outstanding shares, either gradually (a creeping tender offer) or through an offer to all shareholders simultaneously (a tender offer). Once a sufficient number of shares have been acquired, the acquirer can elect a new board and implement a second step merger. Management responsible for the inadequate share prices is replaced.

Tender offers are regulated under the federal securities laws, specifically the Williams Act. 15 U.S.C. §78n(d) & (e). Adopted in 1968, the Act imposes extensive disclosure requirements and substantive obligations on acquirers in order to ensure equal treatment of shareholders. More gradual acquisitions are regulated by the disclosure regime contained in Section 13(d) of the Exchange Act. 15 U.S.C. §78m(d).

Although tender offers involve an appeal directly to shareholders, the boards of the target companies play a critical if not decisive role in the success or failure of the effort. They may resort to defensive tactics that can slow or even prevent consummation of an offer, with poison pills the most common. Mostly exempt from the federal regulatory regime, boards responding to a hostile acquisition must meet their fiduciary obligations imposed under state law. Recognizing the "omnipresent specter that a board may be acting primarily in its own interests, rather than those of the corporation and its shareholders ..." *Unocal Corp. v. Mesa Petroleum Co.*, 493 A.2d 946, 954 (Del. 1985), state courts have modified the traditional fiduciary standards and apply the "modified" business judgment rule to defensive tactics. Under the standard, management of a target company has wide discretion to rely on defensive tactics.

More than defining fiduciary standards, states have played a proactive role in the takeover process. In the 1980s, a number of states adopted statutes designed to provide management with additional discretion to resist hostile offers or to raise the cost of any acquisition attempt. For a time, there was uncertainty about the constitutionality of these laws. These issues were largely resolved when the Supreme Court upheld one type of anti-takeover statute in *CTS Corp. v. Dynamics Corp. of America*, 481 U.S. 69 (1987).

The prevalence of defensive tactics, particularly poison pills, has made hostile tender offers difficult to effectuate. As a result, acquirers wanting to take control of a company over the opposition of incumbent management must typically resort to a proxy contest. These require the nomination of a competing slate of directors in an effort to obtain control of the board. Once elected, the insurgent board will often (but not always) look more favorably on the acquirers' efforts to purchase the business.

Proxy contests are regulated under the federal securities laws. *See* Section 14(a), 15 U.S.C. §78n(a). Insurgents must draft and distribute proxy statements to the shareholders they solicit. The expense associated with a proxy contest, particularly in large public companies, can be substantial and run into the millions of dollars. Insurgents engaging in a proxy contest must pay these amounts from their own pocket while management of the target company can use the corporate treasury to support its candidates.

Boards may resort to a number of tactics and devices designed to discourage proxy contests or to tilt the playing field once one is underway. These may include staggered boards, which generally break the board into three classes with one elected each year. Insurgents seeking to gain control of the board must wait for at least two consecutive elections.

Poison pills also can affect proxy contests. They are triggered not only by acquisitions but also by agreements among shareholders. A poison pill with a low trigger can, therefore, interfere with the ability of insurgents to reach an agreement with other shareholders on a common slate of directors or a sharing of expenses associated with the contest.

Given the costs, proxy contests are relatively rare, although they are increasing in frequency. Moreover, hedge funds and other activist shareholders may use the threat of a proxy contest to induce companies to include their representatives in the slate proposed by management. These sorts of interactions have been on the increase.

I. Hostile Tender Offers

A. Federal Regulation of Tender Offers

One way to acquire control of a company is to purchase a majority of the outstanding shares. Success in doing so will allow the acquirer to elect a majority of directors to the board and have enough shares to implement a second step merger, eliminating remaining shareholders. When the securities laws were adopted in the 1930s, tender offers were not subjected to federal regulation. The result was an assortment of perceived abuses, including "Saturday night specials," those offers made for a short period of time (over the weekend) on a first-come first-served basis, effectively forcing investors to make rushed and uninformed decisions.

That changed with the adoption of the Williams Act in 1968.

Steven M. Davidoff, *The SEC and the Failure of Federal Takeover Regulation*

34 Fla. St. U.L. Rev. 211, 215–218 (2007)[1]

Merger activity in the United States has historically occurred in waves. The "third wave" of U.S. merger activity transpired between 1960 and 1971 and was largely caused by that generation's bubble, the conglomerate acquisition craze. At the wave's height, from 1967–69, over 10,000 companies were acquired, with approximately 25,000 firms disappearing throughout the entire period. It was in response to this flurry of activity and the consequent emergence of the cash tender offer that modern-day federal takeover regulation originated. Previously, takeovers were staid events conducted primarily through proxy solicitations regulated by both state and federal proxy law. In the mid-1960s, however, at the crest of this third wave, there was a sharp comparative rise in unsolicited or "hostile" takeover attempts. These unsolicited bidders typically preferred to evade the federal and state regulatory apparatus applicable to proxy contests and instead often made their takeover attempts via cash tender offer. The rise of the tender offer is evidenced numerically: in 1966, there were over 100 tender offers involving companies listed on national securities exchanges as contrasted with just eight in 1960.

These early tender offers were largely unregulated affairs, and bidder conduct was often egregious. The "Saturday Night Special" was a favorite: in one form, a bidder would embark on a pre-offer buying raid to establish a substantial beachhead of ownership at a reduced price. This would be followed by a short-period, first-come, first-served public tender offer. Disclosure by bidders in these offers was also cramped: target stockholders oftentimes did not know the bidder's future intentions for the corporation, the source or availability of the bidder's capital, or even the bidder's true identity. In the wake of these new and unfamiliar tactics, stockholders and target corporations were relatively helpless. Takeover defenses at the time were in their infancy and virtually non-existent. Indeed, when surveying takeover manuals published during this time period, one marvels at the breadth of subsequent developments.

* * *

In light of the states' failure to respond, the SEC became the principal governmental actor in the drive to regulate cash tender offers. The SEC, led by its Chairman, Manuel F. Cohen, began a vocal campaign in favor of such regulation and to spotlight abuse. The first fruits of the SEC's labor were reaped in 1965, when Senator Harrison A. Williams introduced a bill to regulate tender offers. This first bill, however, headlined in the Congressional Record with the portentous title "Protection Against Corporate Raiders," had an avowedly antitakeover slant. It would, among other things, have required a twenty-day notice period before bidder commencement of a tender offer. The SEC, maintaining its activist approach, conse-

---

1. Copyright © 2007 Florida State University Law Review. Reprinted with permission.

quently took a public stance in opposition to many of the provisions of the bill, including the notice period.

Largely because of this SEC opposition, in 1967 Senator Williams introduced a revised, more neutral bill. One of its stated main purposes was "to avoid tipping the balance of regulation either in favor of management or in favor of the person making the takeover bid." The final bill, signed into law on July 29, 1968, and known as the Williams Act, was almost entirely in the form recommended by the SEC.

The Williams Act itself both substantively and procedurally regulated tender offers, and its terms were keyed specifically to respond to the perceived abuses of the time. First, new section 14(d) obligated bidders to file on Schedule 14D [now Schedule TO] and circulate a disclosure document in connection with a tender offer. Second, new section 14D attempted to curb coercive practices in tender offers by spelling out substantive governing rules. More specifically, new section 14(d) (5) required a bidder to provide withdrawal rights during the first seven days of the offer and thereafter past the sixtieth day, effectively establishing a seven-day minimum offer period; new section 14(d) (6) required a bidder to accept shares tendered during the first ten days of a partial offer on a pro rata basis; and new section 14(d) (7) required a bidder to offer and pay the same consideration to all tendering stockholders. Finally, new section 14(e) prohibited misrepresentations, misleading omissions and "fraudulent, deceptive, or manipulative acts or practices" in connection with a tender offer.

Comments and Questions

1. As the article notes, bidders in hostile tender offers are regulated primarily under federal law. The original scheme in the Williams Act has been significantly altered through SEC rulemaking. First, withdrawal rights have been extended to the length of the offering period (which must be at least 20 days). *See* Rules 14d-7 & 14e-1, 17 C.F.R. 240.14d-7, 14e-1. Similarly, in the case of a partial offer, all shares tendered during the offering period must be purchased on a pro rata basis. *See* Rule 14d-8, 17 C.F.R. 240.14d-8.

2. What is the underlying purpose for withdrawal rights and pro-rationing? What might happen that would cause a rational shareholder to withdraw his/her shares?

3. Bidding companies must file with the Commission a lengthy disclosure document on a Form TO. In addition to considerable information that can include such items as pro-forma financial statements of the entities assuming they ultimately combine, the form is subject to the disclosure requirements of the antifraud provisions and must, therefore, be accurate and complete.

4. The tender offer rules contain their own antifraud provision that prohibit false statements "in connection with any tender offer or request or invitation for tenders, or any solicitation of security holders in opposition to or in favor of any such offer, request, or invitation." Section 14(e), 15 U.S.C. §78n(e). How is this provision different from the more general antifraud provision in Rule 10b-5?

5. Can you make a case that this type of regulation is actually harmful to shareholders?

B. Section 13(d) and Creeping Tender Offers

Tender offers, while not defined in the Williams Act, traditionally involve an offer to all shareholders at substantially above the market price. *See Hanson Trust PLC v. SCM Corp.*, 774 F.2d 47, 54 (2d Cir. 1985). This is not the only way, however, to acquire a controlling interest in a company. Shares can be purchased gradually in the open market, an approach sometimes referred to as a creeping tender offer. *See Telvest, Inc. v. Bradshaw*, 547 F. Supp. 791, 798 (E.D. Va. 1982) (defining a creeping tender offer as "an acquisition strategy where, by achieving a substantial position in a company through open market purchases, an acquiring company can achieve a blocking position which enables them to purchase the remaining shares by tender or exchange offer at a cost that would be substantially less than if a formal tender offer had been made earlier.") (quoting brief of defendant).

Purchases other than through a tender offer are regulated by Section 13(d). 15 U.S.C. §78m(d). Owners with more than 5% of the outstanding voting shares must publicly report their ownership interest on a Schedule 13D within ten days. *See* Rule 13d-1, 17 CFR 240.13d-1. Material changes in ownership must be disclosed promptly. *See* Rule 13d-2, 17 CFR 13d-2 (presumptively defining as material any ownership change of 1% or more). The threshold applies to shares owned directly or indirectly and as part of a "group." In addition, shareholders must state the purpose of the acquisition, something ordinarily reduced to investment or control. The requirement puts other investors on notice of a possible acquisition attempt, something that may influence investment decisions.

Yet what happens if large shareholders violate the provision?

Rondeau v. Mosinee Paper Corp.

United States Supreme Court
422 U.S. 49 (1975)

BURGER, CHIEF JUSTICE:

In April 1971 petitioner Francis A. Rondeau, a Mosinee businessman, began making large purchases of respondent's common stock in the over-the-counter market. Some of the purchases were in his own name; others were in the name of businesses and a foundation known to be controlled by him. By May 17, 1971, petitioner had acquired 40,413 shares of respondent's stock, which constituted more than 5% of those outstanding. He was therefore required to comply with the disclosure provisions of the Williams Act, by filing a Schedule 13D with respondent and the Securities and Exchange Commission within 10 days. That form would have disclosed, among other things, the number of shares beneficially owned by petitioner, the source of the funds used to purchase them, and petitioner's purpose in making the purchases.

Petitioner did not file a Schedule 13D but continued to purchase substantial blocks of respondent's stock. By July 30, 1971, he had acquired more than 60,000 shares.

On that date the chairman of respondent's board of directors informed him by letter that his activity had "given rise to numerous rumors" and "seems to have created some problems under the Federal Securities Laws...." Upon receiving the letter petitioner immediately stopped placing orders for respondent's stock and consulted his attorney. On August 25, 1971, he filed a Schedule 13D which, in addition to the other required disclosures, described the "Purpose of Transaction" as follows:

> "Francis A. Rondeau determined during early part of 1971 that the common stock of the Issuer [respondent] was undervalued in the over-the-counter market and represented a good investment vehicle for future income and appreciation. Francis A. Rondeau and his associates presently propose to seek to acquire additional common stock of the Issuer in order to obtain effective control of the Issuer, but such investments as originally determined were and are not necessarily made with this objective in mind. Consideration is currently being given to making a public cash tender offer to the shareholders of the Issuer at a price which will reflect current quoted prices for such stock with some premium added."

Petitioner also stated that, in the event that he did obtain control of respondent, he would consider making changes in management "in an effort to provide a Board of Directors which is more representative of all of the shareholders, particularly those outside of present management...." One month later petitioner amended the form to reflect more accurately the allocation of shares between himself and his companies.

* * *

As in the District Court and the Court of Appeals, it is conceded here that petitioner's delay in filing the Schedule 13D constituted a violation of the Williams Act. The narrow issue before us is whether this record supports the grant of injunctive relief, a remedy whose basis "in the federal courts has always been irreparable harm and inadequacy of legal remedies." Beacon Theatres, Inc. v. Westover, 359 U.S. 500, 506–507 (1959).

The Court of Appeals' conclusion that respondent suffered "harm" sufficient to require sterilization of petitioner's stock need not long detain us. The purpose of the Williams Act is to insure that public shareholders who are confronted by a cash tender offer for their stock will not be required to respond without adequate information regarding the qualifications and intentions of the offering party. By requiring disclosure of information to the target corporation as well as the Securities and Exchange Commission, Congress intended to do no more than give incumbent management an opportunity to express and explain its position. The Congress expressly disclaimed an intention to provide a weapon for management to discourage takeover bids or prevent large accumulations of stock which would create the potential for such attempts. Indeed, the Act's draftsmen commented upon the "extreme care" which was taken "to avoid tipping the balance of regulation either in favor of management or in favor of the person making the takeover bid." S. Rep. No. 550, 90th Cong., 1st Sess., 3 (1967); H.R. Rep. No. 1711, 90th Cong., 2d Sess., 4 (1968). *See also* Electronic Specialty Co. v. International Controls Corp., 409 F. 2d 937, 947 (CA2 1969).

The short of the matter is that none of the evils to which the Williams Act was directed has occurred or is threatened in this case. Petitioner has not attempted to obtain control of respondent, either by a cash tender offer or any other device. Moreover, he has now filed a proper Schedule 13D, and there has been no suggestion that he will fail to comply with the Act's requirement of reporting any material changes in the information contained therein. 15 U.S.C. § 78m (d) (2); 17 C.F.R. § 240.13d-2 (1974). On this record there is no likelihood that respondent's shareholders will be disadvantaged should petitioner make a tender offer, or that respondent will be unable to adequately place its case before them should a contest for control develop. Thus, the usual basis for injunctive relief, "that there exists some cognizable danger of recurrent violation," is not present here. United States v. W. T. Grant Co., 345 U.S. 629, 633 (1953). *See also* Vicksburg Waterworks Co. v. Vicksburg, 185 U.S. 65, 82 (1902).

Nor are we impressed by respondent's argument that an injunction is necessary to protect the interests of its shareholders who either sold their stock to petitioner at predisclosure prices or would not have invested had they known that a takeover bid was imminent. Brief for Respondent 13, 20–21. As observed, the principal object of the Williams Act is to solve the dilemma of shareholders desiring to respond to a cash tender offer, and it is not at all clear that the type of "harm" identified by respondent is redressable under its provisions. In any event, those persons who allegedly sold at an unfairly depressed price have an adequate remedy by way of an action for damages, thus negating the basis for equitable relief. *See* Youngstown Sheet & Tube Co. v. Sawyer, 343 U.S. 579, 595 (1952) (Frankfurter, J., concurring). Similarly, the fact that the second group of shareholders for whom respondent expresses concern have retained the benefits of their stock and the lack of an imminent contest for control make the possibility of damage to them remote at best. *See* Truly v. Wanzer, 5 How. 141, 142–143 (1847).

Comments and Questions

1. What does this case indicate about the types of remedies that a court will impose for violations of Section 13(d)? To the extent ordering corrective disclosure, courts may also enjoin additional purchases until the market has had time to digest the accurate information. *See General Aircraft Corp. v. Lampert*, 556 F.2d 90, 97 (1st Cir. 1977) (upholding lower court injunction prohibiting acquisition of additional shares "until the Schedule 13D is amended to reflect accurately their intentions.").

2. A number of courts have found that there is no private right of action for damages under Section 13(d). *See Motient Corp. v. Dondero*, 529 F.3d 532, 536 (5th Cir. 2008). Such courts have generally found that actions may only be brought for equitable

relief. The SEC can, however, seek disgorgement. *See* SEC v. Teo, 746 F.3d 90 (3rd Cir. 2014) (obtaining disgorgement of $17,422,054.13 in profits in case involving violation of Section 13d).

3. In most cases, the remedy for a violation of Section 13(d) is corrective disclosure. Does this provide sufficient "incentive" to ensure compliance? What advantages will a shareholder obtain by failing to comply with the requirement? Had management in this case been alerted in a timely fashion could it have done anything to affect additional acquisitions?

4. The Commission has been petitioned to "close" the ten day window in Section 13(d), asserting that "[i]n today's world, ten days is an eternity." *See* Petition for Rulemaking Under Section 13 of the Securities Exchange Act of 1934 from Wachtell Lipton Rosen & Katz, Mar. 7, 2011. The petition noted that the proposal to close the window had generated "vocal opposition." Is the ten day window to file a Schedule 13D too long or too short? What can happen during that period? Should the change is the threshold also be considered in conjunction with the percentage triggers used in poison pills?

5. Disclosure on a Schedule 13D must be made by beneficial owners who own more than 5% of the outstanding equity shares. *See* Rule 13d-1(a), 17 C.F.R. 240.13d-1(a). Beneficial ownership includes anyone with voting or investment power over the shares. *See* Rule 13d-3, 17 C.F.R. 240.13d-3. In the 1980s, the Commission (and criminal authorities) brought a number of actions alleging that purchasers "parked" shares with other investors in order to avoid triggering the 5% disclosure requirement. *See SEC v. Bilzerian*, Litigation Release No. 2104 (D.C. Cir. July 25, 1994). The purchaser would typically agree to later acquire the parked shares or, if not acquired, to hold investor harmless for any losses.

6. One difficult issue with respect to beneficial ownership concerns equity swaps. In *CSX Corp. v. The Children's Investment Fund Management*, 2011 U.S. App. LEXIS 14653 (2d Cir., July 18, 2011), the defendant purchased swaps from a number of large banks that referenced shares of CSX. To avoid any risk of loss, the banks bought shares of CSX, something CSX described in its suit as "inevitable." Once the Fund closed out the swap position, the shares would be sold and available for purchase by the Fund. The district court found that the swaps were designed to avoid the disclosure requirements in Section 13(d). Even if that was the intended purpose, one judge on the panel disagreed that this resulted in the Fund beneficially owning the shares. As Judge Winter concluded:

> In the absence of some other agreement governing the disposition of shares purchased to hedge a swap position, merely having a long position in a cash-settled total-return equity swap does not constitute having the power, directly or indirectly, to direct the disposition of shares that a counterparty purchases to hedge its swap positions, and thus does not constitute having "investment power" for purposes of Rule 13d-3(a).

Id. What do you make of this analysis? What is the other side of the argument?

7. Once a Schedule 13D is filed, material changes must be filed promptly. The term is undefined but the Commission has concluded that "any delay beyond the time the amendment could reasonably have been filed may not be deemed to be prompt." *In the Matter of Cooper Laboratories, Inc.*, Admin. Proc. File No. 3-6535 (June 26, 1985).

C. Substantive Regulation of Tender Offers

Federal regulation of tender offers is designed to provide shareholders with adequate disclosure and adequate time to make an informed investment decision. A tender offer must stay open for a minimum of 20 business days. *See* Rule 14e-1, 17 C.F.R. 240.14e-1. During the offering period, shareholders can withdraw tendered shares at any time. *See* Rule 14d-7, 17 CFR 240.14d-7. This might occur because of a change of heart about the offer or because a better, competing deal surfaced. For tender offers seeking less than all of the outstanding shares, those submitted during the offering period must be purchased on a pro-rata basis. *See* Rule 14d-8, 17 C.F.R. 240.14d-8. As a result, those shares tendered on the last day of the offering period are treated the same as those tendered on the first, eliminating any ability to stampede shareholders into tendering early.

One of the more controversial aspects of tender offers has been the so called "all holders and best price" rule. *See* Rule 14d-10, 17 C.F.R. 240.14d-10. The Rule requires that any tender offer be open to all shareholders of the same class and that all tendering shareholders receive the "best price" paid in the offer. The latter requirement effectively prohibits price discrimination among tendering shareholders.

In regulating tender offers, Congress did not expressly require equal treatment of shareholders. Nonetheless, the Commission did so by rule, contending that the requirement was necessary to implement the goals of the Act.

> Without the all-holders and best-price requirements, the investor protection purposes of the Williams Act would not be fully achieved because tender offers could be extended to some security holders but not to others. Such discriminatory tender offers could result in the abuses inherent in "Saturday Night Specials," "First-Come First Served" offers and unconventional tender offers since security holders who are excluded from the offer may be pressured to sell to those in the included class in order to participate, at all, in the premium offered. These excluded security holders would not receive the information required by the Williams Act, would have their shares taken up on a first-come first-served basis and would have no withdrawal rights. There is nothing in the Williams Act or its legislative history to suggest that Congress intended to permit such selective protection of target company security holders.

Exchange Act Release No. 23421 (July 11, 1986). Despite some regulatory uncertainty, courts have uniformly upheld the Commission's authority to adopt the rule.

The rules also include a prohibition on insider trading applicable specifically to tender offers. Rule 14e-3 prohibits the use of material non-public information once a "substantial step" has been taken towards the commencement of a tender offer. 17 CFR 240.14e-3. The boundaries of that requirement have been subject to judicial scrutiny.

Allergan, Inc. v. Valeant Pharmaceuticals International, Inc.

United States District Court, Central District of California
No. SACV 14-1214 DOC(ANx) (Nov. 4, 2014)

CARTER, DISTRICT JUDGE:

This case arises from a live battle for corporate control that has spilled over into the courts. In February 2014, Canadian-based pharmaceutical company Valeant and hedge fund management company Pershing Square teamed up to help Valeant pursue a combination with Irvine-based pharmaceutical company Allergan. Between February and April, Pershing Square acquired 9.7% of Allergan's shares. In June 2014, Valeant publicly announced a tender offer for Allergan shares after Allergan's board of directors had rebuffed an unsolicited merger proposal. Valeant and Pershing Square then went directly to Allergan's shareholders to urge them to call a special shareholder meeting to replace Allergan's current directors with directors friendlier to Valeant. At the much-publicized urging of Pershing Square and some other shareholders, and after settling litigation in Delaware, Allergan agreed to hold a special shareholders meeting on December 18, 2014.

* * *

Section 14(e) prohibits "fraudulent, deceptive, or manipulative acts or practices, in connection with any tender offer." Under Rule 14e-3(a), once an "offering person" "has taken a substantial step or steps to commence ... a tender offer," "any other person who is in possession of material information relating to such tender offer" that he knows or has reason to know is nonpublic and that he received directly or indirectly from the offering person must either abstain from trading or disclose the information to the public before trading. 17 C.F.R. § 240.14e-3(a). Relatedly, Rule 14e-3(d) makes it unlawful for an "offering person" to communicate "material, nonpublic information relating to a tender offer to any other person under circumstances in which it is reasonably foreseeable that such communication is likely to result in a violation of this section." 17 C.F.R. 240.14e-3(d).

Here, there is no dispute that Pershing Square possessed nonpublic information and did not disclose that information to the public before causing PS Fund 1 [an entity formed by Pershing to acquire Allergan shares] to purchase Allergan shares between February 25 and April 21, 2014. The parties dispute only whether any substantial steps toward a tender offer were taken by then, i.e., whether the nonpublic information in Pershing Square's possession was related to a tender offer at that point. Even if substantial steps were taken, the parties dispute whether it was unlawful for PS Fund 1 to buy Allergan shares because it is unclear whether PS Fund 1 and other Pershing Square Defendants were "offering person[s]." The Court addresses each area of disagreement in turn.

a. Whether Substantial Steps Were Taken to Commence a Tender Offer

In order for Rule 14e-3's "disclose or abstain" requirement to be triggered, there must have been "a substantial step or steps to commence ... a tender offer" before PS Fund 1 began purchasing Allergan equity. To determine whether a "substantial step or steps" toward a tender offer were taken, a court looks mainly to the offering person's objective conduct. The SEC chose an objective standard in order to avoid "the difficulty of identifying when a person has actually determined to make a tender offer." Tender Offers, 45 Fed Reg. 60,410, 60,413 n. 33 (Sept. 12, 1980) ("SEC Adopting Release"). In adopting the "substantial step or steps" standard, the SEC stated:

> [S]ubstantial step or steps to commence a tender offer include, but are not limited to, voting on a resolution by the offering person's board of directors relating to the tender offer; the formulation of a plan or proposal to make a tender offer by the offering person or the person(s) acting on behalf of the offering person; or activities which substantially facilitate the tender offer such as: arranging financing for a tender offer; preparing or directing or authorizing the preparation of tender offer materials; or authorizing negotiations, negotiating or entering into agreements with any person to act as a dealer manager, soliciting dealer, forwarding agent or depository in connection with the tender offer.

Id.

Courts have interpreted this list as only a list of examples and have found that other actions are sufficient to constitute substantial steps.... The courts in *Ginsburg* and *Mayhew* both found that substantial steps toward a tender offer had taken place even though the offeror had not yet settled on a tender offer as the form of the merger....

Here, the Court must determine whether a substantial step was taken toward a tender offer before PS Fund 1's purchases of Allergan stock between February 25 and April 21, 2014. Before February 25, Valeant's board of directors met multiple times and discussed a potential combination with Allergan. Board meeting materials reflect that Valeant knew there was a high likelihood that a transaction with Allergan would involve a "[h]ostile cash and stock merger." Valeant hired three law firms and reached out to bankers to begin doing due diligence and lining up financing for the potential Allergan transaction. Valeant representatives met with Mr. Ackman and others from Pershing Square, who were known for their experience in handling unsolicited bids, and signed a confidentiality agreement with Pershing Square in order for Valeant to reveal the name of its proposed target to Pershing Square.

Valeant and Pershing Square also negotiated and ultimately agreed on a plan pursuant to which Pershing Square would purchase Allergan stock, would commit to voting in favor of any bid for Allergan stock by Valeant, and would accept shares and not cash if the Allergan-Valeant transaction was consummated in a way that gave Allergan shareholders the option to choose stock or cash. Feb. 25 Relationship Agreement §2(b). The February 25 Relationship Agreement specifically provided that Valeant and Pershing Square would form a "Co-Bidder Entity" and would be named as "co-bidders" if a tender offer was launched for Allergan's shares. *Id.* § 1(a), 1(d). Internal emails indicate that their lawyers were concerned about regulators being offended by a person who is not a co-bidder acquiring a toehold. Smith Decl. Ex. 83.

Defendants argue that, before May, they had taken substantial steps toward a negotiated merger with Allergan, which included a strategy of using Allergan's shareholders to pressure Allergan's board to negotiate, but had taken no steps toward a tender offer to Allergan's shareholders. They argue that they took substantial steps toward a tender offer only after the Sanford Bernstein conference on May 29, 2014, where Allergan shareholders urged Valeant and Pershing Square to make a tender offer. Defendants point to provisions of Valeant's and Pershing Square's February 25 Relationship Agreement, in which both sides acknowledged that no steps have been taken toward a tender offer and which required both sides to consent before launching a tender offer. They also point to a resolution by Valeant's board on April 7, 2014 which provided that "the Authorized Officers are not authorized [to] commence a tender offer or a proxy solicitation without the approval of the Board," as well as the fact that they did not line up financing for a tender offer or hire an exchange agent or dealer manager until late May and early June. Opp'n at 25–27.

Defendants stating in a contract that they had not taken any steps toward a tender offer does not necessarily make it so. Evidence that Defendants took more definite steps toward a tender offer in May does not necessarily mean that a "substantial step" did not happen in February. Defendants have not adequately explained why the February 25 Relationship Agreement used the term "Co-Bidder Entity" and required Pershing Square and Valeant to identify themselves as "co-bidders" in the event that Valeant launched a tender offer if there was no plan for a tender offer at that time, or at least a strong possibility at that time that their actions would lead toward and facilitate a tender offer. With further discovery and upon presentation of the evidence to the jury, a jury could find for Defendants on the substantial steps issue. However, based on this record, the Court concludes that Plaintiffs have at least raised serious questions as to whether substantial steps to commence a tender offer were taken before PS Fund 1 began purchasing Allergan shares.

b. Whether Rule 14e-3 Contains a "Co-Offering Person" Exception

Even if Pershing Square purchased Allergan shares based on confidential information about a forthcoming tender offer, Defendants argue that their conduct was not illegal. There are two potential theories under which Pershing Square would be permitted to trade on confidential information that it received from Valeant: (1) if Pershing Square is Valeant's "broker" or "agent" within the meaning of Rule 14e-3(c)(1) or fits into the exception under Rule 14e-3(b), or (2) if Pershing Square and Valeant are collectively an "offering person" and it is possible for two persons to work together as one "offering person" within the meaning of Rule 14e-3. Since Defendants do not argue that Pershing Square fits into Rule 14e-3(b) or (c), the Court addresses the second theory, the "co-offering person" theory. Plaintiffs argue based on the text and legislative and regulatory history of Rule 14e-3, an "offering person" cannot be more than one person. Mot. at 17–23. However, the Court concludes from its review of the relevant statutory and regulatory text that the term "offering person" can include multiple persons.

* * *

c. Who is a Co-Offering Person

The Court's conclusion that Rule 14e-3 allows multiple persons to act as one "offering person" does not end the analysis. If a co-offering person exception is not to swallow the general rule that an offering person cannot tip off another person and other persons cannot then trade on that confidential tip, there must be certain characteristics that distinguish a co-offering person from "any other person" for Rule 14e-3 purposes. The parties have not cited nor has the Court been able to find any legal authority directly addressing how to distinguish between a cooffering person and "any other person" for Rule 14e-3 purposes. Neither Congress nor the SEC has provided guidance directly on point.

Defendants urge the Court to equate "offering person" with "bidder" and "offeror" as the SEC already defines them for disclosure purposes, that is, as "any person who makes a tender offer or on whose behalf a tender offer is made." SEC Regulation M-A; 17 C.F.R. §229.1000(d); Rule 14d1 (g)(2); 17 C.F.R. 240.14d1 (g)(2). When the SEC analyzes "bidder" status for Regulation 14D purposes, the staff consider factors such as:

Did the person play a significant role in initiating, structuring, and negotiating the tender offer?

- Is the person acting together with the named bidder?
- To what extent did or does the person control the terms of the offer?
- Is the person providing financing for the tender offer, or playing a primary role in obtaining financing?
- Does the person control the named bidder, directly or indirectly?
- Did the person form the nominal bidder, or cause it to be formed?, and
- Would the person beneficially own the securities purchased by the named bidder in the tender offer or the assets of the target company?

One or two of these factors may control the determination, depending on the circumstances. These factors are not exclusive.

We also consider whether adding the person as a named bidder means shareholders will receive material information that is not otherwise required under the control person instruction....

In addition, we would consider the degree to which the other party acted with the named bidder, and the extent to which the other party benefits from the transaction.

Excerpt from Current Issues and Rulemaking Projects Outline (Nov. 14, 2000), §II.D.2. Mergers & Acquisitions—Identifying the Bidder in a Tender Offer, http://www.sec.gov/divisions/corpfin/guidance/ci111400ex_tor.htm.

This fact-specific, case-by-case inquiry is also used by the courts. Based on the Court's review of the sparse case law, if there is any clear principle from the case law, it is that bankers who do no more than supply the tender offeror with money to make the tender offer in return for a fee or in return for a security interest in the post-transaction company's stock are not co-bidders. *Van Dusen Air, Inc. v. APL Ltd. Partnership*, 1985 WL 56596, at *1–3 (D.Minn.1985); *Revlon, Inc. v. Pantry Pride, Inc.*, 621 F.Supp. 804, 816–17 (D.Del.1985). Beyond that, "there is no bright, hard-line test" for distinguishing a co-bidder from the "rest of humanity." *MAI Basic Four, Inc. v. Prime Computer, Inc.*, 871 F.2d 212, 221 (1st Cir.1989); *Koppers Co., Inc. v. American Exp. Co.*, 689 F.Supp. 1371, 1387 (W.D.Pa.1988). Courts have considered many different factors in determining whether the person alleged to be a bidder is a "principal participant" who is "central to the offer," *Koppers*, 689 F.Supp. at 1388, including the alleged bidder's role in planning and financing the tender offer and the extent of their interest in and relationship with their co-bidding entities. Defendants rely heavily on the "principal participant" language to distinguish Pershing Square's role from a mere banker's role and to bring Pershing Square within the "co-bidder" safety zone despite the fact that Pershing Square does not appear to have as dense a relationship with Valeant or as deep an interest in the surviving entity as the co-bidders in *MAI Basic Four* and *Koppers*.

Plaintiffs argue that "offering person" cannot be defined identically as "bidder" or "offeror" because effecting the purpose of the Williams Act — to ensure that investors have access to the material information they need to decide how they will respond to a tender offer — requires defining "bidder" broadly to ensure broad disclosures under Sections 13(d) and 14(d) while defining "offering person" narrowly to restrict the number of persons allowed to trade on insider information about tender offers. The Court finds Plaintiffs' argument persuasive because, in promulgating Rule 14e-3, the SEC was concerned about the practice of "warehousing" (the practice of the tender offeror intentionally leaking information to institutional investors to allow those other entities to make early trades before other investors heard about the tender offer) because such a practice is unfair to investors who are trading at an informational disadvantage ...

Although Plaintiffs did not explicitly frame it as such, the Court also finds compelling their proposed test for distinguishing an "offering person" from a "bidder" or "offeror." Plaintiffs argue that an offering person should be more than a financier, and should actually make an offer to purchase shares and should have some degree of control over the terms of the tender offer and over the surviving entity. These factors are included among the factors used by the SEC to determine whether someone is a "bidder" or "offeror" for disclosure purposes. Thus, in essence, Plaintiffs would use the same test as that proposed by Defendants. The only difference is that, similar to how the SEC considers whether adding a person as a named bidder for Regulation 14D purposes would result in more material information being disclosed to shareholders, in determining whether someone is an "offering person," Plaintiffs would add the consideration of whether labeling the person an "offering person" would be consistent with Rule 14e-3's purpose of limiting the universe of persons permitted to trade on inside information only to the person making the tender offer. This may involve emphasizing control factors, such as control over the terms of the offer, control over the surviving entity, and control over and identity with the named bidder.

In adopting this test, the Court is aware that the SEC may one day issue a clarifying interpretation or even promulgate an amended rule that imposes a different test. However, in the absence of action by the SEC and Congress, the Court must do its best to interpret existing laws and regulations and to apply them to the cases before the Court in a manner faithful to their text and purpose. With these considerations in mind, the Court must determine if Pershing Square was a co-offering person within the meaning of Rule 14e-3.

d. Whether Pershing Square Was a Co-Offering Person

In crafting the February 25 Relationship Agreement, Defendants appear to have been trying to fit their relationship into what they hoped would be recognized as a co-offering person or "co-bidder" exception to Rule 14e-3. Neither the SEC nor the Congress has provided clear guidance in this area. Based on the existing legal authorities and the factual record currently before the Court, the Court concludes that, in this case, Plaintiffs have raised serious questions as to whether Pershing Square is a co-offering person.

In reaching this conclusion, the Court considers the following factors. First, the Court recognizes that Pershing Square did play an active role from the beginning in helping Valeant craft its acquisition strategy. It is likely that the tender offer could not have been launched without Pershing Square's assistance in strategizing the bid, financing it by acquiring a toehold through PS Fund 1, agreeing to accept Valeant shares if the Allergan-Valeant transaction included an offer for cash and shares to Allergan's shareholders, and agreeing to buy $400 million of Valeant shares at Valeant's request. The Court also recognizes that, technically, PS Fund 1 was a creature of both Valeant and Pershing Square at the time that it crossed the 5% threshold and triggered Schedule 13D disclosure obligations because, pursuant to the February 25 Relationship Agreement, Valeant was added as a member of the LLC and made a small $75.9 million contribution shortly before that point. (Prior to that point, PS Fund 1's only members and funders were Pershing Square entities.) Additionally, Pershing Square was listed as an "offeror" on the Schedule TO at the SEC's request, Defs.' App'x Ex. 37 at 1, and thus may be jointly and severally liable if Valeant fails to pay the consideration offered to Allergan's shareholders. *See* Rule 14e-1(c); 17 C.F.R. §240.14e1 (c).

However, although Pershing Square was active as a strategist and financier to Valeant and even listed itself as an "offeror," the Court is doubtful that Congress and the SEC meant for these factors to be sufficient to exempt an entity like Pershing Square from the "disclose or abstain" rule of Rule 14e-3. While the February 25 Relationship Agreement required Pershing Square to give its consent before a tender offer could be formally launched, Pershing Square had no control over the price to be offered to Allergan's shareholders, whether the tender offer would involve cash and/or an exchange of stock, or even whether to call off the tender offer at some point. Pershing Square is helping to finance the tender offer; however, there is no evidence that it will actually acquire any Allergan stock through the tender offer. In fact, Defendants' Form S-4 Registration Statement states the opposite:

> Q: WHO IS OFFERING TO ACQUIRE MY SHARES OF ALLERGAN COMMON STOCK?
>
> A: This offer is being made by Valeant through [AGMS], a wholly owned subsidiary of Valeant....
>
> Q: WHAT DOES IT MEAN THAT PERSHING SQUARE AND PS FUND 1, A PERSHING SQUARE AFFILIATE, ARE CO-BIDDERS?
>
> A: .... [N]one of Pershing Square, PS Fund 1 or any of Pershing Square's affiliates is offering to acquire any shares of Allergan common stock in the offer....

In addition, there is no evidence that Pershing Square has any interest or involvement with AGMS, Inc., the wholly-owned subsidiary of Valeant listed as the "Purchaser" on the Schedule TO. There is also no requirement that Pershing Square be involved in the surviving entity beyond the requirement that Pershing Square hold an equity interest in the surviving entity for at least one year. *See supra* note 8; Feb. 25 Relationship Agreement § 2(c). Given that Defendants took care to explain in their tender offer materials that Pershing Square and PS Fund 1 were "co-bidder[s]" only "for SEC purposes," Defs. App'x Ex. 44, it appears that even Defendants do not really see Pershing Square and PS Fund 1 as the persons actually making an offer to pay Allergan shareholders consideration in exchange for their shares.

Based on these considerations, the Court finds that Plaintiffs have, at minimum, raised serious questions regarding whether Pershing Square is an "offering person" or "co-offering person" exempt from Rule 14e-3's "disclose or abstain" rule.

e. Conclusion

In conclusion, the Court finds that Plaintiffs have raised serious questions going to the merits of their Rule 14e-3 claim.

Comments and Questions

1. Pershing purchased an almost 10% interest in Allergan while Valeant made the tender offer. Why do you think the two firms structured the transaction in this manner? Is this type of relationship a harbinger for future offers?

2. What are some of the drawbacks to this structure, both practical and legal?

3. The court states that "there is no dispute that Pershing Square possessed non-public information and did not disclose that information to the public" before purchasing shares. The court analyzed the behavior under Rule 14e-3. What about Rule 10b-5, the traditional insider trading provision? Is it possible that the alleged behavior in this case violated this provision?

4. Ultimately Pershing and Valeant proved unsuccessful in the acquisition attempt. Allergan successfully negotiated a merger with a white knight, Actavis, that paid a higher price. Public reports indicated that Pershing was set to earn more than $2 billion from his investment in Allergan.

5. The tender offer remained in abeyance with the adoption of a poison pill by Allergan. As a result, Pershing sought to replace a majority of the board at a special meeting of shareholders. In order to call the special meeting, Pershing needed the support of 25% of the outstanding voting shares. The bylaws, adopted by the board of Allergan, imposed significant restrictions on the right to call meetings. For example, shareholders were disqualified to the extent refusing to agree to hold their shares through the date of the meeting. Nonetheless, despite the restrictions, Pershing managed to obtain the requisite support and, once done, brought suit to force the board of Allergan to call the special meeting. In a hearing on the action, the Vice Chancellor was reputed to have commented that the provision was a "horse-choker of a bylaw." Ultimately, Allergan agreed to hold the meeting and the lawsuit was dropped. Why might Pershing have opted for this tactic and why might shareholders have supported the efforts to call a special meeting?

II. State Law and the Regulation of Defensive Tactics

Much of the state law applicable to tender offers developed in the 1980s when a wave of hostile acquisitions swept through the markets. The responses took two distinct forms. On the one hand, management tried to impede the acquisitions through the use of an assortment of defensive tactics, with poison pills ultimately emerging as the most popular (and effective).

As the courts struggled to address the appropriate standard for reviewing defensive tactics, states intervened more directly. In general, they did not take kindly to hostile tender offers. An acquisition could result in the relocation of a company's headquarters or a raft of cost cutting measures (including layoffs), all of which could have a detrimental effect on the state's economy. Some responded by adopting statutes designed to make takeovers more difficult.

A. Anti-Takeover Statutes

The first generation of statutes merely obligated acquirers to give target companies advance notice of an impending tender offer. Thus, the Illinois Business Take-Over Act required an offeror to provide target companies with certain connections to the state with twenty days advance notice before the offer could become effective. In *Edgar v. Mite*, 457 U.S. 624 (1982), the Court struck down the statute, concluding that it violated the Commerce Clause. A plurality of Justices also found these first generation statutes were preempted under the Williams Act.

States did not give up. In the aftermath of *Edgar v. Mite*, a second generation of statutes arose. Labeled control share acquisition statutes, they were drafted in a manner that more closely resembled traditional governance provisions. The statutes applied only to companies incorporated in the adopting state. Moreover, they effectively required large shareholders seeking to acquire control to first obtain approval of either disinterested directors or disinterested shareholders. Most commentators and practitioners probably expected these statutes to suffer the same fate as the anti-takeover statutes struck down in *Edgar v. Mite*. The Supreme Court, however, had other ideas.

CTS Corp. v. Dynamics Corp. of America

United States Supreme Court
481 U.S. 69 (1987)

POWELL, JUSTICE:

These cases present the questions whether the Control Share Acquisitions Chapter of the Indiana Business Corporation Law, Ind. Code § 23-1-42-1 *et seq.* (Supp.1986), is pre-empted by the Williams Act, 82 Stat. 454, as amended, 15 U.S.C. §§ 78m(d)-(e) and 78n(d)-(f) (1982 ed. and Supp. III), or violates the Commerce Clause of the Federal Constitution, Art. I, § 8, cl. 3.

I

A

On March 4, 1986, the Governor of Indiana signed a revised Indiana Business Corporation Law, Ind. Code § 23-1-17-1 et seq. (Supp. 1986). That law included the Control Share Acquisitions Chapter (Indiana Act or Act). Beginning on August 1, 1987, the Act will apply to any corporation incorporated in Indiana, § 23-1-17-3(a), unless the corporation amends its articles of incorporation or bylaws to opt out of the Act, § 23-1-42-5. Before that date, any Indiana corporation can opt into the Act by resolution of its board of directors. § 23-1-17-3(b). The Act applies only to "issuing public corporations." The term "corporation" includes only businesses incorporated in Indiana. *See* § 23-1-20-5. An "issuing public corporation" is defined as:

"a corporation that has:

"(1) one hundred (100) or more shareholders;

"(2) its principal place of business, its principal office, or substantial assets within Indiana; and

"(3) either:

"(A) more than ten percent (10%) of its shareholders resident in Indiana;

"(B) more than ten percent (10%) of its shares owned by Indiana residents; or

"(C) ten thousand (10,000) shareholders resident in Indiana."

§ 23-1-42-4(a).

The Act focuses on the acquisition of "control shares" in an issuing public corporation. Under the Act, an entity acquires "control shares" whenever it acquires shares that, but for the operation of the Act, would bring its voting power in the corporation to or above any of three thresholds: 20%, 33 1/3%, or 50%. § 23-1-42-1. An entity that acquires control shares does not necessarily acquire voting rights. Rather, it gains those rights only "to the extent granted by resolution approved by the shareholders of the issuing public corporation." §23-1-42-(a). Section 23-1-42-9(b) requires a majority vote of all disinterested shareholders holding each class of stock for passage of such a resolution. The practical effect of this requirement is to condition acquisition of control of a corporation on approval of a majority of the pre-existing disinterested shareholders.

The shareholders decide whether to confer rights on the control shares at the next regularly scheduled meeting of the shareholders, or at a specially scheduled meeting. The acquirer can require management of the corporation to hold such a special meeting within 50 days if it files an "acquiring person statement," requests the meeting, and agrees to pay the expenses of the meeting. *See* §23-1-42-7. If the shareholders do not vote to restore voting rights to the shares, the corporation may redeem the control shares from the acquirer at fair market value, but it is not required to do so. §23-1-42-10(b). Similarly, if the acquirer does not file an acquiring person statement with the corporation, the corporation may, if its bylaws or articles of incorporation so provide, redeem the shares at any time after 60 days after the acquirer's last acquisition. §23-1-42-10(a).

B.

On March 10, 1986, appellee Dynamics Corporate of America (Dynamics) owned 9.6% of the common stock of appellant CTS Corporation, an Indiana corporation. On that day, six days after the Act went into effect, Dynamics announced a tender offer for another million shares in CTS; purchase of those shares would have brought Dynamics' ownership interest in CTS to 27.5%. Also on March 10, Dynamics filed suit in the United States District Court for the Northern District of Illinois, alleging that CTS had violated the federal securities laws in a number of respects no longer relevant to these proceedings. On March 27, the board of directors of CTS, an Indiana corporation, elected to be governed by the provisions of the Act, *See* §23-1-17-3.

* * *

The Act does not impose an absolute 50-day delay on tender offers, nor does it preclude an offeror from purchasing shares as soon as federal law permits. If the offeror fears an adverse shareholder vote under the Act, it can make a conditional tender offer, offering to accept shares on the condition that the shares receive voting rights within a certain period of time. The Williams Act permits tender offers to be conditioned on the offeror's subsequently obtaining regulatory approval. E.g., Interpretive Release Relating to Tender Offer Rules, SEC Exchange Act Rel. No. 34-16623 (Mar. 5, 1980), 3CCH Fed. Sec. L. Rep. para. 24,284I, p. 17,758, quoted in MacFadden Holdings, Inc. v. JB Acquisition Corp., 802 F.2d 62, 70 (CA2 1986). There is no reason to doubt that this type of conditional tender offer would be legitimate as well.

Even assuming that the Indiana Act imposes some additional delay, nothing in *MITE* suggested that *any* delay imposed by state regulation, however short, would create a conflict with the Williams Act. The plurality argued only that the offeror should "be free to go forward without *unreasonable* delay." 457 U.S. at 639 (emphasis added). In that case, the Court was confronted with the potential for indefinite delay and presented with no persuasive reason why some deadline could not be established. By contrast, the Indiana Act provides that full voting rights will be vested—if this eventually is to occur—within 50 days after commencement of the offer. This period is within the 60-day period Congress established for reinstitution of withdrawal rights in 15 U. S. C. §78n(d) (5). We cannot say that a delay within that congressionally determined period is unreasonable.

Finally, we note that the Williams Act would pre-empt a variety of state corporate laws of hitherto unquestioned validity if it were construed to pre-empt any state statute that may limit or delay the free exercise of power after a successful tender offer. State corporate laws commonly permit corporations to stagger the terms of their directors. *See* Model Business Corp. Act §37 (1969 draft) in 3 Model Business Corp. Act Ann. (2d ed. 1971) (hereinafter MBCA); American Bar Foundation, Revised Model Business Corp. Act §8.06 (1984 draft) (1985) (hereinafter RMBCA). By staggering the terms of directors, and thus having annual elections for only one class of directors each year, corporations may delay the time when a successful offeror gains control of the board of directors. Similarly, state corporation laws commonly provide for cumulative voting. *See* 1 MBCA §33, para. 4; RMBCA §7.28. By enabling minority shareholders to assure themselves of representation in each class of directors, cumulative voting provisions can delay further the ability of offerors to gain untrammeled authority over the affairs of the target corporation. *See* Hochman & Folger, Deflecting Takeovers: Charter and By-Law Techniques, 34 Bus. Law. 537, 538–539 (1979).

In our view, the possibility that the Indiana Act will delay some tender offers is insufficient to require a conclusion that the Williams Act pre-empts the Act. The longstanding prevalence of state regulation in this area suggests that, if Congress had intended to pre-empt all state laws that delay the acquisition of voting control following a tender offer, it would have said so explicitly. The regulatory conditions that the Act places on tender offers are consistent with the text and the purposes of the Williams Act. Accordingly, we hold that the Williams Act does not pre-empt the Indiana Act.

* * *

The principal objects of dormant Commerce Clause scrutiny are statutes that discriminate against interstate commerce. *See*, e. g., Lewis v. BT Investment Managers, Inc., 447 U.S. 27, 36–37 (1980); Philadelphia v. New Jersey, 437 U.S. 617, 624 (1978). *See* generally Regan, The Supreme Court and State Protectionism: Making Sense of the Dormant Commerce Clause, 84 Mich. L. Rev. 1091 (1986). The Indiana Act is not such a statute. It has the same effects on tender offers whether or not the offeror is a domiciliary or resident of Indiana. Thus, it "visits its effects equally upon both interstate and local business," Lewis v. BT Investment Managers, Inc., supra, at 36.

… Because nothing in the Indiana Act imposes a greater burden on out-of-state offerors than it does on similarly situated Indiana offerors, we reject the contention that the Act discriminates against interstate commerce.

* * *

The Court of Appeals did not find the Act unconstitutional for either of these threshold reasons. Rather, its decision rested on its view of the Act's potential to hinder tender offers. We think the Court of Appeals failed to appreciate the significance for Commerce Clause analysis of the fact that state regulation of corporate governance is regulation of entities whose very existence and attributes are a product of state law.... Every State in this country has enacted laws regulating corporate governance. By prohibiting certain transactions, and regulating others, such laws necessarily affect certain aspects of interstate commerce. This necessarily is true with respect to corporations with shareholders in States other than the State of incorporation. Large corporations that are listed on national exchanges, or even regional exchanges, will have shareholders in many States and shares that are traded frequently. The markets that facilitate this national and international participation in ownership of corporations are essential for providing capital not only for new enterprises but also for established companies that need to expand their businesses. This beneficial free market system depends at its core upon the fact that a corporation—except in the rarest situations—is organized under, and governed by, the law of a single jurisdiction, traditionally the corporate law of the State of its incorporation.

These regulatory laws may affect directly a variety of corporate transactions. Mergers are a typical example. In view of the substantial effect that a merger may have on the shareholders' interests in a corporation, many States require supermajority votes to approve mergers. *See, e. g.,* 2 MBCA § 73 (requiring approval of a merger by a majority of all shares, rather than simply a majority of votes cast); RMBCA § 11.03 (same). By requiring a greater vote for mergers than is required for other transactions, these laws make it more difficult for corporations to merge. State laws also may provide for "dissenters' rights" under which minority shareholders who disagree with corporate decisions to take particular actions are entitled to sell their shares to the corporation at fair market value. *See, e. g.,* 2 MBCA §§ 80, 81; RMBCA § 13.02. By requiring the corporation to purchase the shares of dissenting shareholders, these laws may inhibit a corporation from engaging in the specified transactions.

It thus is an accepted part of the business landscape in this country for States to create corporations, to prescribe their powers, and to define the rights that are acquired by purchasing their shares. A State has an interest in promoting stable relationships among parties involved in the corporations it charters, as well as in ensuring that investors in such corporations have an effective voice in corporate affairs.

There can be no doubt that the Act reflects these concerns. The primary purpose of the Act is to protect the shareholders of Indiana corporations. It does this by affording shareholders, when a takeover offer is made, an opportunity to decide collectively whether the resulting change in voting control of the corporation, as they perceive it, would be desirable. A change of management may have important effects on the shareholders' interests; it is well within the State's role as overseer of corporate governance to offer this opportunity. The autonomy provided by allowing shareholders collectively to determine whether the takeover is advantageous to their interests may be especially beneficial where a hostile tender offer may coerce shareholders into tendering their shares.

* * *

Dynamics' argument that the Act is unconstitutional ultimately rests on its contention that the Act will limit the number of successful tender offers. There is little evidence that this will occur. But even if true, this result would not substantially affect our Commerce Clause analysis. We reiterate that this Act does not prohibit any entity—resident or nonresident—from offering to purchase, or from purchasing, shares in Indiana corporations, or from attempting thereby to gain control. It only provides regulatory procedures designed for the better protection of the corporations' shareholders. We have rejected the "notion that the Commerce Clause protects the particular structure or methods of operation in a ... market." Exxon Corp. v. Governor of Maryland, 437 U.S. at 127. The very commodity that is traded in the securities market is one whose characteristics are defined by state law. Similarly, the very commodity that is traded in the "market for corporate control"—the corporation—is one that owes its existence and attributes to state law. Indiana need not define these commodities as other States do; it need only provide that residents and nonresidents have equal access to them. This Indiana has done. Accordingly, even if the Act should decrease the number of successful tender offers for Indiana corporations, this would not offend the Commerce Clause.

Comments and Questions

1. The analysis in *CTS* may have been influenced by disagreement between the Securities and Exchange Commission and the Department of Justice over the preemption analysis provided to the Supreme Court. *See* Neal Devins, *Unitariness and Independence: Solicitor General Control over Independent Agency Litigation*, 82 Cal. L. Rev. 255, 292 (1994) ("In the 1987 CTS v. Dynamics litigation, the Solicitor General agreed with the SEC that the Indiana Control Share Acquisition Act violated the Commerce Clause but disagreed with the SEC's assertion that the law also failed under federal preemption doctrine."). Although an independent federal agency, the SEC has no authority to directly litigate before the Supreme Court.

2. The Illinois statute at issue in *Edgar v. Mite* applied to corporations not incorporated in the state as long as they had their principal executive offices in the state or shareholders in the state owned at least 10% of the shares of the company. How was the statute at issue in *CTS* different? How did this difference influence the Court's decision?

3. Ohio is generally given credit for developing the first control share acquisition statute. *See* Robert A. Prentice, *The Role of States in Tender Offers: An Analysis of CTS*, 1988 Colum. Bus. L. Rev. 1, 27. This was not, however, the only model employed by the states. Some adopted "fair price" provisions that are essentially designed to ensure adequate consideration in the second step of a takeover. The statute mostly protected against two-tier tender offers by ensuring that the shareholders not tendering in the front end transaction would nonetheless receive the same consideration on the back end. Shareholder redemption (or cash out) statutes required acquirers obtaining more than a specified percentage of shares to make an offer to the remaining shareholders.

4. Some states, including New York and Delaware, adopted a business combination statute. *See* Del. Code Ann. tit. 8, §203. These statutes, sometimes referred to as merger moratorium statutes, prohibit "business combinations" with interested shareholders (those owning a specified percentage of shares, often 20%) absent board or shareholder approval for a specified number of years. How might these statutes discourage takeovers?

5. Anti-takeover statutes have become widespread. *See* Roberta Romano, *The States as a Laboratory: Legal Innovation and State Competition for Corporate Charters*, 23 Yale J. on Reg. 209, 215 (2006) (determining that 43 states have "second" generation anti-takeover statutes in place). Given the widespread use of poison pills and other anti-takeover tactics, are these statutes necessary?

B. The Role of the Target Board in Hostile Takeovers

Most resistance to hostile tender offers, however, occurs at the board level. Boards have a dizzying array of potential responses to unwanted acquisition attempts. They range from lock-up options for the crown jewels, to scorched earth, to poison pills. The tactics are designed to induce the acquirer to give up, thereby denying shareholders the right to sell their shares, typically for a significant premium.

Board resistance at one time generated a serious academic debate over the appropriate role of directors in the takeover process. The debate provided two extreme positions: those who argued for a role of passivity for the board and a prohibition on all defensive measures and those who argued for almost unlimited discretion in the board's ability to resist.

Frank H. Easterbrook & Daniel R. Fischel, *The Proper Role of a Target's Management in Responding to a Tender Offer*
94 Harv. L. Rev. 1161, 1173–75 (1981)[2]

Tender offers are a method of monitoring the work of management teams. Prospective bidders monitor the performance of managerial teams by comparing a corporation's potential value with its value (as reflected by share prices) under current management. When the difference between the market price of a firm's shares and the price those shares might have under different circumstances becomes too great, an outsider can profit by buying the firm and improving its management. The outsider reduces the free riding problem because it owns a majority of the shares. The source of the premium is the reduction in agency costs, which makes the firm's assets worth more in the hands of the acquirer than they were worth in the hands of the firm's managers.

All parties benefit in this process. The target's shareholders gain because they receive a premium over the market price. The bidder obtains the difference between the new value of the firm and the payment to the old shareholders. Nontendering shareholders receive part of the appreciation in the price of the shares.

---

2. Copyright © 1981 Harvard Law Review Association. Reprinted with permission.

More significantly for our purposes, shareholders benefit even if their corporation never is the subject of a tender offer. The process of monitoring by outsiders poses a continuous threat of takeover if performance lags. Managers will attempt to reduce agency costs in order to reduce the chance of takeover, and the process of reducing agency costs leads to higher prices for shares. We now explore how different responses to takeover bids influence the size of the benefit derived from monitoring by outsiders in advance of any offer.

B. The Consequences of Management's Defensive Tactics

i. Resistance and Agency Costs. — The argument presented above establishes that takeovers are beneficial to both shareholders and society. It follows that any strategy designed to prevent tender offers reduces welfare. If the company adopts a policy of intransigent resistance and succeeds in maintaining its independence, the shareholders lose whatever premium over market value the bidder offered or would have offered but for the resistance or the prospect of resistance. This lost premium reflects a foregone social gain from the superior employment of the firm's assets.

The target's managers, however, have a substantial interest in preserving their company's independence and thus preserving their salaries and status; the less effective they have been as managers, the greater their interest in preventing a takeover. They may disguise a policy of resistance to all offers as a policy of searching for a better offer than any made so far. Extensive manuals describe both the stratagems of resistance and the methods of disguise. There is no signal that separates intransigent resistance from honest efforts to conduct an auction for the shareholders' benefit. The fact that the first tender offer or any subsequent offer is defeated supplies little information, because any auctioneer understands that determined efforts to collect the highest possible price may lead to no sale at all in the short run.

Even resistance that ultimately elicits a higher bid is socially wasteful. Although the target's shareholders may receive a higher price, these gains are exactly offset by the bidder's payment and thus by a loss to the bidder's shareholders. Shareholders as a group gain nothing; the increase in the price is simply a transfer payment from the bidder's shareholders to the target's shareholders. Indeed, because the process of resistance consumes real resources, shareholders as a whole lose by the amount targets spend in resistance plus the amount bidders and any rivals spend in overcoming resistance. These additional costs can be substantial.

Martin Lipton, *Takeover Bids in the Target's Boardroom*
35 Bus. Law. 101 (1979)[3]

Assuming that a raider makes a firm takeover offer at a substantial premium, must the directors ignore questions as to the adequacy of the price, the legality of the acquisition, the impact on employees, customers, suppliers, communities and national policy and let the shareholders decide for themselves?

---

3. Reprinted by permission of the author.

In pursuing this discussion it will be assumed that the holders of a majority of the shares of the target would accept the offer. This has been the experience in almost every tender offer during the past five years.... The failure of management to convince shareholders not to accept a tender offer is the result of several factors. First, the special dynamics of a tender offer are such that the decision of shareholders is almost always a foregone conclusion—they will tender, therefore, it is misleading to speak of a free shareholder choice at all. The existence of an offer to acquire a controlling interest in a company makes it almost impossible for a shareholder in the target to prudently retain his shares unless he does so for the purpose of exchanging them in a promised subsequent tax-free exchange. Once a raider has acquired control—and target shareholders must assume that the raider will acquire control—it is highly unlikely that shareholders will receive a higher price than that initially offered: since there is no possibility of a competing offer at a higher price, the public trading market (if one still exists) will have been capped at the price offered in the tender offer and the raider is not likely to offer more for the target's shares once it has achieved control. Retaining the target's shares in the face of a tender offer will bring the shareholder no benefit. He is likely to be forced out through a merger at a later date for the same price he could have realized upon the initial offer. The outcome of a shareholder referendum conducted in the form of a tender offer cannot realistically be said to reflect a careful appraisal of the merits or demerits of the offer. Each individual shareholder must look to his own interest and must pragmatically assume that most other shareholders will tender with the result that the nontendering shareholder will be left in a minority, illiquid investment position. Thus, any uncoerced decision *against* acceptance of a tender offer can *only* be made at the board of directors level.

The second factor which accounts for acceptance of tender offers by shareholders is the shift of equities from individuals to professional investment managers during the last 30 years; a shift that has closely paralleled the growth of institutions such as pension funds, private foundations and mutual funds. Today, practical control, *i.e.*, 20 percent to 50 percent of the stock of a large number of major corporations is held by professional investors. As predicted by A.A. Berle, we have now reached the tertiary stage of capitalism. Control of American business passed from the founder-shareholders to the professional managers who held sway until the 1970s and now, at least in the sense of ability to control in the event of a tender offer or proxy contest, to the professional managers of pension funds, foundations and mutual funds. In addition to the holdings of the institutional investors, professional and amateur arbitrageurs will frequently purchase 10 percent to 50 percent of the shares of a target. While some of the arbitrage stock comes from the institutions, it is not infrequent that the institutions and arbitrageurs together quickly end up with a greater than 50 percent interest in a target and thus have the ability to determine its destiny. It is rare for a target to survive as an independent company after such a situation develops.

The only interest of the arbitrageur is in a quick sale at a profit. Some of the institutions may have a longer investment perspective, but in the competition to demonstrate performance among professional investment managers, the lure of improving performance and the ability of tax-exempt funds to realize gains without incurring any tax almost always results in a decision to sell even when there is no more attractive long-term investment available. Frequently this decision to sell is motivated in part by a desire to avoid becoming a minority holder—often with a loss of market liquidity—in a target that will be controlled by the raider. This is so even where the control is less than 50%.

* * *

Even in the face of such an *ad hoc* consortium, the necessity from technological, social and economic standpoints for long-term planning by business requires a policy decision in favor of not mandating decisions that ignore or penalize long-term planning. Rather than forcing directors to consider only the short-term interests of certain shareholders, national policy requires that directors also consider the long-term interests of the shareholders and the company as a business enterprise with all of its constituencies in addition to the short-term and institutional shareholders. There would be a compelling argument for this result even if experience had proven that all takeovers turned out better for the shareholders of the target if they sold at the takeover price. Since experience proves that the decision to sell or remain independent is not clear, and that even when measured by comparing the rejected offer price with the market price, in more than 50 percent of the rejected takeovers the shareholders did better by the target remaining independent. There is no reason to remove the decision on a takeover from the reasonable business judgment of the directors. On the contrary, the policy considerations are overwhelmingly in favor of specific recognition that the directors not only have the right to make takeover decisions based on their reasonable business judgment, but that macrosocioeconomic issues must be considered along with the long-term interests of the shareholders and the company as a business enterprise.

If the shareholders are dissatisfied with the directors' rejection of a takeover bid, they have the right, through the normal proxy machinery, to replace the directors or to instruct the directors to accept a takeover bid. This right, however, should not be translated into an absolute requirement that the directors pass to the shareholders the direct right to accept or reject any takeover bid. To do so would be the equivalent of mandating sale whenever an unsolicited takeover bid is made.

Comments and Questions

1. Professor Fischel and now Judge Easterbrook were renowned for their role in the law and economics movement and in the application of economic analysis to corporate law. What do you make of the application of these principles to the market for corporate control?

2. The assertion that hostile takeovers were necessary to discipline inefficient management was a widely repeated and much accepted view in academia. Do you agree with the perspective? What critique might you offer?

3. The statistics on the economic benefits of hostile acquisitions are mixed. They clearly benefited shareholders of the target company. *See* Gregg A. Jarrell et al., *The*

Market for Corporate Control: The Empirical Evidence Since 1980, 2 J. Econ. Persp. 49, 51 (1988) (noting that "from 1980 to 1985 the average premium was 30 percent."). *See also* Jensen & Ruback, *The Market for Corporate Control*, 11 J. Fin. Econ. 5, 10 (1983) ("The thirteen studies [discussed in the article] indicate that targets of successful takeover attempts release substantial and statistically significant increases in their stock prices."). The evidence with respect to shareholders of the bidder, however, is less clear. Jensen and Ruback, for example, conclude that the "returns to *successful bidding* firms in *mergers* are zero." *Id.* at 22 (emphasis in original) (although noting a "small positive abnormal return" for successful bidding firms in tender offers). Why might shares of the bidder not increase?

4. Do you agree with Mr. Lipton that shareholders need the protection of management from hostile acquisitions? Is it a "foregone conclusion" that they will always tender, irrespective of the merits of the offer? What critique might be offered of the alternative position that defensive tactics should be entirely up to the discretion of the board?

5. Mr. Lipton seems to argue that management should be allowed to "just say no" to an offer under the theory that management has a duty to protect the long term interests of the company. Do you agree with this reasoning? To the extent shareholders object, Mr. Lipton asserts that the proxy machinery provides an effective avenue for shareholders. Is he correct on this point?

6. A great deal has changed since this debate occurred. Do you think circumstances in the intervening years have provided empirical evidence to support one position over the other? Compare the opinions written by Judges Posner and Easterbrook in *Jones v. Harris* that are excerpted in Chapter 6. What do you make of these opinions?

7. In an article written a quarter of a century after the seminal piece excerpted here, Mr. Lipton again raised concerns about a possible weakening of the boards' role in the governance process, although not as a result of hostile takeovers. As he stated:

> Proposals to over-engineer board composition, adopt stricter definitions of director independence, limit the amount and form of executive compensation and increase "shareholder power," coupled with increasing displays of influence by special-interest shareholders (through, for example, withhold-the-vote campaigns and insistence on personal contributions by directors to the settlement of derivative lawsuits), once again threaten to erode the fundamental principles that underlie the business judgment rule and that enable the board to function in an entrepreneurial manner.

Martin Lipton, *Twenty-Five Years After Takeover Bids in the Target's Boardroom: Old Battles, New Attacks and the Continuing War*, 60 Bus. Law. 1369, 1370 (2005). Do you agree? What does this suggest about the dynamics taking place in the corporate governance debate?

In the end, the debate fell to the Delaware courts to resolve. The Delaware Supreme Court did so in *Unocal.*

Unocal Corp. v. Mesa Petroleum Co.

Delaware Supreme Court
493 A.2d 946 (1985)

MOORE, JUSTICE:

On April 8, 1985, Mesa, the owner of approximately 13% of Unocal's stock, commenced a two-tier "front loaded" cash tender offer for 64 million shares, or approximately 37%, of Unocal's outstanding stock at a price of $54 per share. The "back-end" was designed to eliminate the remaining publicly held shares by an exchange of securities purportedly worth $54 per share. However, pursuant to an order entered by the United States District Court for the Central District of California on April 26, 1985, Mesa issued a supplemental proxy statement to Unocal's stockholders disclosing that the securities offered in the second-step merger would be highly subordinated, and that Unocal's capitalization would differ significantly from its present structure. Unocal has rather aptly termed such securities "junk bonds."

Unocal's board consists of eight independent outside directors and six insiders. It met on April 13, 1985, to consider the Mesa tender offer. Thirteen directors were present, and the meeting lasted nine and one-half hours.... Despite the nine and one-half hour length of the meeting, no formal decision was made on the proposed defensive self-tender.

On April 15, the board met again with four of the directors present by telephone and one member still absent.... Based upon this advice, and the board's own deliberations, the directors unanimously approved the exchange offer. Their resolution provided that if Mesa acquired 64 million shares of Unocal stock through its own offer (the Mesa Purchase Condition), Unocal would buy the remaining 49% outstanding for an exchange of debt securities having an aggregate par value of $72 per share. The board resolution also stated that the offer would be subject to other conditions that had been described to the board at the meeting, or which were deemed necessary by Unocal's officers, including the exclusion of Mesa from the proposal (the Mesa exclusion). Any such conditions were required to be in accordance with the "purport and intent" of the offer.

* * *

We begin with the basic issue of the power of a board of directors of a Delaware corporation to adopt a defensive measure of this type. Absent such authority, all other questions are moot. Neither issues of fairness nor business judgment are pertinent without the basic underpinning of a board's legal power to act.

The board has a large reservoir of authority upon which to draw. Its duties and responsibilities proceed from the inherent powers conferred by 8 Del. C. § 141(a), respecting management of the corporation's "business and affairs". Additionally, the powers here being exercised derive from 8 Del. C. § 160(a), conferring broad authority upon a corporation to deal in its own stock. From this it is now well established that in the acquisition of its shares a Delaware corporation may deal selectively with its stockholders, provided the directors have not acted out of a sole or primary purpose to entrench themselves in office.... Finally, the board's power to act derives from its fundamental duty and obligation to protect the corporate enterprise, which includes stockholders, from harm reasonably perceived, irrespective of its source.... Thus, we are satisfied that in the broad context of corporate governance, including issues of fundamental corporate change, a board of directors is not a passive instrumentality.

* * *

When a board addresses a pending takeover bid it has an obligation to determine whether the offer is in the best interests of the corporation and its shareholders. In that respect a board's duty is no different from any other responsibility it shoulders, and its decisions should be no less entitled to the respect they otherwise would be accorded in the realm of business judgment. *See also* Johnson v. Trueblood, 629 F.2d 287, 292–293 (3d Cir. 1980). There are, however, certain caveats to a proper exercise of this function. Because of the omnipresent specter that a board may be acting primarily in its own interests, rather than those of the corporation and its shareholders, there is an enhanced duty which calls for judicial examination at the threshold before the protections of the business judgment rule may be conferred.

... In the face of this inherent conflict directors must show that they had reasonable grounds for believing that a danger to corporate policy and effectiveness existed because of another person's stock ownership. Cheff v. Mathes, 199 A.2d at 554–55. However, they satisfy that burden "by showing good faith and reasonable investigation...." Id. at 555. Furthermore, such proof is materially enhanced, as here, by the approval of a board comprised of a majority of outside independent directors who have acted in accordance with the foregoing standards.

* * *

A.

In the board's exercise of corporate power to forestall a takeover bid our analysis begins with the basic principle that corporate directors have a fiduciary duty to act in the best interests of the corporation's stockholders. Guth v. Loft, Inc., Del. Supr., 23 Del. Ch. 255, 5 A.2d 503, 510 (1939). As we have noted, their duty of care extends to protecting the corporation and its owners from perceived harm whether a threat originates from third parties or other shareholders. But such powers are not absolute. A corporation does not have unbridled discretion to defeat any perceived threat by any Draconian means available.

The restriction placed upon a selective stock repurchase is that the directors may not have acted solely or primarily out of a desire to perpetuate themselves in office. See Cheff v. Mathes, 199 A.2d at 556; Kors v. Carey, 158 A.2d at 140. Of course, to this is added the further caveat that inequitable action may not be taken under the guise of law. Schnell v. Chris-Craft Industries, Inc., Del. Supr., 285 A.2d 437, 439 (1971). The standard of proof established in Cheff v. Mathes and discussed supra at page 16, is designed to ensure that a defensive measure to thwart or impede a takeover is indeed motivated by a good faith concern for the welfare of the corporation and its stockholders, which in all circumstances must be free of any fraud or other misconduct. Cheff v. Mathes, 199 A.2d at 554–55. However, this does not end the inquiry.

B.

A further aspect is the element of balance. If a defensive measure is to come within the ambit of the business judgment rule, it must be reasonable in relation to the threat posed. This entails an analysis by the directors of the nature of the takeover bid and its effect on the corporate enterprise. Examples of such concerns may include: inadequacy of the price offered, nature and timing of the offer, questions of illegality, the impact on "constituencies" other than shareholders (i.e., creditors, customers, employees, and perhaps even the community generally), the risk of nonconsummation, and the quality of securities being offered in the exchange. *See* Lipton and Brownstein, *Takeover Responses and Directors' Responsibilities: An Update*, p.7, ABA National Institute on the Dynamics of Corporate Control (December 8, 1983). While not a controlling factor, it also seems to us that a board may reasonably consider the basic stockholder interests at stake, including those of short term speculators, whose actions may have fueled the coercive aspect of the offer at the expense of the long term investor. Here, the threat posed was viewed by the Unocal board as a grossly inadequate two-tier coercive tender offer coupled with the threat of greenmail.

Specifically, the Unocal directors had concluded that the value of Unocal was substantially above the $54 per share offered in cash at the front end. Furthermore, they determined that the subordinated securities to be exchanged in Mesa's announced squeeze out of the remaining shareholders in the "back-end" merger were "junk bonds" worth far less than $54. It is now well recognized that such offers are a classic coercive measure designed to stampede shareholders into tendering at the first tier, even if the price is inadequate, out of fear of what they will receive at the back end of the transaction. Wholly beyond the coercive aspect of an inadequate two-tier tender offer, the threat was posed by a corporate raider with a national reputation as a "greenmailer".

In adopting the selective exchange offer, the board stated that its objective was either to defeat the inadequate Mesa offer or, should the offer still succeed, provide the 49% of its stockholders, who would otherwise be forced to accept "junk bonds", with $72 worth of senior debt. We find that both purposes are valid.

However, such efforts would have been thwarted by Mesa's participation in the exchange offer. First, if Mesa could tender its shares, Unocal would effectively be subsidizing the former's continuing effort to buy Unocal stock at $54 per share. Second, Mesa could not, by definition, fit within the class of shareholders being protected from its own coercive and inadequate tender offer.

Thus, we are satisfied that the selective exchange offer is reasonably related to the threats posed. It is consistent with the principle that "the minority stockholder shall receive the substantial equivalent in value of what he had before." Sterling v. Mayflower Hotel Corp., Del. Supr., 33 Del. Ch. 293, 93 A.2d 107, 114 (1952). *See also* Rosenblatt v. Getty Oil Co., Del.Supr., 493 A.2d 929, 940 (1985). This concept of fairness, while stated in the merger context, is also relevant in the area tender offer law. Thus, the board's decision to offer what it determined to be the fair value of the corporation to the 49% of its shareholders, who would otherwise be forced to accept highly subordinated "junk bonds", is reasonable and consistent with the directors' duty to ensure that the minority stockholders receive equal value for their shares.

Comments and Questions

1. How did the court resolve the debate between Mr. Lipton and (then) professors Easterbrook and Fischel? Did one side come out better than the other? One commentator concluded that "the Delaware Supreme Court chose the middle ground that had been championed by no one." Ronald J. Gilson, *Unocal Fifteen Years Later (and What We Can Do About It)*, 26 Del. J. Corp. L. 491, 496 (2001). Do you agree?

2. The court commented specifically on the position taken by Professors Easterbrook and Fischel. *See* 493 A.2d at 955 n. 10 ("It has been suggested that a board's response to a takeover threat should be a passive one. Easterbrook & Fischel, *supra*, at 1750. However, that clearly is not the law of Delaware, and as the proponents of this rule of passivity readily concede, it has not been adopted either by courts or state legislatures.").

3. The defensive tactic in this case was a self tender offer. How did it work to ward off Mesa?

4. The court imposed the initial burden on the board of the target company. Defensive tactics were only permitted if directors first identified a threat to the company. What was the threat in this case? Could Mesa have done anything to alleviate the "threat"? What other types of threats might justify the adoption of defensive tactics under the standard set out in *Unocal*?

5. The tactic also must be "reasonable in relation to the threat posed." Is this a balancing test? How might this work in practice?

6. The venerable decision still can elicit strong reactions. As one author wrote two decades after the decision: "Over the last twenty years, academics and others have subjected *Unocal* to unrelenting criticism." Stephen M. Bainbridge, *Unocal at 20: Director Primacy in Corporate Takeovers*, 31 Del. J. Corp. L. 769, 772 (2006). Why do you think this is the case?

After *Unocal*, speculation arose that the Delaware courts would go even further and allow boards to "just say no" to a hostile tender offer.

Paramount Communications, Inc. v. Time Inc.

Delaware Supreme Court
571 A.2d 1140 (1989)

HORSEY, JUSTICE:

As early as 1983 and 1984, Time's executive board began considering expanding Time's operations into the entertainment industry....

* * *

On March 3, 1989, Time's board, with all but one director in attendance, met and unanimously approved the stock-for-stock merger with Warner. Warner's board likewise approved the merger. The agreement called for Warner to be merged into a wholly-owned Time subsidiary with Warner becoming the surviving corporation. The common stock of Warner would then be converted into common stock of Time at the agreed upon ratio. Thereafter, the name of Time would be changed to Time-Warner, Inc.

* * *

At its March 3, 1989 meeting, Time's board adopted several defensive tactics. Time entered an automatic share exchange agreement with Warner. Time would receive 17,292,747 shares of Warner's outstanding common stock (9.4%) and Warner would receive 7,080,016 shares of Time's outstanding common stock (11.1%). Either party could trigger the exchange. Time sought out and paid for "confidence" letters from various banks with which it did business.... Time also agreed to a "no-shop" clause, preventing Time from considering any other consolidation proposal, thus relinquishing its power to consider other proposals, regardless of their merits. Time did so at Warner's insistence. Warner did not want to be left "on the auction block" for an unfriendly suitor, if Time were to withdraw from the deal.

* * *

[On June 7, 1989, Paramount made an all-cash offer for the shares of Time for $175 and said that the offer was "fully negotiable." The board met three times over eight days to discuss the offer.] ... The board's prevailing belief was that Paramount's bid posed a threat to Time's control of its own destiny and retention of the "Time Culture." Even after Time's financial advisors made another presentation of Paramount and its business attributes, Time's board maintained its position that a combination with Warner offered greater potential for Time.... Finally, [on June 16,] Time's board formally rejected Paramount's offer.

* * *

At the same meeting, Time's board decided to recast its consolidation with Warner into an outright cash and securities acquisition of Warner by Time; and Time so informed Warner. Time accordingly restructured its proposal to acquire Warner as follows: Time would make an immediate all-cash offer for 51% of Warner's outstanding stock at $70 per share. The remaining 49% would be purchased at some later date for a mixture of cash and securities worth $70 per share. To provide the funds required for its outright acquisition of Warner, Time would assume 7–10 billion dollars worth of debt, thus eliminating one of the principal transaction-related benefits of the original merger agreement. Nine billion dollars of the total purchase price would be allocated to the purchase of Warner's goodwill.

Warner agreed but insisted on certain terms. Warner sought a control premium and guarantees that the governance provisions found in the original merger agreement would remain intact. Warner further sought agreements that Time would not employ its poison pill against Warner and that, unless enjoined, Time would be legally bound to complete the transaction. Time's board agreed to these last measures only at the insistence of Warner. For its part, Time was assured of its ability to extend its efforts into production areas and international markets, all the while maintaining the Time identity and culture. The Chancellor found the initial Time-Warner transaction to have been negotiated at arms length and the restructured Time-Warner transaction to have resulted from Paramount's offer and its expected effect on a Time shareholder vote.

On June 23, 1989, Paramount raised its all-cash offer to buy Time's outstanding stock to $200 per share. Paramount still professed that all aspects of the offer were negotiable. Time's board met on June 26, 1989 and formally rejected Paramount's $200 per share second offer. The board reiterated its belief that, despite the $25 increase, the offer was still inadequate. The Time board maintained that the Warner transaction offered a greater long-term value for the stockholders and, unlike Paramount's offer, did not pose a threat to Time's survival and its "culture." Paramount then filed this action in the Court of Chancery.

* * *

We turn now to plaintiffs' *Unocal* claim. We begin by noting, as did the Chancellor, that our decision does not require us to pass on the wisdom of the board's decision to enter into the original Time-Warner agreement. That is not a court's task. Our task is simply to review the record to determine whether there is sufficient evidence to support the Chancellor's conclusion that the initial Time-Warner agreement was the product of a proper exercise of business judgment. Macmillan, 559 A.2d at 1288.

* * *

In *Unocal*, we held that before the business judgment rule is applied to a board's adoption of a defensive measure, the burden will lie with the board to prove (a) reasonable grounds for believing that a danger to corporate policy and effectiveness existed; and (b) that the defensive measures adopted was reasonable in relation to the threat posed. Unocal, 493 A.2d 946. Directors satisfy the first part of the Unocal test by demonstrating good faith and reasonable investigation. We have repeatedly stated that the refusal to entertain an offer may comport with a valid exercise of a board's business judgment. See, e.g., Macmillan, 559 A.2d at 1285 n.35; Van Gorkom, 488 A.2d at 881; Pogostin v. Rice, Del. Supr., 480 A.2d 619, 627 (1984).

Unocal involved a two-tier, highly coercive tender offer. In such a case, the threat is obvious: shareholders may be compelled to tender to avoid being treated adversely in the second stage of the transaction. *Accord Ivanhoe*, 535 at 1344. In subsequent cases the Court of Chancery has suggested that an all-cash, all-shares offer, falling within a range of values that a shareholder might reasonably prefer, cannot constitute a legally recognized "threat" to shareholder interests sufficient to withstand a *Unocal* analysis. AC Acquisitions Corp. v. Anderson, Clayton Co., Del. Ch., 519 A.2d 103 (1986); See Grand Metropolitan, PLC v. Pillsbury Co., Del. Ch., 558 A.2d 1049 (1988); City Capital Associates v. Interco, Inc., Del. Ch., 551 A.2d 787 (1988). In those cases, the Court of Chancery determined that whatever threat existed related only to the shareholders and only to price and not to the corporation.

From those decisions by our Court of Chancery, Paramount and the individual plaintiffs extrapolate a rule of law that an all-cash, all-shares offer with values reasonably in the range of acceptable price cannot pose any objective threat to a corporation or its shareholders. Thus, Paramount would have us hold that only if the value of Paramount's offer were determined to be clearly inferior to the value created by management's plan to merge with Warner could the offer be viewed—objectively—as a threat.

Implicit in the plaintiffs' argument is the view that a hostile tender offer can pose only two types of threats: the threat of coercion that results from a two-tier offer promising unequal treatment for nontendering shareholders; and the threat of inadequate value from an all-shares, all-cash offer at a price below what a target board in good faith deems to be the present value of its shares. See, e.g., Interco, 551 A.2d at 797; see also BNS, Inc. v. Koppers, D. Del., 683 F. Supp. 458 (1988). Since Paramount's offer was all-cash, the only conceivable "threat," plaintiffs argue, was inadequate value. We disapprove of such a narrow and rigid construction of Unocal for the reasons which follow.

Plaintiffs' position represents a fundamental misconception of our standard of review under Unocal principally because it would involve the court in substituting its judgment as to what is a "better" deal for that of a corporation's board of directors. To the extent that the Court of Chancery has recently done so in certain of its opinions, we hereby reject such approach as not in keeping with a proper Unocal analysis. See, e.g., Interco, 551 A.2d 787, and its progeny; but see TW Services, Inc. v. SWT Acquisition Corp., Del. Ch., C.A. No. 10427, 1989 Del. Ch. LEXIS 19, Allen, C. (March 2, 1989).

The usefulness of Unocal as an analytical tool is precisely its flexibility in the face of a variety of fact scenarios. Unocal is not intended as an abstract standard; neither is it a structured and mechanistic procedure of appraisal. Thus, we have said that directors may consider, when evaluating the threat posed by a takeover bid, the "inadequacy of the price offered, nature and timing of the offer, questions of illegality, the impact on 'constituencies' other than shareholders, the risk of nonconsummation and the quality of securities being offered in the exchange." 493 A.2d at 955. The open-ended analysis mandated by Unocal is not intended to lead to a simple mathematical exercise: that is, of comparing the discounted value of Time-Warner's expected trading price at some future date with Paramount's offer and determining which is the higher. Indeed, in our view, precepts underlying the business judgment rule militate against a court's engaging in the process of attempting to appraise and evaluate the relative merits of a long-term versus a short-term investment goal for shareholders. To engage in such an exercise is a distortion of the Unocal process and, in particular, the application of the second part of Unocal's test, discussed below.

In this case, the Time board reasonably determined that inadequate value was not the only legally cognizable threat that Paramount's all-cash, all-shares offer could present. Time's board concluded that Paramount's eleventh hour offer posed other threats. One concern was that Time shareholders might elect to tender into Paramount's cash offer in ignorance or a mistaken belief of the strategic benefit which a business combination with Warner might produce. Moreover, Time viewed the conditions attached to Paramount's offer as introducing a degree of uncertainty that skewed a comparative analysis. Further, the timing of Paramount's offer to follow issuance of Time's proxy notice was viewed as arguably designed to upset, if not confuse, the Time stockholders' vote. Given this record evidence, we cannot conclude that the Time board's decision of June 6 that Paramount's offer posed a threat to corporate policy and effectiveness was lacking in good faith or dominated by motives of either entrenchment or self-interest.

* * *

We turn to the second part of the *Unocal* analysis. The obvious requisite to determining the reasonableness of a defensive action is a clear identification of the nature of the threat. As the Chancellor correctly noted, this "requires an evaluation of the importance of the corporate objective threatened; alternative methods of protecting that objective; impacts of the 'defensive' action, and other relevant factors." In Re: Time Incorporated Shareholder Litigation, Del. Ch., C.A. No. 10670, Allen, C. (July 14, 1989). It is not until both parts of the Unocal inquiry have been satisfied that the business judgment rule attaches to defensive actions of a board of directors. Unocal, 493 A.2d at 954. As applied to the facts of this case, the question is whether the record evidence supports the Court of Chancery's conclusion that the restructuring of the Time-Warner transaction, including the adoption of several preclusive defensive measures, was a reasonable response in relation to a perceived threat.

Paramount argues that, assuming its tender offer posed a threat, Time's response was unreasonable in precluding Time's shareholders from accepting the tender offer or receiving a control premium in the immediately foreseeable future. Once again, the contention stems, we believe, from a fundamental misunderstanding of where the power of corporate governance lies. Delaware law confers the management of the corporate enterprise to the stockholders' duly elected board representatives. 8 Del. C. § 141(a). The fiduciary duty to manage a corporate enterprise includes the selection of a time frame for achievement of corporate goals. That duty may not be delegated to the stockholders. Van Gorkom, 488 A.2d at 873. Directors are not obliged to abandon a deliberately conceived corporate plan for a short-term shareholder profit unless there is clearly no basis to sustain the corporate strategy. *See,* e.g., Revlon, 506 A.2d 173.

Although the Chancellor blurred somewhat the discrete analyses required under Unocal, he did conclude that Time's board reasonably perceived Paramount's offer to be a significant threat to the planned Time-Warner merger and that Time's response was not "overly broad." We have found that even in light of a valid threat, management actions that are coercive in nature or force upon shareholders a management-sponsored alternative to a hostile offer may be struck down as unreasonable and nonproportionate responses. Macmillan, 559 A.2d 1261; AC Acquisitions Corp., 519 A.2d 103.

Here, on the record facts, the Chancellor found that Time's responsive action to Paramount's tender offer was not aimed at "cramming down" on its shareholders a management-sponsored alternative, but rather had as its goal the carrying forward of a pre-existing transaction in an altered form. Thus, the response was reasonably related to the threat. The Chancellor noted that the revised agreement and its accompanying safety devices did not preclude Paramount from making an offer for the combined Time-Warner company or from changing the conditions of its offer so as not to make the offer dependent upon the nullification of the Time-Warner agreement. Thus, the response was proportionate. We affirm the Chancellor's rulings as clearly supported by the record. Finally, we note that although Time was required, as a result of Paramount's hostile offer, to incur a heavy debt to finance its acquisition of Warner, that fact alone does not render the board's decision unreasonable so long as the directors could reasonably perceive the debt load not to be so injurious to the corporation as to jeopardize its well being.

Comments and Questions

1. The offer by Paramount in this case was an all cash, all shares offer. Moreover, it involved a 58% premium over Time's pre-offer share price. In short, it lacked none of the coercive elements present in a two tiered partial offer of the type used by Mesa Petroleum against Unocal. Given these terms, what "threat" was presented by this offer to Time that justified the assorted defensive measures?

2. How important to the holding do you think it was that Time and Warner had been in discussions about a possible merger or joint venture for years? What role did process play in the court's decision?

3. Did this case validate the "just say no" response to a hostile takeover? Professor Gordon indicates that the decision "came close" to sustaining the defense. *See* Jeffrey N. Gordon, *Corporations, Markets, and Courts*, 91 Colum. L. Rev. 1931, 1932 (1991). Do you agree? Subsequent decisions would come even closer to approval of the "just say no" response. *See Air Products and Chemicals, Inc. v. Airgas, Inc.*, 16 A.3d 48 (Del. Ch. 2011).

4. Whatever this case indicates for the "just say no" response, the Delaware courts have rejected this approach once a decision has been made to sell the company. In those circumstances, the board has a fiduciary obligation to maximize shareholder return. *See Revlon, Inc. v. MacAndrews & Forbes Holdings*, 506 A.2d 173 (Del. 1986).

5. An alternative approach might have been to allow the Paramount offer to go forward while management tried to convince shareholders not to tender because of the long-term advantages that would inure from the merger between Time and Warner. In not allowing this to occur, the board was ostensibly protecting shareholders from, according to this Court, "ignorance or a mistaken belief of the strategic benefit which a business combination with Warner might produce." What do you make of this reasoning?

C. The Potency of the Poison Pill

Defensive tactics by the board often involve a colorful array of practices that seek to make the company practically, legally, or economically unattractive to acquire. Thus, the board might opt to sell the "crown jewels," selling the very assets that motivated the hostile bidder in the first instance. Employment contracts to top officials (aka "golden parachutes") might provide for substantial payments to officers upon a change of control, raising the cost of the acquisition. The era also saw the use of the pac man defense, white knights, white squires, and shark repellant amendments to the articles of incorporation.

No defensive tactic has been more effective than the shareholder rights plan, more colloquially known as a poison pill. The pill can be implemented by board resolution and immediately renders a hostile acquisition financially impracticable.

Julian Velasco, *Just Do It: An Antidote to the Poison Pill*
52 Emory L.J. 849, 857–859 (2003)[4]

Under a typical Shareholder Rights Plan, the company issues a dividend of one "Right" for each share of its common stock. Each Right represents only a conditional right: it is not immediately exercisable; moreover, it is attached to, and cannot be traded independently of, the corresponding share of common stock.

The Rights would become meaningful upon the occurrence of specified triggering events. The key triggering event is the acquisition, by anyone, of a specified percentage of the company's shares of common stock. The threshold ownership level can vary, but it is usually in the ten- to twenty-percent range. Upon the occurrence of a triggering event, the Rights would give their holders the right to acquire additional securities (or other assets) at a discount. The key to the poison pill, and that which makes it so venomous, is that any Rights in the hands of the hostile bidder would become void and nontransferable. Because all other shareholders would acquire additional securities at a discount, the interest of the hostile bidder would be diluted severely. This dilution would make the acquisition of the company prohibitively expensive. The intention is to deter any unwelcome acquisition, and the poison pill has been very successful in that respect.

The exact nature of the dilution varies depending on the specific terms of the Shareholder Rights Plan. The "active ingredient" in the poison pill can take many different forms, but the main variations fall into three categories. The original form of the poison pill featured "flip-over" provisions. These would entitle the shareholders to acquire shares of stock of the hostile bidder at a significant discount, but only under certain circumstances. Shortcomings in the flip-over pill led to the creation of newer versions of the poison pill. For example, "back-end" provisions would entitle the shareholders, other than the acquirer, to receive assets, generally in the form of debt securities

---

4. Copyright © 2003 Emory Law Journal. Reprinted by permission of the Emory Law Journal and the author.

or cash, from the company. However, back-end pills also suffer significant infirmities. "Flip-in" provisions, on the other hand, suffer from no such shortcomings and account for the prevalence of the poison pill. They would entitle shareholders, other than the hostile bidder, to acquire shares of stock of the target company at a significant discount. Each version of the poison pill is discussed in turn below.

If the Shareholder Rights Plans were to stop there, however, they would not be very practical. Such provisions would prevent any acquisition of the company, however beneficial it might be. Directors generally realize that the limitations inherent in a complete ban would be unwise. Thus, Shareholder Rights Plans also include provisions that allow the board of directors to "pull the pill" by redeeming the Rights at a nominal price. These provisions are intended to encourage potential acquirers to negotiate the acquisition with the company's board of directors. If the acquirer were to persuade the board of directors concerning its offer, then the board could vote to pull the pill by redeeming the Rights. However, if the acquirer were unable to persuade the board, then the poison pill would remain intact. Thus, directors would retain maximum flexibility.

However, an unlimited ability to redeem the Rights would also be problematic because it would permit the acquirer to redeem the Rights after gaining control of the company. Shareholder Rights Plans therefore typically provide that the Rights may be redeemed by the board of directors of the company at any time prior to the triggering of a poison pill, but not afterwards. Upon the occurrence of a triggering event, the Rights would become non-redeemable. Thus, the flexibility enjoyed by the original board of directors is not freely available to the hostile bidder.

Comments and Questions

1. Marty Lipton, one of the named partners in the law firm Wachtell Lipton, invented the poison pill in 1982. *See* Martin Lipton, *Pills, Polls, and Professors Redux*, 69 U. Chi. L. Rev. 1037, 1043 (2002).

2. The legality of these devices was initially unclear. They only worked where the triggering shareholder was excluded from participation. Until *Unocal*, the prevailing rule was that shareholders of the same class were to be treated equally. Although *Unocal* involved a self-tender offer, it upheld discrimination and effectively validated the most salient feature of a poison pill.

3. The poison pill was officially upheld by the Delaware Supreme Court in *Moran v. Household International, Inc.*, 500 A.2d 1346 (Del. 1985).

4. In at least three jurisdictions, courts initially chose not to follow the holding in Delaware that poison pills, with their discriminatory aspect, were valid. In all three instances, the state legislature overturned the decision. *See* J. Robert Brown, Jr., *Discrimination, Managerial Discretion and the Corporate Contract*, 26 Wake Forest L. Rev. 541, 573–74 (1991).

———

So far, only one shareholder has triggered a poison pill and suffered the resulting dilution. *See Selectica, Inc. v. Versata Enterprises, Inc.*, 2010 Del. Ch. LEXIS 39 (Mar.

1, 2010), *aff'd*, 5 A.3d 586 (Del. 2010). Sir James Goldsmith also triggered one aspect of a pill in 1985. His purchases resulted in the distribution of rights to shareholders but did not cause them to become exercisable. This relative rarity shows the effectiveness of the pill in the context of hostile acquisitions. Bidders will not go forward unless the pill is either redeemed or invalidated by a court. The role of the courts, therefore, loom large.

Air Products and Chemicals, Inc. v. Airgas, Inc.

Delaware Chancery Court
16 A.3d 48 (2011)

CHANDLER, CHANCELLOR:

[Airgas had in place a staggered board and a poison pill. On Feb. 11, 2010, Air Products made an all cash, all shares offer for Airgas at $60 a share. The price was raised to $63.50 on July 8 and $65.50 on Sept. 6. In each case, the board rejected the offer, concluding that the price was inadequate. On Sept. 15, 2010, Airgas held an annual meeting of shareholders. Because of the staggered board, only three of the nine directors were up for election, including Peter McCausland, the founder, CEO and chairman of Airgas. Air Products ran a competing slate and all three positions, although McCausland was unanimously reappointed to the board after the meeting. On Dec. 9, 2010, Air Products raised its offering price to $70 but announced that this was the "best and final" offer. The offer was again rejected as "clearly inadequate" and the Airgas board reiterated its view that the minimum share value was $78. Thus, by the time the court ruled on the validity of the poison pill, the takeover attempt had been ongoing for more than a year.]

Under the first prong of *Unocal*, defendants bear the burden of showing that the Airgas board, "after a reasonable investigation ... determined in good faith, that the [Air Products offer] presented a threat ... that warranted a defensive response." ...

* * *

2. What is the "Threat"?

Although the Airgas board meets the threshold of showing good faith and reasonable investigation, the first part of *Unocal* review requires more than that; it requires the board to show that its good faith and reasonable investigation ultimately gave the board "grounds for concluding that a threat to the corporate enterprise existed." In the supplemental evidentiary hearing, Airgas (and its lawyers) attempted to identify numerous threats posed by Air Products' $70 offer: It is coercive. It is opportunistically timed. It presents the stockholders with a "prisoner's dilemma." It undervalues Airgas—it is a "clearly inadequate" price. The merger arbitrageurs who have bought into Airgas need to be "protected from themselves." The arbs are a "threat" to the minority. The list goes on.

* * *

a. Structural Coercion

Air Products' offer is not structurally coercive. A structurally coercive offer involves "the risk that disparate treatment of non-tendering shareholders might distort shareholders' tender decisions." *Unocal*, for example, "involved a two-tier, highly coercive tender offer" where stockholders who did not tender into the offer risked getting stuck with junk bonds on the back end. "In such a case, the threat is obvious: shareholders may be compelled to tender *to avoid being treated adversely* in the second stage of the transaction."

Air Products' offer poses no such structural threat. It is for all shares of Airgas with consideration to be paid in all cash. The offer is backed by secured financing. There is regulatory approval. The front end will get the same consideration as the back end, in the same currency, as quickly as practicable. Air Products is committed to promptly paying $70 in cash for each and every share of Airgas and has no interest in owning less than 100% of Airgas Air Products would seek to acquire any non-tendering shares "[a]s quick[ly] as the law would allow." It is willing to commit to a subsequent offering period. In light of that, any stockholders who believe that the $70 offer is inadequate simply *would not tender* into the offer — they would risk nothing by not tendering because if a majority of Airgas shares did tender, any non-tendering shares could tender into the subsequent offering period and receive the exact same consideration ($70 per share in cash) as the front end. In short, if there were an antonym in the dictionary for "structural coercion," Air Products' offer might be it.

As former-Vice Chancellor, now Justice Berger noted, "[c]ertainly an inadequate [structurally] coercive tender offer threatens injury to the stockholders ... [but i]t is difficult to understand how, as a general matter, an inadequate all cash, all shares tender offer, with a back end commitment at the same price in cash, can be considered a continuing threat under *Unocal*." I agree. As noted above, though, the Supreme Court has recognized other "threats" that can be posed by an inadequately priced offer. One such potential continuing threat has been termed "opportunity loss," which appears to be a time-based threat.

b. Opportunity Loss

Opportunity loss is the threat that a "hostile offer might deprive target stockholders of the opportunity to select a superior alternative offered by target management or ... offered by another bidder." ...

As such, Air Products' offer poses no threat of opportunity loss. The Airgas board has had, at this point, over sixteen months to consider Air Products' offer and to explore "strategic alternatives going forward as a company." After all that time, there is no alternative offer currently on the table, and counsel for defendants represented during the October trial that "we're not asserting that we need more time to explore a specific alternative." The "superior alternative" Airgas is pursuing is simply to "continue[] on its current course and execute[] its strategic [five year, long term] plan."

c. Substantive Coercion

Inadequate price and the concept of substantive coercion are inextricably related. The Delaware Supreme Court has defined substantive coercion ... as "the risk that [Airgas's] stockholders might accept [Air Products'] inadequate Offer because of 'ignorance or mistaken belief' regarding the Board's assessment of the long-term value of [Airgas's] stock." In other words, if management advises stockholders, in good faith, that it believes Air Products' hostile offer is inadequate because in its view the future earnings potential of the company is greater than the price offered, Airgas's stockholders might nevertheless reject the board's advice and tender.

* * *

... In essence, Airgas's argument is that "the substantial ownership of Airgas stock by these short-term, deal-driven investors poses a threat to the company and its shareholders" — the threat that, because it is likely that the arbs would support the $70 offer, "shareholders will be coerced into tendering into an inadequate offer." ... The argument is premised on the fact that a large percentage (almost half) of Airgas's stockholders are merger arbitrageurs — many of whom bought into the stock when Air Products first announced its interest in acquiring Airgas at a time when the stock was trading much lower than it is today — who would be willing to tender into an inadequate offer because they stand to make a significant return on their investment even if the offer grossly undervalues Airgas in a sale. "They don't care a thing about the fundamental value of Airgas." In short, the risk is that a majority of Airgas's stockholders will tender into Air Products' offer despite its inadequate price tag, leaving the minority "coerced" into taking $70 as well. The defendants do not appear to have come to grips with the fact that the arbs bought their shares from long-term stockholders who viewed the increased market price generated by Air Products' offer as a good time to sell.

* * *

... [I]f a majority of stockholders *want* to tender into an inadequately priced offer, is that substantive coercion? Is that a threat that justifies continued maintenance of the poison pill? Put differently, is there evidence in the record that Airgas stockholders are so "focused on the short-term" that they would "take a smaller harvest in the swelter of August over a larger one in Indian Summer"? ...

But there is at least some evidence in the record suggesting that this risk may be real. Moreover, both Airgas expert and well as *Air Products' own expert* testified that a large number — if not all — of the arbitrageurs who bought into Airgas stock at prices significantly below the $70 offer price would be happy to tender their shares at that price regardless of the potential long-term value of the company. Based on the testimony of both expert witnesses, I find sufficient evidence that a majority of stockholders might be willing to tender their shares regardless of whether the price is adequate or not — thereby ceding control of Airgas to Air Products. ...

Ultimately, it all seems to come down to the Supreme Court's holdings in *Paramount* and *Unitrin*. In *Unitrin*, the Court held: "[T]he directors of a Delaware corporation have the prerogative to determine that the market undervalues its stock and to protect its stockholders from offers that do not reflect the long-term value of the corporation under its present management plan." When a company is not in *Revlon* mode, a board of directors "is not under any *per se* duty to maximize shareholder value in the short term, even in the context of a takeover." The Supreme Court has unequivocally "endorse[d the] conclusion that it is not a breach of faith for directors to determine that the present stock market price of shares is not representative of true value or that there may indeed be several market values for any corporation's stock." As noted above, based on all of the facts presented to me, I find that the Airgas board acted in good faith and relied on the advice of its financial and legal advisors in coming to the conclusion that Air Products' offer is inadequate. And as the Supreme Court has held, a board that in good faith believes that a hostile offer is inadequate may "properly employ[ ] a poison pill as a proportionate defensive response to protect its stockholders from a 'low ball' bid."

* * *

Turning now to the second part of the *Unocal* test, I must determine whether the Airgas board's defensive measures are a proportionate response to the threat posed by Air Products' offer.

* * *

2. Range of Reasonableness

"If a defensive measure is neither coercive nor preclusive, the *Unocal* proportionality test requires the focus of enhanced judicial scrutiny to shift to the range of reasonableness." The reasonableness of a board's response is evaluated in the context of the specific threat identified—the "specific nature of the threat [] 'sets the parameters for the range of permissible defensive tactics' at any given time."

Here, the record demonstrates that Airgas's board, composed of a majority of outside, independent directors, acting in good faith and with numerous outside advisors concluded that Air Products' offer clearly undervalues Airgas in a sale transaction. The board believes in good faith that the offer price is inadequate by no small margin. Thus, the board is responding to a legitimately articulated threat.

This conclusion is bolstered by the fact that the three Air Products Nominees on the Airgas board have now wholeheartedly joined in the board's determination—what is more, they believe it is their fiduciary duty to keep Airgas's defenses in place. And Air Products' *own directors* have testified that (1) they have no reason to believe that the Airgas directors have breached their fiduciary duties, (2) even though plenty of information has been made available to the stockholders, they "agree that Airgas management is in the best position to understand the intrinsic value of the company," and (3) if the shoe were on the other foot, they would act in the same way as Airgas's directors have.

* * *

... [T]he maintenance of the board's defensive measures must fall within a range of reasonableness here. The board is not "cramming down" a management-sponsored alternative—or *any* company-changing alternative. Instead, the board is simply maintaining the status quo, running the company for the long-term, and consistently showing improved financial results each passing quarter. The board's actions do not *forever* preclude Air Products, or any bidder, from acquiring Airgas or from getting around Airgas's defensive measures if the price is right. In the meantime, the board is preventing a change of control from occurring at an inadequate price. This course of action has been clearly recognized under Delaware law: "directors, when acting deliberately, in an informed way, and in the good faith pursuit of corporate interests, may follow a course designed to achieve long-term value even at the cost of immediate value maximization."

CONCLUSION

Vice Chancellor Strine recently suggested that:

> The passage of time has dulled many to the incredibly powerful and novel device that a so-called poison pill is. That device has no other purpose than to give the board issuing the rights the leverage to prevent transactions it does not favor by diluting the buying proponent's interests.

There is no question that poison pills act as potent anti-takeover drugs with the potential to be abused. Counsel for plaintiffs (both Air Products and Shareholder Plaintiffs) make compelling policy arguments in favor of redeeming the pill in this case—to do otherwise, they say, would essentially make all companies with staggered boards and poison pills "takeover proof." The argument is an excellent sound bite, but it is ultimately not the holding of this fact-specific case, although it does bring us one step closer to that result.

As this case demonstrates, in order to have any effectiveness, pills do not—and can not—have a set expiration date. To be clear, though, this case does not endorse "just say never." What it does endorse is Delaware's long-understood respect for reasonably exercised managerial discretion, so long as boards are found to be acting in good faith and in accordance with their fiduciary duties (after rigorous judicial fact-finding and enhanced scrutiny of their defensive actions). The Airgas board serves as a quintessential example.

Directors of a corporation still owe fiduciary duties to *all stockholders—this undoubtedly includes short-term as well as long-term holders. At the same time, a board cannot be forced into Revlon mode any time a hostile bidder makes a tender offer that* is at a premium to market value. The mechanisms in place to get around the poison pill—even a poison pill in combination with a staggered board, which no doubt makes the process prohibitively more difficult—have been in place since 1985, when the Delaware Supreme Court first decided to uphold the pill as a legal defense to an unwanted bid. That is the current state of Delaware law until the Supreme Court changes it.

For the foregoing reasons, Air Products' and the Shareholder Plaintiffs' requests for relief are denied, and all claims asserted against defendants are dismissed with prejudice....

Comments and Questions

1. The court found that evidence supported a threat of substantive coercion. How did that threat arise and what does it have to do with arbs (arbitrageurs)? How common is this threat likely to be?

2. What role did the directors elected by Air Products play in this case? What do you make of the phrase "Air Products' own directors"? Irrespective of the shareholder who nominated them, what are the legal responsibilities of these directors?

3. Does this case, as the Defendants argued, make the company "takeover proof"? The judge noted that the case "bring[s] us one step closer to that result." What does he mean by that statement?

4. Chancellor Chandler noted the Delaware Supreme Court had on prior occasions stated that a poison pill was "not absolute." Yet, as he notes, the "pill's limits ... still remain open." What does he mean by this? Is he correct?

5. The trial court seemed unhappy with the result, apparently disagreeing with its own determination that the offer by Air Products was a threat. *Id.* ("[T]here seems to be no threat here—the stockholders know what they need to know (about both the offer and the Airgas board's opinion of the offer) to make an informed decision."). How can you reconcile this view with the analysis in the opinion? What does this suggest about the state of the law with respect to defensive tactics, particularly poison pills?

6. The court specifically disclaimed any attempt to validate the right of boards to "just say no" in the face of a hostile tender offer. As the court noted:

> A board cannot "*just* say no" to a tender offer. Under Delaware law, it must first pass through two prongs of exacting judicial scrutiny by a judge who will evaluate the actions taken by, and the motives of, the board. Only a board of directors found to be acting in good faith, after reasonable investigation and reliance on the advice of outside advisors, which articulates and convinces the Court that a hostile tender offer poses a legitimate threat to the corporate enterprise, may address that perceived threat by blocking the tender offer and forcing the bidder to elect a board majority that supports its bid.

Are you convinced by this explanation?

7. In adopting a poison pill, the risk still exists that an acquirer will engage in a proxy contest and elect a majority of the directors who will then withdraw the defensive tactic. Recognizing this possibility, companies have sometimes tried to restrict a new board's right to withdraw pills. A "slow" hand pill, for example, prohibits a new board from removing a poison pill for some specified period of time. Are these features legal? The answer can be found in *Quickturn Design Systems, Inc. v. Shapiro*, 721 A.2d 1281 (Del. 1998).

8. What if shareholders wanted to adopt a bylaw prohibiting poison pills? Do they have the authority? The Delaware courts have so far not resolved the issue. *See Bebchuk v. CA, Inc.*, 902 A.2d 737 (Del. Ch. 2006) (concluding that issue not ripe for resolution).

So where does this leave hostile tender offers as a method of replacing management?

Joseph A. Grundfest, *Just Vote No: A Minimalist Strategy for Dealing with Barbarians Inside the Gates*
45 Stan. L. Rev. 857, 858–62 (1993)[5]

Although hostile tender offers remain technically possible, the legal and financial barriers in their path are far higher today than they were a few short years ago. As a result, it will be difficult for hostile bidders to prevail in takeover battles, even if shareholders support the insurgents' efforts. Future acquisitions will therefore more frequently involve consensual transactions. Hostile bidders who proceed despite these heightened barriers will likely have to couple proxy contests with tender offers, or rely on strategies that otherwise induce target boards to agree to ostensibly friendly transactions.

This remarkable transformation in the market for corporate control resulted from the emergence of the "poison pill" as an effective antitakeover device, the rapid proliferation of state antitakeover statutes, and the development of financial market conditions inimical to hostile control contests. Poison pills are common among publicly traded firms, and a firm without a pill can quickly adopt one should the need arise. Courts have significantly increased managements' latitude in using this weapon, and the danger of triggering a pill renders it irrational for bidders to pursue tender offers without the approval of a target's board. Instead, bidders intent on working around a poison pill must launch and win proxy contests to elect new directors who are willing to redeem the target's poison pill. Only then can a hostile bidder proceed with an offer, and even so the bid will still be subject to the risk that a second bidder will emerge, or that changes in the legal or financial climate will render the transaction unprofitable.

State antitakeover laws present additional hurdles to hostile bidders....

These legal and political barriers constitute a formidable gauntlet in themselves. The emergence of these barriers in mid to late 1989 coincided with a sea change in financial market conditions that tightened the supply of available credit and made capital for hostile takeover activity exceedingly difficult to obtain. This confluence of legal, political, and financial factors caused a precipitous drop in the volume of hostile tender offers, from twenty-seven deals worth $38.5 billion in 1988 to two deals worth only $77.4 million in 1991. In all of 1992, there were no transactions in which a hostile bidder initiated a successful takeover, and the year's single successful hostile bid was made only after the target firm was "in play" because it had already agreed to a friendly transaction with a third party.

Comments and Questions

1. Following *Unocal* and its progeny, the number of hostile takeovers fell dramatically. One commentator put the number of hostile acquisition attempts during the period

---

from 1995 to 2000 at 92. *See* Lucian Arye Bebchuk, John C. Coates IV & Guhan Subramanian, *The Powerful Antitakeover Force of Staggered Boards: Theory, Evidence, and Policy*, 54 Stan. L. Rev. 887, 925 (2002). Hostile tender offers are rarely used today. On the other hand, some have also noted that the line between friendly and hostile bids blurred. *See* Marcel Kahan & Edward B. Rock, *Executive Compensation & Takeovers: How I Learned to Stop Worrying and Love the Pill: Adaptive Responses to Takeover Law*, 69 U. Chi. L. Rev. 871, 881 (2002). In other words, acquisitions ultimately characterized as friendly may have begun as hostile. Who has the better of the argument?

2. The reduction in hostile takeovers has taken away a significant argument that mismanagement and self-dealing will be corrected by the market place. Given the dearth of hostile acquisitions, are there other ways that the market can effectively punish management for engaging in self serving behavior or otherwise failing to act in the best interests of shareholders?

3. To the extent that the market cannot adequately discipline management, what other approaches can be used to ensure that the interests of shareholders are protected?

III. Proxy Contests

As hostile tender offers become less viable, the focus has shifted to proxy contests. Insurgents opposed by management often respond through efforts to replace the board. Doing so requires the nomination of a competing slate of directors and a campaign to capture the votes of unaffiliated shareholders. The campaign plays out during the proxy solicitation process. The contests can, however, be expensive. Insurgents must pay their own expenses while management may rely on the corporate treasury.

A. Proxy Contests and Shareholder Activism

John C. Coffee, Jr. & Darius Palia, *The Wolf at the Door: The Impact of Hedge Fund Activism on Corporate Governance*

Working Paper No. 521, Sept. 4, 2015, available at
http://papers.ssrn.com/sol3/papers.cfm?abstract_id=2656325

II: The Changed Environment: What Factors Have Spurred Enhanced Activism by Hedge Funds?

Once upon a time, institutional investors followed the "Wall Street Rule": if dissatisfied with management, they sold their stock, but they did not attempt to intervene or challenge management. This passivity was probably the consequence of shareholder dispersion (which made activism costly) and conflicts of interest (large banks—both commercial and investment—did not want to alienate corporate clients). With the growth in institutional ownership, however, behavior changed. This was particularly true in the case of hedge funds, which, unlike mutual funds, typically hold concentrated blocks in a limited number of companies (rather than a broadly diversified portfolio). Concentrated ownership makes shareholder activism rational from a cost/benefit standpoint.

The types of activist campaigns run by hedge funds range from modest interventions in corporate governance (e.g., proposals to separate the positions of CEO and Board Chairman) to more intrusive interventions seeking to sell the company, fire the CEO, or spin off divisions. As will be seen, the more intrusive the intervention, the greater the likely positive stock market response. The frequency of such campaigns has skyrocketed, with one recent survey counting 1,115 activist campaigns between 2010 and early 2014. 2014 alone saw a record 347 campaigns by "activist" hedge funds. Clearly, this escalating rate of intervention is in sharp contrast to earlier periods when, for example, only 52 campaigns could be identified over a 20 consecutive month stretch in 2005–2006. That amounts to a more than 1,000% increase between that period and today and again raises the possibility of a bubble: namely, that more and more hedge funds are pursuing fewer and fewer legitimate opportunities for activist interventions.

Historically, hedge fund activism focused on smaller cap companies because it was too costly to assemble a sizeable stake in a larger cap company. But this has changed. In 2013, for the first time, almost one third of activist campaigns focused on companies with a market capitalization of over $2 billion. If we instead use $10 billion as our dividing line for "large cap" stocks, we find that only 17 such companies were targeted by activist investors in 2010, but then in 2011 to 2013, the number of such activist campaigns rose to 21, 23, and 42, respectively. In effect, they have doubled since 2011. Finally, in 2014, Pershing Square Capital Management L.P. joined with a strategic bidder to make an over $60 billion joint tender offer for Allergan, Inc., and Trian Fund Management conducted a proxy campaign that narrowly failed at DuPont, one of the oldest, largest and most iconic of U.S. companies, but, more importantly, a highly profitable firm that had consistently outperformed all relevant benchmarks for corporate performance. In short, whatever their size or profitability, few companies today seem immune from the reach of hedge fund activism. Seemingly, if a credible scenario can be offered to the market that breaking up a company will yield shareholder gains, activist funds will assemble to attack even those companies with a long record of profitability.

Only a specialized group of hedge funds engage in activist campaign and proxy fights, but they have recently done very well. Over a ten year period, activist hedge funds appear to have earned a 13% return, which more than doubled the 5.8% return for all hedge funds as a group. Equally important, the assets managed by "activist" hedge funds have soared, growing over seven times from $23 billion in 2002 to $166 billion in early 2014, and the top ten activist hedge funds alone attracted $30 billion in new investment in 2013.

Hedge funds initiated the majority of proxy contests in 2013, accounting for 24 of the 35 contests conducted with respect to Russell 3000 companies. Although long more active than other investors, hedge-fund initiated proxy contests have represented a steadily increasing percentage of all proxy contests, rising from 39% in 2009 to 69% in 2013.

More importantly, they are winning these fights, securing partial or complete victories in 19 of the 24 contests they initiated in 2013. In 2014, "activists won in a record 73% of battles for board seats, up from 52% in 2012." Revealingly, once the activists win a board seat, 44% of those companies changed their CEO within 18 months thereafter.

To be sure, increased engagement between shareholders and management has entered the mainstream. An Ernst & Young report finds that half of all S&P 500 companies disclosed engaging with investors in 2013, up from only 23% in 2012, and these contacts are often between institutional investors and members of the board outside the presence of management. Yet, even if there is a broader shareholder desire for engagement with management, hedge fund activism is qualitatively different. As others have stressed, traditional institutional investors—basically, pension funds and mutual funds—have long been essentially "defensive" in their activism (e.g., by seeking, for example, to resist a management initiative), while hedge funds are "offensive," deliberately seeking out an underperforming target in which to invest in order to pursue a proactive agenda and change their target's business model.

Comments and Questions

1. What do you make of the role of activist hedge funds? Is the presence of activist shareholders a new phenomenon? How does it compare, for example, to the corporate raiders of the 1980s?

2. Activists often seek minority representation on the board. Some assert that facilitating the election of dissident directors can result in harm the board's decision making process. *See also* Martin Lipton & Steven A. Rosenblum, *Symposium on Corporate Election, Election Contests in the Company's Proxy: An Idea Whose Time Has Not Come*, 59 Bus. Law. 67 (2003) (arguing that presence of "special interest or dissident directors" on the board will "essentially split [the board] into multiple boards" and "the collegiality of the board is typically destroyed, inhibiting the open discussion and give and take of a well-functioning board where the members trust and respect each other."). What do you make of this contention?

3. Directors designated by activist shareholders (or other investors such as private equity investors) are sometimes referred to as "constituency" or "representative" directors. These directors have fiduciary obligations to act in the best interest of the corporation, not the shareholder responsible for their election. Nonetheless, discuss the tension that exists with respect to the election of these directors in the actual application of fiduciary obligations. For a discussion of these directors, see E. Norman Veasey & Christine T. Di Guglielmo, *How Many Masters Can A Director Serve? A Look at the Tensions Facing Constituency Directors*, 63 Bus. Law. 761 (May 2008).

4. Activists typically own a modest percentage of a target's outstanding shares, often under 10%, sometimes under 5%. As a result, their success typically depends upon the ability to marshal support among other institutional shareholders. Why and under what circumstances might pension plans and mutual funds support activist positions? What might management do to minimize this risk?

5. If the board accedes to the demands of an activist investor, including positions on the board and, eventually repurchase of shares, do other shareholders have any recourse? *See Ryan v. Gursahaney*, C.A. No. 9992-VCP (Del. Ch. Apr. 28, 2015) (alleging "director defendants breached their fiduciary duties by appointing the hedge fund's principal to the board, engaging in a stock repurchase plan similar to the one he advocated for, and then ultimately repurchasing the hedge fund's block of [company] stock at the then-prevailing, but allegedly inflated, market price."). What barriers exist to these types of actions?

6. Multiple activists may target the same company, a phenomenon sometimes called a wolf pack. What are some limitations on this approach? Poison pills are triggered at ownership thresholds as low as 5%. They typically apply to persons or group of persons who meet the requisite threshold. When might a "wolf pack" become a group, thereby resulting in the aggregation of shares for purposes of these triggers? *See* Rule 13d-5, 17 C.F.R. 240.13d-5 (a group includes "two or more persons agreeing to act together for the purpose of acquiring, holding, voting or disposing of equity securities of an issuer").

7. Activist shareholders have sometimes sought to supplement the consideration paid to their board nominees following election. Labeled by some as a "golden leash," the compensation is often tied to the performance of the company. What concerns might these types of arrangements raise? How might a company respond?

———

A Debate: Long Term vs. Short Term Effect of Activist Shareholders

The increased role of activist shareholders is clear. A vigorous debate has arisen, however, over the consequences of this increased role. Some contend that activists have a short term horizon that is harmful to companies. Others dispute the contention.

Lucian A. Bebchuk, Alon Brav & Wei Jiang, *The Long-Term Effects of Hedge Fund Activism*
115 Colum. L. Rev. 1085 (2015)[6]

We focus on the "myopic-activists" claim that has been playing a central role in debates over shareholder activism and the legal rules and policies shaping it. According to this claim, ... activist shareholders with short investment horizons, especially activist hedge funds, push for actions that are profitable in the short term but are detrimental to the long-term interests of companies and their long-term shareholders. The problem, it is claimed, results from the failure of short-term performance figures and short-term stock prices to reflect the long-term costs of actions

———

6. Copyright © 2015 Columbia Law Review. Reprinted by permission.

sought by activists. As a result, activists with a short investment horizon have an incentive to seek actions that would increase short-term prices at the expense of long-term performance, such as excessively reducing long-term investments or the funds available for such investments.

* * *

1. *A Clear Pattern.*— … To begin, activists do not generally target well-performing companies. Targets of activism tended to be companies whose operating performance was below industry peers and also their own historical levels at the time of intervention. Moreover, at the time of the intervention, the targets seemed to be in a negative trend with operating performance declining during the three years preceding the intervention.

Furthermore, during the five years following the intervention, we find no evidence supporting concerns that activist interventions are followed by short-term gains that come at the expense of subsequent long-term declines in operating performance. Examining both Q [Tobins's Q, which "is designed to reflect a company's success in turing a given book value of assets into market value accrued to investors"] and ROA [return on assets], and conducting comparisons both to the end of the year following the intervention and the end of the year preceding it, the feared adverse effect on long-term performance is not found in the data. Indeed, in each of the years three, four, and five following the intervention, we find improvements that are statistically significant. Thus, overall, the evidence on firm performance does not support the myopic-activists claim.

2. *Adverse Effect on the Post-Acquisition Performance of Acquired Firms?*—As is the case with peer companies, a significant percentage of targeted firms are no longer public by the end of the five-year period, having been acquired or otherwise delisted, and are thus no longer part of the Compustat dataset of public company data. Because our results indicate that targets' operating performance improves for as long as they remain public, it might still be argued that activism has an adverse effect on targets that stop being public during the five-year period, that this effect occurs after these targets are no longer public and thus is not detected by our analysis, and that this adverse effect is sufficiently large to make the effects of activism overall negative in the aggregate.

However, there is no reason to expect that the operating performance of targets that are acquired will be more likely to decline rather than improve post-acquisition. Indeed, acquisitions can often be expected to be motivated by the acquirer's expectation that it will be able to improve the performance of the purchased assets through synergies or otherwise. To the extent that this is the case, it can be expected that the performance of assets of activism targets that are acquired will tend to improve, rather than decline, after the targets are acquired and stop having their operating performance reported on Compustat.

Furthermore, as explained below, this concern is directly addressed by a recent empirical study, co-authored by two of us and Hyunseob Kim, that tracks the operating performance of activism targets after they are acquired. That study uses U.S. Census Bureau's longitudinal databases of manufacturing businesses to study activism at targets engaged in manufacturing. A key attribute of the Census data is that the Census continues to record data on manufacturing assets previously belonging to a public company even after the company stops being public due to an acquisition or otherwise. The study is therefore able to assess directly, for targets in the manufacturing sector, what changes in operating performance took place in targets that stopped being public.

The study documents that plants belonging to targets that eventually drop from the Compustat database perform better than those plants whose firms are still covered by Compustat. Thus, to the extent that the targets out the manufacturing sector exhibit a similar pattern, the evidence provided by the study indicates that focusing on target firms that remain public should not be expected to result in an overstatement—and indeed might well generate an understatement—of the postintervention performance of targets.

3. *Stock Picking?*—Finally, critics of hedge fund activism might argue that the identified association between activist interventions and subsequent improvements in operating performance does not by itself demonstrate a causal link. It could merely reflect the activists' tendency to choose targets whose operating performance is expected to increase in any event. Under such a scenario, the improvement in long-term performance experienced by targets reflects the activists' "stock picking" ability rather than the activists' impact on the company's operating performance.

We would like to stress at the outset that accepting that activist interventions are followed by improvements in operating performance, and merely questioning whether activists should "get credit" for these improvements, would already concede that the long-term consequences of activism provide no basis for calls to limit the influence of activism and to insulate boards from such influence. Such calls have been premised on the claim that activist interventions are followed by (and bring about) declines in long-term operating performance. To the extent that interventions are followed by improvements in operating performance, there is no reason to limit the influence of activists regardless of how much credit they should be getting for these improvements. Stock pickers who successfully bet on future improvements might not deserve a medal, but they do not warrant opposition and resistance.

However, there are at least three reasons to believe that the identified improvements in operating performance are at least partly due to the activist interventions. First, activist engagements involve significant costs, and activist investors would have strong incentives to avoid bearing them if they believed that the improvements in performance would ensue in any event, even without engaging with target companies. In such a case, these investors would just buy a stake, avoid any intervention, and capture the benefits of the improved performance expected to take place without incurring costs. Thus, activists' willingness to bear the significant costs of engagement likely reflects their judgment that their activities contribute to the subsequent improvements in operating performance.

Second, ... improvements in operating performance follow activist interventions not just in our dataset as a whole but also in the subset of activist interventions that employ adversarial tactics. Such tactics are used when activists expect companies to resist the activists' suggested course of action. This finding is in tension with the view that the improvements in operating performance following activist interventions are due to corporate actions that incumbents would choose to take even without any intervention.

Furthermore, the view that the interventions contribute to subsequent improvements is consistent with the finding in earlier work coauthored by two of us (together with Hyunseob Kim) that such improvements do not take place after outside blockholders pursuing a passive strategy announce the purchase of a block of shares, but do occur when blockholders switch from passive to activist stance. This finding is also consistent with the view that the patterns we identify above are at least partly a product of the activists' work and not merely a reflection of their foresight in choosing targets.

We therefore conclude that the identified improvements in performance should be expected to be at least partly due to the activist intervention. Of course, causality issues in corporate governance and finance are notoriously difficult to resolve with absolute confidence, and we do not aim at precise identification of the extent to which the improvements are due to activist interventions. Our chief interest in this Article is in investigating empirically whether the long-standing and influential claim that activist interventions are followed by declines in long-term operating performance is backed by the evidence. Our results provide a clear answer: This long-standing claim is not supported by the data.

John C. Coffee, Jr. & Darius Palia, *The Wolf at the Door: The Impact of Hedge Fund Activism on Corporate Governance*

Working Paper No. 521, Sept. 4, 2015, available at
http://papers.ssrn.com/sol3/papers.cfm?abstract_id=2656325

Does Hedge Fund Activism Create Value? For ease of exposition, in this sub-section, we subdivide the evidence into two parts, based on whether the measurement period is the short run (a few days) or the long run (a few years).

(1.) Short-horizon event studies of stock returns: Many studies have examined what happens to targets firm's stock price when there is a Schedule 13D filing with the SEC. The date of filing is called the event date, and the studies examine whether a target firm earns abnormal returns (generally defined as actual returns less returns adjusted for market movements) in the few days before and after the event date (called the "event window"). Most studies have found that target firms of activist hedge funds earn on average positive abnormal returns in the event window, although differences exist in the studies in their definition of event windows and the economic magnitude of the abnormal returns earned.

There are two interpretive issues with the above results. First, although it is generally true that the average stock return performance around the event date is positive, substantial differences exist in the distribution of abnormal returns earned by target firms. A significant proportion of firms actually earned negative abnormal returns in the above studies. This finding implies a significant conflict between the goals of activists and corporations. Activists typically invest in many firms concurrently, resulting in superior fund performance even if only some of their targets earn substantial return performance. Corporations do not have this luxury of diversification, as they are invested only in themselves. Thus, the possibility of a negative return (particularly when the upside return may be only modest) may reasonably cause a board of directors to reject a strategy favored by a group of hedge funds.

Probably the best known example of such a financial disaster caused by aggressive intervention by hedge funds was the joint acquisition by Pershing Square and Vornado Realty Trust of over 26% of the stock of J.C. Penney. Most of this stock was purchased during the ten-day window under Section 13(d), and the two activists obtained board representation, forced the resignation of J.C. Penney's incumbent CEO, and announced a new marketing philosophy. Although J.C. Penney's stock rose initially, customers fled in droves, and J.C. Penney's stock price fell some 59.5% over the period between the initial Schedule 13D filing and Ackman's eventual resignation from the board.

Beyond the distribution of returns (and the risk inherent in running an operating company without prior experience in the field), the second problem with much of the data on hedge fund activism is the missing evidence as to what causes the stock price gains that are observed. If the positive abnormal stock returns are attributable to actions by activists that reduce managerial agency problems, they should leave some trail. That is, there should be evidence about changed capital structure, reduced executive compensation, dividend payouts, or altered investments. Yet, most of the studies find that the positive abnormal returns are not statistically significantly related to changes in real variables that occur subsequently to the activists' intervention.

(2.) Long-horizon stock return studies: Two studies, each published in 2015, merit special attention. First, Bebchuk, Brav and Jiang find that buy and hold stock returns are on average positive in the three-years and five-years after the Schedule 13D filing. In doing so, they control for the returns on the market portfolio and the returns on small size, value and momentum portfolios (often referred to as the four-factor model of stock returns). These positive average long-horizon abnormal returns have also been found in other studies. However, when Bebchuk, Brav and Jiang examine the three-year and five-year calendar year returns before and after the filing date, they find them to be statistically insignificant from zero. This suggests that an activist investor cannot beat the performance of the four-factor stock return model.

A second study by Becht, Franks, Grant and Wagner provides a significantly different perspective. Going beyond simply reporting the impact of the announcement of a block's formation (which in the U.S. occurs on the filing of the Schedule 13D), they uniquely focus on the outcome of the activists' intervention. Unsurprisingly, they find that a successful outcome counts, but more surprisingly, they find that the market appears to value only a limited number of successful outcomes. When the outcome announced was a takeover, this announcement produced abnormal returns averaging 9.7%; similarly, announcement of restructuring produced abnormal returns of 5.6%; but changes in board composition yielded only a more modest average abnormal return of 4.5%. Finally payout changes (whether achieved through dividends or stock buybacks) resulted in a negative abnormal return of -0.2%.

Much depended on whether there was a successful outcome; in the case of North American activist engagements, the value-weighted annualized returns were 6.6% for engagements with successful outcomes but minus 1.2% for engagements without such outcomes. In short, even though the majority of North American engagements do produce a successful outcome, there is clearly a downside. Unless the activist is pursuing a takeover or a restructuring, even successful activist engagements appear to yield only modest, if any, value for shareholders.

Finally, in all these studies, focusing only on the average abnormal returns may miss much of the story. A significant fraction of target firms earn negative long-horizon abnormal returns. In fact, one study finds that a small majority of target firms (52%) earn negative abnormal returns in the one-month before to one-year after the filing period, and another study (which has one author overlapping with the above Bebchuk study) corroborates this finding that a significant fraction of target firms earn negative abnormal returns.

Comments and Questions

1. What do you make of this debate? The data suggests that there are positive returns in the short term. At the same time, however, Professor Coffee, et al., conclude that hedge fund targets typically experience a "sharp decline" in research and development. Why might this be the case and can you reconcile these two statistics?

2. Activist involvement can at least sometimes result in negative long term returns. In some ways, the same was true of hostile takeovers in the 1980s. *See* J. Robert Brown, Jr., *In Defense of Management Buyouts*, 65 Tulane L. Rev. 57, 101 (1990) (noting that "[a] number of long-term studies on the effect of hostile acquisitions have concluded that, on average, bidders incur a negative gain.").

3. The debate over activists has primarily focused on their impact on the target company. Is this the appropriate focus? Do activists also change the behavior of companies that they have not targeted? How might that be the case? As the Chairman of Blackrock observed in a letter to clients: "In the face of these pressures, more and more corporate leaders have responded with actions that can deliver immediate returns to shareholders, such as buybacks or dividend increases, while underinvesting in innovation, skilled workforces or essential capital expenditures necessary to sustain long-term growth." Does this resolve the case over the benefits and harms of activist investors?

B. Proxy Contests and State Law

Proxy contests mostly play out in the context of state law requirements that regulate shareholder meetings and voting rights. In general, a contest entails an attempt by both sides to convince unaffiliated shareholders to support their slate. Management, however, has a number of devices available that can affect the contest. Some are structural. One of the most important is the staggered board.

Lucian Arye Bebchuk, John C. Coates IV & Guhan Subramanian, *The Powerful Antitakeover Force of Staggered Boards: Theory, Evidence, and Policy*
54 Stan. L. Rev. 887, 893–99 (2002)[7]

The default law in all states requires that all directors stand for election at each annual shareholder meeting. However, all states provide an exemption from this requirement if the board is staggered. In a company with a staggered board, directors are grouped into classes (typically three), with each class elected at successive annual meetings. For example, a board with twelve directors might be grouped into three classes, with four directors standing at the 2001 annual meeting, four more directors standing for reelection in 2002, and the remaining four directors standing for reelection in 2003. With three classes, directors in each class would be elected to three-year terms.

Thirty-nine jurisdictions, including Delaware and California, permit a maximum of three classes. New York permits as many as four classes of directors, and Arizona allows three "or to the extent not inconsistent with cumulative voting rights, more." Ten other states have not addressed this issue.

* * *

Though staggered boards have been a part of the corporate law landscape for decades, they gained popularity during the 1980s takeover wave. Today, among a sample of 2,421 large public U.S. companies, 59% have staggered boards. In addition, there was a dramatic increase in staggered board incidence among companies going public in 1991–92 (34%) versus 1999–2000 (82%). The IPO statistics suggest that, barring any major shifts in the legal or political environment, staggered board incidence will only increase further among major U.S. corporations in the years to come.

* * *

Two nontakeover-related justifications have been put forward to justify staggered boards. First, they facilitate the independence of outside directors. Independent directors, goes this argument, will be less influenced by executives if they have a term of three years rather than one year. Second, they reduce annual turnover on the board, thereby promoting board stability. It is generally good, goes the argument, to always have some experienced and seasoned directors, who have the perspective that only time on the board can provide. If the board were not staggered, there is in theory some chance that

---

7. Copyright © 2002 Stanford Law Review. Reprinted by permission.

all board members in a given year will be rookies. A staggered board prevents this outcome by ensuring that at most one-third of the board members will be new.

However, a staggered board imposed through the charter is an unnecessarily blunt instrument to achieve these two benefits. On board independence, a bylaw establishing a staggered board would be sufficient to provide independent directors autonomy from management so that they could effectively monitor. Because officers cannot amend the bylaws without approval of a majority of the whole board, a majority-independent board would not be de-staggered against the will of the independent directors. A bylaw would thus accomplish the independence goal without, as will be made clear below, in any way impeding a hostile bidder.

Similarly, on board stability, a staggered board bylaw would achieve the goal of preventing excessive turnover, and even a company without a staggered board could have a convention or policy requiring that annual slates include at least two-thirds incumbent directors in the ordinary course of business. Such a policy or bylaw would be followed in the normal course of events. As an empirical matter, even in companies that do not have any policy or rule against replacing more than one third of the board in any given year, such high turnover rarely, if ever, happens outside the change of control context. In the normal course of business, most of the candidates running on the insiders' slate are usually those who are already serving on the board. Thus a convention, policy, or bylaw should provide the desired board independence and board stability in the normal course of events in a more focused way than a staggered board.

Of course, in one situation a convention, policy, or bylaw would be insufficient — in the case of a hostile change of control. When a buyer acquires a controlling interest, it would be natural for it to replace the directors with a new slate of directors, assuming that it were not stopped by the charter. Thus, alternatives that stop short of a charter amendment would not likely prevail in the case of a hostile takeover.

But a desire for board stability no longer makes sense in the case of a hostile change of control. The argument for continuity presupposes that there is some team working largely in harmony, and that such a team would benefit from retaining a majority of experienced members from whom new members could and would be willing to learn. But in the case of a hostile takeover, old and new directors are not going to form a harmonious team. In such a case, board stability indeed might be quite harmful. In fact, arguments for board stability, through "dead hand" and "no hand" pills, have already been rejected by the Delaware Chancery Court and the Delaware Supreme Court. Thus charter-based staggered boards are over-encompassing because they provide board stability when business justification and support in the Delaware case law are both at their weakest.

2. Antitakeover justifications.

The third reason often given to explain staggered boards is that they make hostile takeovers more difficult.... [T]his justification may have been unintended when staggered boards first appeared, but the key point is that the interaction between a staggered board and a poison pill puts up a potent defense against a hostile bidder. A pill provides relatively weak takeover protection if the target is vulnerable to a rapid proxy fight, because the target's board can redeem the pill at any time; a staggered board without a pill is likewise ineffective against a bid, given the unlikelihood that target directors will continue to resist if a bidder has acquired a majority of the target's stock. In combination with an effective staggered board, however, a pill provides significant antitakeover protection: the pill blocks any stock acquisition beyond the trigger level, and the staggered board forces the bidder to go through two proxy contests in order to gain control of the board and redeem the pill.

Statistics on staggered board incidence are consistent with the view that staggered boards are at least partly motivated by antitakeover considerations.... [S]taggered boards are relatively less common among smaller firms, where ownership is typically more concentrated and hostile takeovers may be more difficult or impossible (if insiders own a controlling stake). Furthermore, staggered boards were far less common before the 1980s takeover wave, even though the board stability and board independence arguments (presumably) applied with equal force before 1980 as after.

Comments and Questions

1. Staggered boards have declined significantly in recent years, particularly among larger companies. By the end of 2014, only 7% of the S&P 500 had classified boards, down from 45% in 2004. What explains this change? Despite the decrease, there is some evidence that shareholders may benefit from the provisions. *See* Alicia J. Davis, *The Institutional Appetite for "Quack Corporate Governance,"* 2015 Colum. Bus. L. Rev. 1, 41–42 (noting evidence in the literature suggesting that "classified boards can provide value-enhancing continuity and stability.").

2. Staggered board provisions often appear in the articles of incorporation. Article amendments must be approved by shareholders. Doesn't this give shareholders sufficient authority to prevent the use of staggered boards?

3. How might the presence of a staggered board actually encourage a proxy contest? Is it the case that insurgents always seek a majority of the board? Why or why not?

4. Some states have entered the fray. Oklahoma and Indiana have adopted statutes that require staggered boards. Thus, in Indiana, a company must provide a staggered board unless, within 30 days of registering with the SEC under Section 12(g), the board opts out of the requirement. *See* Ind. Code Ann. § 23-1-33-6(c). Why might a state want to impose this type of requirement? What are the advantages? What are the disadvantages? For a discussion of the provision in Oklahoma, see Steven J. Cleveland, *A failure of Substance and a Failure of Process: The Circular Odyssey of Oklahoma's Corporate Law Amendments in 2010, 2012 and 2013*, 67 Okla. L. Rev. 221 (2015).

5. What other structural mechanisms can be used to affect a proxy contest? Companies routinely rely on advance notice bylaws which require insurgents to provide boards with notice 90 or 120 days before the meeting. How might these devices have an impact on a proxy contest?

In addition to structural provisions such as staggered boards, management has a variety of other tactics that can be used in a proxy contest. Perhaps the most practical is the ability to negotiate and reach agreements with insurgents or their prospective allies. The legality of such approaches depends upon the application of a board's fiduciary duties.

Portnoy v. Cryo-Cell International

Delaware Chancery Court
940 A.2d 43 (2008)

STRINE, VICE CHANCELLOR:

This case involves a challenge to the results of a contested corporate election. Cryo-Cell International, Inc. ("Cryo-Cell" or the "Company") is a small public company that has struggled to succeed. By early 2007, several of its large stockholders were considering mounting a proxy contest to replace the board.

One of those stockholders, Andrew Filipowski, used management's fear of replacement to strike a deal for himself to be included in the management slate for the 2007 annual meeting. Another stockholder, plaintiff David Portnoy, filed a dissident slate (the "Portnoy Slate").

Going into the week of the annual meeting, Cryo-Cell's chief executive officer, defendant Mercedes Walton, was desperate because, in her words, "the current board and management [were] losing by huge margins." Aside from actually asking the FBI to intervene in the proxy contest on the side of management, Walton ginned up a plan with Filipowski. That plan involved Walton acting as a "matchmaker" by finding stockholders willing to sell their shares to Filipowski. In exchange for this alliance, Walton promised Filipowski that if their "Management Slate" prevailed, Cryo-Cell's board would, using their power as corporate directors, expand the board to add another seat that Filipowski's designee would fill. That designee was a subordinate who had within the recent past resolved an SEC insider trading investigation by agreeing to disgorge trading profits and to be jointly liable for trading profits made by his tippees. This plan was not disclosed to the Cryo-Cell stockholders, who did not realize that if they voted for management, they would in fact be electing a seven, not six member board, with two, not one, Filipowski representatives.

* * *

Even after employing these methods, Walton and her board went into the day of the annual meeting fearing defeat. They had rented the meeting room from the 11 a.m. start time only until 1 p.m. But Walton did not want to close the polls and count the vote when the scheduled presentations at the meeting were over. So she had members of her management team make long, unscheduled presentations to give her side more time to gather votes and ensure that they had locked in two key blocs. She overruled motions to close the polls.

Even after the filibusters, Walton still harbored doubt that the Management Slate would prevail if the vote was counted and the meeting was concluded. So, at around 2 p.m., Walton declared a very late lunch break, supposedly in response to a request made much earlier.

In fact, Walton desired the break so that she would have more time to seek votes and so that she could confirm that the major blockholders had switched their votes to favor the Management Slate. Only after confirming the switches did Walton resume the meeting at approximately 4:45 p.m., declare the polls closed, and have the vote counted.

The post-meeting vote count resulted in the Management Slate squeaking out a victory by an extremely small margin. Immediately after that, Walton began preparing to add Filipowski's designee to the Cryo-Cell board. Only after this challenge was brought to the election by Portnoy did that process slow down, and only for the obvious reason that the litigation was brought.

* * *

Portnoy claims that all aspects of the incumbents' dealings with Filipowski are tainted by fiduciary misconduct. As he sees it, the incumbents had already marked out the key characteristics they were looking for in additional board members — healthcare industry and stem cell industry experience — and that Filipowski did not have those. Walton, and a board that Portnoy rightly portrays as having every appearance of largely following her lead without much question, simply made a bargain to add Filipowski to the Management Slate, not because they thought his service would help Cryo-Cell but because it would ensure that the large bloc of votes Filipowski controlled would vote for their re-election. That is, this was an entrenchment-motivated decision. Portnoy contends that the deal struck between Walton and the other incumbents, on the one hand, and Filipowski, on the other, to add Filipowski to the Management Slate in exchange for his support in the proxy fight constituted an illegal vote-buying arrangement.

On this claim, which has some color, I find in favor of the defendants. My conclusion rests on several grounds. Initially, I note that an arrangement of this kind fits comfortably, as a linguistic matter, within the traditional definition of so-called "vote buying" used in our jurisprudence. As defined by Vice Chancellor Hartnett in his important decision in Schreiber v. Carney, "[v]ote-buying ... is simply a voting agreement supported by consideration personal to the stockholder, whereby the stockholder divorces his discretionary voting power and votes as directed by the offeror." In this case, I have no doubt that the voting agreement between the Filipowski Group and the incumbents was only assented to by Filipowski after he was offered a candidacy on the Management Slate. What I am more doubtful about is whether an arrangement of this kind — where the incumbents offer a potential insurgent a seat on the management slate in exchange for the potential insurgent's voting support — should trigger the sort of heightened scrutiny rightly given to more questionable arrangements.

To say that the law of corporations has struggled with how to address the subject of so-called "vote buying" is no insult to judges or corporate law scholars, the question of what inducements and agreements may legitimately be forged to cement a voting coalition is doubtless as old as the concept of a polity itself. For these very real-world reasons, Schreiber refused to say that any sort of arrangement involving the exchange of consideration in connection with a stockholder's agreement to vote a particular way was forbidden vote buying. Indeed, distinguished scholars have anguished (the adjective I take away from their work) over how to deal with such arrangements, with most concluding that flat-out prohibitions are neither workable nor of utility to diversified stockholders. The absence of a per se ban on such arrangements is unsurprising for another obvious reason, voting agreements with respect to corporate stock are actually contemplated by our statutory corporate law. Often such agreements have the intended effect of forming a voting coalition between stockholders that involves the requirement that the contracting parties vote to elect each other to the board.

* * *

But being on the inside track is different than being on the board, and that difference suggests that employing an entire fairness standard to such arrangements is overkill. If the only arrangement at issue is a promise to add a potential insurgent to the management slate in exchange for the insurgent's voting support, then the arrangement is subject to stockholder policing in an obvious, but nonetheless, potent form. That policing occurs at the ballot box itself.

Here, to be specific, the Cryo-Cell stockholders went to the polls knowing that Filipowski had been added to the Management Slate. Those stockholders also knew that Filipowski had contracted to vote the Filipowski Group's shares for the Management Slate. Although it was not publicly disclosed that Filipowski's agreement to vote for the Management Slate had been conditioned on his addition to that Slate, and that the incumbents had added Filipowski to the Management Slate in exchange for his support, that inference was, I think, unmistakable to any rational stockholder. Surely it was known by Portnoy, who knew that Filipowski had been unhappy about the Company's performance, and had flirted with running a slate with Portnoy, only to secure a place for himself on the Management Slate. Therefore, Portnoy was well-positioned to point out that Filipowski had committed to support incumbents whose wisdom and fidelity to stockholders Filipowski himself had only recently called into serious question.

Given that the electorate's own opportunity to decide for itself whether Filipowski should serve, I think it unwise, as a matter of our common law, to apply the intrinsic fairness test to this situation. As Portnoy would have it, I should make a judgment about whether Walton and the other incumbents would have ever thought Filipowski a board member beneficial to Cryo-Cell *but for* their entrenchment-motivated desire to secure his vote. I have little hesitancy in concluding that Walton was not anxious to have Filipowski on her board. She and her colleagues warmed to that idea only when confronted with the reality of almost certain defeat if Filipowski joined Portnoy in running a dissident slate, and were at great risk even if Filipowski supported the Management Slate. In other words, I have no doubt Filipowski was added to the

Management Slate primarily to secure his vote. But I also have no doubt that Walton and the board determined that Filipowski was a credible candidate with some useful attributes.

The notion that judges should chew over the complicated calculus made by incumbent boards considering whether to add to the management slate candidates proposed by a large blockholder whose velvety suggestions were cloaking an unmistakably clenched fist seems to run against many of the sound reasons for the business judgment rule. There is, thankfully, a practical and civic dynamic in much of our nation's human relations, including in commerce, by which clashes of viewpoint are addressed peaceably through give and take. When stockholders can decide for themselves whether to seat a candidate who obtained a place on a management slate by way of such bargaining, it seems unwise to formulate a standard that involves the potential for excessive and imprecise judicial involvement.

* * *

In my view, a mere offer of a position on a management slate should not be considered a vote-buying arrangement subject to a test of entire fairness, and for that reason, I see no reason to condemn the addition of Filipowski to the Management Slate. As an alternative matter, the defendants have convinced me that there was nothing unfair about joining forces with Filipowski in this manner. In this regard, I note that there is not a hint that Filipowski sought to receive financial payments from Cryo-Cell in the form of contracts or consulting fees or other such arrangements. What he sought was influence on the board of a company in which he owned a large number of shares, an ownership interest that gave him an incentive to increase the company's value. Stockholders knew he sought a seat and he had to obtain their votes to get on the board.

For all these reasons, I conclude that Portnoy's attack on this aspect of the incumbents' dealings with Filipowski fails.

B. The Promise Of A Second Board Seat For The Filipowski Group

I reach a different conclusion, however, about the later arrangement that was reached with Filipowski shortly before the annual meeting. As I found previously, Walton (acting at the very least with the apparent authority of her board colleagues, who were extremely deferential to her leadership) promised Filipowski that if the Management Slate won, the incumbent board majority would use its powers under the Company's bylaws to expand the Cryo-Cell board from six members to seven and to fill the new seat with Filipowski's designee, Roszak. That promise was made in response to Roszak's request—as Filipowski's negotiator—and made in exchange for Filipowski's promise to go out and buy more shares (and therefore votes).

* * *

"[D]irectors of Delaware corporations are under a fiduciary duty to disclose fully and fairly all material information within the board's control when it seeks shareholder action." That disclosure "obligation attaches to proxy statements and any other disclosures in contemplation of stockholder action." "An omitted fact is material if there is a substantial likelihood that a reasonable shareholder would consider it important in deciding how to vote."

On the day they voted, the Cryo-Cell stockholders knew that a vote for the Management Slate would seat six directors, including Filipowski. They had to know that Filipowski's support for the Management Slate was in large measure motivated by his own inclusion.

What the Cryo-Cell stockholders did not know was that Walton had promised that the board would use its fiduciary powers to expand the board to seven members and seat another person designated by Filipowski. Problematically, the Cryo-Cell stockholders did not know that Filipowski clearly intended to designate Roszak, a person whose recent past would have weighed heavily on the mind of a rational stockholder considering whether to seat him as a fiduciary. Indeed, at trial, the defendants went out of their way to say that they decided to include Filipowski only after concluding that Roszak's conduct in the Blue Rhino situation did not cast doubt on Filipowski's own good character.

In so concluding, I do not hesitate to note my belief that Walton knew that Roszak was going to be Filipowski's designee before the meeting, but also that my ultimate conclusion that this was a material agreement that should have been disclosed would not change if that was not so. Stockholders would have found it material to know that corporate management's cooperation with Filipowski had now extended to a bargain whereby he would buy up more shares and votes in exchange for having two seats on the board. A reasonable stockholder could have come to the conclusion that they did not want Filipowski to have so much influence—and certainly not if Roszak, his employee with a dubious track record, was going to be his guaranteed echo on the board.

* * *

I now come to Portnoy's last complaint. That is about how Walton conducted the meeting.

As an initial matter, I decline to use this as an excuse to probe the difference between a lunch break and a formal adjournment. The language of the Cryo-Cell bylaws creates a colorable argument that a formal adjournment could not have been declared without stockholder approval and there is doubt whether Walton had sufficient proxies in hand for that purpose. In my view, Portnoy is not positioned to contest Walton's authority to "decide all procedural issues regarding the conduct of the meeting, including adjournment," so long as she did so in good faith....

What, however, is more uncertain is that Walton acted inequitably in her conduct of the meeting. The reality is that she did not take a "lupper" break of nearly three hours at 2 p.m. so that the attendees at the meeting could eat. Because Walton undertook action that affected the conduct of an election of directors in a potentially important way, the defendants bear the burden to show that Walton's actions were "motivated by a good faith concern for the stockholders' best interests, and not by a desire to entrench [herself.]" They have failed to prove that Walton's tactics were undertaken in selfless good faith.

Walton"s behavior during the day was analogous to a corrupted soccer referee, intent on adding extra time so that the game would end only when her favored team had a sure lead. Very early in the meeting, the scheduled course of events had run and all stockholder questions had been answered.

* * *

The defendants, of course, say that the Portnoy Slate should have recognized the need to keep searching for votes during the period when Walton was delaying, and that the Portnoy Slate was less than assiduous in ensuring that its early lead was secured by faithful tending of its proxy-giving flock. And one cannot be but reluctant to set a precedent that helps creates justiciable issues out of delays measured in hours, rather than days or weeks.

Nonetheless, it is impossible to ignore the unfairness of Walton's behavior, a justification by reference to effect being no defense to actions affecting a director election that are undertaken for "an inequitable purpose" and in an inequitably deceptive manner. If an electoral contestant assumes the role of presiding over the meeting, she has an obligation to do so fairly. Walton did not do so. She stalled so that her side could win the game, knowing that if the game ended when it was scheduled to end, her side would lose. Then she was dishonest about the reasons for delay.

For all these reasons, I find that Portnoy has proven that serious breaches of fiduciary duty tainted the election. Before considering what remedy to impose, I must briefly address the defendants' contention that the inequitable conduct of their side should be ignored because Portnoy has unclean hands. After doing that, I address the remedial implications of my findings.

* * *

I come now to the question of the appropriate remedy. Although Portnoy would have me simply declare his slate the victor, I do not believe that is the most appropriate remedy. Given how close the contest was and the reality that Filipowski actually acquired beneficial ownership of the shares he voted, I think the remedy that best vindicates the interests of Cryo-Cell stockholders as a class is to order a prompt special meeting at which a new election will be held and presided over by a special master. Until that time, the incumbents who sat on the Cryo-Cell board before the 2007 annual meeting will continue in office; Filipowski's claim to office has no pre-existing legitimacy and he shall leave the board until he is elected by the stockholders.

* * *

A more fitting way to address the cost concerns is to require the Management Slate to bear the costs of their own proxy solicitation efforts, the costs to the corporation of holding the meeting, and the costs of a special master to conduct the meeting. This will ensure that the Cryo-Cell stockholders are not injured by the requirement for an extra meeting. Given the misconduct by the Management Slate, this is a fitting and proportionate remedy. Nor will the remedy place the Management Slate at a disadvantage to any insurgent slate, it will simply level the playing field.

* * *

In terms of the financial obligations imposed on the defendants, I note that I focus their responsibilities on remediating the harm they have caused to the corporation in a proportionate and constructive manner. I reject Portnoy's request to have the defendants or Cryo-Cell pay his litigation and proxy solicitation costs. I do so in deference both to the traditional American Rule approach our jurisprudence embraces and as a fitting consequence for Portnoy's dalliance with Archibald, a course of conduct that I do not believe disentitles him to a remedy but that ought to have some consequence. By rejecting Portnoy's request for reimbursement of his litigation and proxy costs, I limit the defendants' exposure to paying the costs of holding a special meeting, which should not be onerous if the parties are sensible, which the special master will ensure.

The parties shall collaborate on the appropriate date and location for a prompt special meeting and present a conforming order, in advance of seeking a conference this week with the court at which the order will be finalized and a special master appointed.

Comments and Questions

1. Who really won this case? What position did the respective parties have upon resolution of this case?

2. What do you make of the vote-buying analysis in this case? Plaintiff argued that the agreement between management and Filipowski was entrenchment-motivated and therefore an "illegal vote-buying arrangement." Rather than subject the arrangement to entire fairness, however, the court concluded that adequate "policing occurs at the ballot box itself." Do you agree with this approach?

3. In concluding that the vote-buying arrangement was proper, the court noted that Filipowski had not received any financial payments but instead merely received a position on the board, providing him influence on a company where he held a sizeable number of shares. Given the court's reasoning that policing can occur at the ballot box, does the form of consideration (money or influence) matter? Assume for the question that the amount of any payments had been disclosed.

4. The court suggested that it would not be willing to consider procedural issues regarding the conduct of the meeting but did indicate concern with the equity of a "lupper" break. On that matter, the Defendant had the burden of showing that the action was "motivated" by good faith. Since the "lupper" break was also a procedural issue, what is the dividing line between those matters that the court will consider and those it will not?

5. Management knew that it was about to lose the vote and, as a result, delayed the meeting to obtain additional votes. How does management know the tally at this stage of the proxy contest? Does the insurgent shareholder have the same information?

6. What do you make of the remedy in this case? What were Portnoy's choices following the decision? In fact, Portnoy in fact did not run a competing slate of directors and those nominated by management were elected without opposition.

7. The court denied Portnoy's request that Defendants pay his fees. What was the basis for the denial? What impact might that have on future challenges of managerial behavior in proxy contests?

C. Proxy Contests and Interim Voting Results

Most shares of public companies are held by street name owners. They vote their shares for the most part not by executing a proxy card but by returning voting instructions to Broadridge, an agent that acts on behalf of brokers and banks. Broadridge tabulates the instructions and inserts them on a proxy card that is submitted to the company. Broadridge, therefore, is aware of the results as they are submitted. The information can influence the proxy process.

Red Oak Fund, L.P. v. Digirad Corporation

Delaware Chancery Court
C.A. No. 8559-VCN (Oct. 23, 2013)

Red Oak, a Delaware limited partnership based in New York City, invests in public and private companies that generally have a market capitalization less than $200 million. Leading up to the proxy contest, Red Oak was Digirad's fourth-largest stockholder, owning 5.6% of its common stock. David Sandberg ("Sandberg") is the managing member of Red Oak Partners, LLC, which is the general partner of Red Oak.

Digirad, a Delaware corporation based in Poway, California, is a national provider of "in-office nuclear cardiology and ultrasound imaging services to physician practices and hospitals." It also operates a "nuclear camera sales and product services business."

Digirad has five directors: Eberwein, who serves as chairman, as well as Gillman, Climaco, Hawkins, and Sayward (collectively, the "Board"). The Board was up for reelection at Digirad's 2013 annual stockholder meeting, held on May 3, 2013 (the "Election").

III. BACKGROUND

At the time of the Election, Digirad's Chief Executive Officer was Todd Clyde ("Clyde"), and its Chief Financial Officer was Jeffrey Keyes ("Keyes"). These two executives were the most involved in the conduct at issue in this action.

After taking a 5.6% position in Digirad, Red Oak announced on February 27 that it would nominate a slate of five directors to replace the Board at the Election. Digirad filed its definitive proxy statement with the Securities and Exchange Commission ("SEC") on April 4. From then until the Election, both Digirad and Red Oak issued press releases and fight letters encouraging stockholders to vote for their respective nominees.

A. *The Alleged Material Misstatements Touting the Preliminary Election Results*

The first alleged material misstatement involves information potentially shared between John Grau ("Grau"), Digirad's proxy solicitor, and Tyson Bauer ("Bauer"), a sell-side stock research analyst at Kansas City Capital Associates. Eberwein understood Bauer to be familiar with Digirad's stockholder base, including several of its larger stockholders. On April 23, Eberwein asked Gillman to speak with Bauer and Ross Taylor ("Taylor"), a Portfolio Manager at Somerset Capital Advisors ("Somerset"), about persuading Somerset, a Digirad stockholder, to support management in the Election based on a commitment to improve Digirad's on-going stock buyback program. In late March, Digirad had increased the buyback from $4 million to $12 million.

Bauer testified that Gillman told him that management believed it could not lose the Election if it received the support it expected from the proxy advisor firms. Soon thereafter, on April 24, Bauer asked for "indisputable proof" or some other evidence supporting why Digirad was "so confident" that it was "going to win," which was information he was ultimately seeking on behalf of Taylor. Gillman apparently told Bauer that Grau would contact him. Bauer testified that, over the course of these limited conversations, Gillman did not provide him with any stockholder names, voting percentages, or other preliminary proxy tally details.

In the meantime, and after presentations by Digirad and Red Oak, both Institutional Shareholder Services ("ISS") and Glass, Lewis & Co., L.L.C. ("Glass Lewis") recommended on April 22 that Digirad stockholders vote to reelect the Board. Management soon touted this recommendation publicly, issuing a press release by the morning of April 23.

Within a day, Grau and Bauer began a series of three phone conversations. Grau thought that Bauer was "somebody working with the [c]ompany who was going to assist ... in reaching out to shareholders that may be clients of his." The first call with Bauer on April 24, Grau testified, left him "very confused" because "[Bauer] wanted to know more information than [Grau] would have ever expected anyone to be interested in." But Grau, believing "at the time[ ] that [Bauer] was an agent of Digirad's," nonetheless shared "some back-of-the-envelope numbers on where [he] thought the vote was ... factoring in ... where the vote would be given the ISS recommendation." Bauer's notes from the three conversations with Grau list a series of percentage breakdowns showing management first ahead 34% to 12%, then 45% to 10%, and finally management at just under 50% with 63% of shares included. These percentages, Bauer testified, reflected Grau and Digirad's opinion of expected votes—particularly based on the recently announced recommendations of ISS and Glass Lewis in support of management—and not an official tally or a list of stockholders who had submitted proxies.

Bauer and Grau offer competing views on the reasons why the expected vote percentages were shared. Bauer assumed that "there's no purpose for [Grau] to call [him] with those numbers" unless Grau wanted him to share them with stockholders. In stark contrast, Grau testified that it was Bauer who "wanted to know" the information. Consistent with his thinking that "Bauer was working for [Digirad]," Grau further testified that he did not know Bauer was having conversations with Somerset's Taylor; that he did not intend for Bauer to communicate these numbers to stockholders; and that he would not have given to Bauer the expected vote numbers had he known Bauer would share that information with stockholders.

The second alleged material misstatement about the preliminary proxy tallies occurred during a conversation between Eberwein and Taylor. The testimony directly conflicts over whether Eberwein described the preliminary election results as a "landslide," with Taylor testifying that Eberwein said it and Eberwein testifying that he did not. Regardless of whether Eberwein ever said "landslide," the evidence is consistent in showing that Eberwein did not reveal to Taylor specific numbers, aside from a disputed reference to a few index funds, or the specific source of his information on preliminary voting tallies.

Somerset, along with three other of Digirad's five largest stockholders (including Red Oak), voted for Red Oak's slate.

B. *The Proxy Submitted for Digirad Treasury Stock*

In early April, the competing proxy solicitors—Grau of InvestorCom, Inc. for Digirad and Peter Casey ("Casey") of Alliance Advisors for Red Oak—noticed an issue with how much stock was entitled to vote at the Election. Grau compared the March 12 record date list from the Depository Trust Company ("DTC") with Digirad's proxy statement, which revealed what he described as a DTC "overhang of approximately 1,075,000 shares." An overhang meant that the DTC list of Digirad stock held in street name included more stock than the number of shares that Digirad identified in its proxy as eligible to vote. Casey also recognized the overhang and asked Grau's team whether the difference was due to Digirad's treasury stock. Grau's team confirmed on April 8 that treasury stock was the cause of the discrepancy, but, when Casey asked in a response email that same day where Digirad held its treasury stock, no one replied.

Digirad held the repurchased treasury stock from its buyback program at broker Raymond James & Co. ("Raymond James"), apparently in street name. By March 12, the record date for the Election, Digirad held 1,073,641 shares of treasury stock with the broker. Dan Warnock ("Warnock"), a member of Keyes' financial team, was the Digirad accounting manager in charge of "making sure that the financial activity through the [Raymond James treasury stock] account was appropriate." Warnock's responsibilities included receiving regular statements from Raymond James about the account.

On April 9, Warnock received "an e-mail from Raymond James routed through Broadridge," soliciting a proxy for the Election. Under the impression that he may have personally owned Digirad stock at Raymond James, Warnock clicked an electronic link in the email, which presumably directed him to a webpage through which he then submitted a proxy in favor of management. As Keyes testified, "it wasn't apparent to [Warnock] when he pulled up the link how many shares were … to be voted or the fact that they might have been the company's treasury shares."

By at least April 15, just under three weeks before the Election, the proxy solicitors were receiving preliminary reports from Broadridge. During the Election, Broadridge's function was to be an independent third party that received proxies and shared its tabulations of these proxies in periodic reports with Digirad and Red Oak. Of course, as more stockholders submitted new proxies, the preliminary Broadridge reports changed.

Broadridge provided preliminary reports about the Election to only the proxy solicitors, not Digirad's stockholders. Grau reformatted the Broadridge reports before sending them to Digirad, while Casey either just forwarded or similarly reformatted the reports before sharing them with Red Oak. The reports from Broadridge did not name the beneficial owners who had submitted proxies; instead, they listed by street name custodian the proxies submitted for management, for Red Oak's slate, and for withhold. Armed with the preliminary Broadridge reports, Grau and Casey, working independently, were generally able to figure out how Digirad's larger, institutional stockholders were voting.

Digirad and Red Oak used the preliminary Broadridge reports and the stockholder information gleaned by their proxy solicitors in developing and refining their solicitation strategies. Grau admitted that his strategy advice may slightly change in a particular vote if his client had a large lead in the preliminary reports, but he testified that, in general, he "would never stop soliciting proxies because it ain't over until it's over." In contrast, Sandberg described Red Oak's solicitation strategy during the Election as a "fluid process" and a "cost[-]benefit" analysis that depended in large part on the preliminary results. For example, Sandberg testified that it would have been a "game changer" had Red Oak known that the Broadridge reports leading up to the Election were inaccurate.

After Warnock had inadvertently and unknowingly voted the treasury stock, the preliminary reports from Broadridge sent to Digirad and to Red Oak reflected that a large block at Raymond James—over one million shares, around 6% of Digirad's outstanding stock—had voted for management. Reading the Broadridge reports, both Grau and Casey likely recognized that such a significant stockholder (or group of stockholders) could be valuable to their respective clients, and each set about trying to identify who beneficially owned those shares.

By April 25, Casey was still unable to identify the unknown stockholder. On April 26, he again asked Grau's team where Digirad held its treasury stock, but Grau affirmatively declined to provide that information. Grau later testified that, at the time of that response, he did not yet think that the treasury stock had been voted, and, moreover, it was not industry practice to provide such additional information.

Around this time, Grau was starting to have some luck in discovering who owned the Raymond James stock. On April 24, he had inquired about where Clyde held his personal stock, thinking that the large block might be owned by an insider. Clyde noted that he held some stock with one broker and the rest was held at Raymond James. Grau then asked for Clyde to put him in touch with someone at Raymond James who might answer some of his questions.

Separately, in an email the morning of April 26, Grau asked Keyes if Digirad held its treasury stock at Raymond James. Before Keyes answered the question, Grau emailed Eberwein, Clyde, and Keyes to inform them that he was becoming "concerned that for some reason Raymond James voted the 1,000,000 shares being held in treasury as part of the buyback." In an April 27 email to Keyes, Grau seems to have concluded that Raymond James did vote Digirad's treasury stock. None of Eberwein, Clyde, or Keyes appears at that time to have informed anyone else at Digirad about the proxy submitted for the treasury stock.

In the same email to Keyes, Grau explained that he would "exclude[ ]" the treasury stock from the future updates, based on the preliminary Broadridge reports, that he would send to Digirad. To be clear, the preliminary Broadridge reports that Grau and Casey received still reflected approximately one million shares of treasury stock at Raymond James voting for management, but Grau "removed it from [his] vote report and any other correspondence that went to [Digirad]." Casey did not have the same insight; he and Red Oak still operated under the assumption that the Broadridge reports reflected proxies submitted for stock entitled to vote.

Keyes repeatedly testified that he did not know for sure at any point before the Election that a proxy had been submitted for the treasury stock. However, Grau's decision to remove the Raymond James block from his future updates to Digirad shows that at least he was fairly confident that treasury stock had been voted, and Keyes and Digirad continued to rely on Grau throughout the Election.

Keyes soon thereafter had a conversation with the independent inspector of elections, memorialized in a May 1 letter, in which he informed the inspector that Digirad had 1,073,641 shares of treasury stock held at Raymond James that "should not be considered outstanding for purposes of [Digirad's] 2013 Annual Meeting." Keyes testified that he assumed informing the independent inspector was an appropriate way to yield "an accurate vote result"; he also testified that Digirad still had not informed Broadridge, Red Oak, or Casey about the suspected voting of treasury stock.

The May 2 contest vote issued by Broadridge still included treasury stock voting for management. Based on that contest vote and the supplemental report the morning of the Election, Sandberg emailed his slate of nominees on May 3 to let them know they had lost "by approx[imately] 46% to 34%." The email attributed the loss "due to losing ISS"; yet, as Sandberg testified, he did not know until after the Election about the alleged "game changer"—that the Broadridge reports had listed a proxy submitted for Digirad's treasury stock. At trial, although Sandberg did admit the importance of the ISS recommendation in the proxy contest, he insisted that "had [Red Oak] known that the vote was closer than the [Broadridge] information [it was] receiving and [it] had pushed harder, [he] think[s] [Red Oak] would have won."

On May 10, Digirad announced the final results of the Election. The independent inspector certified that the Board had been reelected over Red Oak's slate by a vote of 40% to 34%. The 6% difference between Sandberg's May 3 email listing a result of 46%–34% and the May 10 final vote tally of 40%–34% is the Digirad treasury stock that may not lawfully be counted in a stockholder vote.

* * *

A. *The Preliminary Results of the Election*

Red Oak argues that the Defendants made materially misleading statements before the Election by sharing non-public information about the preliminary results in two ways: by Grau's sharing of voting expectations with Bauer and by Eberwein's making of confident predictions to Taylor.

The Court first finds that the statements by Grau were not material. Both Grau and Bauer acknowledged that they were reflective of Digirad's expected proxy votes, not actual votes. Grau testified that he did not "inflate the lead" in these conversations by including the treasury stock. The preponderance of the evidence shows that the conversations were not intended to be shared with stockholders and were not made with any knowledge that Bauer would share the information with stockholders. They were made with just the opposite intent—Grau thought Bauer was working for Digirad.

Likewise, the Court finds Eberwein's statements were not material. The testimony conflicts over whether any "landslide" comment was made, and although Eberwein may have mentioned certain funds by name, the preponderance of the evidence does not show that Eberwein told Taylor about the actual proxies submitted by any particular stockholder.

Red Oak's final argument is that these statements created an unfair election process because of Digirad's status as a microcap company. Sandberg testified that even suggestions to stockholders about strong preliminary results for management in an election for a public company the size of Digirad can have at least two prejudicial effects: they can "pressure certain shareholders not to want to vote against what's clearly the winning side," and they can even "dissuade shareholders from voting at all." This potentially difficult management-stockholder dynamic does not warrant subjecting microcap companies to additional fiduciary duties or requiring additional protections against an unfair election process.

Because the integrity of the election process is an essential part of the foundation of Delaware corporate law, the Court takes very seriously claims of an unfair election process because of misleading or inadequate disclosures. But, the Court also does not take lightly either finding an election invalid or imposing the equitable remedy of ordering a new one. Fair elections should be based on the disclosure of all material information to stockholders, but the Court here cannot find the Election invalid for want of adequate disclosure based on speculation about alleged misstatements that is unsupported by a preponderance of the evidence. These alleged misstatements do not render the Election invalid.

B. *The Treasury Stock Proxy and the Preliminary* Broadridge *Reports*

Next, Red Oak argues that the Defendants breached their fiduciary duties and created an unfair election process by failing to disclose affirmatively to Red Oak, individually, or along with the rest of Digirad's stockholders, that the Broadridge reports were inaccurate. In the opinion of Sandberg, it would have been a "game changer" for Red Oak's proxy solicitation strategy had it known that the preliminary 12% lead for management should have been just 6%.

The evidence does not demonstrate that the Defendants caused the treasury stock held at Raymond James to be voted. Only after Red Oak commenced this action and the resulting discovery did the Defendants even learn how a proxy was submitted for the treasury stock. What remains unanswered, or at least not revealed during this proceeding, is how exactly Raymond James came to solicit a proxy for the Digirad treasury stock. But, what is clear from the evidence is that the Defendants cannot be said to have directly caused the voting of the treasury stock. Keyes testified that no one instructed Warnock to vote the treasury stock. As Red Oak conceded, the voting was "accidental[ ]," and no evidence contradicts this conclusion. To be sure, it is less than "best practices" of governance for a corporation to hold treasury stock in street name at a retail brokerage firm which then solicits a proxy for its treasury stock, but even the "highly unusual policy of maintaining its [treasury] shares in street name at a retail brokerage account" is not a *per se* unlawful corporate act.

The overriding legal question here is whether the Defendants breached their fiduciary duties or created an unfair election process by failing to inform Red Oak of their suspicion. According to Red Oak, this duty would have attached when the Defendants knew, or at least began to operate under the assumption, that Raymond James voted the treasury stock, which the Court finds to be at the time of Grau's April 27 email to Keyes. The alleged "misleading" of Red Oak, the theory goes, calls into question the fairness of the election. This framed a novel question.

The argument for a duty to disclose such information to one stockholder to use in its proxy contest strategy is unpersuasive. It clashes with the well-established principles that teach that disclosure of material information, when required under Delaware law because the directors seek stockholder action, must be to all stockholders to inform their voting decisions. Thus, if the Board owed Red Oak a duty to disclose that the Broadridge reports were inaccurate, it would have to have been a duty the Board owed to all stockholders.

No cited Delaware authority supports the proposition that the Board was under a fiduciary duty to disclose to its stockholders either the Broadridge reports or the voting of the treasury stock, which could be seen only in the reports. Red Oak conceded that Broadridge did not provide these preliminary reports to the public or to Digirad's stockholders. Proxy contests happen all the time without management disclosure of preliminary proxy tabulation reports, and the Court is loath to find a breach of fiduciary duty under the circumstances for such a customary and inoffensive practice without an exceedingly compelling argument rooted in Delaware law, which Red Oak has not presented. Because Digirad never affirmatively disclosed the preliminary Broadridge reports to all stockholders, or even to some stockholders (such as Red Oak), Digirad also cannot be said to have assumed a duty to disclose whether the reports remained accurate. This type of asymmetry of information appears to be an honest and unfortunate mistake, not anything approaching intentional misconduct.

Accordingly, the Board did not owe a fiduciary duty to disclose to Red Oak that some of them may have known, or at least assumed, that the preliminary Broadridge reports did not accurately reflect the number of shares that could actually be voted at the Election. The preliminary Broadridge reports were "preliminary" by their very terms—meaning that they were subject to change and thus possibly inaccurate. The Court is not convinced that ensuring the accuracy of these reports, without a showing of something akin to intentional misconduct or self-initiated disclosure to the stock-holders, is a matter of Delaware law. Therefore, the Defendants did not breach their fiduciary duties here in any way that would warrant a new election.

Moreover, Red Oak has not demonstrated why the Court should find an unfair election process because of Red Oak's reliance on the inaccurate, preliminary Broad-ridge reports. It is far too speculative a basis to invalidate an election by arguing that one's solicitation strategy would have been different if one knew then what one knows now. Relief under Section 225 that is not based on a breach of fiduciary duty would require proof of an unfair election process for the stockholders—and Red Oak has not demonstrated by a preponderance of the evidence how a proxy solicitation strategy based on preliminary Broadridge reports inaccurately listing Digirad's inadvertently submitted treasury stock proxy amounts to an unfair election process for the stock-holders at large, even if the information asymmetry disadvantaged Red Oak. The ac-cidental voting of the treasury stock and the nondisclosure that the Broadridge reports were inaccurate do not invalidate the Election.

* * *

VI. CONCLUSION

For the foregoing reasons, the Court finds that the Board did not breach its fiduciary duties by making any material misstatements or omissions during the Election. In addition, the Court finds that Red Oak did not establish that the Defendants in some other way created an unfair election process. Therefore, the Court finds the Election valid, and the Defendants are entitled to judgment in their favor.

An implementing order will be entered.

Comments And Questions

1. What exactly is "interim voting" results? Who owns the information and how does it end up in the hands of Broadridge?

2. What is the value of interim voting information in a contest? How can it po-tentially influence the outcome of a proxy fight?

3. Do you agree with the court's decision? Who created the error in this the interim data in this case? Were there ways to ensure the accuracy of the information without requiring the company to disclose the error to Red Oak?

4. In this case, Broadridge provided the interim voting information to both sides in the proxy contest. Should there be any limits on the right of shareholders to receive interim or preliminary voting information? Brokers are exempt from the proxy rules in connection with the forwarding of materials to street name owners under Rule 14a-2(a). The exemption, however, is contingent upon the broker (and its agent) doing no more than "impartially" requesting voting instructions. Does this require-ment of impartiality apply to the disclosure of interim voting information that results from the collection of voting instructions? The Investor Advisory Committee of the SEC has taken the position that it does. *See* Recommendations of the Investor as

Owner Subcommittee: Impartiality in the Disclosure of Preliminary Voting Results, Investor Advisory Committee, Oct. 9, 2014, available at http://www.sec.gov/spotlight/investor-advisory-committee-2012/investor-as-owner-impartiality.pdf.

D. Proxy Contests and Poison Pills

The Disciplinary Effects of Proxy Contests

Poison pills were originally put in place to prevent hostile takeovers. The defensive tactics have, however, increasingly been used in the context of proxy contests. The analytical framework for challenging poison pills remains the modified business judgment rule first set out in *Unocal*. Nonetheless, the courts have shaped the analysis to fit the circumstances of a proxy contest, as the next case illustrates.

Unitrin Inc. v. American General Corp.

Delaware Supreme Court
651 A.2d 1361 (1995)

HOLLAND, JUSTICE:

[American General made an offer to purchase Unitrin. Unitrin responded by adopting a poison pill and a share repurchase program. The repurchase program involved the acquisition by Unitrin of up to 10 million of its own shares. As a result of the repurchases, the percentage of shares held by the directors of Unitrin would increase from 23% to 28%. The Chancery Court found that, under *Unocal*, the repurchase plan was not reasonable in relation to the threat posed. In effect the lower court reasoned that, with the poison pill in place, the repurchase plan was "unnecessary." On appeal, the Supreme Court disagreed and reversed.]

* * *

An examination of the cases applying Unocal reveals a direct correlation between findings of proportionality or disproportionality and the judicial determination of whether a defensive response was draconian because it was either coercive or preclusive in character. In Time, for example, this Court concluded that the Time board's defensive response was reasonable and proportionate since it was not aimed at 'cramming down' on its shareholders a management-sponsored alternative, i.e., was not coercive, and because it did not preclude Paramount from making an offer for the combined Time-Warner company, i.e., was not preclusive. See Paramount Communications, Inc. v. Time, Inc., Del. Supr., 571 A.2d 1140, 1154–55 (1990) (citing for comparison as coercive or preclusive disproportionate responses Mills Acquisition Co. v. Macmillan, Inc., Del. Supr., 559 A.2d 1261 (1989), and AC Acquisitions Corp. v. Anderson, Clayton & Co., Del. Ch., 519 A.2d 103 (1986)).

* * *

If a defensive measure is not draconian, however, because it is not either coercive or preclusive, the Unocal proportionality test requires the focus of enhanced judicial scrutiny to shift to "the range of reasonableness." Paramount Communications, Inc. v. QVC Network, Inc., Del. Supr., 637 A.2d 34, 45–46 (1994). Proper and proportionate defensive responses are intended and permitted to thwart perceived threats. When a corporation is not for sale, the board of directors is the defender of the metaphorical medieval corporate bastion and the protector of the corporation's shareholders. The fact that a defensive action must not be coercive or preclusive does not prevent a board from responding defensively before a bidder is at the corporate bastion's gate.

The ratio decidendi for the "range of reasonableness" standard is a need of the board of directors for latitude in discharging its fiduciary duties to the corporation and its shareholders when defending against perceived threats. The concomitant requirement is for judicial restraint. Consequently, if the board of directors' defensive response is not draconian (preclusive or coercive) and is within a "range of reasonableness," a court must not substitute its judgment for the board's. Paramount Communications, Inc. v. QVC Network, Inc., 637 A.2d at 45–46.

*　*　*

A limited nondiscriminatory self-tender, like some other defensive measures, may thwart a current hostile bid, but is not inherently coercive. Moreover, it does not necessarily preclude future bids or proxy contests by stockholders who decline to participate in the repurchase. Cf. AC Acquisitions Corp. v. Anderson, Clayton & Co., Del. Ch., 519 A.2d 103 (1986) (enjoining a coercive self-tender and restructuring plan). A selective repurchase of shares in a public corporation on the market, such as Unitrin's Repurchase Program, generally does not discriminate because all shareholders can voluntarily realize the same benefit by selling. See Larry E. Ribstein, Takeover Defenses and the Corporate Contract, 78 Geo. L.J. 71, 129–31 (1989). See also Michael Bradley & Michael Rosenzweig, Defensive Stock Repurchases, 99 Harv. L. Rev. 1377 (1986). Here, there is no showing on this record that the Repurchase Program was coercive.

We have already determined that the record in this case appears to reflect that a proxy contest remained a viable (if more problematic) alternative for American General even if the Repurchase Program were to be completed in its entirety. Nevertheless, the Court of Chancery must determine whether Unitrin's Repurchase Program would only inhibit American General's ability to wage a proxy fight and institute a merger or whether it was, in fact, preclusive because American General's success would either be mathematically impossible or realistically unattainable. If the Court of Chancery concludes that the Unitrin Repurchase Program was not draconian because it was not preclusive, one question will remain to be answered in its proportionality review: whether the Repurchase Program was within a range of reasonableness?

The Court of Chancery found that the Unitrin Board reasonably believed that American General's Offer was inadequate and that the adoption of a poison pill was a proportionate defensive response. Upon remand, in applying the correct legal standard to the factual circumstances of this case, the Court of Chancery may conclude that the implementation of the limited Repurchase Program was also within a range of reasonable additional defensive responses available to the Unitrin Board. In considering whether the Repurchase Program was within a range of reasonableness the Court of Chancery should take into consideration whether: (1) it is a statutorily authorized form of business decision which a board of directors may routinely make in a non-takeover context; (2) as a defensive response to American General's Offer it was limited and corresponded in degree or magnitude to the degree or magnitude of the threat, (i. e., assuming the threat was relatively "mild," was the response relatively "mild?"); (3) with the Repurchase Program, the Unitrin Board properly recognized that all shareholders are not alike, and provided immediate liquidity to those shareholders who wanted it.

Comments and Questions

1. *Unitrin* involved a challenge to a repurchase program. Yet the court discussed the impact of the action on proxy contests. Why?

2. A defensive tactic, according to the court, cannot be coercive or preclusive. Given the analysis in this case, how would a repurchase plan or poison pill preclude a proxy contest? What showing might a shareholder have to make?

3. Although the repurchase program would increase the number of shares likely to support management, the court reasoned that the outcome depended upon the "merit of American General's issues, not the size of its stockholdings." The court went on to conclude that "[i]f American General presented an attractive price as the cornerstone of a proxy contest, it could prevail, irrespective of whether the shareholder directors' absolute voting power was 23% or 28%." Do you agree with this analysis? Is victory in a proxy contest simply a matter of having the better argument?

4. In assessing the impact of a defensive tactic on a proxy contest, is the *Unocal* standard the correct approach? To the extent the tactic discourages or prevents a proxy contest, should the courts rely on an even higher standard of review such as the *Blasius* standard? One answer can be found in *Yucaipa Am. Alliance Fund II, L.P. v. Riggio*, 1 A.3d 310 (Del. Ch. 2010).

5. Assuming a defensive tactic is not "preclusive," can these acts "tilt" the contest in management's favor? How might a poison pill that remains in place do so?

6. The court in this case described the poison pill as "an effective takeover device has resulted in such a remarkable transformation in the market for corporate control that hostile bidders who proceed when such defenses are in place will usually have to couple proxy contests with tender offers." Explain what the court means by this statement.

———————

Poison pills prevent acquisitions above the designated threshold. They therefore prevent an acquirer from buying a controlling block of shares. In addition to limiting purchases, the defensive tactics can have a significant impact on a proxy contest as the next case shows.

Yucaipa American Alliance Fund II, LP v. Riggio

Delaware Chancery Court
1 A.3d 310 (2010), *aff'd*, 15 A.3d 218 (Del. 2011)

STRINE, VICE CHANCELLOR:

Less than two years ago, billionaire investor Ronald Burkle called Leonard Riggio, the founder of Barnes & Noble, Inc. to indicate that Burkle's funds, Yucaipa American Alliance Fund II, L.P. and Yucaipa American Alliance (Parallel) Fund II, L.P. (collectively, "Yucaipa"), were going to invest in Barnes & Noble. [Riggio and his brother at the time of this suit owned 28.91% of Barnes & Noble's outstanding stock.] The two men knew each other well, having participated in a joint investment under Burkle's leadership. Because that endeavor had not gone well for Riggio and because Riggio generally preferred not to have other large holders in Barnes & Noble, he tried to persuade Burkle to take his money elsewhere. But Burkle was not dissuaded, and invested in Barnes & Noble.

As in their previous venture, Burkle and Riggio soon were at odds. Burkle touted several ideas for Barnes & Noble to Riggio, which Riggio did not cause Barnes & Noble to pursue. But what really fueled Burkle's ire was when he learned in August 2009 that Barnes & Noble was to acquire a college bookstore chain that had been wholly-owned by Riggio. Burkle communicated his disappointment with how Barnes & Noble was governed, and his fund, Yucaipa, began to increase its stake in the company. Over a four day period in November 2009, Yucaipa approximately doubled its stake in Barnes & Noble to nearly 18%.

In response to the rapid accumulation of shares in Barnes & Noble by Yucaipa, the Barnes & Noble board of directors adopted a poison pill. That pill is triggered when a shareholder acquires over 20% of Barnes & Noble's outstanding stock, or when two or more shareholders, who combined own over 20%, enter into an "agreement, arrangement or understanding ... for the purpose of acquiring, holding, voting ... or disposing of any voting securities of the Company." Notably, however, the pill's 20% threshold does not apply to Riggio or his family, whose approximately 30% stake was grandfathered under the terms of the pill. The pill, however, also limited Riggio from further increasing that stake. [In addition to the shares owned by the Riggios, officers of Barnes & Noble owned another 3.26% and its employees another 6%. This provided a block of shares of around 37% to 38% of the expected vote that the court found would likely support the management slate.]

* * *

Under the familiar *Unocal* standard, adoption of a defensive measure will be protected by the business judgment rule so long as: (1) the board that adopts the measure in question had "reasonable grounds for believing that a danger to corporate policy and effectiveness existed"; and (2) the "defensive response was reasonable in relation to the threat posed." The Supreme Court's *Unitrin* decision helpfully emphasized the utility of the concepts of preclusion and coercion in addressing the question of whether a pill was an unreasonable response. Precisely because *Moran's* approval of the pill was premised on the ability to get around the pill through a proxy contest, *Unitrin* recognized the importance of examining whether the company's defensive arsenal as a whole, including the pill, was preclusive in the precise sense of making it unrealistic for an insurgent to win a proxy contest. Thus, this court has recognized that directors must "show that their actions were reasonable in relation to their legitimate objective, and did not preclude the stockholders from exercising their right to vote or coerce them into voting a particular way." Even if a defense is not preclusive, the court must strike down the defense if the directors fail to persuade the court that that defense was within the "range of reasonableness." That is, *Unitrin* left room for a determination that a non-preclusive, non-coercive defensive measure was nonetheless unreasonable in light of the threat faced by the corporation. As we shall soon see, this "range" comes into play in this case, according to Yucaipa.

* * *

... I now address the question of whether the Barnes & Noble board was responding to a legitimate threat. Yucaipa frames its argument that it poses no serious threat in a very convenient and self-serving way. Although Yucaipa must acknowledge that there is nothing novel about a rights plan's trigger applying to agreements between stockholders to run a joint proxy slate, and that a trigger of 20% has been held to be reasonable on several prior occasions, Yucaipa emphasizes that its case is distinct because all it seeks to do is to elect three directors this year, not a controlling slate, and that it has not announced a tender offer to acquire all the company's shares and has never made a hostile tender offer in its prior investing history. All Yucaipa desires, it says, is to have a little voice, in the form of electing three new directors, and therefore to apply to it the full force of a traditional rights plan designed to address a bidder for control is unreasonable.

The problems with this argument are several. For starters, the argument ignores the reality that the election of three directors to a classified board is not a trifling event, which gives the prevailing party no influence. Although much has been made of the minor number of instances in which a classified board has impeded a committed acquirer willing to pay an attractive price, the reality is that even the combination of a classified board and a rights plan are hardly show-stoppers in a vibrant American M & A market. Once an insurgent has won one election, the incumbent board majority's ability to be intransigent in the face of stockholder sentiment is greatly limited.

And in this case, Yucaipa also has not only the challenge, but also the opportunity, to make a more important point. Although only three directors are up for reelection at the next Barnes & Noble annual meeting, these directors include the founder and Chairman, Leonard Riggio himself, the lead independent director Del Giudice, and Riggio's personal financial advisor, Zilavy. Thus, Yucaipa can make it a referendum about whether the future of the company should follow Riggio's vision or the vision Yucaipa articulates. This is a high-stakes contest, no doubt, but one in which Yucaipa, if it can make a convincing case, can come out of the election with great influence. The potency Yucaipa would gain by winning is also enhanced by the fact that the Rights Plan will be put to a vote this calendar year. If Yucaipa wins a proxy contest, the incumbent board, while having the legal authority to adopt a new pill if the share-holders vote not to renew the Rights Plan, would by doing so be walking with open eyes right into a whirling helicopter blade.

Another major and related problem with Yucaipa's argument is that its portrayal of itself as an "aw shucks, purely friendly" investor is at odds with its own behavior and public disclosures.... More specifically, the record makes clear that Yucaipa's leader, Burkle, has pondered various fundamental strategy changes for Barnes & Noble, including: (1) making major asset purchases from Borders, Barnes & Noble's major rival; (2) a joint venture with HP to introduce Barnes & Noble into the consumer electronics market; and (3) a going private transaction. Burkle was serious enough about these options that he took meetings with key HP executives and investment bankers, and the board was entitled to view him as having an interest in exploring these and the other options the Yucaipa 13Ds left open. In sum, the board had a reasonable basis to conclude that Burkle was potentially planning to acquire a controlling stake in Barnes & Noble, or form a governing bloc with another large stockholder like Aletheia [Aletheia Research and Management, Inc., a California-based investment advisor, that owned 17.44% of the shares of Barnes & Noble.]

* * *

No doubt our law provides substantial protections for other investors in the event that a large stockholder with board representation proposes a going private transaction or engages in other forms of unfair value extraction, but that does not mean that the Barnes & Noble board was not entitled to take reasonable, non-preclusive action to ensure that an activist investor like Yucaipa did not amass, either singularly or in concert with another large stockholder, an effective control bloc that would allow it to make proposals under conditions in which it wielded great leverage to seek advantage for itself at the expense of other investors. Precisely by cabining Yucaipa at a substantial, but not overwhelming, level of voting influence, the board preserved for itself greater authority to protect the company's public stockholders.

Comments and Questions

1. What do you make of the court's discussion of the threat posed by Yucaipa? Should the analysis have been impacted by the presence of a staggered board? What do you make of the court's conclusion that, had Yucaipa won the election, the board's ability to be "intransigent in the face of stockholder sentiment is greatly limited"? 1 A.3d at 347.

2. Yucaipa, according to the court, abandoned any attempt to assert that the poison pill was preclusive. Given that Yucaipa controlled about 20% of the shares while the Riggios were credited with a block of about 38% (which included the shares owned by employees and other directors), what does this suggest about the standard for showing preclusion?

3. Did the poison pill "tilt the playing field" in favor of management? What about the fact that the board was not subject to the limitation on agreements with other

shareholders? The court acknowledged the authority but concluded that the fiduciary obligations of the board were sufficient to prevent behavior that exclusively benefited the Riggios. *See id.* ("To the extent the board, for example, sought to act as an instrument to protect the Riggios rather than for a proper purpose, they would be acting disloyally. That is, the board owes fiduciary duties to the company, something Yucaipa, as a stockholder, generally does not."). Do you agree?

4. Yucaipa ultimately lost the proxy contest. None of its three candidates were elected to the board. *See* Barnes & Noble, Current Report on Form 8-K, Oct. 13, 2010 (disclosing tallies; management directors each received about 26 million votes; Yucaipa candidates received about 23 million).

5. The poison pill applied to any "agreement, arrangement or understanding" among shareholders. Yucaipa argued that the language was ambiguous and would cause other shareholders to refuse to discuss the proxy contest. The court described the interpretation as "an unreasonable one that is based on unrealistic and absurd premises." Do you agree? From the perspective of other shareholders, what risks might they incur in discussing the proxy contest with Yucaipa?

6. The court discussed the role of proxy advisory firms. The court noted that the poison pill did not prevent shareholders from negotiating with these firms. What role do these firms play in a proxy contest?

7. In *Airgas*, the court noted that the standard for preclusiveness was that the poison pill would make a proxy contest "realistically unobtainable." The court noted that in the context of a staggered board "no bidder to my knowledge has ever successfully stuck around for two years and waged two successful proxy contests to gain control of a classified board in order to remove a pill." Nonetheless, the court noted that "clear precedent" in Delaware refused to find a pill preclusive "so long as obtaining control at some point in the future is realistically attainable." Are these positions consistent?

Poison pills prevent both acquisitions of shares and agreements among shareholders. When the trigger is at 15 or 20%, insurgent shareholders can at least acquire a sizeable block from which to launch a proxy contest. But what happens if the company adopts a poison pill with a very low threshold, say 5%? That is what happened in the next case.

Selectica, Inc. v. Versata Enterprises, Inc.

Delaware Supreme Court
5 A.3d 586 (2010)

HOLLAND, JUSTICE:

This is an appeal from a final judgment entered by the Court of Chancery. On November 16, 2008 the Board of Directors of Selectica Inc. ("Selectica") reduced the trigger of its "poison pill" Shareholder Rights Plan from 15% to 4.99% of Selectica's outstanding shares and capped existing shareholders who held a 5% or more interest to a further increase of only 0.5% (the "NOL Poison Pill"). Selectica's reason for taking such action was to protect the company's net operating loss carry forwards ("NOLs"). When Trilogy, Inc. ("Trilogy") subsequently purchased shares above this cap, Selectica filed suit in the Court of Chancery on December 21, 2008, seeking a declaration that the NOL Poison Pill was valid and enforceable. On January 2, 2009, Selectica implemented the dilutive exchange provision (the "Exchange") of the NOL Poison Pill, which reduced Trilogy's interest from 6.7% to 3.3%, and adopted another Rights Plan with a 4.99% trigger (the "Reloaded NOL Poison Pill"). Selectica then amended its complaint to seek a declaration that the Exchange and the Reloaded NOL Poison Pill were valid.

Since it became a public company in March 2000, Selectica has lost a substantial amount of money and failed to turn an annual profit, despite routinely projecting near-term profitability. Its IPO price of $30 per share has steadily fallen and now languishes below $1 per share, placing Selectica's market capitalization at roughly $23 million as of the end of March 2009. By Selectica's own admission, its value today "consists primarily in its cash reserves, its intellectual property portfolio, its customer and revenue base, and its accumulated NOLs." By consistently failing to achieve positive net income, Selectica has generated an estimated $160 million in NOLs for federal tax purposes over the past several years.

* * *

Trilogy's Offers Rejected

On July 15, 2008, Trilogy's President, Joseph Liemandt, called Zawatski to inquire generally about the possibility of an acquisition of Selectica by Trilogy. On July 29, Trilogy Chief Financial Officer Sean Fallon, Trilogy Director of Finance Andrew Price, and Versata Chief Executive Officer Randy Jacops participated in a conference call with Selectica Co-Chairs Zawatski and Thanos on the same topic. During the call, Thanos inquired as to how Trilogy would calculate a value for the Company's NOLs. Fallon replied that Trilogy, "really [did not] pursue them with as much vigor as other[s] might since that is not our core strategy."

The following evening, Fallon contacted Zawatski and outlined two proposals for Trilogy to acquire Selectica's business: (1) Trilogy's purchase of all of the assets of Selectica's sales configuration business in exchange for the cancellation of the $7.1 million in debt Selectica still owed under the October 2007 settlement with Trilogy; or (2) Trilogy's purchase of Selectica's entire operations for the cancellation of the debt plus an additional $6 million in cash. Fallon subsequently followed up with an e-mail reiterating both proposals and suggesting that either proposal would allow Selectica to still make use of its NOLs through the later sale of its corporate entity.

Shortly thereafter, the Board rejected both proposals, made no counterproposal, and there were no follow-up discussions. On October 9, 2008, Trilogy made a second bid to acquire all of the Selectica's assets for $10 million in cash plus the cancellation of the debt, which the Board also rejected. Although Trilogy was invited to participate in the sale process being overseen by Needham, Trilogy was apparently unwilling to sign a non-disclosure agreement, which was a prerequisite for participation. Around this same time, Trilogy had begun making open-market purchases for Selectica stock, although the Board apparently was not aware of this fact at the time.

Trilogy Buys Selectica Stock

On the evening of November 10, Fallon contacted Zawatski and informed her that Trilogy had purchased more than 5% of Selectica's outstanding stock and would be filing a Schedule 13D shortly, which it did on November 13. On a subsequent call with Zawatski and Reilly, Fallon explained that Trilogy had begun buying because it believed that "the company should work quickly to preserve whatever shareholder value remained and that we were interested in seeing this process that they announced with Needham, that we were interested in seeing that accelerate...." Within four days of its 13D filing, Trilogy had acquired more than 320,000 additional shares, representing an additional 1% of the Company's outstanding shares.

* * *

At the request of the Board, Delaware counsel reviewed the Delaware law standards that apply for adopting and implementing measures that have an anti-takeover effect. The Board then discussed amending the existing Shareholder Rights Plan, and the possible terms of such an amendment. These included: the pros and cons of providing a cushion for preexisting 5% holders, the appropriate effective date of the new Shareholder Rights Plan, whether the Board should have authority to exclude purchases by specific stockholders from triggering the Rights Plan, and whether a review process should be implemented to determine periodically whether the Rights Plan should remain in effect.

The Board then unanimously passed a resolution amending Selectica's Shareholder Rights Plan, by decreasing the beneficial ownership trigger from 15% to 4.99%, while grandfathering in existing 5% shareholders and permitting them to acquire up to an additional 0.5% (subject to the original 15% cap) without triggering the NOL Poison Pill.

* * *

On December 18, Trilogy purchased an additional 30,000 Selectica shares, and Trilogy management verified with Liemandt his intention to proceed with "buying through" the NOL Poison Pill. The following morning, Trilogy purchased an additional 124,061 shares of Selectica, bringing its ownership share to 6.7% and thereby becoming an "Acquiring Person" under the NOL Poison Pill....

* * *

The [Independent Director Evaluation] Committee [of the Board] concluded that Trilogy should not be deemed an "Exempt Person," that its purchase of additional shares should not be deemed an "Exempt Transaction," that an exchange of rights for common stock (the "Exchange") should occur, and that a new rights dividend on substantially similar terms should be adopted. The Committee passed resolutions implementing those conclusions, thereby adopting the Reloaded NOL Poison Pill and instituting the Exchange.

The Exchange doubled the number of shares of Selectica common stock owned by each shareholder of record, other than Trilogy or Versata, thereby reducing their beneficial holdings from 6.7% to 3.3%. The implementation of the Exchange led to a freeze in the trading of Selectica stock from January 5, 2009 until February 4, 2009, with the stock price frozen at $0.69. The Reloaded NOL Poison Pill will expire on January 2, 2012, unless the expiration date is advanced or extended, or unless these rights are exchanged or redeemed by the Board some time before.

* * *

[After finding that the possible loss of the NOLs constituted a sufficient threat to justify the defensive tactic, the court addressed whether the 5% threshold was preclusive.]

The second part of the *Unocal* test requires an initial evaluation of whether a board's defensive response to the threat was preclusive or coercive and, if neither, whether the response was "reasonable in relation to the threat" identified. Under *Unitrin*, a defensive measure is disproportionate and unreasonable *per se* if it is draconian by being either coercive or preclusive. A coercive response is one that is "aimed at 'cramming down' on its shareholders a management-sponsored alternative."

A defensive measure is preclusive where it "makes a bidder's ability to wage a successful proxy contest and gain control either 'mathematically impossible' or 'realistically unattainable.'" A successful proxy contest that is mathematically impossible is, *ipso facto*, realistically unattainable. Because the "mathematically impossible" formulation in *Unitrin* is subsumed within the category of preclusivity described as "realistically unattainable," there is, analytically speaking, only one test of preclusivity: "realistically unattainable."

* * *

Trilogy argues that, even if a 4.99% shareholder could realistically win a proxy contest "the preclusiveness question focuses on whether a challenger could realistically attain sufficient board control to remove the pill." Here, Trilogy contends, Selectica's charter-based classified board effectively forecloses a bid conditioned upon a redemption of the NOL Poison Pill, because it requires a proxy challenger to launch and complete two successful proxy contests in order to change control. Therefore, Trilogy argues that even if a less than 5% shareholder could win a proxy contest, Selectica's Rights Plan with a 4.99% trigger in combination with Selectica's charter-based classified board, makes a successful proxy contest for control of the board "realistically unattainable."

Trilogy's preclusivity argument conflates two distinct questions: first, is a successful proxy contest realistically attainable; and second, will a successful proxy contest result in gaining control of the board at the next election? Trilogy argues that unless both questions can be answered affirmatively, a Rights Plan and a classified board, viewed collectively, are preclusive. If that preclusivity argument is correct, then it would apply whenever a corporation has both a classified board and a Rights Plan, irrespective whether the trigger is 4.99%, 20%, or anywhere in between those thresholds.

Classified boards are authorized by statute and are adopted for a variety of business purposes. Any classified board also operates as an anti-takeover defense by preventing an insurgent from obtaining control of the board in one election. More than a decade ago, in *Carmody*, the Court of Chancery noted "because only one third of a classified board would stand for election each year, a classified board would *delay—but not prevent—a hostile acquiror from obtaining control of the board*, since a determined acquiror could wage a proxy contest and obtain control of two thirds of the target board over a two year period, as opposed to seizing control in a single election." The fact that a combination of defensive measures makes it more difficult for an acquirer to obtain control of a board does not make such measures realistically unattainable, i.e., preclusive.

In *Moran*, we rejected the contention "that the Rights Plan strips stockholders of their rights to receive tender offers, and that the Rights Plan fundamentally restricts proxy contests." We explained that "the Rights Plan will not have a severe impact upon proxy contests and it will not *preclude* all hostile acquisitions of Household." In this case, we hold that the combination of a classified board and a Rights Plan do not constitute a preclusive defense.

Range of Reasonableness

If a defensive measure is neither coercive nor preclusive, the *Unocal* proportionality test "requires the focus of enhanced judicial scrutiny to shift to 'the range of reasonableness.'" Where all of the defenses "are inextricably related, the principles of *Unocal* require that such actions be scrutinized collectively as a unitary response to the perceived threat." Trilogy asserts that the NOL Poison Pill, the Exchange, and the Reloaded NOL Poison Pill were not a reasonable collective response to the threat of the impairment of Selectica's NOLs.

* * *

Under part two of the *Unocal* test, the Court of Chancery found that the combination of the NOL Poison Pill, the Exchange, and the Reloaded NOL Poison Pill was a proportionate response to the threatened loss of Selectica's NOLs. Those findings are not clearly erroneous. They are supported by the record and the result of a logical deductive reasoning process. Accordingly, we hold that the Selectica directors satisfied the second part of the *Unocal* test by showing that their defensive response was proportionate by being "reasonable in relation to the threat" identified.

Context Determines Reasonableness

Under a *Unocal* analysis, the reasonableness of a board's response is determined in relation to the "specific threat," at the time it was identified. Thus, it is the specific nature of the threat that "sets the parameters for the range of permissible defensive tactics" at any given time. The record demonstrates that a longtime competitor sought to increase the percentage of its stock ownership, not for the purpose of conducting a hostile takeover but, to intentionally impair corporate assets, or else coerce Selectica into meeting certain business demands under the threat of such impairment. Only in relation to that specific threat have the Court of Chancery and this Court considered the reasonableness of Selectica's response.

The Selectica Board carried its burden of proof under both parts of the *Unocal* test. Therefore, at this time, the Selectica Board has withstood the enhanced judicial scrutiny required by the two part *Unocal* test. That does not, however, end the matter.

As we held in *Moran*, the adoption of a Rights Plan is not absolute. In other cases, we have upheld the adoption of Rights Plans in specific defensive circumstances while simultaneously holding that it may be inappropriate for a Rights Plan to remain in place when those specific circumstances change dramatically. The fact that the NOL Poison Pill was reasonable under the specific facts and circumstances of this case, should not be construed as generally approving the reasonableness of a 4.99% trigger in the Rights Plan of a corporation with or without NOLs.

To reiterate *Moran*, "the ultimate response to an actual takeover bid must be judged by the Directors' actions at that time." If and when the Selectica Board "is faced with a tender offer and a request to redeem the [Reloaded NOL Poison Pill], they will not be able to arbitrarily reject the offer. They will be held to the same fiduciary standards any other board of directors would be held to in deciding to adopt a defensive mechanism." The Selectica Board has no more discretion in refusing to redeem the Rights Plan than it does in enacting any defensive mechanism. Therefore, the Selectica Board's future use of the Reloaded NOL Poison Pill must be evaluated if and when that issue arises.

Comments and Questions

1. Exercise of the poison pill illustrates the show-stopping nature of the defensive tactic. Prior to the exercise of the poison pill, Selectica had 28.7 million shares outstanding. Afterwards, the number increased to 55.5 million. With Trilogy excluded from the exchange, the effect was severe. Trilogy saw its holdings as a percentage of outstanding shares fall from 6.7% to 3.3%. Presumably the dollar amount of the investment went through a similar dilution.

2. The Chancery Court below noted that poison pills with triggers at 15–20% made up "at least" 90% of the examples studied and that those with a trigger below 5% were "quite rare." Testimony further indicated that "more than fifty publicly held companies that have implemented NOL poison pills with triggers at roughly 5%, including several large, well-known corporations, some among the Fortune 1000." Will this likely change in the aftermath of this decision? *See* Lucian A. Bebchuk et al., *Pre-Disclosure Accumulation by Activist Investors: Evidence and Policy*, 39 J. Corp. L. 1, 27 (2013) (estimating that in one sampling of more than 800 poison pills, about 15% included a triggering threshold of less than 10%).

3. What is the reasoning used by the court in considering the low threshold in the context of a company with a staggered board? What do you make of this analysis? Is it correct? Argue both sides.

4. The poison pill in this case was not preclusive. In other words, it did not make a proxy contest "realistically unattainable." Given the holding, what would a shareholder have to show to have a court find that a poison pill had a preclusive effect on a proxy contest?

5. What do you make of the contextual discussion provided by the court at the end of the decision? What does it suggest? If you were advising the board of Selectica, what would you advise the directors as a result of the analysis?

6. Some commentators have suggested that *Selectica* and the use of poison pills with lower thresholds will simply increase the power of proxy advisory services and "effectively turn every contested corporate election into a trial before powerful proxy voting advisors." Paul H. Edelman & Randall S. Thomas, *Resetting the Trigger on the Poison Pill: Selectica's Unanticipated Consequences*, Vanderbilt University Law School Law & Economics, Research Paper No. 10-16, June 28, 2010. How might this be the case? What do you think of this result?

7. Compare this system to the one used in Great Britain. Management may not engage in defensive tactics. Acquirers, however, must make an offer for all shares within a specified period of time. Kraft took advantage of the system to successfully acquire control of Cadbury, the confectionery company. On the other hand, offers, even for a premium over market, sometimes fail. The attempt by Nasdaq to acquire control of the London Stock Exchange failed. For a discussion of the system used in Britain, see Christopher M. Bruner, *Power and Purpose in the "Anglo-American" Corporation*, 50 Va. J. Int'l L. 579 (2010).

Poison pills typically have triggers that apply to all shareholders, although they may grandfather existing large investors. In this area, however, practices evolve. Some pills single out activist investors, imposing lower thresholds.

Third Point LLC v. Ruprecht

C.A. No. 9469-VCP, Delaware Chancery, May 2, 2014

PARSONS, VICE CHANCELLOR:

The primary plaintiff is an activist hedge fund and stockholder of the corporation. According to the hedge fund, the corporation's board violated their fiduciary duties by adopting the rights plan and refusing to provide it with a waiver from the rights plan's terms, so that the Board could obtain an impermissible advantage in an ongoing proxy contest with the hedge fund. The hedge fund avers further that, regardless of the board's intent in adopting and refusing to waive certain features of the rights plan, the fund does not pose a legally cognizable threat to the corporation and that, in any event, the rights plan is not a proportionate response to any threat the board might have perceived. The other plaintiffs in this litigation are institutional stockholders who purport to represent the interests of the corporation's stockholders other than the hedge funds. The stockholder plaintiffs largely join in the arguments made by the hedge fund with a particular emphasis on the effect the rights plan is likely to have on the stockholder franchise both for the near and long term.

In response, the defendant directors, who comprise the corporation's board, assert that, at all relevant times, the hedge fund posed a number of different legally cognizable threats to the corporation, and that the board responded proportionately to those threats in both adopting the rights plan and refusing to grant the hedge fund a waiver from certain of its provisions. The defendants also argue that the rights plan's two-tiered structure is reasonable based on the source of the threats to the corporation.

* * *

Sotheby's is a global art business and primarily focuses on acting as an agent for high-end art sales. The Company operates in an essentially duopolistic market with Christie's, a privately-held enterprise, as its predominant competitor. Thus, when it comes to attracting business or key employees, the Company and Christie's largely are enmeshed in a "zero sum" game, in which a loss for one often translates into a gain for the other.

* * *

3. Hedge funds, including Third Point, begin to purchase Sotheby's stock

On May 15, 2013, in a Form 13F filed with the SEC, Third Point disclosed that it had acquired 500,000 shares of Sotheby's stock. On June 11, 2013, Morrow & Company ("Morrow"), the Company's proxy solicitor, notified Jennifer Park, Sotheby's Investor Relations director, that Trian Fund Management, L.P. ("Trian"), an activist hedge fund with ties to Nelson Peltz, had acquired 250,000 shares in the Company....

On July 30, 2013, another activist fund, Marcato Capital Management LLC ("Marcato"), filed a Schedule 13D disclosing its acquisition of 6.61% of Sotheby's common stock ... ;

On August 9, 2013, Sotheby's management met separately with both Marcato and Third Point. At the Marcato meeting, Richard "Mick" McGuire, Marcato's CEO, urged the Company to return much of its cash-on-hand to investors and showed the Sotheby's delegates materials he had prepared before the meeting to that effect....

On August 14, 2013, Trian filed a Form 13F, revealing that as of June 30, 2013, it had acquired over 2 million shares of Sotheby's, or approximately 3% of the Company's outstanding common stock. The same day, the Company also learned that Third Point had quintupled its stake in Sotheby's (from approximately 500,000 shares to 2.5 million shares), increasing its ownership in the Company to approximately 3.6%....

Less than two weeks later, on August 26, Third Point filed its initial Schedule 13D, disclosing it had acquired a 5.7% stake in the Company. According to the filing, Third Point intended to "engage in a dialogue with members of the Board or management," and also might pursue discussions with other stockholders or "knowledgeable industry or market observers (including art market participants)." ...

On October 2, 2013, Third Point filed an amended Schedule 13D revealing that the fund had increased its stake in Sotheby's to 6.35 million shares, or approximately 9.4% of the Company. Attached to the Schedule 13D was a letter from Loeb to Ruprecht. In the letter, Loeb raised several concerns about Sotheby's, including "the

Company's chronically weak operating margins and deteriorating competitive position relative to Christie's," "Management's lack of alignment with shareholders," Ruprecht's "generous package of cash, pay, perquisites, and other compensation," "a sleepy board and overpaid executive team," and "lack of expense discipline." ...

On October 3, 2013, the Board held a special meeting, which included Goldman and Wachtell, to discuss Third Point's updated Schedule 13D and Loeb's letter.... [and discussed the possibility of adopting a poison pill]

On October 4, the Board held its regularly scheduled meeting. The first item of business was another "Activist Investor Update." After continuing the discussion from the previous day, the Board unanimously approved the adoption of the Rights Plan....

Under the Rights Plan's definition of "Acquiring Person," those who report their ownership in the Company pursuant to Schedule 13G may acquire up to a 20% interest in Sotheby's. A person is eligible to file a Schedule 13G only if, among other things, they have "not acquired the securities with any purpose, or with the effect of, changing or influencing the control of the issuer, or in connection with or as a participant in any transaction having that purpose or effect" and they own less than 20% of the issuer's securities. All other stockholders, including those who report their ownership pursuant to Schedule 13D, such as Third Point and Marcato, are limited to a 10% stake in the Company before triggering the Rights Plan or "poison pill." ...

On March 13, 2014, the Company announced that Dodge would not stand for re-election at the upcoming annual meeting. The same day, Third Point again amended its Schedule 13D, revealing that it owned, directly or beneficially, 9.62% of Sotheby's stock. In addition, Third Point sent a letter to Sotheby's requesting that the Company grant it a waiver from the Rights Plan's 10% trigger, and allow it to purchase up to a 20% stake in the Company....

Two days later, on March 21, 2014, Sotheby's notified Third Point that the Board had denied its request to waive the 10% trigger....

II. ANALYSIS

To obtain a preliminary injunction a plaintiff must demonstrate: (1) a reasonable probability of success on the merits; (2) that absent injunctive relief, they will suffer irreparable harm; and (3) that the balance of the parties' harms weighs in favor of injunctive relief. An injunction will not issue unless all three elements are satisfied....

* * *

The well-known *Unocal* standard consists of two prongs. The first is "a reasonableness test, which is satisfied by a demonstration that the board of directors had reasonable grounds for believing that a danger to corporate policy and effectiveness existed." In other words, a board must articulate a legally cognizable threat. This first prong "is essentially a process-based review." "Directors satisfy the first part of the *Unocal* test by demonstrating good faith and reasonable investigation." A good process standing alone, however, is not sufficient if it does not lead to the finding of an objectively reasonable threat. "[N]o matter how exemplary the board's process, or how independent the board, or how reasonable its investigation, to meet their burden under the first prong of *Unocal* defendants must actually articulate some legitimate threat to corporate policy and effectiveness."

The second prong of *Unocal* is a "proportionality test, which is satisfied by a demonstration that the board of directors' defensive response was reasonable in relation to the threat posed." Proportionality review itself consists of two parts. First, the Court must consider whether a board's defensive actions were "draconian, by being either preclusive or coercive." Next, if the board's response to the threat was not draconian, the Court then must decide whether its actions fell "within a range of reasonable responses to the threat" posed. The defendant board bears the burden of proving the reasonableness of its actions under *Unocal*.

2. The October 2013 adoption of the Rights Plan and the March 2014 refusal to grant Third Point a waiver

As *Moran* makes clear, the Board's decision to adopt the Rights Plan in October 2013 and its subsequent election to refuse to provide Third Point with a waiver from the plan's conditions each independently must pass muster under *Unocal*. Consequently, I begin my analysis with the October 2013 adoption.

a. The October 2013 adoption of the Rights Plan

1. Plaintiffs do not have a reasonable probability of success as to the first prong of *Unocal*

Plaintiffs here make no serious argument that the Sotheby's Board will be unlikely to meet its burden of demonstrating that it conducted a good faith and reasonable investigation into the threat posed by Third Point. The Board undeniably is comprised of a majority of independent directors. In addition, it is undisputed that the Board retained competent outside financial and legal advisors, which it appears to have utilized and relied on frequently. "The presence of a majority of outside directors, coupled with a showing of reliance on advice by legal and financial advisors, 'constitute[s] a *prima facie* showing of good faith and reasonable investigation.'"

Having determined that the Board probably can demonstrate on a full record that it conducted the requisite investigation, the next relevant inquiry is whether the Board determined that Third Point presented an objectively reasonable and legally cognizable threat to Sotheby's. While the Board has asserted that, at all relevant times, Third Point has presented a multitude of threats to the Company, for purposes of the October 2013 adoption, I need focus only on one: "creeping control." At the time the Board elected to adopt the Rights Plan in October 2013, it had several hedge funds accumulating its stock simultaneously, and at least as to Third Point, the accumulation was occurring on a relatively rapid basis. The Board also was informed by its advisors that it was not uncommon for activist hedge funds to form a group or "wolfpack," for the purpose of jointly acquiring large blocks of a target company's stock. Based on these facts, and the profiles of Third Point and Marcato presented to the Board in materials prepared by its financial and legal advisors, I cannot conclude that there is a reasonable probability that the Board did not make an objectively reasonable determination that Third Point posed a threat of forming a control block for Sotheby's with other hedge funds without paying a control premium. That is, on the record before me, there is sufficient support for the Board's assertion that its good faith investigation led it to determine that Third Point posed a legally cognizable threat, and I consider that threat objectively reasonable. Thus, Plaintiffs have not demonstrated a reasonable probability of success with respect to the first prong of the *Unocal* analysis for the October 2013 adoption of the Rights Plan.

2. The "primary purpose" of the October 2013 adoption of the Rights Plan was not to interfere with the stockholder franchise

For the reasons stated previously, the role of *Blasius* in the stockholder rights plan context is not entirely clear. Nevertheless, I address Plaintiffs' argument regarding the Board's intent in adopting the Rights Plan because, at a minimum, the use of the *Unocal* standard is intended to "smoke out" impermissible pre-textual justifications for defensive actions.

On this truncated record, there is sufficient evidence to support a reasonable inference that the Company has been concerned with the prospect of a proxy fight with an activist stockholder since the Summer of 2013. But the facts here do not support the conclusion that Plaintiffs have a reasonable probability of demonstrating that the Board adopted the Rights Plan in October 2013 for the *primary purpose* of interfering with the franchise of any stockholder, including Third Point, several months later. As stated previously, the Company was facing a rapid increase in hedge fund ownership in its stock that at least one Sotheby's insider believed was "collusive." Based on the advice of its outside legal and financial advisors, it appears, at least at this stage of the proceedings, that the Company believed certain hedge funds were attempting to gain effective control of the Company without paying a premium, and that it was objectively reasonable for the Company to perceive that threat. Because it is reasonably likely that the Board will be able to show that they were motivated to adopt the Rights Plan in response to this control threat and that "any effect of electoral rights was an incident to that end," Plaintiffs have not shown that it is reasonably probable that Plaintiffs will be able to establish that interference with the franchise was a major, let alone primary, purpose behind the Board's decision.

There are additional factors that, on the present record, also weigh against the argument that Plaintiffs have a reasonable probability of demonstrating that the Board's primary motivation was impeding the voting rights of any Sotheby's stockholder. First, the record is nearly devoid of facts that would support an inference of entrenchment on the part of the Board. The Board is not staggered, turns over at an above-average rate, and is dominated by outside, independent directors. Moreover, with the possible exception of Ruprecht, there has been no showing that serving on the Sotheby's Board is material, financially or otherwise, to any director such that they have a disabling personal incentive to quash a proxy contest. Although potentially there are reasons beyond entrenchment that would drive an independent, well-advised board to act for the primary purpose of impeding the stockholder franchise, the fact that no discernable entrenchment motive exists here weighs against a finding that the Board acted with such a "primary purpose."

* * *

3. Plaintiffs have not shown they have a reasonable probability of success as to the second prong of *Unocal*

For the reasons stated *supra,* the Rights Plan at issue here is neither preclusive nor coercive. Because it is not draconian, proportionality review turns on whether the Rights Plan adopted by the Board falls within the "range of reasonableness." "The reasonableness of a board's response is evaluated in the context of the specific threat identified — the 'specific nature of the threat [ ] 'sets the parameters for the range of permissible defensive tactics' at any given time.'" When evaluating whether a defensive measure falls within the range of reasonableness, the role of the Court is to decide "whether the directors made a reasonable decision, not a perfect decision." Courts applying enhanced scrutiny under *Unocal* should "not substitute their business judgment for that of the directors" and if, on balance, "a board selected one of several reasonable alternatives, a court should not second-guess that choice."

In this case there is a reasonable probability that the Board will be able to show that in October 2013 it was faced with the legally cognizable and objectively reasonable threat that Third Point, alone or with others, could acquire a controlling interest in the Company without paying Sotheby's other stockholders a premium. Thus, the relevant inquiry is whether the adoption of the Rights Plan was a reasonable and proportionate response to that threat of creeping control.

I consider it reasonably probable that the Board will be able to meet its burden to demonstrate that the adoption of the Rights Plan in October 2013 was a proportionate response to the control threat posed by Third Point. Plaintiffs here have not litigated the issue of or whether a 10% rights plan comports with Delaware law. Because the entire Board, collectively, owns less than 1% of Sotheby's stock, a 10% threshold allows activist investors to achieve a substantial ownership position in the Company. This is supported further by the fact that at its current ownership level just below 10%, Third Point is the Company's largest single stockholder. When the Rights Plan was adopted there also was the objectively reasonable possibility that Third Point was working in connection with one or more other hedge funds in an attempt to create a control block within the Company's stockholder base. A trigger level much higher than 10% could make it easier for a relatively small group of activist investors to achieve control, without paying a premium, through conscious parallelism. This factor also supports my conclusion the Board has a reasonable probability of being able to show that the Rights Plan was a proportionate response to the control threat posed by Third Point.

The gravamen of Plaintiffs' argument that the Rights Plan is disproportionate pertains mostly to its two-tier structure which permits "passive" investors to buy 20% of the Company shares while "activist" stockholders cannot purchase more than 10%.

As an initial matter, I note that while the Rights Plan is "discriminatory" in that sense, it also arguably is a "closer fit" to addressing the Company's needs to prevent an activist or activists from gaining control than a "garden variety" rights plan that would restrict the ownership levels for every stockholder, even those with no interest in obtaining control or asserting influence. In any event, the importance of the "discriminatory" nature of the challenged Rights Plan appears to be overstated in the circumstances of this case. Because I already have determined that the Board is likely to be able to show that the Rights Plan's 10% trigger for activist stockholders is reasonable and proportionate, the reason the discriminatory nature of the Rights Plan would be most likely to be found unreasonable or disproportionate is that it allows Schedule 13G filers, who may be more inclined to vote with the Company's management, to acquire up to 20% of the Company's shares, and not because a 10% cap on activist stockholders is, itself, unreasonable or disproportionate.

* * *

b. The refusal to waive the 10% trigger in March 2014
1. Plaintiffs have not shown they have a reasonable probability of success as to the first prong of *Unocal*

As with the Board's October 2013 decision to adopt the Rights Plan, I find that the Board likely will be able to meet its burden of demonstrating that it undertook a good faith and reasonable investigation in response to Third Point's request to waive the 10% trigger in the Rights Plan. The majority of the Board still were independent and disinterested directors and had utilized their outside legal and financial advisors continuously since the adoption of the Rights Plan in October 2013. Thus, the key inquiry in terms of the first prong of *Unocal* is whether the Board determined there was an objectively reasonable and legally cognizable threat to the Company in March 2014 when Third Point made its waiver request.

This presents a much closer question than the Board's original decision to adopt the Rights Plan in October 2013. Had Third Point asked the Board to waive the Rights Plan in its entirety, rather than just the 10% trigger, based on the record before me, it would have been relatively easy to determine that Third Point posed at least the same threat to the Company that it did when the plan was adopted in the first place. That, however, is not what happened.

Third Point asked only for a waiver of the 10% trigger for Schedule 13D filers so that it could buy up to a 20% interest in the Company. Third Point did not ask, for example, that the Rights Plan be redeemed or that the Company waive the Rights Plan's proscription of concerted action. It is not clear, therefore, that the Board did or should have had the exact same concerns in March 2014 that it did in October 2013 when it adopted the Rights Plan. As a result, I am skeptical that there is a reasonable probability that the Board could establish that when it rejected the request for a waiver, it had an objectively reasonable belief that Third Point continued to pose a "creeping control" risk to the Company, either individually or as part of a "wolf pack."

Nevertheless, despite the change in circumstances, I am persuaded that Sotheby's has made a sufficient showing as to at least one objectively reasonable and legally cognizable threat: negative control. Plaintiffs are correct that the Delaware case law relating to the concept of negative control addresses situations in which a person or entity obtains an explicit veto right through contract or through a level of share ownership or board representation at a level that does not amount to majority control, but nevertheless is sufficient to block certain actions that may require, for example, a supermajority vote. The evidence currently available indicates that Sotheby's may have had legitimate real-world concerns that enabling individuals or entities, such as Loeb and Third Point, to obtain 20% as opposed to 10% ownership interests in the Company could effectively allow those persons to exercise disproportionate control and influence over major corporate decisions, even if they do not have an explicit veto power.

The notion of effective, rather than explicit, negative control obviously raises some significant concerns, chief among them being where does one draw the line to ensure that "effective negative control" does not become a license for corporations to deploy defensive measures unreasonably. In this case, however, on the preliminary record developed to date there appears to be an objectively reasonable basis to believe that Third Point could exercise effective negative control over the Company. If Third Point was given the waiver it requested and achieved 20% ownership it would, by far, be Sotheby's largest single stockholder. That fact, combined with the aggressive and domineering manner in which the evidence suggests Loeb has conducted himself in relation to Sotheby's, provides an adequate basis for legitimate concern that Third Point would be able to exercise influence sufficient to control certain important corporate actions, such as executive recruitment, despite a lack of actual control or an explicit veto power. Therefore, I find that Plaintiffs have not satisfied their burden of showing that there is a reasonable probability that the Board will not be able to demonstrate that it identified an objectively reasonable and legally cognizable threat to Sotheby's corporate policy and effectiveness. Based on that finding, I turn next to an evaluation of whether the Board's refusal to waive the 10% trigger level satisfies the second *Unocal* prong.

2. Plaintiffs have not shown they have a reasonable probability of success as to the second prong of *Unocal*

For the reasons already discussed *supra*, the Rights Plan does not implicate issues of preclusion or coercion. Consequently, the relevant inquiry is whether the Board's refusal to grant Third Point a waiver from the 10% trigger falls within the range of reasonableness. The Board's refusal to grant Third Point a waiver was a response to the threat that it posed to the Company of obtaining, at least, negative control and threatening corporate policy and effectiveness. The refusal to waive the Rights Plan's 10% trigger level is consistent with the Board's stated purposes, and the operation of the Rights Plan at the 10% level would help the Board achieve that end. While it is of course conceivable that there is some level of ownership between 10% and 20% that the Board could have allowed Third Point to increase its stake in the Company to without allowing it to obtain negative control, the 10% cap must be reasonable, not perfect. Based on the record before me, I find that Plaintiffs have not shown that there is a reasonable probability that the Board will be unable to demonstrate that its refusal to waive the 10% trigger in the Rights Plan was within the "range of reasonable" responses to the negative control threat posed by Third Point. Therefore, Plaintiffs have not established a likelihood of success on the merits of their claim that the Board breached its fiduciary duties by refusing to allow Third Point in March 2014 to acquire up to 20% of the Company's stock.

Comments and Questions

1. As was the case in *Yucaipa*, the poison pill put in place by Sothebys included in the definition of beneficial ownership the shares held by any person subject to an "agreement, arrangement or understanding … for the purpose of acquiring, holding, voting … or disposing" of the company's shares. How might this provision have reduced the risk of ThirdPoint actively participating in a wolf pack?

2. This case opens the door to poison pills that apply separate standards to activist shareholders. Can you imagine other possible ways poison pills can be used to single out these investors?

3. Shortly before the meeting, Sotheby's negotiated a settlement, providing Third-Point with three board seats and the right to buy up to 15% of the shares. The contest illustrated that poison pills, even when affirmed, are no panaceas.

E. Solving the Problem of the Costs of a Proxy Contest

One of the impediments to proxy contests is the cost. Proxy solicitations to more than ten shareholders can be expensive. Shareholders must draft a proxy statement and card and distribute the materials to those solicited. To address the cost problem with respect to proxy contests, shareholders have sometimes proposed bylaws that called for reimbursement of solicitation expenses in certain circumstances. Uncertain about the validity of such proposals under state law, the Commission in 2009 certified a question to the court concerning the legality of a bylaw providing for mandatory reimbursement. The SEC received a response in the opinion below.

CA, Inc. v. AFSCME Employees Pension Plan

Delaware Supreme Court
953 A.2d 227 (2008)

JACOBS, JUSTICE:

AFSCME, a CA stockholder, is associated with the American Federation of State, County and Municipal Employees. On March 13, 2008, AFSCME submitted a proposed stockholder bylaw (the "Bylaw" or "proposed Bylaw") for inclusion in the Company's proxy materials for its 2008 annual meeting of stockholders. The Bylaw, if adopted by CA stockholders, would amend the Company's bylaws to provide as follows:

RESOLVED, that pursuant to section 109 of the Delaware General Corporation Law and Article IX of the bylaws of CA, Inc., stockholders of CA hereby amend the bylaws to add the following Section 14 to Article II:

The board of directors shall cause the corporation to reimburse a stockholder or group of stockholders (together, the "Nominator") for reasonable expenses ("Expenses") incurred in connection with nominating one or more candidates in a contested election of directors to the corporation's board of directors, including, without limitation, printing, mailing, legal, solicitation, travel, advertising and public relations expenses, so long as (a) the election of fewer than 50% of the directors to be elected is contested in the election, (b) one or more candidates nominated by the Nominator are elected to the corporation's board of directors, (c) stockholders are not permitted to cumulate their votes for directors, and (d) the election occurred, and the Expenses were incurred, after this bylaw's adoption. The amount paid to a Nominator under this bylaw in respect of a contested election shall not exceed the amount expended by the corporation in connection with such election.

* * *

The first question presented is whether the Bylaw is a proper subject for shareholder action, more precisely, whether the Bylaw may be proposed and enacted by shareholders without the concurrence of the Company's board of directors....

* * *

It is well-established Delaware law that a proper function of bylaws is not to mandate how the board should decide specific substantive business decisions, but rather, to define the process and procedures by which those decisions are made....

Examples of the procedural, process-oriented nature of bylaws are found in both the DGCL and the case law. For example, 8 Del. C. § 141(b) authorizes bylaws that fix the number of directors on the board, the number of directors required for a quorum (with certain limitations), and the vote requirements for board action. 8 Del. C. § 141(f) authorizes bylaws that preclude board action without a meeting. And, almost three decades ago this Court upheld a shareholder-enacted bylaw requiring unanimous board attendance and board approval for any board action, and unanimous ratification of any committee action. Such purely procedural bylaws do not improperly encroach upon the board's managerial authority under Section 141(a).

* * *

The context of the Bylaw at issue here is the process for electing directors—a subject in which shareholders of Delaware corporations have a legitimate and protected interest. The purpose of the Bylaw is to promote the integrity of that electoral process by facilitating the nomination of director candidates by stockholders or groups of stockholders. Generally, and under the current framework for electing directors in contested elections, only board-sponsored nominees for election are reimbursed for their election expenses. Dissident candidates are not, unless they succeed in replacing at least a majority of the entire board. The Bylaw would encourage the nomination of non-management board candidates by promising reimbursement of the nominating stockholders' proxy expenses if one or more of its candidates are elected. In that the shareholders also have a legitimate interest, because the Bylaw would facilitate the exercise of their right to participate in selecting the contestants....

The shareholders of a Delaware corporation have the right "to participate in selecting the contestants" for election to the board. The shareholders are entitled to facilitate the exercise of that right by proposing a bylaw that would encourage candidates other than board-sponsored nominees to stand for election. The Bylaw would accomplish that by committing the corporation to reimburse the election expenses of shareholders whose candidates are successfully elected. That the implementation of that proposal would require the expenditure of corporate funds will not, in and of itself, make such a bylaw an improper subject matter for shareholder action. Accordingly, we answer the first question certified to us in the affirmative.

* * *

In answering the first question, we have already determined that the Bylaw does not facially violate any provision of the DGCL or of CA's Certificate of Incorporation. The question thus becomes whether the Bylaw would violate any common law rule or precept.... we must necessarily consider any possible circumstance under which a board of directors might be required to act. Under at least one such hypothetical, the board of directors would breach their fiduciary duties if they complied with the Bylaw. Accordingly, we conclude that the Bylaw, as drafted, would violate the prohibition, which our decisions have derived from Section 141(a), against contractual arrangements that commit the board of directors to a course of action that would preclude them from fully discharging their fiduciary duties to the corporation and its shareholders.

* * *

... This case involves a binding bylaw that the shareholders seek to impose involuntarily on the directors in the specific area of election expense reimbursement. Although this case is distinguishable in that respect, the distinction is one without a difference. The reason is that the internal governance contract—which here takes the form of a bylaw—is one that would also prevent the directors from exercising their full managerial power in circumstances where their fiduciary duties would otherwise require them to deny reimbursement to a dissident slate. That this limitation would be imposed by a majority vote of the shareholders rather than by the directors themselves, does not, in our view, legally matter.

AFSCME contends that it is improper to use the doctrine articulated in QVC and Quickturn as the measure of the validity of the Bylaw. Because the Bylaw would remove the subject of election expense reimbursement (in circumstances as defined by the Bylaw) entirely from the CA's board's discretion (AFSCME argues), it cannot fairly be claimed that the directors would be precluded from discharging their fiduciary duty. Stated differently, AFSCME argues that it is unfair to claim that the Bylaw prevents the CA board from discharging its fiduciary duty where the effect of the Bylaw is to relieve the board entirely of those duties in this specific area.

That response, in our view, is more semantical than substantive. No matter how artfully it may be phrased, the argument concedes the very proposition that renders the Bylaw, as written, invalid: the Bylaw mandates reimbursement of election expenses in circumstances that a proper application of fiduciary principles could preclude. That such circumstances could arise is not far fetched. Under Delaware law, a board may expend corporate funds to reimburse proxy expenses "[w]here the controversy is concerned with a question of policy as distinguished from personnel o[r] management." But in a situation where the proxy contest is motivated by personal or petty concerns, or to promote interests that do not further, or are adverse to, those of the corporation, the board's fiduciary duty could compel that reimbursement be denied altogether.

It is in this respect that the proposed Bylaw, as written, would violate Delaware law if enacted by CA's shareholders. As presently drafted, the Bylaw would afford CA's directors full discretion to determine what amount of reimbursement is appropriate, because the directors would be obligated to grant only the "reasonable" expenses of a successful short slate. Unfortunately, that does not go far enough, because the Bylaw contains no language or provision that would reserve to CA's directors their full power to exercise their fiduciary duty to decide whether or not it would be appropriate, in a specific case, to award reimbursement at all.

In arriving at this conclusion, we express no view on whether the Bylaw as currently drafted, would create a better governance scheme from a policy standpoint. We decide only what is, and is not, legally permitted under the DGCL. That statute, as currently drafted, is the expression of policy as decreed by the Delaware legislature. Those who believe that CA's shareholders should be permitted to make the proposed Bylaw as drafted part of CA's governance scheme, have two alternatives. They may seek to amend the Certificate of Incorporation to include the substance of the Bylaw; *or* they may seek recourse from the Delaware General Assembly.

Accordingly, we answer the second question certified to us in the affirmative.

Comments and Questions

1. The question was certified to the Delaware Supreme Court pursuant to the State Constitution, Article IV, Section 11(8). The provision had been amended in 2007 to allow the Commission to certify questions to the court. There is an argument that the court violated its own requirements since it accepted a question about an informal position taken by the staff rather than a formal position taken by the Commission.

2. The use of the certification authority was the first and only time so far that the Commission has sought formal advice from the Delaware Supreme Court. Had the Commission not done so, could the bylaw still have been challenged? What would need to happen before a legal challenge could occur?

3. Had this bylaw been implemented, would it likely have encouraged proxy contests? What risks would nominating shareholders still confront with respect to reimbursement?

4. The court gave only two examples of reimbursement that would have been required under the bylaw that would result in a violation of the board's fiduciary obligations, including payment where a "proxy contest is motivated by personal or petty concerns" or designed "to promote interests that do not further, or are adverse to, those of the corporation...." Both points went to the reason for the proxy contest. The bylaw at issue in CA, however, only provided for reimbursement to the extent that the shareholder nominated directors were actually elected to the board. Does their actual election eliminate concerns over the motivation for their nomination?

5. The bylaw required reimbursement of "reasonable" expenses. Does this effectively amount to a fiduciary out? Could the board argue that expense requiring a violation of fiduciary duties were *per se* unreasonable?

6. To the extent seeking to conform to this Court's reasoning, what modification would shareholders need to make to reimbursement bylaws in order for them to be legal under Delaware law? What would be the impact of these types of changes on the bylaw? *See Bebchuk v. CA, Inc.*, 902 A.2d 737 (Del. Ch. 2006) (concluding that suit to test the validity of a bylaw that would require board to withdraw a poison pill was "unripe").

 In the aftermath of the decision, the Delaware legislature amended the law to authorize reimbursement bylaws.

§ 113. Proxy expense reimbursement.

(a) The bylaws may provide for the reimbursement by the corporation of expenses incurred by a stockholder in soliciting proxies in connection with an election of directors, subject to such procedures or conditions as the bylaws may prescribe, including:

(1) Conditioning eligibility for reimbursement upon the number or proportion of persons nominated by the stockholder seeking reimbursement or whether such stockholder previously sought reimbursement for similar expenses;

(2) Limitations on the amount of reimbursement based upon the proportion of votes cast in favor of one or more of the persons nominated by the stockholder seeking reimbursement, or upon the amount spent by the corporation in soliciting proxies in connection with the election;

(3) Limitations concerning elections of directors by cumulative voting pursuant to § 214 of this title; or

(4) Any other lawful condition.

(b) No bylaw so adopted shall apply to elections for which any record date precedes its adoption.

Comments and Questions

1. What impact does Section 113 have on *CA v. AFSCME*, 953 A.2d 227 (Del. 2008)?

2. The provision provides clarity to the area by noting that reimbursement bylaws can be conditioned upon the number of nominees, whether the nominating shareholder has sought reimbursement in the past, and limited in the amount of reimbursement that will be provided. The provision, therefore, allows for significant restrictions on those eligible for reimbursement.

3. At the time of the writing of this textbook, only one company had adopted a reimbursement bylaw. *See* Section 3.4(c), Bylaws of UnitedHealth, attached to Quarterly Report on Form 10-Q, filed Nov. 2009. The bylaw provided that shareholders could be reimbursed only if the election involved a contest of "fewer than 30% of the Directors to be elected," the nominating shareholders owned shares of the company for at least one year, and the nominee received at least 40% of the votes cast (calculated based upon all votes voted for, against, and withheld). In addition, the amount of reimbursement could in no case exceed the expenses incurred by the company.

4. The bylaw imposed significant restrictions on the nominating shareholder. They could not engage in solicitations on behalf of candidates for the board other than their own nominees or otherwise have a purpose of changing control. They were ineligible if they received reimbursement during any of the preceding three years or if their nominees appeared on the company's proxy card. Finally, the bylaw contained an out for the board of directors. As the bylaw provided:

> Notwithstanding any other provision hereof, there shall be no reimbursement under this Section 3.4(c) in the event the Board of Directors determines that any such reimbursement is not in the best interests of the Corporation or would result in a breach of the fiduciary duties of the Board of Directors to the Corporation and its stockholders or that making such a payment would render the Corporation insolvent or cause it to breach a material obligation incurred without reference to the obligations imposed by this Section 3.4(c).

If you were a shareholder considering a proxy contest, how much comfort would you take from this bylaw? What impact, if any, would it have on your decision to engage in a proxy contest?

Other potential solutions to the issue of cost have emerged at the federal level. The SEC has, for example, implemented rules designed to permit distribution of proxy materials electronically. *See* Rule 14a-16, 17 C.F.R. 240.14a-16. By avoiding much of the hard copy costs, distribution expenses by the company and insurgent shareholders will be reduced.

The most controversial proposal has been to allow shareholders to include their nominees in management's proxy statement. Known as "shareholder access," proposals in this area date back to the 1940s. Access would effectively reduce the costs of a proxy solicitation by requiring companies to distribute information on the candidate and include the nominee's name on the company's proxy card.

The SEC proposed in 2002 and again in 2007 a rule that would allow shareholders at least some access to the proxy statement for their own nominees. In general, the authority drew support from shareholder groups (although they raised objections to some of the limitations that would be required under the proposals) and strong opposition from the issuer community. The Commission ultimately chose not to adopt either proposal.

In 2009, however, another proposal surfaced. *See* Exchange Act Release No. 60089 (June 10, 2009). Among the many objections made to the Rule, some asserted that the SEC lacked the authority to adopt the rule. Those concerns were allayed when Congress adopted the Dodd-Frank Act. Section 971 of the Dodd-Frank Act amended Section 14(a) of the Exchange Act and gave the SEC something approaching plenary authority to adopt rules governing shareholder access to the company's proxy statement for their nominees. With that authority in hand, the Commission promptly adopted Rule 14a-11.

Facilitating Shareholder Director Nominations

Exchange Act Release No. 62764 (Aug. 25, 2010)

... One of the key tenets of the federal proxy rules on which the Commission has consistently focused is whether the proxy process functions, as nearly as possible, as a replacement for an actual in-person meeting of shareholders. This is important because the proxy process represents shareholders' principal means of participating effectively at an annual or special meeting of shareholders. In our Proposal we noted our concern that the federal proxy rules may not be facilitating the exercise of shareholders' state law rights to nominate and elect directors. Without the ability to effectively utilize the proxy process, shareholder nominees do not have a realistic prospect of being elected because most, if not all, shareholders return their proxy cards in advance of the shareholder meeting and thus, in essence, cast their votes before the meeting at which they may nominate directors. Recognizing that this failure of the proxy process to facilitate shareholder nomination rights has a practical effect on the right to elect directors, the new rules will enable the proxy process to more closely approximate the conditions of the shareholder meeting. In addition, because companies will be required to include shareholder-nominated candidates for director in company proxy materials, shareholders will receive additional information upon which to base their voting decisions. Finally, we believe these changes will significantly enhance the confidence of shareholders who link the recent financial crisis to a lack of responsiveness of some boards to shareholder interests.

* * *

Commenters opposed to our Proposal believed that recent corporate governance developments, including increased use of a majority voting standard for the election of directors and certain state law changes, already provide shareholders with meaningful opportunities to participate in director elections. These commenters viewed the amendments as inappropriately intruding into matters traditionally governed by state law or imposing a "one size fits all" rule for all companies and expressed concerns about "special interest" directors, forcing companies to focus on the short-term rather than the creation of long-term shareholder value, and other perceived negative effects of the amendments, if adopted, on boards and companies. Finally, commenters worried about the impact of the proposed amendments on small businesses.

* * *

While we recognize that some states, such as Delaware, have amended their state corporate law to enable companies to adopt procedures for the inclusion of shareholder director nominees in company proxy materials, as was highlighted by a number of commenters, other states have not. These commenters noted that, as a result, companies not incorporated in Delaware could frustrate shareholder efforts to establish procedures for shareholders to place board nominees in the company's proxy materials by litigating the validity of a shareholder proposal establishing such procedures, or possibly repealing shareholder-adopted bylaws establishing such procedures. In addition, due to the difficulty that shareholders could have in establishing such procedures, we believe that it would be inappropriate to rely solely on an enabling approach to facilitate shareholders' ability to exercise their state law rights to nominate and elect directors. Even if bylaw amendments to permit shareholders to include nominees in company proxy materials were permissible in every state, shareholder proposals to so amend company bylaws could face significant obstacles.

We also considered whether the move by many companies away from plurality voting to a general policy of majority voting in uncontested director elections should lead to a conclusion that our actions are unnecessary or whether we should premise our actions on the failure of a company to adopt majority voting. We agree with commenters who argued that a majority voting standard in director elections does not address the need for a rule to facilitate the inclusion of shareholder nominees for director in company proxy materials. While majority voting impacts shareholders' ability to elect candidates put forth by management, it does not affect shareholders' ability to exercise their right to nominate candidates for director.

* * *

We recognize that many commenters advocated that shareholders' ability to include nominees in company proxy materials should be determined exclusively by what individual companies or their shareholders affirmatively choose to provide, or that companies or their shareholders should be able to opt out of Rule 14a-11 or otherwise alter its terms for individual companies (the "private ordering" arguments). After careful consideration of the numerous comments advocating this perspective, we believe that the arguments in favor of this perspective are flawed for several reasons.

First, corporate governance is not merely a matter of private ordering. Rights, including shareholder rights, are artifacts of law, and in the realm of corporate governance some rights cannot be bargained away but rather are imposed by statute.

There is nothing novel about mandated limitations on private ordering in corporate governance.

Second, the argument that there is an inconsistency between mandating inclusion of shareholder nominees in company proxy materials and our concern for the rights of shareholders under the federal securities laws mistakenly assumes that basic protections of, and rights of, particular shareholders provided under the federal proxy rules should be able to be abrogated by "the shareholders" of a particular corporation, acting in the aggregate. The rules we adopt today provide individual shareholders the ability to have director nominees included in the corporate proxy materials if state law and governing corporate documents permit a shareholder to nominate directors at the shareholder meeting and the requirements of Rule 14a-11 are satisfied. Those rules similarly facilitate the right of individual shareholders to vote for those nominated, whether by management or another shareholder, if the shareholder has voting rights under state law and the company's governing documents. The rules we adopt today reflect our judgment that the proxy rules should better facilitate shareholders' effective exercise of their traditional state law rights to nominate directors and cast their votes for nominees. When the federal securities laws establish protections or create rights for security holders, they do so individually, not in some aggregated capacity. No provision of the federal securities laws can be waived by referendum. A rule that would permit some shareholders (even a majority) to restrict the federal securities law rights of other shareholders would be without precedent and, we believe, a fundamental misreading of basic premises of the federal securities laws. In addition, allowing some shareholders to impair the ability of other shareholders to have their director nominees included in company proxy materials cannot be reconciled with the purpose of the rules we are adopting today. In our view, it would be no more appropriate to subject a federal proxy rule that provides the ability to include nominees in the company proxy statement to a shareholder vote than it would be to subject any other aspect of the proxy rules—including the other required disclosures—to abrogation by shareholder vote.

Third, the net effect of our rules will be to expand shareholder choice, not limit it. Our rules will result in a greater number of nominees appearing on a proxy card. Shareholders will continue to have the opportunity to vote solely for management candidates, but our rules will also give shareholders the opportunity to vote for director candidates who otherwise might not have been included in company proxy materials.

In addition to these basic conclusions, we note that there are other significant concerns raised by a private ordering approach. A company-by-company shareholder vote on the applicability of Rule 14a-11 would involve substantial direct and indirect, market-wide costs, and it is possible that boards of directors, or shareholders acting with their explicit or implicit encouragement, might seek such shareholder votes, perhaps repeatedly, at no financial cost to themselves but at considerable cost to the company and its shareholders. Another concern relates to the nature of the shareholder vote on whether to opt out of Rule 14a-11: specifically, in that context management can draw on the full resources of the corporation to promote the adoption of an opt-out, while disaggregated shareholders have no similarly effective platform from which to advocate against an opt-out.

In addition, the path to shareholder adoption of a procedure to include nominees in company proxy materials is by no means free of obstructions. While shareholders may ordinarily have the state law right to adopt bylaws providing for inclusion of shareholder nominees in company proxy materials even in the absence of an explicit authorizing statute like Delaware's, the existence of that right in the absence of such a statute may be challenged. Moreover, we understand that under Delaware law, the board of directors is ordinarily free, subject to its fiduciary duties, to amend or repeal any shareholder-adopted bylaw. In addition, not all state statutes confer upon shareholders the power to adopt and amend bylaws, and even where shareholders have that power it is frequently limited by requirements in the company's governing documents that bylaw amendments be approved by a supermajority shareholder vote.

Comments and Questions

1. What are some advantages or disadvantages of shareholder access? One of the common objections is that this will facilitate the election of "special interest" directors. What does this mean? How serious is the risk that this will occur?

2. The premise of shareholder access is that the proxy process has effectively replaced the annual meeting and should therefore as closely as possible replicate the meeting. Is this true? What are the implications of this approach?

3. The SEC gave as one of the reasons for adopting the rule the concern about the board's responsiveness during the financial crisis that occurred in 2008 and 2009. The implication is that had access been in place, the financial crisis might have been averted or at least reduced in severity. How can these two concepts be linked together? Do you agree?

4. In the debate on access, many opponents argued that the matter should not be mandated for public companies (one size fits all) but should instead be left to private ordering. They in particular pointed to Section 112 of the Delaware General Corporation Law which expressly allowed for the adoption of bylaws that would permit "one or more individuals nominated by a stockholder" to be included in the company's proxy statement. What are the benefits and objections to a private ordering model?

5. Does the wide spread use of majority vote provisions obviate the need for shareholder access? Provide analysis for both positions.

6. The rule does not permit companies to "opt out" of the requirement but does provide that a company need not accept director nominees where the shareholder does not have the right to nominate under state law or a provision in the charter. Are there any such limitations under state law? Could companies put in their articles of incorporation a provision that bars shareholders owning less that 20% of the outstanding shares from having the right to nominate directors?

7. The SEC can require the inclusion of nominees in the proxy materials. Can the SEC also determine whether the nominees are actually elected to the board? According

to the Brief filed by the agency in *Business Roundtable v. SEC*, No. 10-1305, D.C. Cir., Jan. 19, 2011, a case challenging the validity of the shareholder access rule, the Commission asserted that "[i]f a candidate who does not meet a company's director qualifications is elected, state law would determine whether the candidate is seated." Given this position, what ability does a company have to refuse to seat a nominee submitted and elected by shareholders? What practical limitations might exist on the exercise of this authority?

Business Roundtable v. SEC

United States Court of Appeals, District of Columbia Circuit
647 F.3d 1144 (2011)

GINSBURG, CIRCUIT JUDGE:

* * *

I. Background

The proxy process is the principal means by which shareholders of a publicly traded corporation elect the company's board of directors. Typically, incumbent directors nominate a candidate for each vacancy prior to the election, which is held at the company's annual meeting. Before the meeting the company puts information about each nominee in the set of "proxy materials"—usually comprising a proxy voting card and a proxy statement—it distributes to all shareholders. The proxy statement concerns voting procedures and background information about the board's nominee(s); the proxy card enables shareholders to vote for or against the nominee(s) without attending the meeting. A shareholder who wishes to nominate a different candidate may separately file his own proxy statement and solicit votes from shareholders, thereby initiating a "proxy contest."

Rule 14a-11 provides shareholders an alternative path for nominating and electing directors. Concerned the current process impedes the expression of shareholders' right under state corporation laws to nominate and elect directors, the Commission proposed the rule, see Facilitating Shareholder Director Nominations, 74 Fed. Reg. 29,024, 29,025–26 (2009) (hereinafter Proposing Release), and adopted it with the goal of ensuring "the proxy process functions, as nearly as possible, as a replacement for an actual in-person meeting of shareholders," 75 Fed. Reg. 56,668, 56,670 (2010) (hereinafter Adopting Release). After responding to public comments, the Commission amended the proposed rule and, by a vote of three to two, adopted Rule 14a-11. Id. at 56,677. The rule requires a company subject to the Exchange Act proxy rules, including an investment company (such as a mutual fund) registered under the Investment Company Act of 1940 (ICA), to include in its proxy materials "the name of a person or persons nominated by a [qualifying] shareholder or group of shareholders for election to the board of directors." Id. at 56,682–83, 56,782/3.

To use Rule 14a-11, a shareholder or group of shareholders must have continuously held "at least 3% of the voting power of the company's securities entitled to be voted" for at least three years prior to the date the nominating shareholder or group submits notice of its intent to use the rule, and must continue to own those securities through the date of the annual meeting. Id. at 56,674–75. The nominating shareholder or group must submit the notice, which may include a statement of up to 500 words in support of each of its nominees, to the Commission and to the company. Id. at 56,675–76. A company that receives notice from an eligible shareholder or group must include the proffered information about the shareholder(s) and his nominee(s) in its proxy statement and include the nominee(s) on the proxy voting card. Id. at 56,676/1.

The Commission did place certain limitations upon the application of Rule 14a-11. The rule does not apply if applicable state law or a company's governing documents "prohibit shareholders from nominating a candidate for election as a director." Id. at 56,674/3. Nor may a shareholder use Rule 14a-11 if he is holding the company's securities with the intent of effecting a change of control of the company. Id. at 56,675/1. The company is not required to include in its proxy materials more than one shareholder nominee or the number of nominees, if more than one, equal to 25 percent of the number of directors on the board. Id. at 56,675/2.

* * *

Under the APA, we will set aside agency action that is "arbitrary, capricious, an abuse of discretion, or otherwise not in accordance with law." 5 U.S.C. § 706(2)(A). We must assure ourselves the agency has "examine[d] the relevant data and articulate[d] a satisfactory explanation for its action including a rational connection between the facts found and the choices made." Motor Vehicle Mfrs. Ass'n of U.S., Inc. v. State Farm Mut. Auto. Ins. Co., 463 U.S. 29, 43, 103 S. Ct. 2856, 77 L. Ed. 2d 443 (1983) (internal quotation marks omitted). The Commission also has a "statutory obligation to determine as best it can the economic implications of the rule." Chamber of Commerce v. SEC, 412 F.3d 133, 143, 366 U.S. App. D.C. 351 (D.C. Cir. 2005).

Indeed, the Commission has a unique obligation to consider the effect of a new rule upon "efficiency, competition, and capital formation," 15 U.S.C. §§ 78c(f), 78w(a)(2), 80a-2(c), and its failure to "apprise itself—and hence the public and the Congress—of the economic consequences of a proposed regulation" makes promulgation of the rule arbitrary and capricious and not in accordance with law. Chamber of Commerce, 412 F.3d at 144; Pub. Citizen v. Fed. Motor Carrier Safety Admin., 374 F.3d 1209, 1216, 362 U.S. App. D.C. 384 (D.C. Cir. 2004) (rule was arbitrary and capricious because agency failed to consider a factor required by statute).

* * *

1. Consideration of Costs and Benefits

In the Adopting Release, the Commission recognized "company boards may be motivated by the issues at stake to expend significant resources to challenge shareholder director nominees." 75 Fed. Reg. at 56,770/2. Nonetheless, the Commission believed a company's solicitation and campaign costs "may be limited by two factors": first, "to the extent that the directors' fiduciary duties prevent them from using corporate funds to resist shareholder director nominations for no good-faith corporate purpose," they may decide "simply to include the shareholder director nominees ... in the company's proxy materials"; and second, the "requisite ownership threshold and holding period" would "limit the number of shareholder director nominations that a board may receive, consider, and possibly contest." *Id.* at 56,770/2–3.

The petitioners object that the Commission failed to appreciate the intensity with which issuers would oppose nominees and arbitrarily dismissed the probability that directors would conclude their fiduciary duties required them to support their own nominees. The petitioners also argue it was arbitrary for the Commission not to estimate the costs of solicitation and campaigning that companies would incur to oppose candidates nominated by shareholders, which costs commenters expected to be quite large. The Chamber of Commerce submitted a comment predicting boards would incur substantial expenditures opposing shareholder nominees through "significant media and public relations efforts, advertising..., mass mailings, and other communication efforts, as well as the hiring of outside advisors and the expenditure of significant time and effort by the company's employees." *Id.* at 56,770/1. It pointed out that in recent proxy contests at larger companies costs "ranged from $14 million to $4 million" and at smaller companies "from $3 million to $800,000." *Id.* In its brief the Commission maintains it did consider the commenters' estimates of the costs, but reasonably explained why those costs "may prove less than these estimates."

We agree with the petitioners that the Commission's prediction directors might choose not to oppose shareholder nominees had no basis beyond mere speculation. Although it is possible that a board, consistent with its fiduciary duties, might forgo expending resources to oppose a shareholder nominee—for example, if it believes the cost of opposition would exceed the cost to the company of the board's preferred candidate losing the election, discounted by the probability of that happening—the Commission has presented no evidence that such forbearance is ever seen in practice. To the contrary, the American Bar Association Committee on Federal Regulation of Securities commented:

> If the [shareholder] nominee is determined [by the board] not to be as appropriate a candidate as those to be nominated by the board's independent nominating committee..., then the board will be compelled by its fiduciary duty to make an appropriate effort to oppose the nominee, as boards now do in traditional proxy contests. Letter from Jeffrey W. Rubin, Chair, Comm. on Fed. Regulation of Secs., Am. Bar Ass'n, to SEC 35 (August 31, 2009)...

The Commission's second point, that the required minimum amount and duration of share ownership will limit the number of directors nominated under the new rule, is a reason to expect election contests to be infrequent; it says nothing about the amount a company will spend on solicitation and campaign costs when there is a contested election. Although the Commission acknowledged that companies may expend resources to oppose shareholder nominees, *see* 75 Fed. Reg. at 56,770/2, it did nothing to estimate and quantify the costs it expected companies to incur; nor did it claim estimating those costs was not possible, for empirical evidence about expenditures in traditional proxy contests was readily available. Because the agency failed to "make tough choices about which of the competing estimates is most plausible, [or] to hazard a guess as to which is correct," Pub. Citizen, 374 F.3d at 1221, we believe it neglected its statutory obligation to assess the economic consequences of its rule, see Chamber of Commerce, 412 F.3d at 143.

The petitioners also maintain, and we agree, the Commission relied upon insufficient empirical data when it concluded that Rule 14a-11 will improve board performance and increase shareholder value by facilitating the election of dissident shareholder nominees. See 75 Fed. Reg. at 56,761–62. The Commission acknowledged the numerous studies submitted by commenters that reached the opposite result. Id. at 56,762/2 & n.924. One commenter, for example, submitted an empirical study showing that "when dissident directors win board seats, those firms underperform peers by 19 to 40% over the two years following the proxy contests." Elaine Buckberg, NERA Econ. Consulting, & Jonathan Macey, Yale Law School, Report on Effects of Proposed SEC Rule 14a-11 on Efficiency, Competitiveness and Capital Formation 9 (2009), available at www.nera.com/upload/Buckberg_Macey_Report_FINAL.pdf. The Commission completely discounted those studies "because of questions raised by subsequent studies, limitations acknowledged by the studies' authors, or [its] own concerns about the studies' methodology or scope." 75 Fed. Reg. at 56,762–63 & n.926–28.

The Commission instead relied exclusively and heavily upon two relatively unpersuasive studies, one concerning the effect of "hybrid boards" (which include some dissident directors) and the other concerning the effect of proxy contests in general, upon shareholder value.... Indeed, the Commission "recognize[d] the limitations of the Cernich (2009) study," and noted "its long-term findings on shareholder value creation are difficult to interpret." Id. at 56,760/3 n.911. In view of the admittedly (and at best) "mixed" empirical evidence, id. at 56,761/1, we think the Commission has not sufficiently supported its conclusion that increasing the potential for election of directors nominated by shareholders will result in improved board and company performance and shareholder value, id. at 56,761/1; see id. at 56,761/3.

Moreover, as petitioners point out, the Commission discounted the costs of Rule 14a-11—but not the benefits—as a mere artifact of the state law right of shareholders to elect directors. For example, with reference to the potential costs of Rule 14a-11, such as management distraction and reduction in the time a board spends "on strategic and long-term thinking," the Commission thought it "important to note that these costs are associated with the traditional State law right to nominate and elect directors, and are not costs incurred for including shareholder nominees for director in the company's proxy materials." Id. at 56,765/1–2. As we have said before, this type of reasoning, which fails to view a cost at the margin, is illogical and, in an economic analysis, unacceptable. See Chamber of Commerce, 412 F.3d at 143 (rejecting Commission's argument that rule would not create "costs associated with the hiring of staff because boards typically have this authority under state law," and assuming that "whether a board is authorized by law to hire additional staff in no way bears upon" the question whether the rule would "in fact cause the fund to incur additional staffing costs").

2. Shareholders with Special Interests

The petitioners next argue the Commission acted arbitrarily and capriciously by "entirely fail[ing] to consider an important aspect of the problem," Motor Vehicle Mfrs. Ass'n, 463 U.S. at 43, to wit, how union and state pension funds might use Rule 14a-11. Commenters expressed concern that these employee benefit funds would impose costs upon companies by using Rule 14a-11 as leverage to gain concessions, such as additional benefits for unionized employees, unrelated to shareholder value. The Commission insists it did consider this problem, albeit not in haec verba, along the way to its conclusion that "the totality of the evidence and economic theory" both indicate the rule "has the potential of creating the benefit of improved board performance and enhanced shareholder value." 75 Fed. Reg. at 56,761/1. Specifically, the Commission recognized "companies could be negatively affected if shareholders use the new rules to promote their narrow interests at the expense of other shareholders," id. at 56,772/3, but reasoned these potential costs "may be limited" because the ownership and holding requirements would "allow the use of the rule by only holders who demonstrated a significant, long-term commitment to the company," id. at 56,766/3, and who would therefore be less likely to act in a way that would diminish shareholder value. The Commission also noted costs may be limited because other shareholders may be alerted, through the disclosure requirements, "to the narrow interests of the nominating shareholder." Id.

The petitioners also contend the Commission failed to respond to the costs companies would incur even when a shareholder nominee is not ultimately elected. These costs may be incurred either by a board succumbing to the demands, unrelated to increasing value, of a special interest shareholder threatening to nominate a director, or by opposing and defeating such nominee(s). The Commission did not completely ignore these potential costs, but neither did it adequately address them.

Notwithstanding the ownership and holding requirements, there is good reason to believe institutional investors with special interests will be able to use the rule and, as more than one commenter noted, "public and union pension funds" are the institutional investors "most likely to make use of proxy access." Letter from Jonathan D. Urick, Analyst, Council of Institutional Investors, to SEC 2 (January 14, 2010).... Nonetheless, the Commission failed to respond to comments arguing that investors with a special interest, such as unions and state and local governments whose interests in jobs may well be greater than their interest in share value, can be expected to pursue self-interested objectives rather than the goal of maximizing shareholder value, and will likely cause companies to incur costs even when their nominee is unlikely to be elected.... By ducking serious evaluation of the costs that could be imposed upon companies from use of the rule by shareholders representing special interests, particularly union and government pension funds, we think the Commission acted arbitrarily.

3. Frequency of Election Contests

In the Proposing Release, the Commission estimated 269 companies per year, comprising 208 companies reporting under the Exchange Act and 61 registered investment companies, would receive nominations pursuant to Rule 14a-11. 74 Fed. Reg. at 29,064/1. In the Adopting Release, however, the Commission reduced that estimate to 51, comprising only 45 reporting companies and 6 investment companies, in view of "the additional eligibility requirements" the Commission adopted in the final version of Rule 14a-11. 75 Fed. Reg. at 56,743/3–56,744/1. (As originally proposed, Rule 14a-11 would have required a nominating shareholder to have held the securities for only one year rather than the three years required in the final rule. *See id. at 56,755*/1.) In revising its estimate, the Commission also newly relied upon "[t]he number of contested elections and board-related shareholder proposals" in a recent year, which it believed was "a better indicator of how many shareholders might submit a nomination" than were the data upon which it had based its estimate in the Proposing Release. *Id.* at 56,743/3.

The petitioners argue the Commission's revised estimate unreasonably departs from the estimate used in the Proposing Release, conflicts with its assertion the rule facilitates elections contests, and undermines its reliance upon frequent use of Rule 14a-11 to estimate the amount by which shareholders will benefit from "direct printing and mailing cost savings," id. at 56,756 & n.872. The petitioners also contend the estimate is inconsistent with the Commission's prediction shareholders will initiate 147 proposals per year under Rule 14a-8, a rule not challenged here. See id. at 56,677/2.

The Commission was not unreasonable in predicting investors will use Rule 14a-11 less frequently than traditional proxy contests have been used in the past. As Commission counsel pointed out at oral argument, there would still be some traditional proxy contests; the total number of efforts by shareholders to nominate and elect directors will surely be greater when shareholders have two paths rather than one open to them. In any event, the final estimated frequency (51) with which shareholders will use Rule 14a-11 does not clearly conflict with the higher estimate in the Proposing Release (269), or the estimate of proposals under Rule 14a-8 (147), both of which were based upon looser eligibility standards.

In weighing the rule's costs and benefits, however, the Commission arbitrarily ignored the effect of the final rule upon the total number of election contests. That is, the Adopting Release does not address whether and to what extent Rule 14a-11 will take the place of traditional proxy contests. Cf. 75 Fed. Reg. at 56,772/2. Without this crucial datum, the Commission has no way of knowing whether the rule will facilitate enough election contests to be of net benefit. See id. at 56,761/1 (anticipating "beneficial effects" because rule will "mak[e] election contests a more plausible avenue for shareholders to participate in the governance of their company").

We also agree with the petitioners that the Commission's discussion of the estimated frequency of nominations under Rule 14a-11 is internally inconsistent and therefore arbitrary. In discussing its benefits, the Commission predicted nominating share-holders would realize "[d]irect cost savings" from not having to print or mail their own proxy materials. Id. at 56,756/2. These savings would "remove a disincentive for shareholders to submit their own director nominations" and otherwise facilitate elec-tion contests. Id. The Commission then cited comment letters predicting the number of elections contested under Rule 14a-11 would be quite high. See id. at 56,756/3 n.872. One of the comments reported, based upon the proposed rule and a survey of directors, that approximately 15 percent of all companies with shares listed on ex-changes, that is, "hundreds" of public companies, expected a shareholder or group of shareholders to nominate a director using the new rule. Letter from Kenneth L. Altman, President, The Altman Group, Inc., to SEC 3 (January 19, 2010), available at http://www.sec.gov/comments/s7-10-09/s71009-605.pdf. Thus, the Commission anticipated frequent use of Rule 14a-11 when estimating benefits, but assumed in-frequent use when estimating costs. *See, e.g., supra* at 10 (SEC asserted solicitation and campaign costs would be minimized because of limited use of the rule).

III. Conclusion

For the foregoing reasons, we hold the Commission was arbitrary and capricious in promulgating Rule 14a-11. Accordingly, we have no occasion to address the peti-tioners' First Amendment challenge to the rule. The petition is granted and the rule is hereby *Vacated*.

Comments and Questions

1. For a discussion of the history of shareholder access, starting in the 1940s, see J. Robert Brown, Jr., *The SEC, Corporate Governance and Shareholder Access to the Board Room*, 2008 Utah L. Rev. 1339.

2. At the time this rule was proposed, a number of commentators questioned whether the Securities and Exchange Commission has the regulatory authority to adopt a shareholder access rule. Much of the argument that the Commission did not arose from the analysis in *Business Roundtable v. SEC*, 905 F.2d 406 (D.C. Cir. 1990). What do you make of this argument? Congress largely eliminated the uncertainty in the Dodd-Frank Act adopted in 2010. In that Act, Section 14(a) of the Exchange Act was amended to give the SEC the authority to adopt a shareholder access rule. *See* Section 971 of the Dodd Frank Act (amending 15 U.S.C. §78n(a)).

3. The court takes the position that the SEC acted in an arbitrary fashion by failing to respond to the arguments made by commentators that "special interest" shareholders would use the threat of director nominations to obtain non-shareholder benefits (such as wage concessions). Does the APA require the SEC to address every comment made? What evidence did the court cite for the proposition that this could occur? Is the evidence convincing?

4. The court struck down the mandatory rule but left untouched the change to Rule 14a-8 that permitted shareholder proposals seeking access. This left open the possibility of private ordering. The area has proved relatively popular. For example,

in 2014, the Comptroller of the City of New York submitted proposals to 75 companies, at least some of which were targeted because of concern over executive compensation and diversity issues. A significant number received majority support from shareholders and by early 2016, over 200 companies had put in place an access bylaw. Discuss the benefits and weaknesses of a private ordering approach with respect to shareholder access.

Chapter 9

The Role of Disclosure in the Governance Process

Disclosure plays a critical role in the corporate governance process. Shareholders cannot make informed decisions or enforce their rights without sufficient information on the activities of the board and the corporation. As a result, public companies are subject to a rich legal regime that requires disclosure of a myriad of information about managerial behavior.

Disclosure, however, does more than provide market participants with material information. It has also been used to affect substantive behavior. Management may prefer to alter its behavior rather than trigger uncomfortable disclosure. Board attendance, for example, likely improved once the SEC required companies to identify any director who missed an excessive number of meetings. Similarly, the obligation to reveal any "disagreement" on the board that results in a director resignation likely creates an incentive to resolve disputes rather than publicize the dispute.

Two separate legal regimes provide for disclosure to shareholders and investors. State law does so through inspection rights. Under that system, the onus rests on shareholders to seek out the information. As a precondition for exercising these rights, shareholders must have a "proper purpose." The elements have been interpreted narrowly and impose significant barriers to access.

Federal law takes a different approach. Public companies must comply with the disclosure regime implemented and administered by the Securities and Exchange Commission under the Exchange Act. *See* Section 12(g), 15 USC § 78l(g). Those with at least 500 shareholders of record and $10 million in assets must file periodic reports on a quarterly basis. *See* Rule 12g-1, 17 CFR § 240.12g-1.

In addition, shareholders receive each year a proxy or information statement that contains full disclosure about matters to be addressed at the annual meeting. Sections 14(a) & 14(c), 15 USC § 78n(a) & (c). The documents include substantial disclosure about the company's corporate governance practices; *see* Item 407 of Regulation S-K, 17 CFR § 229.407, and the background on officers and directors. Item 401 of Regulation S-K, 17 CFR § 229.401. Among other things, shareholders will learn the compensation paid to directors and to the top officers.

Disclosure under the federal system is highly influenced by the antifraud provisions, particularly Rule 10b-5. 17 C.F.R. 240.10b-5. The rules impose an obligation for completeness whenever a company speaks. Under the antifraud provisions, companies are sometimes required to reveal information that relates to the integrity of management. These might include the payment of an illegal campaign contribution or the misstatement of academic credentials. Courts and the SEC have struggled over the application of the antifraud provisions to these types of matters, particularly those relating to the materiality of the information.

Although the Commission has traditionally sought to limit disclosure to information material to investors and shareholders, this has begun to change. Pressure has increased on the SEC to require disclosure that may benefit investors but is also of considerable interest to the general public. Climate change and political contributions are two examples. Moreover, Congress has made the SEC, what one commentator described as a "dumping ground" for disclosure designed primarily to promote social rather than economic goals. This could be seen most clearly with the decision by Congress in Dodd-Frank to require the SEC to oversee the disclosure process in connection with the use of "conflict minerals."

I. The State Regime: Inspection Rights

State law does not require companies to make meaningful affirmative disclosure to shareholders, although Delaware does recognize an obligation of complete honesty whenever the company speaks. *See Malone v. Brincat*, 722 A.2d 5 (Del. 1998). Instead, shareholders wanting information about the activities of management must invoke their statutory right to inspect. 8 Del. Gen. Corp. L. §220.

A. Process

Section 220 imposes a number of procedural hurdles as a precondition for acquiring documents. The shareholder must submit the request in writing. The writing must include a proper purpose. In addition, to the extent that the records are sought by street name and other beneficial owners, the request must be accompanied by proof of beneficial ownership. The courts construe these "form and manner" requirements strictly.

Central Laborers Pension Fund v. News Corporation

Delaware Supreme Court
45 A.3d 139 (2012)

HOLLAND, JUSTICE:

The plaintiff-appellant, Central Laborers Pension Fund ("Central Laborers"), instituted this action, under section 220 of the Delaware General Corporation Law, to compel the defendant-appellee, News Corporation ("News Corp."), to produce News Corp.'s books and records (the "220 Action") related to its acquisition of Shine Group Ltd. (the "Shine Transaction"). Central Laborers seeks to inspect News Corp.'s books and records to investigate potential breaches of fiduciary duty in connection with the

Shine Transaction. The same day that it filed this 220 Action, Central Laborers, joined by another plaintiff, commenced a derivative action against News Corp.'s directors and News Corp., as a nominal defendant (the "Derivative Action"), claiming that the Shine Transaction was consummated at an unfair price as the result of an unfair process.

In the Court of Chancery, News Corp. moved to dismiss the 220 Action on three grounds. First, it argued that Central Laborers' inspection request failed to comply with the statutory procedural requirements of section 220. Second, News Corp. submitted that the simultaneous filing of the Derivative Action and the 220 Action refutes any claim of a proper purpose for its inspection request. Third, it contended that the scope of the inspection relief requested is overbroad.

* * *

Inspection Rights

"Stockholders of Delaware corporations enjoy a qualified right to inspect the corporation's books and records." These rights originated at common law and were recognized because "[a]s a matter of self-protection, the stockholder was entitled to know how his agents were conducting the affairs of the corporation of which he or she was a part owner." Stockholder inspection rights are codified in title 8, section 220(b) of the Delaware Code. That section provides, in part, that "[a]ny stockholder, in person or by attorney or other agent, shall, upon written demand under oath stating the purpose thereof, have the right ... to inspect for any proper purpose ... [t]he corporation's ... books and records...."

The original statutory inspection right was restricted to stockholders of record. After section 220's enactment in 1967, "stockholders of record" were the only persons entitled to inspect the books and records of a corporation for over thirty-five years. In 2003, section 220 was amended to extend inspection rights to beneficial owners.12 In its present form, section 220(b) imposes the following demand requirements upon beneficial stockholders seeking to inspect books and records:

In every instance where the stockholder is other than a record holder of stock in a stock corporation, ... the demand under oath shall [1] state the person's status as a stockholder, [2] be accompanied by documentary evidence of beneficial ownership of the stock, and [3] state that such documentary evidence is a true and correct copy of what it purports to be.

These three requirements are an "important element of the statutory scheme" that extended inspection rights to beneficial owners. Indeed, they "protect[ ] corporations from improper demands by requiring that evidence of beneficial ownership be both furnished with the demand and provided under oath."

The first and third statutory requirements are not at issue here. It is undisputed, however, that Central Laborers Inspection Demand failed to satisfy the second statutory procedural requirement.

Section 220's Balance

"Delaware law allows a stockholder a statutory right to inspect the books and records of a corporation so long as certain formal requirements are met, and the inspection is for a proper purpose." Section 220(c) provides that stockholders seeking to inspect the corporation's books and records "*shall first establish* that: (1) [s]uch stockholder is a stockholder; (2) [s]uch stockholder has *complied with [section 220] respecting the form and manner of making demand for inspection of such documents;* and (3) [t]he inspection such stockholder seeks is for a proper purpose." This statutory language makes it clear that a stockholder must comply with the "form and manner" of making the demand *before* the corporation determines whether the inspection request is for a proper purpose. Absent such procedural compliance, the stockholder has not properly invoked the statutory right to seek inspection, and consequently, the corporation has no obligation to respond.

The requirement that the corporation receive an inspection demand in proper form recognizes the importance of striking an appropriate balance between the rights of stockholders and corporations. In *Seinfeld v. Verizon Communications,* this Court observed the long-standing principle that a stockholder's right to obtain information based upon credible allegations of corporation mismanagement must be balanced against the rights of directors to manage the business of the corporation without undue interference from stockholders. Reaffirming our prior holdings in *Security First Corp. v. U.S. Die Casting & Development Co.* and *Thomas & Betts Corp. v. Leviton Manufacturing Co.,* this Court held that stockholders have a right to inspect books and records when they have established some "credible basis" to believe that there has been wrongdoing. We concluded that such a standard achieves an "appropriate balance between providing stockholders who can offer some evidence of possible wrongdoing with access to corporate records and safeguarding the right of the corporation to deny requests for inspections that are based only upon suspicion or curiosity."

Section 220's requirement that stockholders seeking document inspection first comply with the "form and manner" of making a demand to inspect the corporation's records, achieves the same appropriate balance between the interests of the stockholders and the corporation. The requirements in section 220 protect "corporations from improper demands by requiring that *evidence of beneficial ownership be both furnished with the demand and provided under oath.*" Accordingly, Delaware courts require strict adherence to the section 220 inspection demand procedural requirements.

Statute Not Followed

In this case, Central Laborers' Inspection Demand did not comply with the procedural requirements in section 220(b). Indeed, it contained several errors. First, the Inspection Demand identified the wrong corporation, stating that it seeks "to inspect and copy the ... books and records of *Viacom* and its subsidiaries," rather than that of *News Corp.* Second, the supporting materials filed in support of the Inspection Demand were inconsistent. The affidavit of Dan Koeppel, Central Laborers' Executive Director (the "Koeppel Affidavit"), asserted that Central Laborers' *beneficially* owned

14,110 shares of News Corp. However, the Power of Attorney signed by Koeppel characterized Central Laborers as the *record* owner of the same 14,110 News Corp. shares. Third, evidence of Central Laborers' beneficial ownership of News Corp.'s stock was not included with the Inspection Demand. The Koeppel Affidavit stated that "Central Laborers beneficially owned and held 14,110 shares of News Corporation common stock, *as shown by the annexed document* which is a true and correct copy of the original record." However, no documents were annexed to the Koeppel Affidavit.

In the Court of Chancery, Central Laborers' attorney acknowledged that no documentary evidence of Central Laborers' stock ownership in News Corporation had been included with the Inspection Demand and characterized it as a "clerical error." Nevertheless, Central Laborers contends, it has satisfied the procedural requirements of section 220 by submitting an account statement evidencing its beneficial ownership in News Corp. stock and a revised Koeppel Affidavit, together with its brief in opposition to News Corp.'s motion to dismiss. That contention is without merit.

Strict adherence to the section 220 procedural requirements for making an inspection demand protects "the right of the corporation to receive and consider a demand in *proper form before litigation is initiated.* That right of the corporation is defeated and an integral part of the statute rendered nugatory when ... the demand does not satisfy the statutory mandate and an effort to comply with the requirements of form is made during the course of the litigation without delivering a new form of demand."

In *Mattes v. Checkers Drive-In Restaurants, Inc.,* as in this case, the stockholder plaintiff submitted a defective inspection demand. After suing on his defective demand, the plaintiff "submitted an affidavit in the litigation verifying the demand and confirming that the lawyer who made the demand was acting as his authorized attorney." There, as here, the plaintiff "did not make a new demand conforming to the statute and [then] sue on it." The Court of Chancery refused to accept the plaintiff's demand because "the express statutory requirements of §220 as to the form of a stockholder demand should be strictly followed." The *ratio decidendi* of *Mattes* applies with equal force in this case.

Central Laborers' submission of the account statement as part of its filing in the 220 Action did not effectively cure the statutory defect in the Inspection Demand. Section 220(b) provides that "the demand under oath *shall ... be accompanied by* documentary evidence of beneficial ownership of the stock" and "*shall be directed to the corporation at its registered office ... or at its principal place of business.*" That was not done in this case. Central Laborers furnished the account statement in its response to News Corp.'s motion to dismiss. The statute requires the documentary evidence to accompany the demand for inspection. Therefore, Central Laborers' subsequent filing would comply with the statute only if it was submitted with either a new or an amended demand, directed at News Corp.'s registered office or principal place of business. That was not done here. Accordingly, Central Laborers' was unsuccessful in its attempt to rectify the defect in its Inspection Demand.

Comments and Questions

1. Do you agree with the outcome of the decision? Is it a principle of statutory construction that form and manner requirements be strictly construed? What about the requirement that a director's resignation be in writing? *See* 8 *Del. C.* § 141(b) ("Any director may resign at any time upon notice given in writing or by electronic transmission to the corporation."). Should that be strictly construed? For the answer, see *Biolase Inc. v. Oracle Partners, LP*, 97 A.3d 1029, 1034 (Del. 2014) ("The Court of Chancery's interpretation of § 141(b) as taking a permissive approach that authorizes resignation by the means specified, but not ruling out a resignation by other means, is a sensible and reasonable one.").

2. The Chancery Court dismissed the request, taking the view that having filed a derivative suit, the plaintiff could not use inspection rights as a substitute for discovery. The Court did not affirm on that basis but also did not overturn the analysis. To the extent an accurate interpretation of Section 220, what impact might the lower court's analysis have on inspection rights?

3. Who ought to have the right to inspect records? Delaware originally limited inspection rights to record owners, requiring street name owners to submit a request through Cede & Co., the depository that holds most shares on behalf of brokers and banks. That, however, was changed, and now street name owners can make the request directly. *See* 8 Del. C. § 220(a) (2) (defining "stockholder" as "a person who is the beneficial owner of shares of such stock"). As this case illustrates, however, inspection requests must be accompanied by adequate evidence of beneficial ownership.

4. Obtaining documents of a subsidiary can raise thorny questions. Section 220 permits a request for records of a subsidiary but only if the parent "has actual possession and control of such records." Del. Gen. Corp. L. § 220(b)(2). *See Weinstein Enters. v. Orloff*, 870 A.2d 499 (Del. 2005) (holding that parent owning 45.16% did not have requisite control over subsidiary's books and records).

5. In addition to establishing a proper purpose, shareholders also must show that "each category of the books and records requested is essential and sufficient to the stockholder's stated purpose." *Thomas & Betts Corp. v. Leviton Mfg. Co.*, 681 A.2d 1026 (Del. 1996). What is the practical effect of this requirement?

6. In permitting inspections, courts can impose "limitations or conditions" in connection with inspections. Often, this takes the form of an obligation to keep matters confidential. What about limiting the use of any materials obtained from a company to actions brought in Delaware, at least where the company had a forum selection bylaw designating Delaware as the forum? For an answer, take a look at *United Technologies Corp. v. Treppel*, 109 A.3d 553 (Del. 2014).

B. Proper Purpose

Shareholders seeking to inspect must have a proper purpose. A proper purpose is one "reasonably related to such person's interest as a stockholder." *See* Section 220(b).

As a practical matter, however, this type of interest has generally been limited to allegations of corporate waste, mismanagement, or other wrongdoing. In effect, shareholders are limited to information relating to a possible breach of a fiduciary obligation. Yet these are not, as the next case illustrates, the only types of interests held by shareholders.

City of Westland Police & Fire Retirement System v. Axcelis Technologies, Inc.

Delaware Supreme Court
1 A.3d 281 (2010)

JACOBS, JUSTICE:

Axcelis is a Delaware corporation specializing in the manufacture of ion implantation and semiconductor equipment. Axcelis' stock is publicly traded on the NASDAQ. Westland is a Michigan pension fund, that beneficially owns Axcelis common stock.

In 1983, Axcelis and Sumitomo Heavy Industries, Ltd. ("SHI"), a Japanese company, established, as equal partners, a joint venture called "SEN." That joint venture develops, manufactures and sells semiconductor equipment and licenses technology from Axcelis.

At all relevant times, Axcelis' board of directors (the "Board") consisted of seven members. Chairwoman Mary G. Puma was Axcelis' President and CEO. The remaining six directors—Stephen R. Hardis, Patrick H. Nettles, H. Brian Thompson, William C. Jennings, R. John Fletcher, and Geoffrey Wild—were outside, non-employee directors and were "Independent Directors" under the NASDAQ listing standards.

B. SHI's Acquisition Proposals

On February 4, 2008, SHI (together with TPG Capital LLP) made an unsolicited bid to acquire Axcelis for $5.20 per share. That day, Axcelis shares closed at a price of $4.18 per share. On February 7, Axcelis informed SHI that it would respond to its acquisition proposal after consulting with Axcelis' advisors. On February 25, 2008, the Board issued a press release announcing its rejection of SHI's proposal. The Board determined that the $5.20 per share offered price materially discounted Axcelis' true worth, because it did not assign any value for Axcelis' opportunity to retrieve market share from its competitors, or for the synergistic value of Axcelis' 50% interest in SEN.

On March 10, 2008, SHI made a second bid to acquire Axcelis, this time for $6 per share. That day, Axcelis shares closed at a price of $5.45 per share. On March 17, the Board rejected SHI's second proposal, stating that "the proposal undervalues Axcelis and is not in the best interests of Axcelis and its shareholders." The Board expressed its willingness to meet with SHI privately, however, to explore whether the parties could reach an agreement on a transaction involving SEN.

C. The May 2008 Axcelis Shareholder Meeting

On May 1, 2008, Axcelis held its annual shareholders' meeting. Axcelis had a classified board and the three directors standing for reelection—Messrs. Hardis, Fletcher and Thompson—were unopposed. Axcelis follows the plurality voting provisions of Delaware statutory law, under which a director may be elected without receiving a majority of the votes cast. Importantly, however, the Axcelis Board also had adopted a "plurality plus" governance policy, which provides that:

> At any shareholder meeting at which Directors are subject to an uncontested election, any nominee for Director who receives a greater number of votes "withheld" from his or her election than votes "for" such election shall submit to the Board a letter of resignation for consideration by the Nominating and Governance Committee. The Nominating and Governance Committee shall recommend to the Board the action to be taken with respect to such offer of resignation. The Board shall act promptly with respect to each such letter of resignation and shall promptly notify the Director concerned of its decision.[1]

All three directors seeking reelection at the 2008 annual meeting received less than a majority of the votes cast, which triggered the "plurality plus" governance policy. Therefore, in accordance with that policy, the three directors tendered letters of resignation. The Board, however, decided not to accept the resignations, and in a May 23, 2008 press release, explained why:

> [T]the board considered a number of factors relevant to the best interests of Axcelis. The Board noted that the three directors are experienced and knowledgeable about [the Company], and that if their resignations were accepted, the Board would be left with only four remaining directors. One or more of the three directors serves on each of the key committees of the Company and Mr. Hardis serves as a lead director. The Board believed that losing this experience and knowledge would harm the Company. The Board also noted that retention of these directors is particularly important if Axcelis is able to move forward on discussions with SHI following finalization of an appropriate non-disclosure agreement.

The Board also expressed its intention to be responsive to the shareholder concerns that gave rise to the withhold votes. The Board is seeking to engage in confidential discussions with SHI and, prior to next year's Annual Meeting, the Board will consider recommending in favor of a declassification proposal at that meeting.

ANALYSIS

A. Westland's Claims on Appeal

Westland claims that the Court of Chancery erred as a matter of law by misapplying the applicable legal standard. Westland concedes that the Court of Chancery opinion invokes the proper standard—namely, that a plaintiff seeking inspection of books and records must present some evidence, "through documents, logic, testimony or

---

1. [4] This type of governance policy is sometimes referred to as a "Pfizer-style" policy (because Pfizer, Inc. pioneered its use) or a "plurality plus" policy. See City of Westland Police & Fire Retirement Sys. v. Axcelis Tech., Inc., 2009 Del. Ch. LEXIS 173, 2009 WL 3086537, at *2 n.11 (Del. Ch. Sep. 28, 2009). The Axcelis "plurality plus" policy was adopted by Board resolution, as distinguished from being adopted as a by-law or as part of the certificate of incorporation.

otherwise," to suggest a credible basis from which the Court of Chancery could infer that wrongdoing may have occurred. Westland claims, however, that the Court misapplied that standard by requiring Westland to provide affirmative evidence of wrongdoing. Westland urges that the undisputed facts are sufficient to discharge its burden because those facts, standing alone, established a credible basis to infer wrongdoing. Additionally, Westland urges this Court to adopt the *Blasius* standard in reviewing the Board's decision to reject the three directors' tendered resignations.

B. Standard of Review

This Court reviews de novo whether or not a party's stated purpose for seeking inspection under 8 Del. C. §220(b) (here, to investigate possible mismanagement) is a "proper purpose." A trial judge's determination that a credible basis does (or does not) exist to infer managerial wrongdoing is a mixed finding of fact and law that is entitled to considerable deference.

The standard applicable to a Section 220(b) demand is well established. A stockholder seeking to inspect the books and records of a corporation must demonstrate a "proper purpose" for the inspection. A "proper purpose" is one that is "reasonably related to such person's interest as a stockholder."

Our law recognizes investigating possible wrongdoing or mismanagement as a "proper purpose." To obtain Section 220 relief based on that purpose, the plaintiff-stockholder must present "some evidence" to suggest a "credible basis" from which a court could infer possible mismanagement that would warrant further investigation. In *Seinfeld v. Verizon Comm'n, Inc.*, this Court reaffirmed the "credible basis" standard as striking the appropriate balance between (on the one hand) affording shareholders access to corporate records that may provide some evidence of possible wrongdoing and (on the other) safeguarding the corporation's right to deny requests for inspection based solely upon suspicion or curiosity. Thus, a "mere statement of a purpose to investigate possible general mismanagement, without more, will not entitle a shareholder to broad §220 inspection relief."

A plaintiff may establish a credible basis to infer wrongdoing "through documents, logic, testimony or otherwise." Such evidence need not prove that wrongdoing, in fact, occurred. Because the "credible basis" standard "sets the lowest possible burden of proof," any reduction of that burden would be tantamount to permitting inspection based on the plaintiff-stockholder's mere suspicion of wrongdoing.

C. Westland Failed to Establish a Credible Basis to Infer Wrongdoing

Westland's books and records demand identified two allegedly "suspect" incidents of "wrongdoing." The first was Axcelis' Board's handling of SHI's two acquisition proposals. The second was the Board's refusal to accept the resignations of the three directors who failed to receive an affirmative majority vote at the May 2008 annual meeting. Westland's evidence to support its purpose consisted of (1) the parties' Joint Stipulation of Uncontested Facts and exhibits thereto, and (2) Westland's "logical conclusions" from those facts and exhibits that the Axcelis Board had acted out of improper entrenchment motives. The Vice Chancellor, however, drew different "logical conclusions" from those same uncontested facts, and determined that there was "no support in the record of any entrenchment motive" other than Westland's "bare accusations" suggesting such a motive.

Westland claims that the Court of Chancery incorrectly applied the "credible basis" standard by requiring Westland to present "affirmative evidence" of wrongdoing. For support, Westland offers only its proposed interpretation of the uncontested facts, which (Westland asserts) create a "legitimate basis to believe" that the Board's decisions *might* have been the product of improper entrenchment motives. By way of example, Westland conclusorily asserts that "[i]t cannot seriously be disputed ... that SHI's acquisition proposals could have been deemed a 'threat' to the Axcelis Board's control over the Company," and that the Board's rejection of the three directors' resignations and denial of SHI's request for a "modest" extension, were made "[i]n the face of this threat." Essentially, Westland disagrees with the Vice Chancellor's inferences from the undisputed facts. Westland's disagreement, without any further affirmative showing, is insufficient. The Vice Chancellor concluded that Axcelis' rejection of SHI's unsolicited acquisition proposals, without more, was not a "defensive action" under *Unocal.* That conclusion must stand, because the record provides no credible basis to infer that the Board's rejections of those proposals, and its refusal to extend the deadline for SHI to submit a revised acquisition bid, were other than good faith business decisions.

D. Proper Purpose to Investigate Suitability of Directors

Westland's second claim on appeal is that this Court should adopt the *Blasius* standard when reviewing a board of directors' decision to reject director resignations in cases where a "plurality plus" governance policy (or by-law) is triggered and requires that resignations be tendered. Under *Blasius,* a corporation's board must demonstrate a "compelling justification" for board-adopted measures that interfere with, or frustrate, a shareholder vote. Westland claims that by withholding their votes in the May 2008 director elections—thereby triggering Axcelis' "plurality plus" governance policy—a majority of Axcelis shareholders expressed their will that the three directors should be removed. Because the Board's non-acceptance of the three directors' resignations frustrated that shareholder will and vote (Westland urges), the Axcelis Board must be required to show a "compelling justification" for its decision.

The Court of Chancery rejected Westland's *Blasius* argument. We have concluded that Westland's *Blasius* argument lacks merit, because it improperly attempts to shift to Axcelis Westland's burden to establish a "proper purpose' for a Section 220 inspection. Accordingly, we agree with the Court of Chancery's decision not to adopt the *Blasius* standard when reviewing a board of directors' discretionary decision to reject director resignations in cases where a "plurality plus" governance policy is triggered and requires that resignations be tendered.

Although we conclude that the Court of Chancery properly rejected Westland's *Blasius* argument, the fact that this dispute arises in connection with a shareholder vote requires a further elaboration of the "proper purpose" requirement of our Section 220 jurisprudence in that context. At common law a stockholder of a Delaware corporation had a qualified right to inspect or examine the books and records of the corporation. The shareholder had to show that the requested inspection was for a "proper purpose," which at common law was a purpose relating to the interest the shareholder sought to protect by seeking inspection.

The shareholder's right of inspection is currently codified in Title 8, Section 220 of the Delaware Code. With fidelity to its common law origins, Section 220(b) defines "proper purpose" as "a purpose reasonably related to such person's interest as a stockholder." Over time, that concept has expanded as Delaware courts have interpreted the statutory term "proper purpose" to reconcile legitimate interests of shareholders with the ever-changing dynamics and technology of corporate governance. A leading treatise on Delaware law has compiled a nonexclusive list of judicially recognized proper purposes under Section 220. One of those purposes is "to determine an individual's suitability to serve as a director," which the Court of Chancery recognized in *Pershing Square, L.P. v. Ceridian Corp.* There, the Court of Chancery stated:

> It is difficult for me to understand how determining an individual's suitability to serve as a corporate director is not reasonably related to a person's interest as a stockholder. After all, stockholders elect directors to represent their interests in the corporation and have few other avenues by which they may influence the governance of their companies. Once elected, stockholders may express dissatisfaction only through the electoral check.

The Chancellor recognized, however, that merely stating that purpose does not automatically entitle a shareholder to Section 220 inspection relief:

> Inspection under § 220 is not automatic upon a statement of a proper purpose. First, a defendant may defeat demand by proving that while stating a proper purpose, plaintiff's true or primary purpose is improper. Second, a plaintiff who states a proper purpose must also present some evidence to establish a credible basis from which the Court of Chancery could infer there are legitimate concerns regarding a director's suitability. That is, a stockholder must establish a credible basis to infer that a director is unsuitable, thereby warranting further investigation. Third, a plaintiff must also prove that the information it seeks is necessary and essential to assessing whether a director is unsuitable to stand for reelection. Finally, access to board documents may be further limited by the need to protect confidential board communications. Thus, accepting that a desire to investigate the 'suitability of a director' is a proper purpose does not necessarily expose corporations to greater risk of abuse.

We agree that the purpose articulated in Pershing Square is a "proper purpose" for seeking inspection of corporate books and records under Section 220. Although that does not change the outcome of this case—because Westland did not rely on that purpose as a basis for seeking relief—nonetheless the relationship between the shareholder inspection right and the "plurality plus" policy adopted by the Axcelis board merits sharper focus for future guidance.

In this case, the Axcelis "plurality plus" policy was adopted unilaterally as a resolution of the Board, rather than as a by-law or as part of the certificate of incorporation, both of which would require shareholder approval. Here, the Axcelis Board unilaterally conferred upon the shareholders the right to elect directors by majority vote. But, the Board also conditioned that right upon the board's discretionary power to accept (or reject) the resignations of those directors who were elected by a plurality, but not a majority, shareholder vote.

There is a relationship between the shareholders' inspection right and a unilaterally adopted "plurality plus" policy whereby the directors confer upon themselves the discretion to reject resignations tendered by candidates who fail to receive a majority vote. The less-than-majority shareholder vote may be viewed as a judgment by the holders of a voting majority that those director-candidates were no longer suitable to serve (or continue to serve) as directors. Correspondingly, the Board's decision not to accept those resignations may be viewed as a contrary, overriding judgment by the Board. At stake, therefore, is the integrity of the Board decision overriding the determination by a shareholder majority. Stated differently, the question arises whether the directors, as fiduciaries, made a disinterested, informed business judgment that the best interests of the corporation require the continued service of these directors, or whether the Board had some different, ulterior motivation.

Where, as here, the board confers upon itself the power to override an exercised shareholder voting right without prior shareholder approval (as would be required in the case of a shareholder-adopted by-law or a charter provision), the board should be accountable for its exercise of that unilaterally conferred power. In this specific context, that accountability should take the form of being subject to a shareholder's Section 220 right to seek inspection of any documents and other records upon which the board relied in deciding not to accept the tendered resignations.

That is not to say that the making of a Section 220 demand, or the filing of a Section 220 action, for the purpose of investigating the suitability of directors whose tendered resignations were rejected, will automatically entitle the plaintiff shareholder to relief. It is to say that a showing that enough stockholders withheld their votes to trigger a corporation's (board-adopted) "plurality plus" policy satisfies the *Pershing Square* requirement that "a stockholder must establish a credible basis to infer that a director is unsuitable, thereby warranting further inspection." Nevertheless, to be entitled to relief, the plaintiff must still make the additional showing articulated by the Chancellor in *Pershing Square*. That, in our view, strikes the appropriate balance between the shareholders' entitlement to information and the directors' entitlement to make decisions in the corporation's best interest free from abusive litigation.

CONCLUSION

For the reasons set forth, the judgment of the Court of Chancery is affirmed.

Comments and Questions

1. *Axcelix* involved an inspection request designed to look into the board's reasons for refusing to accept the letters of resignation submitted by three directors who did not receive sufficient support under a majority vote bylaw. The plaintiff sought the following documents:

> All minutes of agendas for meetings (including all draft minutes and exhibits to such minutes and agendas) of the Board at which the Board discussed, considered or was presented with information concerning or related to the Board's decision not to accept the resignations of [the three directors].

> All documents reviewed, considered, or produced by the Board in connection with the Board's decision not to accept the resignations of Directors ...

Why did the company not simply provide shareholders with these documents? What reasons might there have been for refusing the request? What are some possible consequences of making the information available?

2. Plaintiffs asserted that the non-acceptance of the resignations should be tested under the *Blasius* standard, which requires a board seeking to disenfranchise shareholders to establish a "compelling justification" for its actions. The *Blasius* doctrine is discussed in Chapter 7. Could the actions by the board have been undertaken with the goal of disenfranchising shareholders? Was the court's resolution of this issue correct?

3. What was the proper purpose found in this case? How does this differ from the types of purposes usually accepted by the courts in Delaware in inspection cases? Provide some examples of director qualification issues that might generate a request to inspect records.

4. The court noted that the failure of directors to receive majority approval did not automatically mean shareholders were entitled to request records but that they still had to make the "additional showing" required by the court in *Pershing Square.* What are these additional showings and what impact are they likely to have in inspection requests in these circumstances?

5. Does a shareholder have a proper purpose where a derivative claim based upon the same allegations of mismanagement is barred by the statute of limitations? Apparently not. *See Wolst v. Monster Beverage Corp.*, Case No. 9154-VCN (Del. Ch. Oct. 3, 2014).

6. Does the type of information sought affect the analysis? What if the request seeks a list of shareholders? In those circumstances, shareholders are presumed to have a proper purpose. The burden rests with the board to show that they do not. *See* 8 Del. C. §220(c). With respect to shareholder lists, what type of information would the company be required to disclose? Should the list include, for example, email addresses or participants in the depository?

C. Credible Basis

The proper purpose requirement is in the statute. In addition, however, courts have grafted onto the request the need to produce a "credible basis" of support for the proper purpose.

Seinfeld v. Verizon Communications, Inc.

Delaware Supreme Court
909 A.2d 117 (2006)

HOLLAND, JUSTICE:

The plaintiff-appellant, Frank D. Seinfeld ("Seinfeld"), brought suit under section 220 of the Delaware General Corporation Law to compel the defendant-appellee, Verizon Communications, Inc. ("Verizon"), to produce, for his inspection, its books and records related to the compensation of Verizon's three highest corporate officers from 2000 to 2002. Seinfeld claimed that their executive compensation, individually and collectively, was excessive and wasteful....

Facts

Seinfeld asserts that he is the beneficial owner of approximately 3,884 shares of Verizon held in street name through a brokerage firm. His stated purpose for seeking Verizon's books and records was to investigate mismanagement and corporate waste regarding the executive compensations of Ivan G. Seidenberg, Lawrence T. Babbio, Jr. and Charles R. Lee. Seinfeld alleges that the three executives were all performing in the same job and were paid amounts, including stock options, above the compensation provided for in their employment contracts. Seinfeld's section 220 claim for inspection is further premised on various computations he performed which indicate that the three executives' compensation totaled $205 million over three years and was, therefore, excessive, given their responsibilities to the corporation.

During his deposition, Seinfeld acknowledged he had no factual support for his claim that mismanagement had taken place. He admitted that the three executives did not perform any duplicative work. Seinfeld conceded he had no factual basis to allege the executives "did not earn" the amounts paid to them under their respective employment agreements. Seinfeld also admitted "there is a possibility" that the $205 million executive compensation amount he calculated was wrong.

The issue before us is quite narrow: should a stockholder seeking inspection under section 220 be entitled to relief without being required to show some evidence to suggest a credible basis for wrongdoing? We conclude that the answer must be no.

Stockholder Inspection Rights

Delaware corporate law provides for a separation of legal control and ownership. The legal responsibility to manage the business of the corporation for the benefit of the stockholder owners is conferred on the board of directors by statute. The common law imposes fiduciary duties upon the directors of Delaware corporations to constrain their conduct when discharging that statutory responsibility.

Stockholders' rights to inspect the corporation's books and records were recognized at common law because "[a]s a matter of self-protection, the stockholder was entitled to know how his agents were conducting the affairs of the corporation of which he or she was a part owner." The qualified inspection rights that originated at common law are now codified in Title 8, section 220 of the Delaware Code, which provides, in part:

> (b) Any stockholder, in person or by attorney or other agent, shall, upon written demand under oath stating the purpose thereof, have the right during the usual hours for business to inspect for any proper purpose.

Section 220 provides stockholders of Delaware corporations with a "powerful right." By properly asserting that right under section 220, stockholders are able to obtain information that can be used in a variety of contexts. Stockholders may use information about corporate mismanagement, waste or wrongdoing in several ways. For example, they may: institute derivative litigation; "seek an audience with the board [of directors] to discuss proposed reform or, failing in that, they may prepare a stockholder resolution for the next annual meeting, or mount a proxy fight to elect new directors."

Seinfeld Denied Inspection

The Court of Chancery determined that Seinfeld's deposition testimony established only that he was concerned about the large amount of compensation paid to the three executives. That court concluded that Seinfeld offered "no evidence from which [it] could evaluate whether there is a reasonable ground for suspicion that the executive's compensation rises to the level of waste." It also concluded that Seinfeld did not "submit any evidence showing that the executives were not entitled to [the stock] options." The Court of Chancery properly noted that a disagreement with the business judgment of Verizon's board of directors or its compensation committee is not evidence of wrongdoing and did not satisfy Seinfeld's burden under section 220....

Evidentiary Barrier Allegation

In this appeal, Seinfeld asserts that the "Court of Chancery's ruling erects an insurmountable barrier for the minority shareholder of a public company." Seinfeld argues that:

> This Court and the Court of Chancery have instructed shareholders to utilize 220 as one of the tools at hand. Yet, the Court of Chancery at bar, in requiring *evidence* makes a 220 application a mirage. If the shareholder had evidence, a derivative suit would be brought. Unless there is a whistle blower, or a video cassette, the public shareholder, having no access to corporate records, will only have suspicions.

Investigations of meritorious allegations of possible mismanagement, waste or wrongdoing, benefit the corporation, but investigations that are "indiscriminate fishing expeditions" do not. "At some point, the costs of generating more information fall short of the benefits of having more information. At that point, compelling production of information would be wealth-reducing, and so shareholders would not want it produced." Accordingly, this Court has held that an inspection to investigate possible wrongdoing where there is no "credible basis," is a license for "fishing expeditions" and thus adverse to the interests of the corporation:

> Stockholders have a right to at least a limited inquiry into books and records when they have established some credible basis to believe that there has been wrongdoing.... Yet it would invite mischief to open corporate management to indiscriminate fishing expeditions.

A stockholder is "not required to prove by a preponderance of the evidence that waste and [mis]management are actually occurring." Stockholders need only show, by a preponderance of the evidence, a credible basis from which the Court of Chancery can infer there is possible mismanagement that would warrant further investigation— a showing that "may ultimately fall well short of demonstrating that anything wrong occurred." That "threshold may be satisfied by a credible showing, through documents, logic, testimony or otherwise, that there are legitimate issues of wrongdoing."

Although the threshold for a stockholder in a section 220 proceeding is not insubstantial, the "credible basis" standard sets the lowest possible burden of proof. The only way to reduce the burden of proof further would be to eliminate any requirement that a stockholder show *some evidence* of possible wrongdoing. That would be tantamount to permitting inspection based on the "mere suspicion" standard that Seinfeld advances in this appeal. However, such a standard has been repeatedly rejected as a basis to justify the enterprise cost of an inspection.

In Delaware and elsewhere, the "credible-basis-from-some-evidence" standard is settled law. Under the doctrine of *stare decisis*, settled law is overruled only "for urgent reasons and upon clear manifestation of error." A review of the cases that have applied the "credible basis" standard refutes Seinfeld's premise that requiring "some evidence" constitutes an insurmountable barrier for stockholders who assert inspection rights under section 220.

Requiring stockholders to establish a "credible basis" for the Court of Chancery to infer possible wrongdoing by presenting "some evidence" has not impeded stockholder inspections. Although many section 220 proceedings have been filed since we decided *Security First* and *Thomas & Betts*, Verizon points out that Seinfeld's case is only the second proceeding in which a plaintiff's demand to investigate wrongdoing was found to be *entirely* without a "credible basis." In contrast, there are a myriad of cases where stockholders have successfully presented "some evidence" to establish a "credible basis" to infer possible mismanagement and thus received some narrowly tailored right of inspection.

We remain convinced that the rights of stockholders and the interests of the corporation in a section 220 proceeding are properly balanced by requiring a stockholder to show "some evidence of possible mismanagement as would warrant further investigation." The "credible basis" standard maximizes stockholder value by limiting the range of permitted stockholder inspections to those that might have merit. Accordingly, our holdings in *Security First* and *Thomas & Betts* are ratified and reaffirmed.

Comments and Questions

1. The "credible basis" standard is a court created requirement, an example of the common law in action. What is the purpose of the requirement? What impact does it have in inspection requests? Is the standard necessary, as the court suggests here, to avoid a "fishing expedition?"

2. What burden does the standard impose on shareholders? The court described the evidentiary standard as setting "the lowest possible burden of proof." That suggests it is an easy standard to meet. Do you agree?

3. What type of evidence would shareholders have needed in order to inspect the relevant documents concerning executive compensation? How likely will it be to have this type of information at the pleading stage?

4. How does the credible basis standard work in the context of the need to show a proper purpose through allegations of breach of fiduciary duty? What sort of evidence would be necessary to show such a breach? Is such information typically available?

5. Is there a better way to accomplish the same end? Ought, for example, there to be a requirement that inspections be limited to large shareholders owning more than a specified percentage of shares (say 5% or 10%) without requiring a proper purpose?

In an era of global concerns over child labor, the environment, and other related matters, the need for a proper purpose and credible basis would seem to impose barriers to the acquisition of information about a corporation's involvement in, or awareness of, these types of activities. The next case demonstrates that this is not always the case.

Louisiana Municipal Police Employees Retirement System v. The Hershey Co.

Delaware Chancery Court
Civ. Action No. 7996-ML, March 18, 2014

Laster, Vice Chancellor:

[Plaintiffs sought to inspect certain documents. A Master assigned to the case denied the request. Plaintiff took exception to the report of the Master and appealed to the Chancery Court. For the Report of the Master, see Louisiana Mun. Police Emp. Ret. Sys. v. Hershey, DEFAX Case No. D66011 (Del. Ch. Nov. 8, 2013)].

The complaint seeks an order permitting LAMPERS to inspect and make copies of certain books and records set forth in its demand letter. Essentially, the complaint seeks more information.

Here, what I view as the key factual allegations of the complaint: Hershey controls 42 percent of the market for chocolate products in the United States and is a major player in the chocolate industry worldwide. Cocoa is the key ingredient used to manufacture chocolate. West African countries, including Ghana and the Ivory Coast, supply 70 percent of the world's cocoa. Hershey's major sourcing countries include Ghana and the Ivory Coast, as well as other West African nations.

Hershey is well aware of the pervasive use of child-enforced labor in Ghana and the Ivory Coast. And I don't say that in a bad way. Part of what the allegations of the complaint show is that Hershey is engaged in steps to try to address these issues. But that said, it is established for purposes of this motion that Hershey is aware of the pervasive use of child and forced labor in Ghana and the Ivory Coast.

The laws of Ghana and the Ivory Coast forbid employers from forcing children to engage in dangers activities such as carrying heavy loads, clearing land, things like that which require the use of sharp tools such as machetes, all things that are endemic to the production of cocoa. Those laws are routinely violated; hence, the use of child and forced labor is, indeed, pervasive.

In 2001 Hershey and other companies signed the Harkin-Engel Protocol, which established a goal of eliminating the worst forms of child labor in the cocoa sectors in Ghana and the Ivory Coast. There was a goal that by July 1, 2005, this consortium would develop and implement credible mutually acceptable voluntary industry-wide standards for public certification that cocoa beans and the derivative products have been grown and/or processed without any of the worst forms of child labor.

Note the date. 2001. Now, there's discussion in the briefing from Hershey that says "Hey, protocol's been changed. You can't allege a violation of the protocol," et cetera. That's not what the plaintiff is relying on it for. The plaintiff is citing the protocol for the fact of Hershey's long-standing awareness of this problem and unsuccessful efforts to address this problem. And, again, I'm going to say this all the way through. This doesn't necessarily mean that Hershey is a bad company. What we're dealing with here is a request for more information, as I'll get to, based on the possibility of wrongdoing. So the protocol I just referenced was 2001.

On March 31, 2011, the Payson Center for International Development at Tulane University released a report on the continued prevalence of child labor in the cocoa industry. This is 10 years after the protocol. Basically the Payson Report documents all the worst ills that one could imagine about this problem. Nearly 2 million children work illegally on cocoa farms. There's evidence of widespread violations of human trafficking laws. According to the Payson Report, Ghana and the Ivory Coast are common destinations for trafficked children. Again, this is all material for which the purpose of a motion to dismiss supports the inference of pervasive use of child and forced labor in Ghana and the Ivory Coast and Hershey's awareness of the issue.

Now, despite the effort starting in 2001 to come up with voluntary standards so that people could certify that their cocoa was used without the worst forms of child labor, there's still no certification process. There's an indication that one supplier, Cadbury's, has done some form of certification. Hershey's has not. On October 3rd, 2012, Hershey's announced that it would certify that its chocolate products were free of cocoa tainted with child labor and human trafficking violations by 2020. As I discussed with counsel, I think from all this, it is quite reasonable to infer at the pleading stage—and counsel ultimately does not dispute—that right now Hershey's has to acknowledge that some of its cocoa is produced through child labor and as a result of individuals who were the victims of human trafficking.

If I call up, you know, my daughter's school and I say, "Can you confirm for me that there's no one on the payroll with a criminal record?" and they say to me, "We're not going to do that now, but we hope to be able to do so in 2020," I'm going to draw the inference that they can't do it right now and there's probably someone at the school with a criminal record. Now, that may or may not be a bad thing. Hopefully the person has paid their debt to society and is no longer a threat, et cetera. But I'm going to draw that inference, and I think it's a reasonable inference to draw.

Hershey's stockholders also have brought concerns about the use of child labor within Hershey's supply chain, as are other people who are drawing that inference. Despite these concerns, Hershey has declined to provide any details about its sources of cocoa or to disclose its suppliers or to provide information from which one can evaluate the nature of Hershey's involvement in the supply chain.

As I discussed with counsel, however, one can infer at the pleading stage that it is reasonably tight because Hershey's extols the fact that it monitors its suppliers, that it has multi-part programs to ensure that its suppliers are doing the best they can to adhere to Hershey's code of conduct, which it requires suppliers to sign, and that Hershey's kicks out suppliers when it finds out about violations.

All those are really good things, don't get me wrong. But all those also support a reasonable inference at the pleading stage that Hershey's has deep involvement in and control over its supply chain. That is not a radical inference, given the market-leading status and dominant market share that Hershey's has and commands.

… As the Delaware Supreme Court held in Central Mortgage versus Morgan Stanley, the governing pleading standard is reasonable conceivability. …

The conceivability standard, thus, asks whether there is "a possibility" that the allegations of the complaint could support relief. … That possibility standard intersects with another possibility standard to create at this procedural stage double possibility. Section 220 of the DGCL allows a stockholder to inspect a corporation's books and records for any proper purpose. It's well-established that investigation of mismanagement is a proper purpose. One can consult many Supreme Court decisions for that. The operative test as to what a stockholder has to show to establish a basis to inspect books and records to explore possible wrongdoing is Seinfeld versus Verizon Communications. Seinfeld said the following:

> "A stockholder is not required to prove by a preponderance of the evidence that waste and mismanagement are actually occurring. Stockholders need only show by a preponderance of the evidence a credible basis from which the Court of Chancery can infer that there is possible mismanagement that would warrant further investigation, a showing that may ultimately fall well

short of demonstrating that anything wrong occurred. That threshold may be satisfied by a credible showing through documents, logic, testimony or otherwise that there are legitimate issues of wrongdoing." ...

So, again, we've already got possible and inferences going to the plaintiff because of the motion to dismiss standard. Then the merits standard is that, to reiterate, "A stockholder is not required to prove that waste and mismanagement are actually occurring." A stockholder need only provide a reasonable basis from which I can infer—here I'm quoting—"possible mismanagement." And in the words of the Delaware Supreme Court, the standard for possible mismanagement requires a showing that may, ultimately "fall well short"—not my words; their words—"well short of demonstrating that anything wrong occurred."

Now, sadly, I think the Master's recommendation and the defendant's brief repeatedly focus on whether actual wrongdoing has occurred. I know they say they didn't, but let me give you some quotes. So page 15 of the Master's report and one of the key bases for the recommendation of dismissal, she's just reviewed some of the facts that I outlined for you, and then it states this: "Notably, none of these sources or any other source identified in the complaint states that Hershey has violated the law or is under investigation for possible legal violations, nor do they identify any illegal conduct within the company." That's the end of the quote.

"Has violated the law." "under investigation" "any illegal conduct within the company." That's very different from "possible mismanagement," which may "fall well short of actual wrongdoing." ... Although the sources in the complaint—I'm going to quote—"detail at length very serious legal violations on many farms in the Ivory Coast and Ghana, none of the articles directly implicate Hershey in that conduct." Not the standard. "Directly implicate" is not the standard. "Possibly," "possible wrongdoing" is the standard. ...

"The statistical correlation, i.e. the idea that Hershey buys a lot of cocoa and lot of cocoa comes from Ghana and Ivory Coast and a lot of cocoa is tainted"—actually, I don't think that's a statistical correlation. It's a chain of inferences. But regardless, it is "vastly different from what LAMPERS offers in this case, which is little more than the logical fallacy that because some cocoa is produced using child labor and Hershey purchases a large amount of cocoa or cocoa-derived products, Hershey's must use cocoa products tainted by child labor."

And it's not a "must." It's "may use," "possibly use." Right below that, the recommendation says, "Even if I could draw that inference"—I actually think you can draw that inference at the pleading stage. "Even if I could draw that inference, LAMPERS has not alleged a credible basis from which I can infer wrongdoing." The point is not whether you can infer wrongdoing. The point is whether you can infer possible wrongdoing.

"Neither the evidence nor the other sources on which LAMPERS relies provides any basis from which the Court could conclude that Hershey has violated the law." You guys are getting tired of the refrain by now. It's not "has violated the law."

It's "possibly could violate the law." Now, this is not something that came out of whole cloth from the Master. It's because Hershey has consistently made this argument. So even though Hershey's, like the Master's recommendation, recites the Seinfeld standard, whenever they get into the application, they always talk about whether Hershey is actually violating the law. That's not the test.

So on page 2 of their brief below—and I won't give you as many of these—"The issue for the Court"—I'm going to skip over some words—"is whether plaintiff has alleged any credible basis to believe that Hershey is violating any applicable laws, rules or regulations." Not the test.…."LAMPERS fails to supply a credible basis from which the Court may infer any violation of law on the part of Hershey." Not the test.

"The complaint not only fails to supply a credible basis to believe that Hershey's directors or officers allowed any wrongdoing, its allegations and documents it incorporates affirmatively demonstrate the active role that the board takes in the oversight and concern for Hershey's legal compliance." "[A]llowed any wrongdoing." Not the test.…

"What is missing from the complaint is any credible basis to infer that Hershey as opposed to certain cocoa farmers in Ghana and the Ivory Coast or others has violated any federal, state or foreign law or that Hershey officers or directors engaged in any mismanagement." Not the test.

"The complaint, which relies solely on press coverage, the Payson Report and statements by Hershey, does not supply any credible basis to infer that Hershey has violated any law or used any child labor." Not the test.

"Missing from these reports is any allegation that Hershey itself has violated any applicable law or uses child or forced labor." Not the test.

"LAMPERS supplies no credible basis from which to infer any violations of law were committed by Hershey." I think you know what I'm going to say. That was in the briefs before the Master.…

So let's apply the actual test, whether there's a possibility of mismanagement and whether it's conceivable, based on the allegations of the complaint, that there is a possibility of mismanagement, because, recall, we're here on a motion to dismiss.

What that means, I think, is if there are two competing inferences from the allegations in the complaint at this stage, the plaintiff gets the inference. Moreover, the inference that the allegations have to support is not that there is actual wrongdoing, but that there is possible wrongdoing. The point of this lenient standard, I believe, is to drive Section 220 to a prompt merits hearing where the Court can actually make determinations about the sufficiency of the evidence and do the type of balancing that Hershey says is required by the credible basis standard.

Our Chief Justice, while he was Chancellor, has authored several opinions saying that, "Look, motion to dismiss practice in Section 220 actions is really inefficient for precisely these reasons." I think I may have said it a couple times, too. We're not the only ones. This case is a prime example of that. This complaint was filed on November

1, 2012, 16, 17 months ago. As a summary proceeding, this should have gone to a merits hearing in 60 days and been resolved. Instead, we're here still plodding along through motions to dismiss.

In my view, the allegations in the complaint, read in the doubly plaintiff-friendly manner that is required in this procedural posture, support a reasonable inference of possible violations of law in which Hershey may be involved. And those possibilities are sufficient, in the words of our Supreme Court, "to warrant further investigation."

It may, indeed, prove that the documents that Hershey produces show that they are not involved in violations of law at all. That's part of the purpose of a Section 220 investigation, so that a lawyer like Mr. Barry and his client can get the information, evaluate it and say, "You know what. We had suspicions. We had reasonable suspicions, but we were wrong." That's one of the reasons you have Section 220.

So what is the credible basis for wrongdoing? As I've said, the allegations of the complaint support a reasonable inference that Hershey's products contain cocoa and cocoa-derived ingredients that were the result of child labor and human trafficking. There's also a reasonable inference, one possible inference, that the board knows some of its cocoa and cocoa-derived ingredients are sourced from farms that exploit child labor and use trafficked persons.

The laws of Ghana prohibit exploitative child labor and human trafficking. The Children's Act prohibits the use of exploitive child labor, defining children as persons below the age of 18. The Human Trafficking Act prohibits the use of a trafficked person and also includes a duty to inform. One possible inference from the complaint is that Hershey's cocoa sustainability efforts, which admittedly and necessarily put Hershey in contact with farmers in West Africa, results in Hershey knowing of instances involving the use of trafficked children on cocoa farms in Ghana that would have triggered the duty to inform. That is not the only possible inference, but it's one possible inference. And at this procedural stage, I have to credit it.

Hershey has not provided any information about its suppliers. One possible inference — not the only inference, but one possible inference is that Hershey's relationships with its suppliers could support a finding of the use of labor for an aiding and abetting claim. Not the only possible inference, but one possible inference. The laws of the Ivory Coast similarly prohibit exploitative child labor and human trafficking. And courts in the United States, most notably in the recent Doe v. Nestle decision recognized that it is possible for a U.S. corporation to be held liable for aiding and abetting violations of international law, such as the principle, hopefully universally acknowledged, against the use of child labor and human trafficking. Now, as I've already said, Hershey's response has been to argue that plaintiff hasn't proved wrongdoing.

That's not the test. Hershey's has also said that there's no evidence related directly to it, i.e., directly to Hershey's involvement. I think you can draw the inference from Hershey's inability to represent that it currently uses only certified cocoa and its undertaking to do so by 2020. I think you can draw the inference of knowledge from

Hershey's cocoa sustainability efforts, which include its eight "on-the-ground programs" through which Hershey has contact with farmers in West Africa and high-level visits, such as visits by Hershey's chairman.

You can draw the inference from a decision referenced in the complaint by Whole Foods to stop carrying Hershey's Scharffen Berger brand because of Hershey's inability to certify. Again, what you don't need for 220—and certainly not at the motion to dismiss stage—is a report that says Hershey itself has violated this applicable law. It's the possibility, which, as our Delaware Supreme Court said, falls well short of actual wrongdoing.

Comments and Questions

1. To the extent the opinion has an informal feel, that is no mistake. The judge in this case issued the ruling from the bench. The opinion in this case is, therefore, taken from the transcript.

2. What is the "proper purpose" in this case? What is the evidence that provides a "reasonable basis" for this purpose? How might the reasoning in this case be applied to other areas of international human rights or matters of corporate social responsibility?

3. In finding the presence of a credible basis, the court relied on what it viewed as a plausible inferences drawn from the complaint. One inference was that Hershey acquired cocoa that resulted from child labor. But is this enough to establish a credible basis? Doesn't the plaintiff have to provide a credible basis for the assertion that the board knew about the violations? The court found that the complaint gave rise to an inference that the board knew "some of its cocoa and cocoa-derived ingredients are sourced from farms that exploit child labor and use trafficked persons." Based upon the evidence discussed in the opinion, do you agree?

4. The court also found as an inference of wrongdoing that Hershey had "not provided any information about its suppliers." Do you see any problems that might arise from the use of silence as evidence of a credible basis?

5. One commentator has suggested that this case "went beyond the traditional approach taken by Delaware courts". Gabrielle Palmer, Stockholder Inspection Rights and an "Incredible" Basis: Seeking Disclosure Related to Corporate Social Responsibility, 92 Denv. U. L. Rev. Online 125 (April 29, 2015). Does this case suggest that inspection rights will generally be available for shareholders seeking information on human rights activities and other matters of socially responsible behavior?

D. Costs

Shareholders seeking to exercise their inspection rights often have to litigate before receiving the requested documents. This adds considerable cost to the inspection process.

Norman v. US Mobilcomm, Inc.

Delaware Chancery Court

2006 Del. Ch. LEXIS 81 (Apr. 28, 2006)

PARSONS, VICE CHANCELLOR:

Beginning in October 2002 [Jeffrey] Norman [a shareholder] sent USM several requests for books and records. USM produced some information, but Norman found its response to his requests unsatisfactory and filed suit against it under 8 Del C. § 220 on November 16, 2004.

Norman's demand letter seeks to inspect USM's books and records "to determine whether [USM] acted properly in disposing of assets of the Company, whether the Company acted properly in distributing proceeds from sale transactions and otherwise to assess the propriety of management decisions." USM moved to dismiss Norman's complaint on December 20, 2004, asserting that it did not allege mismanagement or facts establishing a credible basis from which the Court could infer the possibility of mismanagement. Instead of filing an opposition to USM's motion to dismiss Norman filed an Amended Complaint pursuant to Court of Chancery Rule 15(aaa).

USM responded by filing another motion to dismiss (the "Second Motion to Dismiss") on February 16, 2005. It again argued that Norman had no basis to support even a suspicion that USM acted improperly. Further, the Second Motion to Dismiss asserted that Norman included unsupported allegations in the Amended Complaint designed to cast aspersions upon David Elkin, USM's president, and that those allegations could not cure the deficiencies of the Demand Letter.

Shortly thereafter USM voluntarily produced approximately 350 pages of documents. Norman considered the production inadequate and sent USM a detailed deficiency letter on March 11, 2005. In that letter Norman claimed to have the following three purposes for inspecting USM's books and records: (1) to investigate mismanagement; (2) to determine whether assets were properly transferred; and (3) to determine whether any distribution or dividends should have been paid given the sales of assets. Norman later sent USM several letters requesting a response to his March 11, 2005 letter. Although no one at USM responded to Norman in writing, they allegedly engaged in telephone conversations about the March 11, 2005 letter and produced an additional 117 pages of documents on April 13, 2005 and 300 pages of documents on May 3, 2005.

After hearing argument, I denied USM's Second Motion to Dismiss on June 17, 2005. Trial was held on August 23, 2005. At the end of trial I did not issue a ruling, but advised the parties that "I'm very much inclined to be granting the 220 relief in pretty broad form."

Thereafter the parties agreed to settle this matter and, on September 30, 2005, entered into a stipulated order and final judgment (the "Order and Judgment"). As a result, USM gave Norman over 4,000 pages of additional documents as well as electronic accounting records and spreadsheet files. Plaintiff subsequently filed the present motion for attorneys' fees and costs, requesting $5,760.38 in costs and attorneys' fees of at least $45,000.00.

II. ANALYSIS

A. Standards

This Court has broad discretion to award attorneys' fees. Normally, however, parties bear their own attorneys' fees pursuant to the American Rule. An exception exists in equity when it appears that a party, or its counsel, has proceeded in bad faith, has acted vexatiously, or has relied on misrepresentations of fact or law in connection with advancing a claim in litigation. There is not a single standard of bad faith that gives rise to an award of attorneys' fees; rather, bad faith turns on the particular facts of each case.

"A subset of this bad faith exception is that attorneys' fees may be awarded if it is shown that the defendant's conduct forced the plaintiff to file suit to secure a clearly defined and established right." "This Court does not invoke the bad faith exception lightly and imposes the stringent evidentiary burden of producing clear evidence of bad faith conduct on the party seeking an award of fees."

B. Costs

The Court of Chancery is authorized under 10 Del. C. § 5106 to "make such order concerning costs in every case as is agreeable to equity." Court of Chancery Rule 54(d) provides:

> Except when express provision therefor is made either in a statute or in [the Court of Chancery Rules], costs shall be allowed as of course to the prevailing party unless the Court otherwise directs. The costs in any action shall not include any charge for the Court's copy of the transcript of the testimony or any depositions.

In this case the parties do not dispute that Norman prevailed in the litigation and USM therefore should pay Norman's costs. Consequently, I will award costs in the requested amount of $5,760.38.

C. Attorneys' Fees

Plaintiff asserts that he should receive attorneys' fees because he had a clear right to certain documents. In particular, Norman contends that USM never challenged his valuation purpose, which is well recognized as a proper purpose, and that due to the sufficiency of his pleadings he also had a clear right to documents to investigate corporate mismanagement and waste. He further asserts that he should receive attorneys' fees because USM acted in bad faith by raising a merits defense to the 220 action and by promising documents which it failed to produce. I will address each of these arguments in turn.

1. The valuation purpose

Norman asserts that he should receive attorneys' fees because USM knew that Norman had a proper valuation purpose for inspecting its books and records and never challenged that purpose. USM responds that it continually challenged all aspects of

Norman's case and that Norman did not state a valuation purpose in his Demand Letter or the Amended Complaint. In particular, USM asserts that Norman's Demand Letter only states that he seeks to inspect USM's books and records dating back to 1997 to determine the propriety of various actions of the Company and management's decisions generally, which implies a purpose of investigating potential waste or mismanagement. Further, USM asserts that Norman did not even raise the issue of obtaining documents for a valuation purpose until he answered USM's Second Motion to Dismiss.

Norman's Demand Letter stated that he sought to inspect USM's books and records to determine whether the Company "acted properly in disposing of assets of the Company, whether the Company acted properly in distributing proceeds from sale transactions and otherwise to assess the propriety of management decisions." As I observed at the argument, I do not believe this statement in the Demand Letter fairly apprised USM that Norman was asserting a valuation purpose.

According to Norman, he also asserted a valuation purpose in his March 11, 2005 deficiency letter. That letter identified three purposes for investigating USM's books and records: (1) to investigate mismanagement; (2) to determine whether assets were properly transferred; and (3) to determine whether any distribution or dividends should have been paid based on the sales of assets. I again question whether this statement reasonably provides notice of a valuation purpose. In any event, Norman contends that USM never responded to this deficiency letter. I disagree.

First, USM asserts that it had telephone conversations with Norman or his representatives regarding the March 11, 2005 deficiency letter. Norman does not appear to contest this statement. Second, and more importantly, USM produced documents to Norman on April 13 and May 3, 2005. In my opinion, therefore, USM's failure to respond formally in writing to the March 11, 2005 letter does not signify bad faith warranting an award of attorneys' fees.

Also both of USM's motions to dismiss contested the sufficiency of Norman's entire case, including any reliance on a valuation purpose. Norman has not shown that USM filed either of these motions in bad faith. Indeed, the fact that Norman amended his complaint after the first motion to dismiss suggests that the motion had at least some merit. The Second Motion to Dismiss challenged the entire 220 action and, at argument on Norman's pending motion, I rejected the contention that the Second Motion to Dismiss was made in bad faith.

Nor has Norman presented clear evidence that any of the actions USM took after I denied its Second Motion to Dismiss constitutes bad faith conduct. In fact, at the pretrial conference I expressed doubt as to which side would win. In particular I stated "at this point, I can't tell which side ... has [ ] the better of this. And it sounds like the most efficient thing we can do is ... go forward." I reaffirmed this position at the beginning of trial. Thus, Norman has not shown that he had a clear right to all the documents he requested based on the alleged valuation purpose or that USM acted in bad faith in opposing his requests. Consequently, I will not award him attorneys' fees on that ground.

2. Norman's purpose to investigate waste and mismanagement

Plaintiff further asserts that he should receive attorneys' fees because he had a clear right to the requested documents to investigate corporate waste and mismanagement. USM disputes that premise.

It is well settled that an investigation of corporate waste and mismanagement is a proper purpose for the inspection of books and records under Section 220. This does not mean, however, that a stockholder who demands books and records for the purpose of investigating corporate waste and mismanagement has a clear right to those documents.

McGowan provides an example of a plaintiff who had a clear right to documents in a Section 220 case. In *McGowan* a director requested the company's books and records. The company promised to produce specific documents on numerous occasions, but failed to do so. In concluding that the director had a clear right, the court noted that a director's rights to inspect books and records are virtually unfettered. There is no requirement that a director make a written demand for inspection. Moreover, if a company refuses a director's request for documents, the company has the burden to prove "that the inspection such director seeks is for an improper purpose."

Norman does not serve as a director of USM; consequently, he had to send a demand letter to USM and had the burden of proving the existence of a proper purpose for his request. Unlike a director, a stockholder, such as Norman, frequently encounters challenges to his purpose for a Section 220 demand. Therefore, I do not consider *McGowan* supportive of Norman's claim for fees.

I also find that USM had a good faith basis for resisting Norman's Section 220 action. The issues presented at trial involved whether Norman had a proper purpose for his requests and whether the scope of those requests was appropriate in the circumstances of this case. Although I ultimately concluded Norman had a proper purpose, I did not reach a firm decision on that issue until after I heard the evidence at trial. In addition, on numerous occasions I expressed concern over the breadth of Norman's requests. At argument on the motion for attorneys' fees I stated that Norman "had incredibly broad requests, probably the broadest I've ever seen, everything since 1997 ... the way it's written, it would cover the sale of a chair, the sale of an old TV, everything." Thus, in my opinion, Norman had not established a clear right to the requested documents for the purpose of determining whether USM engaged in corporate waste or mismanagement until late in the litigation, if at all.

3. Did USM promise to produce documents and fail to do so?

Norman also accuses USM of bad faith for allegedly having promised to produce documents and then failing to do so. Based on those failures, he contends USM should pay his attorneys' fees. USM replies that it never agreed to produce specific documents and did not make any misrepresentations to the Court.

Again, the *McGowan* case provides an example of a court awarding attorneys' fees due to counsel breaking their promise to produce a document. Although the *McGowan* court granted attorneys' fees based in large part on plaintiff's clear right to the documents in question, the opinion also discussed in detail several promises defendant made, and broke, to produce specific documents. In particular, defendant wrote two letters promising to produce the minutes of the company's board meetings to *McGowan*, who served on the company's board of directors. In one letter the defendant's attorney stated, "I acknowledge that I still owe you minutes for 1999 which I will get to you at my earliest convenience this week." Despite that promise the defendant never produced the board minutes. The court held plaintiff "has shown by clear evidence that [defendant] acted in subjective bad faith, both before and after this § 220 action was filed, by falsely promising to produce corporate records that [plaintiff] was clearly entitled to inspect."

In this case not only did Norman not have a clear right from the outset to inspect the USM books and records he requested, but also USM never promised to produce specific documents that it failed to produce. Therefore, *McGowan* is distinguishable. Furthermore, USM produced documents on multiple occasions before trial and I am not aware of any instance in which USM intentionally misrepresented material facts to the Court. Thus, I will not award attorneys' fees on USM's failure to produce documents as quickly or completely as Norman considered necessary.

4. Did USM improperly litigate the merits of the waste and mismanagement allegation?

Finally, Norman claims he is entitled to attorneys' fees because USM engaged in a merits defense to defeat his purpose of investigating suspected waste or mismanagement. Specifically, Norman contends that "despite a prior recognition of the sufficiency of Plaintiff's allegations concerning mismanagement and clear record evidence demonstrating a basis to suspect such mismanagement, the Company nonetheless resisted further production based on its belief that Plaintiff would be defeated at a trial on the merits." USM denies having presented a merits defense to Norman's waste or mismanagement purpose.

This Court has looked with disfavor on a company attempting to litigate the merits of alleged misconduct underlying a claimed purpose for inspecting books and records in a 220 action. In fact, the Court has characterized a company's merits defense to a stockholder's stated purpose as "inequitable and subversive of Section 220." A company engages in a merits defense when it seeks to rebut the plaintiff's allegations as to purpose by arguing that the alleged conduct never occurred or was proper.

Based on my review of the record, I do not believe USM engaged to any material extent in an improper merits defense to any of Norman's claimed purposes for inspecting USM's books and records. Thus, I will not award attorneys' fees on that basis.

Comments and Questions

1. What does this case suggest about the true costs associated with the invocation of inspection rights? What types of shareholders would be willing to incur these costs?

Will the possibility of paying fees act as a deterrent from improper denials of inspection rights?

2. Although designed to be summary proceedings, actions invoking the right to inspect can be anything but summary. A review by Bloomberg BNA of the 206 complaints filed in books and records cases in Delaware in 2013, 2014, and 2015 revealed that 70% of the cases took more than three months to resolve and 20% took more that a year. What impact might this have on the costs of these actions and, as a collateral matter, the willingness of investors to bring the actions in advance of a derivative suit?

3. What reasons did the court give for concluding that USM had a good faith basis for resisting the inspection request? The court noted its own concerns over the breadth of the inspection request. Do these expressions of concern better support the position of Norman or USM?

4. Is the bad faith standard the appropriate standard? What are the problems with the standard? What are the benefits?

5. Assuming that the shareholder obtains the sought after documents and succeeds in showing bad faith (thereby recovering fees), does the company still benefit from the resort to litigation?

6. The Model Act applies a different standard with respect to the recovery of fees. The Act provides that if the shareholders prevail, the court:

> shall also order the corporation to pay the shareholder's costs (including reasonable counsel fees) incurred to obtain the order unless the corporation proves that it refused inspection in good faith because it had a reasonable basis for doubt about the right of the shareholder to inspect the records demanded.

MBCA 16.04(c). The provision, in other words, places the burden on the board. Moreover, the commentary suggests that evidence of good faith will be construed narrowly.

> The corporation must be able to point to some objective basis for its doubt that the shareholder was acting in good faith or had a purpose that was proper. For example, a corporation may point to earlier conduct of the shareholder involving improper use of information obtained from the corporation in the past as indicating that reasonable doubt existed as to his present purpose. A corporation may not avoid the imposition of costs under this section merely by showing it had no information one way or the other about the issues in controversy.

How is this standard different from the one employed in Delaware? Does the distinction make any practical difference?

7. The difficulty in recouping attorneys' fees also potentially adds to the cost of a derivative suit. Delaware courts have all but required shareholders to incur the costs of an inspection as a precondition for a derivative action. *See Seinfeld*, 909 A.2d at

120 ("The rise in books and records litigation is directly attributable to this Court's encouragement of stockholders, who can show a proper purpose, to use the "tools at hand" to obtain the necessary information before filing a derivative action."). What if shareholders choose to forego the expense, file the derivative suit, and only undertake an inspection if the case is dismissed? Some have argued that in these circumstances, shareholders should not be allowed to refile the action. What are the prevailing arguments on each side of that issue? As for the rule in Delaware, the courts addressed the issue in *King v. VeriFone Holdings, Inc.*, 12 A.3d 1140 (Del. 2011).

II. The Federal Disclosure Regime

Overview

In adopting the Securities Act of 1933, Congress was mostly concerned with the primary offering process. Under Section 5 of the Act, companies selling shares to the public were required to file a registration statement with the appropriate regulator (in 1933, that was the Federal Trade Commission, later it was the SEC) absent an applicable exemption. 15 USC § 77e. The document was meant to include all of the information that shareholders would need to make an informed decision at the time of the purchase.

As the legislative history plainly reveals, regulators were not given the authority to approve or disapprove a particular offering, something usually described as merit review. So long as accurate and complete disclosure was made, the offering could go forward. There is an animated discussion in the legislative history to the securities laws about the right of promoters to sell shares in a company that extracted gold from seawater, the rough equivalent back then of alchemy. The sponsor of the legislation responded in the affirmative, indicating that as long as the risks of the business (presumably inevitable failure) were disclosed, the shares could be offered to the public.

The Securities Act, therefore, sets a tone. Those responsible for the securities laws would largely be limited to disclosure, without any right to regulate substantive behavior. Registration statements effectively provided complete disclosure at the time of the offering. The Securities Exchange Act of 1934 sought to put in place the elements needed for an active secondary market, including a system of periodic disclosure by public companies. *See* Section 13(a), 15 USC m(a).

The Commission put in place a disclosure system that centered on quarterly reporting. Public companies were required to file three quarterly reports on a Form 10-Q and an annual report on Form 10-K. Certain material developments that occur between the reports must be filed contemporaneously on a current report on Form 8-K. The system has been characterized as "one of its most important tools for protecting investors and safeguarding the capital markets." In *re Alcohol Sensors Int'l, Ltd.*, Initial Decision Release No. 257 (admin proc Sept. 22, 2004).

The Exchange Act also gave to the SEC responsibility for overseeing the proxy process. The Commission did so primarily (but not exclusively) through the imposition of disclosure requirements. In connection with the annual meeting at which directors will be elected, public companies must distribute a proxy statement and an annual report (a document different from the annual report on Form 10-K) to all shareholders (including beneficial owners). *See* Rule 14a-3, 17 CFR § 240.14a-3. The proxy materials must include the information needed by investors to make an informed decision at the meeting.

Disclosure and Governance

Much of the governance structure of a public company is subject to disclosure. Independent directors must be identified; committees and their functions described; attendance of directors revealed. In connection with the election of directors, the proxy statement includes considerable background information on the nominees for the board. To assess the performance of the incumbent board, the proxy materials also include audited financial statements (typically attached to the annual report). In addition, shareholders are entitled to certain types of information regarding management, including the compensation paid to the top officers.

A. Board Committees

The proxy statement also must disclose information about the governance practices of the board. Specifically, the proxy statement must include substantial disclosure about the committees of the board. Of particular importance is the audit committee.

Item 407(c)(2) of Regulation S-K: Corporate Governance
17 CFR § 229.407(c)(2)

(d) *Audit committee.*

(1) State whether or not the audit committee has a charter. If the audit committee has a charter, provide the disclosure required by Instruction 2 to this Item regarding the audit committee charter.[1]

(2) If a listed issuer's board of directors determines, in accordance with the listing standards applicable to the issuer, to appoint a director to the audit committee who is not independent (apart from the requirements in § 240.10A-3 of this chapter), including as a result of exceptional or limited or similar circumstances, disclose the nature of the relationship that makes that individual not independent and the reasons for the board of directors' determination.

(3)

(i) The audit committee must state whether:

(A) The audit committee has reviewed and discussed the audited financial statements with management;

---

1. Instruction 2 provides that the company must either post the Charter on its Web site or include a copy in an appendix to the proxy/information statement at least once every three years.

(B) The audit committee has discussed with the independent auditors the matters required to be discussed by the statement on Auditing Standards No. 61, as amended (AICPA, *Professional Standards*, Vol. 1. AU section 380), 1 as adopted by the Public Company Accounting Oversight Board in Rule 3200T;

(C) The audit committee has received the written disclosures and the letter from the independent accountant required by applicable requirements of the Public Company Accounting Oversight Board regarding the independent accountant's communications with the audit committee concerning independence, and has discussed with the independent accountant the independent accountant's independence; and

(D) Based on the review and discussions referred to in paragraphs (d)(3)(i)(A) through (d)(3)(i)(C) of this Item, the audit committee recommended to the board of directors that the audited financial statements be included in the company's annual report on Form 10-K (17 CFR 249.310)..., for the last fiscal year for filing with the Commission.

(ii) The name of each member of the company's audit committee (or, in the absence of an audit committee, the board committee performing equivalent functions or the entire board of directors) must appear below the disclosure required by paragraph (d)(3)(i) of this Item.

Standards Relating to Listed Company Audit Committees
Exchange Act Release No. 47654 (Apr. 9, 2003)

Effective oversight of the financial reporting process is fundamental to preserving the integrity of our markets. The board of directors, elected by and accountable to shareholders, is the focal point of the corporate governance system. The audit committee, composed of members of the board of directors, plays a critical role in providing oversight over and serving as a check and balance on a company's financial reporting system. The audit committee provides independent review and oversight of a company's financial reporting processes, internal controls and independent auditors. It provides a forum separate from management in which auditors and other interested parties can candidly discuss concerns. By effectively carrying out its functions and responsibilities, the audit committee helps to ensure that management properly develops and adheres to a sound system of internal controls, that procedures are in place to objectively assess management's practices and internal controls, and that the outside auditors, through their own review, objectively assess the company's financial reporting practices.

* * *

An issuer subject to the proxy rules is currently required to disclose additional information about its audit committee in its proxy statement or information statement, if action is to be taken with respect to the election of directors. First, the audit committee must provide a report disclosing whether the audit committee has reviewed and discussed the audited financial statements with management and discussed certain matters with the independent auditors. Second, issuers must disclose whether the audit committee is governed by a charter, and if so, include a copy of the charter as an appendix to the proxy statement at least once every three years. Finally, the issuer must disclose whether the members of the audit committee are independent....

... If the registrant is a listed issuer, it will still be required to disclose whether the members of its audit committee are independent. The listed issuer must use the definition of independence for audit committee members included in the listing standards applicable to the listed issuer....

Non-listed issuers that have separately designated audit committees will still be required to disclose whether their audit committee members are independent. In determining whether a member is independent, these registrants will be allowed to choose any definition for audit committee member independence of a national securities exchange or national securities association that has been approved by the Commission.

Comments and Questions

1. In addition to the audit committee, Item 407 requires disclosure with respect to the compensation and nominating committees of the board. The provision also requires companies to identify any director who fails to attend 75% of the board and committee meetings (aggregated together). Is attendance information material? What is the likely impact of the disclosure? Shareholders sometimes engage in "vote no" campaigns against directors with poor attendance records.

2. What is the purpose of the disclosure about the audit committee? For example, is the obligation to disclose whether the committee reviewed and discussed the audited financial statements likely to be material to investors? If not, what other purpose might it have?

3. The disclosure requirements in Item 407 should be considered in the context of other requirements governing audit committees of listed companies. Thus, Item 407 merely requires companies to disclose the charter of the audit committee if one has been adopted. The listing standards of the NYSE on the other hand requires that audit committees of listed companies have a charter that addresses among other things oversight of the financial statements and the performance of the independent auditors. *See* NYSE 303A.07. Listing standards for audit committees are influenced by Rule 10A-3, 17 CFR § 240.10A-3. The Rule mandates that the exchanges adopt listing standards that regulate the responsibilities of audit committees. These include the obligation to appoint and dismiss the outside auditor.

4. Can the failure to properly disclose the information required by Item 407 result in a private action under the securities laws? A private right of action does exist in

the antifraud provision contained in the proxy rules. *See* Rule 14a-9, 17 CFR § 240.14a-9. Who would bring the suit and what would be the most significant impediments to any action for violations?

In the Matter of Kiang

Exchange Act Release No. 71824 (Mar. 27, 2014)

II.

In anticipation of the institution of these proceedings, Respondent has submitted an Offer of Settlement (the "Offer") which the Commission has determined to accept. Solely for the purpose of these proceedings and any other proceedings brought by or on behalf of the Commission, or to which the Commission is a party, and without admitting or denying the findings herein, except as to the Commission's jurisdiction over her and the subject matter of these proceedings, which are admitted, Respondent consents to the entry of this Order Instituting Cease-and-Desist Proceedings Pursuant to Section 21C of the Securities Exchange Act of 1934, Making Findings, and Imposing a Cease-and-Desist Order ("Order"), as set forth below.

* * *

2. Beginning in approximately April 2008, L&L did not have a CFO, as its prior CFO had just resigned. L&L, led by Lee, wanted to hire an Acting CFO and, to that end, thought of the purported Acting CFO, who had previously been associated with the company as an accountant from 1997 to 2004, and as a director until 2006.

3. In a July 14, 2008 email to Lee, the purported Acting CFO rejected an offer to become L&L's Acting CFO.

4. Notwithstanding this rejection, L&L falsely represented that the purported Acting CFO was the company's actual Acting CFO in four separate public filings with the Commission, including the company's Form 10-K for fiscal year 2008, and three subsequent Form 10-Qs for fiscal year 2009. Each filing included a Sarbanes-Oxley certification with the purported Acting CFO's digital signature that she had, among other things, attested to the accuracy of the company's financial statements and the appropriateness of the company's disclosure controls and procedures. The purported Acting CFO, however, never performed any such functions.

5. In May 2009, the purported Acting CFO became aware that L&L had falsely represented her as the company's actual Acting CFO in the above-described filings and sent various emails to Lee, demanding an explanation. In a May 19, 2009 email, Lee wrote to the purported Acting CFO that she "did not perform the work of the Acting CFO."

6. On May 21, 2009, the purported Acting CFO emailed Kiang, who was then the Chair of the company's three person Audit Committee and member of the company's Board of Directors. Prior to this email, Kiang had no interaction with the purported Acting CFO with regard to any L&L business. In the email, the purported Acting

CFO told Kiang that she had a "serious and urgent" matter related to L&L's filings that were made without her knowledge and asked her to investigate.

7. Kiang subsequently contacted Lee and asked whether the purported Acting CFO had actually served as the company's Acting CFO, and was informed that the purported Acting CFO had actually served as the company's Acting CFO and was making false allegations in an attempt to obtain money from the company. Kiang contacted no one else, including anyone at the company or the company's external auditors, to investigate whether the purported Acting CFO had actually served as the company's Acting CFO.

8. On June 4, 2009—after receiving no response from Kiang—the purported Acting CFO emailed her again. The purported Acting CFO asked whether Kiang had investigated the allegations that she had not actually served as the company's Acting CFO, and in the email, included her July 14, 2008 email in which she rejected the offer to be L&L's Acting CFO.

9. After receiving the email, Kiang asked Lee for an explanation. Lee told Kiang that the purported Acting CFO had not actually served as the company's Acting CFO; that he had used the purported Acting CFO's name on L&L's public filings without the purported Acting CFO's permission; told Kiang not to worry about it because it was in the past2; told Kiang to not tell anyone about the purported Acting CFO, including the company's Board of Directors or the public; and that, if she shared this information with anyone, L&L's reputation would be affected negatively and its stock price would drop.

10. On August 12, 2009, L&L filed its 2009 Form 10-K, which contained a false Sarbanes-Oxley certification that—based on Lee's and the other certifying officer's most recent evaluation of the company's internal control over financial reporting—any fraud, whether or not material, involving management had been disclosed to the company's auditors and to the company's Audit Committee. Kiang signed L&L's 2009 Form 10-K as Audit Committee Chair and a Director, when she knew or should have known that any fraud, whether or not material, involving management had not been disclosed to the company's auditors and the company's Audit Committee.

Violation

11. Under Section 21C of the Exchange Act, the Commission may impose a cease and-desist order upon, among others, any person that is, was, or would be a cause of the violation, due to an act or omission the person knew or should have known would contribute to such violation of any provision of the Exchange Act.

12. Section 13(a) of the Exchange Act requires issuers that have securities registered pursuant to Section 12 of the Exchange Act to file such periodic and other reports as the Commission may prescribe and in conformity with such rules as the Commission may promulgate. Exchange Act Rule 13a-1 requires the filing of annual reports. In addition to the information expressly required to be included in such reports, Rule 12b-20 under the Exchange Act requires issuers to add such further material information, if any, as may be necessary to make the required statements, in the light of

the circumstances under which they are made, not misleading. "The reporting provisions of the Exchange Act are clear and unequivocal, and they are satisfied only by the filing of complete, accurate, and timely reports." *SEC v. Savoy Industries*, 587 F.2d 1149, 1165 (D.C. Cir. 1978) (citing *SEC v. IMC Int'l, Inc.*, 384 F. Supp. 889, 893 (N.D. Tex. 1974)). A violation of the reporting provisions is established if a report is shown to contain materially false or misleading information. *SEC v. Kalvex, Inc.*, 425 F. Supp. 310, 316 (S.D.N.Y. 1975).

13. L&L violated Exchange Act Section 13(a) and Rules 12b-20 and 13a-1 thereunder by filing an annual report—the 2009 Form 10-K—that included a false Sarbanes-Oxley certification that—based on the CEO's and the other certifying officer's most recent evaluation of the company's internal control over financial reporting—any fraud, whether or not material, involving management had been disclosed to the company's auditors and the company's Audit Committee.

14. By engaging in the conduct described above, Kiang caused L&L's violations of Exchange Act Section 13(a) and Rules 12b-20 and 13a-1 thereunder.

IV.

In view of the foregoing, the Commission deems it appropriate to impose the sanctions agreed to in the Respondent's Offer.

Accordingly, pursuant to Section 21C of the Exchange Act, it is hereby ORDERED that:

A. Respondent Kiang cease and desist from committing or causing any violations and any future violations of Exchange Act Section 13(a) and Rules 12b-20 and 13a-1 promulgated thereunder.

B. To effect compliance with the above-referenced provision and rules of the Exchange Act, Kiang permanently refrain from signing any Commission public filing that contains any certification required pursuant to the Sarbanes-Oxley Act of 2002.

By the Commission.

Comments and Questions

1. As is typical of a settled administrative proceeding, the respondent in the case did not admit or deny the findings. Why might that be the case? Do you think it is good policy to accept settlements without factual admissions?

2. Isn't a violation of a director's duties generally a matter of state law? What gave the SEC authority to bring an action in this case? What advice might you give a board in the aftermath of this decision?

3. Would the chair have known about the violation had she not participated on that audit committee? What does this suggest about the risk of liability for those serving on the audit committee?

4. Is there anything the SEC can do to reduce this risk of liability for those serving on the audit committee? For directors designated as a "financial expert," the SEC has stated that such a designation "does not impose on such persons any duties, obligations

or liability that are greater than the duties, obligations and liability imposed on such person as a member of the audit committee and board of directors in the absence of such designation and identification." Item 407(d)(5)(ii) of Regulation S-K. What affect might this language have on liability?

5. Why did the director in this case sign the annual report on Form 10-K? For those required to sign the form, see General Instruction D to Form 10-K. What role did the execution of the form play in the imposition of liability?

B. Board Diversity

Item 407 requires other types of disclosure about board structure. Disclosure also must address issues relating to board diversity.

Item 407 of Regulation S-K: Corporate Governance
17 CFR § 229.407

(vi) Describe the nominating committee's process for identifying and evaluating nominees for director, including nominees recommended by security holders, and any differences in the manner in which the nominating committee evaluates nominees for director based on whether the nominee is recommended by a security holder, and whether, and if so how, the nominating committee (or the board) considers diversity in identifying nominees for director. If the nominating committee (or the board) has a policy with regard to the consideration of diversity in identifying director nominees, describe how this policy is implemented, as well as how the nominating committee (or the board) assesses the effectiveness of its policy....

Proxy Disclosure Enhancements
Exchange Act Release No. 61175 (Dec. 16, 2009)

B. Enhanced Director and Nominee Disclosure

We proposed to amend Item 401 of Regulation S-K to expand the disclosure requirements regarding the qualifications of directors and nominees, past directorships held by directors and nominees, and the time period for disclosure of legal proceedings involving directors, nominees and executive officers. We are adopting the changes generally as proposed, but have made revisions in response to comments.

* * *

In the Proposing Release, we also requested comment on whether we should amend our rules to require disclosure of additional factors considered by a nominating committee when selecting someone for a board position, such as board diversity. A significant number of commenters responded that disclosure about board diversity was important information to investors. Many of these commenters believed that requiring this disclosure would provide investors with information on corporate culture and governance practices that would enable investors to make more informed voting and investment decisions. Commenters also noted that there appears to be a meaningful relationship between diverse boards and improved corporate financial performance, and that diverse boards can help companies more effectively recruit talent and retain staff. We agree that it is useful for investors to understand how the board considers and addresses diversity, as well as the board's assessment of the implementation of its diversity policy, if any. Consequently, we are adopting amendments to Item 407(c) of Regulation S-K to require disclosure of whether, and if so how, a nominating committee considers diversity in identifying nominees for director. In addition, if the nominating committee (or the board) has a policy with regard to the consideration of diversity in identifying director nominees, disclosure would be required of how this policy is implemented, as well as how the nominating committee (or the board) assesses the effectiveness of its policy. We recognize that companies may define diversity in various ways, reflecting different perspectives. For instance, some companies may conceptualize diversity expansively to include differences of viewpoint, professional experience, education, skill and other individual qualities and attributes that contribute to board heterogeneity, while others may focus on diversity concepts such as race, gender and national origin. We believe that for purposes of this disclosure requirement, companies should be allowed to define diversity in ways that they consider appropriate. As a result we have not defined diversity in the amendments.

Comments and Questions

1. With respect to diversity, what impact might these disclosure practices have on corporate governance practices? Why might companies change their practices as a result of these disclosure requirements? *See* Speech by Commissioner Luis A. Aguilar, Diversity in the Boardroom Is Important and, Unfortunately, Still Rare, SAIS Center for Transatlantic Relations, Sept. 16, 2010 ("While the SEC's new rule focuses only on disclosure, an indirect effect of putting a focus on a board's diversity is that boards may decide to add, or add more, minorities and women as directors. It is reasonable to expect that the process of focusing on their diversity policy and its effectiveness could likely result in greater diversity.").

2. What is the risk that this type of disclosure will become boilerplate, with no real substance? A year after the adoption of the requirements for disclosure on diversity, Commissioner Aguilar noted that "there is a great deal of room for improvement." What needs to happen for this to be avoided?

3. What are alternatives to using disclosure to encourage reform in this area? Norway adopted a law that requires boards to consist of at least 40% of each gender. What do you make of this approach?

4. While the approach in Norway may not be something readily transferable to the United States, there have been other places where Congress has gone beyond disclosure in the regulation of board practices. In SOX, Congress banned loans by the company to executive officers and directors. What was the governance concern that led to this provision? Was a categorical approach the right way to handle the problem? To the extent that a company cannot lend the CEO the money needed for a mortgage, for example, can it simply buy the house and give it to the CEO?

5. Is there a point at which shareholders (and the market) are receiving too much information? Some have referred to this as "information overload." Troy A. Paredes, *Blinded by the Light: Information Overload and Its Consequences for Securities Regulation*, 81 Wash. U. L.Q. 417, 419 (2003). What are the consequences of information overload?

C. Disclosure and Substantive Behavior

Disclosure requirements arguably go beyond the goal of providing shareholders with information necessary to make informed voting decisions. Instead, the disclosure requirements are intended to encourage companies to improve their governance practices. Item 5.02 of Form 8-K specifically deals with the departure of officers and directors. For the most part, companies must disclose the departure of directors and certain key officers. 17 CFR § 229.5.02(b). It is enough to identify the individual and the date of the departure.

Item 5.02, however, requires more fulsome disclosure where a director departs as a result of a "disagreement" with the company over "any matter relating to ... operations, policies or practices". 17 CFR § 229.5.02(a). In these circumstances, however, the resulting disclosure must be more fulsome and intrusive. The Form 8-K must reveal "a brief description of the circumstances representing the disagreement" and include "any written correspondence" received from the director concerning the departure. This difference in the disclosure obligation can require the company to air some uncomfortable information.

In re Hewlett-Packard Co.

Exchange Act Release No. 55801 (admin. proc. May 23, 2007)

A. Summary

1. This matter involves Hewlett-Packard's failure to disclose the circumstances surrounding a board member's resignation amidst the company's controversial investigation into boardroom leaks. On May 18, 2006, HP's Board of Directors learned the findings of the company's leak investigation and voted to request the resignation of a director believed to have violated HP's policies by providing confidential information to the press. Silicon Valley venture capitalist and fellow director Thomas Perkins (not the source of the leak) voiced his strong objections to the handling of the matter, announced his resignation, and walked out of the Board meeting. Contrary to the reporting requirements of the federal securities laws, HP failed to disclose to investors the circumstances of Mr. Perkins' disagreement with the company.

B. Respondent

2. Hewlett-Packard is a Delaware corporation headquartered in Palo Alto, California. HP sells computers, computer equipment, and support services. HP's common stock is registered with the Commission pursuant to Section 12(b) of the Exchange Act and is listed on the New York Stock Exchange under the stock symbol "HPQ."

C. Facts

Legal Background

3. Under the Exchange Act, a public company must file with the Commission a report on Form 8-K when a director resigns from the board. If a director has resigned because of a disagreement with the company, known to an executive officer, on any matter relating to the company's operations, policies, or practices, the company must, among other things, disclose a brief description of the circumstances of the disagreement. In addition, the company must give the director the opportunity to timely review and respond to the company's disclosure about the director's resignation, and the company is required to file any letter written by the director to the company in response to the company's disclosure. Absent such a disagreement, the company must report the resignation, but need not provide the reasons.

HP's Leak Investigation

4. In or around January 2006, in response to apparent unauthorized disclosures of confidential information about HP Board meetings to the press, HP initiated an investigation to determine the source of the leaks. HP Board member Thomas Perkins, Chairman of the Board's Nominating and Governance Committee (which was responsible for, among other things, establishing board member qualifications and evaluating board operations), was generally informed of the inquiry. Mr. Perkins believed that he and HP's Chairman had agreed that, upon completion of the investigation, they would approach any individual implicated privately, obtain an assurance that it would not happen again, and inform the full Board that the matter had been resolved without identifying the source of the leak.

5. By April 2006, HP investigators tentatively concluded that a long-standing HP director had leaked information in connection with a January 23, 2006 press article. After consulting with HP's Chief Executive Officer, General Counsel, outside counsel, and Chairman of the Audit Committee, the Chairman of the Board determined that the leak investigation findings should be presented to the full Board.

Mr. Perkins Resigns During the May 18, 2006 Board Meeting

6. HP's Board of Directors met beginning at 12:30 p.m. on May 18, 2006 at HP's headquarters in Palo Alto, California. All but one of the directors attended, including the CEO (who is a director), as did the company's General Counsel (acting as the Board secretary).

7. At the start of the meeting, the head of HP's Audit Committee discussed the leak investigation and its findings. After some discussion, the identity of the director who provided information for the January 2006 article was revealed. The director addressed the Board, explained his actions, and left the room to permit additional deliberations. The Board discussed HP's policy on unauthorized public disclosures, and considered measures that could be taken in response to the director's actions, including asking him to resign.

8. During the course of the Board's deliberations, which lasted approximately 90 minutes, Mr. Perkins voiced his strong objections to the manner in which the matter

was being handled. Among other things, he repeatedly told the Board that the source of the leak should have been approached "off-line" for an explanation and a warning, rather than identified to the whole Board. He affirmed his belief that the matter should have been handled confidentially by the Chairman of the Board and himself as Chairman of the Nominating and Governance Committee. He also questioned the wisdom of requesting the director to resign over what he perceived to be a relatively minor offense, noting that the director had made significant contributions to HP.

9. After a lengthy and heated discussion, the Board, by a secret written ballot, passed a motion to ask the director to resign from the Board. When HP's General Counsel announced the results of the vote on whether to ask the director to resign, Mr. Perkins continued to voice disagreement. As noted in the Board minutes, Mr. Perkins "restated his strong objections to the process, specifically [the Chairman's] decision to bring the matter to the full Board and the manner in which the meeting was conducted." Mr. Perkins then resigned from the Board and departed the meeting at approximately 2:00 p.m. The director identified by the leak investigation was asked to resign following the vote, but declined to resign at that time.

HP Fails to Disclose the Reasons for Mr. Perkins' Resignation

10. HP executives understood that, in the event a director resigned over a disagreement with the company on a matter relating to its operations, policies, or practices, the company would need to report to the Commission (and thereby disclose to investors) the circumstances of the disagreement.

11. On May 22, 2006, HP filed a report on Form 8-K, pursuant to Item 5.02(b), reporting Mr. Perkins' resignation, but did not comply with Item 5.02(a) by failing to disclose that there had been a disagreement with the company. HP also filed with the Form 8-K a May 19 press release, which announced that Mr. Perkins had resigned without disclosing the circumstances of his disagreement.

12. HP concluded, with the advice of outside legal counsel and the General Counsel, that it need not disclose the reasons for Mr. Perkins' resignation because he merely had a disagreement with the company's Chairman, and not a disagreement with the company on a matter relating to its operations, policies, or practices. Contrary to HP's conclusion, the disagreement and the reasons for Mr. Perkins' resignation should have been disclosed, pursuant to Item 5.02(a), in the May 22 Form 8-K. Mr. Perkins resigned as a result of a disagreement with HP on the following matters: (1) the decision to present the leak investigation findings to the full Board; and (2) the decision by majority vote of the Board of Directors to ask the director identified in the leak investigation to resign. Mr. Perkins' disagreement related to important corporate governance matters and HP policies regarding handling sensitive information, and thus constituted a disagreement over HP's operations, policies or practices.

13. HP did not disclose further information relating to Mr. Perkins' resignation until September 6, 2006, after Mr. Perkins (and the staff of the Securities and Exchange Commission) had begun to raise questions about the adequacy of the company's disclosures.

D. Violations

14. Section 13(a) of the Exchange Act and Rule 13a-11 promulgated thereunder require issuers of securities registered pursuant to Section 12 of the Exchange Act to file with the Commission current reports on Form 8-K upon the occurrence of certain events, including the departure of directors or principal officers. Item 5.02(a) of Form 8-K specifies that if a director has resigned because of a disagreement with the registrant, known to an executive officer of the registrant, on any matter relating to the registrant's operations, policies, or practices, the registrant must, among other things, disclose a brief description of the circumstances representing the disagreement that the registrant believes caused, in whole or in part, the director's resignation. In addition, the registrant must provide the resigning director with a copy of the disclosure no later than the day the company files the disclosure with the Commission. Also, the registrant must provide the director with the opportunity to furnish a response letter stating whether the director agrees with the disclosure in the registrant's Form 8-K. In the event that the registrant receives a response letter from the former director, the letter must be filed by the registrant as an amendment to its Form 8-K within two business days of its receipt. No showing of scienter is required to establish a violation of Section 13(a) of the Exchange Act. SEC v. Savoy, 587 F.2d 1149, 1167 (D.C. Cir. 1978).

15. On May 18, 2006, director Thomas Perkins resigned because of a disagreement with HP regarding the decision to present the leak investigation findings to the full Board and the decision by the Board to ask the director identified in the leak investigation to resign. The disagreement was known to HP executive officers. Mr. Perkins' disagreement with HP related to the operations, policies, or practices of HP. Consequently, HP was required by Item 5.02(a) of Form 8-K to disclose a brief description of the circumstances representing the disagreement, and was required to provide Mr. Perkins with a copy of this disclosure no later than the day of filing. By disclosing the resignation of Mr. Perkins pursuant to Item 5.02(b) in a Form 8-K filed on May 22, 2006, HP failed to disclose the circumstances of Mr. Perkins' disagreement with HP and also failed to provide the director with a copy of such a filing. As a result, HP violated Section 13(a) of the Exchange Act and Rule 13a-11 thereunder.

IV.

In view of the foregoing, the Commission deems it appropriate to impose the sanctions agreed to in Respondent HP's Offer.

Accordingly, it is hereby ORDERED that Respondent HP cease and desist from committing or causing any violations and any future violations of Section 13(a) of the Exchange Act and Rule 13a-11 thereunder.

By the Commission.

Comments and Questions

1. Many of the developments that trigger disclosure on a current report implicate corporate governance issues. They include any amendments to the articles, bylaws or code of ethics, *see* Item 5.03 & 5.04 of Form 8-K, and the results of any action

taken by shareholders at annual or special meetings. *See* Item 5.07 of Form 8-K. What is the benefit of this disclosure and why must it be given out on an accelerated basis in a current report?

2. As a practical matter, what additional leverage does Item 5.02 afford the dissenting director? Do you think this was an intended purpose of the disclosure requirement? When would disagreements in the board room that result in resignation most likely arise?

3. If the HP board could go back and do it again, do you think it would have so readily accepted Perkin's resignation, given what followed? To prevent him from resigning, what might the directors have done?

4. A current report also must also be filed upon the resignation/removal of a CEO or CFO. *See* Item 5.02(b) of Form 8-K. In those circumstances, companies need not air disagreements but are only required to disclose the event and the date it occurred. Why are these transactions treated differently from director resignations?

J. Robert Brown, Jr., *Corporate Governance, the Securities and Exchange Commission and the Limits of Disclosure*
57 Cath. U. L. Rev. 45, 45–48, 62–65, 71–73 (2007)[2]

States regulate the substance of corporate governance. Fiduciary duties, director qualifications, and the rights of shareholders all emanate from state law. Regulation of disclosure, on the other hand, falls to the Securities and Exchange Commission (SEC or the Commission), at least for public companies. It is the Commission that ensures investors and shareholders have the information necessary to make informed decisions.

This neat dichotomy has been long accepted but little examined. In fact, it is not a particularly accurate description. In the public company arena, disclosure means little, absent adequate governance. No matter how many accounting standards are implemented, enforcement proceedings brought, or items added to Regulation S-K, the quality of disclosure hinges on management's commitment to, and involvement in, the process.

The division of authority did not arise from a comprehensive analysis of the optimal method of promoting governance or a deliberate decision to keep the Commission out of the substance of corporate governance, but rather as a consequence of path dependence. When Congress adopted the Securities Exchange Act in 1934, the central issue of corporate governance was the absence of adequate disclosure. Management took advantage of secrecy to self perpetuate, pay excessive salaries, and engage in other abusive practices. With such secrecy, the substantive corporate governance standards mattered far less.

Congress sought to fix the corporate governance process by addressing the deficiencies this secrecy created. The disinfectant effect of disclosure had a corresponding

---

2. Copyright © 2007 Catholic University Law Review. Reprinted by permission.

impact on the substantive standards, but not the one expected. The pressure of self interest did not abate; it merely lost the protection of secrecy. Instead, pressure built on states to loosen substantive standards. Over time, the duty of care evolved into little more than a wooden process, and the duty of loyalty into a standard largely unmoored from fairness.

At the same time, the disclosure regime implemented by the Commission itself impacted the substance of corporate governance....

With the link between disclosure and substance increasingly clear, the Commission embarked on an effort to regulate substance using a variety of mechanisms, including disclosure. In the 1970s, Congress provided increased authority to regulate the internal process of assembling financial statements. Efforts were also made to influence governance through the imposition of listing standards, an avenue largely foreclosed by the courts. Enforcement proceedings and regulatory admonitions were other avenues employed by the Commission.

* * *

Other disclosure requirements sought to improve the governance process by increasing the leverage of dissenting directors. Companies were made to disclose any disagreement that resulted in a director resigning or deciding not to stand for re-election. This information was ostensibly designed to assist shareholders in assessing the "quality of management." More to the point, the information "could enhance the effectiveness of directors by assuring them a forum in which to express differences of opinion on matters that are sufficiently serious to result in termination of the director's association with the issuer."

In other words, the provision gave the dissenting director leverage. Any resignation over a disagreement would result in public disclosure of the underlying conflict, potentially generating bad publicity and inviting legal scrutiny. This threat, therefore, provided the dissenting director additional bargaining power in connection with any disagreement at the board level.

The structure of the provision made clear that it was designed to provide leverage rather than material information to investors. As originally adopted, the rules gave the resigning director sole discretion to determine whether disclosure of the disagreement should occur. Thus, disclosure depended not upon its importance to investors or shareholders but upon the predilections of the departing director. Only in 2004 did the Commission finally eliminate this discretion and impose an affirmative duty to disclose a disagreement, irrespective of the wishes of the resigning director.

The impact of the provision is hard to assess since it sought to use the threat of disclosure to encourage resolution of differences at the board level. The potential impact on governance, however, has always been limited. The provision applies only to conflicts at the board level. It does nothing to ensure that the board has any particular information about the activities of the company, or that conflicts or problems are addressed at the board level in the first instance.

C. Disclosure and Attendance

Other efforts focused more generally on altering board behavior. Board involvement in the disclosure process meant little if directors did not participate in the governance process by attending the meetings. State law, however, imposed no specific obligations on director attendance. In response, the Commission adopted rules requiring disclosure of any director who attended fewer than seventy-five percent of the combined total of board and committee meetings. The Commission noted that this information would assist shareholders in evaluating the director's performance.

In fact, the disclosure requirement was designed to affect director behavior. Directors would presumably attend meetings more often rather than confront the embarrassment associated with poor attendance. This requirement may or may not have increased attendance, but in any case it did little to affect the actual process of deliberations within the boardroom, a matter determined under state law. Nor did the requirement ensure that directors take greater ownership of corporate disclosure issues or engage in more protracted deliberations on matters of concern to shareholders.

* * *

With respect to the nomination of directors, the proxy statement must disclose the *method* used to identify and evaluate director nominees. This includes identifying the source of the nominee by category, with the categories encompassing "security holder, non-management director, chief executive officer, other executive officer, third-party search firm, or other, specified source" and the function of any firm hired to "identify or evaluate" potential nominees.

The disclosure extends to shareholder nominees. The company must reveal any policies regarding the consideration of these nominees, including the procedures for submission. The company must disclose any minimum qualifications, including any specific qualities or skills deemed necessary by the committee, and to the extent a nominee comes from a shareholder with more than five percent of the voting stock, the company should identify the shareholder (or group of shareholders), the nominee, and the board's decision with respect to the nomination. The company is not, however, required to disclose the reasons for rejecting a nominee.

The disclosure of the process used to identify nominees was ostensibly designed to increase transparency. In fact, the approach was meant to encourage consideration of shareholder nominees and reveal the role of the CEO in the process. Neither is likely to result from the disclosure requirements. Nothing in the disclosure process requires substantive consideration of shareholder nominees or prevents the nomination committee from seeking opinions from the CEO with respect to a nominee.

Comments and Questions

1. What do you think of this approach to regulation? Should the SEC use disclosure to alter the substantive behavior of officers and directors? Does this approach even work? What are the limits of using disclosure to affect governance practices?

2. The Commission's express regulatory mission includes ensuring complete disclosure for investors and shareholders. What role does corporate governance have in ensuring this goal?

3. What does this approach to regulation suggest about the tension between state and federal law in the corporate governance area? In the corporate governance area, does it make sense to have different regulators determining governance standards and fiduciary duty standards? Is it possible to have adequate disclosure if fiduciary duty standards are weak?

4. The Commission could simply be given the authority to regulate substantive practices of the board directly. Increasingly that seems to be the approach used by Congress. In the Sarbanes-Oxley Act, the SEC was given substantive authority to regulate audit committees. In the Dodd-Frank Act, the SEC received the substantive authority to regulate compensation committees of the board and to require public companies to provide an advisory vote on executive compensation (say on pay). What might explain this drift away from disclosure in favor of substantive regulation? Does this mean that the Commission no longer has to use disclosure to affect substantive behavior?

III. Disclosure and Management Integrity

Companies may also need to disclose information that relates to the integrity of management. Some of the disclosure is express. Item 401 of Regulation S-K requires the disclosure of a director's age, business experience and involvement in certain legal proceedings such as the filing of a petition for bankruptcy or conviction in a criminal proceeding. 17 C.F.R. 229.401. The background information may be relevant to shareholders in deciding whether to elect the director to the board.

Beyond the express disclosure requirements, however, companies also need to provide shareholders and investors with any other information about the directors that is needed by shareholders in making an informed voting or investment decision. This comes under the general rubric of completeness, an obligation imposed mostly under the rules that prohibit fraud. *See* Rules 10b-5 and 14a-9, 17 CFR § 240.10b-5 &.14a-9. The information must be material and must have "caused" any injury. Both requirements have resulted in a number of interpretive issues. Both impose a state of mind requirement. Rule 14a-9 requires a finding of negligence; Rule 10b-5 a finding of scienter. In other words, innocent and immaterial misstatements are not actionable.

One of the more difficult legal issues related to issues of managerial integrity concern the materiality of any misstatement or omission. Inaccurate statements about an officer's educational background or the failure to reveal a serious health condition may provide insight into the relevant official but will not necessarily affect an investment decision.

Materiality, as the next two cases illustrate, requires a highly fact intensive analysis.

TSC Industries, Inc. v. Northway, Inc.

United States Supreme Court
426 U.S. 438 (1976)

MARSHALL, JUSTICE:

* * *

The question of materiality, it is universally agreed, is an objective one, involving the significance of an omitted or misrepresented fact to a reasonable investor. Variations in the formulation of a general test of materiality occur in the articulation of just how significant a fact must be or, put another way, how certain it must be that the fact would affect a reasonable investor's judgment.

* * *

The general standard of materiality that we think best comports with the policies of Rule 14a-9 is as follows: An omitted fact is material if there is a substantial likelihood that a reasonable shareholder would consider it important in deciding how to vote. This standard is fully consistent with *Mills'* general description of materiality as a requirement that "the defect have a significant *propensity* to affect the voting process." It does not require proof of a substantial likelihood that disclosure of the omitted fact would have caused the reasonable investor to change his vote. What the standard does contemplate is a showing of a substantial likelihood that, under all the circumstances, the omitted fact would have assumed actual significance in the deliberations of the reasonable shareholder. Put another way, there must be a substantial likelihood that the disclosure of the omitted fact would have been viewed by the reasonable investor as having significantly altered the "total mix" of information made available.

Comments and Questions

1. What do you make of the test in *Northway*? How difficult is it to apply? The court emphasized that materiality depends upon the "total mix" of available information. What exactly does that mean?

2. How might this test be applied to issues of management integrity? What if a company misstates the educational background of its CEO? Does *Northway* provide an answer to the materiality of that type of information?

3. Could a "glowing description of the Company's environmental spirit, performance, and sense of responsibility" be considered material and actionable if inaccurate? According to at least one court it can. *See United Paperworkers Int'l Union v. International Paper*, 985 F.2d 1190, 1198 (2d Cir. 1993).

4. *Northway* defines materiality in the proxy context. The same definition has been extended to other provisions in the securities laws. *See Basic Inc. v. Levinson*, 485 US 224 (1988) (applying *Northway* definition to actions for securities fraud under Rule 10b-5). Nonetheless, that does not mean the same information is always material,

irrespective of the context. What is an example of information that might not be material to investors but would be to shareholders voting to elect directors?

5. *Northway* relies on the concept of a "total mix" of information. How does this concept work in practice? Does the information about managerial integrity have to actually appear in the proxy solicitation materials?

6. The proxy rules dictate the disclosure of certain types of information about management. These rules, however, are viewed as a "minimum." Companies must include any other material information necessary to make the proxy materials accurate and complete. In the governance area, this can trigger some unusual disclosure issues. In 2009, Steven Jobs, the CEO of Apple, announced that he had health problems and would be taking a medical leave of absence. Once Jobs voluntarily disclosed the information, did this create an obligation to disclose all material information about his health to the market?

7. What is the downside of this test? The court noted in the opinion that some information was "of such dubious significance that insistence on its disclosure may accomplish more harm than good." Is it clear that this test avoids that result?

———————

The total mix standard requires an analysis of all other available information known to the market. Seemingly important information could be rendered immaterial depending upon what the market already knows. Mostly, though, the issue comes up in the context of seemingly unimportant information treated as material once the context has been examined.

Matrixx Initiatives, Inc. v. Siracusano

United States Supreme Court
563 U.S. 27 (2011)

SOTOMAYOR, JUSTICE:

This case presents the question whether a plaintiff can state a claim for securities fraud under § 10(b) of the Securities Exchange Act of 1934, 48 Stat. 891, as amended, 15 U.S.C. § 78j(b), and Securities and Exchange Commission (SEC) Rule 10b-5, 17 CFR § 240.10b-5 (2010), based on a pharmaceutical company's failure to disclose reports of adverse events associated with a product if the reports do not disclose a statistically significant number of adverse events....

A

Through a wholly owned subsidiary, Matrixx develops, manufactures, and markets over-the-counter pharmaceutical products. Its core brand of products is called Zicam. All of the products sold under the name Zicam are used to treat the common cold and associated symptoms. At the time of the events in question, one of Matrixx's products was Zicam Cold Remedy, which came in several forms including nasal spray and gel. The active ingredient in Zicam Cold Remedy was zinc gluconate. Respondents allege that Zicam Cold Remedy accounted for approximately 70 percent of Matrixx's sales.

Respondents initiated this securities fraud class action against Matrixx on behalf of individuals who purchased Matrixx securities between October 22, 2003, and February 6, 2004. The action principally arises out of statements that Matrixx made during the class period relating to revenues and product safety. Respondents claim that Matrixx's statements were misleading in light of reports that Matrixx had received, but did not disclose, about consumers who had lost their sense of smell (a condition called anosmia) after using Zicam Cold Remedy.

* * *

II

Section 10(b) of the Securities Exchange Act makes it unlawful for any person to "use or employ, in connection with the purchase or sale of any security ... any manipulative or deceptive device or contrivance in contravention of such rules and regulations as the Commission may prescribe as necessary or appropriate in the public interest or for the protection of investors." 15 U.S.C. § 78j(b). SEC Rule 10b-5 implements this provision by making it unlawful to, among other things, "make any untrue statement of a material fact or to omit to state a material fact necessary in order to make the statements made, in the light of the circumstances under which they were made, not misleading." 17 CFR § 240.10b-5(b). We have implied a private cause of action from the text and purpose of § 10(b). See Tellabs, Inc. v. Makor Issues & Rights, Ltd., 551 U.S. 308, 318, 127 S. Ct. 2499, 168 L. Ed. 2d 179 (2007).

To prevail on their claim that Matrixx made material misrepresentations or omissions in violation of § 10(b) and Rule 10b-5, respondents must prove "(1) a material misrepresentation or omission by the defendant; (2) scienter; (3) a connection between the misrepresentation or omission and the purchase or sale of a security; (4) reliance upon the misrepresentation or omission; (5) economic loss; and (6) loss causation." Stoneridge Investment Partners, LLC v. Scientific-Atlanta, Inc., 552 U.S. 148, 157, 128 S. Ct. 761, 169 L. Ed. 2d 627 (2008). Matrixx contends that respondents have failed to plead both the element of a material misrepresentation or omission and the element of scienter because they have not alleged that the reports received by Matrixx reflected statistically significant evidence that Zicam caused anosmia. We disagree.

A

We first consider Matrixx's argument that "adverse event reports that do not reveal a statistically significant increased risk of adverse events from product use are not material information." Brief for Petitioners 17 (capitalization omitted).

1

To prevail on a § 10(b) claim, a plaintiff must show that the defendant made a statement that was "misleading as to a material fact." Basic, 485 U.S., at 238, 108 S. Ct. 978, 99 L. Ed. 2d 194. In Basic, we held that this materiality requirement is satisfied when there is " 'a substantial likelihood that the disclosure of the omitted fact would have been viewed by the reasonable investor as having significantly altered the "total mix" of information made available.' " Id., at 231–232, 108 S. Ct.

978, 99 L. Ed. 2d 194 (quoting TSC Industries, Inc. v. Northway, Inc., 426 U.S. 438, 449, 96 S. Ct. 2126, 48 L. Ed. 2d 757 (1976)). We were "careful not to set too low a standard of materiality," for fear that management would "'bury the share-holders in an avalanche of trivial information.'" 485 U.S., at 231, 108 S. Ct. 978, 99 L. Ed. 2d 194 (quoting TSC Industries, 426 U.S., at 448–449, 96 S. Ct. 2126, 48 L. Ed. 2d 757).

Basic involved a claim that the defendant had made misleading statements deny-ing that it was engaged in merger negotiations when it was, in fact, conducting preliminary negotiations. See 485 U.S., at 227–229, 108 S. Ct. 978, 99 L. Ed. 2d 194. The defendant urged a bright-line rule that preliminary merger negotiations are material only once the parties to the negotiations reach an agreement in principle. Id., at 232–233, 108 S. Ct. 978, 99 L. Ed. 2d 194. We observed that "[a]ny approach that designates a single fact or occurrence as always determinative of an inherently fact-specific finding such as materiality, must necessarily be overinclusive or underinclusive." Id., at 236, 108 S. Ct. 978, 99 L. Ed. 2d 194. We thus rejected the defendant's proposed rule, explaining that it would "artificially exclud[e] from the definition of materiality information concerning merger discussions, which would otherwise be considered significant to the trading decision of a reasonable investor." Ibid.

Like the defendant in Basic, Matrixx urges us to adopt a bright-line rule that reports of adverse events 5 associated with a pharmaceutical company's products cannot be material absent a sufficient number of such reports to establish a statistically significant risk that the product is in fact causing the events. Absent statistical significance, Ma-trixx argues, adverse event reports provide only "anecdotal" evidence that "the user of a drug experienced an adverse event at some point during or following the use of that drug." Brief for Petitioners 17. Accordingly, it contends, reasonable investors would not consider such reports relevant unless they are statistically significant because only then do they "reflect a scientifically reliable basis for inferring a potential causal link between product use and the adverse event." Id., at 32.

As in Basic, Matrixx's categorical rule would "artificially exclud[e]" information that "would otherwise be considered significant to the trading decision of a reasonable investor." 485 U.S., at 236, 108 S. Ct. 978, 99 L. Ed. 2d 194. Matrixx's argument rests on the premise that statistical significance is the only reliable indication of causation. This premise is flawed: As the SEC points out, "medical researchers ... consider mul-tiple factors in assessing causation." Brief for United States as Amicus Curiae 12. Sta-tistically significant data are not always available. For example, when an adverse event is subtle or rare, "an inability to obtain a data set of appropriate quality or quantity may preclude a finding of statistical significance." Id., at 15; see also Brief for Medical Researchers as Amici Curiae 11. Moreover, ethical considerations may prohibit re-searchers from conducting randomized clinical trials to confirm a suspected causal link for the purpose of obtaining statistically significant data. See id., at 10–11.

A lack of statistically significant data does not mean that medical experts have no reliable basis for inferring a causal link between a drug and adverse events. As Matrixx itself concedes, medical experts rely on other evidence to establish an inference of causation. See Brief for Petitioners 44–45, n. 22. We note that courts frequently permit expert testimony on causation based on evidence other than statistical significance. See, e.g., Best v. Lowe's Home Centers, Inc., 563 F.3d 171, 178 (CA6 2009); Westberry v. Gislaved Gummi AB, 178 F.3d 257, 263–264 (CA4 1999) (citing cases); Wells v. Ortho Pharmaceutical Corp., 788 F.2d 741, 744–745 (CA11 1986). We need not consider whether the expert testimony was properly admitted in those cases, and we do not attempt to define here what constitutes reliable evidence of causation. It suffices to note that, as these courts have recognized, "medical professionals and researchers do not limit the data they consider to the results of randomized clinical trials or to statistically significant evidence." Brief for Medical Researchers as Amici Curiae 31.

The FDA similarly does not limit the evidence it considers for purposes of assessing causation and taking regulatory action to statistically significant data. In assessing the safety risk posed by a product, the FDA considers factors such as "strength of the association," "temporal relationship of product use and the event," "consistency of findings across available data sources," "evidence of a dose-response for the effect," "biologic plausibility," "seriousness of the event relative to the disease being treated," "potential to mitigate the risk in the population," "feasibility of further study using observational or controlled clinical study designs," and "degree of benefit the product provides, including availability of other therapies." 8 FDA, Guidance for Industry: Good Pharmacovigilance Practices and Pharmacoepidemiologic Assessment 18 (2005) (capitalization omitted), http://www.fda.gov/downloads/RegulatingInformation/Guidances/UCM126834.pdf (all Internet materials as visited Mar. 17, 2011, and available in Clerk of Court's case file); see also Brief for United States as Amicus Curiae 19–20 (same); FDA, The Clinical Impact of Adverse Event Reporting 6 (1996) (similar), http://www.fda.gov/downloads/safety/MedWatch/UCM168505.pdf. It "does not apply any single metric for determining when additional inquiry or action is necessary, and it certainly does not insist upon 'statistical significance.'" Brief for United States as Amicus Curiae 19.

Not only does the FDA rely on a wide range of evidence of causation, it sometimes acts on the basis of evidence that suggests, but does not prove, causation. For example, the FDA requires manufacturers of over-the-counter drugs to revise their labeling "to include a warning as soon as there is reasonable evidence of an association of a serious hazard with a drug; a causal relationship need not have been proved." 21 CFR § 201.80(e). More generally, the FDA may make regulatory decisions against drugs based on postmarketing evidence that gives rise to only a suspicion of causation. See FDA, The Clinical Impact of Adverse Event Reporting, supra, at 7 ("[A]chieving certain proof of causality through postmarketing surveillance is unusual. Attaining a prominent degree of suspicion is much more likely, and may be considered a sufficient basis for regulatory decisions" (footnote omitted)).

This case proves the point. In 2009, the FDA issued a warning letter to Matrixx stating that "[a] significant and growing body of evidence substantiates that the Zicam

Cold Remedy intranasal products may pose a serious risk to consumers who use them." App. 270a. The letter cited as evidence 130 reports of anosmia the FDA had received, the fact that the FDA had received few reports of anosmia associated with other intranasal cold remedies, and "evidence in the published scientific literature that various salts of zinc can damage olfactory function in animals and humans." Ibid. It did not cite statistically significant data.

Given that medical professionals and regulators act on the basis of evidence of causation that is not statistically significant, it stands to reason that in certain cases reasonable investors would as well. As Matrixx acknowledges, adverse event reports "appear in many forms, including direct complaints by users to manufacturers, reports by doctors about reported or observed patient reactions, more detailed case reports published by doctors in medical journals, or larger scale published clinical studies." Brief for Petitioners 17. As a result, assessing the materiality of adverse event reports is a "fact-specific" inquiry, Basic, 485 U.S., at 236, 108 S. Ct. 978, 99 L. Ed. 2d 194, that requires consideration of the source, content, and context of the reports. This is not to say that statistical significance (or the lack thereof) is irrelevant—only that it is not dispositive of every case.

Application of Basic's "total mix" standard does not mean that pharmaceutical manufacturers must disclose all reports of adverse events. Adverse event reports are daily events in the pharmaceutical industry; in 2009, the FDA entered nearly 500,000 such reports into its reporting system, see FDA, Reports Received and Reports Entered in AERS by Year (as of Mar. 31, 2010), http://www.fda.gov/Drugs/Guidance ComplianceRegulatoryInformation/Surveillance/AdverseDrugEffects/ucm070434.htm. The fact that a user of a drug has suffered an adverse event, standing alone, does not mean that the drug caused that event. See FDA, Annual Adverse Drug Experience Report: 1996, p. 2 (1997), http://druganddevicelaw.net/Annual%20Adverse%20Drug %20Experience%20Report%201996.pdf. The question remains whether a reasonable investor would have viewed the nondisclosed information "'as having significantly altered the "total mix" of information made available.'" Basic, 485 U.S., at 232, 108 S. Ct. 978, 99 L. Ed. 2d 194 (quoting TSC Industries, 426 U.S., at 449, 96 S. Ct. 2126, 48 L. Ed. 2d 757; emphasis added). For the reasons just stated, the mere existence of reports of adverse events—which says nothing in and of itself about whether the drug is causing the adverse events—will not satisfy this standard. Something more is needed, but that something more is not limited to statistical significance and can come from "the source, content, and context of the reports," supra, at 15. This contextual inquiry may reveal in some cases that reasonable investors would have viewed reports of adverse events as material even though the reports did not provide statistically significant evidence of a causal link.

Moreover, it bears emphasis that § 10(b) and Rule 10b-5(b) do not create an affirmative duty to disclose any and all material information. Disclosure is required under these provisions only when necessary "to make ... statements made, in the light of the circumstances under which they were made, not misleading." 17 CFR § 240.10b-5(b); see also Basic, 485 U.S., at 239, n. 17, 108 S. Ct. 978, 99 L. Ed. 2d

194 ("Silence, absent a duty to disclose, is not misleading under Rule 10b-5"). Even with respect to information that a reasonable investor might consider material, companies can control what they have to disclose under these provisions by controlling what they say to the market.

2

Applying Basic's "total mix" standard in this case, we conclude that respondents have adequately pleaded materiality. This is not a case about a handful of anecdotal reports, as Matrixx suggests. Assuming the complaint's allegations to be true, as we must, Matrixx received information that plausibly indicated a reliable causal link between Zicam and anosmia. That information included reports from three medical professionals and researchers about more than 10 patients who had lost their sense of smell after using Zicam. Clarot told Linschoten that Matrixx had received additional reports of anosmia. (In addition, during the class period, nine plaintiffs commenced four product liability lawsuits against Matrixx alleging a causal link between Zicam use and anosmia.) Further, Matrixx knew that Linschoten and Dr. Jafek had presented their findings about a causal link between Zicam and anosmia to a national medical conference devoted to treatment of diseases of the nose. Their presentation described a patient who experienced severe burning in his nose, followed immediately by a loss of smell, after using Zicam—suggesting a temporal relationship between Zicam use and anosmia.

Critically, both Dr. Hirsch and Linschoten had also drawn Matrixx's attention to previous studies that had demonstrated a biological causal link between intranasal application of zinc and anosmia. Before his conversation with Linschoten, Clarot, Matrixx's vice president of research and development, was seemingly unaware of these studies, and the complaint suggests that, as of the class period, Matrixx had not conducted any research of its own relating to anosmia. See, e.g., App. 84a (referencing a press report, issued after the end of the class period, noting that Matrixx said it would begin conducting "'animal and human studies to further characterize these post-marketing complaints'"). Accordingly, it can reasonably be inferred from the complaint that Matrixx had no basis for rejecting Dr. Jafek's findings out of hand.

We believe that these allegations suffice to "raise a reasonable expectation that discovery will reveal evidence" satisfying the materiality requirement, Bell Atlantic Corp. v. Twombly, 550 U.S. 544, 556, 127 S. Ct. 1955, 167 L. Ed. 2d 929 (2007), and to "allo[w] the court to draw the reasonable inference that the defendant is liable for the misconduct alleged," Iqbal, 556 U.S., at ___, 129 S. Ct. 1937, 173 L. Ed. 2d 868, 884. The information provided to Matrixx by medical experts revealed a plausible causal relationship between Zicam Cold Remedy and anosmia. Consumers likely would have viewed the risk associated with Zicam (possible loss of smell) as substantially outweighing the benefit of using the product (alleviating cold symptoms), particularly in light of the existence of many alternative products on the market. Importantly, Zicam Cold Remedy allegedly accounted for 70 percent of Matrixx's sales. Viewing the allegations of the complaint as a whole, the complaint alleges facts suggesting a significant risk to the commercial viability of Matrixx's leading product.

It is substantially likely that a reasonable investor would have viewed this information "'as having significantly altered the "total mix" of information made available.'" Basic, 485 U.S., at 232, 108 S. Ct. 978, 99 L. Ed. 2d 194 (quoting TSC Industries, 426 U.S., at 449, 96 S. Ct. 2126, 48 L. Ed. 2d 757). Matrixx told the market that revenues were going to rise 50 and then 80 percent. Assuming the complaint's allegations to be true, however, Matrixx had information indicating a significant risk to its leading revenue-generating product. Matrixx also stated that reports indicating that Zicam caused anosmia were "'completely unfounded and misleading'" and that "'the safety and efficacy of zinc gluconate for the treatment of symptoms related to the common cold have been well established.'" App. 77a–78a. Importantly, however, Matrixx had evidence of a biological link between Zicam's key ingredient and anosmia, and it had not conducted any studies of its own to disprove that link. In fact, as Matrixx later revealed, the scientific evidence at that time was "'insufficient … to determine if zinc gluconate, when used as recommended, affects a person's ability to smell.'" Id., at 82a.

Assuming the facts to be true, these were material facts "necessary in order to make the statements made, in the light of the circumstances under which they were made, not misleading." 17 CFR § 240.10b-5(b). We therefore affirm the Court of Appeals' holding that respondents adequately pleaded the element of a material misrepresentation or omission.

* * *

For the reasons stated, the judgment of the Court of Appeals for the Ninth Circuit is Affirmed.

Comments and Questions

1. The case focused on a relatively small number of reports from users of the product at issue that they had suffered adverse health effects. As the court in this case noted, the reports themselves were not material. Yet the court ultimately decided that the omitted information was something that would be important to a reasonable investor. What are some of the factors that caused the court to decide that the information was in fact material?

2. How might this same analysis be applied to information that has a relatively small impact on earnings? What sorts of factors may cause small shifts in earnings to be material? The SEC has noted a number of the factors in SAB 99.

3. The Company in this case tried to avoid a finding of materiality by arguing for a bright line test, one of statistical significance. What are the advantages of such a standard? While the approach does result in costs (some information important to reasonable investors becoming immaterial), can you argue that they are outweighed by the benefits? Would a bright line standard be useful with respect to issues concerning the health of a CEO for example?

4. The court noted that a finding of materiality does not mean the information must be disclosed. Instead, companies "can control what they have to disclose …" What does the court mean by this? As a practical reality, is it true? How long, for ex-

ample, could a company keep from the market information about serious health issues connected to the CEO?

Issues of management integrity raise difficult issues under the definition of materiality. Officers or directors could misstate their qualifications or omit legal violations such as DUI convictions. The information would in some cases seem important to investors and shareholders but, at the same time, lack a direct relationship to the earnings of the company. Courts and the SEC have struggled with the application of the materiality standard in these circumstances.

In re Franchard Corp.

Securities and Exchange Commission
42 S.E.C 163 (1964)

On October 14, 1960 — two days after the effective date of registrant's 1960 filing — Glickman began secretly to transfer funds from the registrant to Venada, his wholly owned corporation. Within two months the aggregate amount of these transfers amounted to $296,329. By October 2, 1961, the effective date of registrant's first 1961 filing, Glickman had made 45 withdrawals which amounted in the aggregate to $2,372,511. Neither the 1961 prospectuses nor any of the effective amendments to the 1960 filing referred to these transactions.

* * *

[When the directors learned of the withdrawals, they retained a former judge to conduct an investigation]. In a report submitted on August 20, 1962, Judge Rifkind found that Glickman had on many occasions withdrawn substantial sums from registrant; that Bernard Mann, who was registrant's as well as Venada's treasurer but not a member of registrant's board of directors, was the only one of registrant's officers who had known of the withdrawals and had collaborated with Glickman in effecting them; that registrant's inadequate administrative procedures had to some extent facilitated Glickman's wrongdoing; and that all of the withdrawals had been made good with 6% interest. Judge Rifkind also found that 6% was an inadequate interest rate because Glickman and Venada had been borrowing at appreciably higher interest rates from commercial finance companies and others. Accordingly, he concluded that registrant was entitled to additional interest from Glickman and from Venada in the amount of $145,279. Registrant has not thus far been able to collect any part of this sum.

* * *

Of cardinal importance in any business is the quality of its management. Disclosures relevant to an evaluation of management are particularly pertinent where, as in this case, securities are sold largely on the personal reputation of a company's controlling person. The disclosures in these respects were materially deficient. The 1960 prospectus failed to reveal that Glickman intended to use substantial amounts of registrant's funds for the benefit of Venada, and the 1961 prospectuses made no reference to

Glickman's continual diversion of substantial sums from the registrant. Glickman's pledges were not discussed in either the effective amendments to the 1960 filings or in the two 1961 filings.

In our view, these disclosures were highly material to an evaluation of the competence and reliability of registrant's management—in large measure, Glickman. In many respects, the development of disclosure standards adequate for informed appraisal of management's ability and integrity is a difficult task. How do you tell a "good" business manager from a "bad" one in a piece of paper? Managerial talent consists of personal attributes, essentially subjective in nature, that frequently defy meaningful analysis through the impersonal medium of a prospectus. Direct statements of opinion as to management's ability, which are not susceptible to objective verification, may well create an unwarranted appearance of reliability if placed in a prospectus. The integrity of management—its willingness to place its duty to public shareholders over personal interest—is an equally elusive factor for the application of disclosure standards.

Evaluation of the quality of management—to whatever extent it is possible—is an essential ingredient of informed investment decision. A need so important cannot be ignored, and in a variety of ways the disclosure requirements of the Securities Act furnish factual information to fill this need. Appraisals of competency begin with information concerning management's past business experience, which is elicited by requirements that a prospectus state the offices and positions held with the issuer by each executive officer within the last five years. With respect to established companies, management's past performance, as shown by comprehensive financial and other disclosures concerning the issuer's operations, furnish a guide to its future business performance. To permit judgments whether the corporation's affairs are likely to be conducted in the interest of public shareholders, the registration requirements elicit information as to the interests of insiders which may conflict with their duty of loyalty to the corporation. Disclosures are also required with respect to the remuneration and other benefits paid or proposed to be paid to management as well as material transactions between the corporation and its officers, directors, holders of more than 10 percent of its stock, and their associates.

Glickman's withdrawals were material transactions between registrant and its management, and the registration forms on which registrant's filings were made called for their disclosure. Registrant's argument that the withdrawals were not material because Glickman's undisclosed indebtedness to registrant never exceeded 1.5% of the gross book value of registrant's assets not only minimizes the substantial amounts of the withdrawals in relation to the stockholders' equity and the company's cash flow, but ignores the significance to prospective investors of information concerning Glickman's managerial ability and personal integrity. Registrant as such had no operating history. It concedes that the initial public offering in 1960 was made primarily, if not solely, on Glickman's name and reputation as a successful real estate investor and operator, and it is equally clear that the 1961 offerings were also predicted on his reputation. All of the prospectuses spoke of Glickman's many years of experience "in the creation and development of real estate investment opportunities" as "an investor in real property for his own account." The prospectuses also made it clear that Glickman would dominate and control registrant's operations, and prospective investors in registrant's securities were, in effect, being offered an opportunity to "buy" Glickman management of real estate investments.

A description of Glickman's activities was important on several grounds. First, publication of the facts pertaining to Glickman's withdrawals of substantial funds and of his pledges of his control stock would have clearly indicated his strained financial position and his urgent need for cash in his personal real estate ventures. In the context here, these facts were as material to an evaluation of Glickman's business ability as financial statements of an established company would be to an evaluation of its management's past performance.

Second, disclosure of Glickman's continual diversion of registrant's funds to the use of Venada, his wholly owned corporation, was also germane to an evaluation of the integrity of his management. This quality is always a material factor. In the circumstances of this case the need for disclosure in this area is obvious and compelling. We have spoken of Glickman's dominance. Moreover, Venada was registrant's most important tenant and Glickman would constantly be dealing with himself on behalf of registrant in the context of pressures created by his personal strained financial condition. Even aside from the issues relating to Glickman's character, publication of the fact that he was diverting funds to Venada to bolster that company's weak financial condition was important in evaluating registrant's own operations.

In view of Glickman's dominant role in the management of registrant's affairs, the ambiguity of the purchase agreement should have been more fully discussed in registrant's post-effective amendments which disclosed the transaction. Since cash distributions on shares held by Venada depended on whether the specified amount of vacant MIC space was "rented," the facts necessary to an appraisal of this conflict of interest were material to investors, particularly since Glickman was in a strained financial position. However, the amendments have not become effective, the distribution restriction has never in fact been lifted, and the deficiencies in the earlier filings have been corrected by a satisfactory discussion in the most recent amendment.

Third, Glickman's need for cash as indicated by withdrawals from registrant and his substantial borrowings and pledges of registrant's shares gave him a powerful and direct motive to cause registrant to pursue policies which would permit high distribution rates and maintain a high price for registrant's A shares. The higher that price, the greater his borrowing power; a decline in that price, on the other hand, would lead to the defaults and the consequent loss of control that eventually came to pass. Since prices of cash flow real estate stocks were directly responsive to changes in cash distribution policies, and since, in any event, Glickman needed to derive as much cash as possible from registrant's operations, his financial involvements gave him a peculiarly strong personal interest in setting registrant's current cash distribution rate at the highest possible level and to overlook or to minimize the long-term impact on registrant of an unduly generous distribution policy. Investors were entitled to be apprised of these facts and such potential conflicts of interest.

Finally, the possibility of a change of control was also important to prospective investors. As we have noted, registrant's public offerings were largely predicated on Glickman's reputation as a successful real estate investor and operator. Disclosure of Glickman's secured loans, the relatively high interest rates that they bore, the secondary sources from which many of the loans were obtained, and the conditions under which lenders could declare defaults would have alerted investors to the possibility of a change in the control and management of registrant and apprised them of the possible nature of any such change.

* * *

We also cannot agree with registrant's contention that disclosure of Glickman's borrowings and pledges of registrant's stock would have been an "unwarranted revelation" of Glickman's personal affairs. An insider of a corporation that is asking the public for funds must, in return, relinquish various areas of privacy with respect to his financial affairs which impinge significantly upon the affairs of the company. That determination was made by the Congress over thirty years ago when it expressly provided in the Securities Act for disclosure of such matters as remuneration of insiders and the extent of their shareholdings in and the nature of their other material transactions with the company.

Comments and Questions

1. The amount of money withdrawn was relatively modest (never more than 1.5% of the gross book value of the assets). Yet the SEC seemed to view the amount as irrelevant. Instead, the decision focused almost entirely upon what the diversions suggested about the quality of management. Is this approach consistent with the analysis in *Northway* and *Matrixx*?

2. The SEC's decision also noted that the information was material because the withdrawals indicated a "need for cash" and that this provided an incentive to manage the company in a manner that would emphasize "high distribution rates." What argument is the SEC trying to make? Is it related to the integrity of management? What do you make of the analysis?

3. In determining the materiality of the information, the SEC emphasized the undisclosed nature of the withdrawals. Yet the decision seems to be influenced at least in part by the internal secrecy that accompanied the payments (the board for example was unaware). What if the withdrawals had been accompanied by a valid loan document, had been approved by the board, and were all eventually repaid? Would the case have come out differently? The board may have viewed the transactions differently, but would they have become any less important to reasonable investors?

4. What about Glickman's privacy? How did the disclosure obligations potentially implicate his personal affairs? Does the concept of materiality take this into account?

5. The note to Rule 14a-9 provides examples of what "may be misleading" and includes statements that "directly or indirectly impugns character, integrity or personal reputation, or directly or indirectly makes charges concerning improper, illegal or

immoral conduct or associations, without factual foundation." 17 CFR § 240, 14a-9 note. Does this provision adequately address issues of managerial integrity? The language was adopted back in 1956, well before the decision in *Franchard. See* Exchange Act Release No. 5276 (Jan. 17, 1956).

6. In the aftermath of *Franchard*, management integrity proved to be a convenient doctrine that was widely put into use. During the Watergate Era, the Commission uncovered instances of illegal campaign contributions and bribes paid to foreign officials. They were widespread. *See* Exchange Act Release No. 15570 (Feb. 15, 1979) (noting that more than 400 corporations had made "questionable or illegal payments"). The payments were, in general, modest in amount relative to the earnings of the companies involved. Moreover, unlike the withdrawals in *Franchard*, they arguably had a positive impact on the company's business. It was, therefore, difficult to argue under conventional analysis that shareholders were in any way harmed over the failure to disclose the payments. In arguing that the omissions were material, the staff relied on the management integrity doctrine. *See* Exchange Act Release No. 10673 (March 8, 1974) (with respect to convictions for illegal campaign contributions, "[s]uch a conviction is material to an evaluation of the integrity of the management of the corporation as it relates to the operation of the corporation and the use of corporate funds.").

7. The doctrine, perhaps unsurprisingly, engendered considerable criticism. The concept was vague and often disconnected from earnings and other financial metrics. John Fedders, the former head of the Division of Enforcement at the Securities and Exchange Commission had this to say:

> "The qualitative materiality standard has come and gone. It died at the bar of common sense. It was a standard that had no standards. Outside of its SEC proponents, it had no champion. Its intended beneficiaries—investors— ignored corporate qualitative disclosures. Moreover, the standard was pronounced unfit for use by the courts because it licensed the Commission to allege disclosure failures for unadjudicated misconduct, or the like, based on its own discretion, not by the rule of law."

John M. Fedders, *Qualitative Materiality: The Birth, Struggles, and Demise of an Unworkable Standard*, 48 Cath. U.L. Rev. 41 (Fall 1998).

The issue, however, has not gone away. Cases arise where shareholders or investors allege that companies did not accurately disclose information relevant to the quality and integrity of officers or directors.

Greenhouse v. MCG Capital

United States Court of Appeals, Fourth Circuit
392 F.3d 650 (2004)

GREGORY, CIRCUIT JUDGE:

MCG is an Arlington, Virginia-based venture capital firm that makes debt and equity investments in small and mid-sized private businesses in the media, communications, technology, and information services sectors. The company has been traded publicly since its Initial Public Offering ("IPO") in late 2001.

Following about a decade of experience at two banks, in 1998 Mitchell helped found MCG and began his tenure as the company's CEO and Chairman of the Board. The Appellees admit that Mitchell held himself out as having earned a bachelor's degree in economics from Syracuse University. The truth, however, is that Mitchell attended Syracuse for three years and studied economics, but left before getting his degree.

MCG included Mitchell's purported educational background in various forms filed with the SEC in preparation for its IPO. As an example, the "biographical information" section of the registration statements and prospectus ("Prospectus") stated:

> Bryan J. Mitchell has served as our Chief Executive Officer since 1998 and as the Chairman of our board of directors since May 2001. Mr. Mitchell has served as a member of our board of directors since 1998 and also served as our President from 1998 to May 2001. From 1997 to 1998, Mr. Mitchell was a Senior Vice president for First Union National Bank. From 1988 to 1997, Mr. Mitchell was employed by Signet Bank where he served as a Senior Vice President. Mr. Mitchell serves on the board of directors of MCG Finance Corporation and MCG Finance Corporation II. *Mr. Mitchell earned a B.A. in Economics from Syracuse University.*

Prospectus at 79 (emphasis added). The brief biographical statements about MCG's managers were, of course, merely one part of MCG's filings; other extensive information existed. Aside from this single sentence, repeated in various forms, however, Appellants allege no other misstatements.

After apparent pressure by Herb Greenberg ("Greenberg"), a reporter with the website "TheStreet.Com" who questioned Mitchell's actual history, Mitchell told the truth to MCG's board on November 1, 2002. Later that same day, MCG publicly corrected Mitchell's misrepresentation through a press release, which read:

> MCG Capital Corporation announced today that its Chairman and Chief Executive Officer, Bryan J. Mitchell, informed the Company's Board of Directors this morning that contrary to prior disclosures, he does not hold a Bachelor of Arts degree from Syracuse University. The Board of Directors has requested the Chairman of the Company's Audit Committee, Wallace B. Millner, III, to review the facts relating to these matters and to report to the full board as promptly as possible.

J.A. 74. Appellants assert that this announcement brought MCG negative attention in the investment world. Specifically, they allege that an analyst for Wachovia Securities downgraded MCG to "Hold" from "Buy" on the day of the announcement, noting a worry that this misrepresentation foreshadowed larger "credibility issues" and that two reporters on CNN's Lou Dobbs Moneyline discussed the stock shortly after the company's correction, noting that Mitchell was "another CEO that lied about his resume". J.A. 28–29. Appellants also note that Greenberg questioned on "TheStreet.com" whether other "corrections" were forthcoming. Specifically, on November 1, 2002

Greenberg wrote that, "… if the CEO's disclosure isn't correct, you can't help but wonder … what else isn't?" J.A. 76. He repeated this refrain in a November 3d post: "Can't help but wonder why [sic] credibility an admitted liar, of a CEO, will have going forward. (And can't help but wonder what else at the company has been, shall we say, embellished.)". J.A. 81. Finally, on November 12th, Greenberg opined in an article about MCG that, "when a CEO lies about his educational background … you have to wonder what else might not be right." J.A. 84.

It is plainly plausible that, at least temporarily, investors ingested or shared these financial pundits' concerns about the company's credibility in the wake of the corrective announcement. The stock dipped to $8.40 from $11.85 per share on November 1, 2002. The full price history of the stock, however, complicates the case: the next day, the stock regained approximately half of the previous day's loss, and the remainder of its losses were recovered within about a month.

While Mitchell was an undoubtedly important person for MCG, he was by no means above its punishment. On November 3d, the Board withheld Mitchell's 2001 and 2002 bonuses, made him repay monies loaned to him by MCG, and removed his title as Chairman of the Board. Mitchell remains stripped of his title as Chairman; he retained (and retains) his position as CEO.

* * *

In order to prevail on a claim for securities fraud under either S.E.C. Rule 10b-5 ("Rule 10b-5") or Section 11(a) of the Securities Act of 1933, 15 U.S.C. §77k ("Section 11(a)"), the plaintiff must prove, inter alia, "materiality." Specifically, Rule 10b-5 makes it unlawful to "… make any untrue statement of a material fact or to omit to state a material fact necessary in order to make the statements made, in the light of the circumstances under which they were made, not misleading …" and carries with it a private right of action for the Rule's enforcement. Likewise, Section 11(a) creates a right of action for purchasers when a registration statement "contained an untrue statement of a material fact" or omits a material fact.

* * *

Appellants make a number of arguments, the best of which can be summarized roughly into three main points: (A) as a key manager, Mitchell's education is a material fact; (B) "management's integrity" is always material; and (C) the district court erred by confusing causation with materiality and by taking into account the price of the stock after November 1st, the day of disclosure. We address, and dismiss, each contention in turn.

A.

The misrepresentation of an executive's educational credentials has seldom been addressed in published cases. Even the closest case analogies seem somewhat difficult to apply here because, as noted above, materiality is a fact-specific determination. Those few cases (notably, none from circuit courts) discussing misrepresentation of an educational degree even obliquely, however, do not support Appellants' argument that misstatements about managers' academic backgrounds are material.

Indeed, no binding precedent exists, and the only case of which we are aware that deals explicitly with such a fraud by an executive dismisses that allegation as immaterial and takes pains to distinguish it from truly material facts. *See* New Equity Sec. Holders Comm. for Golden Gulf, Ltd. v. Phillips, 97 B.R. 492, 496–97 (E.D. Ark. 1989) (distinguishing misrepresentation of a business degree, as immaterial, from the omission of recent felony conviction of director, prior and pending litigation against the company, and SEC investigation of the company, as all material).

Appellants, however, cite two district court cases in support of their claim that an individual's education is material: SEC v. Physicians Guardian Unit Inv. Trust, 72 F. Supp. 2d 1342 (M.D. Fla. 1999) and SEC v. Suter, No. 81 C 3865, 1983 WL 1287 (N.D. Ill. 1983). These cases are distinguishable. Physicians Guardian denies, in a notably conclusory fashion, a motion to dismiss an eight-count, 59-paragraph action by the SEC requesting emergency relief and alleging a remarkable multitude of outlandishly fraudulent activity. One of these many fraudulent activities by repeat offenders included that a manager falsely claimed to have a law degree and 27 years of experience as a lawyer. 72 F. Supp. 2d at 1344–51. *Suter* grants injunctive relief in a securities fraud action that contained, hiding among many other falsehoods that are clearly more important, a claim that an investment adviser falsely claimed to have an MBA. 1983 WL 1287 at *3.

Appellants contend that the failure of the courts in these two cases to tease out as immaterial the educational credential from the other frauds, as did the *New Equity* court, is evidence that the courts found such misrepresentations material. This may be facially reasonable, but quickly becomes unpersuasive once one examines the opinions. In both cases the SEC sought and obtained emergency injunctive relief from a long litany of ongoing fraudulent activity by repeat players in the fraud game. In each case, the courts appear overwhelmed with the wide-ranging fraudulent behavior alleged of the defendants. In short, neither court addresses in any specific fashion the materiality of the individual education-related claim within the entire, wide-ranging action, but rather rules against the defendants *en masse*. Here, in contrast, we are presented with the unusual circumstance that *only one* misrepresentation is alleged among uncountable other pieces of information in the prospectus, other filings, and elsewhere, making up the "total mix" of information.

While we do *not* hold as a matter of law that a key manager's education could *never* be material, we do find that Mitchell's education is immaterial here. Even limiting our view, as we must, to those materials relied upon by the Appellants in formulating their complaint and those materials publicly available to reasonable investors, and viewing them in the light most favorable to the Appellants, Mitchell's educational background could not be said to alter the "total mix" of this information. For example, a reasonable investor would likely value information found in MCG's publicly filed statements and elsewhere including: Mitchell's years of management in financial institutions; the other board members' and key managers' similar track record; the years of MCG's earnings statements as a private company; the firm's debt/equity ratio; the general costs of capital and macroeconomic trends; the strength of MCG's potential competitors; etc. In comparison, Appellants have advanced no credible theory as to why a reasonable investor would consider what Mitchell did (or, as the case may be, did not do) during what would have been his fourth year at Syracuse to constitute something so important that it would alter this large body of information. In short, the unavoidable conclusion one reaches is that, in an age of heightened sensitivity to corporate scandal some investors found, for a very short period of time, MCG's stock to be damaged goods because the company's credibility was suddenly suspect, and investors were concerned that revelations of other, more important fabrications were soon forthcoming.

B.

Happily, this realization affords us the opportunity to address Appellants' next argument. Appellants cite a number of ultimately unavailing cases in their attempt to argue that MCG's disclosure about Mitchell implicated management's integrity. Nobody—even MCG—disputes the idea that Mitchell's integrity was brought into question by the revelation that he lied. But this is only a distraction from the real issue: whether the actual fact misrepresented—that is the basis for this suit and that caused investors to question management's integrity—was, in and of itself, material.

In support of their integrity argument, Appellants present the case of Gebhardt v. ConAgra Foods, Inc., 335 F.3d 824 (8th Cir. 2003). But in Gerhardt, unlike here, there plainly was a misrepresented fact that was actually material: management violated generally accepted accounting principles and significantly overstated their earnings. Id. at 830 ("The keystone of plaintiffs' materiality argument is their allegation that UAP's misrepresentations caused ConAgra to appear to be earning more than it was."). If ConAgra's leaders knowingly misrepresented their earnings, of course one byproduct might be that investors would reasonably question the integrity of the company's management; like here, the "integrity concerns" in Gerhardt are merely derivative of the misrepresentation that was the basis for the suit. The key difference, however, is that the fact misrepresented in Gerhardt—the company's earnings—might plausibly alter the total mix of information to a reasonable investor; here, Mitchell's failure to complete his fourth year in college could not.

Likewise, Appellants cite Zell v. Intercapital Income Secur., Inc., 675 F.2d 1041 (9th Cir. 1982), for the same proposition. But again, Zell dealt with a fact of an indisputably different quantum: the defendant's proxy statement failed to disclose "a score of lawsuits charging violations of state and federal securities laws." Id. at 1043. That both misrepresentations call management's integrity into question follows almost necessarily from the fact that they are lies; it does not, however, aid in the determination of whether Mitchell's lie was about *a material fact*.

Finally, Appellants cite a 40-year old SEC case for the proposition that integrity is "always a material factor." In the Matter of Franchard Corp., 42 S.E.C. 163, Release No. 33-4710, 1964 WL 6754 (S.E.C. July 31, 1964). In addition to the fact that it predates the Supreme Court's pronouncement in Basic and other key cases on materiality, Appellants fail to note that this statement is, yet again, ancillary to concerns growing from actual material facts that were not disclosed (and thus were at issue) in the case. Reading the full context out of which Appellants pluck their quote that integrity "is always a material factor," one learns that the underlying fact at issue was that the company's registration statements continually failed to disclose transfers of large sums from the company to the controlling stockholder and chief executive officer, which he used in his own ventures. Id. at *2–*4, *6. This, in turn, created a likelihood of shift in control and caused clear conflicts of interest with the company and its shareholders. *Id.*

In short, in each of these "integrity" cases, and unlike this case, a real, live, material *fact* was at issue. Appellants seem to have chosen these cases because the courts appear to have noted, offhandedly, that management's integrity is important and necessarily implicated with such revelations. Of course, to some extent, "management's integrity" will *always* be implicated in *any* falsehoods. But as this Circuit and the Court in *Basic* noted, not all lies are actionable; the securities laws are only concerned with lies about *material facts.* Reading the law otherwise, as Appellants would have us do, simply reads materiality out of the statute. Under their theory, almost *any* misrepresentation by a CEO — including, perhaps, one about his or her marital fidelity, political persuasion, or golf handicap — that might cause investors to question management's integrity could, as such, serve as a basis for a securities-fraud class action. The law simply does not permit such a result.

* * *

IV.

In conclusion, while we acknowledge that Mitchell's lie is indefensible, it does not follow invariably that it is illegal. We hold that, viewed properly, it is *not* substantially likely that reasonable investors would devalue the stock knowing that Mitchell skipped out on his last year at Syracuse. That is, if one imagines a parallel universe of affairs where the one and only thing different was that MCG's filings made no mention of Mitchell's education (or, instead, said simply that he "attended" Syracuse or "studied economics" there), we find it incredible to believe that MCG's stock would be worth even a penny more to a reasonable investor.

Comments and Questions

1. Materiality is a mixed question of fact and law ordinarily left to a jury. Yet the court in this case found as a matter of law that the information was immaterial. Do you agree? Did the court correctly characterize the misstatement as to what the officer "did" (or, as the case may be, did not do) during what would have been his fourth year at Syracuse?

2. What do you make of the argument that information relating to the qualitative materiality of management is always material? What problems might arise with such an approach? What inroads might it make into the privacy of officers and directors?

3. Although finding that the misstatement about the officer's educational background was immaterial, the court specifically declined to find a per se rule with respect

to this type of information. Under this court's reasoning, when would this type of misstatement be considered material? In *SEC v. Reys*, 712 F. Supp. 2d 1170, 1177 (WD Wash. 2010), the SEC brought an action alleging certain misstatements with respect to the CEO's work history and qualifications. Specifically, the SEC asserted that the officer had

> falsely stated that he had been part of the executive team that took a pharmaceutical company through an initial public offering and subsequent acquisition by a large multinational company, when, in fact, he had only been a sales manager for the pharmaceutical company and had left the company years before its IPO and subsequent acquisition; and ... falsely represented that he had taken one of the privately-held biotechnology companies for which he previously served as CEO from conception to early human clinical trials in 18 months, when, in reality, the company had terminated [the CEO], and [the CEO] had not led the company to human clinical trials.

The court concluded that the information could be material and found the result in *Greenhouse* not to be controlling. Are the two cases really different? How might the materiality analysis result in different outcomes?

4. The court here seems to reject the argument that the materiality of the information is enhanced by the asserted dishonesty of the officer. Is that a correct approach? In Staff Accounting Bulletin No. 99 (1999), the staff listed factors that should be taken into account in determining the materiality of earnings misstatements. In a Q&A portion of the Bulletin, the staff was asked whether a company could "make intentional immaterial misstatements in its financial statements?" The response? "No. In certain circumstances, intentional immaterial misstatements are unlawful." Is the staff's position consistent with the reasoning of this court?

5. With respect to issues of management integrity, do the express disclosure requirements contained in Regulation S-K provide any comfort in determining what is material? In *United States v. Bachynsky*, 2011 U.S. App. LEXIS 3377 (11th Cir., Feb. 18, 2011), the defendant argued that his criminal conviction was immaterial because it occurred outside the time periods specified in Item 401 of Regulation S-K. What do you think is the correct resolution of that argument?

6. Does pending litigation against a company implicate the integrity of management? Sometimes, apparently. *See Zell v. Intercapital Income Securities, Inc.*, 675 F.2d 1041 (9th Cir. 1982) ("Obviously, pending litigation may be relevant to the quality of a corporation's management. Prior breaches of fiduciary duties or violations of securities statutes and regulations may have a direct bearing on managerial integrity."). What does this suggest about the breadth of the management integrity doctrine?

Greenhouse demonstrates that false statements about management's background will not always be treated as material. Does that suggest information relating to the integrity or personnel affairs of management will not be material?

Joan MacLeod Heminway, *Personal Facts about Executive Officers: A Proposal for Tailored Disclosures to Encourage Reasonable Investor Behavior*

42 Wake Forest L. Rev. 749, 750, 762–65 (2007)[3]

... [C]ommon circumstances involving executives' personal lives ... raise questions as to whether (and if so, to what extent) public company executive officers should be required, through federal securities regulation, to publicly disclose (or facilitate corporate public disclosure of) personal facts, including events and conduct.

* * *

2. Personal Facts About Executives May Be Material on Several Different Bases

Given that disclosure questions with respect to executives' personal facts generally involve compliance with gap-filling and antifraud rules and that materiality is vital in disclosure determinations under these rules, it is important to understand the possible bases for materiality of personal facts about executives. Personal facts about an executive may be important to a reasonable investor or have a significant impact on available public information because they may indicate the possibility that the corporation will be without the executive's services either temporarily or permanently. For example, if an executive will be involved as a party in a criminal or civil trial, the executive will lose time away from his or her duties to the corporation during that time. And a conviction in a criminal trial may result in the executive serving jail time or other detention that will keep him or her away from the office, perhaps for a more extended period of time. Similarly, serious or terminal illness requires treatment and time for recovery, and if treatment fails to completely cure the condition, permanent disability, incapacity, or death may result. These effects of illness limit or terminate the executive's ability to render services to the corporation. Investors may find an executive's unavailability especially important in making an investment decision as to a corporation's securities if the executive has a unique expertise or specialized skill critical to the corporation's successful operations. Generally, an executive's absence is more likely to be considered important by a reasonable investor if his or her management or other functions are not adequately covered by others or the executive continues to earn compensation from the corporation during a period of absence from his or her corporate duties.

However, service limitations are not the only potential bases for the materiality of personal facts about executives. Personal information about executive officers also may be important to a reasonable investor or have a significant impact on available public information because the executive has unique attributes that benefit the corporation independent of his or her overall service availability and capabilities. For example, when the reputation of the executive and the corporation are tied, especially

---

because the executive's identity effectively is the corporation's brand or the executive is otherwise iconic, personal facts about the executive may be more important to investors or have a more significant informational effect. Also, the reliability or integrity of certain key members of management may form the basis of a materiality determination, depending on the personal information at issue.

Ultimately, the materiality of personal facts about executive officers determined on any of these bases should depend on an assessment of the specific capabilities or attributes of the executive, their importance (financially or otherwise) to the value of the public company that the executive serves, and the market for executive talent. If the executive is more fungible (easily replaceable without considerable cost to the corporation), his or her personal information should be less important to investors or less significant to the total mix of available information. Although almost every public company undoubtedly would, if prompted, indicate that its chief executive officer and other key executives are important to its business, many will not, without significant thought, be able to indicate precisely why. In many cases, executives are relatively fungible, even if they are talented, intelligent, and knowledgeable about the corporation and its business.

3. Personal Facts About Executives Are Less Likely to Be Material than Corporate Facts

Even where an executive is not fungible, personal facts about the executive are less likely to be important to the reasonable investor or less significant to the total mix of available information than corporate facts. Executives' personal facts are less likely to be directly related to fundamental corporate value and are less apt to impact corporate behavior (apart from the potential for a change in the executive's management responsibilities or a termination of the executive's management or employment status). The value of a public company to its shareholders and others is comprised of many components and can be measured in numerous ways. But it is safe to say that most personal facts about executives have little impact on the corporation's assets, profitability, stability, earnings or growth potential, efficiency (by any measure), or any other fundamental internal value metric when compared with information about the corporation's products or services, financial condition, or results of operations. Of course, public disclosure of a personal fact about an executive may affect the short-term price of the corporation's stock, but that price effect does not necessarily indicate that the personal fact is material.

Personal facts about public executive officers also are less likely to be qualitatively important to the public company. Although the SEC has promoted the possibility that facts related to management competence, reliability, and integrity may be material, there are few court cases expressly endorsing qualitative materiality. In fact, at least one case appears to outright reject qualitative materiality, noting that the SEC can and should provide for mandatory disclosure in areas raising the potential for qualitative materiality claims. Based on existing decisional law, qualitative materiality is most likely to exist where the facts include concealment of self-dealing transactions or illegal activities. However, self-dealing claims cannot be converted from state law fiduciary duty claims to federal securities fraud claims without allegations of manipulation or deception (including principally false or misleading disclosures).

Comments and Questions

1. What do you make of this debate? Has the managerial integrity doctrine died a death of "common sense"?

2. What are some examples of "facts about executives" that could cross the materiality threshold? What are some examples of CEOs that are uniquely important to companies and therefore raise heightened concerns over the materiality? Does a proxy statement have to disclose the personal finances of the CEO where he owns more than 5% of the shares of the company and reveals that the shares are in a margin account? Such information would presumably relevant to whether he or she can meet a margin call without having to sell the shares. The answer, in *United Food and Commercial Workers Union v. Chesapeake Energy Corp.*, 726 F.3d 1158 (10th Cir. 2014) (CEO sold shares over several day period to meet margin call).

3. How about misstatements arising out of backdated stock options? While backdating is not per se illegal, it was often accompanied by falsified documents and misstatements. To the extent the backdating actually had a meaningful impact on the company's earnings, the courts have had little difficulty finding the information material. *See U.S. v. Reyes*, 2009 U.S. App. LEXIS 24575 (9th Cir. Nov. 5, 2009) (failing to expense backdated options resulted in company reporting a profit rather than a loss). What if the misstatement has an insignificant impact on earnings? Might they implicate the integrity of management?

4. What about the tension between this type of information and privacy. Ought the securities laws to do a better job in respecting the privacy of corporate managers? What impact would that have on investors and shareholders?

5. The Commission may not refer to "management integrity" but it does make considerable use of qualitative materiality. Qualitative materiality looks to all of the facts and circumstances surrounding the omitted or misstated information to determine whether to omitted information would be important to a reasonable investor. Thus, for example, the Commission has taken the position that relying solely on quantitative thresholds for determining materiality "has no basis in the accounting literature or the law." Staff Accounting Bulletin No. 99 (Aug. 19, 1999). Can one argue that this is the management integrity doctrine by another name?

6. Indeed, the broad approach to materiality in SAB 99 has caused some tension within the Commission itself. Some commissioners have disagreed with the approach. *See* Speech by SEC Commissioner: Remarks to the 'SEC Speaks in 2008' Program of the Practising Law Institute, by Commissioner Paul S. Atkins, *U.S. Securities and Exchange Commission*, Washington, D.C., February 8, 2008, (describing SAB 99 as having "muddied" the materiality analysis and resulted in the disclosure of "an avalanche of trivial information"). What do you make of this division within the Commission and the comment itself?

7. Courts, on the other hand, have been less conflicted and have generally approved of the reasoning in SAB 99. *See ECA & Local 134 IBEW Joint Pension Trust of Chi. v. JP Morgan Chase*, 553 F.3d 187, 197–98 (2d Cir. 2009) (describing SAB 99 as providing "qualitative factors" and applying them to the facts of the case).

IV. Disclosure and Corporate Social Responsibility

The SEC has always viewed its disclosure mission as cabined by the interests of shareholders and investors. The goal of disclosure has fundamentally been a matter of ensuring informed decision making, whether in the context of purchasing/selling securities or voting on matters submitted to shareholders. The Commission has not viewed disclosure to other stakeholders, including the public, as part of this mission. Disclosure, therefore, has largely focused on "information about the company, its business, and its management periodically and upon the occurrence of specified events." Alison B. Miller, *Navigating the Disclosure Dilemma: Corporate Illegality and the Federal Securities Laws*, 102 Geo. L.J. 1647, 1652 (2014).

For the most part, this has been an accepted understanding of the SEC's role, although exceptions have always existed. Congress gave the SEC the authority to police foreign bribes in the Foreign Corrupt Practices Act. The role was less about the interests of shareholders and investors and more about imposing substantive standards of behavior on corporations and their agents. Similarly, the SEC has long allowed rigorous debate to occur over matters of important public policy through the shareholder proposal rule. *See* Rule 14a-8, 17 CFR 240.14a-8.

Nonetheless, pressure has continued to grow for increased disclosure about matters of importance to the public. In part, the pressure has arisen from shareholders, particularly those that invest in companies meeting socially responsible criteria. Pressure has also arisen from the public. Moreover, because members of the public may also be investors or shareholders, the distinction between the two sets of interests has not always been easy to discern.

Adopting disclosure requirements in these areas raises concerns. First, to the extent divorced from the interests of shareholders and investors, the SEC effectively lacks a guiding set of principles that limit the nature and breadth of its disclosure mission. Second, matters less related to the economic activities of a company but important to some segments of the public can raise issues of significant political sensitivity. The result may be pushback from Congress that can take the shape of legislative penalties, including restrictive legislation or inadequate funding of the agency's budget. Third, to the extent the disclosure requirements emanate from Congress, they may reflect the interests of voters rather than owners and managers. As such, they may not be in the best interests of shareholders.

The Commission has addressed these issues in at least three contexts: (1) disclosure over the impact of climate change; (2) disclosure of political contributions and lobbying expense by public companies; and (3) disclosure of the use of minerals that may have been supplied by combatants in the Democratic Republic of the Congo. The Commission has responded to each of these examples in a very different fashion.

A. Climate Change

The Commission has found itself under increasing pressure to mandate additional disclosure with respect to climate change. In 2007, a broad coalition of organizations and institutional investors petitioned the SEC to adopt an interpretive release "clarifying that material climate-related information must be included in corporate disclosures under existing law." *See* Petition No. 4-547 (Sept. 18, 2007). In 2010, the Commission responded to the petition.

Commission Guidance Regarding Disclosure Related to Climate Change

Exchange Act Release No. 61469 (Feb. 2, 2010)

IV. Climate change related disclosures

* * *

C. Indirect consequences of regulation or business trends.

Legal, technological, political and scientific developments regarding climate change may create new opportunities or risks for registrants. These developments may create demand for new products or services, or decrease demand for existing products or services. For example, possible indirect consequences or opportunities may include:

- Decreased demand for goods that produce significant greenhouse gas emissions;
- Increased demand for goods that result in lower emissions than competing products;
- Increased competition to develop innovative new products;
- Increased demand for generation and transmission of energy from alternative energy sources; and
- Decreased demand for services related to carbon based energy sources, such as drilling services or equipment maintenance services.

These business trends or risks may be required to be disclosed as risk factors or in MD&A. In some cases, these developments could have a significant enough impact on a registrant's business that disclosure may be required in its business description under Item 101 [of Regulation S-K].

For example, a registrant that plans to reposition itself to take advantage of potential opportunities, such as through material acquisitions of plants or equipment, may be required by Item 101(a)(1) to disclose this shift in plan of operation. Registrants should consider their own particular facts and circumstances in evaluating the materiality of these opportunities and obligations.

Another example of a potential indirect risk from climate change that would need to be considered for risk factor disclosure is the impact on a registrant's reputation. Depending on the nature of a registrant's business and its sensitivity to public opinion, a registrant may have to consider whether the public's perception of any publicly available data relating to its greenhouse gas emissions could expose it to potential adverse consequences to its business operations or financial condition resulting from reputational damage.

D. Physical impacts of climate change.

Significant physical effects of climate change, such as effects on the severity of weather (for example, floods or hurricanes), sea levels, the arability of farmland, and water availability and quality, have the potential to affect a registrant's operations and results. For example, severe weather can cause catastrophic harm to physical plants and facilities and can disrupt manufacturing and distribution processes. A 2007 Government Accountability Office report states that 88% of all property losses paid by insurers between 1980 and 2005 were weather-related. As noted in the GAO report, severe weather can have a devastating effect on the financial condition of affected businesses. The GAO report cites a number of sources to support the view that severe weather scenarios will increase as a result of climate change brought on by an overabundance of greenhouse gases.

Possible consequences of severe weather could include:

- For registrants with operations concentrated on coastlines, property damage and disruptions to operations, including manufacturing operations or the transport of manufactured products;

- Indirect financial and operational impacts from disruptions to the operations of major customers or suppliers from severe weather, such as hurricanes or floods;

- Increased insurance claims and liabilities for insurance and reinsurance companies;

- Decreased agricultural production capacity in areas affected by drought or other weather-related changes; and

- Increased insurance premiums and deductibles, or a decrease in the availability of coverage, for registrants with plants or operations in areas subject to severe weather.

Registrants whose businesses may be vulnerable to severe weather or climate related events should consider disclosing material risks of, or consequences from, such events in their publicly filed disclosure documents.

Comments and Questions

1. The climate change guidance was not the first effort by the SEC to increase environmental related disclosure. The Commission began providing guidance in the area in the 1970s. *See* Securities Act Release No. 5170 (July 19, 1971) (guidance discussing obligation to disclose capital outlays and litigation relating to environmental matters). Rules were adopted a decade later. *See* Securities Act Release No. 6383

(March 3, 1982). Regulation S-K contains a modest number of explicit requirements in the area, including: Item 103 (obligation to disclose material legal proceedings arising under provisions designed to regulate "the discharge of materials into the environment or primary for the purpose of protecting the environment").

2. Who really wants this information? How important is it to investors? What are the limits on climate change disclosure when relying on existing SEC requirements?

3. How has this worked to improve disclosure relating to the impact of climate change? In setting out the guidance on climate change disclosure, the Commission stated that it would "monitor the impact of this interpretive release on company filings as part of our ongoing disclosure review program." How important is the idea of continuous monitoring?

4. According to one report that analyzed climate change disclosure in public filings in the aftermath of the guidance quoted above, SEC efforts have not improved the quality of the disclosure.

> While more companies started making climate-related disclosures in 2010 after the SEC's interpretive guidance was issued, there has been little improvement since 2010. In fact, the average score assigned to 10-K climate disclosures has dropped off since 2010 showing that, while more companies are saying something about climate change, they were less specific in disclosures made in 2013 compared with 2010 reporting. A large number of companies fail to say anything about climate change in their 10-K filings. Forty-one percent of S&P 500 companies failed to address climate change in their 2013 filing. Climate-related disclosures made by S&P 500 companies in 10-K filings were highly variable in length and quality.

See Fact Sheet, Reducing Systemic Risks: The Securities & Exchange Commission, Ceres (2014). What do you make of these conclusions? What does it suggest about the limits of the SEC guidance in this area? Is it likely to eliminate pressure for additional disclosure requirements in the area?

5. What are some other avenues for increasing disclosure with respect to climate change? How about shareholder proposals? In 2014, proposals on climate change ranked third, with more than 50 proposals submitted. What impact is this likely to have?

B. Disclosure of Political Contributions and Lobbying Expenses

Another area where the Commission has been subjected to significant pressure to adopt disclosure requirements that may benefit shareholders but are also favored by segments of the public has been with respect to political contributions and lobbying expenses. Pressure began to build in the aftermath of the Supreme Court's decision in *Citizens United* striking down restrictions on campaign contributions. A 5–4 decision, the Court suggested that political expenditures were better addressed through "corporate democracy."

Citizens United v. Federal Election Comm'n

Supreme Court of the United States

558 U.S. 310 (2010)

The Government contends further that corporate independent expenditures can be limited because of its interest in protecting dissenting shareholders from being compelled to fund corporate political speech. This asserted interest, like *Austin*'s antidistortion rationale, would allow the Government to ban the political speech even of media corporations. See *supra*, at 905—906. Assume, for example, that a shareholder of a corporation that owns a newspaper disagrees with the political views the newspaper expresses. See *Austin*, 494 U.S., at 687, 110 S.Ct. 1391 (SCALIA, J., dissenting). Under the Government's view, that potential disagreement could give the Government the authority to restrict the media corporation's political speech. The First Amendment does not allow that power. There is, furthermore, little evidence of abuse that cannot be corrected by shareholders "through the procedures of corporate democracy." *Bellotti*, 435 U.S., at 794, 98 S.Ct. 1407; see *id.*, at 794, n. 34, 98 S.Ct. 1407.

* * *

Shareholder objections [to political contributions by corporations] raised through the procedures of corporate democracy, see *Bellotti, supra*, at 794, and n. 34, 98 S.Ct. 1407, can be more effective today because modern technology makes disclosures rapid and informative. A campaign finance system that pairs corporate independent expenditures with effective disclosure has not existed before today. It must be noted, furthermore, that many of Congress' findings in passing BCRA were premised on a system without adequate disclosure. See *McConnell*, 540 U.S., at 128, 124 S.Ct. 619 ("[T]he public may not have been fully informed about the sponsorship of so-called issue ads"); *id.*, at 196–197, 124 S.Ct. 619(quoting *McConnell I*, 251 F.Supp.2d, at 237). With the advent of the Internet, prompt disclosure of expenditures can provide shareholders and citizens with the information needed to hold corporations and elected officials accountable for their positions and supporters. Shareholders can determine whether their corporation's political speech advances the corporation's interest in making profits, and citizens can see whether elected officials are "'in the pocket' of so-called moneyed interests." 540 U.S., at 259, 124 S.Ct. 619 (opinion of SCALIA, J.); see **371MCFL, supra*, at 261, 107 S.Ct. 616. The First Amendment protects political speech; and disclosure permits citizens and shareholders to react to the speech of corporate entities in a proper way. This transparency enables the electorate to make informed decisions and give proper weight to different speakers and messages.

Lucian A. Bebchuk & Robert J. Jackson, Jr., *Shining Light on Corporate Political Spending*

101 Geo. L.J. 923 (2013)

Public companies' political spending, and whether it serves the interests of shareholders, is the subject of considerable debate. Currently, however, this debate is conducted in the absence of critical facts. Under current law, public companies are not required to, and commonly do not, report their political spending to shareholders. Thus, it is impossible for shareholders to know whether their companies spend investors' money on politics—and, if so, how much is spent and for whom.

* * *

Public companies can, and do, engage in political spending that is never disclosed by channeling that spending through intermediaries. Corporations contribute to entities that spend significant sums on politics, yet these intermediaries do not have to disclose either the identity of the corporations that make these contributions or the amounts that they contribute. As a result, there is no information in the public domain on how much of an intermediary's funds, if any, was provided by a given public company. Even a determined individual shareholder willing to collect all available public information on a company's political spending would be unable to measure any spending through these intermediaries. In this section, we show that intermediaries spend substantial sums on politics, that the level of intermediary spending on politics has been growing over time, and that there is reason to conclude that a significant source of the intermediaries' funding comes from large public companies.

* * *

In addition to spending through intermediaries, corporations are free to spend investor funds on indirect support of political candidates—for example, advertisements urging the election of a particular candidate. Existing election-law rules, such as regulations promulgated by the Federal Election Commission (FEC), may require that information about this type of corporate political spending be available in the public domain. These rules, however, are designed to provide the public with information about the funding sources for particular politicians—not to allow investors to assess whether public companies are using shareholder money to advance political causes.

Thus, the information about corporate political spending that is currently in the public domain is scattered throughout separate filings with the FEC, tax authorities, and state officials, presented in widely varying formats, and is ill-suited to giving shareholders a good picture of a particular corporation's political spending. Putting together all such public data for a given company is a demanding task. Investors in public companies should not have to bear the costs of assembling this information when the corporation, which already has the information, can easily provide it to shareholders. The corporation, rather than individual investors, is in the best position to assemble this information efficiently.

* * *

C. MATERIALITY

In addition, opponents of the Petition have argued that the Commission lacks the statutory authority to adopt the proposed disclosure rules because the magnitude of corporate political spending is not sufficient to meet the securities-law standard of materiality. This argument has been advanced forcefully by the U.S. Chamber of Commerce, which has claimed that the Commission's authority is limited to mandating disclosure of material matters and that "there is no basis whatever for finding [information on political spending] material."

This argument provides little support for opposing rules requiring disclosure of corporate political spending. First, the claim simply asserts a contestable empirical proposition — that public companies' spending on politics is not financially significant — but fails to provide any factual basis for this assertion. Indeed, the evidence presented in this Article suggests that the amounts companies spend on politics might be significant; ... spending by just eight of the most active intermediaries between public companies and politics exceeded $1.5 billion between 2005 and 2010, which is hardly a trivial sum. Of course, until companies are required to disclose political spending, it is impossible to know the full amount of corporate spending on politics. Opponents of transparency in this area should not rely on the lack of disclosure to assert that the amounts not disclosed are not economically significant.

Second, even assuming that the amounts public companies spend on politics do not significantly affect financial results, a finding that political spending is financially significant is not a necessary condition to SEC rules mandating disclosure of that spending. Indeed, many SEC rules have long mandated disclosure of amounts that are unlikely to be financially significant for most large public companies. For example, the SEC's rules on executive pay require disclosure of "[a]ll compensation" paid to executives, including elements of compensation that are not financially significant for the company; indeed, the rules expressly mandate disclosure of amounts as small as $25,000 in some cases. Similarly, the SEC's rules on related-party transactions require disclosure of amounts as small as those exceeding $120,000, although such sums are not financially significant for most large public companies.

The SEC requires these disclosures because the Commission has long recognized that investors may well have an interest in matters beyond the issue's direct relevance to the company's profits and losses. As we have explained, public company investors have expressed considerable interest in having additional information on political spending at the companies they own. Consistent with this evidence, the SEC has previously recognized that political activity is among the issues that may be "significant to an issuer's business, even though such significance is not apparent from an economic viewpoint." Thus, even if opponents.... are correct that the financial magnitude of corporate political spending is not by itself sufficient to meet the standard of securities-law materiality, that fact would provide no basis for concluding that the SEC lacks authority to mandate disclosure of corporate spending on politics.

Comments and Questions

1. The authors of this article were two of the signatories on a petition to the SEC calling for the adoption of a rule that would require disclosure of political related expenses. *See* SEC Petition 4-637 (Aug. 3, 2011) ("We all share, however, the view that information about corporate spending on politics is important to shareholders — and that the Commission's rules should require this information to be disclosed.").

By 2014, the SEC had received over a million comments calling for disclosure. *See* Corporate Reform Coalition, *One Million Comments Urge the SEC to Stop Secret Corporate Political Spending*, Sept. 4, 2014.

2. Given the support for rulemaking, why do you think the Commission has not acted?

3. What do you make of the materiality analysis in the article? Does this information meet the materiality standard set out in *Northway*? Assume that it does, what would be the basis for opposition to disclosure?

4. Would rulemaking efforts in this area generate adverse political ramifications? *See* Financial Services and General Government Appropriations, H. Rep. 113-508, 113th Cong., July 2, 2014 ("The Committee includes language prohibiting funds for the Securities and Exchange Commission to require the disclosure of political contributions, contributions to tax exempt organizations, or dues paid to trade associations.").

5. Could disclosure of this type of information actually harm shareholders? What about bribes paid to government officials in other countries?

C. Disclosure, Conflict Minerals, and the First Amendment

Then there are the instances where disclosure mostly addresses social problems and the SEC is simply instructed to adopt disclosure requirements. In Dodd-Frank, Congress required the imposition of disclosure requirements on issues arguably of only marginal importance to investors. Disclosure was designed to address such matters as human rights violations and corruption. Moreover, it was anticipated that disclosure would alter corporate behavior. This was the case, for example, with respect to the use of conflict minerals.

In the challenges that surfaced after the adoption of the conflicts mineral rule (Rule 13p-1, 17 CFR 240.13p-1), plaintiffs argued that aspects of the rule violated the First Amendment.

National Association of Manufacturers v. SEC
United States Court of Appeals, D.C. Circuit
748 F.3d 359 (2014)

RANDOLPH, SENIOR CIRCUIT JUDGE:

I.

For the last fifteen years, the Democratic Republic of the Congo has endured war and humanitarian catastrophe. Millions have perished, mostly civilians who died of starvation and disease. Communities have been displaced, rape is a weapon, and human rights violations are widespread.

Armed groups fighting the war finance their operations by exploiting the regional trade in several kinds of minerals. Those minerals — gold, tantalum, tin, and tungsten — are extracted from technologically primitive mining sites in the remote eastern

Congo. They are sold at regional trading houses, smelted nearby or abroad, and ultimately used to manufacture many different products. Armed groups profit by extorting, and in some cases directly managing, the minimally regulated mining operations.

In 2010, Congress devised a response to the Congo war. Section 1502 of the Dodd-Frank Wall Street Reform and Consumer Protection Act, Pub.L. No. 111-203, 124 Stat. 1376 (relevant parts codified at 15 U.S.C. §§ 78m(p), 78mnote ('Conflict Minerals')), requires the Securities and Exchange Commission—the agency normally charged with policing America's financial markets—to issue regulations requiring firms using "conflict minerals" to investigate and disclose the origin of those minerals. *See* 15 U.S.C. § 78m(p)(1)(A).

The disclosure regime applies only to "person[s] described" in the Act. *See id.* A "person is described ... [if] conflict minerals are necessary to the functionality or production of a product manufactured by such person." *Id.* § 78m(p)(2). A described person must "disclose annually, whether [its necessary] conflict minerals ... did originate in the [Congo] or an adjoining country." *Id.* § 78m(p)(1)(A). If those minerals "did originate" in the Congo or an adjoining country (collectively, "covered countries") then the person must "submit [a report] to the Commission." *Id.* The report must describe the "due diligence" measures taken to establish "the source and chain of custody" of the minerals, including a "private sector audit" of the report. *Id.* The report must also list "the products manufactured or contracted to be manufactured that are not DRC conflict free." *Id.* A product is "DRC conflict free" if its necessary conflict minerals did not "directly or indirectly finance or benefit armed groups" in the covered countries. *Id.*

In late 2010, the Commission proposed rules for implementing the Act. Conflict Minerals, 75 Fed.Reg. 80,948 (Dec. 23, 2010). Along with the proposed rules, the Commission solicited comments on a range of issues. In response, it received hundreds of individual comments and thousands of form letters. Conflict Minerals, 77 Fed.Reg. 56,274, 56,277–78 (Sept. 12, 2012) ("final rule") (codified at 17 C.F.R. §§ 240.13p-1, 249b.400). The Commission twice extended the comment period and held a round-table for interested stakeholders. *Id.* By a 3–2 vote, it promulgated the final rule, which became effective November 13, 2012. *Id.* at 56,274. The first reports are due by May 31, 2014. *Id.*

The final rule adopts a three-step process, which we outline below, omitting some details not pertinent to this appeal. At step one, a firm must determine if the rule covers it. *Id.* at 56,279, 56,285. The final rule applies only to securities issuers who file reports with the Commission under sections 13(a) or 15(d) of the Exchange Act. *Id.* at 56,287. The rule excludes issuers if conflict minerals are not necessary to the production or functionality of their products. *Id.* at 56,297–98. The final rule does not, however, include a *de minimis* exception, and thus applies to issuers who use very small amounts of conflict minerals. *Id.* at 56,298. The rule also extends to issuers who only contract for the manufacture of products with conflict minerals, as well as issuers who directly manufacture those products. *Id.* at 56,290–92.

Step two requires an issuer subject to the rule to conduct a "reasonable country of origin inquiry." *Id.* at 56,311. The inquiry is a preliminary investigation reasonably designed to determine whether an issuer's necessary conflict minerals originated in covered countries. *Id.* at 56,312. If, as a result of the inquiry, an issuer either knows that its necessary conflict minerals originated in covered countries or "has reason to believe" that those minerals "may have originated" in covered countries, then it must proceed to step three and exercise due diligence. *Id.* at 56,313.

An issuer who proceeds to step three must "exercise due diligence on the source and chain of custody of its conflict minerals." *Id.* at 56,320. If, after performing due diligence an issuer still has reason to believe its conflict minerals may have originated in covered countries, it must file a conflict minerals report. The report must describe both its due diligence efforts, including a private sector audit,4 *id.*, and those products that have "not been found to be 'DRC conflict free,'" *id.* at 56,322 (quoting 15 U.S.C. § 78m(p)(1)(A)(ii)). The report must also provide detailed information about the origin of the minerals used in those products. *Id.* at 56,320.

The final rule does offer a temporary reprieve. During a two-year phase-in period (four years for smaller issuers), issuers may describe certain products as "DRC conflict undeterminable" instead of conflict-free or not conflict-free. *Id.* at 56,321–22. That option is available only if the issuer cannot determine through due diligence whether its conflict minerals originated in covered countries, or whether its minerals benefitted armed groups. *Id.* An issuer taking advantage of the phase-in by describing its products as "DRC conflict undeterminable" must still perform due diligence and file a conflict minerals report, but it need not obtain a private sector audit. *Id.*

* * *

This brings us to the Association's First Amendment claim. The Association challenges only the requirement that an issuer describe its products as not "DRC conflict free" in the report it files with the Commission and must post on its website. 15 U.S.C. § 78m(p)(1)(A)(ii) & (E). That requirement, according to the Association, unconstitutionally compels speech.

The Commission argues that rational basis review is appropriate because the conflict free label discloses purely factual non-ideological information. We disagree. Rational basis review is the exception, not the rule, in First Amendment cases. *See Turner Broad. Sys., Inc. v. FCC*, 512 U.S. 622, 641–42, 114 S.Ct. 2445, 129 L.Ed.2d 497 (1994). The Supreme Court has stated that rational basis review applies to certain disclosures of "purely factual and uncontroversial information." *Zauderer v. Office of Disciplinary Counsel*, 471 U.S. 626, 651, 105 S.Ct. 2265, 85 L.Ed.2d 652 (1985). But as intervenor Amnesty International forthrightly recognizes, we have held that *Zauderer* is "limited to cases in which disclosure requirements are 'reasonably related to the State's interest in preventing deception of consumers.'"

* * *

Having established that rational basis review does not apply, we do not decide whether to use strict scrutiny or the *Central Hudson* test for commercial speech. That is because the final rule does not survive even *Central Hudson's* intermediate standard.

Under *Central Hudson,* the government must show (1) a substantial government interest that is; (2) directly and materially advanced by the restriction; and (3) that the restriction is narrowly tailored. 447 U.S. at 564–66, 100 S.Ct. 2343; *see R.J. Reynolds,*696 F.3d at 1212. The narrow tailoring requirement invalidates regulations for which "narrower restrictions on expression would serve [the government's] interest as well." *Cent. Hudson,* 447 U.S. at 565, 100 S.Ct. 2343. Although the government need not choose the "least restrictive means" of achieving its goals, there must be a "reasonable" "fit" between means and ends. *Bd. of Trs. v. Fox,* 492 U.S. 469, 480, 109 S.Ct. 3028, 106 L.Ed.2d 388 (1989). The government cannot satisfy that standard if it presents no evidence that less restrictive means would fail. *Sable Commc'ns v. FCC,* 492 U.S. 115, 128–32, 109 S.Ct. 2829, 106 L.Ed.2d 93 (1989).

The Commission has provided no such evidence here. The Association suggests that rather than the "conflict free" description the statute and rule require, issuers could use their own language to describe their products, or the government could compile its own list of products that it believes are affiliated with the Congo war, based on information the issuers submit to the Commission. The Commission and Amnesty International simply assert that those proposals would be less effective. But if issuers can determine the conflict status of their products from due diligence, then surely the Commission can use the same information to make the same determination. And a centralized list compiled by the Commission in one place may even be more convenient or trustworthy to investors and consumers. The Commission has failed to explain why (much less provide evidence that) the Association's intuitive alternatives to regulating speech would be any less effective.

The Commission maintains that the fit here is reasonable because the rule's impact is minimal. Specifically, the Commission argues that issuers can explain the meaning of "conflict free" in their own terms. But the right to explain compelled speech is present in almost every such case and is inadequate to cure a First Amendment violation. *See Nat'l Ass'n of Mfrs.,* 717 F.3d at 958. Even if the option to explain minimizes the First Amendment harm, it does not eliminate it completely. Without any evidence that alternatives would be less effective, we still cannot say that the restriction here is narrowly tailored.

We therefore hold that 15 U.S.C. §78m(p)(1)(A)(ii) & (E), and the Commission's final rule, 77 Fed.Reg. at 56,362–65, violate the First Amendment to the extent the statute and rule require regulated entities to report to the Commission and to state on their website that any of their products have "not been found to be 'DRC conflict free.'"

———————

The Commission sought rehearing by the panel and rehearing en banc of the decision. In the interim, the DC Circuit en banc decided *American Meat Institute v. US Dept. of Agriculture,* 760 F.3d 18 (DC Cir. 2014). The case held that Zauderer applied to disclosures that went beyond concerns over deception. In the aftermath of the decision, the majority in NAM declined to change its reasoning.

National Association of Manufacturers v. SEC

DC Circuit
800 F.3d 518 (2015) (petition for rehearing en banc denied, Nov. 9, 2015)
On Petitions For Panel Rehearing.

RANDOLPH, SENIOR CIRCUIT JUDGE:

* * *

Justice White, writing for the majority in *Zauderer,* expressed the Court's holding with his customary precision: we "hold," he wrote, "that an advertiser's [First Amendment] rights are adequately protected *as long as* disclosure requirements are reasonably related to the State's interest in preventing deception of consumers." *Zauderer,* 471 U.S. at 651, 105 S.Ct. 2265 (italics added). In several opinions, our court therefore treated *Zauderer* as limited to compelled speech designed to cure misleading advertising. Government regulations forcing persons to engage in commercial speech for other purposes were evaluated under *Central Hudson Gas & Electric Corp. v. Public Service Commission,* 447 U.S. 557, 564–66, 100 S.Ct. 2343, 65 L.Ed.2d 341 (1980), rather than *Zauderer.* . . .

Our initial opinion in this case adhered to circuit precedent and declined to apply *Zauderer* on the ground that the "conflict minerals" disclosures, compelled by the Dodd-Frank law and the implementing regulations of the Securities and Exchange Commission, were unrelated to curing consumer deception. NAM, 748 F.3d at 370–71.

After our opinion in *NAM* issued, the en banc court in *AMI* decided that *Zauderer* covered more than a state's forcing disclosures in order to cure what would otherwise be misleading advertisements. *AMI,* 760 F.3d at 21–23. Some other governmental interests might suffice. Using *Zauderer*'s relaxed standard of review, *AMI* held that the federal government had not violated the First Amendment when it forced companies to list on the labels of their meat cuts the country in which the animal was born, raised, and slaughtered. *Id.* at 23, 27. It was of no moment that the governmental objective the *AMI* court identified as sufficient—enabling "consumers to choose American-made products," *id.* at 23—was one the government disavowed not only when the Department of Agriculture issued its regulations, but also when the Department of Justice defended them in our court, *id.* at 25; *id.* at 46–47 (Brown, J., dissenting). The *AMI* court therefore overruled the portion of our decisions in *NAM, R.J. Reynolds,* and *National Association of Manufacturers v. NLRB* holding that the analysis in *Zauderer* was confined to government compelled disclosures designed to prevent the deception of consumers.

In light of the *AMI* decision, we granted the petitions of the Securities and Exchange Commission and intervenor Amnesty International for rehearing to consider what effect, if any, *AMI* had on our judgment that the conflict minerals disclosure requirement in 15 U.S.C. §78m(p)(1)(A)(ii) & (E), and the Commission's final rule, 77 Fed.Reg. 56,274, 56,362–65, violated the First Amendment to the Constitution. *See* Order of November 18, 2014. For the reasons that follow we reaffirm our initial judgment.

* * *

Conflict minerals disclosures are to be made on each reporting company's website and in its reports to the SEC. In the rulemaking, the SEC acknowledged that the statute—and its regulations—were "directed at achieving overall social benefits," that the law was not "intended to generate measurable, direct economic benefits to investors or issuers," and that the regulatory requirements were "quite different from the economic or investor protection benefits that our rules ordinarily strive to achieve." 77 Fed.Reg. at 56,350.

The SEC thus recognized that this case does not deal with advertising or with point of sale disclosures. Yet the Supreme Court's opinion in *Zauderer* is confined to advertising, emphatically and, one may infer, intentionally. In a lengthy opinion, the Court devoted only four pages to the issue of compelled disclosures. *Zauderer,* 471 U.S. at 650–53, 105 S.Ct. 2265. Yet in those few pages the Court explicitly identified advertising as the reach of its holding no less than thirteen times. Quotations in the preceding footnote prove that the Court was not holding that any time a government forces a commercial entity to state a message of the government's devising, that entity's First Amendment interest is minimal. Instead, the *Zauderer* Court—in a passage *AMI* quoted, 760 F.3d at 22—held that the advertiser's "constitutionally protected interest in *not* providing any particular factual information *in his advertising* is minimal." *Zauderer,* 471 U.S. at 651, 105 S.Ct. 2265 (last italics added).

* * *

[W]e therefore hold that *Zauderer* has no application to this case....

But given the flux and uncertainty of the First Amendment doctrine of commercial speech, and the conflict in the circuits regarding the reach of *Zauderer,* we think it prudent to add an alternative ground for our decision. It is this. Even if the compelled disclosures here are commercial speech and even if *AMI*'s view of *Zauderer* governed the analysis, we still believe that the statute and the regulations violate the First Amendment.

To evaluate the constitutional validity of the compelled conflict minerals disclosures, the first step under *AMI* (and *Central Hudson*) is to identify and "assess the adequacy of the [governmental] interest motivating" the disclosure requirement. *AMI,* 760 F.3d at 23. Oddly, the SEC's Supplemental Brief does not address this subject. In the first round of briefing the SEC described the government's interest as "ameliorat[ing] the humanitarian crisis in the DRC." Appellee Br. 26. We will treat this as a sufficient interest of the United States under *AMI* and *Central Hudson.*

After identifying the governmental interest or objective, we are to evaluate the effectiveness of the measure in achieving it. *AMI,*760 F.3d at 26; *see, e.g., Ibanez v. Fla. Dep't of Bus. & Prof. Reg.,* 512 U.S. 136, 146, 114 S.Ct. 2084, 129 L.Ed.2d 118 (1994);*Central Hudson,* 447 U.S. at 564–66, 100 S.Ct. 2343. Although the burden was on the government, *see Ibanez,* 512 U.S. at 146, 114 S.Ct. 2084, here again the SEC has offered little substance beyond citations to statements by two Senators and members of the executive branch, and a United Nations resolution. The government asserts that this is a matter of foreign affairs and represents "the type of 'value judgment based on the common sense of the people's representatives' for which this Court has not required more detailed evidence." Appellee Br. 64 (quoting *Nat'l Ass'n of Mfrs. v. Taylor*, 582 F.3d 1, 16 (D.C.Cir.2009)). As the government notes, in the area of foreign relations, "conclusions must often be based on informed judgment rather than concrete evidence." *Holder v. Humanitarian Law Project*, 561 U.S. 1, 34–35, 130 S.Ct. 2705, 177 L.Ed.2d 355 (2010).

But in the face of such evidentiary gaps, we are forced to assume what judgments Congress made when crafting this rule. The most obvious stems from the cost of compliance, estimated to be $3 billion to $4 billion initially and $207 million to $609 million annually thereafter, *see* 77 Fed.Reg. at 56,334, and the prospect that some companies will therefore boycott mineral suppliers having any connection to this region of Africa. How would that reduce the humanitarian crisis in the region? The idea must be that the forced disclosure regime will decrease the revenue of armed groups in the DRC and their loss of revenue will end or at least diminish the humanitarian crisis there. But there is a major problem with this idea—it is entirely unproven and rests on pure speculation.

Under the First Amendment, in commercial speech cases the government cannot rest on "speculation or conjecture." *Edenfield v. Fane*, 507 U.S. 761, 770, 113 S.Ct. 1792, 123 L.Ed.2d 543 (1993). But that is exactly what the government is doing here. Before passing the statute, Congress held no hearings on the likely impact of § 1502. The SEC points to hearings Congress held on prior bills addressing the conflict in the DRC, but those hearings did not address the statutory provisions at issue in this case.When Congress held hearings after § 1502's enactment, the testimony went both ways—some suggested the rule would alleviate the conflict, while others suggested it had "had a significant adverse effect on innocent bystanders in the DRC." *The Unintended Consequences of Dodd-Frank's* Conflict Minerals *Provision: Hearing Before the Subcomm. on Monetary Policy and Trade of the H. Comm. on Financial Services*, 113th Cong. (May 21, 2013) (Statement of Rep. Campbell).

Other post-hoc evidence throws further doubt on whether the conflict minerals rule either alleviates or aggravates the stated problem. As NAM points out on rehearing, the conflict minerals law may have backfired. Because of the law, and because some companies in the United States are now avoiding the DRC, miners are being put out of work or are seeing even their meager wages substantially reduced, thus exacerbating the humanitarian crisis and driving them into the rebels' camps as a last resort. Appellants Supp. Br. 17; *see, e.g.*, Sudarsan Raghavan, *How a Well-Intentioned U.S. Law Left Congolese Miners Jobless*, WASH. POST, Nov. 30, 2014; Lauren Wolfe, *How Dodd-Frank is Failing Congo*, FOREIGN POL'Y, Feb. 2, 2015.

Our original opinion pointed out that the SEC was unable to quantify any benefits of the forced disclosure regime itself. *NAM*, 748 F.3d at 364. *See* 77 Fed.Reg. at 56,335 ("The statute therefore aims to achieve compelling social benefits, which we are unable to readily quantify with any precision."). The Government Accountability Office has refrained from addressing the issue, even though the conflict minerals statute required it to assess the effectiveness of the required disclosures in relieving the humanitarian crises.15 U.S.C. §78m(p)(1)(A)(ii) & (E); *see* U.S. G.A.O., CONFLICT MINERALS: STAKEHOLDER OPTIONS FOR RESPONSIBLE SOURCING ARE EXPANDING, BUT MORE INFORMATION ON SMELTERS IS NEEDED 3 (June 26, 2014) ("[W]e have not yet addressed the effectiveness of SEC's conflict minerals rule as required under the legislation.").

That is not to say that we know for certain that the conflict minerals rule will not help—other sources contend the rule will do so. But it is to say that whether §1502 will work is not proven to the degree required under the First Amendment to compel speech.

All of this presents a serious problem for the SEC because, as we have said, the government may not rest on such speculation or conjecture. *Edenfield v. Fane,* 507 U.S. at 770, 113 S.Ct. 1792. Rather the SEC had the burden of demonstrating that the measure it adopted would "in fact alleviate" the harms it recited "to a material degree." *Id.* at 771, 113 S.Ct. 1792; *see, e.g., Ibanez,* 512 U.S. at 146, 114 S.Ct. 2084; *Turner Broad. Sys., Inc. v. FCC,* 512 U.S. 622, 664, 114 S.Ct. 2445, 129 L.Ed.2d 497 (1994) (plurality opinion); *Pearson v. Shalala,* 164 F.3d 650, 659 (D.C.Cir.1999); *Action for Children's Television v. FCC,* 58 F.3d 654, 665 (D.C.Cir.1995) (en banc). The SEC has made no such demonstration in this case and, as we have discussed, during the rulemaking the SEC conceded that it was unable to do so.

This in itself dooms the statute and the SEC's regulation. If that were not enough, we would move on to evaluate another aspect of *AMI,* an aspect of the opinion on which two of the supplemental briefs on rehearing (those of the SEC and NAM) focus—namely, whether the compelled disclosures here are "purely factual and un-controversial," *AMI,* 760 F.3d at 26 (quoting *Zauderer,* 471 U.S. at 651, 105 S.Ct. 2265)....

We see no way to read *AMI* except as holding that—to quote *AMI*—*Zauderer* "requires the disclosure to be of 'purely factual and uncontroversial information' about the good or service being offered. "*AMI,* 760 F.3d at 27. We are therefore bound to follow that holding. *See LaShawn A. v. Barry,* 87 F.3d 1389, 1393 (D.C.Cir.1996) (en banc).

Even so, the intervenors are correct that the *AMI* majority "made no attempt to define those terms precisely." Intervenors Supp. Br. 9....

One clue is that "uncontroversial," as a legal test, must mean something different than "purely factual." Hence, the statement in *AMI* we just quoted, describing "controversial in the sense that [the compelled speech] communicates a message that is controversial for some reason other than [a] dispute about simple factual accuracy." *AMI,* 760 F.3d at 27. Perhaps the distinction is between fact and opinion. But that line is often blurred, and it is far from clear that all opinions are controversial. Is Einstein's General Theory of Relativity fact or opinion, and should it be regarded as controversial? If the government required labels on all internal combustion engines stating that "USE OF THIS PRODUCT CONTRIBUTES TO GLOBAL WARMING" would that be fact or opinion? It is easy to convert many statements of opinion into assertions of fact simply by removing the words "in my opinion" or removing "in the opinion of many scientists" or removing "in the opinion of many experts." *Cf. Omnicare, Inc. v. Laborers Dist. Council Constr. Indus. Pension Fund,* ___ U.S. ___, 135 S.Ct. 1318, 191 L.Ed.2d 253 (2015); Frederick Schauer, *Facts and the First Amendment,* 57 UCLA L. REV. 897 (2010). It is also the case that propositions once regarded as factual and uncontroversial may turn out to be something quite different. What time frame should a court use in assessing this? At the time of enactment of the disclosure statute? At the time of an agency's rulemaking implementing the disclosure statute? Or at some later time when the compelled disclosures are no longer considered "purely factual" or when the disclosures have become "controversial"?

* * *

In our initial opinion we stated that the description at issue—whether a product is "conflict free" or "not conflict free"—was hardly "factual and non-ideological." *NAM,* 748 F.3d at 371. We put it this way: "Products and minerals do not fight conflicts. The label '[not] conflict free' is a metaphor that conveys moral responsibility for the Congo war. It requires an issuer to tell consumers that its products are ethically tainted, even if they only indirectly finance armed groups. An issuer, including an issuer who condemns the atrocities of the Congo war in the strongest terms, may disagree with that assessment of its moral responsibility. And it may convey that 'message' through 'silence.' *See Hurley,* 515 U.S. at 573, 115 S.Ct. 2338. By compelling an issuer to confess blood on its hands, the statute interferes with that exercise of the freedom of speech under the First Amendment. *See id.*" *NAM,* 748 F.3d at 371.

We see no reason to change our analysis in this respect. And we continue to agree with NAM that "[r]equiring a company to publicly condemn itself is undoubtedly a more 'effective' way for the government to stigmatize and shape behavior than for the government to have to convey its views itself, but that makes the requirement more constitutionally offensive, not less so." Appellants Reply Br. 27–28.

For all these reasons, we adhere to our original judgment "that 15 U.S.C. § 78m(p)(1)(A)(ii) & (E), and the Commission's final rule, 77 Fed.Reg. at 56,362–65, violate the First Amendment to the extent the statute and rule require regulated entities to report to the Commission and to state on their website that any of their products have 'not been found to be "DRC conflict free."'" *NAM,* 748 F.3d at 373.

So ordered.

SRINIVASAN, Circuit Judge, dissenting:

Issuers of securities must make all sorts of disclosures about their products for the benefit of the investing public. No one thinks that garden-variety disclosure obligations of that ilk raise a significant First Amendment problem. So here, there should be no viable First Amendment objection to a requirement for an issuer to disclose the country of origin of a product's materials—including, say, whether the product contains specified minerals from the Democratic Republic of the Congo (DRC) or an adjoining country, the site of a longstanding conflict financed in part by trade in those minerals. Such a requirement provides investors and consumers with useful information about the geographic origins of a product's source materials. Indeed, our court, sitting en banc, recently relied on "the time-tested consensus that consumers want to know the geographical origin of potential purchases" in upholding a requirement for companies to identify the source country of food products. *Am. Meat Inst. v. U.S. Dep't of Agric.*, 760 F.3d 18, 24 (D.C.Cir.2014) (internal quotation marks omitted). It is hard to see what is altogether different about another species of "geographical origin" law requiring identification of products whose minerals come from the DRC or adjoining countries.

If an issuer's products contain minerals originating in those conflict-ridden countries, the Conflict Minerals Rule requires the issuer to determine whether the products are "DRC conflict free," where "DRC conflict free" is a statutorily defined term of art denoting products that are free of "conflict minerals that directly or indirectly finance or benefit armed groups" in the DRC or adjoining countries. 15 U.S.C. §78m(p)(1)(D). If the issuer cannot conclude, after investigating the sourcing of its minerals, that a product is "DRC conflict free" under the statutory definition, it must say so in a report disclosing that the product has "not been found to be 'DRC conflict free.'" The requirement to make that disclosure, in light of the anticipated reaction by investors and consumers, aims to dissuade manufacturers from purchasing minerals that fund armed groups in the DRC region. That goal is unique to this securities law; but the basic mechanism—disclosure of factual information about a product in anticipation of a consumer reaction—is regular fare for governmental disclosure mandates. Many disclosure laws, including the law upheld in *AMI*, operate in just that way.

Appellants raise no First Amendment objection to the obligation to find out which of their products fail to qualify as "DRC conflict free" within the meaning of the statutory definition. Nor do they challenge the obligation to list those products in a report for investors. Appellants also presumably would have no problem with a requirement to list the products by parroting the statutory definition, *i.e.*, as products that have not been determined to be free of conflict minerals that "directly or indirectly finance or benefit armed groups" in the DRC region. At least some issuers in fact have been making essentially that sort of disclosure, without apparent objection, under the partial stay of the Rule in effect since our original panel decision. *See* Exchange Act Rule 13p-1 and Form SD, Exchange Act Release No. 72,079 (May 2, 2014); *e.g.*, Canon Inc., Conflict Minerals Report (Form SD Ex. 1.01) §5 (May 29, 2015).

Appellants' challenge instead is a more targeted one: they object only to the Rule's requirement to describe the listed products with the catchphrase "not been found to be 'DRC conflict free.'" But if there is no First Amendment problem with an obligation to identify and list those products, or to describe them by quoting the statutory definition, it is far from clear why the prescribed use of a shorthand phrase for that definition—in lieu of the technical definition itself—would materially change the constitutional calculus.

Perhaps one might object that the meaning of the shorthand description "DRC conflict free" would not necessarily be known to a reader. But that descriptor comes amidst a set of mandated disclosures about the measures undertaken to determine the source of minerals originating in the DRC or adjoining countries. So the meaning of "DRC conflict free" would seem quite apparent in context. And even if otherwise, an investor or consumer coming across that term for the first time would, with little effort, learn that it carries a specific meaning prescribed by law.

But that's not all. To eliminate any possibility of confusion, the Rule's disclosure obligation enables the issuer to elaborate on the prescribed catchphrase however it sees fit. So, for example, the issuer could say that the listed products have "not been found to be 'DRC conflict free,' *which is a phrase we are obligated to use under federal securities laws to describe products when we are unable to determine that they contain no minerals that directly or indirectly finance or benefit armed groups in the DRC or an adjoining country.*" At that point, there would seem to be nothing arguably confusing or misleading about the content of the Rule's mandated disclosure.

The First Amendment, under the Supreme Court's decisions, poses no bar to the Rule's disclosure obligation. The Court has emphasized that "the extension of First Amendment protection to commercial speech is justified principally by the value to consumers of the information such speech provides." *Zauderer v. Office of Disciplinary Counsel*, 471 U.S. 626, 651, 105 S.Ct. 2265, 85 L.Ed.2d 652 (1985). Correspondingly, when the government requires disclosure of truthful, factual information about a product to consumers, a company's First Amendment interest in withholding that information from its consumers is "minimal." *Id.* That is why countless disclosure mandates in the commercial arena — country of origin of products and materials, calorie counts and nutritional information, extensive reporting obligations under the securities laws, and so on — raise no serious First Amendment question.

The sum of the matter is this: in the context of commercial speech, the compelled disclosure of truthful, factual information about a product to consumers draws favorable review. That review takes the form of the permissive standard laid down by the Supreme Court in *Zauderer*. I would apply that approach here. Like the mine-run of uncontroversial requirements to disclose factual information to consumers in the commercial sphere, the descriptive phrase "not been found to be 'DRC conflict free'" communicates truthful, factual information about a product to investors and consumers: it tells them that a product has not been found to be free of minerals originating in the DRC or adjoining countries that may finance armed groups.

Appellants challenge the prescribed catchphrase for such a product — "not been found to be 'DRC conflict free'" — on the ground that it ostensibly brands issuers with a "scarlet letter." Appellant Br. 52. Appellants' invocation of a "scarlet letter" is out of place. If they mean to suggest that issuers would prefer to avoid the label "not found to be 'DRC conflict free'" because it invites public scrutiny, the same is true of all sorts of entirely permissible requirements to disclose factual information to consumers (high calorie counts or low nutritional value, for instance). When a law mandates disclosure of that sort of "particular factual information" about a company's product, the Supreme Court has said, the company has only a "minimal" cognizable interest in withholding public disclosure. *Zauderer*, 471 U.S. at 651, 105 S.Ct. 2265.

By contrast, the scarlet "A" affixed to Hester Prynne's gown conveyed personal information that she had a strong and obvious interest in withholding from the public. In that sense, requiring a company to disclose product information in the commercial market-place is not the same as requiring Hester Prynne to "show [her] scarlet letter in the [town] marketplace." Nathaniel Hawthorne, The Scarlet Letter 63 (Laird & Lee 1892).

I would therefore hold that the favored treatment normally afforded to compelled factual disclosures in the commercial arena applies to the Conflict Minerals Rule. The obligation to use the term "not been found to be 'DRC conflict free'" should be subject to relaxed *Zauderer* review, which it satisfies. Even under the less permissive test for restrictions on commercial speech established in *Central Hudson Gas & Electric Corp. v. Public Service Commission,* 447 U.S. 557, 100 S.Ct. 2343, 65 L.Ed.2d 341 (1980), I would find that the Rule survives. Because I would conclude that the Conflict Minerals Rule works no violation of the First Amendment, I respectfully disagree with the contrary decision reached by my colleagues.

Comments and Questions

1. The litigation was not a complete loss for the Commission. The original opinion unanimously rejected a variety of challenges to the Rule under the Administrative Procedure Act. In particular, the court found that the cost benefit analysis employed by the Commission in connection with the adoption of Rule 13p-1 was adequate. As the panel reasoned:

> [W]e find it difficult to see what the Commission could have done better. The Commission determined that Congress intended the rule to achieve "compelling social benefits," *id.* at 56,350, but it was "unable to readily quantify" those benefits because it lacked data about the rule's effects. *Id.* That determination was reasonable. An agency is not required "to measure the immeasurable," and need not conduct a "rigorous, quantitative economic analysis" unless the statute explicitly directs it to do so. *Inv. Co. Inst. v. Commodity Futures Trading Comm'n,* 720 F.3d 370, 379 (D.C.Cir.2013) (internal quotation marks omitted); *see Chamber of Commerce,* 412 F.3d at 142. Here, the rule's benefits would occur half-a-world away in the midst of an opaque conflict about which little reliable information exists, and concern a subject about which the Commission has no particular expertise. Even if one could estimate how many lives are saved or rapes prevented as a direct result of the final rule, doing so would be pointless because the costs of the rule — measured in dollars — would create an apples-to-bricks comparison.

Other rules had been invalidated on the basis of an inadequate cost benefit analysis (*see Business Roundtable v. SEC,* 647 F.3d 1144 (DC Cir. 2011)). The analysis suggested that either the Commission was doing a better job at cost benefit analysis or the court was imposing a less exacting standard. Which do you think is more likely?

2. Discuss the implications of the conflict mineral disclosure requirement. Should companies be required to make this type of disclosure? Is it appropriate for the SEC

to implement the requirement? Does this suggest a significant change in the regulatory mission of the SEC?

3. The majority found that the challenged phrase implicated commercial speech. The majority could have chosen to apply the "relaxed" standard in *Zauderer* or the intermediate standard in *Central Hudson*. Instead, the opinion determined that the required disclosure in this case did not meet either standard. What was the basis for this determination? Do you agree?

4. What implications might this have for other areas of the federal securities laws? To the extent compelled disclosure must be supported by a government interest that is not speculative, can you make the case that other provisions may be subject to challenge under the First Amendment?

5. In the dissent, Judge Srinivasan viewed the disclosure as "truthful factual information" about a product. On the other hand, he notes that appellants characterized the disclosure as a "scarlet letter." This suggests that the two sides in the litigation view the disclosure very differently. What do you make of this disparity in view? Does it explain the outcome in the case?

6. Who appointed the judges on this panel? Does this matter in considering the outcome of the decision?

7. Dodd Frank also instructed the SEC to draft rules requiring disclosure by "resource extraction companies" of payments to government governments in return for the right to develop oil, gas, or mineral concessions. 15 U.S.C. §78m(q)(2)(A). Senator Lugar described the provision as addressing "oil money intended for a nation's poor ends up lining the pockets of the rich or is squandered on showcase projects instead of productive investments." 156 Cong. Rec. S3816 (May 17, 2010). For an analysis of the rule adopted by the Commission (and struck down by the court), see *American Petroleum Institute v. SEC*, 953 F.Supp.2d 5 (D DC 2013).

Whatever the merits with respect to the disclosure of conflict minerals, the task effectively expanded the SEC's obligations beyond its traditional boundaries. The Agency was made responsible for disclosure that primarily benefited the public rather than shareholders. Not everyone has agreed with this shift.

Celia R. Taylor, *Drowning in Disclosure: The Overburdening of the Securities & Exchange Commission*
8 Va. L. & Bus. Rev. 85 (Winter 2014)

II. The SEC as a Disclosure Dumping Ground

D. Why Are These Types of Disclosures Ending up at the SEC?

The conflict minerals and resource extractive industries provisions are only two examples of Congressional delegation of responsibility to the SEC to craft rules for the disclosure of issues that touch upon political or social policies rather than on the regulation of markets or protection of investors. Given the at best awkward fit of these sections into the securities laws framework, it is worth considering why they ended up there in the first place. A simple explanation may be that legislators default to the SEC when delegating disclosure authority out of habit and out of the not entirely misplaced perception that regulating disclosure is one of the strengths of the SEC. The result is not always a bad one—many disclosure issues properly do belong under SEC jurisdiction. However, the default nature of the decision-making process is problematic. Just as agencies engaging in rulemaking are required to use detailed processes, the delegation of rulemaking authority should also be required to be the result of careful decision-making.

Ideally, disclosure provisions and their locus in a regulatory framework would be the subject of careful thought. Assume that an issue has been identified and deemed worthy of being the subject of a disclosure requirement. The next step taken by those interested in imposing a disclosure obligation should be a careful institutional choice analysis. Institutional choice theory asserts that when crafting public policy or rules, it is important to consider not only the end-goal, but also the mechanism of reaching that goal. Therefore, it is critical to consider what institution will be tasked with pursuing that goal. To make that decision requires comparing the available institutions and assessing their strengths and weakness with regard to the task at hand. Factors in the decision-making process might include, among others, relative expertise, coordination, capture, accountability, and funding.

With this in mind, next consider how conflict minerals disclosure regulation ended up in the SEC's bailiwick. Section 1502 of Dodd-Frank was not the first attempt by legislators to regulate conflict minerals, but earlier attempts proved fruitless because Congress lacked the political will to address the issue. Representative Jim McDermott (D-WA.) tried for years to pass a free-standing bill regulating conflict minerals, and on November 19, 2009, introduced the Conflict Minerals Trade Act in the House. Similarly, on April 23, 2009, Senators Sam Brownback (R-KS), Dick Durbin (D-IL), and Russ Feingold (D-WI) introduced the Congo Conflict Minerals Act of 2009 to "require annual disclosure to the Securities and Exchange Commission of activities involving columbite-tantalite, cassiterite and wolframite for the Democratic Republic of Congo." Neither of these legislative efforts ultimately prevailed as there was insufficient support from fellow politicians.

The rush to adopt Dodd-Frank, coupled with the length and complexity of its provisions, enabled Senator Brownback to slip the conflict minerals provision into the Act with little attention....

While it is puzzling to me that section 1502 falls completely outside the scope of the Dodd-Frank Act, that legislation was passed as a result of the financial crisis to add stability to the financial system. section 1502 does nothing to "provide for financial regulatory reform, to protect consumers and investors, to enhance Federal understanding of insurance issues, or to regulate over-the-counter derivatives markets," which were the stated purpose of the Dodd-Frank Act. Section 1502 does nothing to address the cause of the financial crisis.

Additionally, section 1502 will cause regulation by the SEC. This is a complex matter beyond the SEC's normal area of expertise. The SEC's mission is to protect investors; maintain fair, orderly, and efficient markets; and to facilitate capital formations. This section does not protect investors or provide information about the financial health of companies. So development of this well-intended law—and I will say it was a well-intended law—seems quite irregular. And its impacts on companies are expected to be massive. We have been hearing from a number of companies and trade associations expressing concern about the costs and magnitude of this provision. Now is not the time to be placing additional burden on the American companies.

I am incredulous that Congress would pass a mandate down on businesses that the National Association of Manufacturers estimates to be between $9 billion and $16 billion. While the provision only applies to the SEC-listed companies, the truth is it will affect non-SEC companies and small businesses all over this country. Members of Congress were not the only ones taken by surprise by the inclusion of the conflicts minerals provision and the resulting rulemaking responsibility handed to the SEC. Then-Chairman Mary Shapiro acknowledged that the Commission lacked expertise on the mining of conflict minerals and the disclosure matters mandated by the statute. To be clear, the SEC did not want the responsibility for crafting conflict mineral disclosure regulation and knew that it was not the best choice of entity to take on that responsibility—but, of course, had to do so when faced with a Congressional mandate. The final locus of conflict mineral disclosure regulation within the SEC was far from being the outcome of rational and thoughtful institutional choice.

It seems likely that the inclusion of sections 1502 and 1504 in Dodd-Frank and the resulting delegation of rulemaking authority to the SEC resulted from inattention on the part of many legislators and from a well-founded bias on the part of those members of Congress who were paying attention. That bias led them to default to the SEC because it is viewed as the agency of choice when disclosure matters are involved. While tasking the SEC with disclosure regulation is entirely sensible in many situations, it is not always the agency best suited to the task. As is discussed below, there are other institutions that could better handle certain disclosure matters. It is time to stop reflexively dumping disclosure on the SEC. Instead, we should consider alternative allocations to institutions better situated for the job.

III. Disclosures Could Be Handled By Another Entity

If we are to stop overburdening the SEC with responsibility over disclosure regulations, some change must happen. Either the amount of disclosure required (an idea explored below) must be decreased, or the responsibility for such requirements must be better allocated (or some combination thereof). While the topic of the "correct" level of disclosure is an important and fruitful one, we must first consider whether the SEC must be the disclosure dumping ground. While the SEC is often the default agency to handle disclosure, more thoughtful consideration demonstrates that there are other agencies and institutions that are better positioned to handle disclosure regulations that are currently being allocated to the SEC. Consider the examples of the conflict minerals and the resource extractive industries provisions.

A. Conflict Minerals

As discussed above, there is wide agreement that conflict mineral disclosure has little to do with the core mission of the SEC and ended up under its jurisdiction due largely to inattention and institutional bias. When conflict minerals disclosure was being considered as part of the Conflict Minerals Trade Act (the "CMTA"), rather than as part of Dodd-Frank, disclosure would have been regulated the trade through United States Customs and Border Protection ("Customs"). Although the CMTA died in committee, its provisions are worth noting. The CMTA would have created an auditing mechanism for facilities processing tin, tantalum, and tungsten, a means of identifying and labeling shipments potentially containing conflict minerals, and entrusted to Customs the responsibility of prohibiting shipments from unaudited facilities, beginning two years after the enactment of the legislation.

Delegating to Customs the task of monitoring conflict mineral disclosure is a much better fit than delegating that responsibility to the SEC. One of Customs' stated goals is to "[e]nsure the efficient flow of legitimate trade and travel across the borders of the United States." To achieve this goal, Customs "plays a central role in preventing the entry of unsafe or illegitimate goods into the United States." Customs' primary duties include processing shipments, identifying shipments not imported according to trade regulations, and seizing illegal shipments—functions that make it well-suited to monitor the import of products incorporating conflict minerals. Not only is the maintenance of legitimate trade a stated goal and important function of Customs in a general sense, the agency has experience regulating the import of other conflict resources. It is the agency responsible for enforcing the Kimberley Process, a joint governmental diamond industry and civil society initiative to stem the flow of conflict diamonds. As the responsible agency, Customs must monitor all United States' diamond retailers to endure that they buy diamonds from manufacturers who have the proper documentation and that their merchandise was obtained through legitimate channels. Customs reviews all rough diamond import documentation, flags rough diamond shipments for review, and enters each shipment's information into a computer system. These processes could be adapted to apply to conflict minerals and would allow Customs to capitalize on institutional learning already in place rather than expanding the mandate of the SEC to cover an issue it lacks knowledge in confronting or the capacity to handle effectively.

* * *

Comments and Questions

1. The article illustrates that the disclosure authority given to the SEC over conflict minerals was not part of a significant policy decision to expand the agency's mission. Instead, the SEC ended up with the authority almost by accident.

2. What are some strengths and weaknesses of having Customs address the issues raised by Congress with respect to conflict minerals?

3. Had the SEC been asked if it wanted the authority, what do you think the answer would have been? One chair of the SEC who was not in office when the provision

was adopted described the obligations as "more directed at exerting societal pressure on companies to change behavior, rather than to disclose financial information that primarily informs investment decisions." Mary Jo White, Chair, SEC, *The Importance of Independence*, 14th Annual AA Sommer, Jr. Corporate Securities and Financial Law Lecture, Fordham Law School (Oct. 3, 2013). She went on to say that, "as the Chair of the SEC, I must question, as a policy matter, using the federal securities laws and the SEC's powers of mandatory disclosure to accomplish these goals."

4. What do you make of the argument that the SEC lacks expertise for this type of disclosure? Does the SEC have expertise with respect to all areas of disclosure under its jurisdiction? Where it does not, how does the agency compensate?

5. Should the SEC be traveling down this path? Why might it be the case that Congress will likely repeat the conflict minerals experience at some point in the future by mandating disclosure of other matters of social responsibility? Where is the pressure coming from for such disclosure?

V. Equal Access to Information

While the periodic reports and proxy material remain a critical source of information for investors and shareholders, companies rely increasingly on informal, less regulated methods of notifying the market of important developments, including press release, discussions with analysts, and the Internet. These methods of disclosure are, however, not subject to express regulation by the SEC.

One concern that can arise with this type of informal disclosure is selective dissemination to specific shareholders or market professionals. With the information, the recipients have an informational advantage that they may use in purchasing or selling shares. At one time, selective disclosure was thought to violate the proscriptions on insider trading. In *SEC v. Dirks*, 463 U.S. 646 (1983), however, the Supreme Court essentially held that the selective disclosure of material information by a corporate insider to an analyst was not insider trading absent some type of pecuniary benefit to the insider. The case arguably validated the practice of selective disclosure.

The SEC addressed that concern through the adoption of Regulation FD, a controversial rulemaking endeavor. Regulation FD essentially prohibited deliberate selective disclosure to those likely to use the information for trading purposes. The prohibition on deliberate selective disclosure may seem like a reasonable requirement but it also has the potential to reduce the amount of disclosure available to the market, depending in part upon how the provision is enforced.

In re Office Depot

Exchange Act Release No. 63152 (admin. proc. Oct. 21, 2010)

ORDER INSTITUTING CEASE-AND-DESIST PROCEEDINGS PURSUANT TO SECTION 21C OF THE SECURITIES EXCHANGE ACT OF 1934, MAKING FINDINGS, AND IMPOSING A CEASE-AND-DESIST ORDER

I.

The Securities and Exchange Commission ("Commission") deems it appropriate that cease-and-desist proceedings be, and hereby are, instituted pursuant to Section 21C of the Securities Exchange Act of 1934 ("Exchange Act"), against Office Depot, Inc. ("Respondent").

II.

In anticipation of the institution of these proceedings, Respondent has submitted an Offer of Settlement ("Offer") which the Commission has determined to accept. Solely for the purpose of these proceedings and any other proceedings brought by or on behalf of the Commission, or to which the Commission is a party, and without admitting or denying the findings herein, except as to the Commission's jurisdiction over it and the subject matter of these proceedings, which are admitted, Respondent consents to the entry of this Order Instituting Cease-and-Desist Proceedings Pursuant to Section 21C of the Securities Exchange Act of 1934, Making Findings, and Imposing a Cease-and-Desist Order ("Order"), as set forth below.

III.

On the basis of this Order and Respondent's Offer, the Commission finds that:

Summary

1. Office Depot violated Regulation FD in 2007 by selectively communicating to analysts that it would not meet analysts' quarterly earnings estimates for Office Depot. After a discussion between the company's Chief Executive Officer ("CEO") and then-Chief Financial Officer ("CFO"), Office Depot conducted one-on-one calls with the analysts late in the second quarter of 2007. The company did not directly tell the analysts that it would not meet their expectations; rather, this message was signaled through its references to recent public statements of comparable companies about the impact of the slowing economy on their earnings, and reminders of Office Depot's prior cautionary public statements. The analysts promptly lowered their estimates for the period. The CFO assisted in preparing the talking points for the calls. The CFO and the CEO were aware of the declining estimates while the company made the calls, and they encouraged the calls to be completed. The company also continued to make the calls despite the CFO being notified of some analysts' concerns of, among other things, the lack of public disclosure. Six days after the calls began, Office Depot filed a Form 8-K announcing to the market, among other things, that its sales and earnings would be negatively impacted due to a continued soft economy. Prior to that Form 8-K, Office Depot's share price had significantly dropped on increased trading volume.

* * *

Respondent

3. Office Depot a Delaware corporation based in Boca Raton, Florida, is an office products supplier. Office Depot's common stock is registered with the Commission pursuant to Section 12(b) of the Exchange Act and is traded on the New York Stock Exchange.

Background

A. Regulation FD Violation

4. Office Depot, as a company policy, did not offer specific quarterly earnings guidance during the relevant time period. In late 2006 and early 2007, the CEO and the CFO believed the significant earnings per share ("EPS") growth the company achieved in 2005 and early 2006 was not sustainable and set out to temper analysts' expectations. In February 2007, during a publicly broadcasted earnings conference call, the CEO and the CFO described Office Depot's business model, which contemplated mid to upper teens EPS growth over the long-term. On another public conference call in late April 2007, the company warned investors that its largest business segments were facing a softening in demand that was continuing into the second quarter. Shortly following the analysts' publication of EPS estimates for Office Depot in late April (when most analysts lowered their estimates for Office Depot), the company reiterated at a publicly available investor conference in early May that its business model contemplated only mid to upper teens EPS growth over the long-term and that the company faced a softening demand environment.

5. On May 31, 2007, the CEO alerted Office Depot's board of directors and the executive committee that the company would not likely meet the analysts' consensus $0.48 EPS estimate for the second quarter and that senior management was discussing a strategy for advance communication to avoid a complete surprise to the market.

6. Office Depot did not have written Regulation FD policies or procedures at the time. The company had also never conducted any formal Regulation FD training prior to June 2007, although its general counsel had occasionally distributed guidance and updates on Regulation FD.

Office Depot's Selective Disclosures to Analysts

7. In early June 2007, in response to the CEO's May 31, 2007 notice to the board of directors, the CFO instructed the director of investor relations and his immediate supervisor to prepare a draft press release for her review previewing certain second quarter earnings information should the company later determine to issue one. By mid June 2007, certain of the company's preliminary internal estimates forecasted up to $0.44 EPS for the quarter. The CFO and CEO were uncomfortable with issuing a press release because the company's internal estimates were incomplete at this point.

8. On June 20, 2007, ten days prior to the close of Office Depot's second quarter for 2007, the CEO and the CFO, both of whom had investor relations experience,

discussed how to encourage analysts to revisit their analysis of the company. The CEO, in an attempt to get analysts to lower their estimates, proposed to the CFO that the company talk to the analysts and refer them to recent earnings announcements by two comparable companies that had recently publicly announced results which were impacted by the slowing economy. The CEO further suggested that Office Depot point out on the calls what the company had said to the market in April and May 2007. The CEO and the CFO jointly decided to adopt this approach. The CEO believed that if the analysts looked at Office Depot again in that light, they would come to the point of view that their estimates were too high and likely would lower them.

9. The CFO, the director of investor relations, and the director's immediate supervisor drafted talking points, based in part on the CEO's suggestions, for use as a guide for the calls with analysts. The CEO was not asked to review the talking points and did not do so. The agreed upon talking points are set forth below.

- Haven't spoken in a while, just want to touch base.
- At beg. of Qtr we've talked about a number of head winds that we were facing this quarter including a softening economy, especially at small end.
- I think the earnings release we have seen from the likes of [Company A], [Company B], and [Company C] have been interesting.
- On a sequential basis, [Company A] and [Company B] domestic comps were down substantially over prior quarters.
- [Company C] mentioned economic conditions as a reason for their slowed growth.
- Some have pointed to better conditions in the second half of the year—however who knows?
- Remind you that economic model contemplates stable economic conditions— that is midteens growth

10. On Friday, June 22, 2007, and the following Monday, June 25, 2007, the director of investor relations spoke individually with all 18 analysts covering Office Depot and conveyed to them the information contained in the talking points. Office Depot did not regularly initiate calls of this type to all 18 analysts covering the company. Word of these calls quickly spread among analysts, some of whom believed that Office Depot was "talking down" analysts' earnings estimates.

11. The CFO and the CEO were in communication with the director of investor relations during and after the calls. On Saturday, June 23, 2007, the CFO emailed the analysts' revised estimates to the CEO and advised that the director of investor relations had spoken to most of the company's analysts and that two had reduced their estimates. The CEO responded positively and encouraged the calls to continue so that additional analysts would lower their estimates. On Monday, June 25, 2007, the CFO asked the director of investor relations' immediate supervisor whether the director of investor relations had contacted a particular analyst whose EPS estimate was the highest and had not yet been revised. Also on Monday, the CEO requested

and received an update, which showed that the analysts' consensus estimate was still $0.46. With the CFO's knowledge, the CEO then commented to the director of investor relations that they still needed conversations with a few more analysts.

12. Office Depot's calls influenced many analysts to revise and lower their second quarter 2007 forecasts. By the end of the second day of the calls, fifteen of the eighteen analysts lowered their estimates, bringing the consensus estimate down from $0.48 to $0.45.

Analyst and Investor Reaction to Calls and Calls to Institutional Investors

13. During a call on Friday, June 22, 2007, one analyst expressed concern to the director of investor relations about the lack of a press release. That same day, the director of investor relations conveyed to the CFO this concern and that one other analyst was informing his customers that he expected Office Depot's earnings to be down based on his call.

14. On Monday, June 25, 2007, the director of investor relations notified the CFO that another analyst told him that he was surprised at the lack of a press release and indicated that several of his clients were also surprised. Also, late Monday evening, the CFO instructed the director of investor relations to call the company's top twenty institutional investors and relay the same talking points to them, which he did the following day.

Office Depot Files an 8-K

15. After the close of the market on Thursday, June 28, 2007, six days after the calls to analysts began, Office Depot filed a Form 8-K publicly disclosing, among other things, that its earnings would be "negatively impacted due to continued soft economic conditions."

Market Reaction

16. Between Friday, June 22, 2007 (the day Office Depot began calling analysts) and June 28, 2007 (the last market close before Office Depot filed its 8-K), the company's stock dropped 7.7%. On the first day of the calls, Office Depot's stock closed at $33.49 per share. This was a decrease of 2.8% from the previous close, on trading volume of almost 7.5 million shares, which was two and half times the average volume for the remainder of that week. On the second day of calls, the stock dropped another 3.5% to $32.32 per share on trading volume of 7 million shares.

* * *

Violations

Violations of Regulation FD and Section 13(a) of the Exchange Act

22. Regulation FD prohibits issuers or persons acting on their behalf from disclosing material nonpublic information to securities analysts, institutional investors, or other enumerated persons without disclosing that information to the public. See generally Regulation FD, Rule 100; Final Rule: Selective Disclosure and Insider Trading, Exchange Act Rel. No. 43154, 65 Fed. Reg. 51,716 (Aug. 15, 2000) ("Adopting Release").

Where a selective disclosure of material nonpublic information is "intentional," issuers must make a public disclosure simultaneously with the selective disclosure. Regulation FD, Rule 100(a)(1). Intentional means "when the person making the disclosure either knows, or is reckless in not knowing, that the information he or she is communicating is both material and nonpublic." Regulation FD, Rule 101(a). Where the selective disclosure is "non-intentional," Regulation FD requires issuers to make a public disclosure of the information promptly after a senior official of the issuer learns of the non-intentional disclosure. Rules 100(a)(2) & 101(d). Regulation FD defines "promptly" to mean "as soon as reasonably practicable (but in no event after the later of 24 hours or the commencement of the next day's trading on the New York Stock Exchange)." Rule 101(d).

23. An issuer's failure to make a required public disclosure pursuant to Regulation FD constitutes a violation of both Regulation FD and Section 13(a) of the Exchange Act. See Adopting Release, 65 Fed. Reg. at 51,726.

24. The Commission adopted Regulation FD out of concern that issuers were "disclosing important nonpublic information, such as advance warnings of earnings results, to securities analysts or selected institutional investors or both, before making full disclosure of the same information to the general public." Id. at 51,716. The Commission explained in the Adopting Release:

> When an issuer official engages in a private discussion with an analyst who is seeking guidance about earnings estimates, he or she takes on a high degree of risk under Regulation FD. If the issuer official communicates selectively to the analyst nonpublic information that the company's anticipated earnings will be higher than, lower than, or even the same as what analysts have been forecasting, the issuer likely will have violated Regulation FD. This is true whether the information about earnings is communicated expressly or through indirect "guidance," the meaning of which is apparent though implied.

Id. at 51,721.

25. Furthermore, the Division of Corporation Finance has stated in its interpretations of Regulation FD that "a confirmation of expected quarterly earnings made near the end of a quarter might convey information about how the issuer actually performed. In that respect, the inference a reasonable investor may draw from such a confirmation may differ significantly from the inference he or she may have drawn from the original forecast early in the quarter." Division of Corporation Finance: Manual of Publicly Available Telephone Interpretations, Regulation FD, Item 1 (4th supp., May 2001) ("Telephone Interpretations"). (On August 14, 2009, the Telephone Interpretations regarding Regulation FD were migrated over to the Compliance & Disclosure Interpretation format.)

26. As a result of the conduct described above, Office Depot violated Regulation FD and Section 13(a) of the Exchange Act.

* * *

Remedial Efforts

In determining to accept the Offer, the Commission considered remedial acts promptly undertaken by Respondent and cooperation afforded the Commission staff.

IV.

In view of the foregoing, the Commission deems it appropriate to impose the sanctions agreed to in Respondent's Offer.

Accordingly, it is hereby ORDERED that pursuant to Section 21C of the Exchange Act, Respondent Office Depot cease and desist from committing or causing any violations and any future violations of Sections 13(a), 13(b)(2)(A), and 13(b)(2)(B) of the Exchange Act and Rules 12b-20, 13a-1, and 13a-13 thereunder, and Regulation FD.

By the Commission.

Comments and Questions

1. What type of information would ordinarily be susceptible to selective disclosure? Would this provision apply, for example, to information selectively revealed about the health of the CEO?

2. What exactly did the Company in this case do wrong? The SEC brought the action. Would aggrieved investors also be able to maintain a claim?

3. What impact might this Regulation have on corporate governance? For example, sometimes companies might want to discuss compensation packages with key shareholders before disclosing them in the proxy statement. Would this sort of discussion trigger obligations under Regulation FD?

4. How might a company discuss these matters with key constituencies (such as large investors) without triggering an obligation to reveal the information to the market? Would an oral promise from the shareholder to keep the information confidential be sufficient? Perhaps some of the answer can be found in *SEC v. Cuban*, 620 F.3d 551 (5th Cir. 2010).

5. When the SEC adopted the provision, some critics argued that it would lead to a decline in the amount of disclosure. How would that occur? Is that a likely result from the requirement? *See* Jill E. Fisch & Hillary A. Sale, *The Securities Analyst as Agent: Rethinking the Regulation of Analysts*, 88 Iowa L. Rev. 1035, 1067 (2003) (noting that "initial research suggests that the purported negative effects of Regulation FD on information flow and volatility may be overstated.").

How might public disclosure occur? The SEC has made clear that the filing of a current report on form 8-K will be sufficient. *See* Rule 101(e), 17 CFR § 243.101(e). In addition, however, a company may disseminate the information "through another method (or combination of methods) of disclosure that is reasonably designed to provide broad, non-exclusionary distribution of the information to the public." *Id.* What might this mean? Does it include disclosure through social media?

Report of Investigation Pursuant to Section 21(A) of the Securities Exchange Act of 1934: Netflix, Inc. and Reed Hastings

Exchange Act Release No. 69279 (April 2, 2013)

III. Facts

Netflix is an on-line entertainment service that provides movies and television programming to subscribers by streaming content through the internet and by distributing DVDs through the mail. Over the last two years, Netflix has stated that it is increasingly focused on expanding its internet streaming business.

On January 4, 2012, Netflix announced by press release that it had streamed two billion hours of content in the fourth quarter of 2011. Netflix also featured the two billion hours streaming metric in the opening paragraph of the January 25, 2012, letter to shareholders signed by Hastings that accompanied Netflix's quarterly financial results included in its earnings release, a copy of which was also furnished on EDGAR on a Current Report on Form 8-K. During Netflix's 2011 year-end and fourth quarter earnings conference call on January 25, 2012, Hastings was asked why this streaming metric was relevant (since Netflix's revenues are derived through fixed subscriber fees, not based on the number of hours of programming viewed). Hastings explained that streaming was "a measure of an engagement and scale in terms of the adoption of our service and use of our service.... It [two billion hours streaming in a quarter] is a great milestone for us to have hit. And like I said, shows widespread adoption and usage of the service." He also stated that although he did not anticipate that Netflix would regularly report the number of hours of streamed content, Netflix would update the metric "on a milestone basis."

In an early June posting on Netflix's official blog, Netflix made a brief reference to people "enjoying nearly a billion hours per month of movies and TV shows from Netflix." The blog was technical in nature, announcing a new content delivery network available to Internet Service Providers, and there was no further detail given about the streaming metric. Beyond that, Netflix did not make any milestone announcements regarding streaming hours between January 25, 2012 and the beginning of July 2012.

On July 3, 2012, just before 11:00 a.m. Eastern time, Hastings posted the following message on his personal Facebook page:

> Congrats to Ted Sarados, and his amazing content licensing team. Netflix monthly viewing exceeded 1 billion hours for the first time ever in June. When House of Cards and Arrested Development debut, we'll blow these records away. Keep going, Ted, we need even more!

This announcement represented a nearly 50% increase in streaming hours from Netflix's January 25, 2012 announcement that it had streamed 2 billion hours over the preceding three-month quarter.

Prior to his post, Hastings did not receive input from Netflix's chief financial officer, the legal department, or investor relations department. Netflix did not file with or furnish to the Commission a Current Report on Form 8-K, issue a press release through its standard distribution channels, or otherwise announce the streaming milestone. Also on July 3, 2012, and after the Facebook post, Netflix issued a press release announcing the date of its second quarter 2012 earnings release but did not mention Hastings's Facebook post. Netflix's stock continued a rise that began when the market opened on July 3, increasing from $70.45 at the time of Hastings's Facebook post to $81.72 at the close of the following trading day.

The announcement of the streaming milestone reached the securities market incrementally. The post was picked up by a technology-focused blog about an hour later and by a handful of news outlets within two hours. Approximately an hour after the post, Netflix sent it to several reporters, but did not disseminate it to the broader mailing list normally used for corporate press releases. After the markets closed early at 1:00 p.m., several articles in the mainstream financial press picked up the story. Research analysts also wrote about the streaming milestone, describing the metric as a positive measure of customer engagement, indicative of a reduction in the rate Netflix is losing customers, or "churn," and possibly suggesting that quarterly subscriber numbers would be at the high end of guidance.

Facebook members can subscribe to Hastings's Facebook page, which had over 200,000 subscribers at the time of the post, including equity research analysts associated with registered broker-dealers, shareholders, reporters, and bloggers. Neither Hastings nor Netflix had previously used Hastings's Facebook page to announce company metrics. Nor had they taken any steps to make the investing public aware that Hastings's personal Facebook page might be used as a medium for communicating information about Netflix. Instead, Netflix has consistently directed the public to its own Facebook page, Twitter feed, and blog and to its own web site for information about Netflix. In early December 2012, Hastings stated for the public record that "we [Netflix] don't currently use Facebook and other social media to get material information to investors; we usually get that information out in our extensive investor letters, press releases and SEC filings."

IV. Discussion

A fundamental question raised during the staff's investigation was the application of Regulation FD and the 2008 Guidance to issuer disclosures through rapidly changing forms of communication, including social media channels. We do not wish to inhibit the content, form, or forum of any such disclosure, and we are mindful of placing additional compliance burdens on issuers. In fact, we encourage companies to seek out new forms of communication to better connect with shareholders. We also remind issuers that the analysis of whether Regulation FD was violated is always a facts-and-circumstances analysis based on the specific context presented.

We take this opportunity to clarify and amplify two points. First, issuer communications through social media channels require careful Regulation FD analysis comparable to communications through more traditional channels. Second, the principles outlined in the 2008 Guidance—and specifically the concept that the investing public should be alerted to the channels of distribution a company will use to disseminate material information—apply with equal force to corporate disclosures made through social media channels.

A. Disclosures Triggering Regulation FD

Regulation FD applies when an issuer discloses material, non-public information to certain enumerated persons, including shareholders and securities professionals. It prohibits selective disclosure "[w]henever an issuer, or any person acting on its behalf, discloses any material nonpublic information regarding that issuer *to any person* described in paragraph (b)(1) of this section." Although the Regulation FD Adopting Release highlights the Commission's special concerns about selective disclosure of information to favored analysts or investors, the identification of the enumerated persons within Regulation FD is inclusive, and the prohibition does not turn on an intent or motive of favoritism. Nor does the rule suggest that disclosure of material, non-public information to a broader group that includes both enumerated and non-enumerated persons but that still falls short of a public disclosure negates the applicability of Regulation FD. On the contrary, the rule makes clear that public disclosure of material, nonpublic information must be made in a manner that conforms with Regulation FD whenever such information is disclosed to any group that includes one or more enumerated persons.

Accordingly, we emphasize for issuers that all disclosures to groups that include an enumerated person should be analyzed for compliance with Regulation FD. Specifically, if an issuer makes a disclosure to an enumerated person, including to a broader group of recipients through a social media channel, the issuer must consider whether that disclosure implicates Regulation FD. This would include determining whether the disclosure includes material, nonpublic information. Further, if the issuer were to elect not to file a Form 8-K, the issuer would need to consider whether the information was being disseminated in a manner "reasonably designed to provide broad, non-exclusionary distribution of the information to the public."

B. Broad, Non-Exclusionary Distribution of Information to the Public

Our 2008 Guidance was directed primarily at the use of corporate web sites for the disclosure of material, non-public information. Like web sites, corporate social media pages are created, populated, and updated by the issuer. The 2008 Guidance, furthermore, specifically identified "push" technologies, such as email alerts and RSS feeds and "interactive" communication tools, such as blogs, which could enable the automatic electronic dissemination of information to subscribers. Today's evolving social media channels are an extension of these concepts, whereby information can be disseminated to those with access. Thus, the 2008 Guidance continues to provide a relevant framework for applying Regulation FD to evolving social media channels of distribution.

Specifically, in light of the direct and immediate communication from issuers to investors that is now possible through social media channels, such as Facebook and Twitter, we expect issuers to examine rigorously the factors indicating whether a particular channel is a "recognized channel of distribution" for communicating with their investors. We emphasize for issuers that the steps taken to alert the market about which forms of communication a company intends to use for the dissemination of material, non-public information, including the social media channels that may be used and the types of information that may be disclosed through these channels, are critical to the fair and efficient disclosure of information. Without such notice, the investing public would be forced to keep pace with a changing and expanding universe of potential disclosure channels, a virtually impossible task.

Providing appropriate notice to investors of the specific channels a company will use for the dissemination of material, nonpublic information is a sensible and expedient solution. It is not expected that this step would limit the channels of communication a company could use after appropriate notice or the opportunity for a company and investors to benefit from technological innovation and changes in communications practices. The 2008 Guidance encourages issuers to consider including in periodic reports and press releases the corporate web site address and disclosures that the company routinely posts important information on that web site. Similarly, disclosures on corporate web sites identifying the specific social media channels a company intends to use for the dissemination of material non-public information would give investors and the markets the opportunity to take the steps necessary to be in a position to receive important disclosures—e.g., subscribing, joining, registering, or reviewing that particular channel. These are some, but certainly not all, of the methods a company could use, with minimal burden, to enable evolving social media channels of corporate disclosure to be used as recognized channels of distribution in compliance with Regulation FD and the 2008 Guidance.

Although every case must be evaluated on its own facts, disclosure of material, nonpublic information on the personal social media site of an individual corporate officer, without advance notice to investors that the site may be used for this purpose, is unlikely to qualify as a method "reasonably designed to provide broad, non-exclusionary distribution of the information to the public" within the meaning of Regulation FD. This is true even if the individual in question has a large number of subscribers, friends, or other social media contacts, such that the information is likely to reach a broader audience over time. Personal social media sites of individuals employed by a public company would not ordinarily be assumed to be channels through which the company would disclose material corporate information. Without adequate notice that such a site may be used for this purpose, investors would not have an opportunity to access this information or, in some cases, would not know of that opportunity, at the same time as other investors.

V. Conclusion

There has been a rapid proliferation of social media channels for corporate communication since the issuance of the Commission's 2008 Guidance. An increasing number of public companies are using social media to communicate with their shareholders and the investing public. We appreciate the value and prevalence of social media channels in contemporary market communications, and the Commission supports companies seeking new ways to communicate and engage with shareholders and the market. This Report is not aimed at inhibiting corporate communication through evolving social media channels. To the contrary, we seek to remind issuers that disclosures to persons enumerated in Regulation FD, even if made through evolving social media channels, must still be analyzed for compliance with Regulation FD. Moreover, we emphasize that the Commission's 2008 Guidance, though largely focused on the use of web sites, is equally applicable to current and evolving social media channels of corporate communication. The 2008 Guidance explained that issuers must take steps sufficient to alert investors and the market to the channels it will use for the dissemination of material, nonpublic information. We believe that adherence to this guidance will help, with minimal burden, to assure compliance with Regulation FD and the fair and efficient operation of the market.

Comments and Questions

1. *In re Netflix* is a Report filed under Section 21(a) of the Exchange Act. 15 U.S.C. § 78u(a). These types of reports are rarely issued by the Commission (from 1996 through 2014, the Commission issued 14 of these reports). The provision allows the SEC to "publish information" disclosing the results of any investigation. The reports are not admissions by the parties involved. What is the purpose of these reports? Why do you think one was issued in this case?

2. Based upon this case, what advice would you give to corporations seeking to meet their obligations under Regulation FD through the use of social media? How much did it matter in this case that the relevant disclosure took place over the CEO's personal Facebook page rather than over a similar site operated by Netflix?

3. Netflix subsequently posted on its corporate web site a social media disclosure policy. The policy notified investors that the company used "social media to communicate with our subscribers and the public about our company, our services and other issues and that investors were encouraged ... to review the information we post on the [listed] U.S. social media channels ... The listed channels included Facebook, Twitter, the Netflix Investor Relations YouTube Page, and the Facebook page for the CEO." Had the policy already been in place, would the SEC have issued the Section 21(a) Report in this case?

4. What are some other possible limitations imposed by social media? Does the analysis change whether the applicable social media involves push technology? What about the limitation on the number of characters in Twitter? The SEC has indicated in other contexts that where disclosure occurs over a platform that "has technological limitations on the number of characters or amount of text," the issuer does not have to include certain required legends but can include a hyperlink to the relevant language. Is the same authority be available with respect to disclosure under Regulation FD?

5. The SEC has taken the position that simultaneous broadcast of a shareholder meeting or analyst conference can constitute public disclosure under Regulation FD so long as investors are given adequate notice of the conference/call and the means for accessing it. As the Commission noted:

> First, issue a press release, distributed through regular channels, containing the information; Second, provide adequate notice, by a press release and/or website posting, of a scheduled conference call to discuss the announced results, giving investors both the time and date of the conference call, and instructions on how to access the call; and Third, hold the conference call in an open manner, permitting investors to listen in either by telephonic means or through Internet webcasting.

Exchange Act Release No. 43154 (Aug. 21, 2000). Note, however, that this approach does not actually require anyone to attend the conference call. In other words, the company can make selective disclosure as long as there is an opportunity for others to participate. What do you make of this? Should there be additional requirements such as an obligation by the company to post the broadcast on the Internet for some specified period of time?

Chapter 10

Shareholders' Derivative Litigation

What can shareholders do if they believe that the corporation's directors or officers have engaged in wrongdoing, shirked their responsibilities, or otherwise injured the firm? The conventional answer is that shareholders can sell their shares (the "Wall Street Walk"), vote to replace directors, or sue the responsible corporate fiduciaries to enforce their duties. However, we have seen that, absent proof of fraud or self-dealing, courts rarely find corporate fiduciaries liable for breaching their legal duties. The law of Delaware, where most large public companies are incorporated, affords broad legal protection to directors so long as they act in good faith and in a manner that they believe to be in the best interests of the corporation. Nevertheless, shareholders sometimes attempt to redress alleged malfeasance through litigation. For example, in 2002 and 2003, shareholders of dozens of public companies filed lawsuits after revelations of egregious financial frauds also exposed gross failures of corporate governance systems. In addition to suing for damages, plaintiff investors also may seek injunctive relief, reforms to the company's governance structure or practices, and payment of their counsel's fees and costs.

While a corporate fiduciary's dereliction of his duties generally gives rise to one or more causes of action held by the firm rather than its shareowners, corporate law (initially developed by courts exercising their equitable authority) allows one or more of the company's shareholders to maintain a derivative action to enforce the corporation's claims. Shareholders have standing to sue on behalf of the corporation "in the interests of justice"[1] — that is, to hold directors and officers accountable for breaching their legal duties to the corporation. However, legislators and courts have imposed severe restrictions on shareholder derivative litigation. Why? One concern is that shareholders will bring claims against directors and officers for losses attributable to market forces or other external factors. Also, according to critics of shareholders' lawsuits, plaintiffs' attorneys will prosecute meritless claims in order to extract settlements that benefit lawyers but not corporations or shareholders. Because companies often choose to avoid engaging in lengthy, expensive litigation by offering to settle claims, even weak claims, corporate directors and officers may become the targets of strike suits.

Nonetheless, directors' actual exposure to liability from such complaints is quite limited. The business judgment rule insulates directors from many claims for breach of fiduciary duty. Furthermore, as discussed in Chapter 4, corporations often can limit the financial liability of their directors prospectively by including exculpation

---

1. *Schoon v. Smith*, 953 A.2d 196 (Del. 2008).

clauses in their articles of incorporation. Recall that Delaware added Section 102(b)(7) to the General Corporation Law in response to the *Smith v. Van Gorkom* decision. In substance, Section 102(b)(7) authorizes a corporation to restrict or even eliminate a director's personal liability for many breaches of fiduciary duty, and it acts as one of the most significant restrictions on recoveries produced by shareholder litigation. Of course, Section 102(b)(7) prohibits corporations from eliminating directors' liability for breach of the duty of loyalty, or for acts or omissions which are in bad faith, intentional, or knowing violations of law. Nor can exculpatory clauses limit liability for wrongful corporate distributions or for any transaction from which the director derived an improper personal benefit.

The Delaware courts continue to establish the precise contours of Section 102(b)(7). In 2009, the Delaware Supreme Court held that officers of Delaware corporations owe the same fiduciary duties as directors, but the court emphasized that neither Section 102(b)(7) nor any other Delaware statute authorizes the prospective limitation of an officer's personal liability. Indeed, Delaware courts have not yet resolved important questions concerning the extent to which the law may expose non-director executives to greater fiduciary liability. Recent cases do highlight the importance of pleading non-exempt conduct; namely, duty of loyalty claims that will withstand defendants' inevitable dispositive motions. Assuming corporations have utilized Section 102(b)(7) to eliminate directors' liability to the fullest extent, shareholders' complaints to enforce fiduciary duties must allege that defendants' conduct falls within one of Section 102(b)(7)'s exceptions. Although courts often dismiss duty of care claims, plaintiffs may be allowed to proceed if they somehow can characterize defendants' misconduct as disloyal.

I. Preliminary Consideration—
Direct or Derivative Claims

When presented with a complaint filed by a corporation's shareholders against its directors and officers, the court initially must determine whether that lawsuit is direct or derivative in nature. A direct suit alleges that an officer or director breached a duty owed to shareholders specifically. In a direct action, the shareholder sues to enforce that duty or redress his own injury. By contrast, a derivative suit alleges that the defendant officers and directors breached a duty owed to the corporation. The plaintiff-shareholder sues to enforce the rights of the corporation, derivatively.

This fundamental distinction has significant implications. Although we later consider procedural requirements for derivative actions in more depth, it is important to note here that those requirements impose substantial obstacles for lawsuits classified as derivative. If a derivative action manages to clear these hurdles and produce some recovery, that recovery is for the benefit of the corporation, to be shared only indirectly with the firm's shareholders. Recovery in a direct suit, by contrast, inures to the benefit of the shareholders who prosecute the suit. And while a derivative suit precludes further action for the same breach of duty, a direct suit has no such effect, except to the extent that the direct suit is brought as a class action on behalf of the named plaintiff and other shareholders similarly situated.

Traditionally, courts have distinguished the two types of actions with a "special injury" inquiry. If the plaintiff-shareholder suffered a special injury, then the action was deemed direct. If every shareholder suffered the same injury equally, then the action was deemed derivative. More recent decisions center on whether the shareholder can prevail without showing an injury or breach of duty to the corporation. If he can, then the action is direct; otherwise, it is derivative. The Delaware Supreme Court ultimately clarified the relevant test under Delaware law in the following case.

Tooley v. Donaldson, Lufkin & Jenrette, Inc.

Delaware Supreme Court
845 A.2d 1031 (2004)

VEASEY, CHIEF JUSTICE:

Plaintiff-stockholders brought a purported class action in the Court of Chancery, alleging that the members of the board of directors of their corporation breached their fiduciary duties by agreeing to a 22-day delay in closing a proposed merger. Plaintiffs contend that the delay harmed them due to the lost time-value of the cash paid for their shares. The Court of Chancery granted the defendants' motion to dismiss on the sole ground that the claims were, "at most," claims of the corporation being asserted derivatively. They were, thus, held not to be direct claims of the stock-holders, individually. Thereupon, the Court held that the plaintiffs lost their standing to bring this action when they tendered their shares in connection with the merger.

We set forth in this Opinion the law to be applied henceforth in determining whether a stockholder's claim is derivative or direct. That issue must turn *solely* on the following questions: (1) who suffered the alleged harm (the corporation or the suing stockholders, individually); and (2) who would receive the benefit of any recovery or other remedy (the corporation or the stockholders, individually)?

Patrick Tooley and Kevin Lewis are former minority stockholders of Donaldson, Lufkin & Jenrette, Inc. (DLJ), a Delaware corporation engaged in investment banking. DLJ was acquired by Credit Suisse Group (Credit Suisse) in the Fall of 2000. Before that acquisition, AXA Financial, Inc. (AXA), which owned 71% of DLJ stock, controlled DLJ. Pursuant to a stockholder agreement between AXA and Credit Suisse, AXA agreed to exchange with Credit Suisse its DLJ stockholdings for a mix of stock and cash. The consideration received by AXA consisted primarily of stock. Cash made up one-third of the purchase price. Credit Suisse intended to acquire the remaining minority interests of publicly-held DLJ stock through a cash tender offer, followed by a merger of DLJ into a Credit Suisse subsidiary.

The tender offer price was set at $90 per share in cash. The tender offer was to expire 20 days after its commencement. The merger agreement, however, authorized two types of extensions. First, Credit Suisse could unilaterally extend the tender offer if certain conditions were not met, such as SEC regulatory approvals or certain payment obligations. Alternatively, DLJ and Credit Suisse could agree to postpone acceptance by Credit Suisse of DLJ stock tendered by the minority stockholders.

Credit Suisse availed itself of both types of extensions to postpone the closing of the tender offer. The tender offer was initially set to expire on October 5, 2000, but Credit Suisse invoked the five-day unilateral extension provided in the agreement. Later, by agreement between DLJ and Credit Suisse, it postponed the merger a second time so that it was then set to close on November 2, 2000.

Plaintiffs challenge the second extension that resulted in a 22-day delay. They contend that this delay was not properly authorized and harmed minority stockholders while improperly benefitting AXA. They claim damages representing the time-value of money lost through the delay.

The Decision of the Court of Chancery

Plaintiffs argue that they have suffered a "special injury" because they had an alleged contractual right to receive the merger consideration of $90 per share without suffering the 22-day delay arising out of the extensions under the merger agreement. But the trial court's opinion convincingly demonstrates that plaintiffs had no such contractual right that had ripened at the time the extensions were entered into:

> Because Credit Suisse Group and DLJ did in fact agree to extend the tender offer period, any right to payment plaintiffs could have did not ripen until this newly negotiated period was over. The merger agreement only became binding and mutually enforceable at the time the tendered shares ultimately were accepted for payment by Credit Suisse Group.

It is at that moment in time, November 3, 2000, that the company became bound to purchase the tendered shares, making the contract mutually enforceable. DLJ stockholders had no individual contractual right to payment until November 3, 2000, when their tendered shares were accepted for payment.

The Court of Chancery correctly noted that "[t]he Court will independently examine the nature of the wrong alleged and any potential relief to make its own determination of the suit's classification.... Plaintiffs' classification of the suit is not binding." The trial court's analysis was hindered, however, because it focused on the confusing concept of "special injury" as the test for determining whether a claim is derivative or direct. The trial court's premise was as follows:

> In order to bring a *direct* claim, a plaintiff must have experienced some 'special injury.' A special injury is a wrong that 'is separate and distinct from that suffered by other shareholders, ... or a wrong involving a contractual right of a shareholder, such as the right to vote, or to assert majority control, which exists independently of any right of the corporation.' [citations omitted].

In our view, the concept of "special injury" that appears in some Supreme Court and Court of Chancery cases is not helpful to a proper analytical distinction between direct and derivative actions. We now disapprove the use of the concept of "special injury" as a tool in that analysis.

The Proper Analysis to Distinguish Between Direct and Derivative Actions

The analysis must be based solely on the following questions: Who suffered the alleged harm—the corporation or the suing stockholder individually—and who would receive the benefit of the recovery or other remedy?

In the context of a claim for breach of fiduciary duty, the Chancellor articulated the inquiry as follows: "Looking at the body of the complaint and considering the nature of the wrong alleged and the relief requested, has the plaintiff demonstrated that he or she can prevail without showing an injury to the corporation?" We believe that this approach is helpful in analyzing the first prong of the analysis: what person or entity has suffered the alleged harm? The second prong of the analysis should logically follow.

A Brief History of Our Jurisprudence

Because a derivative suit is being brought on behalf of the corporation, the recovery, if any, must go to the corporation. A stockholder who is directly injured, however, does retain the right to bring an individual action for injuries affecting his or her legal rights as a stockholder. Such a claim is distinct from an injury caused to the corporation alone. In such individual suits, the recovery or other relief flows directly to the stockholders, not to the corporation.

Determining whether an action is derivative or direct is sometimes difficult and has many legal consequences, some of which may have an expensive impact on the parties to the action. For example, if an action is derivative, the plaintiffs are then required to comply with the requirements of Court of Chancery Rule 23.1, that the stockholder: (a) retain ownership of the shares throughout the litigation; (b) make presuit demand on the board; and (c) obtain court approval of any settlement. Further, the recovery, if any, flows only to the corporation. The decision whether a suit is direct or derivative may be outcome-determinative. Therefore, it is necessary that a standard to distinguish such actions be clear, simple and consistently articulated and applied by our courts.

Two confusing propositions have encumbered our caselaw governing the direct/derivative distinction. The "special injury" concept can be confusing in identifying the nature of the action. The same is true of the proposition that an action cannot be direct if all stockholders are equally affected or unless the stockholder's injury is separate and distinct from that suffered by other stockholders.

A court should look to the nature of the wrong and to whom the relief should go. The stockholder's claimed direct injury must be independent of any alleged injury to the corporation. The stockholder must demonstrate that the duty breached was owed to the stockholder and that he or she can prevail without showing an injury to the corporation.

Standard to Be Applied in This Case

In this case it cannot be concluded that the complaint alleges a derivative claim. There is no derivative claim asserting injury to the corporate entity. There is no relief that would go the corporation. Accordingly, there is no basis to hold that the complaint states a derivative claim.

But, it does not necessarily follow that the complaint states a direct, individual claim. While the complaint purports to set forth a direct claim, in reality, it states no claim at all. The trial court analyzed the complaint and correctly concluded that it does not claim that the plaintiffs have any rights that have been injured. Their rights have not yet ripened. The contractual claim is nonexistent until it is ripe, and that claim will not be ripe until the terms of the merger are fulfilled, including the extensions of the closing at issue here. Therefore, there is no direct claim stated in the complaint before us.

Accordingly, the complaint was properly dismissed. But, due to the reliance on the concept of "special injury" by the Court of Chancery, the ground set forth for the dismissal is erroneous, there being no derivative claim. That error is harmless, however, because, in our view, there is no direct claim either.

Comments and Questions

1. Why did Tooley and Lewis insist that their claims were derivative? Wouldn't the opportunity to recover damages directly lead all but the most altruistic shareholders to plead their claims as direct in nature?

2. In its Principles of Corporate Governance, the ALI adopted a direct-derivative test based on the essential elements of the claim. Under Section 7.01, if the shareholder can prevail only by showing an injury to the corporation or the breach of a duty owed to the corporation, then the action is derivative. If that proof is not essential to the claim, then the action may be maintained as direct. Where both direct and derivative claims are possible, the shareholder should be allowed to maintain both simultaneously. The ALI also has provided four relevant policy considerations for courts reviewing close cases:

> (1) The recovery in a derivative action will be shared broadly with all shareholders and creditors of the corporation, while recovery in a direct action will be limited to the plaintiffs;
>
> (2) A derivative action will have preclusive effect while a direct action will not;
>
> (3) In a derivative action the plaintiff may recover attorney's fees directly from the corporation but cannot do so in a direct action; and
>
> (4) Characterizing the action as derivative may entitle the board to take over the action or seek dismissal.

In a close case, would these factors favor a direct suit or a derivative suit? Would *Tooley*'s two-part test necessarily produce the same result?

II. Derivative Litigation

Although shareholders' derivative litigation began as an equitable remedy for minority shareholders, the actions evolved into a mechanism for shareholders to hold management accountable for malfeasance. In a derivative action, the shareholder who initiates the suit represents the interests of the firm and, indirectly, the interests of other shareholders. Thus, the plaintiff must establish standing.

A. Standing

Schoon v. Smith

Delaware Supreme Court
953 A.2d 196 (2008)

RIDGELY, JUSTICE:

Appellant Richard W. Schoon is a director, but not a stockholder, of Troy Corporation, a privately held Delaware corporation. He filed a derivative action in the Court of Chancery on behalf of Troy, alleging breaches of fiduciary duties by his fellow directors.

Schoon argues on appeal that this Court should hold that a director has the right to bring a derivative action for the same reasons that equity has traditionally granted stockholders the right to do so. He contends that an extension of standing to a director will promote Delaware public policy. Although the Delaware General Assembly has the prerogative to confer standing upon directors by statute, it has not chosen to do so. Because a stockholder derivative action is available to redress any breach of fiduciary duty, we decline to extend the doctrine of equitable standing to allow a director to bring a similar action.

Facts and Procedural Background

Troy Corporation is a privately held Delaware corporation whose capital structure consists of three series of common stock. Series A shares are entitled to elect four of the five Troy directors. Daryl Smith, the CEO and Chairman of Troy, owns a majority of the Series A shares, which he voted to elect himself and three others to the board of directors. Series B stockholders have the right to elect the final member of the board. Another privately held Delaware Corporation, Steel, owns a majority of Series B shares, which it voted to elect Schoon, who owns no stock in Troy, to the Troy board of directors. Series C shares have no voting rights.

Schoon alleges that shortly after he became a director of Troy, he discovered that the other three board members were "beholden to Smith," which enabled Smith to dominate and control the board. Schoon alleges that Smith has taken actions on several occasions that were designed to entrench himself in power and, in turn, thwart potential value-maximizing transactions for the benefit of Troy and its stockholders....

Standing and the Rationale for Equitable Standing of Stockholders

"Standing is the requisite interest that must exist in the outcome of the litigation at the time the action is commenced." We have previously explained the concept:

> The concept of 'standing,' in its procedural sense, refers to the right of a party
> to invoke the jurisdiction of a court to enforce a claim or redress a grievance.

It is concerned only with the question of *who* is entitled to mount a legal challenge and not with the merits of the subject matter of the controversy. In order to achieve standing, the plaintiff's interest in the controversy must be distinguishable from the interest shared by other members of a class or the public in general. Unlike the federal courts, where standing may be subject to stated constitutional limits, state courts apply the concept of standing as a matter of self-restraint to avoid the rendering of advisory opinions at the behest of parties who are 'mere intermeddlers.'

The traditional concept of standing confers upon the corporation the right to bring a cause of action for its own injury.

As "a creature of equity," the derivative action has generally served as a vehicle to enforce a corporate right. There has been a singular purpose for this grant of equitable standing to a stockholder:

The stockholder does not bring such a suit because *his* rights have been *directly* violated, or because the cause of action is *his*, or because *he* is entitled to the relief sought; he is permitted to sue in this manner *simply in order to set in motion the judicial machinery of the court*.... In fact, the plaintiff has no such *direct* interest; the defendant corporation alone has a direct interest; the plaintiff is permitted, notwithstanding his want of interest, to maintain the action *solely to prevent an otherwise complete failure of justice.*

Statutory Restrictions Upon Equitable Standing of Stockholders

Over time, the stockholder derivative action became stigmatized as a "refuge of strike suit artists specializing in corporate extortion." In response, statutes to authorize and regulate this type of action were passed. In Delaware, the General Assembly enacted Section 327 of the Delaware General Corporation Law, titled "Stockholder's derivative action; allegation of stock ownership." Section 327 provides:

In any derivative suit instituted by a stockholder of a corporation, it shall be averred in the complaint that the plaintiff was a stockholder of the corporation at the time of the transaction of which such stockholder complains or that such stockholder's stock thereafter devolved upon such stockholder by operation of law.

This provision and its predecessor were enacted solely "to prevent what has been considered an evil, namely, the purchasing of shares in order to maintain a derivative action designed to attack a transaction which occurred prior to the purchase of the stock." Further, "while the statute should be construed so as to reasonably effectuate its primary purpose — to discourage a type of strike suit — it should not be construed so as to unduly encourage the camouflaging of transactions and thus prevent reasonable opportunities to rectify corporate aberrations."

Section 327 "*does not create the right to sue derivatively, but rather restricts that right.*" The equitable standing of a stockholder to bring a derivative action was judicially created but later restricted by a statutory requirement that a stockholder plaintiff must either have been a stockholder at the time of the transaction of which she complains or her stock must have devolved upon her thereafter by operation of law. The judicial creation of equitable standing for a stockholder to bring a derivative action demonstrates that equitable doctrine can be judicially extended to address new circumstances. Accordingly, we cannot agree with the Court of Chancery's categorical conclusion that "any decision" to extend equitable standing to a director is for the General Assembly to make. That decision is one the judiciary is empowered to make as well. We conclude, however, that there is no reason to do so at this time.

The Extension of Equitable Doctrine

As this Court has noted, "it is well settled law that the judiciary has the power to overturn *judicially-created doctrine*, so long as that doctrine has not been codified in statute." Here, we are dealing with judicially-created equitable doctrine that also has been embodied in a statute. We are asked to exercise our inherent authority to extend the doctrine of equitable standing to include a director at a time when the General Assembly has not spoken on the subject. Judicially-created equitable doctrines may be extended so long as the extension is consistent with the principles of equity.

Having these principles and the rationale for the original grant of equitable standing to stockholders in mind, we examine the role of corporate directors and whether new exigencies require extending the doctrine of equitable standing to allow a director to bring a derivative action.

Director Independence

We begin with the bedrock statutory principle that "[t]he business and affairs of every corporation ... shall be managed by or under the direction of a board of directors...." In discharging their management function, "directors owe fiduciary duties of care and loyalty to the corporation and its shareholders."

As *Aronson* and *Beam* demonstrate, director "independence" does not require that a director remove the debate from the boardroom to the courtroom to resolve his or her differences with the board. Nor have we defined "independence" to enlarge a director's fundamental fiduciary duties so as to include a duty to sue on behalf of the corporation in his or her capacity as a director.

Notwithstanding these considerations, Schoon advances a practical argument for his standing to sue. He contends that to protect the interests of the corporation and the stockholders, a director should be permitted to sue derivatively because the director is in a better position to know and to make his allegations against the board without waiting for a stockholder to do so. This proposed efficiency overlooks the reason why the equitable standing doctrine was adopted, which (to reiterate) is to prevent a complete failure of justice on behalf of the corporation.

No such complete failure is presented in this case. Here, the stockholder who elected Schoon (Steel) is not only aligned with him, but also is actively litigating other matters involving Troy before the Court of Chancery. We take judicial notice that Steel has already begun using the "tools at hand" to obtain books and records information from Troy. Given the well-established duties of a director and the ability and the right of Steel, as a stockholder, to bring a derivative action if Steel deems it necessary, we perceive no new exigencies that require an extension of equitable standing to Schoon, as a director.

The ALI Proposal for Director Standing

In arguing that a grant of standing to directors will further the policy of protecting against misconduct by fiduciaries, Schoon urges us to adopt the 1994 proposal of the American Law Institute ("ALI") that relates to director standing.

Section 7.02(c) of the ALI Principles provides: "A director of a corporation has standing to commence and maintain a derivative action unless the court finds that the director is unable to represent fairly and adequately the interests of the shareholders." The commentary to this provision recognizes that this is a "special right" because "most directors will already have standing to sue as shareholders." The ALI Principles also acknowledge that normally a director will bring his or her concerns regarding illegal or fraudulent conduct to the board and that the preference is for the entire board to provide "a collegial response" to a director's concerns regarding potential misconduct. The ALI Principles justify the creation of director derivative standing only for those occasions "when the board is dominated by a controlling shareholder, in which the board will fail to act even when clear evidence of misbehavior or illegality has been presented to it...." The ALI Principles further reason that procedural requirements for maintaining a shareholder derivative suit, such as contemporaneous ownership and continuing ownership, do not apply to directors because "the director's fiduciary obligation entitles the director to seek to rectify wrongs to the corporation that do not directly injure the director." ...

Given the absence of statutory authority for his standing to sue as a director, Schoon's argument must succeed or fail on the merits of extending the doctrine of equitable standing judicially. We have explained the rationale for this equitable doctrine and decline to enlarge it by embracing a policy that will divert the doctrine from its original purpose: to prevent a complete failure of justice. Schoon has not shown that a complete failure of justice will occur unless he is granted standing to sue as a director. A stockholder derivative action would fully and adequately redress any injuries to Troy resulting from a breach of fiduciary duty by its board. Accordingly, we decline to extend equitable standing to Schoon to sue derivatively in his capacity as a director.

Comments and Questions

1. Under the so-called contemporaneous ownership requirement in Section 327 of Delaware's statute, a shareholder lacks standing to bring a derivative claim unless she owned stock at the time the alleged wrong was committed. In practice, the contemporaneous ownership requirement may affect the ability of entrepreneurial lawyers to find shareholders willing to act as representative plaintiffs. Before his appointment to the Chancery Court, Vice Chancellor Travis Laster urged that the Delaware General Assembly amend Section 327 to require that a derivative plaintiff hold stock only at the time the complaint is filed, and that she not voluntarily divest the shares during the action's pendency.[2] In 2014, Vice Chancellor Laster refused to apply the contemporaneous ownership requirement to creditor plaintiffs who had filed a derivative

action, reasoning that by its plain language, Section 327 applied only to stockholders.[3] Other courts have refused to disqualify contemporaneous shareholders from acting as plaintiffs in derivative suits, even when they demonstrate very little knowledge of the claims asserted.[4]

2. In addition to contemporaneous ownership, state law also may require derivative plaintiffs to comply with other rules in order to maintain their standing. Some states, for example, mandate that the shareholder plaintiff hold a continuing interest in the corporation until the derivative lawsuit concludes. The plaintiff, then, may lose standing to pursue her derivative claims if the corporation in which the plaintiff holds shares merges with another firm. However, the lawsuit may proceed "if the merger itself is the subject of a claim of fraud, being perpetrated merely to deprive stockholders of the standing to bring a derivative action."[5]

3. Did the court's decision in *Schoon* turn on anything other than the activities of Steel? What if the only other shareholders had been those who were under the "domination and control" of Smith?

4. Under ALI Principles, directors' fiduciary duties provide them with standing to pursue harms inflicted on the corporation. Should state procedural rules designed to restrict shareholders' derivative claims (e.g., the contemporaneous ownership requirement) also apply if directors wish to sue on behalf of the corporation? Why or why not?

B. The Demand Requirement

The demand requirement for derivative litigation forces shareholders to appeal to corporate directors for action before involving the courts in the governance dispute. The Federal Rules of Civil Procedure governing derivative litigation, reprinted below, mandate that the plaintiff attempt to resolve the dispute privately before the matter can proceed in court.

Federal Rule of Civil Procedure 23.1. Derivative Actions

(b) Pleading Requirements. The complaint must be verified and must:

(1) allege that the plaintiff was a shareholder or member at the time of the transaction complained of, or that the plaintiff's share or membership later devolved on it by operation of law;

(2) allege that the action is not a collusive one to confer jurisdiction that the court would otherwise lack; and

---

2. J. Travis Laster, *Goodbye to the Contemporaneous Ownership Requirement*, 33 Del. J. Corp. L. 673 (2008) (arguing that the rule arbitrarily mandates dismissal of potentially meritorious claims and is unnecessary in light of the numerous alternatives available to defendants seeking to dismiss strike suits).

3. *Quadrant Structured Prod. Co. v. Vertin*, 2014 WL 5099428 (Del. Ch. Oct. 1, 2014).

4. *See, e.g.,* In re Fuqua Indus., Inc. Shareholder Litig., 752 A.2d 126 (Del. Ch. 1999).

5. *See Lewis v. Anderson*, 477 A.2d 1040 (Del. 1984).

    (3) state with particularity:

        (A) any effort by the plaintiff to obtain the desired action from the directors or comparable authority and, if necessary, from the shareholders or members; and

        (B) the reasons for not obtaining the action or not making the effort.

Delaware Court of Chancery Rule 23.1 substantially follows the federal analog. The complaint must describe the "efforts, if any, made by the plaintiff to obtain the action the plaintiff desires from the directors or comparable authority and the reasons for the plaintiff's failure to obtain the action or for not making the effort."

The rule requiring stockholder plaintiffs to make efforts to obtain the desired action from the board is commonly called the "demand requirement." Before a stockholder can maintain a derivative claim, she must "demand" that the board assert the rights of the corporation. As the Delaware Supreme Court explained in *Grimes v. Donald*:

> A stockholder filing a derivative suit must allege either that the board rejected his pre-suit demand that the board assert the corporation's claim or allege with particularity why the stockholder was justified in not having made the effort to obtain board action.[6]

Furthermore, the plaintiff stockholder must include these allegations in her complaint when filed, without the benefit of discovery.

In reality, the derivative action is two distinct actions: one to compel the board of directors to assert the corporation's rights, and a second to actually assert those rights. Because the nature of a derivative action is such that the rights ultimately forming the basis of recovery belong to the corporation, the board's right to control the business and affairs of the corporation entitles it to manage the litigation. Insistence that the board of directors consider the merits of the potential litigation preserves the corporation's interests in keeping business decisions within management's control. The courts also have pointed to two policies — both intended to deter lawsuits and reduce litigation costs — underlying the demand requirement. First, compelling plaintiffs to make demand promotes intracorporate dispute resolution; shareholders must seek action by the board of directors and exhaust their internal remedies before pursuing their complaint in court. Second, the demand requirement serves to discourage the filing of baseless claims, non-meritorious complaints filed for the purpose of extracting nuisance value settlements from the corporation. Thus, the demand requirement promotes resolution of corporate disputes outside the courtroom and eliminates frivolous cases from judicial dockets.

Unless the culpable directors or officers have left the company, boards almost always refuse shareholders' demands. For a host of reasons that we explore next, di-

---

6. *Grimes v. Donald*, 673 A.2d 1207, 1216 (Del. 1996).

rectors are loath to pursue claims against their board colleagues or the non-director executives to whom the board delegated management responsibility. After receiving the company's decision and considering its stated reasons for refusing the demand, the shareholder may choose not to pursue the matter further, or the shareholder may seek to enforce the corporation's claims derivatively and plead that the board wrongfully refused the demand. At that point, the corporation likely will respond by moving to dismiss the shareholder's complaint, and the court likely will grant that motion. Indeed, courts very rarely deny motions to dismiss in demand refused cases. The shareholder plaintiff making the demand has conceded, by law, the board's independence and disinterestedness and has waived the right to argue that demand was futile or otherwise excused.[7] Furthermore, the business judgment rule protects the board's decision to refuse demand.[8] In other words, "[w]here the board considers a demand, and determines that pursuit of the litigation demanded is not in the corporate interest, the stockholder thereafter lacks standing to bring the litigation derivatively, unless the board's refusal is wrongful; that is, the refusal itself is in breach of the directors' fiduciary duties."[9] Plaintiff, then, not only must allege sufficient facts to state a claim against the defendants, but plaintiff also must plead with particularity facts giving rise to reasonable doubt that the board exercised due care by refusing plaintiff's demand. This double pleading burden is nearly insurmountable if well-advised boards investigate shareholder demands in good faith.

Experienced shareholders' counsel, then, rarely advise their clients to make demand on the board before filing their derivative complaint. Instead, shareholders will plead demand futility. If the reviewing judge agrees, the court will excuse demand. Since compliance with the demand requirement involves delay and some added expense, and because shareholders who initiate demands waive their rights to later allege demand futility, shareholders regularly elect to sue without doing so. In their study of shareholder litigation filed in Delaware courts from 1999 to 2000, Professors Robert Thompson and Randall Thomas reported that plaintiffs plead demand futility (demand excused) in nearly all derivative cases litigated during that period.[10] However, shareholder plaintiffs still must satisfy onerous pleading requirements. Fed. R. Civ. P. 23.1 and its Delaware counterpart require that the complaint "allege with particularity … the reasons for the plaintiff's failure to obtain the action or for not making the effort."

When will the courts excuse demand as futile? The following principal case decided by the Delaware Supreme Court sets out the test for demand futility under Delaware law.

---

7. *See Spiegel v. Buntrock*, 571 A.2d 767, 774–75 (Del. 1990).

8. *See Levine v. Smith*, 591 A.2d 194, 212 (Del. 1991).

9. *Ironworkers Dist. Council of Philadelphia & Vicinity Retirement & Pension Plan v. Andreotti*, 2015 WL 2270673 (Del. Ch. May 8, 2015).

10. *See* Robert B. Thompson & Randall S. Thomas, *The Public and Private Faces of Derivative Lawsuits*, 57 Vand. L. Rev. 1747 (2004).

Aronson v. Lewis

Delaware Supreme Court
473 A.2d 805 (1984)

MOORE, JUSTICE:

[W]hen is a stockholder's demand upon a board of directors, to redress an alleged wrong to the corporation, excused as futile prior to the filing of a derivative suit? We granted this interlocutory appeal to the defendants, Meyers Parking System, Inc. (Meyers), a Delaware corporation, and its directors, to review the Court of Chancery's denial of their motion to dismiss this action, pursuant to Chancery Rule 23.1, for the plaintiff's failure to make such a demand or otherwise demonstrate its futility. The Vice Chancellor ruled that plaintiff's allegations raised a "reasonable inference" that the directors' action was unprotected by the business judgment rule. Thus, the board could not have impartially considered and acted upon the demand.

We cannot agree with this formulation of the concept of demand futility. In our view demand can only be excused where facts are alleged with particularity which create a reasonable doubt that the directors' action was entitled to the protections of the business judgment rule. Because the plaintiff failed to make a demand, and to allege facts with particularity indicating that such demand would be futile, we reverse the Court of Chancery and remand with instructions that plaintiff be granted leave to amend the complaint.

The issues of demand futility rest upon the allegations of the complaint. The plaintiff, Harry Lewis, is a stockholder of Meyers. The defendants are Meyers and its ten directors, some of whom are also company officers.

This suit challenges certain transactions between Meyers and one of its directors, Leo Fink, who owns 47% of its outstanding stock. Plaintiff claims that these transactions were approved only because Fink personally selected each director and officer of Meyers.

On January 1, 1981, the defendants approved an employment agreement between Meyers and Fink for a five year term with provision for automatic renewal each year thereafter, indefinitely. Meyers agreed to pay Fink $150,000 per year, plus a bonus of 5% of its pre-tax profits over $2,400,000. Fink could terminate the contract at any time, but Meyers could do so only upon six months' notice. At termination, Fink was to become a consultant to Meyers and be paid $150,000 per year for the first three years, $125,000 for the next three years, and $100,000 thereafter for life. Death benefits were also included. Fink agreed to devote his best efforts and substantially his entire business time to advancing Meyers' interests. The agreement also provided that Fink's compensation was not to be affected by any inability to perform services on Meyers' behalf. Fink was 75 years old when his employment agreement with Meyers was approved by the directors. There is no claim that he was, or is, in poor health.

Additionally, the Meyers board approved and made interest-free loans to Fink totalling $225,000. These loans were unpaid and outstanding as of August 1982 when the complaint was filed. At oral argument defendants' counsel represented that these loans had been repaid in full.

The complaint charges that these transactions had "no valid business purpose", and were a "waste of corporate assets" because the amounts to be paid are "grossly excessive," that Fink performs "no or little services," and because of his "advanced age" cannot be "expected to perform any such services." The plaintiff also charges that the existence of the Prudential consulting agreement with Fink prevents him from providing his "best efforts" on Meyers' behalf. Finally, it is alleged that the loans to Fink were in reality "additional compensation" without any "consideration" or "benefit" to Meyers.

The complaint alleged that no demand had been made on the Meyers board because:

> … such attempt would be futile for the following reasons:
>
> (a) All of the directors in office are named as defendants herein and they have participated in, expressly approved and/or acquiesced in, and are personally liable for, the wrongs complained of herein.
>
> (b) Defendant Fink, having selected each director, controls and dominates every member of the Board and every officer of Meyers.
>
> (c) Institution of this action by present directors would require the defendant-directors to sue themselves, thereby placing the conduct of this action in hostile hands and preventing its effective prosecution.

The trial judge correctly noted that futility is gauged by the circumstances existing at the commencement of a derivative suit. This disposed of plaintiff's argument that defendants' motion to dismiss established board hostility and the futility of demand.

The Vice Chancellor then dealt with plaintiff's contention that Fink, as a 47% shareholder of Meyers, dominated and controlled each director, thereby making demand futile. After noting the presumptions under the business judgment rule that a board's actions are taken in good faith and in the best interests of the corporation, the Court of Chancery ruled that mere board approval of a transaction benefiting a substantial, but non-majority, shareholder will not overcome the presumption of propriety.

Turning to plaintiff's allegations of board approval, participation in, and/or acquiescence in the wrong, the trial court focused on the underlying transaction to determine whether the board's action was wrongful and not protected by the business judgment rule.

The trial court then stated that board approval of the Meyers-Fink agreement, allowing Fink's consultant compensation to remain unaffected by his ability to perform any services, may have been a transaction wasteful on its face. Consequently, demand was excused as futile, because the Meyers' directors faced potential liability for waste and could not have impartially considered the demand....

A cardinal precept of the General Corporation Law of the State of Delaware is that directors, rather than shareholders, manage the business and affairs of the corporation. A stockholder is not powerless to challenge director action which results in harm to the corporation. The derivative action developed in equity to enable shareholders to sue in the corporation's name where those in control of the company refused to assert a claim belonging to it. The nature of the action is two-fold. First, it is the equivalent of a suit by the shareholders to compel the corporation to sue. Second, it is a suit by the corporation, asserted by the shareholders on its behalf, against those liable to it.

By its very nature the derivative action impinges on the managerial freedom of directors. Hence, the demand requirement of Chancery Rule 23.1 exists at the threshold, first to insure that a stockholder exhausts his intercorporate remedies, and then to provide a safeguard against strike suits. Thus, by promoting this form of alternate dispute resolution, rather than immediate recourse to litigation, the demand requirement is a recognition of the fundamental precept that directors manage the business and affairs of corporations.

In our view the entire question of demand futility is inextricably bound to issues of business judgment and the standards of that doctrine's applicability. The business judgment rule is an acknowledgment of the managerial prerogatives of Delaware directors. It is a presumption that in making a business decision the directors of a corporation acted on an informed basis, in good faith and in the honest belief that the action taken was in the best interests of the company. Absent an abuse of discretion, that judgment will be respected by the courts. The burden is on the party challenging the decision to establish facts rebutting the presumption.

The function of the business judgment rule is of paramount significance in the context of a derivative action. It comes into play in several ways—in addressing a demand, in the determination of demand futility, in efforts by independent disinterested directors to dismiss the action as inimical to the corporation's best interests, and generally, as a defense to the merits of the suit. However, in each of these circumstances there are certain common principles governing the application and operation of the rule.

First, its protections can only be claimed by disinterested directors whose conduct otherwise meets the tests of business judgment. From the standpoint of interest, this means that directors can neither appear on both sides of a transaction nor expect to derive any personal financial benefit from it in the sense of self-dealing, as opposed to a benefit which devolves upon the corporation or all stockholders generally. Thus, if such director interest is present, and the transaction is not approved by a majority consisting of the disinterested directors, then the business judgment rule has no application whatever in determining demand futility.

Second, to invoke the rule's protection directors have a duty to inform themselves, prior to making a business decision, of all material information reasonably available to them. Having become so informed, they must then act with requisite care in the discharge of their duties. While the Delaware cases use a variety of terms to describe the applicable standard of care, our analysis satisfies us that under the business judgment rule director liability is predicated upon concepts of gross negligence.

However, it should be noted that the business judgment rule operates only in the context of director action. Technically speaking, it has no role where directors have either abdicated their functions, or absent a conscious decision, failed to act. But it also follows that under applicable principles, a conscious decision to refrain from acting may nonetheless be a valid exercise of business judgment and enjoy the protections of the rule.

The gap in our law, which we address today, arises from this Court's decision in *Zapata Corp. v. Maldonado.* Under *Zapata,* the Court of Chancery, in passing on a committee's motion to dismiss a derivative action in a demand excused case, must apply a two-step test. First, the court must inquire into the independence and good faith of the committee and review the reasonableness and good faith of the committee's investigation. Second, the court must apply its own independent business judgment to decide whether the motion to dismiss should be granted.

After *Zapata* numerous derivative suits were filed without prior demand upon boards of directors. The complaints in such actions all alleged that demand was excused because of board interest, approval or acquiescence in the wrongdoing. In any event, the *Zapata* demand-excused/demand-refused bifurcation, has left a crucial issue unanswered: when is demand futile and, therefore, excused?

Delaware courts have addressed the issue of demand futility on several earlier occasions. The rule emerging from these decisions is that where officers and directors are under an influence which sterilizes their discretion, they cannot be considered proper persons to conduct litigation on behalf of the corporation. Thus, demand would be futile.

However, those cases cannot be taken to mean that any board approval of a challenged transaction automatically connotes "hostile interest" and "guilty participation" by directors, or some other form of sterilizing influence upon them. Were that so, the demand requirements of our law would be meaningless, leaving the clear mandate of Chancery Rule 23.1 devoid of its purpose and substance.

The trial court correctly recognized that demand futility is inextricably bound to issues of business judgment, but stated the test to be based on allegations of fact, which, if true, "show that there is a reasonable inference" the business judgment rule is not applicable for purposes of a pre-suit demand.

The problem with this formulation is the concept of reasonable inferences to be drawn against a board of directors based on allegations in a complaint. As is clear from this case, and the conclusory allegations upon which the Vice Chancellor relied, demand futility becomes virtually automatic under such a test. Bearing in mind the presumptions with which director action is cloaked, we believe that the matter must be approached in a more balanced way.

Our view is that in determining demand futility the Court of Chancery in the proper exercise of its discretion must decide whether, under the particularized facts alleged, a reasonable doubt is created that: (1) the directors are disinterested and independent and (2) the challenged transaction was otherwise the product of a valid exercise of business judgment. Hence, the Court of Chancery must make two inquiries, one into the independence and disinterestedness of the directors and the other into the substantive nature of the challenged transaction and the board's approval thereof. As to the latter inquiry the court does not assume that the transaction is a wrong to the corporation requiring corrective steps by the board. Rather, the alleged wrong is substantively reviewed against the factual background alleged in the complaint. As to the former inquiry, directorial independence and disinterestedness, the court reviews the factual allegations to decide whether they raise a reasonable doubt, as a threshold matter, that the protections of the business judgment rule are available to the board. Certainly, if this is an "interested" director transaction, such that the business judgment rule is inapplicable to the board majority approving the transaction, then the inquiry ceases. In that event futility of demand has been established by any objective or subjective standard.* This includes situations involving self-dealing directors.

However, the mere threat of personal liability for approving a questioned transaction, standing alone, is insufficient to challenge either the independence or disinterestedness of directors, although in rare cases a transaction may be so egregious on its face that board approval cannot meet the test of business judgment, and a substantial likelihood of director liability therefore exists. In sum, the entire review is factual in nature. The Court of Chancery in the exercise of its sound discretion must be satisfied that a plaintiff has alleged facts with particularity which, taken as true, support a reasonable doubt that the challenged transaction was the product of a valid exercise of business judgment. Only in that context is demand excused....

Having outlined the legal framework within which these issues are to be determined, we consider plaintiff's claims of futility here: Fink's domination and control of the directors, board approval of the Fink-Meyers employment agreement, and board hostility to the plaintiff's derivative action due to the directors' status as defendants.

Plaintiff's claim that Fink dominates and controls the Meyers' board is based on: (1) Fink's 47% ownership of Meyers' outstanding stock, and (2) that he "personally selected" each Meyers director. Plaintiff also alleges that mere approval of the employment agreement illustrates Fink's domination and control of the board. In addition, plaintiff argued on appeal that 47% stock ownership, though less than a majority, constituted control given the large number of shares outstanding, 1,245,745.

Such contentions do not support any claim under Delaware law that these directors lack independence. In the demand context even proof of majority ownership of a company does not strip the directors of the presumptions of independence, and that their acts have been taken in good faith and in the best interests of the corporation. There must be coupled with the allegation of control such facts as would demonstrate that through personal or other relationships the directors are beholden to the con-

---

* We recognize that drawing the line at a majority of the board may be an arguably arbitrary dividing point. Critics will charge that we are ignoring the structural bias common to corporate boards throughout America, as well as the other unseen socialization processes cutting against independent discussion and decisionmaking in the boardroom. The difficulty with structural bias in a demand futile case is simply one of establishing it in the complaint for purposes of Rule 23.1. We are satisfied that discretionary review by the Court of Chancery of complaints alleging specific facts pointing to bias on a particular board will be sufficient for determining demand futility.

trolling person. To date the principal decisions dealing with the issue of control or domination arose only after a full trial on the merits. Thus, they are distinguishable in the demand context unless similar particularized facts are alleged to meet the test of Chancery Rule 23.1.

The requirement of director independence inheres in the conception and rationale of the business judgment rule. The presumption of propriety that flows from an exercise of business judgment is based in part on this unyielding precept. Independence means that a director's decision is based on the corporate merits of the subject before the board rather than extraneous considerations or influences. While directors may confer, debate, and resolve their differences through compromise, or by reasonable reliance upon the expertise of their colleagues and other qualified persons, the end result, nonetheless, must be that each director has brought his or her own informed business judgment to bear with specificity upon the corporate merits of the issues without regard for or succumbing to influences which convert an otherwise valid business decision into a faithless act.

Thus, it is not enough to charge that a director was nominated by or elected at the behest of those controlling the outcome of a corporate election. That is the usual way a person becomes a corporate director. It is the care, attention and sense of individual responsibility to the performance of one's duties, not the method of election that generally touches on independence....

We conclude that in the demand-futile context a plaintiff charging domination and control of one or more directors must allege particularized facts manifesting "a direction of corporate conduct in such a way as to comport with the wishes or interests of the corporation (or persons) doing the controlling." The shorthand shibboleth of "dominated and controlled directors" is insufficient. We stress that the plaintiff need only allege specific facts; he need not plead evidence. Otherwise, he would be forced to make allegations which may not comport with his duties under Chancery Rule 11.

Here, plaintiff has not alleged any facts sufficient to support a claim of control. The personal-selection-of-directors allegation stands alone, unsupported. At best it is a conclusion devoid of factual support. The causal link between Fink's control and approval of the employment agreement is alluded to, but nowhere specified. The director's approval, alone, does not establish control, even in the face of Fink's 47% stock ownership. The claim that Fink is unlikely to perform any services under the agreement, because of his age, and his conflicting consultant work with Prudential, adds nothing to the control claim. Therefore, we cannot conclude that the complaint factually particularizes any circumstances of control and domination to overcome the presumption of board independence, and thus render the demand futile.

Turning to the board's approval of the Meyers-Fink employment agreement, plaintiff's argument is simple: all of the Meyers directors are named defendants, because they approved the wasteful agreement; if plaintiff prevails on the merits all the directors will be jointly and severally liable; therefore, the directors' interest in avoiding personal liability automatically and absolutely disqualifies them from passing on a shareholder's demand.

Such allegations are conclusory at best. In Delaware mere directorial approval of a transaction, absent particularized facts supporting a breach of fiduciary duty claim, or otherwise establishing the lack of independence or disinterestedness of a majority of the directors, is insufficient to excuse demand. Here, plaintiff's suit is premised on the notion that the Meyers-Fink employment agreement was a waste of corporate assets. So, the argument goes, by approving such waste the directors now face potential personal liability, thereby rendering futile any demand on them to bring suit. Unfortunately, plaintiff's claim falls in its initial premise. The complaint does not allege particularized facts indicating that the agreement is a waste of corporate assets. Indeed, the complaint as now drafted may not even state a cause of action, given the directors' broad corporate power to fix the compensation of officers.

In essence, the plaintiff alleged a lack of consideration flowing from Fink to Meyers, since the employment agreement provided that compensation was not contingent on Fink's ability to perform any services. The bare assertion that Fink performed "little or no services" was plaintiff's conclusion based solely on Fink's age and the *existence* of the Fink-Prudential employment agreement. As for Meyers" loans to Fink, beyond the bare allegation that they were made, the complaint does not allege facts indicating the wastefulness of such arrangements. Again, the mere existence of such loans, given the broad corporate powers conferred by Delaware law, does not even state a claim.

Plaintiff's final argument is the incantation that demand is excused because the directors otherwise would have to sue themselves, thereby placing the conduct of the litigation in hostile hands and preventing its effective prosecution. This bootstrap argument has been made to and dismissed by other courts. Its acceptance would effectively abrogate Rule 23.1 and weaken the managerial power of directors. Unless facts are alleged with particularity to overcome the presumptions of independence and a proper exercise of business judgment, in which case the directors could not be expected to sue themselves, a bare claim of this sort raises no legally cognizable issue under Delaware corporate law.

In sum, we conclude that the plaintiff has failed to allege facts with particularity indicating that the Meyers directors were tainted by interest, lacked independence, or took action contrary to Meyers' best interests in order to create a reasonable doubt as to the applicability of the business judgment rule. Only in the presence of such a reasonable doubt may a demand be deemed futile. Hence, we reverse the Court of Chancery's denial of the motion to dismiss, and remand with instructions that plaintiff be granted leave to amend his complaint to bring it into compliance with Rule 23.1 based on the principles we have announced today.

Comments and Questions

1. Recall from Chapters 5 and 6 that disinterestedness turns on provable facts; that is, whether the board member in question received any direct personal financial

benefit from the challenged transaction. Independence, however, turns on the board member's state of mind; that is, whether the director could decide objectively about pursuing the corporation's claims, based solely on the merits, and impartially, without regard to her relationship with any interested director. How can complaining shareholders detect and assess possible sources of influence that cast doubt as to directors' independence?

2. Can a shareholder evade the demand requirement by naming every board member as a defendant? Why or why not?

3. The *Aronson* court opined that "in rare cases a transaction may be so egregious on its face that board approval cannot meet the test of business judgment, and a substantial likelihood of director liability therefore exists." What does this statement indicate about the relationship of the business judgment rule and the standard for demonstrating demand futility?

4. One oft-stated rationale for the business judgment rule is that judges are less qualified than boards to make business decisions. Are judges similarly less qualified than boards to decide the merits of fiduciary duty claims alleged against corporate directors and officers? Why or why not?

5. When is the *Aronson* test inapplicable? The Delaware Supreme Court answered this question in *Rales v. Blasband*.[11] Pleading demand futility, stockholder Blasband alleged that the board of directors of Easco misused over $61.9 million of proceeds from a public note offering. During the period between the alleged wrong and Blasband's suit, however, Easco merged with another corporation. The Delaware Supreme Court concluded that the *Aronson* test for demand futility did not apply in that context because the board that would have reviewed Blasband's demand did not commit the wrong alleged in his complaint. Instead, reviewing courts "must determine whether or not the particularized factual allegations of a derivative stockholder complaint create a reasonable doubt that, as of the time the complaint is filed, the board of directors could have properly exercised its independent and disinterested business judgment in responding to a demand." If the plaintiff satisfies this burden, the court will excuse demand as futile.

The *Rales* test generally applies in three circumstances: (1) when the majority of the directors that made the business decision no longer serve on the board of directors; (2) when the derivative action does not challenge a business decision made by the board of directors (e.g., *Caremark* claims); and (3) when the derivative action challenges a decision made by the board of directors of a different corporation. When a board delegates decisions about which the directors have no personal interest and are otherwise independent, the question is whether the corporation's charter includes an exculpatory clause and, if so, whether the claimed action is covered.

6. Do exculpatory charter provisions adopted pursuant to Section 102(b)(7) create a gap between the spirit of *Aronson* and application of its second prong? By asking whether the underlying decision was the product of a valid business judgment, the

---

11. 634 A.2d 927 (Del. 1993).

test attempts to reach those claims that actually may subject directors to personal liability. However, exculpatory charter provisions protect directors from liability for money damages for breaching their duty of care, regardless of whether the business judgment rule protects the challenged decision from judicial review. In other words, the *Aronson* test may create situations in which demand is deemed futile, yet directors face no true threat of personal liability. For an argument that this circumstance improperly restricts board authority, see Andrew C.W. Lund, *Rethinking* Aronson, 11 U. Pa. J. Bus. L. 703 (2009).

7. Unlike Delaware, many states no longer recognize the demand futility doctrine. Instead, the jurisdictions require that the shareholder plaintiff make a demand prior to filing any derivative suit. This rule, the so-called universal demand requirement, is now the law in about half of the states. Why do you think state lawmakers have enacted universal demand statutes? What are the arguments against universal demand? Can you think of a way to improve the demand futility doctrine without eliminating it?

8. The pleading with particularity requirements applicable to derivative suits differ significantly from the more permissive notice pleading rules applied to other fiduciary litigation. Shareholder plaintiffs cannot satisfy Rule 23.1 with conclusory statements. Instead, the complaint must allege particularized factual statements (sometimes called "ultimate facts") essential to the claim. Nevertheless, Delaware judges not infrequently admonish plaintiffs and their counsel that they also must draft "simple, concise and direct" pleadings.

C. Special Litigation Committees

1. Selection, Composition, and Duties

The special litigation committee is a powerful device used by corporations to address shareholder derivative lawsuits. SLCs investigate the merits of shareholders' allegations and determine whether pursuing litigation against one or more company fiduciaries would be in the best interest of the corporation. Indeed, the SLC is the "only instance in American Jurisprudence where a defendant can free itself from a suit by merely appointing a committee to review the allegations of the complaint...."[12] More precisely, appointment of a special litigation committee isolates interested directors (usually defendants in the lawsuit) from managing the litigation for the corporation, thereby increasing the likelihood that the court will apply the business judgment rule to decide the company's inevitable motion to dismiss plaintiff's claims. Even where pre-suit demand is futile or excused on other grounds, the board of directors may maintain control over a derivative action by delegating oversight of the complaint to a special litigation committee of disinterested directors.

Delaware law does not specify the number of board members necessary to form functional special litigation committees, nor does the law impose restrictions on directors' qualifications to serve on SLCs. If most or all board members are named as

---

12. *Lewis v. Fuqua*, 502 A.2d 962, 967 (Del. Ch. 1985).

defendants or otherwise not independent or disinterested, one or more new directors may join the board in order to form a disinterested SLC. At the pre-suit demand stage, the board benefits from a presumption of independence. However, the SLC has the burden of establishing its independence. Furthermore, plaintiffs may conduct limited discovery concerning the committee's independence as well as the depth and breadth of its investigation and related matters.

Once established, the SLC will investigate the merits of the plaintiffs' claims to make a decision about whether the corporation should pursue the litigation or seek dismissal of the lawsuit. In deciding whether or not to pursue litigation, SLCs generally will consider the merits of the claims, the amount of potential money damages or other relief, the likelihood of recovering a judgment, the possible detriment to the company from asserting claims, the indirect costs of litigation (e.g., effects on other potential litigation), the impact on relationships with customers, suppliers, or other stakeholders, and remedial steps already taken or planned by the company to address the challenged actions and prevent their reoccurrence. The SLC usually retains independent counsel and other experts to assist with the factual investigation, to help evaluate the legal claims, and to draft an extensive, non-confidential report detailing its findings and recommendation. If (as is more common) the SLC determines that pursuing the lawsuit is not in the best interests of the corporation, it will seek dismissal of the complaint.

Exculpatory charter provisions often play an important role in an SLC's decision. If plaintiffs have sued directors for monetary damages based on claims covered by Section 102(b)(7), then the SLC probably will be charged with evaluating the corporation's exculpatory provision as it applies to those claims. Assuming that the SLC is advised adequately about the applicable law, it may conclude that plaintiffs' suit should be dismissed because any recovery of money damages will be barred. An SLC that relies improperly on an exculpatory charter provision as a basis for dismissal, or fails to investigate its applicability adequately, will undermine its credibility with the court and risk continuation of the suit, contrary to the SLC's recommendation.

2. Judicial Review of SLC Decisions

Mindful that the board's statutory authority to manage corporate affairs must include the power to decide whether to enforce the firm's claims against directors and officers, courts nonetheless recognize that directors' natural bias may inhibit them from pursuing meritorious complaints against their colleagues and peers. Thus, judges have strained to safeguard the board's control while still providing to shareholders a mechanism for holding corporate fiduciaries accountable for disloyalty and intentional wrongdoing. Applying the business judgment rule, some courts, including courts in New York, readily accept SLCs' recommendations to dismiss shareholders' suits. Other courts, however, have demonstrated a willingness to make independent appraisal of the lawsuits' merits. What standard of review should courts apply in evaluating the decisions of SLCs to terminate derivative lawsuits? Should reviewing judges defer to the SLC's business judgments? In the following case, the Delaware Supreme Court established a two-part test for evaluating the recommendations of SLCs, providing judges with discretion to examine the merits and determine whether the lawsuit should proceed.

Zapata Corp. v. Maldonado

Delaware Supreme Court
430 A.2d 779 (1980)

QUILLEN, JUSTICE:

In June, 1975, William Maldonado, a stockholder of Zapata, instituted a derivative action in the Court of Chancery on behalf of Zapata against ten officers and/or directors of Zapata, alleging, essentially, breaches of fiduciary duty. Maldonado did not first demand that the board bring this action, stating instead such demand's futility because all directors were named as defendants and allegedly participated in the acts specified. In June, 1977, Maldonado commenced an action in the United States District Court for the Southern District of New York against the same defendants, save one, alleging federal security law violations as well as the same common law claims made previously in the Court of Chancery.

By June, 1979, four of the defendant-directors were no longer on the board, and the remaining directors appointed two new outside directors to the board. The board then created an "Independent Investigation Committee" (Committee), composed solely of the two new directors, to investigate Maldonado's actions, as well as a similar derivative action then pending in Texas, and to determine whether the corporation should continue any or all of the litigation. The Committee's determination was stated to be "final, ... not ... subject to review by the Board of Directors and ... in all respects ... binding upon the Corporation."

Following an investigation, the Committee concluded, in September, 1979, that each action should "be dismissed forthwith as their continued maintenance is inimical to the Company's best interests."

On March 18, 1980, the Court of Chancery denied Zapata's summary judgment motion, holding that Delaware law does not sanction this means of dismissal. More specifically, it held that the "business judgment" rule is not a grant of authority to dismiss derivative actions and that a stockholder has an individual right to maintain derivative actions in certain instances. We limit our review in this interlocutory appeal to whether the Committee has the power to cause the present action to be dismissed.

Corporations, existing because of legislative grace, possess authority as granted by the legislature. Directors of Delaware corporations derive their managerial decision making power, which encompasses decisions whether to initiate, or refrain from entering, litigation, from Section 141(a). This statute is the fount of directorial powers. The "business judgment" rule is a judicial creation that presumes propriety, under certain circumstances, in a board's decision. Viewed defensively, it does not create authority. In this sense the "business judgment" rule is not relevant in corporate decision making until after a decision is made. It is generally used as a defense to an attack on the decision's soundness. The board's managerial decision making power, however, comes from Section 141(a). The judicial creation and legislative grant are related because the "business judgment" rule evolved to give recognition and deference to directors' business expertise when exercising their managerial power under Section 141(a).

In the case before us, although the corporation's decision to move to dismiss or for summary judgment was, literally, a decision resulting from an exercise of the directors' (as delegated to the Committee) business judgment, the question of "business judgment", in a defensive sense, would not become relevant until and unless the decision to seek termination of the derivative lawsuit was attacked as improper.

We turn first to the Court of Chancery's conclusions concerning the right of a plaintiff stockholder in a derivative action. We find that its determination that a stockholder, once demand is made and refused, possesses an independent, individual right to continue a derivative suit for breaches of fiduciary duty over objection by the corporation, as an absolute rule, is erroneous.

A demand, when required and refused (if not wrongful), terminates a stockholder's legal ability to initiate a derivative action. But where demand is properly excused, the stockholder does possess the ability to initiate the action on his corporation's behalf.... Even in this situation, it may take litigation to determine the stockholder's lack of power, i.e., standing. These conclusions, however, do not determine the question before us. Rather, they merely bring us to the question to be decided. Derivative suits enforce corporate rights and any recovery obtained goes to the corporation. "The right of a stockholder to file a bill to litigate corporate rights is, therefore, solely for the purpose of preventing injustice where it is apparent that material corporate rights would not otherwise be protected." We see no inherent reason why the "two phases" of a derivative suit, the stockholder's suit to compel the corporation to sue and the corporation's suit should automatically result in the placement in the hands of the litigating stockholder sole control of the corporate right throughout the litigation. To the contrary, it seems to us that such an inflexible rule would recognize the interest of one person or group to the exclusion of all others within the corporate entity.

The question to be decided becomes: When, if at all, should an authorized board committee be permitted to cause litigation, properly initiated by a derivative stockholder in his own right, to be dismissed? As noted above, a board has the power to choose not to pursue litigation when demand is made upon it, so long as the decision is not wrongful. If the board determines that a suit would be detrimental to the company, the board's determination prevails. Even when demand is excusable, circumstances may arise when continuation of the litigation would not be in the corporation's best interests. Our inquiry is whether, under such circumstances, there is a permissible procedure under Section 141(a) by which a corporation can rid itself of detrimental litigation. If there is not, a single stockholder in an extreme case might control the destiny of the entire corporation. But, when examining the means, including the committee mechanism examined in this case, potentials for abuse must be recognized. This takes us to the second and third aspects of the issue on appeal.

Before we pass to equitable considerations as to the mechanism at issue here, it must be clear that an independent committee possesses the corporate power to seek the termination of a derivative suit. Section 141(c) allows a board to delegate all of its authority to a committee. Accordingly, a committee with properly delegated authority would have the power to move for dismissal or summary judgment if the entire board did.

Even though demand was not made in this case and the initial decision of whether to litigate was not placed before the board, Zapata's board, it seems to us, retained all of its corporate power concerning litigation decisions. If Maldonado had made demand on the board in this case, it could have refused to bring suit. Maldonado could then have asserted that the decision not to sue was wrongful and, if correct, would have been allowed to maintain the suit. The board, however, never would have lost its statutory managerial authority. The demand requirement itself evidences that the managerial power is retained by the board. When a derivative plaintiff is allowed to bring suit after a wrongful refusal, the board's authority to choose whether to pursue the litigation is not challenged although its conclusion — reached through the exercise of that authority — is not respected since it is wrongful. Similarly, Rule 23.1, by excusing demand in certain instances, does not strip the board of its corporate power. It merely saves the plaintiff the expense and delay of making a futile demand resulting in a probable tainted exercise of that authority in a refusal by the board or in giving control of litigation to the opposing side. But the board entity remains empowered under Section 141(a) to make decisions regarding corporate litigation. The problem is one of member disqualification, not the absence of power in the board.

The corporate power inquiry then focuses on whether the board, tainted by the self-interest of a majority of its members, can legally delegate its authority to a committee of two disinterested directors. We find our statute clearly requires an affirmative answer to this question. As has been noted, under an express provision of the statute, a committee can exercise all of the authority of the board to the extent provided in the resolution of the board.

We do not think that the interest taint of the board majority is per se a legal bar to the delegation of the board's power to an independent committee composed of disinterested board members. The committee can properly act for the corporation to move to dismiss derivative litigation that is believed to be detrimental to the corporation's best interest.

If, on the one hand, corporations can consistently wrest bona fide derivative actions away from well-meaning derivative plaintiffs through the use of the committee mechanism, the derivative suit will lose much, if not all, of its generally-recognized effectiveness as an intra-corporate means of policing boards of directors. If, on the other hand, corporations are unable to rid themselves of meritless or harmful litigation and strike suits, the derivative action, created to benefit the corporation, will produce the opposite, unintended result. It thus appears desirable to us to find a balancing point where bona fide stockholder power to bring corporate causes of action cannot be unfairly trampled on by the board of directors, but the corporation can rid itself of detrimental litigation.

The context here is a suit against directors where demand on the board is excused. We think some tribute must be paid to the fact that the lawsuit was properly initiated. It is not a board refusal case. Moreover, this complaint was filed in June of 1975 and, while the parties undoubtedly would take differing views on the degree of litigation activity, we have to be concerned about the creation of an "Independent Investigation Committee" four years later, after the election of two new outside directors. Situations could develop where such motions could be filed after years of vigorous litigation for reasons unconnected with the merits of the lawsuit.

Moreover, notwithstanding our conviction that Delaware law entrusts the corporate power to a properly authorized committee, we must be mindful that directors are passing judgment on fellow directors in the same corporation and fellow directors, in this instance, who designated them to serve both as directors and committee members. The question naturally arises whether a "there but for the grace of God go I" empathy might not play a role. And the further question arises whether inquiry as to independence, good faith and reasonable investigation is sufficient safeguard against abuse, perhaps subconscious abuse.

Finally, if the committee is in effect given status to speak for the corporation as the plaintiff in interest, then it seems to us there is an analogy to Court of Chancery Rule 41(a)(2) where the plaintiff seeks a dismissal after an answer. Certainly, the position of record of the litigating stockholder is adverse to the position advocated by the corporation in the motion to dismiss. Accordingly, there is perhaps some wisdom to be gained by the direction in Rule 41(a)(2) that "an action shall not be dismissed at the plaintiff's instance save upon order of the Court and upon such terms and conditions as the Court deems proper."

Whether the Court of Chancery will be persuaded by the exercise of a committee power resulting in a summary motion for dismissal of a derivative action, where a demand has not been initially made, should rest, in our judgment, in the independent discretion of the Court of Chancery. We thus steer a middle course between those cases which yield to the independent business judgment of a board committee and this case as determined below which would yield to unbridled plaintiff stockholder control. In pursuit of the course, we recognize that "the final substantive judgment whether a particular lawsuit should be maintained requires a balance of many factors—ethical, commercial, promotional, public relations, employee relations, fiscal as well as legal." But we are content that such factors are not "beyond the judicial reach" of the Court of Chancery which regularly and competently deals with fiduciary relationships, disposition of trust property, approval of settlements and scores of similar problems. We recognize the danger of judicial overreaching but the alternatives seem to us to be outweighed by the fresh view of a judicial outsider. Moreover, if we failed to balance all the interests involved, we would in the name of practicality and judicial economy foreclose a judicial decision on the merits. At this point, we are not convinced that is necessary or desirable.

After an objective and thorough investigation of a derivative suit, an independent committee may cause its corporation to file a pretrial motion to dismiss in the Court of Chancery. The basis of the motion is the best interests of the corporation, as determined by the committee. The motion should include a thorough written record of the investigation and its findings and recommendations. Under appropriate Court supervision, akin to proceedings on summary judgment, each side should have an opportunity to make a record on the motion. As to the limited issues presented by the motion noted below, the moving party should be prepared to meet the normal burden under Rule 56 that there is no genuine issue as to any material fact and that the moving party is entitled to dismiss as a matter of law.

First, the Court should inquire into the independence and good faith of the committee and the bases supporting its conclusions. Limited discovery may be ordered to facilitate such inquiries. The corporation should have the burden of proving independence, good faith and a reasonable investigation, rather than presuming independence, good faith and reasonableness. If the Court determines either that the committee is not independent or has not shown reasonable bases for its conclusions, or, if the Court is not satisfied for other reasons relating to the process, including but not limited to the good faith of the committee, the Court shall deny the corporation's motion. If, however, the Court is satisfied under Rule 56 standards that the committee was independent and showed reasonable bases for good faith findings and recommendations, the Court may proceed, in its discretion, to the next step.

The second step provides, we believe, the essential key in striking the balance between legitimate corporate claims as expressed in a derivative stockholder suit and a corporation's best interests as expressed by an independent investigating committee. The Court should determine, applying its own independent business judgment, whether the motion should be granted. This means, of course, that instances could arise where a committee can establish its independence and sound bases for its good faith decisions and still have the corporation's motion denied. The second step is intended to thwart instances where corporate actions meet the criteria of step one, but the result does not appear to satisfy its spirit, or where corporate actions would simply prematurely terminate a stockholder grievance deserving of further consideration in the corporation's interest. The Court of Chancery of course must carefully consider and weigh how compelling the corporate interest in dismissal is when faced with a non-frivolous lawsuit. The Court of Chancery should, when appropriate, give special consideration to matters of law and public policy in addition to the corporation's best interests.

If the Court's independent business judgment is satisfied, the Court may proceed to grant the motion, subject, of course, to any equitable terms or conditions the Court finds necessary or desirable.

Comments and Questions

1. Why does the *Zapata* court opt for a standard that is less deferential to boards of directors than the business judgment rule? Why might courts be entrusted with weighing corporate interests in this context (review of a demand excused shareholder derivative lawsuit), whereas directors' authority to decide the best interests of the firm is inviolable many other circumstances?

2. Compare the opinion in *Zapata* with the decision in *Auerbach v. Bennett*.[13] In that case, the board of directors of General Telephone & Electronics formed a special litigation committee to investigate derivative claims arising from GTE's disclosure that it paid more than $11 million in bribes and kickbacks to foreign officials and political parties. The SLC ultimately determined that it was not in GTE's best interest to pursue the claims alleged against certain members of the board of directors and the company's outside auditor. Applying the business judgment rule, the New York Court of Appeals deferred to the decision of the SLC. According to the court, the SLC's determination not to prosecute the claims "falls squarely within the embrace of the business judgment doctrine, involving as it did the weighing and balancing of legal, ethical, commercial, promotional, public relations, fiscal and other factors familiar to the resolution of many if not most corporate problems. To this extent the conclusion reached by the special litigation committee is outside the scope of our review. Thus, the courts cannot inquire as to which factors were considered by that committee or the relative weight accorded them in reaching that substantive decision." What policies support the deferential approach adopted in *Auerbach*? Which decision, *Zapata* or *Auerbach*, do you find more persuasive? Why?

3. What is structural bias? How might structural bias influence decisions made by special litigation committees? Do you think the Delaware Supreme Court's concern with structural bias, as articulated in *Zapata*, is justified? Why or why not? Does concern with structural bias rationalize step two of the inquiry announced in *Zapata*; that is, a decision by the reviewing court to apply its own independent business judgment to determine whether the corporation should pursue claims against directors? Why didn't structural bias influence the Delaware Supreme Court in *Aronson* to give similar discretion (to examine the substantive merits of plaintiffs' claims) to judges tasked with deciding demand futility?

4. Insofar as a reviewing court may exercise its discretion to conduct a substantive review of a good faith decision to dismiss derivative claims made by an independent SLC, why should the court first inquire into the independence and good faith of the committee and the bases supporting its conclusions? In other words, does the reviewing court's discretion to conduct the second stage analysis make the first step a nullity?

5. In practice, courts applying Delaware law rarely have exercised their discretion to engage in the second prong of the *Zapata* test. Can you think of reasons that reviewing judges might be reticent to apply its own independent business judgment and decide whether the lawsuit should continue? Even if courts usually decline to examine the claims substantively, why might the potential for a second stage analysis nonetheless affect the behavior of boards of directors and their special litigation committees?

6. As indicated by the opinion in *Zapata*, courts and commentators have expressed skepticism about whether directors ever decide that corporations should prosecute shareholders' derivative suits. Skeptics view the SLC process as a method by which

13. 393 N.E.2d 994 (N.Y. Ct. App. 1979).

766
10 · SHAREHOLDERS' DERIVATIVE LITIGATION
otherwise predisposed directors legitimize their decisions to oppose shareholders' complaints. Legal scholars who investigated this criticism in the 1980s found that SLCs almost invariably decide that it is not in their corporations' best interest to pursue plaintiffs' claims.[14]

More recently, however, the research findings raise some doubts. Professor Minor Myers, who studied the decisions of 106 SLCs formed during the period 1995–2004, found that over forty percent of the time, SLCs decided to settle claims or to pursue at least some allegations against one or more defendants.[15] Furthermore, the decisions to pursue or settle claims often resulted in substantial financial recoveries for the corporations, indicating that SLCs do not invariably "take it easy" on defendants. However, analyzing a hand-collected, original dataset of over 180 shareholder derivative suits filed in the federal courts from 2005–06, Professor Jessica Erickson found only one case in which the SLC recommended that the firm pursue claims against a defendant. In every case, SLCs recommended dismissal of claims against at least one (and usually more than one) defendant.[16]

What might explain the apparently conflicting findings? Are shareholders' derivative claims more meritorious? Could corporate boards have become more independent?

7. Regardless of the independence of the special litigation committee and the reasonableness of its investigation, other jurisdictions require reviewing courts to determine whether the special litigation committee reached a reasonable and principled decision on the basis of the evidence presented. In *Houle v. Low*,[17] for example, the Massachusetts Supreme Judicial Court ordered judges to determine the merits of the lawsuit, but the Court restricted the lower courts' substantive analysis of the merits, directing that they consider factors such as the likelihood of a judgment in the plaintiff's favor, the expected recovery as compared to out-of-pocket costs, whether the corporation itself took corrective action, whether the balance of corporate interests warrants dismissal, and whether dismissal would allow any defendant who has control of the corporation to retain a significant improper benefit. According to *Houle*, such a limited review "avoid[s] the problem in the second level of the *Zapata* test, which requires the judge to exercise his or her own business judgment. The courts are better able to determine the merits of a lawsuit than whether a decision is correct based on a subjective evaluation of the business policies involved." Do you agree?

---

14. *See, e.g.*, James D. Cox, *Searching for the Corporation's Voice in Derivative Suit Litigation: A Critique of* Zapata *and the ALI Project*, 1982 Duke L.J. 959 (in all but one of twenty reported cases, SLCs concluded suit not in company's best interest).

15. Minor Myers, *The Decisions of Corporate Special Litigation Committees: An Empirical Investigation*, 84 Ind. L. Rev. 1309 (2009).

16. Jessica M. Erickson, *Corporate Governance in the Courtroom: An Empirical Analysis*, 51 Wm. & Mary L. Rev. 1749 (2010).

17. 556 N.E.2d 51 (Mass. 1990) (citing ALI Principles of Corporate Governance Section 7.08 (Tent. Draft No. 8, 1988)).

3. When Are Directors "Independent"?

Directors' independence matters during at least two stages of a derivative lawsuit. First, courts analyze directors' independence in deciding a motion by defendants to dismiss the complaint for plaintiff's failure to make demand on the board. The court will examine plaintiff's particularized allegations and determine whether the pleading creates a reasonable doubt as to the directors' independence to evaluate a demand. Again, at this stage of the proceedings, the plaintiff shareholder has the burden on the independence question, but without the availability of discovery, plaintiff must use the "tools at hand"—such as documents obtained from inspecting the corporation's books and records—to plead facts sufficient to defeat defendants' motion to dismiss. Second, assuming demand is excused and the board has delegated management of the lawsuit to a special litigation committee, courts deciding defendants' motion to dismiss must analyze the independence of the SLC. In the following case, the Delaware Supreme Court considered when business and social relationships between disinterested directors and defendant directors create reasonable doubt about the directors' independence.

Beam ex rel. Martha Stewart Living Omnimedia, Inc. v. Stewart

Delaware Supreme Court
845 A.2d 1040 (2004)

Veasey, Chief Justice:

The single issue before us is that of demand futility. But, pursuant to our plenary appellate review, we undertake a further explication of certain points covered by the Chancellor, including the matter of director independence.

The plaintiff, Monica A. Beam, owns shares of Martha Stewart Living Omnimedia, Inc. (MSO). Beam filed a derivative action in the Court of Chancery against Martha Stewart, the five other members of MSO's board of directors, and former board member L. John Doerr.

In the single claim at issue on appeal, Beam alleged that Stewart breached her fiduciary duties of loyalty and care by illegally selling ImClone stock in December of 2001 and by mishandling the media attention that followed, thereby jeopardizing the financial future of MSO. The Court of Chancery dismissed under Court of Chancery Rule 23.1 because Beam failed to plead particularized facts demonstrating presuit demand futility.

When Beam filed the complaint in the Court of Chancery, the MSO board of directors consisted of six members: Stewart, Sharon L. Patrick, Arthur C. Martinez, Darla D. Moore, Naomi O. Seligman, and Jeffrey W. Ubben. The Chancellor concluded that the complaint alleged sufficient facts to support the conclusion that two of the directors, Stewart and Patrick, were not disinterested or independent for purposes of considering a presuit demand.

The Court of Chancery found that Stewart's potential civil and criminal liability for the acts underlying Beam's claim rendered Stewart an interested party and therefore unable to consider demand. The Court also found that Patrick's position as an officer and inside director, together with the substantial compensation she receives from the company, raised a reasonable doubt as to her ability objectively to consider demand. The defendants do not challenge the Court's conclusions with respect to Patrick and Stewart.

We now address the plaintiff's allegations concerning the independence of the other board members. We must determine if the following allegations of the complaint, and the reasonable inferences that may flow from them, create a reasonable doubt of the independence of either Martinez, Moore or Seligman:

> Defendant Arthur C. Martinez ("Martinez") is a director of the Company, a position that he has held since January 2001. Martinez is a longstanding personal friend of defendants Stewart and Patrick. While at Sears, Martinez established a relationship with the Company, which marketed a substantial volume of products through Sears. Martinez was recruited for the board by Stewart's longtime personal friend, Charlotte Beers. Defendant Patrick was quoted in an article dated March 22, 2001 appearing in *Directors & Board* as follows: 'Arthur is an old friend to both me and Martha.'

> Defendant Darla D. Moore ("Moore") is a director of the Company, a position she has held since September 2001. Moore is a longstanding friend of defendant Stewart. In November 1995, she attended a wedding reception hosted by Stewart's personal lawyer, Allen Grubman, for his daughter. Also in attendance were Stewart and Stewart's friend, Samuel Waksal. In August 1996, *Fortune* carried an article highlighting Moore's close personal relationship with Charlotte Beers and defendant Stewart. When Beers, a longtime friend and confidante to Stewart, resigned from the Company's board in September 2001, Moore was nominated to replace her.

> Defendant Naomi O. Seligman ("Seligman") is a director of the Company, a position that she has held since September 1999. According to a story appearing on July 2, 2002 in *The Wall Street Journal*, Seligman contacted the Chief Executive Officer of John Wiley & Sons (a publishing house) at defendant Stewart's behest last year to express concern over its planned publication of a biography that was critical of Stewart.

> Martinez, Moore, Seligman, and Ubben are hereinafter referred to collectively as the Director Defendants. By reason of Stewart's overwhelming voting control over the Company, each of the Director Defendants serves at her sufferance. Each of the Director Defendants receives valuable perquisites and benefits by reason of their service on the Company's Board.

DEMAND ALLEGATIONS

> 73. ... No demand on the Board of Directors was made prior to institution of this action, as a majority of the Board of Directors is not independent or disinterested with respect to the claims asserted herein.

> 77. Defendant Martinez is not disinterested in view of his longstanding personal friendship with both Patrick and Stewart.

78. Defendant Moore is not disinterested in view of her longstanding personal relationship with defendant Stewart.

79. Defendant Seligman is not disinterested; she has already shown that she will use her position as a director at another corporation to act at the behest of defendant Stewart when she contacted the Chief Executive Officer of John Wiley & Sons in an effort to dissuade the publishing house from publishing a biography that was critical of Stewart.

80. The Director Defendants are not disinterested as they are jointly and severally liable with Stewart in view of their failure to monitor Stewart's actions. Moreover, pursuit of these claims would imperil the substantial benefits that accrue to them by reason of their service on the Board, given Stewart's voting control.

Decision of the Court of Chancery

The Chancellor found that Beam had not alleged sufficient facts to support the conclusion that demand was futile because he determined that the complaint failed to raise a reasonable doubt that these outside directors are independent of Stewart. Because Patrick and Stewart herself are not independent for demand purposes, all the plaintiff need show is that one of the remaining directors is not independent, there being only six board members.

It is appropriate here to quote the Chancellor's analysis of the allegations regarding these three directors:

> ... [T]he amended complaint does not give a single example of any action by Martinez that might be construed as evidence of even a slight inclination to disregard his duties as a fiduciary for any reason. In this context, I cannot reasonably infer, on the basis of several years of business interactions and a single affirmation of friendship by a third party, that the friendship between Stewart and Martinez raises a reasonable doubt of Martinez's ability to evaluate demand independently of Stewart's personal interests.

> The allegations regarding the friendship between Moore and Stewart are somewhat more detailed, yet still fall short of raising a reasonable doubt about Moore's ability properly to consider demand. To my mind, this is quite a close call. Perhaps the balance could have been tipped by additional, more detailed allegations about the closeness or nature of the friendship, details of the business and social interactions between the two, or allegations raising additional considerations that might inappropriately affect Moore's ability to impartially consider pursuit of a lawsuit against Stewart. On the facts pled, however, I cannot say that I have a reasonable doubt of Moore's ability to properly consider demand....

> There is no allegation that Seligman made any inappropriate attempt to prevent the publication of the biography. Nor does the amended complaint indicate whether the biography was ultimately published and, if so, whether Seligman's inquiry is believed to have resulted in any changes to the content

gationationve

Of the book. As alleged, this matter does not serve to raise a reasonable doubt of Seligman's independence or ability to consider demand on Count I....

Demand Futility and Director Independence

This Court reviews de novo a decision of the Court of Chancery to dismiss a derivative suit under Rule 23.1. The scope of this Court's review is plenary. The Court should draw all reasonable inferences in the plaintiff's favor....

Under the first prong of *Aronson*, a stockholder may not pursue a derivative suit to assert a claim of the corporation unless: (a) she has first demanded that the directors pursue the corporate claim and they have wrongfully refused to do so; or (b) such demand is excused because the directors are deemed incapable of making an impartial decision regarding the pursuit of the litigation. The issue in this case is the quantum of doubt about a director's independence that is "reasonable" in order to excuse a presuit demand. The parties argue opposite sides of that issue.

The key principle upon which this area of our jurisprudence is based is that the directors are entitled to a presumption that they were faithful to their fiduciary duties. In the context of demand, the burden is upon the plaintiff in a derivative action to overcome that presumption. The Court must determine whether a plaintiff has alleged particularized facts creating a reasonable doubt of a director's independence to rebut the presumption at the pleading stage. If the Court determines that the pleaded facts create a reasonable doubt that a majority of the board could have acted independently in responding to the demand, the presumption is rebutted for pleading purposes and demand will be excused as futile.

A director will be considered unable to act objectively with respect to a presuit demand if he or she is interested in the outcome of the litigation or is otherwise not independent. A director's interest may be shown by demonstrating a potential personal benefit or detriment to the director as a result of the decision. "In such circumstances, a director cannot be expected to exercise his or her independent business judgment without being influenced by the ... personal consequences resulting from the decision." The primary basis upon which a director's independence must be measured is whether the director's decision is based on the corporate merits of the subject before the board, rather than extraneous considerations or influences.

Independence Is a Contextual Inquiry

Independence is a fact-specific determination made in the context of a particular case. The court must make that determination by answering the inquiries: independent from whom and independent for what purpose? To excuse presuit demand in this case, the plaintiff has the burden to plead particularized facts that create a reasonable doubt sufficient to rebut the presumption that either Moore, Seligman or Martinez was independent of defendant Stewart.

In order to show lack of independence, the complaint of a stockholder-plaintiff must create a reasonable doubt that a director is not so "beholden" to an interested director (in this case Stewart) that his or her "discretion would be sterilized." Our jurisprudence explicating the demand requirement:

is designed to create a balanced environment which will: (1) on the one hand, deter costly, baseless suits by creating a screening mechanism to eliminate claims where there is only a suspicion expressed solely in conclusory terms; and (2) on the other hand, permit suit by a stockholder who is able to articulate particularized facts showing that there is a reasonable doubt either that (a) a majority of the board is independent for purposes of responding to the demand, or (b) the underlying transaction is protected by the business judgment rule.

The "reasonable doubt" standard "is sufficiently flexible and workable to provide the stockholder with 'the keys to the courthouse' in an appropriate case where the claim is not based on mere suspicions or stated solely in conclusory terms."

Personal Friendship

A variety of motivations, including friendship, may influence the demand futility inquiry. But, to render a director unable to consider demand, a relationship must be of a bias-producing nature. Allegations of mere personal friendship or a mere outside business relationship, standing alone, are insufficient to raise a reasonable doubt about a director's independence. In this connection, we adopt as our own the Chancellor's analysis in this case:

> Some professional or personal friendships, which may border on or even exceed familial loyalty and closeness, may raise a reasonable doubt whether a director can appropriately consider demand. This is particularly true when the allegations raise serious questions of either civil or criminal liability of such a close friend. Not all friendships, or even most of them, rise to this level and the Court cannot make a *reasonable* inference that a particular friendship does so without specific factual allegations to support such a conclusion.

The facts alleged by Beam regarding the relationships between Stewart and these other members of MSO's board of directors largely boil down to a "structural bias" argument, which presupposes that the professional and social relationships that naturally develop among members of a board impede independent decisionmaking....

In the present case, the plaintiff attempted to plead affinity beyond mere friendship between Stewart and the other directors, but her attempt is not sufficient to demonstrate demand futility. Even if the alleged friendships may have preceded the directors' membership on MSO's board and did not necessarily arise out of that membership, these relationships are of the same nature as those giving rise to the structural bias argument.

Allegations that Stewart and the other directors moved in the same social circles, attended the same weddings, developed business relationships before joining the board, and described each other as "friends," even when coupled with Stewart's 94% voting power, are insufficient, without more, to rebut the presumption of independence. They do not provide a sufficient basis from which to infer that Martinez, Moore and Seligman may have been beholden to Stewart. Whether they arise before board membership or later as a result of collegial relationships among the board of directors, such affinities — standing alone — will not render presuit demand futile.

The Court of Chancery in the first instance, and this Court on appeal, must review the complaint on a case-by-case basis to determine whether it states with particularity facts indicating that a relationship — whether it preceded or followed board membership — is so close that the director's independence may reasonably be doubted. This doubt might arise either because of financial ties, familial affinity, a particularly close or intimate personal or business affinity or because of evidence that in the past the relationship caused the director to act non-independently vis à vis an interested director. No such allegations are made here. Mere allegations that they move in the same business and social circles, or a characterization that they are close friends, is not enough to negate independence for demand excusal purposes.

That is not to say that personal friendship is always irrelevant to the independence calculus. But, for presuit demand purposes, friendship must be accompanied by substantially more in the nature of serious allegations that would lead to a reasonable doubt as to a director's independence. That a much stronger relationship is necessary to overcome the presumption of independence at the demand futility stage becomes especially compelling when one considers the risks that directors would take by protecting their social acquaintances in the face of allegations that those friends engaged in misconduct. To create a reasonable doubt about an outside director's independence, a plaintiff must plead facts that would support the inference that because of the nature of a relationship or additional circumstances other than the interested director's stock ownership or voting power, the non-interested director would be more willing to risk his or her reputation than risk the relationship with the interested director.

Specific Allegations Concerning Seligman and Moore

1. Seligman

Beam's allegations concerning Seligman's lack of independence raise an additional issue not present in the Moore and Martinez relationships. Those allegations are not necessarily based on a purported friendship between Seligman and Stewart. Rather, they are based on a specific past act by Seligman that, Beam claims, indicates Seligman's lack of independence from Stewart. Beam alleges that Seligman called John Wiley & Sons (Wiley) at Stewart's request in order to prevent an unfavorable publication reference to Stewart. The Chancellor concluded, properly in our view, that this allegation does not provide particularized facts from which one may reasonably infer improper influence.

Indeed, the reasonable inference is that Seligman's purported intervention on Stewart's behalf was of benefit to MSO and its reputation, which is allegedly tied to Stewart's reputation, as the Chancellor noted. A motivation by Seligman to benefit the company every bit as much as Stewart herself is the only reasonable inference supported by the complaint, when all of its allegations are read in context.

2. Moore

The Court of Chancery concluded that the plaintiff's allegations with respect to Moore's social relationship with Stewart presented "quite a close call" and suggested ways that the "balance could have been tipped." Although we agree that there are ways that the balance could be tipped so that mere allegations of social relationships would become allegations casting reasonable doubt on independence, we do not agree that the facts as alleged present a "close call" with respect to Moore's independence. These allegations center on: (a) Moore's attendance at a wedding reception for the daughter of Stewart's lawyer where Stewart and Waksal were also present; (b) a *Fortune* magazine article focusing on the close personal relationships among Moore, Stewart and Beers; and (c) the fact that Moore replaced Beers on the MSO board. In our view, these bare social relationships clearly do not create a reasonable doubt of independence.

A Word About the Oracle Case

In his opinion, the Chancellor referred several times to the Delaware Court of Chancery decision in *In re Oracle Corp. Derivative Litigation*. Oracle involved the issue of the independence of the Special Litigation Committee (SLC) appointed by the Oracle board to determine whether or not the corporation should cause the dismissal of a corporate claim by stockholder-plaintiffs against directors. The Court of Chancery undertook a searching inquiry of the relationships between the members of the SLC and Stanford University in the context of the financial support of Stanford by the corporation and its management. The Vice Chancellor concluded, after considering the SLC Report and the discovery record, that those relationships were too close for purposes of the SLC analysis of independence.

An SLC is a unique creature that was introduced into Delaware law by *Zapata v. Maldonado* in 1981. The SLC procedure is a method sometimes employed where presuit demand has already been excused and the SLC is vested with the full power of the board to conduct an extensive investigation into the merits of the corporate claim with a view toward determining whether—in the SLC's business judgment—the corporate claim should be pursued. Unlike the demand-excusal context, where the board is presumed to be independent, the SLC has the burden of establishing its own independence by a yardstick that must be "like Caesar's wife"—"above reproach." Moreover, unlike the presuit demand context, the SLC analysis contemplates not only a shift in the burden of persuasion but also the availability of discovery into various issues, including independence.

Section 220

Beam's failure to plead sufficient facts to support her claim of demand futility may be due in part to her failure to exhaust all reasonably available means of gathering facts. As the Chancellor noted, had Beam first brought a Section 220 action seeking inspection of MSO's books and records, she might have uncovered facts that would have created a reasonable doubt. For example, irregularities or "cronyism" in MSO's process of nominating board members might possibly strengthen her claim concerning Stewart's control over MSO's directors. A books and records inspection might have revealed whether the board used a nominating committee to select directors and maintained a separation between the director-selection process and management. A books and records inspection might also have revealed whether Stewart unduly controlled the nominating process or whether the process incorporated procedural safeguards to ensure directors' independence. Beam might also have reviewed the minutes of the board's meetings to determine how the directors handled Stewart's proposals or conduct in various contexts. Whether or not the result of this exploration might create a reasonable doubt would be sheer speculation at this stage. But the point is that it was within the plaintiff's power to explore these matters and she elected not to make the effort.

In general, derivative plaintiffs are not entitled to discovery in order to demonstrate demand futility. The general unavailability of discovery to assist plaintiffs with pleading demand futility does not leave plaintiffs without means of gathering information to support their allegations of demand futility, however. Both this Court and the Court of Chancery have continually advised plaintiffs who seek to plead facts establishing demand futility that the plaintiffs might successfully have used a Section 220 books and records inspection to uncover such facts....

Because Beam did not even attempt to use the fact-gathering tools available to her by seeking to review MSO's books and records in support of her demand futility claim, we cannot know if such an effort would have been fruitless, as Beam claimed on appeal. Beam's failure to seek a books and records inspection that may have uncovered the facts necessary to support a reasonable doubt of independence has resulted in substantial cost to the parties and the judiciary.

Conclusion

Because Beam did not plead facts sufficient to support a reasonable inference that at least one MSO director in addition to Stewart and Patrick was incapable of considering demand, Beam was required to make demand on the board before pursuing a derivative suit. Hence, presuit demand was not excused. The Court of Chancery did not err by dismissing Count 1 under Rule 23.1.

Comments and Questions

1. Plaintiff Beam unsuccessfully relied on a decision from the Chancery Court in the *Oracle Derivative Litigation*.[18] Before *Oracle*, Delaware courts generally examined only the "economically consequential relationships" between the deciding directors and the defendants to determine whether the defendants "dominated and controlled" their colleagues, corrupting their independence. In *Oracle*, however, Vice Chancellor Strine also scrutinized the personal, charitable, and business rela-

---

18. *In re Oracle Corp. Deriv. Litig.*, 824 A.2d 917 (Del. Ch. 2003) *appeal denied, Oracle Corp. ex rel. Special Litig. Comm. v. Barone*, 829 A.2d 141 (Del. 2003), *summary judgment granted, In re Oracle Corp., Derivative Litig.*, 867 A.2d 904 (Del. Ch. 2004), *aff'd*, 872 A.2d 960 (Del. 2005).

tionships between the defendants and the SLC directors (denominated by the court as the "'thickness' of the social and institutional connections") to determine whether the SLC members might have felt "beholden" to the defendant directors. The court noted that "the question of independence turns on whether a director is, for any substantial reason, incapable of making a decision with only the best interests of the corporation in mind."

The procedural context of *Beam* and *Oracle*, and hence the burdens of proof, differed. In reviewing a demand futility dispute, as in *Beam*, courts presume that a majority of the board of directors could have acted independently in responding to a pre-suit demand by the plaintiff stockholder. The plaintiff, then, must plead particularized facts sufficient to create a reasonable doubt as to the directors' independence. Unlike the dispute in *Beam*, the matter before the reviewing court in *Oracle* was the defendants' motion to dismiss a demand-excused derivative suit. Oracle's board of directors had formed a special litigation committee (comprised of two new directors not named as defendants) to investigate the complaint filed by plaintiff stockholders. Following its investigation, the SLC recommended that the corporation move to dismiss the derivative claims. In that context, the decision of the SLC is not entitled to any presumption of independence, good faith, or reasonableness. Instead, the corporation bears the burden to establish the absence of any disputed material fact concerning the SLC's independence. Oracle failed to meet its burden.

2. *Beam* affirmed that judicial review of director independence is highly fact specific. Delaware law does not specify which relationships between defendant directors and other board members create conflicts that are disqualifying. What are the advantages and disadvantages of this contextual approach for boards of directors?

3. Plaintiff Beam failed to persuade the Delaware Supreme Court that the majority of MSO directors were biased by their personal friendships with Stewart, such that Beam's complaint raised a reasonable doubt as to their independence. Under what circumstances might personal friendships between defendant directors and their colleagues on the board become disqualifying? Why do think the Supreme Court highlighted the standing of the three directors in the business community?

4. The Court noted that plaintiff Beam failed to initiate a Section 220 action under Delaware's General Corporation Law in order to inspect of MSO's books and records. While the Court conceded that whether such an action would have uncovered facts creating a reasonable doubt is a matter of "sheer speculation," do you think plaintiff's failure to exhaust her statutory rights of inspection before filing her complaint persuaded the court to dismiss the claims? Indeed, the Delaware courts have encouraged stockholders repeatedly to use Section 220 before filing a derivative action to investigate, among other things, the independence of directors for purposes of evaluating a pre-suit demand. Although plaintiff stockholders may seek to inspect the company's books and records by making written demands pursuant to Section 220, is it likely that they will uncover enough evidence to satisfy the heightened demand futility pleading requirements? Or will the courts' decisions regarding of the SLC's independence necessarily depend on the "contextual inquiry"?

5. Commentators have suggested that plaintiffs' entitlement to discovery regarding the independence of SLC members often is outcome-determinative. In *Oracle*, for example, the plaintiffs uncovered during discovery a "series" of ties between the defendant directors and the SLC, relationships that the SLC failed to disclose in its report. In his opinion, then-Vice Chancellor Strine expressed "some shock" about the SLC's omissions: "[T]he plain facts are a striking departure from the picture presented in the [SLC's] Report." At the very least, the SLC's failure to disclose these sources of potential bias called into question the competency of the committee. However, the court also seemed to believe that the ties were too significant to simply have been overlooked. To repeat the allusion adopted by Chief Justice Veasey in *Beam*, the Oracle SLC was not, like Caesar's wife, above reproach.

6. Regardless of the legal merits of the shareholders' claims, couldn't a special litigation committee always decide that it is not in the best interest of the corporation to pursue the shareholders' claims based on other business considerations, such as the expense of litigation, the lawsuit's distraction to key executives, the impact of negative publicity on relationships with customers, suppliers, and employees, the effect of litigation uncertainty on the company's share price, and even the uncertainty of collecting a judgment? Under what circumstances would you expect that a SLC would decide to continue litigating breach of duty claims against directors still sitting on the board or non-director executives still employed by the firm?

———

Just over a decade after the Delaware Supreme Court decided *Beam*, and about a dozen years after he decided *Oracle* in the Chancery Court, now Chief Justice Leo Strine, writing for the Delaware Supreme Court, had another opportunity to consider how personal relationships influence director independence.

Delaware County Employees' Retirement Fund v. A.R. Sanchez, Jr.

Supreme Court of Delaware
2015 WL 5766264

Strine, Chief Justice:

INTRODUCTION

Determining whether a plaintiff has pled facts supporting an inference that a director cannot act independently of an interested director for purposes of demand excusal under *Aronson* can be difficult. And this case illustrates that. But in that determination, it is important that the trial court consider all the particularized facts pled by the plaintiffs about the relationships between the director and the interested party in their totality and not in isolation from each other, and draw all reasonable inferences from the totality of those facts in favor of the plaintiffs. In this case, the plaintiffs pled not only that the director had a close friendship of over half a century with the interested party, but that consistent with that deep friendship, the director's primary employment (and that of his brother) was as an executive of a company over which the interested party had substantial influence. These, and other facts of a similar nature, when taken together, support an inference that the director could not act independently of the interested party. Because of that, the plaintiffs pled facts supporting an inference that a majority of the board who approved the interested transaction they challenged could not consider a demand impartially. Therefore, we reverse and remand so that the plaintiffs can prosecute this derivative action.

BACKGROUND

This case involves an appeal from a complicated transaction between a private company whose equity is wholly owned by the family of A.R. Sanchez, Jr., Sanchez Resources, LLC (hereinafter, the Private Sanchez Company"), and a public company in which the Sanchez family constitutes the largest stockholder bloc with some 16% of the shares and that is dependent on the Private Sanchez Company for all of its management services, Sanchez Energy Corporation (the "Sanchez Public Company"). The transaction at issue required the Sanchez Public Company to pay $78 million to: i) help the Private Sanchez Company buy out the interests of a private equity investor; ii) acquire an interest in certain properties with energy-producing potential from the Private Sanchez Company; iii) facilitate the joint production of 80,000 acres of property between the Sanchez Private and Public Companies; and iv) fund a cash payment of $14.4 million to the Private Sanchez Company. In this derivative action, the plaintiffs allege that this transaction involved a gross overpayment by the Sanchez Public Company, which unfairly benefited the Private Sanchez Company by allowing it to use the Sanchez Public Company's funds to buy out their private equity partner, obtain a large cash payment for itself, and obtain a contractual right to a lucrative royalty stream that was unduly favorable to the Private Sanchez Company and thus unfairly onerous to the Sanchez Public Company. As to the latter, the plaintiffs allege that the royalty payment was not only unfair, but was undisclosed to the Sanchez Public Company stockholders, and that it was the Sanchez family's desire to conceal the royalty obligation that led to what can be fairly described as a convoluted transaction structure.

The Court of Chancery dismissed the complaint, finding that the defendants were correct in their contention that the plaintiffs had not pled demand excusal under *Aronson*. In a thorough and careful opinion, the Court of Chancery examined both prongs of *Aronson* and concluded that the plaintiffs had not satisfied their pleading burden to show that demand was excused under either. On appeal, the plaintiffs argue that the Court of Chancery was wrong on both scores.

But, in resolving this appeal, we focus on only one issue, which is outcome-determinative. The parties agree that two of the five directors on the Sanchez Public Company board were not disinterested in the transaction: A.R. Sanchez, Jr., the Public Company's Chairman; and his son, Antonio R. Sanchez, III, the Sanchez Public Company's President and CEO. For the sake of clarity, we refer to the patriarch of the Sanchez family, A.R. Sanchez, Jr., as Chairman Sanchez.

The question for *Aronson* purposes was therefore whether the plaintiffs had pled particularized facts raising a pleading-stage doubt about the independence of one of the other Sanchez Public Company directors. If they had, the defendants and the

Court of Chancery itself recognized that the plaintiffs would have pled grounds for demand excusal under *Aronson*.

ANALYSIS

To plead demand excusal under Rule 23.1, a plaintiff in a derivative action must plead particularized facts creating a reasonable doubt" that either "(1) the directors are disinterested and independent or (2) the challenged transaction was otherwise the product of a valid exercise of business judgment." Although there is a heightened burden under Rule 23.1 to plead particularized facts, when a motion to dismiss for failure to make a demand is made, all reasonable inferences from the pled facts must nonetheless be drawn in favor of the plaintiff in determining whether the plaintiff has met its burden under *Aronson*.

The closest question below centered on director Alan Jackson. The complaint bases its challenge to Jackson's independence on two related grounds. First, it pleads that "[Chairman] Sanchez and Jackson have been close friends for more than five decades." Consistent with this allegation, the complaint indicates that when Chairman Sanchez ran for Governor of Texas in 2012, Jackson donated $12,500 to his campaign.

Second, the complaint pleads facts supporting an inference that Jackson's personal wealth is largely attributable to business interests over which Chairman Sanchez has substantial influence. According to the complaint, Jackson's full-time job and primary source of income is as an executive at IBC Insurance Agency, Ltd. IBC Insurance provides insurance brokerage services to the Sanchez Public Company and other Sanchez affiliates. But even more importantly, IBC Insurance is a wholly owned subsidiary of International Bancshares Corporation ("IBC"), a company of which Chairman Sanchez is the largest stockholder and a director who IBC's board has determined is not independent under the NASDAQ Marketplace Rules. Not only does Jackson work full-time for IBC Insurance, so too does his brother. Both of them service the work that IBC Insurance does for the Sanchez Public and Private Companies. The complaint also alleges that the approximately $165,000 Jackson earned as a Sanchez Public Company director constituted "30–40% of Jackson's total income for 2012."

The plaintiffs contend that these pled facts support an inference that Jackson cannot act independently of Chairman Sanchez, because he is Sanchez's close friend of a half century, derives his primary employment from a company over which Sanchez has substantial control, has a brother in the same position, and that the coincidence of these personal and business ties are, well, no coincidence. In its opinion, the Court of Chancery disagreed with the plaintiffs. After examining all of these factors, the Court of Chancery concluded that the plaintiffs had not pled facts overcoming the presumption that Jackson was independent. The defendants defend the Court of Chancery's reasoning on appeal, and stress that it relied on precedent such as *Beam v. Stewart,* and reflected a careful assessment of the pled facts and whether they were sufficient to compromise Jackson's independence under *Aronson*. They also note, as did the Court of Chancery, that this Court has admonished derivative plaintiffs to use the books and record process to aid them in satisfying *Aronson* 's stringent pleading test and that, if the plaintiffs came up short, it was their own fault for not using this avenue.

We agree with the defendants that the Court of Chancery diligently grappled with this close question and justified its decision that the plaintiffs had not pled facts supporting an inference that Jackson could not act independently of Sanchez in terms of relevant precedent. But, employing the *de novo* review that governs this appeal, we do not come to the same conclusion as the Court of Chancery. The reason for that is that the Court of Chancery's analysis seemed to consider the facts the plaintiffs pled about Jackson's personal friendship with Sanchez and the facts they pled regarding his business relationships as entirely separate issues. Having parsed them as categorically distinct, the Court of Chancery appears to have then concluded that neither category of facts on its own was enough to compromise Jackson's independence for purposes of demand excusal.

The problem with that approach is that our law requires that all the pled facts regarding a director's relationship to the interested party be considered in full context in making the, admittedly imprecise, pleading stage determination of independence. In that consideration, it cannot be ignored that although the plaintiff is bound to plead particularized facts in pleading a derivative complaint, so too is the court bound to draw all inferences from those particularized facts in favor of the plaintiff, not the defendant, when dismissal of a derivative complaint is sought.

Here, the plaintiffs did not plead the kind of thin social-circle friendship, for want of a better way to put it, which was at issue in *Beam*. In that case, we held that allegations that directors "moved in the same social circles, attended the same weddings, developed business relationships before joining the board, and described each other as 'friends,'… are insufficient, without more, to rebut the presumption of independence." In saying that, we did not suggest that deeper human friendships could not exist that would have the effect of compromising a director's independence. When, as here, a plaintiff has pled that a director has been close friends with an interested party for a half century, the plaintiff has pled facts quite different from those at issue in *Beam*. Close friendships of that duration are likely considered precious by many people, and are rare. People drift apart for many reasons, and when a close relationship endures for that long, a pleading stage inference arises that it is important to the parties.

The plaintiffs did not rely simply on that proposition, however. They pled facts regarding the economic relations of Jackson and Chairman Sanchez that buttress their contention that they are confidantes and that there is a reasonable doubt that Jackson can act impartially in a matter of economic importance to Sanchez personally. It may be that it is entirely coincidental that Jackson's full-time job is as an executive at a subsidiary of a corporation over which Chairman Sanchez has substantial influence, as the largest stockholder, director, and the Chairman of an important source of brokerage work. It may be that it is also coincidental that Jackson's brother also works there. It may be coincidental that Jackson and his brother both work on insurance brokerage work for the Sanchez Public and Private Companies there. And it may be coincidental that Jackson finds himself a director of the Sanchez Public Company. But rather certainly, there arises a pleading stage inference that Jackson's economic positions derive in large measure from his 50-year close friendship with Chairman Sanchez, and that he is in these positions because Sanchez trusts, cares for, and respects him. If that is true, there is of course nothing wrong with that. Human relationships of that kind are valuable. In this context, however, where the question is whether the plaintiffs have met their pleading burden to plead facts suggesting that Jackson cannot act independently of Chairman Sanchez, these obvious inferences that arise from the pled facts require that the defendants' motion to dismiss be denied.* In other words, using the precise parlance of *Aronson*, the plaintiffs pled particularized facts, that when considered in the plaintiff-friendly manner required, create a reasonable doubt about Jackson's independence.

As to this point, we also think it useful to note that although, like the Court of Chancery, we agree that it would have been ideal for the plaintiffs to use the books and records tool, as our prior cases have encouraged, that instrument may have been of limited utility on this particular point. It may be that the Sanchez Public Company has a file of the disclosure questionnaires for the board that would provide more detail about the thickness of the relationship between Chairman Sanchez and Jackson. But we cannot hold the plaintiffs' failure to undertake additional investigation against them when, as here, the facts pled in the complaint support an inference that a majority of the board lacked independence.

Because we conclude that the plaintiffs pled demand excusal under the first prong of *Aronson*, we need not and therefore do not reach the other issues presented on ap-

---

* The Court of Chancery decided that the plaintiffs had not compromised Jackson's independence because they had not pled facts showing that Chairman Sanchez had the unilateral power to cause Jackson's termination as an executive at IBC because Chairman Sanchez was only one of nine directors at the parent company and the plaintiffs did not plead precisely how much of the stock of IBC Chairman Sanchez and his family controlled. Although it is true that the plaintiffs did not plead the percentage of IBC shares the Sanchez family owned, the plaintiffs i) pled that Chairman Sanchez was the "largest stockholder" of IBC; ii) pled that Chairman Sanchez had been a non-independent director of IBC; and iii) cited to a proxy statement that acknowledged Chairman Sanchez's interest in IBC by noting that he was not an independent director "as defined in the applicable NASDAQ Marketplace Rules," which define a non-independent director as someone "having a relationship which, in the opinion of the Company's board of directors, would interfere with the exercise of independent judgment in carrying out the responsibilities of a director."... NASDAQ Marketplace Rule 5605(a)(2). The plaintiffs also pled that "[i]f Jackson ... were to act against the interests of Sanchez Jr., he faces the threat of termination at IBC, the loss of promotion opportunities, and the loss or decrease of his salary—his very livelihood—because of Sanchez Jr.'s position on IBC's board and significant influence through his substantial equity stake." One natural inference from these pled facts is that Chairman Sanchez is very influential at IBC as a whole, including its wholly owned subsidiary. And the fact that "both Jackson and his brother received a portion of the commissions paid to IBC by [Sanchez Energy] and its affiliates," and that their employment is their primary source of income, is pled. A lack of independence does not turn on whether the interested party can directly fire a director from his day job. It turns on, at the pleading stage, whether the plaintiffs have pled facts from which the director's ability to act impartially on a matter important to the interested party can be doubted because that director may feel either subject to the interested party's dominion or beholden to that interested party. At the very least, the pled facts suggest an inference that Jackson might feel strongly beholden to Chairman Sanchez as the source of his primary job, and that of his brother.

peal. Therefore, the judgment of the Court of Chancery of November 25, 2014 dismissing this case is reversed, and this case is remanded for further proceedings consistent with this opinion.

Comments and Questions

1. How did Chief Justice Strine distinguish the friendships among the MSO directors in *Beam* from the friendship that allegedly threatened Jackson's independence in this case?

2. At the pleading stage, a lack of independence turns on "whether the plaintiffs have pled facts from which the director's ability to act impartially on a matter important to the interested party can be doubted because that director may feel either subject to the interested party's dominion or beholden to that interested party." As in *Beam*, the Delaware Supreme Court continues to reference two ways that directors may be disqualified by bias: (1) directors lack independence because they are *dominated* by another party; and (2) directors lack independence because they are *beholden* to another party with an interest in the transaction. Having read both cases, what is the distinction between dominated directors and beholden directors?

3. Recall that in *Beam*, the Delaware Supreme Court announced a "risk of reputation" test for determining when allegations of friendship could raise questions of independence:

> To create a reasonable doubt about an outside director's independence, a plaintiff must plead facts that would support the inference that because of the nature of a relationship or additional circumstances other than the interested director's stock ownership or voting power, the non-interested director would be more willing to risk his or her reputation than risk the relationship with the interested director.

Did the *Sanchez* court apply this test? Support your answer.

4. After *Sanchez*, should boards and their nominating/governance committees investigate and take into account personal friendships when selecting directors and making committee assignments, even in the absence of any regulatory mandate requiring that they to do so? Should personal friendships be considered potentially disqualifying if and only if a director or director candidate also has a significant business tie with the CEO?

London v. Tyrrell

Delaware Chancery Court
2010 Del. Ch. LEXIS 54 (Mar. 11, 2010)

CHANDLER, CHANCELLOR:

After a four-month investigation of plaintiffs' claims in this derivative action, a special litigation committee formed by nominal defendant iGov has recommended dismissal of plaintiffs' suit. I deny the SLC's motion to dismiss because there are material questions of fact regarding (1) the SLC's independence, (2) the good faith of its investigation, and (3) whether the grounds upon which it recommended dismissal of this lawsuit are reasonable. Accordingly, plaintiffs may continue to pursue this action.

Facts

This dispute springs from the approval and implementation of an equity incentive plan on January 30, 2007 (the "2007 Plan"). iGov is a government contracting firm that initially focused on the reseller market for information technology hardware, primarily selling to federal military and civilian agencies. After nine years in the low margin, highly competitive reseller market, however, the Company decided to change its focus from product sales to the higher-margin government services market. This shift in focus, which occurred in 2005, was driven by management's view that iGov could not sustain itself over the long term in the reseller business because of increasing competition from larger players.

At some point in 2006 defendants decided that it would be advisable to implement the 2007 Plan for the benefit of key members of management. Defendants caused iGov to retain Chessiecap Securities, Inc. to value iGov stock for purposes of setting the exercise price of options under the 2007 Plan. Plaintiffs complaint alleges that defendants "secretly decided to implement [the 2007 Plan] at an unfair price to benefit themselves at the expense of the other stockholders."

Under the 2007 Plan, 300,000 stock options were to be issued to various directors and senior executives. Collectively, defendants were to be given 60% of the options granted under the 2007 Plan. In addition, the 2007 Plan contemplated the sale of 65,000 shares of stock to Tyrrell [the CFO]. In contrast, plaintiffs were not to be given any options or shares under the 2007 Plan, presumably because they had been removed from their director and management positions.

Plaintiffs allege that the 2007 Plan was designed to substantially reduce their ownership interests in iGov and increase defendants' interests to a level that would permit defendants to entrench themselves as iGov directors and managers. In support of this theory, plaintiffs assert that implementation of the 2007 Plan immediately reduced their collective ownership interests from 44% to 40%. On a fully diluted basis, the 2007 Plan allegedly reduced plaintiffs' collective ownership interests from 42.3% to 28.7%. At the same time, the 2007 Plan allegedly increased defendants' collective ownership interests from 50.1% to 54.1% and, on a fully diluted basis, defendants' collective ownership interests allegedly increased from 48.2% to 54.2%.

Plaintiffs contend that defendants manipulated the Final Valuation by excluding positive developments which occurred after July 31, 2006. Plaintiffs also contend that defendants wrongfully declined to update either the Revised Forecast or the Final Valuation before approving the 2007 Plan, falsely representing that no material change had occurred between July 31, 2006 and January 30, 2007.

After the 2007 Plan was approved, plaintiffs made a books and records request under 8 Del. C. §220. The ground for the request was plaintiffs' objection to iGov using the Final Valuation as the basis for the strike price. Plaintiffs also engaged the McLean Group, a valuation firm, to conduct separate valuations of iGov's equity as of October 31, 2006 and December 31, 2006.

While the McLean Valuations were being conducted, iGov expanded the size of its board from three members to five. In August 2007, Vincent Salvatori and John Vinter became iGov directors. Both men were first approached by Tyrrell and both had connections to him. Both men also had extensive experience in government contracting that understandably made them attractive candidates for iGov's board.

On October 31, 2007, after attempts to resolve the dispute failed, plaintiffs filed their complaint. The counts in the complaint are characterized as derivative and individual, alleging harm to iGov as a company and to plaintiffs in their personal capacity.

In my June 24, 2008 Opinion, I found that plaintiffs' complaint "easily survived" defendants' motion to dismiss; demand being excused because a majority of the board was interested in the transaction. Thereafter, on November 21, 2008, the iGov board voted to form a two-member SLC comprised of Salvatori and Vinter to consider whether it was in iGov's best interest to pursue the derivative claims in plaintiffs' complaint.

After its formation, the SLC obtained advisors. From April 2009 to July 2009 the SLC conducted its investigation. Discovery was stayed during this time. In conducting the investigation the SLC interviewed twelve witnesses and reviewed relevant documentation produced by the parties. To inform their investigation, the SLC sought counsel's advice as to the legal principles that determine whether defendants complied with their fiduciary duties.

The SLC concluded that it could make a recommendation respecting this suit and iGov's best interests without declaring a winner in the battle between plaintiffs' and defendants' experts. The SLC Report concludes that the suit is not in the best interests of the Company and recommends that it be dismissed. The SLC believes that the discovery that will resume if the suit is allowed to continue will be extremely disruptive to iGov's operations. The SLC also believes that negative publicity associated with the suit will immediately damage the Company's goodwill and reputation in the government contracting community.

As to the actual claims asserted in plaintiffs' complaint, the SLC Report concludes as follows. First, as to Count I, the SLC concluded that defendants acted properly in adopting the 2007 Plan and did not breach their duties of care or loyalty. The SLC concluded that a duty of care claim should not be pursued because defendants breach of care conduct, if it occurred, would be covered by the § 102(b)(7) provision in iGov's certificate of incorporation. As to the duty of loyalty, the SLC concluded that defendants' approval of the 2007 Plan and actions leading to that approval would satisfy the entire fairness standard because the process employed was fair and the $4.92 strike price was fair.

After reviewing the SLC Report, plaintiffs filed an opposition brief arguing that the SLC has not met the standard required by *Zapata Corporation v. Maldonado* and its progeny for dismissal of a claim based on an SLC's recommendation in a demand-excused case. I now consider whether the SLC has met the *Zapata* standard and, consequently, whether the suit should be dismissed or permitted to proceed.

Standard

In *Zapata*, the Supreme Court rejected the notion that the SLC's recommendation, made in the form of a motion to dismiss, should be subject to business judgment review. Rather, the Supreme Court established a two-step analysis that must be applied to the SLC's motion to dismiss. The first step of the analysis is mandatory. The Court reviews the independence of SLC members and considers whether the SLC conducted a good faith investigation of reasonable scope that yielded reasonable bases supporting its conclusions. The second step of the analysis is discretionary. The Court applies its own business judgment to the facts to determine whether the corporation's best interests would be served by dismissing the suit. The second step is designed for situations in which the technical requirements of step one are met but the result does not appear to satisfy the spirit of the requirements.

The Court treats the SLC's motion in a manner akin to a Rule 56 motion for summary judgment; the SLC bears the burden of demonstrating that there are no genuine issues of material fact as to its independence, the reasonableness and good faith of its investigation, and that there are reasonable bases for its conclusions. If the Court determines that a material fact is in dispute on any of these issues it must deny the SLC's motion.

Analysis

Were the SLC Members Independent?

Whether an SLC member is independent "is a fact-specific determination made in the context of a particular case." When an SLC member has no personal interest in the disputed transactions, the Court scrutinizes the members' relationship with the interested directors, as that would be the source of any independence impairment that might exist.

An SLC member does not have to be unacquainted or uninvolved with fellow directors to be regarded as independent. But an SLC member is not independent if he or she is incapable, for any substantial reason, of making a decision with only the best interests of the corporation in mind.

Unlike a board in the pre-suit demand context, SLC members are not given the benefit of the doubt as to their impartiality and objectivity. They, rather than plaintiffs, bear the burden of proving that there is no material question of fact about their independence. Thus, it is conceivable that a court might find a director to be independent in the pre-suit demand context but not independent in the *Zapata* context based on the same set of factual allegations made by the two parties.

It is undisputed that neither SLC member had a personal stake in the challenged transactions. Neither Salvatori nor Vinter received shares of stock or options under the 2007 Plan and neither faces any risk of personal liability in this suit. Moreover,

Salvatori and Vinter were not appointed to the board until after the 2007 Plan was adopted. In addition, plaintiffs do not allege that any of the defendants dominate or control Salvatori or Vinter. Thus, the focus must be on whether the relationships Salvatori and Vinter have with defendants are of such a nature that they might have caused Salvatori and Vinter to consider factors other than the best interests of the corporation in making their decision to move for dismissal. Such a relationship would raise a material question as to the SLC's independence. After carefully reviewing the evidence produced by the limited discovery thus far permitted, I conclude that there is a material question of fact as to the independence of both SLC members based on their relationships to Tyrrell.

Plaintiffs argue that Vinter's independence is impaired by one simple fact; Vinter's wife is Tyrrell's cousin. According to plaintiffs, it was that association that caused Tyrrell to approach Vinter about joining the iGov board.

The Company, not plaintiffs, must do the explaining in the first instance if there are associations that cast a shadow on independence. Frankly, appointing an interested director's family member to an SLC will always position a corporation on the low ground. From there, the corporation must fight an uphill battle to demonstrate that, notwithstanding kinship, there is no material question as to the SLC member's objectivity.

I admit that it is not possible, at this stage of the proceedings, to say unequivocally that Vinter's independence is impaired. On the one hand, the relationship between Vinter's wife and Tyrrell does not seem to be particularly close. They do not frequently associate with one another as some cousins are wont to do. On the other hand, they do see each other regularly, albeit infrequently, at family functions. For example, each year Vinter and his wife attend a large family party at Tyrrell's in honor of Tyrrell's mother, who has passed away.

Now to Salvatori. Like Vinter, Salvatori's contact with iGov was based on an association with Tyrrell. In 1993, Tyrrell was hired by Salvatori to work as an internal auditor for a company called QuesTech. Salvatori was a QuesTech co-founder and served as its President, CEO, and Chairman while Tyrrell was employed there for six years. During that time, Salvatori promoted Tyrrell to CFO, in which role he reported directly to Salvatori. Tyrrell worked as QuesTech's CFO until it was sold in 1998.

In this case, I believe there is a material question of fact as to Salvatori's independence because his earlier associations with Tyrrell may have given rise to a sense of obligation or loyalty to him. Salvatori appears to have been satisfied with the price he received for QuesTech, and he continues to feel that Tyrrell was an important factor in securing that price. In saying this, I do not find that Salvatori in fact does feel a sense of obligation to Tyrrell, but there is certainly a strong possibility that he does, and that is enough under *Zapata* to preclude dismissal.

Before moving on I note a few pieces of evidence that buttress my conclusion that there is a material question of fact regarding the SLC's independence. First, the SLC members appear to have reviewed the merits of plaintiffs' claims before the SLC was ever formed. In September 2007, plaintiffs' counsel sent a letter to iGov outlining many of the allegations that ultimately appeared in plaintiffs' complaint and requesting a meeting to begin resolving the dispute. When SLC members are simply exposed to or become familiar with a derivative suit before the SLC is formed this may not be enough to create a material question of fact as to the SLC's independence. But if evidence suggests that the SLC members prejudged the merits of the suit based on that prior exposure or familiarity, and then conducted the investigation with the object of putting together a report that demonstrates the suit has no merit, this will create a material question of fact as to the SLC's independence. In this case, that is what has occurred.

Salvatori was asked in his deposition about the SLC's efforts to investigate the allegations in plaintiffs' complaint. Salvatori responded "I know we read it all over and I know we *attacked* it all." Plaintiffs' counsel followed up with "[y]ou did what it all?" to which Salvatori answered "*[a]ttacked* it all." Salvatori's counsel then repeated "*[a]ttacked* it all" after which Salvatori changed his answer to "[w]e considered it."

Given the SLC members' relationships to Tyrrell, their exposure to the merits of plaintiffs' suit well before the SLC was formed, and the unsatisfactory scope of the investigation conducted, Salvatori and Vinter's use of the word "attack" does not help to fully convince me that the SLC was independent.

Did the SLC Conduct an Investigation of Reasonable Scope in Good Faith and Did the SLC Have Reasonable Bases for its Conclusions?

To conduct a good faith investigation of reasonable scope, the SLC must investigate all theories of recovery asserted in the plaintiffs' complaint. If the SLC fails to investigate facts or sources of information that cut at the heart of plaintiffs' complaint this will usually give rise to a material question about the reasonableness and good faith of the SLC's investigation. A total failure to explore the less serious allegations in plaintiffs' complaint may cast doubt on the reasonableness and good faith of an SLC's investigation when exploring those less serious allegations, at least in summary fashion, would have helped the SLC gain a full understanding of the more serious allegations in plaintiffs' complaint.

To demonstrate that its recommendations are supported by reasonable bases, the SLC must show that it correctly understood the law relevant to the case. If the SLC's recommendation is based on an error of law then the basis for that recommendation is not reasonable. Moreover, if the SLC gets the undisputed facts wrong in its report, and then relies on its erroneous recitation of the undisputed facts in making its dismissal recommendation, it also goes without saying that the basis for the recommendation is not reasonable.

The SLC Report identifies the SLC's recommendations for each of the three counts in plaintiffs' complaint. As we have seen, Count I alleges that defendants breached their fiduciary duties of care and loyalty by adopting the 2007 Plan. The duty of care claims are based on the allegation that defendants approved the 2007 Plan knowing that the Final Valuation was based on stale and incomplete information. The duty of loyalty claims are based on the allegation that defendants intentionally provided misleading and incomplete information to artificially depress iGov's value so that defendants would receive underpriced options and shares when the 2007 Plan was implemented. Count II seeks rescission of the 2007 Plan and is essentially dependent on the success of Count I. Count III is styled as an individual claim, the personal harm being that defendants improperly diluted plaintiffs' ownership interests, thereby expropriating economic value and voting power from them.

1. The Duty of Care Claims in Count I

The SLC first addressed Count I, ultimately concluding that it should be dismissed. As to the duty of care claims in Count I, the SLC found that the 8 Del. C. § 102(b)(7) provision in iGov's corporate charter exculpates directors from personal liability for monetary damages so long as the director did not engage in intentional misconduct or knowing violations of the law.... *On that basis alone*, the SLC concluded that duty of care claims against defendants should not be pursued. I find this to be an unreasonable conclusion because the SLC failed to consider that the requested relief in plaintiffs' complaint is not limited to money damages; it specifically requests that the 2007 Plan be rescinded. Under Delaware law, exculpatory provisions do not bar duty of care claims "in remedial contexts..., such as in injunction or rescission cases." Thus, if I became convinced at the summary judgment stage or after a trial on the merits that defendants breached their duty of care the exculpatory provision in the iGov charter would not preclude me from ordering rescission of the 2007 Plan, even though it might preclude me from entering a judgment for monetary damages against defendants. It was unreasonable, therefore, for the SLC to conclude that the duty of care claims in Count I should not go forward solely on the basis of iGov's § 102(b)(7) provision. The SLC simply fails to understand that Delaware law permits a suit seeking rescission to go forward despite a § 102(b)(7) provision protecting directors against monetary judgments.

2. The Duty of Loyalty Claims in Count I

The SLC's investigation of plaintiffs' duty of loyalty claims, as well as its conclusion that those claims should be dismissed, merits the most discussion in my analysis of the *Zapata* requirements. The SLC concluded that plaintiffs' duty of loyalty claims should be dismissed because it believes the 2007 Plan was entirely fair to iGov.

a. Fair Process

I begin by analyzing whether the SLC's investigation of defendants' process was reasonable in scope. I also analyze whether the SLC's conclusion that the process was fair is supported by reasonable bases. My findings here relate only to the SLC's investigation.

In concluding that defendants would be able to show fair dealing, the SLC first determined that plaintiffs' claims can be distilled to *one key issue.* Can a CFO have one forecasting model for the purpose of seeking an increase in the Company's credit availability and for [internal] goal-setting while, at the same time, have a *substantially lower* forecast for the purpose of valuing the Company's equity?

As is evident from the SLC Report, the SLC concluded that the process of adopting the 2007 Plan was fair primarily because the SLC believes it was perfectly normal for Tyrrell to provide "optimistic" and "art of the possible" forecasts and use those forecasts internally, while at the same time providing a forecast to its valuation expert that was "substantially lower" but something the Company could "actually achieve," rather than being "wishful."

I need not rest my decision solely on the merits of this crucial conclusion, because, broadly speaking, I do not believe that the SLC's investigation was sufficient in scope to adequately address plaintiffs' duty of loyalty claims. Nor do I believe the SLC developed reasonable bases for concluding plaintiffs' duty of loyalty claims should be dismissed.

As we have seen, Tyrrell's own emails suggest that he believed these higher internal forecasts where achievable, in direct contradiction to the testimony he provided the SLC, but the SLC does not appear to have questioned him thoroughly about these emails. Instead, the SLC explains away these internal forecasts with its finding that they were used to motivate and inspire management by demonstrating what *might* be achievable, rather than what Tyrrell actually believed was achievable. The SLC's finding on this point appears to be completely based on Tyrrell's assertions about the purpose of the internal forecasts. Nothing in the SLC Report suggests that management was questioned to see if they understood that the internal projections being circulated were not what the CFO believed was actually achievable.

An objective SLC would have been *duty bound* at this point to thoroughly explore why management pervasively used forecasts it did not believe were realistic, but the SLC failed to do this....

The SLC Report characterizes plaintiffs' removal from the board as the product of a disagreement between plaintiffs and defendants over the direction that iGov should take. Conspicuously absent from the SLC Report are any citations to interview notes or other evidence supporting the SLC's finding that this disagreement was the cause of plaintiffs' removal from the board. In fact, there is evidence in the record that shows defendants may have been just as interested in maximizing short-term profits from iGov as plaintiffs' purportedly were, but the SLC Report fails to investigate or explain this. The biggest problem, though, is that the SLC Report wholly fails to analyze or explain why plaintiffs were removed from the board only three days after objecting to the Final Valuation and a little less than two weeks before the 2007 Plan was adopted. This does not demonstrate that the SLC conducted an investigation of reasonable scope.

I could go on, but I decline to. What I have written is sufficient to demonstrate that there is a material question of fact as to whether the SLC conducted a good faith investigation of reasonable scope into the fairness of the 2007 Plan's adoption process.

b. Fair Price

Having determined that the SLC did not conduct a reasonably thorough investigation into defendants' process for adopting the 2007 Plan and did not have reasonable bases for concluding that the process was fair, I could dispense with the remainder of the entire fairness inquiry. Nevertheless, to be thorough, I will briefly explore the SLC's investigation of price and whether it had reasonable bases to conclude that $4.92 per share was a fair price.

Disagreement about the effect of iGov's cash position on value, combined with the SLC's hunches about the Company's value, led the SLC to conclude that even the SRR Valuations missed the mark. Thus, the SLC is left with no professional valuation upon which to hang its hat entirely. That is certainly enough to create a material question of fact about whether the SLC had a reasonable basis to conclude that $4.92 was a fair price.

3. Counts II and III

I briefly address Counts II and III before concluding my *Zapata* step-one analysis. The SLC recommended that Count II be dismissed because it believed adoption of the 2007 Plan was entirely fair to iGov and, therefore, plaintiffs would not prevail on Count I. Because the SLC failed to meet the *Zapata* standard its recommendation to dismiss Count I is denied. Accordingly, Count II, which seeks rescission of the 2007 Plan, will not be dismissed for the obvious reason that rescission may be the appropriate remedy if plaintiffs ultimately prevail on the merits of Count I.

With respect to Count III, the SLC concluded it was a derivative claim and should be dismissed along with Count I (and for the same reasons). Plaintiffs assert that this is an individual claim over which the SLC has no power. Because I am permitting plaintiffs to continue piloting derivative claims through this litigation, I will not spend time at this juncture attempting to resolve whether Count III alleges individual or derivative claims. Either way the claims survive. We can leave determination of the exact nature of Count III for another day. In fact, a more accurate determination may be made at a later time when the benefits of full discovery have enlarged the record.

The Court's Independent Business Judgment

Having determined that I will not grant the SLC's motion to dismiss after fully applying the first step of the *Zapata* standard to the motion, I find it unnecessary to apply the second step of *Zapata*. In my view, this is not a case where application of the second step will add anything of value, and so I exercise my discretion not to apply this step.

Conclusion

Because there are material questions of fact as to the SLC's independence, the reasonableness of its investigation, and whether it had reasonable bases for its conclusions, the SLC's motion to dismiss plaintiffs' complaint is DENIED.

Comments and Questions

1. As in *Oracle*, when a special litigation committee moves to dismiss a demand-excused derivative suit, the SLC has the burden of demonstrating the absence of gen-

uine issues of material fact regarding the committee's independence. Consider, then, the context of Chancellor Chandler's opinion in this case. The court already had concluded in 2008 that plaintiffs' demand on the board was excused, and that plaintiffs' derivative claims "easily survived" defendants' motion to dismiss. Having lost that initial motion to dismiss, iGov's board of directors expanded the board and formed the SLC, appointing its two new directors Salvatori and Vinter to the committee. The SLC hired advisers and conducted its investigation of plaintiffs' claims over the four months that followed. At the conclusion of its probe, the SLC issued a written report finding that the claims lacked merit and recommending that it was not in iGov's best interest to pursue the lawsuit. The company again moved to dismiss the complaint, this time relying on the recommendation of the SLC.

Chancellor Chandler emphasized in his opinion that because plaintiffs previously had established demand futility, the iGov SLC had the burden of proving that there was no material question of fact concerning its independence. Do you agree with Chancellor Chandler that the very same facts that precluded a finding of independence in this context (distant familial connections and prior business associations) might militate the opposite conclusion at the demand-futility stage? Recall the applicable standard of review from *Aronson*.

2. Why should it be "nigh unto impossible" for a special litigation committee to show independence where "the SLC member and a director defendant have a family relationship"? Although director Vinter's wife was defendant Tyrrell's cousin, there was little evidence that their relationship was close. Indeed, defendants asserted that "they only occasionally cross paths at large family functions once or twice each year." The Court was further troubled by deposition testimony and notes suggesting that the SLC members viewed their job as "attacking" the plaintiffs' complaint.

3. If factually applicable, plaintiffs also argue that family relationships affect directors' independence. It is difficult to predict how courts judge the effect of family ties on independence. "Different decisions take a different view about the bias-producing potential of familial relationships, not all of which can be explained by mere degrees of consanguinity."[19] Vinter's wife was Tyrell's cousin, and the couple attended an annual party hosted by Tyrell in his mother's honor. While these facts did not persuade the court to conclude "unequivocally that Vinter's independence was impaired," the evidence did create a material issue of fact. Do you agree?

4. What lessons can future SLCs learn from Chancellor Chandler's opinion about how to conduct their investigations and draft their reports in demand-excused actions?

D. Resolving Shareholders' Lawsuits

Because shareholders seeking to prosecute claims on behalf of the corporation face considerable legal obstacles, as we have seen, derivative litigation seldom succeeds in holding fiduciaries liable for breaching their duties to the firm. Not surprisingly,

---

19. *In re Oracle Corp. Deriv. Litig.*, 824 A.2d 917, 939 (Del. Ch. 2003).

boards rarely authorize lawsuits against themselves and their colleagues, nor do they cause the corporation to sue firm executives. In the exceptional case that directors approve such litigation, the board already terminated the wrongdoing executive. An example of such a lawsuit is the shareholders' winning prosecution of derivative claims against Richard Scrushy. Following a 2009 bench trial, an Alabama court entered a nearly $2.9 billion judgment against the former HealthSouth Chairman and CEO,[20] purportedly the largest derivative suit judgment ever obtained by shareholders seeking damages for breach of fiduciary duty from a former company executive on behalf of the corporation. In 2011, the Alabama Supreme Court upheld the judgment on appeal.[21] Shareholders prevail even less frequently when, as is common, the corporation objects to their pusuit of claims against defendant fiduciaries. Recently, however, shareholders overcame procedural and substantive hurdles in a well-publicized Delaware case. Following a trial on the merits, shareholders persuaded then-Chancellor Leo Strine to enter a $1.263 billion judgment for the benefit of Southern Peru Copper Corporation in a derivative action relating to the company's acquisition of Minerva Mexico from Groupo México, Southern Peru's controlling shareholder. Chancellor Strine found that in a "manifestly unfair transaction," Southern Peru overpaid for the mining company.

Despite such results, shareholder derivative suits rarely end with judgments for monetary damages. Indeed, cases not dismissed by the courts usually settle without payment of any significant monetary award to the corporation. Shareholder derivative suits more commonly resolve with the parties agreeing to corporate governance enhancements. In these settlements, corporations agree to reform their corporate governance practices, from the number of independent directors on their boards to the method by which they compensate their top executives. Whether these governance settlements have effected meaningful changes on corporate internal affairs is a matter of some controversy.

1. Empirical Evidence

Empirical research demonstrates that shareholders rarely obtain judgments holding executives liable for violating their fiduciary duties. A well-publicized study by Professor Bernard Black and other scholars determined that, from 1985 through 2000, only six derivative actions against outside directors of public companies went to trial, and plaintiffs won just two of those suits.[22] Professors Robert Thompson and Randall Thomas examined all Delaware derivative suits filed during 1999 and 2000. They found that, out of the fifty lead cases that were resolved, only six resulted in monetary recovery for the corporations.[23]

---

20. *See* Valerie Bauerlein & Mike Esterl, *Judge Orders Scrushy to Pay $2.88 Billion in Civil Suit*, Wall St. J., June 19, 2009, at B1.

21. *See Scrushy v. Tucker*, 70 So.3d 289 (2011) (affirming judgment in its entirety).

22. *See* Bernard Black, et al., *Outside Director Liability*, 58 Stan. L. Rev. 1055, 1090–91 (2006).

23. *See* Robert B. Thompson & Randall S. Thomas, *The Public and Private Faces of Derivative Lawsuits*, 57 Vand. L. Rev. 1747, 1775–76 (2004). *See also* Robert B. Thompson & Randall S. Thomas, *The New Look of Shareholder Litigation: Acquisition-Oriented Class Actions*, 57 Vand. L. Rev. 133 (2004).

In 2009, Professor Black and his colleagues published another article, this time comparing shareholder litigation against public company directors in the United States and the United Kingdom.[24] Examining lawsuits filed in state and federal courts between 2000 and 2007, they found that directors face even less risk from shareholder litigation than previously thought. Only a small percentage of shareholders' lawsuits were sufficiently contentious that courts issued written decisions; indeed, courts dismissed a substantial fraction of those cases. When the researchers compared their U.S. lawsuit data to the data from Thompson and Thomas' Delaware studies, they determined that only one in seven complaints filed against directors in Delaware produced a written decision. Most written decisions favored defendants, but, more often than not, judges simply dismissed the complaints without any written opinion. Indeed, the researchers found just six written decisions (three percent of all written decisions) entering judgments against defendants and awarding damages following trials on the merits.

Not only do nonmanagement directors seldom incur liability for breaching their fiduciary duties, but they rarely contribute any funds to settle such claims. Thus, when individual defendants agree to make out-of-pocket payments to help resolve shareholders' complaints, such exceptional settlements create anxiety in public company boardrooms. In 2005, for example, Corporate America winced when former outside directors of Enron and WorldCom contributed personal millions to settle federal securities claims brought by investors in class action lawsuits. Ten Enron directors contributed a total of $13 million of their own funds (representing five percent of the gains they made selling Enron stock before the company's true financial condition was revealed). The settlement of similar claims required eleven WorldCom outside directors to pay a total of $20 million (representing about 20 percent of the directors' net worth, excluding their primary residences, retirement funds, and certain marital property). As experienced commentators had predicted, however, these settlements did not prove to be a "harbinger of new exposure" for personal liability to directors.[25]

Indeed, shareholders seldom recover substantial monies for the corporation ... at least historically. In recent years, however, a number of shareholder derivative actions made headlines for their significant settlements. In 2014, directors of videogame company Activision Blizzard agreed to pay $279 million to settle a derivative suit arising from a stock buyback. That settlement bested the $139 million paid by News Corp's directors in 2013 to resolve claims that they failed to avert the company's hacking scandal.

Defendants often agree to settle shareholders' derivative claims for non-pecuniary relief, including negotiated reforms to corporate governance systems or enhancements to corporate compliance programs designed to prevent the alleged malfeasance or

---

24. John Armour et al., *Private Enforcement of Corporate Law: An Empirical Comparison of the United Kingdom and the United States*, 6 J. Empir. L. Stud. 687, 705–10 (2009).

25. Ira M. Millstein & E. Norman Veasey, *Some Thoughts on Director Protection In Light of the WorldCom and Enron Settlements: Suggestions for Directors*, Metro. Corp. Counsel (June 2005).

wrongdoing from recurring. As part of the Activision settlement, for example, the company agreed, among other corporate governance changes, to add two independent directors to its board. Nonetheless, when plaintiff shareholders agree to dismiss derivative actions and release claims in exchange for governance reforms and payment of attorneys' fees only, such resolutions provide support to critics' arguments that plaintiffs' lawyers abuse the legal system for their personal gain at the expense of the best interests of shareholders and corporation. "Tagalong" derivative actions — complaints repeating allegations made in previously-filed securities class actions, regulatory enforcement actions, or criminal cases — are especially likely settle for corporate "therapeutics" only, with no monetary recovery to the company.

2. Judicial Review of Settlements

Parties to shareholders' lawsuits must obtain judicial approval to settle and dismiss derivative claims. This requirement is "intended to guard against surreptitious buy-outs of representative plaintiffs, leaving other [shareholders] without recourse" when the settlement, by design, releases their claims.[26] Under Delaware law, the reviewing court must determine whether, in the exercise of its own business judgment and in light of the facts and circumstances presented, the proposed settlement is a fair and reasonable resolution of the litigation. *See* Del. Ch. Ct. Rule 23.1. Federal law is substantially similar. Courts have broad discretion to consider the terms of the settlement, including recovery by the corporation and any reimbursement of expenses to the plaintiff and the individual defendants, as well as the outcome that might have resulted from trial, discounted by the uncertainty of litigation, the costs caused by delay of the resolution, disruption of business, possible negative publicity, and increased insurance premiums if recovery at trial is higher.

Settlement negotiations may reveal a divergence between the interests of shareholder-plaintiffs and the interests of the lawyers who represent them in derivative litigation. Because shareholders' attorneys agree to prosecute most derivative suits on a contingent fee basis, plaintiffs' counsel likely has a more direct and substantial financial interest in the case outcome than the named plaintiffs. Moreover, under the contingent fee arrangement, the plaintiff's attorney will receive compensation only on the successful prosecution of the suit or by its settlement. Should the parties agree to settle derivative claims, courts generally approve plaintiffs' attorneys upon a showing that the settlement provided "substantial benefit" to the corporation.

While shareholders have different investment goals and time horizons, they presumably file suit seeking the largest monetary recovery possible for the corporation, accounting for the risk of continuing the litigation through trial and, potentially, appeal. Shareholders who continue to own stock in the firm also may benefit from settlements that include reforms to the corporation's governance systems, and empirical studies have found that these so-called "corporate governance settlements" have become increasingly common in recent years. While the value received by the cor-

---

26. *Wied v. Valhi, Inc.*, 466 A.2d 9, 15 (Del. 1983).

poration from governance settlements may be difficult to quantify, the law is clear that "a corporation may receive a 'substantial benefit' from a derivative suit, justifying an award of counsel fees, regardless of whether the benefit is pecuniary in nature."[27]

Regardless of whether the parties' proposed resolution provides the corporation and, indirectly, its shareholders with monetary compensation, non-monetary benefits, or both, reviewing courts "must balance the policy preference for settlement against the need to insure that the interests of the class have been fairly represented."[28] When presenting a settlement to a court for approval, the proponents of the settlement bear the burden of persuading the court that the settlement is fair and reasonable. The Delaware Supreme Court has instructed that reviewing judges consider:

1. the probable validity of the claims;
2. the apparent difficulties in enforcing the claims through the courts;
3. the collectibility of any judgment recovered;
4. the delay, expense and trouble of litigation;
5. the amount of compromise as compared with the amount and collectibility of a judgment; and
6. the views of the parties involved, pro and con.[29]

These factors seem to contemplate that the settlement provides for an exchange of monetary amounts, or at least consideration that can be valued. Derivative litigation is an instrument of equity, however, and chancery courts have significant discretion to approve corporate governance reforms in lieu of, or in addition to, monetary settlements. Governance reforms may include increasing the number of outside directors, restricting the number of boards on which corporate directors can sit, or installing an independent lead director on the board. While some commentators applaud these settlements and endorse derivative litigation as a tool for shareholder voice, other observers question whether the reforms are merely cosmetic. Some commentators argue that settlements of derivative lawsuits impose reputational penalties on defendant officers and directors, thereby deterring future fiduciary breaches. Other scholars contend that the plaintiffs' lawyers are the primary beneficiaries of shareholders' derivative litigation.[30] Cognizant of the potential divergence between the interests of plaintiffs' attorneys and the interests of the shareholders they represent, the Delaware Supreme Court has instructed that "the Court of Chancery must ... play the role of fiduciary in its review of these settlements...." In re Resorts Int'l S'holders Litig. Appeals, 570 A.2d 259, 266 (Del. 1990). to encourage stockholder champions to bring meritorious litigation but not to confer unwholesome windfalls that result in excessive and unwarranted lawsuits."

27. *Mills v. Elec. Auto-Lite Co.*, 396 U.S. 375, 395 (1970).
28. *Barkan v. Amsted Indus., Inc.*, 567 A.2d 1279, 1283 (Del. 1989).
29. *Polk v. Good*, 507 A.2d 531, 536 (Del. 1986).
30. *See* Jessica Erickson, *Corporate Governance in the Courtroom: An Empirical Analysis*, 51 Wm. & Mary L. Rev. 1749, 1816–25 (2010) (concluding that mounting empirical evidence indicates that the vast majority of derivative lawsuits benefit the parties' lawyers rather than the corporations).

3. Litigation Challenging Corporate Mergers and Acquisitions

Since 2010, courts and commentators have focused increasing attention on the proliferation of shareholders' lawsuits opposing corporate mergers, acquisitions, and going private transactions. Often filed shortly after management announces the deal, shareholders of the selling corporation typically sue that firm's directors (as well as any non-director officers substantially involved in negotiating the transaction), alleging that the defendant fiduciaries breached their duties and committed fraud by agreeing to sell the company for insufficient consideration. These lawsuits, whether instituted as derivative actions, class actions, or both, frequently seek injunctive relief to block transactions from closing on the terms announced, but plaintiffs' complaints also include prayers for other equitable relief and damages as well.

More specifically, shareholders usually claim that the board of directors failed to maximize shareholders' value because (1) the sale was insufficiently competitive, (2) the board approved restrictive deal protections, discouraging further bids, and/or (3) conflicts of interest tainted the transaction. Often, plaintiffs also allege that the defendant directors misrepresented or failed to disclose to shareholders material information concerning the sale process, valuations by financial advisors, and conflicts of interest corrupting the board's decision making. In addition, plaintiffs sue the buyer and, increasingly, financial advisors who provided services facilitating the transaction, claiming that these defendants aided and abetted the directors' breach of their fiduciary duties.

While not the primary defendants in most shareholder litigation, financial advisors also have become attractive targets to shareholders challenging public company mergers, as plaintiffs' lawyers achieved successful resolutions of several noteworthy cases. In 2011, for example, Del Monte and Barclays Capital paid $89.4 million to settle stockholders' derivative litigation arising from the leveraged buyout of Del Monte by Kohlberg Kravis Roberts, Vestar Capital Partners, and Centerview Partners. The stockholders, who alleged that Barclays had conflicts of interest in providing buy-side financing while advising Del Monte, successfully obtained a preliminary injunction delaying the sale. More recently, the Delaware Supreme Court affirmed a $76 million judgment against RBC Capital Markets, finding that the bank manipulated Rural/Metro's 2011 sale process in an attempt to win a lucrative financing deal from the ambulance company's private equity acquirer. *RBC Capital Markets, LLC v. Jervis*, __ A.3d __, 2015 WL 7721882 (Del. Nov. 30, 2015). Although the justices declined to characterize the investment bank as a "gatekeeper" responsible for the integrity of the sale process, the decision marked the first time that Delaware's highest court upheld liability of a financial adviser for aiding and abetting a corporate board's breach of duty. Not only will *Rural/Metro* likely prompt corporate boards to examine bankers' conflicts more closely, but the Court's opinion will likely affect investment banks' fees, their conflict disclosures, and the indemnification terms in their engagement letters.

Public companies object not only the prevalence of this litigation,[31] but corporate managers also protest that stockholders with small stakes, represented by competing

---

31. In 2014, for example, disgruntled stockholders filed lawsuits alleging management wrongdoing in 93 percent of all M&A deals valued over $100 million. Cornerstone Research, *Shareholder Litigation*

entrepreneurial lawyers, file duplicative lawsuits alleging essentially the same claims against the same defendants in multiple state and federal courts. Generally, public company stockholders may sue directors and officers of the firm in its state of incorporation (usually Delaware) as well as in the state where the firm maintains its headquarters, assuming the defendant directors and officers have a legal presence in that jurisdiction. Both complaints (or groups of complaints) arise from the same corporate transaction and allege nearly identical claims under the law of the state of incorporation (typically Delaware). Moreover, public company stockholders enjoy some rights under federal law that they may enforce in state courts, and federal courts may exercise diversity jurisdiction over state law claims in specified circumstances. Prosecuting claims in federal courts as well as two (or more) states' courts further inflates the inefficiencies and expense associated with multiforum M&A litigation.

At bottom, it is competition among plaintiffs' lawyers for representation of shareholders that generates the filing of duplicative complaints in multiple fora. Because the plaintiffs' counsel who negotiate a broad settlement release in one jurisdiction may control subsequent settlements in cases filed in other jurisdictions,[32] lawyers for shareholders not included in a first-filed case have incentives to sue in another jurisdiction, establish control of the litigation in the second forum, and attempt to negotiate a settlement with the defendants that releases all claims alleged in both cases. Simply put, plaintiffs' law firms file copycat complaints to gain leverage with their competitors (lawyers who have filed similar claims on behalf of other plaintiff stockholders) in an effort to extract a share of the attorneys' fees awarded to stockholders' counsel following settlement with the defendants. Delaware Vice Chancellor J. Travis Laster described the jockeying among plaintiffs' lawyers to lead the litigation, and the parties' prompt agreements to settle the lawsuits thereafter, as a "Kabuki dance."[33] For their part, defendants—who strongly prefer global settlements, dismissal of all complaints, and the broadest release of claims for the least cost possible—have incentives play plaintiffs' lawyers against one another in settlement negotiations.

Most shareholder complaints arising from M&A deals settle at an early stage in the litigation; defendants have strong incentives to resolve plaintiffs' claims before the transactions close. Furthermore, the terms of such settlements follow a similar construct: in exchange for a comprehensive release of claims, the corporation agrees to disclose additional information about the deal, perhaps alter some deal terms, and pay a fee to plaintiffs' lawyers in an amount approved by the court. Defendants also often agree that they will not object to plaintiffs' request for attorneys' fees. One study

---

Involving Acquisitions of Public Companies: Review of 2014 M&A Litigation 2 (2014), *available at* http://www.cornerstone.com. The frequency of M&A litigation swelled from just under 40 percent of transactions in 2005 to over 92 percent by 2011. Matthew D. Cain & Steven Davidoff Solomon, *A Great Game: The Dynamics of State Competition and Litigation*, 100 Iowa L. Rev. 465, 469 (2015).

32. *Matsushita Electric Industrial Co. v. Epstein*, 516 U.S. 367 (1996).

33. *In re Revlon, Inc. Shareholders Litig.*, 990 A.2d 940, 946 (Del. Ch. 2010) ("[A] controller made a merger proposal. A series of actions were filed with a brief flurry of activity until the [plaintiffs' counsel] leadership structure was settled. Real litigation activity then ceased.").

of shareholders' lawsuits challenging M&A transactions in 2010 and 2011 found that two-thirds of the cases had settled, and in some 83 percent of those settlements, defendants simply agreed to supplement their disclosures in the merger proxy statement without paying monies to the corporation or its shareholders.[34] In 2014, as in previous years, nearly 80 percent of settlements provided only additional disclosures, and just six settlements provided some payment to shareholders.[35] Insofar as plaintiff shareholders challenge most large public company mergers, but usually it is the plaintiffs' attorneys who receive the only monetary consideration from resolving the litigation, the parties' so-called "disclosure only" settlements have come under increased scrutiny.

Prodded by shareholders' objections,[36] courts in Delaware and other jurisdictions have questioned and even rejected these settlements.[37] Delaware courts announced in 2015 that they intend to examine more closely the value of supplemental disclosures negotiated by settling parties, the breadth of plaintiffs' release of claims, and plaintiffs' attorneys' requests for fees.[38] In October 2015, Vice Chancellor Laster refused to approve a disclosure-only settlement of shareholders' complaints challenging Hewlett-Packard's $2.7 billion acquisition of Aruba Networks, lamenting that such proposed resolutions are a "systemic" problem.

Critics argue that the costs of defending shareholders' M&A lawsuits and the fees paid to plaintiffs' lawyers to settle the complaints amount to a "deal tax" assessed on corporate transactions, regardless of whether management breached its duties or engaged in any fraud or other wrongdoing. Detractors also contend that corporations benefit by entering into "sweetheart settlements" of meritorious claims that fail to deter fiduciary disloyalty, bad faith, and fraud. Indeed, there is danger that weak claims are overcompensated, but there also is danger that strong claims are undercompensated. Unlike an arm's-length compromise negotiated between litigating parties, arguably a reasonable measure of the value of the claims asserted, neither the

---

34. Robert M. Daines & Olga Kouminan, Cornerstone Research, *Recent Dev. in Shareholder Litig. Involving Mergers and Acquisitions*, 2012 Update 9, 11 (2012), *available at* http://www.cornerstone.com.

35. Olga Kouminan, Cornerstone Research, *Shareholder Litigation Involving Acquisitions of Public Companies: Review of 2014 M&A Litigation* (2014), *available at* http://www.cornerstone.com.

36. In advance of a judicial hearing on the fairness of their proposed settlement, both the plaintiffs and the defendants submit to the court extensive briefs advocating for approval of their negotiated resolution, and the parties provide notice to shareholders. The adversarial arguments filed by objecting shareholders may provide reviewing courts with new information concerning the fairness and reasonableness of settlements negotiated by plaintiffs' counsel and defendants. *In re Jefferies Grp., Inc. S'holders Litig.*, 2015 WL 3540662, at *2 n.5 (Del. Ch. Jun. 5, 2015) (explaining how adversarial briefing provides "salutary" benefits). Objectors to disclosure-only settlements have complained that the low value consideration provided by defendants cannot justify the plaintiffs' broad release of claims, especially future claims arising from the same transaction.

37. *See, e.g., In re Rural/Metro Corp. Shareholders Litig.*, CA No. 6350-VCL, tr. at 134 (Del. Ch. Jan. 17, 2012) (rejecting disclosure-only settlement); *Gordon v. Verizon Comm., Inc.*, 2014 WL 7250212 (Sup. Ct. N.Y. Dec. 19, 2014) (same).

38. *See, e.g., In re Riverbed Tech., Inc.*, 2015 WL 5458041 (Del. Ch. Sept. 17, 2015) (reluctantly approving settlement because parties reasonably relied on prior settlement practices of the court, but expressing concern about breadth of release).

shareholder plaintiff nor the director/officer defendants in a derivative action fully represent the interests of the corporation and its shareholders on whose behalf the lawsuit is brought. The plaintiffs' lawyers may sue and settle quickly, not investing resources in investigations necessary to detect actual breaches of loyalty, fraud, or other wrongdoing but, nonetheless, trading away the rights of other shareholders to pursue direct or derivative claims.

As for the defendants, so long as directors' and officers' liability insurance funds the settlement costs, they need not concern themselves with the amounts paid to plaintiffs' attorneys. The legal fees incurred by defendants actually exceed the insignificant monetary recovery paid to the corporation in many settled cases. Still, defense counsel have satisfied their clients by negotiating a comprehensive global release, eliminating defendants' exposure to liability from any and all claims related to the underlying facts, including any theories and claims that plaintiffs' counsel failed to raise in the lawsuit. Understanding the incentives of the named plaintiff, the defendants, and the parties' attorneys, it is not surprising that defendants often agree in settlement to take no position regarding the application of plaintiffs' counsel for attorneys' fees.

4. Attorneys' Fees

Pursuant to the traditional "American rule" of litigation, each party pays its own attorneys' fees and costs. However, to encourage stockholders to bring meritorious actions, recognizing that their enforcement efforts will benefit the corporation rather than themselves, the law recognizes an exception to the American rule. If the lawsuit has produced a substantial benefit for the corporation, either through judgment on the merits or by settlement, plaintiffs' counsel may petition the court to recover fees and costs from the corporation. In fact, attorneys for stockholder plaintiffs prosecute derivative litigation with the expectation that the courts will award them fees and costs at the (successful) conclusion of the case. Courts will approve an award of attorneys' fees and costs to plaintiffs under the corporate benefit doctrine, if: (1) plaintiff filed a meritorious complaint; (2) the defendants took action benefiting the corporation or its stockholders prior to the judicial resolution of the lawsuit; and (3) the resulting corporate benefit was related causally to the lawsuit.[39] The defendant has the burden to demonstrate that there was no causal connection between the suit and the action taken by the corporation.[40]

Recognizing that their decisions on fee petitions influence the behavior of plaintiffs' counsel, "[the] court's goal in setting a fee award should be to avoid windfalls to

---

39. *Alaska Elec. Pension Fund v. Brown*, 988 A.2d 412, 417 (Del. 2010). The corporate benefit doctrine is actually a variant of earlier court decisions awarding attorneys' fees out of common funds in cases in which the lawsuits produced recoveries for the benefit of corporations or plaintiff classes. Sean J. Griffith, *Correcting Corporate Benefit: How to Fix Shareholder Litigation by Shifting the Doctrine on Fees*, 56 B.C. L. Rev. 1, 37–41 (2015).

40. *Tandycrafts, Inc. v. Initio Partners*, 562 A.2d 1162 (Del. 1989).

counsel while encouraging future meritorious lawsuits."[41] Judges generally calculate the amount of attorneys' fees awarded to plaintiffs' attorneys in one of two ways. If a percentage-of-recovery method is used, then the attorney usually keeps 20–35 percent of the award up to a certain amount. Beyond that amount—typically $100 million—the attorney still will share in the award, but to a lesser degree. Alternatively, the lodestar method awards fees based on a reasonable hourly rate for the counsel's services and the number of hours dedicated to the case. The reasonable hourly rate accounts for the experience, reputation, and qualifications of the attorney. Sometimes a multiplier is applied to reflect the risk assumed or the particular quality of the work on the case. Of course, the percentage-of-recovery method has the potential to result in a fee that far exceeds the amount the attorney would have earned charging an hourly rate. Courts may apply the lodestar method as a "cross-check" on the reasonableness of a percentage-based fee award and reduce the requested fee if the percentage method would result in excessive compensation relative to the lodestar method.[42]

Today, a majority of appellate courts permit or, in some jurisdictions, direct lower courts to use the percentage-of-recovery method to calculate attorneys' fees in shareholder litigation. The Delaware Supreme Court adopted this approach in *Sugarland Indus., Inc. v. Thomas*[43] and instructed reviewing courts to consider five factors in awarding fees to plaintiffs' counsel: (1) the results achieved; (2) the time and effort of counsel; (3) the relative complexities of the litigation; (4) any contingency factor; and (5) the standing and ability of counsel involved. Although the last four *Sugarland* factors relate to the value of the legal services provided by plaintiffs' counsel, Delaware courts have stated repeatedly that they consider the first factor—the value of the results achieved—most important in deciding fee applications.

The attorneys' fees awarded to plaintiffs' counsel in derivative cases vary significantly. On the high end, the Delaware Supreme Court in 2012 affirmed an award of attorneys' fees totaling more than $304 million to plaintiff's lawyers who had obtained a $2 billion judgment on behalf of Southern Peru Copper in a derivative suit against the company's controlling shareholder and directors.[44] Although his fee award represented only 15 percent of the judgment (plaintiff's counsel originally petitioned for 22.5 percent of the recovery), then-Chancellor Leo Strine effectively approved payment to counsel of some $35,000 per hour billed. Nonetheless, the Supreme Court declined to set a cap or institute a formula limiting attorneys' fees in large cases, holding that Chancellor Strine properly applied the *Sugarland* factors and did not abuse his discretion in light of the extraordinary benefit achieved on behalf of the corporation. Following the decision, some commentators contended that Delaware judges awarded more generous attorneys' fees in order to continue to attract corporate litigation to

---

41. *In re Cox Radio, Inc. Shareholders Litig.*, 2010 WL 1806616, at *20 (Del. Ch. May 6, 2010), *aff'd*, 9 A.3d 475 (Del. 2010).

42. *In re Cendant Corp. Litig.*, 264 F.3d 201 (3d Cir. 2001).

43. 420 A.2d 142 (Del. 1980) (disapproving lodestar method).

44. *Americas Mining Corp. v. Theriault*, 51 A.3d 1213, 1252–62 (Del. 2012).

the state. Other observers posited that judges, as lawyers themselves, generally are inclined to grant generous fee awards, even in settled cases when plaintiffs' attorneys seem to have provided de minimus benefits to the corporation.

Critics of derivative actions have argued for many decades that these lawsuits benefit attorneys at the expense of corporations, their shareholders, and the public interest. Members of the plaintiffs' bar, in particular, stand accused of exploiting the legal system for their personal gain. To the extent that courts overcompensate share-holders' attorneys—approving larger fees than fully informed clients would have agreed to pay before authorizing the lawsuit—judges not only bestow on plaintiffs' counsel financial windfalls (fees not justified by the benefits obtained for the corpo-ration), but courts also distort the incentives for plaintiffs' counsel to prosecute mer-itorious claims. Delaware courts, and other courts as well, understand and readily acknowledge that their fee application decisions affect the incentives of plaintiffs' counsel and, thus, the quality and quantity of shareholders' claims. In fact, experts have documented that judicial fee awards in derivative cases have declined in recent years,[45] the *Southern Peru* award to the contrary. Courts in Delaware and elsewhere deny or reduce fee requests where the efforts of plaintiffs' counsel do not produce much value for shareholders or the corporation or, alternatively, where the benefit to the corporation resulted from influences other than the efforts of plaintiffs' counsel. In disclosure-only settlements, for example, the average fee awarded has declined, as has the average requested fee award.

If trial or settlement of derivative claims results in a monetary recovery for the corporation, calculation of attorneys' fees is not likely to pose difficulties for reviewing courts. However, courts encounter valuation uncertainties when the parties resolve their dispute by agreeing to corporate governance modifications or supplemental dis-closures, as discussed above. While this consideration may justify an award of attor-neys' fees under Delaware law (insofar as such reforms benefit the corporation and/or its shareholders and result from plaintiff's meritorious suit), courts must grapple with how to value the non-pecuniary benefits in order to calculate plaintiffs' attorneys' fees. Analyzing fee applications in connection with disclosure-only settlements, Delaware courts have expressed increasing skepticism about the benefits achieved for the corporation and its shareholders.[46] Consistent with academic research suggesting that shareholders receive little value from supplemental disclosures in M&A cases,[47]

45. *See* Elaine Buckberg, et al., *"Recent Trends in Shareholder Class Action Litigation: Bear Market Cases Bring Big Settlements" How Markets Work*, National Econ. Research Assoc. (Feb. 2005).

46. *See In re Sauer-Danfoss Inc. S'holders Litig.*, 2011 WL 2519210 (Del. Ch. Apr. 29, 2011) (an-alyzing fee awards in other disclosure-only settlements and awarding $75,000 to plaintiffs' attorneys who had requested $750,000, finding that just one of eleven supplemental disclosures provided share-holders with meaningful additional information to shareholders).

47. *See, e.g.,* Jill E. Fisch, Sean J. Griffith & Steven Davidoff Solomon, *Confronting the Peppercorn Settlement in Merger Litigation: An Empirical Analysis and a Proposal for Reform*, 93 Tex. L. Rev. 557 (2015) (reporting results of research finding that supplemental disclosures negotiated in settlements of shareholder litigation did not affect shareholders' voting on challenged transactions).

Delaware chancery court judges seem to be reducing the fees requested by plaintiffs' attorneys who have negotiated such settlements.[48]

5. Indemnification and Insurance

Were corporate directors and officers held personally accountable for actions taken in their official capacities, the liability undoubtedly would bankrupt them. Without a system in place to indemnify fiduciaries and insure against these liability risks, only the wealthiest and least risk-averse individuals would accept positions of corporate authority. Indemnification and insurance are the two primary ways by which high-level corporate service is made viable for more than this limited population.

To be sure, Section 102(b)(7) protects corporate directors from liability for violations of the duty of care. However, the statute does not provide directors protection for breaching a duty of loyalty.[49] And although corporate officers and other non-director executives do not enjoy the statutory liability protections set forth in Section 102(b)(7), both directors and officers may (and typically do) receive the protective benefits of indemnification agreements, included in charter documents and/or employment contracts, as well as liability insurance.

The corporation may provide indemnification to management pursuant to Section 145 of the DGCL. Subsections 145(a) and (b) allow corporations to indemnify corporate officers, directors, employees, and agents for litigation costs from actual or threatened legal action arising out of their relationship with the corporation. The corporation has the option of indemnifying these individuals for reasonable attorneys' fees, judgments, fines, and settlement costs, so long as the litigated conduct of the individual seeking indemnification was in good faith and in accordance with the business judgment rule. Just as with Section 102(b)(7), the Delaware legislature is not willing to shield corporate officers from bad faith conduct when either the corporation itself or its shareholders seek redress.

The primary difference between Section 145(a) and Section 145(b) is that Section 145(b) prohibits indemnification when the defendant is found liable to the corporation itself. It would make sense for a corporation to sue an officer to recover losses if the corporation itself bears the cost of the judgment or settlement. Corporate officers who lose on the merits under Section 145(a) still can be indemnified, but this is a discretionary matter for the board. Section 145(c) mandates indemnification for corporate officers and directors who succeed on the merits in a suit, provided that the corporation is willing to confirm that the defendant acted in good faith under Section 145(d). A determination of good faith must be made by: a majority

---

48. *See In re Riverbed Tech., Inc.*, 2015 WL 5458041 (Del. Ch. Sept. 17, 2015) (awarding fee of $200,000, though counsel requested $500,000). Fee awards in disclosure-only settlements range from $250,000 to $450,000. *See In re Sauer-Danfoss Inc. S'holders Litig.*, 2011 WL 2519210 (Del. Ch. Apr. 29, 2011) (appending chart identifying ten disclosure-only settlements and documenting Delaware courts awarded fees from $250,000 to $450,000, with two exceptions).

49. *Emerald Partners v. Berlin*, 787 A.2d 85, 90 (Del. 2001).

of directors not subject to the litigation at hand; a committee of directors designated for just such a purpose; independent legal counsel; or the stockholders. Corporations can determine, through their bylaws or through contracts with individual officers, how such proceedings would take place. This mandatory indemnification is available to whatever extent the officer or director is successful, meaning that if a director or officer is successful in defending against one element of a suit, he is entitled to indemnification for costs associated with that claim even if he is found liable under other claims.

Corporations also have the option to advance legal fees to defendant officers and directors. Under Delaware law, the legal right to advancement is separate from and not dependent upon the right to indemnification. Litigation cost advancement essentially provides the defendant with a line of credit, with the expectation of repayment unless indemnification would apply. Provisions for advancement are made in the certificate of incorporation, corporate bylaws, and/or in individual executive contracts. Corporations must take care when structuring advancement policies, as defense costs for derivative suits and criminal trials for executives can run into the millions and even tens of millions of dollars. Section 145(j) ensures that indemnification and advancement provided under Section 145 continues even when a defendant has severed her ties with the corporation, preventing corporations from mitigating costs simply by terminating the defendant. Section 145(h) provides similar assurances of continuity for rights to indemnification and advancement in the event of mergers and acquisitions.

Indemnification is an important protection for directors, even at companies that have purchased directors' and officers' insurance. D&O insurance has limits of liability, while indemnification is really only limited by the financial realities of the corporation. Like any insurance policy, D&O insurance contains many exclusions and limitations. Indemnification, on the other hand, is likely to be granted via broad decree in the corporate charter or bylaws, often to the fullest extent permitted by law. Indemnification also may be separately negotiated in the contract of a director or officer, but in either instance, it is unlikely to change from year to year. Insurance coverage likely will have to be renewed each year, possibly subject to changes in exclusions and limitations. While indemnification protects directors and officers, insurance provides protection for the corporation itself. Section 145(g) of Delaware's statute allows corporations to purchase this insurance for anyone "who is or was a director, officer, employee or agent of the corporation, or is or was serving at the request of the corporation as a director, officer, employee or agent of another corporation, partnership, joint venture, trust or other enterprise."

Individual D&O insurance, or "Side A" coverage, provides coverage for directors and officers only, not the corporation itself. Why, then, would a corporation choose to pay potentially costly premiums in order to protect its officers and directors from lawsuits instituted to make the corporation itself whole from their malfeasance? Providing insurance to fill in some of the gaps in protection enhances the corporation's ability to attract and retain top-tier talent. Executives will be wary of joining a corporation that will not protect them against suits by disgruntled shareholders. Corporations that indemnify and insure executives and directors to the fullest extent permitted by law have a competitive advantage in the executive recruitment market.

There are coverage options for D&O insurance that directly benefit the corporation, often referred to as "entity" or "Side B" coverage. Entity coverage allows a corporation to insure itself against both indemnification costs for which it might be liable and litigation costs when the corporation itself is a defendant in a shareholder suit. This kind of coverage provides a benefit to shareholders as well, as it protects corporate assets rather than the assets of individual directors or officers. Insurers also offer customization options that allow a corporation to secure a policy best suited to its size (small-cap corporations are likely to need far less coverage than large-cap firms), risk profile, statutory circumstances (40 percent of major American corporations are not incorporated in Delaware and thus may face different liability and indemnification structures), and industry (highly-regulated industries conceivably bear a greater litigation risk than other less regulated industries due to the heightened probability of government action).

Corporations that require high coverage limits (over $50 million) can purchase "towers of coverage" that limit the risk to any single carrier. Towers establish a primary policy through one company that agrees to provide a certain amount of coverage, and then one or more excess policies are stacked on top of the primary policy to create a higher total coverage limit. For example, if the primary policy offers $20 million in coverage and the secondary policy provides an additional $30 million, the secondary policy would not owe anything until the coverage limits on the primary policy are exhausted. The same applies to tertiary policies and so on across the full extent of the tower. Stacking primary and secondary policies into towers spreads the risk of loss across multiple carriers and increases the number of carriers from which a corporation can purchase a policy, since a potentially prohibitive single coverage limit no longer applies. D&O insurance policies also may include a "Side C" coverage, which provides protection when the corporation itself is held liable. For public companies, this protection usually covers liability under the securities laws.

For many if not most public companies, the amount of coverage available in a single D&O policy is likely to be inadequate relative to the extraordinary liability exposure. To afford sufficient protection, corporations may purchase excess liability coverage from other insurers, essentially stacking policies to provide higher levels of protection. The primary insurer will pay up to a certain dollar amount, at which point the excess coverage will kick in up to its dollar limit. Generally, the excess coverage is only implicated if the policy limit on the primary policy is surpassed. Excess "Side A" insurance often provides certain additional protection for actions or events not covered by the primary "Side A" insurance. These additional coverages "drop down," in that they will pay starting from the first dollar of liability when the primary policy does not cover the claim.

Unlike other forms of insurance (commercial general liability, for example), there is no standard D&O policy. Each carrier has forms that differ from their competitors' forms and most policies are negotiated. D&O insurance also has the potential to involve a new party in corporate governance practices: the insurance carrier. Policy provisions allow carriers to become involved with, and to some extent control, the litigation defense for covered parties. Insurance carriers also may develop close relationships with firms seeking coverage in order to provide risk data to its underwriters.

Prior to issuing policies, D&O carriers investigate applicant companies. D&O carriers might examine corporate financials, internal controls, corporate litigation history, shareholder-board-executive relations, loss prevention practices, executive turnover rate, and regulatory compliance measures within a given corporation in order to quote an accurate premium. These pre-policy inquiries familiarize carriers with the risk management practices and legal personnel employed by applicant corporations. For a discount, the carrier could offer consultation on risk management practices that pertain to executive and board action. Such activity could reduce the exposure to loss for both the corporation and the carrier, providing a dispassionate evaluation of the firm's governance systems.

However, evidence suggests that D&O carriers do not necessarily investigate and monitor their insureds' corporate governance systems; competition is not based on services or future operational gains but on premium price.[50] Some corporations, in fact, carry individual D&O coverage in an effort to reduce premium costs, not to insure the corporation itself against loss. Corporate executives may not welcome excessive involvement in corporate affairs from outside parties, so long as they are covered themselves.

At the beginning of the new millennium, financial frauds and related scandals at Enron, WorldCom, and other public companies led to massive litigation as well as regulatory and even criminal cases against the directors, officers, and other senior executives. Defense costs alone totaled hundreds of millions of dollars. For example, Jeffrey Skilling racked up $70 million in defense fees in the Enron case. Former HealthSouth CEO Richard Scrushy's defense in the HealthSouth case cost $21 million, and former Tyco CEO Dennis Kozlowski incurred $26 million in defense costs. Such expenses are staggering by any account, but the obligation to pay them typically arises at a time of great turbulence—financial and otherwise—for the corporation. Not surprisingly, then, former directors and officers may find themselves at odds with corporations about their entitlement to indemnification and/or advancement of costs.

Because many corporate indemnification provisions simply reproduce the language of Section 145, questions concerning coverage often require construction of the statutory language. Section 145 provides that a corporation *may* indemnify any person who incurs liability "*by reason of the fact*" that the person is or was a "*director, officer, employee or agent of the corporation*" or "*is or was serving at the request of*" the corporation. If there is a nexus or causal connection between any of the underlying proceedings and the individual's official capacity, those proceedings are 'by reason of the

---

50. Tom Baker & Sean J. Griffith, *The Missing Monitor in Corporate Governance: The Directors' & Officers' Liability Insurer*, 95 Geo. L.J. 1795, 1808–13 (2007).

fact' that he was a corporate officer or director, without regard to any motivation for engaging in that conduct. *Homestore, Inc. v. Tafeeen*, 888 A.2d 204, 215 (Del. 2005).

If a present or former director or officer is "successful" in defending a claim, then Section 145(c) requires indemnification for expenses. Yet, even this apparently straight-forward provision can give rise to litigation, as it often is unclear whether the director or officer has been "successful." When a complaint is dismissed without prejudice, it is possible that it could be reinstituted in the future. Likewise, plaintiffs often have multiple claims, and the dismissal of one claim does not guarantee any particular result with respect to the others.

Another source of contention is the word "defending." Defense has been given a broad meaning, including affirmative defenses and counterclaims. *Citadel Holding Corp. v. Roven*, 603 A.2d 818 (Del. 1992). While counterclaims technically are separate causes of action, counterclaims arising from the same transaction or occurrence must be plead or lost, so they are advanced to defeat or offset the claim against the officer or director. Despite the basis of the holding, permissive counterclaims were not explicitly excluded from "defending." From there, the analysis has become muddled further, with some courts holding that the true test for "defending" is whether a counterclaim defeats or offsets the original claim, and other courts holding that all compulsory counterclaims are part of a defense. Of course, corporations remain free to use more precise language than that contained in Section 145. The firm could include or exclude expenses relating to counterclaims explicitly.

Litigation also may ensue should the corporation refuse to indemnify its (usually former) director or officer. Generally, Delaware courts enforce corporations' indemnification and advancement bargains. Indeed, under Delaware law, a director or officer denied indemnification not only may recover indemnification of the judgment, fines, or other costs at issue, but she also may recover the attorneys' fees and other expenses incurred to collect the monies owing.[51] The right to "fees on fees" is limited by the extent to which the director or officer is successful in collecting against the corporation. In other words, directors and officers can collect "fees on fees" only in proportion to their success on the underlying indemnification or advancement action.

Effective August 1, 2011, the Delaware General Assembly amended Section 145(f) to clarify that corporations may not impair or eliminate indemnification or advancement rights retroactively. Specifically, an indemnification or advancement right provided by the certificate of incorporation or bylaws cannot be eliminated or impaired by any amendment to the documents after the occurrence of the act or omission to which indemnification or advancement of expenses relates, unless that provision contains, at the time of the act or omission, an explicit authorization of such elimination

---

51. *Stifel Fin. Corp. v. Cochran*, 809 A.2d 555 (Del. 2002) ("giving full effect to Section 145 prevents a corporation from using its 'deep pockets' to wear down a former director, with a valid claim to indemnification, through expensive litigation."). *See also Reddy v. Elec. Data Sys. Corp.*, 2002 Del. Ch. LEXIS 69 (June 18, 2002), *aff'd*, 820 A.2d 371 (Del. 2003) (applying "fees on fees" principal to advancement case).

or limitation. Under current law, then, a corporation may not circumvent an indemnification or expense advancement obligation contained in a charter provision by adopting, retroactively, an amendment to its bylaws.

The following case from the Second Circuit Court of Appeals explores the policy-based limits of indemnification, as affected by the clawback provisions of the Sarbanes-Oxley Act.

Cohen v. Viray

United States Court of Appeals, Second Circuit
622 F.3d 188 (2010)

HALL, CIRCUIT JUDGE:

On appeal, intervenor-appellant argues principally that the district court erred by approving the settlement of the shareholders' derivative litigation brought on behalf of DHB Industries, Inc. against a number of its former officers and directors because the settlement agreement impermissibly releases and indemnifies DHB's former Chief Executive Officer and Chief Financial Officer against all liability arising under § 304 of the Sarbanes-Oxley Act, 15 U.S.C. § 7243.* We agree.

BACKGROUND

We recount only such facts as are necessary to explain our decision. In the fall of 2005, DHB Industries, Inc.'s stock price plummeted following revelations that the body armor manufactured by the company contained an inferior material prone to rapid deterioration. Numerous derivative and class action lawsuits were subsequently filed against DHB and a number of its former officers and directors. In January 2006, the United States District Court for the Eastern District of New York (Seybert, J.) consolidated the derivative actions and class actions and appointed derivative counsel and class counsel. The settlement of the consolidated derivative action is the subject of this appeal, though the Settlement is a joint settlement that settled both the consolidated derivative action and the consolidated class action.

In the district court, intervenor-appellant D. David Cohen and the Department of Justice Civil Litigation Division, in consultation with the Securities and Exchange Commission, presented objections to the Settlement. As relevant to our decision, Cohen and the United States objected to the provisions in which DHB agreed to release David H. Brooks, DHB's former Chairman and Chief Executive Officer, and Dawn M. Schlegel, DHB's former Chief Financial Officer, from any liability under § 304 of the Sarbanes-Oxley Act, 15 U.S.C. § 7243* ("§ 304"),

---

* 15 U.S.C. § 7243 provides in full:
  (a) Additional compensation prior to noncompliance with Commission financial reporting requirements
      If an issuer is required to prepare an accounting restatement due to the material non-compliance of the issuer, as a result of misconduct, with any financial reporting requirement under the securities laws, the chief executive officer and chief financial officer of the issuer shall reimburse the issuer for—

and to indemnify them against any liability they may incur under § 304.**
Over these objections, on July 8, 2008, the district court entered final judgment approving the Settlement. The court subsequently entered an order
granting derivative counsel's application for attorneys' fees and rejecting
Cohen's application for attorneys' fees. This appeal followed.

PROCEDURAL HISTORY

It was in December 2006 that the district court was first presented with the proposed
Settlement, which had been agreed to by derivative counsel, class counsel, the named
defendants, and DHB. The following month, Cohen moved to intervene in the consolidated class and derivative actions pursuant to Federal Rule of Civil Procedure
24(a)(2) and, inter alia, objected to preliminary approval of the proposed Settlement.
Cohen subsequently filed a memorandum of law in opposition to that approval and,
in May 2007, appeared at a court hearing held to review it. The court made a preliminary finding in favor of the Settlement and subsequently entered an order to that
effect.

In September 2007, Cohen filed objections to final approval of the Settlement.

On October 1, 2007, DHB filed restated financial statements for 2003, 2004, and
the first three quarters of 2005. Three days later, on October 4, 2007, the DOJ petitioned the district court pursuant to the Class Action Fairness Act, 28 U.S.C. §§ 1715
et seq., for an extension of time to evaluate the proposed Settlement.

The following month, the United States filed objections to the Settlement, principally on the grounds that it: (i) limited the remedies available to the government
in pending criminal cases against the individual defendants, and (ii) undermined ef-

---

(1) any bonus or other incentive-based or equity-based compensation received by
that person from the issuer during the 12-month period following the first public
issuance or filing with the Commission (whichever first occurs) of the financial document embodying such financial reporting requirement; and
(2) any profits realized from the sale of securities of the issuer during that 12-month
period.
(b) Commission exemption authority
The Commission may exempt any person from the application of subsection (a) of this section, as
it deems necessary and appropriate.

** Section 1.27 of the Settlement provides in relevant part:
Released Derivative Claims includes, without limitation, a release by DHB of David H.
Brooks and Dawn M. Schlegel, and each of them, from any and all liability under § 304 of
the Sarbanes-Oxley Act of 2002 to reimburse DHB for any bonus or other incentive-based
or equity based compensation received by them or either of them, or for any profits realized
by them or either of them from the sale of any securities of DHB.
Section 4.7 provides in relevant part:
DHB shall indemnify defendants David H. Brooks and Dawn M. Schlegel, and each of
them, against any liability under § 304 of the Sarbanes-Oxley Act of 2002 incurred by them,
or either of them, in any action brought by a third party under § 304, and to pay to them,
and to each of them, an amount equal to any payment made by them, or either of them,
to DHB pursuant to any judgment in any such action.

forts by the SEC to hold the individual defendants liable for disgorgement under § 304. In letters to the district court in December 2007 and June 2008, the United States Attorney for the Eastern District of New York expressed concern regarding its ability to seek restitution in connection with pending criminal cases and noted that Brooks' contribution to the Settlement was funded at least in part with the proceeds of insider trading.

In response to the United States' objections, the settling parties offered to add the following language to the Settlement: "Nothing contained in this Settlement is intended to limit the United States' ability to pursue forfeiture, restitution or fines in any criminal, civil or administrative proceeding." Brooks conditioned his acceptance of the proposed language on the addition of the phrase "except that ¶ 4.7 of the [Settlement] shall remain in full force and effect," thus seeking to ensure that Brooks and Schlegel were indemnified against liability under § 304. See n. 3, supra. Cohen and the United States continued to object to the Settlement.

In June 2008, the district court held a hearing for final approval of the Settlement. Cohen and the United States each appeared in opposition to the Settlement, and each reiterated the objections relating to § 304. As already noted, the court granted final approval of the Settlement, and on July 8, 2008, entered final judgment to that effect. Paragraph twelve of the final judgment provides that the Settlement includes a new paragraph 4. 10, which states, in part, that "[n]othing contained in this Stipulation is intended to limit the United States' ability to pursue forfeiture, restitution or fines in any criminal, civil or administrative proceeding, except that Paragraph 4.7 of this Stipulation [regarding indemnification for § 304 liability] shall remain in full force and effect." ...

DISCUSSION

On appeal, Cohen principally asserts that the district court erred by approving the Settlement, awarding attorneys' fees to derivative plaintiffs' counsel, and denying his application for attorneys' fees. Because we hold that the indemnification and release provisions of the Settlement violate § 304, our discussion is limited to that single issue, and we decline to address the remaining issues argued on appeal.

As a preliminary matter, we note there is no merit to the suggestion that Cohen waived any objection to the Settlement's indemnification of Brooks against § 304 liability on the grounds that indemnification is violative of § 304 and public policy. As already noted, Cohen repeatedly raised objections on these grounds to the district court. Appellees' argument that Cohen's objections were untimely is precluded, moreover, as this argument was not made in the district court, and appellees do not assert that it is "necessary [that we nevertheless consider the argument] to serve an 'interest of justice.'"

Standard of Review

Although the district court normally has discretion to approve a settlement, we may review that court's decision de novo where an appellant's challenge to the authority of the district court to approve the settlement raises novel issues of law. This is such a case. We have not, and indeed no court has, yet addressed whether by private agreement parties may indemnify a CEO or CFO against liability imposed by § 304.

SOX Section 304

Before reaching the ultimate issue—i.e., whether the Settlement's provisions releasing and indemnifying DHB's former CEO and CFO against liability imposed by § 304 violate that section—we must first determine whether § 304 provides a private cause of action. If it does, the SEC would have no claim that the Settlement usurps its sole authority to exempt persons from § 304 liability....

The Ninth Circuit, the only other Court of Appeals to have directly confronted the issue, has held that no such private right of action exists. *See In re Digimarc Corp. Derivative Litig.*, 549 F.3d 1223, 1233 (9th Cir. 2008). ("[W]e conclude that section 304 does not create a private right of action."). The Court of Appeals for the District of Columbia addressed this issue in dicta, and came to the same conclusion—that no private cause of action exists. *See Pirelli Armstrong Tire Corp. Retiree Med. Benefits Trust ex rel. Fed. Nat'l Mortg. Ass'n v. Raines*, 534 F.3d 779, 793 (D.C. Cir. 2008) (holding that defendant's directors' decision not to bring suit under § 304 for disgorgement by CEO and CFO was within the business judgment rule, as "§ 304 does not create a private right of action").

Since the plain language of the statute does not answer the question of whether a private right of action exists under § 304, we begin our inquiry by analyzing congressional intent. *See Bellikoff v. Eaton Vance Corp.*, 481 F.3d 110, 116 (2d Cir. 2007).

> Congressional intent is the keystone as to whether a federal private right of action exists for a federal statute. Without a showing of congressional intent, a cause of action does not exist. This Court must begin its search for Congress's intent with the text and structure of the statute, and cannot ordinarily conclude that Congress intended to create a right of action when none was explicitly provided.

Id. Section 304 by its terms requires CEOs and CFOs to reimburse their company for any bonus or similar compensation, or any profits realized from the sale of company stock, for the 12-month period following a false financial report, if the company "is required to prepare an accounting restatement due to the material noncompliance of the [company], as a result of misconduct." 15 U.S.C. § 7243(a). It also permits the SEC to exempt "any person" from this mandatory duty, "as it deems necessary and appropriate." *Id.* § 7243(b). The statute makes no explicit provision of a private cause of action for violations of § 304. We therefore presume that Congress did not intend to create one. Under § 3(b)(1) of SOX, moreover, the SEC has authority to enforce § 304 pursuant to its authority to enforce any provision of the Securities Exchange Act of 1934, 15 U.S.C. § 78u(d)(1).

> A violation by any person of this Act, any rule or regulation of the Commission issued under this Act, or any rule of the Board shall be treated for all purposes in the same manner as a violation of the Securities Exchange Act of 1934 (15 U.S.C. 78a et seq.) or the rules and regulations issued thereunder,

consistent with the provisions of this Act, and any such person shall be subject to the same penalties, and to the same extent, as for a violation of that Act or such rules or regulations.

Id.

As in *Bellikoff,* our presumption that Congress did not intend to create a private cause of action is supported by the text and structure of the statute at issue. *See id.* It is clear from the text of the statute that § 304 imposes a mandatory duty on those subject to it, see 15 U.S.C. § 7243(a) (CEO and CFO "shall reimburse" (emphasis added)), and that it vests the SEC with the authority to exempt any person from the obligation to reimburse the issuer under § 304(a), "as it deems necessary and appropriate." *Id.* § 7243(b) (emphasis added). Congress thus provided only the SEC authority to exempt persons from § 304(a), indicating that only the SEC has that authority and that other parties do not. Other provisions in SOX, moreover, do provide a private cause of action—e.g., § 306 expressly creates a private cause of action to recover profits made by officers and directors from insider trading during pension fund blackout periods. The inclusion of a specific provision to this effect elsewhere in the statute "'suggests that omission of any explicit private right to enforce other sections was intentional.'" *Bellikoff,* 481 F.3d at 116. We therefore join our sister circuits in holding that § 304 does not create a private cause of action.

We now turn to whether the Settlement's provisions releasing and indemnifying DHB's former CEO and CFO against liability under § 304 violate that statute. Cohen argues that the indemnification and release provisions of the Settlement violate SOX and public policy "[b]ecause Congress vested authority to 'exempt' CEOs and CFOs from application of § 304(a) solely in the SEC, and did not grant such discretion to the public companies themselves," Appellant's Br. 25, and because the indemnification and release provisions "would nullify the right and remedy that Congress expressly provided in the statute." *Id.* 27. The United States, as amicus, similarly asserts that the Settlement's release and indemnification provisions are illegal and effectively "[n]ullif[y]" the SEC's authority to pursue the § 304 remedy or to grant exemptions from the statute. We agree. The district court erred when it approved the Settlement's provisions requiring DHB to release and indemnify Brooks and Schlegel against any liability imposed under § 304.

As noted, only the SEC has authority to enforce § 304, ... and to "exempt" CEOs and CFOs from liability under § 304. The Settlement's release and indemnification provisions attempt an end-run around § 304 that vitiates the SEC's role and is inconsistent with the law. If allowed to stand, it would effectively bar the relief the SEC is authorized to seek. It is true the SEC could order disgorgement. The terms of the indemnification agreement, however, would allow Brooks and Schlegel to pass that claim on to DHB so that they, individually, would suffer no penalty at all. The Supreme Court has held that agreements of private parties cannot frustrate the power of a federal agency to pursue the public's interests in litigation. Here, the Settlement's release and indemnification provisions would accomplish exactly that, flying in the face of Congress's efforts to make high ranking corporate officers of public companies directly responsible for their actions that have caused material noncompliance with financial reporting requirements.

The SEC's decision to pursue § 304 relief is not solely intended to reimburse a company; it also furthers important public purposes. The § 304 remedy is an enforcement mechanism that ensures the integrity of the financial markets. As the Supreme Court recently observed, Congress enacted SOX in the wake of "a series of celebrated accounting debacles." *Free Enterprise Fund v. Public Co. Accounting Oversight Bd.*, 130 S. Ct. 3138, 3147 (2010). In sum, companies themselves do not have the authority effectively to exempt persons from § 304 liability.

Our holding is further supported by our jurisprudence addressing similar situations under comparable statutes. While no court has previously addressed whether a company may indemnify an officer subject to a § 304 remedy, courts have addressed indemnification against liability under other provisions of federal securities law and have concluded that indemnification cannot be permitted where it would effectively nullify a statute. For example, § 29(a) of the Exchange Act, which provides that any "condition, stipulation, or provision binding any person to waive compliance with any provision of this chapter or of any rule or regulation thereunder, or of any rule of an exchange required thereby shall be void," is instructive. This Court, citing § 29(a), has refused to "give effect to contractual language purporting to be a general waiver or release of Rule 10b-5 liability altogether." *Vacold LLC v. Cerami*, 545 F.3d 114, 122 (2d Cir. 2008).

CONCLUSION

Because we conclude that the indemnification and release provisions of the Settlement violate § 304 of the Sarbanes-Oxley Act, we do not reach the question of whether the Settlement is substantively and procedurally fair, reasonable, and adequate. Nor do we reach the issues pertaining to attorneys' fees. The district court will need to reexamine those issues in any event, either in the context of a revised settlement or the outcome of further litigation.

For the foregoing reasons, the judgment of the district court is VACATED and the case is REMANDED to the district court for proceedings consistent with this opinion.

Comments and Questions

1. Since the 1980s, regulators and federal lawmakers—relying on the work of economists and other compensation experts—have pressed boards of directors to align executives' pay with corporate performance. In Chapter 6, we examined some of the myriad of laws, rules, and regulations governing executive compensation, including disclosure mandates, accounting standards, tax policies, and, most recently, direct legislation requiring shareholders to approve executive compensation by nonbinding votes every three years. Often imposed following revelations of corporate abuses and economic declines, intrusions into corporate executives' compensation arrangements, like SOX Section 304, have sparked considerable controversy. Having studied the language of Section 304 and read the Second Circuit's decision interpreting

the statute, why did Congress include Section 304 in Sarbanes-Oxley? Other than seeking indemnification, how might corporate executives avoid potential losses under the statute?

2. Insofar as Section 304 makes no mention of indemnification for executive officers, what arguments persuaded the Second Circuit to void the indemnification provisions of the Settlement? Applying the court's reasoning, could corporations arrange for or provide insurance protecting executives against the risk that they will have forfeit their incentive-based compensation? In the alternative, could executives purchase insurance themselves to protect against this risk? If so, would it be permissible for the corporation to increase the executives' salaries in order to facilitate their purchase of insurance?

3. Section 304 compels CEOs and CFOs to reimburse their firms for any bonuses or equity-based compensation received, and any profits realized from selling shares, in the twelve months commencing with the filing of financial statements that are subsequently restated "due to material noncompliance of the issuer as a result of misconduct." Notably, Section 304 does not define "misconduct," nor does the provision specify whose misconduct triggers the restatement (and, thus, the clawback). Having read the court's analysis in *Cohen v. Viray*, what is the argument that Section 304 establishes a standard of strict liability for CEOs and CFOs whose companies have issued restated financial statements? Does Section 304 permit the clawback of bonuses, incentive-based compensation, or stock sale proceeds not alleged to have been tied to, or affected by, the misstatements?

4. The SEC failed to bring any Section 304 cases until 2007, five years after SOX became law. According to research published in 2011, the SEC utilized Section 304 very infrequently for nearly a decade after Congress enacted Sarbanes-Oxley, and when the Commission did so, it usually initiated its clawback action only after the executives targeted already had been convicted of criminal fraud.[52] Does the SEC's apparent reticence to use Section 304 undermine the policy argument supporting Second Circuit's reasoning in *Cohen v. Viray*? Can you think of reasons that the Commission might opt to overlook violations of the statute? Do you agree with critics who argue that Section 304 is only a deterrent if the SEC uses it? In light of the SEC's failure to bring cases under Section 304, should Congress amend the statute to provide an express private right of action allowing shareholders to enforce the statute? Why or why not?

5. When the SEC eventually began to enforce Section 304, it targeted CEOs and CFOs allegedly involved in the misconduct that caused the financial statements to be misleading; indeed, the SEC alleged that the executives violated other securities laws. However, in the immediate aftermath of the financial crisis, the SEC invoked Section 304 to clawback monies from CEOs and CFOs not alleged to have had any involvement in the misconduct. Although the executives charged moved to dismiss the SEC's complaint, arguing that liability under the statute requires wrongdoing, federal courts disagreed. In 2012, for example, U.S. District Judge Sam Sparks refused to dismiss

---

52. Jesse Fried & Nitzan Shilon, *Excess-Pay Clawbacks*, 36 J. Corp. L. 722 (2011).

a complaint filed by the SEC against the CEO and CFO of ArthroCare, seeking to recover on behalf of the firm cash bonuses, incentives, and equity-based compensation paid to them for financial reporting periods that the company restated. Neither executive had any involvement in or even awareness of the misconduct that led to the restatements. Rejecting the defendants' arguments for dismissing the Section 304 action, the court emphasized that Congress had "good policy reasons" for requiring that executive officers reimburse corporations, even in the absence of allegations that they committed conscious wrongdoing:

> Apologists for the extraordinarily high compensation given to corporate officers have long-justified such pay as asserting CEOs take 'great risks,' and so deserve great rewards. For years, this has been a vacuous saw, because corporate law, and private measures such as wide-spread indemnification of officers by their employers, and the provisions of Directors & Officers insurance, have ensured any 'risks' taken by these fearless captains of industry almost never impact their personal finances. In enacting Section 304 of Sarbanes Oxley, Congress determined to put a modest measure of real risk back into the equation. This was a policy decision, and while its fairness or wisdom can be debated, its legal effect cannot. Section 304 creates a powerful incentive for CEOs and CFOs to take their corporate responsibilities very seriously indeed.

SEC v. Baker, 2012 WL 5499497 at *11 (W.D. Tex. Nov. 13, 2012).

6. Although the SEC made infrequent use of Section 304, the financial crisis in 2008 and subsequent federal bailout of financial institutions spawned new popular support for government regulation of executive compensation and, in particular, restrictions on pay received by then-current or departing execs of financial institutions. The Emergency Economic Stabilization Act of 2008, enacted in October 2008, regulated executive compensation at financial institutions that accepted bailout funds from the federal government. That statute provided for, among other directives, recovery of bonuses and other incentive compensation awarded on the basis of materially inaccurate financial data.

When it then enacted Dodd-Frank in July 2010, Congress extended the financial crisis legislation to cover public company executives more broadly. Among other new laws, Section 954 of Dodd-Frank, the "Recovery of Erroneously Awarded Compensation" provision, added Section 10D to the Securities Exchange Act of 1934. Section 954 requires the SEC to promulgate rules directing public (exchange-listed) companies "to develop and implement a policy" providing:

> [T]hat, in the event that the issuer is required to prepare an accounting restatement due to the material noncompliance of the issuer with any financial reporting requirement under the securities laws, the issuer will recover from any current or former executive officer of the issuer who received incentive-based compensation (including stock options awarded as compensation) during the three-year period preceding the date on which the issuer is required to prepare an accounting restatement, based on the erroneous data, in excess

of what would have been paid to the executive officer under the accounting restatement.

How does Section 954 of Dodd-Frank differ from SOX Section 304?

7. In July 2015, a full five years after Congress enacted Dodd-Frank, the SEC finally proposed rules to effect executive compensation clawbacks under Section 954. Rule 10D-1, as proposed, would prohibit listed companies from indemnifying any executive officer or former executive officer against the loss of erroneously awarded compensation. Furthermore, the rule would prohibit the corporation from paying or reimbursing the executive for premiums for a third-party insurance policy purchased to fund potential recovery obligations. Do you think that the SEC should bar listed companies from indemnifying their executive officers and/or funding the purchase of insurance to protect executive officers against the risk that they forfeit excess compensation back to the firm, as proposed? Why or why not? Should Rule 10D-1 also prohibit companies from indemnifying executive officers' litigation expenses in recovery actions?

III. Debating Derivative Litigation

Because of its representative nature, shareholder derivative actions give rise to agency problems. Corporate executives and other critics of shareholders' litigation contend that the impetus for derivative lawsuits comes from the "greedy" plaintiffs' bar, "extortionist" lawyers motivated by the potential for recovering "windfall" legal fees, who file questionable claims against corporate fiduciaries and their advisors. When shareholder litigation does produce a monetary recovery for the corporation, detractors argue, the action simply transfers company assets from one corporate pocket to another corporate pocket, less the substantial "transfer fee" taken by the attorneys. While D&O insurance shifts some of the costs of derivative lawsuits from the corporation to insurance companies, the availability of insurance does not resolve whether or not derivative suits actually benefit corporations and their shareholders. The following article excerpt explains the questionable value of derivative litigation.

Reinier Kraakman, Hyun Park, & Steven Shavell, *When Are Shareholder Suits in Shareholder Interests?*
82 Geo. L.J. 1733 (1994)[53]

Shareholder suits are the primary mechanism for enforcing the fiduciary duties of corporate managers. Such suits often allege that an officer or director has breached his duty of loyalty; in other words, that the manager has effectively "cheated" the company by self-dealing, accepting kickbacks, appropriating a corporate opportunity, wasting corporate assets, or entrenching his position to avoid removal. Less frequently, because the odds of success are lower, shareholder suits assert that an officer or director

---

53. Reprinted with permission of the publisher, Georgetown Law Journal © 1994.

has breached his duty of care by harming the corporation through his negligent—or grossly negligent—failure to exercise appropriate business judgment.

The procedural form of a shareholder suit depends on whether managers are said to have harmed the corporation or instead its shareholders in the first instance. In the usual case, where the injury is corporate (for example, where directors are accused of self-dealing), a shareholder must sue "derivatively" on behalf of the corporation. If a derivative suit succeeds, any recoveries go to the corporation, while the plaintiff-shareholder (or his attorney) receives legal fees from the company that typically exceed the out-of-pocket costs of prosecuting suit. Sometimes, however, a manager's breach of duty injures shareholders directly—as, for example, where directors are alleged to have wrongfully approved the sale of the company at an unfair price. In this case, a public shareholder can sue directly as the named plaintiff on behalf of the shareholder class, and any recoveries will go to the plaintiff class directly rather than to the corporation.

The legal rules that currently govern both forms of shareholder suits are widely discussed and frequently criticized in the legal literature. Many authors have explored the related problems of frivolous shareholder suits ("strike suits") and of "sweetheart" settlements between plaintiffs' attorneys and corporate defendants that disregard the interests of the corporation and the shareholder body as a whole. Partly in response to these problems, commentators have also addressed the comparative competence of courts and corporate boards to screen shareholder suits. Finally, there is a promising new literature on the empirical effects of such suits on corporate performance.

Somewhat surprisingly, however, few authors have investigated the fundamental relationship of shareholder suits to shareholder welfare. Shareholder suits are generally acknowledged to generate both significant corporate costs and significant potential benefits. Yet, except in the context of discussing fee awards to plaintiffs' attorneys, almost no one has explored how these opposing effects compare.

We undertake such an inquiry here, with particular attention to derivative suits against corporate managers. The central contribution of our article is the development of a model contrasting the circumstances in which derivative suits tend to increase corporate value with those in which the immediate incentives of self-interested share-holders will lead them to bring derivative suits.

As we develop below, a derivative suit increases corporate value in two circumstances: if the prospect of suit deters misconduct or, alternatively, if the suit itself yields a positive recovery net of all costs that the corporation must bear as a consequence of suit. These are the circumstances in which suit is in the interest of the corporation. But we find that *a shareholder's interest in bringing suit can diverge from the corporation's interest in either direction.* On one hand, a shareholder may rationally decide not to sue when willingness to do so would raise corporate value. This can occur because, even though suit is discouraged by an expected recovery that is small relative to litigation costs, the prospect of suit would have served to deter costly misconduct. On the other hand, a shareholder may elect to bring a derivative suit when this will be likely to lower corporate value. The reason, in essence, is that the expected recovery from managers that motivates suit may be only an apparent gain for the corporation: it will be offset, at least in part, by increases in liability insurance premia, indemnification payments made by the corporation on managers' behalf, and managerial compensation. Indeed, for these reasons, we demonstrate that under a broad class of regimes for allocating the costs and benefits of derivative suits among shareholders—including the typical American contingent fee regime—shareholder incentives to sue may be either excessive or insufficient, relative to the criterion of maximizing corporate value.

To avoid any misunderstanding, we emphasize at the outset that our analysis of litigation incentives does not imply that the institution of shareholder suits is categorically flawed. Indeed, as we discuss below, identifying the incentive problems in shareholder litigation also suggests possible reform measures. But if the institution of shareholder suits is not intrinsically flawed, many existing (and proposed) legal rules perpetuate the misalignment of incentives that we model here. To highlight the generality of the problem and its locus in the motives of initiators of shareholder litigation, we refer to the parties who decide to initiate suit generically as "shareholder plaintiffs." Under some legal regimes, these are ordinary shareholders. Under the American regime, they are more likely to be attorneys (with nominal shareholders in tow) in search of legal fees. But both classes of actors may be shareholder plaintiffs in our terminology because both may face similar distortions in their incentives to bring suit as measured by the yardstick of increasing corporate value.

A Model of Derivative Suits Against Corporate Managers

In this Part, we examine when derivative suits against managers would be expected to increase corporate value in our model. We then show that even though the shareholders' goal is assumed to be the maximization of corporate value, their incentives whether or not to bring suit may not advance corporate value. As we will see, the essential reason for this conclusion is that the decision whether or not to sue is by its nature made only after a wrongful act has been committed, not before.

We stress that the analysis in this Part concerns the rational behavior of shareholders in the world of the model. When we predict that shareholders will behave in a particular way or when we make a judgment about the desirability (or lack thereof) of an outcome, we will be referring in strict logic only to the model. Moreover, the model is spare. It supposes that a corporation is in business for a single period, at the end of which misconduct may or may not be discovered; that all suits are adjudicated; and that managers' salaries adjust to accurately reflect the personal costs and benefits of prospective litigation.

The Costs and Benefits of Derivative Suits

Whatever the nature of a derivative claim, bringing suit can increase corporate value in two ways. First, successful suit may confer monetary benefits on shareholders: corporations may recover damages from errant managers for past harms and undo or avert corrupt transactions. Second, suit—or, more precisely, the prospect of suit— can add to corporate value by deterring wrongdoing.

On the other hand, derivative suits impose two types of costs on corporations. First, they generate litigation costs. A corporation and its shareholders together must pay for both defending and prosecuting derivative suits—in time and energy, as well as in dollars. Second, derivative suits can raise the expenses that corporations must incur in order to attract managers. In theory, a manager's net return from his job must equal some "reservation" level for him to be willing to work for the corporation. Hence, if managers face a risk of suit, a corporation must either supply them with adequate liability insurance or raise their salaries by an offsetting amount to induce them to stay on the job. Moreover, if the threat of a derivative suit deters misconduct from which a manager would otherwise benefit, the corporation must raise his salary accordingly. Of course, actual adjustments of salary for this reason may not often occur in real markets for managerial services. Nevertheless, for the purpose of clarity, we assume here that the salaries of managers fully adjust to the anticipated effects of derivative suits.

When Derivative Suits Increase Corporate Value

To determine when the bringing of derivative suits will increase corporate value, it is useful to consider a hypothetical breach of fiduciary duty. Suppose that managers in a certain industry have an ownership interest in supply companies that attempt to overcharge corporations for their products. Specifically, suppose that a manager's authorized overcharges will cost a corporation $3,000,000, $1,000,000 of which he will earn as a co-owner of the supplier. Suppose further that the going reservation salary for managers is $2,000,000.

If no derivative suits are brought, a typical manager will anticipate earning $1,000,000 from self-dealing. Accordingly, this manager will be willing to accept a salary of only $1,000,000, rather than $2,000,000. On these assumptions, a corporation will incur $4,000,000 in total manager-related costs: a $3,000,000 loss on the purchase of overpriced products and a $1,000,000 salary.

By contrast, if shareholders bring derivative suits, and these suits succeed in deterring managers from engaging in self-dealing transactions, corporations will be better off. Corporations will not suffer $3,000,000 losses from purchases of overpriced products, but will have to pay managers $2,000,000 in salary. Thus, a corporation's total manager-related costs will be $2,000,000, rather than $4,000,000.

The reason that corporations will be better off if derivative suits deter misconduct is that the $3,000,000 loss that they thereby avoid exceeds the $1,000,000 increase in salary that they must pay. To express the point somewhat differently, permitting self-dealing is an inefficient way for corporations to pay managers $1,000,000 because self-dealing transactions cost corporations $3,000,000 in overcharges; it is cheaper for corporations to pay $1,000,000 in salary directly to their managers and to deter self-dealing. Note, too, that when deterrence is successful, there is no actual litigation of derivative suits (assuming that suits are brought only in response to misconduct).

Finally, if shareholders bring derivative suits that do not deter managerial misconduct, corporations may or may not be better off. For example, suppose that shareholders detect misconduct fifty percent of the time and that if misconduct is detected, a suit is certain to succeed. Suppose too that when a suit succeeds, an offending manager will pay damages of $500,000 and no overcharge will be incurred, saving the corporation $3,000,000 (and denying the manager his $1,000,000). Then managers will not be deterred: a manager's expected gain from self-dealing will be $500,000 (that is, .5 × $1,000,000), whereas his expected penalty will be less, $250,000 (that is, .5 × $500,000).

In this case, where misconduct is not deterred, how does suit affect corporate value? Because the probability is fifty percent that shareholders will bring suit and the corporation will reverse a $3,000,000 loss and collect $500,000 in damages, the corporation's expected gain will be $1,750,000 (that is, 0.5 × $3,500,000). But, the corporation must also raise its manager's salary by $750,000 to offset both his loss of $500,000 in expected gains from self-dealing and his expected liability of $250,000. Hence, the net expected gain to the corporation from suit is not $1,750,000, but only $1,000,000, exclusive of litigation costs. It follows that if expected litigation costs are less than $1,000,000—which is to say, if actual litigation costs are less than $2,000,000—derivative suits raise corporate value, but not otherwise. In general, suits that do not deter are worthwhile for corporations if, but only if, expected litigation costs are less than expected recoveries *net* of expected liabilities of managers, which equal the increase in managerial salaries (or in liability insurance premia). The important point here is that a part of a corporation's recovery—namely, the liability of its manager—is not an actual gain to the corporation because it must compensate the manager for his expected losses (or bear higher liability insurance premia).

The Market for Managers and D&O Insurance

Our model assumes a well-functioning market for the services of risk neutral managers who demand (and receive) full compensation ex ante for the expected personal costs and forgone benefits that result from prospective liability. Thus, an important issue concerns how far recoveries from managers—as well as illicit benefits that they give up—are actually offset by corporations through insurance, indemnification, or salary.

Looking first to the expected recoveries from managers in derivative suits, the answer seems straightforward. Liability insurers absorb most out-of-pocket losses in shareholder suits, which strongly implies that corporations pay indirectly for much of the expected cost of their managers' liability. To be sure, shareholders in the simple world of our model would prefer to compensate managers for their expected liability costs in the form of salary increases rather than subsidized insurance. Insurance is attractive only in the real world where managers are risk averse and courts sometimes err in imposing liability. But the form of the ex ante cost imposed on the corporation by managers' prospective liability—whether payments to managers or insurers—leaves our conclusion unchanged. If the insurance premia paid by corporations roughly mirror the liability expenses of insurers, corporations cannot gain in any systematic sense when they recover from liability insurers. And, obviously, corporations cannot gain when they must indemnify the liability expenses of their managers, even if they are insured against such indemnification costs.

Of course, insurance cannot cushion managers against all losses from suit, nor can it reimburse the illicit gains that managers forgo under threat of suit. The remaining question, then, is whether managers' salaries increase by the expected value of these uninsurable losses. Although managers who expect to spend time and energy defending themselves and their reputations in derivative suits probably will want some increase in salary as compensation, it is doubtful that salaries will rise to compensate managers for corrupt gains that they are denied by the threat of suit. There are several grounds for such skepticism.

First, only a minority of managers may be of the type that would engage in intentional misconduct. Were these managers to bargain openly about the benefits from misconduct that they would enjoy in the absence of the threat of derivative suits, they would reveal their dishonesty and thus invite unwelcome scrutiny or dismissal. Second, explicit bargaining about the benefits from misconduct might reflect badly on the corporation if, as seems likely, shareholders were to suspect the firm of tolerating immoral behavior that ought to be punished instead. Consequently, the corporation would probably avoid explicit bargaining about gains from misconduct. Third, opportunities for misconduct may be episodic, low-probability events. If so, managers who are not risk neutral would attach only small value to such opportunities. For example, the value a manager would attach to a two percent chance of making an extra $100,000 through misconduct might be only several hundred dollars, significantly less than its expected value of $2,000. Hence, even full salary adjustments to such opportunities would be small relative to their expected value. Together, we suspect, these three factors ordinarily prevent salaries from rising to offset the expected value of uninsured recoveries against managers.

We therefore believe that our model may overstate the ex ante costs to the corporation of imposing liability on managers. Shareholder suits can impose some costs on managers that should be counted as gains to corporations because they are not offset by corporate expenses; illicit gains to managers that are deterred by the prospect of suit may fall into this category, as may the occasional noninsurable monetary recoveries from managers. But in the real world, as in the model, corporations pay ex ante in insurance premia for the bulk of their own monetary recoveries from derivative suits. In any event, to the extent that our model overstates the ex ante costs to the corporation of imposing liability on managers (or of denying them illicit gains), litigation incentives are not necessarily less distorted in the real world. Rather, what follows is a shift in the form of distortion. Relative to the results we expect from the model, shareholders will bring value-decreasing suits less often, but they will fail to bring value-increasing suits more often (because the value to the corporation of deterrence is greater than it would be in the model).

Fee Reform, Agency Problems, and D&O Insurance

A proposal to award attorney fees only when suits appear to be value-increasing addresses incentive problems in shareholder litigation that are logically distinct from the agency problems widely discussed in the literature. Thus, awarding fees as we propose would not directly bar either frivolous suits or sweetheart settlements. But a revised fee rule might plausibly mitigate both agency problems by altering the incentives of plaintiffs' attorneys. Frivolous suits that produced, at most, small insurance settlements would yield no net recoveries under our analysis, and hence no fee awards. Similarly, sweetheart settlements of meritorious suits that induced insurers to fund large settlements without penalizing managers would generate neither deterrent benefits nor net corporate recoveries. As a consequence, plaintiffs' attorneys would reject such settlements. Under our proposal, they could earn fees only by imposing real penalties on errant managers or obtaining uninsured recoveries, whether by going to trial or by negotiating settlements to the same effect.

Commentators frequently observe that the agency problems endemic to shareholder litigation are closely linked to prevailing settlement and insurance practices. Boards settle dubious suits (and hence lawyers bring them) not only to avoid legal costs and the outside risk of personal liability, but also because insurance funding disguises the true costs of settlement. Similarly, easy access to insurance funds permits culpable managers to buy off strong shareholder claims at little visible cost to their companies. In effect, our proposal for fee reform would limit both uses of insurance funds by forcing plaintiffs' attorneys to reject settlements that provided for insurer contributions and little else.

Of course, viewing our proposal as a constraint on D&O insurance raises substantive questions about how much liability risk managers should bear. At one extreme, it is logically possible—although highly unlikely—that restricting fee awards does not go far enough: D&O insurance itself should be limited, or even prohibited outright, to maximize deterrent benefits and net recoveries from shareholder suits. At the opposite extreme, it is also possible that constraining D&O insurance in even the minimal and indirect fashion that we suggest would impose too much risk on managers. Again, however, we are skeptical.

Although our proposed reform of fee awards might well increase managers' liability risk, two considerations suggest that this effect would be small relative to the potential deterrent and recovery benefits of suit. First, limiting fee awards to value-increasing actions would eliminate the incentive to bring large numbers of weak or dubious suits. Second, companies would continue to retain considerable control over legal risk under our proposal. They could choose to litigate derivative actions or to settle on terms that combined insurance contributions with value-increasing measures. For example, a plausible settlement might impose private penalties on suspect managers (such as dismissal or demotion) but rely on insurers to pay monetary claims. These terms could generate a deterrent benefit (and hence fees for plaintiff's attorney) but would nonetheless limit the risks of defending managers by shielding them from massive damage claims.

Comments and Questions

1. In the typical derivative lawsuit, the shareholder plaintiff stands to gain, if successful, some increase in the value of his or her company stock. Because the

plaintiff sues on behalf of the firm, any monetary recovery will inure to the corporation itself. Corporate governance reforms, too, will benefit the shareholder plaintiff only indirectly. Since most shareholders also have a limited amount of their investment portfolio (and overall wealth) invested in any given corporation, why would any shareholder agree to serve as the representative plaintiff in a derivative case?

2. Because any benefit that they would receive from a successful lawsuit is limited and indirect, it is not economically rational for most shareholders to investigate potential causes of action against corporate fiduciaries, nor is it cost effective for them to initiate litigation. For this reason, shareholder litigation often is "lawyer-driven" insofar as plaintiffs' lawyers recognize the potential claims against directors and officers, investigate their merits, decide whom to sue and where, and file the complaint after identifying and selecting one or more shareholders willing sue and serve as the named plaintiff(s). Incentivized by contingent fees, it is plaintiffs' lawyers—usually attorneys specializing in the monitoring of corporate fiduciaries—who assume the risk that a court will dismiss the derivative claims for failure to make demand or on other grounds. What are the problems with entrepreneurial lawyers acting as the primary watchdogs for shareholders, identifying breaches of duty and other wrongdoing by corporate fiduciaries?

3. Does the mere imposition of fiduciary duties on directors and officers deter their disloyalty, bad faith, and fraud without a credible threat of liability for breaching those duties? Why or why not?

4. Some academics and practitioners argue that meritorious derivative lawsuits fail because judges and their management-friendly doctrines, like the business judgment rule, protect corporate directors and officers from liability for disloyalty, malfeasance, bad faith, and/or glaringly deficient oversight. As we have seen, courts frequently dismiss shareholders' complaints at the initial stages of litigation by applying demand doctrines or by affirming the decisions of special litigation committees. Even on the rare occasion when a shareholders' derivative action proceeds to trial, Delaware and other state courts do not allow juries to hear shareholders' claims. In Delaware, plaintiffs must file derivative lawsuits in the Chancery Court, where judges sit without juries. Should Delaware judges, who have received criticism for their pro-management bias, also act as the ultimate factfinders, deciding the merits of shareholders' claims at trial? Professor Ann Scarlett has argued no, observing that if the corporation, rather than its shareholders, pursued its legal claims against fiduciaries for monetary damages, the corporation would receive a jury trial.[54] However, when the corporation's board of directors cannot or will not sue its fiduciaries, requiring shareholders to bring suit on behalf of the corporation in a derivative action, Delaware and many other states refuse to permit juries to hear the legal claims. Do you think juries should decide derivative claims at trial? Why or why not?

---

54. *See* Ann M. Scarlett, *Shareholders in the Jury Box: A Populist Check Against Corporate Mismanagement*, 78 U. Cin. L. Rev. 127 (2009).

5. In 2015, the Delaware Chancery Court approved a unique resolution of shareholder derivative claims, allowing shareholders of Freeport-McMoRan to receive direct benefits from their settlement. The derivative litigation arose from the company's 2013 acquisition of two affiliated energy firms for $9 billion. Plaintiff shareholders complained that Freeport's directors overpaid for the companies, that a majority of Freeport's directors received significant personal benefits from the deals, and that conflicts of interest tainted the transactions, insofar as several Freeport directors also served on the boards and owned equity in the acquired companies. In addition to stipulating to corporate governance enhancements, the director and officer defendants agreed to settle by payment of $137.5 million, funded by $115 million from D&O insurers and $22.5 million from Freeport. Freeport's financial advisor, Credit Suisse Securities, also agreed to settle with plaintiffs by contributing an additional $10 million in cash and $6.5 million in credit against future services to Freeport. Not only did the plaintiffs negotiate one of the largest cash settlements of a Delaware derivative action, but, apparently for the first time in any derivative action, all of the cash recovered on behalf of the Freeport ($147.5 million less attorneys' fees and costs) was distributed to Freeport's shareholders in the form of a special dividend. Following announcement of the special dividend, pundits debated whether this form of settlement, providing proceeds directly to shareholders, might become a model for resolving derivative cases going forward. What do you think? Does the payment of settlement proceeds directly to shareholders as a special dividend send a stronger message of accountability to directors? Does this settlement structure enhance deterrence?

IV. Reforming Shareholders' Litigation

Not surprisingly, the most recent wave of M&A lawsuits has generated calls from Corporate America and Wall Street for new restrictions on shareholders' litigation. As evidence of abuse, directors, officers, and their advisors point to plaintiffs' attorneys racing to state and federal courthouses to file multiple lawsuits objecting to transactions within just days, if not hours, after announcement of the deals. According to the U.S. Chamber of Commerce, most of these shareholder actions lack any merit, but corporations offer to settle "the extortionate claims," usually by making "irrelevant additional disclosures," in order to close the transactions.[55] Published opinions indicate that judges have similar concerns.[56] The problem of shareholders' strike suits—meritless claims filed for their nuisance value—is not new. Academics have studied and

---

55. Victor E. Schwartz & Cary Silverman, U.S. Chamber Institute for Legal Reform, *The New Lawsuit Ecosystem: Trends, Targets & Players* 3 (Oct. 2013), *available at* www.instituteforlegalreform.com.

56. *See, e.g., In re Cox Comm'ns, Inc. S'holders Litig.*, 879 A.2d 604, 608 (Del. Ch. 2005) ("[H]astily-filed, first-day complaints … serve no purpose other than for a particular law firm and its client to get into the medal round of the filing speed (also formerly known as the lead counsel selection) Olympics."); *In re Revlon, Inc. S'holders Litig.*, 990 A.2d 940, 945–64 (Del. Ch. 2010) (replacing as lead counsel "frequent fliers" who did not litigate the claims before agreeing to settlement with defense counsel).

written extensively on the agency costs associated with shareholders' litigation for nearly four decades. Their work and testimony influenced federal lawmakers to pass the Private Securities Litigation Reform Act (PSLRA) in 1995. Enacted over the veto of President Bill Clinton, the PSLRA restricted shareholders' rights, as well as the incentives of plaintiffs' counsel, to file securities class actions in federal court. The PSLRA and its later sister statute, the Securities Litigation Uniform Standards Act of 1998, limited the exposure of companies and their directors, officers, and advisors to liability for violating the antifraud provisions of the federal securities laws.

Rather than waiting for state or federal lawmakers to regulate shareholders' M&A lawsuits, however, corporate directors and officers have focused on private ordering solutions. Specifically, corporate boards have attempted to use bylaw provisions to restrict shareholders' litigation. The following Delaware Supreme Court decision, examining a fee-shifting bylaw, sparked intense debate about the enforceability of such provisions as well as the benefits and costs of shareholder lawsuits.

ATP Tour, Inc. v. Deutscher Tennis Bund

Supreme Court of Delaware
91 A.3d 554 (2014)

BERGER, JUSTICE:

This Opinion constitutes the Court's response to four certified questions of law concerning the validity of a fee-shifting provision in a Delaware non-stock corporation's bylaws. The provision, which the directors adopted pursuant to their charter-delegated power to unilaterally amend the bylaws, shifts attorneys' fees and costs to unsuccessful plaintiffs in intra-corporate litigation. The United States District Court for the District of Delaware found that the bylaw provision's validity was an open question under Delaware law and certified four questions to this Court, asking it to decide whether, and under what circumstances, such a provision is valid and enforceable. Although we cannot directly address the bylaw at issue, we hold that fee-shifting provisions in a non-stock corporation's bylaws can be valid and enforceable under Delaware law. In addition, bylaws normally apply to all members of a non-stock corporation regardless of whether the bylaw was adopted before or after the member in question became a member.

Factual And Procedural Background

The following undisputed facts are drawn from the District Court's Certification of Questions of Law. ATP Tour, Inc. (ATP) is a Delaware membership corporation that operates a global professional men's tennis tour (the Tour). Its members include professional men's tennis players and entities that own and operate professional men's tennis tournaments. Two of those entities are Deutscher Tennis Bund (DTB) and Qatar Tennis Federation (QTF, and collectively, the Federations). ATP is governed by a seven-member board of directors, of which three are elected by the tournament owners, three are elected by the player members, and the seventh directorship is held by ATP's chairman and president.

Upon joining ATP in the early 1990s, the Federations "agreed to be bound by ATP's Bylaws, as amended from time to time." In 2006, the board amended ATP's bylaws to add an Article 23, which provides, in relevant part:

> (a) In the event that (i) any [current or prior member or Owner or anyone on their behalf ("Claiming Party")] initiates or asserts any [claim or counterclaim ("Claim")] or joins, offers substantial assistance to or has a direct financial interest in any Claim against the League or any member or Owner (including any Claim purportedly filed on behalf of the League or any member), and (ii) the Claiming Party (or the third party that received substantial assistance from the Claiming Party or in whose Claim the Claiming Party had a direct financial interest) does not obtain a judgment on the merits that substantially achieves, in substance and amount, the full remedy sought, then each Claiming Party shall be obligated jointly and severally to reimburse the League and any such member or Owners for all fees, costs and expenses of every kind and description (including, but not limited to, all reasonable attorneys' fees and other litigation expenses) (collectively, "Litigation Costs") that the parties may incur in connection with such Claim.

In 2007, ATP's board voted to change the Tour schedule and format. Under the board's "Brave New World" plan, the Hamburg tournament, which the Federations own and operate, was downgraded from the highest tier of tournaments to the second highest tier, and was moved from the spring season to the summer season. Displeased by these changes, the Federations sued ATP and six of its board members in the United States District Court for the District of Delaware, alleging both federal antitrust claims and Delaware fiduciary duty claims.

After a ten-day jury trial, the District Court granted ATP's and the director defendants' motion for judgment as a matter of law on all of the fiduciary duty claims, and also on the antitrust claims brought against the director defendants. The jury then found in favor of ATP on the remaining antitrust claims. Thus, the Federations did not prevail on any claim. ATP then moved to recover its legal fees, costs, and expenses under Rule 54 of the Federal Rules of Civil Procedure. ATP grounded its motion on Article 23.3(a) of ATP's bylaws. The District Court denied ATP's Rule 54 motion because it found Article 23.3(a) to be contrary to the policy underlying the federal antitrust laws.4 The District Court effectively ruled that "federal law preempts the enforcement of fee-shifting agreements when antitrust claims are involved."

ATP appealed, and the United States Court of Appeals for the Third Circuit vacated the District Court's order. The Third Circuit found that the District Court should have decided whether Article 23.3(a) was enforceable as a matter of Delaware law before reaching the federal preemption question. On remand, the District Court reasoned that the question of Article 23.3(a)'s enforceability was a novel question of Delaware law that should be addressed in the first instance by this Court. The District Court certified the following four questions of law:

1. May the Board of a Delaware non-stock corporation lawfully adopt a bylaw (i) that applies in the event that a member brings a claim against another member, a member sues the corporation, or the corporation sues a member (ii) pursuant to which the claimant is obligated to pay for "all fees, costs, and expenses of every kind and description (including, but not limited to, all reasonable attorneys' fees and other litigation expenses)" of the party against which the claim is made in the event that the claimant "does not obtain a judgment on the merits that substantially achieves, in substance and amount, the full remedy sought"?

2. May such a bylaw be lawfully enforced against a member that obtains no relief at all on its claims against the corporation, even if the bylaw might be unenforceable in a different situation where the member obtains some relief?

3. Is such a bylaw rendered unenforceable as a matter of law if one or more Board members subjectively intended the adoption of the bylaw to deter legal challenges by members to other potential corporate action then under consideration?

4. Is such a bylaw enforceable against a member if it was adopted after the member had joined the corporation, but where the member had agreed to be bound by the corporation's rules "that may be adopted and/or amended from time to time" by the corporation's Board, and where the member was a member at the time that it commenced the lawsuit against the corporation?

We accepted the certified questions based on principles of comity, and will address each question in turn.

Discussion

Fee-shifting bylaws are permissible under Delaware law

The first certified question asks whether the board of a Delaware non-stock corporation may lawfully adopt a bylaw that shifts all litigation expenses to a plaintiff in intra-corporate litigation who "does not obtain a judgment on the merits that substantially achieves, in substance and amount, the full remedy sought." Under Delaware law, a corporation's bylaws are "presumed to be valid, and the courts will construe the bylaws in a manner consistent with the law rather than strike down the bylaws." To be facially valid, a bylaw must be authorized by the Delaware General Corporation Law (DGCL), consistent with the corporation's certificate of incorporation, and its enactment must not be otherwise prohibited. That, under some circumstances, a bylaw might conflict with a statute, or operate unlawfully, is not a ground for finding it facially invalid.

A fee-shifting bylaw, like the one described in the first certified question, is facially valid. Neither the DGCL nor any other Delaware statute forbids the enactment of fee-shifting bylaws. A bylaw that allocates risk among parties in intra-corporate litigation would also appear to satisfy the DGCL's requirement that bylaws must "relat[e] to the business of the corporation, the conduct of its affairs, and its rights or powers or the rights or powers of its stockholders, directors, officers or employees." The corporate charter could permit fee-shifting provisions, either explicitly or implicitly by silence. Moreover, no principle of common law prohibits directors from enacting fee-shifting bylaws.

Delaware follows the American Rule, under which parties to litigation generally must pay their own attorneys' fees and costs. But it is settled that contracting parties may agree to modify the American Rule and obligate the losing party to pay the prevailing party's fees. Because corporate bylaws are "contracts among a corporation's shareholders," a fee-shifting provision contained in a nonstock corporation's validly-enacted bylaw would fall within the contractual exception to the American Rule. Therefore, a fee-shifting bylaw would not be prohibited under Delaware common law.

Whether the specific ATP fee-shifting bylaw is enforceable, however, depends on the manner in which it was adopted and the circumstances under which it was invoked. Bylaws that may otherwise be facially valid will not be enforced if adopted or used for an inequitable purpose. In the landmark *Schnell v. Chris-Craft Industries* decision, for example, this Court set aside a board-adopted bylaw amendment that moved up the date of an annual stockholder meeting to a month earlier than the date originally scheduled. The Court found that the board's purpose in adopting the bylaw and moving the meeting was to "perpetuat[e] itself in office" and to "obstruct [ ] the legitimate efforts of dissident stockholders in the exercise of their rights to undertake a proxy contest against management." The *Schnell* Court famously stated that "inequitable action does not become permissible simply because it is legally possible."

More recently, in *Hollinger Int'l, Inc. v. Black,* the Court of Chancery addressed bylaw amendments, enacted by a controlling shareholder, that prevented the board "from acting on any matter of significance except by unanimous vote" and "set the board's quorum requirement at 80%," among other changes. The Court of Chancery found, and this Court agreed, that the bylaw amendments were ineffective because they "were clearly adopted for an inequitable purpose and have an inequitable effect." That finding was based on an extensive review of the facts surrounding the controller's decision to amend the bylaws.

Conversely, this Court has upheld similarly restrictive bylaws that were enacted for proper purposes. In *Frantz Manuf. Co. v. EAC Indus.,* a majority stockholder amended the corporation's bylaws by written consent in order to "limit the [ ] board's anti-takeover maneuvering after [the stockholder] had gained control of the corporation." The amended bylaws, like those invalidated in *Hollinger,* increased the board quorum requirement and mandated that all board actions be unanimous. The Court found that the bylaw amendments were "a permissible part of [the stockholder's] attempt to avoid its disenfranchisement as a majority shareholder" and, thus, were "not inequitable under the circumstances."

In sum, the enforceability of a facially valid bylaw may turn on the circumstances surrounding its adoption and use. The Certification does not provide the stipulated facts necessary to determine whether the ATP bylaw was enacted for a proper purpose or properly applied. Moreover, because certifications by their nature only address questions of law, we are able to say only that a bylaw of the type at issue here is facially valid, in the sense that it is permissible under the DGCL, and that it may be enforceable if adopted by the appropriate corporate procedures and for a proper corporate purpose.

The bylaw, if valid and enforceable, could shift fees if a plaintiff obtained no relief in the litigation.

The second certified question essentially asks whether a more limited version of the ATP bylaw would be valid. Article 23.3(a) states that it can be invoked against any plaintiff who does not obtain a judgment "that substantially achieves, in substance and amount, the full remedy sought." Since there might be difficulty applying the "substantially achieves" standard, the District Court asks whether the bylaw would be enforceable, at least, where plaintiff obtains "no relief at all against the corporation." Subject to the limitations set forth in our answer to the first certified question, we answer the second question in the affirmative.

The bylaw would be unenforceable if adopted for an improper purpose

The third certified question asks whether the bylaw is "rendered unenforceable as a matter of law if one or more Board members subjectively intended the adoption of the bylaw to deter legal challenges by members to other potential corporate action then under consideration." Again, we are unable to respond fully. Legally permissible bylaws adopted for an improper purpose are unenforceable in equity. The intent to deter litigation, however, is not invariably an improper purpose. Fee-shifting provisions, by their nature, deter litigation. Because fee-shifting provisions are not *per se* invalid, an intent to deter litigation would not necessarily render the bylaw unenforceable in equity.

Generally, a bylaw amendment is enforceable against members who join the corporation before its enactment

The fourth certified question asks whether a fee-shifting bylaw provision is enforceable against members who joined the corporation before the provision's enactment and who agreed to be bound by rules "that may be adopted and/or amended from time to time" by the board. Assuming the provision is otherwise valid and enforceable, as a statutory matter the answer is yes. The DGCL permits a corporation to, "in its certificate of incorporation, confer the power to adopt, amend or repeal bylaws upon the directors." If directors are so authorized, "stockholders will be bound by bylaws adopted unilaterally by their boards."

CONCLUSION

Under Delaware law, a fee-shifting bylaw is not invalid *per se,* and the fact that it was adopted after entities became members will not affect its enforceability. But we cannot say, as a matter of law, that the ATP fee-shifting provision was adopted for a proper purpose or is enforceable in the circumstances presented.

Comments and Questions

1. This case came to the Delaware Supreme Court as a series of certified questions from the federal district court in Delaware, which heard the plaintiff's state law

claim following remand of the case from the Third Circuit. The Third Circuit's decision noted:

> [T]he by-law provision here imposes fees on a plaintiff who 'does not obtain a judgment on the merits that substantially achieves, in substance and amount, the full remedy sought.' This is not your average fee-shifting provision. Its language seems to suggest that a plaintiff would have to pay the defendant's fees even if the plaintiff receives a favorable settlement, because the plaintiff in such a case failed to 'obtain a judgment on the merits.' Further, if a plaintiff prevailed at trial and won $10,000,000, but sought $20,000,000, this by-law theoretically could require the plaintiff to pay the defendant's fees because the judgment the plaintiff received arguably did not 'substantially achieve[ ], in substance and amount, the full remedy sought.'[57]

Does this fee-shifting bylaw serve the interests of the courts? Why or why not? How might widespread adoption of fee-shifting bylaws affect the development of corporate law? How, if at all, might fee-shifting bylaws affect shareholders' incentives to file meritorious stockholder claims?

2. Corporate directors, officers, and their advisors argue that fee-shifting bylaws are necessary in order to deter abusive stockholders' litigation challenging M&A transactions. They contend that the litigation is frivolous and imposes significant costs, monetary and otherwise, on corporations. What remedies does the law provide already to defendants harmed by frivolous litigation? Why might those remedies be insufficient?

3. While noting that legally permissible bylaws are unenforceable in equity if adopted for an improper purpose, the Delaware Supreme Court held that the board of directors' intent to deter litigation is not "invariably an improper purpose." When would directors' intent to deter litigation render a bylaw unenforceable in equity? What is an improper purpose?

4. Delaware Governor Jack Markell signed Senate Bill 75 in June 2015, which, among other things, amended Sections 102 and 109 of the General Corporation Law, effective August 1, 2015, as follows:

Amend § 102, Title 8 of the Delaware Code, by adding a new section, § 102(f), shown by underline as follows:

(f) The certificate of incorporation may not contain any provision that would impose liability on a stockholder for the attorneys' fees or expenses of the corporation or any other party in connection with an internal corporate claim, as defined in § 115 of this title.

Amend § 109(b), Title 8 of the Delaware Code, by making insertions as shown by underline and deletions as shown by strike through as follows:

(b) The bylaws may contain any provision, not inconsistent with law or with the certificate of incorporation, relating to the business of the corporation,

---

57. *Deutscher Tennis Bund v. ATP Tour Inc.*, 480 F.3d 124, 128 (3d Cir. 2012).

the conduct of its affairs, and its rights or powers or the rights or powers of its stockholders, directors, officers or employees. The bylaws may not contain any provision that would impose liability on a stockholder for the attorneys' fees or expenses of the corporation or any other party in connection with an internal corporate claim, as defined in § 115 of this title.

For purposes of both of these provisions, the term "intracorporate claims" is defined to mean claims arising under Delaware's statutory laws, including claims of breach of fiduciary duty by current or former directors or officers or controlling shareholders of the corporation, or persons who aid or abet such a breach. Because the amendments apply only to Delaware stock corporations, the new laws do not invalidate the *ATP Tour* decision.

What interests do you think motivated Delaware's lawmakers to ban fee-shifting bylaws?

5. Although the 2015 legislation banned fee-shifting bylaws by Delaware stock corporations, the new law also validated bylaw (and charter) provisions selecting the Delaware — but not any other state — courts as the exclusive forum for litigating "internal corporate claims." Pursuant to newly-added Section 115 of the DGCL, "internal corporate claims" are those claims "(i) that are based upon a violation of a duty by a current or former director or officer or stockholder in such capacity, or (ii) as to which the title confers jurisdiction upon the Court of Chancery." Provisions of the certificate of incorporation or bylaws selecting a forum other than Delaware for internal corporate claims are neither expressly authorized nor prohibited under the new statute. The law does, however, invalidate any such provision selecting courts outside of Delaware, or any arbitral forum, to the extent that the bylaw would prohibit litigation of intra-corporate claims in Delaware courts.

The 2015 legislation was enacted after two Delaware decisions sanctioned forum selection (or sole forum) bylaws as an important tool for use by corporations seeking to avoid multijurisdictional litigation. In *Boilermakers Local 154 Retirement Fund v. Chevron Corp.*, 73 A.3d 934 (Del. Ch. 2013), then-Chancellor Leo Strine upheld the statutory and contractual validity of bylaws selecting Delaware as the exclusive forum for intra-corporate disputes. In 2014, Chancellor Andre Bouchard upheld a bylaw that designated an exclusive forum other than Delaware for intra-corporate disputes. *City of Providence v. First Citizens BancShares, Inc.*, 99 A.3d 229, 234 (Del. Ch. 2014).

Chapter 11

Philanthropy, Social Responsibility, and Stakeholder Rights

Boards are legally obligated to act in the best interest of the corporation and shareholders. Some equate this motivation with profit maximization. As the court noted in *Dodge v. Ford Motor Co.*, 170 N.W. 668 (Mich. 1919):

> A business corporation is organized and carried on primarily for the profit of the stockholders. The powers of the directors are to be employed for that end. The discretion of directors is to be exercised in the choice of means to attain that end, and does not extend to a change in the end itself, to the reduction of profits, or to the nondistribution of profits among stockholders in order to devote them to other purposes.

The language suggests that corporations should not be in the business of redistributing wealth to any group other than shareholders.

The concept of profit maximization rests uneasily with notions of philanthropy and social responsibility. Some courts initially considered these types of activities to be beyond the authority of the corporation. Over time, the view evolved but the nexus with the need for a business benefit remained. In short, social responsibility and philanthropy were permitted but only if they added to the bottom line.

This cramped view has been challenged. Some states have addressed the issue by adopting statutes that permit charitable contributions without the need to establish benefit. Yet in doing so, they have created another set of problems. The removal of the benefit requirement potentially allows for contributions unmoored by any objective standard or limit. In these circumstances, the risk arises that management will engage in philanthropy that promotes not the interests of shareholders or even the community but their own self-interest.

Beyond charitable contributions, some have argued that corporations ought to have a mandatory obligation to take other, non-shareholder interests into account. They assert that boards, in making decisions, should consider the concerns of a basket of stakeholders, ranging from suppliers to employees to the community. Proponents of this view often seek to give stakeholders a greater role in management. This may include representation on the board of directors or the creation of specialty companies that expressly eliminate the need to profit maximize or act solely in the interests of shareholders.

States have intervened in this area through the adoption of shareholder constituency statutes. They allow directors to at least sometimes consider stakeholders in making decisions. These statutes have, however, been controversial and their import unclear. They arose initially in an effort to provide management with greater flexibility to resist hostile takeovers by taking into account the impact on groups other than shareholders. Some have also challenged the central premise of the statutes, questioning whether fiduciary duties are the best way to maximize the rights of stakeholders. Finally, others have suggested that the statutes, by allowing, but not requiring, consideration of stakeholders, did not significantly enhance consideration of the interests of stakeholders.

Some change has come from private ordering. Companies increasingly put in place codes of conduct and ethics for employees. While most merely ensure conformity with existing legal requirements, some embody more aspirational goals such as bans on child labor or reductions in global warming. Other companies adhere to the Global Compact, a set of voluntary standards developed by the United Nations that seeks to elevate corporate behavior with regard to human rights, labor standards, the environment, and corruption.

All such standards raise concern over compliance and verification. In some cases, pressure from customers and risk to reputation may be enough to ensure that companies adhere to their commitments. Nonetheless, the area is not entirely devoid of enforcement. Under the Alien Tort Claims Act, a statute adopted by the first Congress, actions can sometimes be brought in U.S. courts against corporations that violate internationally accepted standards of human rights. Some related actions have also been brought under the Antiterrorism Act of 1991. The federal securities laws have represented another avenue of enforcement, at least where companies misrepresent their socially responsible behavior.

I. The Purpose of the Corporate Form

Corporations are said to represent the interests of shareholders. Yet they operate in a more complex environment and affect other constituencies. The debate has long been lodged over the proper role of corporations and their obligations to the broader community.

William W. Bratton & Michael L. Wachter, *Shareholder Primacy's Corporatist Origins: Adolf Berle and The Modern Corporation*
34 J. Corp. L. 99, 124–26, 129, 131 (2008)[1]

Dodd's *For Whom Are Corporate Managers Trustees?* started by paying brief homage to Berle's desire to constrain managers from transferring the assets of the corporation to their own pocket. But Dodd quickly switched to the attack, stating that Berle's

---

1. Copyright © 2008 The Journal of Corporation Law. Reprinted by permission.

shareholder trustee view was problematic because "it was undesirable ... to give increased emphasis at the present time to the view that business corporations exist for the sole purpose of making profits for their stockholders." Instead, corporations should act as social institutions.

* * *

Dodd believed that the corporatist policy for the United States should be based on the presumption that the managerial elite, given the appropriate mandate, would act as trustees for the community and use their corporations to resolve the economic and social problems of the Great Depression. Extensive regulation would be unnecessary, and "the principal object of legal compulsion might then be to keep those who failed to catch the new spirit up to the standards which their more enlightened competitors would desire to adopt voluntarily."

Dodd professed the utmost faith in managers and their sense of professional responsibility. He proclaimed that "power over the lives of others tends to create on the part of those most worthy to exercise it a sense of responsibility." He noted:

> Some of our business leaders and students of business tell us, there is in fact a growing feeling not only that business has responsibilities to the community but that our corporate managers who control business should voluntarily and without waiting for legal compulsion manage it in such a way as to fulfill those responsibilities.

* * *

Berle's answer to Dodd, *For Whom Corporate Managers Are Trustees: A Note*, appeared in the next issue of the Harvard Law Review. It was a brief but forceful counterpunch that avoided responding to Dodd's corporatism broadly, and focused only on mechanics. Berle attacked the idea that managers could be trusted to use discretionary power for the welfare of others as the naive and out-of-touch thinking of an ivory tower academic. Berle caustically remarked that Dodd's argument "is theory, not practice" and "[corporate lawyers] know what the social theorist does not." The key insight that Berle attributed to these corporate lawyers is that a management-coordinated, multiple constituency system simply would not work.

The problem was that unconstrained managers would maximize their own welfare. Specifically: "It must be conceded, at present, that relatively unbridled scope of corporate management has, to date, brought forward in the main seizure of power without recognition of responsibility—ambition without courage." The danger was that "when the fiduciary obligation of the corporate management and 'control' to stockholders is weakened or eliminated, the management and 'control' become for all practical purposes absolute." To make managers trustees for the community would free them of any meaningful constraint because almost all corporate activity could be justified in the interests of one group or another.

* * *

Dodd's solution is surprising to us moderns but is true to the business commonwealth view. The answer was to free management from shareholder constraints and to make managers servants of the community. But how could managers be trusted to advance social welfare when they could not be trusted with their own shareholders' capital? Dodd played the public/private card. Faithfulness of managers in the wider context could be relied on because of the "strong emotional appeal" of public service. "Service to one's fellow workers, to those who have need of one's products, or to the social and political community of which one is a member would seem a less abnormal aim than vicarious profit-seeking."

Dodd believed management would become a form of civil service, driven by the managers' desire for prestige rather than pecuniary interests.

Comments and Questions

1. The debate between Dodd and Berle has long been viewed as a proxy for the debate over the role of the corporation in society. Dodd gets credit for proposing a broader social role of the corporation while Berle is characterized as the father of shareholder primacy, that is that management should run the corporation focused on the interests of shareholders. Is that an accurate characterization of the two views?

2. Dodd wanted to benefit the community by freeing managers from the oversight of shareholders. Yet without the pressure from shareholders, what ensures that management will act in the best interests of the community rather than its own-self interest? What solution does Dodd postulate? Do you think he is correct? Are there any alternatives?

3. What do you think of Berle's view that broad managerial discretion will simply result in self-serving behavior by the directors? What does he mean by this? Do you agree with this position?

4. Those who pursue a shareholder primacy model generally equate the board's duties with profit maximization. *See Kurz v. Holbrook*, 989 A.2d 140 (Del Ch.), *aff'd in part, rev'd in part, Crown Emak Partners, LLC v. Kurz*, 992 A.2d 377 (Del. 2010) (noting that shareholders pursue a "corporate goal of stockholder wealth maximization"). Not everyone, however, agrees with this characterization. *See* Antony Page, *Review: Has Corporate Law Failed? Addressing Proposals for Reform*, 107 Mich. L. Rev. 979, 987 (April 2009) ("There is evidence that corporations are not in fact limited to maximizing shareholder wealth."). What do you think?

5. Berle ultimately backed away from his view. The profit maximization position, however, was taken up by others. *See* Milton Friedman, Capitalism and Freedom 133–34 (1962). For a more recent defense of these arguments see, *e.g.*, Stephen M. Bainbridge, *In Defense of the Shareholder Wealth Maximization Norm: A Reply to Professor Green*, 50 Wash. & Lee L. Rev. 1423 (Fall 1993).

II. Corporate Philanthropy

Any discussion of the broader role of the corporation must foremost address the practice of philanthropy. The idea of giving away profits would seem, at first blush, to conflict with the goal of maximizing returns for shareholders. Indeed, corporate law principles initially restricted philanthropy. Courts typically gave one of two reasons.

First, giving away corporate funds was viewed as inconsistent with the wealth maximization goal required of corporations. Second, a separate strain of cases viewed the expenditures as *ultra vires* and outside the purpose clause contained in the articles of incorporation. *See Davis v. Old Colony R.R. Co.*, 131 Mass. 258, 275 (1881) ("The holding of a 'world's peace jubilee and international musical festival' is an enterprise wholly outside the objects for which a railroad corporation is established; and a contract to pay, or to guarantee the payment of, the expenses of such an enterprise, is neither a necessary nor an appropriate means of carrying on the business of the railroad corporation").

Gradually, however, the law in this area evolved. Cases began to validate charitable contributions, at least those that had some kind of benefit to the business. *See A. P. Smith Mfg. Co. v. Barlow*, 98 A.2d 581 (N.J. 1953). The cases blended the notion of philanthropy with the obligation to profit maximize. In other instances, states intervened directly. Most have authorized charitable contributions by statute. In some cases, the statutes specifically abrogate the need for a corporate benefit. *See* Cal Corp Code § 207(e) (providing that corporations could make donations "regardless of specific corporate benefit, for the public welfare or for community fund, hospital, charitable, educational, scientific, civic or similar purposes.").

Delaware, however, has merely provided that corporations have the authority to "[m]ake donations for the public welfare or for charitable, scientific or educational purposes, and in time of war or other national emergency in aid thereof." 8 Del. C. § 122(9). The statute is silent on whether the contribution must be supported by a business purpose. The matter has, therefore, been left to the courts.

Theodora Holding Corp. v. Henderson
Delaware Chancery Court
257 A.2d 398 (1969)

MARVEL, VICE CHANCELLOR:

Alexander Dawson, Inc. has functioned as a personal holding company since 1935 when Mr. Henderson's mother exchanged a substantial number of shares held by her in a company which later became Avon Products, Inc., for all of the shares of her own company known as Alexander Dawson, Inc. Mr. Henderson and a brother later succeeded to their mother's interest in Alexander Dawson, Inc., the brother thereafter permitting his shares to be redeemed by the corporation. As noted earlier, Mr. Henderson, by reason of his combined holdings of common and preferred stock of the corporate defendant, is in clear control of the affairs of such corporation, which, for the most part, has been operated informally by Mr. Henderson with scant regard for the views of other board members.... Through exercise of such control, Mr. Henderson has, since 1957, caused the corporate defendant to donate varying amounts to a charitable trust organized in that year by Mr. Henderson, namely the Alexander Dawson Foundation [a Foundation under the control of Mr. Henderson]. In 1957, $10,610 was donated to such trust. From 1960 to 1966 (except for the year 1965) gifts were in the range of approximately $63,000 to $70,000 or higher in each year other than 1963 when $27,923 was donated. In 1966, however, a gift in the form of a large tract of land in Colorado, having a value of some $467,750, was made. All of these gifts through 1966 were unanimously approved by all of the stockholders of Alexander Dawson, Inc., including Mrs. Theodora G. Henderson.

The gift now under attack, namely one of the shares of stock of the corporate defendant having a value of some $528,000, was made to the Alexander Dawson Foundation in December of 1967.... It is significant, however, as noted above, that the 1966 corporate gift, consisting of a ranch located in Colorado, had been approved by all of the directors and stockholders of the corporate defendant, and that the gift here under attack was apparently intended to be a step towards consummation of the purpose behind such grant of land, namely to provide a fund for the financing of a western camp for under privileged boys, particularly members of the George Junior Republic, a self-governing institution which has served the public interest for some seventy-five years at a school near Freeville, New York. Thus, in the summer of 1967, a small group of under privileged children had enjoyed the advantages of such camp in a test of the feasibility of such an institution. However, it is apparently Mr. Henderson's intention to continue and expand his interest in such camp where he maintains an underground home which he occupies at a $6,000 rental per annum, such house being occupied by him during some three months of the year.

* * *

The next matter to be considered is the propriety of the December 1967 gift made by Alexander Dawson, Inc. to the Alexander Dawson Foundation of shares of stock of the corporate defendant having a value in excess of $525,000, an amount within the limits of the provisions of the federal tax law having to do with deductible corporate gifts, Internal Revenue Code of 1954 §§ 170(b) (2), 545(b) (2).

Title 8 Del. C. § 122 provides as follows:

"Every corporation created under this chapter shall have power to—

(9) Make donations for the public welfare or for charitable, scientific or educational purposes, and in time of war or other national emergency in aid thereof."

There is no doubt but that the Alexander Dawson Foundation is recognized as a legitimate charitable trust by the Department of Internal Revenue. It is also clear that it is authorized to operate exclusively in the fields of "* * * religious, charitable, scientific, literary, or educational purposes, or for the prevention of cruelty to children or animals * * *". Furthermore, contemporary courts recognize that unless corporations carry an increasing share of the burden of supporting charitable and educational causes that the business advantages now reposed in corporations by law may well prove to be unacceptable to the representatives of an aroused public. The recognized obligation of corporations towards philanthropic, educational and artistic causes is reflected in the statutory law of all of the states, other than the states of Arizona and Idaho.

* * *

I conclude that the test to be applied in passing on the validity of a gift such as the one here in issue is that of reasonableness, a test in which the provisions of the Internal Revenue Code pertaining to charitable gifts by corporations furnish a helpful guide. The gift here under attack was made from gross income and had a value as of the time of giving of $528,000 in a year in which Alexander Dawson, Inc.'s total income was $19,144,229.06, or well within the federal tax deduction limitation of 5% of such income. The contribution under attack can be said to have "cost" all of the stockholders of Alexander Dawson, Inc. including plaintiff, less than $80,000, or some fifteen cents per dollar of contribution, taking into consideration the federal tax provisions applicable to holding companies as well as the provisions for compulsory distribution of dividends received by such a corporation. In addition, the gift, by reducing Alexander Dawson, Inc.'s reserve for unrealized capital gains taxes by some $130,000, increased the balance sheet net worth of stockholders of the corporate defendant by such amount. It is accordingly obvious, in my opinion, that the relatively small loss of immediate income otherwise payable to plaintiff and the corporate defendant's other stockholders, had it not been for the gift in question, is far out-weighed by the overall benefits flowing from the placing of such gift in channels where it serves to benefit those in need of philanthropic or educational support, thus providing justification for large private holdings, thereby benefiting plaintiff in the long run. Finally, the fact that the interests of the Alexander Dawson Foundation appear to be increasingly directed towards the rehabilitation and education of deprived but deserving young people is peculiarly appropriate in an age when a large segment of youth is alienated even from parents who are not entirely satisfied with our present social and economic system.

Comments and Questions

1. What is the test adopted by this court for assessing charitable contributions? Does the test impose meaningful limits on contributions?

2. Does there need to be a business justification for the contribution? At least one commentator has concluded that the Delaware statute does not require evidence of a business benefit. *See* Einer Elhauge, *Sacrificing Corporate Profits in the Public Interest*, 80 N.Y.U. L. Rev. 733 (2005). Based upon the analysis in *Theodora*, do you agree? Does this mean that business benefit has become irrelevant?

3. While the court stressed the gift was likely to assist under privileged boys, in fact, the case does not find that this was its actual purpose. 257 A.2d at 402 (noting only that defendant "apparently intended" to use the contribution for this purpose). Should the precise purpose of the funds enter into the court's analysis or is it enough that they were donated to a "legitimate" charity?

4. Who decides whether to make a charitable contribution? Must there be board oversight or can the CEO make the determination unilaterally? *See* R. Franklin Balotti & James J. Hanks, Jr., *Giving at the Office: A Reappraisal of Charitable Contributions by Corporations*, 54 Bus. Law. 965, 973 (1999) ("More importantly, because very few statutes demand board oversight of charitable contributions, corporate executives have been permitted to pursue personal interests in their philanthropic decisionmaking on behalf of the corporation."). As a practical matter, what difference does this make?

5. Even in jurisdictions that do not require benefit, do these provisions effectively encourage philanthropy? Should they? Should the statutes be rewritten to make mandatory some level of philanthropy?

6. Corporate philanthropy often takes the form of in kind contributions. Food, pharmaceutical and computer companies are among the most generous in that regard. Thus, for example, Pfizer gave away $2.3 billion in pharmaceuticals in 2009. Cash, on the other hand, is less common. The largest donor in 2009 was Wal-Mart, contributing almost $290 million. What do these statistics suggest about corporate philanthropy?

Under the reasonableness standard articulated in *Theodora Holding*, what limits, if any, apply to charitable contributions? Said another way, if directors are not acting in the best interests of shareholders, whose interests are they advancing?

Kahn v. Sullivan

Delaware Supreme Court
594 A.2d 48 (1990)

HOLLAND, JUSTICE:

At the time of his death on December 10, 1990, Dr. Hammer was Occidental's chief executive officer and the chairman of its board of directors. Since the early 1920's, Dr. Hammer had been a serious art collector. When Dr. Hammer died, he personally and The Armand Hammer Foundation (the "Foundation"), owned three major collections of art (referred to in their entirety as "the Art Collection"). The Art Collection, valued at $300–$400 million included: "Five Centuries of Art," more than 100 works by artists such as Rembrandt, Rubens, Renoir and Van Gogh; the Codex Hammer, a rare manuscript by Leonardo da Vinci; and the world's most extensive private collection of paintings, lithographs and bronzes by the French satirist Honore Daumier. See The Armand Hammer Collection (J. Walker 2d ed. 1982).

* * *

On January 19, 1988, at a meeting of the executive committee of Occidental's board of directors ("the Executive Committee"), Dr. Hammer proposed that Occidental, in conjunction with the Foundation, construct a museum for the Art Collection. After discussing Occidental's history of identification with the Art Collection, the Executive Committee decided that it was in Occidental's best interest to accept Dr. Hammer's proposal. The Executive Committee approved the negotiation of arrangements for the preliminary design and construction of an art museum. It would be located adjacent to Occidental's headquarters, on the site of an existing parking garage used by Occidental for its employees. The Executive Committee also decided that once the art museum project was substantially defined, a final proposal would be presented to the Board or the Executive Committee for approval and authorization.

The art museum concept was announced publicly on January 21, 1988. On February 11, 1988, the Board approved the Executive Committee's prior actions. Occidental informed its shareholders of the preliminary plan to construct The Armand Hammer Museum and Cultural Center of Art ("the Museum") in its 1987 Annual Report. In accordance with the January 19, 1988 resolutions passed by the Executive Committee, construction of a new parking garage for Occidental began in the fall of 1988. The Board approved a construction bond on November 10, 1988. [At a meeting held on February 16, 1989, the board appointed a Special Committee of eight independent and disinterested directors to consider and act on the Museum proposal.]

* * *

On February 16, 1989, the Special Committee unanimously approved the Museum proposal, subject to certain conditions. The proposal approved by the Special Committee included the following provisions [the proposal included, among other things, construction costs of about $50 million, an annuity for the museum with an estimated cost of $35.6 million; four floors of the corporate headquarters rent free; and the Museum would be named "The Armand Hammer Museum of Art and Culture Center"]

* * *

[After disclosure of the proposal, at least two groups of shareholders sued: The Kahn action and the Sullivan action. The Kahn plaintiffs moved to enjoin the settlement. While denying the motion, the Chancery Court expressed a number of concerns with the settlement, including: "(1) the failure of the Special Committee appointed by the directors of Occidental to hire its own counsel and advisors or even to formally approve the challenged acts; (2) the now worthlessness of a prior donation by Occidental to the Los Angeles County Museum; (3) the huge attorney fees which the parties have apparently decided to seek or not oppose; (4) the egocentric nature of some of Armand Hammer's objections to the Los Angeles County Museum being the recipient of his donation; (5) the issue of who really owns the art; and (6) the lack of any direct substantial benefit to the stockholders." The Special Committee considered these concerns and ultimately negotiated another settlement with the Sullivan plaintiffs.]

* * *

The parties to the Sullivan action presented the Court of Chancery with a fully executed Stipulation of Compromise, Settlement and Release agreement ("the Settlement") on January 24, 1990. This agreement was only slightly changed from the June 3, 1989 Memorandum of Understanding. The Settlement, inter alia, provided:

(1) The Museum building shall be named the "Occidental Petroleum Cultural Center Building" with the name displayed appropriately on the building.

(2) Occidental shall be treated as a corporate sponsor by the Museum for as long as the Museum occupies the building.

(3) Occidental's contribution of the building shall be recognized by the Museum in public references to the facility.

(4) Three of Occidental's directors shall serve on the Museum's Board (or no less than one-third of the total Museum Board) with Occidental having the option to designate a fourth director.

(5) There shall be an immediate loan of substantially all of the art collections of Dr. Hammer to the Museum and there shall be an actual transfer of ownership of the collections upon Dr. Hammer's death or the commencement of operation of the Museum—whichever later occurs.

(6) All future charitable contributions by Occidental to any Hammer-affiliated charities shall be limited by the size of the dividends paid to Occidental's common stockholders. At current dividend levels, Occidental's annual contributions to Hammer-affiliated charities pursuant to this limitation could not exceed approximately three cents per share.

(7) Any amounts Occidental pays for construction of the Museum in excess of $50 million and any amounts paid to the Foundation upon Dr. Hammer's death must be charged against the agreed ceiling on limitations to Hammer-affiliated charities.

(8) Occidental's expenditures for the Museum construction shall not exceed $50 million, except that an additional $10 million may be expended through December 31, 1990 but only if such additional expenditures do not enlarge the scope of construction and if such expenditures are approved by the Special Committee. Amounts in excess of $50 million must be charged against the limitation on donations to Hammer-affiliated charities.

(9) Occidental shall be entitled to receive 50% of any consideration received in excess of a $55 million option price for the Museum property or 50% of any consideration the Museum receives from the assignment or transfer of its option or lease to a third party.

(10) Plaintiffs' attorneys' fees in the Sullivan action shall not exceed $1.4 million.

* * *

On August 7, 1990, the Court of Chancery found the Settlement to be reasonable under all of the circumstances. The Court of Chancery concluded that the claims asserted by the shareholder plaintiffs would likely be dismissed before or after trial. While noting its own displeasure with the Settlement, the Court of Chancery explained that its role in reviewing the proposed Settlement was restricted to determining in its own business judgment whether, on balance, the Settlement was reasonable. The Court opined that although the benefit to be received from the Settlement was meager, it was adequate considering all the facts and circumstances.

* * *

In an appeal from the Court of Chancery, following the approval of a settlement of a class action, the function of this Court is more limited in its nature. Id.; see also Polk v. Good, 507 A.2d at 536. This Court does not review the record to determine the intrinsic fairness of the settlement in light of its own business judgment. Nottingham Partners v. Dana, 564 A.2d at 1102. This Court reviews the record "solely for the purpose of determining whether or not the Court of Chancery abused its discretion by the exercise of its business judgment." Id. (citing Polk v. Good, 507 A.2d at 536).

* * *

First, the Objectors submitted that the business judgment rule would probably not protect the actions of the Special Committee because the independence of the Special Committee was questionable. In support of that argument, the Objectors assert that at least four members of the Special Committee had close ties to Dr. Hammer and personal business dealings with him. After examining the record, the Court of Chancery found that the Objectors had not established any facts that the Special Committee had any self-interest in the transaction either from a personal financial interest or from a motive for entrenchment in office. See Grobow v. Perot, Del. Supr., 539 A.2d 180, 188 (1988). The Court of Chancery also concluded that there was no evidence in the record indicating that any of the members of the Special Committee were in fact dominated by Dr. Hammer or anyone else.

Second, in a related argument, the Objectors argued that the presumption of the business judgment rule would have been overcome because the Special Committee proceeded initially without retaining independent legal counsel. In fact, that was a concern identified by the Court of Chancery in its July 19, 1989 opinion. However, in approving the Settlement, the Court of Chancery noted that the Special Committee had retained independent counsel, and "subsequently, and for the first time, formally approved the challenged charitable contributions." Thus, the Court of Chancery specifically found that the Special Committee had the advice of independent legal counsel before it finally approved the Museum proposal.

In this appeal, with respect to the aforementioned finding, the Objectors submit that the Court of Chancery's eventual approval of the Settlement was based upon its mistaken belief that a major judicial concern, i.e., the failure of the Special Committee to retain independent counsel prior to its formal approval of the Museum proposal, had been rectified. In particular, the Objectors contend that the Special Committee formally approved the Museum proposal at its July 20, 1989 meeting. The parties all agree that the Special Committee retained its independent legal counsel on August 4, 1989. Therefore, the Objectors argue that the Court of Chancery's conclusion that the business judgment rule would apply was based upon an erroneous premise.

In response to that argument by the Objectors, the proponents of the Settlement submit the record reflects that the Special Committee reviewed and ratified all of its prior actions on September 20, 1989, after retaining independent legal counsel. Accordingly, the proponents of the Settlement contend that, whether the September

20, 1989 action by the Special Committee is characterized as the first final approval of the Museum proposal or as a re-approval of its action taken on July 20, 1989, the Special Committee's ultimate decision to proceed with the Museum proposal was based upon the advice of independent counsel.

The Objectors' third argument in the Court of Chancery, challenging the viability of the business judgment rule as a successful defense, was based upon *Van Gorkom* and contended that the Special Committee and other directors were grossly negligent in failing to inform themselves of all material information reasonably available to them. Thus, the Objectors argued that even if, arguendo, the Special Committee was itself independent and formally approved the Museum proposal after its retention of independent legal counsel, such approval would not have cured the Special Committee's prior failure to exercise due care. The Court of Chancery found the record showed that the Special Committee had given due consideration to the Museum proposal and rejected the Objectors' argument to the contrary. See generally Smith v. Van Gorkom, Del. Supr., 488 A.2d 858 (1985).

The Court of Chancery carefully considered each of the Objectors' arguments in response to the merits of the suggested business judgment rule defense. It concluded that if the Sullivan action proceeded, it was highly probable in deciding a motion to dismiss, a motion for summary judgment, or a post-trial motion, the actions of "the Special Committee would be protected by the presumption of propriety afforded by the business judgment rule." Specifically, the Court of Chancery concluded that it would have been decided that the Special Committee, comprised of Occidental's outside directors, was independent and made an informed decision to approve the charitable donation to the Museum proposal. These conclusions by the Court of Chancery are supported by the record and are the product of an orderly and logical deductive process. Barkan v. Amsted Industries Inc., Del. Supr., 567 A.2d 1279, 1284 (1989); Nottingham Partners v. Dana, 564 A.2d at 1102; Polk v. Good, 507 A.2d at 536; cf. Rome v. Archer, 197 A.2d at 54.

Following its analysis and conclusion that the business judgment rule would have been applicable to any judicial examination of the Special Committee's actions, the Court of Chancery considered the shareholder plaintiffs' claim that the Board and the Special Committee's approval of the charitable donation to the Museum proposal constituted a waste of Occidental's corporate assets. In doing so, it recognized that charitable donations by Delaware corporations are expressly authorized by 8 Del. C. § 122(9). It also recognized that although § 122(9) places no limitations on the size of a charitable corporate gift, that section has been construed "to authorize any reasonable corporate gift of a charitable or educational nature." Theodora Holding Corp. v. Henderson, Del. Ch., 257 A.2d 398, 405 (1969). Thus, the Court of Chancery concluded that the test to be applied in examining the merits of a claim alleging corporate waste "is that of reasonableness, a test in which the provisions of the Internal Revenue Code pertaining to charitable gifts by corporations furnish a helpful guide." Id. We agree with that conclusion.

The Objectors argued that Occidental's charitable contribution to the Museum proposal was unreasonable and a waste of corporate assets because it was excessive.

The Court of Chancery recognized that not every charitable gift constitutes a valid corporate action. Nevertheless, the Court of Chancery concluded, given the net worth of Occidental, its annual net income before taxes, and the tax benefits to Occidental, that the gift to the Museum was within the range of reasonableness established in Theodora Holding Corp. v. Henderson, Del. Ch., 257 A.2d 398, 405 (1969). Therefore, the Court of Chancery found that it was "reasonably probable" that plaintiffs would fail on their claim of waste. That finding is supported by the record and is the product of an orderly and logical deductive process. Barkan v. Amsted Industries Inc., 567 A.2d at 1284; Nottingham Partners v. Dana, 564 A.2d at 1102; Polk v. Good, 507 A.2d at 536; cf. Rome v. Archer, 197 A.2d at 54.

* * *

... [A]fter considering the legal and factual circumstances of the case sub judice, the Court of Chancery examined the value of the Settlement. The proponents of the Settlement argued that the monetary value of having the Museum building called the "Occidental Petroleum Cultural Center Building" was approximately ten million dollars. The Court of Chancery noted that, in support of their valuation arguments, the proponents also argued that the Settlement: (1) reinforced and assured Occidental's identification with and meaningful participation in the affairs of the Museum; (2) reinforced and protected the charitable nature and consequences of Occidental's gifts by securing the prompt delivery and irrevocable transfer of the Art Collection to the Museum; (3) imposed meaningful controls upon the total construction costs that Occidental will pay, which had already forced the reduction of the construction budget by $19.4 million; (4) placed meaningful restrictions upon Occidental's future charitable donations to "Hammer" affiliated entities and avoided increases in posthumous payments to the Foundation or any other designated recipient after Dr. Hammer's death; (5) restored to Occidental an equitable portion of any appreciation of the properties in the event the Museum exercised its option and disposed of the properties or transferred its option for value; and (6) guaranteed that the Art Collection would continue to be located in the Los Angeles area and remain available for the enjoyment of the American public rather than dissipated into private collections or sold abroad.

The Court of Chancery characterized the proponents' efforts to quantify the monetary value of most of the Settlement benefits as "speculative." The Court of Chancery also viewed the estimate that naming the building for Occidental would have a ten million dollar value to Occidental with "a good deal of skepticism." Nevertheless, the Court of Chancery found that Occidental would, in fact, receive an economic benefit in the form of good will from the charitable donation to the Museum proposal. It also found that Occidental would derive an economic benefit from being able to utilize the Museum, adjacent to its corporate headquarters, in the promotion of its business.

Finally, the Court of Chancery applied its own independent business judgment in deciding whether the Settlement was fair and reasonable. In doing so, the Court of Chancery was called upon to function in its special role as the so-called third party to the Settlement. Barkan v. Amsted Industries Inc., 567 A.2d at 1283–84; Nottingham

Partners v. Dana, 564 A.2d at 1102 (quoting Rome v. Archer, 197 A.2d at 53–54). This required it to balance the policy preference for settlement against the need to insure that the interests of the shareholders, as a class, had been fairly represented. Barkan v. Amsted Industries, Inc., 567 A.2d at 1283 (citing Rome v. Archer, 197 A.2d at 53).

In discharging its special role in the case sub judice, the Court of Chancery properly evaluated the value of the Settlement in the context of the strength of the claims which were being compromised.... The Court of Chancery found that "the benefit [of the Settlement] to the stockholders of Occidental is sufficient to support the Settlement and is adequate, if only barely so, when compared to the weakness of the plaintiffs' claims." The Court of Chancery concluded that "although the Settlement is meager, it is adequate considering all the facts and circumstances."

* * *

Conclusion

The reasonableness of a particular class action settlement is addressed to the discretion of the Court of Chancery, on a case by case basis, in light of all of the relevant circumstances. Evans v. Jeff D., 475 U.S. 717, 742, 106 S. Ct. 1531, 89 L. Ed. 2d 747, reh'g denied, 476 U.S. 1179, 106 S.Ct. 2909, 90 L.Ed.2d 995 (1986). In this case, we find that all of the Court of Chancery's factual findings of fact are supported by the record. We also find that all of the legal conclusions reached by the Court of Chancery were based upon a proper application of well established principles of law. Consequently, we find that the Court of Chancery did not abuse its discretion in deciding to approve the Settlement in the Sullivan action. Barkan v. Amsted Industries, Inc., 567 A.2d at 1285; Nottingham Partners v. Dana, 564 A.2d at 1104; Polk v. Good, 507 A.2d at 536–39; Rome v. Archer, 197 A.2d at 58. Therefore, the decision of the Court of Chancery is

AFFIRMED.

Comments and Questions

1. The Armand Hammer Museum of Art and Culture Center opened in November 1990. The Museum's web site indicated that it was "founded" by Armand Hammer and "financed" by Occidental. From the terms of the settlement, how much benefit did Occidental get from its contribution?

2. Dr. Hammer had originally planned to donate his collection to the Los Angeles County Museum of Art. The Museum named a wing after the Hammers and Occidental contributed $2 million to expand and refurbish the space. Negotiations were terminated between Dr. Hammer and the Museum in January 1988. The same month, Dr. Hammer proposed to the Executive Committee of the Board that Occidental consider participating in the construction of a museum for his art collection.

3. What does this case suggest about corporate philanthropy? What were the "benefits" to the corporation? Make the case that the board's decision with respect to the museum was and was not in the best interests of shareholders.

4. Are these contributions more appropriately analyzed under the duty of care or the duty of loyalty? As commentators have described:

> There are several ways officers can engage in "self-dealing" or personal aggrandizement with respect to corporate charitable contributions. These include: (i) contributions made to further officers' own political or ideological preferences; (ii) contributions made to achieve a higher social status; (iii) contributions made to pet charities of fellow executives in hopes of reciprocity; (iv) contributions made as a "payment" for membership on the board of directors of nonprofit corporations; and (v) contributions to charities of which the officers, or relatives or friends of the officers, are insiders.

R. Franklin Balotti & James J. Hanks, Jr., *Giving at the Office: A Reappraisal of Charitable Contributions by Corporations*, 54 Bus. Law. 965 (May 1999). Were any of these factors present? What difference would it have made had this case been analyzed under the duty of loyalty?

5. How much was this case determined by the process and how much was it determined by the substance of the transaction? Would the outcome have been different had there been fewer corporate benefits or had the amount paid by Occidental been significantly greater?

6. Were the directors on the Special Committee independent? The Chancery Court found that none of the directors were dominated by Dr. Hammer. Would it influence your opinion to know that according to one commentator, Dr. Hammer had undated letters of resignation from each director? *See* Nell Minow, *Corporate Charity: An Oxymoron?* 54 Bus. Law. 997, 1001 (1999).

7. Some have called for SEC disclosure of charitable contributions. *See* Faith Stevelman Kahn, *Pandora's Box: Managerial Discretion and the Problem of Corporate Philanthropy*, 44 UCLA L. Rev. 579 (February 1997). What impact might this have on the contributions?

———————

In any event, the decision with respect to charitable contributions may be more complex than just the best interests of shareholders or directors.

M. Todd Henderson & Anup Malani,
Essay: Corporate Philanthropy and the Market for Altruism
109 Colum. L. Rev. 571, 577–81 (2009)[2]

Prominent scholars such as Michael Porter argue that philanthropy helps a firm's bottom line and can be a source of competitive advantage. Numerous studies claim to support the link between giving and profit. The mechanisms by which this link operates include generating good feelings among customers, suppliers, or employees;

———————

2. Copyright © 2009 Columbia Law Review. Reprinted by permission.

attracting high quality employees; or decreasing the risk of government or activist action. Whether the source of the goodwill and increased profits is the advertising benefits of doing good or something else is beside the point. All that matters is that the firm is actually doing some public good and that the act of doing this helps not only strangers to the firm but also its shareholders. Even Milton Friedman, who famously claimed that the "only ... responsibility of business [is] to use its resources and engage in activities designed to increase its profits," acknowledged that corporate philanthropy may be justified when it is necessary to maximize long-run profits.

Other scholars argue that philanthropy is simply managerial graft, no different from a CEO using a fancy corporate jet for personal purposes. Managers are spending other people's money, and, because monitoring by shareholders is imperfect, managers will do so in ways that maximize their own utility rather than that of the shareholders. Numerous studies claim to support this view. The agency costs account is supported by the facts that the law does not require firms to disclose to shareholders corporate charitable gifts and that many firms do not do so. Proponents of this view call into question the causal connection between donations and profits relied on by the opposing camp. They argue that profits, or the expectation of profits, may allow corporations to be more generous—thus explaining the observed correlation between corporate success and philanthropy.

The empirical research is not conclusive, but suggests that corporate philanthropy reflects a blend of motives. Even studies finding evidence consistent with profit-maximizing motives also find that companies with lower agency costs—greater monitoring by creditors, more independent boards, less free cash available to managers—gave less to charity than other firms. We think these studies fairly capture reality: Both positive theories are more or less true and will be present at various levels in most cases. Just as a CEO's decision about the use of a corporate jet may be motivated by both personal and shareholder concerns, it would be surprising if decisions about doing good for others were not mostly based on mixed motives.

In light of the inevitable mixed motives and the inability of courts to distinguish ex post between "good" and "bad" philanthropic decisions made by firms, the law takes a very agnostic view. This was not always the case. Prior to about 1960, donations to charity were often considered beyond the power of firms. But how is a court to determine whether a donation to Princeton University, a commitment to pay higher wages to autoworkers, or a decision not to install lights at Wrigley Field is a profit-maximizing decision or a charitable one? After all, a firm's decision to limit pollution to a greater extent than that required by law is as much charity as a gift to the opera, and if courts are in the business of making these distinctions, regulatory laws become not only minimums but maximums. In this way, the law's permissive attitude toward corporations doing good (in all forms) is an inevitable result of the business judgment rule: Courts avoid second guessing business decisions in an attempt to minimize the sum of decision costs and error costs, and the decision to act charitably, whether it is by donating money or not acting badly, is a quintessential business decision.

Comments and Questions

1. This excerpt suggests that the law remains largely "agnostic" when it comes to charitable contributions. Is this the right outcome? What are the consequences of this approach?

2. What do you make of the observation that charitable contributions decline when agency costs are lower? What does this suggest about the profit maximizing benefits of these contributions from the perspective of shareholders and creditors? If they are less enamored with the expenses, why do they occur anyway?

III. Stakeholders

Corporate philanthropy is permitted but not required. Some view this as not going far enough. They have sought to require directors to consider the interests of all stakeholders, not just shareholders. While there is no definitive list of applicable constituencies, they often include employees, creditors, and the community. How might corporate governance be altered to give these constituencies a voice in the operation of the corporation?

Larry E. Ribstein, *Accountability and Responsibility in Corporate Governance*

81 Notre Dame L. Rev. 1431, 1439–42 (2006)[3]

Whether corporate governance should be restructured to enable or require managers to respond to the interests of stakeholders in the firm other than shareholders implicates an analysis of existing corporate structure. Executives make day-to-day management decisions in a publicly held corporation. The board of directors monitors these decisions through their power to approve major transactions or initiate them for shareholder approval, and to hire, fire, and compensate the managers. The owners exercise control through their power to elect the board and to approve extraordinary matters such as mergers and charter amendments that the board has initiated. Nonshareholder stakeholders exercise power under specific agreements, such as credit and employment agreements and supply contracts, as well as by their ability to decide whether to deal with the firm.

This general structure suggests three potential legal tools for increasing managers' social responsibility. First, nonshareholder stakeholders can be given power to control managers. For example, employees might vote equally with shareholders and serve on the board of directors. The primary alternative to giving owners exclusive powers of control is the European system of codetermination, which gives employees some representation on the board.

---

3. Reprinted with permission © by *Notre Dame Law Review*, University of Notre Dame. Publisher bears responsibility for any errors which have occurred in reprinting or editing.

While such proposals might seem the most obvious routes to corporate social responsibility, radical restructuring favoring nonshareholder stakeholders may entail high costs and obscure benefits. Because equity holders have a claim only to what is left after other stakeholders have been paid off, shareholders gain more than other stakeholders from voting powers and fiduciary duties. Restructuring corporate governance to favor nonshareholder stakeholders therefore could significantly increase these stakeholders' ability to extract wealth from shareholders. Shareholders could be expected to pay less for their shares to reflect this appropriation risk. In other words, shifting power to stakeholders solves the problem of shareholder opportunism to stakeholders by creating a potentially more serious problem of stakeholder opportunism to shareholders.

Stakeholders also might gain little from their increased power. Given stakeholders' heterogeneous objectives, internal dissension might seriously compromise their effectiveness in governing the firm. By contrast, shareholders simply want to maximize risk-adjusted profits, perhaps qualified by generalized social objectives. Thus, empowering stakeholders might effectively leave managers accountable to nobody.

Second, courts or legislatures could adjust managers' judicially enforced fiduciary duties. Managers might have an affirmative duty to serve the interests of groups other than the shareholders, or their basic duty to serve shareholders' interests might be qualified by giving managers some discretion to act in nonshareholders' interests. However, as discussed below, courts are inherently constrained in the extent to which they can supervise corporate managers. This limits what can be accomplished by fine-tuning fiduciary duties.

Third, shareholders' power to control managers can be reduced. For example, the law might loosen shareholders' control over the board by giving directors five-year terms. Short of such radical suggestions, the limits of shareholder control are built into the logistics of the publicly held firm. For example, managers' ability to fend off takeovers is inherent in their ability to exercise control in other ways, and courts are no more able to monitor exercise of this power than they are to supervise other managerial activities.

Finally, any legal moves to reform corporate governance in the U.S. must confront the constraints imposed by the federal system. The "internal affairs rule" lets firms choose the particular state's law that applies to their internal governance irrespective of where the business conducts its operations. Accordingly, if a state restricts the extent to which a firm can provide for management accountability to shareholders, the firm is free to incorporate in any other state. This means in effect that restrictions on managerial accountability to shareholders must be provided for either by a radical move to federal internal governance law, a radical rejection at the state level of the internal affairs rule, federal securities laws that apply to firms irrespective of where they are incorporated, or by nonorganization law such as tax law or regulation of business practices that are not subject to the internal affairs rule. Indeed, this is why the corporate tax emerges as a major factor in corporate governance.

Comments and Questions

1. Stakeholders are protected from a variety of mechanisms, including legal requirements and contractual provisions. The issue in the corporate governance context is whether their interests should be further enhanced through greater consideration by directors in the exercise of their fiduciary obligations. One way to do so, as Professor Ribstein notes, is to expand the board's fiduciary obligations to include stakeholders. What impact might this have on board decision making?

2. Are all stakeholders created equal? For example, a board deciding to close an old factory might improve the environment (by reducing pollution) but harm employees (as a result of layoffs). Should the duties of the board specify which stakeholder ought to receive greater consideration? Incidentally, how would this decision be resolved under the existing fiduciary standards of the board?

3. Professor Ribstein mentions the constraints imposed by the internal affairs doctrine. This is discussed at length in Chapter 2. What is this doctrine and what impact might it have on reform efforts in this area? Would boards want to move to states that restricted or enhanced their ability to consider stakeholders when making decisions?

4. According to one commentator, most large public companies "espouse stakeholder rhetoric." Lisa M. Fairfax, *Easier Said Than Done? A Corporate Law Theory for Actualizing Social Responsibility Rhetoric*, 59 Fla. L. Rev. 771 (2007). In other words, they already claim to take stakeholders into account. Given this widespread acceptance of the stakeholder model, is reform even needed?

Placing stakeholders on the board of directors is one possible way to increase their voice in the corporate governance process, as Professor Ribstein notes. Germany, for example, requires large public companies to include employee representatives on its board of directors. What are some of the benefits that might arise from such a system?

Kent Greenfield & D. Gordon Smith,
Debate: Saving the World with Corporate Law?
57 Emory L.J. 947, 978–84 (2008)[4]

[This excerpt was written by Professor Greenfield.]

The best way to realize the potential of the corporation as a progressive force is to adjust the composition of the board so that it contains directors who represent those who invest in the firm in addition to shareholders. At present, shareholders occupy not only a supreme position within the legal framework, being the only beneficiary of management's fiduciary duties, but also within the board itself. Only shareholders vote in elections for corporate directors, and votes are weighed according to the number of shares they own. Once we recognize, however, that corporations are to serve

---

4. Copyright © 2008 Emory Law Journal. Reprinted by permission of Emory Law Journal and the authors.

all their stakeholders, it becomes clear that the dominance of shareholders within corporate management is a mistake.

Why would a stakeholder board be beneficial? The answer is twofold. First, such a change will inevitably mean that the corporate surplus will be more equitably and efficiently shared, which will help ensure the sustainability (and profitability) of the enterprise over time. Second, a more pluralistic board will improve corporate decisionmaking, which will also help ensure the sustainability (and profitability) of the enterprise over time.

a. Benefit #1: More Fairness

The first benefit is straightforward. When the board decides how to allocate the corporate surplus, a stakeholder board will behave differently than a shareholder board. The market will be a constraint, to be sure, but the goal of the board will be to allocate the surplus so as to maintain the firm as a going concern. Shareholders will get their proportion, but so will others. In a sense, this conception would use the corporation not only as the mechanism for creation of wealth but its distribution as well.

This is not as jarring as it might seem at first. In the United States, and indeed in most industrialized countries, one of the most important tasks of the state is to redistribute wealth. Mechanisms include the tax and welfare system, minimum wage, and the Social Security program. At base, my proposal is simply to adjust the structure of corporate law so that it can better serve this purpose as well.

The strength of this argument is bolstered by evidence from other nations. In a recent study, Sigurt Vitols measured the macroeconomic implications of worker participation in corporate management throughout Europe. On a countrywide level, European countries with strong "codetermination" (i.e., worker participation on boards) had lower income inequality than countries that have no or weak worker participation. Moreover, countries with strong codetermination had higher labor productivity, fewer days lost to strikes, and lower unemployment rates.

The stakeholder board, in an ironic sense, is a genuine realization of the "nexus of contracts" view of the firm. If the firm is best seen as a microcosm of the market, then let us be honest about recognizing all contracts by putting the most important market participants in a position where they can be heard at the decisionmaking level of the firm. The specifics will be difficult, but not impossible: employees could elect a proportion of the board; communities in which the company employs a significant percentage of the workforce could be asked to propose a representative for the board; long-term business partners and creditors could be represented as well.

The specifics do not matter as much as the notion that the board itself should be a place where more than just a shareholder perspective will be heard. As they participate on the board, each stakeholder representative will have the incentive to build and maintain profitability in order to sustain the company over time. Moreover, the board will be the locus of the real negotiations among the various stakeholders about the allocation of the corporate surplus. Even though board members might be selected for their positions in different ways and from different constituencies, each would be held to fiduciary duties to the firm as a whole. Decisions that affect major stakeholders would no longer be made cavalierly without someone on the board being able to anticipate and articulate the likely impact that such a decision would have on the workers, creditors, and other interested stakeholders.

b. Benefit #2: Better Decisions

This proposal for board pluralism will strike most readers, at least in the United States, as outlandish. But codetermination is common in many countries in Europe and is used to good effect. Perhaps the reason for its success is that, overall, board pluralism makes for better decisions.

Recall the discussion in Part I about the success of corporations being based in part on their dependence on a group decisionmaker at the top of the hierarchy. But the benefits of group decisionmaking are drastically mitigated, and sometimes undermined completely, when the group is too homogeneous. In fact, more and more studies show that good decisionmaking requires diversity of viewpoints. As Cass Sunstein has detailed in his recent book Why Societies Need Dissent, conformity among people in a decisionmaking group inevitably breeds error. Dissent is essential, and sometimes "social bonds and affection" can suppress dissent. Sunstein notes, "If strong bonds make even a single dissent less likely, the performance of groups and institutions will be impaired." He extends the points to corporate boards: "The highest performing companies tend to have extremely contentious boards that regard dissent as a duty and that 'have a good fight now and then.'"

If homogeneity is a flaw, then corporate boards are blemished indeed. At present, corporate boards are among the least diverse institutions in America. A 2002 survey found that 82% of the director positions on Fortune 1000 companies were held by white men, while only 11% were held by white women, 3% by African Americans, 2% by Asian-Americans, and 2% by Hispanics. Adding perspectives other than those of rich, white men will almost certainly improve the quality of business decisions made by the board.

This idea is hardly as radical as it might seem at first. Even mainstream scholars are sometimes found to recognize the benefits of board pluralism. For example, Stephen Bainbridge has said, in the context of suggesting that larger boards are better than smaller boards, that "more directors will usually translate into more interlocking relationships with other organizations that may be useful in providing resources such as customers, clients, credit, and supplies." Note that Bainbridge sees the benefits of including persons on the board who can speak for and offer insight from various non-equity investors, even though he notably does not include workers in his list. He describes the benefits of this kind of board pluralism as including the ability to address information asymmetries and thus aiding in the creation of strategic alliances. That insight, which seems right, would be true not only for business partners but also for all non-equity investors, including workers. Workers are also, in effect, entering into a strategic alliance with a firm when they invest their time, energy, and futures with the company. Thus, they too "need access to credible information about the competencies and reliability of prospective partners," just as the firm needs credible information about their "competencies and reliability."

The worries often expressed about codetermination are overblown. No constituency would have an incentive to hurt the company in order to gain a larger piece of the pie. Even if they did, they would be violating their fiduciary duties to the firm as a whole and could be held to account for their behavior. Second, the possibility of strategic, "rent-seeking" behavior already exists in the firm. Directors are currently elected by shareholders only, and shareholders already have incentives in certain circumstances to put their interests ahead of the interests of the firm as a whole. A pluralistic board could actually retard those selfish impulses, because any behavior that benefits one stakeholder at the expense of the firm must be done in full view of the others.

To be sure, making the board less homogeneous will make decisions less tidy, since more views will have to be taken into account and the board will be forced to compromise so that decisions are acceptable to a majority or plurality of stakeholders. But the fact that decisions will be more difficult is not in itself a reason to refuse to improve boards by having them listen to a range of views and perspectives. The real question is whether additional diversity results in decisions that are worth the extra effort. A greater diversity in perspectives and backgrounds within the boardroom will create material benefits to the firm by lessening the risk over time that the board will engage in the defects and systematic mistakes of "groupthink."

On this point, we can gather insight from our experiences outside of business. The notion that decisions produced by a finely wrought process of dialogue and compromise are better than decisions made unilaterally by a uniform group of individuals is widely accepted by institutions other than corporate boards. We recognize in legislative bodies, administrative agencies, school faculties, and non-profit boards that diversity of viewpoints and people increases the likelihood that dissent will be welcomed, important perspectives will be heard, and decisions will be more fully vetted. As Madison argued in the Federalist Papers, a pluralistic federal government where power is balanced among many different groups actually weakens factions. To make important decisions, one must build coalitions; individual factions cannot act on their own. The same is likely true in corporate governance.

… These principles of good decisionmaking are not new or earth-shaking. They are just systematically ignored in corporate governance. If we imported these insights into corporate law, the strengths of the corporate form could be maintained and then harnessed for a purpose higher than the aggregation of shareholder profit. Social wealth could be built; social interests could be internalized into firm decisionmaking; wealth could be more fairly distributed. Perhaps the world will not be saved. But it would be better.

Comments and Questions

1. What might a stakeholder board look like? What interest groups would have representation on the board under the proposed model? Professor Greenfield notes

that in resolving these issues, "[t]he specifics do not matter as much as the notion that the board itself should be a place where more than just a shareholder perspective will be heard." Do you agree with this observation?

2. Professor Greenfield contends that in allocating the corporate surplus, "a stakeholder board will behave differently than a shareholder board." How is it likely to behave differently? Does this depend at all on the number and manner of electing stakeholder representatives to the board?

3. Do you agree that a less homogeneous board would result in better decision making? Even if that is the case, is it correct to think that stakeholders such as employees would be the right category of non-homogeneous directors to avoid the problem of groupthink? How else might a board be structured to avoid homogeneity without necessarily embracing a stakeholder representation model?

4. Why is not the answer to simply expand the board's fiduciary obligations to include stakeholders (a controversial enough proposal)? Do the stakeholders actually need to have positions on the board?

There is plenty of room to disagree with a stakeholder representation model, as the next two articles demonstrate.

Antony Page, *Review: Has Corporate Law Failed?* *Addressing Proposals for Reform*
107 Mich. L. Rev. 979, 996–97 (2009)[5]

This proposal [of putting stakeholders on the board] is interesting but unfortunately underdeveloped. The uncertainty lies in the board's composition and voting rules. Would shareholders' directors still have a majority? Greenfield states that his proposal is about allowing stakeholders to "be heard at the decision-making level of the firm" and giving stakeholders a "meaningful way to participate in corporate decision making". However, he also suggests something more radical: "boards will be forced to compromise on a decision that is acceptable to a majority or plurality of stakeholders". If there must be compromise, nonshareholder stakeholders would, at a minimum, have veto power. Having a voice is a very different matter from having the power to block or make substantive decisions. Even Germany's system, the model of codetermination where employee representatives make up half of a large company's supervisory board, gives the tie-breaking vote to management.

Greenfield believes that "in most cases, no stakeholder would have an incentive to hurt the company in order to gain a larger piece of the pie", but every decision involving the allocation of wealth (wages, subcontracting, capital structure, production methods, etc.) could involve such a conflict. A larger piece of a smaller pie may well

---

5. Reprinted by permission from *Michigan Law Review*, April 2009, Vol. 107, No. 6. Copyright © 2009 by Antony Page.

be attractive. Although the board might "benefit from a greater openness and diversity", the result might also be a factionalized board, able to perform its monitoring role but unable to adequately perform an advisory role. In addition, even though directors would still owe fiduciary duties to all stakeholders and not merely those that they represent, their discretion would not be cabined because, under the business-judgment rule, there is little risk of legal liability regardless of the decision's merits. Furthermore, a director who failed to zealously support her constituency's interests would likely face reduced chances of reelection.

Overall, Greenfield's proposed means to better aggregate social welfare seem unlikely to achieve very much. Unconstrained directors would remain unconstrained and a board with directors representing stakeholders besides shareholders might well result in no change, or worse, even a less effectively run corporation. Given the success of the status quo, at least in creating wealth, we should be wary of change absent more persuasive reasons.

George W. Dent, Jr., *Stakeholder Theory and the Relationships between Host Communities and Corporations: Stakeholder Governance: A Bad Idea Getting Worse*
58 Case W. Res. L. Rev. 1107, 1115–17 (2008)[6]

Apart from economic theory, there is another and perhaps more telling problem with the stakeholder concept: If stakeholder governance can produce a bigger pie, and a larger piece for each constituency, why has it not happened through private arrangements? Sometimes pie-increasing solutions cannot be reached privately because the transaction costs of negotiation are too high. But at least for employees with collective bargaining that should not be so—they are negotiating with management already.

Professor Greenfield suggests that firms do not act voluntarily because they "simply do not see the potential long-term profitability of stakeholder governance." This explanation is unpersuasive. Businesses constantly seek new ways to increase profits. Stakeholder theory has been around for a long time; it is not so novel an idea that it simply has not occurred to investors and entrepreneurs. If it held any promise, some firms would try it. But even if we assumed that he is right about this, it would follow that after stakeholder governance was forced on investors, they would discover they liked it. He should, then, be willing to let shareholders of a company vote to end stakeholder governance and institute shareholder primacy after some period of time (one year?), since they would not do so unless experience showed that stakeholder governance materially injured them.

* * *

---

6. Copyright © 2008. Reprinted by permission of the author.

Actually, we do see this, but not at all in the way stakeholder advocates want. In fact, most companies are controlled by employees, but only by a small, elite group of employees. Law firms are run by their partners. Even in industrial, non-professional firms employee control, where it exists, tends to be concentrated in a homogeneous subset of workers, not shared among all. The reason for this is that the interests of different groups of employees conflict. In general, labor-controlled firms grow more slowly and create fewer new jobs than other public firms. When outside equity capital is needed, venture capitalists provide it, but only on conditions that are not at all what stakeholder theorists envision.

American organized labor has also shown little interest in board representation. And Europe is moving toward the shareholder model and may have passed the United States in protecting investors.

In addition to this "negative" empirical evidence, there is positive empirical evidence that employee participation in corporate governance does not "grow the pie." In France and Norway, law requires employee representation on certain boards. The conditions and exceptions permit a good comparison of firms with and without such representation. Recent studies in both countries found that employee representation significantly injured firm performance. Other studies have made similar findings in other countries, even when labor representation is granted voluntarily.

Voluntary action may in fact be moving in the opposite direction. Employee stock ownership plans ("ESOP") were originally adopted mostly in nonunionized firms, but by the 1990s they became just as prevalent in unionized firms. The adoption of an ESOP in a unionized firm causes a reduction in strikes and of the proportion of labor disputes that lead to strikes. Giving employees stock changes their incentives and brings their interests closer to those of the shareholders. This is a more promising path than stakeholder governance.

When other stakeholders are tossed into the recipe, the conflicts become glaring and overwhelming. Employees want the highest compensation and job security and the easiest working conditions. Customers want the best products at the lowest prices. Creditors want the highest assurance of prompt payment of their claims. Suppliers want the largest orders at the highest prices. Environmentalists want to minimize pollution. These preferences make irreconcilable demands on corporate resources.

Comments and Questions

1. One criticism of the approach taken by Professor Greenfield concerns logistics. As Professor Page notes, the approach does not address the logistics, including voting rules and composition requirements. How might these matters be solved? What would be an appropriate set of composition and voting requirements?

2. To the extent that stakeholders have a veto, but not control, is this enough to ensure that their interests are represented? In Germany, employees control half of the board of the largest companies. In the case of a tie, however, the chairperson (typically a shareholder elected director) is the deciding vote. Moreover, employee

representatives often do not sit on important board committees such as the compensation committee.

3. Assuming stakeholders are included on the board, should they still have an obligation to act in the best interests of shareholders? If the fiduciary obligations remain unchanged, won't the stakeholder directors be powerless to ensure greater consideration of the interests of their constituencies?

4. Creditors are often listed as a stakeholder. Yet some have taken the position that they have considerable ability to influence the governance process. *See* Douglas G. Baird & Robert K. Rasmussen, *Essay: Private Debt and the Missing Lever of Corporate Governance*, 154 U. Pa. L. Rev. 1209, 1211 (2006) ("When a business trips one of the wires in a large loan, the lender is able to exercise de facto control rights—such as replacing the CEO of a company—that shareholders of a public company simply do not have."). Do creditors need any additional protections as a stakeholder? What about public versus private debt holders?

5. With stakeholders on the board, presumably they will want a greater share of the corporate resources. Shareholders will only benefit if the approach results in increased profitability, with owners receiving more overall, albeit a smaller piece of a larger pie. Contrast the views of Professors Greenfield and Dent on this issue.

6. Professor Dent notes that much of the stakeholder analysis focuses on employees but that when the category is broadened, the "conflicts become glaring and overwhelming." How so? Can this ultimately be overcome or is it, in the end, the Achilles Heel of any governance model designed to promote the interests of stakeholders?

7. Despite the thoughtful reasoning of Professor Greenfield, the impact of a stakeholder model of governance must be viewed as uncertain. Does Professor Page have it right when he suggests that given the success of the existing model, "we should be wary of change absent more persuasive reasons"?

8. Do all stakeholders even want representation on the board? Douglas Fraser, the president of the United Automobile Workers, joined the board of directors of Chrysler in 1980, becoming the first union representative to sit on the board of a major U.S. corporation. Professor Dent concludes that, in the eyes of some union officials, the appointment "tainted" Fraser and that unions have shown little interest in board representation. *See* George W. Dent, Jr., *Stakeholder Theory and the Relationships Between Host Communities and Corporations: Stakeholder Governance: A Bad Idea Getting Worse*, 58 Case W. Res. L. Rev. 1107 (2008).

Many states have intervened in this area. They have done so by tampering with the fiduciary duties of directors. They have allowed boards to take into account the interests of non-shareholder groups. Thus, Pennsylvania law provides that the board "may, in considering the best interests of the corporation, consider to the extent they deem appropriate" the following:

> (1) The effects of any action upon any or all groups affected by such action, including shareholders, members, employees, suppliers, customers and cred-

itors of the corporation, and upon communities in which offices or other establishments of the corporation are located.

(2) The short-term and long-term interests of the corporation, including benefits that may accrue to the corporation from its long-term plans and the possibility that these interests may be best served by the continued independence of the corporation.

(3) The resources, intent and conduct (past, stated and potential) of any person seeking to acquire control of the corporation.

(4) All other pertinent factors.

See 15 Pa. C. S. §515(a). At some level, these statutes can have a radical impact. They no longer require that boards consider only the best interests of shareholders. Despite broad language, some have argued that the statutes do no such thing.

Committee on Corporate Laws, *Report on Other Constituencies Statutes: Potential for Confusion*

45 Bus. Law. 2253, 2261–63, 2265–66, 2268–70 (1990)[7]

All of the statutes incorporate one or more of the following provisions:

1. The directors may consider the interests of, or the effects of their action on, various non-stockholder constituencies.

2. These constituencies may include employees, customers, creditors, suppliers, and communities in which the corporation has facilities.

3. The directors may consider the national and state economies and other community and societal considerations.

4. The directors may consider the long-term as well as the short-term interests of the corporation and its shareholders.

5. The directors may consider the possibility that the best interests of the corporation and its stockholders may best be served by remaining independent.

6. The directors may consider any other pertinent factor.

7. Officers may also be covered.

In most of the statutes, the recital of the interests directors may consider is qualified by the prefatory clause, "... in considering the best interests of the corporation...." The significance of this language is discussed below.

* * *

---

7. "Report on Other Constituencies Statutes: Potential for Confusion," by the Committee on Corporate Laws, 1990, *Business Lawyer,* 45:4. © Copyright 1990 by the American Bar Association. Reprinted with permission. This information or any portion thereof may not be copied or disseminated in any form or by any means or stored in an electronic database or retrieval system without the express written consent of the American Bar Association.

ANALYSIS OF THE STATUTES

The critical analytical question is whether, indeed, the other constituency statutes effect a change in the existing law of the states where they have been enacted; more particularly, do they change in any fashion the fiduciary obligation that directors have to shareholders?

Most of the other constituency statutes state by one formulation or another that the directors *in considering the best interests of the corporation* [emphasis added] may take into account other constituencies. The classical formulation of the directors' duty of care has as one of its elements a requirement that the director perform his duties "in a manner he reasonably believes to be in the best interests of the corporation." The Commentary to section 4.01 of the current draft of ALI Principles of Corporate Governance states that, "In general, the principles stated in section 2.01 and the 'best interests of the corporation' (as stated in section 4.01(a)) will be in harmony." Section 2.01 states that "[a] business corporation should have as its objective the conduct of business activities with a view to enhancing corporate profit and shareholder gain ..." The Commentary to section 2.01 suggests this is in general a statement of present law. Thus the "best interests of the corporation" are equated with "corporate profit and shareholder gain." In some instances taking into consideration other constituencies, unless that consideration must be related to shareholder benefits, may result in actions which are inconsistent with corporate profit and shareholder gain.

Unlike the Delaware judicial articulations of the extent to which directors may take into consideration the interests of other constituencies, statutes of the Illinois type do not explicitly require that such consideration be related to shareholder benefits. However, if the understanding of "best interests of the corporation" stated in the ALI Principles of Corporate Governance is accepted, then such a limiter is built into the typical statutory formulation.

Some of the statutes are restricted in their operation to decision-making by directors in the control context, but most, like the Illinois statute, apply to the full range of board decision-making. The circumstances in which the statutes were adopted, however, indicate that the enacting legislatures expected that they would have their principal relevance in contests for control....

The issue then becomes whether state corporation laws, and, in particular, a broadening of the interests that directors may consider, constitute an efficient and desirable way to provide protections for non-shareholder groups. The Committee has concluded that permitting—much less requiring—directors to consider these interests without relating such consideration in an appropriate fashion to shareholder welfare (as the Delaware courts have done) would conflict with directors' responsibility to shareholders and could undermine the effectiveness of the system that has made the corporation an efficient device for the creation of jobs and wealth.

The Committee believes that the better interpretation of these statutes, and one that avoids such consequences, is that they confirm what the common law has been:

directors may take into account the interests of other constituencies but only as and to the extent that the directors are acting in the best interests, long as well as short term, of the shareholders and the corporation. While the Delaware courts have related the consideration directors may give other constituencies to the interests of shareholders by stating there must be "rationally related benefits to shareholders," it may well be that other courts may choose other words with which to express the nexus.

The confusion of directors in trying to comply with such statutes, if interpreted to require directors to balance the interests of various constituencies without according primacy to shareholder interests, would be profoundly troubling. Even under existing law, particularly where directors must act quickly, it is often difficult for directors acting in good faith to divine what is in the best interests of shareholders and the corporation. If directors are required to consider other interests as well, the decision-making process will become a balancing act or search for compromise. When directors must not only decide what their duty of loyalty mandates, but also to whom their duty of loyalty runs (and in what proportions), poorer decisions can be expected.

If directors have, or may have, recognized legal duties to other constituencies, perhaps a new class or classes of plaintiffs will have access to the courts to redress perceived breaches of those duties or to challenge directors' failures to take various competing interests into account. An interpretation of these statutes to the effect that directors owe enforceable duties to constituencies other than shareholders would signal a major shift in the premises underlying traditional corporation law and might deter suitable candidates from undertaking board responsibilities.

Furthermore, any articulation of a director's duties that extended them to other constituencies without primacy being accorded shareholder interests would diminish the ability of shareholders to monitor appropriately the conduct of directors. Dean Robert C. Clark has said,

> [a] single objective goal like profit maximization is more easily monitored than a multiple, vaguely defined goal like the fair and reasonable accommodation of all affected interests.... Assuming shareholders have some control mechanisms, better monitoring means that corporate managers will be kept more accountable. They are more likely to do what they are supposed to do and do it efficiently.

As was recently pointed out in the *Columbia Business Law Review*, the reallocation of wealth is a function for which directors are not especially suited and one beyond the general pale of their perceived mandate from society. Such allocations of wealth (which essentially a balancing of the interests of various constituencies would be) are *political* decisions. Absent the vesting of enforceable rights in those whose interests would have to be acknowledged, directors would not be accountable for their conduct in preferring the interests of one constituency over others.

Finally, it is important to note that other constituencies legislation reinforces the contentions of those who would impose on corporations goals that transcend traditional business considerations and the profit motive. Those who argue for increased control of corporations at the federal level routinely point to the multiple interests that corporate activities affect as a basis for urging the exercise of increased corporate governance powers by agencies outside the corporation. Other constituencies provisions may lend support to this movement.

Comments and Questions

1. To the extent that this analysis is correct, what do these types of statutes add? Does not the board already have the authority to consider any stakeholder interest if in the best interests of the corporation and shareholders?

2. Assuming these statutes in fact expand the board's fiduciary responsibilities, do you agree that the attendant consequences of balancing the interests of stakeholders "would be profoundly troubling"? What about the possibility that the duties "might deter suitable candidates from serving on the board"? To the extent that these duties in fact discouraged some candidates from serving, what might a company do in response?

3. In some cases, these statutes require consideration of other constituencies, but in limited circumstances. Connecticut, for example, requires consideration of assorted constituencies during certain changes of control transactions. *See* Conn. Gen. Stat. 33-756(d) (2004) ("a director ... shall consider, in determining what he reasonably believes to be in the best interests of the corporation ... the interests of the corporation's employees, customers, creditors and suppliers, and ... community and societal considerations"). What impact might the mandatory nature of the provision have on the board's decision making in the change of control context?

4. The article notes problems of monitoring. It contends that profit maximization, as a singular motive, is easier to monitor than a multiple of other goals and duties. In fact, how easy is it to monitor profit maximization? Does this standard impose any meaningful limits on board behavior?

––––––––––

Although often allowing the board to consider stakeholder interests in a myriad of circumstances, these statutes originally arose in the context of corporate takeovers. By broadening the board's fiduciary duties to include stakeholders, directors had a wider set of justifications for opposing a hostile acquisition attempt.

Baron v. Strawbridge & Clothier

United States District Court, Eastern District of Pennsylvania
646 F. Supp. 690 (1986)

Kelly, Judge:

FACTUAL BACKGROUND AND FINDINGS

Defendant Strawbridge & Clothier is a corporation organized under the laws of Pennsylvania with its principal place of business at Philadelphia, Pennsylvania. Although Strawbridge & Clothier's shares have been publicly held since the 1930's, approximately 40% of its stock continues to be owned directly or beneficially by descendants of the two founders, Justus C. Strawbridge and Isaac H. Clothier. Five members of the third and fourth generations of the Strawbridge family are engaged full-time in the management of the Company, and other Strawbridge descendants, as well as one Clothier descendant, serve as directors. The Company's Board of Directors ("board") is composed of twelve individuals, (the individual defendants in this action) eleven of whom are the company's current or former senior officers or their relatives.

In the last decade, many retail chains have been acquired by national or international chains or conglomerates. Strawbridge & Clothier has avoided this trend. The Company's management ("management") and its board view this independence to be a predominant factor in the company's success. Each manager and director who testified in this matter emphasized that in his or her view, the company's independence is its most highly prized asset. Two reasons were repeatedly articulated for supporting this conclusion: that the influence of continuous, local family management (1) fosters a unique relationship, based on loyalty and dedication, between the company's employees and managers, and (2) makes it possible for the Company to plow earnings back into the business and opt for greater long term growth instead of smaller, more immediate short-term profits. An expert witness from the retail business, who is not associated with the Company, also testified to these benefits of local, independent management.

Plaintiff Ronald Baron, a resident and citizen of New York and plaintiff BCI, a New York corporation, have both owned common stock of Strawbridge & Clothier continuously for the past four years. Plaintiff Berry, a corporation organized under Delaware laws with its principal place of business at New York, was organized in 1986 for the purpose of making a tender offer for Strawbridge & Clothier's shares.

In 1984, management perceived that Ronald Baron was mounting an attempt either to take over the Company or to "put the company in play" and enable his shares to be sold at a premium. Baron's early steps included demands that the Company sell off or mortgage important assets, that it consider selling out to a third party, and that Baron be named as a director. Baron also publicly announced that he considered the Company "ripe for a takeover."

Management proposed to its shareholders that they approve various measures designed to discourage a hostile takeover. These measures (the "1984 proposals") included the elimination of cumulative voting; an increase in the percentage of shares necessary to call a special meeting of shareholders; the requirement of two-thirds shareholder approval of actions not proposed by a majority of the board; and a requirement that candidates for election to the board be nominated at least 45 days prior to a meeting of shareholders. The "anti-takeover" purpose of these proposals was disclosed in the 1984 proxy materials. Management had been planning these proposals for some time, but accelerated their presentation in direct response to the threat presented by Baron's activities; this, too, was fully disclosed in the proxy materials. All of the antitakeover proposals were approved by the shareholders at a special meeting held on April 10, 1984.

Thereafter, Baron made other overtures, culminating in Berry's April 21, 1986 tender offer (the "tender offer"). The tender offer has a two-tiered structure: it proposes to buy two-thirds of the Company's outstanding common stock at a price of $60 per share and total purchase price of $276.25 million; if successful, the purchasers plan to then buy out the remaining shareholders for cash, or for debt securities of unspecified terms.

2. *The reclassification plan, and other anti-takeover actions, serve legitimate corporate purposes*

The company was faced with a generalized threat, dating to 1984, to its long-standing corporate policies. Testimony has shown that the plaintiff Ronald Baron disagrees fundamentally with nearly every major management decision the Company makes. The Company was also faced with a particularized threat to its corporate policies in the form of Berry's two-tiered tender offer. The Company and its directors have dealt with these threats properly, without breaching fiduciary duties to shareholders. The board acted with due deliberation and care, and did not act hastily. It was proper for the company to consider the effects the Berry tender offer would have, if successful, on the Company's employees, customers and community. Pa. Stat. Ann. tit. 15 § 1408 (Purdon 1967 + Supp.). The Company concluded these effects would be detrimental to its success.

The company solicited experts to provide a financial evaluation of the offer. The experts concluded the offer was financially inadequate. Under the law of Pennsylvania, as in other jurisdictions, Enterra Corp. v. SGS Associates, 600 F. Supp. 678, 686 (E.D. Pa. 1985), the fiduciary duty of corporate directors "to act in the best interests of the corporation's shareholders ... requires the directors to attempt to block takeovers that would [in their judgment] be harmful to the target company," and "directors are obliged to oppose tender offers deemed to be 'detrimental to the well-being of the corporation even if that [opposition] is at the expense of the short-term interests of the individual shareholders.'"

Defensive proposals and alternatives were considered over many months. The evidence shows that the Board of Directors considered and rejected the so-called "poison pill" rights plan as unfair and also determined not to pursue a "time phased" voting plan, in part because the shareholders would have no choice of the sort offered by the instant reclassification plan. Expert, independent advice was also solicited to provide an analysis of various plans, as well as an analysis of the effect of the proposed reclassification plan on the price of stock. In short, the Company weighed the interests of all shareholders in responding to the takeover threats posed by the plaintiffs, and the Company's responses, including the proposed reclassification plan, served legitimate corporate purposes.

The evidence showed that the directors were conscious of their duty to consider each future takeover effort from outsiders, including tender offers, on the merits, and the plaintiffs' reliance on isolated portions of the testimony of the two most recently elected directors did not establish the contrary proposition.

Comments and Questions

1. Constituency statutes were not born out of a broad reconsideration of the fiduciary obligations of the directors and the need to protect stakeholders. They mostly arose during the hostile acquisition era in the 1980s and were designed to facilitate management's ability to impede takeovers. As one court noted, the Pennsylvania statute, the first stakeholder statute, was adopted "[i]n reaction to a rise of hostile takeover bids." *Stilwell Value Partners I, L.P. v. Prudential Mutual Holding Co., et al.*, 2007 U.S. Dist. LEXIS 59653 (E.D. Pa., Aug. 15, 2007).

2. How might stakeholders be harmed in a hostile acquisition attempt? Will there be any hostile acquisitions that do not have a detrimental impact on at least some stakeholders? Assuming this is true, what kind of discretion does it really provide management in resisting a takeover?

3. What role did the statute play in this case? Given the development of the law since then (particularly with respect to poison pills), what role are these types of statutes likely to play in the hostile acquisition context?

––––––

Another approach is to permit the creation of entities with boards that no longer have as an exclusive purpose the interests of shareholders. A number of states, including Delaware, have adopted statutes that permit the creation of Benefit Corporations. Benefit corporations make mandatory the board's consideration of interests held by a number of non-shareholder constituencies. In these types of entities, therefore, "the concept of shareholder primacy vanishes …" Celia R. Taylor, *Berle and Social Businesses: A Consideration*, 34 Seattle U. L. Rev. 1501, 1507 (2011).

Joseph Karl Grant, *When Making Money and Making a Sustainable and Societal Difference Collide: Will Benefit Corporations Succeed or Fail?*
46 Ind. L. Rev. 581 (2013)

II. Benefit Corporations: The Model Statutory Landscape

Benefit corporations are very similar to standard corporations, but they differ from their traditional cousins in four main ways. First, the purpose section of the Articles of Incorporation requires specific items not found in traditional purpose sections. Second, the Articles of Incorporation for benefit corporations are statutorily mandated to provide a specific level of accountability to certain stakeholders not found in most traditional corporate codes. Third, benefit corporations have unique transparency requirements unheard of in traditional corporate codes. Finally, specific rights of action are granted to particular stakeholders based on breach of the benefit corporation charter.

Newly formed corporations may elect to be recognized as benefit corporations. Existing corporations may become benefit corporations under prescribed procedures: amendment of their articles of incorporation by a two-thirds shareholder vote.

A. Purpose

Pennsylvania provides a good example of a state's recent legislative adoption of the Model Benefit Corporation Legislation. In order to create a benefit corporation in Pennsylvania, the incorporators are required to mandate the following in the Articles of Incorporation:

(a) The "corporation shall have [the] purpose of creating [a] general public benefit;"

(b) The corporation shall have the right to name "one or more specific public benefit[]" purposes; and

(c) "The creation of [a] general public benefit and specific public benefit.... [must be] in the best interests of the benefit corporation."

At a minimum, a benefit corporation must have a "general public benefit." "General public benefit" means the corporation must have "[a] material positive impact on society and the environment, taken as a whole" by "operations of [the] benefit corporation" as measured using "a third-party standard," through activities that promote some combination of specific public benefits. Additionally, and at the benefit corporation's option, the corporation could pursue a "specific public benefit purpose[,]" which could include the following:

(1) providing low-income or underserved individuals or communities with beneficial products or services;

(2) promoting economic opportunity for individuals or communities beyond the creation of jobs in the normal course of business;

(3) protecting or restoring the environment;

(4) improving human health;

(5) promoting the arts, sciences, or advancement of knowledge;

(6) increasing the flow of capital to entities with a purpose to benefit society or the environment; and

(7) conferring any other particular benefit on society or the environment.

B. Accountability

The accountability standards that directors of benefit corporations must meet include the following:

In discharging the duties of their respective positions and in considering the best interests of the benefit corporation, the board of directors, committees of the board, and individual directors of a benefit corporation, in considering the interests of the benefit corporation:

(1) shall consider the effects of any action upon:

(i) the shareholders of the benefit corporation;

(ii) the employees and work force of the benefit corporation, its subsidiaries, and its suppliers;

(iii) the interests of customers as beneficiaries of the general public benefit or specific public benefit purposes of the benefit corporation;

(iv) community and societal factors, including those of each community in which offices or facilities of the benefit corporation, its subsidiaries, or its suppliers are located;

(v) the local and global environment;

(vi) the short-term and long-term interests of the benefit corporation, including benefits that may accrue to the benefit corporation from its long-term plans and the possibility that these interests may be best served by the continued independence of the benefit corporation; and

(vii) the ability of the benefit corporation to accomplish its general public benefit purpose and any specific public benefit purpose; and

(2) may consider:

[(i) the interests referred to in [cite constituencies provision of the business corporation law if it refers to constituencies not listed above]; and

(ii)] other pertinent factors or the interests of any other group that they deem appropriate; but

(3) need not give priority to the interests of a particular person or group referred to [above] over the interests of any other person or group unless the benefit corporation has stated in its articles of incorporation its intention to give priority to certain interests related to its accomplishment of its general public benefit purpose or of a specific public benefit purpose identified in its articles.

Generally, standards of accountability are identical for operating and liquidity/change of control decisions. A director is not personally liable, as such, for monetary damages for any action taken as a director if the director performed the duties of his or her office under the applicable duty of care.

C. Transparency

Benefit corporations are required to publish an annual benefit report prepared in accordance with recognized "third-party standard[s]" "for defining, reporting, and assessing corporate social and environmental performance." Additionally, the Benefit Report must assess the successes and failures of the corporation in achieving the general and specific public benefit purposes of the corporation, and consider the effects of decisions on stakeholders....

(5) The statement of the benefit director described in [the annual compliance statement provision].

* * *

The benefit corporation must deliver the report to all shareholders "(1) within 120 days following the end of the fiscal year of the benefit corporation; or (2) at the same time that the benefit corporation delivers any other annual report to its shareholders." Also, in an effort to foster transparency, the benefit report must be posted "on the public portion of its Internet website, if any; but the compensation paid to directors and financial or proprietary information ... may be omitted from the benefit reports as posted."

Comments and Questions

1. What types of companies might use a "benefit" corporation? Patagonia, the clothing retailer, is one example of an early convert to benefit corporation status. Why do you think the company to take this step? What other types of companies are likely to replicate this model?

2. What are the benefits that come from this structure? Would, for example, consumers be more likely to buy products made by a benefit corporation? According to Professor Grant:

> Benefit corporations, due to their mandate of a general public benefit, accountability, and transparency, now offer a formal, tangible, and verifiable base for consumers to judge and reward corporations that are truly committed to sustainability. Over time, benefit corporations will succeed because consumers will have a yardstick by which to measure the claims and successes of corporations that say they are committed to achieving sustainability. As benefit corporations take hold, flashy and sometimes deceptive marketing will no longer work. Corporations will have to back up their claims with results and clearly demonstrate the areas in which they are having an impact. Because consumer demand is driving the need for the benefit corporation, benefit corporations likely will succeed.

Do you agree with this observation?

3. The real key is whether investors will buy shares in for-profit companies that do not have as their exclusive purpose the goal of shareholder primacy. Certainly, there are investors, including institutions, that seek to invest in companies with a strong record of corporate social responsibility. But these investors currently invest in companies that promote corporate social responsibility while continuing to have an obligation to profit maximize. As a practical matter, what is the likely outcome with respect to capital raising?

4. Some have expressed concern that benefit corporations create fiduciary standards that that impose no meaningful limits on board behavior. As one commentator wrote:

> From either perspective, orthodox Blabs benefit corporations permit directors and officers to take an enormous number of interests and factors into account, many of which are unspecified by the shareholders who adopt the benefit corporation posture. General public benefit is a mish-mash and directors, all of whom have personal interests and some of whom may have personal

agendas, are simply tossed into the middle of the mess. For example, if directors conclude that electric car promotion is a social good, Teslas can be acquired for all corporate executives. If directors think that polar bear preservation is good, the corporation can spend large fortunes to maintain ice in Greenland. From the contractarian perspective, further specification of fiduciary duties by contract is not contemplated and the gap-fillers are not sufficiently robust. From the fiduciarian perspective, there are fundamentally no restrictions that hamper the freedom of directors whose actions involve the risk of injury to others.Benefit corporations open the door for irresponsible directors to justify their actions (including self-interested actions) by pointing to some public benefit justification (or alternatively when public benefit is involved, to some private shareholder benefit justification).

J. William Callison, *Putting New Sheets on a Procrustean Bed: How Benefit Corporations Address Fiduciary Duties, the Dangers Created, and Suggestions for Change*, 2 Am. U. Bus. L. Rev. 85, 108 (2012). Do you agree with this analysis?

5. Is the benefit corporation even necessary? Could, for example, a corporation abandon the shareholder primacy model in its articles of incorporation? The New York Times provides in its articles that the company's purpose, among other things, is to engage in the "business of printing, publishing and selling newspapers, books, pamphlets and other publications, gathering, transmitting and supplying news reports, general job printing, and any and all other business incidental to the foregoing or any of them or thereunto pertaining or proper in connection therewith." Does this effectively terminate the obligation to profit maximize, at least where it conflicts with the newspaper business? Alternatively, could language requiring the board to take into account non-shareholder interests be inserted in an operating agreement for an LLC?

IV. Corporate Social Responsibility

For profit corporations generally operate under a shareholder primacy model. Socially responsible behavior, therefore, must generally support this objective. Nonetheless, pressure from both shareholders and the public have put pressure on companies to engage in socially responsible behavior. Sometimes the actions have a clear nexus to the bottom line. In other circumstances, the commitments are more likely designed to promote the company's overall reputation.

A. Corporate Social Responsibility and Private Ordering

Short of mandatory legal requirements, corporate social responsibility remains dependent upon private ordering. Companies often engage in socially responsible activity on a voluntary and informal basis. They may codify these responsibilities in codes of behavior or ethics. They may also agree to adhere to preexisting standards, including for example, the Global Compact on Governance promulgated by the United Nations.

Private ordering, however, raises a number of concerns. There may be a gap between public commitments to corporate social responsibility and actual practice. To assess compliance, investors and stakeholders will need adequate disclosure, something not always forthcoming. In a small number of instances, corporate behavior may be actionable. The Alien Tort Statute, for example, provides for actions by those injured in violation of international law. 28 USC § 1350. The Antiterrorism Act of 1991 (*see* 18 USC prec. § 2331) allows for suits against companies that aid terrorist organizations. These laws are narrow but they arguably impose outer limits on some types of behavior implicating social responsibility.

CODES OF CONDUCT

Private ordering can be increasingly seen through the use of codes of conduct and ethics by most large public companies. In the narrowest sense, the codes address specific legal requirements. They often reiterate the ban on insider trading or set out restrictions on practices that might otherwise violate the Foreign Corrupt Practices Act. 15 USC § 78dd-1. Implementation of these types of codes provides advantages under the sentencing guidelines and in settling cases with the Securities and Exchange Commission. *See* Exchange Act Release No. 44969 (Oct. 23, 2001) (adopting so called "Seaboard standards" and noting that in assessing corporate penalties, SEC would take into consideration the "compliance procedures [that] were in place to prevent the misconduct").

Corporate codes of conduct received additional impetus with the adoption of the Sarbanes Oxley Act. Section 406 of the Act instructed the Commission to adopt rules for reporting companies that required them to disclose whether they had a code of ethics and any changes to, or waivers of, the code. Item 406 of Regulation S-K defines a code of ethics. According to the SEC, the code should be designed to "deter wrongdoing" and to promote:

1. Honest and ethical conduct, including the ethical handling of actual or apparent conflicts of interest between personal and professional relationships;

2. Full, fair, accurate, timely, and understandable disclosure in reports and documents that a registrant files with, or submits to, the Commission and in other public communications made by the registrant;

3. Compliance with applicable governmental laws, rules and regulations;

4. The prompt internal reporting of violations of the code to an appropriate person or persons identified in the code; and

5. Accountability for adherence to the code.

Item 406(b) of Regulation S-K, 17 CFR 240.406(b). In addition, the NYSE requires listed companies to have a code of conduct and ethics. *See* NYSE 303A.10.

———

While the codes often have common attributes, they vary considerably as the excerpt from the next article illustrates.

Joshua A. Newberg, *Corporate Codes of Ethics, Mandatory Disclosure, and the Market for Ethical Conduct*

29 Vt. L. Rev. 253, 258–64 (2005)[8]

2. What Codes Say

The typical CCOE [corporate code of ethics] of a large public company is a hybrid that combines some general statements of the firm's commitment to broadly expressed normative formulations of principled business conduct—such as acting with "integrity" or adherence to "the highest ethical standards"—with a number of specific pronouncements or rules addressing discrete areas of unlawful and/or unethical conduct. Provisions of the latter type may be articulated as statements of corporate policy from which management and employee duties may be inferred. Alternatively, such provisions may be expressed as admonitions to employees either to act in a certain way ("do's") or to refrain from engaging in specific types of prohibited conduct ("don'ts"). These specific corporate policy statements/admonitions generally fall within one or more of five overlapping categories: (a) follow the law; (b) be honest; (c) be loyal to the company (i.e., avoid conflicts of interest); (d) keep the company's secrets; and (e) treat corporate stakeholders and competitors with fairness and respect.

a. *Follow the law*: Many CCOEs include both general exhortations to follow the law and references to specific types of legal violations that employees are to avoid. Among the most commonly mentioned areas of law with which employees are called upon to comply are: the antitrust laws; health, safety, and environmental regulations; the Foreign Corrupt Practices Act; intellectual property protections; export controls; and prohibitions against insider trading, employment discrimination, and sexual harassment.

b. *Be honest*: In addition to general admonitions to be honest, codes typically include directives to keep accurate corporate records, and to report company information truthfully within the organization and without. Many codes specifically promise that information submitted to the Securities and Exchange Commission will be accurate, timely, and complete. It is common, moreover, for codes to articulate commitments to truthful advertising and the avoidance of deceit in relationships with customers, suppliers, and competitors. Another recurring CCOE provision, within the rubric of "honesty," is the admonition to employees to use company assets solely for company business.

c. *Be loyal to the company*: The vast majority of codes prohibit conflicts of interest. However, the documents vary substantially in the level of detail with which the employees' duty of loyalty to the company is articulated. Codes typically define conflicts of interest broadly and then list specific types of potentially problematic conduct,

---

8. Copyright © 2005 Vermont Law Review. Reprinted by permission.

such as working for another firm, steering company business to a relative, or maintaining a personal financial interest in a company transaction.

d. *Keep the company's secrets*: Corporate ethics codes typically require employees to protect the secrecy of the company's confidential information. Many also explicitly oblige employees to keep the secrets of customers, clients, and others with whom the company conducts business.

e. *Treat stakeholders and competitors with fairness and respect*: This is, in a sense, a residual category that could be understood to encompass some or all of the content already discussed under the first four headings. Corporate "stakeholders" include investors, employees, suppliers, customers, and the communities in which firms operate. Nevertheless, the "treatment-of-stakeholders" category reflects the actual language of many CCOEs that specifically address the interests of certain stakeholder groups and the standards to be observed when dealing with them. Indeed, some codes are essentially structured as a series of promises to discrete stakeholder constituencies. Other codes address stakeholder issues less systematically by means of general commitments to "fair dealing" and/or "good corporate citizenship."

B. Management Structures for Implementation & Enforcement

In addition to the types of content described in the previous section, many corporate codes of ethics include provisions governing code administration and enforcement. Although such provisions take different forms, the CCOEs of large public companies typically give some indication of: (1) who is responsible for administering the code; (2) basic procedures to be followed for reporting and evaluating possible code violations; and (3) sanctions that may be imposed upon those who are found to have violated the code.

For the administration and enforcement of their CCOEs, large public companies are likely to rely on a combination of employees' personal responsibility, managerial oversight, and specialized in-house personnel (such as in-house counsel or designated compliance and/or ethics officers). Many codes expressly state that all employees are responsible for their own compliance and for reporting suspected violations. Indeed, it is not uncommon for CCOEs to set forth a "when-in-doubt" inquiry for employees to follow when deciding whether a given course of conduct is consistent with the letter and spirit of the company's code. Employees are typically admonished, moreover, to raise questions regarding ethics and compliance with their supervisors, in-house counsel, or corporate ethics and/or compliance officers (who may or may not be attorneys).

Some CCOEs indicate that managers bear a special responsibility for implementing the company code by setting a good example, educating employees under their supervision, and/or seeing to it that the code is followed. Other CCOEs refer to "ethics committees," "ethics officers," or other management structures for code implementation and enforcement. However, it is relatively rare for CCOEs to describe code administration, enforcement, or the punishment of violations in any depth. With regard to enforcement and punishment, CCOEs typically state that violators are subject to disciplinary sanctions up to and including dismissal, but offer little more in the way of specifics.

Comments and Questions

1. Do these codes advance the goal of social responsibility by corporations?

2. Like many of the provisions in SOX, Section 406 of SOX had its impetus in perceived abuses at Enron. As the Senate Report noted:

> The problems surrounding Enron Corp. and other public companies raise concerns about the ethical standards of corporations and their senior financial managers. The Committee believes that investors have a legitimate interest in knowing whether a public company holds its financial officers to certain ethical standards in their financial dealings. The bill requires issuers to disclose whether or not they have adopted a code of ethics for senior financial officers and, if not, why not.

Senate Comm. on Banking, Housing & Urban Affairs Public Company Accounting Reform and Investor Protection Act of 2002, S. Rep. No. 107-205, at 32. Given this concern, why did Congress not require the implementation of these types of codes?

3. The approach taken by Congress in Section 406 of SOX has sometimes been referred to as "comply or explain." Companies must adopt a code of ethics or explain why they have not. What do you make of this approach to regulation? How might it encourage the use of codes of ethics?

4. Are these codes enforceable? What is the consequence if a company does not adhere to its own code of conduct/ethics?

5. Waivers of the applicability of the code of ethics must be disclosed. *See* Item 5.05 of Form 8-K. What is the purpose of this requirement? What impact might it have on waivers?

6. Some have suggested that these codes are merely window-dressing. *See* Usha Rodrigues, *From Loyalty to Conflict: Addressing Fiduciary Duty at the Officer Level*, 61 Fla. L. Rev. 1, 31 (2009) (noting a "generalized fear that compliance codes and corporate codes of conduct are mere window-dressing"). Do you agree?

———

Codes can and often do go further than compliance with specific legal obligations. Some companies use them to set out ethical obligations and socially responsible goals. These "aspirational" codes may contain prohibitions on child labor or restrictions on greenhouse gas emissions. Yet aspirational codes are not without risk.

Elizabeth F. Brown, *No Good Deed Goes Unpunished: Is There a Need for a Safe Harbor for Aspirational Corporate Codes of Conduct?*

26 Yale L. & Pol'y Rev. 367, 385–86, 393–95 (2008)[9]

Some business leaders are deterred from adopting aspirational codes of conduct—and compliance programs to ensure that they are met—out of fear that such codes and programs will increase the potential liabilities of the business. Ramon Mullerat echoes these concerns:

> A related issue is to determine whether the violation of self-imposed standards of conduct ([i.e.,] codes of conduct) engenders legal liability or, in other words, the violator can be legally sued for damages. Can a corporation that has publicised, internally and externally, that it complies with high labour, environmental and human rights standards, just break one of them with impunity, or would it have some sort of economic sanction?

The answer to Mullerat's question is that corporations will sometimes be held liable for violating the voluntary standards that they adopt in their codes of conduct, even if those standards are higher than the obligations imposed on the corporations by the law. These legal liabilities can arise in several contexts, including suits for false and deceptive advertising and breach of contract.

* * *

In April 1998, Marc Kasky sued Nike and five of its corporate officers claiming that Nike's corporate social responsibility reports and advertising violated California's prohibitions on unfair business practices and false advertising under California's Unfair Business Practices Act and California's Business and Professions Code § 17500. Kasky alleged that Nike and the individual defendants made numerous false and misleading statements in an effort to respond to the adverse publicity and maintain Nike's sales. Nike made these statements in press releases, letters to newspapers, letters to university presidents and athletic directors, and in other documents. In addition, Nike bought advertisements in leading newspapers to publicize the report by Good-Works International LLC. Nike had contracted with GoodWorks to have Andrew Young, the former U.S. Ambassador to the United Nations under President Carter, evaluate the conditions at the factories of its contracting partners. Ambassador Young visited twelve of the factories as part of the evaluation of labor practices at the facilities and declared that he found no evidence of mistreatment or abuse of workers.

* * *

In September 2003, Nike settled the lawsuit with Marc Kasky. Nike agreed to donate to the Fair Labor Association $1.5 million. As a result of this settlement, no court ever ruled on whether Nike's statements regarding the conditions in the factories were truthful. During the discovery phase of the case, Nike turned over a wide range of

---

9. Copyright © 2008 Yale Law & Policy Review. Reprinted by permission.

internal documents discussing the conditions in factories, and some news stories speculated that the contents of those documents led Nike to settle, rather than shoulder the costs of pursuing the litigation. In the settlement announcement, Nike commented: "Due to the potential difficulties posed by the application of California Statute section 17200, Nike has decided not to issue its corporate responsibility report externally for its fiscal year 2002 and will continue to limit its participation in public events and media engagements in California."

The Nike case sent ripples of unease throughout the worldwide CSR community, which feared that it would deter other businesses from incorporating CSR principles in their codes of conduct. Unfortunately, no empirical evidence appears to exist that measures how many corporations reconsidered adopting CSR principles in their codes of conduct in the wake of the Nike case.

Comments and Questions

1. Are "aspirational" codes of conduct an effective method of promoting social responsibility? What are their strengths and weaknesses? Should there be some kind of safe harbor for obligations contained in an aspirational code?

2. What are some reasons why companies might or might not commit to socially responsible behavior in these types codes? Nike found itself mired in a law suit because of representations in its code. Yet why might companies implement these codes, even if some risk of liability can result?

3. Can the antifraud provisions of the securities laws result in liability for misrepresentations about a company's commitment to corporate social responsibility? *See In re: Ford Motor Co. Sec. Litig.*, 381 F.3d 563 (6th Cir. 2004) (characterizing statement that company "is going to lead in corporate social responsibility" as mere puffery). What would be the toughest elements to meet in establishing a claim under Rules 10b-5 or 14a-9 for misstatements about a company's record with respect to social responsibility?

4. Could a benefit corporation be a better alternative to voluntary codes? At least one commentator suggests they may be. See Joseph Karl Grant, *When Making Money and Making A Sustainable and Societal Difference Collide: Will Benefit Corporations Succeed or Fail?*, 46 Ind. L. Rev. 581 (2013) ("the Articles of Incorporation for benefit corporations are statutorily mandated to provide a specific level of accountability to certain stakeholders not found in most traditional corporate codes" and are subject to "unique transparency requirements unheard of in traditional corporate codes"). Do you agree?

GLOBAL COMPACTS

Assuming companies want to adhere to more "aspirational" standards, one concern is defining those goals. An increasingly common source is the U.N. Global Compact on Governance. The Compact has been developed under the auspices of the United Nations and is voluntary.

Introduced in 2000, the Global Compact originally consisted of nine principles, with one addressing corruption added in 2004. The Principles include:

Human Rights

- Principle 1: Businesses should support and respect the protection of internationally proclaimed human rights; and
- Principle 2: make sure that they are not complicit in human rights abuses.

Labor Standards

- Principle 3: Businesses should uphold the freedom of association and the effective recognition of the right to collective bargaining;
- Principle 4: the elimination of all forms of forced and compulsory labor;
- Principle 5: the effective abolition of child labor; and
- Principle 6: the elimination of discrimination in respect of employment and occupation.

Environment

- Principle 7: Businesses should support a precautionary approach to environmental challenges;
- Principle 8: undertake initiatives to promote greater environmental responsibility; and
- Principle 9: encourage the development and diffusion of environmentally friendly technologies.

Anti-Corruption

- Principle 10: Businesses should work against corruption in all its forms, including extortion and bribery.

———————

Adherence to the Global Compact is, however, voluntary. Moreover, the provisions are broad and permit considerable discretion. Nor are there remedies for violations. The result has been a mix of criticism and praise.

Surya Deva, *Global Compact: A Critique of the U.N.'s "Public-Private" Partnership for Promoting Corporate Citizenship*

34 Syracuse J. Int'l L. & Com. 107, 129–30, 132, 141–43 (2006)[10]

A. Compact, General and Vague Principles

In order to keep it simple and attractive for corporations, the ten principles of the Global Compact are basically "one-liners," at best an example of a "minimalist code" of corporate conduct. Therefore, the principles hardly provide adequate and concrete

———————

10. Copyright © 2006 Syracuse Journal of International Law & Commerce. Reprinted by permission.

guidance to corporations about the conduct expected from them: "Many of the [Global Compact's] principles cannot be defined at this time with the precision required for a viable code of conduct." The generality-cum-vagueness of the Compact principles is counter-productive from the perspective of both sincere and insincere corporate citizens. The language of these principles is so general that insincere corporations can easily circumvent or comply with them without doing anything to promote human rights or labor standards. On the other hand, even a sincere corporate citizen like Novartis finds the language too general to be implemented: "The generality of the Global Compact principles needed to be particularized for the specific Novartis environment as a first step in implementation." A certain level of generality or flexibility in guiding principles of any international initiative is a desirable virtue, but not if it could be taken to include or exclude anything as per the individual corporate convenience.

Also, we may recall that the Compact principles are subject to a general rider, that is, companies need to take measures only "within their sphere of influence." What constitutes the "sphere of influence" of a given corporation, though fundamental to the efficacy of Compact principles, is a matter of uncertainty and speculation. For example, will it include the subsidiary and affiliate concerns of a parent corporation? Furthermore, will it include the supply chains of a corporation? If yes, to what extent? Point twelve of the Shanghai Declaration seems to address this issue vis-a-vis the supply chains as corporations agree to "ensure that supply chain capacities are built to effectively implement the U.N. Global Compact." But the extent to which corporations would go to ensure that their supply chains have the required capacity to implement the Compact principles is still to be seen. Also, it cannot be said with certainty whether all the subsidiaries of a parent corporation will be treated as entities within the sphere of influence of the parent. Logically, they should be so treated.

* * *

3. Where Do the World's Top Corporations Stand?

Finally, it may be relevant to find out how the world's largest corporations have responded to the challenge of embracing the Global Compact. A list of the world's top corporations is compiled by several financial magazines or newspapers, such as Fortune, Forbes and the Financial Times. Based on the ranking of the Financial Times Global 500, the Compact Office takes pride in stating that 106 of the world's largest 500 companies have signed to the Global Compact. The "CG Global 106," as the Compact's website calls them, come from twenty-five countries, directly employ around ten million people, and have a market value of about USD $3.5 trillion. The support of Global 106 (21.20% of the total Financial Times Global 500) to the Compact is undoubtedly an encouraging sign, also because of these companies, only one (Johnson Controls Inc.) has been listed as a non-communicating company.

In addition to the Financial Times Global 500, it is also examined how Fortune Global 500 has shown an interest to participate in the U.N.'s "public-private" partnership for corporate citizenship. Since the Compact applies the leadership principle, a Fortune Global 500 is considered a participant to the Global Compact only if the parent corporation is a participant. In some cases, although the parent has not signed to the Global Compact, one or more of its subsidiaries has become a participant in its own right. For example, although Ford Motor is missing from the list of Compact participants, Ford Argentina and Ford Malaysia are parties to the Compact. Similarly, Fiat France and Fiat Argentina have signed, but not Fiat, the parent corporation. Also, GlaxoSmithKline Romania and GlaxoSmithKline Bulgaria are participants of the Global Compact, but not their UK parent.

Of these 500 corporations, 131 (about 26% of the total number) were participants of the Global Compact on March 18, 2006.... On the other hand, around 74% of the top 500 global corporations (369 corporations) have not yet become signatory to the Global Compact. Many of the world's well-known corporations are part of this missing list of Compact participants, ...

The objective of this survey was not to suggest that all the Compact participants ipso facto become good corporate citizens, or that embracing the Global Compact is the litmus test for responsible corporate conduct. Several Compact participants such as Coca-Cola, BHP, Shell, L'Oreal, and Cisco have been the subject matter of public criticism or even legal actions for their policies/actions that violate human rights, labor standards, or pollute the environment. Conversely, even without participating in the Compact, corporations could join other initiatives and fulfill their social responsibilities in an effective manner. Rather, the objective was to measure the extent to which the world's largest corporations were buying the idea of the Global Compact.

On the basis of above findings, it can be reasonably concluded that the world's leading corporations have found joining the Compact an attractive proposition. As most of these corporations have already adopted some kind of code of conduct, and may have assigned the responsibility of looking after CSR issues to someone within the organization, joining the Compact is not likely to put much additional burden on them. Conversely, signing to the Compact provides direct access to the U.N. Therefore, it is expected that more Global 500 corporations will become Compact participants in coming years. The extent to which these corporations take and would continue to take the Compact commitments seriously is, however, an altogether separate issue.

Comments and Questions

1. Has the Global Compact been a success or a failure? Certainly based upon the number of companies agreeing to abide by the principles, it would seem to be a success. See David Weissbrodt, *Human Rights Standards Concerning Transnational Corporations and Other Business Entities*, 23 Minn. J. Int'l L. 135, 166 (2014) (noting that in 2012, the Global Compact had "over 10,000 participants, including over 7000 businesses, from 145 different countries"). At the same time, those figures need to be tempered. See Id. at 166–67 (noting that by 2013, "only 512 of those companies consider their implementation of the Global Compact to be at an 'advanced level,' while over 1,500 were identified as 'non-communicating participants,' and over 4,000 had been expelled for 'failure to communicate progress by the required deadline.'").

2. What are the limits of the Compact? Companies adhering to the Global Compact must "embrace, support, and enact, within their sphere of influence, a set of core values" in the enumerated areas. Is it specific enough to provide meaningful standards for assessing compliance?

3. According to one commentator: "Signatories to the Global Compact make a visible and public commitment to implement the ten principles of a responsible business, publish an annual report describing the measures they have enacted in furtherance of these principles, and publicly advocate for others to join in support of the Compact's principles." Janet E. Kerr, *The Creative Capitalism Spectrum: Evaluating Corporate Social Responsibility Through A Legal Lens*, 81 Temp. L. Rev. 831, 866 (2008). Is this enough to ensure at least a degree of compliance?

4. Failure to meet voluntary standards may result in reputational harm. *See* Kevin T. Jackson, *Global Corporate Governance: Soft Law and Reputational Accountability*, 35 Brook. J. Int'l L. 41, 105 (2010) ("Any attempt to deceive the public, in today's age of far-reaching, decentralized media, will quickly cause reputational harm."). Is this enough to ensure compliance with voluntary standards?

5. Even for those companies that agree to adhere to the Compact, can compliance be verified? Participants are expected to produce an annual report discussing implementation. Is this enough to permit verification? What impact would a strict system of disclosure and verification have on the popularity of the Compact?

6. To the extent there are issues with compliance, can the Compact have negative consequences? Does it allow for corporations to create the appearance of social responsibility without actually engaging in the behavior?

7. Teaching about corporate social responsibility in a traditional corporations or securities class is not always a self evident proposition. Professor Stevelman, however, notes that:

> [A]s CSR is attaining critical mass as a social movement, there is likely to be sustained pressure from consumers and investors for businesses to take fuller account of what had been deemed externalities. Law schools that fail to prepare their students for this new environment—fail to alert them to this broader dimension of corporate counseling—will fall behind.

Faith Stevelman, *Globalization and Corporate Social Responsibility: Challenges for the Academy, Future Lawyers, and Corporate Law*, 53 N.Y.L. Sch. L. Rev. 817, 852 (2008/2009). Do you agree? Is it a disservice not to teach this doctrine in more traditional legal courses?

B. Corporate Social Responsibility and Private Enforcement of Human Rights

The Global Compact seeks to promote a number of principles, including those related to human rights, but presents serious concerns over compliance and enforcement. One possible form of enforcement, at least for violations of international human rights, has been lawsuits in the United States. The most widely used statute is probably the Alien Tort Statute (aka the Alien Tort Claims Act). The Act provides jurisdiction over tort actions "committed in violation of the law of nations or a treaty of the United States." 28 U.S.C. § 1350.

Although adopted in the first Congress in 1789, the statute was largely moribund until the Supreme Court reinvigorated the law in the new millennium.

Sosa v. Alvarez-Machain

United States Supreme Court
542 U.S. 692 (2004)

SOUTER, JUSTICE:

Judge Friendly called the ATS [Alien Tort Statute, 28 USC § 1350] a "legal Lohengrin," IIT v. Vencap, Ltd., 519 F.2d 1001, 1015 (CA2 1975); "no one seems to know whence it came," *ibid.*, and for over 170 years after its enactment it provided jurisdiction in only one case. The first Congress passed it as part of the Judiciary Act of 1789, in providing that the new federal district courts "shall also have cognizance, concurrent with the courts of the several States, or the circuit courts, as the case may be, of all causes where an alien sues for a tort only in violation of the law of nations or a treaty of the United States." Act of Sept. 24, 1789, ch. 20, § 9, 1 Stat. 77.

* * *

... [T]he First Congress understood that the district courts would recognize private causes of action for certain torts in violation of the law of nations, though we have found no basis to suspect Congress had any examples in mind beyond those torts corresponding to Blackstone's three primary offenses: violation of safe conducts, infringement of the rights of ambassadors, and piracy. We assume, too, that no development in the two centuries from the enactment of § 1350 to the birth of the modern line of cases beginning with Filartiga v. Pena-Irala, 630 F.2d 876 (CA2 1980), has categorically precluded federal courts from recognizing a claim under the law of nations as an element of common law; Congress has not in any relevant way amended § 1350 or limited civil common law power by another statute. Still, there are good reasons for a restrained conception of the discretion a federal court should exercise in considering a new cause of action of this kind. Accordingly, we think courts should require any claim based on the present-day law of nations to rest on a norm of international character accepted by the civilized world and defined with a specificity comparable to the features of the 18th-century paradigms we have recognized....

* * *

... Whatever the ultimate criteria for accepting a cause of action subject to jurisdiction under § 1350, we are persuaded that federal courts should not recognize private claims under federal common law for violations of any international law norm with less definite content and acceptance among civilized nations than the historical paradigms familiar when § 1350 was enacted. See, e.g., United States v. Smith, 18 U.S. 153, 5 L. Ed. 57, 5 Wheat. 153, 163–180 (1820) (illustrating the specificity with which the law of nations defined piracy). This limit upon judicial recognition is generally consistent with the reasoning of many of the courts and judges who faced the issue before it reached this Court. See Filartiga, supra, at 890 ("[F]or purposes of civil liability, the torturer has become—like the pirate and slave trader before him—hostis humani generis, an enemy of all mankind"); Tel-Oren, supra, at 781 (Edwards, J., concurring) (suggesting that the "limits of section 1350's reach" be defined by "a handful of heinous actions—each of which violates definable, universal and obligatory norms"); see also In re Estate of Marcos Human Rights Litigation, 25 F.3d 1467, 1475 (CA9 1994) ("Actionable violations of international law must be of a norm that is specific, universal, and obligatory"). And the determination whether a norm is sufficiently definite to support a cause of action should (and, indeed, inevitably must) involve an element of judgment about the practical consequences of making that cause available to litigants in the federal courts.

* * *

JUSTICE SCALIA, with whom the CHIEF JUSTICE and JUSTICE THOMAS join, concurring in part and concurring in the judgment.

There is not much that I would add to the Court's detailed opinion, and only one thing that I would subtract: its reservation of a discretionary power in the Federal Judiciary to create causes of action for the enforcement of international-law-based norms.

Comments and Questions

1. Adopted as part of the Judiciary Act by the first Congress in 1789, the Alien Tort Statute was viewed by some as a "dead letter." Vassilis P. Tzevelekos, *In Search of Alternative Solutions: Can the State of Origin Be Held Internationally Responsible for Investors' Human Rights Abuses that Are Not Attributable to it?*, 35 Brook. J. Int'l L. 155, 209 (2010). Indeed, as the Court noted in *Sosa*, "for over 170 years after its enactment it provided jurisdiction in only one case." *Sosa v. Alvarez-Machain*, 542 U.S. 692, 741 (2004). The Supreme Court's decision, however, reinvigorated the statute and its use has increased dramatically.

2. According to the majority, Congress, in adopting the ATS, was aware of three primary offenses: violation of safe conducts, infringement of the rights of ambassadors, and piracy. Ought the statute to be limited to these claims?

3. Justice Souter suggests that the common law will play a role in determining the conduct ensnared by the provision. The reference suggests that the law in the area will be determined by the courts. What sorts of concerns might this raise? Is this what Justice Scalia is addressing in his dissent?

4. The Court indicated that claims for violations of international law under the ATS should not be recognized unless "definite." How might one prove that a principle of international law is sufficiently "definite" to sustain a cause of action?

5. Justice Breyer, in his concurring opinion, argued that comity should be part of the analysis. "I would ask whether the exercise of jurisdiction under the ATS is con-

sistent with those notions of comity that lead each nation to respect the sovereign rights of other nations by limiting the reach of its laws and their enforcement." Do you agree?

6. What does Judge Friendly mean in his reference to the statute as a legal Lohengrin? Lohengrin was a knight of the Holy Grail who, when asked his name by his spouse, disappeared, never to return.

7. In many ways, the Alien Tort Statute is unique. As one commentator noted: "[N]o domestic court in the European Union has per se civil jurisdiction over violations of international law committed abroad by corporations." Jan Wouters & Cedric Ryngaert, *Litigation for Overseas Corporate Human Rights Abuses in the European Union: The Challenge of Jurisdiction*, 40 Geo. Wash. Int'l L. Rev. 939, 944 (2009). What do you make of this? Ought the statute to be applied in other jurisdictions? What impact might this have?

———————

Although *Sosa* involved an individual, the Alien Tort Statute has increasingly been used against corporations. This can raise difficult issues, particularly where corporate participation in the alleged human rights violations is indirect.

Kiobel v. Royal Dutch Petroleum Co.

Supreme Court of the United States
133 S.Ct. 1659 (2013)

Chief Justice Roberts delivered the opinion of the Court:

Petitioners were residents of Ogoniland, an area of 250 square miles located in the Niger delta area of Nigeria and populated by roughly half a million people. When the complaint was filed, respondents Royal Dutch Petroleum Company and Shell Transport and Trading Company, p.l.c., were holding companies incorporated in the Netherlands and England, respectively. Their joint subsidiary, respondent Shell Petroleum Development Company of Nigeria, Ltd. (SPDC), was incorporated in Nigeria, and engaged in oil exploration and production in Ogoniland. According to the complaint, after concerned residents of Ogoniland began protesting the environmental effects of SPDC's practices, respondents enlisted the Nigerian Government to violently suppress the burgeoning demonstrations. Throughout the early 1990's, the complaint alleges, Nigerian military and police forces attacked Ogoni villages, beating, raping, killing, and arresting residents and destroying or looting property. Petitioners further allege that respondents aided and abetted these atrocities by, among other things, providing the Nigerian forces with food, transportation, and compensation, as well as by allowing the Nigerian military to use respondents' property as a staging ground for attacks.

Following the alleged atrocities, petitioners moved to the United States where they have been granted political asylum and now reside as legal residents. See Supp. Brief for Petitioners 3, and n. 2. They filed suit in the United States District Court for the

Southern District of New York, alleging jurisdiction under the Alien Tort Statute and requesting relief under customary international law.…

II

Passed as part of the Judiciary Act of 1789, the ATS was invoked twice in the late 18th century, but then only once more over the next 167 years. Act of Sept. 24, 1789, § 9, 1 Stat. 77; … The statute provides district courts with jurisdiction to hear certain claims, but does not expressly provide any causes of action. We held in *Sosa v. Alvarez-Machain*, 542 U.S. 692, 714, 124 S.Ct. 2739, 159 L.Ed.2d 718 (2004), however, that the First Congress did not intend the provision to be "stillborn." The grant of jurisdiction is instead "best read as having been enacted on the understanding that the common law would provide a cause of action for [a] modest number of international law violations." *Id.,* at 724, 124 S.Ct. 2739. We thus held that federal courts may "recognize private claims [for such violations] under federal common law." *Id.,* at 732, 124 S.Ct. 2739. The Court in *Sosa* rejected the plaintiff's claim in that case for "arbitrary arrest and detention," on the ground that it failed to state a violation of the law of nations with the requisite "definite content and acceptance among civilized nations." *Id.,* at 699, 732, 124 S.Ct. 2739.

The question here is not whether petitioners have stated a proper claim under the ATS, but whether a claim may reach conduct occurring in the territory of a foreign sovereign. Respondents contend that claims under the ATS do not, relying primarily on a canon of statutory interpretation known as the presumption against extraterritorial application. That canon provides that "[w]hen a statute gives no clear indication of an extraterritorial application, it has none," *Morrison v. National Australia Bank Ltd.,* 561 U.S. 247, ___, 130 S.Ct. 2869, 2878, 177 L.Ed.2d 535 (2010), and reflects the "presumption that United States law governs domestically but does not rule the world," *Microsoft Corp. v. AT & T Corp.,* 550 U.S. 437, 454, 127 S.Ct. 1746, 167 L.Ed.2d 737 (2007).

This presumption "serves to protect against unintended clashes between our laws and those of other nations which could result in international discord.".…

We typically apply the presumption to discern whether an Act of Congress regulating conduct applies abroad.… The ATS, on the other hand, is "strictly jurisdictional." *Sosa,* 542 U.S., at 713, 124 S.Ct. 2739. It does not directly regulate conduct or afford relief. It instead allows federal courts to recognize certain causes of action based on sufficiently definite norms of international law. But we think the principles underlying the canon of interpretation similarly constrain courts considering causes of action that may be brought under the ATS.

Indeed, the danger of unwarranted judicial interference in the conduct of foreign policy is magnified in the context of the ATS, because the question is not what Congress has done but instead what courts may do. This Court in *Sosa* repeatedly stressed the need for judicial caution in considering which claims could be brought under the ATS, in light of foreign policy concerns. As the Court explained, "the potential [foreign policy] implications … of recognizing.… causes [under the ATS] should make courts particularly wary of impinging on the discretion of the Legislative and Executive Branches in managing foreign affairs." *Id.*, at 727, 124 S.Ct. 2739; see also *id.*, at 727–728, 124 S.Ct. 2739 ("Since many attempts by federal courts to craft remedies for the violation of new norms of international law would raise risks of adverse foreign policy consequences, they should be undertaken, if at all, with great caution"); *1665 id.*, at 727, 124 S.Ct. 2739 ("[T]he possible collateral consequences of making international rules privately actionable argue for judicial caution"). These concerns, which are implicated in any case arising under the ATS, are all the more pressing when the question is whether a cause of action under the ATS reaches conduct within the territory of another sovereign.

These concerns are not diminished by the fact that *Sosa* limited federal courts to recognizing causes of action only for alleged violations of international law norms that are "'specific, universal, and obligatory.'" *Id.*, at 732, 124 S.Ct. 2739 (quoting *In re Estate of Marcos, Human Rights Litigation,* 25 F.3d 1467, 1475 (C.A.9 1994)). As demonstrated by Congress's enactment of the Torture Victim Protection Act of 1991, 106 Stat. 73, note following 28 U.S.C. § 1350, identifying such a norm is only the beginning of defining a cause of action. See *id.*, § 3 (providing detailed definitions for extrajudicial killing and torture); *id.*, § 2 (specifying who may be liable, creating a rule of exhaustion, and establishing a statute of limitations). Each of these decisions carries with it significant foreign policy implications.

The principles underlying the presumption against extraterritoriality thus constrain courts exercising their power under the ATS.

III

Petitioners contend that even if the presumption applies, the text, history, and purposes of the ATS rebut it for causes of action brought under that statute....

To begin, nothing in the text of the statute suggests that Congress intended causes of action recognized under it to have extraterritorial reach. The ATS covers actions by aliens for violations of the law of nations, but that does not imply extraterritorial reach — such violations affecting aliens can occur either within or outside the United States. Nor does the fact that the text reaches "*any* civil action" suggest application to torts committed abroad; it is well established that generic terms like "any" or "every" do not rebut the presumption against extraterritoriality....

Petitioners make much of the fact that the ATS provides jurisdiction over civil actions for "torts" in violation of the law of nations. They claim that in using that word, the First Congress "necessarily meant to provide for jurisdiction over extraterritorial transitory torts that could arise on foreign soil." Supp. Brief for Petitioners 18. For support, they cite the common-law doctrine that allowed courts to assume jurisdiction over such "transitory torts," including actions for personal injury, arising abroad. See *Mostyn v. Fabrigas,* 1 Cowp. 161, 177, 98 Eng. Rep. 1021, 1030 (1774) (Mansfield, L.) ("[A]ll actions of a transitory nature that arise abroad may be laid as happening in an English county"); *Dennick v. Railroad Co.,* 103 U.S. 11, 18, 26 L.Ed. 439 (1881) *1666* ("Wherever, by either the common law or the statute law of a State, a right of action has become fixed and a legal liability incurred, that liability may be enforced and the right of action pursued in any court which has jurisdiction of such matters and can obtain jurisdiction of the parties").

Under the transitory torts doctrine, however, "the only justification for allowing a party to recover when the cause of action arose in another civilized jurisdiction is a well founded belief that it was a cause of action in that place." *Cuba R. Co. v. Crosby,* 222 U.S. 473, 479, 32 S.Ct. 132, 56 L.Ed. 274 (1912) (majority opinion of Holmes, J.). The question under *Sosa* is not whether a federal court has jurisdiction to entertain a cause of action provided by foreign or even international law. The question is instead whether the court has authority to recognize a cause of action under U.S. law to enforce a norm of international law. The reference to "tort" does not demonstrate that the First Congress "necessarily meant" for those causes of action to reach conduct in the territory of a foreign sovereign. In the end, nothing in the text of the ATS evinces the requisite clear indication of extraterritoriality.

Nor does the historical background against which the ATS was enacted overcome the presumption against application to conduct in the territory of another sovereign. See *Morrison, supra,* at ___, 130 S.Ct., at 2883 (noting that "[a]ssuredly context can be consulted" in determining whether a cause of action applies abroad). We explained in *Sosa* that when Congress passed the ATS, "three principal offenses against the law of nations" had been identified by Blackstone: violation of safe conducts, infringement of the rights of ambassadors, and piracy. 542 U.S., at 723, 724, 124 S.Ct. 2739; see 4 W. Blackstone, Commentaries on the Laws of England 68 (1769). The first two offenses have no necessary extraterritorial application. Indeed, Blackstone—in describing them—did so in terms of conduct occurring within the forum nation....

* * *

Nor does the historical background against which the ATS was enacted overcome the presumption against application to conduct in the territory of another sovereign. See *Morrison, supra,* at ___, 130 S.Ct., at 2883 (noting that "[a]ssuredly context can be consulted" in determining whether a cause of action applies abroad). We explained in *Sosa* that when Congress passed the ATS, "three principal offenses against the law of nations" had been identified by Blackstone: violation of safe conducts, infringement of the rights of ambassadors, and piracy.542 U.S., at 723, 724, 124 S.Ct. 2739; see 4 W. Blackstone, Commentaries on the Laws of England 68 (1769). The first two offenses have no necessary extraterritorial application. Indeed, Blackstone—in describing them—did so in terms of conduct occurring within the forum nation. See *ibid.* (describing the right of safe conducts for those "who are here"); 1 *id.,* at 251 (1765) (explaining that safe conducts grant a member of one society "a right to intrude into another"); *id.,* at 245–248 (recognizing the king's power to "receiv[e] ambassadors at home" and detailing their rights in the state "wherein they are appointed to reside"); see also E. De Vattel, Law of Nations 465 (J. Chitty et al. transl. and ed. 1883) ("[O]n his entering the country to which he is sent, and making himself known, [the ambassador] is under the protection of the law of nations ...")....

The third example of a violation of the law of nations familiar to the Congress that enacted the ATS was piracy. Piracy typically occurs on the high seas, beyond the territorial jurisdiction of the United States or any other country. See 4 Blackstone, *supra*, at 72 ("The offence of piracy, by common law, consists of committing those acts of robbery and depredation upon the high seas, which, if committed upon land, would have amounted to felony there"). This Court has generally treated the high seas the same as foreign soil for purposes of the presumption against extraterritorial application. See, *e.g., Sale v. Haitian Centers Council, Inc.,* 509 U.S. 155, 173–174, 113 S.Ct. 2549, 125 L.Ed.2d 128 (1993) (declining to apply a provision of the Immigration and Nationality Act to conduct occurring on the high seas); *Argentine Republic v. Amerada Hess Shipping Corp.,* 488 U.S. 428, 440, 109 S.Ct. 683, 102 L.Ed.2d 818 (1989) (declining to apply a provision of the Foreign Sovereign Immunities Act of 1976 to the high seas). Petitioners contend that because Congress surely intended the ATS to provide jurisdiction for actions against pirates, it necessarily anticipated the statute would apply to conduct occurring abroad.

Applying U.S. law to pirates, however, does not typically impose the sovereign will of the United States onto conduct occurring within the territorial jurisdiction of another sovereign, and therefore carries less direct foreign policy consequences. Pirates were fair game wherever found, by any nation, because they generally did not operate within any jurisdiction. See 4 Blackstone, *supra*, at 71. We do not think that the existence of a cause of action against them is a sufficient basis for concluding that other causes of action under the ATS reach conduct that does occur within the territory of another sovereign; pirates may well be a category unto themselves. See *Morrison,* 561 U.S., at ___, 130 S.Ct., at 2883 ("[W]hen a statute provides for some extraterritorial application, the presumption against extraterritoriality operates to limit that provision to its terms"); see also *Microsoft Corp.,* 550 U.S., at 455–456, 127 S.Ct. 1746.

* * *

We therefore conclude that the presumption against extraterritoriality applies to claims under the ATS, and that nothing in the statute rebuts that presumption. "[T]here is no clear indication of extraterritoriality here," *Morrison,* 561 U.S., at ___, 130 S.Ct., at 2883, and petitioners' case seeking relief for violations of the law of nations occurring outside the United States is barred.

IV

On these facts, all the relevant conduct took place outside the United States. And even where the claims touch and concern the territory of the United States, they must do so with sufficient force to displace the presumption against extraterritorial application. See *Morrison,* 561 U.S. 247, 130 S.Ct., at 2883–2888. Corporations are often present in many countries, and it would reach too far to say that mere corporate presence suffices. If Congress were to determine otherwise, a statute more specific than the ATS would be required.

The judgment of the Court of Appeals is affirmed.

It is so ordered.

Comments and Questions

1. Some saw the decision as a significant blow to the protection of international human rights. *See* Robert C. Bird, Daniel R. Cahoy & Lucien J. Dhooge, *Corporate Voluntarism and Liability for Human Rights in a Post-Kiobel World*, 102 Ky. L.J. 601 (2013–2014) ("Kiobel struck a blow to human rights jurisprudence, disabling one of the few viable remaining vehicles in the world for victims of human rights to seek redress through a national court."). Do you agree?

2. Is the reasoning persuasive? The Court gave a number of historical examples that involve behavior in the United States but one that did not, piracy. Is the Court's explanation of this example convincing in finding that the statute was not intended to have extraterritorial application?

3. Four Justices (Breyer, Ginsburg, Sotomayor, and Kagan) agreed with the conclusions of the majority but not the reasoning. In a concurring opinion, written by Justice Breyer, he asserted that the statute provided "jurisdiction only where distinct American interests are at issue." Because the corporate defendants had a "minimal and indirect American presence" (both had New York offices), Justice Breyer concluded that the action did not help to "vindicate a distinct American interest." What difference in application would this standard have made?

4. What sorts of challenges to corporate behavior may survive the reasoning of this decision? Does the relevant behavior have to occur in the United States or can a claim be brought for some behavior that occurs overseas? Will it, for example, be enough to allege violations by a subsidiary in another country and allege that the subsidiary was subject to "general corporate supervision" by the parent in the US? For one circuit's answer, see *Balintulo v. Ford Motor Co.*, 796 F.3d 160, 168 (2nd Cir. 2015).

———

Assuming the plaintiffs can survive the barriers created by *Kiobel*, they still must allege a violation of the law of nations. Despite the concerns expressed in the concurring opinion by Justice Scalia in *Sosa* and the cautionary admonitions in the majority opinions, courts have been willing to expand the concept of the law of nations beyond those in place in 1789.

Doe v. Nestle USA, Inc.

United States Court of Appeals. Ninth Circuit
766 F.3d 1013 (2014) (rehearing and rehearing en banc denied, May 6, 2015)

D.W. Nelson, Senior Circuit Judge:

I. Background

The use of child slave labor in the Ivory Coast is a humanitarian tragedy. Studies by International Labour Organization, UNICEF, the Department of State, and numerous other organizations have confirmed that thousands of children are forced to work without pay in the Ivorian economy. Besides the obvious moral implications, this widespread use of child slavery contributes to poverty in the Ivory Coast, degrades its victims by treating them as commodities, and causes long-term mental and physical trauma.

The plaintiffs in this case are three victims of child slavery. They were forced to work on Ivorian cocoa plantations for up to fourteen hours per day six days a week, given only scraps of food to eat, and whipped and beaten by overseers. They were locked in small rooms at night and not permitted to leave the plantations, knowing that children who tried to escape would be beaten or tortured. Plaintiff John Doe II witnessed guards cut open the feet of children who attempted to escape, and John Doe III knew that the guards forced failed escapees to drink urine.

Though tarnished by these atrocities, the Ivory Coast remains a critical part of the international chocolate industry, producing seventy percent of the world's supply of cocoa. The defendants in this case dominate the Ivorian cocoa market. Although the defendants do not own cocoa farms themselves, they maintain and protect a steady supply of cocoa by forming exclusive buyer/seller relationships with Ivorian farms. The defendants are largely in charge of the work of buying and selling cocoa, and import most of the Ivory Coast's cocoa harvest into the United States. The defendants' involvement in the cocoa market gives them economic leverage, and along with other large multinational companies, the defendants effectively control the production of Ivorian cocoa.

To maintain their relationships with Ivorian farms, the defendants offer both financial assistance and technical farming assistance designed to support cocoa agriculture. The financial assistance includes advanced payment for cocoa and spending money for the farmers' personal use. The technical support includes equipment and training in growing techniques, fermentation techniques, farm maintenance, and appropriate labor practices. The technical support is meant to expand the farms' capacity and act as a quality control mechanism, and either the defendants or their agents visit farms several times per year as part of the defendants' training and quality control efforts.

The defendants are well aware of the child slavery problem in the Ivory Coast. They acquired this knowledge firsthand through their numerous visits to Ivorian farms. Additionally, the defendants knew of the child slave labor problems in the Ivorian cocoa sector due to the many reports issued by domestic and international organizations.

Despite their knowledge of child slavery and their control over the cocoa market, the defendants operate in the Ivory Coast "with the unilateral goal of finding the cheapest sources of cocoa." The defendants continue to supply money, equipment, and training to Ivorian farmers, knowing that these provisions will facilitate the use of forced child labor. The defendants have also lobbied against congressional efforts to curb the use of child slave labor. In 2001, the House of Representatives passed a bill that would have required United States importers and manufacturers to certify and label their products "slave free." The defendants and others in the chocolate industry rallied against the bill, urging instead the adoption of a private, voluntary enforcement mechanism. A voluntary enforcement system was eventually adopted, a result that, according to the plaintiffs, "in effect guarantee[d] the continued use of the cheapest labor available to produce [cocoa] — that of child slaves."

The plaintiffs filed a proposed class action in the United States District Court for the Central District of California, alleging that the defendants were liable under the ATS for aiding and abetting child slavery in the Ivory Coast. The district court granted the defendants' motion to dismiss in a detailed opinion, which concluded that corporations cannot be sued under the ATS, and that even if they could, the plaintiffs failed to allege the elements of a claim for aiding and abetting slave labor. The plaintiffs declined to amend their complaint, and appeal the district court's order.

* * *

A. Corporate Liability under the ATS

The primary focus of international law, although not its exclusive focus, is the conduct of states. *Kiobel v. Royal Dutch Petroleum Co.,* 621 F.3d 111, 165 (2d Cir.2010) (Leval, J., concurring) ("*Kiobel I* "). Many of its prohibitions therefore only apply to state action, and an important issue in ATS litigation can be determining whether the norm asserted by the plaintiff is applicable to both state actors and private actors. This issue is illustrated by the contrasting decisions of the D.C. Circuit in *Tel-Oren v. Libyan Arab Republic* and the Second Circuit in *Kadic v. Karadzic.* In *Tel-Oren,* Judge Edwards concluded that the plaintiffs' ATS claim was barred because there was no consensus that international law applied to torture carried out by non-state actors. 726 F.2d 774, 791–95 (D.C.Cir.1984). In *Kadic,* by contrast, the Second Circuit held that international law's prohibition on genocide applies regardless of whether the perpetrator is acting on behalf of a state. 70 F.3d 232, 241–42 (2d Cir.1995).

The Supreme Court's only allusion to corporate liability occurred in a footnote that referenced these discussions in *Tel-Oren* and *Kadic. Sosa,* 542 U.S. at 732 n. 20, 124 S.Ct. 2739. In the footnote, the Court directed federal courts contemplating the recognition of new ATS claims to consider "whether international law extends the scope of liability for a violation of a given norm to the perpetrator being sued, if the defendant is a *private actor such as a corporation or individual." Id.* (emphasis added).

The issue of corporate liability has been more thoroughly examined in the circuit courts, which have disagreed about whether and under what circumstances corporations can face liability for ATS claims. *Kiobel I,* 621 F.3d at 145; *Doe v. Exxon Mobil Corp.,* 654 F.3d 11, 57 (D.C.Cir.2011), *vacated on other grounds by* 527 Fed.Appx. 7 (D.C.Cir.2013); *Sarei v. Rio Tinto, PLC,* 671 F.3d 736, 747 (9th Cir.2011), *vacated on other grounds by* ___ U.S. ___, 133 S.Ct. 1995, 185 L.Ed.2d 863 (2013); *Flomo,* 643 F.3d at 1020–21. Here, we reaffirm the corporate liability analysis reached by the en banc panel of our circuit in *Sarei v. Rio Tinto.*

In *Sarei,* the plaintiffs sought to hold corporate defendants liable for aiding and abetting genocide and war crimes. We first rejected the defendants' argument that corporations can never be sued under the ATS. Rather than adopting a blanket rule of immunity or liability, the *Sarei* court held that for each ATS claim asserted by the plaintiffs, a court should look to international law and determine whether corporations are subject to the norms underlying that claim. *Id.* at 748 ("*Sosa* expressly frames the relevant international-law inquiry to be the scope of liability of private actors for a violation of the 'given norm,' i.e. an international-law inquiry specific to each cause of action asserted."). Thus, we adopted a norm-by-norm analysis of corporate liability.

The *Sarei* court then conducted corporate liability analyses for the two norms underlying the plaintiffs' claims, the norm against genocide and the norm against war crimes. *Id.* at 759–61, 764–65. The en banc panel observed that both norms apply to states, individuals, and groups, and that the applicability of the norms turns on the "specific identity of the *victims* rather than the identity of the *perpetrators.*" *Id.* at 760, 764–65 (emphasis added). Thus, we concluded that the norms were "universal" or applicable to "all actors," and, consequently, applicable to corporations. *Id.* at 760, 765. We reasoned that allowing an actor to "avoid liability merely by incorporating" would be inconsistent with the universal quality of these norms. *See id.* at 760 (discussing genocide).

In *Sarei* we also explained that a norm could form the basis for an ATS claim against a corporation even in the absence of a decision from an international tribunal enforcing that norm against a corporation. *Id.* at 761 ("We cannot be bound to find liability only where international fora have imposed liability."). *Contra* Kiobel *I,* 621 F.3d at 131–45. We explained that the absence of decisions finding corporations liable does not imply that corporate liability is a legal impossibility under international law, and also noted that the lack of decisions holding corporations liable could be explained by strategic considerations. *Sarei,* 671 F.3d at 761 (citing Jonathan A. Bush,*The Prehistory of Corporations and Conspiracy in International Criminal Law: What Nuremberg Really Said,* 109 Colum. L.Rev. 1094, 1149–68 (2009)). Rejecting an analysis that focuses on past enforcement, *Sarei* reaffirmed that corporate liability ultimately turns on an analysis of the norm underlying the ATS claim. *Id.* at 760–61 ("We ... believe the proper inquiry is not whether there is a specific precedent so holding, but whether international law extends its prohibitions to the perpetrators in question.").

We thus established three principles about corporate ATS liability in *Sarei,* that we now reaffirm. First, the analysis proceeds norm-by-norm; there is no categorical rule of corporate immunity or liability. *Id.* at 747–48. Second, corporate liability under an ATS claim does not depend on the existence of international precedent enforcing legal norms against corporations. *Id.* at 760–61. Third, norms that are "universal and absolute," or applicable to "all actors," can provide the basis for an ATS claim against a corporation. *Id.* at 760. To determine whether a norm is universal, we consider, among other things, whether it is "limited to states" and whether its application depends on the identity of the perpetrator. *Id.* at 764–65.

We conclude that the prohibition against slavery is universal and may be asserted against the corporate defendants in this case. Private, non-state actors were held liable at Nuremberg for slavery offenses. *The Flick Case,* 6 Trials of War Criminals (T.W.C.) 1194, 1202. Moreover, the statutes of the International Criminal Tribunals for Rwanda and the former Yugoslavia are broadly phrased to condemn "persons responsible" for enslavement of civilian populations. ICTY Statute Art. 5(c), U.N. S/RES/827 (May 25, 1993); ICTR Statute Art. 3(c), U.N. S/RES/955 (Nov. 8, 1994). The prohibition against slavery applies to state actors and non-state actors alike, and there are no rules exempting acts of enslavement carried out on behalf of a corporation. Indeed, it would be contrary to both the categorical nature of the prohibition on slavery and the moral imperative underlying that prohibition to conclude that incorporation leads to legal absolution for acts of enslavement. *Kiobel I,* 621 F.3d at 155 (Leval, J., concurring) ("The majority's interpretation of international law, which accords to corporations a free pass to act in contravention of international law's norms, conflicts with the humanitarian objectives of that body of law.").

A final point of clarification is in order about the role of domestic and international law. Although international law controls the threshold question of whether an international legal norm provides the basis for an ATS claim against a corporation, there remain several issues about corporate liability which must be governed by domestic law. This division of labor is dictated by international legal principles, because international law defines norms and determines their scope, but delegates to domestic law the task of determining the civil consequences of any given violation of these norms. *Id.* at 172 (Leval, J., concurring); *Exxon,* 654 F.3d at 42–43; *Flomo,* 643 F.3d at 1020. Thus, when questions endemic to tort litigation or civil liability arise in ATS litigation — such as damages computation, joint and several liability, and proximate causation — these issues must be governed by domestic law. Many questions that surround corporate liability fall into this category, including, most importantly, the issue of when the actions of an individual can be attributed to a corporation for purposes of tort liability. Determining when a corporation can be held liable therefore requires a court to apply customary international law to determine the nature and scope of the norm underlying the plaintiffs' claim, and domestic tort law to determine whether recovery from the corporation is permissible.

Our holding that the norm against slavery is universal and thus may be asserted against the defendants addresses only the international legal issues related to corporate liability in this case. We do not address other domestic law questions related to corporate liability, and leave them to be addressed by the district court in the first instance.

B. Aiding and Abetting Liability

We next consider whether the plaintiffs' complaint alleges the elements of a claim for aiding and abetting slavery. Customary international law — not domestic law — provides the legal standard for aiding and abetting ATS claims. *Sarei,* 671 F.3d at 765–66. When choosing between competing legal standards, we consider which one best reflects a consensus of the well-developed democracies of the world. *See Sosa,* 542 U.S. at 732, 124 S.Ct. 2739 (directing federal courts to apply legal norms in ATS litigation that are accepted by "civilized nations"); *Khulumani,* 504 F.3d at 276 (Katzmann, J., concurring) (consulting the Rome Statute's aiding and abetting legal standard in part due to its wide acceptance among "most of the mature democracies of the world").

1. *Mens Rea*

The plaintiffs argue that the required *mens rea* for aiding and abetting is knowledge, specifically, knowledge that the aider and abetter's acts would facilitate the commission of the underlying offense. This knowledge standard dates back to the Nuremberg tribunals, and is well illustrated by the *Zyklon B Case,* 1 Law Reports Of Trials Of War Criminals 93 (1946). There, the defendants supplied poison gas to the Nazis knowing that it would be used to murder innocent people, and were convicted of aiding and abetting war crimes. *Id.* at 101. An analogous knowledge standard is applied in *The Flick Case,* where a defendant was convicted of aiding and abetting war crimes for donating money to the leader of the SS, knowing that it would be used to support a criminal organization. 6 T.W.C. 1216–17, 1220–21; *see also The Ministries Case,* 14 T.W.C. 622 (concluding that the defendant's knowledge regarding the intended use of a loan was sufficient to satisfy the *mens rea* requirement, but declining to find that the defendant satisfied the *actus reus* requirement).

As plaintiffs contend, this knowledge standard has also been embraced by contemporary international criminal tribunals. The International Criminal Tribunals for Rwanda and the former Yugoslavia consistently apply a knowledge standard. In *Prosecutor v. Blagojevic,* for instance, the tribunal stated that "[t]he requisite mental element of aiding and abetting is knowledge that the acts performed assist the commission of the specific crime of the principal perpetrator." No. IT-02-60-A, ¶ 127 (ICTY, May 9, 2007) ("*Blagojevic* "); *see also Prosecutor v. Kayishema,* No. ICTR-95-1-T, ¶ 205 (ICTR, May 21, 1999); *Khulumani,* 504 F.3d at 277–79 (Katzmann, J., concurring) (observing that the ICTY and ICTR decisions apply a knowledge standard); *Exxon,* 654 F.3d at 33–34 (same). Additionally, after conducting an extensive review of customary international law, the Appeals Chamber of the Special Court for Sierra Leone recently affirmed this knowledge standard, concluding that "an accused's knowledge of the consequence of his acts or conduct—that is, an accused's 'knowing participation' in the crimes—is a culpable *mens rea* standard for individual criminal liability." *Taylor,* ¶ 483.

However, two of our sister circuits have concluded that knowledge is insufficient and that an aiding and abetting ATS defendant must act with the *purpose* of facilitating the criminal act, relying on the Rome Statute of the International Criminal Court, 37 I.L.M. 999 (1998) ("Rome Statute"). *See Aziz v. Alcolac, Inc.,* 658 F.3d 388, 399–400 (4th Cir.2011); *Presbyterian Church of Sudan v. Talisman Energy, Inc.,* 582 F.3d 244, 259 (2d Cir.2009). These circuits have interpreted the Rome Statute to bar the use of a knowledge standard because it uses the term "purpose" to define aiding and abetting liability:

> [A] person shall be criminally responsible and liable for punishment for a crime within the jurisdiction of the Court if that person ... [f]or the *purpose* of facilitating the commission of such a crime, aids, abets, or otherwise assists in its commission....

Rome Statute, art. 25(3)(c) (emphasis added). Taking this text at face value, as the Second and Fourth Circuits did, it appears that the Rome Statute rejects a knowledge standard and requires the heightened *mens rea* of purpose, suggesting that a knowledge standard lacks the universal acceptance that *Sosa* demands.

Here, we need not decide whether a purpose or knowledge standard applies to aiding and abetting ATS claims. We conclude that the plaintiffs' allegations satisfy the more stringent purpose standard, and therefore state a claim for aiding and abetting slavery. All international authorities agree that "*at least* purposive action ... constitutes aiding and abetting [.]" *Sarei,* 671 F.3d at 765–66 (declining to determine whether the *mens rea* required for an aiding and abetting claim is knowledge or purpose).

Reading the allegations in the light most favorable to the plaintiffs, one is led to the inference that the defendants placed increased revenues before basic human welfare, and intended to pursue all options available to reduce their cost for purchasing cocoa. Driven by the goal to reduce costs in any way possible, the defendants allegedly supported the use of child slavery, the cheapest form of labor available. These allegations explain how the use of child slavery benefitted the defendants and furthered their operational goals in the Ivory Coast, and therefore, the allegations support the inference that the defendants acted with the purpose to facilitate child slavery.

The defendants' alleged plan to benefit from the use of child slave labor starkly distinguishes this case from other ATS decisions where the purpose standard was not met. *See Talisman,* 582 F.3d at 262–64; *Aziz,* 658 F.3d at 390–91, 401. According to the allegations here, the defendants have not merely profited by doing business with known human rights violators. Instead, they have allegedly sought to accomplish their own goals by supporting violations of international law. In *Talisman,* by contrast, the defendant did not in any way benefit from the underlying human rights atrocities carried out by the Sudanese military, and in fact, those atrocities ran contrary to the defendant's goals in the area, and even forced the defendant to abandon its operations. *Talisman,* 582 F.3d at 262. Similarly, in *Aziz,* the plaintiffs alleged that the defendants sold chemicals knowing they would be used to murder Kurds in northern Iraq, but failed to allege that the defendants had anything to gain from the use of chemical weapons. *Aziz,* 658 F.3d at 394, 401. Thus, in *Talisman* and *Aziz,* the purpose standard was not satisfied because the defendants had nothing to gain from the violations of international law, and in *Talisman,* the violations actually ran counter to the defendants' interest. Here, however, the complaint alleges that the defendants obtained a direct benefit from the commission of the violation of international law, which bolsters the allegation that the defendants acted with the purpose to support child slavery.

The defendants' control over the Ivory Coast cocoa market further supports the allegation that the defendants acted with the purpose to facilitate slavery. According to the complaint, the defendants had enough control over the Ivorian cocoa market that they could have stopped or limited the use of child slave labor by their suppliers. The defendants did not use their control to stop the use of child slavery, however, but instead offered support that facilitated it. Viewed alongside the allegation that the defendants benefitted from the use of child slavery, the defendants' failure to stop or limit child slavery supports the inference that they intended to keep that system in place. The defendants had the means to stop or limit the use of child slavery, and had they wanted the slave labor to end, they could have used their leverage in the cocoa market to stop it. Their alleged failure to do so, coupled with the cost-cutting benefit they allegedly receive from the use of child slaves, strongly supports the inference that the defendants acted with purpose.

The defendants' alleged lobbying efforts also corroborate the inference of purpose. According to the complaint, the defendants participated in lobbying efforts designed to defeat federal legislation that would have required chocolate importers and manufacturers to certify and label their chocolate as "slave free." As an alternative to the proposed legislation, the defendants, along with others from the chocolate industry, supported a voluntary mechanism through which the chocolate industry would police itself. The complaint also alleges that when the voluntary enforcement system was eventually put into practice instead of legislation, it "in effect guaranteed the continued use of the cheapest labor available to produce [cocoa] — that of child slaves."

Despite these detailed allegations, the dissent contends that the complaint should be dismissed as implausible under *Ashcroft v. Iqbal*, 556 U.S. 662, 129 S.Ct. 1937, 173 L.Ed.2d 868 (2009). The allegation of purpose is not, however, a bare and conclusory assertion that is untethered from the facts underlying the plaintiffs' claims. Instead, the complaint specifically ties the defendants' alleged purpose to the defendants' economic goals in the Ivory Coast, their control over the cocoa market, and their lobbying efforts. The factual allegations concerning the defendants' goals and business operations give rise to a reasonable inference that the defendants acted with purpose, and that is enough to satisfy *Iqbal. Id.* at 678–79, 129 S.Ct. 1937; *Moss v. U.S. Secret Serv.*, 572 F.3d 962, 969 (9th Cir.2009) ("In sum, for a complaint to survive a motion to dismiss, the non-conclusory 'factual content,' and reasonable inferences from that content, must be plausibly suggestive of a claim entitling the plaintiff to relief.").

We also disagree with the dissent's assertion that the plaintiffs have conceded that their allegations fail to satisfy the purpose standard. The plaintiffs have maintained throughout this appeal that the purpose standard has been satisfied. They only conceded that the defendants did not have the subjective motive to harm children. Indeed, the complaint is clear that the defendants' motive was finding cheap sources of cocoa; there is no allegation that the defendants supported child slavery due to an interest in harming children in West Africa.

This is not to say that the purpose standard is satisfied merely because the defendants intended to profit by doing business in the Ivory Coast. Doing business with child slave owners, however morally reprehensible that may be, does not by itself demonstrate a purpose to support child slavery. Here, however, the defendants allegedly intended to support the use of child slavery as a means of reducing their production costs. In doing so, the defendants sought a legitimate goal, profit, through illegitimate means, purposefully supporting child slavery.

Thus, the allegations suggest that a myopic focus on profit over human welfare drove the defendants to act with the purpose of obtaining the cheapest cocoa possible, even if it meant facilitating child slavery. These allegations are sufficient to satisfy the *mens rea* required of an aiding and abetting claim under either a knowledge or purpose standard.

2. Actus Reus

We next consider whether the plaintiffs have alleged the *actus reus* elements of an aiding and abetting claim. The *actus reus* of aiding and abetting is providing assistance or other forms of support to the commission of a crime. *Blagojevic*, ¶ 127; *Taylor*, ¶ 362; Rome Statute, art. 25(3)(c). As both parties agree, international law further requires that the assistance offered must be substantial. *Blagojevic*, ¶ 127; *Taylor*, ¶ 362. The parties dispute, however, whether international law imposes the additional requirement that the assistance must be specifically directed towards the commission of the crime.

The "specific direction" requirement appears to have originated in decisions issued by the International Criminal Tribunal for the former Yugoslavia. *See Prosecutor v. Tadic*, Case No. IT-94-1-A (ICTY July 15, 1999); *Prosecutor v. Perisic*, Case No. IT-04-81-A, (ICTY Feb. 28, 2013) ("*Perisic*"). In *Tadic*, the Appeals Chamber used the phrase "specifically directed" to distinguish joint criminal enterprise liability from aiding and abetting liability. *Tadic*, ¶¶ 227–29. While joint criminal enterprise liability only requires an individual to engage in conduct that "in some way" assisted the commission of a crime, the Appeals Chamber stated that aiding and abetting liability requires an individual to engage in conduct that is "specifically directed" towards the commission of a crime. *Id.* ¶ 229(ii). In *Perisic*, a later panel of the Appeals Chamber clarified that the specific direction requirement relates to the "link" between the assistance provided and the principal offense, and requires that "assistance must be 'specifically'— rather than 'in some way'—directed towards the relevant crimes." *Perisic*, ¶ 27, 37 (quoting *Tadic*, ¶ 229).

Some Appeals Chamber panels and other international tribunals have explicitly rejected the specific direction requirement. *Prosecutor v. Mrksic*, Case No. IT-95-13/1-A, ¶ 159 (ICTY May 5, 2009) ("[T]he Appeals Chamber has confirmed that 'specific direction' is not an essential ingredient of the *actus reus* of aiding and abetting."); *Blagojevic*, ¶ 189 ("[S]pecific direction has not always been included as an element of the *actus reus* of aiding and abetting."); *Taylor*, ¶ 481. Beneath this controversy, however, there is widespread substantive agreement about the *actus reus* of aiding and abetting. As the Special Court for Sierra Leone Appeals Chambers recently affirmed, "[t]he actus reus of aiding and abetting liability is established by assistance that has a substantial effect on the crimes, not the particular manner in which such assistance is provided." *Taylor*, ¶ 475. What appears to have emerged is that there is less focus on specific direction and more of an emphasis on the existence of a causal link between the defendants and the commission of the crime. However, we decline to adopt an *actus reus* standard for aiding and abetting liability under the ATS. Instead, we remand to the district court with instructions to allow plaintiffs to amend their complaint in light of *Perisic* and *Taylor,* both of which were decided after the complaint in this case was dismissed and this appeal had been filed.

C. Extraterritorial ATS Claims

The defendants' final argument contends that the plaintiffs' ATS claim seeks an extraterritorial application of federal law that is barred by the Supreme Court's recent decision in *Kiobel II,* 133 S.Ct. at 1669. We decline to resolve the extraterritoriality issue, and instead remand to allow the plaintiffs to amend their complaint in light of *Kiobel II.*

* * *

Rather than attempt to apply the amorphous touch and concern test on the record currently before us, we conclude that the plaintiffs should have the opportunity to amend their complaint in light of *Kiobel II.* It is common practice to allow plaintiffs to amend their pleadings to accommodate changes in the law, unless it is clear that amendment would be futile. *Moss,* 572 F.3d at 972 ("Having initiated the present lawsuit without the benefit of the Court's latest pronouncements on pleadings, Plaintiffs deserve a chance to supplement their complaint ..."). Here, the plaintiffs seek to amend their complaint to allege that some of the activity underlying their ATS claim took place in the United States. On the record before us, we are unable to conclude that amendment would be futile, because unlike the claims at issue in *Kiobel II,* the plaintiffs contend that part of the conduct underlying their claims occurred within the United States. *See* Kiobel *II,* 133 S.Ct. at 1669. Moreover, it would be imprudent to attempt to apply and refine the touch and concern test where the pleadings before us make no attempt to explain what portion of the conduct underlying the plaintiffs claims took place within the United States.

We therefore decline to determine, at present, whether the plaintiffs' ATS claim is barred by the Supreme Court's holding in *Kiobel II,* and remand this case to allow the plaintiffs to amend their complaint.

IV. Conclusion

The district court's order is REVERSED, and we VACATE for further proceedings consistent with this opinion.

IT IS SO ORDERED.

Comments and Questions

1. The court did not determine whether the standard should be knowledge or action with the purpose of facilitating the criminal act because both were sufficiently alleged. What would be the impact of a knowledge over an action test? What are the "actions" alleged to have met the standard in this case?

2. The court did not resolve how Kiobel might affect the decision. Speculate. What is likely to happen when the trial court applies the analysis in that case?

3. The decision was put to a vote of the judges on the 9th Circuit for reconsideration en banc. The request did not receive support of a majority of the active judges and,

as a result, was not heard en banc. Nonetheless, a dissent to the denial en banc was issued and joined by eight judges. They opened with the following:

> Unfortunately, the panel majority here has substituted sympathy for legal analysis. I quite agree plaintiffs are deserving of sympathy. They are alleged former child slaves of Malian descent, dragooned from their homes and forced to work as slaves on cocoa plantations in the Ivory Coast. But they do not bring this action against the slavers who kidnapped them, nor against the plantation owners who mistreated them. Instead the panel majority concludes that defendant corporations, who engaged in the Ivory Coast cocoa trade, did so with the *purpose* that plaintiffs be enslaved, hence aiding and abetting the slavers and plantation owners. By this metric, buyers of Soviet gold had the purpose of facilitating gulag prison slavery.

788 F.3d 946 (9th Cir. 2015). Given the analysis in *Kiobel*, is this analysis correct?

The majority notes that the claim is "premised on the existence of a norm of customary international law prohibiting medical experimentation on non-consenting human subjects" and concludes that there is. How does a court determine the existence of a norm of customary international law?

4. Most cases under the ATS involve allegations of some type of state action. *See Kadic v. Karadzic,* 70 F.3d 232, 243 (2d Cir. 1995) ("Torture and summary execution — when not perpetrated in the course of genocide or war crimes — are proscribed by international law only when committed by state officials or under color of law."). How did the court deal with that issue in this case? To the extent that actions can be brought in the absence of state action, what impact might that have on actions under the ATS?

Another statute that has been used to police international behavior by corporations has been the Antiterrorism Act of 1991. *See* 18 U.S.C.S. §2331. The Act provides an express civil cause of action on behalf of any "national of the United States injured in his or her person, property, or business by reason of an act of international terrorism." 18 U.S.C.S. §2333. The provisions of the Act have sometimes been used against corporations.

In re Chiquita Brands International

United States District Court, Southern District of Florida
690 F. Supp. 2d 1296 (2010)

MARRA, DISTRICT JUDGE:

The FARC, established in 1964 by the Colombia Communist Party as its "military wing," is Colombia's largest rebel group and has committed thousands of ransom kidnapings in Colombia, often targeting innocent civilians. Compl. PP 173, 174, 176, 180. FARC is a union of communist militants and peasant self-defense groups. FARC is comprised of 15,000 to 18,000 members, organized into approximately 64 "frentes" or fronts, and operating primarily in sparsely populated areas in Colombia. Compl. P 174. FARC claims to represent the rural poor against Colombia's wealthy classes, and opposes the influence of the United States in Colombia, the privatization of natural resources, and multinational corporations. Compl. P 175.

FARC supports its operations through kidnapings, extortion, drug trafficking and "war taxes" it collects from residents, businesses and landowners. Compl. PP 177–78. In addition to kidnaping twenty-three Americans between 1994 and 1997 alone, FARC has also committed many murders, including killing Americans. Compl. PP 180–82. During the period relevant to this action, FARC held significant influence over, controlled, or was fighting other terrorist organizations for control of labor unions in Colombia's banana growing regions. Compl. PP 179, 198.

On October 8, 1997, the U.S. Secretary of State designated FARC a Foreign Terrorist Organization ("FTO"), a designation that still remains today. This designation was based in part on the U.S. Department of State's conclusion that FARC committed "bombings, murder, kidnaping, extortion, hijacking, as well as terrorist and conventional military action against Colombian political, military and economic targets." Compl. P 185. At the same time, the European Union and Colombian governments also designated FARC as a terrorist organization. Compl. P 183–85.

* * *

Chiquita's Payments and Provisions to FARC: 1989–1997

Chiquita is a multinational corporation incorporated in New Jersey and headquartered in Cincinnati, Ohio. Compl. P 44. Chiquita produces, markets, and distributes bananas and other fresh produce. Compl. P 46. Chiquita is one of the largest banana producers in the world and is a major supplier of bananas throughout North America and Europe. Compl. P 46. It has operations throughout the world, including in Colombia, where it operated through its wholly-owned subsidiary, C.I. Bannanos de Exportacion, S.A. ("Banadex") until approximately May 2004. Compl. P 44. At all times relevant hereto, Banadex was Chiquita's controlled subsidiary, agent and/ or alter ego. Compl. P 45. At all relevant times, Chiquita had over 200 farms in Colombia dedicated to banana production. Compl. P 48.

From 1989 through at least 1997, Chiquita knowingly and intentionally made numerous and substantial secret payments to FARC, and also provided FARC with weapons, ammunition and other supplies through its transportation contractors. Chiquita did so knowing, or consciously avoiding, the fact that FARC was a violent terrorist organization. Compl. P 191. Chiquita's payments to FARC, which began as cash at FARC's request, escalated into regular monthly payments ranging from $20,000.00 to $100,000.00. Over time, the payments were fixed to a percentage of Banadex's gross revenues, with as much as ten percent being diverted to FARC. Compl. P 192.

Chiquita went to great lengths to hide its relationship with FARC. Compl. PP 191–96. The payments were often delivered by a former American military pilot known as "Kaiser," who held a management position with Chiquita in Colombia. Compl. P 193. In order to conceal the payments, Chiquita placed false names and non-existent employees on its payroll, providing the funds on local paydays to regional FARC commanders. Compl. P 194. Chiquita also assisted and/or advised FARC terrorists on how to create front organizations, enabling Chiquita to continue to channel funds to FARC and to mislead law enforcement, regulators, auditors, and anyone else who [*21] might examine Chiquita and Banadex's books and records. Compl. P 195. Chiquita also drew up fictitious contracts with legitimate operating organizations or, alternatively, overvalued existing contracts it maintained with such organizations. This was done for the express purpose of hiding its secret payments to FARC. Compl. P 194–96.

Chiquita also worked with FARC-controlled labor unions, such as Sintrabanano, as another means of channeling payments to FARC. Compl. P 197. Chiquita also collaborated with FARC and assisted FARC in subverting many local labor unions, and wresting control of local labor unions from other terrorist organizations. Compl. PP 198. In doing so, Chiquita anticipated and strived to obtain a competitive advantage over other banana growers facing less accommodating unions. Compl. P 198. FARC also helped Chiquita by harassing its competitors in the region. Compl. P 199. In addition, Chiquita funneled weapons to FARC (and assisted FARC in the transport of weapons) through Chiquita's local transportation contractors. Compl. P 202.

Chiquita's March 19, 2007 Guilty Plea

On March 19, 2007, Chiquita pled guilty to violating U.S. anti-terrorism laws by funding another Colombian terrorist organization, the AUC. In so doing, Chiquita acknowledged that it had for years made payments to FARC as well. Compl. PP 201, 205. Chiquita admitted to using many tactics similar to those alleged above as a means of disguising and hiding its AUC payments. Later, in 2007, as part of the sentence imposed on it pursuant to the guilty plea, Chiquita agreed to pay a $25 million fine to the U.S. government....

* * *

Plaintiff's Allegations of Civil Claims Under the ATA

Enacted as part of the Antiterrorism Act of 1991 ("ATA"), 18 U.S.C. § 2333 provides a cause of action for American nationals injured in their person, property, or business by reason of an act of international terrorism. The statute reads, in relevant part:

> (a) Action and jurisdiction.—Any national of the United States injured in his or her person, property, or business by reason of an act of international terrorism, or his or her estate, survivors, or heirs, may sue therefor in any appropriate district court of the United States and shall recover threefold the damages he or she sustains and the cost of the suit, including attorney's fees. 18 U.S.C. § 2333(a).

International Act of Terrorism

Chiquita argues that Plaintiffs' allegations are insufficient because they fail to plead "an act of international terrorism," as required by 18 U.S.C. § 2333(a). The Court rejects Chiquita's contention.

Section 2333(a) provides that any national of the United States injured "by reason of an act of international terrorism" may sue for damages. Contrary to Chiquita's argument, Plaintiffs need not allege that Chiquita committed the act of terrorism. While ultimately Chiquita's liability will depend on whether its alleged conduct in assisting the FARC can be said to have caused Plaintiffs' injuries, there can be no dispute that Plaintiffs have adequately pled that they were injured by acts of international terrorism. See Linde v. Arab Bank, PLC, 384 F.Supp.2d 571, 581 (E.D.N.Y. 2005).

Section 2331(1) of the ATA defines "international terrorism" as activities that:

(A) involve violent acts or acts dangerous to human life that are a violation of the criminal laws of the United States or of any State, or that would be a criminal violation if committed within the jurisdiction of the United States or of any State;

(B) appear to be intended—

(i) to intimidate or coerce a civilian population;

(ii) to influence the policy of a government by intimidation or coercion; or

(iii) to affect the conduct of a government by mass destruction, assassination or kidnaping; and

(C) occur primarily outside the territorial jurisdiction of the United States, or transcend national boundaries in terms of the means by which they are accomplished, the persons they appear intended to intimidate or coerce, or the locale in which their perpetrators operate or seek asylum.

Plaintiffs allege that FARC was designated in 1997 as a Foreign Terrorist Organization ("FTO") pursuant to 8 U.S. C. § 1189 by the United States Secretary of State and currently remains a designated FTO. Comp. P 183–84. When the Secretary of State issued FARC's FTO designation, the U.S. State Department concluded that FARC committed "'bombings, murder, kidnaping, extortion, highjacking, as well as terrorist and conventional military action against Colombian political, military and economic targets.'" Comp. P 185. Plaintiffs allege that FARC opposes the influence of the United States in Colombia. Comp. P 175. Plaintiffs also allege that FARC has been responsible for most of the ransom kidnapings in Colombia, targeting wealthy landowners, foreign tourists, prominent international and domestic officials and ordinary civilians. Comp. P 176. Plaintiffs claim that FARC has a history of kidnaping Americans, specifically that it kidnaped twenty-three Americans between 1994 and 1997. Comp. P 181. Plaintiffs further assert that all five American missionaries in this case were kidnaped, held hostage, and eventually murdered by FARC, which was confirmed by the Colombian National Prosecutor's Office in 2007. Comp. P 49–148, 171. Plaintiffs allegations are sufficient to state predicate acts of international terrorism pursuant to section 2331(1) of the ATA.

* * *

The Restatement (Second) of Torts § 876(b) provides that, "[f]or harm resulting to a third person from the tortious conduct of another, one is subject to liability if he … knows that the other's conduct constitutes a breach of duty and gives substantial assistance or encouragement to the other so to conduct himself." The United States

Court of Appeals for the District of Columbia Circuit set forth the scope of civil aiding and abetting liability in Halberstam v. Welch, 705 F.2d 472, 227 U.S. App. D.C. 167 (D.C. Cir. 1983). The United States Supreme Court has described Halberstam as a "comprehensive opinion on the subject." See Central Bank, 511 U.S. at 181. To support a civil aiding and abetting claim, Plaintiffs must show:

> (1) the party whom the defendant aids must perform a wrongful act that causes an injury; (2) the defendant must be generally aware of his role as part of an overall illegal or tortious activity at the time that he provides the assistance; (3) the defendant must knowingly and substantially assist the principal violation. Halberstam, 705 F.2d at 477; Cox v. Administrator U.S. Steel & Carnegie, 17 F.3d 1386 (11th Cir. 1994). See also Burnett v. Al Baraka Inv. & Dev. Corp., 274 F.Supp.2d 86, 105 (D.D.C.2003) (finding plaintiffs sufficiently alleged aiding and abetting under ATA where complaint stated that defendant knowingly provided funds directly to terrorist organization in furtherance of terrorist activities).

Additionally, the Eleventh Circuit held in Schneberger v. Wheeler, 859 F.2d 1477 (11th Cir. 1988) that knowledge of the violation and of one's own role in the violation are required to satisfy the test for aider and abetter. Id. at 1480. "This knowledge may be inferred from circumstantial evidence." Id. In particular, "if the method or transaction is atypical or lacks business justification, it may be possible to infer the knowledge necessary for aiding and abetting liability." Woodward v. Metro Bank of Dallas, 522 F.2d 84, 97 (5th Cir. 1975)

Here, Plaintiffs' allegations support aiding and abetting liability. The Amended Complaint alleges that the monetary instruments and weapons provided to FARC by Chiquita provided substantial assistance to international terrorism. Plaintiffs' Amended Complaint describes the wrongful acts performed by the FARC, Chiquita's general awareness of its role as part of an overall illegal activity, and Chiquita's knowing and substantial assistance to the principal violations. These allegations are well within the mainstream of aiding and abetting liability. See Halberstam, 705 F.2d at 477. Moreover, Plaintiffs' make detailed allegations of "atypical practices" from which it is possible to infer knowledge necessary for aiding and abetting liability pursuant to Woodward, 522 F.2d at 97. These allegations include Chiquita making furtive, secret payments, including large sums of cash personally transported and made by a senior Chiquita employee on a regular basis; falsification of names and non-existent employees on Chiquita's payroll to provide funds to regional FARC commanders on local paydays; assistance in creating false front organizations and dummy corporations to channel funds; creation of fictitious contracts with legitimate organizations or overvaluation of existing contracts to bury secret payments in its bookkeeping; cooperation with FARC-controlled labor unions, including Sintrabanano, to channel payments to FARC, funneling weapons to FARC and assistance of the transport of weapons through Chiquita's local transportation contractors; payments to AUC through intermediaries known as "convivirs"; making false and misleading entries on its books and records; and filing false and/or misleading documents with the

Colombian and United States governments. See Compl. PP 193–198, 202–206, 208, 212. Plaintiffs have sufficiently alleged aiding and abetting liability.

Comments and Questions

1. Chiquita did not actually commit any acts of terrorism. Instead, the claims arose out of the alleged assistance provided by Chiquita to an organization designated by the State Department as a Foreign Terrorist Organization. In short, the cause of action was for aiding and abetting. How does the standard adopted in this case compare to the one adopted by the court in *Talisman* under the Alien Tort Statute?

2. In a criminal case arising out of the payments, Chiquita agreed to a plea of one count of Engaging in Transactions with a Specially-Designated Global Terrorist, 50 U.S.C.S. § 1705(b). The Company agreed to pay a fine of $25 million and be on corporate probation for five years. *See* Sarah A. Altschuller & Amy Lehr, *Corporate Social Responsibility*, 43 Int'l Law. 577, 582 n.31 (2009). As part of the agreement, Chiquita agreed to maintain a "permanent compliance and ethics office" and ensure that the head of the office report "directly to the Chief Executive Officer and to the Board of Directors" at least annually.

3. Why did Chiquita make payments to FARC? In the criminal case, the Company was represented by, among others, Eric Holder, who later became attorney general under Barak Obama. In the response to the Sentencing Memorandum filed by the U.S. Government, Chiquita had this to say about its actions.

> Chiquita ... paid the A.U.C. to prevent its Colombian employees from being kidnapped, injured, or murdered. The threats facing Chiquita were very real, a point the government does not—and cannot—contest. When Chiquita learned in 2003 (and not earlier as the government implies) that the U.S. government had designated the A.U.C. as a foreign terrorist organization, thereby making the payments illegal under U.S. law, Chiquita voluntarily disclosed its intolerable dilemma to the Department of Justice and sought its guidance— guidance that, despite the government's acknowledgment of the "complicated" nature of the life-and-death situation facing Chiquita, was never provided.

Defendant's Response to Government's Sentencing Memorandum, *United States v. Chiquita Brands International, Inc.*, Crim. No. 07-055, Sept. 14, 2007. What do you make of this explanation?

4. Payments made directly to terrorist organizations will likely be rare. Nonetheless, these organizations may try to directly or indirectly access the global financial system, providing potential exposure for financial institutions. Section 2333B prohibits "material support" to terrorist organizations but requires knowledge that the organization was providing the support. What would it take to show knowledge? For some insight into this issue, see *Weiss v. National Westminster Bank PLC*, 768 F.3d 301 (2nd Cir. 2014) (allegations that financial institution provided "material support" to organization that raised funds for a terrorist organization). Assuming knowledge, is it enough that a financial institution provide typical banking services?

C. Corporate Social Responsibility and Private Enforcement under the Federal Securities Laws

Corporations may disclose that they engage in socially responsible behavior. What happens if these activities are misrepresented?

Miriam A. Cherry, *The Law and Economics of Corporate Social Responsibility and Greenwashing*
14 U.C. Davis Bus. L.J. 281 (2014)[11]

One of the most significant challenges to achieving corporate social responsibility (CSR) in business today is the threat of greenwashing. As green technology becomes increasingly common, and consumers request or, in some instances, even demand green products and services, many businesses have become financially incentivized to improve their social and environmental reputations. A firm can increase its reputation legitimately, by investing in sustainable practices or engaging in corporate social responsibility with its emphasis on the triple bottom line—people, profit, planet. Some firms, however, have responded to this new move toward CSR by cultivating a green image without evidencing genuine commitment to change or investing the (sometimes quite considerable) money that such a change would entail. As such, greenwashing may ultimately undermine the credibility of even the most well-meaning and well-implemented CSR efforts.

Greenwashing occurs when a corporation increases its sales or boosts its brand image through environmental rhetoric or advertising, but in reality does not make good on these environmental claims. In an earlier article, my co-author Judd Sneirson and I analyzed the 2011 BP oil spill disaster as a case study of greenwashing in the energy sector. While BP compiled a record rife with safety and environmental violations, at the same time the company mounted a highly successful advertising campaign, portraying itself as environmentally friendly, or at the very least, not as bad as other oil companies, and cast itself as the champion of alternative energy and environmental causes. This disconnect between myth and reality caused us to question whether the law could be more effective in establishing a cause of action for consumers and investors who have been led astray by dubious claims of greenwashing or Faux CSR. Other forms of what Judd Sneirson and I have termed "Faux CSR" involve claims of corporate social responsibility toward workers or investment in local communities that by objective evidentiary standards fail to measure up to reality.

As currently structured in the United States, CSR is a voluntary endeavor that largely relies on the alignment of environmental consciousness and long-term firm reputation with shareholder value, the consciences of corporate managers and direc-

---

11. This work, copyright 2014 by Miriam A. Cherry, was originally published in the *UC Davis Business Law Journal*, vol. 14, pp. 281–303, copyright 2014 by The Regents of the University of California. All rights reserved. Reprinted with permission.

tors, and the goodwill of consumers and investors toward a planet and people-friendly vision. While ideally, the aspects of the triple bottom line would align, the reality at times is far more complicated. Furthermore, the challenge that greenwashing poses to CSR strikes at its very core and indeed, may threaten to undermine its existence. As CSR depends on the support of consumers and investors, if these groups suspect they are being defrauded, they will be more inclined to dismiss all such claims of CSR and corporate environmentalism, regardless of whether those claims are accurate. Such dismissal and cynicism could be seriously detrimental to the CSR endeavor.

In re Ford Motor Co. Secur. Litigation
United States Court of Appeals, Sixth Circuit
381 F.3d 563 (2004)

KENNEDY, CIRCUIT JUDGE:

Plaintiffs allege, not that Ford had an independent duty to disclose the dangerousness of ATX equipped Explorers or the possible loss contingency regarding it, but that Ford made misrepresentations or statements that are misleading absent the disclosure of such material information. In their complaint, plaintiffs allege that Ford made many statements about Ford having experienced earnings improvement and the Explorer having set various sales records that were misleading because Ford knew that such profits and sales were due to its sale of a defective product and that the eventual public revelation of the defect would affect adversely Ford's financial status. However, we have held that "[t]he disclosure of accurate historical data does not become misleading even if ... [the company might predict] less favorable results ... in the future." *In re Sofamor Danek Group*, 123 F.3d 394, 401 n. 3 (6th Cir.1997). Because plaintiffs have not alleged the historical inaccuracy of Ford's financial and earnings' statements, such statements are not misrepresentations.

A misrepresentation or an omission is material only if there is a substantial likelihood that "a reasonable investor would have viewed the misrepresentation or omission as 'having significantly altered the total mix of information made available.'" *In re Sofamor*, 123 F.3d at 400 (quoting *Basic, Inc.*, 485 U.S. at 232, 108 S.Ct. 978). We may properly dismiss a complaint on the ground that the alleged misrepresentations or omissions are immaterial only if "they are so obviously unimportant to a reasonable investor that reasonable minds could not differ on the question of their unimportance." *Helwig*, 251 F.3d at 563 (internal quotation marks, citation and emphasis omitted). "Immaterial statements include vague, soft, puffing statements or obvious hyperbole" upon which a reasonable investor would not rely. *In re K-tel Int'l, Inc. Sec. Litig.*, 300 F.3d 881, 897 (8th Cir.2002). Statements that are "mere puffing" or "corporate optimism" may be forward-looking or "generalized statements of optimism that are not capable of objective verification." *Grossman v. Novell, Inc.* 120 F.3d 1112,1119 (10th Cir.1997). In their complaint, plaintiffs allege that Ford made many misleading statements regarding its commitment to quality, safety, and corporate citizenship, such as: 1) "[A]t Ford quality comes first."; 2) "We aim to be the quality leader"; 3) "Ford has its best quality ever"; 4) Ford is "taking across-the-board actions to improve ... [its] quality."; 5) Ford has made "quality a top priority"; 6) "Ford is a worldwide leader in automotive safety"; 7) Ford has made "quality a top priority"; 8) Ford is "designing safety into ... [its] cars and trucks" because it wants its "customers to feel safe and secure in their vehicles at all times"; 9) Ford "want[s] to make customers' lives ... safer"; 10) Ford has "dedicated ... [itself] to finding even better ways of delivering ... safer vehicles to [the] consumer"; 11) Ford "want[s] to be clear leaders in corporate citizenship"; 12) Ford's "greatest asset is the trust and confidence ... [it] has earned from ... [its] customers"; 13) Ford "is going to lead in corporate social responsibility." Such statements are either mere corporate puffery or hyperbole that a reasonable investor would not view as significantly changing the general gist of available information, and thus, are not material, even if they were misleading. All public companies praise their products and their objectives. Courts everywhere "have demonstrated a willingness to find immaterial as a matter of law a certain kind of rosy affirmation commonly heard from corporate managers and numbingly familiar to the marketplace—loosely optimistic statements that are so vague, so lacking in specificity, or so clearly constituting the opinions of the speaker, that no reasonable investor could find them important to the total mix of information available."....

Comments and Questions

1. What do you make of the court's analysis that the statement Ford "is going to lead in corporate social responsibility" is not actionable as puffery? Does this analysis provide insight into the difficulties of bringing a cause of action for false disclosure relating to corporate social responsibility under the federal securities laws?

2. In contrast, the court in *In re Massey Energy Co. Secur. Litigation*, 883 F. Supp. 2d 597, 617 (W. Va. 2013), addressed the materiality of statements evidencing a commitment to mine safety (that safety was a "first priority every day" and that the company was an "industry leader" in safety). The defendants asserted that statements "regarding its commitment to corporate values, or its claim of industry leadership in safety and compliance" were puffery and therefore not actionable. The court, however, found that "the truth or falsity of Defendants' statements can be determined." The statements of commitment to safety were "closely aligned" to the company's "productivity and success."

3. When might a claim for greenwashing be actionable under the antifraud provisions of the federal securities laws? Are these actions appropriate for shareholders? Would they be better brought by other interest groups such as consumers? Green is not the only possible color at issues. How about "bluewashing?" *See* Robert C. Bird, Daniel R. Cahoy & Lucien J. Dhooge, *Corporate Voluntarism and Liability for Human Rights in A Pot-Kiobel World*, 102 Ky. L.J. 601 (2013–2014) (noting that false reports concerning human rights may be described as "bluewashing" "to note a firm's attempt to cloak itself in the flag of United Nations' principles.").

4. What will be the impact on fraud actions of any increase in mandatory disclosure related to corporate social responsibility? Dodd-Frank, for example, required disclosure about mining safety. *See* Section 1503 of Dodd-Frank. California adopted the Transparency in Supply Chains Act that requires "certain companies to report on their specific actions to eradicate slavery and human trafficking in their supply chains."

Chapter 12

Comparative Corporate Governance

Comparative law has sometimes been defined as a method of "looking at legal problems, legal institutions, and entire legal systems" in order to "gain insights" otherwise unavailable when focusing on a single system. Rudolph B. Schlesinger, et al., Comparative Law 1 (5th ed. 1988). Comparative corporate governance likewise can provide considerable insight.

To some degree, the topic can be addressed by examining the myriad of variations that inevitably emerge among different nation states. Some of these differences can, however, be examined in a more systemic fashion, involving comparisons by geography, by legal system (whether civil and common law), or by stages of development. Yet while often convenient starting points, these broad categories are themselves overgeneralizations that often mask considerable internal differences. Thus, Great Britain and the United States share the same common law roots, yet they diverge significantly in some aspects of corporate governance.

Other variables matter. The problem of monitoring management can vary depending upon a company's ownership configuration. In the United States, most large public companies have a dispersed ownership model, with the largest shareholder often holding no more than a few percent of the outstanding voting shares. Corporate governance in these circumstances has as a central goal the reduction in rent seeking behavior by management.

In contrast, most other countries have an ownership structure premised upon controlling shareholders, whether a family or an investment group. Governance in these circumstances focuses on the need to reduce the rent seeking behavior by large shareholders. At the same time, however, the configuration has advantages. Large owners have a greater incentive to monitor management and ensure shareholder oriented behavior.

Similarly, some countries rely on capital markets as an important if not talismanic mechanism to discipline management. For those that do, the markets are expected to exact a penalty on inefficient management, typically in the form of lower share prices. Jurisdictions that look to capital markets may likewise need to have a rigorous system of disclosure. Only with adequate information can investors react and apply the appropriate penalty or reward.

Yet active and efficient capital markets is often the exception rather than the rule. In their absence, the corporate governance structure may need to be very different.

In those circumstances, disclosure, a critical component of the US system of governance, may not play quite the same role.

Finally, no comparison of corporate governance practices can be complete without at least some consideration of the impact of culture and history. A country's particular development may have considerable impact on the system of corporate governance. The impact of culture (including religion) and history can be difficult to quantify or assess. Nonetheless, they must be examined in determining the appropriate approach to governance and in determining their effectiveness.

I. Corporate Governance Hegemony

As the new millennium dawned, some viewed the evolution of corporate governance as finished. All countries would ultimately adopt the Anglo-American model with a shareholder centric approach to governance.

Henry Hansmann & Reinier Kraakman, *The End of History for Corporate Law*
89 Geo. L.J. 439, 439–41, 450–51, 468 (2001)[1]

Much recent scholarship has emphasized institutional differences in corporate governance, capital markets, and law among European, American, and Japanese companies. Despite very real differences in the corporate systems, the deeper tendency is toward convergence, as it has been since the nineteenth century. The basic law of corporate governance—indeed, most of corporate law—has achieved a high degree of uniformity across developed market jurisdictions, and continuing convergence toward a single, standard model is likely. The core legal features of the corporate form were already well established in advanced jurisdictions one hundred years ago, at the turn of the twentieth century. Although there remained considerable room for variation in governance practices and in the fine structure of corporate law throughout the twentieth century, the pressures for further convergence are now rapidly growing. Chief among these pressures is the recent dominance of a shareholder-centered ideology of corporate law among the business, government, and legal elites in key commercial jurisdictions. There is no longer any serious competitor to the view that corporate law should principally strive to increase long-term shareholder value. This emergent consensus has already profoundly affected corporate governance practices throughout the world. It is only a matter of time before its influence is felt in the reform of corporate law as well.

*   *   *

Recent years, however, have brought strong evidence of a growing consensus on these issues among the academic, business, and governmental elites in leading juris-

---

1. Reprinted with permission of the publisher, Georgetown Law Journal © 2001.

dictions. The principal elements of this emerging consensus are that ultimate control over the corporation should rest with the shareholder class; the managers of the corporation should be charged with the obligation to manage the corporation in the interests of its shareholders; other corporate constituencies, such as creditors, employees, suppliers, and customers, should have their interests protected by contractual and regulatory means rather than through participation in corporate governance; non-controlling shareholders should receive strong protection from exploitation at the hands of controlling shareholders; and the market value of the publicly traded corporation's shares is the principal measure of its shareholders' interests.

* * *

The increasing internationalization of both product and financial markets has brought individual firms from jurisdictions adhering to different models into direct competition. It is now widely thought that firms organized and operated according to the shareholder-oriented model have had the upper hand in these more direct encounters as well. Such firms can be expected to have important competitive advantages over firms adhering more closely to other models. These advantages include access to equity capital at lower cost (including, conspicuously, start-up capital), more aggressive development of new product markets, stronger incentives to reorganize along lines that are managerially coherent, and more rapid abandonment of inefficient investments.

These competitive advantages do not always imply that firms governed by the standard model will displace those governed by an alternative model in the course of firm-to-firm competition, for two reasons. First, firms operating under the standard model may be no more efficient than other firms in many respects. For example, state-oriented Japanese and Korean companies have demonstrated great efficiency in the management and expansion of standardized production processes, while German and Dutch firms such as Daimler Benz and Philips (operating under labor- and management-oriented models, respectively) have been widely recognized for engineering prowess and technical innovation. Second, even when firms governed by the standard model are clearly more efficient than their nonstandard competitors, the cost-conscious standard-model firms may be forced to abandon particular markets for precisely that reason. Less efficient firms organized under alternative models may overinvest in capacity or accept abnormally low returns on their investments in general, and thereby come to dominate a product market by underpricing their profit-maximizing competitors. But if the competitive advantages of standard-model firms do not necessarily force the displacement of nonstandard firms in established markets, these standard-model firms are likely, for the reasons offered above, to achieve a disproportionate share among start-up firms, in new product markets, and in industries that are in the process of rapid change.

The ability of standard-model firms to expand rapidly in growth industries is magnified, moreover, by access to institutional investors and the international equity markets, which understandably prefer shareholder-oriented governance and are influential advocates of the standard model. Those equity investors, after all, are exclusively interested in maximizing the financial returns on their investments. Over time, then, the standard model is likely to win the competitive struggle on the margins, confining other governance models to older firms and mature product markets. As the pace of technological change continues to quicken, this competitive advantage should continue to increase.

* * *

The triumph of the shareholder-oriented model of the corporation over its principal competitors is now assured, even if it was problematic as recently as twenty-five years ago. Logic alone did not establish the superiority of this standard model or of the prescriptive rules that it implies, which establish a strong corporate management with duties to serve the interests of shareholders alone, as well as strong minority shareholder protections. Rather, the standard model earned its position as the dominant model of the large corporation the hard way, by out-competing during the post-World War II period the three alternative models of corporate governance: the managerialist model, the labor-oriented model, and the state-oriented model.

If the failure of the principal alternatives has established the ideological hegemony of the standard model, though, perhaps this should not come as a complete surprise. The standard model has never been questioned for the vast majority of corporations. It dominates the law and governance of closely held corporations in every jurisdiction. Most German companies do not participate in the codetermination regime, and most Dutch companies are not regulated by the managerialist "structure" regime. Similarly, the standard model of shareholder primacy has always been the dominant legal model in the two jurisdictions where the choice of models might be expected to matter most: the U.S. and the U.K. The choice of models matters in these jurisdictions because large companies often have highly fragmented ownership structures. In continental Europe, where most large companies are controlled by large shareholders, the interests of controlling shareholders traditionally dominate corporate policy no matter what the prevailing ideology of the corporate form.

We predict, therefore, that as equity markets evolve in Europe and throughout the developed world, the ideological and competitive attractions of the standard model will become indisputable, even among legal academics. And as the goal of shareholder primacy becomes second nature even to politicians, convergence in most aspects of the law and practice of corporate governance is sure to follow.

Comments and Questions

1. The article was published in early 2001. By late 2001, Enron had filed for bankruptcy, with Worldcom following less than a year later. In the aftermath, Congress passed the Sarbanes-Oxley Act, the most far reaching reform of the securities laws since the Great Depression. Broadly speaking, the Act sought to reform the corporate governance process. What do these developments, if anything, say about the positions taken by Professors Hansmann and Kraakman?

2. What do the authors mean by a "shareholder-centered ideology of corporate law"? Is this an ethno-centric approach to comparative corporate governance? At least

one professor apparently thinks so. *See* Douglas M. Branson, *The Very Uncertain Prospect of "Global" Convergence in Corporate Governance*, 34 Cornell Int'l L.J. 321, 330–31 (2001) (analysis represented "a chauvinistic statement of the Americanocentric convergence thesis."). We address this topic at the end of this chapter.

3. The shareholder centered system is described as one where the managers of the corporation are "charged with the obligation to manage the corporation in the interests of its shareholders." Is that an accurate description of the corporate governance system in the United States?

4. Convergence, the authors contend, arises in part from the competitive advantages that inure to companies adhering to the shareholder-centric model. One of the main advantages is lower cost capital. How does this model promote that goal? Can this only be accomplished through implementation of the shareholder model?

5. The article describes one aspect of the shareholder centric model as a shift in power from controlling to public shareholders. The premise presumably is that a dispersed ownership pattern (such as the one prevalent in the United States) is more efficient than the controlling shareholder model prevalent in most other countries. Is this true? Are there advantages that come with controlling shareholders? *See* Karl Hofstetter, *One Size Does Not Fit All: Corporate Governance for "Controlled Companies,"* 31 N.C. J. Int'l L. & Com. Reg. 597, 614 (2006) ("There is no question that the most obvious advantage of a controlling shareholder lies in the fact that he has interests that are generally aligned with those of the shareholders as a class."). What are the disadvantages?

6. Can you reconcile the argument for convergence with path dependency and the role of history or culture? For a discussion of these issues in the governance context, *see* Lucian Arye Bebchuk & Mark J. Roe, *A Theory of Path Dependence in Corporate Ownership and Governance*, 52 Stan. L. Rev. 127 (1999). For example, a large part of the governance process in the U.S. is a byproduct of self-regulation. Is this a deliberate or accidental form of regulation?

II. Monitoring Management

Corporate governance broadly speaking seeks to reduce agency costs. In some countries, the task is largely left to the market. Self-serving or inefficient management will cause shareholders to vote with their feet. The resulting decline in share prices can reduce the compensation paid to executive officers or potentially generate a takeover that results in the replacement of inefficient management.

Not all countries, however, rely on capital markets as a primary mechanism for monitoring management. The alternatives may arise because of the absence of active capital markets. Alternatively, governance may be explained by path dependency or as a consequence of a different ownership configuration. In those countries, banks and controlling shareholders are often alternative sources for monitoring the behavior of management.

A. Capital Markets and Monitoring

In the United States, the system for monitoring management relies extensively on capital markets as a disciplinary mechanism. Managers that act in an inefficient manner will see share prices drop. That might adversely affect executive compensation, particularly where bonuses and other payment are keyed to share performance. In addition, if the shares are cheap enough, the company may become ripe for a takeover.

In short, management that fails to act in the best interests of shareholders will suffer at the hands of the market. But this method of monitoring management requires the presence of capital markets capable of imposing the requisite penalties. We start the topic with an examination of the largest exchanges by market capitalization.

Franklin Allen & Jun "QJ" Qian,
China's Financial System and the Law
47 Cornell Int'l L.J. 499 (2014)[2]

A Comparison of the Largest Stock Markets in the World in December 2013

Ranking	Stock Exchange	2013 Dec market cap US bn	2013 Dec share turnover
1	NYSE Euronext (US)	17,950	70.9%
2	NASDAQ OMX (US)	6,085	144.6%
3	Tokyo SE Group	4,543	129.6%
4	London SE Group	4,428	46.5%
5	NYSE Euronext (Europe)	3,584	355.2%
6	**Hong Kong Stock Exchange**	**3,101**	**40.9%**
7	**Shanghai SE**	**2,497**	**151.6%**
8	TMX Group	2,114	62.6%
9	Deutsche Börse	1,936	67.8%
10	SIX Swiss Exchange	1,541	45.4%
11	**Shenzhen SE**	**1,452**	**269.3%**
12	Australian SE	1,387	57.7%

Comments and Questions

1. How might capital markets effectively monitor management? What elements need to be present to maximize the effectiveness of capital markets as a monitoring tool? Does a strong disciplining role automatically follow from the existence of an active stock market?

---

2. Copyright © 2014 Cornell International Law Journal. Reprinted with permission.

2. What do you make of this table? The market capitalization of companies listed on the NYSE and NASDAQ almost equal the market capitalization of all other exchanges set out in the table. On the other hand, if you together the market capitalization of the three bolded exchanges from China, they would rank second, ahead of NASDAQ. Given these observations, can you equate size (based upon market capitalization) with ability to discipline?

3. How might the absence of active capital markets affect a system of corporate governance? Is there any way that capital markets in developed countries can improve governance in less developed countries? Data shows that foreign companies listing on a US stock exchange undergo an increase in share prices in their home country. Why might this be the case? The same phenomenon does not occur for foreign companies listed on the LSE. Can you explain this difference in effect?

4. A strong premise of the use of capital markets as a disciplinary mechanism is the requirement of full disclosure. *See* Jill E. Fisch, *Confronting the Circularity Problem in Private Securities Litigation*, 2009 Wis. L. Rev. 333, 335 ("Capital-market discipline through the efficient incorporation and pricing of firm-specific information depends critically upon the existence of informed trading."). Only with such disclosure can the share prices accurately reflect the activities and practices of the company. Does disclosure play the same role in countries without active capital markets?

5. With respect to financial disclosure, Germany has been described as less transparent than the United States. On the other hand, German companies have traditionally looked to banks or controlling shareholders rather than capital markets to monitor management's activities. *See* Katherine V. Jackson, *Towards A Stakeholder-Shareholder Theory of Corporate Governance: A Comparative Analysis*, 7 Hastings Bus. L.J. 309, 365 (2011). To the extent this is the case, would more rigorous disclosure requirements have the same effect in Germany as in the United States? Could they be harmful?

6. Capital markets have historically been more active in common law (rather than civil code) jurisdictions. As a result, some have argued that common law systems are more conducive to capital raising. Yet as one commentator contends, the highest return of any stock market in the period of 1900 to 2000 is Sweden, a civil law country. Brian B. Kim, *Stock Returns, Corporate Governance, and Long-Term Economic Growth*, 35 Ohio N.U. L. Rev. 685, 702 (2009) (noting that "four of the top seven countries with the highest stock returns from 1900 to 2000 were shareholder-oriented economies" but that the list was topped by Sweden). What do you make of this analysis?

7. Capital markets can discipline inefficient management through hostile takeovers. When share prices fall sufficiently, an acquirer will step in, buy the company, and replace inefficient management. What if such a market does not exist? For example, a hostile takeover market really does not exist in Japan. Similarly, with the advent of poison pills, the market has been weakened in the United States. In the absence of such a mechanism, how else might capital markets effectively monitor management?

8. A number of developing countries have tried to use disclosure to affect the behavior of management. In South Africa, for example, the King Code, a voluntary code of corporate governance, recommends that companies employ the triple bottom line, which requires consideration in decision making not only of economic interests, but also social and environmental factors. *See* Philip C. Aka, *Corporate Governance in South Africa: Analyzing the Dynamics of Corporate Governance Reforms in the "Rainbow Nation,"* 33 N.C.J. Int'l L. & Com. Reg. 219, 250 (2007). To encourage its use, the Johannesburg Stock Exchange implemented the Social Responsible Investment Index, a trading index that seeks to measure companies' "policies, performance and reporting in relation to the three pillars of the triple bottom line (environmental, economic and social sustainability), as well as corporate governance practice." In other words, the JSE will provide investors with an easy method of determining compliance. What impact might this have on the behavior of managers?

Corporate disclosure can have multiple purposes. In efficient and active markets, disclosure can directly impact governance. Disclosure can alter share prices, potentially affecting executive compensation or even a company's independence. In that respect, disclosure intersects with the capital markets. Appropriate disclosure may alert shareholders to issues that must be addressed by management, a form of corporate transparency. In those circumstances, disclosure is a sub-category of the governance process that facilitates shareholder governance on a company specific basis. In the latter case, however, the approach has limitations.

Iris H-Y Chiu, *Reviving Shareholder Stewardship: Critically Examining the Impact of Corporate Transparency Reforms in the UK*
38 Del. J. Corp. L. 983 (2014)[3]

Compared to the U.S., the regulatory framework for the exercise of shareholders' corporate governance role in the UK is much more empowering. However, shareholder derivative or securities litigation for publicly-listed companies are not the norm, whether as an expression in corporate governance or as a form of market discipline. Shareholder monitoring in corporate governance, is predominantly expressed in informal forms of dialogue and engagement with management. Such has been the norm in the 1980s and 1990s, and the nature of such engagement may be attributed to the shareholder base of the UK corporate sector, which is characterized by high levels of institutional ownership....

* * *

For the last two decades, the shareholders' corporate governance role in the UK may be regarded as adequately empowered in company law, and enhancements to

---

3. Copyright © 2014 Delaware Journal of Corporate Law. Reprinted with permission.

corporate transparency does not serve the same purpose in the U.S. as a substitutive platform for corporate governance in lieu of rights and powers based in company law. UK policy-makers frown upon the exercise of the shareholders' role in corporate governance via the mechanism of private securities litigation based on defective corporate disclosure. Hence, when the UK had to implement the EU legislation on enhanced corporate transparency requirements relating to periodic securities reporting, the UK made a policy decision to restrict the opportunities for civil litigation in respect of defective periodic securities reporting, only allowing investors to sue if the defective securities disclosure was material and was known or deceitfully concealed. The requirement imposed on investors to prove knowledge or dishonesty is much more onerous than the fraud-on-the-market assumption made in favor of investors in the U.S.

In sum, the corporate governance role of shareholders in the UK is seen as a distinct realm from market discipline in the securities markets. This allows it to be legitimately viewed as a role to be exercised in the private paradigm of the company's internal relations, and is not narrowly framed around corporate transparency and market discipline for securing integrity in corporate accountability. Corporate transparency is therefore a servant to corporate governance in the UK, and provides an informed basis for shareholders to decide how to engage-whether informally or through the exercise of corporate powers provided in the Companies Act 2006. In the U.S., however, a significant part of corporate governance is framed around corporate transparency itself, and the nature of such governance may be regarded as narrowly framed. But such governance, expressed in private securities litigation, provides a visible and vibrant form of market discipline.

2. Lack of Shareholder Monitoring

In the wake of the global financial crisis, faith in the corporate governance role of shareholders in the UK has been shaken. Policy-makers in the UK have articulated their concern that there is a persistent lack of shareholder monitoring of their investee companies. The empowering legal framework for shareholders' rights and enhanced corporate transparency in corporate governance, directors' remuneration, and narrative reporting in the business review have not sustained a vibrant landscape of shareholder monitoring. First, it may be argued that institutional shareholders, being diversified, do not have a keen interest in exercising governance rights and vote with their feet if they need to. Hence, although there has always been evidence of institutional shareholder engagement in the UK, such levels are not particularly vibrant.

Second, the ownership landscape has changed dramatically in the UK in the last decade or so, with institutional ownership falling to approximately 13 percent from over 26 percent in 2008 and over 40 percent in 1998, while foreign ownership has increased to over 40 percent. The decrease in institutional ownership of the corporate sector has weakened the little informal shareholder engagement that has taken place thus far. The change in the dynamics in corporate governance relations has made policy-makers realize the assumption that there is a working regime of informal shareholder engagement led by UK institutions may be increasingly misplaced. Further, the last decade is marked by a noted lack of shareholder engagement, as investors have become much more focused on short-term market gains than on underlying corporate value, in an era characterized by the explosion of financial innovation and development of myriad forms of financial instruments. That said, occurrences of intense shareholder activism carried out in the UK have been due to hedge-fund activism, which is an investment strategy that facilitates "value-extraction." Such shareholder activism is questionably beneficial for the long-term stability of the corporation.

* * *

... [T]he corporate governance role of shareholders in the UK is seen as a distinct realm from market discipline in the securities markets. This allows it to be legitimately viewed as a role to be exercised in the private paradigm of the company's internal relations, and is not narrowly framed around corporate transparency and market discipline for securing integrity in corporate accountability. Corporate transparency is therefore a servant to corporate governance in the UK, and provides an informed basis for shareholders to decide how to engage — whether informally or through the exercise of corporate powers provided in the Companies Act 2006. In the U.S., however, a significant part of corporate governance is framed around corporate transparency itself, and the nature of such governance may be regarded as narrowly framed. But such governance, expressed in private securities litigation, provides a visible and vibrant form of market discipline.

Comments and Questions

1. This article suggests that in Britain, disclosure has traditionally been seen as a subcategory of governance, designed to provide shareholders with information needed to play a meaningful role in the governance process but not necessarily to facilitate market discipline. What are the strengths and weaknesses of this approach?

2. Does this approach work for any ownership configuration? What were some of the factors that facilitated the use of this model in Britain and how are they changing? What impact are these changes having on this model?

3. How might these varying approaches to disclosure actually affect the disclosure regime? Can you come up with some examples of matters important to shareholders wanting to interact with management but not necessary important for efficient trading markets (and vice versa)?

4. What are some of the issues that have arisen in the UK that might provide an impetus to become less reliant on "institutional shareholder engagement" as a means of disciplining management? Can you make the case that the regulatory regime in the US is moving towards a model of "institutional shareholder engagement?"

To the extent that active capital markets play a role in disciplining management, does that mean all countries should strive for these types of markets? Is the goal a viable one? To the extent that they do not, there are alternatives. Companies in one country can list on the exchanges of another.

Yuliya Gusevaa, *Cross-Listings and the New World of International Capital: Another Look at the Efficiency and Extraterritoriality of Securities Law*

44 Geo. J. Int'l L. 411 (2013)[4]

B. The Costs and Benefits of Cross-Listings

... [A] more puzzling question is why a foreign issuer would wish to come specifically to a U.S. market even though, as mentioned earlier in this Article, (a) other global exchanges offer comparable liquidity, execution, and the overall efficiency of trading and (b) the rigorous standards of U.S. securities law and liability may apply to a cross-listed FPI [Foreign Private Issuer].

Historically, there were several incentives for companies to cross-list. The first derived from a deep segmentation of the global capital market and germane information problems preventing cross-border capital flows. For these reasons, cross-listings conveyed information to U.S. investors and positively affected a firm's cost of capital. Second, cross-listings have been traditionally associated with better liquidity of FPI securities. Third, foreign managers believe that through cross-listings they can simultaneously achieve not only better liquidity but also capital raising, marketing, and other corporate objectives. Specifically, many issuers, particularly firms from developing economies, directly raise capital through cross-listings. Others, like issuers from developed European economies, have used cross-listings to establish a foothold in the United States for further acquisitions.

Fourth, for multinational companies cross-listings on major stock exchanges have been traditionally associated with better cross-border "marketability" of not only shares but also their products, which in the opinion of managers outweighs the direct costs of compliance with registration and reporting requirements, especially in cases where share trading volumes are sufficiently high. Finally, some scholars believe that, by coming to the United States, foreign issuers signal to the world that they are willing to be subject to the scrutiny of the U.S. market, private plaintiff-shareholders, and regulatory agencies, and, by thus "bonding" themselves to the United States, are rewarded with a certain valuation premium.

Comments and Questions

1. Cross-listings occur where a company lists on more than one stock exchange. This In the US, it is not unusual for companies based in China and Israel to cross-list in the US. What are some of the reasons companies do this? Are companies from these two countries likely to have the same or different motivations?

2. A number of studies have suggested that cross-listings on US stock exchanges can give rise to significant valuation premiums. What are some possible explanations for this premium? What factors might affect this premium?

---

3. Does the home country of the company engaging in the cross-listing matter? A Staff Report from Federal Reserve Board of NY concluded that "firms cross listing in a more prestigious market enjoy significant valuation gains over the five-year period following the listing." *See* Nicola Cetorelli & Stavros Peristiani, Staff Report No. 747, FRB of NY (Sept. 2010). What does the study mean by "more prestigious"? Why would there be an increase in those instances? Assume you are the CEO of the NYSE. What does this determination suggest about the director regulatory reform for the NYSE?

4. Not all foreign exchanges provide a valuation premium. *See* John C. Coffee, Jr., *Law and the Market: The Impact of Enforcement*, 156 U. Pa. L. Rev. 229 (2007) (noting that "foreign firms incur no listing premium when cross-listing on the London Stock Exchange"). Why might this be the case? Given this, why would companies choose to list on the LSE instead of the NYSE?

5. Do exchanges compete for these cross-listings? What are some possible consequences of this competition? What impact might this have on an exchange's approach to regulation?

B. Controlling Shareholders and Monitoring

In contrast to the United States, public companies in other countries do not typically have a dispersed ownership pattern. Instead, they commonly have a controlling shareholder that has the power to elect at least a majority of directors to the board. *See* Ronald J. Gilson, *Controlling Shareholders and Corporate Governance: Complicating the Comparative Taxonomy*, 119 Harv. L. Rev. 1641 (2006). Controlling shareholders can be investors, industrial groups, or families. They may own their shares directly or indirectly, often through a pyramid ownership structure.

The presence of controlling shareholders can have some benefits. *See* Lucian A. Bebchuk & Assaf Hamdani, *The Elusive Quest for Global Governance Standards*, 157 U. Pa. L. Rev. 1263, 1281 (2009) ("controlling shareholders commonly have both the effective means to monitor management and the incentives to do so."). At the same time, the ownership configuration can allow for controlling shareholder to engage in rent seeking behavior.

Erica Gorga, *Changing the Paradigm of Stock Ownership from Concentrated towards Dispersed Ownership? Evidence from Brazil and Consequences for Emerging Countries*
29 Nw. J. Int'l L. & Bus. 439, 498–99 (2009)[5]

I. Controlling Shareholders' Preferences and Incentives

Controlling shareholders bear significant costs maintaining concentration of ownership and voting rights. They incur the opportunity cost of holding a non-diversified portfolio, costs associated with the lack of liquidity of their investment, and costs of

---

5. Reprinted by special permission of Northwestern University School of Law, *Northwestern Journal of International Law and Business*.

monitoring the operation of the company so as to assure that they will derive profits from their investment. Controlling shareholders benefit by extracting private benefits from the corporation in exchange for incurring these costs.

Some level of benefits extraction by controlling shareholders may be efficient for the corporation and the non-controlling shareholders as well. The controlling shareholders may do a better job in policing the management of public corporations than what market-oriented techniques would achieve in firms with dispersed ownership. The controlling shareholders have lower information costs and have incentives to watch closely what is happening in the corporation, and therefore may be best-situated to recognize problems that could impair corporate results. In light of this, controlling shareholders could serve as an efficient solution to the agency problems that arise in widely-held companies. The controlling shareholders would increase productivity, generating gains to non-controlling shareholders as well. Therefore, non-controlling shareholders should prefer having controlling shareholders manage the corporation, provided that the gains from the "reduction in managerial agency costs" justify the private benefits that controlling shareholders extract. This balancing is what Professors Gilson and Gordon have called "the controlling shareholder trade off."

Using this framework, it appears that a corporate governance system should achieve a positive trade off from controlling shareholder structures. To put it differently, the problem is transforming a structure featuring inefficient controlling shareholders accustomed to extracting many private benefits of control, into a structure featuring efficient controlling shareholders whose monitoring generates benefits exceed the costs of private benefits extraction. This would cause minority shareholders to be better off under the controlling shareholders' management, raising the overall level of confidence in the capital markets.

Gilson hypothesizes that "an efficient controlling shareholder system supports a diversity of shareholder distribution[]" structures among companies. He gives examples from Sweden and Italy, showing that Sweden (a "good law" nation) has considerably more widely-held ownership than Italy (a "bad law" nation), despite the fact that both systems are considered dominated by controlling shareholders. According to Gilson's hypothesis, inefficient controlling shareholders systems show less diversity of shareholding distribution.

Comments and Questions

1. Benefits extracted by controlling shareholders has been referred to as "tunneling." *See* Simon Johnson, et al., *Tunneling*, 90 Am. Econ. Rev. 22 (2000). Self-dealing is a more common way of putting it. What are some mechanisms that a controlling shareholder might use to extract benefits from the company at the expense of shareholders? What sorts of governance requirements might minimize this type of activity?

2. As noted, the controlling shareholder model is common outside the United States. According to one commentator, "between 80 percent and 95 percent of listed firms in Austria, Belgium, Germany, and the Netherlands, there is a single shareholder that commands more than 25 percent of votes. In Italy, Spain and Sweden,

the figure is around two-thirds of companies. In contrast, in the UK the figure is 16 percent and in the U.S. between 5 percent and 7 percent." MARCH BECHT & COLIN MAYER, MARKET DISCIPLINE ACROSS COUNTRIES AND DISCIPLINES, Ch. 21, Corporate Governance in Europe: Competition v. Harmonization 257 (MIT Press 2004). What difference does this make in the discussion of comparative corporate governance?

3. What are the advantages of the controlling shareholder model? How about the disadvantages? When will the use of controlling shareholders as monitors benefit non-controlling investors? According to Professor Gilson: "[A] controlling shareholder may police the management of public corporations better than the standard panoply of market-oriented techniques employed when shareholdings are widely held." Ronald J. Gilson, *Controlling Shareholders and Corporate Governance: Complicating the Comparative Taxonomy, 119 HARV. L. REV. 1641* (2006). When might this be the case? Professor Gilson, as the piece above notes, distinguishes the role of controlling shareholders in countries with "good" law and "bad" law. What distinguishes the two and why does the "law" matter?

4. Who are these controlling shareholders? "Families are the most important group of largest shareholders in France, Spain and Italy." Christoph Van der Elst, *Shareholder Mobility in Five European Countries*, ECGI-Law Working Paper No. 104, at 30 (2008). In contrast, "foreign shareholders are the most important class of largest shareholders in the UK ... Almost 30% of the British companies had this type of shareholder as largest shareholder in 2007." *Id.* at 31. What about banks? *Id.* ("The number of Spanish companies with a bank as largest shareholder decreased since 1999 from 15% to 12% in 2007. Banks are negligible as largest shareholder in other countries."). What impact might the type of controlling shareholder have on the monitoring process?

5. What if the controlling shareholder is the government? The government of China owns a sizable portion of most listed companies. *See* Benjamin L. Liebman & Curtis J. Milhaupt, *Reputational Sanctions in China's Securities Market*, 108 Colum. L. Rev. 929, 938 (2008) (stating that about 60% of the share of exchange traded companies in China were owned by the state or state affiliates). What impact might this have on minority shareholders? *See* Chenxia Shi, *Protecting Investors in China Through Multiple Regulatory Mechanisms and Effective Enforcement*, 24 Ariz. J. Int'l & Comp. Law 451, 483 (2007) ("The interests of minority shareholders [in China] are not adequately protected because the state is the controlling shareholder in most listed companies."). How might this effect the system of governance in Chinese companies?

C. Banks and Monitoring

Banks can also be an important source of monitoring. Particularly in countries with underdeveloped capital systems, financial institutions often represent an important source of long term funding for public companies. As lenders, banks have an incentive to monitor. They will seek to ensure that management acts in a manner most likely to ensure repayment of any loan.

Banks often have better access to information than the market. Borrowers may provide information under the terms of the loan. Banks also sometimes place agents directly on the board of directors. This may be true even when they own a negligible portion of the outstanding equity.

In at least some economies, management has an incentive to follow the advice meted out by banks. Sometimes they are required to do so under the terms of the lending agreement. In other cases, the influence is more subtle. Companies do so in order to maintain close relationships with particular banks and ensure a constant supply of long term funding.

The most widely studied example of bank monitoring occurred in Japan. For much of the post-war period, public companies relied on their main or lead bank for most of their capital needs.

Dan W. Puchniak, *The Efficiency of Friendliness: Japanese Corporate Governance Succeeds Again without Hostile Takeovers*
5 Berkeley Bus. L.J. 195, 206–208 (2008)[6]

… Although Japanese companies borrowed from many banks, most companies had a special relationship with only one: their main bank. Typically, main banks held the major payment settlement accounts, and were both the largest single lenders and the principal shareholders of the company. This made main banks the central repository of accurate real time information about corporations' financial health and business ventures. Another key facet to main banks' relationships with their company clients was that main banks made an implicit promise to restructure failing corporations in times of financial or managerial crisis, rather than foreclosing on their loans—a promise made feasible because of the government's implied promise to prevent main bank failure.

… [T]his long-term intimate relationship between main banks and client companies was seen as the zenith of efficiency. Having ready access to a wealth of accurate information about client corporations allowed these main banks to evaluate managerial performance effectively. Further, main banks' substantial debt and equity positions with client companies gave them the leverage to use their information to influence managerial decisions and, when necessary, to control agency costs by replacing senior management and placing members of the bank on company boards. The main bank's promise to attempt to restructure underperforming clients allowed companies to pursue long-term goals and invest in human capital, which was a central component of Japan's competitive advantage over the United States during Japan's high growth era (1950–1973).

In addition, main bank monitoring avoided many of the deficiencies in the hostile takeovers-based American corporate governance model. Main banks did not suffer from the same collective action and information asymmetry problems as dispersed shareholders and, unlike hostile takeovers, did not force managers to focus myopically on short-term quarterly profits. The main bank's promise to help restructure failing client firms also prevented valuable firm-specific assets from being squandered by premature liquidation and avoided the significant costs associated with formal bankruptcy.

Keiretsu and stable shareholdings were the second fundamental element of the main bank model that provided an efficient substitute for hostile takeovers. Keiretsu is the name given essentially to the six major corporate groups in Japan, composed almost entirely of Japan's "blue chip" companies. These corporate groups were highly interconnected, not only by interlocking or cross-shareholding, but also by reciprocal directors, product market exchanges, information exchanges and a shared central main bank. In the postwar period, at the high point of this form of corporate organization, approximately two-thirds of all company shares in Japan were held by stable corporate shareholders friendly to management.

Keiretsu specifically, and stable shareholding relationships more generally, buttressed the stability and long-term managerial focus that main banks bestowed upon their company clients. This was because stable shareholdings eliminated the threat of hostile takeovers—allowing managers to focus on long-term investments, bolster human capital and ensure themselves and fellow employees long-term employment. This made white-collar and blue-collar employees quasi-owners of the firm, which was an extremely effective way to minimize the agency costs that hostile takeovers are said to address in the American model. In addition, the keiretsu corporate structure (by allowing information and market exchanges between firms) made it possible for companies to capture many of the synergetic efficiency gains of hostile takeovers, without the significant costs associated with the complete integration of companies after a hostile takeover.

Comments and Questions

1. What are some of the benefits that might arise out of a main bank system? What are some of the concerns? How does a system of bank monitoring compare with the monitoring function of the capital markets or controlling shareholders?

2. Are the interests of banks in alignment with the interests of shareholders? *See* Katherine V. Jackson, *Towards A Stakeholder-Shareholder Theory of Corporate Governance: A Comparative Analysis*, 7 Hastings Bus. L.J. 309, 364 (2011) (noting that banks play multiple roles, including "stockholder, board member, lender, and financial service provider" and may not always monitor in a manner that is on "behalf of all shareholders"). What if the banks have a close relationship with the government? How much do these differences matter?

3. What link if any does share ownership play in a system of bank monitoring? For most of the post-war period, Japanese banks could not own more than 5% of a public company. Nonetheless, main banks were typically part of industrial networks called keiretsu. The networks collectively owned a controlling block of the participating companies. Germany has also used a bank monitoring system during the post-war period. In addition to direct ownership, banks were allowed to act as a proxy and

vote the shares deposited by their customers. As a result, banks in Germany have often exercised considerable influence over the supervisory board. That, however, has changed. *See* Bruce E. Aronson, *Japanese Corporate Governance Reform: A Comparative Perspective*, 11 Hastings Bus. L.J. 85 (2015) ("Shareholdings of listed companies by main banks (i.e., city and regional banks) declined from a steady fifteen percent during the 1990s to an insignificant level today. They have been replaced by foreign shareholders, whose share of the stock market has increased from five percent in 1990 to twenty-eight percent today.").

4. What sorts of circumstances are necessary to give rise to a strong system of bank monitoring? In Japan, for example, banks largely had a monopoly on long term financing for public companies for much of the post-war period. While the country had capital markets, they were, according to some, a matter of "decorative appeal." Yoshiro Miwa & J. Mark Ramseyer, *Debt as a Lever of Control: The Beguiling Appeal of Banks*, 75 U. Cin. L. Rev. 1005, 1009 (2007). How might this have affected the bank monitoring system in Japan? Does it suggest that bank monitoring only works in the absence of active capital markets?

5. How likely is it that a bank monitoring system will occur in other developing countries? *Compare* Franklin Allen & Jun "QJ" Qian, *China's Financial System and the Law*, 47 Cornell Int'l L.J. 499, 552 (2014) ("the large banking sector dominated by state-owned banks has played a much more important role in funding the growth of many types of firms than the financial markets"), *with* Donald C. Clarke, *Law Without Order in Chinese Corporate Governance Institutions*, 30 Nw. J. Int'l L. & Bus. 131, 156 (2010) (noting that banks in China "have historically had neither the capacity nor the incentive to play this monitoring role"). What might explain some of the variations in developing countries?

6. The main bank system in Japan provided a mechanism for the government to influence the economy. For much of the post-war period, bank loans mostly went to companies approved by the government. *See* J. Robert Brown, Jr., *Industrial Policy and the Dangers of Emulating Japan*, 27 Geo. Wash. J. Int'l L. & Econ. 1 (1993). Japan was not the only country that used its banking system in this fashion. *See* Christopher Hale, *Addressing the Incentive for Expropriation within Business Groups: The Case of the Korean Chaebol*, 30 Fordham Int'l L.J. 1, 25 n.110 (2006) (noting that the government in Korea "effectively told the banks to make loans to certain entities"). Do you think the risk of government influence is inherent in a system of bank monitoring? Is government involvement always problematic? How did Japan's economy fair in the post-war period?

7. The bureaucracy in Japan is perceived to be the successors to the Samurai. During the post-war period, a career in the bureaucracy is considered among the most prestigious, with none more exalted than the Ministry of Finance. Indeed, when the doyens at the Ministry of Finance retire, they often embark on second careers in government entities (such as the Bank of Japan) or financial institutions. The process is termed *amakudari*, or descent from heaven, as if these post-ministry careers are a step down. Can you imagine a role played by *amakudari* in the bank monitoring system used by Japan?

8. In a bank dominated system, what role does the board play in the corporate governance process? In Japan, board membership often went to employees at the end of their careers. Meetings were often viewed as "ceremonial." *See* Mizuki Hayashi, Corporate Ownership and Governance Reforms in Japan: Influence of Globalization and U.S. Practice, 26 Colum. J. Asian L. 315 (2013) (describing board meetings as "somewhat ceremonial and noting that boards in Japanese companies mostly consists of employees). Is this an inevitable result of system that relies significantly on banks as a primary monitoring mechanism?

———————

Japan also represents a good example of a country undergoing a transition from one system of governance to another. The main bank system in Japan has begun to break down. While there are a number of explanations for the change, the most significant is the loss of leverage by financial institutions. Public companies were subject to significant bank influence when they had few alternative sources of capital. By the 1980s, however, they could obtain funds from a wide array of sources, whether overseas or from non-lead banks in Japan. With banks no longer able to adequately monitor management, another source had to be developed.

Bruce E. Aronson, *The Olympus Scandal and Corporate Governance Reform: Can Japan Find a Middle Ground between the Board Monitoring Model and Management Model?*
30 UCLA Pac. Basin L.J. 93 (2012)[7]

B. Monitoring of Management under Japan's Corporate Governance System

When initially examining Japan's tremendous economic success in the 1980s, commentators in both the U.S. and Japan developed a familiar, if now somewhat faded, model of Japanese corporate governance. The model emphasized economic analysis over law, and key features included lifetime employment; large, insider-dominated boards that directly operated the business (i.e., no separation of directors and officers); close cooperation among businesses, including membership in an industrial group (keiretsu); and large shareholdings by main banks and other group companies. In terms of monitoring management, this account paid little attention to the formal legal duties under corporate law of directors and company auditors, and instead emphasized the practical monitoring role of main banks, as well as the monitoring roles of affiliated business partners and product markets.

However, the collapse of Japan's economic bubble around 1990 undermined this traditional model. The subsequent financial crisis reduced the role of the main banks and other supporting features of the system. Since 1996, an ongoing debate on corporate governance reform has spurred numerous amendments to Japanese corporate laws. To some Japanese and many foreign commentators, the fundamental question is whether there should be at least a partial shift from an employee-dominated firm

———————

7. Copyright © 2012 UCLA Pacific Basin Law Journal. Reprinted with permission.

to one where a more independent board of directors and/or company auditors more actively monitor management on behalf of shareholders.

In attempting to improve the monitoring function in Japanese corporate governance, amendments to Japan's corporate law have emphasized strengthening the role of company auditors rather than the role of directors. Under Japanese corporate law, directors have fiduciary duties generally similar to those mandated in the U.S. Company auditors, who have no managerial duties, have the role of checking management performance of the directors. Their role, which was loosely derived from the German Supervisory Board, has expanded over time from financial auditing to include compliance and, arguably, monitoring of management. Since 1993, large companies are required to have a board of audit composed of company auditors; since 2001, at least half of their company auditors must be outsiders. Beginning in 2010, at least one of the outside company auditors or outside directors must satisfy the definition of independence under TSE listing standards. In addition, the term of office for company auditors has been gradually lengthened to four years in an effort to enhance their independence.

Japanese corporate law also added an optional alternative to this traditional system in 2002. This system allows Japanese companies to replace the traditional, German-inspired representative director and company auditor positions with an American-inspired alternative: a representative executive officer and three board committees (audit, compensation, and nomination committees), with a majority of outside directors required for each committee. However, only 2.2% of listed Japanese companies have given up their traditional company with auditors structure and adopted this new, American-inspired company with committees structure.

It is widely recognized in Japan that the company auditor system is "difficult to explain" to global investors and that issues remain concerning its effectiveness. Nevertheless, most Japanese businesses seem reluctant to abandon the company auditor system for a number of reasons, including its widespread use by the vast majority of Japanese companies and the decades-long effort to strengthen its effectiveness.

Over the last few years there has also been modest progress in increasing the role of independent directors. As noted above, the TSE added a new requirement at the end of 2009 that every listed corporation must have one independent (as opposed to outside) director or company auditor. However, most listed companies have fulfilled this requirement by appointing an independent company auditor rather than an independent director. At present, roughly half of Japanese listed companies still have no outside directors.

Comments and Questions

1. Japan is struggling to find a system of monitoring that replaces the traditional role of the main bank. The 2002 reforms essentially allowed for the implementation of a western style form of corporate governance. Japan did not entirely commit to this approach, however. Companies were permitted to "opt in" and, so far, only a modest number of public companies have done so. Chien-Chung Lin, *The Japanese Independent Director Mechanism Revisited: The Corporate Law Setting, Current Status, and Its Explanations*, 24 Temp. Int'l & Comp. L.J. 65, 99 (2010) ("The ratio on the

Tokyo Stock Exchange Second Section is less than one percent (four out of 457). In total, almost seven years after the 2002 amendment, only 2.3 percent of all TSE-listed companies have adopted committee structure."). What explains the unwillingness of Japanese companies to opt for a different model?

2. The article notes that Japan has looked to the US for "inspiration" with respect to governance reform, something that has resulted in particular emphasis on the use of independent directors. What are some difficulties that arise from this source of inspiration? Do independent directors function the same way in Japan as in the US?

3. According to Professor Aronson, the number of First Section listed companies with at least one outside director has increased from 74% in 2014 to 92% in 2015; those with two from 21.5% 50 46.5%. Moreover, the 2015 version of the Corporate Governance Code recommends that listed companies include two "independent" rather than outside directors. Assuming the focus in Japan remains on increasing the number of independent directors, will this result in improved governance or are there other changes that also must occur? *See* Bruce E. Aronson, *Japanese Corporate Governance Reform: A Comparative Perspective*, 11 Hastings Bus. L.J. 85 (2015) (independent directors need to operate in an environment with "sufficient access to information, greater litigation risk, or some other incentive to encourage monitors to raise issues that may challenge the views of corporate management and additional outside monitors, such as professional service providers functioning as gatekeepers").

4. Reforms have continued. Board size, for example, has shrunk. *See* Bruce E. Aronson, *Japanese Corporate Governance Reform: A Comparative Perspective*, 11 Hastings Bus. L.J. 85 (2015) ("Nearly all large Japanese companies have taken voluntary action to significantly reduce the size of their board from large boards of twenty to forty directors a few decades ago to an average of 8.13 directors for listed companies today."). What does this suggest about the evolution of the role of the board?

5. What is the role of the statutory auditor (kansayaku) in Japanese companies? They are elected by shareholders and can attend board meetings. They do not, however, have voting rights and cannot dismiss officers. They have been described as "completely ineffective with respect to performance monitoring" but more effective at "compliance monitoring." Bruce E. Aronson, *Corporate Governance Models and Practices in Japan and East Asia*, 27 Colum. J. Asian L. 221 (2014) (comments by Professor Kozuka). What do you make of this approach? Is it an adequate substitute for structural reforms to the board of directors?

6. In February 2014, Japan adopted a "Stewardship Code." The Code "defines principles considered to be helpful for institutional investors who behave as responsible institutional investors in fulfilling their stewardship responsibilities with due regard both to their clients and beneficiaries and to investee companies." Principles for Responsible Institutional Investors, The Council of Experts Concerning the Japanese Version of the Stewardship Code (Feb. 26, 2014). As Professor Aronson describes, the Code "encourages Japan's institutional investors to become more active shareholders and engage in 'constructive dialogue' with their portfolio companies to improve such companies' governance." What impact might this have on Japanese governance?

III. Civil Code vs. Common Law Jurisdictions

A significant number of countries, particularly in Europe, operate under the civil code system. Although not uniform in their approach, these jurisdictions resort to a statutory framework that sets out applicable legal requirements, preferring a legislative rather than judicial solution to most legal issues. With respect to corporate governance, civil code jurisdictions are more prone to a governance structure that involves two boards of directors and are more likely to impose duties on directors that favor multiple stakeholders rather than only shareholders.

Likewise, civil code jurisdictions often favor a non-mandatory approach to governance (although this is also used in many common law jurisdictions). Employing the rubric of "comply or explain," they tend to rely on voluntary codes where companies can opt in or opt out. The approach eschews uniformity and allows public companies greater flexibility to determine the system of corporate governance most suited to their interests. On the other hand, this approach typically has no enforcement mechanism other than moral suasion.

Common law jurisdictions represent the alternative model. These countries are typically more comfortable with a legal structure more reliant on judicial interpretation and imposition. A likely effect of a heightened judicial role is that governance requirements can be more easily changed, arguably providing both increased flexibility and increased uncertainty. In the governance area, common law jurisdictions generally favor a shareholder centric model. Nonetheless, within this broad parameter, significant differences in approach exist.

A. The Common Law Model and Its Variations

The U.S. and UK are often lumped together in any discussion of corporate governance. Both have active capital markets. They also have in place a shareholder centric approach to corporate governance. As a result, there is a tendency to view the two systems as the essentially same, particularly when comparing them to those used on the continent. Nonetheless, they have a number of differences, with Britain sometimes referred to as a "shareholder's paradise."

Christopher M. Bruner, *Power and Purpose in the "Anglo-American" Corporation*

50 Va. J. Int'l L. 579, 603–06, 610–11 (2010)[8]

In contrast with the position of shareholders in a U.S. public corporation, U.K. shareholders possess substantial powers to intervene directly in corporate governance, and benefit from directors' duties and a conception of corporate purpose focusing far more intently on their interests. (For the sake of clarity, the contrasts discussed below are summarized in Figure 1.) The result is a decidedly shareholder-centric gov-

---

8. Copyright © 2010 Virginia Journal of International Law. Reprinted by permission.

Figure 1: Shareholders' Default Powers and Directors'
Duties in Public Corporations

	U.S. (Del.)	U.K.
Call special meetings	No	Yes
Remove directors without cause	No, if board is classified	Yes
Initiate charter amendments	No	Yes
Compel board action	No	Yes
Approve takeover defenses	No	Yes
Beneficiaries of directors' efforts	Corporation & Shareholders	Shareholders

ernance system exhibiting little of the ambivalence that characterizes U.S. corporate governance.

Unlike in the United States, shareholders in a U.K. public corporation can, under the Companies Act (2006), unilaterally amend the company's constitution (its core governance document) by special resolution of a seventy-five percent majority. This differs enormously from the Delaware approach, which permits the board to play a gatekeeping role by requiring that any change to the charter be proposed by the board before the shareholders may approve it. Additionally, U.K. shareholders possess far greater capacity to replace directors. Shareholders representing five percent voting power can demand a meeting, at which directors can be removed by ordinary resolution of a simple majority. It should also be noted that U.K. shareholders do not encounter the sorts of regulatory impediments to coordinated action that U.S. securities regulation imposes.

As in the United States, the model articles that apply to U.K. public companies by default state that generally "the directors are responsible for the management of the company's business, for which purpose they may exercise all the powers of the company." Thus, as in U.S. corporations, the board is clearly "the most important decision-making body within the company." However, there is a critical difference: the model articles permit U.K. shareholders literally to "direct the directors," by special resolution, "to take, or refrain from taking, specified action." This notion of directing the directors is utterly foreign to Delaware law and, at least in theory, would appear to give the shareholders a very strong card to play in discussions with management.

As a practical matter, the removal power, which requires only an ordinary resolution, is far more significant. As Paul Davies observes, "the disgruntled shareholders can say, in effect, to the directors: if you choose not to follow our views, we will by ordinary majority seek to remove you from office" — a "powerful inducement" to follow the shareholders' wishes. In general, British institutional shareholders have been content to leave governance entirely to the board, but when trouble arises, the removal power gives them tremendous leverage in discussions with management over the future of the company. The power to "direct the directors," however, does remain significant at a theoretical level, vividly illustrating that the board's powers in a U.K. corporation are fundamentally a matter of "private ordering." U.K. directors' powers emanate solely from "delegation via the articles and not from a separate and free-standing grant of authority from the State," a fact that, in Davies' view, "helps to underline the shareholder-centred nature of British company law."

* * *

Overall, it would appear that the U.K. corporate governance system is substantially more compatible with theories emphasizing shareholders' interests than the U.S. corporate governance system is. In particular, the U.K. approach would appear broadly compatible with the nexus view of the corporation. The default corporate governance arrangement resembles the nexus corporation in granting relatively broad managerial authority to a board elected by the shareholders. This mode of accountability is bolstered by the clarity of the board's duty to shareholders under section 172, as well as by the U.K.'s relatively unfettered market for corporate control. Moreover, the Companies Act explicitly characterizes the corporation as contractual in nature, stating that the company's constitution "binds the company and its members to the same extent as if there were covenants on the part of the company and of each member to observe those provisions." Whether the nexus theory can, in fact, be said to provide a compelling description of U.K. corporate governance is questioned below, but there is certainly evidence that the nexus view carries some sway among scholars and practitioners in the United Kingdom. The steering group for the comprehensive company law review that culminated in the 2006 Companies Act even stated in a consultation document that this structure "serves the interests of shareholders by conferring on them ultimate control of the undertaking," citing Easterbrook and Fischel's The Economic Structure of Corporate Law for "economic justification."

As this overview of U.S. and U.K. corporate governance demonstrates, the "Anglo-American" corporation is, at best, a stylized fact. As such, its utility in global comparative analysis comes at a cost: a lack of nuance that obscures the substantial and fundamental differences that emerge on closer analysis....

Comments and Questions

1. What do you make of the differences in the two systems? Do you agree that "at close range" the two systems "do not look similar at all"? David A. Skeel, Jr., *Book Review, Corporate Governance and Social Welfare in the Common-Law World*, 92 Tex. L. Rev. 973, 975 (2014).

2. Given these differences, make the case that in fact it is proper to treat the UK and US system as similar? After all, both in fact rely on common law more that civil code jurisdictions and both do not have an ownership configuration that is premised upon the existence of controlling shareholders. Is that enough to group these systems together?

3. As noted, shareholders in Britain have the right to propose amendments to the articles of incorporation, while those in the U.S. do not. Shareholders in the U.S. cannot, therefore, initiate changes in the articles with provisions that they oppose. How important is this difference? For a more detailed discussion of consequences of the board alone having the authority to propose amendments, see J. Robert Brown, Jr. & Sandeep Gopalan, *Opting Only In: Contractarians, Waiver of Liability Provisions, and the Race to the Bottom*, 42 Ind. L. Rev. 285 (2009).

4. Shareholders in Great Britain also have the right to approve a wider array of transactions, particularly those involving potential conflicts of interest with board members. Thus, for example, the Companies Act permits loans to management but only if first approved by shareholders. *See* Section 197 of the Companies Act of 2006. Contrast this with the system in the US. Most matters, even those involving a conflict of interest with directors, do not have to be submitted to shareholders. When Congress had concern with loans given to management, it did not expand shareholder rights but instead simply prohibited the practice. *See* Section 13(k), 15 U.S.C.S. § 78m(k). What explains these differences in approach? Which is the better approach?

5. Can the US learn from the British system? Britain gave shareholders the right to an advisory vote on executive compensation in 2002. It took until the adoption of the Dodd-Frank Act in 2010 before shareholders of public companies in the US received similar authority. Britain has since adopted a "second generation" say on pay statute that seeks to provide shareholders with some binding authority over the compensation process. See Randall S. Thomas & Christopher Van der Elst, Say on Pay Around the World, 92 Wash. U. L. Rev. 653 (2015). Why might Great Britain have done this and is there any likelihood the US will follow suit?

6. A significant difference in the systems used by the two countries concerns private enforcement. Shareholders in Great Britain rarely bring derivative actions. *See* John Armour, *"Enforcement Strategies in UK Corporate Governance: A Roadmap and Empirical Assessment"* (Apr. 2008). ECGI-Law Working Paper No. 106/2008 (describing the number of actions against directors) ("The number of instances of formal private enforcement, as far as we are able to estimate, is practically zero in relation to listed companies."). What are the reasons for this? One of them is the application of the English rule with respect to fees, with the losing shareholders obligated to pay the costs incurred by the directors in defending the suit, something mitigated somewhat by the right of shareholders to obtain indemnification for bringing the suit. *Id.* (Describing these costs as a "significant deterrent" to bringing the suits). Is it possible that, given the other rights possessed by shareholders, derivative actions are less necessary?

7. Would a more shareholder centric approach in the US operate in the same manner as in Britain? How much does this depend upon variations in the ownership configuration of most public companies? While controlling shareholders are not common in the US or the UK, companies in the UK tend to have a smaller number of institutions and "their impact is much greater there than in any other country, even the United States." Klaus J. Hopt, *Comparative Corporate Governance: The State of the Art and International Regulation*, 59 Am. J. Comp. L. 1, 33 (2011). What dif-

ference might this make in both the establishment and impact of increased rights for shareholders?

8. What about other law common countries? One analysis of Australia concluded that the country has stronger protections for shareholders than either the US or the UK. *See* Richard Mitchell, et al., *Shareholder Protection in Australia: Institutional Configurations and Regulatory Evolution*, 38 Melb. U. L. Rev. 68, 73 (2014) ("While having more in common with the United Kingdom than the United States since 1980, the level of shareholder protection in Australia was higher than both the United Kingdom and the United States for the entire period of the study from 1970–2005."). What is the explanation for this? Does ownership configuration provide a possible answer? *Id.* at 95 (noting studies that suggest that "ownership of Australian companies has been characterised by a notable degree of concentration, persisting across time, which calls into question any categorisation of the Australian system of corporate ownership and control as unequivocally a dispersed or outsider system.").

9. How much does the system function in the UK only because shareholders are rarely expected to use this authority? *See* Brian R. Cheffins, *Does Law Matter? The Separation of Ownership and Control in the United Kingdom*, 30 J. Legal Stud. 459, 465 (2001) ("British institutional investors are reluctant to respond to poor corporate performance by intervening in order to try to rectify matters."). In an era of shareholders activists, a trend that has gone international, these same rights provide activists with powerful mechanisms for pressuring directors. For example, shareholders in the UK owning 5% of the voting shares could call a special meeting and ask to have the entire board replaced. This possibility is discussed in Dionysia Katelouzou, *Worldwide Hedge Fund Activism: Dimensions and Legal Determinants*, 17 U. Pa. J. Bus. L. 789 (2015). Does this act as a possible catalyst for governance changes?

B. Civil Code Jurisdictions

Much of the world eschews the vagaries of the common law system in favor of a civil code approach to regulation. Civil codes often provide greater certainty and uniformity. The civil code approach is the norm in continental Europe.

Comparing common law and civil law systems in the realm of corporate governance has limitations. For one thing, there is often a tendency to treat civil law countries collectively. Yet some of the most noticeable differences in governance are applicable in only a subset of civil law jurisdictions. Thus, Germany and Scandinavia rely on a dual board structure, with a management board consisting mostly of officers and a supervisory board elected by shareholders (and sometimes employees). Nonetheless, not all European companies rely on the dual board system and, indeed, "[i]nternationally, the most prevalent board structure is the one-tier board." Klaus J. Hopt, *Comparative Corporate Governance: The State of the Art and International Regulation*, 59 Am. J. Comp. L. 1, 21 (2011).

Similarly, civil law countries sometimes use a stakeholder approach to governance, effectively allowing boards to consider the interests of groups other than shareholders. Germany, which gives employees the right to select half of the board of the largest public companies, is the common example of this approach. Yet many civil law jurisdictions do not rely on codetermination and, those that do, rarely grant employees half of the positions on the board of directors. Moreover, stakeholder rights have taken hold in places like South Africa which, while probably a hybrid jurisdiction, has strong common law roots resulting from the period of British rule.

At the same time, some attributes of civil law systems are also relatively typical within common law jurisdictions. The use of voluntary corporate codes is popular among civil law countries. The codes also exist, however, in such common law stalwarts as the United Kingdom and Australia. Moreover, while civil code countries are typified by detailed laws, the most recent revision of the Companies Act in Great Britain resulted in a massive piece of legislation that goes on for hundreds of pages.

Yet there may be some unifying themes. Perhaps those are less about differences in objective requirements and more about differences in the philosophical approach towards regulation.

1. Background

Civil law jurisdictions ostensibly have their roots in the legal codifications undertaken during the Roman Empire. The more modern progenitor is the Napoleonic Code.

Mark J. Roe, *Legal Origins, Politics, and Modern Stock Markets*
120 Harv. L. Rev. 460, 469–70 (2006)[9]

The Emperor Justinian had Roman law compiled and, when the compilation was completed in the year 533, barred future decisionmakers from referring to the work of judges and from citing authorities other than his Code. All law was reflected in his Corpus Juris Civilis, all else extraneous. Napoleon, seeking to control the judges in post-revolutionary France as the revolutionaries had sought in 1791 — by requiring judges, if the legislative text was ambiguous or silent, to ask the legislature its meaning — promulgated his famous Code. The common law, on the other hand, grows as judges decide cases and precedents evolve, without the judges' referring to a central code. A code centralizes authority; common law judges disperse it.

Civil law and common law judges read the text of the governing code differently, it is said. Civil law judges read its plain meaning; if the text is incomplete, it is said, a classic civil law judge does not fill in gaps where a common law judge would. Hence, the civil law judge deters insider corporate schemes ineptly, while the wily common law judge adapts and stops insider thievery. Common law judges follow precedent, thereby building a cohesive system of law from the ground up. Civil law judges, in contrast, do not follow prior opinions, often do not write down their reasoning, and do not tightly tie their decisions to the facts of the case.

---

9. Copyright © 2006 Harvard Law Review Association. Reprinted by permission.

The civil law tends toward deductive thinking—"to making plans, to regulating things in advance, ... to drawing up rules and systematizing them." In contrast, "the Englishman improvises, never making a decision until he has to.... Only experience counts ... and so he is not given to abstract rules of law."

The civil law plans, the common law reacts.

Comments and Questions

1. The Roman roots notwithstanding, the modern civil code began with France. Moreover, it spread initially not on the merits but as a result of military fiat. *See* Guy Canivet, *French Civil Law Between Past and Revival*, 20 Conn. J. Int'l L. 111, 111–12 (2004) ("And no one disputes that if, from the moment of its promulgation, the Civil Code transcended national boundaries, it was via military conquests and through the Emperor's hegemonic ambitions. For it was, indeed, the force of arms that propagated the Civil Code in Europe in Napoleon's time.").

2. Some countries have deliberately opted to be civil law jurisdictions. Japan, in its opening to the West, borrowed extensively from the German civil code. Turkey, when it became a republic in the 1920s, more or less adopted wholesale the civil code used in Switzerland. Given Professor Roe's description, what is the attraction of a civil law approach?

3. What do you make of the conclusion that civil code jurisdictions plan while common law countries react? What impact might this have on the corporate governance process? Which is more consistent with a market economy?

4. For emerging or developing markets, is there any real alternative to a civil law approach? What would be the consequence of eschewing a civil code approach? What type of infrastructure needs to be in place to effectively implement a common law system?

5. Studies have examined differences in attributes of common and civil law jurisdictions with respect to corporate governance and effective capital markets. In general, those studies tend to view common law jurisdictions more favorably, at least when judged by the quality of their securities markets. To the extent differences exist, it may have less to do with the characterization of civil and common and more to do with the philosophical approach to regulation and enforcement. See John C. Coffee, Jr., *Law and the Market: The Impact of Enforcement, 156 U. Pa. L. Rev. 229* (2007) ("The key contrast here is that in civil law jurisdictions the role of the central government is greater and more intrusive, with far less discretion being accorded to private or self-regulatory bodies."). Assuming the accuracy of this observation, what steps might a civil law country take to promote the development of active securities markets?

2. Comply or Explain

Comply or explain entails the development of corporate governance practices through the use of non-mandatory codes of best practices. Sometimes referred to as "soft law," these codes often contain detailed and specific standards. Companies may pick and choose the applicable provisions, although they must sometimes "explain" the rejection of particular practices. Investors and the capital markets, rather than the government, are the ultimate arbiters of the choices made by these companies.

These codes exist in both common and civil law jurisdictions. Indeed, their roots can largely be traced to the Cadbury Report, a set of voluntary governance standards developed in the UK in 1992.

Klaus J. Hopt, *Comparative Corporate Governance: The State of the Art and International Regulation*
59 Am. J. Comp. L. 1 (2011)[10]

More recently, corporate governance in the form of soft law in various forms has gained ground. Prominent examples include the host of corporate governance codes; non-binding recommendations of various sources such as chambers of commerce, business and banking associations, and international committees; best practice standards; and other forms of self-regulation and market discipline. Today most countries have corporate governance codes. These codes are not law and thus lack binding force. The prototype and current international model for these instruments is the UK Corporate Governance Code that goes back to the Combined Code of the Cadbury Committee 1992. In the meantime there has been a whole wave of corporate governance codes, and today practically all relevant countries have one or more of them. These codes stem from various sources, including stock exchanges, business organizations, special governmental or similar public committees, supervisory agencies, and a few from academics and practitioners. Usually these codes address only listed corporations. But there are also specific corporate governance codes for family enterprises, or for businesses in which the state or other public bodies hold an important block of shares. Sometimes particular sectors of the economy such as banking or even individual corporations like, for a while, the Deutsche Bank, have issued special corporate governance codes or similar recommendations.

The content of these corporate governance codes varies considerably. Some are very sophisticated: the UK Code, for example, contains high-level Main Principles, mid-level Supporting Principles and low-level Provisions. Others are shorter, and much less explicit or rigorous. The content of each code depends on financial traditions and the possibility of the individual country and its institutions having and credibly supporting self-regulation. In the City of London, of course, this is much more evident to all participants than in a federal state with diverse economic centers and participants, as is traditional in Germany. In Germany and some other countries the respective corporate governance codes are meant also to inform foreign investors on the national rules on corporate governance, whether stemming from actual formal law or from good corporate governance practice as recommended in the code. In general, corporate governance codes primarily regulate the board and its committees,

---

10. Cited in the American Journal of Comparative Law. Reprinted with permission.

or in the case of a two-tier board, both boards and the relationship between them. But there are also rules on shareholder rights and auditing practices. All of these corporate governance codes contain provisions concerning internal corporate governance, with particular emphasis on the board. Rules of external corporate governance, especially concerning takeovers, have traditionally developed separately, both in law and under self-regulation. The prime example is the Takeover Code of the Takeover Panel in the United Kingdom, which was formerly fully self-regulatory, but following the EU Takeover Directive now has legislative backing under the Companies Act of 2006. The coexistence of these regimes—corporate governance law and codes and takeover regulation (through takeover law and takeover codes)—can lead to gaps and inconsistencies regarding rules and recommendations.

The rate of adherence to these codes is different—high in the United Kingdom and Germany, for example, but lower in other countries—but a clear link between observance of the codes and the stock price of the corporation has not yet been empirically established. In any case, the relevance of the codes for focusing attention on the practice of good corporate governance and also for research and academic debate is high.

3. Administration and Enforcement of the Codes

The administration and enforcement of corporate governance codes differ considerably. In some countries there are no permanent code commissions or similar bodies, with the result that the code remains a mere recommendation; it is not enforced other than by peer pressure and self-interest, and is not regularly revised in light of new needs and insights. A mild form of disclosure is provided for in the countries of the European Union where the mandatory corporate governance statement must indicate whether the corporation is subject to a corporate governance code and, if so, to which one.

Stock exchanges may require more, namely asking companies in their listing conditions to observe the code, as in the United Kingdom and other countries.... If observance of the code is a condition for listing, this leaves the corporation and its directors no choice but to agree to those terms. Hence observance of the code is no longer voluntary except for non-listed companies.

In other countries, special corporate governance commissions are in charge of issuing, administering and enforcing the code. Enforcement can be simple self-regulation, i.e., basically by peer pressure or through disclosure, usually on a "comply or disclose" basis. In some countries—such as the Netherlands, Germany, Austria, Denmark, Portugal and Spain—this disclosure, but not the code and its content, is supported by law, for example by a provision in the stock corporation act that listed companies must "comply or disclose" or "comply or explain." This is an interesting technique that lies between self-regulation and regulation by law, and may be described as "self-regulation in the shadow of the law." The extent to which non-observance must be explained varies considerably. Some codes do not detail what "explain" means; others distinguish between the main principles and the lower-level principles of the code. Experience shows that such a requirement may lead to thorny legal problems, not only with regard to the reach and content of the rule, but also the responsibility for such disclosure and the legal consequences of non-disclosure. In some countries, courts attach legal consequences to false or omitted disclosure, provided that the corporation has declared that it complies with the code. An example is the voidability of a shareholder resolution on ratification of an action taken by the management board. False or non-disclosure is also a violation of a director's duty that can carry internal and/or legal consequences, including censure by the shareholders, measures taken by a supervisory agency or the stock exchange, and possibly even personal liability.

A further variation concerns the extent to which corporate governance disclosure must be verified or even audited. As seen before, the "comply or explain" disclosure declaration is usually issued by the board as a whole. Yet, if the company is obliged or chooses to publish information concerning it being subject to a corporate governance code, or its observance or non-observance of such a code, and if this declaration is part of its annual report, this declaration is also subject to the annual audit. This is why most companies prefer to issue a separate declaration as an annex to the annual management report that is therefore not subject to the auditing requirement.

Comments and Questions

1. The codes employed in over 70 countries can be found at the web site for the European Corporate Governance Institute. *See* http://www.ecgi.org/codes/all_codes.php.

2. What are the strengths and weaknesses of a system premised around voluntary corporate codes? Does the risk that these codes could have a detrimental effect on corporate governance militate against their use? Are there circumstances where these effects are less likely to occur?

3. Comply or explain has sometimes been described as a system that relies on principles rather than mandatory rules. *See* Exchange Act Release No. 61175 (Dec. 16, 2009) (adoption of compensation disclosure requirements and noting that disclosure of compensation policies and practices done in a manner consistent with a "principles based approach"). What are some problems with this approach? What about the explanation for non-compliance? As the Combined Code in the UK describes:

> [T]he company has to report on how it applies the principles in the Code. This should cover both main and supporting principles. The form and content of this part of the statement are not prescribed, the intention being that companies should have a free hand to explain their governance policies in the light of the principles, including any special circumstances applying to them which have led to a particular approach.

What flexibility does this give with respect to the disclosure required under a "comply or explain" approach?

4. Can these codes really work without enforcement? What about a company that misstates the level of compliance? As one commentator described: "Whilst it is therefore a breach of the Listing Rules for a firm to fail to state *whether* they comply, or *why* they do not comply, in practice there are no reported instances of the [govern-

ment] taking action against companies for non-compliance with these requirements." Armour, John, *Enforcement Strategies in UK Corporate Governance: A Roadmap and Empirical Assessment* (April 2008). ECGI-Law Working Paper No. 106/2008.

5. Although discussed as an attribute of civil law systems, the United States has on rare occasions employed the comply or explain approach. *See* Item 407 of Regulation S-K, 17 CFR 229.407 (requiring disclosure of financial expert on audit committee or an explanation why company "does not have an audit committee financial expert."). The U.S. has, however, increasingly relied on listing standards to implement mandatory requirements. Can you make the argument that this represents a middle ground between comply or explain and mandatory standards?

3. Dual Board Structure

In a number of continental countries, public companies rely on a dual board structure. Some such as Germany require the structure. Others, including France and Italy, allow but do not mandate its use. Under the typical dual board structure, the supervisory board is elected by shareholders (except where employee representation is required). The supervisory board in turn appoints the internal, executive board which has responsibility for the day to day management of the company.

Brian R. Cheffins & Bernard S. Black,
Outside Director Liability Across Countries
84 Tex. L. Rev. 1385, 1421–22 (2006)[11]

The two-tier board is another feature that distinguishes Germany not only from common law countries, but also from many civil law jurisdictions. All German public companies must take the Aktiengesellachaft (AG) stock corporation legal form, though many AGs do not go public. An AG's board of directors is divided into two tiers: the management board (Vorstand) and the supervisory board (Aufsichtstrat). The management board has sole responsibility for managing the company and is composed of full-time executives. The supervisory board includes only non-executives, who appoint and monitor the management board. Under a policy of "codetermination," labor representatives must comprise one-third of the supervisory board of an AG with over 500 workers, and one-half of the board of an AG with over 2,000 workers. Labor nominees excepted, the supervisory board of a typical German public company will be a mix of former executives of the company, professional business advisers (e.g., bankers or lawyers), and representatives of key suppliers or customers, with few executives from unaffiliated companies.

The German Stock Corporation Act (Aktiengesetz or "AktG") provides that the management board must report regularly to the supervisory board on the company's affairs and immediately inform the supervisory board chair of developments that

---

11. Copyright © 2006 Texas Law Review Association. Reprinted by permission. English version only.

may have a material impact on the company. The supervisory board also customarily approves the company's annual audited financial statements and may inspect the company's books and records at any time. In addition, the supervisory board has the discretion to specify transactions that require its approval.

* * *

AktG § 116 stipulates that the duties of management board members, specified in 93, apply analogously to the supervisory board. As a result, supervisory directors must perform their duties with the care of a "diligent and conscientious" businessperson holding such a position. While a supervisory board director is not expected to have expertise in a company's particular industry, general business knowledge is required, and courts likely will impose more exacting standards on directors with special qualifications (e.g., bankers, lawyers and accountants). A director who lacks important information could be in breach of duty by not seeking appropriate advice, yet German courts have been reluctant to accept reliance on others as a defense.

Comments and Questions

1. What are some advantages and disadvantages of the supervisory board model? How does it compare to the unitary board structure in the United States?

2. How "independent" is a supervisory board? While management is not allowed to serve as directors, the prohibition does not generally apply to past managers or officers. It is not unusual for the retiring chair of the management board to serve as the chair of the supervisory board. Moreover, the management board may have considerable influence over the selection of members to the supervisory board. *See* Hans van Ees & Theo J.B.M. Postma, *Dutch Boards and Governance A Comparative Institutional Analysis of Board Roles and Member (S)election Procedures*, 34 Int. Studies of Mgt. & Org. 90, 104 (2002).

3. One of the difficulties has been the attempt to delineate the oversight role of the supervisory board. *See* Klaus J. Hopt & Patrick C. Leyens, *Board Models in Europe—Recent Developments of Internal Corporate Governance Structures in Germany, the United Kingdom, France, and Italy*, ECGI-Law Working Paper No. 18/2004 ("While the clear responsibility of the management board is the running of the business, the role of the supervisory board is not easy to describe. Its legal functions are primarily the appointment, supervision, and removal of members of the management board.").

4. Are the criticisms really about the dual board system or are they more about how the system is structured in practice? Often the boards are large, with as many as twenty-one members, reducing efficiency and making decision making more difficult. Without members of management, supervisory boards can also have difficulty obtaining necessary information about the operations of the company.

5. Some emerging markets have embraced the dual board structure, including China. *See* Chao Xi, *In Search of an Effective Monitoring Board Model: Board Reforms*

and the Political Economy of Corporate Law in China, 22 Conn. J. Int'l L. 1 (2006). In China, however, both the supervisory board and the board of directors are elected by shareholders. Moreover, while the supervisory board has the obligation to supervise the board of directors, the board of directors must include independent directors. These two approaches arguably conflict. As one commentator described:

> Both the supervisory board and independent directors are conceptualized as insider monitoring mechanisms. In terms of oversight, the powers and duties vested with board of supervisors and independent directors significantly overlap. Specifically, supervisory boards in China hold all of the powers vested in audit committees in the United States. This overlap in authority creates both tension and discord between the independent director system and the supervisory system.

Jie Yuan, *Formal Convergence or Substantial Divergence? Evidence from Adoption of the Independent Director System in China*, 9 Asian-Pacific L. & Pol'y J. 71, 102 (2007). Is this conflict inevitable?

6. Once elected, directors on both the management and supervisory board are not easy to remove. As one commentator described:

> The supervisory board elects and dismisses management board members, but premature dismissal requires a showing of cause, which includes a vote of no confidence by shareholders. Thus, dismissal requires agreement between major shareholders and the supervisory board. Supervisory board members are elected by shareholders, have a period in office of up to five years, and normally can only be dismissed prematurely by a supermajority of three quarters.

Martin Gelter, *The Dark Side of Shareholder Influence: Managerial Autonomy and Stakeholder Orientation in Comparative Corporate Governance*, 50 Harv. Int'l L.J. 129, 158 (2009). Of course, as Professor Gelter notes, these limits largely become meaningless in the context of companies owned by a controlling shareholder. In those circumstances, they have the ability to control both the supervisory board and, by extension, the management board.

7. Some emerging markets have embraced the dual board structure, including China. *See* Chao Xi, *In Search of an Effective Monitoring Board Model: Board Reforms and the Political Economy of Corporate Law in China*, 22 Conn. J. Int'l L. 1 (2006). In China, however, both the supervisory board and the board of directors are elected by shareholders. Moreover, while the supervisory board has the obligation to supervise the board of directors, the board of directors must include independent directors. These two approaches arguably conflict. As one commentator described:

> Both the supervisory board and independent directors are conceptualized as insider monitoring mechanisms. In terms of oversight, the powers and duties vested with board of supervisors and independent directors significantly overlap. Specifically, supervisory boards in China hold all of the powers vested in audit committees in the United States. This overlap in authority

creates both tension and discord between the independent director system and the supervisory system.

Jie Yuan, *Formal Convergence or Substantial Divergence? Evidence from Adoption of the Independent Director System in China*, 9 Asian-Pacific L. & Pol'y J. 71, 102 (2007). Is this conflict inevitable?

———

What is the function of a supervisory board beyond designating the members of the management board? Some attribute to the board a networking with shareholders and other corporate constituencies. What about the role of the supervisory board in protecting the company?

Seybold v. Groenink

United States District Court, Southern District of New York
2007 U.S. Dist. Lexis 16994 (Mar. 12, 2007)

DENISE COTE, DISTRICT JUDGE:

This litigation raises the issue of whether an American holder of American Depository Receipts (ADRs)[12] in a bank incorporated in the Netherlands has standing to bring a shareholder derivative action against the corporation's directors for common law claims of breach of fiduciary duty and indemnification. It arises in the aftermath of the corporation's deficient compliance with federal anti-money laundering laws, deficiencies which have resulted in the corporation paying hundreds of millions of dollars to federal authorities. Finding that in this diversity action New York choice of law rules require that the law of the Netherlands determine whether plaintiff has standing to bring a derivative claim, the defendants' motion to dismiss is granted.

In order for a foreign corporation to trade on an American stock exchange, the foreign corporation must issue and deposit American Depository Shares ("ADSs") with an American financial institution. E.ON v. Acciona, No. 06 Civ. 8720 (DLC), 468 F. Supp. 2d 537, 2006 U.S. Dist. LEXIS 84179, 2006 WL 3357261, at *1 n.2 (S.D.N.Y. Nov. 20, 2006). The depository institution then issues American Depository Receipts ("ADRs") to the beneficial owners of the ADSs, who may sell the ADSs on American securities exchanges. Id. The ADR system is the means by which American investors hold and trade equity interests in foreign companies. Id.

* * *

———

12. [1] In order for a foreign corporation to trade on an American stock exchange, the foreign corporation must issue and deposit American Depository Shares ("ADSs") with an American financial institution. E.ON v. Acciona, No. 06 Civ. 8720 (DLC), 468 F. Supp. 2d 537, 2006 U.S. Dist. LEXIS 84179, 2006 WL 3357261, at *1 n.2 (S.D.N.Y. Nov. 20, 2006). The depository institution then issues American Depository Receipts ("ADRs") to the beneficial owners of the ADSs, who may sell the ADSs on American securities exchanges. Id. The ADR system is the means by which American investors hold and trade equity interests in foreign companies. Id.

ABN is a foreign bank, as defined in Section 3101(7) of the International Banking Act, 12 U.S.C. 3101(7), that is incorporated in Amsterdam, the Netherlands as an "N.V.", a public company with limited liability. It maintains a New York branch ("New York Branch") through which it offers banking services and financial products. Since 2003, ABN has come under investigation by federal and state regulatory authorities for deficiencies in its internal controls to ensure compliance with banking law and federal anti-money laundering laws, and for alleged violations of United States sanctions laws arising from transactions originating in the bank's office in Dubai, United Arab Emirates.

* * *

E) The Netherlands' Company Law

According to Professor Kroeze, corporations in the Netherlands must be governed by two separate bodies: a Managing Board and a Supervisory Board. Managing Board members are responsible for the management and business affairs of the company and owe fiduciary duties to the corporation, not to the corporation's shareholders. These fiduciary duties include a duty to the company to "properly perform" management tasks. Supervisory Board members serve in an advisory role to oversee the Managing Board. Members of both boards "have a duty of good faith which requires them to behave reasonably and equitably toward one another."

As a public company with limited liability, ABN is subject to the rules set forth in the Dutch Civil Code (the "Code"). The Code provides at least three mechanisms to commence suits on behalf of the corporation for injuries sustained as a result of the breach of duties by members of the Managing or Supervisory Boards. First, it authorizes the Managing Board to initiate legal proceedings on behalf of the company, including proceedings for mismanagement against current or former members of either board. Second, the Code also permits "a Managing Board to delegate its representative authority to one or more directors, or a non-director signatory, acting individually or in concert." ABN's Articles of Association delegate the authority to represent the company as follows:

> 1. The authority to represent the Company shall either reside with two members of the Managing Board acting jointly, or with one member of the Managing Board and *one duly authorized signatory* acting jointly.

> 2. The Company may also be represented by authorized signatories with due observance of any restrictions imposed upon their representative authority. The Managing Board shall decide on their authority, their job title and the terms of appointment, on the understanding that the title of Senior Executive Vice President may only be granted in consultation with the Supervisory Board. (Emphasis supplied.) ABN's Articles of Association do not generally permit an individual shareholder or group of shareholders to commence a legal action on behalf of the corporation to obtain damages for alleged injuries to the corporation. Third, the "[p]revailing opinion among Dutch legal scholars" is that under the Code, the Supervisory Board may also initiate legal proceedings against Managing Board members on behalf of the corporation when

there are conflicts of interest between these individuals and the company, absent any contrary provision in the corporation's articles of association.

The Code does not, however, permit a shareholder or group of shareholders to bring a derivative action on behalf of the corporation to redress injuries caused by Managing Board members' breach of their duties to the corporation. It considers "the company [to be] an independent judicial entity whose legitimate interests are ... distinct, and at times even divergent, from the interests of the company's shareholders." For this reason, Dutch jurists and legal scholars have concluded that "the law of the Netherlands does not recognise shareholder derivative suits that allow a shareholder of a company to sue on behalf of the company for an action that the company has acquired."

Professor Kroeze reports that only one lower court decision in the Netherlands has allowed an action resembling a shareholder derivative suit. In 2000, the District Court of the Hague permitted a 50% shareholder and director of a closely held company to amend a claim in which he alleged harm to the value of his shares due to fraud by the defendant, the other 50% shareholder and director. District Court of The Hague, Den Haag, 12 July 2000, JOR 2001, 90 (ann. MJK) (Neth.). The plaintiff sought compensation for the company from the defendant due to his breach of duties against the company. This lower court decision does not comport with the Supreme Court of the Netherlands' earlier holding in Poot/ABO, Hoge Raad der Nederlanden [HR] [Supreme Court of the Netherlands], 2 December 1994, NJ 288 (ann. Maeijir) (Neth.), that [t]he property of the company is separate from that of its shareholders. In the event that the company incurs a loss because a third party violates a contractual obligation or commits a tort vis-a-vis the company, only the company can bring an action against such a third party in order to seek compensation. Id.

The Code does offer shareholders other means for addressing Managing and Supervisory Board members' malfeasance. First, shareholders may vote to suspend or remove members of either board or even the entire Managing or Supervisory Board. Second, the shareholders may pass a simple majority resolution recommending that the company initiate a legal proceeding against one or more members of the Managing Board. Leading Dutch scholars maintain that the company must follow such a directive. Third, shareholders may apply in writing to the Enterprise Chamber of the Amsterdam Court of Appeal for an inquiry into the management and state of affairs of public companies like ABN which maintain corporate headquarters in the Netherlands. The Enterprise Chamber is authorized to make such an inquiry and take appropriate restorative action.

ABN's Articles of Association permit a two-thirds vote of the general meeting of shareholders to take such action, provided that the voted shares comprise at least half of the company's issued share capital. The Supervisory Board may accomplish the same result by majority vote.

* * *

The expert declaration of Professor Kroeze establishes, and plaintiff concedes, that the law of the Netherlands affords shareholders no right to bring a claim on behalf of a corporation against members of its Managing or Supervisory Boards for breach of duties owed to shareholders since, under Dutch law, members of these boards do not owe fiduciary duties directly to shareholders. While Dutch law and the ABN Articles of Association do provide several avenues which, if followed, would grant a minority shareholder standing to bring a derivative suit on behalf of the corporation, the plaintiff has not pled that she has brought her suit through any of these means. Seybold has not pleaded that a majority of ABN shareholders voted at a General Meeting to grant her authority to bring a derivative action. Nor has she pleaded that the ABN Managing Board delegated its representative authority to her by designating her an "authorized signator[y]" with the power to bring an action on behalf of the corporation either independently or with a member of the Managing Board. Finally, Seybold has not pointed to any provision of the ABN Articles of Association that provides an exception to these rules....

Comments and Questions

1. This case is being brought in the United States. Why is the court applying the law of the Netherlands? Refer to the discussion of the internal affairs doctrine in Chapter 2.

2. As this court notes, supervisory boards, rather than shareholders, have the authority to bring actions against the managing board. What does this suggest about the role of the supervisory board in the governance process?

3. How much choice do shareholders really have in electing members to the supervisory board? *See* Winfried van den Muijsenbergh, *Corporate Governance: The Dutch Experience*, 16 Transnat'l Law. 63, 72 (2002) ("Since the Dutch corporate governance system allows the supervisory board to nominate [its] own members as well as the CEO, the desires of the shareholders are not necessarily important to the board members."). What impact might this have on the supervisory board's role in litigating against managers?

4. An alternative in the Netherlands is for shareholders to petition the government to investigate the actions of management. *See Windt v. Qwest Communs. Int'l, Inc.*, 529 F.3d 183, 193 (3d Cir. 2008) ("Indeed, Dutch shareholders of KPN Qwest have successfully petitioned the Enterprise Chamber in the Netherlands to investigate the alleged mismanagement of the company."). How effective do you think this approach might be?

5. What are some of the reasons to believe that a supervisory board might not be rigorous in bringing legal actions for failings of the management board? Scholars have noted that while derivative suits are commonly allowed in European countries, they are rarely filed. Some attribute this to the high ownership thresholds usually required to bring a suit. *See* Kristoffel R. Grechenig & Michael Sekyra, *No Derivative Shareholder Suits in Europe—A Model of Percentage Limits and Collusion*, Columbia University Law Economics Working Paper No. 312, at 1, 7 (2010) (noting that "in a large number of European countries" shareholders must own "a minimum state of typically 5% to 10% to bring a derivative action and concluding that this explains

"the lack of derivative lawsuits in continental Europe."). The paper does note, however, that there are "few or no lawsuits" in Switzerland or France, two countries with no percentage limits. *Id.* at 8. Others have argued for a wider range of explanations, including the rules governing litigation costs. *See* Pavlos E. Masouros, *Is the EU Taking Shareholder Rights Seriously?: An Essay on the Impotence of Shareholdership in Corporate Europe*, 7 Eur. Company L. 195, 202 (2010) (asserting that shareholders in derivative suits in Europe are "less likely" to be awarded attorneys fees). Is the risk of liability for failure to supervise the management board another possible explanation?

What happens when companies with different board structures merge? Daimler-Benz and Chrysler presented the issue.

Tracinda Corp. v. Daimlerchrysler AG

United States Court of Appeals, Third Circuit
502 F.3d 212 (2007)

Roth, Circuit Judge:

Tracinda Corporation is a holding company, involved primarily in private investment. Its chairman, chief executive officer, and sole shareholder is multi-billionaire Kirk Kerkorian. Prior to the merger of Daimler-Benz and Chrysler Corporation in 1998, Tracinda was the largest holder of Chrysler stock at approximately 14%. Between 1992 and 1996, Kerkorian had a contentious relationship with Chrysler's managers. He frequently pressured them for stock buybacks, stock splits, and dividend increases, and he threatened to initiate a proxy fight in 1995. In 1996, Chrysler and Kerkorian settled their differences with various agreements. Among other things, Chrysler agreed to appoint a Tracinda designee, James Aljian, to the Chrysler Board of Directors.

* * *

On May 6, 1998, the Chrysler Board of Directors unanimously approved the merger and recommended that the Chrysler shareholders do the same. On that same day, simultaneously with the execution of the BCA [Business Combination Agreement], Tracinda, Kerkorian, Chrysler, and Daimler-Benz executed the Stockholder Agreement (SHA), which obligated Tracinda to vote its shares in favor of the merger. The SHA contained a jury waiver clause: Each of the parties hereto ... agrees to waive any right to a trial by jury with respect to any claim, counterclaim or action arising out of or in connection with this Agreement or the transactions completed hereby. Schrempp signed the SHA on behalf of Daimler-Benz; he did not sign in his individual capacity. The agreement was negotiated at arm's length with both sides represented by counsel and other advisors.

Substantively, the SHA did not use the term "merger of equals" and contained no representations concerning corporate governance. Rather, the SHA referred to the BCA, which described the shared governance structure of the new company. Although the BCA used the term "merger of equals" and contained a lengthy definition section, the BCA did not define that term.

On August 6, 1998, the proxy statement and prospectus (Proxy)—which described the proposed merger between Daimler-Benz and Chrysler and sought shareholder approval for the transaction—was filed with the SEC.... The Proxy stated, among other things, that "DaimlerChrysler AG" would be the surviving entity, it would be incorporated in Germany, and it would have two headquarters (in Auburn Hills, Michigan, and Stuttgart, Germany). The Proxy explained that the German AG form was chosen primarily for its tax advantages. The Proxy described various risks relating to the merger, including the difficulties inherent in integrating two large corporations from different countries and business cultures. The Proxy reiterated the terms of the BCA's corporate governance provisions, noting among other things that (1) the DaimlerChrysler Supervisory Board would consist of 5 shareholder representatives designated by Daimler-Benz, another 5 from Chrysler, and 10 labor representatives; (2) the DaimlerChrysler Management Board would initially consist of 8 members designated by Daimler-Benz, another 8 from Chrysler, and 2 members from Daimler's non-automotive group; and (3) Schrempp and Eaton would serve as co-CEOs of DaimlerChrysler for three years. The Proxy included a clear standalone clause that stated these initial management structures could change after the merger was consummated. Kerkorian did not concern himself with the Proxy because he had already committed in the SHA to voting for the merger.

German law requires publicly-owned companies to have two boards—a board of supervisors and a board of management that is supervised by the board of supervisors.

* * *

For two years, the composition of the DaimlerChrysler Supervisory Board did not change; 5 of the 10 shareholder representatives were former Chrysler directors. As provided for in the BCA, the DaimlerChrysler Management Board initially consisted of 10 designees from Daimler-Benz and 8 from Chrysler. Because the Management Board acted by consensus rather than through formal votes, the initial disparity between Chrysler and Daimler-Benz designees was not significant. The managers from Chrysler were able to provide their input with regard to all operations of Daimler-Chrysler and their opinions were taken seriously. The Integration Committee, a transitional body provided for in the BCA, was formed with 50% of its members from Chrysler and 50% from Daimler-Benz, pursuant to the terms of the BCA. This committee was later renamed the Shareholder Committee. Aljian was a member of the Shareholder Committee until Kerkorian directed him to resign on November 24, 2000. Consistent with the BCA, DaimlerChrysler maintained two operational headquarters, in Stuttgart and Auburn Hills.

Because both Daimler-Benz and Chrysler designees considered the 18-person Management Board to be too large, approximately a year after the merger the Board was reduced to 14 members. Five of the remaining members were Chrysler designees. At the time, neither Aljian nor Kerkorian was concerned about this imbalance.... At the time of trial, only one executive from Chrysler, Tom Sidlik, remained on the Management Board; four former Chrysler directors served on the Supervisory Board.

* * *

Was it clearly erroneous then for the District Court to find the term "merger of equals," as defined in relation to the BCA, not to be false or misleading? In order to make this determination, we must assess whether DaimlerChrysler followed the corporate governance structure set forth in the BCA. Pursuant to German law, the BCA provided for a DaimlerChrysler Supervisory Board responsible for appointing members to the Management Board and overseeing their operations. The BCA states that the Supervisory Board shall consist of 20 members, including 10 labor representatives (pursuant to German law), 5 shareholder representatives designated by Daimler-Benz, and 5 shareholder representatives designated by Chrysler. The District Court found that this provision was followed; Tracinda does not assert otherwise. At the time the District Court issued its post-trial opinion, the Supervisory Board was about evenly split between Daimler-Benz and Chrysler designees.

DaimlerChrysler's handling of the Management Board, however, is a more contentious issue. The post-merger changes to that board's composition, as colored by Schrempp's comments in the *Financial Times* and *Barron's* are what prompted Tracinda to bring its suit. With respect to the Management Board's composition, the BCA states (with emphasis added):

> The Management Board … of DaimlerChrysler AG shall consist of 18 members. *In general*, 50% of such members shall be those designated by Chrysler, and 50% of such members shall be those designated by Daimler-Benz, and there will be two additional members with responsibility for Daimler-Benz's non-automotive businesses. For three years following the Effective Time, Jurgen E. Schrempp and Robert J. Eaton shall be the Co-CEOs and Co-Chairmen … of the Management Board … of DaimlerChrysler AG and members of the Office of the Chairmen of DaimlerChrysler AG. If any person designated as a member of the Office of the Chairmen or the Management Board of DaimlerChrysler AG ceases to be a full-time employee of either Chrysler or Daimler-Benz at or before the Effective Time, Daimler-Benz, in the case of any such employee of Daimler-Benz on the date hereof or any such employee to be designated by Daimler-Benz, or Chrysler, in the case of any such employee of Chrysler on the date hereof or any such employee to be designated by Chrysler, shall designate another person to serve in such person's stead.

As highlighted by the District Court, the 50-50 split between Daimler-Benz and Chrysler designees was meant to be understood in general, initial terms. The BCA provided for the right of Chrysler and Daimler-Benz to replace a designee to the Management Board or Office of the Chairman if that individual ceased to be a full-time employee of the company *prior* to the effective date of the merger, but no such provision exists for the departure of executives *after* the merger closed. Other than the time frames placed on the co-chairmanship, no provision of the BCA specified how long the composition of the Management Board was to last after the merger closed. Indeed, the Proxy explicitly stated that the Management Board members chosen by Daimler-Benz and Chrysler pursuant to the BCA were "initial" designees. Further, as noted by the District Court, the BCA provides that the post-merger governance structure is based on "recommendations" and is subject to the powers of the DaimlerChrysler shareholders and the Supervisory and Management Boards. As made clear in the Proxy, the BCA "contains no provision that would bar governance changes after the [merger has] been consummated." Therefore, the District Court found that the post-merger changes to the Management Board composition, resulting in more Daimler-Benz designees sitting on the Board than Chrysler designees, were permitted under the BCA. The District Court explicitly found that "[t]he Merger closed consistent with the provisions in the BCA." Tracinda Corp. v. DaimlerChrysler AG, 364 F. Supp. 2d 362, 380 (D. Del. 2005).

Consequently, the District Court concluded that Tracinda had not proved, by a preponderance of the evidence, a misrepresentation based on use of the term "merger of equals," as defined by the BCA's corporate governance provisions....

Comments and Questions

1. Given that Chrysler would have no more than five directors out of 20 on the supervisory board, was it accurate to call this a merger of equals, at least to the extent this suggested equal right to manage?

2. This was, at the time, the largest cross-border industrial merger. It presented some unique issues, not the least of which was the role of employees in the management structure. German employees had the right to select half of the supervisory board. The United Auto Workers Union received one of the ten labor slots. Lawrence A. Cunningham, *Paradigm or Paradox? Commonalities and Prescriptions in the Vertical Dimension of Global Corporate Governance*, 84 Cornell L. Rev. 1133, 1167 (1999). A member of the UAW remained on the supervisory board until 2007, when the Chrysler was sold to Cerberus, a private equity fund.

3. The management board was originally divided 50-50 between Chrysler and Daimler Benz. What was likely to happen to this configuration over time? Would Chrysler have been able to maintain its equal membership on this board?

4. Although Daimler shareholders held a controlling interest after the merger, there were actually more U.S. than German shareholders. *See* Jeffrey N. Gordon, *Pathways to Corporate Convergence? Two Steps on the Road to Shareholder Capitalism in Germany*, 5 Colum. J. Eur. L. 219, 230 (1999) (immediate post-merger period held 44% of the outstanding "ordinary" stock, while German shareholders held only 37%). This occurred because U.S. shareholders owned approximately 10% of Daimler before the merger. *See* Dennis E. Logue & James K. Seward, *Challenges to Corporate Governance: Anatomy of a Governance Transformation: The Case of Daimler-Benz*, 62 Law & Contemp. Prob. 87, 106 (1999). Nonetheless, the percentage of U.S. ownership quickly dropped, in part, apparently because the company was not included in the S&P Index.

5. The CEO of Daimler, Jürgen Schrempp, indicated that the merger would create "the first German company with a North American culture." One place where the North American culture apparently prevailed was with respect to executive compensation. Chrysler paid substantially higher amounts than Daimler. Statements from Daimler indicated that the matter would be resolved by adopting the Chrysler approach. *See* Cunningham, *supra*, 84 Cornell L. Rev. at 1295.

———————

Are the two systems really that different? Some have asserted that the two systems are in fact converging. *See* Paul L. Davies & Klaus J. Hopt, *Corporate Boards in Europe—and Convergence, Accountability*, 61 Am. J. Comp. L. 301 (2013) ("not only the supervisory boards but also the one-tier boards are dependent on management for information and advice, sometimes to the extent that management takes over."). Make the case for and against convergence.

4. The Role of Stakeholders

Continental systems also sometimes provide for an explicit role in the governance process for non-shareholders. Employees are the most commonly represented stakeholder group. In Germany, companies with 500 or more employees must provide workers with the right to elect representatives to the supervisory board. In the case of companies with more than 2000 employees, half the board must be chosen by employees. Numerous other countries in Europe require employee representation, although not to the same extent as Germany.

Paul L. Davies & Klaus J. Hopt,
Corporate Boards in Europe—Accountability and Convergence
61 Am. J. Comp. L. 301 (2013)[13]

3. Proportion of Employee Representatives

The extent of codetermination at the board level varies considerably. Most often the codetermination laws provide for one-third of the board to be elected by labor. This is the case for many E.U. Member States. In some countries such as Sweden, under certain circumstances labor gets up to two or three seats on the board. A parity form of boardroom codetermination exists only in Germany. It also existed, in a co-optative form, until 2004 in the Netherlands. The German codetermination regime, although best known outside Europe, is in fact an exception since, for large companies it is more exactly at quasi-parity since the shareholder-elected chairman has a casting vote. Yet this casting vote is hardly ever used because of its very negative consequences for the working climate in the company and possible clashes with the unions. This far-reaching codetermination system is path-dependent and has its origins in the post-World War I (1922) and post-World War II (1950, 1952 and 1976) years when the forces of capital and labor had to jointly rebuild Germany's industry. The extent

———————

13. Cited in the American Journal of Comparative Law. Reprinted with permission.

of the codetermination depends on the legal form of the company and its size (below 500 employees: no mandatory employee representation; from 500 to 2000 employees: one-third representation, which applies to about 3,000 companies; more than 2,000 employees: parity, applying to about forty companies). The employee representatives are elected by the workforce either directly or indirectly. Some board seats are reserved for representatives of the trade unions. This regime and its accompanying vested interests are so deeply rooted in tradition that Germany has held up E.U. efforts to harmonize national company laws on board composition or to provide E.U. forms of incorporation—for fear on the part of trade unions that German companies would avoid the national codetermination rules by re-incorporating in other Member States or as E.U. companies. To date, all efforts of reform within Germany have failed.

4. Impact of Mandatory Employee Representation

The most challenging, controversial, and least empirically confirmed question is what impact mandatory employee representation at the board level has. Apart from a problematic impact on the size of the board, felt most acutely under parity codetermination in Germany, and of the costs and the slowing down of the decision-making process, much of the information from companies and trade unions remains anecdotal and is often contradictory.

As to possible impacts on the company and its corporate governance, the impact on the information streams is the most probable. The presence of employee representatives on the board may improve the information available to the board because the information the (supervisory) board receives from the company is filtered by the management. The employee representatives are usually members of the works council, and as such have thorough information about what is going on at the grassroots level. But information goes both ways. Some seats on the labor side, at least in Germany, are filled directly by trade unions, and most of the other employee representatives are trade union members. The labor constituency and the trade unions expect to be informed by their representatives. While there is a mandatory rule on boardroom secrecy, in practice this is often not respected. Even inside information slips out to employees and trade unions, though the European Court of Justice has clearly stated that codetermination cannot justify leaks. This danger may make the management reluctant to inform the (supervisory) board of inside data. Whether an increased flow of (non-inside) information about corporate strategy to trade unions reduces the likelihood of management and union misunderstanding their respective positions in collective bargaining remains a matter of speculation.

Another impact on decision-making occurs because labor issues are most likely to be brought to the board from the workforce in the company as well as from the trade unions. This may be helpful because critical labor issues may be discussed and solved at the board level instead of looming unresolved or coming up only during collective bargaining. But there is also a quid pro quo: the management and the board may omit or delay decisions that would be useful for the company, such as more investment in foreign countries that would have consequences for the workforce at home. Yet, if measures, including drastic ones, need to be taken in the interest of the company, they may actually be facilitated by codetermination, as the experience of rescues, layoffs, and close-downs of companies after the German reunification has shown. Some expect that codetermination will enable better board control over management risk-taking and management remuneration. But experiences from the financial crisis and incidents like the Mannesmann case cast doubt on that theory. Nevertheless, recent decisions in Germany about the compensation of directors have been taken away from the remuneration committees and mandatorily assigned to the board as a whole.

Codetermination may have a distorting impact on the general corporate governance function of the board. Codetermination, at least codetermination at parity, leads to a division between two camps ("benches"). The employee members regularly meet previously in a caucus and tend to discuss and vote as a single body, unless there is a special representative for leading employees. This has been different for the shareholder side, though the German Corporate Governance Code recommended that they also have separate pre-meetings. The distorting effect may be even stronger if the unions have their own representatives on the board. While the unions tend to have a broader view that may be useful for the board in some cases, they may bring in labor interests from outside the company that may not be in the interest of the company and the shareholders. On the whole, this polarization by cementing "benches" is rather negative. Whether this distorting effect can be avoided by having independent directors is doubtful, even if the employee side were to have independent directors as well.

Codetermination may also have an effect on external corporate governance, i.e., on the takeover market. Indeed, codetermination is sometimes considered to be one of the many structural obstacles to the development of a lively takeover market. This is because both management and labor have an incentive to fight off (hostile) takeovers that may result in installing new management and cutting down labor costs and jobs at home.

Evidence about the consequences of codetermination beyond the company is even more anecdotal and speculative. Codetermination in Germany is said to have contributed to a more peaceful climate between capital and labor, to fewer strikes, and to better cooperation between both sides in the interest of the economy as a whole. Some have called codetermination an early social monitoring system.

Comments and Questions

1. What are the advantages and disadvantages of having employee representation on the board? Are there alternative methods of enhancing employee influence without necessarily placing them on the board? Some countries such as the Netherlands have employed work councils. These bodies are selected by employees and have the right to consent to certain practices (particularly labor related matters) and the right to consultation on others (such as a change in control). *See* Tom R. Ottervanger & Ralph M. Pais, *Employee Participation in Corporate Decision Making: The Dutch Model*, 15 Int'l Law. 393 (1981).

2. Is the codetermination structure really beneficial for employees? Some suggest that the record is mixed. *See* Klaus J. Hopt, *Comparative Corporate Governance: The State of the Art and International Regulation*, 59 Am. J. Comp. L. 1 (2011) (noting doubts about whether system provides benefits beyond good labor relations and the avoidance of strikes). Assuming this is true, does codetermination have negative consequences? *See id.* ("The true effect of such a rule might only be greater discretion by the board to act, which in turn makes it more difficult to hold the board accountable.").

3. Not all civil law countries, however, provide employee representation. Eleven of the 27 countries in the EU do so (Austria, the Czech Republic, Denmark, Finland, Germany, Hungary, Luxembourg, the Netherlands, Slovakia, Slovenia and Sweden). Another six do so only for state owned companies (Belgium, France, Greece, Ireland, Poland and Spain). Ten countries provide for no employee representation of any kind (Bulgaria, Cyprus, Estonia, Italy, Latvia, Lithuania, Malta, Portugal, Romania and the United Kingdom). For those requiring representation, one-third of the supervisory board is the most common maximum percentage set aside for employees. Board membership may also be accompanied by restrictions. Thus, for example, in Sweden, union representatives on the board may not participate in bargaining related issues that result in a conflict of interest.

4. What impact does the guaranteed right of employee representatives have on the development of qualifications for the board, including director independence? Should, for example, any independence requirement apply, as is the case with Sweden, only to directors elected by shareholders? What impact would this have on eligibility?

———

As the prior article points out, the practice in Germany of allowing an equal number of employee directors on the supervisory boards of the largest companies is an exception.

Aditi Bagchi, *Varieties of Employee Ownership: Some Unintended Consequences of Corporate Law and Labor Law*
10 U. Pa. J. Bus. & Emp. L. 305, 327–28 (2008)[14]

Labor representatives to supervisory boards are chosen by workers, or workers' electors, in a very complex and heavily regulated election process. Some seats are guaranteed to persons nominated by trade unions, rather than by workers at the company. The 1976 law also gives at least one seat on the supervisory board to each class of employee (blue-collar, white-collar and upper-middle managers) and leaves other labor seats on the board proportional to payroll. The supervisory board elects one person to be chairman by a two-thirds vote. If no one gets two-thirds, separate votes are held by labor and shareholder representatives, with the labor side electing

———

14. Copyright © 2008 University of Pennsylvania Journal of Business & Employment Law. Reprinted by permission.

the vice chairman and the shareholder side electing the chairman. The rule ensures that no labor candidate for the chair can win without shareholder consent. The chair and the chairman's extra vote therefore goes to shareholders.

The Biedenkopf Commission found that German worker-directors emphasized the social aspects of board decisions but had little effect on investment decisions, dividends, and takeovers. Nevertheless, the informational role of codetermination is significant in allowing unions to expand the scope of their influence. This informational advantage of codetermination is undercut by the informal processes firms use, perhaps to avoid the law's intended consequences. Decisions may be negotiated in advance of (infrequent) board meetings and there are indications that the information flow to the supervisory board is limited in anticipation of labor's access. But the informality of the process takes place on both the labor and the shareholder sides, as well as across sides. One of the effects is to limit accountability, which enhances the ability of worker representatives to negotiate compromises.

Unions are able to dominate codetermination. Although workers may not want to delegate their codetermination rights to unions completely, in the sense that they will vote for non-union candidates in the supervisory board primaries, in the actual election they vote overwhelmingly for union candidates. The main effect of non-union candidacies in the primaries is therefore to steer the union in the "right direction" rather than to jeopardize union control. The multi-step process by which board members are elected works to the unions' advantage, because "the selection, nomination, and election of electors ... is more easily controlled by the union apparatus than in direct elections...."

Comments and Questions

1. What does this structure—both formal and informal—suggest about the role of labor in the corporate governance practice? What are some practical implications?

2. While large companies may have an equal division on the board, German law does not require equal division within board committees. It is not unusual to see committee membership consisting of a majority of non-employee directors. What is the significance of this practice?

3. In addition to employees, some German companies have government designated directors. Volkswagen is an example. *See Legal Liability of Directors and Company Officials Part 1: Substantive Grounds for Liability (Report to the Russian Securities Agency)*, 2007 Colum. Bus. L. Rev. 628 (2007) (discussing VW-Gesetz (Volkswagen Act) that provides Lower Saxony with representation on the Volkswagen supervisory board as long as they remain shareholders). Lower Saxony retained its two slots following the merger between Volkswagen and Porsche. What impact might this have on the decision of the supervisory board?

4. China also provides for employees on the supervisory board, although typically less than a majority. *See* Chao Xi, *In Search of an Effective Monitoring Board Model: Board Reforms and the Political Economy of Corporate Law in China*, 22 Conn. J. Int'l L. 1

(2006). They have not been particularly effective. *Id.* (describing union representatives as "a weak junior partner vis-a-vis management" and as "powerless and passive.").

C. Case Study: Italy

Italy represents a useful case study on the evolution of corporate governance in continental Europe. Like other continental countries, Italy is a civil code jurisdiction. The ownership configuration of public companies is also dominated by controlling shareholders, another common attribute outside the United States. At the same time, the country has gone through an almost continuous process of governance reform as a result of multiple catalysts.

Reforms have taken a variety of shapes. They have sought to strengthen traditional Italian governance structures. They have increasingly turned to independent directors as a source of oversight. Perhaps most interestingly, Italy has sought to ensure the presence of independent directors by allowing minority shareholders to nominate and elect their own candidates. Unlike the US, therefore, "independent" directors are not screened by the board of directors. Finally, Italy has also adopted legislation that will allow companies to select their governance structure, including the single and dual board structure.

None of this has been in a straight line fashion. Reforms have had a variety of catalysts, including scandal. Moreover, while corporate governance in Italian companies has strengthened, the efforts operate in a legal environment that makes enforcement sometimes problematic. Governance reform in Italy, therefore, has to address not only the relationship between owners and managers but also the broader cultural context.

Carlo Drago, Francesco Millo, Roberto Ricciuti, Paolo Santella, *Corporate Governance Reforms, Interlocking Directorship and Company Performance in Italy*
41 Int'l Rev. L. & Econ. 38 (2015)[15]

In Italy corporate control is exerted by "industrial families" through alliances based on cross participations, yielding stability in control, in a context in which pyramidal groups have been exploited as a way to separate ownership from control, using capital provided by third parties in order to fund growth. This allows controlling families not only to keep control over the group but also to control the majority of shares in all companies belonging to the pyramid with direct ownership concentrated at the highest level of the control chain, minimizing the amount of capital invested in order to control the whole group. Italian listed companies also issued shares with limited or without voting rights in order to increase capital without diluting the control of the parent company.... Furthermore, when additional capital was required, control

---

15. Copyright © 2015 International Review of Law and Economics. Reprinted with permission.

has been maintained by forming coalitions with other groups.... This is a long-standing feature of the Italian corporate system ...

In addition to controlling families, another "tradition" of Italian companies has been reliance on a single board of directors and a "board of statutory auditors" ("collegio sindaci"). Statutory auditors were elected by shareholders and had some authority to oversee the activities of the board of directors. To the extent, however, that the Italian companies were dominated by controlling shareholders, as the prior article indicates, they could determine the membership of the board of directors and the board of statutory auditors. The first serious effort at governance reform coincided with the government's efforts to reduce its role in the economy by privatizing a significant segment of industry.

Reforms were undertaken in an effort to improve the rights of minority shareholders. Although taking a variety of shapes, they specifically stressed changes to the board of statutory auditors.

Lorenzo Segato, *A Comparative Analysis of Shareholder Protections in Italy and the United States:* Parmalat *as a Case Study*
26 Nw. J. Int'l L. & Bus. 373, 380–81, 400–01 (2006)[16]

The board of statutory auditors has the duty to monitor the company from the inside. Article 148 of the Legislative Decree n. 58/98 (the so-called "Testo Unico della Intermediazione Finanziaria" or "T.U.I.F.") establishes that a company's charter must indicate the number of auditors (not less than three) and ensure that one (or two, depending upon whether the board is composed of more than three auditors) of the auditors is appointed by the minority shareholders. In this way the board can express the will of all the shareholders.... The number of members on the board of statutory auditors directly affects the level of protection for minority shareholders. In fact some powers (for instance, the power to call a shareholders' meeting as a consequence of a director's decision) can be exercised only by at least two members of the board in concert. In a board composed of five members, minority shareholders can elect two statutory auditors and thus have the ability to call a shareholder meeting.

* * *

The board of auditors, in the traditional model of the Italian *società per azioni*, is composed of three or five members and is elected by the meeting of the shareholders. The board of auditors has the duty to control the lawfulness and efficiency of the company; more specifically, to supervise the observance of the law and the by-laws, and comply with the principles of proper management. In particular, the board of auditors has the power to supervise the adequacy of the organization and the admin-

---

istrative and accounting structure adopted by the company and its functioning (article 2403 of the Civil Code).

Article 2407 of the Civil Code establishes that the auditors shall fulfill their duties with the professionalism and diligence required by the nature of the appointment; they are liable for the truth of their statements, and shall keep secret the facts and documents of which they have knowledge by reason of their office. Auditors are liable both to the company and the creditors of the company for the correct fulfillment of their duties. Auditors are also liable in solido with the directors for acts and omissions of the latter, when the injury would not have occurred if they had exercised vigilance in conformity with the duties of their office.

Auditors of listed companies have further duties and powers. Article 149 of the T.U.I.F. requires them to immediately inform the CONSOB about any irregularities discovered and also to send CONSOB the minutes of the board meetings, the assessments made, and any other documents deemed useful. Auditors, even as individuals, may ask the directors about the state of the company's management or about other specific matters. They can also call a meeting both of the shareholders and of the directors. Finally, auditors can also report the facts to the court when they discover serious irregularities in the management by the directors in violation of their duties (article 151 of the T.U.I.F.).

Comments and Questions

1. The reforms in 1998, known as the Draghi Law, were traced to privatization by the government. How might privatization act as a catalyst for governance reform?

2. The reforms sought to, among other things, strengthen the role of the statutory auditors. Despite the name, the board of statutory auditors does not conduct audits, at least for public companies. That task falls to an outside auditor. Broadly speaking, the board of statutory auditors is assigned "to monitor the directors' performance in the discharge of their duties ..." Andrea Melis, *On the Role of the Board of Statutory Auditors in Italian Listed Companies*, 12 Corp. Governance 74, 77 (2004). The ability to oversee depends at least in part on the ability to learn of concerns or wrongdoing. Members are allowed to attend board meetings and are entitled to regular reports from the board. TUIF, Article 150. Is this enough to assess the conduct of management?

3. What happens when the board of statutory auditors becomes aware of any kind of irregularity or improper activity by management? One option is to report the matter to the CONSOB, the Italian Securities and Exchange Commission. *See* TUIF, Article 149. Assuming a referral requires a majority vote of the board of statutory auditors, what are some reasons why this might not occur even when improprieties are uncovered?

4. Statutory auditors exist in other countries. We have already seem something similar in Japan. Likewise, Swiss companies rely on the structure. The duties of the body, however, can vary. In Switzerland, the statutory auditor is responsible for auditing the company's financial statements. The primary role of the statutory auditor

in Japan is to ensure legal compliance. The effectiveness of the body may depend upon the system of election.

5. The reforms adopted in 1998 went beyond changes to the board of statutory auditors. In addition, derivative suits were permitted for the first time, although they could only be brought by shareholders with 5% or more of the shares. The percentage of shares necessary to call a special meeting was reduced (from 20% to a still significant 5%) and the proxy process was liberalized. For a discussion of these reforms, see Bianchi L. Enriques, *Corporate Governance in Italy After the 1998 Reform: What Role for Institutional Investors?*, Studie Ricerche (Jan. 2001). Do you think these reforms significantly increased the rights of minority shareholders?

6. Italy in 1998 also adopted the Preda Code, a voluntary code of corporate governance drafted under the auspices of Stefano Preda, the chairman of the Borsa Italiana. As with other governance codes, adherence is voluntary. Built around the principle of comply or explain, listed companies must, however, annually report on their conformity with the Code. The Preda Code has since gone through a number of revisions.

Another series of reforms were motivated by a very different set of considerations. As business became more global and Italian companies interacted and merged with foreign business, pressure arose for a more flexible governance structure. The government addressed these concerns in 2004.

Marco Ventoruzzo, *Experiments in Comparative Corporate Law: The Recent Italian Reform and the Dubious Virtues of a Market for Rules in the Absence of Effective Regulatory Competition*
40 Tex. Int'l L.J. 113, 146–148 (2004)[17]

The Reform [that came into effect on Jan. 1, 2004] introduced, in addition to this traditional model of corporate governance, new variations that permit at least three, and potentially four, separate possible models of corporate governance. The first possible model is the classic, traditional model [relying on a board of statutory auditors], which is similar to the ones adopted in France, Spain, and most South and Central American countries. In addition, it is now also possible (as will be discussed below) to adopt either a "dualistic" model, inspired by the German system of corporate governance, or a "monistic" system, inspired by Anglo-American systems of corporate governance.

Even within the traditional model, there are some revisions. As noted above, prior to the Reform, the board of auditors in nonlisted corporations controlled the cor-

---

17. Copyright © 2004 Texas International Law Journal. Reprinted by permission.

poration's accounting and balance sheet, while in listed corporations, the internal board of auditors controlled only the corporation's system of information, with external auditors controlling the accounting and balance sheet. Under the Reform, it is now possible for both listed and nonlisted corporations to assign to external auditors control over the accounting and balance sheet, leaving to the internal board of auditors the task of controlling the corporation's system of information.

In addition to the traditional model, a corporation can adopt a "dualistic" system, inspired by German corporate law. Under this model, the corporation does not appoint two different bodies, a board of directors and a board of auditors. Instead under this model, the shareholders' meeting appoints only a supervisory board, which under German law is called the Aufsichtsrat. This supervisory board is charged with appointing the board of managing directors, which under German law is called the Vorstand. In effect, there are two boards of directors, the supervisory board and the board of managing directors. The shareholders' meeting does not directly appoint and cannot remove the board of managing directors, but that power is instead vested in the supervisory board, which is appointed by the shareholders' meeting.

One important feature of this model is that the board of supervisory directors has responsibility for some of the controlling functions that in the traditional model are assigned to the board of auditors and also for some of the functions traditionally reserved to shareholders' meeting in the traditional model. One example is that the balance sheet is approved by the supervisory board. This is a change from the traditional system, in which the balance sheet was generated by the board of directors but approved by the shareholders' meeting.

In the third model, the "monistic" system based on Anglo-American systems, the shareholders' meeting appoints only a board of directors, but one-third of the members of the board must possess independence requirements similar to the ones prescribed for the members of the board of auditors in the traditional model and provided by Article 2399 of the Civil Code. The board of directors then appoints, within the board itself, an audit committee among the directors possessing the independence requirements mentioned above. There is not a separate body that controls the activities of the managing directors, but instead an internal body of independent directors.

From this brief overview, it is clear that the Reform dramatically expands contractual freedom in structuring corporate governance. Instead of one model, there are now three, four if retention of the original traditional model is considered, and each model has significantly different rules. The new models create the possibility for more precise tailoring of corporate governance structures to the specific needs of particular corporations. For example, the dualistic model, with its supervisory and managing board, can be used by a very large corporation in which it is necessary to have a board that deals only with general issues, as well as a more executive board for day-by-day managing of the corporation. This system might also render a corporation more resistant to hostile takeovers because the incumbent controlling shareholders would have to change not only one board of directors, but two separate boards. It would first be necessary to terminate the members of the supervisory board, and then to have the newly appointed members of the supervisory board appoint new members of the board of managing directors. While this hurdle is probably not technically a defensive measure, it can nevertheless make it more difficult and more expensive to take over a corporation, at least in comparison to the monistic model.

Comments and Questions

1. Globalization likely played an important role in the adoption of these reforms. The flexibility to select an appropriate governance model allowed a parent in Italy and a subsidiary incorporated in other countries to have the same governance structure. Similarly, the approach enabled Italian companies listed in other jurisdictions to adopt a governance structure more recognizable in those markets. An Italian company listed on the NYSE, for example, could opt for a unitary board system.

2. Why might a company favor one model over the other? What are the advantages and disadvantages of each? Professor Ventoruzzo notes that the dual board structure might be useful for the transfer of ownership of a family business. "The heirs of a corporation's founders could be members of the managing board of directors, while the founders can be members of the controlling supervisory board."

3. Most public companies in Italy continue to rely on the traditional structure (a board and a board of statutory auditors), with few listed companies opting for other variations. *See* 2014 Report on Corporate Governance of Italian Listed Companies, CONSOB (Dec. 2014) ("The evidence on corporate boards of Italian listed companies confirms the predominance of the traditional management and control system, with only 7 companies out of 244 envisaging an alternative system at the end of 2013"). Some banks initially adopted the supervisory board structure, although the structure remains relatively unpopular. Mediobanca, an Italian investment bank, did so then switched back to the traditional board structure with a Board of Statutory Auditors. What do you think explains the resistance?

4. Italy is not alone in providing flexibility in the selection of the appropriate governance structure. We have already noted the example of Japan. Other countries have done the same. *See* Klaus J. Hopt, *Comparative Corporate Governance: The State of the Art and International Regulation*, 59 Am. J. Comp. L. 1, 23 (Winter 2011) (noting that France, the Netherlands, Belgium, Luxembourg, Finland, Portugal and Denmark allow some choice on governance structure). Is this perhaps an alternative to convergence? Alternatively, will this approach result in convergence?

Italy in the new millennium suffered corporate scandals on the magnitude of Enron and Worldcom. In December 2003, Parmalat, Italy's 8th largest company and one dominated by a family, defaulted on bond payments and, shortly afterwards, filed for bankruptcy. The collapse raised a number of questions about the governance structure in Italy, particularly the role of the board of statutory auditors.

In re Parmalat Securities Litigation

United States District Court, Southern District of New York

376 F. Supp. 2d 449 (2005)

KAPLAN, DISTRICT JUDGE:

Maria Martellini is a citizen and resident of Italy. She is a professor of economics at the Universita degli Studi de Brescia where she has taught business and economics for nearly 15 years. She is a defendant in this case because she was a minority shareholder representative on the Board of Statutory Auditors ("Statutory Board") of Parmalat's holding company, Parmalat Finanziaria, S.p.A ("Finanziaria") during the period commencing with the Statutory Board's 1999 Half-Year Report and concluding with its 2001 Annual Report. She never was an officer or director of Finanziaria or any of its subsidiaries.

The complaint alleges in substance that reports issued by the Statutory Board during Prof. Martellini's tenure stated that the Board (1) had "verified the adequacy of the administrative/accounting and internal audit systems" as well as "compliance with legal provisions concerning the drawing up and layout of the statutory and consolidated financial statements and the directors' report through direct checks and information received from" Deloitte, (2) had "carried out the checks required by law in accordance with the principles for boards of statutory auditors established by the Italian accounting profession," (3) was unaware of any atypical or unusual related party or intercompany transactions and that the notes to the financial statements relating to such transactions were adequate, (4) had carried out its obligation to supervise the administration of the company and had checked the adequacy of the internal controls and administrative and accounting system, and (5) Parmalat had complied substantially with the Voluntary Code of Best Practice set up by the Italian stock exchange. Plaintiffs allege that the Board in fact was under the control of company management, that it recklessly failed to oversee the accuracy of Parmalat's financial statements and to see to it that internal controls were working effectively, that it recklessly failed to recognize that Parmalat's web of affiliates and special purpose entities were not accounted for properly, that the Board members and others "individually and collectively were responsible for the ... preparation and review of [Parmalat's] audited and unaudited financial statements," that the members of the Board were reckless in not knowing of—or directed or participated in—Parmalat's fraudulent overstatement of assets and earnings and understatement of liabilities, and that they recklessly or deliberately issued false reports.

* * *

Plaintiffs argue that the complaint adequately alleges that members of the Statutory Board, including Prof. Martellini, recklessly failed to oversee the accuracy of financial controls and otherwise to serve as a check on improper financial practices. More specifically, they contend that the Board, including Prof. Martellini, (1) failed to investigate claims made by shareholders on April 14, 2003, (2) failed to investigate concerns expressed by CONSOB, the Italian securities regulator, "in 2002 or 2003" concerning the Epicurum Fund, and (3) swept under the rug questions raised by local Deloitte partners concerning a Parmalat Argentine subsidiary. These contentions, however, fail.

To begin with, the complaint alleges that Prof. Martellini's term on the Statutory Board ended with the 2001 Annual Report, which appears to have been issued in April 2002. Thus, there is no basis for supposing that Prof. Martellini had anything to do with shareholder complaints in 2003.

The assertion relating to the CONSOB concerns is equally specious. Plaintiffs' memorandum says that the Statutory Board "in 2002 or 2003" ignored an "obvious red flag" raised by a CONSOB inquiry relating to allegedly suspicious transactions involving the Epicurum fund. The complaint, however, alleges that Epicurum was incorporated in September 2002 and, contrary to the statement in plaintiffs' memorandum, does not date the CONSOB inquiry. Given the fact that the complaint alleges that Prof. Martellini left the Statutory Board months before Epicurum even was incorporated, there is simply nothing here to support an allegation of recklessness or worse on her part.

Finally, plaintiffs' argument concerning the concerns raised by Deloitte with respect to the Argentine subsidiary takes liberties with the record. Their memorandum states:

> "Additionally, during Martellini's tenure on the Board of Statutory Auditors in 2000, local Deloitte partners raised questions about the accounting of Parmalat's Argentinian operations, but when they requested certain information, Tonna angrily revoked Deloitte's auditing contract in Argentina. Mamoli, the Deloitte partner in Italy, met with Tonna *and with Parmalat's Board of Statutory Auditors—which at the time, included Martellini.* The issues raised by the local Deloitte auditor in Argentina were never addressed, and Martellini and the Statutory Auditors swept them under the rug. PP 1033–39."

In fact, the complaint tells a somewhat different story.

According to the complaint, problems arose between Deloitte's regional auditor in Argentina and Deloitte's Italian office and Parmalat. Following a request for information from unspecified Deloitte partners, Tonna revoked Deloitte's Argentine contract. Mamoli, the engagement partner at Deloitte Italy, then expressed the hope that Deloitte Argentina and Deloitte Italy would be more cooperative to avoid offending Parmalat. Esteban, evidently the Argentine partner, nevertheless reaffirmed his position. The complaint then states that "after a meeting with Tonna and Parmalat's Board of Statutory Auditors, but without addressing the issues Esteban had raised..., Mamoli informed Esteban that the Argentina issue had been resolved...."

The important point to note here is that the plaintiffs' memorandum—by stating that the Statutory Board swept the issue under the rug—implies that the Board knew of the concerns raised by Esteban and Deloitte Argentina. But the complaint says no such thing. It says only that Mamoli, after a meeting with the Board that is not described in any respect, announced to Esteban that the issue had been resolved. It does not allege that the facts ever came to the attention of the Board.

Finally, plaintiffs contend that *scienter* may be inferred from the fact that Prof. Martellini failed to review or check information that she had a duty to monitor and had access to information suggesting the Statutory Board's public statements were inaccurate. Although plaintiffs here quote from the Second Circuit's opinion in *Novak v. Kasaks*, they do not address the court's explanation there that such allegations would be sufficient where the plaintiffs alleged that the defendant ignored specific instances of obvious fraud or suspicious behavior, or, in the case of access to contrary information, where the plaintiff identified the reports supposedly containing the contrary information. Plaintiffs make no such specific allegations here. In consequence, there is no permissible basis for concluding that the members of the Board acted recklessly.

Comments and Questions

1. The scandal at Parmalat was not subtle. *See* David A. Skeel, Jr., *Book Review: Governance in the Ruins: Law and Capitalism: What Corporate Crises Reveal About Legal Systems and Economic Development Around the World*, 122 Harv. L. Rev. 696, 728 (2008) ("Parmalat's fraud was remarkable more for its audacity and scope than for its complexity."). One court described the activities of Parmalat as "something akin to a Ponzi scheme." *In re Parmalat Sec. Litig.*, 594 F. Supp. 2d 444, 448 (S.D.N.Y. 2009). What sorts of concerns does this raise about the system of governance in Italy?

2. As part of the oversight function, the board of statutory auditors has a role in the financial disclosure process. It is usually responsible, for example, for ensuring the independence of the outside auditing firm and monitoring any non-accounting related services provided by the firm. Moreover, listed companies with an internal control committee (sometimes referred to as an audit committee) are expected to report their activities to the board of statutory auditors and to allow the chair to "participate" in the meetings. Finally, the board of statutory auditors and outside auditors are expected to exchange information although they are independent of each other. Given this authority, why might the fraud at Parmalat not have been uncovered by the board of statutory auditors? *See* Guido Ferrarini & Paolo Giudici, *Financial Scandals and the Role of Private Enforcement: The Parmalat Case*, *in* After Enron: Improving Corporate Law And Modernising Securities Regulation in Europe and the U.S. 187 (John Armour & Joseph A. McCahery eds., 2006) (describing board of statutory auditors as inefficient "in discovering mismanagement and fraud," as well as complacent).

3. The collapse of Parmalat illustrated how reforms designed to ensure proper governance can be circumvented. Italian law at the time required the outside auditor to be rotated every nine years. Article 159. Consistent with that requirement, Parmalat dutifully replaced its existing auditor but not the auditor for all of the subsidiaries. How might this undermine the obligation to rotate accounting firms? *See In re Parmalat Sec. Litig.*, 594 F. Supp. 2d 444, 448 (S.D.N.Y. 2009) (assertions that, in anticipation of the change in auditor, allegedly "fictitious financing transactions" were moved to jurisdictions not scheduled to be audited by Deloitte).

4. Parmalat was a family controlled business. Family ownership, as already noted, has historically been a common feature of Italian governance. Do you think, in light of Parmalat, globalization, and other factors buffeting the traditional approach to governance, this might be changing? See 2014 Report on Corporate Governance of Italian Listed Companies, CONSOB, Dec. 2014 ("Families play the major role as 'ultimate controlling shareholders' in 61 percent of the firms (around 30 percent of total market capitalisation), especially smaller companies operating in the industrial sector."). What does this suggest about the direction of governance reform in Italy?

———————

The lessons of Parmalat generated pressure for reform designed to strengthen the system of governance. In particular, the changes were intended to increase the role of both minority investors and independent directors in the governance process.

David A. Skeel, Jr. et al., *Inside-Out Corporate Governance*
37 J. Corp. L. 147 (2011)[18]

... On the basis of the 2005 law, all listed corporations were required to amend their bylaws to give force to this provision and ensure that at least one director on their boards was elected by means of a so-called alternative list to represent the interests of minority shareholders. The law gave companies flexibility in determining the minimum amount of stock a minority shareholder or group needed to have to present its own "slate" of directorial nominees, but required that the percentage be not greater than 2.5%.

It is worth pausing to note how far the Italian approach to protecting minority shareholders diverges from U.S. corporate governance. In the United States, the watchword is shareholder power and proxy access is designed to make shareholder voting more meaningful. In Italy, by contrast, shareholder voting is secondary; the objective is to put minority representatives on the board. The most obvious explanation for the distinction is the prevalence of controlling shareholder blocks in Italy, as compared to the more fluid nature of shareholdings in the United States. But the distinction also seems to reflect different emphases in the two countries: voting is privileged in the United States, negotiation (with minority shareholders given a seat at the table) in Italy.

Prior to a March 2006 revision of the Italian Stock Exchange's corporate governance code, election of directors was conducted by means of secret ballot. This caused a serious problem in ensuring that the minority shareholder chose the minority representative as it was impossible to ascertain which shareholders were voting for the different slates of directors. In March 2006, the Italian Stock Exchange revised its Corporate Governance Code to recommend that: "(a) Italian listed companies, while complying with the secret ballot requirement, still 'ensure transparency in the selection and appointment process of directors' and (b) qualified shareholders of Italian listed

———————

companies (including controlling shareholders and institutional investors) sponta-neously declare their votes in the shareholders' meetings for the appointment of the directors."

An issue that has generated widespread discussion in Italy, and may also have rel-evance for the United States, is the question whether minority shareholders will in fact place directors on the boards of most large Italian companies. The number of minority directors remains quite small; some observers suspect that the controlling shareholders of some companies have struck deals with the largest minority share-holders in return for the shareholders' promise not to propose a slate of directors. This observation echoes concerns that proxy access in the United States will be used strategically, though the concerns are in sense mirror images: in Italy, the issue is hidden deals; in the United States it is, as discussed in the next Part, strategic use by outsiders of the "megaphone" of a public directorial election process.

Comments and Questions

1. The reforms essentially provided for a system that allowed minority share-holders to nominate and elect candidates to the board. The article notes, however, that it is an open question as to whether minority shareholders will actually use the authority. Indeed, most listed companies do not have directors nominated by mi-nority shareholders. *See* 2014 Report on Corporate Governance of Italian Listed Companies, CONSOB (Dec. 2014) (92 out of 237 listed companies with available data had a minority director). Why is that the case? What are some impediments to minority shareholders availing themselves to authority designed to protect their own interests?

2. Ordinarily, countries seeking to increase board independence simply require the inclusion of independent directors on the board. In such a system, it is manage-ment that locates and nominates these directors. Why do you think Italy did not opt for that approach? What are the advantages and disadvantages to the approach taken in Italy?

3. Discuss the tension between the use of a secret ballot and the requirement that minority shareholders have the right to elect their own candidates. Does the solution fully address these concerns?

4. Italy is not the only country to have given minority shareholders representation on the board. *See* Marco Ventoruzzo, *Empowering Shareholders in Directors' Elections: A Revolution in the Making*, ECGI Working Paper Series in Law, Working Paper No. 147/2010, Mar. 2010, at 35 (noting that in addition to Italy, Iceland, Russia and Spain "have adopted some form of minority shareholders' representation on the board"). Nonetheless, the list is rather short. Why might this be the case?

5. Reforms in the aftermath of Parmalat also sought to strengthen the position of minority shareholders with respect to the board of statutory auditors. First, minority shareholders have the right to elect at least one representative to the BSA. Moreover, the chair must be selected from the minority members of the BSA. The chair has the

authority to attend meetings of the internal control (audit) committee of the company. In addition, the board of statutory auditors was given the right to file a derivative suit, although only upon a two thirds approval of the members. What will be the likely impact of these reforms? Will the mere presence of independent directors on the board improve governance?

6. Is it enough to include minority representatives on the board? They obviously cannot control the outcome of decisions. How might their authority be enhanced?

7. The controlling shareholder model of ownership differentiates Italy from the US. Could this be a comparative advantage? *See* Maria DiMeo Calvelli, *In Defense of the Business Cultural Values Reflected in the Italian Securities Markets: What the US 2008 Financial Meltdown Can Teach Us*, 5 Brook. J. Corp. Fin & Com. L. 317, 338 (2011) ("Although there is room for the continued improvement of its corporate governance, the time has come for Italy to focus its reforms so as to capitalize on both the unique advantages offered by the controlling or dominant shareholder system and the improvements already made in protecting the investing minority."). How might this be the case?

8. Additional reforms have sought to increase the role of independent directors in the area of executive compensation. The Preda Code recommends the formation of a remuneration committee that is made up of non-executive directors, a majority of which should be independent. At least one director must have "adequate knowledge and experience in finance or remuneration policies ..." What impact is this structure likely to have in companies with controlling shareholders?

Other reforms have sought to empower minority investors by eliminating barriers to private enforcement.

Luca Enriques, *Corporate Governance Reforms in Italy: What Has Been Done and What Is Left to Do*
10 Eur. Bus. Org. L. Rev. 477–513 (2009)[19]

Private enforcement is a necessary evil for effective corporate governance regimes, unless and until control over listed companies is in the hands of institutional investors (as in the UK). Without private enforcement, self-enforcement (shareholders' voice) is itself emasculated, because there can be no credible commitment to obtain justice via formal enforcement, and even public enforcement is less effective, because of the lower "competitive" pressure on supervisors.

* * *

---

19. Copyright © 2009. Reprinted by permission of the author.

The problem is that Italian private enforcement institutions are currently in such a bad shape that one is reluctant to push for greater access to justice for minority shareholders before those institutions are improved. At the same time, no serious improvement of private enforcement institutions can be expected if rules remain in place that basically discourage plaintiffs from bringing suits or, in other words, if private enforcement institutions are not given a chance to gain experience on the field. To break this deadlock, shareholders' access to justice should be encouraged with the very purpose of making the longer-term reform efforts that are needed to improve private enforcement institutions politically salient.

Repeal of the ban on contingency fees in 2006 was a first, important step in the direction of removing obstacles to shareholder suits, but much more can be done before we come even close to the excesses of U.S. private enforcement. A simple list is sufficient for present purposes: no thresholds for derivative suits (possibly with an "opt-up" clause allowing to impose threshold lower than the current ones), discovery mechanisms, notice pleading as opposed to fact pleading, a selective American rule preventing judges from burdening losing plaintiff shareholders with defendants' fees and costs other than in case of strike suits, better cooperation mechanisms between supervisors, such as Consob, and private enforcers (in the form of *amicus curiae* briefs and assistance to courts in the gathering of evidence). All of these measures would encourage shareholders to bring suit in case of corporate insiders' wrongdoing while at the same time stopping short of sparking the problems associated with U.S. excesses.

* * *

Of course, a reform-minded policymaker should start as soon as possible tackling the chronic malaise of the Italian civil justice system, i.e. the length of trials and the average low level of specialization of its courts, and of course not just to improve listed companies' corporate governance. To do so, reforms should tackle the very governance of civil justice institutions, so that judges' incentives are more aligned to citizens' interests in a speedier and higher-quality justice service.

A more market-friendly political culture would have a much greater impact on Italian capital markets' competitiveness than any corporate law reform ever could. In fact, the persistent and bi-partisan meddling of politicians with the allocation of control rights in listed companies and their clear and credible commitment to keep control in Italian hands, should a foreigner launch a hostile (or even a friendly) bid on any large Italian company, intuitively make investment in Italian listed companies less attractive.

From another perspective, the central role politics still has in economic activities, whether via regulation or via informal interference, makes it valuable for listed companies to have dominant shareholders who mediate with politicians in the interest of minority shareholders too. In other words, in such an environment dominant shareholders are the lesser evil: because they can better resist the State's grabbing hand than non-owner managers could, ownership (together with political connections) grants dominant shareholders the social and political legitimacy that is needed to defend the firm. That it is thus impossible to dispense with (politically well-connected) dominant shareholders is also detrimental to the efficient allocation of control and to the functioning of the market for corporate control as a disciplining device, because no outsider (i.e. no foreigner) can aspire to play that role, let alone to play it effectively.

Finally, legal formalism and doctrinal legal thought are still predominant in courts, law faculties, and the legal professions. That negatively affects the quality of corporate governance institutions, because in order for the law to effectively protect equity holders, substance has always to trump form and standards need to be applied creatively (albeit with a market-friendly approach). In fact, dominant shareholders have a number of ways to evade bright line rules or to formally adhere to the letter of the law. If courts, as I have argued elsewhere, tend to be formalistic and deferential to corporate insiders' decisions even when these are tainted by conflicts of interest, then even shareholder plaintiff-friendly procedural rules will prove insufficient to protect minority shareholders. Similarly, for Consob to effectively perform its investor protection functions, it should be possible for it to go beyond the formalistic interpretation of its own rules. However, such is not a realistic course of action, because formalistic courts review its resolutions.

Is there any chance to move in the direction of a more common law style, equity-friendlier legal and political culture in Italy? Unfortunately, little if anything can be done to change the broadly prevailing market-hostile political culture, but something can indeed be thought out to modernize Italian legal culture in the long run. First, public, semi-public (like banking foundations'), and private funds could be channeled to send Italian law graduates in the U.S. or the UK to attend LLM programs. Second, and much more ambitiously, a bottom-up reform of Italian legal education could be given a try. By bottom-up, I mean that a good start would be if groups of academics, however small, and preferably within the same few above-average law faculties, invested in teaching law to students from a functional perspective. Again, private, semi-private and perhaps public funds could be used to give those academics the incentives to invest in such endeavor, compensating them for their high opportunity costs.

Comments and Questions

1. The article by Professor Enriques suggests the need for greater private enforcement, particularly through the expanded use of derivative suits. Yet he also notes that the private enforcement institutions in the country are weak and specifically references problems with the Italian civil justice system. Can one work without the other? What does this suggest about the complexity of governance reform?

2. What about the problem of judicial delay? *See* Marco Ventoruzzo, *Issuing New Shares and Preemptive Rights: A Comparative Analysis*, 12 Rich. J. Global L. & Bus. 517, 535–35 (2013) (describing as impediments to litigation for breach of fiduciary duties "the extremely long duration of civil litigation"). How does this interfere with private enforcement and what are some possible solutions?

3. What does this article suggest about the role of culture and politics in the system of corporate governance? How might one go about instituting a more "market-friendly political culture"? Do you agree that one solution (albeit a partial one) would be to send more students to the U.S. and UK for LLMs? What would this accomplish?

IV. What Role for the European Union?

Governance reform often occurs as a result of catalysts. Some, such as the collapse of Parmalat, are domestic. Others, however, are external. In the European Union, reform can occur because of the need to implement the strictures of a relevant directive.

The EU has been undertaking a broad experiment in harmonizing the approach to governance among member states. The complex task must address a wide array of approaches to corporate governance, whether common or civil law, stakeholder or shareholder, developed or developing. In what can often be a slow task, the directives that emerge from the process must then be implemented by the member nations.

Arthur R. Pinto, *The European Union's Shareholder Voting Rights Directive from an American Perspective: Some Comparisons and Observations*
32 Fordham Int'l L.J. 587, 604–09 (2009)[20]

III. THE COMPANY LAW HARMONIZATION PROCESS

Up until 1989, there were nine company law directives and one regulation implemented. From 1989 until 2001, the period has been described as one of stagnation with controversies over a variety of issues of company law such as regulation of takeovers and the SE and with no significant company law adopted at the EU level.

But in the late 1990s, there was a strong EU push to improve the capital markets and improve the single market for financial services through its financial service action plan. Given that success, in 2001 the Commission set up the High Level Group of Company Law Experts—also referred to as the "Winter Group"—to develop an action plan for company law. It was "to define new priorities for the broader future development of company law in the European Union." In addition there was the need to deal with the rejection of the Takeover Directive by the European Parliament after more than a decade of attempts to enact it. In the midst of its work there were the corporate scandals in the United States and the enactment of Sarbanes-Oxley. The recommendations of the Winter Group became the basis of the EU Commission publishing in 2003 "Modernising Company Law and Enhancing Corporate Governance in the European Union—A Plan to Move Forward," ("CLAP").

---

20. Copyright © 2009 Fordham International Law Journal. Reprinted by permission of Fordham International Law Journal and the author.

CLAP dealt with a number of broad issues including: 1) corporate governance, 2) legal capital maintenance and alteration, 3) company groups, 4) restructuring and mobility, 5) new European business forms, and 6) enhancing transparency. But the main concern of the Commission was corporate governance.

IV. THE VOTING RIGHTS DIRECTIVE

There were several proposals on corporate governance issues that were part of CLAP and some were quickly enacted including the Voting Rights Directive. There are a number of different reasons behind the enactment of this Directive. In much of Europe there is no long tradition of easy proxy voting directly by shareholders without a variety of constraints, and the Voting Rights Directive may now enhance that voting. There was the promotion of good corporate governance through shareholder participation in voting, the protection of EU shareholders who do not reside in the home country where their company resides, the protection of small individual shareholders, the concern that increased ownership by foreign investors could create firms with passive investors, the recognition of increased cross border investing and the importance of integrated markets.

The Voting Rights Directive recognized that prior securities EU directives have provided disclosure to shareholders, but there was also a need for certain minimum standards for protecting investors and promoting the free exercise of voting. Of particular concern to the Commission and those consulted were the obstacles to cross-border voting such as "the requirement to block shares before a general meeting..., difficult and late access to information that is relevant to the general meeting and the complexity of cross-border proxy voting." Thus the Directive was designed to provide some minimum standards.

The Voting Rights Directive is a mix of principles, mandatory rules and rules that provide companies with options. The key provisions include:

1. Equal treatment of shareholders as to participation and voting in the general meeting;

2. Required notice of general meeting of at least 30 days and certain required information;

3. The right to put items on the agenda of the general meeting and table draft resolutions;

4. Removal of requirements of any blocking mechanism such as share deposits that restricted shareholder participation in the general meeting;

5. The right of shareholders to ask questions on agenda items which must be answered; and

6. Allowing and facilitating proxy voting individually and through securities accounts.

The Directive also attempts to deal with the potential of the internet and thus one of its goals was to "remove all legal obstacles to electronic participation in general meetings." Because of concerns with technology and security, it was not made oblig-atory. The Directive does call for the posting of some information on the internet, such as meeting notice, number of shares and voting rights, text of proposed reso-lutions and related documents and forms that can be used to vote. Questions can also be asked by electronic means prior to the meeting and response can be given if the relevant information is available on the company's internet site. Proxy holders may be appointed by electronic means and Member States shall prohibit requirements, which hinder the exercise of voting rights by electronic means except if necessary for shareholder identification.

Comments and Questions

1. The adoption of directives has been described as a "complicated and time-consuming process." Michael C. Schouten, *The Political Economy of Cross-Border Voting in Europe*, 16 Colum. J. Eur. L. 1, 9 (2009–10). The formative process for the Directive began in 2003 but it took until 2007 and a "lengthy consultation process" before the Directive emerged. Luca Enriques & Matteo Gatti, *EC Reforms of Corporate Governance and Capital Markets Law: Do They Tackle Insiders' Opportunism?*, 28 Nw. J. Int'l L. & Bus. 1, 27 (2007).

2. Member states were given until August 2009 to comply with the Voting Rights Directive. Nonetheless, compliance was slow. Germany implemented changes in 2009; Italy in 2010. Nonetheless, by early 2010, the European Commission sent notices of noncompliance to a number of countries, including Belgium, Spain, France, the Netherlands, and Sweden. What does this suggest about the difficulties associated with the harmonization of corporate governance requirements in the EU?

3. The Directive provides that "[s]hareholders should, in principle, have the pos-sibility to put items on the agenda of the general meeting and to table draft resolutions for items on the agenda." The Directive specifically allows the right to be restricted based upon an ownership threshold not exceeding 5%. *See* Voting Right Directive, Council Directive No. 2007/36, O.J. L 184/17 (2007). How does this compare to the rights of shareholders in the United States? Given the high threshold, is the right likely to have much effect?

4. Although much discussed, the Directive did not mandate one share one vote. Why not? For one possible explanation, *see* Jennifer G. Hill, *What We Can Learn From Other Statutory Schemes: Regulatory Show and Tell: Lessons from International Statutory Regimes*, 33 Del. J. Corp. L. 819, 827 n.60 (2008) ("It appears that countries with a high proportion of family-owned companies, such as the Scandinavian coun-tries, France, and Spain, were the principal opponents to the proposal."). Note also that Sweden makes extensive use of dual class voting, something that would not be consistent with one share one vote.

Nonetheless, there is a more fundamental question about EU regulation of cor-porate governance: Does it matter?

Luca Enriques, *EC Company Law Directives and Regulations: How Trivial Are They?*

27 U. Pa. J. Int'l Econ. L. 1, 12–17 (2007)[21]

The [European] Commission has traditionally lacked the resources to monitor Member States' compliance with corporate law directives; no significant enforcement "from the bottom," in the form of European Court of Justice ("ECJ") preliminary reference procedures from national courts has ever made up for this. Thus far, the ECJ (which has no docket control) has decided upon fewer than twenty-five preliminary reference procedures dealing with secondary EC corporate law.

Of course, Member States do implement directives, although often with considerable delay. However, major instances of implementing rules that are clearly at odds with the text of the directives can be found throughout the EU....

More insidiously, Member States have sometimes failed to enforce implementing rules. Again, Germany provides a case in point with respect to the obligation to disclose annual accounts as imposed by the Fourth Council Directive. Although most private companies ("GmbHs") failed to comply, no sanction ever followed, because the rules on sanctions had been crafted in such a way as to make them practically impossible to apply. Fifteen years after the deadline for the implementation of the relevant EC provisions, the ECJ finally declared that Germany had failed to comply with its obligations under EC law. Despite changes in the rules governing the disclosure obligation so as to make it easier for sanctions to be applied, most German companies still fail to disclose their accounts. This warrants the suspicion (admittedly, only the suspicion) that the accounting rules implementing the Fourth Council Directive may also be commonly violated: in the absence of disclosure to the public, there is definitely less incentive to provide true and fair accounts.

EC securities law, as the Lamfalussy Report recognized, is also a field in which Member States have often violated Community law with very little subsequent EC enforcement. It is too early to tell whether the new wave of securities directives, together with the Lamfalussy architecture and especially its Level 3 and Level 4 regulatory tools, will change this state of affairs.

A process of "intentional or unintentional erosion" may also take place, by which new national laws modify rules implementing EC directives in a way inconsistent with the latter, a phenomenon "which may well occur without the Community authorities being aware of it or being in a position to evaluate its impact."

Good examples of erosion can be found in recent corporate law developments in Italy. The comprehensive corporate law reform of 2003 blatantly violates the Second Council Directive in several respects. For instance, contrary to article 18, paragraph 1 of the Second Council Directive, which bans subscription of own shares outright, article 2357-ter, paragraph 2 of the Italian Civil Code now provides that the share-

---

holders' meeting may authorize the company to exercise the preemptive rights pertaining to its treasury shares and thus to subscribe its own shares. Additionally, against the Second Council Directive's article 13, the provisions on conversion of companies do not require an expert report assessing that the value of the net assets of a private limited liability company ("societa a responsabilita limitata") being converted into a public company ("societa per azioni") corresponds at least to the transformed entity's legal capital.

Finally, the fact that directives have no direct horizontal effect further dulls the impact of EC legislation on corporate law within the Member States. As the ECJ has frequently reiterated, directives are addressed to Member States, and private parties cannot invoke them in relationships with other private parties. This means that national company laws that conflict with a directive remain in effect with regard to private parties until they are repealed by the national legislature, even if in the meantime the ECJ finds that they are in violation of the directive. To be sure, the Court has also held that, in applying national law, national courts must construe the national law, "as far as possible, in the light of the wording and the purpose of the directive in order to achieve the result pursued by the latter." ...

Comments and Questions

1. What explains the resistance to harmonization often apparent once a directive has been issued? How realistic is it to expect the members of the EU to harmonize their laws with Directives such as the one on shareholder rights?

2. While a number of countries had not implemented the Directive on Shareholder Rights by the appointed deadline, many had. What explains the variations in the level of compliance? Does it have anything to do with the topics addressed? For example, why had the EU not issued a directive on fiduciary duties or derivative suits?

3. Is there a better way to encourage uniformity? What about a competition among European countries for charters, much the way states in the US compete. Could this result in harmonization? Has it resulted in harmonization in the US?

4. European countries have a version of the internal affairs doctrine, although the tests vary. Some apply the law of the country of incorporation. Others apply the law where the company has its headquarters (the so called "real seat" theory). What impact might these different theories have on the goal of harmonization?

5. Assuming some application of the internal affairs doctrine in the EU, will it be effective without a right to reincorporate? Reincorporation had been prohibited or limited in a number of European countries, although this is apparently undergoing slow change. *See* Federico M. Mucciarelli, *Freedom of Reincorporation and the Scope of Corporate Law in the U.S. and the E.U.*, NYU Center for Law, Economics and Organization, Law & Economics Research Paper Series, Working Paper No. 11-07 (Mar. 2011). What impact might this have on the goal of harmonization of corporate law in the EU?

Difficulties in the EU's approach to the harmonization of governance practices have not gone unnoticed. Efforts have been made to undertake a more flexible approach that will allow for harmonization as a result of a "race to the top."

Shuangge Wen, *Less Is More—A Critical View of Further EU Action towards a Harmonized Corporate Governance Framework in the Wake of the Crisis*
12 Wash. U. Global Stud. L. Rev. 41 (2013)[22]

Recognizing many Member States' calls for more flexibility, a combination of legislation and soft law enabling a "bottom-up" convergence and a broader use of alternative instruments to primary legislation have been stated as a main theme of EU action on corporate governance in the new millennium. It is suggested that a harmonized framework should be achieved over time via "a certain coordination" of national codes of practices based on "best practices," reflecting the tremendous growth in voluntary codes and guidelines in Member States during the past few decades. Compared to traditional directives, which produced "a certain 'petrifaction'" of corporate performances, these corporate governance codes are generally developed on a national basis and "bring a firm considerable legitimacy" by reflecting what public or private organizations consider to be best practices. As described by the recent comprehensive EU report on corporate governance codes, "[t]he codes—together with market pressures—may serve as a converging force, by focusing attention and discussion on governance issues, articulating best practice recommendations and encouraging companies to adopt them."

When delineating the new code-based approach, sweeping uniform European corporate governance code was rejected on the grounds that the specificities of Member States' corporate governance systems are so influential that a common EU code would either be meaninglessly abstract, or would become a very complex document aiming to be inclusive of all contingencies arising from diverse local practices and rules, which would not bring significant changes to the current landscape. This accords with the well-accepted idea that European integration would work best when it supports, rather than undermines, the idiosyncratic values of Member States. To put this in a broader context, one might suggest that this code-based approach is one of the many responses to the forceful academic criticism of the excessive supranationalism exhibited in early Union harmonization practice. Indeed, few would now disagree that a positive interventionist role should only be assumed by the Union in a cautious fashion, when its superiority over national or local action can be demonstrated. The principles of subsidiarity and proportionality contained in Article 5 of TEU are precisely constructed to tackle this issue by acknowledging the necessity of penetrating Union intervention in certain areas.

To facilitate the anticipated trend of bottom-up convergence, the European Commission turned its attention to positively harmonizing not the substance, but rather

---

22. Copyright © 2013 Washington University Global Studies Law Review. Reprinted with permission.

the enforcement mechanisms, which, as will become clear, has been a rather disappointing process. Two further moves were introduced by the European Commission to accompany the code-based harmonization efforts. These were the establishment of the European Corporate Governance Forum in 2004 and the enshrinement of the Comply-or-Explain approach as imposed by Directive 2006/46/EC. Under Article 46(a) of the directive, it is compulsory for a listed company to include a corporate governance statement in its annual report with reference to the national corporate governance code to which the company is subject. While directives and recommendations continue to be introduced in specific areas, the code-based approach supported by mandatory application of the comply-or-explain principle is now scholarly termed "procedural harmonization," and it operates as the major European approach to corporate governance.

* * *

The EU's experience with the comply-or-explain approach, however, again challenges the effectiveness of the Union's integration activities regarding corporate governance. It further proves the point that a good national rule for corporate governance does not necessarily work as efficiently at the European level. Before being adopted into the EU corporate governance framework, the comply-or-explain approach was known as "the trademark of corporate governance in the UK," and it has been in place since the beginning of voluntary codes. In the United Kingdom, where the comply-or-explain principle originated and has flourished, the approach has been well received by businesses and is highly praised for its flexibility. Data also shows satisfactorily high rates of compliance with most provisions of the UK Corporate Governance Code by companies of all sizes. When companies do deviate from the Code, most manage to clearly set out their reasons and the arrangements that they put in place to provide alternative safeguards. The efficiency of the comply-or-explain principle has been nevertheless challenged ever since its arrival in European law. Recent studies described by the Green Paper cast doubt on its efficacy as an EU policy, referring to it as "reduc[ing] the efficiency of the EU's corporate governance framework and limit[ing] the system's usefulness."

Much of the criticism so far has been pinpointed at the inherent flaws of comply-or-explain without challenging the unnecessary Union regulatory intervention. The flexible code-based system has been championed by the UK over the past fifteen years because of the prosperity of the UK's market-based economy and the strong role played by the London Stock Exchange as a self-regulatory body. The comply-or-explain principle, reflecting its embedded environment, is principally based on the strong role played by the market in corporate control, primarily disciplining non-compliant companies by lowering their share prices. This market-based economic background and self-regulatory tradition are not present in many of the other Member States, which calls into question the suitability of this approach in other nations. In practice, the sweeping implementation of comply-or-explain across Europe has had a more disruptive effect on national enforcement systems, which were established and operated in a coherent manner before the community measure. In over 60% of deviations, the principle has been abused by companies failing to provide sufficient explanation when they chose not to apply recommendations from the codes; "they either simply stated that they had departed from a recommendation without any further explanation, or they provided only a general or limited explanation." It was suspected that many companies supported the comply-or-explain concept merely because they could easily get away with deviations. With regard to the requirement of the German Corporate Governance Code to disclose the remuneration of company executive directors on an individual basis, only a small minority of firms (10 out of 126 in a 2002 sample and 22 out of 146 in a 2003 sample) actually complied with the suggestion.

The efficiency of the comply-or-explain principle in European harmonization becomes even more questionable because the EU mandates the implementation, yet fails to cater for the complementary need for proper monitoring and disciplining mechanisms. This issue, according to Article 60(a) of the directive, is tackled by way of "self-governance" in Member States, which generates a multifaceted picture. A number of different schemes have so far been employed by Member States in applying the comply-or-explain idea, including: assimilating into the local listing rules, self-embodiment in the codes, or enshrining in a mixture of public and private regulations—the listing rules make reference to the code and the law, whilst securities regulation imposes the comply-or-explain approach. To add to this complexity, national implementation methods are further differentiated by ambits of national codes customized for diverse company types. Currently, some Member States have specific corporate governance codes tailored to small and medium-sized listed companies. In other jurisdictions, however, codes are designed to apply to all listed companies, with specific provisions devoted to smaller companies. Local differences in the application of the comply-or-explain approach inevitably lead to diverse enforcement results, and thereby contribute to the continuing fragmented landscape of European corporate governance.

Comments and Questions

1. The article suggests a move away from proscriptive requirements, to be replaced by the goal of convergence through coordination of national codes. What are some advantages and disadvantages of this approach?

2. Given that most countries already have corporate governance codes in place, what exactly is the role of the EU in encouraging convergence?

3. Reliance on a system of comply or explain is presumably premised upon accurate disclosure of deviations from any code. The EU has stepped into this space. *See* Article 20(1) of Directive 2013/34/EU (requiring listed companies to explain departures from governance codes). The quality of disclosure, however, has been an issue. Recognizing that companies "do not provide appropriate explanations when they depart" from these codes, the EU adopted a recommendation designed to "improve the overall quality of corporate governance statements". The guidance was not, however, "legally binding." *See* Commission Recommendation on the Quality of Corporate Governance

Reporting ('Comply or Explain'), 2014/208/EU (Apr. 9, 2014). As a result, member states were merely advised to "draw" the interpretation "to the attention of the bodies responsible for national corporate governance codes, listed companies and other parties concerned." How effective is this approach likely to be?

4. Not every area has been left to comply or explain. In 2014, the European Parliament has adopted a directive that will require listed companies to "disclose information on policies, risks and results as regards environmental matters, social and employee-related aspects, respect for human rights, anti-corruption and bribery issues, and diversity on boards of directors."

V. Corporate Governance and Developing Countries

Developing countries arguably have unique issues in the development of appropriate systems of governance. The catalysts for reform may be the same. Sometimes change arises out of corporate scandal; other times it is a byproduct of incorporation into the global marketplace. Pressure also may arise from the need to encourage domestic investment.

Whatever the reason, developing countries confront a number of problems that potentially interfere with the development of an effective system of corporate governance. Often they lack the necessary institutions, whether effective regulators or courts. They typically lack robust capital markets. Corruption, while present in all markets, can be a particular concern in developing countries. Culture and history, including a colonial heritage, may also present unique variables.

A. Does the Law Matter?

These issues raise a fundamental question at the outset. Does the law even matter?

Ali Adnan Ibrahim, *Developing Governance and Regulation for Emerging Capital and Securities Markets*
39 Rutgers L.J. 111, 138 (2007)[23]

Although some disagree with the universal applicability of the "law matters thesis," its significance has been considered relevant for the transition economies. However, some scholars have convincingly argued that law alone is not relevant for developing strong and deep securities markets in the transition economies, and without the help of surrounding private institutions, the task might not be possible. Other arguments regard "society's social and political organization" to be crucial, in addition to the suggested institutions, for creation of public firms and a deep securities market and to have more room for private action.

---

23. Copyright © 2007 Rutgers Law Journal. Reprinted by permission.

As for the "law matters thesis," its essence "is about strong shareholder property rights, as reflected in the control that shareholders are allocated over the enterprise and the legal limitations that constrain managerial and directorial discretion; all of which point in the direction of ensuring that shareholders do not have their wealth expropriated." The "law matters thesis," therefore, suggests that minority shareholders will emerge pursuant to laws safeguarding their property rights. However, potential shareholders may need more than protective laws. A legal framework encouraging entrepreneurs to raise capital through the securities market is more important. That is, a well-conceived combination of foreign investment strategy and modernization of customary law will better serve minority shareholders.

Comments and Questions

1. As this author notes, the law matters in developing countries but it is not the only variable. What else is needed to ensure strong corporate governance and active capital markets?

2. Independent directors and disclosure are common attributes of most systems of corporate governance. Will these concepts apply in the same manner in developed and developing economies?

3. Often, companies in developing economies do not make robust disclosure of their financial condition. They may view transparency as a detriment, for example by alerting the tax authorities to additional sources of revenue. As a consequence, however, minority investors will lack the information needed to make informed decision making. What advice might you provide to a country seeking to deal with this practical problem in its corporate code?

4. Some developing nations have attempted to harmonize governance practices. The Organization for Harmonization in Africa of Business Laws has, for example, attempted to do so among a group of west and central African countries. *See* Claire Moore Dickerson, *Harmonizing Business Laws in Africa: OHADA Calls the Tune*, 44 Colum. J. Transnat'l L. 17 (2005). What advantages might this approach have for that region of the world?

5. What role does corruption play in the governance process? Some view the problem as singular. *See* Naomi Cahn, *Corporate Governance Divergence and Sub-Saharan Africa: Lessons from Out Here in the Fields*, 33 Stetson L. Rev. 893, 924 (2004) ("In developing countries, the critical issues are corruption and inefficient, dishonest governments. Only when these issues have been resolved can companies, multilaterals, and governments turn their attention to how best to structure capital markets."). Is it possible to have a system of governance that protects investors in countries where corruption is rife?

6. Can corruption be viewed as, at least in part, a cultural phenomenon? As one article described:

> The culture of the country in which a business transaction occurs often determines the character of the transaction. As examples, political payments

are a feature of Middle Eastern life, where the payment of *baksheesh* in the Arabic and Turkish-speaking countries, and of *roshveh* in Iran is embedded in the social and cultural fabric of these countries. In Nigeria and other former British West African colonies, functionaries often expect or seek a tip, referred to as "dash," for services rendered to the public.... Bribery in some nations is so entwined in normal business practice that many of the home countries of active corporate bribers had, until recently, laws making the bribes tax deductible.

Barbara Crutchfield George & Kathleen A. Lacey, *A Coalition of Industrialized Nations, Developing Nations, Multilateral Development Banks, and Non-Governmental Organizations: A Pivotal Complement to Current Anti-Corruption Initiatives*, 33 Cornell Int'l L.J. 547, 554–55 (2000). It may also occur because of economic necessity, given the inadequate salaries paid to employees of the government. What difference does the underlying source of corruption make in drafting an appropriate legal regime?

7. Needless to say, corruption is not limited to developing countries. The SEC in the United States uncovered widespread examples of bribes paid by public companies to foreign government officials in the 1970s, ultimately resulting in the adoption of the Foreign Corrupt Practices Act, which prohibited the practice. Despite the adoption of this law, the SEC routinely brings actions for violations of the FCPA. *See SEC v. IBM*, Litigation Release No. 21889 (D.D.C. Mar. 18, 2011) (company paid $10 million fine for violations of the FCPA).

B. The Problem of Enforcement in Emerging Markets

One critical issue in developing countries concerns enforcement. This issue became particularly clear in the context of the demise of the Soviet Union in the early 1990s. The Soviet Union had promoted central planning and eschewed private property. There were no corporations and or corporation laws. As pieces of the former Soviet Union became independent, they had to put in place the requisite legal infrastructure that would permit business formation.

The laws, however, were not enough. Even with rights legally guaranteed, shareholders needed some mechanism for enforcement. The courts, however, lacked sufficient capacity and the regulators arguably lacked sufficient will, if not authority. This led to a more radical proposal: A system of corporate governance that to some degree sought to sidestep these institutions.

Bernard Black & Reinier Kraakman,
A Self-Enforcing Model of Corporate Law
109 Harv. L. Rev. 1911, 1916–17 (1996)[24]

What kind of corporate law should govern publicly owned companies in emerging markets, including newly privatizing economies? This important question has no

---

ready answer. Corporate law, we believe, should have the same principal goal in developed and emerging economies—succinctly stated, to provide governance rules that maximize the value of corporate enterprises to investors. However, emerging economies cannot simply copy the corporate laws of developed economies. These laws depend upon highly evolved market, legal, and governmental institutions and cultural norms that often do not exist in emerging economies. Developed country corporate laws also reflect the idiosyncratic history of their country of origin. They are not necessarily efficient at home, let alone when transplanted to foreign soil. Moreover, in many emerging markets, corporate law must serve a second central goal that is less pressing in mature market economies: fostering public confidence in capitalism and in private ownership of large business enterprises.

Thus, corporate law must be designed substantially from scratch to work within the infrastructure available in an emerging market. Fortunately, this can be politically feasible. Precisely because existing institutions (to which the law must adapt) are often weak or missing, one can rethink from first principles what corporate law ought to look like and what related institutions it ought to rely on and promote.

Beyond producing a new model for emerging markets, the effort to develop corporate law from scratch can expose weaknesses and idiosyncracies in the corporate laws of developed countries. The model can highlight the ways in which these laws did not simply evolve toward efficiency, but instead evolved from historically contingent starting places to ending places shaped by preexisting institutions, by the inertial power of the status quo, and by the preferences of key participants in the corporate enterprise. For example, German corporate law adapted to strong banks and labor unions, while American law adapted to strong capital markets, weak financial institutions, and strong corporate managers.

In this Article, we sketch the basic elements of a "self-enforcing" model of corporate law, designed for an emerging economy. The model is grounded in a case study: the effort, in which we participated, to develop a new corporate law for Russia. We begin with three central claims. First, effective corporate law is context-specific, even if the problems it must address are universal. The law that works for a developed economy, when transplanted to an emerging economy, will not achieve a sensible balance among company managers' need for flexibility to meet rapidly changing business conditions, companies' need for low-transaction-cost access to capital markets, large investors' need to monitor what managers do with the investors' money, and small investors' need for protection against self-dealing by managers and large investors. The defects in the law will increase the cost of capital and reduce its availability.

In developed countries, corporate law combines with other legal, market, and cultural constraints on the actions of corporate managers and controlling shareholders to achieve a sensible balance among these sometimes competing needs. Corporate law plays a relatively small, even "trivial" role. In emerging economies, these other constraints are weak or absent, so corporate law is a much more central tool for motivating managers and large shareholders to create social value rather than simply transfer wealth to themselves from others. The "market" cannot fill the regulatory gaps that an American-style "enabling" corporate law leaves behind.

Further, corporate law in developed countries evolved in tandem with supporting legal institutions. For example, the United States relies on expert judges to assess the reasonableness of takeover defenses and the fairness of transactions in which managers have a conflict of interest. When necessary, these judges make decisions literally overnight to ensure that judicial delay does not kill a challenged transaction. A company law that depends on fast and reliable judicial decisions is simply out of the question in many emerging markets. In Russia, for example, courts function slowly if at all, some judges are corrupt, and many are Soviet-era holdovers who neither understand business nor care to learn. Better judges and courts will emerge only over several decades, as the old judges die or retire. In the meantime, Russian corporate law must rely on courts as little as possible.

More generally, every emerging economy has some legal and market institutions, some norms of behavior, some distribution of share ownership, and some financial institutions. Corporate law must reflect these background facts. For example, if (as in Russia) employees often own large stakes in their companies, but are vulnerable to having their votes controlled by corporate managers, company law needs special rules that safeguard the rights of employee-shareholders. Company law must also limit the influence of dysfunctional background features, such as widespread corruption.

Our second central claim is that despite the context-specificity of effective corporate law, there is a large class of emerging capitalist economies (including formerly Communist countries) that are sufficiently similar to permit generalization about the type of corporate law that will be useful for them. Russia is perhaps an extreme case, but it is hardly alone in having insider-controlled companies, malfunctioning courts, weak and sometimes corrupt regulators, and poorly developed capital markets. For example, an acute problem in Russia is protecting minority investors against exploitation by managers or controlling shareholders. Protection of minority investors has also emerged as a central political issue in the most successful post-Communist economy, the Czech Republic, and is at the core of recent reforms in Israeli corporate law.

Our third claim is that our task is not impossible. Despite weak markets and institutions, one can design a company law that prevents a significant fraction of the corporate governance failures that would otherwise occur. Even developed country corporate governance systems fail with uncomfortable frequency. We can expect still more failures in emerging markets. Nonetheless, it is possible to design a law that works tolerably well—that vests substantial decisionmaking power in large outside shareholders, who have incentives to make good decisions; that reduces, though it cannot eliminate, fraud and self-dealing by corporate insiders; that minimizes, though it cannot altogether avoid, the need for official enforcement through courts; that gives managers and controlling shareholders incentives to obey the rules even when they could often get away with ignoring them; that reinforces desirable cultural attitudes about proper managerial behavior; and that still leaves managers with the flexibility they need to take risks and make quick decisions. Such a law can add far more value than corporate law adds in developed economies, precisely because other institutions that could shape corporate behavior are weak in developing economies.

The central features of our "self-enforcing" model of corporate law are:

(i) Enforcement, as much as possible, through actions by direct participants in the corporate enterprise (shareholders, directors, and managers), rather than indirect participants (judges, regulators, legal and accounting professionals, and the financial press).

(ii) Greater protection of outside shareholders than is common in developed economies, to respond to a high incidence of insider-controlled companies, the weakness of other constraints on self-dealing by managers and controlling shareholders, and the need to control self-dealing to strengthen the political credibility of a market economy.

(iii) Reliance on procedural protections—such as transaction approval by independent directors, independent shareholders, or both—rather than on flat prohibitions of suspect categories of transactions. The use of procedural devices balances the need for shareholder protection against the need for business flexibility.

(iv) Whenever possible, use of bright-line rules, rather than standards, to define proper and improper behavior. Bright-line rules can be understood by those who must comply with them and have a better chance of being enforced. Standards, in contrast, require judicial interpretation, which is often unavailable in emerging markets, and presume a shared cultural understanding of the regulatory policy that underlies the standards, which may also be absent.

(v) Strong legal remedies on paper, to compensate for the low probability that the sanctions will be applied in fact. Enforcement takes place primarily through a combination of voting rules and transactional rights. The central voting elements include: shareholder approval (including in some cases supermajority approval or approval by a majority of outside shareholders) for broad classes of major transactions and self-interested transactions; approval of self-interested transactions by a majority of outside directors; mandatory cumulative voting for directors, which empowers large minority shareholders to select directors (this power is protected by requirements of one common share, one vote; minimum board size; and no staggering of board terms); and a unitary ballot on which both managers and large shareholders can nominate directors. The honesty of the vote is protected through confidential voting and independent vote tabulation, while the quality of voting decisions is buttressed by mandatory disclosure rules.

Shareholders also receive transactional rights (put and call options) triggered by specified corporate actions. These include preemptive rights when a company issues new shares; appraisal rights for shareholders who do not approve major transactions; and takeout rights when a controlling stake in the firm is acquired (that is, minority shareholder rights to sell their shares to the new controlling shareholder).

The self-enforcing model seeks to build legal norms that managers and large share-holders will see as reasonable and comply with voluntarily. The need to induce voluntary compliance reinforces our preference for procedural rather than substantive protections. For example, managers may evade a flat ban on self-interested transactions, yet comply with a procedural requirement for shareholder approval because they think that they can obtain approval. Once they decide to obtain shareholder approval, the managers may make the transaction more favorable to shareholders, to ensure approval and avoid embarrassment. The model often relies not only on bright-line rules, but also on relatively simple rules. Managers can't comply with, and judges can't enforce, rules that they don't understand. Nor will managers respect an unduly complex statute.

———————

Is the self-enforcing model something that can work in the former Soviet Union? The proposal drew objections and proposed alternatives.

J. Robert Brown, Jr. & Kostyantyn Shkurupiy, *Corporate Governance in the Former Soviet Union: The Failure of the Self-Enforcing Model*
7 Colum. J. E. Eur. L. 629 (2000)[25]

Increasing investment in the emerging markets of the former Soviet Union requires increased assurances that managers, whether white or red, will engage in behavior motivated by the best interest of the enterprise. Perforce, this will require a reduction in self dealing. In particular, it will require a reduction in stealing and other dishonest behavior, any law seeking to increase investor confidence must address three things. First, directors need to be subjected to clear limitations on their ability to steal. Second, there must be an adequate enforcement mechanism. Third, the system must contain adequate benefits to make the risk of loss of management position a significant enough penalty to ensure compliance with prohibitions on dishonest behavior.

* * *

The Soviet experience suggests the possibility of a top down system of regulation, with the government imposing penalties for dishonest behavior. The approach does not require reduced attention to the plight of outside shareholders or the need for statutory protections of their interests. Nor does it suggest that shareholders will ul-timately prove unable to monitor managers effectively. It does suggest, however, that under current circumstances, shareholders are not the most effective method of doing so in most cases. An alternative mechanism is required.

For the system to work in the near term, the legal regime needs to track the system from the Soviet days more closely. This requires three things. First, the position of director must be attractive and lucrative. In other words, the position must be sought after, with dismissal a serious consequence. Second, the obligations imposed on di-

———————

25. Copyright © 2000 Columbia Journal of Eastern European Law. Reprinted by permission.

rectors and officers must be absolutely clear. In contrast to the "self-enforcing" model of corporate law, they should go much further, prohibiting behavior that facilitates dishonest behavior or limits detection.

Finally, a new system of monitoring of managers must be implemented. Instead of shareholders, the power to monitor management should be given to the government; in most cases the agency responsible for regulating the securities markets. Securities commissions in the former Soviet Union are typically (though not always) professionally trained, lithe bureaucracies, less beholden to the traditional bureaucratic practices prevalent in a planned economy. In this regard, however, steps would need to be taken to protect against corruption. In effect, the system must be structured to make positions at the commission valuable commodities, with either corruption or the appearance of corruption an automatic basis for dismissal.

Comments and Questions

1. How are the two approaches to corporate governance different? How do they address the problems associated with developing economies? How successful are they likely to be?

2. Both models draw on the experiences of countries emerging after the fall of the Soviet Union. Specifically, the self-enforcing model was developed in the context of the development of Russia in the aftermath of the break-up of the Soviet Union. Ultimately, Professors Black and Kraakman posit that all emerging markets "are sufficiently similar to permit generalization about the type of corporate law that will be useful to them." Do you agree?

3. Some view the self-enforcing model as not going far enough. *See* Troy A. Paredes, *A Systems Approach to Corporate Governance Reform: Why Importing U.S. Corporate Law Isn't the Answer*, 45 Wm. & Mary L. Rev. 1055, 1127 (2004) ("Ultimately, what developing countries need is a more mandatory model of corporate law, still comprising bright-line rules, that gives shareholders additional 'negative' and 'positive' control rights.").

4. What are the concerns with government involvement in the enforcement of corporate government requirements? Are these concerns more acute in the context of developing countries? Are there other countries where government involvement and ideology may play a role in the governance process? *See* Jiangyu Want, *The Political Logic of Corporate Governance in China's State-Owned Enterprises*, 47 Cornell Int'l L. J. 631, 654 (2014) (noting that executives in state owned companies are mostly members of the Chinese Communist Party ("CCP") and that party obligations form a "general and ideological control on the minds and behaviors of CCP members, who, from the CEO to the factory workers, must, at least in theory, implement Party policies and execute Party orders faithfully when performing their duties").

5. Why is it insufficient to simply allow shareholders with the right to bring derivative suits in court? What impediments might exist to such an approach in a developing economy?

6. The second model calls for greater government intervention to protect the rights of shareholders. What problems can arise with such an approach? How might you try to avoid some of these problems? Is it realistic to think that the government in a developing economy would do a better job than shareholders in ensuring proper behavior by directors?

7. A great deal has been written about the effectiveness (or ineffectiveness) of the independent director requirement in China. Sometimes labeled "vase" directors (decorative items that merely adorn the board room), the largest category of independent directors in China (44%) according to one study, is academics, not always for the most complimentary reasons. *See* Jie Yuan, *Formal Convergence or Substantial Divergence? Evidence from Adoption of the Independent Director System in China*, 9 Asian-Pacific L. & Pol'y J. 71 (2007) ("In addition, insiders favor scholars precisely because scholars may not be very familiar with corporate operations and therefore will tend not to interfere."). Perhaps unsurprisingly, one study "indicates that the performance of companies with independent directors is not significantly different from companies without independent directors." *Id.* at 91.

8. Are these directors really independent? *See* Chao Xi, *In Search of an Effective Monitoring Board Model: Board Reforms and the Political Economy of Corporate Law in China*, 22 Conn. J. Int'l L. 1, 17 (2006) ("Surveys have shown that a vast majority of independent directors are nominated by the majority shareholder and management. Minority shareholders have little input in the process. The prevailing practice has been that the controlling shareholder and the management appoint their social friends to be independent directors.").

VI. Corporate Governance and Culture

There is growing acknowledgement in the context of comparative corporate governance that "culture matters." It is, however, a notoriously difficult subject to study, at least with any hope of practical application. For one thing, it is not an easy term even to define. For another, application of culture generally defies quantification. Analysis, therefore, often devolves down to a matter of "general intuition." Amir N. Licht, *Legal Plug-Ins: Cultural Distance, Cross-Listing, and Corporate Governance Reform*, 22 Berkeley J. Int'l L. 195, 216 (2004).

At some level, culture involves an examination of a country's shared values and understandings. Literature has arisen that seeks to broadly characterize national cultures. Some have been classified as hierarchical and others as egalitarian. Cultures can vary based upon the degree of communal versus individual values. Moreover, culture has both national and individual components. Investors in the United States are sometimes said to be more risk tolerant than in other countries, a potential explanation for dynamic equity markets. The explanations for the differences may be historical, tracing back to Pliny, Plato or Confucius. They may arise out of philosophical or religious differences. Geography may even play a role.

Identifying differences is the easy part. Examining how they may actually impact corporate governance is more difficult. Nonetheless, there are some places where cultural differences can be observed in practice. Attitudes about executive compensation vary among cultures. In a country like the United States, characterized as more individualist and less egalitarian, the reigning culture tolerates higher levels of compensation. A system of governance cannot count on social pressure, therefore, to impose effective limits. In more egalitarian cultures, in contrast, shaming and other forms of social pressure may effectively limit these amounts. As a result, the regulation of executive compensation may vary considerably.

Sometimes culture can be observed by examining differences in legal regimes applicable to corporate governance. In other cases, however, the impact is more subtle. Thus, most systems of corporate governance to some degree rely on the presence at the board level of non-management directors. Yet independent directors are to some degree intended to provide a discordant viewpoint in the board room. Purportedly representing the interests of shareholders, they are expected to at least sometimes object to the path selected by management. This is particularly true in the U.S. with efforts to increase the opportunities for the election of non-management nominated directors.

In more egalitarian or communal societies, this expectation for independent director can often conflict with social values. As a result, these directors (and the process of selecting the directors) may not put significant weight on the need for dissident viewpoints.

Comments and Questions

1. What impact might a culture characterized as hierarchical have on corporate governance? For example, in societies with clear hierarchies, what impact might that have on any system of enforcement?

2. Do shareholder configurations have a cultural explanation? In Italy, pyramid structures, often created by families, are common. In the US, dispersed ownership is the common pattern. Are there cultural explanations for these structures? If so, what does that suggest about the likelihood of their changing? Might culture explain a preference for a civil law versus common law system?

3. Uncertainty avoidance or risk tolerance is said to vary among cultures. *See* Michael H. Lubetsky, *Cultural Difference and Corporate Governance*, 17 Transnat'l L. & Contemp. Probs. 187, 190–91 (2008) ("Uncertainty avoidance (UA) measures a culture's comfort with unpredictable events. Higher values suggest a more conformist, risk-averse, and generally inflexible society, while lower values suggest a greater tolerance for risk, change, diversity, and ambiguity. Japan, Belgium, and Greece all feature high levels of uncertainty avoidance while Singapore, Sweden, and the United Kingdom have relatively low levels."). How might this affect a country's system of governance?

4. Professor Milhaupt asserts, for example, that risk tolerance is necessary for an active venture capital market and that risk tolerance is "nurtured in the American

system of corporate governance." Curtis J. Milhaupt, *The Market for Innovation in the United States and Japan: Venture Capital and the Comparative Corporate Governance Debate*, 91 Nw. U.L. Rev. 865, 893 (1997). Do you agree? He notes that this cultural trait is not found in Japan. What difference might this make in the development of a system of corporate governance?

5. Traditionally, U.S. CEOs make higher salaries than their counterparts in other countries. Moreover, the U.S. system is based in large part upon performance, with much of the compensation paid to executives in the form of equity. As share prices appreciate, so does their compensation. Some use culture as a critical explanation for the difference. Yet there is evidence that compensation practices are converging, with greater global use of incentive based payments. What does this suggest about the application of culture? Does the increasingly global nature of the economy have an impact on cultural norms? Is, for example, the market for top management in large companies global or national?

6. How might cultural differences explain varying legal regimes with respect to self-dealing beyond executive compensation? *See* Erica Gorga, *Culture and Corporate Law Reform: A Case Study of Brazil*, 27 U. Pa. J. Int'l Econ. L. 803 (2006) ("There are no strong social norms to support effective sanctions because society does not strongly condemn self-dealing practices.").

What about the introduction of an economic system based upon private ownership to a culture that largely eschewed such an approach? Ought the governance structure to reflect these differences or can the conventional model be transplanted wholesale to a country despite these cultural and historical differences?

J. Robert Brown, Jr., *Culture, Chaos and Capitalism: Privatization in Kazakhstan*

19 U. Pa. J. Int'l Econ. L. 909, 909–910, 912, 962–64 (1998)[26]

Those countries arising out of the remnants of the Soviet Union immediately confronted a number of serious political and economic problems. Each had to wrestle with issues of sovereignty and democracy and, in some cases, civil war. In the economic realm, they had to address the problems of dismantling the command economy. Independence left these states owning the pieces of the centralized economy that happened to be in their territory when the Soviet Union collapsed. The result was more chaos than cohesion.

Most of the newly independent states tried, with varying degrees of seriousness, to abandon the Soviet style of economic management in favor of a more open market-

---

26. Copyright © 1998 University of Pennsylvania Journal of International Economic Law. Reprinted by permission.

driven approach. As part of the process, these countries privatized industries, shifting ownership from public to private. The programs typically involved a mix of cash sales and outright transfers, usually in return for coupons or vouchers.

The widespread nature of privatization efforts in the former Soviet Union has become a common enough topic in legal literature, although critical analysis of the success or failure of these efforts remains woefully underdeveloped. To the extent assessment has occurred, it has usually centered on the speed with which the government has placed state assets into the hands of private owners.

Often missed are the pronounced differences among the various parts of the former Soviet Union and the need to consider the cultural effects of a new economic order. Open markets and capitalism contained values inimical to some cultures in the former Soviet Union. Moreover, they had to address the consequences of installing an open market economy at the very time they were trying to construct a nation state. This was particularly true in connection with Kazakhstan.

* * *

Located in Central Asia, the territory of Kazakhstan had been inhabited largely by nomadic peoples for 2,500 years. The explanation was, in large part, geographic. Containing vast open spaces, Kazakhstan consisted mostly of steppe and desert/semi-desert, with mountains dominating the south. The result was an open, sparsely populated territory highly receptive to cultures which ranged over large areas, primarily in search of grazing land.

Unlike the more settled "oasis" people, Kazakhs relied on animal husbandry rather than crop cultivation as their primary economic activity. They lived a migratory existence, ranging over large swathes of territory in search of adequate grazing lands. "Unfettered by belongings," Kazakhs were "organized by uninterrupted movement." A culture not based on stone and mortar, Kazakhs built no great cities and left behind no massive monuments like those found in the Uzbek city of Samarkand.

* * *

Nomadic societies were generally tolerant and egalitarian, with little class stratification. Family ties were strong, and political control was weak. Moreover, although these societies were patriarchal, women played a central role in Kazakh society. In addition, they had a highly dependent relationship with the surrounding environment. Herd size ultimately depended upon the productivity of the pasture lands used by migrating Kazakhs. Some trade did develop with neighboring sedentary populations, but generally did not constitute a large part of the nomadic economy.

This description should not, however, suggest a romantic existence. Dependent upon herding, periodic droughts or long winters resulted in hardship and famine. War was a constant threat, with rich pasture lands inevitably coveted by others. For all of the difficulties, however, Central Asian nomads had rich and deeply imbued qualities. They recognized "martial prowess, hospitality, respect for elders, love for children, and ready aid to kinsmen as virtues."

* * *

Inexorable Russian expansion into Central Asia had a profound effect on Kazakh culture and life style. In particular, the decentralized and unstratified nature of the Kazakh society came under assault, as did the growing emphasis on land ownership and agriculture. Some aspects of nomadic culture survived; many did not.

[Absorption of Kazakhstan into the Soviet Union] was followed by aggressive efforts to restructure Kazakh life. Considered the last great nomadic people, many Kazakhs had continued to live a migratory existence through the 1920s. Even those who opted for farming often viewed the activity as an adjunct to animal husbandry, cultivating crops to provide winter-feed for herds. Stalin, however, ordered collectivization and, in 1928, instituted a five-year plan designed to accomplish the task.

The catastrophe of collectivization resulted in Kazakhs becoming a minority in their own country. Between 1926 and 1939, the number of Kazakhs fell from 3.7 million to 2.3 million. At the same time, the Russian population increased to 2.5 million, representing 40% of the total population compared with Kazakhs representing 38% of the population. It would be fifty years before Kazakhs would again constitute a plurality.

Economic transformation [in a post-Soviet era] had to occur. Moreover, some amount of privatization was inevitable. The government lacked the resources to retain ownership of all economic assets. Privatization, if nothing else, would reduce the continued drain on the treasury caused by these money-losing businesses. In addition, some portion of state-owned assets could be returned to the population as a whole, a symbolic reversal of the excesses of collectivization and the nationalization of the means of production.

* * *

Criticism [of the privatization process] is easy to levy. Dislocation would have followed the implementation of any economic system. Nonetheless, it was probably unrealistic to expect a rapid and successful adoption of a capitalist economy. In part, Kazakhstan was unprepared, both practically and psychologically, to wholly abandon an economic system based upon government control and to completely embrace open markets. Moreover, the anomalies created by the demise of the command economy meant that market principles prevalent in more developed countries would not function in post-independent Kazakhstan.

This suggests that economic reform should have emphasized a regime better suited to the unique conditions in Kazakhstan. In part, this meant recognition of the lack of training in capitalist principles and familiarity with open markets. It meant recognition that Kazakhstan was not a developing nation, but a misdeveloped nation. It also meant a recognition of unique cultural and historical aspects of the country's development.

Despite the horrors of the Stalin era, with forced collectivization of herds and mass starvation, attributes of nomadic culture had survived and even flourished during the Soviet era. Kazaks still had not developed a culture centering on the ownership of real property and the rapacious collection of personal possessions. Moreover, the Soviet era did little to change the strong family ties shared among Kazakhs and a fundamental hospitality that seemed universal. In the transforming economy, however, these attributes were placed under considerable strain.

Nor did the privatization program make any effort to take advantage of traditional Kazakh strengths. Kazakh lifestyle had a number of attributes that, in a properly designed process of economic transformation, could solve some of the inevitable problems that would arise. Strong family ties, developed in the days when Kazakh families traveled together in *auls* over migratory routes, remained largely intact. So did the sense of mutual obligation and cooperation, a quality necessary for survival on the steppe. Privatization could, therefore, take into account these values and inclinations, perhaps by encouraging family units to pool resources.

Instead, privatization made little use of these values. To the extent that cultural considerations surfaced, it usually centered on chauvinistic efforts to force Kazakh on the non-Kazakh population. Moreover, as one Kazakh noted, "not one scholarly study is dedicated" to the subject of oral literature. As capitalism descended, the attempts to mandate Kazakh were running into conflict with the desire to learn English, the language of international business.

A more effectively run privatization would not have eliminated the conflict between a new economic order and the surviving vestiges of nomadic culture. Even with a smoother and more rapid recovery, Kazakh had to adapt. Nonetheless, reducing the period of economic debilitation—something that could have occurred with a more effective privatization process—would have created an environment more susceptible to a revival of Kazakh culture, history and traditions.

This suggests that in devising a program of privatization, the need exists to consider the transformation in economical, cultural and psychological terms. In doing so, it is clear that one size does not fit all. Nor does the speed with which assets are shifted from the public sector to the private represent the only or even the best method of ascertaining the success of a privatization program.

Comments and Questions

1. If you were asked to provide expert advice in a developing country on an appropriate corporate code, how would you begin? What are some of the issues that you would need to address? How important is it to know the local culture?

2. Kazakhstan was absorbed by Russia relatively late, with the process completed in the 1800s. Until the 1930s and the forced settlement, a significant number of Kazakhs remained nomadic. This was a life "organized by uninterrupted movement." It was not, in other words, a culture built around private ownership of businesses and land.

3. While it is always dangerous to characterize entire cultures, nomadic societies were often viewed as tolerant and egalitarian. As one commentator described, nomads in Central Asia were imbued "martial prowess, hospitality, respect for elders, love for

children, and ready aid to kinsmen as virtues." Might these qualities affect a corporate governance regime?

4. Kazakhs were divided into three groups or Juz (sometimes translated as clans): Great, Middle and Small. Each was concentrated in a specific part of Kazakhstan. The first president of independent Kazakhstan, Nursultan Nazarbayev, was from the Great Juz. How might the presence of these groups influence an approach to corporate governance?

5. What difference might this culture and history make in the development of a system of corporate governance? One commentator noted positions of other scholars suggesting that "Kazakhstani people would not support anticorruption legislation because it would infringe on their tradition of gift giving." Philip M. Nichols, *The Fit Between Changes to the International Corruption Regime and Indigenous Perceptions of Corruption in Kazakhstan*, 22 U. Pa. J. Int'l Econ. L. 863, 903 (Winter 2001). How might this impact the development of an appropriate system of governance?

6. Does the self-enforcing model respond to these cultural differences? How might the system of regulation address the unique cultural differences evidenced by Kazakhs?

———————

How might culture affect corporate governance in practice? For example, should culture be taken into account when formulating the definition of independent director?

Yu-Hsin Lin, *Do Social Ties Matter in Corporate Governance? The Missing Factor in Chinese Corporate Governance Reform*

5 Geo. Mason J. Int'l Com. L. 39 (2013)[27]

IV. SOCIAL TIES IN CHINESE CORPORATE BOARDS

Central to Chinese culture is the concept of *guanxi*, which roughly translates into personal connections, or interpersonal relationships. This component of Chinese culture dominates every aspect of social life in Chinese societies, including in the business world. In contemporary Chinese societies, *guanxi* remains so powerful that, if left unregulated, it could endanger the core value of independent directors—independence.

Another central feature of Chinese societies is the extraordinary degree to which harmony is prized and conflict is avoided. This cultural respect for harmony can, like *guanxi*, powerfully affect group cohesion, which is an important source of structural bias. This section reviews the process by which Taiwan and China undertook a legal transplantation of independent directors, and analyzes the effects that inde-

———————

27. Copyright © 2013 George Mason University Journal of International Commerical Law. Reprinted with permission.

pendent directors' social ties to controlling shareholders or corporate insiders can have on corporate governance.

* * *

B. The Reform

Introducing the institution of independent directors to the boards of Chinese listed companies is one of the major regulatory measures that the Chinese government has taken to address the issue that most corporate boards are dominated and controlled by single-shareholders and insiders. On August 16, 2001, the CSRC issued its *Guidance Opinion on the Establishment of an Independent Director System in Listed Companies* (the "CSRC Independent Director Opinion"), which is the most comprehensive regulatory measure taken by the Chinese government so far regarding its imposition of independent directors on listed companies. According to the CSRC Independent Director Opinion, all listed companies were required to have at least two independent directors by June 30, 2002 and such directors were to constitute at least one-third of each board by June 30, 2003. The CSRC further provides detailed regulation of the qualifications, independence, nomination, election, obligations, and responsibilities of independent directors.

Following the CSRC Independent Director Opinion, the CSRC issued several regulatory rules guiding the operation of the independent-director mechanism in Chinese listed companies. A 2005 amendment to the PRC Company Law formally stipulated that all listed companies should have independent directors on their boards. Although the 2005 amendment did not identify specific requirements and responsibilities of independent directors, it confirmed the requirement for independent directors in Chinese listed companies.

C. Renqing Dongshi (Favor Directors)

In the years since 2001, when CSRC published the CSRC Independent Director Opinion, the most notable criticism of independent directors in China has centered on their independence—or, more appropriately, their *lack* of independence—from controlling shareholders and other corporate insiders. Since most nominations of independent directors still lie in the hands of boards controlled by dominant shareholders under the current corporate-ownership structure, most independent directors are beholden to dominant shareholders. In a survey by the Listed Companies Association of Shanghai, fifty-five percent of independent directors were nominated by major shareholders and twenty-seven percent by corporate executives. Since major shareholders have controlled most corporate executives in recent years, we can calculate that major shareholders have nominated over eighty percent of independent directors during this same timeframe. With the largest major shareholder in Chinese capital markets being the state, "China's corporate governance regime can never wholeheartedly sanction a system in which independent directors can obstruct the wishes of dominant shareholders."

Commentators have coined the term *"renqing dongshi"* (roughly translated as "favor directors") in referring to independent directors who join a board simply because of their close personal relationships with corporate insiders, and have coined another term, "*huaping dongshi*" (roughly translated as "vase directors") in referring to independent directors whose function is no more than window-dressing. The popularity of these two terms reflects not only the ineffectiveness of Chinese independent directors but also public concerns over social ties among independent directors and corporate insiders.

Culture has also helped reinforce the social ties among independent directors and controlling shareholders or corporate insiders. *Guanxi* and *renqing* (favor) are core concepts and practical principles in Chinese social relationships. *Guanxi* is more close to the concept of social ties or personal relationships. On the other hand, the concept of *renqing* operates more like the rules of *guanxi*, such as how you should treat someone you know. The rule of *renqing* actually operates beyond the rule of reciprocity and it can be manifested in an old Chinese saying, "If you have received a drop of beneficence from other people, you should return to them a fountain of beneficence." Therefore, if you receive a favor from other people, you should return them not just a favor but much more than that.

If we understand that a component of traditional and contemporary Chinese culture is the belief that one favor deserves another—and perhaps even better—favor, then we can see that the term "*renqing dongshi*" (favor directors) refers to those independent directors who join a board because they owe controlling shareholders or corporate insiders a favor and they return those corporate insiders a favor by being nominally independent directors. In this situation, we cannot expect these "favor directors" to act with impartiality in the best interests of the corporation. It was reported in 2011 that China's top fifty listed companies collectively employed a total of thirty-four independent directors who were retired government officials. By retaining former government officials, these enterprises want not only to take advantage of these government officials' *guanxi* in the public sector, but also to use the independent-director position as a kind of gift, presented to these retired officials as a *renqing* (i.e., a favor); that is, as a way of thanking the retirees for various benefits they might have bestowed on the given enterprise during their time in elected or appointed office.

Ping Jiang, a well-known law professor and former President of China University of Political Science and Law, once said in a conference that, from his practical experience of serving as an independent director in various posts, independent directors in China are basically window-dressing. He also confessed that the corporate insiders who invited him to serve as an independent director had all been his close friends basically asking him to do them a "favor."

> As far as I see it, independent directors in the companies where I participated are no more than a "vase" or "decoration." The CSRC has made the independent-director system mandatory, and I think boards in general truly don't want independent directors. Personally, the people who invited me to serve as an independent director were all close friends asking me to do them a favor. We're close, so I wouldn't turn my back on them.

It is commonplace for independent directors in China to have close personal relationships with controlling shareholders or corporate insiders. With boards dominated and controlled by insiders (the so-called "insider-control problem"), the given corporate environment seems to not encourage truly independent directors. Reported interviews from China have yielded findings similar to those stemming from Taiwan: companies there have tended to hire independent directors who have *guanxi* with controlling shareholders or corporate insiders and who would not vote against controlling shareholders.

* * *

The problem of transplanting independent directors to other countries lies in the lack of complementary institutions that make such arrangements meaningful in the transplanting countries. These complementary institutions cannot be built in one night but the regulations can. Therefore, the fastest way for policy-makers to institute change is to change the related laws and regulations. Many Asian countries have changed their laws and regulations, but have undertaken no changes to critical institutional settings related to the transplantation of independent directors. Therefore, it is the case that not only would companies lack an incentive to appoint truly independent directors, but also no institution would check on the true independence of directors. Asian countries are sacrificing the core value of system, independence.

The situation is even worse in Chinese societies, whose shared traditional and contemporary culture prizes harmony and interpersonal relations. In the business world, social ties among board members further enhance collegial board culture, facilitating boards' advisory function but weakening their monitoring function. The main legislative objective of importing the institution of independent directors from the United States to China and Taiwan has been to decrease insider control over boards and to provide a checks-and-balances system capable of controlling private benefits of control enjoyed by controlling shareholders. However, the current Taiwanese and Chinese regulatory regimes' failure to address the issue of social ties, whether through *ex ante* regulation or *ex post* judicial review, strongly suggests that the legislative objective of the institution of independent directors will remain unachieved and unachievable.

This article urges Chinese policy-makers to rethink the current definition of "independence" and the effect of independent directors' social ties to controlling shareholders or corporate insiders. Social ties, on the one hand, can serve as an effective source of information for independent directors, who in turn can be more effective in providing advice to the management. But on the other hand, social ties can be detrimental to independent directors' monitoring capabilities. All countries that transplant independent directors should be aware that the institution of independent directors will most likely lose its core value to the firm if there is no legal control over social ties.

Comments and Questions

1. What does this article suggest about the role of culture in transplanting concepts from one country to another?

2. The issue of "favor directors" may be more pronounced in China than in the US but nonetheless illustrate a tension that exists with the designation of independent directors in all countries? What is the tension? Do officers really want a board that can exercise significant oversight and perhaps overturn their decision?

3. How might a board location "favor directors?" To the extent you were designing a system to reduce the presence of these types of directors, how would you do it? Would process reforms be enough?

4. You have been asked to advise the Chinese government in the drafting of a definition of director independence. What are the typical types of relationships that impair independence and would, therefore, be covered by any definition you might suggest?

5. How important is it to understand the specifics of Chinese culture to adopt an adequate definition? After all, the concern that boards in the US consist of friends and persons from the CEO's social network has been much discussed. Are there aspect of Chinese culture that made the analysis more unique?

Religion is another aspect of culture that can impact corporate governance. One place where religion has had a direct and observable impact on finance and capital markets has been in connection with the application of Islam. Islam contains a number of prohibitions and practices that affect these areas. Islamic law, for example, bans the payment and receipt of riba, or interest. The prohibition extends to bank deposits, mortgages, corporate bonds, and other debt instruments.

Principles embodied in *Shariah* are viewed as divine. They have their roots in the word of God contained in the Koran and the acts and sayings of Mohammed, the Prophet.

Ali Adnan Ibrahim, *The Rise of Customary Businesses in International Financial Markets: an Introduction to Islamic Finance and the Challenges of International Integration*
23 Am. U. Int'l L. Rev. 661, 675 (2008)[28]

In general, the sources in Islamic law may be categorized as revealed and non-revealed. The Quran is the first revealed source. Being the word of God in its letter and spirit, the Quran is communicated through the Prophet Muhammad. "All that is narrated from the Prophet, his acts, his sayings and whatever he has tacitly approved" (the "Prophetic traditions") represent the second revealed source because the Quran declared the Prophet's acts, sayings, and tacit approvals to be divinely inspired. Both revealed sources are considered primary. In contrast, non-revealed sources were developed by Islamic law scholars, and represent the "methodology and

----

28. Copyright © 2008 American University International Law Review. Reprinted by permission.

procedural guidelines to ensure correct utilization [sic]" of the revealed sources. Such sources include consensus of juristic opinion, analogical or juristic reasoning, previously revealed laws, legal opinions from companions of the Prophet ("companions"), equitable considerations, public interest, customs, presumptions of continuity, and blocking the means to evil. All of the secondary sources derive their authority in the Quran, the Prophetic traditions, or both.

Comments and Questions

1. Because the source of Islamic rules and principles are divine in nature, noncompliance has additional potential consequences. *See* Craig C. Briess, Esq., *The Crescent and the Corporation: Analysis and Resolution of Conflicting Positions between the Western Corporation and the Islamic Legal System*, 8 Rich. J. Global L. & Bus. 453, 481–82 (2009) ("Therefore, a company officer will always be responsible for his actions, regardless of whether the regulators catch his false reporting, and certainly the punishment of eternal fire in hell is worse than several years in jail."). Does this provide sufficient incentive, making other forms of enforcement unnecessary?

2. There are a number of Islamic principles that have a direct impact on corporate activities. The most obvious may be the prohibition on the receipt or payment of interest (*riba*). Similarly, Islam also prohibits the practice of *gharar*, something translated as excessive uncertainty or risk. The term embraces matters of pure chance such as gambling. Nonetheless, the term entails a continuum. The concept has been extended to insurance. In the business environment, the prohibition includes policies designed to protect assets used as security for loans and products intended to protect critical personnel, such as key man life policies. At a more systemic level, the ban extends to deposit insurance.

3. The ban on uncertainty likewise applies to speculative transactions such as naked options and derivatives. In the global financial crisis that began at the end of 2008, Islamic financial institutions were perceived to be in a better position to ride out the downturn in part because they had stayed away from high risk areas such as derivatives.

4. A number of Islamic alternatives to western financial products have arisen. Sukuk bonds, for example, are Islamic compliant fixed income instruments. They involve the creation of a special purpose entity (SPV) that sells certificates to raise capital. In one form of these bonds, the funds are used to buy an income producing asset. Investors are not paid interest but are paid a return on investment. Nonetheless, depending upon the income stream from the underlying asset (rental income, for example), investors may receive a payment that is similar in amount to a similarly rated bond. At the expiration of a fixed term, the SPV sells the asset back to the original seller and repays the certificate holders.

5. Islamic alternatives have also arisen in the insurance area. Built around the concept of *takaful*, these products involve the formation of something akin to a mutual benefit society, with members pooling their funds in an effort to assist those suffering a loss of property.

6. The practice of developing Islam-compliant products that resembles a non-compliant counterpart has been criticized. Thus, Professor Hamoudi describes the ban on insurance as something that, while arising from "a central prohibition within Islamic finance, more often than not it is conveniently ignored, less through formalist artifice and more through semantic reclassification." Haider Ala Hamoudi, *The Muezzin's Call and the Dow Jones Bell: On the Necessity of Realism in the Study of Islamic Law*, 56 Am. J. Comp. L. 423, 447 (2008). What do you make of this criticism?

7. Islam also imposes obligations on shareholders. In general, they are prohibited from purchasing shares in companies that primarily engage in activities deemed sinful. These include companies that are primarily involved in the manufacturing or distribution of alcohol, pork, and pornography. The prohibition also extends to tobacco and weapons. Likewise, investing in banks and insurance companies will violate Islamic principles because they derive most of their profits from interest, a prohibited activity. The prohibitions apply to individuals and to Islam-compliant mutual funds.

8. It is not always possible, however, to purchase shares of companies that do not derive at least some revenues from prohibited activities. Most companies receive and pay some interest. In these circumstances, shareholders have an obligation to "cleanse" any dividend payment by giving away the portion generated from the prohibited activities. Investors may also have an obligation to vote against these activities at shareholders meetings.

9. Capital markets can also be judged for their compliance with Islamic principles. *See* Hikmahanto Juwanqa, Yeni Salma Barlinti & Yetty Komalasari Dewi, *Sharia Law as a System of Governance in Indonesia: The Development of Islamic Financial Law*, 25 Wis. Int'l L.J. 773 (2008) ("The only main difference lies in the type of business activities, where in the *sharia* capital market, every economic activity must be halal (allowed by religion), both in terms of products as well as in terms of the object, the manner of acquiring and using such products or objects."). Markets that represent themselves as Islam-compliant (Sudan for example) would not permit the listing of companies that engage in prohibited activities. The Sudan stock exchange, therefore, does not list any companies that primarily engage in the business of manufacturing alcohol.

Islamic law does not expressly address corporations. Nonetheless, principles applicable to individuals may also be relevant at the entity level. Activities deemed sinful to the individual may be deemed sinful to a business. Affirmative obligations on individuals to give alms (*zakat*) may also apply at the corporate level. In addition, companies may want to issue Islam-compliant bonds or sell products (such as credit cards) that require review and even approval of *Shariah* experts.

To ensure compliance with relevant religious precepts, businesses, particularly financial institutions, often employ *Shariah* Boards, a group of scholars who review practices and transactions to ensure that they meet Islamic requirements.

Wafik Grais & Matteo Pellegrini,
Corporate Governance and Shariah Compliance in Institutions Offering Islamic Financial Services
WORLD BANK POLICY RESEARCH WORKING PAPER No. 4054 (2006)[29]

Each institution offering Islamic financial services has in-house religious advisers, who are collectively known as the *Shariah* Supervisory Board (SSB). In principle, the role of the SSB covers five main areas: certifying permissible financial instruments through *fatwas* (ex-ante *Shariah* audit), verifying that transactions comply with issued *fatwas* (ex-post *Shariah* audit), calculating and paying *Zakat*, disposing of non-*Shariah* compliant earnings, and advising on the distribution of income or expenses among shareholders and investment account holders. The SSB issues a report to certify that all financial transactions comply with the above-mentioned principles. This report is often an integral part of the Annual Report of the Islamic financial institution.

* * *

The functioning of SSBs raises five main issues of corporate governance: independence, confidentiality, competence, consistency, and disclosure. The first concerns the *independence* of the SSB from management. Generally members of the SSB are appointed by the shareholders of the bank, represented by the Board of Directors. As such, they are employed by the financial institution, and report to the Board of Directors. Their remuneration is proposed by the management and approved by the Board. The SSB members' dual relationship with the institution as providers of remunerated services and as assessors of the nature of operations could be seen as creating a possible conflict of interest.

In principle, SSB members are required to submit an unbiased opinion in all matters pertaining to their assignment. However, their employment status generates an economic stake in the financial institution, which can negatively impact their independence. The opinions of the SSB may, for example, prohibit the bank engaging in certain profitable transactions or impose a reallocation of illicit income to charity, resulting in a poorer overall financial performance. Under these circumstances, the bank managers may be tempted to use their leverage to influence SSB members, producing what is commonly referred to as "*Fatwa* shopping" or "*Shariah* advisory *à la carte*".

In practice, the risk of such conflict of interest is mitigated by the ethical standards of the SSB members, and the high cost that a stained reputation would inflict on them and on the financial institution. Generally, members of SSBs are highly regarded *Shariah* scholars and guardians of its principles. Therefore, a less than truthful assessment and disclosure of *Shariah* compliance by an SSB would seem to be highly unlikely. In the event that it does occur and comes to light, it would seriously damage the concerned scholars' reputation and the prospect for further recourse to their serv-

---

ices. Similarly, managerial interference in compliance assessments can lead to a loss of shareholders' and stakeholders' confidence. Management may be penalized and face dismissal. All that being said, and the heavy costs of untruthful assessments notwithstanding, a potential conflict of interest is inherent in existing corporate arrangements regarding SSBs.

The issue of *confidentiality* is intertwined with that of independence. Often, some *Shariah* scholars sit on the SSBs of more than one financial institution. This association with multiple IIFS may be seen as a strength in as much as it could enhance an SSB's independence vis-à-vis a particular institution. However, it does give the particular individual access to proprietary information of other, possibly competing institutions. Thus SSB members may find themselves in another type of potential conflict of interest. In the current practice, Malaysia has attempted to deal with this issue by discouraging jurists from sitting on the SSB of more than one IIFS. While this eliminates confidentiality concerns, the practice poses other potential problems. First, it would exacerbate lack of competence where there is a scarcity of *Fiqh al-Muamalat* jurists. Second, it may prevent the formation of an efficient labor market for *Shariah* audit, by decreasing the economic appeal of the profession. Lastly, it may create a symbiotic relationship between the auditor and the financial institution that could undermine impartiality.

The third issue relates to the nature of the *competence* required of SSB members. Due to the unique role that they are called upon to fulfill, SSB members should ideally be knowledgeable in both Islamic law and commercial and accounting practices (*Fiqh al-Muamalat*). In practice, it would appear that very few scholars are well-versed in both disciplines. The issue has been addressed by including members from different backgrounds in most SSBs. However, the combination of experts rather than expertise creates the challenge of overcoming different perspectives as well as the risk of potential failure of communication. Over time, the demand gap for combined *Shariah* and financial skills is likely to be reduced through public policy and normal labor market operations. Progress in this direction is already noticeable in countries where the Islamic financial industry is well established. For instance, the Securities Commission of Malaysia has certified a total of 27 individuals and 3 companies eligible for *Shariah* advisory on unit trust funds, for a total of 24 companies offering such funds. However, in countries where Islamic finance is less developed, other transitional arrangements may be needed.

The fourth issue concerns *consistency* of judgment across banks, over time, or across jurisdictions within the same bank. In essence the activities of SSBs are in the nature of creating jurisprudence by the interpretation of legal sources. It should therefore not be surprising to find conflicting opinions on the admissibility of specific financial instruments or transactions. In reality, however, the diversity of opinions is less widespread than might be expected. The CIBAFI sampled about 6000 *fatwas*, and found that 90% were consistent across banks. The fact that over one hundred *Shariah* scholars around the world issued these *fatwas* would suggest an overall consistency in the interpretation of the sources. Further, this high degree of consistency between the *fatwas* would also point to a substantial independence of SSBs. Nevertheless, as the industry expands, the number of conflicting *fatwas* on the permissibility of an instrument is likely to increase. This could undermine customer confidence in the industry and have repercussions on the enforceability of contracts.

The last and overarching issue relates to *disclosure* of all information relating to *Shariah* advisories. In addition to the positive aspects of thus empowering stakeholders, disclosure could be the means to addressing some of the issues discussed in the preceding paragraphs. A transparent financial institution would ideally disclose the duties, decisionmaking process, areas of competence, and the composition of its SSB, as well publish all *fatwas* issued by the SSB. This would strengthen stakeholders' confidence in the credibility of SSB assessments. In addition, public disclosure of such information would provide a forum for educating the public, thus paving the way for a larger role for market discipline in regard to *Shariah* compliance. Finally, it would decrease the costs that external agents may face in assessing the quality of internal *Shariah* supervision.

Comments and Questions

1. Approval by a *Shariah* Board effectively telegraphs to investors, clients, and customers, that the practice is *Shariah* compliant, alleviating their obligation to make an independent determination. The boards may have a continuing responsibility for ensuring compliance throughout the life of the matter. *See* Shaykh Yusuf Talal DeLorenzo, *Islamic Business and Commercial Law: Shari'ah Compliance Risk*, 7 Chi. J. Int'l L. 397, 400 (2007) ("Throughout the product lifecycle, it is the responsibility of the SSB to work with management to ensure that everything about the financial product or service is in compliance with the principles and precepts of the Shari'ah").

2. What are some concerns that can arise out of the structure? Members of these boards may represent different schools of thought in *Shariah* interpretation. Why do *Shariah* boards employ this type of diversity?

3. For financial institutions, board members need to be versed both in the precepts of Sharia and in modern finance. This has resulted in a shortage of qualified scholars. *See* David Yerushalmi, Esq., *Shari'ah's "Black Box": Civil Liability and Criminal Exposure Surrounding Shari'ah-Compliant Finance*, 2008 Utah L. Rev. 1019, 1086 ("There are only approximately 20–25 sufficiently trained Shari'ah authorities, and each of these exclusive club members sits on dozens of Shari'ah supervisory boards around the world."). What impact might this have on the use of these boards?

4. As this article notes, members of these boards are typically paid by the institution that hires them. This, in the mind of some, creates an unacceptable conflict of interest. *See* Scott R. Anderson, *Forthcoming Changes in the Shari'ah Compliance Regime for Islamic Finance*, 35 Yale J. Int'l L. 237, 240 (2010) ("While shari'ah supervisory boards have become prevalent, the fact that they are paid and maintained by the same institutions that they supervise raises concerns regarding their independence and reliability."). Do you agree?

5. There is not a uniformity of opinion when it comes to interpretations of *Shariah*. Even when a practice is approved by a particular *Shariah* board, others may have a different view. Moreover, even after approval occurs, opinions can change. Something deemed non-compliant will affect its treatment by the market. This possibility is sometimes referred to as *Shariah* compliance risk.

6. Differences sometimes have a geographical component. Scholars from the Middle-East are generally viewed as more conservative than those in Southeast Asia, particularly Malaysia. Approval of a product or practice by a *Shariah* board of scholars from Malaysia will not, therefore, necessarily suffice for investors in the Middle East.

7. One of the pillars of Islam is Zakat, or the payment of alms. In some Islamic countries, corporations must make these payments. In Saudi Arabia, for example, companies must annually pay 2.5% of capital and income to the Department of Zakat. The funds are then used for charitable and social causes determined by the government.

8. What role might competitive pressures have on the future direction of Islamic interpretations? J. Robert Brown, Jr., Secularism, Sharia and the Turkish Financial Markets, 40 Brook. J. Int'l L. 407 (2015) ("While better able to reach customers who selected banking relationships primarily on the basis of religious compliance, Islamic banks did not limit their activities to this modest segment of the market. They also competed for customers who relied on the traditional commercial banks. Success, therefore, depended upon an ability to match rates of return as well as the quality and variety of services. The need to do so was particularly important with respect to credit cards.").

VII. Corporate Governance Hegemony (Redux)

After reviewing some of the differences in approach to corporate governance, we can return to the article that you read at the beginning of this chapter, the one by Professors Hansmann and Kraakman. Are they correct? Is global corporate governance converging towards the Anglo-American model?

Douglas M. Branson, *The Very Uncertain Prospect of "Global" Convergence in Corporate Governance*
34 Cornell Int'l L.J. 321, 332 (2001)[30]

This section makes five points,.... They are: (1) the existing convergence scholarship engages in a high degree of pontification, with little evidence in support of assertions made and seemingly consciously unmindful of authority to the contrary; (2) the existing scholarship is highly inbred, ignoring work of scholars at lesser known institutions or in other fields and citing almost exclusively work by a few scholars at a

---

30. Copyright © 2001 Cornell International Law Journal. Reprinted by permission.

handful of elite institutions; (3) when the convergence scholars do assemble evidence in support of their thesis the sample is an extremely narrow one from which to postulate "global" anything; (4) the advocacy of the United States model as global demonstrates an extreme lack of cultural understanding and sensitivity, ignoring countless cultures and billions of persons for whom United States style corporate governance would never be acceptable; and (5) implicit in this advocacy scholarship is the assumption that only one economic model, that which places efficiency and profit in the ascendancy, is acceptable. The reality is that in most of the world other economic models, grouped generically under "embedded capitalism," govern human and fictional beings' (corporations') lives, goals and aspirations.

Chapter 13

How Does Corporate Governance Matter?

Although corporate governance has received extensive attention from federal law-makers, shareholder advocates, and the media, little empirical evidence conclusively establishes how, or even whether, so-called "best" corporate governance practices affect firm profitability, much less other results important to investors and the public. However, following the enactment of the Sarbanes-Oxley Act in 2002, more scholars have attempted to answer these questions. This chapter begins by considering how to measure the value of corporate governance reforms enacted at the federal level. The next section presents both sides of a pointed exchange about the Sarbanes-Oxley Act and, more recently, the Dodd-Frank Act. Did Congress legislate "quack" corporate governance reforms? Both of these sections offer brief glimpses into the vast empirical research published on corporate governance questions during the past fifteen years. The chapter ends with a more in-depth presentation of one facet of this research: the impact of independent directors on corporate performance.

I. Does Good Governance Enhance Firm Performance?

One way to measure the effectiveness of corporate governance is to consider the effect of best practices on overall firm performance. In theory, shareholders would expect that companies that have adopted good governance practices would enjoy superior returns. However, scholars examining the effects of various corporate governance practices on firm performance have not reported conclusive findings. For example, numerous researchers have studied the effects of board composition on firm performance, but many researchers have found no significant relation between director independence and company profits. The following provocative article discusses various attempts by scholars to link specific board governance practices to corporate performance.

Sanjai Bhagat, Brian Bolton & Roberta Romano,
The Promise and Peril of Corporate Governance Indices
108 Colum. L. Rev. 1803 (2008)[1]

Corporate governance took on a new urgency in the aftermath of Enron's collapse and a succession of accounting scandals. It became a topic of intense media and activist institutional investor interest, in the hope that closer scrutiny of firms' governance could prevent further Enrons. At the same time, corporations were being forced to reconsider their governance by federal legislation and stock exchange listing requirements that were enacted in reaction to the scandals and that emphasized corporate governance solutions. And mutual funds were pushed to become more involved in governance under regulation adopted by the U.S. Securities and Exchange Commission (SEC), which required funds to adopt written policies on proxy voting and to disclose their specific votes. In turn, the heightened attention accorded corporate governance increased the demand for third-party corporate-governance-related services — by institutional investors for research and advice on proxy voting and by corporations for advice on how to improve their governance ratings.

Shortly before the surge in interest in corporate governance, a team of financial economists — Paul Gompers, Joy Ishii, and Andrew Metrick (GIM) — wrote a seminal paper in which they constructed an index of corporate governance quality for a large number of publicly traded U.S. firms. They found that higher-quality governance as defined by their index was associated with improved future stock performance. The focus on corporate governance following Enron's collapse made GIM's findings of great interest to a far wider audience than corporate governance scholars.

In particular, the relation between governance and performance identified in GIM's paper offered intellectual support for commercial governance-ranking services. This connection was not lost on commercial governance service providers. Although GIM had been assiduously careful in interpreting their data and did not draw causal connections between good governance and superior performance, commercial governance service providers, and some institutional investor activists, exercised no such caution. This incaution fed the demand for and supply of governance services, which accelerated post-Enron. Today, a market for corporate governance ratings exists, with proxy-advising firms — such as the dominant market leader, Institutional Shareholder Services, Inc. (ISS) — using ratings to formulate voting recommendations and other governance-rating providers using them to advise on investment decisions.

The idea underlying ratings construction is to benchmark a firm's governance features against what the index constructor considers to be best practices. Accordingly, a firm's score on the index or rating is intended to provide a readily comparable, summary measure of governance quality. However, establishing a relation between governance and performance is technically difficult. The two variables, governance

---

1. Copyright © 2008 Columbia Law Review. Reprinted by permission.

and performance, are plausibly endogenous, meaning that their relationship is bidirectional rather than unidirectional. And using existing indices can magnify that problem because their construction is based on two factually incorrect assumptions: one, that good governance components do not vary across firms; and, two, that such components are always complements and never substitutes.

The aim of this Article is twofold: first, to analyze the performance of corporate governance indices as predictors of corporate performance; and, second, to consider the public policy implications that follow from that assessment. This Article examines methodological issues in the construction and interpretation of governance indices and their relation to performance not so much to critique the foundational work of GIM, although we do that, but rather to criticize the use to which corporate governance indices such as GIM's have been put. Because the precise construction of commercial indices is viewed as proprietary information by their owners and thus is not publicly disclosed, our analysis focuses on the relation between corporate performance and existing academic indices, some of which are, fortunately for our purposes, closely linked to commercial ones. Nevertheless, we believe that conclusions from this analysis are equally applicable to the use of commercial indices. This judgment is bolstered by a recent study that finds no systematic relation between commercial governance ratings and firms' future performance.

Our core conclusion is that there is no consistent relation between the academic and related commercial governance indices and corporate performance. In short, there is no one "best" measure of corporate governance: The most effective governance institution depends on context and on firms' specific circumstances. It would therefore be difficult for an index, or any one variable, to capture critical nuances necessary for making informed regulatory, investing, or proxy voting decisions. As a consequence, we also conclude that governance indices are highly imperfect and that investors and policymakers should exercise utmost caution in attempting to draw inferences regarding a firm's quality or future stock market performance from its ranking on any particular governance measure. If we had to make a choice between using an index and one variable to predict performance from the quality of a firm's governance, we would in fact select one variable: the median independent director's stockholdings. We conclude from the research that two of us have undertaken that this one variable performs better overall with respect to evaluating corporate performance.

Most important, our analysis implies that corporate governance is an area where a flexible regulatory regime allowing ample variation across firms is particularly desirable as there is considerable variation in the relation between different governance indices and different measures of performance. In essence, mandatory governance terms are the functional equivalent of a governance index that has the force of law, because such terms impose on all firms, without allowance for customization to a firm's specific circumstances, governance characteristics that a legislature or regulator considers to be best practices, just as is done by an index constructor in selecting his index's components.

Comments and Questions

1. How can the findings of Professors Bhagat, Bolton, and Romano be incorporated into any future corporate governance regulation? Keep this question in mind while reading Professor Romano's characterization of the Sarbanes-Oxley Act as "quack" corporate governance in the next section.

2. Do you think this critique of governance indices is more relevant to federal and state legislators or to firms considering employing outside governance consultants? As the article observes, governance consultants thrived in the wake of SOX. If governance consultants set aside governance indices as benchmarks and instead engage in in-depth, firm-specific analyses, the costs of such governance consultations seem likely to increase. If indices truly provide little to no useful guidance in structuring corporate governance, wouldn't the market ultimately react?

The next article also examines market responses to corporate governance. However, instead of studying stock performance in relation to governance indices, Professors Larcker, Ormazabal, and Taylor measure market responses to proposed governance regulations. In reviewing this selection from their paper, consider the weight that lawmakers should give to how the market responds in the short-term to governance reforms intended to protect shareholders over time.

David F. Larcker, Gaizka Ormazabal & Daniel J. Taylor, *The Market Reaction to Corporate Governance Regulation*
available at www.ssrn.com/abstract=1650333 (2010)[2]

The Securities and Exchange Commission, the state of Delaware, and various senators and congressmen have recently proposed substantial regulations that would limit executive pay, limit the firm's control of the proxy process (i.e. proxy access), and ban specific corporate governance provisions (e.g., staggered boards and CEO-chairman duality). Given the nature of these proposed changes, it is not surprising that organizations such as the U.S. Chamber of Commerce, the Business Roundtable, and other similar organizations have reacted in a negative manner, whereas CalPERS, CalSTRS, and other activist shareholders have praised the proposals. Employing standard event study methodologies, this paper examines the stock market's reaction to the announcement of these and other recent actions pertaining to the regulation of corporate governance.

There is an ongoing debate in the literature on whether existing governance practices are characterized by rent extraction or shareholder wealth maximization. In an attempt to provide insight on this debate, a vast literature correlates measures of corporate governance with various measures of shareholder value. However, given the endogenous nature of corporate governance, it is not surprising that many of the results

---

2. Copyright © 2010. Reprinted by permission.

linking governance and shareholder value are mixed. Because governance choices are endogenous decisions made by managers and shareholders, the value maximizing governance choices for one firm may be very different from the value maximizing governance choices of another firm. As a result, in equilibrium, the relation between governance choices and shareholder value will be ambiguous.

Recent corporate governance regulations represent an exogenous shock to equilibrium governance practices. Thus, the market's reaction to recent corporate governance regulation provides a novel setting to examine the relation between governance and shareholder value that is less subject to the endogeneity, or "within equilibrium" critique, of existing research. If existing governance practices are, on average, characterized by rent extraction, we expect regulation of these practices to increase shareholder value. In contrast, if existing governance practices are, on average, value-maximizing, we expect regulation of these practices to decrease shareholder value.

Schwert (1981), Binder (1985), and many others note that the stock market's reaction to a proposed regulation is a function of (i) the change in the probability that the regulation will be adopted and (ii) the dollar value of the expected impact of the regulation on shareholder wealth. Accordingly, we expect that the reaction to corporate governance regulations will be most pronounced for those firms affected by the regulation. In particular, we expect those firms whose existing governance practices are inconsistent with the regulation (e.g., firms with highly paid executives and firms with staggered boards) to have a more pronounced reaction than those firms whose governance practices are consistent with regulation.

In conducting our tests, we take a broad sampling of legislative and regulatory events related to governance regulation, rather than focusing on any single event, or only those events that are associated with significant abnormal returns. We examine the market reaction to eighteen key events related to economy-wide corporate governance regulation from March 2007 to June 2009. We group each of the eighteen events into two non-mutually exclusive categories: *Executive Pay Events* and *Proxy Access Events*. Eight of these events are *Executive Pay Events*, and relate to regulation that would explicitly limit executive pay and/or require annual "say on pay" votes. Interestingly, all eight of these events are related to legislative actions and none of these events are related to the actions of regulators (e.g., the SEC). Thirteen events are *Proxy Access Events*, and relate to regulation that would give increased power to shareholders holding ownership stakes of 1% or more (or shareholder coalitions holding 1% or more) to nominate directors in contested elections and influence the proxy process. Five of these thirteen events are related to decreases in the likelihood of proxy access regulation. Additionally, three events are related to both executive pay and proxy access regulation, and these events also relate to legislation that bans specific governance practices such as staggered boards and CEO-chairman duality. If any event is unassociated with a change in the probability of regulation *or* that regulation is expected to have a trivial impact on value, we expect to observe both an insignificant market reaction and that the reaction is unrelated to the firm's existing governance choices. Because we examine multiple events related to corporate governance regulation, trivial changes in the probability that a regulation will be adopted *or* trivial [e]ffects on shareholder wealth decrease the power of our tests and bias against finding both significant changes in shareholder value for a given event and significant changes in shareholder value on average across all events.

Our results are as follows:

Executive Pay Events. We find an insignificant reaction to events relating to the regulation of executive pay. However, examining cross-sectional variation in the market's reaction, on average, we find a negative relation between abnormal returns on the days of these events and CEO compensation. The higher the CEO's compensation relative to industry and size peers, the more negative the reaction. These results are consistent with a value-maximizing view of current pay practices even for firms with extreme levels of compensation. The results are consistent with critics' arguments that capping or regulating executive pay will result in less efficient contracts and negatively affect shareholder wealth in these firms.

Proxy Access Events. On average, we find a weak negative reaction to proxy access regulation. Examining cross-sectional variation in the market's reaction, we find strong evidence that abnormal returns are increasingly negative for firms with a greater number of large institutional blockholders (i.e., those holding at least 1% of shares outstanding). Additionally, we find strong evidence that abnormal returns are decreasing in the ease by which small institutional investors can access the proxy process. This is consistent with critics' claims that proxy access regulations that give shareholders (or shareholder coalitions) who hold 1% or more the ability to nominate their own slate of directors and/or list proxy proposals increases the power of blockholders who may not act in the interest of other shareholders (e.g., certain activists, bidders with toeholds, or corporate raiders).

Specific Governance Practices. Prior literature argues that staggered boards and CEO-chairman duality allow managers to extract rents from shareholders (e.g., Bebchuk and Cohen, 2005). If this is the case, we expect firms with staggered boards and firms where the CEO is also chairman of the board to respond positively to regulation that would either (i) ban such practices or (ii) give shareholders a greater say in the proxy process (i.e. decrease the cost of changing such practices). Examining cross-sectional variation in the market's reaction, on average, we find a significant *negative* relation between abnormal returns to these events and the presence of a staggered board, and no evidence of a relation between abnormal returns to these events and CEO-chairman duality. This is inconsistent with the market viewing the elimination of staggered boards as value increasing. If anything the results suggest the opposite, the elimination of the option to have a staggered board is value decreasing. One explanation for the lack of cross-sectional variation with respect to CEO-chairman duality is that the market correctly anticipated the portion of the regulation relating to CEO-chairman duality, but not the portion relating to CEO pay and proxy access. An alternative explanation is that regulations relating to CEO-chairman duality were not fully anticipated, but that CEO-chairman duality does not affect shareholder value incremental to the provisions of the regulation related to CEO pay and proxy access. This is consistent with the notion that the firm can use similar, but unregulated, governance provisions to achieve a similar effect as those provisions being banned.

Comparing the results between non-event and event days[] enables us to rule out the possibility that the statistical relations we document are a general phenomenon not specific to the market's reaction to governance regulation. The results of this analysis suggest that the relations we document between governance variables and event returns are unique to the governance regulatory events that we examine.

Examining the market reaction to recent actions pertain to corporate governance regulation provides an opportunity to study the effect of an exogenous shock to equilibrium governance practices on shareholder value. The managerial power view of governance suggests that many existing governance practices are the result of managerial rent extraction. This perspective predicts that the economy-wide regulation that limits rent-extracting governance practices will result in contracts that increase shareholder value. In contrast, another view of governance suggests that existing governance practices are the result of value-maximizing contracts between shareholders and management. This perspective predicts that regulation of corporate governance will result in less-efficient contracts and decrease shareholder value.

With regard to executive pay regulation, the evidence suggests that shareholders react increasingly negative for firms with highly paid CEOs. One possible explanation for this result is that the market perceives that the regulation of executive compensation will ultimately result in less desirable contracts and potentially decreases the supply of high-quality executives to public firms.

With regard to proxy access regulation, the evidence suggests the market reaction is decreasing in the number of large blockholders and decreasing in the number of coalitions small institutional investors can form in order to control a combined 1% of shares outstanding. This is consistent with critics' claims that shareholders (and shareholder coalitions) who hold 1% or more will use the privileges afforded them by proxy access regulation to manipulate the governance process to make themselves better off at the expense of other shareholders. Because the costs and benefits of proxy access vary significantly across firms, our results suggests that shareholders may best be served by voluntary proxy access in which shareholders themselves (rather than the government) to determine the rules that govern proxy access on a company-by-company basis (e.g., Grundfest, 2009).

With regard to specific governance practices, the evidence suggests the market reaction is increasingly negative for firms with staggered boards. This is consistent with the notion that the presence of a staggered board is a value-maximizing governance choice, such that banning staggered boards decreases shareholder value.

Across all tests, we find generally robust evidence of negative stock price reactions for firms whose governance practices would be affected by the proposed regulations. The results support the notion that the proposed governance regulations harm shareholders of affected firms. However, an important caveat is that the results do not rule out the possibility that there exists some form of governance regulation that is wealth increasing for shareholders.

Comments and Questions

1. What are the actual market reactions Professors Larcker, Ormazabal, and Taylor identify as responses to regulatory events? How do single-day responses by market constituents to potential regulation inform the likely actual market effects of those regulatory measures?

2. To what extent should lawmakers consider research such as this study when drafting and debating new corporate governance legislation? Can you identify potential problems with relying on academics' empirical work? Should Congress prioritize shareholders' wealth maximization as its regulatory objective? What about other policy goals, such as market stability, systemic risk reduction, or combating corporate criminality, and other corporate stakeholders? Even assuming that Congress regulates corporate governance for the purpose of maximizing shareholder value, shareholders have differing investment horizons. Should corporate governance favor long-term investors or short-term shareholders? See Jesse M. Fried, *The Uneasy Case for Favoring Long-Term Shareholders*, 124 Yale L. J. 1554 (2015) (challenging popular normative claim that public policy should encourage long-term shareholding).

II. The Quack Corporate Governance Debate

The previous section offered a mix of views on regulating corporate governance. This part begins with Professor Roberta Romano's now famous characterization of SOX as "quack corporate governance" and continues with excerpts from scholars who either have defended the legislation or have added support to Professor Romano's charges. As you read these selections, consider the assumptions underlying the authors' arguments, as compared to the motivations behind the specific legislation in question. Could this exchange have taken place even without the impetus of Congressional efforts to reform corporate governance following the 2008 global financial crisis? The intensity of this dispute is likely to increase as further empirical data becomes available.

Roberta Romano, *The Sarbanes-Oxley Act and the Making of Quack Corporate Governance*
114 Yale L.J. 1521 (2005)[3]

SOX was enacted in a flurry of congressional activity in the run-up to the midterm 2002 congressional elections after the spectacular failures of the once highly regarded firms Enron and WorldCom. Those firms entered bankruptcy proceedings in the wake of revelations of fraudulent accounting practices and executives' self-dealing transactions. But many of the substantive corporate governance provisions in SOX

---

3. Copyright © 2005 Yale Law Journal. Reprinted by permission.

are not in fact regulatory innovations devised by Congress to cope with deficiencies in the business environment in which Enron and WorldCom failed. Rather, they may more accurately be characterized as recycled ideas advocated for quite some time by corporate governance entrepreneurs. In particular, the independent-director requirement and the prohibition of accounting firms' provision of consulting services to auditing clients had been advanced as needed corporate law reforms long before Enron appeared on any politician's agenda. That is not, of course, unique or surprising, because congressional initiatives rarely are constructed from whole cloth; rather, successful law reform in the national arena typically involves the recombination of old elements that have been advanced in policy circles for a number of years prior to adoption.

The substantive corporate governance mandates in SOX that are the focus of this Article consist of the provisions that require independent audit committees, restrict corporations' purchases of non-auditing services from their auditors, prohibit corporate loans to officers, and require executive certification of financial statements. In contrast to provisions in SOX entirely within the bounds of traditional federal securities regulation, such as the direction for increased disclosure of off-balance-sheet transactions, or outside the scope of issuer regulation, such as the creation of a new public board to oversee auditors, the substantive corporate governance provisions overstep the traditional division between federal and state jurisdiction, although they did not have to do so. They could have been formulated as disclosure mandates. Had that been done, those provisions would have fallen within the conventional regulatory apparatus. Instead, they were imposed as substantive mandates, a different and more costly regulatory approach. It is instructive that the SOX initiatives are not to be found in any state corporation codes.

The central policy recommendation of this Article is that the corporate governance provisions of SOX should be stripped of their mandatory force and rendered optional for registrants. The findings of the empirical literature are consistent with the view that the more efficacious corporate and securities law regimes are the product of competitive legal systems, which permit legal innovations to percolate from the bottom up by trial and error, rather than being imposed from the top down by regulators or corporate governance entrepreneurs, who are far removed from the day-to-day operations of firms. In that regard it is important to point out that the bulk of the provisions of competitive corporate codes are enabling, permitting firms to tailor their internal organization to their specific needs. The best path to ameliorating the misguided congressional promulgation of substantive governance mandates through SOX is to conform them to the states' enabling approach to corporate law. A plausible mechanism to reduce the probability of future policy blunders on the scale of SOX is to routinize a requirement of periodic review for any legislation enacted in emergencies or similar crisis-like circumstances.

Evaluating the Substantive Corporate Governance Mandates in SOX

A considerable body of corporate finance and accounting research bears on the efficacy of the substantive corporate governance mandates of SOX. This Part briefly reviews the relevant empirical literature, which indicates that the data do not support the view that the SOX initiatives will improve corporate governance or performance.

Independent Audit Committees

Section 301 of SOX requires all listed companies to have audit committees composed entirely of independent directors, as defined by Congress. The rationale for the rule is that such directors can be expected to be effective monitors of management and thereby reduce the possibility of audit failure, because their financial dependence on the firm is limited to directors' fees (misstating earnings will not, for example, increase their income as could be the case for insiders with bonus compensation related to earnings). Congress also mandated disclosure of whether any of those directors are "financial expert[s]," along with an explanation—for firms with no expert on the audit committee—of why no committee members are experts.

A large literature has developed on whether independent boards of directors improve corporate performance. Across a variety of analytical approaches, the learning of that literature is that independent boards do not improve performance and that boards with too many outsiders may, in fact, have a negative impact on performance. There are fewer studies of the relation between audit committee composition and firm performance (four in total). None of these studies have found any relation between audit committee independence and performance, using a variety of performance measures including both accounting and market measures as well as measures of investment strategies and productivity of long-term assets.

A few studies find that having a director with financial expertise improves performance and, more specifically, that complete independence is less significant than expertise with respect to the relation between audit committee composition and accounting statement quality. These results are notable in that SOX does not mandate the presence of a financial expert on the audit committee (it has only a disclosure requirement regarding financial expertise on the committee), while it does mandate completely independent audit committees.

The compelling thrust of the literature on the composition of audit committees, in short, does not support the proposition that requiring audit committees to consist solely of independent directors will reduce the probability of financial statement wrongdoing or otherwise improve corporate performance. Not only is that the case for the overwhelming majority of studies, but also, and more importantly, that is so for the studies using the more sophisticated techniques.

Provision of Non-Audit Services

Section 201 of SOX prohibits accounting firms from providing specified non-audit services to firms that they audit. The banned services include financial information system design and implementation, appraisal or valuation services, internal auditing services, investment banking services, legal and expert services unrelated to the audit, brokerage services, and actuarial services. Although this provision is included in SOX's cluster of provisions directed at the accounting profession, it is, in fact, a substantive corporate governance mandate. Congress is substituting its judgment regarding what services a company can purchase from its auditor for that of corporate boards or shareholders. The rationale for the ban was that the receipt of high fees for non-audit services compromises auditor independence by providing auditors with a financial incentive to permit managers to engage in questionable transactions or accounting practices in the audit.

The conclusion that audit quality—and hence auditor independence—is not jeopardized by the provision of non-audit services is compelling not only because it is the finding of the vast majority of studies but also because it is the result of the studies using the most sophisticated techniques, as well as those whose findings are most robust to alternative model specifications. The absence of a systematic inverse relation between non-audit fees and audit quality (across all measures of audit quality) in the scholarly literature is consistent with the Panel on Audit Effectiveness's failure to identify a single instance of a compromised audit by auditors providing non-audit services in its field study of auditor independence. That finding no doubt contributed to the Panel's decision, as well as to that of the Independence Standards Board, not to recommend banning the provision of non-audit services and to opt instead for bolstering the audit committee function by proposing that audit committees be composed of independent and financially literate directors.

Executive Loans

Section 402(a) of SOX prohibits corporations from arranging or extending credit to executive officers or directors (unless the corporation is a financial institution offering credit in the ordinary course of business and the terms of the credit are the same as those offered to the public). Loans became a focus of congressional attention in the wake of disclosures that executives at Enron, WorldCom, Tyco International, and Adelphia Communications had obtained extremely large loans (in some cases in the hundreds of millions of dollars), personally benefiting from firms whose shareholders and employees suffered devastating financial losses. The ban was introduced at the end of the legislative process in the Senate as a floor amendment substitute for a provision that was drafted and reported out of the Senate committee as a disclosure measure. The blanket prohibition has engendered concern among practitioners, because it appears to prohibit standard compensation practices thought to be uncontroversial and beneficial, such as the purchase of split-dollar life insurance policies and the arrangement with brokers or other financial institutions for employees' cashless exercise of stock options under incentive compensation plans.

Because executive loans in many cases appear to serve their purpose of increasing managerial stock ownership, thereby aligning managers' and shareholders' interests, the blanket prohibition of executive loans in SOX is self-evidently a public policy error. The provision in the original Senate bill, which was consistent with the conventional federal regulatory approach, required disclosure of executive loans but did not prohibit them. Such an approach would have been far less problematic than the final legislative product from the perspective of shareholder welfare. It would have had the effect of facilitating the termination of loans most unlikely to benefit shareholders, by highlighting their presence to investors who could then put those loans' elimination on a corporate governance agenda (in the many states where they would otherwise not be involved because shareholder approval of loans is not required). Instead, the legislation is a blunderbuss approach that prohibits all loans, whether or not they are useful in facilitating the shareholders' objective of providing a sought-after incentive effect.

Executive Certification of Financial Statements

Section 302 of SOX requires the CEO and CFO to certify that the company's periodic reports do not contain material misstatements or omissions and "fairly present" the firm's financial condition and the results of operations. The certification requirement contains substantive corporate governance mandates. It imposes on the signing officers the responsibility for establishing and maintaining internal controls and for evaluating the effectiveness of those controls, along with the duty to disclose to the audit committee any deficiencies in the internal control design or any fraud involving any officer or employee with a significant role in the company's internal controls. The officers' signature certifies both the undertaking of those tasks and the veracity of the financial information. Section 404 contains a related filing requirement, a management report attested to by the external auditor assessing the internal controls. A third provision, section 906(a), is a new criminal statute that enumerates penalties for knowingly violating a certification requirement similar to that of section 302.

[O]ne policy approach would be to render the certification regime optional. That would permit firms for which there is a benefit to engage in special certifications rather than the conventional financial statement signatures (for example, opaque firms such as bank holding companies) to do so. Such an approach is supported by the considerable compliance costs associated with certification that have been reported or anticipated: Firms would select into the regime when the burden of compliance was more likely to produce a positive payoff to their investors.

Policy Implications

The analysis of the empirical literature and the political dynamics relating to the SOX corporate governance mandates indicates that those provisions were poorly conceived, because there was no basis to believe they would be efficacious. Hence, there is a disconnect between means and ends. The straightforward policy implication of this chasm between Congress's action and the learning bearing on it is that the mandates should be rescinded. The easiest mechanism for operationalizing such a policy change would be to make the SOX mandates optional, i.e., statutory default rules that firms could choose whether to adopt. An alternative and more far-reaching approach, which has the advantage of a greater likelihood of producing the default rules preferred by a majority of investors and issuers, would be to remove corporate governance provisions completely from federal law and remit those matters to the states. Finally, a more general implication concerns emergency legislation. It would be prudent for Congress, when legislating in crisis situations, to include statutory safeguards that would facilitate the correction of mismatched proposals by requiring, as in a sunset provision, revisiting the issue when more considered deliberation would be possible.

Converting Mandates into Statutory Defaults

Were the SOX corporate governance mandates treated as defaults, corporations would be able to opt out by shareholder vote. In this way, for example, small firms for which the audit committee composition, non-audit services, and certification requirements pose substantial costs would be able to sidestep coverage — in contrast to larger firms with lower compliance costs, whose owners might perceive an attractive cost-benefit ratio from the mandates and wish to retain them. This would be the easiest way to revamp Congress's misconceived corporate governance provisions, because it could be done by the SEC under its general exemptive authority, without congressional action.

State corporate law consists principally of enabling provisions that operate as defaults from which firms opt out if tailoring better suits their organizational needs. Firms can therefore particularize their corporate charters, as well as pick the state code that best matches their requirements, so as to minimize the cost of doing business, thereby increasing the return to their investors. The defaults incorporated in state codes are those expected to be selected by the vast majority of firms, which further reduces transaction costs (because most firms need not incur the cost of particularizing their charters). Transforming the SOX mandates into optional defaults for firms would move the federal regime closer to the state law approach to corporate governance.

From a transaction-cost-reducing perspective on corporate governance regulation, it is questionable whether all, or even most, of the SOX mandates would be chosen by a majority of firms and, consequently, whether they should be structured as opt-in or opt-out default provisions. Some pertinent facts lend support to an opt-in approach. States, for instance, could have enacted similar requirements to SOX as statutory defaults, but none chose to do so. Indeed, in the case of executive loans, state corporation codes contained the opposite substantive default rule, specifying the criteria for undertaking such transactions. The most reasonable and straightforward inference to draw is that there was no demand for the SOX mandates: If there had been a significant demand, then the provisions would have appeared in at least some state codes.

In addition, despite state corporation codes' silence, firms could have declined to purchase non-audit services from auditors, refused to make executive loans, and created completely independent audit committees (prior to the stock exchange requirement of such committees). Many firms chose not to do so, and the literature suggests they had good reasons: Completely independent audit committees add no significant benefit over majority-independent committees (and the benefit from even majority-independent committees is an open question), purchasing non-audit services from auditors does not diminish audit quality, and executive loan programs can serve bona fide purposes that benefit shareholders. Were the SOX mandates rendered optional, firms that found them beneficial would be unaffected, because they could continue to follow the SOX strictures. For example, firms that did not wish to purchase non-audit services from their auditors could follow such a policy without its being mandated, and to demonstrate a continuing commitment to that policy, they could opt into the federal default provision.

Comments and Questions

1. Two years after Professor Romano published her assessment of the Sarbanes-Oxley Act, Professors Robert Prentice and David Spence responded to what they characterized as her "savaging" of the law. *See* Robert A. Prentice & David B. Spence, *Sarbanes-Oxley as Quack Corporate Governance: How Wise Is the Received Wisdom?*, 95 Geo. L.J. 1843, (2007). Among other criticisms, the authors questioned Professor Romano's political motivations to label SOX as quackery. What do you think? How would proof of political motivation undermine Professor Romano's arguments?

2. What are the benefits and costs of adopting an optional federal regulatory regime, as proposed by Professor Romano? If all fifty states passed identical versions of SOX, would Professor Romano's objections persist?

3. Professors Prentice and Spence also questioned Professor Romano's contention that emergency legislation is inherently flawed or undesirable. They argued that Congress is better able to legislate in accord with the will of the general public, experiencing what is called a "republican moment," when responding to a crisis that interests the nation as a whole. Professors Prentice and Spence also argue that powerful corporate lobbies more likely will influence legislation enacted in non-emergency situations because the general public has less interest in such legislation. What do you think? Should Congress review enacted laws using sunset provisions and blue ribbon committees, as Professor Romano suggests?

Although the benefits of best governance practices, including their impact on corporate performance, are difficult to measure, the costs of corporate governance reforms are more quantifiable. The Sarbanes-Oxley Act imposed significant new reporting and internal monitoring requirements on public companies. The following selection describes the various costs incurred by public companies in complying with SOX.

Harry N. Butler & Larry E. Ribstein, *The Sarbanes-Oxley Debacle: What We've Learned; How to Fix It*
AEI Press 2006[4]

The current defense of SOX is that, despite its evident costs, at least it helped rid us of the fraud that had taken the capital markets down after Enron. As discussed below, ... the direct costs of SOX are quite high—indeed, high enough to have attracted significant attention in the business press.

Many defenders focus on these direct compliance costs, and reassure us that these costs are temporary, will decline as firms figure out how to comply, and in any event

---

4. Copyright © 2006. Reprinted by permission of the authors.

are worth it if the result is reducing fraud. However, these assessments are based on an overly sanguine view of what SOX compliance actually entails and a failure to realize what a heavy weight it ties around the legs of US firms. Among other things, SOX has diverted executives' attention from the hard work of maximizing shareholder value and distorted executives' incentives and investment decisions. [T]he most extensive and persuasive study of SOX's financial costs estimates the loss in total market value of firms around legislative events leading to the passage of SOX at $1.4 trillion.

Consistent with the disclosure philosophy of the original 1933 and 1934 Acts, SOX increases mandated disclosure in several areas. Perhaps the most troublesome new disclosure provision has been Section 404, which imposes a brand new and extensive obligation on managers to assess the quality of their internal controls. Little discussed or debated in Congress, and little noticed during the whirlwind of July 2002, it provides for SEC rules requiring firms' annual reports

> to contain an internal control report, which shall—(1) state the responsibility of management for establishing and maintaining an adequate internal control structure and procedures for financial reporting; and (2) contain an assessment, as of the end of the most recent fiscal year of the issuer, of the effectiveness of the internal control structure and procedures of the issuer for financial reporting.

SOX also requires external auditors to opine on both managers' assessment and on their own evaluation of control effectiveness....

The SEC initially estimated that its proposed rules implementing SOX Section 404 "would impose an additional 5 burden hours per issuer in connection with each quarterly and annual report." This estimate was sharply rebuked in comments on the proposed rule. The SEC's final rule revised the estimate up to "around ... $91,000 per company," not including "additional cost burdens that a company will incur as a result of having to obtain an auditor's attestation." Moreover, the SEC was way off the mark even after it revised its cost estimates. For example, Financial Executives International estimated compliance costs at $4.36 million per company as of mid-2005. AMR Research has estimated that companies will spend $6 billion to comply with SOX in 2006. One can only wonder how the SEC (or plaintiffs' attorneys) would react to errors and restatements of similar magnitude by a publicly traded corporation.

SOX's drafters and defenders seem to think that managers have plenty of time and energy and that, as long as they do not have much else to do, they may as well spend time on the tasks SOX assigns to them. In fact, management energy and resources are scarce. What is spent on SOX compliance is not spent on other activities that may be more valuable to the firm and to society. This recalls Milton Friedman's admonition memorialized as "TANSTAAFL"—"there ain't no such thing as a free lunch."

SOX has demanded the attention all board members and senior officers of every publicly traded company in America. It is very difficult to measure the opportunity cost of the time devoted to complying with SOX.

The internal controls rule also places a particularly heavy burden on smaller firms, with significantly lesser benefit to investors. This is supported by evidence that smaller and less actively traded firms reacted more unfavorably to events that increased the likelihood of SOX's passage. In particular, smaller firms have relatively higher overhead costs than larger firms, and therefore must struggle to compete with them. Any increase in overhead imposes an extra burden. Smaller firms compete, in part, through flexibility—the ability to rapidly change business plans to meet customer needs, and to combine functions in single individuals.

The heavy burden that SOX imposes on small firms has had the significant side effect of causing these firms to reduce their public ownership to avoid SOX. They can do this by becoming privately held or by "going dark"—that is, reducing the number of nominal public shareholders to below 300, which is the threshold for application of the Securities and Exchange Act of 1934, of which SOX is a part.

Studies also have shown that 200 firms went dark in 2003, the year after SOX was enacted, that more firms went private after SOX, and that 44 of 114 firms that went private in 2004 cited SOX compliance costs as a reason....

Comments and Questions

1. Professors Butler and Ribstein argue that SOX harms shareholders by imposing costs on public companies that well exceed the costs of fraud and other wrongdoing that lawmakers intended to prevent by enacting the law. Similar arguments have been made about other mandatory corporate governance rules. Critics assert that activist shareholders, unlike managers, focus on short-term increases in stock value rather than the "long-term health of the firms, much less with the long-term health and stability of the financial system more broadly." Nicholas Calcina Howson, *When "Good" Corporate Governance Makes "Bad" (Financial) Firms: The Global Crisis and the Limits of Private Law*, 108 Mich. L. Rev. First Impressions 44, 47 (2009). If, in fact, shareholders seek short-term performance rather than long-term value, why might management act contrary to shareholders' interests? How would executives' own stock holdings affect their decisions and behavior?

2. Although enacted with broad bipartisan support, criticism of SOX proliferated after President George W. Bush signed the bill into law in July 2002. While Professors Butler and Ribstein focus on the costs imposed by the regulations, other commentators have argued that SOX simply has not provided the benefits promised. For example, Professor James McConvill has claimed that the "shift towards formal rules in various aspects of corporate governance has not resulted in a tangible improvement in terms of the performance of the corporation and its executives and advisers." James A. McConvill, *Reflections on the Regulation of Contemporary Corporate Governance*, 2 Corp. Gov. L. Rev. 1, 19 (2006). What evidence might point to, or refute, this contention?

3. Many of the arguments made by Professors Butler and Ribstein concern the impact of the law's requirements on smaller public companies. Would the same concerns apply to larger public companies? In fact, many of the provisions of SOX received

the support of the Chamber of Commerce. *See* Remarks by Thomas J. Donohue, President, U.S. Chamber of Commerce, SIA (Mar. 3, 2005). Would it make sense, given these concerns, to exempt small public companies from some or all of the requirements of SOX? Congress did exactly that when it enacted the Dodd-Frank Act in 2010. Section 989G provided an exemption from the attestation requirement in SOX Section 404(b) for companies that are not accelerated filers. In essence, then, companies with a market capitalization of less than $75 million are not required to have auditors attest to the effectiveness of their internal procedures. *See* Rule 12b-2, 17 C.F.R. 240.12b-2 (defining accelerated filer).

4. SOX also mandated new corporate disclosures. Although these reforms potentially reduce the incidents of financial reporting fraud, it is notoriously difficult to quantify this benefit. Data does suggest that shareholders have filed fewer lawsuits alleging such securities fraud, a trend that continued even in the aftermath of the 2008 financial crisis. *See* Securities Class Action Clearinghouse, Stanford Law School, http://securities.stanford.edu (including data for number of securities class action law suits filed since 1997; number filed in 2009 lowest on record, excepting only 2006).

5. How does the analysis of SOX by Professors Butler and Ribstein compare with the evaluation of the law by Professor Cheffins? Who do you think is right? Do subsequent events, like the 2008 financial crisis, affect your views?

———

Professors Butler and Ribstein emphasized the direct costs imposed by SOX. While some expenses may have increased after Congress enacted SOX (which, in turn, affected the ability of some companies to access the public markets), other costs may not be as easy to quantify as critics suggest.

J. Robert Brown, Jr., *Essay: Criticizing the Critics: Sarbanes-Oxley and Quack Corporate Governance*
90 Marq. L. Rev. 309 (2006)[5]

The changes made by SOX in this area generated the most obvious set of costs emanating from the legislation and, as a result, made it the favorite target. Section 404 and its requirement that outside auditors attest to a company's internal controls has been labeled, perhaps wrongly, the most expensive provision added by SOX. Studies have attempted to quantify these costs, with most of the criticism focusing on the disproportionate expenses incurred by smaller companies.

As an initial matter, it seems clear enough that SOX resulted in increased out-of-pocket expenses for public companies. In quantifying the costs, however, the data to date is generally weak and incomplete. First, much of what is used is anecdotal and

———

5. Copyright © 2006 Marquette Law Review. Reprinted by permission.

often relies on extrapolations from small samplings. Second, the amounts overstate the continuing costs of SOX. They do not typically separate out expenses that were a one-time event necessary to bring companies into initial compliance, a process that should become cheaper over time.

Third, some of the costs attributed to section 404 would have occurred anyway, even had the provision never been adopted. To the extent accounting firms were forced into a more distant, gatekeeper role, it is reasonable to assume that their fees would rise, with or without section 404. Moreover, while the gatekeeper role was enhanced by other provisions of SOX, it is likely that even absent legislation, accounting firms, in the aftermath of Enron and WorldCom, would have gone in this direction in order to reduce legal exposure.

Similarly, the impact on smaller companies ignores the fact that these companies are notorious for having poor internal accounting systems. Particularly as they grow in size, they will need to improve these systems. One suspects that SOX accelerated an improvement process at least some of which would have, or should have, occurred anyway.

The other data subset used to demonstrate the high cost of SOX concerns the number of companies "going dark," those allowing the number of shareholders of record to fall below 300. The consequences of going dark are severe. No longer subject to the periodic reporting requirements, the companies cannot be traded on an exchange or the Bulletin Board and are limited to unregulated markets such as the automated pink sheets. In general, only the smallest of companies with limited liquidity allow this to happen.

The number of companies "going dark" because of SOX is hard to discern. A GAO report noted a post-SOX increase in the numbers, with some companies unsurprisingly giving as one explanation the costs (including those imposed by SOX) of maintaining public company status. Nonetheless, the numbers are at best modest, increasing from 143 in 2001, the last full year before the adoption of SOX, to 245 in 2004; less than two percent of all public companies. Moreover, in terms of size, they are small and trade in the least liquid markets.

Others have studied leveraged buyouts ("LBOs") and "going private" transactions. Data suggests that in the first few years after the adoption of SOX the number of these transactions increased, although again, the numbers are modest. These types of transactions occur for a variety of reasons, with the cost of remaining public only one factor. While SOX no doubt played a role on the margins (as did the costs associated with remaining public in general), attributing the increase, or even a significant portion of the increase, to the Act is a stretch.

LBOs typically involve the repurchase of shares from public stockholders at a premium financed mostly by borrowing, using the assets of the company as leverage. Thus, the cost of the shares is the key variable. Even before the adoption of SOX, share prices essentially collapsed, only reaching bottom in late 2002. The decline made LBO transactions more viable and, predictably, the numbers increased. Share prices on the NYSE recovered by late 2005 and 2006. Unsurprisingly, the number of LBOs appears to have declined.

Whether relying on costs associated with compliance or the number of companies "going dark" or engaging in LBOs, the analysis places little or no weight on the benefits associated with the reforms. Certainly, reforming internal controls will not "prevent" all fraud, although reducing the control of the CEO and CFO over the finances by empowering the audit committee and accounting firms will prevent some instances of it. Whether that alone will prove to be enough to justify the reforms and their attendant costs is an empirical question not ready to be answered.

But focusing solely on the prevention of fraud deliberately understates the benefits of SOX. More broadly, the Act also increases investor confidence in the efficacy of corporate disclosure, something that will likely follow from an improvement in the integrity of financial statements. After all, most inaccuracies do not result from fraud. Companies may have inaccurate financial statements because they do not rigorously follow existing requirements or do not have adequate internal controls.

Comments and Questions

1. What does Professor Brown's article suggest about the out-of-pocket costs associated with corporate governance reforms? Why might comparing audit fees and internal control costs just before enactment of SOX with those fees and costs incurred shortly after the statute's requirements became effective exaggerate the law's actual long-term direct costs?

2. Having reviewed the arguments advanced by Professors Romano, Ribstein, and Butler and the counter arguments articulated by Professor Brown, what claims do you find most persuasive and why?

3. If you were a member of Congress reconsidering SOX reforms, what additional empirical evidence would you want to examine concerning the costs and benefits associated with the law?

4. Having surveyed some 120 papers written by accounting, business, and legal scholars who studied the costs and benefits of SOX between 2003 and 2015, Professors John Coates and Suraj Srinivasan determined "the state of research is such that— even after ten years—no conclusions can be drawn about the net costs and benefits of the Act, its effects on net shareholder wealth, or other research relevant to its assessment." John C. Coates IV & Suraj Srinivasan, *SOX After Ten Years: A Multidisciplinary Review*, 28 Acct. Horizons 627 (2014). The evidence does indicate that, despite the high initial costs of complying with the statute's internal control regulations, corporations and markets benefited from those mandates. Indeed, SOX appears to have created a higher level of confidence in corporate financial reporting. Furthermore, companies that went private typically were very small, with market capitalizations generally below $30 million, and evidence that SOX reduced the number of IPOs is "weak at best, and is offset by evidence that IPO pricing improved."

Following the 2008 credit meltdown and resulting global financial crisis, political pressure mounted for Congress to pass a new round of financial reform legislation. Spearheaded by Senator Chris Dodd (D-CT) and Congressman Barney Frank (D-MA), these legislative efforts culminated in Congress passing the Dodd-Frank Act in the summer of 2010. Although the SOX "quack corporate governance" discussion had not concluded, enactment of Dodd-Frank revived the debate. In the following excerpt, Professor Bainbridge proposes several key indicia for "quack corporate governance" that support his indictment of Dodd-Frank's corporate governance reforms. As you read Professor Bainbridge's critique, consider how his criteria and their application relate to Professor Romano's original "quack corporate governance" appraisal.

Stephen M. Bainbridge, *Dodd-Frank: Quack Federal Corporate Governance Round II*
available at http://ssrn.com/abstract=1673575 (2010)[6]

In response to public outrage prompted by stock market losses and seemingly rampant fraud, Congress passed the "Public Company Accounting Reform and Investor Protection Act" of 2002 (popularly known as the Sarbanes-Oxley Act or SOX). When President George W. Bush signed the Act later that month, he praised it for making "the most far-reaching reforms of American business practices since the time of Franklin Delano Roosevelt." In contrast, however, Yale law professor Roberta Romano slammed SOX as "quack corporate governance."

When the economy suffered through an even worse patch at the end of the decade, it was thus perfectly predictable that another round of regulation would be forthcoming. The story of the housing bubble's burst, the subprime mortgage crisis, and the Great Recession is far too complex to recount herein. Suffice it to say that, as was the case with SOX, populist outrage motivated Congress to pass The Wall Street Reform and Consumer Protection Act of 2010 ("Dodd-Frank" or "The Dodd-Frank Act").

Although Dodd-Frank's 2319 pages dwarf SOX in both size and scope, most of the Act deals with issues other the corporate governance. The key provisions pertinent to our inquiry are six in number:

1. Section 951's so-called "say on pay" mandate, requiring periodic shareholder advisory votes on executive compensation.

2. Section 952's mandate that the compensation committees of reporting companies must be fully independent and that those committees be given certain specified oversight responsibilities.

3. Section 953's direction that the SEC require companies to provide additional disclosures with respect to executive compensation.

---

6. Copyright © 2010. Reprinted by permission of the author.

4. Section 954's expansion of SOX's rules regarding clawbacks of executive compensation.

5. Section 971's affirmation that the SEC has authority to promulgate a so-called "shareholder access" rule pursuant to which shareholders would be allowed to use the company's proxy statement to nominate candidates to the board of directors.

6. Section 972's requirement that companies disclose whether the same person holds both the CEO and Chairman of the Board positions and why they either do or do not do so.

The question before us is whether Dodd-Frank's corporate governance provisions, like those of SOX, are mere quackery.

[Q]uack corporate governance regulation will have some or all of the following features:

1. It is a bubble law, enacted in response to a major negative economic event.

2. It is enacted in a crisis environment.

3. It was a response to a populist backlash against corporations and/or markets.

4. It is adopted at the federal rather than state level.

5. It transfers power from the states to the federal government.

6. Interest groups that are strong at the federal level but weak at the Delaware level support it.

7. Typically, it is not a novel proposal, but rather a long-standing agenda item of some powerful interest group.

8. The empirical evidence cited in support of the proposal is, at best, mixed and often shows the proposal to be unwise.

All of Dodd-Frank meets the first four criteria. It was enacted in the wake of a massive populist backlash motivated by one of the worst economic crises in modern history. As we will see in the next Part, the corporate governance provisions each satisfy all or substantially all of the remaining criteria.

Quackery Round II

Compared to some of the proposals floated in Congress following the 2007–2008 financial crisis, Dodd-Frank's corporate governance provisions were relatively modest. Senators Maria Cantwell's and Charles Schumer's Shareholder Bill of Rights, for example, would have mandated the use of majority voting in the election of directors. It also would have banned the use of staggered boards of directors and required creation of board-level risk management committees. None of these provisions made it into the final Dodd-Frank Act. Other provisions of the Cantwell-Schumer bill made it into Dodd-Frank only in a much weakened form. Instead of instructing the SEC to adopt a proxy access rule, Dodd-Frank merely affirms that the SEC has authority to do so. Instead of requiring that companies separate the positions of CEO and

Chairman of the Board, with the latter being an independent director, Dodd-Frank merely requires the companies disclose their policy with respect to filling those positions. Even so, however, the question remains whether the provisions that survived are likely to improve corporate governance.

Therapeutic Disclosures

Therapeutic disclosures are not intended to inform investors. Instead, they are intended to affect substantive corporate behavior. Two such provisions are contained in Dodd-Frank.

Pay Disclosures

Section 953 requires that each reporting company's annual proxy statement must contain a clear exposition of the relationship between executive compensation and the issuer's financial performance. It further requires disclosure of "the median of the annual total compensation of all employees of the issuer," except the CEO, the CEO's annual total compensation, and the ratio of the two amounts. This requirement is expected to be hugely burdensome: [It] means that for every employee, the company would have to calculate his or her salary, bonus, stock awards, option awards, nonequity incentive plan compensation, change in pension value and nonqualified deferred compensation earnings, and all other compensation (e.g., perquisites). This information would undoubtedly be extremely time-consuming to collect and analyze, making it virtually impossible for a company with thousands of employees to comply with this section of the Act.

The Senate Committee cited the Council of Institutional Investors (CII) as having supported this provision. CII's position as a de facto trade association for large, activist investors makes it an important policy entrepreneur. In addition to thus being part of a key interest group's agenda, however, the provision also should be seen as part of the populist backlash against corporations and markets. "The law taps into public anger at the increasing disparity between the faltering incomes of middle America and the largely recession-proof multimillion-dollar remuneration of the typical corporate chief."

Board Structure Disclosure

Section 973 directs the SEC to adopt a new rule requiring reporting companies to disclose whether the same person or different persons holds the positions of CEO and Chairman of the Board. In either case, the company must disclose its reasons for doing so. "The legislation does not endorse or prohibit either method." If this is the effect Section 973 ends up having, it will be without compelling support in the empirical literature. A study by Olubunmi Faleye, for example, finds support for the hypothesis that firms actively weigh the costs and benefits of alternative leadership structures in their unique circumstances and concludes that requiring a one size fits all model separating the CEO and Chairman positions may be counterproductive. Another study by James Brickley, Jeffrey Coles, and Gregg A. Jarrell found "preliminary support for the hypothesis that the costs of separation are larger than the benefits for most firms."

In my view, proponents of a mandatory non-executive Chairman of the Board have overstated the benefits of splitting the positions, while understating or even ignoring the costs of doing so. Michael Jensen identified the potential benefits in his 1993 Presidential Address to the American Finance Association, arguing that: "The function of the chairman is to run the board meetings and oversee the process of hiring, firing, evaluation, and compensating the CEO.... Therefore, for the board to be effective, it is important to separate the CEO and Chairman positions." In fact, however, overseeing the "hiring, firing, evaluation, and compensating the CEO," is the job of the board of directors as a whole, not just the Chairman of the Board.

To be sure, in many corporations, the Chairman of the Board is given unique powers to call special meetings, set the board agenda, and the like. In such companies, a dual CEO-Chairman does wield powers that may impede board oversight of his or her performance. Yet, in such companies, the problem is not that one person holds both posts; the problem is that the independent members of the board of directors have delegated too much power to the Chairman. The solution is to adopt bylaws that allow the independent board members to call special meetings, require them to meet periodically outside the presence of managers, and the like.

Turning from the benefit side to the cost side of the equation, even if splitting the posts makes it easier for the board to monitor the CEO, the board now has the new problem of monitoring a powerful non-executive Chairman. The board now must expend effort to ensure that such a Chairman doesn't use the position to extract rents from the company and, moreover, that the Chairman expends the effort necessary to carry out the post's duties effectively. The board also must ensure that a dysfunctional rivalry does not arise between the Chairman and the CEO, both of whom presumably will be ambitious and highly capable individuals. In other words, if the problem is "who watches the watchers?," splitting the two posts simply creates a second watcher who also must be watched. In addition, a non-executive Chairman inevitably will be less well informed than a CEO. Such a Chairman therefore will be less able to lead the board in performing its advisory and networking roles. Likewise, such a Chairman will be less effective in leading the boards in monitoring top managers below the CEO, because the Chairman will not know those managers as intimately as the CEO.

Proxy Access

Dodd-Frank § 971 affirms that the SEC has authority to adopt proposed proxy access rules. It does not require that the SEC do so. If the SEC does so, however, Congress intends that the SEC "should have wide latitude in setting the terms of such proxy access." In particular, § 971 expressly authorizes the SEC to exempt "an issuer or class of issuers" from any proxy access rule and specifically requires the SEC to "take into account, among other considerations, whether" proxy access "disproportionately burdens small issuers." Proxy access is a long-standing goal of shareholder activists, especially among the institutional investor community. Not surprisingly, it was supported by policy entrepreneurs from the CII and "[a] coalition of state public officials in charge of public investments, AFSCME, CalPERS, and the Investor's Working Group...."

Because proxy access' effect will be to increase the number of short slates, albeit to an uncertain extent, its impact on corporate governance likely will be analogous to that of cumulative voting. Both result in divided boards representing differing constituencies. In turn, while some firms might benefit from the presence of skeptical outsider viewpoints, divided boards are likely to be dominated by adversarial relations between the majority block and the minority of shareholder nominees.

The likely effects of proxy access therefore will not be better governance. It is more likely to be an increase in interpersonal conflict (as opposed to the more useful cognitive conflict). There probably will be a reduction in the trust-based relationships that causes horizontal monitoring within the board to provide effective constraints on agency costs. There may also be an increase in the use by the majority of pre-meeting caucuses and a reduction in information flows to the board as a whole.

In sum, proxy access is bad public policy, unsupported by the empirical evidence, and the pet project of a powerful interest group. As we have seen, these are the characteristics of quack corporate governance.

Executive Compensation

Section 952 contains a number of provisions relating to compensation committees, including a directive that the SEC to direct the self-regulatory organizations (SROs) to adopt listing standards requiring that each member of an issuer's compensation committee be independent. This provision was supported by CII, which argued that the bill should "ensure that compensation committees are free of conflicts and receive unbiased advice." Once again we see another one size fits all model being forced on all public companies. Once again the mandate lacks support in the empirical evidence. Most empirical studies have rejected the hypothesis that compensation committee independence is positively correlated with firm performance or with improved CEO compensation practices.

Dodd-Frank § 954 adds a new § 10D to the Securities Exchange Act, pursuant to which the SEC is instructed to direct the SROs to require their listed companies to disclose company policies for clawing back incentive-based compensation paid to current or former executive officers in the event of a restatement of the company's financials due to material non-compliance with any federal securities law financial reporting requirement. Issuers failing to adopt such a policy must be delisted. The requisite policy must provide for clawing back any "excess" compensation any such executive officer received during the three-year period prior to the date on which the issuer was obliged to issue the restatement. Excess compensation is defined as the difference between what the executive was paid and what the executive would have received if the financials had been correct.

Section 954 is seriously flawed in a number of respects. On the one hand, as a deterrent to financial reporting fraud and error, it is over-inclusive. It encompasses all executive officers, without regard to their responsibility or lack thereof for the financial statement in question. Some innocent executives therefore will have to forfeit significant amounts of pay. On the other hand, it is under-inclusive. Executive officers include an issuer's "president, any vice president ... in charge of a principal business unit, division or function..., any other officer who performs a policy making function or any other person who performs similar policy making functions...." As the Senate committee acknowledged, the policy therefore applies only to a "very limited number of employees...." The trouble with this limitation is that "decisions of individuals such as proprietary traders, who may well not be among" an issuer's executive officers nevertheless "can adversely affect, indeed implode, a firm." Another concern is the high probability of unintended consequences. In response to SOX's much narrower clawback provision, "companies increased non-forfeitable, fixed-salary compensation and decreased incentive compensation, thereby providing insurance to managers for increased risk." Because current federal policy seeks to promote pay for performance, mandatory clawbacks undermine that goal. There is a significant risk, moreover, that other unintended consequences will develop in light the "many ambiguities in the legislative language which will have to be clarified in implementing SEC regulations, e.g. is it retroactive, how to calculate recoverable amount, the dates during which the recovery must be sought."

Dodd-Frank § 951 creates a new § 14A of the Securities Exchange Act, pursuant to which reporting companies must conduct a shareholder advisory vote on specified executive compensation not less frequently than every three years. At least once every six years, shareholders must vote on how frequently to hold such an advisory vote (i.e., annually, biannually, or triannually). The compensation arrangements subject to the shareholder vote are those set out in Item 402 of Regulation S-K. In addition, a shareholder advisory is required of golden parachutes. The vote must be tablulated and disclosed, but is not binding on the board of directors. The vote shall not be deemed either to effect or affect the fiduciary duties of directors. The SEC is given exemption power and is specifically directed to evaluate the impact on small issuers.

Say on pay was highly contentious. Supporters included the CII, "the Consumer Federation of America, AFSCME, and the Investor's Working Group." It's a long-standing goal of the AFL-CIO. Business groups, such as the Business Roundtable156 and the US Chamber of Commerce, have long opposed it.

Is There an Executive Compensation Crisis?

The core argument for say on pay is that executive compensation has been decoupled from the financial performance of their firms. As the Senate committee put it, "[t]he economic crisis revealed instances in which corporate executives received very high compensation despite the very poor performance by their firms."

House Report 110-088, which accompanied an earlier say on pay bill, explained that in FY 2005 the median CEO among 1400 large companies "received $13.51 million in total compensation, up 16 percent over FY 2004." The Report also noted that "in 1991, the average large-company CEO received approximately 140 times the pay of an average worker; in 2003, the ratio was about 500 to 1." Yet, it's difficult to describe those amounts as constituting a crisis in and of themselves when many occupations today carry even larger rewards. The highest paid investment banker on Wall Street in 2006 was Lloyd Blankfein of Goldman Sachs, for example, who "earned $54.3 million in salary, cash, restricted stock and stock options,"161 or about 4 times the median CEO salary from the year before. But the pay of some private hedge fund managers dwarfed even that sum. Hedge fund manager James Simons earned $1.7 billion in 2006, for example, and two other hedge fund managers also cracked the billion dollar level that year.

The effectiveness of say on pay is highly contested. The Senate committee report argued that:

> The UK has implemented "say on pay" policy. Professor John Coates in testimony for the Senate Banking Committee stated that the UK's experience has been positive; "different researchers have conducted several investigations of this kind ... These findings suggest that say-on-pay legislation would have a positive impact on corporate governance in the U.S. While the two legal contexts are not identical, there is no evidence in the existing literature to suggest that the differences would turn what would be a good idea in the UK into a bad one in the U.S."

In contrast, Professor Jeffrey Gordon argues that the U.K. experience with say on pay makes a mandatory vote a "dubious choice." First, because individualized review of compensation schemes at the 10,000-odd U.S. reporting companies will be prohibitively expensive, activist institutional investors will probably insist on a narrow range of compensation programs that will force companies into something close to a one size fits all model. Second, because many institutional investors rely on proxy advisory firms, a very small number of gatekeepers will wield undue influence over compensation. This likely outcome seriously undercuts the case for say on pay. As we have seen, proponents of say on pay claim it will help make management more accountable, but they ignore the probability that say on pay really will shift power from boards of directors not to shareholders but to advisory firms like RiskMetrics. There's good reason to think that boards are more accountable than those firms. "The most important proxy advisor, RiskMetrics, already faces conflict issues in its dual role of both advising and rating firms on corporate governance that will be greatly magnified when it begins to rate firms on their compensation plans." Ironically, the only constraint on RiskMetrics' conflict is the market—i.e., the possibility that they will lose credibility and therefore customers—the very force most shareholder power proponents claim doesn't work when it comes to holding management accountable.

Gordon concludes "that 'say on pay' has some downsides even in the United Kingdom, downsides that would be exacerbated by a simple transplant into the United States." He recommended that any federal rule be limited to an opt-in regime or, if some form of mandatory regime was politically necessary, that it be limited to the very largest firms. As we have seen, Congress went in a different direction, despite the considerable uncertainty as to whether say on pay will be effective.

The Departure from Board Centrism

There is no more basic question in corporate governance than "who decides"? Is a particular decision or oversight task to be assigned to the board of directors, management, or shareholders? Corporate law generally adopts what I have called "director primacy." It assigns decision making to the board of directors or the managers to whom the board has properly delegated authority. Under state law, executive compensation is no exception.

To be sure, the say on pay provision contained in Dodd-Frank is only an advisory vote. Yet, the logic of an advisory vote on pay seems to be the same as that underlying precatory shareholder proposals made pursuant to Rule 14a-8. Even though they are not binding, they are nevertheless expected to affect director decisions.

Say on pay is just one small piece of the shareholder activists' agenda, moreover. As we have seen, Dodd-Frank presages the accomplishment of another of those agenda items by authorizing the SEC to go forward with proxy access. Another of the activists" agenda items was recently achieved when states began changing their corporation statutes to allow the use majority voting in election of directors. Because even an advisory say on pay vote is part of this package of what Cardozo called, albeit in a different context, "the 'disintegrating erosion' of particular exceptions" by which director primacy is slowly being undermined, it is worth reminding ourselves why board centric corporate governance has value.

The case for board centrism is grounded in Kenneth Arrow's work on organizational decision making, which identified two basic decision-making mechanisms: "consensus" and "authority." Organizations use some form of consensus-based decision making when each voting stakeholder in the organization has comparable access to information and similar interests. In the absence of information asymmetries and conflicting interests, collective decision making can take place at relatively low cost. In contrast, organizations resort to authority-based decision-making structures where stakeholders have conflicting interests and asymmetrical access to information. In such organizations, information is funneled to a central agency empowered to make decisions binding on the whole organization.

Small business firms typically use some form of consensus decision making. As firms grow in size, however, consensus-based decision-making systems become less practical and, by the time we reach the publicly held corporation, their use becomes essentially impractical. Hence, it is hardly surprising that "a publicly held corporation's decision-making structure is principally an authority-based one." Shareholders have neither the information nor the incentives necessary to make sound decisions on either operational or policy questions. Overcoming the collective action problems that prevent meaningful shareholder involvement would be difficult and costly. Rather, shareholders should prefer to irrevocably delegate decision-making authority to some smaller group.

Granted, the resulting "separation of ownership from control produces a condition where the interests of owner and of ultimate manager may, and often do, diverge."

Corporate governance therefore necessarily must include measures by which to hold directors and managers accountable, of which shareholder voting is one. In a complete theory of the firm, neither discretion nor accountability can be ignored, because both promote values essential to the survival of business organizations. At the same time, however, the power to hold to account is ultimately the power to decide. Managers therefore cannot be made more accountable without undermining their discretionary authority. Establishing the proper mix of discretion and accountability thus emerges as the central corporate governance question. Unfortunately, it is also a question no one in Congress appears to have pondered in connection with say on pay; instead, only accountability concerns seem to have mattered.

The Suspect Policy Entrepreneurs

Dodd-Frank's corporate governance provisions were included in the legislation because key policy entrepreneurs were able to hijack the legislative process to advance a longstanding political agenda. Specifically, as we have seen, all the major governance provisions were strongly supported by activists in the institutional investor community, especially union and state and local pension funds, for whom such items as proxy access and say on pay were high priority agenda items.

It seems reasonable to assume that these same activist investors will be the shareholders most likely to make use of their new powers. The interests of these activists, however, are likely to differ significantly from those of retail investors or even other institutions. Indeed, union and state and local pension funds are precisely the shareholders most likely to use their position to self-deal—i.e., to take a non-pro rata share of the firm's assets and earnings—or to otherwise reap private benefits not shared with other investors.

What we have in Dodd-Frank thus is a bubble law designed to promote rent seeking by a powerful interest group, which is a defining characteristic of quack corporate governance.

The Illogical Basic Premise

The proposition that Dodd-Frank's corporate governance provisions were a sop to special interests is further confirmed by the odd disconnect between the internal logic of those provisions and the back story of the financial crisis. Consider, for example, the question of executive compensation. Regulators identified executive compensation schemes that focused bank managers on short-term returns to shareholders as a contributing factor almost from the outset of the financial crisis. As was the case with almost all public U.S. corporations, banks and other financial institutions shifted in the 1990s to a much greater reliance on equity-based pay for performance compensation schemes. The rationale for such schemes is that they align the risk preferences of managers and shareholders. Because managers typically hold less well-diversified portfolios than shareholders, having significant investments of both human and financial capital in their employers, they tend to be much more averse to firm specific risk than diversified investors would prefer. Pay for performance compensation schemes that link managerial compensation to shareholder returns are designed to counteract that inherent bias against risk and thus align managerial risk preferences with those of shareholders.

As already noted, shareholder activists long have complained that these schemes provide pay without performance. This was one of the corporate governance flaws Dodd-Frank was intended to address, most notably via say on pay. The trouble, of course, is that shareholders and society do not have the same goals when it comes to executive pay. Society wants managers to be more risk averse. Shareholders want them to be less risk averse, for the reasons just discussed. If say on pay and other shareholder empowerment provisions of Dodd-Frank succeed, manager and shareholder interests will be further aligned, which will encourage the former to undertake higher risks in the search for higher returns to shareholders. Accordingly, as Christopher Bruner aptly observed, "the shareholder-empowerment position appears self-contradictory, essentially amounting to the claim that we must give shareholders more power because managers left to the themselves have excessively focused on the shareholders' interests."

Can Anything be Done?

The federal role in corporate governance thus appears to be a case of what Robert Higgs identified as the ratchet effect. Higgs focused on wars and other major crises. In the case of the former, for example, there is typically a dramatic growth in the size of government, accompanied by higher taxes, greater regulation, and loss of civil liberties. Once the war ends, government may shrink somewhat in size and power, but rarely back to pre-war levels. Just as a ratchet wrench works only in one direction, the size and scope of government tends to move in only one direction—upwards—because the interest groups that favored the changes now have an incentive to preserve the status quo as do the bureaucrats who gained new powers and prestige. Hence, each crisis has the effect of ratcheting up the long-term size and scope of government.

We now observe the same pattern in corporate governance. As we have seen, the federal government rarely intrudes in this sphere except when there is a crisis. At that point, policy entrepreneurs favoring federalization of corporate governance spring into action, hijacking the legislative response to the crisis to advance their agenda. Although there may be some subsequent retreat, such as Dodd-Frank's Section 404 relief for small reporting companies, the overall trend has been for each major financial crisis of the last century to result in an expansion of the federal role.

Comments and Questions

1. Recall the eight factors Professor Bainbridge identified as indicia of "quackery." What evidence does he provide to support the inclusion of each criterion? Professor Bainbridge echoed Professor Romano's disdain for crisis response legislation and apparent threats to federalism, and he decried legislative action in defiance of select empirical analyses. Is Professor Bainbridge more persuasive in establishing these issues as the determinants of inevitably flawed legislation?

2. According to Professor Bainbridge, one indicator of quack corporate governance legislation is its enactment in response to a populist backlash against corporations.

Is a populist backlash against corporate conduct necessarily a faulty motivation for legislative or regulatory action? Why or why not?

3. In the view of Professor Bainbridge, what is the ideal relationship between regulators and corporations? Do you agree?

III. Independent Directors and Corporate Governance

In their attempts to assess the benefits of corporate governance compliance, scholars have focused particular attention the role of independent directors. A large body of literature engages in highly technical analyses of the link between independent outside directors and firm value. The following articles provide a high-level view of this research and its impact on public policy.

Jeffrey N. Gordon, *The Rise of Independent Directors in the United States, 1950–2005: Of Shareholder Value and Stock Market Prices*
59 Stan. L. Rev. 1465 (2007)[7]

The most thorough survey of the empirical evidence on board composition effects is a 1999 paper by Bhagat and Black. In describing efforts to show correlation between firm performance and board independence, they report that "most studies find little correlation, but a number of recent studies report evidence of a negative correlation between the proportion of independent directors and firm performance — the exact opposite of conventional wisdom." They include their own 1999 study in those negative studies, with results driven by negative outcomes in firms that have an especially high fraction of independent directors, firms with only one or two insiders. One criticism of cross-sectional studies that regress board composition on performance measures is the potential lag between good governance and the visible effect on performance. Bhagat and Black attempt to address this in a detailed 2001 follow-on study with a large sample and long horizon, but the conclusion is the same: that increasing the degree of board independence does not improve firm performance.

Bhagat and Black's 1999 survey also takes a dim view as to whether boards with a majority (or supermajority) of independent directors do a better job on important discrete tasks undertaken by boards. A possible exception is avoiding financial fraud, where the studies suggest that a predominance of independent directors on the board may make a difference. Here are some important examples of board decision-making that test whether board composition matters.

---

7. Copyright © 2007 Stanford Law Review. Reprinted by permission.

Executive compensation decisions arguably present the sharpest clash between shareholder and managerial interests. The empirical evidence on the compensation effects of independent directors is equivocal, with "little evidence that independent directors do a better job than inside directors in establishing CEO pay." One surprising result is that boards with more independent directors are more likely to award "golden parachutes" (change-in-control severance payments typically equal to approximately three times annual salary and average bonus). One defense of these plans is that they may reduce managerial resistance to a takeover bid, but a more independent board presumably should be better able to control managers directly.

The best-developed evidence of board composition effects is the positive association between board independence and financial reporting accuracy. The exact channel of this effect is not well-specified, but some studies suggest it could be through the independent audit committee.

Comments and Questions

1. Although agreeing that the evidence suggests that director independence has "only minimal effects on board behavior and shareholder value," Professor Gordon nonetheless asserts that this conclusion "would mostly be wrong." Why might that be?

2. As you learned in Chapter 3, Professor Gordon notes that boards can play both a monitoring role and an advisory role to firm executives. Why might majority and supermajority independent boards spend less time and resources performing an advisory function?

3. To the extent that non-management directors qualify as "independent" under stock exchange listing rules but nonetheless are unwilling or unable to exercise objective judgment, would you expect firm value to suffer? Why or why not?

———————

The following article examines the importance of independent directors serving as a minority presence on a board. What effect do you think the announcement of such a board would have on share value, particularly when independent directors were installed at the behest of activist shareholders? What data would you collect if you were studying the issue yourself?

Chris Cernich et al., *Effectiveness of Hybrid Boards*

Proxy Governance Working Paper,
available at http://ssrn.com/abstract=1410205 (2009)[8]

This study examines whether "hybrid" boards—boards formed when activist shareholders such as hedge funds, through actual or threatened proxy contests, were able

———————

to elect dissident directors but did not win full control of a board—create value for shareholders. The study reviewed the effectiveness of 120 such boards formed from 2005 through 2008. Board effectiveness was evaluated both in terms of changes in corporate governance structures and strategy, as well as through increases or decreases in shareholder value, measured in both absolute returns and relative to peers.

On average, the study found that total shareholder returns at ongoing companies with hybrid boards were 19.1%—16.6 percentage points better than peers—from the beginning of the contest period through the hybrid board's one year anniversary. More than half of these gains came during a three-month period leading up to the formation of the hybrid board, providing strong evidence for a sizeable contest effect increase in share prices, as the market priced in its expectations of changes a hybrid board might bring.

This effect is similar to the "announcement effect"—an increase in share price over a short period after the announcement, via a 13-D filing, that an activist investor has taken a significant position in a company's stock—observed in other studies of shareholder activism. In many cases, however, the contest effect was distinct from a 13-D announcement effect, as it often came a significant period time after the initial 13-D filing, and was clearly related to a specific activist initiative—the proxy contest—rather than a general expectation of productive activism.

Among the 15 ongoing businesses in the sample for which three years of performance data was available following the creation of a hybrid board, total shareholder returns averaged only 0.7% over the three-year period—6.6 percentage points worse than peers. Total share price performance for the 39 months from the beginning of the contest period through the three year anniversary of the hybrid board, however, averaged 21.5%—17.8 percentage points higher than peers—again largely on significant contest period share price appreciation.

Comments and Questions

1. What does this study potentially tell us about the benefits of independent directors? What does it suggest about the importance of who makes the determination concerning director independence?

2. Is the study conclusive? Why or why not? Why might the long-term data not support the conclusions in the study?

3. Is this study consistent with the conclusions presented by Professor Gordon in the prior selection that you read?

4. What policy changes does this study suggest might be necessary to obtain the economic advantages of independent directors? Would these changes be controversial?

The question of independent directors raises more issues than firm profitability and shareholder rights. As Professors Lucien Bebchuk and Michael Weisbach discuss in the next article excerpt, excessive regulation concerns also arise, as do problems associated with the informational advantage enjoyed by insider directors. The authors briefly summarize some of the more recent findings in corporate governance research and identify several important questions still in need of examination as independent directors have become favored by the markets, regulators, and the courts.

Lucian A. Bebchuk & Michael S. Weisbach,
The State of Corporate Governance Research
23 Rev. Fin. Stud. No. 3, 939–961 (2010)[9]

How do we make boards work better? One recipe that has been increasingly suggested by public and private decision-makers is to have independent boards. Indeed, a common policy response to observed 'governance crises' has been to adopt reforms designed to strengthen the independence of boards. For example, following the Enron and WorldCom scandals in 2002, the exchanges increased independence requirements, and the Sarbanes-Oxley Act of 2002 required the independence of audit committees. The financial crisis has similarly led to the consideration of legislation aimed at bolstering the independence of compensation committees.

Why impose regulatory limits on the composition of the board? Hermalin and Weisbach (1998) present a model in which directors imposed on the firm by regulations are likely to be less effective than those picked through the endogenous selection process that would occur in the absence of regulation. At the same time, regulators are typically concerned that, without regulation, opportunism by insiders might lead to insufficient independence of directors.

Nonetheless, given the growing importance of independent directors, whether due to regulation or to choices made by firms, it is important to study empirically the effects of director independence. Initial work on the subject failed to find a link between board independence and higher firm value. However, there is a growing body of empirical research indicating that director independence is associated with improved decisions with respect to some specific types of decisions. In particular, it has been shown that director independence has an impact on CEO turnover, executive compensation decisions, the incidence of fraud, and on the incidence of opportunistic timing of stock option grants.

An important, and necessary, condition for directors to be able to be effective is the amount and nature of information that they have. If directors only have access to publicly-available information, it is hard to imagine that they will be able to evaluate management better than an outside shareholder. In addition, the mere fact that the directors do *not* have superior information would in itself be the consequence of a strained relationship with management, since presumably no information of value would have been transmitted during board meetings. The informational advantage of directors over outsiders thus presumably provides a measure of the potential for these directors to add value.

Comments and Questions

1. Professors Bebchuk and Weisbach identified several discrete board functions that are enhanced by the presence of independent directors. Do these findings justify the radical alterations of board composition required by the Sarbanes-Oxley Act, given the absence of conclusive evidence that firms' bottom-line performance has improved as a result of the governance mandates?

2. If corporate boards included additional insiders (firm executives), would their presence bridge the information gap between management and independent directors? Would Professors Bebchuk and Weisbach object to boards that did not include at least an independent director majority?

3. As between regulators and shareholders, who should decide board composition? Does one size fit all? In other words, does the same board composition make sense for all firms in all industries? What industries might benefit most from majority independent boards or supermajority independent boards? What industries might benefit more from majority insider boards? Why?

————————

Numerous researchers have studied the value of independent directors by examining share performance relative to the number of independent directors on public company boards and the timing of their election. In the next article, the authors consider the operational integration of independent directors in order to evaluate their likely impact on firm value. The authors identify the key functions of the board in order to hypothesize the potential ability of independent directors to perform those functions, the operational differences between insider directors and independent directors, and the impact such differences have on market performance.

Olubunmi Faleye, Rani Hoitash & Udi Hoitash,
The Costs of Intense Board Monitoring
101 J. Fin. Econ. 160 (2011)[10]

Corporate governance and issues of managerial accountability have come under intense scrutiny since the recent spate of corporate scandals. While many solutions have been proffered, the most common cure for corporate woes appears to be increased independence of the board of directors and greater monitoring powers for independent directors. For example, an editorial in *The Economist* called for increases in the number and oversight responsibilities of independent directors. Similarly, the New York Stock Exchange (NYSE) requires the three principal board committees (audit, compensation, and nominating) of listed companies to be composed solely of independent directors. An implication of these expectations is that many independent directors concurrently

————————

10. Copyright © 2011. Reprinted by permission.

serve on multiple oversight committees, resulting in the devotion of significant time to monitoring responsibilities (Heidrick & Struggles, 2007).

In this paper, we study how the devotion of board resources to oversight duties in this manner impacts the board's effectiveness in value creation through its advising and monitoring functions. On one hand, since these committees' primary responsibilities involve overseeing top management, committing significant board resources to them can improve the quality of board monitoring (Vafeas, 2005), leading to reductions in potential agency costs. Furthermore, independent directors serving on multiple monitoring committees can gain a more complete understanding of the firm. This broader view can aid such directors in making more informed decisions, again leading to better outcomes. Nevertheless, oversight improvements obtained through intense monitoring can be costly because of its effects on board advising. Holmstrom (2005) argues that intense monitoring destroys the trust necessary for the chief executive officer (CEO) to share relevant strategic information with directors. Similarly, Adams and Ferreira (2007) propose a model in which the CEO does not communicate with a board that monitors too much, while Adams (2009) presents survey evidence suggesting that independent directors receive less strategic information from management when they monitor intensely. Since independent directors' advisory role depends critically on information provided by the CEO (Song and Thakor, 2006; Adams and Ferreira, 2007), this can result in poor advising. In addition, given that directors' time is a finite resource, increasing the time spent on monitoring reduces the time available for advising. Besides, Adams (2009) suggests that intense monitoring leads directors to perceive their primary function as monitoring management and to shy away from offering strategic advice. Thus, intense monitoring can leave directors with little time, less information, and a poorer focus on advising, thereby compromising the board's ability to create value. Finally, intense monitoring can promote managerial myopia by weakening the CEO's perception of board support, which is necessary to encourage investments in risky but value enhancing ventures such as corporate innovation.

Our objectives are three-fold. First, we examine whether the quality of board monitoring is better when most independent directors serve on multiple oversight committees. Second, we examine whether this is associated with weaker advising. Third, we examine how this potential tradeoff between the quality of board monitoring and advising affects firm value, emphasizing the role of the firm's advising requirements in the process. We study these issues using firms in the S&P 500, S&P MidCap 400, and S&P SmallCap 600 indexes (collectively S&P 1500) over 1998–2006.

We test for monitoring effects by analyzing CEO turnover, executive compensation, and earnings quality. We find that the sensitivity of turnover to firm performance increases with the intensity of board monitoring. We also find improvements in earnings quality, with less discretionary accruals and more informative earnings. Furthermore, we find a significant reduction in excess executive compensation, although there is no evidence of an increase in pay-performance sensitivity. Overall, our results suggest that the quality of board monitoring increases when independent directors devote significant time to oversight responsibilities, which is consistent with several prior studies suggesting that independent directors can be valuable monitors (e.g., Weisbach, 1988; Borokhovich, Parrino, and Trapani, 1996).

Next, we examine how this affects the quality of board advising. We first focus on a strategic event that requires significant board input by analyzing acquisitions. We find that firms with monitoring intensive boards exhibit worse acquisition performance, with announcement returns lower by 48 basis points and a longer time to deal completion. Yet acquisitions are discrete events and worse acquisition performance needs not imply generalized ineffective strategic advising. Hence, we provide further insight by focusing on corporate investments in innovation. Innovation entails the cultivation of firm-specific human capital and tolerance for experimentation and potentially costly mistakes. This requires that the CEO sees the board as supportive, which offers the implicit assurance necessary to induce him to assume strategic risks. Intense monitoring can destroy this perception, causing the CEO to focus more on routine projects with relatively safe outcomes rather than on high-risk innovation. Consistent with this, we find that firms with monitoring intensive boards innovate less, where innovation is measured using research and development (R&D) investments and the quality of patents granted to the company by the U.S. Patent and Trademark Office (USPTO).

Next, we focus on value creation (as measured by Tobin's q) to provide evidence on the net effect of intense board monitoring. Demsetz and Lehn (1985) suggest that, in a frictionless world with no transaction costs, firms will always maintain value-maximizing board structures by speedily adjusting their boards as their circumstances change. For example, they will add more directors to maintain the board's advising capacity when board monitoring increases. Thus, empirical tests will detect no relation between board structure and firm value. Nevertheless, transaction costs and other constraints (e.g., due to public sentiments and/or regulatory requirements) can lead to deviations from optimal board structures and permit a measurable effect on firm value. Consistent with this, we find that firm value is significantly lower when the board monitors intensely. This suggests that the negative advising effects dominate the monitoring improvements on average. It also suggests differential effects based on firm-specific advising requirements since companies with high advising needs should suffer greater value losses if constrained to have monitoring intensive boards when their characteristics demand greater board advising.

Coles, Daniel, and Naveen (2008) and Linck, Netter, and Yang (2008) both argue that complex firms have greater advising requirements. Thus, we perform additional analyses to test whether complex firms with monitoring intensive boards suffer greater negative effects. Following Coles, Daniel, and Naveen (2008), we construct an index of advising needs based on operating complexity and then test whether the effects of intense monitoring are amplified by strategic advising requirements. We find that the reduction in acquisition performance, corporate innovation, and firm value is greater for firms with stronger advising requirements. For example, a firm with significant advising needs whose board monitors intensely experiences an 8.9% reduction in the quality of corporate innovation, compared with no reductions for a low-advising-needs firm with a monitoring intensive board. Similarly, intense monitoring is associated with a reduction of 9.5% in firm value when advising needs are high, compared with a statistically insignificant reduction of 0.8% for firms with low advising needs. Thus, for firms with high advising needs, the benefits of intense monitoring are outweighed by weaknesses in board advising while this does not appear to be the case when advising requirements are low.

This paper makes several important contributions. First, we extend the nascent literature on the board's advising function by providing evidence on the tradeoffs between directors' duty to oversee management and their responsibility to provide strategic counsel that facilitates value creation. Traditionally, academics and regulators tend to focus on directors' oversight duties, and suggestions for governance improvement are often couched in terms of more intense monitoring by independent directors. Recent theoretical papers (e.g., Holmstrom, 2005; Adams and Ferreira, 2007) argue that this can significantly alter board dynamics by disrupting the relationship between the CEO and independent directors. We provide important evidence by showing that while intense monitoring improves board oversight, the quality of board advising deteriorates when independent directors are principally devoted to oversight duties. Furthermore, the negative advising effects appear to outweigh monitoring improvements, resulting in net value losses especially among firms with greater advising needs. Thus, monitoring effectiveness alone is not a sufficient yardstick for good corporate governance.

We also extend the literature on the impact of directors' time commitment on board effectiveness. Fich and Shivdasani (2006) show that firm value suffers when a majority of outside directors are excessively busy through service on multiple corporate boards. Yet the decision to assume additional board appointments is fundamentally different from directors' obligation to sit on additional committees. The prestige and pay associated with board appointments can motivate directors to justify the allocation of incremental time to each additional board. In contrast, if directors rationally allocate time among their major responsibilities, they may not significantly increase the time devoted to one particular board when they receive additional committee assignments from that board. Rather, time spent on additional committees may come at the expense of the time they would otherwise devote to other board responsibilities at the same firm. We extend the literature by showing that this potential tradeoff has significant implications for the effectiveness with which the board performs its advising and monitoring functions.

Finally, our results have important policy implications. Our findings of improved monitoring provide an empirical basis for recommendations of increased independent director involvement in oversight duties. However, the deterioration in advising quality associated with intense monitoring suggests that an exclusive focus on board monitoring can be detrimental. Thus, there is the need to balance directors' monitoring and advising duties in the design of value-maximizing governance structures. More importantly, and in the same spirit as Coles, Daniel, and Naveen (2008), our results on the different effects of intense board monitoring on firms with high and low advising requirements challenge the one-size-fits-all approach often favored by regulators, shareholder activists, and the popular press. We hope that our results will encourage a more nuanced consideration of relevant factors as firms design their governance structures to maximize value.

Comments and Questions

1. The authors' analysis relies on several key assumptions; most notably, that boards of directors serve two functions (monitoring and advising), and that directors have a relatively fixed amount of time to dedicate to these functions. Given these assumptions, are you surprised that if boards must engage in greater monitoring, their performance of the advising function will suffer?

2. The authors cite a study by Fich and Shivdasani finding that outside directors are more likely to serve on multiple boards, reducing their available time. The same study, however, also reported that, despite potentially devoting less attention to board responsibilities than inside directors, outside directors have quashed more fraud as their representation on corporate boards increased. Given this finding, should it matter if senior executives receive less strategic guidance from their boards of directors? What can corporations do to ensure that CEOs and other key executives receive more counsel from outside directors?

––––––

Although board composition research dominates the recent corporate governance literature, it is not the only element of governance that scholars have examined. The authors of the following paper excerpt analyze changes in corporate governance research and propose an alternative measure for judging the quality of firm governance.

Sanjai Baghat & Brian Bolton,
Director Ownership, Governance and Performance
available at papers.ssrn.com/abstract_id=1571323 (2010)[11]

The corporate scandals of the early 2000's, including Enron, WorldCom, Tyco and others, led to a wave of regulation aimed at improving the corporate governance environment. A common feature of this was the implementation of guidelines concerning the independence of the members of the board of directors. For example, the Sarbanes-Oxley Act of 2002 mandates that all members of a listed firm's audit committee must be independent. Soon thereafter, both the New York Stock Exchange and NASDAQ Stock Market required all listed companies to have a majority of independent directors.

The regulatory and institutional focus on board independence is surprising given that most of the prior academic research found no statistical relationship, and, in

––––––

11. Copyright © 2010. Reprinted by permission.

many cases, found a negative relationship, between board independence and firm performance....

While we confirm the negative relationship between board independence and firm performance (that most prior research has identified) for the pre-2002 period, this result is reversed for the post-2002 period. *During the years 2003–2007, greater board independence is positively correlated with operating performance.*

While SOX specifically affects board independence, perhaps the increased scrutiny of all firms' corporate governance environments forces firms to implement better corporate governance practices, regardless of how those governance practices are measured. As such, board independence is not the only measure of governance that we consider. We find that the dollar value of director stock ownership is positively related to operating performance both pre-2002 and post-2002. We also find that whether or not a firm's CEO is also negatively related to operating performance throughout the sample period.

Although most prior research has not found a positive relationship between board independence and firm performance prior to 2002, some research has found support for board independence in specific situations. Hermalin and Weisbach (2005) develop a model predicting that board independence provides greater oversight of managerial actions. Bhagat and Bolton (2008) find that firms with greater firm independence are more likely to replace the CEO following periods of bad performance.

We find a consistent positive performance-governance relationship for director ownership. On average, the median director's stock ownership is 45 percent greater in 2003–2007 than it was in 1998–2001—and the relationship between director ownership and firm performance is consistently positive for both sub-periods. Hence, this study proposes a governance measure—namely, dollar ownership of the board members—that is simple [and] intuitive.

Comments and Questions

1. Long-time critics of independent director mandates, Professors Bhagat and Bolton report that firms with majority independent boards performed better after SOX than firms without majority independent boards. What might explain their finding?

2. Another study reported that independent-majority boards are superior to insider-majority boards for firms that are underperforming and facing restructuring and layoff decisions. *See* Tod Perry & Anil Shivdasani, *Do Boards Affect Performance? Evidence from Corporate Restructuring*, 78 J. Bus. 1403 (2005). An early critical determination of the study found that firms with independent-majority boards were more likely than other firms to restructure assets and lay off employees. However, these same firms also demonstrated the only significant recovery in the few years following the restructuring decision. Why might independent-majority boards be more likely to restructure assets and lay employees off?

3. Why might directors' ownership of company stock affect the quality of board governance? Aside from directors' independence and stock ownership, can you think of other factors impacting the quality of board governance?

4. Professors Bebchuk and Hamdani contend that:

> Academics and practitioners ... should abandon the effort to develop a single governance metric. Rather, they would do better to develop separate methodologies for assessing the governance of companies with and without a controlling shareholder. Such a two-track approach would best serve researchers, investors, and policymakers in assessing investor protection at either the country level or the firm level.

Lucian A. Bebchuk & Assaf Hamdani, *The Elusive Quest for Global Governance Standards*, 157 U. Pa. L. Rev. 1263, 1268 (2009). Do you agree? Why or why not?

Index

[References are to chapters and sections.]